2013
Novel & Short Story Writer's
MARKET®

includes a 1-year online subscription to **Novel & Short Story Writer's Market** on

WritersMarket.com
Where & How to Sell What You Write

THE ULTIMATE MARKET RESEARCH TOOL FOR WRITERS

To register your *2013 Novel & Short ~~Story Writer's~~ Market* book and **start your 1-year online genre only subscription**, ~~scratch~~ below to reveal your activation code, then go to www.WritersMa~~rket~~ ~~link~~ that says "Have an Activation Code?" then click on "Sign ~~Up~~ ~~enter your~~ contact information and activation code. It's that ~~easy~~.

UPDATED MARKET LISTINGS FOR YOUR INTEREST AREA
EASY-TO-USE SEARCHABLE DATABASE • RECORD-KEEPING TOOLS
PROFESSIONAL TIPS & ADVICE • INDUSTRY NEWS

Your purchase of *Novel & Short Story Writer's Market* gives you access to updated listings related to this genre of writing (valid through 12/31/13). For just $9.99, you can upgrade your subscription and get access to listings from all of our best-selling Market books. Visit **www.WritersMarket.com** for more information.

WritersMarket.com
Where & How to Sell What You Write

Activate your WritersMarket.com subscription to get instant access to:

- **UPDATED LISTINGS IN YOUR WRITING GENRE:** Find additional listings that didn't make it into the book, updated contact information and more. WritersMarket.com provides the most comprehensive database of verified markets available anywhere.

- **EASY-TO-USE SEARCHABLE DATABASE:** Looking for a specific magazine or book publisher? Just type in its name. Or widen your prospects with the Advanced Search. You can also search for listings that have been recently updated!

- **PERSONALIZED TOOLS:** Store your best-bet markets, and use our popular recording-keeping tools to track your submissions. Plus, get new and updated market listings, query reminders, and more—every time you log in!

- **PROFESSIONAL TIPS & ADVICE:** From pay rate charts to sample query letters, and from how-to articles to Q&A's with literary agents, we have the resources freelance writers need.

YOU'LL GET ALL OF THIS WITH YOUR INCLUDED SUBSCRIPTION TO

WritersMarket.com
Where & How to Sell What You Write

13 NMI0M

32ND ANNUAL EDITION

2013

Novel & Short Story Writer's MARKET

Scott Francis, Editor

WD
WRITER'S DIGEST
BOOKS
WritersDigest.com
Cincinnati, Ohio

Publisher: Phil Sexton

Writer's Market website: www.writersmarket.com

Writer's Digest website: www.writersdigest.com

Distributed in Canada by Fraser Direct
100 Armstrong Avenue
Georgetown, Ontario, Canada L7G 5S4
Tel: (905) 877-4411

Distributed in the U.K. and Europe by F&W Media International
Brunel House, Newton Abbot, Devon, TQ12 4PU, England
Tel: (+44) 1626-323200, Fax: (+44) 1626-323319
E-mail: postmaster@davidandcharles.co.uk

Distributed in Australia by Capricorn Link
P.O. Box 704, Windsor, NSW 2756 Australia
Tel: (02) 4577-3555

ISSN: 0897-9812
ISBN 13: 978-1-59963-595-8
ISBN 10: 1-59963-595-X

Attention Booksellers: This is an annual directory of F+W Media, Inc.
Return deadline for this edition is December 31, 2013.

Edited by: Scott Francis
Cover designed by: Jessica Boonstra
Interior designed by: Claudean Wheeler
Production coordinated by: Greg Nock
Cover illustration by: Josh Rob

media

CONTENTS

INDEX

FROM THE EDITOR

Hello, fellow writer. It's my pleasure to welcome you to another installment of *Novel & Short Story Writer's Market*. Whether you are new to writing or an old hat, I expect you'll find some worth in these pages. Of course, you'll find all the resources you'd expect in a resource devoted to getting your work published: listings for book publishers, literary journals and magazines, online markets, literary agents, contests and the like. But that's just the foundation. My challenge is to make *NSSWM* something more than just a research tool—this book should be a trusted friend that you meet with regularly to catch up on the latest news, to learn new things, and to be inspired. So this year's installment includes articles and interviews covering a range of fiction-writing topics from helpful insight into craft and technique to insider advice for getting published and marketing your work.

You'll learn how to hone your craft with articles like "Crafting Emotion: How to Make Your Story Resonate With Readers" by renowned literary agent Donald Maass (page 46), and an interview with best-selling novelist Christopher Golden on "Weaving Character, Structure, and Theme" (page 41). You'll then go on to learn how to effectively spread the word about your writing with articles like "Beating the Competition: Insider Tips for Making Your Fiction Stand Out From the Crowd" by longtime *NSSM* contributor Jack Smith (page 65) and "Sell Your Fiction Like Wildfire: Marketing Tips for Fiction Writers" by book-marketing guru Rob Eagar (page 116).

It's an exciting time to be a writer. The publishing industry is ever changing with the increasing popularity of e-books and opportunities to promote your writing via social media. It's important to stay on top of the latest trends, keep up-to-date with changes in submission guidelines, and be vigilant about all of the new information and technologies out there. This resource is a great place to start. I wish you the very best in writing and in all things.

Scott Francis
Content Editor, Writer's Digest Books

HOW TO USE
NSSWM

To make the most of *Novel & Short Story Writer's Market*, you need to know how to use it. And with more than five hundred pages of fiction publishing markets and resources, a writer could easily get lost amid the information. This quick-start guide will help you wind your way through the pages of *Novel & Short Story Writer's Market*, as well as the fiction publishing process, and emerge with your dream accomplished—to see your work in print.

1. READ, READ, READ. Read numerous magazines, fiction collections and novels to determine if your fiction compares favorably with work currently being published. If your fiction is at least the same caliber as what you're reading, then move on to step two. If not, postpone submitting your work and spend your time polishing your fiction. Writing and reading the work of others are the best ways to improve craft.

For help with craft and critique of your work: You'll find advice and inspiration from best-selling authors and top fiction editors in the articles found in the first few sections of this book (**Craft & Technique, Getting Published,** and **Promoting Your Work**). You'll find contest listings in the **Contests & Awards** section and even more listings to help you locate various events where you can hone your craft in the **Conferences & Workshops** section.

2. ANALYZE YOUR FICTION. Determine the type of fiction you write to best target markets most suitable for your work. Do you write literary, genre, mainstream or one of many other categories of fiction? For definitions and explanations of genres and subgenres, check out the **Glossary** and the **Genre Glossary** in the **Resources** section of the book. There are magazines and presses seeking specialized work in each of these areas as well as numerous others.

For editors and publishers with specialized interests, see the **Category Index** in the back of the book.

3. LEARN ABOUT THE MARKET. Read *Writer's Digest* magazine (F+W Media, Inc.); *Publishers Weekly*, the trade magazine of the publishing industry; and *Independent Publisher*, which contains information about small- to medium-sized independent presses. And don't forget the Internet. The number of sites for writers seems to grow daily, and among them you'll find www.writersmarket.com and www.writersdigest.com.

4. FIND MARKETS FOR YOUR WORK. There are a variety of ways to locate markets for fiction. The periodical section in bookstores and libraries is a great place to discover new journals and magazines that might be open to your type of short stories. Read writing-related magazines and newsletters for information about new markets and publications seeking fiction submissions. Also, frequently browse bookstore shelves to see what novels and short story collections are being published and by whom. Check acknowledgment pages for names of editors and agents, too. Online journals often have links to the websites of other journals that may publish fiction. And last but certainly not least, read the listings found here in *Novel & Short Story Writer's Market*.

Also, don't forget to utilize the various category **Indexes** at the back of this book to help you target the market for your fiction.

5. SEND FOR GUIDELINES. In the listings in this book, we try to include as much submission information as we can get from editors and publishers. Over the course of the year, however, editors' expectations and needs may change. Therefore, it is best to request submission guidelines by sending a self-addressed stamped envelope (SASE). You can also check each magazine's and press's website—they usually contain a page with guideline information. And for an even more comprehensive and continually updated online markets list, you can obtain a subscription to www.writersmarket.com.

6. BEGIN YOUR PUBLISHING EFFORTS WITH JOURNALS AND CONTESTS OPEN TO BEGINNERS. If this is your first attempt at publishing your work, your best bet is to begin with local publications or those you know are open to beginning writers. Then, after you have built a publication history, you can try the more prestigious and nationally distributed magazines. For markets most open to beginners, look for the ○ symbol preceding listing titles. Also, look for the ◑ symbol that identifies markets open to exceptional work from beginners as well as work from experienced, previously published writers.

7. SUBMIT YOUR FICTION IN A PROFESSIONAL MANNER. Take the time to show editors that you care about your work and are serious about publishing. By following a publication's or book publisher's submission guidelines and practicing standard submission etiquette, you can increase your chances that an editor will want to take the time to read your work and consider

- ⊕ market new to this edition
- Ⓐ market accepts agented submissions only
- ⊘ market does not accept unsolicited submissions
- ☺ award-winning market
- ☮ Canadian market
- ☚ market located outside of the U.S. and Canada
- ⑂ market pays (in magazine sections)
- ☐ comment from the editor of *Novel & Short Story Writer's Market*
- ◯ actively seeking new writers
- ◐ seeks both new and established writers
- ● prefers working with established writers, mostly referrals
- ◉ market has a specialized focus
- ◉ imprint, subsidiary or division of larger book publishing house (in book publishers section)
- ☻ publisher of graphic novels or comics

it for publication. Remember, first impressions last; a carelessly assembled submission packet can jeopardize your chances before your story or novel manuscript has had a chance to speak for itself.

8. KEEP TRACK OF YOUR SUBMISSIONS. Know when and where you have sent fiction and how long you need to wait before expecting a reply. If an editor does not respond in the time indicated in his or her market listing or guidelines, wait a few more months and then follow up with a letter (and SASE) asking when the editor anticipates making a decision. If you still do not receive a reply from the editor within a month or two, send a letter withdrawing your work from consideration and move on to the next market on your list.

9. LEARN FROM REJECTION. Rejection is the hardest part of the publication process. Unfortunately rejection happens to every writer, and every writer needs to learn to deal with the negativity involved. On the other hand, rejection can be valuable when used as a teaching tool rather than a reason to doubt yourself and your work. If an editor offers suggestions with his or her rejection slip, take those comments into consideration. You don't have to automatically agree with an editor's opinion of your work. It may be that the editor has a different perspective on the piece than you do. Or you may find that the editor's suggestions give you new insight into your work and help you improve your craft.

10. DON'T GIVE UP. The best advice for you as you try to get published is to be persistent and to always believe in yourself and your work. By continually reading other writers' work, constantly working on the craft of fiction writing, and relentlessly submitting your work, you will eventually find that magazine or book publisher that's the perfect match for your fiction. *Novel & Short Story Writer's Market* will be here to help you every step of the way.

GUIDE TO LISTING FEATURES

Below is an example of the market listings contained in *Novel & Short Story Writer's Market* with callouts identifying the various format features of the listings. (For an explanation of the icons used, see the sidebar on the opposite page).

THE SOUTHERN REVIEW

Old President's House, Louisiana State University, Baton Rouge, LA 70803-5001. (225)578-5108. Fax: (225)578-5098. E-mail: southernreview@lsu.edu (**Website:** www.lsu.edu/thesouthern review/.

Contact Cara Blue Adams, editor. Magazine: 6 ¼ × 10; 240 pages; 50 lb. Glatfelter paper; 65 lb. #1 grade cover stock. Quarterly. Circ. 3,000.

    • Several stories published in The Southern Review were Pushcart Prize selections.

NEEDS Literary. "We select fiction that conveys a unique and compelling voice and vision." Receives approximately 300 unsolicited mss/month. Accepts 4-6 mss/issue. Reading period: September-June. Publishes ms 6 months after acceptance. Agented fiction 1%. Publishes 10-12 new writers/year. Recently published work by Jack Driscoll, Don Lee, Peter Levine, and Debbie Urbanski. Also publishes literary essays, literary criticism, poetry and book reviews.

HOW TO CONTACT Mail hard copy of ms with cover letter and SASE. No queries. ("Prefer brief letters giving author's professional information, including recent or notable publications. Biographical info not necessary." Responds within 10 weeks to mss. Sample copy for $8. Writer's guidelines online. Reviews fiction, poetry.

PAYMENT/TERMS Pays $30/page. Pays on publication for first North American serial rights. Sends page proof to author via e-mail. Sponsors awards/contests.

TIPS "Careful attention to craftsmanship and technique combined with a developed sense of the creation of story will always make us pay attention."

EASY-TO-USE REFERENCE ICONS

E-MAIL AND WEBSITE INFORMATION

SPECIFIC CONTACT NAMES

DETAILED SUBMISSION GUIDELINES

EDITOR'S COMMENTS

TEN WRITING PITFALLS

And How to Beat Them

....

I.J. Schecter

There are a number of writing demons just lying in wait to trip up aspiring wordsmiths. You're probably familiar with a number of them (the demons, not the wordsmiths). I'm here to tell you that none of these alleged obstacles are legitimate, and that you're well within your rights to punch each one of them in the nose on your way to literary fame and fortune.

Of course, to be able to overcome an obstacle, you have to be able to recognize it. Here are the top ten excuses I've heard writers offer for not being able to stick with the program, the reasons each of them are totally unfounded, and the steps you need to take to get past them. And by past them, I mean right through the suckers.

EXCUSE #1

I can't tell which of my ideas is the best-selling one.

WHY IT ISN'T LEGIT: All writers are constantly bombarded by story ideas. That's practically what makes you a writer. If you didn't have ideas, you'd have nothing to write. So having too many ideas is not a good excuse.

WHAT YOU NEED TO DO: Stop worrying about which idea is the perfect one and just pick any one. Test it. See if it has legs. You'll know quickly enough. Or maybe you won't. Maybe you won't discover until page 150 that it's dead on the vine. But that's okay. As you write more, not only will your writing get better and better, so will your ability to pick out the great ideas from the average ones.

TIP: If you're having trouble judging the quality of a certain manuscript, put it aside for at least a week and then come back to it. When you look at it with fresh eyes, you'll know.

EXCUSE #2

Writing chapter two seems wickedly intimidating.

WHY IT ISN'T LEGIT: Writing chapter one is like running the first ten minutes of a marathon—you're on adrenaline. After that, it becomes a true test to see whether you have what it takes.

WHAT YOU NEED TO DO: Stop fretting about whether you know the characters well enough or can envision exactly where the plot is going over the next 250 pages. Just write. Write whatever comes. Force yourself to meet a certain number of pages or words per day. Do it. Don't not do it.

TIP: Don't write in chapters. Write the entire manuscript as a complete story first, beginning to end. Don't break it up or assign chapters until you're done. Thinking too much about chapter breaks, scene transitions, and so on can serve as an inadvertent hindrance to the actual writing—which should be paramount.

EXCUSE #3

I don't know what made me think I could write a whole novel.

WHY IT ISN'T LEGIT: After the energetic burst of chapter one, chapter two seems daunting as heck. After the concerted effort to get chapter two down, the rest of the book seems downright impossible. But writer's block, in all its supposed forms, is just plain bogus. If you've written fifty pages, how could it make sense that you can't write another fifty—and another fifty after that? You know the only way to shut up that voice that says "you can't write"? Write.

WHAT YOU NEED TO DO: Remember the true reason you're writing a novel in the first place: the irrepressible need that makes you write whether you like it or not. Take it a chunk at a time; don't let yourself get intimidated by the whole looming beast. A thousand words here, a few pages there. You'll get there. Because, actually, you have no choice.

TIP: Plot the story backwards. I'm serious. Start with the ending and work in reverse. When you're finished, you'll have a full outline.

EXCUSE #4

This all made sense a hundred pages ago. Now I don't know what the hell I'm talking about.

WHY IT ISN'T LEGIT: Every writer in history has had to deal with the psychological roller coaster that is writing, whether it's a 2,000-word short story or sprawling epic. One minute your writing is spellbinding, the next it's a dog's breakfast. On page 50, everything seems cohesive and fluid; on page 100, it seems threadbare and disjointed. It goes with the territory.

WHAT YOU NEED TO DO: Remind yourself that every writer writes to a certain level of ability every time he or she sits down to compose. Yes, to your eyes the writing might seem wonderful one moment and miserable the next, but that's just your perception playing tricks on you. How you evaluate your writing on a given day likely has more to do with how fat or thin you feel, whether your new relationship is going well or poorly, and how many copies of your most loved/hated author's new book just sold in its first week of release. Just get the story down. Later, when you go back to it fresh, you'll have a more objective view. Slightly more objective, anyway.

TIP: Before you get too deep into the manuscript, chart some basic elements to keep you in control: each character's age, general personality, reason for being in the story, and specific motivations; an overall description of the setting, including anything special or unusual about it; and any important date or event references, so that you can always go back and check that you aren't contradicting something you've written earlier.

EXCUSE #5

I don't know how to end it.

WHY IT ISN'T LEGIT: If you started it, you can finish it.

WHAT YOU NEED TO DO: Take a good hard look at whether your story can end before you've currently ended it. It's often said that most stories actually begin on page two, which I firmly believe. I also believe most stories end before the last page. Go have a look and see if I'm right.

TIP: Take half a dozen books you've read before and reread their final twenty pages. Then, if you don't already know where your own story is going to end, sketch out three possible endings. The right denouement will probably make itself obvious.

EXCUSE #6

I can't bring myself to change these words. They're like my babies. Plus, how do I know I won't end up cutting out the best parts?

WHY IT ISN'T LEGIT: Revision aversion is strictly about ego, and the sooner you put that ego aside, the sooner you'll improve your manuscripts by leaps and bounds. Beginning writers often ask me the number one hardest thing for a writer to learn, and I always tell them the same thing: learning to enjoy tearing apart your own work.

WHAT YOU NEED TO DO: When you plunge in and start to edit your manuscript, don't think of it as detraction; think of it as enhancement—because it is. Any first draft is just a prototype. It's the final version of the product that counts. So embrace the editing process. It can be exhilarating, liberating, empowering, and, ultimately—when you sit down to read the improved manuscript—tremendously gratifying. Also, learning to write and learning to revise are two different, but equally important, skills. There isn't a successful writer on the planet who's only a good writer or only a good reviser. Every great writer has worked hard to be both.

TIP: Avoid the edit-as-you-go syndrome. I'm not talking about deleting the word you've just written and replacing it with a better one; I'm talking about scrapping and rewriting entire paragraphs or sections as a substitute for getting words down on the page. There is nothing more important as a writer than conditioning yourself to produce drafts first, then edit them.

EXCUSE #7

I freak out when I think about sending my work anywhere. I don't know if I can stand the rejection.

WHY IT ISN'T LEGIT: You have two choices in this business. Grow a thick hide and start sending your work out, or write material for the rest of your life and never share it with anyone. The thing is, that latter choice is incompatible with the reasons you write in the first place: to express your feelings and opinions, to share them with others, hopefully through publication, and to have lots and lots of people pay money to read them. You don't want to deal with the rejection? Then let me ask you this: What's worse in your mind: having to hear "no" lots of times on the way to publishing success or never having tried?

WHAT YOU NEED TO DO: If you love them, set them free. Get your work to a level you believe is spit-polish fantabulous, listen to the voice in your head when it tells you it's time to submit, take the time to study your *Writer's Market*, proofread a zillion times, make sure your query is short and great (and that you've spelled the editor's name right), inhale deeply, and then let yourself click Send or drop the envelope into the mail. It isn't an easy moment, but you'll survive it. And, like revising your own work, the more often you force yourself to do it, the less of a big deal it will become.

TIP: When your work does get rejected—and it will—it's okay to let yourself get angry, frustrated or mildly homicidal. But it's only okay if you put a time limit on this reaction. I impose on myself a ten-minute limit. When I get a reply I didn't want to hear, I allow my emotions to boil to the surface in whatever form, but I give them only ten minutes to fester. Then I turn them into productive energy.

EXCUSE #8

It's hard to make a living writing.

WHY IT ISN'T LEGIT: It's definitely hard to make enough money from writing to do it full-time. But who says you have to do it full-time to call yourself a writer? If we measured writing success only by the ability to do it professionally, there would be very few writers. More writers than you think have their fingers in other pies.

WHAT YOU NEED TO DO: Put aside any hard-and-fast definitions of "success" you may be clinging to, like "I will write a best-selling novel" or "I will make X amount of dollars from my writing." Those kinds of concrete feats are largely beyond your control. Instead, take control of the things you can influence, like how much you write, when you write, and what ideas you submit when. Build your credentials and your profile over time. Yes, there are the Stephenie Meyer and John Grisham stories that happen every once in a while. And I wish that kind of success for you. But look at your writing career as a long-term thing. Think of all those actors who say "It took me twenty years to become an overnight success." They became overnight successes because they had the right attitude in the first place.

TIP: Whatever your day job is, when you're at work, be about work. When you're writing, be about writing. Try not to spend all your time at work talking about "what you really want to do," because you then preclude yourself from the upward progression you deserve. You might not even think about, or be aware of, how good you actually are at your job, but other people probably recognize it, so, while you're waiting for that big writing strike, allow yourself the possibility of reaping the rewards of your other talents and efforts, too.

EXCUSE #9

It seems impossible to keep track of everything.

WHY IT ISN'T LEGIT: Creative people constantly use the excuse that their creativity is at odds with the instinct for good organization. I don't buy it, and neither should you. Let's look at this simply. As I've often been heard to say, when you're well organized, you can spend more time writing and less time trying to find the stapler. And don't you want to spend your time writing?

WHAT YOU NEED TO DO: Create a simple system of organization. First, buy some folders, hanging files, vertical organizers—whatever works best for your working area—and label them according to logical categories. For example, I use categories like *Contracts*, *Submissions*, and *Correspondence*, and then I have subfolders for each. Next, organize yourself electronically. Create e-mail folders that precisely match the physical folders you've created (or at least align them as closely as possible), and start filing individual e-mails. Do the same for all your manuscripts and other documents. Don't let them sit among a vast pool of stuff, making them difficult to find, reference, and keep track of. If it's warranted, make multiple subfolders. Go as many layers down as you need to until everything is where it belongs and easy to find. It will make your life immensely easier and your writing time infinitely more fruitful.

TIP: The busier you get, the more you'll benefit from following the one-spot-for-one-thing rule. The rule is simple: Designate one spot for each important item you use, and always put it away in that same spot. Oh, sure, it seems easy, but it isn't. Try it. I guarantee you'll adore it once you get good at it. Memory sticks, pens, rulers, stamps, envelopes, CDs, keys, wallets, manuscripts—the list of things we all have to keep track of day-to-day is almost endless. But follow this rule and you'll want to kiss yourself for the ease with which you can locate things. Now if I could just convince my wife to follow it.

EXCUSE #10

I want my writing to be read and adored by millions, but I don't want to have to be an "Author."

WHY IT ISN'T LEGIT: You know how you get all annoyed when you hear movie stars whining about how they don't have any privacy? What do you say to the television when you hear them say these things? Right: "So why did you become an actor in the first place, jerk?"

WHAT YOU NEED TO DO: Understand that writers today need to put themselves out there in order to sell. You need to be a social marketer. You need to be a strategic (read: shameless) self-promoter. You need to force yourself to talk proudly and commercially about your writing at social gatherings. You need to embrace the aspirational spotlight. One of my goals is to change the perception that authors don't make good talk-show guests. Make it one of your goals, too.

TIP: Attend readings by visiting writers—at libraries, community centers, bookstores, auditoriums, wherever. Watching other authors in action will help you learn how some use the public eye to their advantage and some don't. Study the ones who do, and emulate them.

I.J. SCHECTER (www.ijschecter.com) is an award-winning author, interviewer, and essayist based in Toronto. His best-selling collection, *Slices: Observations From the Wrong Side of the Fairway* (John Wiley & Sons) is available in bookstores and online.

READING WITH A WRITER'S EYE

Read to Gain Insight Into Your Craft

....

Tania Casselle

"What's your best tip for new writers?" That's a question I've asked more than fifty authors in radio interviews, and they're often quick to reply: "Read! Read a lot. Read with a writer's eye."

It's advice that newer writers sometimes take with a grain of salt, perhaps suspecting that those already on the publishing ladder are just trying to sell more books. And even if we do take their advice, what does it mean to read with a writer's eye? We don't want to sound like someone else, we have our own voice and style. So how can reading other people's work practically help with our own writing?

First, there's the sheer inspiration of reading wonderful fiction, the motivation it gives us to jump up from the armchair and hit the keyboard. Then there's the osmosis factor—just by reading widely we absorb the art of writing, which emerges intuitively in our work. But when our intuition fails, when we're stuck in a project or realize that we need to polish up a craft area, that's the time to turn our writer's eye to our favorite fiction. Examining objectively what works successfully in a story, and how and why it works, helps us pick up tips, tricks, and techniques we can bring to our own writing problems or just give a gentle nudge to open our minds to possibilities we haven't seen before.

After all, every challenge we face in fiction has already been solved by someone else. Why reinvent the wheel? As author John Nichols says: "See how other people do it, the same way that painters go to museums and reproduce the great masters in order to understand how Rembrandt or Picasso used color and construction. The tools of the writing trade are essentially what's been written before."

DEVELOPING YOUR WRITER'S EYE

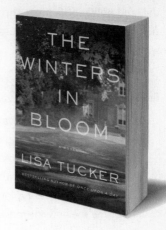

"Read the first pages of five books to see what's in common in the first pages, or the first chapters," says Lisa Tucker, author of *The Promised World* and *The Winters in Bloom*. "This is after you've read the whole book, and you understand what the story is, and you want to see how it's made the nuts and bolts."

Study how the writer creates and establishes her characters. "A lot of new writers think 'If I kill somebody on page one, I'll really have the reader.' But you won't, unless the person you kill is somebody we already care about. You need to bring characters to life quickly, especially if you're going to murder them. Then the threat is so much more important. It's a real person that's going to be killed."

Tucker noticed how Kate Atkinson's *When Will There Be Good News?* created a vivid impression of a family in the first pages, setting up the tragedy that soon befalls them. The mother, for example, is "An artist, divorced, a sort of a wild woman. You get the feeling that she has a passionate personality, there's maybe one sentence about the painting she used to do … and the fact that she used to do it… Why doesn't she do it anymore? You want to give us enough about the character that we're curious about them."

Also consider how the backstory is handled. "How much backstory must be told? Writers feel that they have to introduce everything about their backstory before they can do anything, which is not true." Tucker suggests charting out what we're told in the first pages about front story and backstory, noting the interplay between them, and writing down what we're told about every character.

If your characters feel flat, Robin Romm (*The Mother Garden*) says "Look at the way Andre Dubus or Joy Williams create character. They're using very particular traits, staying consistent, and they don't say very much. It's not a list of 'blonde hair, blue eyes, six foot five.' It's more likely to be the way somebody puts a beer can on the counter."

Romm points to Flannery O'Connor's *The Life You Save May Be Your Own*, when Mr. Shiflet strikes a match. The flame creeps closer to his skin till he puts it out just before it burns him. "O'Connor never says this is a dangerous man, but the fact that he let the match burn that long, that tiny detail is all you need."

"You read a story once and it affects you, it's a great story, but you probably don't know how or why," says Antonya Nelson, author of *Nothing Right* and *Bound*. "So you read it again and again, and you start to see how the writer has been manipulating your experience. How the writer has made conscious decisions about how to place its emphasis, how to inflect certain themes or moments." Nelson suggests looking at why a story ended where it did, and how motifs move through it. "I was struck in an Edith Wharton novel by the patient way she described a character, and realized that I was trying shortcuts with a piece I was working on."

WORD BY WORD

John Nichols (*The Empanada Brotherhood*) observes that we learn by imitation—it's how children learn language and behavior. He's taken chapters from writers he admires and typed them up, word by word. "In the process you demystify them, and you also learn a lot about how that person writes."

Lisa Tucker recalls typing out a scene from Jane Smiley's "A Thousand Acres." "It helped me see how she moved from dialogue to action. I had a problem at first thinking about incorporating gestures into dialogue. Sometimes I'd have floating heads—two characters having a discussion—and I had to remember 'Oh wait, they're doing something!' It made me understand how people look away, pick things up, make expressions, and how to fit that in with dialogue in such a smooth way."

Robert Wilder typed out Ethan Canin's story "The Year of Getting to Know Us" when he was learning to write fiction. He liked Canin's economy and wanted to understand the structure. "I was figuring it out from the inside out. It helped me enormously about scene and summary, and fed into my understanding of what makes a scene, dialogue, description, setting, details. And to literally feel what it's like to have those words coming out of your hands. Hopefully some of the structure of the prose and sentence-making ability will enter into your body." Wilder's two essay collections include *Tales From The Teachers' Lounge*, and his fiction has appeared in *The Greensboro Review*, *Colorado Review*, and *Hayden's Ferry Review*.

MENTORS & MODELS

"A lot of professors in my grad program were not crazy about my work, so I found mentorship in books," says Pam Houston, whose latest novel is *Contents May Have Shifted*. Houston read Ron Carlson, Richard Ford, Lorrie Moore, and Amy Bloom. "My contemporaries, but ahead of me in their careers. Writers who were doing things that seemed similar to what I was trying to do. I studied how they used metaphors, how they structured stories, how they made sentences."

When Houston started writing her novel *Sight Hound*, she was struggling with voice. Her previous books were essentially written in her own personal voice, but she couldn't see that approach working for *Sight Hound*. Yet it was a big leap to imagine it told from a different voice.

Houston laughs as she remembers. "I felt, God, I'm sick to death of this girl. Have you no range, Pam?" Then she saw *The Laramie Project* on stage, based on interviews with people around the murder of Matthew Shepard. "The bartender, the cop, the doctor, his parents, everybody, and they created monologues for all these characters. It's so moving, the idea of a choral community telling the story together." Houston bought the play that night and read it. "Seeing how a bunch of different voices could tell the story in the first person gave me permission to tiptoe into this idea of other voices. That's how *Sight Hound* wound up having twelve first-person narratives."

Novels from two very different writers were helpful studies for Tara Ison's debut novel. "*The Bluest Eye* by Toni Morrison was the first time I was consciously aware of the device of multiple points of view. The texture that gave the story, to use that shifting lens so seamlessly and beautifully... It was really inspiring to me." As a teen, Ison read Stephen King's *Carrie*. "It's a narrative collage, with newspaper articles and interviews, and he takes all of these elements, and weaves them together." Both informed Ison's *A Child Out of Alcatraz*.

Ison's second novel *The List* was originally written in first-person narrative voice, alternating between two characters. "It felt too claustrophobic," says Ison, so she switched gears and revisited Brian Moore's *The Lonely Passion of Judith Hearne* to see how he'd achieved a close third-person voice. (So close, in fact, that on earlier readings Ison had remembered it written in first person; she'd been surprised to realize it was in third person.) "I went back to study how he was able to make me feel so intimate to the character, yet he had the flexibility of third person. He could leave her mind when he needed to, to give us insights that the character could not have on her own."

FIRST IMPRESSIONS

"If you find a writer you love, go back and read their first novel. It's easier to see how they're made, they show their structure more clearly because the writer is not as good at hiding it. If you read *The Song Reader*, my first novel, I think it's more clear how I did it. You could make an outline and think about what I was working with, because I wasn't able to hide the bones." —Lisa Tucker

---

Pamela Erens found a model structure for her first novel *The Understory* in William Trevor's *Reading Turgenev*, where chapters of past story are interspersed with chapters of current story, and the two gradually converge.

"Trevor's book starts with a character in a bad spot, in an institution, but you don't know why. After a short chapter, you immediately jump way back in time, but the past chapters keep getting closer to the present."

Erens' character was in a different kind of institution, a Buddhist monastery, and her past story didn't sprawl back as far as Trevor's, but she immediately intuited that this was a good way to marry her material with form. "It was a very enjoyable way to bring the reader incrementally toward the present moment and explain how he got to where he was when you opened to the first page. It's reassuring to have some sort of structure to follow."

The Understory has an ominous tone which builds turn-the-page tension. Erens had already pared the writing in revisions, but during her final draft she read Camus' *The Stranger*. "It's a very short book, with a creepy sense of omission—what's being left out." Reading that made her trim back even more.

SCENE VS. SUMMARY

"Pay attention to where the writer is slowing down to put us in the moment with the character, versus when the writer is doing a summarizing sweep of time, to move us along. Identify moments of discovery, confrontation, and decision making, because I think those are the moments that express character so well, and those are the moments rich in conflict, and that's when I think it's really valuable to slow down, as opposed to summarizing for the reader." —Tara Ison

OPEN TO ENLIGHTENMENT

John Dufresne (*Requiem, Mass.*) believes that reading writers who don't write the way you do is especially useful to open up new vistas. "It snaps you out of your habitual way you write."

Dufresne's greatest difficulty as a writer is usually in finding his plot. "I start with characters, give them some trouble, then after one hundred pages of the novel ask myself: 'Well, what's the plot?'"

In turning our writer's eye on other authors' story plots, Dufresne suggests a few questions. "The first time you read it you were surprised at everything but when you got to the end you realized it was inevitable, it had to happen this way. So how did he effect that? Do you know why the character is doing what he's doing at any moment? What does he want? Why does he want it? Why is he doing this to get it? The plot emanates from the behavior of the characters … here's where the struggle begins, here's where the character tried to get what she wanted.

"I pay attention to my own emotions. Why do I love this character so much? Why do I feel so sad at this point? The writer made me feel this way or think that way, how did she do it? When was I surprised? How did she pull that surprise off?"

One way to pick up tricks of the trade is to diagram a story you admire. You can even follow that model, using your own characters and story.

"I've done this with Alice Munro," says Dufresne. "I took a story of hers and diagrammed it out and tried to write a story in exactly the same way, as an exercise… just trying to intuit what she was thinking."

INSPIRATIONS

"Dennis Cooper opened my mind on what you can actually do in a novel," says Don Waters, winner of the Iowa Short Fiction Award for his collection *Desert Gothic*. "Cooper began writing as a poet first, a novelist later. I love how in his sentences things are working! Several things can be happening in the same sentence. It's that weird thing that happens when you're striving for something, and then you see somebody else who's already done it, and something in you just physically bursts open and you think: This is it! And Cooper walks a very risky line in what he writes about. It opened my mind to what you could actually write about in terms of subject matter."

Waters recommends reading plays to study dialogue. "Like David Mamet, the master of hyperrealistic dialogue. Everything happens through dialogue in a play, characterization and how to move a plot."

While obviously it's plagiarism to copy other writers' words, there's a difference between form and content, and everyone's techniques and approaches to craft and structure are all up for grabs.

"Hemingway and Fitzgerald, they never had workshops!" says Robert Westbrook, whose novels include the series of Howard Moon Deer Mysteries. "They just read and read and loved books. If you do imitate, consciously or unconsciously, your own effort is going to come out different. It comes out with your own slant."

"What I discovered is the wonderful truth that it never sounds like the other writer," says Pamela Erens. "It sounds like yourself, and learning that really freed me up. While you're working on a story, things mutate so much that you end up with something that's your own. Every writer has a completely different consciousness and inflection. How else are you going to learn? It's a great resource. You have the whole library of literature to go to for help.

TANIA CASSELLE is freelance writer with nearly two decades of experience contributing to magazines and news media in the United States and Europe. She contributed to *Now Write! Fiction Writing Exercises from Today's Best Writers and Teachers* (Tarcher), and her fiction has appeared in lit journals including *New York Stories*, *The Saint Ann's Review*, *South Dakota Review*, *Bitter Oleander*, *Carve Magazine*, and anthologies including *Harlot Red* (Serpent's Tail Press) and *Online Writing: The Best of the First Ten Years* (Snowvigate Press). She hosts the *Writers on Radio* show for NPR-affiliate KRZA in New Mexico and Colorado, also broadcast on other stations.

ALAN DEAN FOSTER

Effective World Building

....

Janice Gable Bashman

Alan Dean Foster knows the importance of effective world building. In his original work, and in the dozens of movie tie-in novelizations he's written, Foster considers the significance of each element in his created world and how it will impact his characters. He states, "there must be a sound scientific/ecological reason for everything you create. If your aliens have tentacles instead of arms, don't just use them as arms. Consider the implications of having one instead of the other." Foster's ability to create effective worlds results in successful storytelling where great characters and their reactions to events reveal the heart of the story.

New York Times bestselling author of more than one hundred books, Alan Dean Foster is not defined by genre. He's written science fiction, fantasy, horror, historical, and contemporary fiction and nonfiction. He's known for his novelizations of numerous films, including *Star Wars*, *Star Trek*, *Transformers*, *Terminator Salvation*, *Alien*, *Clash of the Titans*, and *The Chronicles of Riddick*. His original fiction includes *Body, Inc.*; *Predators I Have Known*; and *The Human Blend*. His short fiction has appeared in all the major science fiction magazines and in several "Best of the Year" compendiums.

Why is effective world building so important?

Nothing breaks a reader's immersion in a story faster than an obvious error in world building. This holds true across all genres but is especially true for science fiction. You can insert anything you please into your imaginary world as long as you maintain the internal logic. The more realistic your invented world appears and the more consistent it becomes, the more the reader will recognize it as a reality, albeit an alternate one. It's why starships aren't powered by magic spells and light sabers have an acknowledged power source beyond potions.

When building worlds, what factors do you consider, and why are they significant?

First and foremost, everything must relate logically to everything else. If you create a jungle world where the life forms are based on something besides chlorophyll, you'd better have at least a cursory scientific explanation ready for how and why it works as it does. Building a world is akin to being a sculptor who works from the ground up: first by sculpting a skeleton, then adding muscles, then flesh, skin, and lastly, color. The great paleoartists who build dinosaur models all work this way. Viewers see only the exterior but instinctively recognize the presence of the underlying work that lends reality to the final build.

Constructing an alien world is no different. What is the world's basic chemistry? How do the life forms interact with the composition of the atmosphere, the surrounding ecology, even the geology? If you describe a world dominated by deep cave dwellers, as I do in *Flinx in Flux*, how do they interact with their surroundings? How do they find their way around? If not by batlike sonar, then what other sense might be employed? This in turn affects the physiology of the creature. If you take them out into the light, how does it affect them (if at all)?

You cannot have alien creatures shooting death rays from their eyes unless you provide a reasonable power source, a reason for them to do so (predation? defense? sexual attractant?), and an explanation of why they do it in the first place.

What happens when a writer does not pay attention to those details?

You immediately lose the reader. Or they start laughing at you. You end up with a book or film that might look wonderful on the surface, but subsequent reflection that reveals its serious flaws tells the reader that the writer did not do his homework. The reader ends up feeling cheated. That's not the emotion you want to leave your reader with after they've just finished pouring through 350 pages or shelling out fifteen bucks to see a film.

Just because a reader might not recognize an error or omission is no excuse for the writer not to address the problem. To ignore it is lazy writing, to miss it is incompetence. Midworld is a planet covered by a forest that reaches a thousand meters in height. Nitrogen is critical to tree growth. Much nitrogen is fixed in the soil by lightning, from whence it is taken up by plants. How to convey lightning three thousand feet to the ground through a dense forest? Via the voltree, which conducts it all the way to the ground. I'm neither a botanist nor a biochemist, but if it was possible to research such things in pre-internet days, it's infinitely easier now. So would-be world-builders no longer have the excuse of not being able to access necessary information.

How does effective world building help you get to the heart of the story?

Everything proceeds from the characters' immediate environment. They not only have to cope with it, they are required to react to it. Every combat story is reaction of the characters to their surroundings. The more realistic the surroundings, the greater the final impact on the story. Ask any video-game designer. Games like *Assassin's Creed*, *Skryim*, or *Lord of War* are nothing without the careful world building that has gone into them. Oftentimes teasing out the details of the invented world *is* the story. *Midworld*, *Sentenced to Prism*, and *Sagramanda* are examples of this in my own oeurve.

Science fiction is replete with hundreds of famous examples where the world is the story. Think of Arthur C. Clarke's *Rendezvous with Rama* which is, essentially, about a world. Or Larry Niven's *Ringworld*. The most famous example, and one of the great classics of science fiction, is Hal Clement's *Mission of Gravity*. In that story the characters and the plot are driven by the act of world building, one of the greatest in the genre.

Why is focusing on the human element so important when writing fiction?

Ultimately your characters are the difference between a competent work of fiction and a great work. Readers who can forget an entire plot, and (less so) the world in which a story takes place, will always remember great characters. Few people can remember the detailed plotlines of *The Three Musketeers* or many of Dickens' novels, but they can call forth the characters in a heartbeat. People may not remember the plotline of *Moby-Dick*, but they can visualize Ahab in an instant.

In the Flinx and Pip sequence of novels, which itself lies within the Commonwealth series, the main character visits dozens of worlds, each of which must be carefully constructed and thought through prior to his visit. But at the end it's the characters of Flinx and Pip whom readers remember first and foremost, no matter how exotic the worlds on which their adventures take place.

You stated that creating interesting and believable characters is the most challenging aspect of writing. What difficulties have you encountered in this process, and how did you address them?

It's easier if you've had a difficult life, if you've suffered. I haven't, and I always worry that the lack of experience with hardships makes it difficult for me to write about flawed characters. So I have to draw upon characters from real life, from devouring the news and from reading history. Heroes are as tough to create as villains, because readers want "real" heroes, and in life most heroes come by that appellation accidentally. Conan, Superman…these are simple heroes and easy to create. A believable analog to Louis Pasteur or Marie Curie is much more difficult to create and make interesting in terms of fiction.

For one book, *Cachalot*, I based every character therein on someone I knew or had met. The two main characters are based on my goddaughter and her grandmother. The polynesian local is drawn from a man named Fredo Tetuamanuhiri, a Tahitian policeman whose family I lived with in the summer of 1973. Needing a powerful industrialist, I based his character on the maitre'd of the Majestic Hotel in Kuala Lumpur. A six-foot-two gentleman of Chinese extraction, he was among the most dignified men I had ever met. And so I populated the novel.

In the case of *Bloodhype* the main character of Kitten Kai-sung, instead of being based on a real person, was created out of whole cloth because, as a fledgling scribe of twenty-six I would have delighted in meeting a six-foot knockout who was half Chinese and half Irish. Alas, she exists only as an invented character.

Is it a lot easier to show atmosphere than describe it?

Again, if the writer does his homework, the book should envelop the reader in his created atmosphere. I recommend Joseph Conrad's short novel *Typhoon*, which is essentially one long description of what it's like to endure a severe storm at sea. I defy any film to match it for creating a particular atmosphere.

Taking the other tack, we humans are visual beings. While it might take pages and pages to give even a hint of what the Grand Canyon or Angel Falls or Blupblup Island (real place) looks like, a simple snapshot does the job as well or better.

When writing novels and film novelizations, you use visualization techniques. Describe that process and why it works so well for you.

As someone who grew up learning to read from comic books and watching the early days of television (Captain Video! Captain Midnight! Rocky Jones, Space Ranger!… the not-a-captain, I guess), I've always tended to visualize everything I intend to write before I set it down in print. Within the theater of my mind I generate images of whatever is involved in the next paragraph. I create an image of a character, then I simply describe what I'm "seeing." I intended to go into film, but ended up with the cheaper medium of print. Unlimited sfx budget, though.

Besides, it's more fun to visualize a character or a scene first. That's where the enjoyment comes from; not from the act of writing. Alfred Hitchcock, when once asked how he liked directing, to the shock of the interviewer replied that he hated it. What he enjoyed was visualizing everything, every scene, in his mind. The act of directing he regarded as heavy labor, since he had already seen the film in his head. I'm the same way when I'm writing a book. It's why I hate rewriting. Perhaps one day we'll have direct mind-to-print or mind-to-video technology and the reader/viewer will be able to follow the act of creation along as it occurs.

What advice can you give to other writers about effective world building?

Find a small place on the globe of the Earth. Research it a bit. Then imagine you're there and try describing it in print. That's step one. Step two…repeat the exercise with an imaginary piece of a new world. Remember what you saw when researching that chosen bit of Earth. Are there rivers, mountains, deserts? What's the weather like? Where does the population live, how does it support itself? Must it, like so many alien worlds, have a unified world government, or is there internal dissention just like on Earth? If this sounds like an exercise in geoeconomics, it is. Everything arises from something. For example, nothing bothers me more than descriptions of advanced alien worlds replete with starships, advanced local transportation, and other wondrous technologies… but no industry, hydrology works, or electric generating plants, among other necessary basics for an advanced civilization.

Watch the film version of Carl Sagan's novel *Contact*. Building an interstellar transportation system is a lot of work. Worlds are the same way. Don't overlook the details. For every new piece of technology you introduce there should be at least a minimal explanation of its support system. For every new piece of ecology there should be an explanation of how it interacts with the rest of your new world. And for Stapeldon's sake, try to be *different*. How many SF worlds have you seen in film that look exactly like slightly altered versions of Earth? Remember: If it looks like Topeka only with funny names, it isn't SF.

Any last thoughts?

Make sure your aliens don't all sound like you. If they have Brooklyn accents, they'd better be from Brooklyn. If they're humanoid and bisymmerical, there'd better be a sound biological reason for it. One reason why *District 9* was so believable was because the aliens were…alien. Love to see their home world.

JANICE GABLE BASHMAN is co-author of *Wanted Undead or Alive*, nominated for a Bram Stoker award. She is the manging editor of *The Big Thrill*, the International Thriller Writer's e-zine. Visit Janice at janicegablebashman.com.

RAISING THE CURTAIN

Bringing Your Characters Onstage

....

Jeff Gerke

Many novelists give little thought to how they're going to lift the curtain on their main character. They begin with the character in a conversation or doing something uncharacteristic of him. Often this is because they're trying to engage the reader with action while also introducing the main character.

FIRST IMPRESSIONS

In fiction, as in life, first impressions are crucial. The first time the reader sees your protagonist, you want her doing the perfect thing, something that instantly typifies her and shows what's wonderful about her.

If you could introduce your main character in the perfect way, how would you do it? What elements differentiate your character from every other character, and consider how you can bring those out in a scene.

It's no mistake that every James Bond film begins with 007 doing something incredible to take down the bad guys or get the information he needs. There's usually a beautiful woman involved in the event as well. We get a terrific sense of who the character is (and what kind of story it's going to be) before anything else has happened.

That's what you want for your book. So let your mind hover over your character and your "story stew" a bit and think about ways you could reveal her essence in an introductory scene.

The best example I know of a great character introduction is the opening sequence from the movie *Raiders of the Lost Ark*. Remember the iconic jungle scenes? With very few words uttered, we get to see exactly what this Indiana Jones person is like. We see that he's a tough hombre who knows his way around a gun and a whip. We learn he knows a lot about ancient traps and treasures. We see his grit and daring. We feel like he could punch our lights out. We see his resourcefulness. We also see his limits, his vanity (the hat), and his fears (the snake). We even meet his nemesis.

By the end of that sequence, when he's swinging through the trees and flying away in the getaway plane, we know not only who this person is but what kind of movie this is going to be.

If it had to, this sequence could stand alone as a short film. It is a self-contained unit in and of itself, with a great story arc. The fact that it's the beginning of the movie sets the viewers' expectations. They know it's going to be a very special ride.

To bring your main character onstage the first time, pretend this is a cameo—the only time she's going to be in the story—but you want to give her an unforgettable moment of glory.

Begin with what you have identified as the essence, the core, of this person, and craft an episode around that. Keep your character's soliloquy in mind, as well as the Indiana Jones and James Bond examples, and see what you can come up with.

What elements differentiate your character from every other character? Consider how you can bring those out in a scene.

Of course it doesn't have to be an action scene. If your story is a romantic comedy, an action scene would be all wrong. Just think about what kind of book this is going to be and write a fun little scene or sequence that allows your main character to reveal who she is at heart.

This introduction is the perfect opportunity to reveal what your character is wanting or trying to achieve *and* what's likable about her. Your reader is thinking of committing days or even months to your book, and if she's going to spend three-hundred-plus pages with this character, she'd better not be a jerk. Even if she *is* a jerk and that's the whole point of her inner journey (eradicating her unpleasantness), you still have to show us something sympathetic about her in these opening moments.

THE ENTIRE CAST

Your protagonist isn't the only character you should craft a special introduction for. If you have an antagonist, that person ought to have a wonderful intro, too—perhaps in the prologue. If there is a romantic interest in your book, that person should be brought on with a carefully crafted scene to give us—and the main character—the right first impression. Sidekicks, henchmen, possible suspects, and anyone else you want to feature should get his or her own well-chosen walk-on scene.

Lesser characters should get less-developed introductory scenes, of course. Maybe it's just a moment, like a character stumbling into a room and dropping a box of doughnuts or a fabulous quick scene of a singing telegram at the door. Who can forget Dickens' introduction in *A Tale of Two Cities* to Marquis Evrémonde, who runs down a plebian child in his carriage and then curses peasants for getting in his way?

Barliman Butterburr has a small part in *The Lord of the Rings,* but it's memorable. The first time we see him he's doing exactly what he does: tending to his tavern guests. But he's kind and affable, and Tolkien created a scene that revealed Butterburr's chief characteristics, and his forgetfulness, which becomes important later.

Use that model as you're constructing introductory scenes for your featured minor characters. Give thought to how you can raise the curtain on them in their essence and doing what characterizes them.

JEFF GERKE is an editor and author of fiction and nonfiction including such books as the Operation: Firebrand novels. He is the founder of Marcher Lord Press, an indie publishing company dedicated to producing Christian science fiction and fantasy.

Excerpted from *Plot Versus Character* © 2010 by Jeff Gerke. Used with the kind permission of Writer's Digest Books, an imprint of F+W Media Inc. Visit www.writersdigestshop.com or call (800)448-0915 to obtian a copy.

RAZOR SHARP(ENING) DIALOGUE

....

Janice Hussein

Dialogue should communicate and entertain. It should be dynamic, brilliant, and fresh. It should seem authentic, and have variety, great pacing, purpose, and conflict. Dialogue is both *what* is said and *how* it's said. It is a means to an end. Novels are usually a balance of dialogue, narrative, and action, so that at least one-third to one-half of your novel could be dialogue scenes, depending on the story. That's why it's important to learn to write great dialogue.

A novel is greater than its parts; it's a stew, not a buffet. Dialogue can add spice to any scene, but remember that it also takes its flavor from the context of the story, the context of the scene, and the characters—their personalities, problems, lifestyle, outlook. Dialogue also depends on which characters the author decides will carry it, the POV that is used in any particular scene, and the story lines that converge in that scene.

HOW TO USE DIALOGUE IN STORYTELLING:

1) To move plot forward: Dialogue can be used for revelations of plot points, reversals, obstacles, and turning points. A classic example occurs in *Star Wars*, when Darth Vader tells Luke Skywalker: "I'm your father."

2) For Characterization: Dialogue can show attitudes, values, worldview, and frame of mind through the characters' speeches and reactions—what the characters say and how they say it, an indication of their tone and speech cadence, the phrases used repeatedly, their mannerisms. Dialogue can show the characters' fields of interest, current and past, of work the characters have done, of experiences which

flavor their speech—at home, in social situations, and in conversation. It can indicate race, age, and gender.

3) To provide background info for readers: Dialogue shows the past influences on the character—friends, family, transformative events, ethnicity, their socioeconomic and educational backgrounds, where they grew up, and where they currently live.

4) For description of other characters: To reveal characteristics that are perceived by those around the characters.

5) To create suspense & build tension.

6) To describe the setting: One of the four ways to reveal setting is through dialogue.

7) For pacing: A dialogue scene must be balanced by other kinds of scenes—contemplative, epiphanies, narrative, and action. Dialogue scenes speed up the pace, just as action scenes do.

8) To show, rather than tell.

TEN THINGS AN AUTHOR SHOULDN'T DO:

1) DON'T REPEAT THE NAMES.

It's distracting and unrealistic to constantly repeat the characters' names in dialogue.

> *"Marcia, the new play is tonight," John said.*
> *"But John, I think I have to work," Marcia said.*
> *"Marcia, it's opening night," John said.*

2) EXCESSIVE DIALECT.

While including dialect in the dialogue is a great way to make the story and characters come alive, the dialogue shouldn't be hard to read or make the reader backtrack to piece together what is being said. Limit the use of contractions, misspellings, slang, and colloquialisms, and be consistent with the words particular characters use. Use the flavor of your characters' dialect used to express identity, liveliness, and to provide a reflection of setting, background, ethnicity, and socioeconomic status, but don't hit them over the head with it. Readers shouldn't have to translate the dialect to understand what's being said. For example, for a Scottish brogue, an author could use the following words: *aye* for *yes*, *nay* for *no*, *dinnae* for *didn't*, *canna* for *cannot*, and *no'* for *not*, and this would help impart the flavor of the brogue, without being hard to decipher. Writers who are particularly great at writing good dialect are Amy Tan, Alice Walker, Sherman Alexie, and Susan Straight.

3) ADVERBS SHOULD BE AVOIDED.

How a phrase is said should be reflected in the context of the scene and through the dialogue itself. Instead of adverbs, use strong nouns and verbs.

There are exceptions to this rule: When the state of mind of the speaker is different from the words spoken, different from what is expected, and there's no other way to state or indicate this, an adverb may be used.

Examples:

> *"You little shit," she said, sweetly.*
> *"A present," she said in a sad, soft voice.*

4) ACTION AND NARRATIVE TAGS.

Tags with a similar format should not be repeated too much.

Examples of participles as tags:

> *"That's silly," she said, looking out the window.*
> *"Why is it silly?" he said, fiddling with his pen.*
> *"Because it's old-fashioned," she said, rising to leave.*

Other examples: "as" phrases.

> *"That's silly," she said, as she looked out the window.*
> *"Why is it silly?" he said, as he fiddled with his pen.*

And,

> *Sidde turned toward him. "Not a chance."*
> *Jeff watched Sidde brandish the Glock. "Is that necessary?"*
> *She glared at him. "You think you could step over to the door?"*

5) TOO MUCH DIALOGUE.

A novel that is written mostly in dialogue doesn't work. Dialogue is a means to an end, not the end in itself.

6) DON'T HAVE EVERYDAY KINDS OF PHRASES IN YOUR DIALOGUE:

> *How are you?*
> *I am fine.*
> *How's the weather out there?*
> *Cold and rainy.*
> *Would you like some coffee?*
> *Yes, please.*
> *Sugar or cream?*

Snore… Plus your readers will begin to skip the dialogue, and the next time your titles are up on the shelves, these same readers may skip your next book. The above dialogue has nothing of real interest going on—no conflict, no character development, no suspense—unless the reader is burning to know if someone wants sugar or cream.

7) DON'T MIX THE ACTION OF ONE CHARACTER WITH THE DIALOGUE OF ANOTHER, WITHOUT A DIALOGUE TAG.

Example:

> *"Have you seen my red high heels?" David walked to the closet to check there.*

Readers "attribute" the dialogue in the paragraph to the first character that is mentioned doing the action—in this case, David. But is David looking for his own red high heels?

8) DON'T HAVE TWO CHARACTERS SPEAKING IN THE SAME PARAGRAPH.

Begin a new paragraph with each new speaker and his or her dialogue. There are exceptions to this rule. For example, when two characters start to speak at the same time:

> *"What color was the car?" the detective asked the couple.*
> *"Grey," Linda answered, while at the same time, Scott said, "Blue."*

9) UNLESS YOU'RE USING SILENCE OR SOME OTHER NONVERBAL RESPONSE, DON'T HAVE JUST ONE CHARACTER TALKING.

Dialogue implies a give-and-take, a back-and-forth exchange, a conversation. Reading the dialogue out loud will help identify passages where another character should be responding and is not.

10) DON'T CLUTTER THE DIALOGUE.

When a dialogue scene becomes unfocused and the pace slows too much, one or more problems may be occurring: uninteresting dialogue that lacks momentum or purpose; too much (or too little) action, setting, backstory, or internal dialogue; too many dialogue tags; or too many narrative or action tags. The author needs to identify the purpose of the particular passage of dialogue, which will help to focus the scene. It might be necessary to cut the passage down to bare bones before you begin to add elements back in.

TEN EASY THINGS TO MAKE DIALOGUE BETTER:

1) Silence: Use gesture, have characters nod in response, or have them make no response, while simply continuing to do what they were doing. This can add a sense of either distance or intimacy to the relationships or conversation.

2) Eavesdropping. Many writing instructors suggest eavesdropping. Listen for how people talk, for the specialized words that are used. For example, listening to teenagers in order to write young adult fiction. At the same time, identify what makes you *want* to listen…or not?

3) Conflict. Dialogue should have conflict. Build tension in the scene until the moment when something important is revealed in the dialogue, something the protagonist must react to.

4) Idiom. Using the jargon of the story world, or of a particular character's world, lends realism to the scene, story, and characters.

5) Omit words from the dialogue. Elmore Leonard does this exceptionally well. His dialogue makes his characters seem real—they come alive on the page. For example, the dialogue omits nouns at the beginning of sentences, and omits pronouns like *who* and *that* within sentences. But much more than that, the characters speak a kind of shorthand, which helps make the author's dialogue swift and razor sharp.

6) Read it out loud, for cadence, for rhythm, for realism.

7) Use dialogue for conveying descriptions, history, and background instead of long narrative passages. Strong details in the dialogue can portray a more realistic sense of the fictional world.

8) Subtext and foreshadowing: What isn't said, what is hinted at, what is avoided, what is lied about—all these reactions create suspense and conflict.

9) Have your characters say what they must say because of who they are, how they would say it.

10) Balance dialogue, narrative, and action in your scenes. Weaving together a combination of the three is the best way to engage readers emotionally in a scene. Use dialogue-only, narrative-only, or action-only scenes only when you want to focus on something of particular importance. Doing so brings the readers' attention to specific actions, events, or characteristics.

PACING WITHIN YOUR DIALOGUE SCENE:

Adding dialogue tags, descriptions, narrative and action are ways to pace the dialogue. Just adding dialogue tags like *said* creates pauses in the dialogue, and slows it down. Straight dialogue is the faster pace. A faster pace can imply danger or it can focus readers on a particular character or event.

Pace can be controlled by whether an author uses regular dialogue like conversations or a narrative dialogue. Regular dialogue puts the readers into the scene and is immediate. It is one of the best ways to pull readers into a scene. But sometimes a longer passage of regular dialogue isn't needed and would take up too much space without any real benefit, depending on the purpose of the scene and dialogue. This is where narrative dialogue can summarize what would otherwise require a longer sequence of spoken dialogue, and speed up the pace. Sometimes a combination of regular and narrative dialogues is effective. An example of this combination:

> "There are three motion detectors near the painting," he said, "and two more in the farthest room there." The curator pointed to a small enclave with glass doors. He then went on [narrative dialogue begins] to describe the most vulnerable areas in the museum, the most valuable artwork, the schedules of the security personnel, and the locations of their three safes.

USING DIALOGUE TAGS & FORMATTING:

Dialogue tags should be kept simple. The word said is the *best* and most used dialogue tag. It fades into the background. Anything else is considered somewhat distracting. Examples:

> "Why did he leave?" she said. "I don't want to be responsible for this."
> "If you're done," he said, "there is other work I should be doing."

However, there are exceptions to this rule. Other dialogue tags have their place, just as adverbs sometimes have a place: when what a character says is different from what is expected, or when there's no other way to state or indicate this within the context of the scene. They also help when you want to impart a value such as humor or sarcasm—an undertone of attitudes within a scene, or in reaction to something that is said or to someone who is speaking. For example: "That's not the point," he muttered. The context of the scene wouldn't indicate the way this character says these words.

Dialogue tags don't have to be used each time someone speaks. If it's obvious who the speaker is, an author can omit the tags for part of the dialogue. This will speed up the pace and is a good technique for introducing conflict or humor, or focusing the readers' attention.

Example:

> "I don't have the keys," Ava said.
> "Where are they?" John said.
> "I think I dropped them on the trail somewhere."
> "Please, don't tell me that!"

Or, if it's first person, then:

> Everyone pauses, then Mary says, "I hear you got engaged."
> "And married. But our pets would like a divorce—he has a cat, I have a dog."

"A case of irreconcilable differences, then."

Other things can affect the pace and dynamic of dialogue. Experiment with varying where the tags appear in the dialogue: first, middle, last. You can make use of shifts in the dialogue—echoing, interruptions, shifts in tone, or changing the subject. Doing so makes the dialogue more dynamic, and also alters the pace. Another technique is to have the characters answer a question with a question.

To illustrate some of these things, I offer an excerpt from my short story, *Ghost of a Chance,* about a ghost (from *his* POV) with a mortal girlfriend and a rival, during an en Plein Air writing function. (Full text of dialogue example: http://bit.ly/rCuoSZ)

> *"Well, you can't say I'm walking 'out of your life' again." Danielle leaned her arms on the white railing, gazing toward Mt. Adams, Mt. Hood. He stood beside her.*
>
> *"Okay, who would you chose if you were on the other side?" he said.*
>
> *"Why do you appear only during the Plein Air?"*
>
> *Ross sighed. "It's all the creativity, openness to possibilities. And a little wine probably doesn't hurt. I'm more likely to be seen."*
>
> *"Liar. Isn't there some rule for ghosts where you must tell the truth?" she said, arching a brow, smiling up at him.*
>
> *"Gees, woman. Why would you think there's another reason?"*

Writing strong dialogue will make your characters and novel much more engaging, as any agent will tell you. When you're writing, ask yourself these questions: "What is the point of this dialogue?" and "What am I trying to achieve in this scene?" Once you have that focus, then above all, be creative with it. Put aside your inner critique. Nothing is set in stone. Then use these techniques and guidelines to razor-sharpen that dialogue.

....

JANICE HUSSEIN has worked nine years as a professional freelance editor and three years for a literary agent. Her published articles on the writing craft have been featured in *Writer's Digest, Novel & Short Story Writer's Market,* and the *Romance Writer's Report.* She offers classes and workshops through her website www.documentdriven.com.

....

KNOW YOUR ANTAGONIST

Jack Smith

You have a protagonist in mind, but what does this protagonist want? What stands in his or her way? The antagonist serves this function of standing in the way, of blocking the protagonist from achieving a particular goal. But what makes a good antagonist? How can you make antagonists come alive in your fiction? What are some principles you can use to develop strong, compelling, and believable antagonists? Do you even need an antagonist?

DEVELOPING COMPELLING, BELIEVABLE ANTAGONISTS

For Catherine Brady, award-winning short story writer and author of *Story Logic and the Craft of Fiction*, a compelling antagonist is one who is as "complicated" as the story's protagonist. Just as the protagonist must be a "round" versus a "flat" character, in E.M. Forster's terms, so must the antagonist, says Brady. "If the antagonist is a stock figure, then readers won't be able to believe that he can generate real conflict for the protagonist." More specifically: "If we can size up the heroine's husband as a manipulative, belligerent drunk right from the start of the story, we won't be able to sympathize with her inability to leave him or to understand her conflict over doing so."

Lise Haines, author of three literary novels, including *Small Acts of Sex and Electricity*, also sees the compelling antagonist as one with complexity of character. She suggests that "compelling, believable antagonists have much at stake, clear flaws and contradictions, and act out a complicated relationship with the protagonist." She cites as an example her "dark, apocalyptic satire, *Girl in the Arena*," which "freights an alternate history in which neogladiator sport is now as big as the NFL. Uber, my antagonist, is a young fighter pitted against an opponent named Tommy, whom he admires and emulates. When Uber slays Tommy, he is expected to marry Tommy's daughter, Lyn, and of course Lyn, my protagonist, hates Uber for taking Tommy away. Uber is both fighter and clumsy suitor; a man trying to get things right yet aware that as a killer, he creates constant sorrow, as a victor, joy."

Geoffrey Clark, author of several novels and story collections, also stresses that the antagonist should be a round character—a realistic one instead of a "consciously symbolic" one. Thus the writer should be careful not "to make an antagonist totally vile and evil; you don't want him/her to be just a kind of case study in pathology." Instead, says Clark, an antagonist "needs a spark of humanity." Looking back on his third book, *Schooling the Spirit*, a novella and six stories, he believes that his antagonist was a flat character: "a very nasty guy, clearly a villain who has no redeeming qualities: he's simply loutish and brutal." In contrast, in his most recent novel, *Two, Two, Lily-White Boys*, Clark feels he has a much stronger antagonist: a young man by the name of Russell "Curly" Norrys, "14 or 15 or maybe 16—everything about him is ambiguous." Capable of contradictory behaviors, Curly "can be moved to tears by the end of Chekhov's 'Grief,' then be unspeakably cruel to his companions, even to the point of murder (though even that is ambiguous)." Clark appreciates such ambiguity, and this he discovered through non-rational, intuitive means: "Though Curly may be beyond definition by the reader (as he is by the writer) I think I got him right: I trusted instinct beyond intellect; imagination rather than will."

Finding humanity in his antagonists is also important to DeWitt Henry, author of *The Marriage of Anna Maye Potts,* winner of the Peter Taylor Prize for the Novel. "Antagonists usually embody my own worst characteristics or impulses, while protagonists, my best, but then in the process of storytelling, I discover humanizing (if not redeeming) characteristics in the person I first meant to condemn." Henry finds Richard Yates's antagonists more to his liking than the "daemonic antagonists" he finds in the work of William Styron "or even Robert Stone." He seeks a deeper ambivalence in the reader: "By nature, I follow Richard Yates when he says: 'I much prefer the kind of story where the reader is left wondering who's to blame until it begins to dawn on him (the reader) that he himself must bear some of the responsibility because he's human and therefore infinitely fallible.' Think of the insufferable Mrs. Givings in Yates's *Revolutionary Road*, whom Yates said he "kinda loved."

Perhaps Ellen Sussman, author of the novel *French Lessons*, has something similar in mind: "I think the challenge for writers is to love their antagonists." This means complexity—a multidimensional character: "We have to find something about this person that is so engaging or compelling," says Sussman, "that we have to get to know them and we love watching them in action. Beginning writers often create villains who are terrible—and that results in a two-dimensional character." In creating her antagonists, Sussman goes for paradox: "I want a villain who is terrible and wonderful! Then you're on your road to creating a believable character and one who will carry the story."

Tim Johnston, author of *Irish Girl: Stories*, winner of the Katherine Anne Porter Prize in Short Fiction, emphasizes another key aspect of Forster's round character: the ability to change. For Johnston, the antagonist must not be a static character, just as the protagonist must not be. This means an element of mystery: "I also happen to believe there should always be some mystery about such characters (mystery about all characters, perhaps); that the antagonist should not be a purely antagonistic force in the story, but ought to change shape, by which I mean behavior, the way all good characters change shape in the course of good stories or novels." This change of behavior must be incremental, not sudden, says Johnston. In great works of fiction, "the revelation of what is antagonistic about the antagonist is a gradual one; a slow unveiling of character from Ordinary Citizen of The Story, to Primary Bad Guy."

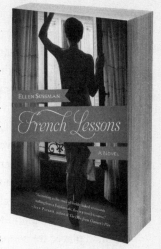

The element of surprise is another aspect of Forster's round character. Steven Schwartz is fiction editor for *Colorado Review* and professor of creative writing at Colorado State University and in the Warren Wilson MFA Program. "Successful antagonists," states Schwartz, "are those who keep you guessing as to their true motivations, their trustworthiness, their capacity for good and ill—and the line between these two behaviors." Kristen-Paige Madonia, author of the young adult novel *Fingerprints of You*, also looks for this element of surprise: "For me, the best antagonists are never predictable, and though we know they are, at their root, working against the successes of the protagonist, an antagonist's behavior should surprise the reader."

Josh Weil is author of *The New Valley*, published by Grove/Atlantic in 2009, and winner of the Sue Kaufman Award for First Fiction from the American Academy of Arts & Letters. Weil makes a distinction between the believable and the compelling antagonist. "An antagonist has to be driven by wounds, wants, and emotions just as organically as any other character. If those wounds are honestly dealt with, and the character's actions are addressing them, then the antagonist will be believable. For an antagonist to be compelling, those wounds, desires, needs have to be in conflict with what the protagonist wants." The antagonist will be compelling if this character acts as "the largest, most threatening obstacle standing in the way of the protagonist's goal."

ANTAGONISTS—FROM STORY TO STORY

Antagonists include a wide range of types, as Lise Haines points out. "In *Fight Club* we see a man pitted against his unleashed self; in *Virgin Suicides* a chorus of sisters go against the fragile yet hard-coated, Crucifix-bearing mother; in *Madame Bovary* we have the boring country doctor and the rake, but isn't this ultimately a story of Emma fighting the antagonist of wealth, stature, and a life filled with beauty; Humbert Humbert confronts the two-headed monster of mother and daughter along with his double, Clare Quilty; and so on."

Given such a wide range of antagonist types, how do you apply a general principle—a complex character with the ability to change and surprise—to varying story dynamics? Do different stories call for different modifications of these principles? For Josh Weil, certain core values won't vary. But the need for an antagonist will: "Some stories—many, in fact—might be better served by not trying to simplify and compress obstacles and thematic elements into one character. So writers working on less traditional narratives might do best to cast a wary eye on the idea of an antagonist." If an antagonist *is* needed, Weil points out a possible exception in the treatment: perhaps "a purposefully cartoonish or flat antagonist played for comic effect." "Though, even then," says Weil, "I think adding depth by grounding the character in core needs and desires will only enrich the antagonist and the story, even the humor."

What will certainly change from story to story, from antagonist to antagonist, is the character arc, states Ellen Sussman. "Does he or she change? Is he or she affected by the plot and transformed in some real way? The deeper the story, the more possibilities there might be for the antagonist to develop as a character." The arc can indeed change, Tim Johnston states, noting an exception to his gradual change idea in Flannery O'Connor's "A Good Man Is Hard to Find." In this story, the Misfit, says Johnston, "arrives on the scene with all his badness already in place, and thereafter is revealed, through O'Connor's extraordinary deftness with character and dialogue, to possess a depth of humanity no other God- and law-abiding character in the story comes close to matching—unless it is the grandmother herself, who undergoes her own astounding transformation in that lovely and grim fable."

Steven Schwartz reminds writers that change depends on character. Antagonists change "as much as one character varies from another. Remember that the biggest mistake a beginning writer makes about antagonists is to presume their guilt from the get-go." He cites as provocative examples Becky Sharp in *Vanity Fair*, the Misfit in O'Connor's story, and O'Brien in *1984*. "Each of these antagonists is distinct from the other, perfectly suited to their often opaque ends. Antagonists may be familiar and warm, cold and aloof, peculiar and mystifying, or any other combination of characteristics. But what they all have in common— and this can't be overstated—is to relentlessly enforce their will on those around them."

THINGS TO AVOID

When you realize what makes a compelling, believable antagonist—what those features are—think oppositely for what to avoid.

One is stereotypes. Stereotypical antagonists present a major problem, says Kristen-Paige Madonia: "A story will fall flat if characters are stereotyped because the reader will lose interest. Of course, a reader doesn't have to like every character in a novel or a story—in fact, it's much more interesting if they don't. But liking a character is different than believing the character and their actions are authentic and motivated by valid emotions."

Illuminating this point further, Steven Schwartz points out that "stereotypical or contrived creations who speak in blisteringly bad dialogue" make for a definite problem. "When people hear *antagonists*, they sometimes think *caricatures*. But antagonists, though they might be villainous, must first be human. As a writer, conceive not of these characters by viewing them from the outside, but from the inside; that is, from one's own being, unpleasant as that may be to recognize."

The good/bad dichotomy, then, needs to be avoided. Catherine Brady puts it this way: "In creating effective antagonists, it's easy to make the mistake of assuming the antagonist must be the 'bad' character, the protagonist the 'good.'" An antagonist, says Brady, "represents a very potent external obstacle for the protagonist, but what the antagonist has to be capable of doing is opposing the protagonist in a way that generates strong internal conflict; his job is to make the hero's choices more difficult." But what if your antagonist *is* absolutely bad—what then? Brady's solution is this: "If your antagonist is genuinely a diabolical creature, then you have to be sure that something else about the dramatic situation generates difficulty for the protagonist: Is the protagonist or the reader seduced by this bad boy? Or does the protagonist mistake what it will cost to defeat him?" For Brady, in most cases, the antagonist should be seen in more complex terms than the simple good/bad category allows. "More often, antagonists are not absolutely evil, only misguided creatures convinced of their own rightness, or creatures whose evil is disturbingly mixed with traits that they share with us—the con artist who always remembers to send flowers to his wife on her birthday." It works well, says Brady, to "grant some credibility" to your antagonist's perspective and "to avoid an ending in which the antagonist is unmasked as unequivocally wrong. You don't want to solve the mystery of this person's moral or spiritual failings for the reader; you want the reader to continue to be troubled by them long after the action ends."

In writing her novel *Towelhead*, Alicia Erian was tempted to create an absolutely evil antagonist. "I really was compelled by my anger toward my abusive father. Having said that, I was also smart enough to know that if I didn't find some way to make the Daddy character multifaceted, my book would stink. So I grudgingly and resentfully tried to round him out. Even I liked him in the end, which made me angry!" But as she points out: "As a reader, I love being tossed around. I love being forced to ask myself why it is that I'm willing to give credit to a jerk. This is an engaging and interesting way to respond to a story, I think." And this is surely because this ambivalence will cause the reader to be more "troubled," as Brady says, than an "unequivocally wrong" antagonist would.

Avoid melodrama, says DeWitt Henry. He admits that it's "always a temptation, with good opposing evil, hero opposing villain." His novel presented this problem: "The template of *Anna Maye* is probably Cinderella, for instance. But the discipline of fiction demands that the author grow past simple oppositions." Henry's solution was for his two major antagonists, Mary and Louie, to become complex versus one-dimensional melodramatic figures: "In their meanest or most selfish acts, both Mary and Louie rationalize. They think they mean well, mostly."

The problem of the one-dimensional antagonist may result from the antagonist being conceived of as a mere contrivance, or a "tool in the narrative," says Josh Weil. For him, it works this way: "If the character arises naturally from the protagonist's struggles then that's a good sign. If the protagonist isn't struggling enough and the writer feels a need to throw another obstacle in there, the temptation to use a character as a tool that way should send up some red flags."

STORIES WITHOUT ANTAGONISTS

Do some stories *not* need an antagonist—as Josh Weil has suggested? Steven Schwartz places the issue in this context: "In the age of voice-driven and lyrical narratives, contemporary short story writers are as reluctant to use such an old-fashioned term as *antagonist,* just as they are *plot.* The fact remains, however, that your main character has to face adversity, which usually comes in the form of an antagonist."

Perspectives on this question do vary. Dennis Vannatta, author of three short story collections, states: "I can't recall ever creating an antagonist in a piece of fiction. I just don't think in those terms." Dennis Must, author of two story collections, makes a similar comment: "When writing a story, I honestly don't think of protagonists or antagonists, finding the definitions too self-limiting. In most of my work where conflict is created between two characters, the denouement often ends up equivocally. The roles of protagonist and antagonist are frequently interchangeable."

Anjali Banerjee, author of several commercial works of fiction, both literary and young adult, doesn't think in terms of protagonist/antagonist either—at least not in the traditional sense. The antagonist becomes a psychic projection of her main character. She states: "Maybe the visible antagonist is a function of the concrete/external plot. In other words, often the protagonist has an internal emotional arc in the story and an external, concrete goal. The antagonist as a concrete character is a way to 'push back' against the concrete goal, but the antagonist also represents the darkest aspect—or weakness—in the hero."

Robert Stewart, editor of *New Letters*, provocatively shifts the attention not only from the protagonist/antagonist issue but from story dynamics and even character: "I have little

interest in a protagonist's function in a story, or the story dynamics. I am interested in how the story uses language, which, of course, includes dialogue, which defines the character. The language (including dialogue) of a story needs to reveal an authentic, honest voice, whether abrasive, endearing, or quirky. Anything conventional or generalized is deadly, to me. Just take a look at Ree Dolly in Daniel Woodrell's *Winter's Bone* or Caulfield in *The Catcher in the Rye*, as characters of different cultures. Each character is on a kind of quest, but that, in itself, is not the reason we care about them. Every word they speak defines them as distinct individuals and also as products of their particular worlds. I don't know how that's done, except that it can't be ordered up easily. The writer learns this trick by reading slowly and deeply."

Thaisa Frank, author of the literary novel *Heidegger's Glasses*, thinks in terms of voice, not character. She states, "As a voice-driven writer, rather than a character-driven writer, I'm not good at thinking about characters. My characters show up after I've fooled around with the story. There are two characters in *Heidegger's Glasses* that are antagonists. One is Stumpf and the other is Mueller. They honestly just came to me as a result of being in the setting and the situation."

Her process goes like this: "Especially in a novel I visualize them and feel them kinesthetically—feel how they move in the world. But I start with a title and have a place or a setting. It's almost as though I have to create a setting so they know where to come. I think of them as out-of-work characters in character-land, just like actors who want a part in a play. I don't know quite how they show up. Some of them have bodies and faces I've never seen, and others look remarkably like people I know. Once I get a sense of how a character moves through space—a sense of embodiment, which is always accompanied by a vision of a face and a body—they start to talk and do things for me. Later, of course, I fill them out by giving them more situations to act in—to be more villainous, to be more heroic, or just to speak more naturally. But by the time I do this, the story is fleshed out and they're reacting to the situation. In some of my short stories and my flash fiction, I only have a kinesthetic sense of them. In both short stories and flash fiction it's easier to construct something by following the voice. Sometimes a visualization comes and at other times they're almost allegorical. However it works—I'm always very grateful to them for showing up and wanting work, even when I don't want to work. And when I live with them for a long time—as I did in *Heidegger's Glasses*—they become very real to me."

For Thaisa Frank, all of her characters "show up" at some point in the process. She doesn't concern herself with the story dynamics, with character as such, but she depends on voice. And so the question of the antagonist's one-dimensionality, or multidimensionality, isn't a question she ever takes up. She trusts the process, hears the voice, and follows it.

SOME FINAL THOUGHTS

For writers who do focus more on character, and on various story dynamics, the role of both protagonist and antagonist becomes quite important. And they generally agree on one thing: Don't reduce the matter to good and bad. Create levels in both protagonist and antagonist. And complicate, perplex. Alicia Erian offers this provocative thought: "The best antagonists are the ones who leave the reader saying, 'Am I supposed to like this person? Because I'm not sure that I do. Maybe I do. But I don't think so." And a great piece of advice: "Practically speaking, I think that a great exercise is to base a character on someone you truly dislike in real life, because then you will be forced to redeem them in some way, in order to make your story work."

JACK SMITH's satirical novel *Hog to Hog* (Texas Review Press) won the George Garrett Fiction Prize. His stories and essays have appeared in many publications, including *North American Review*, *The Southern Review*, *Georgia Review*, and *Ploughshares*. Besides his writing, he co-edits *The Green Hills Literary Lantern*.

CHRISTOPHER GOLDEN

Weaving Character, Structure, and Theme

....

Janice Gable Bashman

For bestselling author Christopher Golden, "every compelling work of fiction is an intricate weave of character, structure, and theme." Readers must identify with the characters, the story structure must take the reader from page to page, and the theme should serve a purpose. Without these three elements in a work of fiction, the reader is "lost."

There are more than eight million copies of Christopher Golden's books in print. He writes novels for adults and teens (*Of Saints and Shadows*, *The Secret Journeys of Jack London*, *Strangewood*, and others) and collaborates with writers on books, comics, and scripts with authors such as Charlaine Harris (*Cemetery Girl* graphic novel trilogy), Tim Lebbon (Jack London books for young adults), Mike Mignola (*Baltimore, Or, The Steadfast Tin Soldier and the Vampire*), and Thomas E. Sniegoski (*Outcast* and *The Menagerie*). Golden is the editor of numerous anthologies, including *The New Dead*, *The Monster's Corner*, and *British Invasion*. He's also written media tie-ins for *Buffy the Vampire Slayer*, *Hellboy*, *Star Wars*, *X-Men*, and others.

How does weaving an intricate web of character, structure, and theme create incredible storytelling?

The point of that statement is that all three things are vital to a compelling story, at least from my perspective. A story or novel must have characters that are engaging and interesting and who are fascinating either because you find yourself identifying and sympathizing with them, or repelled by them. You must present readers with characters they will like, or even love, or with characters they will despise enough to love reading about them. A combination of the two is even better. With structure, you're talking about plot and pacing, and obviously that means you need a story with momentum, a structure that balances quiet and loud, that provides enough heart to carry the reader through the intimate moments, and enough tension to have them turning pages and reluctant to stop reading at the end of a scene or chapter. Some may disagree with me about the necessity of theme, but I don't want a hollow story. I want to read something that is about more than just the plot, about more than just putting the characters through their paces. Theme doesn't have to be evident on the surface, but when the writer is exploring something, you can usually feel the weight behind the words. When you have all three of these things, and they are skillfully balanced, that's when you have a truly memorable reading experience. I'm presently reading *The Night Circus* by Erin Morgenstern, and it's a wonderful example, at least at the one-hundred-page mark I've reached in my reading.

How do you accomplish this in your work?

I'm not sure I always do, but it's certainly something I strive for. I approach the writing process with both my heart and my head. I'm plotting with purpose, but if I feel the story or the characters wanting to go in a different direction, wanting to do something I hadn't considered, I'll gladly follow. Sometimes that works and sometimes it doesn't. Beyond that, I often ask myself what, exactly, I'm writing about. Beyond the superficial, what are these characters going through that speaks to me—that examines something in my own life. I'm not preaching or lecturing anybody, but I think we're all wrestling with questions about our world and living, or dying, in it. If your characters aren't doing the same, they're just not going to be as interesting to me. Even if a character is in the midst of an argument, or a battle, or a moment of self-doubt, I will sometimes close my eyes at my keyboard and try to imagine myself in their shoes. My heart speeds up. I can feel their fear or worry or heartache or anger or disdain, and I try to translate that into print. One of the places where I feel I accomplished this best was in my novel *The Ferryman*. I was going through a period where I obsessed about dying, and I've often said *The Ferryman* is four hundred pages of me coming to terms with that fear. Those who read my upcoming collaboration with Mike Mignola, *Joe Golem and the Drowning City*, will find that in the midst of its horrors and marvels and mystery, it's about humanity.

What happens when one of the elements (character, structure, theme) is not done well, and how does that impact the other two elements, and the story?

Well, certainly there are plenty of novels that are a pleasure to read but don't have perfect execution of all three elements. And I know people will argue about the necessity of theme. But I'm not suggesting that every story must have some didactic lesson. One of the best books I've read this year was *Robopocalypse* by Daniel H. Wilson. It's an incredibly compelling novel, and some might want to chalk that up to the plot and pacing alone. But if you stripped away the wonderful characters and the way that Wilson draws us in and makes us feel what they're feeling or worry for them even when they don't know enough to be worried for themselves, or if you removed the element of the story that is a cautionary tale about how reliant we're becoming on technology and about playing God, you'd be left with a generic "robot fighting video game" of a novel. Having all three elements adds depth and texture; it draws the reader in and connects on different levels, doing something more than simply entertaining.

How can a writer ensure that readers identify with the characters?

A million little ways, but all of them should come from a real place, rather than some shallow interest in constructing a character. If you want the reader to know and feel a character, to believe in them, then you—the writer—must know and feel and believe in them as well. Dean Koontz wrote a nonfiction book, now long out of print, called something like *How to Write Bestselling Fiction*. In that book, he detailed an exercise that consisted of creating a character window, a history for a character that only you—the writer—will know. What is the most embarrassing thing that has ever happened to your character? Their most cherished memory? Best childhood friend? Family members and jobs and favorite colors, pet peeves and secret passions and ambitions? Even if you never use those things in the course of the book, the more you know the character, the more you will be able to make their emotions and behavior feel real and natural. I haven't actively used Koontz's method in fifteen years or more, but I think that you get to the point where you learn how to connect with your characters. That way, if the plot demands they behave one way, you'll just *know* if they really ought to be doing something else. Characters and plot grow organically together, each affecting the other. Does the character's behavior feel genuine? If this was a real person, someone you knew in your own life, and some third person told you they had done or said "X," would you believe it of them? If not, you're not being true to your characters.

You stated, "writing a novel is creating an entire world, with all the textures and visuals and themes and heart contained within the worlds." What difficulties have you encountered during this process, and how did you overcome them?

Honestly, I think we know when we're cutting corners. I certainly do, at least. The writer's worst enemy is laziness, whether it be not wanting to do the research or not fully exploring elements that really require it for the book to be the best it can be. I've caught myself plenty of times, and sometimes I've been frustrated by that, but only for a day. Once I get going on fixing the problem, on making the story what it should have been all along, I always feel better about it, and am glad that I took the time. I wrote a big fat thriller called *The Ocean Dark*, under the pseudonym Jack Rogan. The first draft, it was really a horror novel, but that was not at all the book that I had sold to my editor, and promised her. I had cheated myself. Maybe I doubted my ability to really deliver on my ambition for the book. She did me the biggest favor in the world by coming back and telling me exactly that, and as soon as she did so, it was like a dam giving way. I knew everything that needed doing in that book. It grew 50 percent longer. Characters' backstories were explored; new characters were introduced who became my favorite characters. The scale of the entire novel grew exponentially because I went back and explored all of the textures and visuals and themes and, yes, the heart of the story, and the world I was writing it in.

Although you've written in many genres, and written them well, you prefer writing fantasy and about monsters. Why?

I always have. I grew up on horror movies and scary stories and comic books and fantasy novels. Robert R. McCammon said, many years ago, that what he loved about horror was that in the context of horror, you could write about anything—love, hate, sex, death, loss, etc. I've always subscribed to that belief. I also think that when we write about monsters, it's a wonderful, twisted mirror we're holding up to ourselves, to humanity. And when we write about ghosts and angels and demons, we're exploring the edges of our ability to believe in spirituality and an afterlife. When I was a kid, my mother asked me why I couldn't write something "good," by which she meant something…nicer. I told her that I'd written love stories and westerns and science fiction, but that somebody always dies. And ain't that the truth? I guess I'm just wired like this.

After working together with a lot of writers, what are some great writing tips that you've learned from them along the way?

Tips. Hmm. Tom Sniegoski taught me how to write comics, but that's not a tip, really. Mike Mignola taught me that you don't always have to have an explanation for the magical, and that's a damn fine tip for writing, or just for living your life.

What advice can you give to other writers about weaving character, structure, and theme?

Only that it is a balance of skill and instinct, and both can be developed with work and focus. Don't be afraid to let your characters change, even if that means the structure of the story will also change. You have to be fluid. There is nothing better for a novel than allowing yourself to discover avenues you hadn't even considered exploring and to find facets in your own work that you didn't know were there. Some thematic elements aren't there at the beginning. We often aren't even aware of how much of what we feel is coming out in our work, at least at first. I can't begin to tell you how many times I've been writing a short story or a novel and gotten halfway or two-thirds of the way through before I realized what it was I was *really* writing about, and that can be daunting and thrilling in equal measure. It usually means going back and revising what you've already done, but it makes something entirely new and wonderful out of the finished product. My novel *Strangewood* remains one of my personal favorites, and I know it would be a pale shadow of itself if I had been reluctant to follow the inspiration—no, the revelation—I had when I had already written two-thirds of the book. I realized, quite abruptly, that what I was really writing about was what it meant to me to have had the father I had and to have become a father myself. It's about love and personal sacrifice, and neglect, and what it really means to be a parent. At least, that's what it's about for me.

....

JANICE GABLE BASHMAN is co-author of *Wanted Undead or Alive*, nominated for a Bram Stoker award. She is the manging editor of *The Big Thrill*, the International Thriller Writer's ezine. Visit Janice at janicegablebashman.com.

....

CRAFTING EMOTION

How to Make Your Story Resonate With Readers

....

Donald Maass

A story's action generates in readers excitement and interest. Conflict—especially micro-tension—keeps readers involved. Associative devices like metaphor, simile, symbols, parallels, reversals, and references contribute a sense of meaning. Meaning itself in the form of theme is necessary for high impact.

But what is it that moves readers' hearts? What conjures in readers' imaginations a reality that, for a while, feels more real than their own lives? What glues readers to characters and makes those characters objects of identification: people with whom readers feel intimately involved, about whom they care, and whose outcomes matter greatly?

Emotions. When readers feel little or nothing, then a story is just a collection of words. It's empty. To foster reader involvement and accomplish with a novel that which you desire, it's first critical to map an emotional landscape across which readers will travel. Readers must feel that they are on a journey, one with felt significance and destination that we can sum up as change.

There is in some literary circles a suspicion that emotions on the page are bad. This Hemingway-like way of looking at it values imagery, restraint, subtext, and suggestiveness. Raw emotions written out are artless. Emotions evoked are artful, particularly when a given emotion has no name but nevertheless feels covertly real. You don't need to name it. Indeed, don't. But make your readers experience something "true," as in accurate.

Look, there's nothing wrong with restraint. Working with subtext is artful. Familiar emotions, especially when in neon lights, have little effect on readers. By contrast, going sideways to explore secondary and nuanced emotions can bring a fictional moment ferociously alive. I'm not against artfulness. I'm for it because it works. But eschewing emotions as a style, in the false belief that a drought somehow quenches thirst, is too often an excuse for a novelist to hide behind. Sere writing can be as mannered and false, in its way, as the most purple genre fare.

To create a novel's emotional landscape you must first open yourself to your own. That's hard to do. If it's difficult to confide your feelings to those close to you, consider how much more fearful it is to do that with strangers. But that's what you're doing. Whether you're aware of it or not, there is wired inside you a terror of exposing yourself to embarrassment, shame, and ridicule. But here you are writing fiction. Are you nuts? Or, more to the point, is that what people will think of you when they read your work?

The inhibiting effect of shame cannot be overstated. It explains why some writers slide into genre clichés or literary imitation. To put authentic emotions on the page you need to own them. When you do, readers will respect you. It's when you hide that readers feel short-changed, cheated, and only minimally involved.

....

Emotions evoked are artful, particularly when a given emotion has no name but nevertheless feels covertly real.

....

Set down the emotions that you believe you should and it's pretty much a guarantee that a given passage will feel glib. On the other hand, if you capture emotions that are fresh, genuine, specific to your character, and unique to the situation, then you will overrun readers' defenses. You'll take them by surprise. Readers feel resistance too. They fear high feelings as much as you do. Paradoxically, it's also what they seek in fiction. If you have ever raged or cried when reading a novel and cursed the author for making you feel like that, then you've experienced that resistance.

Recognize that above all things, you likely were hurt in childhood. Unless you've had a lot of psychotherapy, those hurts are with you still. If they hurt enough, you might unconsciously re-create the old painful circumstances in your current relationships. I mention this because it's helpful to the fiction process. Your deepest hurts are a wellspring of passion. Projecting old conflicts onto current relationships probably doesn't work, but projecting it into your stories does. Don't fight it. Many novelists aren't even aware they're doing it. But when there's passion on the page it probably flows from buried rage, the sting of injustice, unhealed trauma, or the ache for love.

Deep stuff. Painful feelings. Beautiful material! One of the joys of writing is the permission it gives you to feel deeply and wide. Your task is to tune yourself to the frequency where honest emotions come through with a crackle and hiss. It can be hard to find them amid the blast of the powerful-but-familiar emotional playlists crowding the dial.

Fortunately, there are tools and techniques to help you sift out what's authentic. Emotions that come in primary colors like anger, fear, desire, resolve, and envy are fine but hammer readers dully because they're familiar. Anything described as "gut-twisting" isn't going to twist readers' guts. Secondary emotions can bring subtlety and nuance to a scene. Sometimes it's also useful to reverse yourself and force onto the page an emotion that's the opposite of what you first thought to write down.

Better still are emotions that surprise. Best of all are emotions that conflict. Work toward building an instinct for emotional originality. When you've got that you'll be painting emotional landscapes that are constantly intriguing and even provocative for travelers.

The more sudden are the turns, the steeper the climbs, and the most astounding the vistas, the more readers will connect to the landscape. The trip you take them on is one they'll take inside. It will feel like a memory, even though you invented it at the keyboard.

DONALD MAASS founded the Donald Maass Literary Agency in New York in 1980. His agency sells more than 150 novels every year to major publishers in the United States and overseas. He is the author of *The Career Novelist* (1996), *Writing the Breakout Novel* (2001), *Writing the Breakout Novel Workbook* (2004), *The Fire in Fiction* (2009), and *The Breakout Novelist* (2011). He is a past president of the Association of Authors' Representatives, Inc.

Excerpted from *Writing 21st Century Fiction*© 2012 by Donald Maass. Used with the kind permission of Writer's Digest Books, an imprint of F+W Media Inc. Visit www.writersdigestshop.com or call (800)448-0915 to obtian a copy.

THE BUSINESS OF FICTION WRITING

//

It's true there are no substitutes for talent and hard work. A writer's first concern must always be attention to craft. No matter how well presented, a poorly written story or novel has little chance of being published. On the other hand, a well-written piece may be equally hard to sell in today's competitive publishing market. Talent alone is just not enough.

To be successful, writers need to study the field and pay careful attention to finding the right market. While the hours spent perfecting your writing are usually hours spent alone, you're not alone when it comes to developing your marketing plan. *Novel & Short Story Writer's Market* provides you with detailed listings containing the essential information you'll need to locate and contact the markets most suitable for your work.

Once you've determined where to send your work, you must turn your attention to presentation. We can help here, too. We've included the basics of manuscript preparation, along with information on submission procedures and how to approach markets. We also include tips on promoting your work. No matter where you're from or what level of experience you have, you'll find useful information here on everything from presentation to mailing to selling rights to promoting your work—the "business" of fiction.

APPROACHING MAGAZINE MARKETS

While it is essential for nonfiction markets, a query letter by itself is usually not needed by most magazine fiction editors. If you are approaching a magazine to find out if fiction is accepted, a query is fine, but editors looking for short fiction want to see how you write. A cover letter can be useful as a letter of introduction, but it must be accompanied by the actual piece. The key here is brevity. A successful cover letter is no more than one page (20-lb. bond paper). It should be single spaced with a double space between paragraphs, proofread carefully and neatly typed in a standard typeface (not script or italic). The writer's name, address, phone number, and e-mail address appear at the top, and the letter is addressed, ideally, to a specific editor. (If the editor's name is unavailable, address to "Fiction Editor.")

The body of a successful cover letter contains the name and word count of the story, a brief list of previous publications if you have any, and the reason you are submitting to this particular publication. Mention that you have enclosed a self-addressed, stamped envelope or postcard for reply. Also let the editor know if you are sending a disposable manuscript that doesn't need to be returned. (More and more editors prefer disposable manuscripts that save them time and save you postage.) Finally, don't forget to thank the editor for considering your story.

Note that more and more publications prefer to receive electronic submissions, both as e-mail attachments and through online submission forms. See individual listings for specific information on electronic submission requirements and always visit magazines' websites for up-to-date guidelines.

APPROACHING BOOK PUBLISHERS

Some book publishers do ask for queries first, but most want a query plus sample chapters or an outline or, occasionally, the complete manuscript. Again, make your letter brief. Include the essentials about yourself—name, address, phone number, e-mail address and publishing experience. Include a three or four sentence "pitch" and only the personal information related to your story. Show that you have researched the market with a few sentences about why you chose this publisher.

BOOK PROPOSALS

A book proposal is a package sent to a publisher that includes a cover letter and one or more of the following: sample chapters, outline, synopsis, author bio, publications list. When asked to send sample chapters, send up to three consecutive chapters. An outline covers the highlights of your book chapter by chapter. Be sure to include details on main characters, the plot, and subplots. Outlines can run up to thirty pages, depending on the length of your novel. The object is to tell what happens in a concise, but clear, manner. A synopsis is a shorter summary of your novel, written in a way that expresses the emotion of the story in addition to just explaining the essential points. Evan Marshall, literary agent and author of *The Marshall Plan for Getting Your Novel Published* (Writer's Digest Books), suggests you aim for a page of synopsis for every twenty-five pages of manuscript. Marshall also advises you write the synopsis as one unified narrative, without section, subheads, or chapters to break up the text. The terms synopsis and outline are sometimes used interchangeably, so be sure to find out exactly what each publisher wants.

A FEW WORDS ABOUT AGENTS

Agents are not usually needed for short fiction and most do not handle it unless they already have a working relationship with you. For novels, you may want to consider working with an agent, especially if you intend to market your book to publishers who do not look at unsolicited submissions. For more on approaching agents and to read listings of agents willing to work with beginning and established writers, see our Literary Agents section and refer to this year's edition of *Guide to Literary Agents*, edited by Chuck Sambuchino.

MANUSCRIPT MECHANICS

A professionally presented manuscript will not guarantee publication. But a sloppy, hard-to-read manuscript will not be read—publishers simply do not have the time. Here's a list of suggested submission techniques for polished manuscript presentation:

- For a short story manuscript, your first page should include your name, address, phone number, and e-mail address (single spaced) in the upper left corner. In the upper right, indicate an approximate word count. Center the name of your story about one-third of the way down, skip a line and center your byline (byline is optional). Skip four lines and begin your story. On subsequent pages, put last name and page number in the upper right-hand corner.

- For book manuscripts, use a separate title page. Put your name, address, phone number, and e-mail address in the lower right corner and word count in the upper right. If you have representation, list your agent's name and address in the lower right. (This bumps your name and contact information to the upper left corner.) Center your title and byline about halfway down the page. Start your first chapter on the next page. Center the chapter number and title (if there is one) one-third of the way down the page. Include your last name and the novel's title in all caps in the upper left and put the page number in the upper right of this page and each page to follow. Start each chapter with a new page.

- Proofread carefully. Keep a dictionary, thesaurus, and stylebook handy and use the spell-check function on your computer.

- Include a word count. If you work on a computer, chances are your word-processing program can give you a word count.

- Suggest art where applicable. Most publishers do not expect you to provide artwork and some insist on selecting their own illustrators, but if you have suggestions, let them know. Magazine publishers work in a very visual field and are usually open to ideas.

- Keep accurate records. This can be done in a number of ways, but be sure to keep track of where your stories are and how long they have been "out." Write down submission dates. If you do not hear about your submission for a long time—about one to two months longer than the reporting time stated in the listing—you may want to contact the publisher. When you do, you will need an accurate record for reference.

Electronic Submissions:

- When sending electronic submissions via e-mail or online submission form, check the publisher's website or contact them first for specific information and follow the directions carefully.

Hard Copy Submissions:

- Use white, 8½ × 11 bond paper, preferably 16- or 20-lb. weight. The paper should be heavy enough so it will not show pages underneath it and strong enough to take handling by several people.

- Type your manuscript on a computer and print it out using a laser or ink-jet printer (or, if you must, use a typewriter with a new ribbon).

- An occasional white-out is okay, but don't send a marked-up manuscript with many typos.

- Always double space and leave a 1-inch margin on all sides of the page.

- Don't forget word count. If you are using a typewriter, there are a number of ways to count the number of words in your piece. One way is to count the words in five lines and divide that number by five to find an average. Then count the number of lines and multiply to find the total words. For long pieces, you may want to count the words in the first three pages, divide by three and multiply by the number of pages you have.

- Always keep a copy. Manuscripts do get lost. To avoid expensive mailing costs, send only what is required. If you are including artwork or photos but you are not positive they will be used, send photocopies. Artwork is hard to replace.

- Enclose a self-addressed, stamped envelope (SASE) if you want a reply or if you want your manuscript returned. For most letters, a business-size (#10) envelope will do. Avoid using any envelope too small for an 8½ × 11 sheet of paper. For manuscripts, be sure to include enough postage and an envelope large enough to contain it. If you are requesting a sample copy of a magazine or a book publisher's catalog, send an envelope big enough to fit.

- Consider sending a disposable manuscript that saves editors time (this will also save you money).

ABOUT OUR POLICIES

We occasionally receive letters asking why a certain magazine, publisher, or contest is not in the book. Sometimes when we contact listings, the editors do not want to be listed because they:

- do not use very much fiction.
- are overwhelmed with submissions.
- are having financial difficulty or have been recently sold.
- use only solicited material.
- accept work from a select group of writers only.
- do not have the staff or time for the many unsolicited submissions a listing may bring.

Some of the listings do not appear because we have chosen not to list them. We investigate complaints of unprofessional conduct in editors' dealings with writers and misrepresentation of information provided to us by editors and publishers. If we find these reports to be true, after a thorough investigation, we will delete the listing from future editions.

There is no charge to the companies that list in this book. Listings appearing in *Novel & Short Story Writer's Market* are compiled from detailed questionnaires, phone interviews, and information provided by editors, publishers, and awards and conference directors. The publishing industry is volatile and changes of address, editor, policies, and needs happen frequently. To keep up with the changes between editions of the book, we suggest you check the market information on the Writer's Market website at www.writersmarket.com or on the Writer's Digest website at www.writersdigest.com. Many magazine and book publishers offer updated information for writers on their websites. Check individual listings for those website addresses.

Organization newsletters and small magazines devoted to helping writers also list market information. Several offer online writers' bulletin boards, message centers and chat lines with up-to-the-minute changes and happenings in the writing community.

We rely on our readers, as well, for new markets and information about market conditions. E-mail us if you have any new information or if you have suggestions on how to improve our listings to better suit your writing needs.

RIGHTS

The Copyright Law states that writers are selling one-time rights (in almost all cases) unless they and the publisher have agreed otherwise. A list of various rights follows. Be sure you know exactly what rights you are selling before you agree to the sale.

Copyright is the legal right to exclusive publication, sale, or distribution of a literary work. As the writer or creator of a written work, you need simply to include your name, date, and the copyright symbol © on your piece in order to copyright it. Be aware, however, that most editors today consider placing the copyright symbol on your work the sign of an amateur and many are even offended by it.

....

Some people are under the mistaken impression that copyright is something they have to send away for.

....

To get specific answers to questions about copyright (but not legal advice), you can call the Copyright Public Information Office at (202)707-3000 weekdays between 8:30 a.m. and 5 p.m. EST. Publications listed in *Novel & Short Story Writer's Market* are copyrighted unless otherwise stated. In the case of magazines that are not copyrighted, be sure to keep a copy of your manuscript with your notice printed on it. For more information on copyrighting your work, see *The Copyright Handbook: How to Protect & Use Written Works, 11th edition,* by Stephen Fishman (Nolo Press, 2011).

Some people are under the mistaken impression that copyright is something they have to send away for and that their writing is not properly protected until they have "received" their copyright from the government. The fact is, you don't have to register your work with the Copyright Office in order for your work to be copyrighted; all piece of writing is copyrighted the moment it is put to paper.

Although it is generally unnecessary, registration is a matter of filling out an application form (for writers, that's Form TX) and sending the completed form, a nonreturnable copy of the work in question and a check for $45 to the Library of Congress, Copyright Office, Register of Copyrights, 101 Independence Ave. SE, Washington DC 20559-6000. If the thought of paying $45 each to register every piece you write does not appeal to you, you can cut costs by registering a group of your works with one form, under one title for one $45 fee.

Most magazines are registered with the Copyright Office as single collective entities themselves; that is, the individual works that make up the magazine are not copyrighted individually in the names of the authors. You'll need to register your article yourself if you wish to have the additional protection of copyright registration.

For more information, visit the United States Copyright Office online at www.copyright.gov.

First Serial Rights

This means the writer offers a newspaper or magazine the right to publish the article, story or poem for the first time in a particular periodical. All other rights to the material remain with the writer. The qualifier "North American" is often added to this phrase to specify a geographical limit to the license.

When material is excerpted from a book scheduled to be published and it appears in a magazine or newspaper prior to book publication, this is also called first serial rights.

One-Time Rights

A periodical that licenses one-time rights to a work (also known as simultaneous rights) buys the nonexclusive right to publish the work once. That is, there is nothing to stop the author from selling the work to other publications at the same time. Simultaneous sales would typically be to periodicals without overlapping audiences.

Second Serial (Reprint) Rights

This gives a newspaper or magazine the opportunity to print an article, poem, or story after it has already appeared in another newspaper or magazine. Second serial rights are nonexclusive; that is, they can be licensed to more than one market.

All Rights

This is just what it sounds like. All rights means a publisher may use the manuscript anywhere and in any form, including movie and book club sales, without further payment to the writer (although such a transfer, or assignment, of rights will terminate after thirty-five years). If you think you'll want to use the material later, you must avoid submitting to such markets or refuse payment and withdraw your material. Ask the editor whether he is willing to buy first rights instead of all rights before you agree to an assignment or sale. Some editors will reassign rights to a writer after a given period, such as one year. It's worth an inquiry in writing.

Subsidiary Rights

These are the rights, other than book publication rights, that should be covered in a book contract. These may include various serial rights; movie, television, audiotape, and other electronic rights; translation rights, etc. The book contract should specify who controls these rights (author or publisher) and what percentage of sales from the licensing of these subrights goes to the author.

Dramatic, Television, and Motion Picture Rights

This means the writer is selling his material for use on the stage, in television or in the movies. Often a one-year option to buy such rights is offered (generally for 10 percent of the total price). The interested party then tries to sell the idea to actors, directors, studios, or television networks. Some properties are optioned over and over again, but most fail to become dramatic productions. In such cases, the writer can sell his rights again and again—as long as there is interest in the material. Though dramatic, TV, and motion picture rights are more important to the fiction writer than the nonfiction writer, producers today are increasingly interested in nonfiction material; many biographies, topical books and true stories are being dramatized.

Electronic Rights

These rights cover usage in a broad range of electronic media, from online magazines and databases to CD-ROM magazine anthologies and interactive games. The editor should specify in writing if—and which—electronic rights are being requested. The presumption is that the writer keeps unspecified rights.

Compensation for electronic rights is a major source of conflict between writers and publishers, as many book publishers seek control of them and many magazines routinely include electronic rights in the purchase of print rights, often with no additional payment. Alternative ways of handling this issue include an additional 15 percent added to the amount to purchase first rights and a royalty system based on the number of times an article is accessed from an electronic database.

MARKETING & PROMOTION

Everyone agrees writing is hard work whether you are published or not. Yet once you achieve publication the work changes. Now not only do you continue writing and revising your next project, you must also concern yourself with getting your book into the hands of readers. It becomes time to switch hats from artist to salesperson.

While even best-selling authors whose publishers have committed big bucks to marketing are asked to help promote their books, new authors may have to take it upon themselves to plan and initiate some of their own promotion, sometimes dipping into their own pockets. While this does not mean that every author is expected to go on tour, sometimes at their own expense, it does mean authors should be prepared to offer suggestions for promoting their books.

Depending on the time, money, and personal preferences of the author and publisher, a promotional campaign could mean anything from mailing out press releases to setting up book signings to hitting the talk-show circuit. Most writers can contribute to their own promotion by providing contact names—reviewers, hometown newspapers, civic groups, organizations—that might have a special interest in the book or the writer.

Above all, when it comes to promotion, be creative. What is your book about? Try to capitalize on it. Focus on your potential audiences and how you can help them connect with your book.

IMPORTANT LISTING INFORMATION

- Listings are not advertisements. Although the information here is as accurate as possible, the listings are not endorsed or guaranteed by the editors of *Novel & Short Story Writer's Market*.
- *Novel & Short Story Writer's Market* reserves the right to exclude any listing that does not meet its requirements.

SUBMISSIONS

Getting Your Foot in the Door

....

Janice Hussein

After spending months writing your novel, you're faced with writing a query and synopsis that you need to push that publishing dream into reality. And then, after writing them, perhaps even after a submissions critique, you may still be left wondering if it will be "enough." This article offers solid information on what to include, what to exclude, and how to distill that 80,000 word novel into an effective one-page query and one- to two-page synopsis—a submissions package that will gain an agent's or editor's interest.

THE QUERY

A query is a marketing tool, designed to be brief yet to give the most pertinent key details about a novel, including a short blurb that sells the idea and some brief info about you, the author. Basically it's a business proposal.

The query should be one page. Most agents and editors don't have time for more than that. And many of them do a three-paragraph-test read—if you haven't captured their interest by that time, your query faces the rejection-pile.

Formatting the Query

The snail-mail submission: The format for snail mail is much like a normal letter: Always use formal business letter format, with the standard 12-point font, 1-inch margins, and 20-lb. paper. The author's name, address, phone number, and e-mail address should be centered at the top of the page. The date should appear, justified left, and then the publisher's/agent's name and address, also justified left—skipping a line in between each of the two. The body of the query should be single spaced, with double spacing between paragraphs.

The closing should include the salutation, four line spaces, and your name—all left justified. Always include a SASE.

The e-mail submission: The format for the query is slightly different. The address line is one line, not a five-liner like the snail-mail version. Your contact info appears at the end of the letter after the closing. Keep the e-mail query professional. That includes the content of the actual e-mail address, the address itself. For example, rather than fluffy@hotstuff.com maybe MacKenzieSanders@romanceforyou.com.

Follow the agent's submissions guidelines for the subject line, but at the same time use this line to engage interest. Don't neglect this important small detail. What you write shouldn't be bland or just factual. It can be a marketing tool.

Starting the Query

You can start a query three different ways by varying the three most important query elements: the details, the hook, and the overview of the book. One is the business way, by introducing the details—introduce your work, including genre, title, setting and word count—and then providing the hook and an overview. Another way is to start with a hook, give the overview of the book, and then provide the details. A third way is to start with the hook, then give the details and then proceed to give the overview of the book. The first and third ways are the most effective, giving the hook and details first, then the overview. Most editors and agents prefer to know the details immediately.

The Query at a Glance:

Your query should be about five or six paragraphs long. The title of your novel should be upper cased.

PARAGRAPH 1: This paragraph should include either the details or the hook. If you start with the details, introduce yourself and your work: genre, title, setting, and word count. Example: "My recently completed 80,000-word romantic suspense novel, THE VENICE CONSPIRACY, is set in New York…" Or if the hook appears in the first paragraph, then the details come in the second paragraph. Example (after the hook): "That's the premise of my recently completed novel, THE VENICE CONSPIRACY, an 80,000-word romantic suspense that takes the reader from New York to London."

State why you're contacting this agent: You met her at a conference; she was recommended; you heard her speak somewhere; or the theme of your book is similar to a book(s) the agent is already representing.

PARAGRAPH 2: The details or the hook. In this case, we've started with the details, so the second paragraph would be the hook.

PARAGRAPHS 3 AND 4: A brief overview, like a backcover blurb. The key is to establish voice.

PARAGRAPH 5: In your second to last paragraph, you should list your credentials and experience, and anything that would establish you as a competent, professional writer. Include:

1) Any publication credits;
2) Awards (for instance, if you've finaled in contests);
3) Teaching or other pertinent experience;
4) Writing degrees; and,
5) Any professional memberships, including memberships in writing groups.

If your story involves something that might require specialized knowledge or experience—you're writing a legal thriller and you are an attorney—then include that info as well. It's another reason you are the right person to write such a story.

If the novel is part of a series, mention the next book and its status. But don't send a letter querying about more than one book. The general rule is to send a separate query for each book.

PARAGRAPH 6: The end paragraph should include something like the following: "Upon your request, I would be happy to provide the complete manuscript. Thank you for taking the time to consider my work (thanks the agent). I have enclosed a SASE (via snail mail) and look forward to hearing from you."

That's the query at a glance, now I'll go more in-depth.

THE HOOK

The query needs to start with a bang, with a one- or two-sentence teaser, to grab the agent or editor's interest. So consider that you have one chance to hook the agent's attention, and if he doesn't read past this paragraph, what then? Then ask yourself…what would you have wanted to say to snag his interest?

The hook is your pitch to the agent or editor. Think of the "elevator pitch" where you have thirty seconds in an elevator, with an important agent, to relate what your book is about and to earn the interest of the agent. The hook details what makes your book exciting, different, or unusual for the agent or editor, and it encapsulates what the book is about.

To help with coming up with that great hook, ask yourself this question: Why would anyone else want to read the novel? The answer to that question will help define your hook. Another suggestion is to write down the major plot points, themes, and whatever makes the book and characters especially intriguing, and then brainstorm over several days, writing down every idea that comes to mind. One of these ideas might not be perfect, but a combination of one or more could be the hook that brings you that request for a full manuscript. Remember: The query is a selling tool—to sell the idea to the agent or editor.

DETAILS

This introduces the novel to agents and editors, so they know what they're reading about, they know that it's something they'd be interested in. Placing the details near the beginning saves them time and some frustration—they don't have to scan the whole query for those details.

OVERVIEW

Condense the 80,000 words to one page: To summarize your novel and plot points in about six sentences, think of how you would tell your story to an acquaintance. You wouldn't tell it blow by blow; you'd summarize it, while also presenting the story in an exciting and intriguing way. I often suggest taking what you have, the query or synopsis, whatever you have written, however long, and editing it down, detail by detail, until you have just the major plot points and major characters. Then tell a friend about the novel to see what that person asks you about afterwards, or record the conversation and listen to what you've said. See what your own reaction is and what might make it clearer and more exciting.

The query letter should not include the ending—save that for the synopsis. The query should be like a backcover blurb that functions to engage the interest of editors and agents, giving some details of the novel. The goal is two-fold: To have them read the query and to make the reader want to know more.

Be sure that you've read the submission guidelines for the particular agent/agency and that you're tracking your submissions—what you sent, when you sent it, who you sent it to.

TAKEAWAY

1) The subject line: Don't neglect this important small detail—make it interesting.
2) In the actual query, have a great hook.
3) Proofread—no typos, punctuation, or grammar errors.
4) Don't use "To Whom it May Concern." Use the agent's name, spelled correctly.
5) Include any marketing hooks.
6) Remember that you're selling the book, not yourself (though secondarily yourself).
7) Don't query multiple projects at the same time, in the same query letter.
8) Show the characters' motivation.
9) Summarize both the main internal and external conflict.
10) Do not query two agents at the same literary agency.
11) Eliminate opinions—let the agent or editor judge.

THE SYNOPSIS

The synopsis is part of the screening process for manuscripts. It should normally be about one- to three- pages long, depending on the agent or editor and their submissions guidelines. For a long novel, such as 120,000 words, the synopsis length could be up to five pages. If the agent or editor likes the proposal, then she will request the first three chapters and maybe a longer synopsis.

FORMATTING: If the synopsis is one page, then it should be single spaced with double spacing between paragraphs. If the synopsis is two or more pages, then it should be double spaced throughout. The formatting should be the standard—Times New Roman, 12-point font—with one-inch margins. The title and first mention of the main characters' names (first and last names) should be formatted in capital letters (JANE DOE).

The Synopsis at a Glance:

1) The hook can be one sentence to one paragraph long. This opening should grab the agent's or editor's interest. Again, the first three paragraphs will likely determine if the rest of the synopsis is read.

2) Introduce the characters, including the villain—something about each, their relationship to the plot, and what makes each character special. What makes the characters different or interesting? What are their goals and motivations?

3) Include the character arcs. This is internal conflict.

4) External conflict: Major plot points, turning points, black moment, and resolution. Include the romantic arc, if there is one.

5) Romantic plot: What is the setup that brings the hero and heroine together and establishes the external conflict that blocks them.

6) Tie up any loose ends for the main plot and romantic plot.

The synopsis should give a rough idea of how the book progresses. The key, again, is voice—a funny book should have a funny synopsis, and so on.

General:

Normally, the synopsis should cover three main elements: setup, major developments, and resolution. A second approach is to include internal conflict, external conflict, and resolution.

Another function of the synopsis is to introduce the characters with first and last names—hero, heroine, and main villain— using uppercase letters. Include only the names of the main characters, keeping the number of names to a minimum—use only as many as will tell the story without revealing names.

The Hook:

You need a hook for the synopsis, something involving and engaging. Here's an example: "The man who attorney Cathy Parker loved, then left fifteen years ago, begs her to defend his son, a young photographer charged with murdering a magazine editor. When another murder occurs, Cathy must challenge her beliefs as she uncovers the truth."

Body of the Synopsis:

Too many scene details or secondary characters or too much backstory will convolute your synopsis, and offer the agent or editor too much detail. Don't present the story scene by scene. Focus on the major events and conflicts. Only include those details that make the main plot hang together and that are necessary for the ending to make sense. But don't hide the major, important details from the agent or editor.

Except for where you are telling backstory, use the present tense, in the third person. Normally a synopsis describes events as they happen in sequence, as if you were telling the story to a friend, with events in order, as they happen. Otherwise, it can be confusing. If you have to include backstory, always indicate where the actual plotline begins for that particular novel.

Takeaway:

1) Develop a great hook
2) Don't include dialogue.
3) Focus on major plot points, not a scene by scene summary.
4) Don't include secondary plots or characters unless they are essential to understand the resolution.
5) Don't use multiple POV.
6) Proofread thoroughly. Don't rely on spell-checker.
7) Make the first three paragraphs strong—most editors do a "three-paragraph" test— if you haven't caught their interest, they won't continue to read.
8) Wait at least a month after the agent's stated "reply by" date, before sending a polite note to an agent or editor, reminding them of your submission and that you hope to hear from them shortly.
9) Watch the transitions—make it a clear, logical flow.
10) Use strong nouns and verbs.
11) Limit adverbs and adjectives.
12) For agent contact information, check the *Writer's Market*, the Writer's Digest *Guide to Literary Agents*, the *Literary Marketplace*, or Publisherslunch.com. Another good website is www.agentquery.com—a free searchable database of over nine hundred agents.

A great query and synopsis can get your foot in the door, so spend the time to make them excellent. Being careless or neglecting to put real effort into this process could mean your wonderful novel won't get the attention it deserves from an agent or editor.

JANICE HUSSEIN has worked nine years as a professional freelance editor and three years for a literary agent. Her published articles on the writing craft have been featured in *Writer's Digest, Novel & Short Story Writer's Market,* and the *Romance Writer's Report*. She offers classes and workshops through her website documentdriven.com.

BEATING THE COMPETITION

Insider Tips for Making Your Fiction Stand Out From the Crowd

Jack Smith

What are the five most important things you can do to get your work accepted at a high-profile literary magazine—or to get your novel published? Answers from professionals vary considerably from submission issues to craft issues, from knowledge of the genre to the highest quality fiction possible, to the right attitude and the need for dogged persistence.

Let's begin with magazine editors at three prestigious magazines. As a writer what should you do if you want to get your stories accepted at these magazines?

WHAT SOME TOP LITERARY MAGAZINE EDITORS SAY

ANTHONY VARALLO, FICTION EDITOR, *CRAZYHORSE*:

"Publishable" Isn't Enough!

If you want to beat out the best fiction submissions, there are, to begin with, some bottom-line things you absolutely must attend to, says Anthony Varallo. First, proofread your work. Second, read the magazine you plan to submit to. Third, if you're submitting fiction, you should read plenty of fiction. "If you wish to write short stories, you must read short stories and read them massively." Fourth, says Varallo, it's important to read your work out loud—especially the opening pages—watching for anything that doesn't "ring true." Fifth, Varallo cautions writers not to submit a first draft—because this is "work that simply isn't ready yet."

But why *these* five? Varallo explains: "The five points above all congregate around a single idea, namely that writing is *work*, and you must work hard if you want your stories to go out into the world. There can be nothing careless, sloppy, inattentive, or thoughtless in the stories you submit—instead, your stories must show, sentence by sentence, that you've done the work of writing."

Yet work can be good—but not *great*. And *Crazyhorse*, Varallo makes clear, is looking for great, memorable work—work that lives on: "A 'publishable' story is perhaps one which gives the editors little to do, but—and this is important—a publishable story is not necessarily the same thing as a story we're going to accept." Out of the hundreds of "publishable stories" *Crazyhorse* receives each year, only a "handful," Varallo says, are accepted for publication. These stories are the ones "that we can't forget, that speak to us, that we love, and that we hope our readers will love, too." What's *publishable*, then, "is too low an ambition for publication" at *Crazyhorse*. "The story has to do more than just be 'publishable.'" What it in fact has to do is linger in the memory of readers for a long time after they put it down.

SUSAN BURMEISTER-BROWN,
CO-EDITOR, *GLIMMER TRAIN STORIES*:

Stories That "Matter"

The story that lingers on, the one several cuts above the merely "publishable," is also what *Glimmer Train* editors are looking for. Susan Burmeister-Brown, co-editor, sums up the editorial criteria succinctly. "The reader cares about the characters, and thinks about them after the story is over. The story is rooted with some detail so that the reader has something to envision and hook into. The dialogue, if there is any, is believable. The story offers a deep and fresh view. It matters and it lingers. At the end of the story, the reader is satisfied. It doesn't mean everything is wrapped up nicely, but that this piece of the journey has come to a sense of closure."

What *Glimmer Train* is looking for, then, is the truly knockout story. And here's why: The first three criteria Burmeister-Brown includes relate to the adept handling of key elements of fictional craft—character, detail, dialogue. The last two editorial standards surely depend on an artistic handling of these elements, though with any story, as any serious student of fiction knows, the sum of the parts is never equal to the whole, and while it's hard to pinpoint *all* of the elements that must be added to the three elements of craft Burmeister-Brown focuses on, it's clear that the finished story must accomplish just what she says it must. The story that provides a "deep and fresh view" is the kind of story that illuminates the intricate meanings integral to felt or lived experience. The writing is "deep" because the story is layered, not surface-level or superficial. The story is "fresh" because it doesn't depend on clichés or platitudes. It's not predictable; it's absolutely new. And for this reason, it gives intelligent readers "satisfaction," both intellectual and emotional. It's indeed the story that "matters" that meets these tough demands, and yet this is high quality literary fiction, and that's what *Glimmer Train* editors want.

SUSAN MASE, FICTION EDITOR, *NIMROD*:

Stories That "Dazzle"

Editors at *Nimrod International Journal*, a prestigious literary journal that is among the oldest in the country, are also looking for that great short story, and Susan Mase, fiction editor, describes what this looks like: "The story that quickly rises above the rest, the sure thing, often grabs our attention at the first sentence, delights or compels in some way after a paragraph or two, and sends us racing to the finish, our senses heightened with the promise of discovering a standout piece." Such a find, says Mase, "speaks to us, dazzles, or connects us."

If Mase admits she cannot provide a precise definition of this "standout piece," it does have certain recognizable qualities, she says—a distinctive voice being one. *Nimrod* editors are sensitive to this voice, the kind "that captures our attention from the first word to the last." They hear it in the story's "rhythm, turn of speech, personality." A second quality is "fully alive characters." Mase emphasizes that editors "see a character emerge from the way he or she talks, gestures, acts, and not necessarily by what we are told by an omniscient narrator." In other words, this is a character that comes alive before them—realized through dramatization: by showing versus telling. Third, regardless of the kind of story, it must be layered, giving the reader something to delve into, or "explore"—or, in Burmeister-Brown's language, it must be "deep." And, as with *Glimmer Train*, descriptive detail is also essential. Mase points out that such sensory detail delivers two payoffs: "Precise, vivid details bring your voice and content and characters to life, and carry us below the surfaces to reveal a keenly observed interior or exterior world." Fifth, a strong sense of place is vital, but it "must be a seamless addition to voice, character, and content, and not included at the expense of narrative interest."

Nimrod editors often find stories that contain most of these qualities, stories that come close, says Mase, and they may reject the piece but suggest some revision. She urges writers to make these revisions promptly and re-submit, that "many of the stories we publish are the result of a second or even third try."

As we've seen, writers hoping to beat out the tough competition at the top literary magazines need to address a number of issues. Pay attention to submission standards. Bottom line: Proofread your work. Know the magazine you're submitting to—a marketing essential. Know the genre. Become a voluminous reader of fiction, especially short fiction. Your work itself needs to be finished, polished—with a strong sense of craft, of storytelling techniques, of story sense, evident from the first page of your manuscript. And go for the great story—not the merely "publishable." A lot of stories fall into this bare-minimum category; they're competent, but they don't "dazzle" the reader. Great stories have the power to linger with the reader long after the story has been read. Maybe it's due to the story's multilayered complexity. Maybe it's the compelling description. Maybe it's the voice the readers remember. Maybe it's all of these. Top literary magazine editors know professional work when they see it, and also when they *hear* it—when they listen to your voice on the printed page. And that's from page one on.

SHORT STORY WRITERS & THE TOUGH COMPETITION

Naturally writers see publication from a different perspective. They're at the creative end, and what makes a work great is often hard to judge, to be totally objective. Still, writers who have been at the game for some time certainly have developed what it takes to get their work accepted in the top markets. They know their craft. They know their genre. They know the submission game well. They know how big the slush pile is—and it's very big at the top literary magazines. They've developed hard-won strategies to beat the odds, and they've also developed the right attitude—a positive one. Rejection doesn't defeat them.

GARY FINCKE:

"Read the Magazine"

Gary Fincke, whose work has been published in innumerable prestigious literary magazines as well as in a number of collections, including *Sorry I Worried You*, winner of the Flannery O'Connor Prize for Short Fiction, hits several of the same issues we've already seen: knowing the magazine, basic proofreading, and story quality.

First, says Fincke, "Read the magazine—it seems so obvious, but it's where to begin—editorial tastes matter to your chances—I began by sending my stories to magazines that had published writers I admired—there's a connection in that equation."

Second, proofreading: "Send a clean copy—again, so obvious, but a large number fail this test—I've judged contests where entries are obviously not proofread."

Third, "Give the story room—don't rush it out the door the day you believe it is finished—it's always revealing to read the story 'later.'"

Fourth, having authored several short story collections, Fincke offers some sound advice to those planning a collection at some point: "For a story collection, pay attention to the order of stories, the points of view and their varieties—the subjects—for example, unless you want the collection to be all coming-of-age stories, make sure that you don't have the bulk of them in that territory or they might seem redundant."

Fincke ends his advice on a familiar and crucial point: persistence counts. But he makes some important distinctions: "Be persistent—as long as when a story is rejected and I can read it again and still believe in it, I'll keep it in circulation; and the other side of that—sometimes when a story is returned I read it again and see it new—revision follows, or even discarding it." Persist with a story as long as you "still believe in it." Otherwise, revise some more—or … just put it away. You should consider "discarding" a story that's fatally flawed, or maybe there's no story there at all. That's not giving up; that's doing something positive. That's putting your energies in work that's worth your time and attention.

KARL HARSHBARGER:

"Write the Highest Quality Stories Possible"

Karl Harshbarger, who has published sixty stories in many of the top literary journals in the country, including *The Atlantic,* knows about beating the odds in literary magazine publication.

"My first suggestion is by far the most obvious," says Harshbarger: "write the highest quality stories possible." His other suggestions, he states, "pale beside this one." He explains: "The editors of the top-ranked magazines are simply looking for the best material they can find (as are, I hasten to add, the editors of most 'lower ranked' magazines). If your writing is of high quality, eventually you will be accepted in one of the best journals."

In other words, it's just a matter of time? Well, no. Because there's certainly more at hand than a mere waiting game, as Harshbarger makes clear. There's the rigorous process of continual submission: "Be diligent and methodical in sending your stories out. This would seem to be an obvious suggestion, but I know a number of writers who work very hard on their writing but are seemingly haphazard in submitting their material. If the journal doesn't get your story they obviously cannot consider accepting it."

In the highly competitive world of publishing, it doesn't hurt to have a sense of realpolitik, notes Harshbarger: "When possible (and, of course, within limits) cultivate some kind of personal relationship with editors and/or members of their staffs. Since there are a lot of fine stories being written, sometimes (as in the rest of life) who you know can make a difference." In other words, a foot in the door can't hurt. Schmoozing might get you a reading with a senior staff member. But the story had better be good.

Fourth, for Harshbarger, read the good journals and know what they want. There's an obvious difference, he points out, "in what the editors of *The New Yorker* seem to want as compared to some other literary journals." That is, magazines reflect different sensibilities, different tones. This is another way of saying know your market.

Finally, Harshbarger warns the writer not to be naïve about the nature of the game: "Be aware that the market is highly capricious and the damndest things happen or (more often) don't happen." The upshot? "It's not your fault! At least 50 percent of the time it's the gods up there!"

And yet, while there's an undeniable subjective component in creative writing, Harshbarger does urge writers to persist in developing the highest quality stories possible. In the midst of a battery of rejections, you can be assured, Harshbarger believes—despite the mysteries of capricious fate—that top quality work will ultimately find a good home.

ROBERT GARNER MCBREARTY:

"Write!"

Robert Garner McBrearty is the author of three story collections, including *Episode*, winner of the prestigious Sherwood Anderson Foundation Fiction Award. His third story collection, *Let the Birds Drink in Peace*, was published in 2011.

First, McBrearty emphasizes being the professional that the business requires: "Write! This sounds obvious, of course, but the writer who writes regularly, who works hard, has a much better chance than the writers who don't." Many advise sending your work out regularly. Make sure you have plenty of it to send out, says McBrearty.

Second, "Develop something distinctive in your work, whether it's the type of stories you tell or your own distinctive writing voice. Easier said than done, but this is where the combination of work and inspiration comes in." Hard work "increases the chances you will become inspired," says McBrearty. If you plod along for a while, uninspired, you need to realize that "writers often make breakthroughs, have sudden insights that transform their writing for the better." It's these insights, surely, that are needed for the story with a "deep and fresh view" that *Glimmer Train* calls for—and for the story that "dazzles" the *Nimrod* editors. Stories without insights are dull. They are flat and one-dimensional and offer no surprises.

Third, McBrearty turns to the opening page, which must absolutely grip and pull the reader in: "You need a strong opening page. If the first page isn't appealing, the story doesn't have much of a chance. I don't mean you have to have a great hook or something extraordinary. I just mean the prose has to be smooth and sharp." It must suggest a page-turner, says McBrearty. You have to gain your editor's interest—and confidence—right off.

Fourth, attitude. "Have a positive attitude but be realistic. (Though a certain amount of fantasizing comes naturally to fiction writers and may be a healthy thing! If one didn't dream big, why bother?). Accept that you're not going to beat out the competition most of the time. For every story published or award won, most writers have many rejections in between." We understand McBrearty correctly when we see the difference between being realistic and being defeatist: Acknowledge the odds, but don't give up.

Fifth, says McBrearty: "Build a backlog of drafts, fragments. That way you always have something to work on. You may have a story or partial story that's been sitting around for years and you pick it up and suddenly see it anew. Inspiration isn't just about creating something new—it can be about finding the treasure in something old. On the other hand, don't spend too long going down a dead-end road. Writers need to sense when it's time to let a story go and move on." There's a time to "discard," as Gary Fincke advises.

BEATING THE COMPETITION WITH BOTH STORIES & NOVELS

Mark Wisniewski can speak to both short story and novel publication. His stories have been published widely in the top magazines in the country, and his novels have been highly acclaimed, though these accolades have required patience on his part. His short story "Straightaway" appeared in both *Antioch Review* and *Best American Short Stories 2008* after having been rejected for nearly two years; his first novel, *Confessions of a Polish Used Car Salesman*, was compared to *Huckleberry Finn* by the *Los Angeles Times* and sold out two printings after having been rejected for ten years; his second novel, *Show Up, Look Good*, was rejected for seven years before its recent publication by Gival Press, after which it was praised nationwide and likened by numerous reviewers to *The Catcher in the Rye* and *Bright Lights, Big City*.

According to Wisniewski, the five things needed to beat the competition for success in the best publishing venues include, first off, a great story. He speaks of his recently published novel: "To beat out the competition, a writer needs to be open to finding a great story. I try to keep my eyes, ears, and mind open. I was lucky to hear *Show Up, Look Good's* narrative voice in my head, and luckier still to have been open to it."

Second, says Wisniewski, the writer needs the "ability to recognize a great story as great." He points out the difficulty of doing this. "There are so many mediocre stories in print that it becomes difficult to recognize a great story as such. Ask yourself: Has this story been told before? What makes it different? Does it make me uncomfortable? If so, maybe that's a good thing."

Third, a writer needs the "guts to write a great story." This might sound a bit odd, but Wisniewski explains: "There are plenty of reasons why a writer might be afraid to write a great story. Political and social agendas of editors, publishers, writing teachers, and English professors affect would-be boldness. It's probably true that to write a great story is to risk failure, loneliness, harassment, and/or ridicule."

Fourth, Wisniewski stresses the "ability to revise optimally." This takes some doing, he points out: "Most writers are too impressed by themselves and their work in general to revise a great story sufficiently. And sometimes the knock-dead core of a great story will exist in the writer's head but not completely on paper. Alternately, a great story can be whittled away by too *much* revision. At times I worry about this regarding *Show Up*, which, thanks to an agent, ended up being only half of its original length, leaving so much of it implied that some readers don't 'get' it. Optimal revision is a matter of balance, and ultimately a matter of serving the story above all else."

The fifth and perhaps most crucial must for Wisniewski is persistence in the face of rejection. "A great story is more or less guaranteed to face significant rejection. This might be because agendas in publishing do indeed result in the success of 'safe' work, but it's also because of huge slush piles, poorly trained or motivated editorial assistants (who are, in their defense, paid little or nothing), editors' desires not to offend sources of funding, and so on. In any case, the writer of a great story might need to withstand rejection for months if not years before publication, and even then, publication might bring modest financial reward."

These are indeed hard-hitting comments about the market from an author who has served his time in the trenches. But what Wisniewski sheds light on here is the average reader's desire to read the great story, and the writer's difficulty in knowing exactly what the "great story" looks like, given the abundance of less-than-stellar work found in print. Whether or not one shares Wisniewski's view of the state of published fiction—and of the lack of good models for the "great story," given the market's frequent opting for the "safe"— his idea about needing *guts* to write the great story must surely resonate with many writers. Greatness, Wisniewski suggests, is revolutionary. It challenges the staid, the conventional. It makes us uncomfortable. And given Wisniewski's experience, trying to get great work published may mean years of rejection. Yet shouldn't writers stick to their guns and write only what they know is absolutely outstanding? Wisniewski believes they should, and he encourages them to both develop and value the guts to do so.

Great fiction means work of very high artistic quality—it meets the kinds of standards we've seen from three top literary magazine editors. If you as author deem a piece of your fiction great, and you've written and revised it to enhance its greatness, don't give up on it, regardless of any apparent scarcity of payoffs. If it's truly great fiction, it will *eventually* find a good home, as Harshbarger tells us. And publication in the best places, the venues with the toughest literary standards, has always been validation for writers. Great work eventually gets there, though the route may be long.

JACK SMITH's satirical novel *Hog to Hog* (Texas Review Press) won the George Garrett Fiction Prize. His stories and essays have appeared in many publications, including *North American Review, The Southern Review, Georgia Review,* and *Ploughshares.* In addition to writing, he co-edits *The Green Hills Literary Lantern.*

EMERGING VOICES

Debut Authors Share Advice for Getting Published

....

Chuck Sambuchino

RAMONA AUSUBEL

No One Is Here Except All of Us

(Literary Fiction, Riverhead)
In 1939, with war looming, the families in a remote Jewish village in Romania decide to reinvent the world, deny any relationship with the known, and start over from scratch.

Where do you write from?

Santa Barbara, California

What did you do prior to writing *No One Is Here Except All of Us*?

I started and gave up on this book a number of times. I also wrote short stories, and some of those were published in journals before I had a publisher for the novel.

What was the time frame for the book?

Eight years passed between conception and publication. The first full draft of the book was written over about five-and-a-half weeks, but it was a terrific, incredible mess. Seventeen drafts later, it's a little more sensible.

How did you meet your agent?

I had a story published in a great journal called *One Story,* and I got some notes from agents and editors. It was through one of those editors that I found my amazing agent, P.J. Mark, who works at Janklow & Nesbit Associates.

What did you learn along the way?

It's really worth it to be patient and wait to find the right agent and publisher. These relationships are very personal, so it matters that you feel like you have the best possible team.

What did you do right?

I focused on the writing. It doesn't matter how good your connections are if you don't have something great to submit.

Would you do anything differently?

I wouldn't have worried so much. I got lots of rejections and disappointments, and for a long time, I thought that meant it was never going to work.

Website?

ramonaausubel.com.

What's next for you?

A collection of short stories called *A Guide to Being Born*, forthcoming from Riverhead.

SERÉ PRINCE HALVERSON

The Underside of Joy
(Mainstream Fiction, Dutton)
For three years, Ella has been the only mother the kids have known. But when Ella's husband dies, his ex-wife re-enters the picture—intent on reclaiming the children.

Where do you write from?

Northern California.

What did you do prior to writing *The Underside of Joy*?

I've been a copywriter for twenty years, but writing fiction has been my passion for just as long.

What was the time frame for the book?

I started the book in 2005. I wrote on and off. But in late 2009, I joined a small telewriting group and took a one-month writing retreat, staying alone in a cabin near the Russian River. These two things made all the difference.

How did you meet your agent?

My agent is Elisabeth Weed [of Weed Literary]. I found her the old-fashioned way—I wrote her a query letter. But before that, I researched. … There's so much information available to writers now. There's no reason to approach an agent blind.

What did you learn along the way?

Yes, the publishing industry is a subjective, imperfect blend of art and commerce trying to find its way through a kooky time. But everyone shares a passion for books and writing. I'm so impressed with everyone I've met and worked with.

Would you do anything differently?

I guess if there were some way to fold back time, I'd tell my younger self, *"Hey, don't stress. It's all going to work out. The kids will graduate. And you, my dear, you will get published."*

Tell us a little about your platform.

I used to say I was virtually shy. I'd never even commented on a blog! But the year before I signed on with my agent, I joined Facebook and began an essay-style blog. I was surprised to discover that I actually enjoy both.

Websites?

sereprincehalverson.com; whomovedmybuddha.blogspot.com.

What's next for you?

A novel set in Saudi Arabia, about a young American artist.

ANNE LYLE

The Alchemist of Souls

(Fantasy, Angry Robot Books)

Assigned to guard an ambassador from the New World, Elizabethan swordsman Mal Catlyn uncovers a conspiracy that could lose England her most powerful ally—and Mal his soul.

Where do you write from?

Cambridge, England.

What did you do prior to writing *The Alchemist of Souls*?

I had one short story published before this book was picked up.

What was the time frame for the book?

I did the first (very rough) draft for NaNoWriMo [National Novel Writing Month] in 2006, then spent the next four years rewriting it from scratch. A week after I began submitting the manuscript to agents, I met my future editor at a convention and pitched to him late one night over a glass of whiskey. Five months and one revision pass later, I had a three-book deal.

How did you meet your agent?

My agent is John Berlyne [at Zeno Literary Agency]. At around the same time I got the request for the full manuscript from Angry Robot, Zeno opened its doors to submissions for the first time in ages. As soon as I got the offer for the novel, I went straight to John and asked him for representation.

What did you learn along the way?

The change of gears from working at my own pace—even on a self-imposed deadline—to working to order. I went into this three-book deal with only one book finished, which means I have to be highly disciplined and write whether I feel like it or not.

What did you do right?

I wrote a story that I really loved and believed in, and I had it ready to pitch when the perfect opportunity came along.

Would you do anything differently?

I would have started knuckling down to serious writing a lot sooner.

Tell us a little about your platform.

I've been active on several writers' forums for years. That gave me the confidence to launch into social media. I'm a big fan of Twitter, as it allows me to stay in touch with friends all over the world.

Website?

annelyle.com.

What's next for you?

I'm currently working on the sequel, *The Merchant of Dreams*, which is due out next year.

ROBIN MELLOM

Ditched: A Love Story

(Humorous Young Adult, Hyperion)
A girl finds herself lying in a ditch with no memory of the last twelve hours, which she soon learns include a disappearing prom date, a Tinker Bell tattoo, and a dog-swapping escapade.

Where do you write from?

Central Coast, California

What did you do prior to writing *Ditched*?

I wrote lighthearted middle-grade fiction for several years, which was how I landed my agent. While submitting, my agent suggested I try writing a funny teen novel.

What was the time frame for the book?

I wrote *Ditched* in about five months. I knew exactly how I wanted it to end but wasn't sure of the specific events that would get me there. I went ahead and wrote an opening chapter, listing five of the most random things I could think of (a three-legged Chihuahua, In-N-Out Burger, etc.), figuring I would change them later, but they all ended up being big plot points.

How did you meet your agent?

I met Jill Corcoran of The Herman Agency several years ago at the Society of Children's Book Writers and Illustrators National Conference. She was looking specifically for humorous middle grade, so we were a perfect match.

What did you do right?

I listened to my agent's advice. It had never occurred to me to try my humorous writing for teens instead of middle grade. She saw something in my writing I didn't realize I had in me.

What did you learn along the way?

The community of writers is such a supportive environment. There's not a sense of competition but rather a feeling that the more books there are available to teen readers, the better. Authors are fans of one another and very often become good friends.

Would you do anything differently?

I wouldn't have stressed quite so much over the rejections.

Website?

robinmellom.com.

What's next for you?

A middle-grade series, The Classroom, debuting in June, as well as the companion novel to *Ditched*, titled *Busted*.

KIM PURCELL

Trafficked

(Young Adult Thriller, Viking Juvenile)
Stranded in a foreign land with no money and nobody who can help her, Hannah must find a way to save herself from her new status as a modern-day slave.

Where do you write from?

Westchester, New York

What did you do prior to writing *Trafficked*?

I worked briefly as a journalist. Later, while I was teaching English as a Second Language, my students talked to me about how they'd been mistreated, and I became interested in the issue of modern-day slavery.

What was the time frame for the book?

From the very beginning stages of researching this book to the final copyedit, it took eight years. In the middle of all that, I gave birth to two children and wrote during their naps.

How did you meet your agent?

My husband met my agent, Kate Lee at [International Creative Management], and asked if I could send her my novel. Fortunately, she called me and said she loved it. I was shocked. I had sent an earlier novel out to a bunch of agents, and even had some personal referrals, but no one took it.

What did you learn along the way?

I always thought if I got a great agent—and Kate Lee is indeed great—I'd be set. It didn't happen this way. Kate sent [my book] out to six editors, and all of them passed on it. I agreed with the editors' comments and didn't want it to keep being rejected, so I reimagined the main character and rewrote the book from scratch.

What did you do right?

I never stopped writing or putting myself out there. I think that's the difference between a published writer and an unpublished writer—the published writer hears the word "No," but interprets it as "Not yet."

Tell us a little about your platform.

I have a website and a blog. Also, I'm using Twitter a lot and building relationships in the literary community.

Website?

kimpurcell.com.

What's next for you?

I'm writing a paranormal thriller.

ASHLEY REAM

Losing Clementine
(Upmarket Fiction, William Morrow)
World-renowned artist Clementine Pritchard has only thirty days left to live, to love, and to paint, and we discover the shocking reasons why.

Where do you write from?

Los Angeles.

How did you meet your agent?

Barbara Poelle of the Irene Goodman Literary Agency is my agent. I had done all the things you are supposed to do when querying agents. I'd met them at conferences. I'd asked my published friends to give me introductions to their agents. But in the end, Barbara was a cold submission.

What did you do prior to writing *Losing Clementine*?

I had written a darkly humorous mystery that got turned down by every publisher in New York. My agent [asked] me to write something nongenre. My voice just didn't fit neatly into one category. When I stopped trying to fit, the next book sold quickly, with two houses bidding on it.

What was the time frame for the book?

It takes me about nine months to write a book.

What did you learn along the way?

Everyone around you—your agent, your editor, the cover designer, the proofreader, everyone—is going to have a slightly different idea of who you are as a writer. It's really important for you to be clear for yourself. Someone has to steer the boat.

What did you do right?

I worked for several years at daily newspapers, which taught me all I'll ever need to know about meeting deadlines and being edited. I also wrote a lot, and I kept writing. *Losing Clementine* is my first published novel, but the fifth one I've written. Also, I remembered my manners. It's amazing how far being nice will get you.

Website?

ahream.com.

What's next for you?

The next novel is *Honey in the Dell*, but I reserve the right to change my mind about the title.

STEPHANIE REENTS

The Kissing List

(Short-Story Collection, Hogarth)

The interlocking stories of The Kissing List *feature young women who navigate the treachery of first dates, temp jobs and roommates, failed relationships and unexpected affairs.*

Where do you write from?
Providence, Rhode Island

What did you do prior to writing *The Kissing List*?
The Kissing List includes stories I wrote more than ten years ago while I was in graduate school.

How did you meet your agent?
I started querying agents as soon as I had published a couple of stories in literary magazines. But I quickly learned that many agents were reluctant to take me on until I had written a chunk of a novel. Short stories, I heard time and again, don't sell. [A friend] put me in touch with a young agent who worked with her agent, Wendy Weil. That young agent was Emily Forland, and she was willing to take a risk on my stories. Emily and I worked together for five years before *The Kissing List* came into the world.

Would you do anything differently?
For a long time, I resisted the idea that story collections need a central focus or a theme. Once I found a focus, it was easier to pull this book together.

Tell us a little about your platform.
Besides using Facebook and Twitter to spread the word about *The Kissing List*, I'm also hoping to do old-fashioned readings.

What's next for you?
I'm working on a surreal novel called *The Claustrophobic House* that explores some big, fun metaphysical questions.

MORGAN CALLAN ROGERS

Red Ruby Heart in a Cold Blue Sea
(Mainstream Fiction, Viking)
Told from the perspective of Florine Gilham in no-nonsense Maine dialect, the story begins right before the center of Florine's world—her mother—disappears forever.

Where do you write from?
Portland, Maine, and western South Dakota.

What did you do prior to writing *Red Ruby Heart in a Cold Blue Sea*?
I worked [on writing] for thirty years in various capacities. I wrote fiction, but never felt that I could make a living at it. Then, one day, I knew that if I didn't honor the best part of me in some way—my imagination—I would regret it for the rest of my

sorry life. ... I applied for admission to a regional master of fine arts program, was accepted, and it changed my life.

What was the time frame for the book?

This book is actually the backstory to a novella I wrote in the MFA program. I finished [it] in a year's time, writing weekend mornings and weekday evenings after my day job.

How did you meet your agent?

I am blessed to have the most fabulous agent in the world, Gail Hochman, of Brandt & Hochman. I am equally blessed to have had one of my MFA mentors suggest that I send my manuscript to Gail, who loved it.

What did you learn along the way?

I think it helps if you're willing to "assist" in any way you can. Ask if there's anything you can do—participate in the process, but don't be a pest.

What did you do right?

I cultivated the friendship and support of positive people. ... I also revised the finished manuscript a dozen times with a journalistic eye.

Website?

greenandgoldenocean.blogspot.com.

What's next for you?

I'm working on two new novels.

JENNY TORRES SANCHEZ

The Downside of Being Charlie
(Young Adult, Running Press)
Charlie's life is spiraling out of control as he struggles with his weight, a girl who may or may not like him, and a mom who mysteriously and repeatedly abandons him.

Where do you write from?

Orlando, Florida

What did you do prior to writing *The Downside of Being Charlie*?

I was writing short stories mostly, but one day I was thinking how your teenage years really are unlike any others in your life. They're wonderful and horrendous and unpredictable. Suddenly, a story started to form. I started typing immediately, although at the time I didn't realize how much it would change.

What was the time frame for the book?

This story took about nine months to write, but afterward, there were revisions.

How did you meet your agent?

I found my agent, Kerry Sparks of the Levine Greenberg Agency, through Casey Mc-Cormick's site Literary Rambles [caseylmccormick.blogspot.com].

What was the biggest surprise?

How supportive the YA community is. It really is amazing how encouraging and helpful other YA writers have been (especially The Apocalypsies—a group of 2012 debut [children's and YA] authors).

What did you do right?

I didn't give up. There were times I stepped outside myself and thought, *You're nuts*—but even then I didn't give up. Also, I finished the manuscript and researched agents before querying them.

Tell us a little about your platform.

I blog, and I'm on Twitter and Facebook. I enjoy connecting with others online.

Website?

jennytorressanchez.com.

What's next for you?

A dark and funny novel about a death-obsessed girl who talks to Emily Dickinson's corpse and is dealing with a secret about a classmate. Stay tuned!

ADAM WILSON

Flatscreen

(Humorous Literary Fiction, Harper Perennial)
A slacker meets a drug addict ex-TV star who likes prostitutes, and all hell breaks loose.

Where do you write from?

Brooklyn, New York

What did you do prior to writing *Flatscreen*?

I had been living in Texas working a terrible job for which I had to spend my days holding up a giant orange arrow at a highway exit ramp. I quit, went to New York for [a master of fine arts] and stayed there. After grad school I made my living as a freelance writer.

What was the time frame for the book?

From conception to completion, the whole thing took roughly five years.

How did you meet your agent?

My agent is the lovely Erin Hosier [of Dunow, Carlson & Lerner]. A [friend] knew her and suggested I get in touch.

What was the biggest surprise?

That someone actually decided to publish the book! I have also considered myself doomed and unlucky, and was thrilled to find out that I'm actually blessed and lucky. For now.

What did you do right?

Not be stubborn about taking outside suggestions on the manuscript. I think some writers become so attached to their own work that they refuse to make substantial edits even when they know the edits will help the manuscript.

Tell us a little about your platform.

I'm all over the Internet—on Twitter, Facebook, etc. [I write] for blogs and webzines (as well as print publications). I also edit a website called *The Faster Times*.

Website?

adamzwilson.com; thefastertimes.com.

What's next for you?

I just finished a story collection and am now at work on a new novel.

....

CHUCK SAMBUCHINO is an editor and a writer. He works for Writer's Digest Books and edits the *Guide To Literary Agents* (guidetoliteraryagents.com/blog) as well as the *Children's Writer's & Illustrator's Market*. He is also the author of *How to Survive a Garden Gnome Attack* and *Red Dog / Blue Dog*.

....

CONFERENCES, WORKSHOPS & RETREATS

Should You Go?

Jack Smith

If you're serious about your craft, you spend a lot of time working at it—alone. Writing, as any writer knows, is a very solitary activity. If you're a member of a writing group or guild, or have writer friends who provide feedback and encouragement, you're already connected to other writers. But still, if you don't attend conferences, you may be missing out on the chance to make important professional contacts. Plus more: valuable information about craft and marketing from presentations and panels; creative writing workshops and professional criticism of your work; an opportunity to meet with agents and publishers. There's the cost, of course, and possibly the time away from work. But if you can swing those two, a good conference may be well worth the investment.

For one thing, there's the spark of inspiration.

"I've often left conferences feeling energized and renewed, committed to completing a writing project," says Anjali Banerjee, a commercial success in both young adult and literary women's fiction. For literary fiction writer Phyllis Westover, "Perhaps one of the biggest benefits of writers conferences is just the stoking of one's own furnace by virtue of being in an energetic writing environment totally protected from all the distractions of business as usual and the many obligations of life."

To make your conference experience this positive, choose well. Banerjee emphasizes that different conferences have different focuses—some on craft, some on marketing and promotion, and some on a combination of craft and marketing. Which one is right for you? Start with the current issue of *Novel & Short Story Writer's Market*, which has a section covering conferences and workshops. Visit the conference website and, if need be, e-mail or call for more information. Check with colleagues for advice on good ones to attend. If you are working in a specific genre (e.g., romance, mystery, Christian, science fiction, and fantasy), it may be best to choose a conference devoted to that area.

What you want out of a conference can probably be boiled down to two basic benefits: personal and professional.

CONNECTING WITH OTHER WRITERS

Tom LaMarr, author of Hallelujah City, sees conferences as a way out of the typical writer's alienated existence: "Like many writers, I produced my first novel in a vacuum. A conference would have been helpful, if only to offset that feeling of isolation." Joe Benevento, co-editor of *The Green Hills Literary Lantern*, notes the sense of camaraderie one sometimes feels in the presence of fellow writers. "Even a few people who I rejected for *GHLL* ended up saying things like, 'Yours was the nicest rejection letter I ever received,' or things of that sort."

Besides the chance to socialize with other writers, there's of course the professional benefit, as Nathan Leslie, author of six volumes of fiction, points out: "One can establish connections through writing conferences that can help advance one's writing career." But with which writers? "Conferences are a great way to meet fellow writers who are a step or two beyond you in your career," says Steven Wingate, author of the prize-winning *Wife-shopping*. "You can learn as much from them about getting where you want to be as you can from people who have already reached the top of the totem pole because they've recently gone through what you're going through."

You should be aware of the hierarchy, especially at large conferences, as far as writers several career notches above you. Wingate cautions against "expecting that you'll hobnob with the big authors," which "isn't realistic because they are inundated with requests from people and want to protect their time just as any other writer does." Benevento has noted the hierarchical nature of such large conferences as the annual AWP. DeWitt Henry, founder of *Ploughshares*, and workshop leader at several conferences, applauds The Squaw Valley Writer's Conference for eliminating this very problem: "The tenor of the entire conference is engaging and egalitarian, rather than hierarchical. Financial aid is available on a merit basis. When a staff member discovers exciting work, word quickly spreads throughout the conference."

PRESENTATIONS, PANELS, BOOKS FAIRS

Depending on the conference, presentations and panels can cover a wide variety of topics, from craft to marketing to promotion in several genres. Nathan Leslie identifies these program elements as "the bread and butter of most conferences." Conference offerings should be available on the conference website. "What an opportunity to learn from those farther along the writing path!" exclaims Mary-Lane Kamberg, author of nonfiction as well as poetry and fiction. "Don't be afraid to ask questions. Writers conferences are also good places to learn what's hot and what's not." Kamberg says of The Maui Writers Conference and Retreat: "Every presenter had multiple bestseller titles and was happy to share the nuts and bolts."

Phyllis Westover appreciates one informative aspect of the Iowa Summer Writing Festival—the "Elevenses": "Between 11 and noon each day, a different member of the teaching staff speaks on a different topic or aspect of writing. Not only is that informative, but it gives you a good taste of presenters/instructors with whom you might want to take a workshop with another year."

Panels are another highlight of conferences, and agents often sit on panels. The tips they offer can sometimes be surprising. Midge Raymond, author of the prize-winning *Forgetting English*, recalls one example: "One thing I remember well was an agent in a panel saying that a first-time author does *not* want a big, six- or seven-figure advance ('you're screwing yourself' were her exact words) because the chances of earning it back in sales were slim, and it would forever be a struggle to sell your next book. This is a surprise to most writers (everyone thinks they want a big advance), but it's such an important thing to consider and I was glad to hear it mentioned."

Janna Cawrse Esarey, author of the memoir *The Motion of the Ocean*, mentions another surprising agent comment: "I remember one agent who announced at an agent/editor panel that the reason they were all here was to meet us, the writers. Don't be shy, she said, about pitching at lunch, in the hall, in the bathroom. She was kidding about the bathroom. But you could almost see the rest of the panel cringe as she spoke. Her point was a good one, though," says Esarey. "Writers who politely approach agents and editors are helping them do their job—regardless of how intently agents and editors may examine their shoes as they walk down the hall."

Of course, you might pick up such tips or comments in a creative writing craft book or magazine article. But when a conference has an agent presence, and agents serve on panels, they're right there to drop nuggets of wisdom—and if you have questions, you can direct these questions right at them.

One advantage of large-scale conferences is book fairs. Simmons Buntin, editor/publisher, *Terrain.org: A Journal of the Built & Natural Environments*, emphasizes the importance of book fairs at large conferences like AWP: "Visiting tables/booths and talking with editorial staff (and sometimes contributors) is the best way to learn about the publication short of actually purchasing it (or, in our case, visiting it online)." But one shouldn't get the idea that this is a forum "for submitting work," says Buntin. Instead, book fairs provide a good opportunity "for identifying publications you're interested in submitting your work to (whether individual literary journals or book publishers), talking with the editors to get a sense of what they're interested in for upcoming issues, and rubbing elbows with other inquiring writers."

WORKSHOPS

Many conferences—as well as workshops and retreats—offer writing workshops. Check to be sure that the one you're interested in does. AWP, for instance, doesn't. If you're planning on participating in a writing workshop, be sure to find out the setup before you go. Robert Garner McBrearty, a winner of the Sherwood Anderson Foundation Fiction Award for his short story collection *Episode* (Pocol Press), has had fellowships at MacDowell Colony and the Fine Arts Work Center, in Provincetown, MA., as well as taught at several conferences. According to McBrearty, one should find out what is meant by the term *workshop* prior to attending a planned-on conference. This may mean directed creative writing exercises—not a critique of your work. Don't disallow craft workshops, though. Midge Raymond has taught revision workshops at Get Lit! in Spokane as well as at the Southern California Writers' Conference in San Diego. "I was happily surprised to find that the revision workshops were very well attended (often when teaching I find that this is a least favorite aspect of writing). But perhaps," says Raymond, "because conferences focus on getting your work sold, attendees see the value in it."

But let's say a craft workshop doesn't meet your present needs. You want professional feedback on a particular story or novel-in-progress. If so, be sure you know the exact workshop setup. Workshops that provide critiques of writers' work may be "run like grad school workshops, where one's work is critiqued by a teacher and fellow students," says McBrearty. If this is the case, you should find out in advance the answers to three basic questions: "How many people will be in the workshop; how many stories will one be able to present to the workshop; and how long and thoroughly will one's story be discussed?"

"Chances are," McBrearty points out, "in many conference workshops, you may only have an opportunity to have one of your stories, or a novel chapter discussed." But this presents another question: "Will the stories be read ahead of time, or will they be read out loud in class?" If the latter, "don't expect the level of critique to be very high. Much of the value of this type of workshop will depend upon the adeptness of the teacher and one's fellow students and also on one's own ability to take and give criticism."

Make sure, says McBrearty, to find out about the workshop leader. "What are his or her credentials? If possible, read some of his or her work. If you're writing a detective novel, and the teacher writes absurdist short stories, it may not be a good fit."

Finally, McBrearty advises writers not to "trust everything that is said, either positively or negatively, about one's work."

Three basic points to keep in mind, then: Know the workshop setup, and decide if it's right for you. Check out the workshop leader's credentials. Go to the workshop hoping to get solid feedback—not "the answer."

Writers have certainly had rewarding experiences from workshop activities. Cliff Garstang, author of *In an Uncharted Country*, states: "The most useful workshops I've attended are those with workshop faculty who are genuinely interested in teaching and helping writers improve their craft. My experiences at Sewanee Writers' Conference and Bread Loaf Writers' Conference have been uniformly positive. Not only are the attendees generally serious about their craft, but the workshops are dedicated." Garstang also attended the Tinker Mountain Writers' Workshop twice. "It's a well-organized smaller conference that attracts good faculty, but the student writers aren't all experienced. The advantage is that the size allows for plenty of interaction with the faculty and sometimes closer attention than you might get at a bigger conference." Under the Volcano, in Tepoztlán, Mexico, was also a good experience, says Garstang. "It's small, with excellent faculty, so you get a lot of face time with them."

Steven Wingate appreciates this face-to-face quality in Sozopol Fiction Seminars, held in Sozopol, Bulgaria. It's "very new and intimate, and it's developing its personality as it moves forward. The founder, Elizabeth Kostova, even workshops her own fiction alongside those of the seminar participants."

Dana Wood, Chicago literary author, explains her definition of a successful workshop: "A successful workshop does not mean that you will walk away signed with an agent or a bona fide contract from an editor. What comes from a successful workshop is that you learned something, something that will help you be a better writer, something imparted to you by the carefully-selected literary professionals in attendance."

MEETING AGENTS & EDITORS

As with workshops, don't go in blind. If the conference blurb or website doesn't mention agents and editors, don't assume they'll be there. If agents and editors will be present, or "participate," what does this mean? If the conference blurb isn't more specific than this, then, says McBrearty, you have to wonder about the various scenarios possible: "Does it mean that writers need to be lucky or aggressive enough to meet one at a cocktail party, or does it mean the agents and editors will be giving talks, or does it mean that there will be some system set up where one can meet the agents/editors and have one's work reviewed? Ideally, one will have a chance to set up an appointment, which may mean paying an extra fee." Check all this out in advance, McBrearty urges.

McBrearty himself had a good experience at the Aspen Summer Words Writing Retreat and Literary Festival. "There was an organized system for signing up to meet agents and editors and to have one's work reviewed. There was an added fee to meet agents or editors, though it seemed quite reasonable. After reading my opening chapter, the agent that I met asked me to send the rest of my novel to her."

Cliff Garstang has found that Sewanee and Bread Loaf are great conferences to meet with agents and editors. "Faculty members have been known to recommend their workshop participants to visiting agents, which is an invaluable foot in the door. And it frequently happens that agents and editors will approach writers whose readings they've heard and liked."

Dana Wood praises Writing Away Retreats: "They differ from other conferences because the publishing professionals are very accessible. Like other retreats, you get consult time with the agents and editors and you get to make your pitch. But at Writing Away Retreats, the professionals are embedded with you all weekend. You eat meals with them, drink wine with them, play Scrabble with them, banter around a bonfire with them. This is unprecedented access compared to other conferences."

Sorche Elizabeth Fairbank, of Fairbank Literary Representation, advises authors to choose wisely amongst the range of agent and editor interactions available across the board: "It may come down to quality versus quantity: the week-long retreat and limited attendance weekend workshops mean much more one-on-one time with fewer agents, whereas mega-conferences and one-day pitch sessions tend to get you a short time with a greater variety of agents."

If you do have the opportunity to pitch your work, regardless of session type, you should consider this sound advice from Mary-Lane Kamberg: "Be sure you're pitching to someone who represents what you have written." And once that matter is settled, says Kamberg, consider what you're getting into in case the agent takes an interest in your work. Two key questions to ask yourself: Is this someone you'd like to work with? Is this "someone you would trust with your money?"

Definitely do not head off to a conference with plans to sign with an agent, cautions Steven Wingate. "Remember that the path to your agent can go through many steps, and remember that your goal in meeting an agent is not an instant 'yes' but an invitation to send a manuscript—that's all you need to do on a first meeting."

Esarey puts it this way: "They don't have to love it. They don't have to gush about it. You simply want the right to put these three words on your correspondence: Requested Materials Enclosed. That will keep you out of the slush pile."

MEETING WITH SMALL PRESS PUBLISHERS

"Writing conferences can be a useful source for finding out about publishers," states Nathan Leslie. "I personally haven't found a publisher per se through this route, but I've discovered publishers who I've later submitted my work to." As to bringing your work "to pass around," Leslie discourages this practice since many editors seem to "frown on this." What he finds most helpful about the small press publisher presence "is the fact that the editors are right there to assist with questions, to clarify what they publish and so on."

Says Barry Kitterman, author of *The Baker's Boy*, "I have connected with editors of magazines and with the publisher of my novel [SMU Press]. I think AWP is a good opportunity to try to talk to the people who are representing small presses. I also see representatives from the self-publishing enterprises there, so I'm sure a writer could arrange for someone to publish a book that way, if that's the sort of thing someone wants to do."

Joe Benevento has also appreciated the small press presence at conferences. "I met the publisher of my second novel, Lynn Price of Behler Publications, just when she was starting out with that press, and so was able to have her agree to look at *The Odd Squad.*" Behler eventually published this novel, and it was a finalist, says Benevento, for the 2006 John Gardner Fiction Book Award.

SOME FINAL THOUGHTS

No two conferences are the same, so you need to be sure the conference you choose satisfies whatever goals or objectives you have. Doug Crandell, author of several works of fiction at commercial presses, cautions writers to be careful in selecting workshops: "Anybody can put up a shingle, but the staff should be people who've published recently, or agents who are actively selling books. There are some scams out there, some that may not technically be scams but are hosted by people who are not actively engaged in writing, publishing, and helping others get published." A second, different kind of caution, from Anjali Banerjee: "Ultimately, writing is a solitary pursuit. I believe that in some ways, conferences can be a distraction from facing the true work of actually completing a manuscript, revising, and sending out your work." The lesson here? Do take advantage of every opportunity to attend a good conference, but be prepared to get back to your cloister, to start cranking again, facing that computer screen alone. Inspired, of course, by all you gained at a valuable conference.

JACK SMITH's satirical novel *Hog to Hog* (Texas Review Press) won the George Garrett Fiction Prize. His stories and essays have appeared in many publications, including *North American Review, The Southern Review, Georgia Review*, and *Ploughshares*. In addition to writing, he co-edits *The Green Hills Literary Lantern*.

THE M-WORD

Marketing Your Fiction Without Selling Out

....

Scott Francis

For many writers, marketing is almost a dirty word—an ugly truth that must be dealt with in order to make money as a writer. But it doesn't have to be that way. Instead, think of marketing your work as a natural extension of your writing—a way of continuing the conversation you're having with your reader.

In today's world it's difficult to go anywhere or do anything without being asked to buy something or sign up. It's a fact of modern life. The result? Lots of people begin tuning out. They ignore most of the advertising they see. So what does that mean for marketing? It means it doesn't really work to push a product into someone's face and ask him or her to "buy now!" Successful marketing involves connecting with an audience by informing, educating, and entertaining them. Now … doesn't that sound like why you got into writing in the first place?

Writing is essentially a conversation with the reader, so think of marketing as striking up a conversation with someone you've just met. Having that interaction with a stranger happen as naturally and genuinely as it might in a pub or on an airplane is the trick. If you can learn how to do that, then you'll not only be more successful, but you might actually enjoy promoting your work.

BUILDING YOUR PLATFORM

As a writer you've probably heard this term thrown around by now, but if you haven't, *platform* essentially means who you are and how you promote yourself. Before taking a chance on your work, publishers want to know how well-known you are: what kind of media attention you've already gotten, what kind of connections you have, the readership for your blog or column (if you have one), how many hits your website gets (if you have one)—things of that nature. Obviously, you can't just write a book and expect publishers to come knocking at your door or snatch up the work you send them and take it to press. Publishers want to know why you should be considered someone worth listening to. Basically they're wondering if you're already perceived as a voice among the audience you're trying to reach. If you are, you have a better chance of getting published because you're a safer bet. At the end of the day, publishers are trying to sell books, and they're looking for authors who are making themselves known—not those who just lock themselves in a room and churn out page after page.

If you're serious about getting published and building your writing career, you need to start thinking about your author platform. Good ways to get started are to start a blog, to join online communities devoted to the kinds of writing you're doing, and to submit your writing to every place you can think of. Many writers "save" their writing, but to get your name known it's important to try to get published as many places as you can, including small or local publications.

Remember, an author platform is more than a bio stating the things you've already done. Think of it as a plan for the way you are promoting your writing career—the steps you're taking to establish your voice as one of expertise about your subject.

UNDERSTANDING WHAT MARKETING MEANS TODAY

Almost every day I talk to book authors who have a variety of ideas about how they think their book should be marketed. Everyone has a different approach to the way they think about "self-promotion." A handful of authors are really interested in doing lots of lectures and readings to promote their books … and that really works to their advantage. On the other hand, many writers think of "self-promotion" as an unsavory part of the business. For them, writing is an art form—an act of creation. It's easy to understand the hesitance one might feel when it comes time to sell the work.

The good news is that marketing doesn't necessarily mean the same thing as it did in the old days. The internet has changed the rules and forced marketers to rethink their old approach of "advertising to the masses." Today, people are wise to traditional marketing and are looking for something more genuine. They want authenticity, not a cheap gimmick.

This message is a hopeful one for anyone who is worried about maintaining the integrity of what he is marketing. As writers, we should all take this to heart. Marketing our writing and promoting our work should be considered an extension of the writing itself. It's another way of connecting with the reader. It's a way to inform and entertain. Marketing is no longer a "sales pitch." It's the sharing of information. Your audience wants to find out about new things and to be entertained. By sharing content (either through excerpts of your writing, information about events or related news topics) you are giving them what they want. You're also getting your work and your name in front of them. Encourage feedback and find ways to make yourself accessible. Just like the act of writing, communication is what marketing your work is all about.

KEEPING UP

In today's fast-paced world it's easy to be quickly forgotten if you don't keep up with constant change. An important part of marketing your work is staying up-to-date. If you're promoting your book (or trying to promote yourself as an author), you need to present yourself as an authority within the subject areas you write about. Make sure you stay apprised of the latest news in your genre and stay active on related forums and message boards. Blog regularly to keep your audience reading, and update your website frequently to keep people coming back for more. If you send out press releases or media kits, make sure you constantly update them to include your latest accomplishments, appearances, or clippings from your most recent work.

Today, people are wise to traditional marketing and are looking for something more genuine. They want authenticity, not a cheap gimmick.

When promoting yourself, its also important to be concise. Audiences (and the media) are growing increasingly impatient, so you need to get your point across quickly. If you're planning to speak on a TV or radio program or a podcast or webcast, prepare by writing down your pitch or your description of your work. Edit it down, and then rehearse it a bit. Don't over polish it—you don't want to sound like a robot—but practice the art of getting your main point across. Your goal is to be quick, clear, and interesting.

ESTABLISHING YOURSELF AS THE EXPERT

Everyone has a different way of presenting themselves to the public, whether the goal is to be authoritative or entertaining (or both). The main thing to keep in mind is to present yourself as an expert within your genre, whether you think you are or not. To be an expert, you don't have to be the world's most informed person about something—you simply need to know what you're talking about. If you research and write regularly about a subject and present yourself in a knowledgeable way, then that makes you an expert.

Bottom line: You have to believe you're an expert before the media or your audience will, so have faith in what you know and present yourself with an authoritative voice.

SETTING REALISTIC GOALS

Start by setting achievable goals for yourself. Having a "pie in the sky" dream is great, but make sure you have a realistic plan for getting there.

I've worked with authors whose first question is when I'll get their book on national talk shows. (Hmmmm. How do I respond to that?) I'm not saying I don't think the book deserves attention. I'm not even saying the book won't eventually get there. But, there is probably a better place to begin publicity efforts—such as local television and radio and relevant blogs and periodicals. By actively approaching these venues first, an author is more likely to gain the attention of broader-reaching media.

Bottom line: Start with realistic and achievable promotional ideas and build from there. Your efforts will help you gain more success and should lead to better and better opportunities.

DEALING WITH REJECTION

When promoting your writing, it's important to deal with rejections or bad news professionally. It's easy to become frustrated or even angry when you have a manuscript rejected, get negative feedback about your work, or have a scheduled public speaking event or bit of media coverage postponed or canceled. But these things are simply going to happen—it's part of the business. Take them in stride. You don't want to close any doors or burn bridges. When an opportunity falls through, be understanding and express an interest in pursuing it at a later date. Showing disappointment is okay, but keep it in check and put forth an optimistic face.

Remember: If writing is your career, then relationship building is an important part of that. Having a good attitude in the face of setbacks is essential. Always think long term.

WORKING WITH PUBLISHERS

A lot of authors I've worked with are confused about or don't really understand exactly what goes on in marketing and publicity departments, and therefore are confused about how much time, effort, and resources will go into promoting their books. If you're already published, then you probably have an idea of what I'm talking about, but if you're soon to be published or are shopping your book around, then I'd like to help you know what to expect.

One harsh reality you should prepare yourself for is that most publishers don't have a large budget to work with for advertising. For this reason, a lot of promotional work publishers do relies on publicity—which is to say they try to come up with creative ways to get positive reviews and mentions of books in newspapers, magazines, online, and elsewhere. This, as you can imagine, can be hit-and-miss. Publicists find themselves at the mercy of the publications they're soliciting for reviews.

Which brings me to the second thing you need to keep in mind (especially if you're working with a larger publisher): Publishers have to divide their time and resources amongst many titles. In my own day-to-day work, this seems to be the primary cause of frustration with authors I talk to. It's easy to feel forgotten or neglected when your publisher has a few main initiatives planned for your book when you're brimming with lots of great ideas.

So where does that leave you? First of all, I advise any author to do a lot of her own work promoting her book. Whether your publisher has a large marketing plan or not, anything extra you can do will help. Set up some local speaking engagements and promote your book on your website or blog. Stay active on online message boards and forums relating to your topic. Consistently update your blog or website with new content. Attend writers conferences, book festivals, and other events relating to the genre you write in. Keep your publisher informed of everything you are doing. This will help them to coordinate their efforts with yours.

The main thing is to keep open lines of communication with your audience as well as with your publisher. By being open, positive, and easily accessible, more opportunities will open up for you.

SCOTT FRANCIS is an editor for Writer's Digest Books. Prior to turning his focus to editing he served as marketing manager for Writer's Digest. He is the author of *Monster Spotter's Guide to North America* and co-author of *The Writer's Book of Matches*. He blogs at seescott write.wordpress.com.

MARKETING YOUR SMALL PRESS BOOK

....

Jack Smith

You know the image: The novelist does the book tour, signs some books, then goes on to pounding the keys on the next one. After all, writers are writers, not marketers. If this was true at one time, writers today are expected to get actively involved in marketing and promotion, especially at small presses, and increasingly at large commercial presses, according to Kim Wright, author of *Your Path to Publication* (Press 53) and a literary novel *Love in Mid Air*. This is not to say that publishers won't get involved; they do—and sometimes quite actively. But the writer mustn't think fiction writing is the writer's only role. There's a lot the writer is expected to do.

Writers today are using several promotional strategies to get their book to the media, marketers, and the reading public. Gearing up can even begin with the submission process itself.

THE SUBMISSION PROCESS

Kim Wright states that small press publishers today expect their potential authors to show that they are "connected to a wider community." They need to demonstrate that they are "prepared to promote the book and understand that it's part of their job to promote the book." They need to have developed a strong Internet presence—which includes Facebook, Twitter, and blogs. If you come off as the "artiste" who is above it all, sporting your MFA, "that can count against you," says Wright. You need to be "part of a team, not an artist who just gives them the book." You need to make clear that you know your "target reader" and the "best way to get your book into the hands of that target reader." Lidia Yuknavitch, memoir-ist and novelist, states that she's "very present in terms of FB, Blogs, and other Internet re-alities," and she encourages writers to "include their level of participation in social media in their cover letters." Or, she says, it's important to at least make it clear, up front, that you "have a platform or the capability of understanding social media presence." Barry Kitter-man discovered the same expectation before SMU Press agreed to publish his novel *The Baker's Boy*. "I didn't have to convince them that I knew what I was doing with Facebook and a personal web page, but I had to promise that I would do my best to figure something out. After I put together a web page and got on line with Facebook, SMU offered to publish my second book, *From the San Joaquin*, and they had every expectation that I would con-tinue to try to promote my work online." Publishers' expectations can certainly vary, but bottom-line: You need to make the publisher confident that you are willing to actively pro-mote and market your book.

ONCE YOUR BOOK IS ACCEPTED

It might seem that you have nothing to market until your book actually comes out. But it's a mistake to think so. The marketing should begin much earlier than that. Lidia Yuknavitch's novel *Dora: A Head Case* is scheduled for publication by Hawthorne Books on September 1, 2012. Yuknavitch says, "I started my engine up Sept. 1st, 2011." There are a number of things that both writer and publisher can do prior to the book's coming out.

Develop a Web Presence

According to Seth Fried, author of the collection *The Great Frustration* (Soft Skull Press), "If you can develop a web presence or a presence in the literary community before your book comes out, things will be that much easier for you down the line." A web presence, says Fried, includes three principal things: maintaining a blog, making use of social media, and cre-ating book trailers. One important caveat, though: "No promotional method will be use-ful to you unless you're willing to use your personality to breathe some sort of life into it."

An author's website is very important. Authors may need to create this on their own, or they may be fortunate enough to get help from publishers. Prior to the release of her novel *Stranger Here Below*, Joyce Hinnefeld developed her own website with the help of a former student, a web designer. Yet she found her publisher, Unbridled Books, quite "helpful in planning and implementing this."

Seek Media Coverage

The author will need to work closely with the publisher on marketing and author press plans, which start as early as a year in advance of publication. A year before her novel *Sleight* came out, Kirsten Kaschock's publisher, Coffee House Press, asked her to fill out a questionnaire about her background in order to decide on the best way to "pitch the book to sellers and reviewers—at least in part." Hawthorne Books began to develop an author press plan for Lidia Yuknavitch's novel nearly a year prior to its release.

The publisher naturally has an important part to play here. Shortly before publication, the press should actively pursue media coverage, says Seth Fried. "Ideally," says Fried, the publisher will take two basic "promotional steps" prior to the book's release. "1) A few months before the book is released, the publisher will produce advanced reading copies (also known as ARCs) and mail them at their own expense to various media outlets along with a press release. 2) If the publisher in question has a publicist, he or she will then follow up with those outlets to see if they have any interest in covering your book."

This media coverage, says Barry Kitterman, means advance copies to all "possible reviewers: hometown newspapers, alumni magazines, publications that come out of any and all religious affiliations, lodges, professional societies." Still, says Kitterman, writers cannot expect the publisher to handle all of this alone. For one thing, writers should contact magazines and journals where they've recently published and let editors know about their new book. "Most editors are happy to at least announce that one of their previous writers is coming out with a new book." Some editors, says Kitterman, will include a review of the book. For second, or subsequent books, the writer should consider contacting those who wrote favorable reviews of the first one. The author's publisher "should be willing," says Kitterman, "to send review copies out, lots of review copies."

Advance Copies to Independent Booksellers

Besides media outlets, publishers should also send advance copies to independent booksellers, says Joyce Hinnefeld. Unbridled Books did this for her novel *In Hovering Flight*, and she found that it "helped the book's reception and sales tremendously." She explains why: "*If the booksellers particularly like the book (or take a particular interest in it—I think, for instance, some booksellers like the idea of promoting a first novel in particular), they'll 'hand sell' it more vigorously; that is, they'll recommend it to customers and just talk it up in general, and in some cases they might also invite the writer to do a signing, etc.*" The writer has a part to play here also—in terms of establishing connections with independent bookstores. Lidia Yuknavitch advises authors to "build personal relationships with booksellers and industry folks. For my own part, I have sent a giant thank-you cake to the back room employees at Powell's City of Books, and other tokens of affection to indie stores that have worked so hard to keep my *COW* (*The Chronology of Water*) alive." She also visits indie stores as often as she can to talk to store personnel, buy books, and ask how she can "promote their stores."

WHEN THE BOOK IS RELEASED

All the advance prepublication promotion is quite important, but now is the time to put things in high gear. Strategies include a strong campaign of web presence as well as direct, personal promotion of the book.

Blogs, Blog Reviews & Facebook Book Pages

A quick search on Google will produce blogs of all kinds on different fiction genres: mysteries, thrillers, chick lit, literary novels, etc. "This is the world that writers need to get connected to," says Kim Wright. Lidia Yuknavitch has. For her memoir, *The Chronology of Water*, she as well as her publisher, Hawthorne Books, sent requests to blogs "that smelled like my readership or ones I already was familiar with." They not only wanted to interview her but also to get her blogging on topics connected to her book—in this case, "gender, sexuality, grief, addiction, relationships, lgbt issues, art, and the writing process." Essays she wrote for The Rumpus "generated a high degree of traffic and interest in my book." Kim Wright advises authors to use Twitter to drive traffic to blogs they're featured on: "Tweet with a link to blogs where you're featured." At the end of a blog interview, the reader can click on a button that sends them right to Amazon to buy the book. "The beauty of the Internet," notes Wright, "is that readers who like your blogpost can buy your book so much faster."

Writers today are expected to get actively involved in marketing and promotion, especially at small presses, and increasingly at large commercial presses.

Lidia Yuknavitch praises the blogosphere for its capacity to get the word out: "Bloggers are connected to other bloggers, and so if they admire your work or take an interest, word spreads like wildfire." Brian Doyle's *Bin Laden's Blind Spot and Other Stories* (Red Hen Press) was reviewed "plenty," by bloggers, says Doyle. Red Hen, he states, was proactive in sending out review copies—"I bet they sent fifty easy." Blog reviews can reach target audiences for your book. Kirsten Kaschock is excited about her novel *Sleight* being reviewed on thinkingdance.net "because it will get the word out to a specialty audience it is more difficult to reach through other channels."

Facebook pages for the book itself are a great promotional tool. Oregon State University Press did a Facebook page for Brian Doyle's novel *Mink River*, including "posting of the best reviews, snippets that were cut from the book, musings from the author, the best notes from readers, etc." Doyle feels that Red Hen Press's Facebook page for his *Bin Laden's Blind Spot* has really made the book come "alive."

Book Tours, Conferences, Book Clubs

"The book tour is dead," says Kim Wright, and she points out that an author can travel a great distance and have only two or three people show up. Today's alternative is the virtual book tour. Through Lit Pub, Lidia Yuknavitch was able to do a virtual tour for her memoir. "Molly Gaudry posted chapter by chapter discussion questions and readers responded, and I responded when I could as well. Deep penetration of your book like in a book club—only people also shared and posted online about the discussions." Yuknavitch did schedule readings for her book, but in addition, she found another great creative alternative: workshops. She set up "a late night series of one-hour workshops at Broadway Books, splitting the fees with the store."

Instead of book tours at independent bookstores, where it's "hard to draw a crowd," says Kim Wright, authors should serve as panelists at conferences, as well as participate in book fairs, where you also have "sheer volume, in the sense there are going to be people there anyway. You can sell a lot of books at a conference." Seth Fried served as a panelist at the Brooklyn Book Festival. "It was a great opportunity for the book and got my work out to a lot of readers." Marcos Villatoro, author of *Blood Daughters: A Romilla Chacon Novel*, published by Red Hen, has acted as panel speaker many times. Whether you sell a lot of books or not, he says, it's an unobtrusive way to get "your face and name out there as much as you can." For Joyce Hinnefeld, there's another attractive, professional feature—"the opportunity to connect (and discuss ideas) with other writers."

Book clubs are another important venue. There are a "tremendous amount of book clubs, and they can lead to more sales," says Kim Wright. "You can meet with them in person or virtually through Skype." Lidia Yuknavitch finds the experience a "wonderfully intimate form/atmosphere where everyone can let their 'author' guard down and just, you know, be a person who loves literature." Joyce Hinnefeld has travelled to "lots of book clubs," from her home in Pennsylvania to the Midwest. She's never used Skype, but she states: "I did talk to one or two book groups by phone."

Using Creativity

Kirsten Kaschock found a truly creative way to promote her novel *Sleight*, which she calls "odd" since it doesn't fall neatly into a particular genre or "class of similar books." At the Book Expo in New York she enlisted the help of dancers and filmmakers "to help represent the art form at the center of the novel." She states: "Three dancers, all pre-professional students at NYC colleges, performed contact improv within Coffee House Press's booth, visually representing the imaginary art form at the heart of the book. Browsers stopped to find out what was going on, and the sense of inquiry created was entirely appropriate for *Sleight*—a novel that doesn't shy away from movement and mystery."

Internet or Personal Exposure—Which Is Better?

Kim Wright puts considerable emphasis on the author's Internet presence; however, as we've seen she also urges writers to do panels at conferences, participate in book fairs, and present at book clubs. Brian Doyle puts most of his emphasis on personal exposure: "The author's energy in doing readings, book club visits, visits to schools, radio interviews, web video snips, is maybe the most important of all. People do read and buy books in great part by word of mouth, and every time you connect in person to twenty people, fifty, one hundred, you ripple the web of people who will talk about and read the book. I have great respect for social networking with electricity, but my experience has been that social networking with your own voice and face and humor and ears and heart is better and deeper." If the jury's still out on this one, one thing is certainly clear: The author who wants to successfully market a book has to consider all the options carefully and do what works best to get the book out there. And yet one might remember Seth Fried's caution about any promotional strategy. If you don't put your personality in it, it won't work.

Whichever strategies you do employ, the most important thing to keep in mind is that once your book is published, you shouldn't decide that the work is over. The publisher can certainly take important steps to help, but the author must get involved. The work of promotion and marketing must go on. "While you're writing your next tome, keep marketing the last book," advises Marcos Villatoro.

PROMOTING AND MARKETING—THE PAYOFF

Small presses, as we've seen, can and do get involved in very important ways in the marketing and promotion of their books. But Marcos Villatoro states that authors need to handle most of the promotion on their own. And, for him, this only makes sense: "Don't spend two years writing the great American novel and only two weeks trying to market it." Villatoro has taken an active part in his own book promotion: "I tweet/Facebook/set up interviews with radio and TV/get into universities."

Lidia Yuknavitch also emphasizes that the writer's work isn't done when the manuscript is finished: "Do not pretend you are 'done' with the work as a writer when you finish your book." "A lot" has to be done by the author to market the book, says Yuknavitch, yet it's a good process with small presses: "The beauty of working with small presses is that you can maintain a great deal of artistic integrity and participate fully in the entire process. The harder side of that is that it is a lot of work—no agent or media team or marketing team . . . to spread your glory nationally."

Without this promotion, you essentially have no audience for your book. It comes down to what you want to get out of your publication, says Seth Fried: "If all you want is to be able to put on your CV that you published something in 2011, then once your book is accepted you don't really need to do anything. But if you want your book to have an audience, then you should expend as much energy promoting your book as you did writing it. In the months since my book came out, I have done eighteen readings, participated in seventeen interviews for various outlets, written twenty blog posts, tweeted five hundred tweets, wrote and published four new short stories, made five trailers, and attended an untold number of literary events. That might not sound like a lot, but it sure felt like it."

Writers tend to resist doing this, but says Barry Kitterman, "Even the most curmudgeonly luddite can have at least a small website or a Facebook page. It's painfully hard for most of us to promote ourselves and our own work. Take a deep breath, grit your teeth, and do it." Get help, says Kitterman, from an assistant: "A student worker, a son or daughter, an indentured servant. If someone reliable offers to help, don't turn anyone down."

The big payoff is a book that really sells, of course. "And a continual, gradual interest in the book," as Marcos Villatoro points out.

And yet, says Seth Fried, there's more at hand than big sales. "As a writer, I think success comes when you find evidence that your book has managed to get into the hands of people who enjoy it. Obviously, there's no objective way to measure if your book is being read or passed around. But you can pick up hints here and there. People will e-mail you random messages, or you'll go into an indie bookstore and find your book under Chuck's Picks."

Or, as Lidia Yuknavitch says: "The personal e-mails I receive from individuals have blown me away. This has never happened to me before, so I take care to respond to every one I receive. I don't ever want to forget or lose sight of the fact that readers and writers really do have a one-on-one relationship with each other."

And what about the publisher? For Brian Doyle, the publisher can do a lot to connect the book to readers. "In my view, the very best marketing a press can do is sing the book as an experience, a stimulation, a deeper play than merely product."

SOME DON'TS

There are a number of things presses can do and a number of good things writers can do to promote and market their books. But is there anything an author shouldn't do? Here are four things to think about:

- Don't approach big media outlets. Seth Fried states: "As an author, you should not approach huge media outlets about the book unless you know someone there who will be happy to hear from you. Writing to *The New York Times* about your book is just going to make you seem like a wackadoo. It's best to leave that stuff to your publisher."

- Don't be narcissistic. Marcos Villatoro states: "Red Hen taught me the finesse of tweeting: for every one tweet you write about yourself, write three tweets about other events/people. Don't let the inherent narcissism (which is fundamental to writing) of a writer entrap you in your own swamp of self-interests." Projecting an image of self-interest is "the sign of a desperate writer."

- Don't assume familiarity. Says Lidia Yuknavitch: "Do not assume familiarity—*ever*—you have to build relationships with people and bookstores and communities of readers, just like in life."

- "It's rarely necessary to spend money on ads, and you may not even need a publicist," says Kim Wright. "Work hard for the things you can do without spending money."

And a final piece of advice about attitude. Don't let disappointments drag you down. Barry Kitterman cautions: "It's easy for a writer to be disappointed with a small crowd at a bookstore event or with a review by someone who clearly hasn't read the book." But like others have noted, Kitterman states, "The measure of a successful book has to be something other than sales and royalties. Each of us figures it out in our own way."

JACK SMITH's satirical novel *Hog to Hog* (Texas Review Press) won the George Garrett Fiction Prize. His stories and essays have appeared in many publications, including *North American Review*, *The Southern Review*, *Georgia Review*, and *Ploughshares*. In addition to writing, he co-edits *The Green Hills Literary Lantern*.

BLOGGING BASICS:

Get the Most Out of Your Blog

....

by Robert Lee Brewer

In these days of publishing and media change, writers have to build platforms and learn how to connect to audiences if they want to improve their chances of publication and overall success. There are many methods of audience connection available to writers, but one of the most important is blogging.

Since I've spent several years successfully blogging—both personally and professionally—I figure I've got a few nuggets of wisdom to pass on to writers who are curious about blogging or who are already doing it.

Here's my quick list of tips:

1. **START BLOGGING TODAY.** If you don't have a blog, use Blogger, WordPress, or some other blogging software to start your blog today. It's free, and you can start off with your very personal "Here I am, world" post.
2. **START SMALL.** Blogs are essentially very simple, but they can get very complicated (for people who like complications). However, I advise bloggers start small and evolve over time.
3. **USE YOUR NAME IN YOUR URL.** This will make it easier for search engines to find you when your audience eventually starts seeking you out by name. For instance, my URL is http://robertleebrewer.blogspot.com. If you try Googling "Robert Lee Brewer," you'll notice that My Name Is Not Bob is one of the top five search results (behind my other blog: Poetic Asides).
4. **UNLESS YOU HAVE A REASON, USE YOUR NAME AS THE TITLE OF YOUR BLOG.** Again, this helps with search engine results. My Poetic Asides blog includes my name in the title, and it ranks higher than My Name Is Not Bob. However, I felt the play on my name was worth the trade-off.

5. **FIGURE OUT YOUR BLOGGING GOALS.** You should return to this step every couple months, because it's natural for your blogging goals to evolve over time. Initially, your blogging goals may be to make a post a week about what you have written, submitted, etc. Over time, you may incorporate guests posts, contests, tips, etc.

6. **BE YOURSELF.** I'm a big supporter of the idea that your image should match your identity. It gets too confusing trying to maintain a million personas. Know who you are and be that on your blog, whether that means you're sincere, funny, sarcastic, etc.

7. **POST AT LEAST ONCE A WEEK.** This is for starters. Eventually, you may find it better to post once a day or multiple times per day. But remember: Start small and evolve over time.

8. **POST RELEVANT CONTENT.** This means that you post things that your readers might actually care to know.

9. **USEFUL AND HELPFUL POSTS WILL ATTRACT MORE VISITORS.** Talking about yourself is all fine and great. I do it myself. But if you share truly helpful advice, your readers will share it with others, and visitors will find you on search engines.

10. **TITLE YOUR POSTS IN A WAY THAT GETS YOU FOUND IN SEARCH ENGINES.** The more specific you can get the better. For instance, the title "Blogging Tips" will most likely get lost in search results. However, the title "Blogging Tips for Writers" specifies which audience I'm targeting and increases the chances of being found on the first page of search results.

11. **LINK TO POSTS IN OTHER MEDIA.** If you have an e-mail newsletter, link to your blog posts in your newsletter. If you have social media accounts, link to your blog posts there. If you have a helpful post, link to it in relevant forums and on message boards.

....

Don't spend a week writing each post. Try to keep it to an hour or two tops and then post.

....

12. **WRITE WELL, BUT BE CONCISE.** At the end of the day, you're writing blog posts, not literary manifestos. Don't spend a week writing each post. Try to keep it to an hour or two tops and then post. Make sure your spelling and grammar are good, but don't stress yourself out too much.

13. **FIND LIKE-MINDED BLOGGERS.** Comment on their blogs regularly and link to them from yours. Eventually, they may do the same. Keep in mind that blogging is a form of social media, so the more you communicate with your peers the more you'll get out of the process.

14. **RESPOND TO COMMENTS ON YOUR BLOG.** Even if it's just a simple "Thanks," respond to your readers if they comment on your blog. After all, you want your readers to be engaged with your blog, and you want them to know you care that they took time to comment.

15. **EXPERIMENT.** Start small, but don't get complacent. Every so often, try something new. For instance, the biggest draw to my Poetic Asides blog are the poetry prompts and challenges I issue to poets. Initially, that was an experiment—one that worked very well. I've tried other experiments that haven't panned out, and that's fine. It's all part of a process.

SEO TIPS FOR WRITERS

Most writers may already know what SEO is. If not, SEO stands for *search engine optimization*. Basically, a site or blog that practices good SEO habits should improve its rankings in search engines, such as Google and Bing. Most huge corporations have realized the importance of SEO and spend enormous sums of time, energy, and money on perfecting their SEO practices. However, writers can improve their SEO without going to those same extremes.

In this section, I will use the terms of *site pages* and *blog posts* interchangeably. In both cases, you should be practicing the same SEO strategies (when it makes sense).

Here are my top tips on ways to improve your SEO starting today:

1. **USE APPROPRIATE KEYWORDS.** Make sure that your page displays your main keyword(s) in the page title, content, URL, title tags, page header, image names and tags (if you're including images). All of this is easy to do, but if you feel overwhelmed, just remember to use your keyword(s) in your page title and content (especially in the first and last fifty words of your page).

2. **USE KEYWORDS NATURALLY.** Don't kill your content and make yourself look like a spammer to search engines by overloading your page with your keyword(s). You don't get SEO points for quantity but for quality. Plus, one of the main ways to improve your page rankings is when you...

3. **DELIVER QUALITY CONTENT.** The best way to improve your SEO is by providing content that readers want to share with others by linking to your pages. Some of the top results in search engines are years old, because the content is so good that people keep coming back. So, incorporate your keywords in a smart way, but make sure it works organically with your content.

4. **UPDATE CONTENT REGULARLY.** If your site looks dead to visitors, then it'll appear that way to search engines, too. So update your content regularly. This should be very easy for writers who have blogs. For writers who have sites, incorporate your blog into your site. This will make it easier for visitors to your blog to discover more about you on your site (through your site navigation tools).

5. **LINK BACK TO YOUR OWN CONTENT.** If I have a post titled Blogging Tips for Writers, for instance, I'll link back to it if I have a platform-building post, because the two complement each other. This also helps clicks on my blog, which helps SEO. The one caveat is that you don't go crazy with your linking and that you make sure your links are relevant. Otherwise, you'll kill your traffic, which is not good for your page rankings.

6. **LINK TO OTHERS YOU CONSIDER HELPFUL.** Back in 2000, I remember being ordered by my boss at the time (who didn't last too much longer afterward) to ignore any competitive or complementary websites—no matter how helpful their content—because they were our competitors. You can try basing your online strategy on these principles, but I'm nearly 100 percent confident you'll fail. It's helpful for other sites and your own to link to other great resources. I shine a light on others to help them out (if I find their content truly helpful) in the hopes that they'll do the same if ever they find my content truly helpful for their audience.

7. **GET SPECIFIC WITH YOUR HEADLINES.** If you interview someone on your blog, don't title your post with an interesting quotation. While that strategy may help get readers in the print world, it doesn't help with SEO at all. Instead, title your post as "Interview With (insert name here)." If you have a way to identify the person further, include that in the title, too. For instance, when I interview poets on my Poetic Asides blog, I'll title those posts like this: Interview With Poet Erika Meitner. Erika's name is a keyword, but so are the terms *poet* and *interview*.

....

If you interview someone on your blog, don't title your post with an interesting quotation. While that strategy may help get readers in the print world, it doesn't help with SEO at all.

....

8. **USE IMAGES.** Many expert sources state that the use of images can improve SEO, because it shows search engines that the person creating the page is spending a little extra time and effort on the page than a common spammer. However, I'd caution anyone using images to make sure those images are somehow complementary to the content. Don't just throw up a lot of images that have no relevance to anything. At the same time...

9. **OPTIMIZE IMAGES THROUGH STRATEGIC LABELING.** Writers can do this by making sure the image file is labeled using your keyword(s) for the post. Using the Erika Meitner example above (which does include images), I would label the file "Erika Meitner headshot.jpg"—or whatever the image file type happens to be. Writers can

also improve image SEO through the use of captions and ALT tagging. Of course, at the same time, writers should always ask themselves if it's worth going through all that trouble for each image or not. Each writer has to answer that question for him (or her) self.

10. **USE YOUR SOCIAL MEDIA PLATFORM TO SPREAD THE WORD.** Whenever you do something new on your site or blog, you should share that information on your other social media sites, such as Twitter, Facebook, LinkedIn, online forums, etc. This lets your social media connections know that something new is on your site/blog. If it's relevant and/or valuable, they'll let others know. And that's a great way to build your SEO.

Programmers and marketers could get much deeper into the dynamics of SEO optimization, but I think these tips will help most writers out immediately and effectively while still allowing plenty of time and energy for the actual work of writing.

BLOG DESIGN TIPS FOR WRITERS

Design is an important element to any blog's success. But how can you improve your blog's design if you're not a designer? I'm just an editor with an English Lit degree and no formal training in design. However, I've worked in media for more than a decade now and can share some very fundamental and easy tricks to improve the design of your blog.

Here are my seven blog design tips for writers:

1. **USE LISTS.** Whether they're numbered or bullet points, use lists when possible. Lists break up the text and make it easy for readers to follow what you're blogging.

2. **BOLD MAIN POINTS IN LISTS.** Again, this helps break up the text while also highlighting the important points of your post.

3. **USE HEADINGS.** If your posts are longer than three hundred words and you don't use lists, then please break up the text by using basic headings.

4. **USE A READABLE FONT.** Avoid using fonts that are too large or too small. Avoid using cursive or weird fonts. Times New Roman or Arial works, but if you want to get "creative," use something similar to those.

5. **LEFT ALIGN.** English-speaking readers are trained to read left to right. If you want to make your blog easier to read, avoid centering or right aligning your text (unless you're purposefully calling out the text).

6. **USE SMALL PARAGRAPHS.** A good rule of thumb is to try and avoid paragraphs that drone on longer than five sentences. I usually try to keep paragraphs to around three sentences.

7. **ADD RELEVANT IMAGES.** Personally, I shy away from using too many images. My reason is that I only like to use them if they're relevant. However, images are very

powerful on blogs, so please use them. Just make sure they're relevant to your blog post.

If you're already doing everything on my list, keep it up! If you're not, then you might want to rethink your design strategy on your blog. Simply adding a header here and a list there can easily improve the design of a blog post.

GUEST POSTING TIPS FOR WRITERS

Recently, I've broken into guest posting as both a guest poster and as a host of guest posts (over at my Poetic Asides blog). So far, I'm pretty pleased with both sides of the guest posting process. As a writer, it gives me access to an engaged audience I may not usually reach. As a blogger, it provides me with fresh and valuable content I don't have to create. Guest blogging is a rare win-win scenario.

That said, writers could benefit from a few tips on the process of guest posting:

1. **PITCH GUEST POSTS LIKE ONE WOULD PITCH ARTICLES TO A MAGAZINE.** Include what your hook is for the post, what you plan to cover, and a little about who you are. Remember: Your post should somehow benefit the audience of the blog you'd like to guest post.

2. **OFFER PROMOTIONAL COPY OF BOOK (OR OTHER GIVEAWAYS) AS PART OF YOUR GUEST POST.** Having a random giveaway for people who comment on a blog post can help spur conversation and interest in your guest post, which is a great way to get the most mileage out of your guest appearance.

3. **CATER POSTS TO AUDIENCE.** As the editor of *Writer's Market* and *Poet's Market*, I have great range in the topics I can cover. However, if I'm writing a guest post for a fiction blog, I'll write about things of interest to a novelist, not a poet.

4. **MAKE PERSONAL, BUT PROVIDE NUGGET.** Guest posts are a great opportunity for you to really show your stuff to a new audience. You could write a very helpful and impersonal post, but that won't connect with readers the way a very helpful and personal post will. Getting more personal makes readers want to learn more about you (and your blog, your book, your Twitter account, etc.). Speaking of which...

5. **SHARE LINKS TO YOUR WEBSITE, BLOG, SOCIAL NETWORKS, ETC.** After all, you need to make it easy for readers who enjoyed your guest post to learn more about you and your projects. Start the conversation in your guest post and keep it going on your own sites, profiles, etc. And related to that...

6. **PROMOTE YOUR GUEST POST THROUGH YOUR NORMAL CHANNELS ONCE THE POST GOES LIVE.** Your normal audience will want to know where you've been and what you've been doing. Plus, guest posts lend a little extra "street cred" to your projects. But don't stop there...

7. **CHECK FOR COMMENTS ON YOUR GUEST POST AND RESPOND IN A TIMELY MANNER.** Sometimes the comments are the most interesting part of a guest post (no offense). This is where readers can ask more in-depth or related questions, and it's also where you can show your expertise on the subject by being as helpful as possible. And guiding all seven of these tips is this one:

8. **PUT SOME EFFORT INTO YOUR GUEST POST.** Part of the benefit to guest posting is the opportunity to connect with a new audience. Make sure you bring your A-game, because you need to make a good impression if you want this exposure to actually help grow your audience. Don't stress yourself out, but put a little thought into what you submit.

ONE ADDITIONAL TIP: Have fun with it. Passion is what really drives the popularity of blogs. Share your passion and enthusiasm, and readers are sure to be impressed.

ROBERT LEE BREWER is the editor of *Writer's Market* and *Poet's Market,* as well as a published poet. He is the former Poet Laureate of the Blogosphere.

TWITTER CHEAT SHEET FOR WRITERS

by Robert Lee Brewer

With the publishing (and/or media) industry changing at the speed of light, so are the roles of writers (or content providers), editors (or content managers), agents (or content strategists), etc. One big change for writers (even in fiction, poetry, and other fields) is that they are expected to take an active role in building their own platforms via online and real-world networking and exposure. One great tool for this online is Twitter.

It's easy enough (and free) to create a Twitter account, but how can writers take advantage of this social networking tool? What can they logically expect to gain from using it? What is a hashtag anyway? Well, hopefully, this cheat sheet will help.

First, let's look at some basic terminology:

- **TWEET** = Any message sent out to everyone on Twitter. Unless you direct message (DM) someone, everything on Twitter is a Tweet and viewable by anyone.
- **RT** = Retweet. Twitter created a RT-ing tool that makes for easy retweets, but the standard convention is to put an RT and cite the source before reposting something funny or useful that someone else has shared. For example, if I tweeted "Nouns are verbs waiting to happen," you could RT me this way: RT @robertleebrewer Nouns are verbs waiting to happen.
- **DM** = Direct message. These are private and only between people who DM each other.
- **# = HASHTAG.** These are used in front a word (or set of letters) to allow people to easily communicate on a specific topic. For instance, I tweet poetry with other poets on Twitter by using the hashtag #poettalk. Poets can click on the "poettalk" after the hashtag (no space) or they can search on the term "poettalk" in Twitter (right-hand toolbar).

- **#FF** = Follow Friday. This is a nice way to show support for other tweeters on Twitter. On Friday.

Second, here are ten things you can do to optimize your use of Twitter:

1. **USE YOUR REAL NAME IF POSSIBLE.** Make it easy for people you know or meet to find you on Twitter.

2. **ADD A PROFILE PICTURE.** Preferably this will be a picture of you. People connect better with other people, not cartoons, book covers, logos, etc.

3. **LINK TO A WEBSITE.** Hopefully, you have a blog or website you can link to in your profile. If you don't have a website or blog, make one. Now. And then link to it from your Twitter profile.

4. **WRITE YOUR BIO.** Make this memorable in some way. You don't have to be funny or cute, but more power to you if you can do this and still make it relevant to who you are.

5. **TWEET REGULARLY.** It doesn't matter if you have only two followers (and one is your mom); you still need to tweet daily (or nearly daily) for Twitter to be effective. And remember: If you don't have anything original to add, you can always RT something funny or useful from someone else.

6. **TWEET RELEVANT INFORMATION.** Don't be the person who tweets like this: "I am making a salad;" "I am eating a salad;" "That salad was good;" "I wonder what I'm going to eat next;" etc. These tweets are not interesting or relevant. However, if your salad-eating experience rocked your world in a unique way, feel free to share: "Just ate the best salad ever. Now, I'm ready to write a novel."

7. **LINK AND DON'T LINK.** It's good to link to other places and share things you're doing or that you've found elsewhere. At the same time, if all you do is link, people may think you're just trying to sell them stuff all the time.

8. **HAVE A PERSONALITY.** Be yourself. You don't have to be overly cute, funny, or smart. Just be yourself and remember that Twitter is all about connecting people. So be a person.

9. **FOLLOW THOSE WORTH FOLLOWING.** Just because you're being followed you don't have to return the follow. For instance, if some local restaurant starts following me, I'm not going to follow them back, because they aren't relevant to me or to my audience.

10. **COMMUNICATE WITH OTHERS.** I once heard someone refer to Twitter as one big cocktail party, and it's true. Twitter is all about communication. If people talk to you or RT you, make sure you talk back and/or thank them. (*Here's a secret: People like to feel involved and acknowledged. I like it; you like it; and so does everyone else.*)

And, of course, if you're not already, please follow me on Twitter @robertleebrewer (http://twitter.com/robertleebrewer).

HERE ARE SOME EXTRA RESOURCES:

- **TwitterGrader.com** (http://twittergrader.com) This site allows you to enter your profile at any given time and find out how you're doing (according to them) in using Twitter effectively. Of course, the grade you receive is bound to not be perfect, but it is a good measuring stick.
- **What the Hashtag?** (http://wthashtag.com) This site allows you to search for hashtags, run reports on them, get transcripts between specific time periods, and more.
- **Hootsuite** (http://hootsuite.com) This is one of many tools that allow you to Tweet and track your account without even going to Twitter. Many (maybe even most) people use these. There are others, such as TweetDeck, Seesmic, etc. Find one that you like and let it make your social networking life easier to manage.
- **bit.ly** (http://bit.ly) This is one of many URL shortening services out there, which is very helpful when tweeting URL links, since they can easily eat into your 140-character limit on Twitter. This particular one makes it easy for you to track clicks, though I'm sure that's fairly standard.

ROBERT LEE BREWER is the editor of *Writer's Market* and *Poet's Market*, as well as a published poet. He is the former Poet Laureate of the Blogosphere.

SELL YOUR NOVEL LIKE WILDFIRE

Marketing Tips for Fiction Writers

....

Rob Eagar

"Informing the reader about facts and events is an important part of what I do. But ultimately that's not enough: I also want you to care. A history book can educate you, but oddly, a novel is much more likely to move you to tears, because it creates empathy. That's the amazing power of fiction."

Barbara Kingsolver—New York Times best-selling author

Fiction authors sometimes see themselves as a different animal within the publishing community. Novelists often bristle at the idea of becoming world-class marketers. For some reason, they harbor the idea that fiction authors shouldn't, or couldn't, promote their books. I've heard excuses, such as:

- "Novelists should just stay home and write. Leave the marketing to the publisher."
- "Radio and TV programs hate interviewing fiction authors and prefer nonfiction."
- "Marketing corrupts the purity of writing, so authors shouldn't promote their work."
- "I'm too introverted to promote my books in public."
- "A few book signings ought to be enough."

If an author holds these kinds of beliefs, it's no wonder she might view book marketing as the emotional equivalent of getting a root canal. Fortunately the process of boosting your book sales doesn't have to be a painful experience. There are plenty of activities to choose from and at least a few should fit your personality.

Having said that, I do agree that there are some distinct differences that separate how you promote fiction versus nonfiction. For example, successful fiction tends to rely more on word of mouth than nonfiction does. Thus many publishers put less emphasis on a novelist's marketing platform and focus more on his skill as a writer. The assumption is that if the story is compelling enough, the book will sell itself.

I partially agree with this idea. My concern is that the publishing industry churns out so many new books each year, even great ones sometimes get crowded out by all of the hubbub. That's why a solid marketing plan is just as crucial for selling fiction as it is for nonfiction.

Here is a list of tips that specifically focus on promoting novels. If you're an introvert, you will be glad to find that most of these tips don't require you to leave your writer's cave or interact with people in public.

1. Create Emotion With Your Author Website

Your author website plays a critical role in helping boost book sales. It's to every author's benefit to achieve these four main goals with their online presence:

> **GOAL #1:** Credibility—Establish your expertise
>
> **GOAL #2:** Content—Offer value-laden information for free
>
> **GOAL #3:** Community—Create a reader fan base
>
> **GOAL #4:** Contact Information—Ask visitors to let you stay in touch

However, there is one important aspect about websites that affects fiction authors more than nonfiction writers. The difference is the ability to create an emotional experience with your website. A fiction author's website should be more than just a boring group of pages that lists facts about you and your book. Your website should provide a visual and emotional connection that relates to the stories within your books.

2. Offer Contests

People love to win stuff. Likewise, whenever a lottery starts reaching an obscenely high number, such as $200 million, people naturally start to talk about it. You can tap into this same principle by creating a contest that really excites people.

3. Activate the Power of Book Clubs and Discussion Groups

One marketing technique particularly useful to fiction authors is to tap the power of book clubs and discussion groups. Millions of readers congregate both in person and online to discuss their favorite novels. Promoting your books to these groups can quickly boost sales by increasing the number of volume orders placed.

4. Create Tools for Bloggers and Social Media

Book reviews can mean life or death to a novel. Getting praise from influential critics is a crucial aspect to promoting fiction. Before the Internet, though, major newspapers, magazines, and Oprah's book club controlled the literary review world. If you couldn't get a book review from the establishment, you were out of luck.

Fortunately the Internet came along and revolutionized the book review process by allowing anyone to evaluate a book and post comments for the world to see. The major sources of influence are no longer consolidated to just a few industry critics. Today there are book review bloggers and social media mavens who have bigger followings than the old "experts." This change has helped level the playing field for authors of all kinds.

It's easier than ever before to market your novel to large audiences. The key is to make it as painless as possible for bloggers to get access to your book. That's why I recommend novelists create a free "toolkit" on their website that simplifies the process for bloggers and social media reviewers. Fill your toolkit with these resources:

- Cover art images of your book in various sizes.
- A brief author bio of around one hundred words.
- A one-paragraph synopsis of your book.
- A website link to your video trailer, if you have one.
- A website link or PDF file to download your first chapter.
- A short "Q&A with the author" article that a blogger can use.
- Your contact information for bloggers to reach you and request a review.

Creating a toolkit for bloggers simplifies the review process on both ends by serving as a one-stop shop for your novel. Bloggers can quickly access all of the information without having to track you down. That kind of speed and convenience makes it easier for them to post a review without waiting to get your information and possibly losing interest. Likewise, there's less work on your part, because the necessary tools are premade and ready to go.

Once you've composed your toolkit, don't sit back and wait for bloggers to find you. Use online search engines to find bloggers that address your book's genre.

5. Maximize the Use of Video

An old adage says that a picture is worth a thousand words. If that's true, a video is worth a million words. That's why the use of video trailers as book commercials has become so popular in the publishing industry.

6. Develop Backstories and Unpublished Writings

Offering exclusive, unpublished writing is a great way to entice readers to return to a fiction author's website. Examples include short stories, backstories, lost chapters, and alternative openings or endings. If you want to drive more people to your website, posting exclusive, unpublished writing is one of the most effective ways to do it.

Hollywood is famous for using this process to create movie prequels, sequels, tie-ins, and spin-offs. Original movies, such as *Star Wars*, *Rocky*, *Batman*, *Star Trek*, and James Bond have been expanded far beyond their initial story lines. Literary phenom Stephenie Meyer developed a novella called *The Short Second Life of Bree Tanner* based on her Twilight book series. She offered the novella as a limited-time free gift to her fans before officially publishing it. The buzz over the story was huge and kept readers engaged with her books.

7. Master Media Interviews

Many fiction authors complain that there is a media bias against their genre. In some cases it's true, because it's easier for a self-help nonfiction author to offer material that fits most radio and TV programs. Plus some novelists worry that they won't have anything to talk about on the air. After all, they don't want to spoil the book for readers.

Still, I believe fiction authors can provide a more interesting interview than a didactic self-help nonfiction author. Keep in mind that fiction routinely outsells nonfiction, and the reading public is enamored with great storytellers. Readers want to see the quirky person who writes the novels that touch their hearts.

ROB EAGAR is the founder of WildFire Marketing, a consulting practice that helps authors and publishers sell more books and spread their message like wildfire. Rob has consulted with numerous publishers and trained over 400 authors. His client list includes several *New York Times* bestselling authors, such as Dr. Gary Chapman, Wanda Brunstetter, and Lysa TerKeurst. Rob is also a successful author who has spoken to over 35,000 people and appeared on the *CBS Early Show*, CNN Radio, the *Los Angeles Times*, and the ABC Family Channel. He resides with his wife, Ashley, in Atlanta, Georgia.

Excerpted from *Sell Your Book Like Wildfire*© 2012 by Rob Eagar. Used with the permission of Writer's Digest Books, an imprint of F+W Media Inc. Visit www.writersdigestshop.com or call (800)448-0915 to obtian a copy.

LITERARY AGENTS

///

Many publishers are willing to look at unsolicited submissions but most feel having an agent is in the writer's best interest. In this section, we include agents who specialize in or represent fiction.

The commercial fiction field is intensely competitive. Many publishers have small staffs and little time. For that reason, many book publishers rely on agents for new talent. Some publishers are even relying on agents as "first readers" who must wade through the deluge of submissions from writers to find the very best. For writers, a good agent can be a foot in the door—someone willing to do the necessary work to put your manuscript in the right editor's hands.

It would seem today that finding a good agent is as hard as finding a good publisher. Yet those writers who have agents say they are invaluable. Not only can a good agent help you make your work more marketable, an agent also acts as your business manager and adviser, protecting your interests during and after contract negotiations.

Still, finding an agent can be very difficult for a new writer. If you are already published in magazines, you have a better chance than someone with no publishing credits. (Some agents read periodicals searching for new writers.) Although many agents do read queries and manuscripts from unpublished authors without introduction, referrals from their writer clients can be a big help. If you don't know any published authors with agents, attending a conference is a good way to meet agents. Some agents even set aside time at conferences to meet new writers.

Almost all the agents listed here have said they are open to working with new, previously unpublished writers as well as published writers. They do not charge a fee to cover the time and effort involved in reviewing a manuscript or a synopsis and chapters, but their time is still extremely valuable. Only send an agent your work when you feel it is as complete and polished as possible.

USING THE LISTINGS

It is especially important that you read individual listings carefully before contacting these busy agents. The first information after the company name includes the address and phone, fax, e-mail address (when available) and website. **Member Agents** gives the names of individual agents working at that company. (Specific types of fiction an agent handles are indicated in parentheses after that agent's name.) The **Represents** section lists the types of fiction the agency represents. Reading the **Recent Sales** gives you the names of writers an agent is currently working with and, very importantly, publishers with which the agent has placed manuscripts. **Writers Conferences** identifies conferences an agent attends (and where you might possibly meet that agent). **Tips** presents advice directly from the agent to authors.

Also, look closely at the openness to submissions icons that precede most listings. They will indicate how willing an agency is to take on new writers.

THE AHEARN AGENCY, INC.

2021 Pine St., New Orleans LA 70118. **E-mail:** pahearn@aol.com. **Website:** www.ahearnagency.com. **Contact:** Pamela G. Ahearn. Other memberships include MWA, RWA, ITW. Represents 35 clients. 20% of clients are new/unpublished writers. Currently handles novels (100%).

REPRESENTS Considers these fiction areas: action, adventure, contemporary issues, crime, detective, ethnic, family saga, feminist, glitz, historical, humor, literary, mainstream, mystery, police, psychic, regional, romance, supernatural, suspense, thriller.

⟞ Handles women's fiction and suspense fiction only. Does not want to receive category romance, science fiction or fantasy.

HOW TO CONTACT Query with SASE. Accepts simultaneous submissions. Responds in 8 weeks to queries. Responds in 10 weeks to mss. Obtains most new clients through recommendations from others, solicitations, conferences.

TERMS Agent receives 15% commission on domestic sales. Agent receives 20% commission on foreign sales. Offers written contract, binding for 1 year; renewable by mutual consent.

RECENT SALES *The Ronin's Mistress*, by Laura Joh Rowland; *How to Woo a Reluctant Lady*, Jeffies; *The Things That Keep Us Here*, by Carla Buckley.

WRITERS CONFERENCES Moonlight & Magnolias; RWA National Conference; Thriller Fest; Florida Romance Writers; Bouchercon; Malice Domestic.

TIPS "Be professional! Always send in exactly what an agent/editor asks for—no more, no less. Keep query letters brief and to the point, giving your writing credentials and a very brief summary of your book. If one agent rejects you, keep trying—there are a lot of us out there!"

MARCIA AMSTERDAM AGENCY

41 W. 82nd St., Suite 9A, New York NY 10024-5613. (212)873-4945. **Contact:** Marcia Amsterdam. Signatory of WGA. Currently handles nonfiction books (15%), novels (70%), movie scripts (5%), TV scripts (10%).

REPRESENTS Novels, movie scripts, feature film, sitcom. **Considers these fiction areas:** adventure, detective, horror, mainstream, mystery, romance (contemporary, historical), science, thriller, young adult.

HOW TO CONTACT Query with SASE. Responds in 1 month to queries.

TERMS Agent receives 15% commission on domestic sales. Agent receives 20% commission on foreign sales. Agent receives 10% commission on film sales. Offers written contract, binding for 1 year. Charges clients for extra office expenses, foreign postage, copying, legal fees (when agreed upon).

RECENT SALES *Hidden Child* by Isaac Millman (FSG); *Lucky Leonardo*, by Jonathan Canter (Sourcebooks).

TIPS "We are always looking for interesting literary voices."

BETSY AMSTER LITERARY ENTERPRISES

6312 SW Capitol Hwy #503, Portland OR 97239. **Website:** www.amsterlit.com. **Contact:** Betsy Amster. Estab. 1992. Member of AAR. Represents more than 65 clients. 35% of clients are new/unpublished writers. Currently handles nonfiction books (65%), novels (35%).

○ Prior to opening her agency, Ms. Amster was an editor at Pantheon and Vintage for 10 years, and served as editorial director for the Globe Pequot Press for 2 years.

REPRESENTS Nonfiction books, novels. **Considers these fiction areas:** ethnic, literary, women's, high quality.

⟞ "Actively seeking strong narrative nonfiction, particularly by journalists; outstanding literary fiction (the next Richard Ford or Jhumpa Lahiri); witty, intelligent commerical women's fiction (the next Elinor Lipman or Jennifer Weiner); mysteries that open new worlds to us; and high-profile self-help and psychology, preferably research based." Does not want to receive poetry, children's books, romances, western, science fiction, action/adventure, screenplays, fantasy, techno-thrillers, spy capers, apocalyptic scenarios, or political or religious arguments.

HOW TO CONTACT For adult titles: b.amster.assistant@gmail.com. See submission requirements online at website. The requirements have changed and only e-mail submissions are accepted. Accepts simultaneous submissions. Responds in 1 month to queries. Responds in 2 months to mss. Obtains most new clients through recommendations from others, solicitations, conferences.

TERMS Agent receives 15% commission on domestic sales. Agent receives 20% commission on foreign sales.

Offers written contract, binding for 1 year; 3-month notice must be given to terminate contract. Charges for photocopying, postage, long distance phone calls, messengers, galleys/books used in submissions to foreign and film agents and to magazines for first serial rights.

WRITERS CONFERENCES USC Masters in Professional Writing; San Diego State University Writers' Conference; UCLA Extension Writers' Program; Los Angeles Times Festival of Books; The Loft Literary Center; Willamette Writers Conference.

❶ ARTISTS AND ARTISANS INC.

244 Madison Ave., Suite 334, New York NY 10016. **Website:** www.artistsandartisans.com. **Contact:** Adam Chromy and Jamie Brenner. Represents 70 clients. 80% of clients are new/unpublished writers. Currently handles nonfiction books (50%), fiction 50%.

MEMBER AGENTS Adam Chromy (fiction and narrative nonfiction); Jamie Brenner (thrillers, commercial and literary fiction, memoir, narrative nonfiction, Young Adult); Gwendolyn Heasley (Young Adult).

REPRESENTS Nonfiction books, novels. **Considers these fiction areas:** confession, family, humor, literary, mainstream.

⚷ "My education and experience in the business world ensure that my clients' enterprise as authors gets as much attention and care as their writing." Working journalists for nonfiction books. No scripts, photo or childrens' books.

HOW TO CONTACT Query by e-mail only. Start subject line with "query." No unsolicted submissions. All fiction queries must include a brief author's bio, and the setup or premise for the book. Accepts simultaneous submissions. Responds to queries only if interested. Obtains most new clients through recommendations from others, solicitations, conferences.

TERMS Agent receives 15% commission on domestic sales. Agent receives 25% commission on foreign sales. Offers written contract; 1-month notice must be given to terminate contract. "We only charge for extraordinary expenses (e.g., client requests check via FedEx instead of regular mail)."

RECENT SALES *New World Monkeys*, (Shaye Areheart); *World Made by Hand* (Grove Atlantic); *House of Cards*, by David Ellis Dickerson (Penguin).

WRITERS CONFERENCES ASJA Writers Conference, Pacific Northwest Writers Conference, Newbury Port Writers Conference.

TIPS "Please make sure you are ready before approaching us or any other agent. If you write fiction, make sure it is the best work you can do and get objective criticism from a writing group. If you write nonfiction, make sure the proposal exhibits your best work and a comprehensive understanding of the market."

○ AVENUE A LITERARY

419 Lafayette St., Second Floor, New York NY 10003. **Fax:** (212)228-6149. **E-mail:** submissions@avenuealiterary.com. **Website:** www.avenuealiterary.com. **Contact:** Jennifer Cayea. Represents 20 clients. 75% of clients are new/unpublished writers. Currently handles nonfiction books (40%), novels (45%), story collections (5%), juvenile books (10%).

◑ Prior to opening her agency, Ms. Cayea was an agent and director of foreign rights for Nicholas Ellison, Inc., a division of Sanford J. Greenburger Associates. She was also an editor in the audio and large print divisions of Random House.

REPRESENTS Nonfiction books, novels, short story collections, juvenile. **Considers these fiction areas:** contemporary issues, family saga, feminist, historical, literary, mainstream, thriller, young adult women's/chick lit.

⚷ "Our authors are dynamic and diverse. We seek strong new voices in fiction and nonfiction, and are fiercely dedicated to our authors." We are actively seeking new authors of fiction and nonfiction.

HOW TO CONTACT Query via e-mail only. Submit synopsis, publishing history, author bio, full contact info. Paste info in e-mail body. No attachments. Include all information *in the body of your e-mail*: submissions sent as attachments will *not* be read. Accepts simultaneous submissions. Responds in 6-8 weeks to queries. Obtains most new clients through recommendations from others, solicitations, conferences.

TERMS Agent receives 15% commission on domestic sales. Agent receives 15% commission on foreign sales. Offers written contract; 30-day notice must be given to terminate contract.

RECENT SALES *Gunmetal Black*, by Daniel Serrano.

TIPS "Build a résumé by publishing short stories if you are a fiction writer."

● THE AXELROD AGENCY

55 Main St., P.O. Box 357, Chatham NY 12037. (518)392-2100. **E-mail:** steve@axelrodagency.com.

Website: www.axelrodagency.com. **Contact:** Steven Axelrod. Member of AAR. Represents 15-20 clients. 1% of clients are new/unpublished writers. Currently handles novels (95%).

REPRESENTS Novels. **Considers these fiction areas:** mystery, romance, women's.

HOW TO CONTACT Query with SASE. Accepts simultaneous submissions. Responds in 3 weeks to queries. Responds in 6 weeks to mss. Obtains most new clients through recommendations from others.

TERMS Agent receives 15% commission on domestic sales. Agent receives 20% commission on foreign sales. No written contract.

WRITERS CONFERENCES RWA National Conference.

● BAKER'S MARK LITERARY AGENCY

P.O. Box 8382, Portland OR 97207. (503)432-8170. E-mail: info@bakersmark.com. **Website:** www.Bakersmark.com. **Contact:** Bernadette Baker-Baughman or Gretchen Stelter. Currently handles nonfiction books (35%), novels (25%), graphic novels (40%).

REPRESENTS Nonfiction books, novels, scholarly books, graphic novels. **Considers these fiction areas:** cartoon, comic books, contemporary issues, crime, detective, erotica, ethnic, experimental, fantasy, feminist, gay, glitz, historical, horror, humor, lesbian, literary, mainstream, mystery, police, psychic, regional, satire, supernatural, suspense, thriller, women's chick literature.

⟝ "Baker's Mark specializes in graphic novels and popular nonfiction with an extremely selective taste in commercial fiction." Actively seeking graphic novels, nonfiction, fiction (YA/Teen and magical realism in particular). Does not want to receive westerns, poetry, sci-fi, novella, high fantasy, or children's picture books.

HOW TO CONTACT Query with 1 page with no attachments and no chapters in the e-mail. Queries sent with attachments will be deleted unread. Send SASE if mailing by post. "If interested, we will request representative materials from you." Accepts simultaneous submissions. Responds in 4-6 weeks. Obtains most new clients through recommendations from others, solicitations.

TERMS Agent receives 15% commission on domestic sales. Agent receives 20% commission on foreign sales. Offers written contract, binding for 18 months; 30-day notice must be given to terminate contract.

RECENT SALES *Never After*, by Dan Elconin (Simon Pulse); *Boilerplate: History's Mechanical Marvel* by Paul Guinan and Anina Bennet (Abrams Image); *War Is Bor-*

ing, by David Axe, with illustration by Matt Bors (New American Library); *The Choyster Generation*, by Amalia mcGibbon, Claire Williams, and Lara Vogel (Seal Press).

WRITERS CONFERENCES New York Comic Convention, BookExpo of America, San Diego Comic Con, Stumptown Comics Fest, Emerald City Comic Con.

TIPS "Baker's Mark is also looking to help pioneer new media models for books, and is especially interested in books that experiment with social media, open source software (and other digital technologies) as we help establish new business paradigms for the ebook revolution."

● BARER LITERARY, LLC

270 Lafayette St., Suite 1504, New York NY 10012. (212)691-3513. **E-mail:** submissions@barerliterary.com. **Website:** www.barerliterary.com. **Contact:** Julie Barer. Estab. 2004. Member of AAR.

Ⓠ Before becoming an agent, Julie worked at Shakespeare & Co. Booksellers in New York City. She is a graduate of Vassar College.

MEMBER AGENTS Julie Barer.

REPRESENTS Nonfiction books, novels, short story collections. Julie Barer is especially interested in working with emerging writers and developing long-term relationships with new clients. **Considers these fiction areas:** contemporary issues, ethnic, historical, literary, mainstream.

⟝ This agency no longer accepts young adult submissions. No Health/Fitness, Business/Investing/Finance, Sports, Mind/Body/Spirit, Reference, Thrillers/Suspense, Military, Romance, Children's Books/Picture Books, Screenplays.

HOW TO CONTACT Query with SASE; no attachments if query by e-mail. We do not respond to queries via phone or fax.

TERMS Agent receives 15% commission on domestic sales. Agent receives 20% commission on foreign sales. Offers written contract. Charges for photocopying and books ordered.

RECENT SALES *The Unnamed*, by Joshua Ferris (Reagan Arthur Books); *Tunneling to the Center of the Earth*, by Kevin Wilson (Ecco Press); *A Disobedient Girl*, by Ru Freeman (Atria Books); *A Friend of the Family*, by Lauren Grodstein (Algonquin); *City of Veils*, by Zoe Ferraris (Little, Brown).

⊕ BARONE LITERARY AGENCY

385 North St., Batavia OH 45103. (513)732-6740. **Fax:** (513)297-7208. **E-mail:** baroneliteraryagency@road-

runner.com. **Website:** www.baroneliteraryagency. com. **Contact:** Denise Barone. Estab. 2010. RWA Represents 7 clients. 100% of clients are new/unpublished writers. Currently handles 80% novels, 20% movie scripts.

REPRESENTS Considers these fiction areas: action, adventure, cartoon, comic books, commercial, confession, contemporary issues, crime, detective, erotica, ethnic, experimental, family saga, fantasy, feminist, frontier, gay, glitz, hi-lo, historical, horror, humor, inspirational, juvenile, lesbian, literary, mainstream, metaphysical, military, multicultural, multimedia, mystery, New Age, occult, plays, psychic, regional, religious, romance, science fiction, sports, thriller, women's, young adult.

> Actively seeking adult contemporary romance. Does not want textbooks.

HOW TO CONTACT Submit query letter, SASE and synopsis. Accepts simultaneous submissions. Obtains new clients by queries/submissions, Facebook, recommendations from others.

TERMS 15% commission on domestic sales, 20% on foreign sales. Offers written contract.

RECENT SALES *The Cinderella Files*, by Rebekah Purdy (Astrea Press); *The Trouble with Charlie*, by Cathy Bennett (Astrea Press).

TIPS "In the immortal words of Sir Winston Churchill, if you want to get published, you must never give up!"

LORETTA BARRETT BOOKS, INC.

220 E. 23rd St., 11th Floor, New York NY 10010. (212)242-3420. **E-mail:** query@lorettabarrettbooks. com. **Website:** www.lorettabarrettbooks.com. **Contact:** Loretta A. Barrett, Nick Mullendore, Gabriel Davis. Estab. 1990. Member of AAR. Currently handles nonfiction books (50%), novels (50%).

> Prior to opening her agency, Ms. Barrett was vice president and executive editor at Doubleday and editor-in-chief of Anchor Books.

MEMBER AGENTS Loretta A. Barrett; Nick Mullendore.

REPRESENTS Nonfiction books, novels. **Considers these fiction areas:** contemporary, psychic, adventure, detective, ethnic, family, historical, literary, mainstream, mystery, thriller, young adult.

> "The clients we represent include both fiction and nonfiction authors for the general adult trade market. The works they produce encompass a

wide range of contemporary topics and themes including commercial thrillers, mysteries, romantic suspense, popular science, memoirs, narrative fiction and current affairs." No children's, juvenile, cookbooks, gardening, science fiction, fantasy novels, historical romance.

HOW TO CONTACT See guidelines online. Use email (no attachments) or if by post, query with SASE. For hardcopy queries, please send a 1-2 page query letter and a synopsis or chapter outline for your project. In your letter, please include your contact information, any relevant background information on yourself or your project, and a paragraph of description of your project. If you are submitting electronically, then all of this material may be included in the body of your e-mail. Accepts simultaneous submissions. Responds in 3-6 weeks to queries.

TERMS Agent receives 15% commission on domestic sales. Agent receives 20% commission on foreign sales. Offers written contract. Charges clients for shipping and photocopying.

FAYE BENDER LITERARY AGENCY

19 Cheever Place, Brooklyn NY 11231. **E-mail:** info@ fbliterary.com. **Website:** www.fbliterary.com. **Contact:** Faye Bender. Estab. 2004. Member of AAR.

MEMBER AGENTS Faye Bender.

REPRESENTS Nonfiction books, novels, juvenile. **Considers these fiction areas:** commercial, literary, women's, young adult (middle-grade).

> "I choose books based on the narrative voice and strength of writing. I work with previously published and first-time authors." Faye does not represent picture books, genre fiction for adults (western, romance, horror, science fiction, fantasy), business books, spirituality, or screenplays.

HOW TO CONTACT Query with SASE and 10 sample pages via mail or e-mail (no attachments). Guidelines online. "Please do not send queries or submissions via registered or certified mail, or by FedEx or UPS requiring signature. We will not return unsolicited submissions weighing more than 16 ounces, even if an SASE is attached. We do not respond to queries via phone or fax."

TIPS "Please keep your letters to the point, include all relevant information, and have a bit of patience."

THE BENT AGENCY

Bent Agency, The, 204 Park Place, Number 2, Brooklyn NY 11238. **E-mail:** info@thebentagency.com.

Website: www.thebentagency.com. **Contact:** Jenny Bent, Susan Hawk, Molly Ker Hawn, Nicole Steen. Estab. 2009.

MEMBER AGENTS Jenny Bent (all adult fiction, except for science fiction); Susan Hawk (young adult and middle grade books; within the realm of kids stories, she likes fantasy, science fiction, historical fiction, and mystery); Molly Ker Hawn (young adult and middle grade books, including contemporary, historical science fiction, fantasy, thrillers, mystery; Nicole Steen (literary and commercial fiction, narrative nonfiction, and memoir).

REPRESENTS Considers these fiction areas: commercial, crime, historical, horror, mystery, picture books, romance, suspense, thriller, women's, young adult literary.

HOW TO CONTACT For Jenney Bent, e-mail queries@thebentagency.com; for Susan Hawk, e-mail kidsqueries@thebentagency.com; for Molly Ker Hawn, e-mail hawnqueries@thebentagency.com; for Nicole Steen, e-mail steenqueries@thebentagency.com. "Tell us briefly who you are, what your book is, and why you're the 1 to write it. Then include the first 10 pages of your material in the body of your e-mail. We respond to all queries; please resend your query if you haven't had a response within 4 weeks." Accepts simultaneous submissions.

RECENT SALES *Worst Laid Plans*, by Laura Kindred and Alexandra Lydon; *The Dark Ink Chronicles*, by Elle Jasper; *What We Don't Tell*, by Desiree Washington; *Bent Road*, by Lori Roy; *The Art of Saying Goodbye*, by Ellyn Bache; *Through Her Eyes*, by Jenny Archer; *You Don't Sweat Much for a Fat Girl*, by Celia Rivenbark; *When Harry Met Molly*, by Kieran Kramer.

BLEECKER STREET ASSOCIATES, INC.

217 Thompson St., #519, New York NY 10012. (212)677-4492. **Fax:** (212)388-0001. **E-mail:** bleeckerst@hotmail.com. **Contact:** Agnes Birnbaum. Member of AAR. Other memberships include RWA, MWA. Represents 60 clients. 20% of clients are new/unpublished writers. Currently handles nonfiction books (75%), novels (25%).

○ Prior to becoming an agent, Ms. Birnbaum was a senior editor at Simon & Schuster, Dutton/Signet, and other publishing houses.

REPRESENTS Nonfiction books, novels. **Considers these fiction areas:** ethnic, historical, literary, mystery, romance, thriller, women's.

✎ "We're very hands-on and accessible. We try to be truly creative in our submission approaches.

We've had especially good luck with first-time authors." Does not want to receive science fiction, westerns, poetry, children's books, academic/scholarly/professional books, plays, scripts, or short stories.

HOW TO CONTACT Query with SASE. No e-mail, phone, or fax queries. Accepts simultaneous submissions. Responds in 2 weeks to queries. Responds in 1 month to mss. "Obtains most new clients through recommendations from others, solicitations, conferences, plus, I will approach someone with a letter if his/her work impresses me."

TERMS Agent receives 15% commission on domestic sales. Agent receives 25% commission on foreign sales. Offers written contract; 1-month notice must be given to terminate contract. Charges for postage, long distance, fax, messengers, photocopies (not to exceed $200).

RECENT SALES Sold 14 titles in the last year. *Following Sarah*, by Daniel Brown (Morrow); *Biology of the Brain*, by Paul Swingle (Rutgers University Press); *Santa Miracles*, by Brad and Sherry Steiger (Adams); *Surviving the College Search*, by Jennifer Delahunt (St. Martin's).

TIPS "Keep query letters short and to the point; include only information pertaining to the book or background as a writer. Try to avoid superlatives in description. Work needs to stand on its own, so how much editing it may have received has no place in a query letter."

◐ BOOKENDS, LLC

136 Long Hill Rd., Gillette NJ 07933. **Website:** www.bookends-inc.com; bookendslitagency.blogspot.com. **Contact:** Kim Lionetti, Jessica Alvarez, Lauren Ruth. Member of AAR. RWA, MWA Represents 50+ clients. 10% of clients are new/unpublished writers. Currently handles nonfiction books (50%), novels (50%).

MEMBER AGENTS Jessica Faust (**no long accepting unsolicited material**) (fiction: romance, erotica, women's fiction, mysteries and suspense; nonfiction: business, finance, career, parenting, psychology, women's issues, self-help, health, sex); Kim Lionetti (Kim is only currently considering romance, women's fiction, and young adult queries. If your book is in any of these 3 categories, please be sure to specify "Romance," "Women's Fiction," or "Young Adult" in your e-mail subject line. Any queries that do not follow these guidelines will not be considered); Jessica

Alvarez (romance, women's fiction, erotica, romantic suspense); Lauren Ruth.

REPRESENTS Nonfiction books, novels. **Considers these fiction areas:** detective, cozies, mainstream, mystery, romance, thrillers, women's.

✂ "BookEnds is currently accepting queries from published and unpublished writers in the areas of romance (and all its sub-genres), erotica, mystery, suspense, women's fiction, and literary fiction. We also do a great deal of nonfiction in the areas of self-help, business, finance, health, pop science, psychology, relationships, parenting, pop culture, true crime, and general nonfiction." BookEnds does not want to receive children's books, screenplays, science fiction, poetry, or technical/military thrillers.

HOW TO CONTACT Review website for guidelines, as they change. BookEnds is no longer accepting unsolicited proposal packages or snail mail queries. Send query in the body of e-mail to only one agent.

● THE BARBARA BOVA LITERARY AGENCY

3951 Gulf Shore Blvd. No. PH 1-B, Naples FL 34103. (239)649-7263. **Fax:** (239)649-7263. **E-mail:** michaelburke@barbarabovaliteraryagency.com. **Website:** www.barbarabovaliteraryagency.com. **Contact:** Ken Bova, Michael Burke. Represents 30 clients. Currently handles nonfiction books (20%), fiction (80%).

REPRESENTS Nonfiction books, novels. **Considers these fiction areas:** adventure, crime, detective, mystery, police, science fiction, suspense, thriller, women's, young adult teen lit.

✂ This agency specializes in fiction and nonfiction, hard and soft science. No scripts, poetry or children's books.

HOW TO CONTACT Query through website. No attachments. We accept short (3-5 pages) e-mail queries. All queries should have the word "query" in the subject line. Include all information as you would in a standard, snail mail query letter, such as pertinent credentials, publishing history, and an overview of the book. Include a word count of your project. You may include a short synopsis. We're looking for quality fiction and nonfiction. Obtains most new clients through recommendations from others.

TERMS Agent receives 15% commission on domestic sales. Agent receives 20% commission on foreign

sales. Charges clients for overseas postage, overseas calls, photocopying, shipping.

RECENT SALES Sold 24 titles in the last year. *The Green Trap* and *The Aftermath*, by Ben Bova; *Empire and a War of Gifts*, by Orson Scott Card; *Radioman*, by Carol E. Hipperson.

TIPS "We also handle foreign, movie, television, and audio rights."

◑ BRADFORD LITERARY AGENCY

5694 Mission Center Rd., #347, San Diego CA 92108. (619)521-1201. **E-mail:** queries@bradfordlit.com. **Website:** www.bradfordlit.com. **Contact:** Laura Bradford, Natalie Lakosil. Member of AAR. RWA, SCBWI, ALA Represents 50 clients. 20% of clients are new/unpublished writers. Currently handles nonfiction books (5%), novels (95%).

REPRESENTS Nonfiction books, novels, novellas, stories within a single author's collection anthology. **Considers these fiction areas:** adventure, detective, erotica, ethnic, historical, humor, mainstream, mystery, romance, thriller psychic/supernatural.

✂ Actively seeking romance (historical, romantic suspense, paranormal, category, contemporary, erotic), urban fantasy, women's fiction, mystery, thrillers, children's (Natalie Lakosil only), and young adult. Does not want to receive poetry, screenplays, short stories, westerns, horror, new age, religion, crafts, cookbooks, gift books.

HOW TO CONTACT Accepts e-mail queries only, send to queries@bradfordlit.com. The entire submission must appear in the body of the e-mail and not as an attachment. The subject line should begin as follows: QUERY: (The title of the ms or any short message that is important should follow). For fiction: e-mail a query letter along with the first chapter of ms and a synopsis. Be sure to include the genre and word count in your cover letter. Nonfiction: e-mail full nonfiction proposal including a query letter and a sample chapter. Accepts simultaneous submissions. Responds in 2-4weeks to queries. Responds in 10 weeks to mss. Obtains most new clients through solicitations.

TERMS Agent receives 15% commission on domestic sales. Agent receives 20% commission on foreign sales. Offers written contract, non-binding for 2 years; 45-day notice must be given to terminate contract. Charges for extra copies of books for foreign submissions.

RECENT SALES Sold 68 titles in the last year. *All Fall Down,* by Megan Hart (Mira Books); *Body and Soul,* by Stacey Kade (Hyperion Children's); *All Things Wicked,* by Karina Cooper (Avon); *Circle Eight: Matthew,* by Emma Lang (Kensington Brava); *Midnight Enchantment,* by Anya Bast (Berkley Sensation); *Outpost,* by Ann Aguirre (Feiwel and Friends); *The One That I Want,* by Jennifer Echols (Simon Pulse); *Catch Me a Cowboy,* by Katie Lane (Grand Central); *Back in a Soldier's Arms,* by Soraya Lane (Harlequin); *Enraptured,* by Elisabeth Naughton (Sourcebooks); *Wicked Road to Hell,* by Juliana Stone (Avon); *Master of Sin,* by Maggie Robinson (Kensington Brava); *Chaos Burning,* by Lauren Dane (Berkley Sensation); *If I Lie,* by Corrine Jackson (Simon Pulse); *Renegade,* by J.A. Souders (Tor).

WRITERS CONFERENCES RWA National Conference; Romantic Times Booklovers Convention.

CURTIS BROWN, LTD.

10 Astor Place, New York NY 10003-6935. (212)473-5400. **E-mail:** gknowlton@cbltd.com. **Website:** www.curtisbrown.com. **Contact:** Ginger Knowlton. Alternate address: Peter Ginsberg, president at CBSF, 1750 Montgomery St., San Francisco CA 94111. (415)954-8566. Member of AAR. Signatory of WGA.

MEMBER AGENTS Ginger Clark; Katherine Fausset; Holly Frederick, VP; Emilie Jacobson; Elizabeth Hardin; Ginger Knowlton, executive vice president; Timothy Knowlton, CEO; Laura Blake Peterson; Mitchell Waters. San Francisco Office: Peter Ginsberg (president).

REPRESENTS Nonfiction books, novels, short story collections, juvenile. **Considers these fiction areas:** contemporary, glitz, New Age, psychic, adventure, comic, confession, detective, erotica, ethnic, experimental, family, fantasy, feminist, gay, gothic, hi lo, historical, horror, humor, juvenile, literary, mainstream, military, multicultural, multimedia, mystery, occult, picture books, plays, poetry, regional, religious, romance, science, short, spiritual, sports, thriller, translation, western, youn, women's.

HOW TO CONTACT Prefers to read materials exclusively. *No unsolicited mss.* Query with SASE. If a picture book, send only one picture book ms. Considers simultaneous queries, "but please tell us." Returns material only with SASE. Responds in 3 weeks to queries; 5 weeks to mss. Obtains most new clients through recommendations from others, solicitations, conferences.

TERMS Agent receives 15% commission on domestic sales; 20% on foreign sales. Offers written contract.

75 days notice must be given to terminate contract. Offers written contract. Charges for some postage (overseas, etc.).

RECENT SALES This agency prefers not to share information on specific sales.

● BROWNE & MILLER LITERARY ASSOCIATES

410 S. Michigan Ave., Suite 460, Chicago IL 60605-1465. (312)922-3063. **E-mail:** mail@browneandmiller.com. **Website:** www.browneandmiller.com. **Contact:** Danielle Egan-Miller. Estab. 1971. Member of AAR. Other memberships include RWA, MWA, Author's Guild. Represents 150 clients. 2% of clients are new/unpublished writers. Currently handles nonfiction books (25%), novels (75%).

REPRESENTS Nonfiction books, most genres of commercial adult fiction and nonfiction, as well as select young adult projects. **Considers these fiction areas:** contemporary issues, crime, detective, erotica, ethnic, family saga, glitz, historical, inspirational, literary, mainstream, mystery, police, religious, romance, sports, suspense, thriller paranormal.

⊶ "We are partial to talented newcomers and experienced authors who are seeking hands-on career management, highly personal representation, and who are interested in being full partners in their books' successes. We are editorially focused and work closely with our authors through the whole publishing process, from proposal to after publication." "We are most interested in commercial women's fiction, especially elegantly crafted, sweeping historicals; edgy, fresh teen/chick/mom/lady lit; and CBA women's fiction by established authors. We are also very keen on literary historical mysteries and literary YA novels. Topical, timely nonfiction projects in a variety of subject areas are also of interest, especially prescriptive how-to, self-help, sports, humor, and pop culture." Does not represent poetry, short stories, plays, original screenplays, articles, children's picture books, software, horror, or sci-fi novels.

HOW TO CONTACT Only accepts e-mail queries. Inquiring authors may initially submit one chapter and a synopsis. *No unsolicited mss.* Prefers to read material exclusively. Put submission in the subject line. Send no attachments. Also has online submission form. Responds in 2-4 months to queries. Obtains most new clients through referrals, queries by professional/marketable authors.

TERMS Agent receives 15% commission on domestic sales. Agent receives 20% commission on foreign sales. Offers written contract, binding for 2 years. Charges clients for photocopying, overseas postage.

WRITERS CONFERENCES BookExpo America; Frankfurt Book Fair; RWA National Conference; ICRS; London Book Fair; Bouchercon, regional writers conferences.

TIPS "If interested in agency representation, be well informed."

ANDREA BROWN LITERARY AGENCY, INC.

1076 Eagle Dr., Salinas CA 93905. (831)422-5925. **Fax:** (831)422-5915. **E-mail:** andrea@andreabrownlit.com; caryn@andreabrownlit.com. **Website:** www.andreabrownlit.com. **Contact:** Andrea Brown, president. Member of AAR. 10% of clients are new/unpublished writers.

Prior to opening her agency, Ms. Brown served as an editorial assistant at Random House and Dell Publishing and as an editor with Knopf.

MEMBER AGENTS Andrea Brown; Laura Rennert (laura@andreabrownlit.com); Kelly Sonnack; Caryn Wiseman; Jennifer Rofé; Jennifer Laughran, associate agent; Jamie Weiss Chilton, associate agent; Jennifer Mattson, associate agent; Mary Kole.

REPRESENTS Juvenile, nonfiction books, novels. **Considers these fiction areas:** juvenile, literary, picture books, women's, young adult middle-grade, all juvenile genres.

Specializes in "all kinds of children's books—illustrators and authors." 98% juvenile books. Considers: Nonfiction (animals, anthropology/archaeology, art/architecture/design, biography/autobiography, current affairs, ethnic/cultural interests, history, how-to, nature/environment, photography, popular culture, science/technology, sociology, sports); fiction (historical, science fiction); picture books, young adult.

HOW TO CONTACT For picture books, submit complete ms, SASE. For fiction, submit short synopsis, SASE, first 3 chapters. For nonfiction, submit proposal, 1-2 sample chapters. For illustrations, submit 4-5 color samples (no originals). "We only accept queries via e-mail. No attachments, with the exception of jpeg illustrations from illustrators." Visit the agents' bios on our website and choose only one agent to whom you will submit your e-query. Send a short e-mail query letter to that agent with QUERY in the subject field. Accepts simultaneous submissions. If we are interested in your work, we will certainly follow up by e-mail or by phone. However, if you haven't heard from us within 6 to 8 weeks, please assume that we are passing on your project. Obtains most new clients through referrals from editors, clients and agents. Check website for guidelines and information.

TERMS Agent receives 15% commission on domestic sales. Agent receives 20% commission on foreign sales. Offers written contract.

RECENT SALES *Chloe*, by Catherine Ryan Hyde (Knopf); Sasha Cohen autobiography (HarperCollins); *The Five Ancestors*, by Jeff Stone (Random House); *Thirteen Reasons Why*, by Jay Asher (Penguin); *Identical*, by Ellen Hopkins (S&S)

WRITERS CONFERENCES SCBWI; Asilomar; Maui Writers' Conference; Southwest Writers' Conference; San Diego State University Writers' Conference; Big Sur Children's Writing Workshop; William Saroyan Writers' Conference; Columbus Writers' Conference; Willamette Writers' Conference; La Jolla Writers' Conference; San Francisco Writers' Conference; Hilton Head Writers' Conference; Pacific Northwest Conference; Pikes Peak Conference.

TRACY BROWN LITERARY AGENCY

P.O. Box 772, Nyack NY 10960. (914)400-4147. **Fax:** (914)931-1746. **E-mail:** tracy@brownlit.com. **Contact:** Tracy Brown. Represents 35 clients. Currently handles nonfiction books (90%), novels (10%).

REPRESENTS Nonfiction books, novels anthologies. **Considers these fiction areas:** contemporary issues, feminist, literary, mainstream, women's.

Specializes in thorough involvement with clients' books at every stage of the process from writing to proposals to publication. Actively seeking serious nonfiction and fiction. Does not want to receive YA, sci-fi or romance.

HOW TO CONTACT Submit outline/proposal, synopsis, author bio. Accepts simultaneous submissions. Responds in 2 weeks to queries. Obtains most new clients through referrals.

TERMS Agent receives 15% commission on domestic sales. Agent receives 20% commission on foreign sales. Offers written contract.

RECENT SALES *Why Have Kids?* by Jessica Valenti (HarperCollins); *Hotel Notell: A Novel,* by Daphne Uviller (Bantam); *Healing Sexual Pain,* by Deborah Coady, MD and Nancy Fish, MSW, MPH (Seal Press).

● **SHEREE BYKOFSKY ASSOCIATES, INC.**
P.O. Box 706, Brigantine NJ 08203. **E-mail:** shereebee@aol.com. **E-mail:** submitbee@aol.com. **Website:** www.shereebee.com. **Contact:** Sheree Bykofsky. Member of AAR. Other memberships include ASJA, WNBA. Currently handles nonfiction books (80%), novels (20%).

○ Prior to opening her agency, Ms. Bykofsky served as executive editor of the Stonesong Press and managing editor of Chiron Press. She is also the author or coauthor of more than 20 books, including *The Complete Idiot's Guide to Getting Published.* Ms. Bykofsky teaches publishing at NYU and SEAK, Inc.

MEMBER AGENTS Janet Rosen, associate.

REPRESENTS Nonfiction books, novels. **Considers these fiction areas:** contemporary issues, literary, mainstream, mystery, suspense.

⌐ This agency specializes in popular reference nonfiction, commercial fiction with a literary quality, and mysteries. "I have wide-ranging interests, but it really depends on quality of writing, originality, and how a particular project appeals to me (or not). I take on fiction when I completely love it—it doesn't matter what area or genre." Does not want to receive poetry, material for children, screenplays, Westerns, horror, science fiction, or fantasy.

HOW TO CONTACT We only accept e-queries now and will only respond to those in which we are interested. E-mail short queries to submitbee@aol.com. Please, no attachments, snail mail, or phone calls. One-page query, one-page synopsis, and first page of manuscript in the body of the e-mail. Nonfiction: One-page query in the body of the e-mail. We cannot open attached Word files or any other types of attached files. These will be deleted. Accepts simultaneous submissions. Responds in 1 month to requested mss. Obtains most new clients through recommendations from others.

TERMS Agent receives 15% commission on domestic sales. Agent receives 20% commission on foreign sales. Offers written contract, binding for 1 year. Charges for postage, photocopying, fax.

RECENT SALES *Red Sheep: The Search for My Inner Latina,* by Michele Carlo (Citadel/Kensington); *Bang the Keys: Four Steps to a Lifelong Writing Practice,* by Jill Dearman (Alpha, Penguin); *Signed, Your Student: Celebrities on the Teachers Who Made Them Who They Are Today,* by Holly Holbert (Kaplan); *The Five Ways We Grieve,* by Susan Berger (Trumpeter/Shambhala).

WRITERS CONFERENCES ASJA Writers Conference; Asilomar; Florida Suncoast Writers' Conference; Whidbey Island Writers' Conference; Florida First Coast Writers' Festival; Agents and Editors Conference; Columbus Writers' Conference; Southwest Writers' Conference; Willamette Writers' Conference; Dorothy Canfield Fisher Conference; Maui Writers' Conference; Pacific Northwest Writers' Conference; IWWG.

TIPS "Read the agent listing carefully and comply with guidelines."

● **KIMBERLEY CAMERON & ASSOCIATES**
1550 Tiburon Blvd., #704, Tiburon CA 94920. **Fax:** (415)789-9177. **E-mail:** info@kimberleycameron.com. **Website:** www.kimberleycameron.com. **Contact:** Kimberley Cameron. Member of AAR. 30% of clients are new/unpublished writers. Currently handles nonfiction books 50%; fiction 50%.

○ Kimberley Cameron & Associates (formerly The Reece Halsey Agency) has had an illustrious client list of established writers, including the estate of Aldous Huxley, and has represented Upton Sinclair, William Faulkner, and Henry Miller.

MEMBER AGENTS Kimberley Cameron, Amy Burkhardt, Elizabeth Kracht.

REPRESENTS Nonfiction, fiction. **Considers these fiction areas:** adventure, contemporary issues, ethnic, family saga, historical, horror, mainstream, mystery, interlinked short story collections, thriller, women's, and sophisticated/crossover young adult.

⌐ "We are looking for a unique and heartfelt voice that conveys a universal truth."

HOW TO CONTACT Query via e-mail. "See our website for submission guidelines." Obtains new clients through recommendations from others, solicitations.

TERMS Agent receives 15% on domestic sales; 10% on film sales. Offers written contract, binding for 1 year.

WRITERS CONFERENCES Pacific Northwest Writers Association Conference, Aspen Summer Words, Willamette Writers Conference, San Diego State University Writers Conference, San Francisco Writers Conference, Killer Nashville, Left Coast Crime, Bouchercon, Book Passage Mystery and Travel Writers Conferences, Antioch Writers Workshop, Florida Writers Association Conference, and others.

TIPS "Please consult our submission guidelines and send a polite, well-written query to our e-mail address."

◐ MARIA CARVAINIS AGENCY, INC.

1270 Avenue of the Americas, Suite 2320, New York NY 10019. (212)245-6365. **Fax:** (212)245-7196. **E-mail:** mca@mariacarvainisagency.com. **Contact:** Maria Carvainis, Chelsea Gilmore. Member of AAR. Signatory of WGA. Other memberships include Authors Guild, Women's Media Group, ABA, MWA, RWA. Represents 75 clients. 10% of clients are new/unpublished writers. Currently handles nonfiction books (35%), novels (65%).

○ Prior to opening her agency, Ms. Carvainis spent more than 10 years in the publishing industry as a senior editor with Macmillan Publishing, Basic Books, Avon Books, and Crown Publishers. Ms. Carvainis has served as a member of the AAR Board of Directors and AAR Treasurer, as well as serving as chair of the AAR Contracts Committee. She presently serves on the AAR Royalty Committee. Ms. Gilmore started her publishing career at Oxford University Press, in the Higher Education Group. She then worked at Avalon Books as associate editor. She is most interested in women's fiction, literary fiction, young adult, pop culture, and mystery/suspense.

MEMBER AGENTS Maria Carvainis, president/literary agent; Chelsea Gilmore, literary agent.

REPRESENTS Nonfiction books, novels. **Considers these fiction areas:** contemporary issues, historical, literary, mainstream, mystery, suspense, thriller, women's, young adult middle grade.

⌐⊶ Does not want to receive science fiction or children's picture books.

HOW TO CONTACT Query with SASE. No e-mail accepted. Responds in up to 3 months to mss and to queries 1 month. Obtains most new clients through recommendations from others, conferences, query letters.

TERMS Agent receives 15% commission on domestic sales. Agent receives 20% commission on foreign sales. Offers written contract. Charges clients for foreign postage and bulk copying.

RECENT SALES *A Secret Affair*, by Mary Balogh (Delacorte); *Tough Customer*, by Sandra Brown (Simon & Schuster); *A Lady Never Tells*, by Candace

Camp (Pocket Books); *The King James Conspiracy*, by Phillip Depoy (St. Martin's Press).

WRITERS CONFERENCES BookExpo America; Frankfurt Book Fair; London Book Fair; Mystery Writers of America; Thrillerfest; Romance Writers of America.

◐◑ CASTIGLIA LITERARY AGENCY

1155 Camino Del Mar, Suite 510, Del Mar CA 92014. (858)755-8761. **Fax:** (858)755-7063. **E-mail:** deborah@castigliaagency.com; win@castiglioagency.com. **Website:** home.earthlink.net/~mwgconference/id22.html. Member of AAR. Other memberships include PEN. Represents 65 clients. Currently handles nonfiction books (55%), novels (45%).

MEMBER AGENTS Julie Castiglia; Winifred Golden (science fiction, ethnic, commercial and thriller novels, plus narrative nonfiction and some health books—prefers referrals); Sally Van Haitsma (actively looking for good proposals by way of query letters, and her wish list covers literary and women's fiction, current affairs, architecture, pop culture, and science fiction); Deborah Ritchken (narrative nonfiction, food/cook books, design, France, literary fiction, no genre fiction).

REPRESENTS Nonfiction books, novels. **Considers these fiction areas:** contemporary issues, ethnic, literary, mainstream, mystery, suspense, women's.

⌐⊶ Does not want to receive horror, screenplays, poetry or academic nonfiction.

HOW TO CONTACT No unsolicited submissions. Query with SASE. No e-mail submissions accepted. Obtains most new clients through recommendations from others, solicitations, conferences.

TERMS Agent receives 15% commission on domestic sales. Agent receives 25% commission on foreign sales. Offers written contract; 6-week notice must be given to terminate contract.

RECENT SALES *Germs Gone Wild*, by Kenneth King (Pegasus); *The Insider* by Reece Hirsch (Berkley/Penguin); *The Leisure Seeker*, by Michael Zadoorian (Morrow/HarperCollins); *Beautiful: The Life of Hedy Lamarr*, by Stephen Shearer (St. Martin's Press); *American Libre*, by Raul Ramos y Sanchez (Grand Central); *The Two Krishnas*, by Ghalib Shiraz Dhalla (Alyson Books).

WRITERS CONFERENCES Santa Barbara Writers' Conference; Southern California Writers' Conference; Surrey International Writers' Conference; San Diego State University Writers' Conference; Willamette Writers' Conference.

TIPS "Be professional with submissions. Attend workshops and conferences before you approach an agent."

◑ JANE CHELIUS LITERARY AGENCY

548 Second St., Brooklyn NY 11215. (718)499-0236. **Fax:** (718)832-7335. **E-mail:** queries@janechelius.com. **Website:** www.janechelius.com. Member of AAR.

REPRESENTS Nonfiction books, novels. **Considers these fiction areas:** literary, mystery, suspense.

⇐─ Does not want to receive fantasy, science fiction, children's books, stage plays, screenplays, or poetry.

HOW TO CONTACT Please see website for submission procedures. Does not consider email queries with attachments. No unsolicited sample chapters or mss. Responds in 3-4-weeks usually.

●●◉ ELYSE CHENEY LITERARY ASSOCIATES, LLC

78 Fifth Avenue, 3rd Floor, New York NY 10011. **Website:** www.cheneyliterary.com. **Contact:** Elyse Cheney, Nicole Steen.

REPRESENTS Nonfiction, novels. **Considers these fiction areas:** upmarket commercial fiction, historical fiction, literary, suspense, upmarket women's fiction, and YA novels.

HOW TO CONTACT Query this agency with a referral. Include SASE or IRC. No fax queries. Snail mail or e-mail (submissions@cheneyliterary.com) only.

RECENT SALES *Moonwalking with Einstein: The Art and Science of Remembering Everything*, by Joshua Foer; *The Possessed: Adventures with Russian Books and the People Who Read Them*, by Elif Batuman (Farrar, Strauss & Giroux); *The Coldest Winter Ever*, by Sister Souljah (Atria); *A Heartbreaking Work of Staggering Genius*, by Dave Eggers (Simon and Schuster).

THE CHOATE AGENCY, LLC

1320 Bolton Rd., Pelham NY 10803. **E-mail:** mickey@thechoateagency.com. **Website:** www.thechoateagency.com. **Contact:** Mickey Choate. Estab. 2004. Member of AAR.

REPRESENTS Nonfiction books, novels. **Considers these fiction areas:** historical, mystery, thriller select literary fiction, strong commercial fiction.

⇐─ The agency does not handle genre fiction, chic-lit, cozies, romance, self-help, confessional memoirs, spirituality, pop psychology, religion, how-to, New Age titles, children's books, poetry, self-published works, or screenplays.

HOW TO CONTACT Query with brief synopsis and bio. This agency prefers e-queries, but accepts snail mail queries with SASE.

● DON CONGDON ASSOCIATES INC.

156 Fifth Ave., Suite 625, New York NY 10010-7002. (212)645-1229. **Fax:** (212)727-2688. **E-mail:** dca@doncongdon.com. **Website:** http://doncongdon.com. **Contact:** Don Congdon, Michael Congdon, Susan Ramer, Cristina Concepcion, Maura Kye-Casella, Katie Kotchman, Katie Grimm. Member of AAR. Represents 100 clients. Currently handles nonfiction books (60%), other (40% fiction).

REPRESENTS Nonfiction books, fiction. **Considers these fiction areas:** action, adventure, contemporary issues, crime, detective, literary, mainstream, mystery, police, short story collections, suspense, thriller, women's.

⇐─ Especially interested in narrative nonfiction and literary fiction.

HOW TO CONTACT Query with SASE or via e-mail (no attachments). Responds in 3 weeks to queries. Responds in 1 month to mss. Obtains most new clients through recommendations from other authors.

TERMS Agent receives 15% commission on domestic sales. Agent receives 19% commission on foreign sales. Charges client for extra shipping costs, photocopying, copyright fees, book purchases.

TIPS "Writing a query letter with a SASE is a must. We cannot guarantee replies to foreign queries via standard mail. No phone calls. We never download attachments to e-mail queries for security reasons, so please copy and paste material into your e-mail."

● CRICHTON & ASSOCIATES

6940 Carroll Ave., Takoma Park MD 20912. (301)495-9663. **Fax:** (202)318-0050. **E-mail:** query@crichton-associates.com. **Website:** www.crichton-associates.com. **Contact:** Sha-Shana Crichton. 90% of clients are new/unpublished writers. Currently handles nonfiction books 50%, fiction 50%.

REPRESENTS Nonfiction books, novels. **Considers these fiction areas:** ethnic, feminist, inspirational, literary, mainstream, mystery, religious, romance, suspense chick lit.

⇐─ Actively seeking women's fiction, romance, and chick lit. Looking also for multicultural fiction and nonfiction. Does not want to receive poetry, children's, YA, science fiction, or screenplays.

HOW TO CONTACT In the subject line of e-mail, please indicate whether your project is fiction or nonfiction. Please do not send attachments. Your query letter should include a description of the project and your biography. If you wish to send your query via snail mail, please include your telephone number and e-mail address. We will respond to you via e-mail. For fiction, include short synopsis and first 3 chapters with query. For nonfiction, send a book proposal. Responds in 3-5 weeks to queries.

TERMS Agent receives 15% commission on domestic sales. Agent receives 20% commission on foreign sales. Offers written contract, binding for 45 days. Only charges fees for postage and photocopying.

RECENT SALES *The African American Entrepreneur*, by W. Sherman Rogers (Praeger); *The Diversity Code*, by Michelle Johnson (Amacom); *Secret & Lies*, by Rhonda McKnight (Urban Books); *Love on the Rocks*, by Pamela Yaye (Harlequin). Other clients include Kimberley White, Beverley Long, Jessica Trap, Altonya Washington, Cheris Hodges.

WRITERS CONFERENCES Silicon Valley RWA; BookExpo America.

D4EO LITERARY AGENCY

7 Indian Valley Rd., Weston CT 06883. (203)544-7180. **Fax:** (203)544-7160. **E-mail:** d4eo@optonline.net. **Website:** www.d4eo.com. **Contact:** Bob Diforio. Represents 100+ clients. 50% of clients are new/unpublished writers. Currently handles nonfiction books (70%), novels (25%), juvenile books (5%).

MEMBER AGENTS Kristin Miller, Weronika Janczuk.

REPRESENTS Nonfiction books, novels. **Considers these fiction areas:** adventure, detective, erotica, historical, horror, humor, juvenile, literary, mainstream, mystery, picture books, romance, science, sports, thriller, western, young adult.

HOW TO CONTACT Query with SASE. Accepts and prefers e-mail queries. Prefers to read material exclusively. Responds in 1 week to queries. Obtains most new clients through recommendations from others.

TERMS Agent receives 15% commission on domestic sales. Agent receives 25% commission on foreign sales. Offers written contract, binding for 2 years; 60-day notice must be given to terminate contract. Charges for photocopying and submission postage.

◑ DANIEL LITERARY GROUP

1701 Kingsbury Dr., Suite 100, Nashville TN 37215. (615)730-8207. **E-mail:** submissions@danielliterarygroup.com. **Website:** www.danielliterarygroup.

com. **Contact:** Greg Daniel. Represents 45 clients. 30% of clients are new/unpublished writers. Currently handles nonfiction books (85%), novels (15%).

> Prior to becoming an agent, Mr. Daniel spent 10 years in publishing—six at the executive level at Thomas Nelson Publishers.

REPRESENTS Nonfiction books, novels. **Considers these fiction areas:** action, adventure, contemporary issues, crime, detective, family saga, historical, humor, inspirational, literary, mainstream, mystery, police, religious, satire, suspense, thriller.

> The agency currently accepts all fiction topics, except for children's, romance and sci-fi. "We take pride in our ability to come alongside our authors and help strategize about where they want their writing to take them in both the near and long term. Forging close relationships with our authors, we help them with such critical factors as editorial refinement, branding, audience, and marketing." The agency is open to submissions in almost every popular category of nonfiction, especially if authors are recognized experts in their fields. No screenplays, poetry, science fiction/fantasy, romance, children's, or short stories.

HOW TO CONTACT Query via e-mail only. Submit publishing history, author bio, brief synopsis of work, key selling points. E-queries only. Send no attachments. For fiction, send first 5 pages pasted in e-mail. Check Submissions Guidelines before querying or submitting. Please do not query via telephone. Responds in 2-3 weeks to queries.

● DARHANSOFF & VERRILL LITERARY AGENTS

236 W. 26th St., Suite 802, New York NY 10001. (917)305-1300. **Fax:** (917)305-1400. **E-mail:** chuck@dvagency.com. **Website:** www.dvagency.com. Member of AAR. Represents 120 clients. 10% of clients are new/unpublished writers. Currently handles nonfiction books (25%), novels (60%), story collections (15%).

MEMBER AGENTS Liz Darhansoff; Chuck Verrill, Michele Mortimer.

REPRESENTS Novels, juvenile books narrative nonfiction, literary fiction, mystery & suspense, young adult.

HOW TO CONTACT Queries welcome via website or with SASE. Obtains most new clients through recommendations from others.

⦿ THE JENNIFER DECHIARA LITERARY AGENCY

31 East 32nd St., Suite 300, New York NY 10016. (212)481-8484. **Fax:** (212)481-9582. **E-mail:** jenndec@aol.com; stephenafraser@verizon.net. **Website:** www.jdlit.com. **Contact:** Jennifer DeChiara, Stephen Fraser. Represents 100 clients. 50% of clients are new/unpublished writers. Currently handles nonfiction books (25%), novels (25%), juvenile books (50%).

○ Prior to becoming an agent, Ms. DeChiara was a writing consultant, freelance editor at Simon & Schuster and Random House, and a ballerina and an actress.

MEMBER AGENTS Jennifer DeChiara, Stephen Fraser, Dorothy Spencer (adult fiction and nonfiction).

REPRESENTS Nonfiction books, novels, juvenile. **Considers these fiction areas:** confession, crime, detective, ethnic, family saga, fantasy, feminist, gay, historical, horror, humor, juvenile, lesbian, literary, mainstream, mystery, picture books, police, regional, satire, sports, suspense, thriller, young adult chick lit, psychic/supernatural, glitz.

⸙━ "We represent both children's and adult books in a wide range of ages and genres. We are a full-service agency and fulfill the potential of every book in every possible medium—stage, film, television, etc. We help writers every step of the way, from creating book ideas to editing and promotion. We are passionate about helping writers further their careers, but are just as eager to discover new talent, regardless of age or lack of prior publishing experience. This agency is committed to managing a writer's entire career. For us, it's not just about selling books, but about making dreams come true. We are especially attracted to the downtrodden, the discouraged, and the downright disgusted." Actively seeking literary fiction, chick lit, young adult fiction, self-help, pop culture, and celebrity biographies. Does not want Westerns, poetry, or short stories.

HOW TO CONTACT Query with SASE. Accepts simultaneous submissions. Responds in 3-6 months to queries. Responds in 3-6 months to mss. Obtains most new clients through recommendations from others, conferences, query letters.

TERMS Agent receives 15% commission on domestic sales. Agent receives 20% commission on foreign sales. Offers written contract.

RECENT SALES Sold more than 100 titles in the past year. *The Chosen One*, by Carol Lynch Williams (St. Martin's Press); *The 30-Day Heartbreak Cure*, by Catherine Hickland (Simon & Schuster); *Naptime for Barney*, by Danny Sit (Sterling Publishing); *The Screwed-Up Life of Charlie the Second*, by Drew Ferguson (Kensington); *Heart of a Shepherd*, by Rosanne Parry (Random House); *Carolina Harmony*, by Marilyn Taylor McDowell (Random House); *Project Sweet Life*, by Brent Hartinger (HarperCollins). Movie/TV MOW scripts optioned/sold: *The Elf on the Shelf*, by Carol Aebersold and Chanda Bell (Waddell & Scorsese); *Heart of a Shepherd*, by Rosanne Parry (Tashtego Films); *Geography Club*, by Brent Hartinger (The Levy Leder Company). Other clients include Sylvia Browne, Matthew Kirby, Sonia Levitin, Susan Anderson, Michael Apostolina.

⦿ DEFIORE & CO.

47 E. 19th St., 3rd Floor, New York NY 10003. (212)925-7744. **Fax:** (212)925-9803. **E-mail:** info@defioreandco.com; submissions@defioreandco.com. **Website:** www.defioreandco.com. **Contact:** Lauren Gilchrist. Member of AAR. Represents 75 clients. 50% of clients are new/unpublished writers. Currently handles nonfiction books (70%), novels (30%).

MEMBER AGENTS Brian DeFiore (popular nonfiction, business, pop culture, parenting, commercial fiction); Laurie Abkemeier (memoir, parenting, business, how-to/self-help, popular science); Kate Garrick (literary fiction, memoir, popular non-fiction); Debra Goldstein (health and diet, wellness); Laura Nolan (cookbooks, memoir, non-fiction); Matthew Elblonk (young adult, popular culture, narrative non-fiction); Karen Gerwin (popular culture, memoir); Caryn Karmatz-Rudy (popular fiction, self-help, narrative non-fiction).

REPRESENTS Nonfiction books, novels. **Considers these fiction areas:** ethnic, literary, mainstream, mystery, suspense, thriller.

⸙━ "Please be advised that we are not considering children's picture books, poetry, adult science fiction and fantasy, romance, or dramatic projects at this time."

HOW TO CONTACT Query with SASE or e-mail to submissions@defioreandco.com. Please include the word "Query" in the subject line. All attachments will be deleted; please insert all text in the body of the e-mail. For more information about our agents, their individual interests, and their query guidelines, please visit our "About Us" page. Accepts simultaneous submissions. Responds in 3 weeks to queries. Responds in 2 months to mss. Obtains most new clients through recommendations from others.

TERMS Agent receives 15% commission on domestic sales. Agent receives 20% commission on foreign sales. Offers written contract; 10-day notice must be given to terminate contract. Charges clients for photocopying and overnight delivery (deducted only after a sale is made).

WRITERS CONFERENCES Maui Writers Conference; Pacific Northwest Writers Conference; North Carolina Writers' Network Fall Conference.

● JOELLE DELBOURGO ASSOCIATES, INC.

101 Park St., 3rd Floor, Montclair NJ 07042. (973)783-6800. **Fax:** (973)783-6802. **E-mail:** info@delbourgo. com. **Website:** www.delbourgo.com. **Contact:** Joelle Delbourgo, Molly Lyons, Jacquie Flynn. Represents more than 100 clients. Currently handles nonfiction books (75%), novels (25%).

○ Prior to becoming an agent, Ms. Delbourgo was an editor and senior publishing executive at HarperCollins and Random House.

MEMBER AGENTS Joelle Delbourgo (narrative nonfiction, serious "expert-driven" nonfiction, self-help, psychology, business, history, science, medicine, quality fiction); Molly Lyons (memoir, narrative nonfiction, biography, current events, cultural issues, pop culture, health, psychology, smart, fresh practical nonfiction, fiction, young adult and middle grade); Jacquie Flynn (thought-provoking and practical business, parenting, education, personal development, current events, science and other select nonfiction and fiction titles).

REPRESENTS Nonfiction books, novels. **Considers these fiction areas:** historical, literary, mainstream, mystery, suspense.

8—π "We are former publishers and editors, with deep knowledge and an insider perspective. We have a reputation for individualized attention to clients, strategic management of authors' careers, and creating strong partnerships with publishers for our clients." Actively seeking history, narrative nonfiction, science/medicine, memoir, literary fiction, psychology, parenting, biographies, current affairs, politics,

young adult fiction and nonfiction. Does not want to receive genre fiction, science fiction, fantasy, or screenplays.

HOW TO CONTACT Query by mail with SASE. Accepts simultaneous submissions. Responds in 3 weeks to queries. Responds in 2 months to mss.

TERMS Agent receives 15% commission on domestic sales. Agent receives 20% commission on foreign sales. Offers written contract. Charges clients for postage and photocopying.

RECENT SALES *Alexander the Great*, by Philip Freeman; *The Big Book of Parenting Solutions*, by Dr. Michele Borba; *The Secret Life of Ms. Finkelman*, by Ben H. Wintners; *Not Quite Adults*, by Richard Settersten Jr. and Barbara Ray; *Tabloid Medicine*, by Robert Goldberg, PhD; *Table of Contents*, by Judy Gerlman and Vicky Levi Krupp.

TIPS "Do your homework. Do not cold call. Read and follow submission guidelines before contacting us. Do not call to find out if we received your material. No e-mail queries. Treat agents with respect, as you would any other professional, such as a doctor, lawyer or financial advisor."

● DHS LITERARY, INC.

10711 Preston Road, Suite 100, Dallas TX 75230. (214)363-4422. **Fax:** (214)363-4423. **Website:** www. dhsliterary.com. **Contact:** David Hale Smith, president. Represents 35 clients. 15% of clients are new/unpublished writers. Currently handles nonfiction books (60%), novels (40%).

REPRESENTS Nonfiction books, novels. **Considers these fiction areas:** crime, detective, ethnic, frontier, literary, mainstream, mystery, police, suspense, thriller, westerns.

8—π This agency is not actively seeking clients and usually takes clients on by referral only.

HOW TO CONTACT We accept new material by referral only. Only responds if interested. *No unsolicited mss.*

TERMS Agent receives 15% commission on domestic sales. Agent receives 25% commission on foreign sales. Offers written contract; 10-day notice must be given to terminate contract. This agency charges for postage and photocopying.

RECENT SALES *So Cold The River*, by Michael Koryta; *In The Shadow of Gotham*, by Stefanie Pintoff; *The Body Scoop for Girls*, by Jennifer Ashton, MD; *The Prosperity Plan*, by Laura Berman Fortgang .

TIPS "Remember to be courteous and professional, and to treat marketing your work and approaching an agent as you would any formal business matter. If you have a referral, always query first via e-mail. Sorry, but we cannot respond to queries sent via mail, even with a SASE. Visit our website for more information."

◐◐ JIM DONOVAN LITERARY

4515 Prentice St., Suite 109, Dallas TX 75206-5028. **E-mail:** jdlqueries@sbcglobal.net. **Contact:** Melissa Shultz, agent. Represents 30 clients. 10% of clients are new/unpublished writers. Currently handles nonfiction books (75%), novels (25%).

MEMBER AGENTS Jim Donovan (history—particularly American, military and Western; biography; sports; popular reference; popular culture; fiction—literary, thrillers and mystery); Melissa Shultz (parenting, women's issues, memoir).

REPRESENTS Nonfiction books, novels. **Considers these fiction areas:** action, adventure, crime, detective, literary, mainstream, mystery, police, suspense, thriller.

8—⊶ This agency specializes in commercial fiction and nonfiction. "Does not want to receive poetry, children's, short stories, inspirational or anything else not listed above."

HOW TO CONTACT "For nonfiction, I need a well-thought query letter telling me about the book: What it does, how it does it, why it's needed now, why it's better or different than what's out there on the subject, and why the author is the perfect writer for it. For fiction, the novel has to be finished, of course; a short (2 to 5 page) synopsis—not a teaser, but a summary of all the action, from first page to last—and the first 30-50 pages is enough. This material should be polished to as close to perfection as possible." Accepts simultaneous submissions. Responds in 3 weeks to queries. Responds in 1 month to mss. Obtains most new clients through recommendations from others.

TERMS Agent receives 15% commission on domestic sales. Agent receives 20% commission on foreign sales. Offers written contract, binding for 1 year; 30-day notice must be given to terminate contract. This agency charges for things such as overnight delivery and manuscript copying. Charges are discussed beforehand.

RECENT SALES Sold 27 titles in the last year. *The Last Gunfight*, by Jeff Guinn (Simon and Schuster); *Resurrection* by Jim Dent (St. Martin's Press); *The Battling Bastards of Bataan* by Bill Sloan (Simon and Schuster); *Perfect*, by Lew Paper (NAL); *Honor in the Dust*, by Gregg Jones (NAL); *First in War* by David Clary (Simon and Schuster); *Desperadoes* by Mark Gardner (HarperCollins); *Apocalypse of the Dead* by Joe McKinney (Kensington).

TIPS "Get published in short form—magazine reviews, journals, etc.—first. This will increase your credibility considerably, and make it much easier to sell a full-length book."

◐ DUNHAM LITERARY, INC.

156 Fifth Ave., Suite 625, New York NY 10010-7002. (212)929-0994. **E-mail:** query@dunhamlit.com. **Website:** www.dunhamlit.com. **Contact:** Jennie Dunham. Member of AAR. SCBWI Represents 50 clients. 15% of clients are new/unpublished writers. Currently handles nonfiction books (25%), novels (25%), juvenile books (50%).

MEMBER AGENTS Blair Hewes. Represents authors of literary and commercial fiction, narrative non fiction, and books for children of all ages. She is interested in representing authors of nonfiction books in the categories of pop culture, historical biography, lifestyle, and women's issues. She is not interested in westerns, hard-boiled crime fiction, or political or medical thrillers.

REPRESENTS Nonfiction books, novels, short story collections, juvenile. **Considers these fiction areas:** ethnic, juvenile, literary, mainstream, picture books, young adult.

HOW TO CONTACT Query with SASE. Responds in 1 week to queries; 2 months to mss. Obtains most new clients through recommendations from others, solicitations.

TERMS Agent receives 15% commission on domestic sales. Agent receives 20% commission on foreign sales.

RECENT SALES Sold 30 books for young readers in the last year. *Peter Pan*, by Robert Sabuda (Little Simon); *Flamingos on the Roof*, by Calef Brown (Houghton); *Adele and Simon in America*, by Barbara McClintock (Farrar, Straus & Giroux); *Caught Between the Pages*, by Marlene Carvell (Dutton); *Waiting For Normal*, by Leslie Connor (HarperCollins), *The Gollywhopper Games*, by Jody Feldman (Greenwillow); *America the Beautiful*, by Robert Sabuda; *Dahlia*, by Barbara McClintock; *Living Dead Girl*, by Tod Goldberg; *In My Mother's House*, by Margaret McMulla; *Black Hawk Down*, by Mark Bowden; *Look Back All the Green Valley*, by Fred Chappell;

Under a Wing, by Reeve Lindbergh; *I Am Madame X*, by Gioia Diliberto.

● DUPREE/MILLER AND ASSOCIATES INC. LITERARY

100 Highland Park Village, Suite 350, Dallas TX 75205. (214)559-BOOK. **Fax:** (214)559-PAGE. **Website:** www.dupreemiller.com. Other memberships include ABA. Represents 200 clients. 20% of clients are new/unpublished writers. Currently handles nonfiction books (90%), novels (10%).

MEMBER AGENTS Jan Miller, president/CEO; Shannon Miser-Marven, senior executive VP; Annabelle Baxter; Nena Madonia; Cheri Gillis.

REPRESENTS Nonfiction books, novels, scholarly, syndicated religious.inspirational/spirituality. **Considers these fiction areas:** action, adventure, crime, detective, ethnic, experimental, family saga, feminist, glitz, historical, humor, inspirational, literary, mainstream, mystery, picture books, police, psychic, religious, satire, sports, supernatural, suspense, thriller.

8—➤ This agency specializes in commercial fiction and nonfiction.

HOW TO CONTACT Submit 1-page query, summary, bio, how to market, SASE through U.S. postal service. Obtains most new clients through recommendations from others, conferences, lectures.

TERMS Agent receives 15% commission on domestic sales. Offers written contract.

WRITERS CONFERENCES Aspen Summer Words Literary Festival.

TIPS "If interested in agency representation, it is vital to have the material in the proper working format. As agents' policies differ, it is important to follow their guidelines. Work on establishing a strong proposal that provides sample chapters, an overall synopsis (fairly detailed), and some biographical information on yourself. Do not send your proposal in pieces; it should be complete upon submission. Your work should be in its best condition."

● EAST/WEST LITERARY AGENCY, LLC

1158 26th St., Suite 462, Santa Monica CA 90403. (310)573-9303. **Fax:** (310)453-9008. **E-mail:** dwarren@eastwestliteraryagency.com; mgjames@eastwestliteraryagency.com; rpfeffer@eastwestliteraryagency.com. Estab. 2000. Represents 100 clients. 70% of clients are new/unpublished writers. Currently handles juvenile books (80%), adult books 20%.

MEMBER AGENTS Deborah Warren, founder; Mary Grey James, partner literary agent (special interest: Southern writers and their stories, literary fiction); Rubin Pfeffer, partner content agent and digital media strategist.

HOW TO CONTACT By referral only. Submit proposal and first 3 sample chapters, table of contents (2 pages or fewer), synopsis (1 page). For picture books, submit entire ms. Requested submissions should be sent by mail as a Word document in Courier, 12-pt., double-spaced with 1.20-inch margin on left, ragged right text, 25 lines per page, continuously paginated, with all your contact info on the first page. Only responds if interested, no need for SASE. Responds in 60 days. Obtains new clients through recommendations from others.

TERMS Agent receives 15% commission on domestic sales. Agent receives 25% commission on foreign sales. Offers written contract; 30-day notice must be given to terminate contract. Charges for out-of-pocket expenses, such as postage and copying.

● ANNE EDELSTEIN LITERARY AGENCY

20 W. 22nd St., Suite 1603, New York NY 10010. (212)414-4923. **Fax:** (212)414-2930. **E-mail:** info@aeliterary.com. **Website:** www.aeliterary.com. Member of AAR.

MEMBER AGENTS Anne Edelstein; Krista Ingebretson.

REPRESENTS Nonfiction books, fiction. **Considers these fiction areas:** literary.

8—➤ This agency specializes in fiction and narrative nonfiction.

HOW TO CONTACT Query with SASE; submit 25 sample pages.

RECENT SALES *Confessions of a Buddhist Atheist*, by Stephen Batchelor (Spiegel & Grau); *April & Oliver*, by Tess Callahan (Doubleday).

THE NICHOLAS ELLISON AGENCY

Affiliated with Sanford J. Greenburger Associates, 55 Fifth Ave., 15th Floor, New York NY 10003. (212)206-5600. **Fax:** (212)463-8718. **E-mail:** nellison@sjga.com. **Website:** www.greenburger.com. **Contact:** Nicholas Ellison. Represents 70 clients. Currently handles nonfiction books (50%), novels (50%).

🗩 Prior to becoming an agent, Mr. Ellison was an editor at Minerva Editions and Harper & Row, and editor-in-chief at Delacorte.

MEMBER AGENTS Nicholas Ellison; Chelsea Lindman.

REPRESENTS Nonfiction books, novels literary, mainstream children's books. **Considers these fiction areas:** literary, mainstream.

HOW TO CONTACT Query with SASE. Responds in 6 weeks to queries.

TERMS Agent receives 15% commission on domestic sales. Agent receives 20% commission on foreign sales.

❶ THE ELAINE P. ENGLISH LITERARY AGENCY

4710 41st St. NW, Suite D, Washington DC 20016. (202)362-5190. **Fax:** (202)362-5192. **E-mail:** queries@elaineenglish.com. **E-mail:** elaine@elaineenglish.com. **Website:** www.elaineenglish.com/literary.php. **Contact:** Elaine English, Lindsey Skouras. Member of AAR. Represents 20 clients. 25% of clients are new/unpublished writers. Currently handles novels (100%).

MEMBER AGENTS Elaine English (novels).

REPRESENTS Novels. **Considers these fiction areas:** historical, multicultural, mystery, suspense, thriller, women's romance (single title, historical, contemporary, romantic, suspense, chick lit, erotic), general women's fiction. The agency is slowly but steadily acquiring in all mentioned areas.

⌐► Actively seeking women's fiction, including single-title romances, and young adult fiction. Does not want to receive any science fiction, time travel, or picture books.

HOW TO CONTACT Generally prefers e-queries sent to queries@elaineenglish.com. If requested, submit synopsis, first 3 chapters, SASE. Please check website for further details. Responds in 4-8 weeks to queries; 3 months to requested submissions. Obtains most new clients through recommendations from others, conferences, submissions.

TERMS Agent receives 15% commission on domestic sales. Agent receives 20% commission on foreign sales. Offers written contract; 30-day notice must be given to terminate contract. Charges only for shipping expenses; generally taken from proceeds.

RECENT SALES Have been to Sourcebooks, Tor, Harlequin.

WRITERS CONFERENCES RWA National Conference; Novelists, Inc.; Malice Domestic; Washington Romance Writers Retreat, among others.

❶ FELICIA ETH LITERARY REPRESENTATION

555 Bryant St., Suite 350, Palo Alto CA 94301-1700. (650)375-1276. **Fax:** (650)401-8892. **E-mail:** feliciaeth@aol.com. **Contact:** Felicia Eth. Member of AAR. Represents 25-35 clients. Currently handles nonfiction books (75%), novels (25% adult).

REPRESENTS Nonfiction books, novels. **Considers these fiction areas:** literary, mainstream.

⌐► This agency specializes in high-quality fiction (preferably mainstream/contemporary) and provocative, intelligent, and thoughtful nonfiction on a wide array of commercial subjects.

HOW TO CONTACT Query with SASE. Accepts simultaneous submissions. Responds in 3 weeks to queries. Responds in 4-6 weeks to mss.

TERMS Agent receives 15% commission on domestic sales. Agent receives 20% commission on foreign sales. Agent receives 20% commission on film sales. Charges clients for photocopying and express mail service.

RECENT SALES Sold 7-10 titles in the last year. *Bumper Sticker Philosophy*, by Jack Bowen (Random House); *Boys Adrift* by Leonard Sax (Basic Books); *A War Reporter*, by Barbara Quick (HarperCollins); *Pantry*, by Anna Badkhen (Free Press/S&S).

WRITERS CONFERENCES "Wide Array — from Squaw Valley to Mills College."

TIPS "For nonfiction, established expertise is certainly a plus—as is magazine publication—though not a prerequisite. I am highly dedicated to those projects I represent, but highly selective in what I choose."

❶ FAIRBANK LITERARY REPRESENTATION

P.O. Box 6, Hudson NY 12534-0006. (617)576-0030. **Fax:** (617)576-0030. **E-mail:** queries@fairbankliterary.com. **Website:** www.fairbankliterary.com. **Contact:** Sorche Fairbank. Member of AAR. Represents 45 clients. 20% of clients are new/unpublished writers. Currently handles nonfiction books (60%), novels (22%), story collections (3%), other (15% illustrated).

MEMBER AGENTS Sorche Fairbank (narrative nonfiction, commercial and literary fiction, memoir, food and wine); Matthew Frederick (scout for sports nonfiction, architecture, design).

REPRESENTS Nonfiction books, novels, short story collections. **Considers these fiction areas:** action, adventure, feminist, gay, lesbian, literary, mainstream, mystery, sports, suspense, thriller, women's Southern voices.

☛ "I have a small agency in Harvard Square, where I tend to gravitate toward literary fiction and narrative nonfiction, with a strong interest in women's issues and women's voices, international voices, class and race issues, and projects that simply teach me something new about the greater world and society around us. We have a good reputation for working closely and developmentally with our authors and love what we do." Actively seeking literary fiction, international and culturally diverse voices, narrative nonfiction, topical subjects (politics, current affairs), history, sports, architecture/design and pop culture. Does not want to receive romance, poetry, science fiction, pirates, vampire, young adult, or children's works.

HOW TO CONTACT Query with SASE. Submit author bio. Accepts simultaneous submissions. Responds in 6 weeks to queries. Responds in 10 weeks to mss. Obtains most new clients through recommendations from others, solicitations, conferences, ideas generated in-house.

TERMS Agent receives 15% commission on domestic sales. Agent receives 20% commission on foreign sales. Offers written contract, binding for 12 months; 45-day notice must be given to terminate contract.

WRITERS CONFERENCES San Francisco Writers' Conference, Muse and the Marketplace/Grub Street Conference, Washington Independent Writers' Conference, Murder in the Grove, Surrey International Writers' Conference.

TIPS "Be professional from the very first contact. There shouldn't be a single typo or grammatical flub in your query. Have a reason for contacting me about your project other than I was the next name listed on some website. Please do not use form query software! Believe me, we can get a dozen or so a day that look identical—we know when you are using a form. Show me that you know your audience—and your competition. Have the writing and/or proposal at the very, very best it can be before starting the querying process. Don't assume that if someone likes it enough they'll 'fix' it. The biggest mistake new writers make is starting the querying process before they—and the work—are ready. Take your time and do it right."

FARRIS LITERARY AGENCY, INC.

P.O. Box 570069, Dallas TX 75357. (972)203-8804. **E-mail:** farris1@airmail.net. **Website:** www.farrisliterary.com. **Contact:** Mike Farris, Susan Morgan Farris. Represents 30 clients. 60% of clients are new/unpublished writers. Currently handles nonfiction books (40%), novels (60%).

REPRESENTS Nonfiction books, novels. **Considers these fiction areas:** action, adventure, crime, detective, frontier, historical, humor, inspirational, mainstream, mystery, police, religious, romance, satire, sports, suspense, thriller, westerns.

☛ "We specialize in both fiction and nonfiction books. We are particularly interested in discovering unpublished authors. We adhere to AAR guidelines." Does not want to receive science fiction, fantasy, gay and lesbian, erotica, young adult, or children's.

HOW TO CONTACT Query with SASE or by e-mail. Accepts simultaneous submissions. Responds in 2-3 weeks to queries. Responds in 4-8 weeks to mss. Obtains most new clients through recommendations from others, solicitations, conferences.

TERMS Agent receives 15% commission on domestic sales. Agent receives 20% commission on foreign sales. Offers written contract; 30-day notice must be given to terminate contract. Charges clients for postage and photocopying.

RECENT SALES *The Yard Dog* and The Insane Train, by Sheldon Russell (St. Martin's Press); *Eurostorm*, by Payne Harrison (Variance Publishing); *Relative Chaos*, by Kay Finch (Avalon Books); *Call Me Lucky: A Texan in Hollywood*, by Robert Hinkle and Mike Farris (University of Oklahoma Press); *Sketch Me If You Can* (the first book in a three-book deal for the A Portrait of Crime mystery series), by Sharon Pape (Berkley Books); film rights options for *Balaam Gimble's Gumption*, by Mike Nichols (John M. Hardy Publishing).

WRITERS CONFERENCES The Screenwriting Conference in Santa Fe; La Jolla Writers Conference; East Texas Christian Writers Conference.

DIANA FINCH LITERARY AGENCY

116 W. 23rd St., Suite 500, New York NY 10011. **E-mail:** diana.finch@verizon.net. **Website:** dianafinchliteraryagency.blogspot.com/. **Contact:** Diana Finch. Member of AAR. Represents 40 clients. 20% of clients are new/unpublished writers. Currently han-

dles nonfiction books (85%), novels (15%), juvenile books (5%), multimedia (5%).

REPRESENTS Nonfiction books, novels, scholarly. **Considers these fiction areas:** action, adventure, crime, detective, ethnic, historical, literary, mainstream, police, thriller, young adult.

8—¬ Actively seeking narrative nonfiction, popular science, memoir and health topics. "Does not want romance, mysteries, or children's picture books."

HOW TO CONTACT Query with SASE or via e-mail (no attachments). Accepts simultaneous submissions. Obtains most new clients through recommendations from others.

TERMS Agent receives 15% commission on domestic sales. Agent receives 20% commission on foreign sales. Offers written contract. "I charge for photocopying, overseas postage, galleys, and books purchased, and try to recoup these costs from earnings received for a client, rather than charging outright."

RECENT SALES *Heidegger's Glasses,* by Thaisa Frank; *Genetic Rounds,* by Robert Marion, MD (Kaplan); *Honeymoon in Tehran,* by Azadeh Moaveni (Random House); *Darwin Slept Here* by Eric Simons (Overlook); *Black Tide,* by Antonia Juhasz (HarperCollins); *Stalin's Children,* by Owen Matthews (Bloomsbury); *Radiant Days,* by Michael Fitzgerald (Shoemaker & Hoard); *The Queen's Soprano,* by Carol Dines (Harcourt Young Adult); *What to Say to a Porcupine,* by Richard Gallagher (Amacom); *The Language of Trust,* by Michael Maslansky et al.

TIPS "Do as much research as you can on agents before you query. Have someone critique your query letter before you send it. It should be only 1 page and describe your book clearly—and why you are writing it—but also demonstrate creativity and a sense of your writing style."

FINEPRINT LITERARY MANAGEMENT

240 West 35th St., Suite 500, New York NY 10001. (212)279-1282. **E-mail:** stephany@fineprintlit.com. **Website:** www.fineprintlit.com. Member of AAR.

MEMBER AGENTS Peter Rubie, CEO (nonfiction interests include narrative nonfiction, popular science, spirituality, history, biography, pop culture, business, technology, parenting, health, self help, music, and food; fiction interests include literate thrillers, crime fiction, science fiction and fantasy, military fiction and literary fiction); Stephany Evans, president (nonfiction interests include health and wellness—especially women's health, spirituality, lifestyle, home renovating/decorating, entertaining, food and wine, popular reference, and narrative nonfiction; fiction interests include stories with a strong and interesting female protagonist, both literary and upmarket commercial—including chick lit, romance, mystery, and light suspense); June Clark (nonfiction: entertainment, self-help, parenting, reference/how-to books, teen books, food and wine, style/beauty, and prescriptive business titles); Diane Freed (nonfiction: health/fitness, women's issues, memoir, baby boomer trends, parenting, popular culture, self-help, humor, young adult, and topics of New England regional interest); Meredith Hays (both fiction and nonfiction: commercial and literary; she is interested in sophisticated women's fiction such as urban chick lit, pop culture, lifestyle, animals, and absorbing nonfiction accounts); Janet Reid (mysteries and offbeat literary fiction); Colleen Lindsay; Marissa Walsh; Ward Calhoun; Laura Wood.

REPRESENTS Nonfiction books, novels. **Considers these fiction areas:** crime, detective, fantasy, literary, military, mystery, police, romance, science fiction, suspense, war, women's, young adult.

HOW TO CONTACT Query with SASE. Submit synopsis and first two chapters for fiction; proposal for nonfiction. Do not send attachments or manuscripts without a request. See contact page onilne at website for e-mails. Obtains most new clients through recommendations from others, solicitations.

TERMS Agent receives 15% commission on domestic sales. Agent receives 20% commission on foreign sales.

FOUNDRY LITERARY + MEDIA

33 West 17th St., PH, New York NY 10011. (212)929-5064. **Fax:** (212)929-5471. **Website:** www.foundry-media.com.

MEMBER AGENTS Peter H. McGuigan (smart, offbeat nonfiction, particularly works of narrative nonfiction on pop culture, niche history, biography, music and science; fiction interests include commercial and literary, across all genres, especially first-time writers); Yfat Reiss Gendell (favors nonfiction books focusing on all manners of prescriptive: how-to, science, health and well-being, memoirs, adventure, travel stories and lighter titles appropriate for the gift trade genre. Yfat also looks for commercial fiction highlighting the full range of women's experiences—young and old—and also seeks science fiction, thrillers and historical fiction); Stéphanie Abou (in fiction and nonfiction alike,

Stéphanie is always on the lookout for authors who are accomplished storytellers with their own distinctive voice, who develop memorable characters, and who are able to create psychological conflict with their narrative. She is an across-the-board fiction lover, attracted to both literary and smart upmarket commercial fiction. In nonfiction she leans towards projects that tackle big topics with an unusual approach. Pop culture, health, science, parenting, women's and multicultural issues are of special interest); Chris Park (memoirs, narrative nonfiction, Christian nonfiction and character-driven fiction); David Patterson (outstanding narratives and/or idea-driven works of nonfiction); Hannah Brown Gordon (fiction, YA, memoir, narrative nonfiction, history, current events, science, psychology and pop culture); Lisa Grubka; Mollie Glick (literary fiction, narrative nonfiction, YA, and a bit of practical nonfiction); Stephen Barbara (all categories of books for young readers in addition to servicing writers for the adult market); Brandi Bowles (idea and platform-driven nonfiction in all categories, including music and pop culture, humor, business, sociology, philosophy, health, and relationships. Quirky, funny, or contrarian proposals are always welcome in her in-box, as are big-idea books that change the way we think about the world. Brandi also represents fiction in the categories of literary fiction, women's fiction, urban fantasy, and YA).

REPRESENTS Considers these fiction areas: literary, religious.

HOW TO CONTACT Query with SASE. Should be addressed to one agent only. Submit synopsis, 3 sample chapters, author bio, For nonfiction, submit query, proposal, sample chapter, TOC, bio. Put submissions on your snail mail submission.

FOX LITERARY

168 Second Ave., PMB 180, New York NY 10003. **E-mail:** submissions@foxliterary.com. **Website:** www.foxliterary.com.

REPRESENTS Considers these fiction areas: erotica, fantasy, literary, romance, science, young adult, science fiction, thrillers, historical fiction, literary fiction, graphic novels, commercial fiction, women's fiction, gay and lesbian, erotica historical romance.

8—➤ Does not want to receive screenplays, poetry, category westerns, horror, Christian/inspirational, or children's picture books.

HOW TO CONTACT E-mail query and first 5 pages in body of e-mail. E-mail queries preferred. For snail mail queries, must include an e-mail address for response. Do not send SASE.

● SARAH JANE FREYMANN LITERARY AGENCY

59 W. 71st St., Suite 9B, New York NY 10023. (212)362-9277. **E-mail:** sarah@sarahjanefreymann.com; Submissions@SarahJaneFreymann.com. **Website:** www.sarahjanefreymann.com. **Contact:** Sarah Jane Freymann, Steve Schwartz. Represents 100 clients. 20% of clients are new/unpublished writers. Currently handles nonfiction books (75%), novels (23%), juvenile books (2%).

MEMBER AGENTS Sarah Jane Freymann; (Nonfiction books, novels, illustrated books); Jessica Sinsheimer, Jessica@sarahjanefreymann.com (young adult fiction); Steven Schwartz, steve@sarahjanefreymann.com; Katharine Sands.

REPRESENTS Considers these fiction areas: ethnic, literary, mainstream.

HOW TO CONTACT Query with SASE. Responds in 2 weeks to queries. Responds in 6 weeks to mss. Obtains most new clients through recommendations from others.

TERMS Agent receives 15% commission on domestic sales. Agent receives 20% commission on foreign sales. Offers written contract. Charges clients for long distance, overseas postage, photocopying. 100% of business is derived from commissions on ms sales.

RECENT SALES *How to Make Love to a Plastic Cup: And Other Things I Learned While Trying to Knock Up My Wife*, by Greg Wolfe (Harper Collins); *I Want to Be Left Behind: Rapture Here on Earth*, by Brenda Peterson (a Merloyd Lawrence Book); *That Bird Has My Name: The Autobiography of an Innocent Man on Death Row*, by Jarvis Jay Masters with an Introduction by Pema Chodrun (HarperOne); *Perfect One-Dish Meals*, by Pam Anderson (Houghton Mifflin); *Birdology*, by Sy Montgomery (Simon & Schuster); *Emptying the Nest: Launching Your Reluctant Young Adult*, by Dr. Brad Sachs (Macmillan); *Tossed & Found*, by Linda and John Meyers (Steward, Tabori & Chang); *32 Candles*, by Ernessa Carter; *God and Dog*, by Wendy Francisco.

TIPS "I love fresh, new, passionate works by authors who love what they are doing and have both natural talent and carefully honed skill."

◐ FULL CIRCLE LITERARY, LLC

7676 Hazard Center Dr., Suite 500, San Diego CA 92108. **E-mail:** submissions@fullcircleliterary.com.

Website: www.fullcircleliterary.com. **Contact:** Lilly Ghahremani, Stefanie Von Borstel. Represents 55 clients. 60% of clients are new/unpublished writers. Currently handles nonfiction books (70%), novels (10%), juvenile books (20%).

○ Before forming Full Circle, Ms. Von Borstel worked in both marketing and editorial capacities at Penguin and Harcourt; Ms. Ghahremani received her law degree from UCLA, and has experience in representing authors on legal affairs.

MEMBER AGENTS Lilly Ghahremani (Lilly is only taking referrals: young adult, pop culture, crafts, "green" living, narrative nonfiction, business, relationships, Middle Eastern interest, multicultural); Stefanie Von Borstel (Latino interest, crafts, parenting, wedding/relationships, how-to, self help, middle grade/teen fiction/YA, green living, multicultural/bilingual picture books); Adriana Dominguez (fiction areas of interest: children's books—picture books, middle grade novels, and {literary} young adult novels; on the adult side, she is looking for literary, women's, and historical fiction. Nonfiction areas of interest: multicultural, pop culture, how-to, and titles geared toward women of all ages).

REPRESENTS Nonfiction books, juvenile. **Considers these fiction areas:** ethnic, literary, young adult.

☛ "Our full-service boutique agency, representing a range of nonfiction and children's books (limited fiction), provides a one-stop resource for authors. Our extensive experience in the realms of law and marketing provide Full Circle clients with a unique edge." "Actively seeking nonfiction by authors with a unique and strong platform, projects that offer new and diverse viewpoints, and literature with a global or multicultural perspective. We are particularly interested in books with a Latino or Middle Eastern angle and books related to pop culture." Does not want to receive "screenplays, poetry, commercial fiction or genre fiction (horror, thriller, mystery, Western, sci-fi, fantasy, romance, historical fiction)."

HOW TO CONTACT Agency accepts e-queries. See website for fiction guidelines, as they are in flux. For nonfiction, send full proposal. Accepts simultaneous submissions. Responds in 1-2 weeks to queries. Responds in 4-6 weeks to mss. Obtains most new clients through recommendations from others, solicitations, conferences.

TERMS Agent receives 15% commission on domestic sales. Agent receives 20% commission on foreign sales. Offers written contract; up to 30-day notice must be given to terminate contract. Charges for copying and postage.

TIPS "Put your best foot forward. Contact us when you simply can't make your project any better on your own, and please be sure your work fits with what the agent you're approaching represents. Little things count, so copyedit your work. Join a writing group and attend conferences to get objective and constructive feedback before submitting. Be active about building your platform as an author before, during, and after publication. Remember this is a business and your agent is a business partner."

GELFMAN SCHNEIDER LITERARY AGENTS, INC.

250 W. 57th St., Suite 2122, New York NY 10107. (212)245-1993. **Fax:** (212)245-8678. **E-mail:** mail@gelfmanschneider.com. **Website:** www.gelfmanschneider.com. **Contact:** Jane Gelfman, Deborah Schneider. Member of AAR. Represents 300+ clients. 10% of clients are new/unpublished writers.

REPRESENTS Fiction and nonfiction books. **Considers these fiction areas:** literary, mainstream, mystery, women's.

☛ Does not want to receive romance, science fiction, westerns, or children's books.

HOW TO CONTACT Query with SASE. Send queries via snail mail only. No unsolicited mss. Please send a query letter, a synopsis, and a SAMPLE CHAPTER ONLY. Responds in 1 month to queries. Responds in 2 months to mss.

TERMS Agent receives 15% commission on domestic sales. Agent receives 20% commission on foreign sales. Agent receives 15% commission on film sales. Offers written contract. Charges clients for photocopying and messengers/couriers.

BARRY GOLDBLATT LITERARY, LLC

320 Seventh Ave., #266, Brooklyn NY 11215. **Fax:** (718)360-5453. **Website:** www.bgliterary.com. **Contact:** Barry Goldblatt. Member of AAR. SCBWI

MEMBER AGENTS Barry Goldblatt, Joe Monti, Beth Fleisher (kids work and graphic novels; she is particularly interested in finding new voices in middle grade and young adult fantasy, science fiction, mystery, historicals and action adventure).

REPRESENTS Juvenile books. **Considers these fiction areas:** picture books, young adult middle grade, all genres.

⁫— This agency specializes in children's books of all kinds from picture books to young adult novels, across all over genres.

HOW TO CONTACT E-mail queries query@bgliterary.com, and include the first 5 pages and a synopsis of the novel pasted into the text of the e-mail. No attachments or links.

RECENT SALES *Prophecy: The Dragon King Chronicles*, by Ellen Oh; *Kiss Number Eight*, by Colleen af Venable; The Mysterious Four Series, by Dan Poblocki.

THE SUSAN GOLOMB LITERARY AGENCY

875 Avenue of the Americas, Suite 2302, New York NY 10001. **Fax:** (212)239-9503. **E-mail:** susan@sgolombagency.com; eliza@sgolombagency.com. **Contact:** Susan Golomb. Represents 100 clients. 20% of clients are new/unpublished writers. Currently handles nonfiction books (50%), novels (40%), story collections (10%).

MEMBER AGENTS Susan Golomb (accepts queries); Sabine Hrechdakian (accepts queries); Kim Goldstein (no unsolicited queries).

REPRESENTS Nonfiction books, novels, short story collections, novellas. **Considers these fiction areas:** ethnic, historical, humor, literary, mainstream, satire, thriller, women's, young adult chick lit.

⁫— "We specialize in literary and upmarket fiction and nonfiction that is original, vibrant and of excellent quality and craft. Nonfiction should be edifying, paradigm-shifting, fresh and entertaining." Actively seeking writers with strong voices. Does not want to receive genre fiction.

HOW TO CONTACT Query with SASE. Submit outline/proposal, synopsis, 1 sample chapter, author bio, SASE. Query via mail or e-mail. Responds in 2 week to queries. Responds in 8 weeks to mss. Obtains most new clients through recommendations from others, solicitations.

TERMS Agent receives 15% commission on domestic sales. Agent receives 20% commission on foreign sales. Offers written contract.

RECENT SALES Sold 20 titles in the last year. *Sunnyside*, by Glen David Gold (Knopf); *How to Buy a Love of Reading*, by Tanya Egan Gibson (Dutton);

Telex from Cuba, by Rachel Kushner (Scribner); *The Imperfectionists* by Tom Rachman (Dial).

IRENE GOODMAN LITERARY AGENCY

27 W. 24th Street, Suite 700B, New York NY 10010. **E-mail:** queries@irenegoodman.com. **Website:** www.irenegoodman.com. **Contact:** Irene Goodman, Miriam Kriss. Member of AAR.

MEMBER AGENTS Irene Goodman; Miriam Kriss; Barbara Poelle; Jon Sternfeld.

REPRESENTS Nonfiction books, novels. **Considers these fiction areas:** historical, intelligent literary, modern urban fantasies, mystery, romance, thriller, women's.

⁫— "Specializes in the finest in commercial fiction and nonfiction. We have a strong background in women's voices, including mysteries, romance, women's fiction, thrillers, suspense. Historical fiction is one of Irene's particular passions and Miriam is fanatical about modern urban fantasies. In nonfiction, Irene is looking for topics on narrative history, social issues and trends, education, Judaica, Francophilia, Anglophilia, other cultures, animals, food, crafts, and memoir." Barbara is looking for commercial thrillers with strong female protagonists; Miriam is looking for urban fantasy and edgy sci-fi/young adult. No children's picture books, screenplays, poetry, or inspirational fiction.

HOW TO CONTACT Query. Submit synopsis, first 10 pages. E-mail queries only! See the website submission page. No e-mail attachments. Responds in 2 months to queries.

RECENT SALES *The Ark*, by Boyd Morrison; *Isolation*, by C.J. Lyons; *The Sleepwalkers*, by Paul Grossman; *Dead Man's Moon*, by Devon Monk; *Becoming Marie Antoinette*, by Juliet Grey; *What's Up Down There*, by Lissa Rankin; *Beg for Mercy*, by Toni Andrews; *The Devil Inside*, by Jenna Black.

TIPS "We are receiving an unprecedented amount of e-mail queries. If you find that the mailbox is full, please try again in two weeks. E-mail queries to our personal addresses will not be answered. E-mails to our personal in-boxes will be deleted."

SANFORD J. GREENBURGER ASSOCIATES, INC.

55 Fifth Ave., New York NY 10003. (212)206-5600. **Fax:** (212)463-8718. **E-mail:** queryHL@sjga.com.

Website: www.greenburger.com. Member of AAR. Represents 500 clients.

MEMBER AGENTS Heide Lange; Faith Hamlin; Dan Mandel; Matthew Bialer; Courtney Miller-Callihan, Michael Harriot, Brenda Bowen (authors and illustrators of children's books for all ages as well as graphic novelists); Lisa Gallagher.

REPRESENTS Nonfiction books and novels. **Considers these fiction areas:** action, adventure, crime, detective, ethnic, family saga, feminist, gay, glitz, historical, humor, lesbian, literary, mainstream, mystery, police, psychic, regional, satire, sports, supernatural, suspense, thriller.

⌐ No Westerns. No screenplays.

HOW TO CONTACT Submit query, first 3 chapters, synopsis, brief bio, SASE. Accepts simultaneous submissions. Responds in 2 months to queries and mss. Responds to mss. Obtains most new clients through recommendations from others.

TERMS Agent receives 15% commission on domestic sales. Agent receives 20% commission on foreign sales. Charges for photocopying and books for foreign and subsidiary rights submissions.

◖ THE GREENHOUSE LITERARY AGENCY

11308 Lapham Dr., Oakton VA 22124. **E-mail:** submissions@greenhouseliterary.com. **Website:** www.greenhouseliterary.com. **Contact:** Sarah Davies. Other memberships include SCBWI. Represents 20 clients. 100% of clients are new/unpublished writers. Currently handles juvenile books (100%).

REPRESENTS Juvenile. **Considers these fiction areas:** juvenile, young adult.

⌐ "We exclusively represent authors writing fiction for children and teens. The agency has offices in both the USA and UK, and Sarah Davies (who is British) personally represents authors to both markets. The agency's commission structure reflects this—taking 15% for sales to both US and UK, thus treating both as 'domestic' market.'" All genres of children's and YA fiction—ages 5+. Does not want to receive nonfiction, poetry, picture books (text or illustration) or work aimed at adults; short stories, educational or religious/inspirational work, pre-school/novelty material, or screenplays.

HOW TO CONTACT E-mail queries only; short letter containing a brief outline, biography and any writing 'credentials'. Up to the first five pages of text may be pasted into the email. All submissions are answered Responds in 2-6 week to queries; 6-8 weeks to requested mss. Obtains most new clients through recommendations from others, solicitations, conferences.

TERMS Agent receives 15% commission on domestic sales. Agent receives 25% commission on foreign sales. Offers written contract. This agency charges very occasionally for copies for submission to film agents or foreign publishers.

RECENT SALES *Princess for Hire*, by Lindsey Leavitt (Hyperion); *What Happened on Fox Street*, by Tricia Springstubb (Harpercollins); *The Replacement*, by Brenna Yovanoff (Razorbill); *Just Add Magic*, by Cindy Callaghan (Aladdin).

WRITERS CONFERENCES Bologna Children's Book Fair, SCBWI conferences, BookExpo America.

TIPS "Before submitting material, authors should read the Greenhouse's 'Top 10 Tips for Authors of Children's Fiction,' which can be found on our website."

◖ KATHRYN GREEN LITERARY AGENCY, LLC

250 West 57th St., Suite 2302, New York NY 10107. (212)245-2445. **Fax:** (212)245-2040. **E-mail:** query@kgreenagency.com. **Contact:** Kathy Green. Other memberships include Women's Media Group. Represents approximately 20 clients. 50% of clients are new/unpublished writers. Currently handles nonfiction books (50%), novels (25%), juvenile books (25%).

REPRESENTS Nonfiction books, novels, short story collections, juvenile, middle grade and young adult only). **Considers these fiction areas:** crime, detective, family saga, historical, humor, juvenile, literary, mainstream, mystery, police, romance, satire, suspense, thriller, women's, young adult women's.

⌐ Keeping the client list small means that writers receive my full attention throughout the process of getting their project published. Does not want to receive science fiction or fantasy.

HOW TO CONTACT Query to query@kgreenagency.com. Send no samples unless requested. Accepts simultaneous submissions. Responds in 1-2 months to mss. Obtains most new clients through recommendations from others, solicitations, conferences.

TERMS Agent receives 15% commission on domestic sales. Agent receives 20% commission on foreign sales. No written contract.

RECENT SALES The Touch Series by Laurie Stolarz; *How Do You Light a Fart*, by Bobby Mercer; *Creepiosity*, by David Bickel; *Hidden Facets: Diamonds for the Dead* by Alan Orloff; *Don't Stalk the Admissions Officer*, by Risa Lewak; *Designed Fat Girl*, by Jennifer Joyner.

TIPS "This agency offers a written agreement."

● **JILL GROSJEAN LITERARY AGENCY**

1390 Millstone Rd., Sag Harbor NY 11963-2214. (631)725-7419. **Fax:** (631)725-8632. **E-mail:** Jill-Lit310@aol.com. **Contact:** Jill Grosjean. Represents 40 clients. 100% of clients are new/unpublished writers. Currently handles novels (100%).

REPRESENTS Novels. **Considers these fiction areas:** historical, literary, mainstream, mystery, regional, romance, suspense.

⌐ This agency offers some editorial assistance (i.e., line-by-line edits). Actively seeking literary novels and mysteries.

HOW TO CONTACT E-mail queries only, no attachments. No cold calls, please. Accepts simultaneous submissions. Responds in 1 week to queries. Responds in 1 month to mss. Obtains most new clients through recommendations from others, solicitations.

TERMS Agent receives 15% commission on domestic sales. Agent receives 20% commission on foreign sales. No written contract. Charges clients for photocopying and mailing expenses.

RECENT SALES *Threading the Needle,* by Marie Bostwick (Kensington Publishers); *A Spark Of Death*, by Bernadette Pajer, (Poison Pen Press); *A Single Thread* and *Thread of Truth, A Thread So Thin, Snow Angels,* by Marie Bostwick (Kensington); *Greasing the Pinata* and *Jump*, by Tim Maleeny (Poison Pen Press); *Shame* and *No Idea* by Greg Garrett, David C. Cook; *The Reluctant Journey of David Conners.*

WRITERS CONFERENCES Book Passage's Mystery Writers' Conference; Agents and Editors Conference; Texas Writers' and Agents' Conference.

● **LAURA GROSS LITERARY AGENCY**

39 Chester Street, Suite 301, Newton Highlands MA 02461. (617)964-2977. **Fax:** (617)964-3023. **E-mail:** query@lg-la.com. **Website:** http://lauragrossliteraryagency.com. **Contact:** Laura Gross. Estab. 1988. Represents 30 clients. Currently handles nonfiction books (40%), novels (50%), scholarly books (10%).

REPRESENTS Nonfiction books, novels. **Considers these fiction areas:** historical, literary, mainstream, mystery, suspense, thriller.

HOW TO CONTACT Submit online using submissions manager. Query with SASE or by e-mail. Submit author bio. Responds in several days to queries. Obtains most new clients through recommendations from others.

TERMS Agent receives 15% commission on domestic sales. Agent receives 20% commission on foreign sales. Offers written contract.

THE MITCHELL J. HAMILBURG AGENCY

149 S. Barrington Ave., #732, Los Angeles CA 90049. (310)471-4024. **Fax:** (310)471-9588. **Contact:** Michael Hamilburg. Estab. 1937. Signatory of WGA. Represents 70 clients. Currently handles nonfiction books (70%), novels (30%).

REPRESENTS Nonfiction books, novels. **Considers these fiction areas:** glitz, New Age, adventure, experimental, feminist, humor, military, mystery, occult, regional, religious, romance, sports, thriller crime; mainstream; psychic.

HOW TO CONTACT Query with outline, 2 sample chapters, SASE. Responds in 1 month to mss. Obtains most new clients through recommendations from others, conferences, personal search.

TERMS Agent receives 10-15% commission on domestic sales.

● **HARTLINE LITERARY AGENCY**

123 Queenston Dr., Pittsburgh PA 15235-5429. (412)829-2483. **Fax:** (412)829-2432. **E-mail:** joyce@hartlineliterary.com. **Website:** www.hartlineliterary.com. **Contact:** Joyce A. Hart. Represents 40 clients. 20% of clients are new/unpublished writers. Currently handles nonfiction books (40%), novels (60%).

MEMBER AGENTS Joyce A. Hart, principal agent; Terry Burns: terry@hartlineliterary.com; Tamela Hancock Murray: tamela@hartlineliterary.com; Diana Flegal: diana@hartlineliterary.com.

REPRESENTS Nonfiction books, novels. **Considers these fiction areas:** action, adventure, contemporary issues, family saga, historical, inspirational, literary, mystery, regional, religious, suspense, thriller amateur sleuth, cozy, contemporary, gothic, historical, and regency romances.

⌐ "This agency specializes in the Christian bookseller market." Actively seeking adult fiction, self-help, nutritional books, devotional, and business. Does not want to receive erotica, gay/lesbian, fantasy, horror, etc.

HOW TO CONTACT Submit summary/outline, author bio, 3 sample chapters. Accepts simultaneous submissions. Responds in 2 months to queries. Responds in 3 months to mss. Obtains most new clients through recommendations from others.

TERMS Agent receives 15% commission on domestic sales. Offers written contract.

RECENT SALES *Aurora, An American Experience in Quilt, Community and Craft,* and *A Flickering Light,* by Jane Kirkpatrick (Waterbrook Multnomah); *Oprah Doesn't Know My Name* by Jane Kirkpatric (Zondervan); *Paper Roses, Scattered Petals, and Summer Rains,* by Amanda Cabot (Revell Books); *Blood Ransom,* by Lisa Harris (Zondervan); *I Don't Want a Divorce,* by David Clark (Revell Books); *Love Finds You in Hope, Kansas,* by Pamela Griffin (Summerside Press); Journey to the Well, by Diana Wallis Taylor (Revell Books); *Paper Bag Christmas, The Nine Lessons* by Kevin Milne (Center Street); *When Your Aging Parent Needs Care* by Arrington & Atchley (Harvest House); *Katie at Sixteen* by Kim Vogel Sawyer (Zondervan); *A Promise of Spring,* by Kim Vogel Sawyer (Bethany House); *The Big 5-OH!,* by Sandra Bricker (Abingdon Press); *A Silent Terror & A Silent Stalker,* by Lynette Eason (Steeple Hill); Extreme Devotion series, by Kathi Macias (New Hope Publishers); *On the Wings of the Storm,* by Tamira Barley (Whitaker House); Tribute, by Graham Garrison (Kregel Publications); *The Birth to Five Book,* by Brenda Nixon (Revell Books); *Fat to Skinny Fast and Easy,* by Doug Varrieur (Sterling Publishers).

● JOHN HAWKINS & ASSOCIATES, INC.

71 W. 23rd St., Suite 1600, New York NY 10010. (212)807-7040. **Fax:** (212)807-9555. **E-mail:** jha@jhalit.com; moses@jhalit.com; free@jhalit.com. **Website:** www.jhalit.com. **Contact:** Moses Cardona (rights and translations); Liz Free (permissions). Member of AAR. Represents over 100 clients. 5-10% of clients are new/unpublished writers. Currently handles nonfiction books (40%), novels (40%), juvenile books (20%).

MEMBER AGENTS Moses Cardona; Liz Free.

REPRESENTS Nonfiction books, novels, young adult. **Considers these fiction areas:** action, adventure, crime, detective, ethnic, experimental, family saga, feminist, frontier, gay, glitz, hi-lo, historical, inspirational, lesbian, literary, mainstream, military, multicultural, multimedia, mystery, police, psychic, religious, short story collections, sports, supernatural, suspense, thriller, translation, war, westerns, women's, young adult.

HOW TO CONTACT Submit query, proposal package, outline, SASE. Accepts simultaneous submissions. Responds in 1 month to queries. Obtains most new clients through recommendations from others.

TERMS Agent receives 15% commission on domestic sales. Agent receives 20% commission on foreign sales. Charges clients for photocopying.

RECENT SALES *Celebration of Shoes,* by Eileen Spinelli; *Chaos,* by Martin Gross; *The Informationist,* by Taylor Stevens; *The Line,* by Olga Grushin

◑ RICHARD HENSHAW GROUP

22 West 23rd Street, 5th Floor, New York NY 10010. **E-mail:** submissions@henshaw.com. **Website:** http://www.richh.addr.com. **Contact:** Rich Henshaw. Member of AAR. Other memberships include SinC, MWA, HWA, SFWA, RWA. 20% of clients are new/unpublished writers. Currently handles nonfiction books (35%), novels (65%).

REPRESENTS Nonfiction books, novels. **Considers these fiction areas:** action, adventure, crime, detective, ethnic, family saga, historical, humor, literary, mainstream, mystery, police, psychic, romance, satire, science fiction, sports, supernatural, suspense, thriller.

☛ This agency specializes in thrillers, mysteries, science fiction, fantasy and horror.

HOW TO CONTACT Query with SASE. Accepts multiple submissions. Responds in 3 weeks to queries. Responds in 6 weeks to mss. Obtains most new clients through recommendations from others, solicitations, conferences.

TERMS Agent receives 15% commission on domestic sales. Agent receives 20% commission on foreign sales. No written contract. Charges clients for photocopying and book orders.

RECENT SALES *Though Not Dead,* by Dana Stabenow; *The Perfect Suspect,* by Margaret Coel; *City of Ruins,* by Kristine Kathryn Rusch; *A Dead Man's Tale,* by James D. Doss, *Wickedly Charming,* by Kristine Grayson, History of the World series by Susan Wise Bauer; *Notorious Pleasures,* by Elizabeth Hoyt.

TIPS "While we do not have any reason to believe that our submission guidelines will change in the near future, writers can find up-to-date submission policy information on our website. Always include a SASE with correct return postage."

HIDDEN VALUE GROUP

1240 E. Ontario Ave., Ste. 102-148, Corona CA 92881. (951)549-8891. **Fax:** (951)549-8891. **Website:** www. hiddenvaluegroup.com. **Contact:** Nancy Jernigan. Represents 55 clients. 10% of clients are new/unpublished writers.

MEMBER AGENTS Jeff Jernigan, jjernigan@hiddenvaluegroup.com (men's nonfiction, fiction, Bible studies/curriculum, marriage and family); Nancy Jernigan, njernigan@hiddenvaluegroup.com (nonfiction, women's issues, inspiration, marriage and family, fiction).

REPRESENTS Nonfiction books and adult fiction; no poetry. **Considers these fiction areas:** action, adventure, crime, detective, fantasy, frontier, inspirational, literary, police, religious, thriller, westerns, women's.

> "The Hidden Value Group specializes in helping authors throughout their publishing career. We believe that every author has a special message to be heard and we specialize in getting that message out." Actively seeking established fiction authors, and authors who are focusing on women's issues. Does not want to receive poetry or short stories.

HOW TO CONTACT Query with SASE. Submit synopsis, 2 sample chapters, author bio, and marketing and speaking summary. Accepts queries to bookquery@hiddenvaluegroup.com. No fax queries. Responds in 1 month to queries. Responds in 1 month to mss. Obtains most new clients through recommendations from others, solicitations.

TERMS Agent receives 15% commission on domestic sales. Agent receives 15% commission on foreign sales. Offers written contract.

WRITERS CONFERENCES Glorieta Christian Writers' Conference; CLASS Publishing Conference.

HOPKINS LITERARY ASSOCIATES

2117 Buffalo Rd., Suite 327, Rochester NY 14624-1507. (585)352-6268. **Contact:** Pam Hopkins. Member of AAR. Other memberships include RWA. Represents 30 clients. 5% of clients are new/unpublished writers. Currently handles novels (100%).

REPRESENTS Novels. **Considers these fiction areas:** mostly women's genre romance, historical, contemporary, category, women's.

> This agency specializes in women's fiction, particularly historical, contemporary, and category romance, as well as mainstream work.

HOW TO CONTACT Regular mail with synopsis, 3 sample chapters, SASE. Accepts simultaneous submissions. Responds in 2 weeks to queries. Responds in 1 month to mss. Obtains most new clients through recommendations from others, solicitations, conferences.

TERMS Agent receives 15% commission on domestic sales. Agent receives 20% commission on foreign sales. No written contract.

RECENT SALES Sold 50 titles in the last year. *The Wilting Bloom Series* by Madeline Hunter (Berkley); *The Dead Travel Fast*, by Deanna Raybourn; *Baggage Claim*, by Tanya Michna (NAL).

WRITERS CONFERENCES RWA National Conference.

ANDREA HURST LITERARY MANAGEMENT

For Andrea Hurst and Vickie Motter P.O. Box 1467, for Gordon Warnock P.O. Box 19010, Sacramento CA 95819, Coupeville WA 98239. **E-mail:** andrea@ andreahurst.com. **Website:** www.andreahurst.com. **Contact:** Andrea Hurst, Judy Mikalonis, Gordon Warnock, Vickie Motter. Represents 100+ clients. 50% of clients are new/unpublished writers. Currently handles nonfiction books (50%), novels (50%).

MEMBER AGENTS Andrea Hurst, andrea@andreahurst.com (adult fiction, women's fiction, nonfiction—including personal growth, health and wellness, science, business, parenting, relationships, women's issues, animals, spirituality, women's issues, metaphysical, psychological, cookbooks, and self-help); Judy Mikalonis, judy@andreahurst.com (YA fiction, Christian fiction, Christian nonfiction). Gordon Warnock, gordon@andreahurst.com, P.O. Box 19010, Sacramento, CA 95819. Gordon represents nonfiction: Memoir, political and current affairs, health, humor and cookbooks. Fiction: Commercial narrative with a literary edge. Vickie Motter, vickie@andreahurst. com, P.O.Box 1467, Coupeville, WA 98239. Vickie represents YA fiction and nonfiction and adult nonfiction.

REPRESENTS Nonfiction books, novels, juvenile. **Considers these fiction areas:** inspirational, juvenile, literary, mainstream, psychic, religious, romance, supernatural, thriller, women's, young adult.

> "We work directly with our signed authors to help them polish their work and their platform for optimum marketability. Our staff is always available to answer phone calls and e-mails from our authors and we stay with a

project until we have exhausted all publishing avenues." Actively seeking "well written nonfiction by authors with a strong platform; superbly crafted fiction with depth that touches the mind and heart and all of our listed subjects." Does not want to receive sci-fi, horror, Western, poetry, or screenplays.

HOW TO CONTACT Email query with SASE. Submit outline/proposal, synopsis, 2 sample chapters, author bio. Query a specific agent after reviewing website. Use (agentfirstname)@andreahurst.com. Accepts simultaneous submissions. Obtains most new clients through recommendations from others, solicitations, conferences.

TERMS Agent receives 15% commission on domestic sales. Agent receives 20% commission on foreign sales. Offers written contract, binding for 6 to 12 months; 30-day notice must be given to terminate contract. This agency charges for postage. No reading fees. Visit our new blog: www.andreahurst.com.

RECENT SALES *No Buddy Left Behind,* by Terri Crisp and Cindy Hurn, Lyons Press; *A Year of Miracles* Dr. Bernie Siegel, NWL; *Selling Your Crafts on Etsy* (St. Martin's); *The Underground Detective Agency* (Kensington); *Alaskan Seafood Cookbook* (Globe Pequot); *Faith, Hope and Healing,* by Dr. Bernie Siegel (Rodale); *Code Name: Polar Ice,* by Jean-Michel Cousteau and James Fraioli (Gibbs Smith); *How to Host a Killer Party,* by Penny Warner (Berkley/Penguin).

WRITERS CONFERENCES San Francisco Writers' Conference; Willamette Writers' Conference; PNWA; Whidbey Island Writers Conference.

TIPS "Do your homework and submit a professional package. Get to know the agent you are submitting to by researching their website or meeting them at a conference. Perfect your craft: Write well and edit ruthlessly over and over again before submitting to an agent. Be realistic: Understand that publishing is a business and be prepared to prove why your book is marketable and how you will market it on your own. Be persistent!" "Andrea Hurst is no longer accepting unsolicited query letters. Unless you have been referred by one of our authors, an agent or publisher, please check our website for another appropriate agent. www.andreahurst.com."

● **INTERNATIONAL TRANSACTIONS, INC.**

P.O. Box 97, Gila NM 88038-0097. (845)373-9696. **Fax:** (845)373-7868. **E-mail:** submissions@intltrans.com; submission-fiction@intltrans.com; submission-nonfiction@intltrans.com. **Website:** www.intltrans.com. **Contact:** Peter Riva. Represents 40+ clients. 10% of clients are new/unpublished writers. Currently handles nonfiction books (60%), novels (25%), story collections (5%), juvenile books (5%), scholarly books (5%).

MEMBER AGENTS Peter Riva (nonfiction, fiction, illustrated; television and movie rights placement); Sandra Riva (fiction, juvenile, biographies); JoAnn Collins (fiction, women's fiction, medical fiction).

REPRESENTS Nonfiction books, novels, short story collections, juvenile, scholarly illustrated books, anthologies. **Considers these fiction areas:** action, adventure, crime, detective, erotica, experimental, family saga, feminist, gay, historical, humor, lesbian, literary, mainstream, mystery, police, satire, spiritual, sports, suspense, thriller, women's, young adult chick lit.

➘ "We specialize in large and small projects, helping qualified authors perfect material for publication." Actively seeking intelligent, well-written innovative material that breaks new ground. Does not want to receive material influenced by TV (too much dialogue); a rehash of previous successful novels' themes, or poorly prepared material.

HOW TO CONTACT First, e-query with an outline or synopsis. E-queries only! Responds in 3 weeks to queries. Responds in 5 weeks to mss. Obtains most new clients through recommendations from others, solicitations.

TERMS Agent receives 15% (25% on illustrated books) commission on domestic sales. Agent receives 20% commission on foreign sales. Offers written contract; 120-day notice must be given to terminate contract.

TIPS 'Book'—a published work of literature. That last word is the key. Not a string of words, not a book of (TV or film) 'scenes,' and never a stream of consciousness unfathomable by anyone outside of the writer's coterie. A writer should only begin to get 'interested in getting an agent' if the work is polished, literate and ready to be presented to a publishing house. Anything less is either asking for a quick rejection or is a thinly disguised plea for creative assistance—which is often given but never fiscally sound for the agents involved. Writers, even published authors, have difficulty in being objective about their own work. Friends and family are of no assistance in that process either. Writers should attempt to get their work read by the most unlikely and stern critic as part of the editing process, months before any agent is approached. In another matter: the economics of our job have changed as well. As the publishing world goes through the transition to e-books (much as the music industry went through the change to downloadable music)—a transition we expect to see at 95% within 10 years—everyone is nervous and wants 'assured bestsellers' from which to eke out a living until they know what the new e-world will bring. This makes the sales rate and, especially, the advance royalty rates, plummet. Hence, our ability to take risks and take on new clients' work is increasingly perilous financially for us and all agents."

JABBERWOCKY LITERARY AGENCY

P.O. Box 4558, Sunnyside NY 11104-0558. (718)392-5985. **Website:** www.awfulagent.com. **Contact:** Joshua Bilmes. Other memberships include SFWA. Represents 40 clients. 15% of clients are new/unpublished writers. Currently handles nonfiction books (15%), novels (75%), scholarly books (5%), other (5% other).

MEMBER AGENTS Joshua Bilmes; Eddie Schneider.

REPRESENTS Novels. **Considers these fiction areas:** action, adventure, contemporary issues, crime, detective, ethnic, family saga, fantasy, gay, glitz, historical, horror, humor, lesbian, literary, mainstream, police, psychic, regional, satire, science fiction, sports, supernatural, thriller.

> This agency represents quite a lot of genre fiction and is actively seeking to increase the amount of nonfiction projects. It does not handle children's or picture books. Book-length material only—no poetry, articles, or short fiction.

HOW TO CONTACT We are currently closed to unsolicited queries. No e-mail queries, please. Query with SASE. Please check our website, as there may be times during the year when we are not accepting queries. Query letter only; no manuscript material unless requested. Accepts simultaneous submissions. Responds in 3 weeks to queries. Obtains most new clients through solicitations, recommendation by current clients.

TERMS Agent receives 15% commission on domestic sales. Agent receives 20% commission on foreign sales. Offers written contract, binding for 1 year. Charges clients for book purchases, photocopying, international book/ms mailing.

RECENT SALES Sold 30 US and 100 foreign titles in the last year. *Dead in the Family*, by Charlaine Harris; *The Way of Kings*, by Brandon Sanderson; *The Desert Spear*, by Peter V. Brett; *Oath of Fealty*, by Elizabeth Moon. Other clients include Tanya Huff, Simon Green, Jack Campbell, Kat Richardson, and Jon Sprunk.

TIPS "In approaching with a query, the most important things to us are your credits and your biographical background to the extent it's relevant to your work. I (and most agents) will ignore the adjectives you may choose to describe your own work."

JET LITERARY ASSOCIATES

2570 Camino San Patricio, Santa Fe NM 87505. (505)474-9139. **E-mail:** etp@jetliterary.com. **Website:** www.jetliterary.com. **Contact:** Liz Trupin-Pulli. Represents 75 clients. 35% of clients are new/unpublished writers.

MEMBER AGENTS Liz Trupin-Pulli (adult and YA fiction/nonfiction; romance, mysteries, parenting); Jim Trupin (adult fiction/nonfiction, military history, pop culture); Jessica Trupin, associate agent based in Seattle (adult fiction and nonfiction, children's and young adult, memoir, pop culture).

REPRESENTS Nonfiction books, novels, short story collections. **Considers these fiction areas:** action, adventure, crime, detective, erotica, ethnic, gay, glitz, historical, humor, lesbian, literary, mainstream, mystery, police, romance, suspense, thriller, women's, young adult.

> "JET was founded in New York in 1975, so we bring a wealth of knowledge and contacts, as well as quite a bit of expertise to our representation of writers." Actively seeking women's fiction, mysteries and narrative nonfiction. JET represents the full range of adult and YA fiction and nonfiction, including humor and cookbooks. Does not want to receive sci-fi, fantasy, horror, poetry, children's or religious.

HOW TO CONTACT An e-query only is accepted. Responds in 1 week to queries. Responds in 8 weeks to mss. Obtains most new clients through recommendations from others, solicitations, conferences.

TERMS Agent receives 15% commission on domestic sales. Agent receives 10% commission on foreign sales. Offers written contract, binding for 3 years. This agency charges for reimbursement of mailing and any photocopying.

RECENT SALES Sold 22 books in 2009 including several ghostwriting contracts. *Mom-in-chief*, by Jamie Woolf (Wiley, 2009); *Dangerous Games* by Charlotte Mede (Kensington, 2009); *So You Think You Can Spell!* by David Grambs and Ellen Levine (Perigee, 2009); *Cut, Drop & Die*, by Joanna Campbell Slan (Midnight Ink, 2009).

WRITERS CONFERENCES Women Writing the West; Southwest Writers Conference; Florida Writers Association Conference.

TIPS Do not write cute queries—stick to a straightforward message that includes the title and what your book is about, why you are suited to write this particular book, and what you have written in the past (if anything), along with a bit of a bio.

CAREN JOHNSON LITERARY AGENCY

132 East 43rd St., No. 216, New York NY 10017. E-mail: caren@johnsonlitagency.com. **Website:** www.johnsonliterary.com. **Contact:** Caren Estesen, Elana Roth. Represents 20 clients. 50% of clients are new/unpublished writers. Currently handles nonfiction books 35%, juvenile books 35%, romance/women's fiction 30%.

MEMBER AGENTS Caren Estesen, Elana Roth, Katie Shea.

REPRESENTS Nonfiction books, novels. **Considers these fiction areas:** detective, erotica, ethnic, romance, young adult middle grade, women's fiction.

☞ Does not want to receive poetry, plays, or screenplays/scripts. Elana Roth will consider picture books but is very selective of what she takes on.

HOW TO CONTACT Query via e-mail only, "directing your query to the appropriate person; responds in 12 weeks to all materials sent. Include 4-5 sample pages within the body of your e-mail when pitching us. Accepts simultaneous submissions. Responds in 4-6 weeks to queries. Responds in 6-8 weeks to mss. Obtains most new clients through recommendations from others.

TERMS Agent receives 15% commission on domestic sales. Agent receives 20% commission on foreign sales. Offers written contract; 30-day notice must be given to terminate contract. This agency charges for postage and photocopying, though the author is consulted before any charges are incurred.

RECENT SALES Please check out website for a complete client list.

WRITERS CONFERENCES RWA National; BookExpo America; SCBWI.

VIRGINIA KIDD AGENCY, INC.

538 E. Harford St., P.O. Box 278, Milford PA 18337. (570)296-6205. **Fax:** (570)296-7266. **Website:** www.vk-agency.com. Other memberships include SFWA, SFRA. Represents 80 clients.

MEMBER AGENTS Christine Cohen.

REPRESENTS Novels. **Considers these fiction areas:** fantasy, historical, mainstream, mystery, science fiction, suspense, women's speculative.

☞ This agency specializes in science fiction and fantasy.

HOW TO CONTACT *This agency is not accepting queries from unpublished authors at this time.* Submit synopsis (1-3 pages), cover letter, first chapter, SASE. Snail mail queries only. Responds in 6 weeks to queries.

TERMS Agent receives 15% commission on domestic sales. Agent receives 20-25% commission on foreign sales. Agent receives 20% commission on film sales. Offers written contract; 2-month notice must be given to terminate contract. Charges clients occasionally for extraordinary expenses.

RECENT SALES *Sagramanda*, by Alan Dean Foster (Pyr); *Incredible Good Fortune*, by Ursula K. Le Guin (Shambhala); *The Wizard and Soldier of Sidon*, by Gene Wolfe (Tor); *Voices and Powers*, by Ursula K. Le Guin (Harcourt); *Galileo's Children*, by Gardner Dozois (Pyr); *The Light Years Beneath My Feet* and *Running From the Deity*, by Alan Dean Foster (Del Ray); *Chasing Fire*, by Michelle Welch. Other clients include Eleanor Arnason, Ted Chiang, Jack Skillingstead, Daryl Gregory, Patricia Briggs, and the estates for James Tiptree, Jr., Murray Leinster, E.E. "Doc" Smith, R.A. Lafferty.

TIPS "If you have a completed novel that is of extraordinary quality, please send us a query."

HARVEY KLINGER, INC.

300 W. 55th St., Suite 11V, New York NY 10019. (212)581-7068. **E-mail:** queries@harveyklinger.com. **Website:** www.harveyklinger.com. **Contact:** Harvey Klinger. Member of AAR. Represents 100 clients. 25% of clients are new/unpublished writers. Currently handles nonfiction books (50%), novels (50%).

MEMBER AGENTS David Dunton (popular culture, music-related books, literary fiction, young adult, fiction, and memoirs); Sara Crowe (children's and young adult authors, adult fiction and nonfiction, foreign rights sales); Andrea Somberg (literary fiction, commercial fiction, romance, sci-fi/fantasy, mysteries/thrillers, young adult, middle grade, quality narrative nonfiction, popular culture, how-to, self-help, humor, interior design, cookbooks, health/fitness).

REPRESENTS Nonfiction books, novels. **Considers these fiction areas:** action, adventure, crime, detective, family saga, glitz, literary, mainstream, mystery, police, suspense, thriller.

☞ This agency specializes in big, mainstream, contemporary fiction and nonfiction.

HOW TO CONTACT Use online e-mail submission form, or query with SASE. No phone or fax queries. Don't send unsolicited manuscripts or e-mail attachments. Responds in 2 months to queries and mss. Obtains most new clients through recommendations from others.

TERMS Agent receives 15% commission on domestic sales. Agent receives 25% commission on foreign sales. Offers written contract. Charges for photocopying mss and overseas postage for mss.

RECENT SALES *Woman of a Thousand Secrets*, by Barbara Wood; *I Am Not a Serial Killer*, by Dan Wells; untitled memoir, by Bob Mould; *Children of the Mist*; by Paula Quinn; *Tutored*, by Allison Whittenberg; *Will You Take Me As I Am*, by Michelle Mercer. Other clients include: George Taber, Terry Kay, Scott Mebus, Jacqueline Kolosov, Jonathan Maberry, Tara Altebrando, Alex McAuley, Eva Nagorski, Greg Kot, Justine Musk, Alex McAuley, Nick Tasler, Ashley Kahn, Barbara De Angelis.

◑ KRAAS LITERARY AGENCY

E-mail: irenekraas@sbcglobal.net. **Website:** www.kraasliteraryagency.com. **Contact:** Irene Kraas. Represents 35 clients. 75% of clients are new/unpublished writers. Currently handles novels 100%.

MEMBER AGENTS Irene Kraas, principal.

REPRESENTS Novels. **Considers these fiction areas:** literary, thriller, young adult.

☞ This agency is interested in working with published writers, but that does not mean self-published writers. "The agency is ONLY accepting new manuscripts in the genre of adult thrillers and mysteries. Submissions should be the first ten pages of a completed manuscript embedded in an email. I do not open attachments or go to websites." Does not want to receive short stories, plays, or poetry. This agency no longer represents adult fantasy or science fiction.

HOW TO CONTACT Query and e-mail the first 10 pages of a completed ms. Requires exclusive read on mss. Accepts simultaneous submissions.

TERMS Offers written contract.

TIPS "I am interested in material—in any genre—that is truly, truly unique."

EDITE KROLL LITERARY AGENCY, INC.

20 Cross St., Saco ME 04072. (207)283-8797. **Fax:** (207)283-8799. **E-mail:** ekroll@maine.rr.com. **Contact:** Edite Kroll. Represents 45 clients. 20% of clients are new/unpublished writers. Currently handles nonfiction books (40%), novels (5%), juvenile books (40%), scholarly books (5%), other.

REPRESENTS Nonfiction books, novels, very selective, juvenile, scholarly. **Considers these fiction areas:** juvenile, literary, picture books, young adult middle grade, adult.

☞ "We represent writers and writer-artists of both adult and children's books. We have a special focus on international feminist writers, women writers and artists who write their own books (including children's and humor books)." Actively seeking artists who write their own books and international feminists who write in English. Does not want to receive genre (mysteries, thrillers, diet, cookery, etc.), photography books, coffee table books, romance, or commercial fiction.

HOW TO CONTACT Query with SASE. Submit outline/proposal, synopsis, 1-2 sample chapters, author bio, entire ms if sending picture book. No phone queries. Responds in 2-4 weeks to queries. Responds in 4-8 weeks to mss. Obtains most new clients through recommendations from others.

TERMS Agent receives 15% commission on domestic sales. Agent receives 20% commission on foreign sales. Offers written contract; 30-day notice must be given to terminate contract. Charges clients for photocopying and legal fees with prior approval from writer.

RECENT SALES Sold 12 domestic/30 foreign titles in the last year. This agency prefers not to share information on specific sales. Clients include Shel Silverstein estate, Suzy Becker, Geoffrey Hayes, Henrik Drescher, Charlotte Kasl, Gloria Skurzynski, Fatema Mernissa.

TIPS "Please do your research so you won't send me books/proposals I specifically excluded."

○ KT LITERARY, LLC

9249 S. Broadway, #200-543, Highlands Ranch CO 80129. (720)344-4728. **Fax:** (720)344-4728. **E-mail:**

contact@ktliterary.com. **Website:** http://ktliterary.com. **Contact:** Kate Schafer Testerman. Member of AAR. Other memberships include SCBWI. Represents 20 clients. 60% of clients are new/unpublished writers. Currently handles nonfiction books (5%), novels (5%), juvenile books (90%).

REPRESENTS Nonfiction books, novels, juvenile books. **Considers these fiction areas:** action, adventure, fantasy, historical, juvenile, romance, science fiction, women's, young adult.

8—☛ "I'm bringing my years of experience in the New York publishing scene, as well as my lifelong love of reading, to a vibrant area for writers, proving that great work can be found, and sold, from anywhere." "Actively seeking brilliant, funny, original middle grade and young adult fiction, both literary and commercial; witty women's fiction (chick lit); and pop culture, narrative nonfiction. Quirky is good." Does not want picture books, serious nonfiction, and adult literary fiction.

HOW TO CONTACT E-mail queries only. Ms. Testerman is closed to submissions until June of 2011. Keep an eye on the KT Literary blog for updates. Responds in 2 weeks to queries. Responds in 2 months to mss. Obtains most new clients through recommendations from others, solicitations, conferences.

TERMS Agent receives 15% commission on domestic sales. Agent receives 20% commission on foreign sales. Offers written contract; 30-day notice must be given to terminate contract.

WRITERS CONFERENCES Various SCBWI conferences, BookExpo.

TIPS "If we like your query, we'll ask for (more). Continuing advice is offered regularly on my blog 'Ask Daphne,' which can be accessed from my website."

○ KT PUBLIC RELATIONS & LITERARY SERVICES

1905 Cricklewood Cove, Fogelsville PA 18051. (610)395-6298. **Fax:** (610)395-6299. **Website:** www.ktpublicrelations.com; Blog: http://newliteraryagents.blogspot.com. **Contact:** Jon Tienstra. Represents 12 clients. 75% of clients are new/unpublished writers. Currently handles nonfiction books (50%), novels (50%).

MEMBER AGENTS Kae Tienstra (health, parenting, psychology, how-to, women's fiction, general fiction); Jon Tienstra (nature/environment, history, cooking/

foods/nutrition, war/military, automotive, gardening, science fiction, mystery/crime, thriller).

REPRESENTS Nonfiction books, novels. **Considers these fiction areas:** action, adventure, crime, detective, family saga, historical, literary, mainstream, mystery, police, romance, science fiction, suspense, thriller.

8—☛ "We have worked with a variety of authors and publishers over the years and have learned what individual publishers are looking for in terms of new acquisitions. We are both mad about books and authors and we look forward to finding publishing success for all our clients. Specializes in parenting, history, cooking/foods/nutrition, war, health/medicine, psychology, how-to, gardening, science fiction, contemporary fantasy, women's fiction, and popular fiction." Does not want to see unprofessional material.

HOW TO CONTACT Query with SASE. Prefers snail mail queries. Will accept e-mail queries. Responds in 3 months to chapters; 6-9 months for mss. Accepts simultaneous submissions. Responds in 4 weeks to queries.

TERMS Agent receives 15% commission on domestic sales. Agent receives 20% commission on foreign sales. Offers written contract. Charges clients for long-distance phone calls, fax, postage, photocopying (only when incurred). No advance payment for these out-of-pocket expenses.

● THE LA LITERARY AGENCY

P.O. Box 46370, Los Angeles CA 90046. (323)654-5288. **E-mail:** ann@laliteraryagency.com; mail@laliteraryagency.com. **Website:** www.laliteraryagency.com. **Contact:** Ann Cashman.

MEMBER AGENTS Ann Cashman, Eric Lasher, Maureen Lasher.

REPRESENTS Nonfiction books, novels. **Considers these fiction areas:** action, adventure, crime, detective, family saga, feminist, historical, literary, mainstream, police, sports, thriller.

HOW TO CONTACT Prefers submissions by mail, but welcomes e-mail submissions as well. Nonfiction: query letter and book proposal; fiction: query letter and first 50 (double-spaced) pages. Query with outline, 1 sample chapter.

RECENT SALES *Full Bloom: The Art and Life of Georgia O'Keeffe*, by Hunter Druhojowska-Philp (Norton); *And the Walls Came Tumbling Down*, by H. Caldwell

(Scribner); *Italian Slow & Savory*, by Joyce Goldstein (Chronicle); *A Field Guide to Chocolate Chip Cookies*, by Dede Wilson (Harvard Common Press); *Teen Knitting Club* (Artisan); *The Framingham Heart Study*, by Dr. Daniel Levy (Knopf).

● PETER LAMPACK AGENCY, INC.

551 Fifth Ave., Suite 1613, New York NY 10176-0187. (212)687-9106. **Fax:** (212)687-9109. **E-mail:** alampack@verizon.net. **Contact:** Andrew Lampack. Represents 50 clients. 10% of clients are new/unpublished writers. Currently handles nonfiction books (20%), novels (80%).

MEMBER AGENTS Peter Lampack (president); Rema Delanyan (foreign rights); Andrew Lampack (new writers).

REPRESENTS Nonfiction books, novels. **Considers these fiction areas:** adventure, crime, detective, family saga, literary, mainstream, mystery, police, suspense, thriller contemporary relationships.

8—⚷ "This agency specializes in commercial fiction, and nonfiction by recognized experts." Actively seeking literary and commercial fiction, thrillers, mysteries, suspense, and psychological thrillers. Does not want to receive horror, romance, science fiction, westerns, historical literary fiction or academic material.

HOW TO CONTACT Query via e-mail. *No unsolicited mss.* Responds within 2 months to queries. Obtains most new clients through referrals made by clients.

TERMS Agent receives 15% commission on domestic sales. Agent receives 20% commission on foreign sales.

RECENT SALES *Spartan Gold*, by Clive Cussler with Grant Blackwood; *The Wrecker*, by Clive Cussler with Justin Scott; *Medusa*, by Clive Cussler and Paul Kemprecos; *Silent Sea* by Clive Cussler with Jack Dubrul; *Summertime*, by J.M. Coetzee; *Dreaming in French*, by Megan McAndrew; *Time Pirate*, by Ted Bell.

WRITERS CONFERENCES BookExpo America; Mystery Writers of America.

TIPS "Submit only your best work for consideration. Have a very specific agenda of goals you wish your prospective agent to accomplish for you. Provide the agent with a comprehensive statement of your credentials—educational and professional accomplishments."

◐ LAURA LANGLIE, LITERARY AGENT

63 Wyckoff St., Brooklyn NY 11201. (718)855-8102. **Fax:** (718)855-4450. **E-mail:** laura@lauralanglie.com. **Contact:** Laura Langlie. Represents 25 clients. 50% of clients are new/unpublished writers. Currently handles nonfiction books (15%), novels (58%), story collections (2%), juvenile books (25%).

REPRESENTS Nonfiction books, novels, short story collections, novellas, juvenile. **Considers these fiction areas:** crime, detective, ethnic, feminist, historical, humor, juvenile, literary, mainstream, mystery, police, suspense, thriller, young adult mainstream.

8—⚷ "I'm very involved with and committed to my clients. I also employ a publicist to work with all my clients to make the most of each book's publication. Most of my clients come to me via recommendations from other agents, clients and editors. I've met very few at conferences. I've often sought out writers for projects, and I still find new clients via the traditional query letter." Does not want to receive how-to, children's picture books, science fiction, poetry, men's adventure, or erotica.

HOW TO CONTACT Query with SASE. Accepts queries via fax. Accepts simultaneous submissions. Responds in 1 week to queries. Responds in 1 month to mss. Obtains most new clients through recommendations, submissions.

TERMS Agent receives 15% commission on domestic sales. Agent receives 20% commission on foreign and dramatic sales. No written contract.

RECENT SALES Sold 15 titles in the last year. *Autobiography of Mrs. Tom Thumb*, by Melanie Benjamin (Delacorte Press); *A Body of Water*, by Sarah Dooley (Feiwel & Friends/Macmillan); *Miss Dimple Rallies to the Cause*, by Mignon F. Ballard (St. Martin's Press); *Abandon* by Meg Cabot (Scholastic, Inc.); *Overbite*, by Meg Cabot (William Morrow); *Huntress*, by Malinda Lo (Little, Brown & Co Books for Young Readers); *Everybody Bugs Out*, by Leslie Margolis (Bloomsbury); *The Elite Gymnasts*, by Dominique Moceanu and Alicia Thompson (Disney/Hyperion); *Safe from the Sea*, by Peter Geye (Unbridled Books).

TIPS "Be complete, forthright and clear in your communications. Do your research as to what a particular agent represents."

LANGTONS INTERNATIONAL AGENCY

124 West 60th St., #42M, New York NY 10023. (646)344-1801. **E-mail:** langton@langtonsinternational@com; llangton@langtonsinternational.com. **Website:** www.langtonsinternational.com. **Contact:** Linda Langton, President.

REPRESENTS Nonfiction books and literary fiction. **Considers these fiction areas:** literary, political thrillers, young adult, and middle grade books.

8—π "Langtons International Agency is a multi-media literary and licensing agency specializing in nonfiction, inspirational, thrillers and children's middle grade and young adult books as well as the the visual world of photography."

HOW TO CONTACT Please submit all queries via hard copy to the address aove or e-mail outline/proposal, synopsis, publishing history, author bio. Only published authors should query this agency. Accepts simultaneous submissions.

RECENT SALES *Talking with Jean-Paul Sartre: Conversations and Debates*, by Professor John Gerassi (Yale University Press); *The Obama Presidency and the Politics of Change*, by Professor Stanley Renshon (Routledge Press); *I Would See a Girl Walking*, by Diana Montane and Kathy Kelly (Berkley Books); *Begin 1913-1992*, by Avi Shilon (Yale University Press); *This Borrowed Earth*, by Robert Emmet Hernan (Palgrave McMillan); *The Perfect Square*, by Nancy Heinzen (Temple Uni Press); *The Honey Trail* by Grace Pundyk (St. Martin's Press); *Dogs of Central Park* by Fran Reisner (Rizzoli/Universe Publishing).

MICHAEL LARSEN/ELIZABETH POMADA, LITERARY AGENTS

1029 Jones St., San Francisco CA 94109-5023. (415)673-0939. **E-mail:** larsenpoma@aol.com. **Website:** www.larsen-pomada.com. **Contact:** Mike Larsen, Elizabeth Pomada. Member of AAR. Other memberships include Authors Guild, ASJA, PEN, WNBA, California Writers Club, National Speakers Association. Represents 100 clients. 40-45% of clients are new/unpublished writers. Currently handles nonfiction books (70%), novels (30%).

MEMBER AGENTS Michael Larsen (nonfiction); Elizabeth Pomada (fiction & narrative nonfiction).

REPRESENTS Considers these fiction areas: action, adventure, contemporary issues, crime, detective, ethnic, experimental, family saga, feminist, gay, glitz, historical, humor, inspirational, lesbian, literary, mainstream, mystery, police, religious, romance, satire, suspense chick lit.

8—π We have diverse tastes. We look for fresh voices and new ideas. We handle literary, commercial and genre fiction, and the full range of nonfiction books. Actively seeking commercial, genre, and literary fiction. Does not want to receive children's books, plays, short stories, screenplays, pornography, poetry or stories of abuse.

HOW TO CONTACT Query with SASE. **Elizabeth Pomada** handles literary and commercial fiction, romance, thrillers, mysteries, narrative non-fiction and mainstream women's fiction. If you have completed a novel, **please e-mail the first 10 pages and 2-page synopsis to larsenpoma@aol.com.** Use 14-point typeface, double-spaced, as an e-mail letter with no attachments. For nonfiction, please read Michael's *How to Write a Book Proposal* book—available through your library or bookstore, and through our website—so you will know exactly what editors need. Then, before you start writing, send him the title, subtitle, and your promotion plan via conventional mail (with SASE) or e-mail. If sent as e-mail, please include the information in the body of your e-mail with NO attachments. Please allow up to 2 weeks for a response. Responds in 8 weeks to pages or submissions.

TERMS Agent receives 15% commission on domestic sales. Agent receives 20% (30% for Asia) commission on foreign sales. May charge for printing, postage for multiple submissions, foreign mail, foreign phone calls, galleys, books, legal fees.

RECENT SALES Sold at least 15 titles in the last year. *Secrets of the Tudor Court*, by D. Bogden (Kensington); *Zen & the Art of Horse Training*, by Allan Hamilton, MD (Storey Pub.); *The Solemn Lantern Maker* by Merlinda Bobis (Delta); *Bite Marks*, the fifth book in an urban fantasy series by J.D. Rardin (Orbit/Grand Central); *The Iron King*, by Julie Karawa (Harlequin Teen).

WRITERS CONFERENCES This agency organizes the annual San Francisco Writers' Conference (www.sfwriters.org).

TIPS "We love helping writers get the rewards and recognition they deserve. If you can write books that meet the needs of the marketplace and you can promote your books, now is the best time ever to be a writer. We must find new writers to make a living, so we are very eager to hear from new writers whose work will interest large houses, and nonfiction writers who can promote their books. For a list of recent sales, helpful info, and three ways to make yourself irresistible to any publisher, please visit our website."

THE STEVE LAUBE AGENCY

5025 N. Central Ave., #635, Phoenix AZ 85012. (602)336-8910. **E-mail:** krichards@stevelaube.com.

Website: www.stevelaube.com. **Contact:** Steve Laube. Other memberships include CBA. Represents 60+ clients. 5% of clients are new/unpublished writers. Currently handles nonfiction books (48%), novels (48%), novella (2%), scholarly books (2%).

REPRESENTS Nonfiction books, novels. **Considers these fiction areas:** religious.

☛ Primarily serves the Christian market (CBA). Actively seeking Christian fiction and religious nonfiction. Does not want to receive children's picture books, poetry, or cookbooks.

HOW TO CONTACT Submit proposal package, outline, 3 sample chapters, SASE. No e-mail submissions. Consult website for guidelines. Accepts simultaneous submissions. Responds in 6-8 weeks to queries. Obtains most new clients through recommendations from others, solicitations, conferences.

TERMS Agent receives 15% commission on domestic sales. Agent receives 20% commission on foreign sales. Offers written contract; 30-day notice must be given to terminate contract.

RECENT SALES Sold 80 titles in the last year. Other clients include Deborah Raney, Allison Bottke, H. Norman Wright, Ellie Kay, Jack Cavanaugh, Karen Ball, Tracey Bateman, Susan May Warren, Lisa Bergren, John Rosemond, Cindy Woodsmall, Karol Ladd, Judith Pella, Michael Phillips, Margaret Daley, William Lane Craig, Tosca Lee, Ginny Aiken.

WRITERS CONFERENCES Mount Hermon Christian Writers' Conference; American Christian Fiction Writers' Conference.

◖ ROBERT LECKER AGENCY

4055 Melrose Ave., Montreal QC H4A 2S5 Canada. (514)830-4818. **Fax:** (514)483-1644. **E-mail:** leckerlink@aol.com. **Website:** www.leckeragency.com. **Contact:** Robert Lecker. Represents 20 clients. 20% of clients are new/unpublished writers. Currently handles nonfiction books (80%), novels (10%), scholarly books (10%).

MEMBER AGENTS Robert Lecker (popular culture, music); Mary Williams (travel, food, popular science).

REPRESENTS Nonfiction books, novels, scholarly syndicated material. **Considers these fiction areas:** action, adventure, crime, detective, erotica, literary, mainstream, mystery, police, suspense, thriller.

☛ RLA specializes in books about popular culture, popular science, music, entertainment, food, and travel. The agency responds to articulate, innovative proposals within 2 weeks. Actively seeking original book mss only after receipt of outlines and proposals.

HOW TO CONTACT Query first. Only responds to queries of interest. Discards the rest. Accepts simultaneous submissions. Responds in 2 weeks to queries. Responds in 1 month to mss. Obtains most new clients through recommendations from others, conferences, interest in website.

TERMS Agent receives 15% commission on domestic sales. Agent receives 15-20% commission on foreign sales. Offers written contract, binding for 1 year; 6-month notice must be given to terminate contract.

● LESCHER & LESCHER, LTD.

346 E. 84th St., New York NY 10028. (212)396-1999. **Fax:** (212)396-1991. **E-mail:** cl@lescherltd.com. **Contact:** Carolyn Larson, agent. Member of AAR. Represents 150 clients. Currently handles nonfiction books (80%), novels (20%).

REPRESENTS Nonfiction books, novels. **Considers these fiction areas:** commercial, literary, mystery, suspense.

☛ Does not want to receive screenplays, science fiction, or romance.

HOW TO CONTACT Query with SASE. Obtains most new clients through recommendations from others.

TERMS Agent receives 15% commission on domestic sales. Agent receives 10% commission on foreign sales.

LEVINE GREENBERG LITERARY AGENCY, INC.

307 Seventh Ave., Suite 2407, New York NY 10001. (212)337-0934. **Fax:** (212)337-0948. **E-mail:** submit@levinegreenberg.com. **Website:** www.levinegreenberg.com. Member of AAR. Represents 250 clients. 33% of clients are new/unpublished writers. Currently handles nonfiction books (70%), novels (30%).

MEMBER AGENTS James Levine, Daniel Greenberg, Stephanie Kip Rostan, Lindsay Edgecombe, Danielle Svetcov, Elizabeth Fisher, Victoria Skurnick.

REPRESENTS Nonfiction books, novels. **Considers these fiction areas:** literary, mainstream, mystery, thriller, psychological, women's.

☛ This agency specializes in business, psychology, parenting, health/medicine, narrative nonfiction, spirituality, religion, women's issues, and commercial fiction.

HOW TO CONTACT See website for full submission procedure at "How to Submit." Or use our e-mail address if you prefer, or online submission form. Do not submit directly to agents. Prefers electronic submissions. Cannot respond to submissions by mail. Obtains most new clients through recommendations from others.

TERMS Agent receives 15% commission on domestic sales. Agent receives 20% commission on foreign sales. Offers written contract. Charges clients for out-of-pocket expenses—telephone, fax, postage, photocopying—directly connected to the project.

WRITERS CONFERENCES ASJA Writers' Conference.

TIPS "We focus on editorial development, business representation, and publicity and marketing strategy."

PAUL S. LEVINE LITERARY AGENCY

1054 Superba Ave., Venice CA 90291-3940. (310)450-6711. **Fax:** (310)450-0181. **E-mail:** paul@paulslevinelit.com. **Website:** www.paulslevinelit.com. **Contact:** Paul S. Levine. Other memberships include the State Bar of California. Represents over 100 clients. 75% of clients are new/unpublished writers. Currently handles nonfiction books (60%), novels (10%), movie scripts (10%), TV scripts (5%), juvenile books 5%.

MEMBER AGENTS Paul S. Levine (children's and young adult fiction and nonfiction, adult fiction and nonfiction except sci-fi, fantasy, and horror); Loren R. Grossman (archaeology, art/photography/architecture, gardening, education, health, medicine, science).

REPRESENTS Nonfiction books, novels, episodic drama, movie, TV, movie scripts, feature film, TV movie of the week, sitcom, animation, documentary, miniseries syndicated material, reality show. **Considers these fiction areas:** action, adventure, comic books, confession, crime, detective, erotica, ethnic, experimental, family saga, feminist, frontier, gay, glitz, historical, humor, inspirational, lesbian, literary, mainstream, mystery, police, regional, religious, romance, satire, sports, suspense, thriller, westerns.

⚷ Does not want to receive science fiction, fantasy, or horror.

HOW TO CONTACT Query with SASE. Accepts simultaneous submissions. Responds in 1 day to queries. Responds in 6-8 weeks to mss. Obtains most new clients through conferences, referrals, listings on various websites, and in directories.

TERMS Agent receives 15% commission on domestic sales. Offers written contract. Charges for postage and actual, out-of-pocket costs only.

RECENT SALES Sold 8 books in the last year.

WRITERS CONFERENCES Willamette Writers Conference; San Francisco Writers Conference; Santa Barbara Writers Conference and many others.

TIPS "Write good, sellable books."

LIPPINCOTT MASSIE MCQUILKIN

27 West 20th Street, Suite 305, New York NY 10011. **Fax:** (212)352-2059. **E-mail:** info@lmqlit.com. **Website:** www.lmqlit.com.

MEMBER AGENTS Maria Massie (fiction, memoir, cultural criticism); Will Lippincott (politics, current affairs, history); Rob McQuilkin (fiction, history, psychology, sociology, graphic material); Jason Anthony (young adult, pop culture, memoir, true crime, and general psychology).

REPRESENTS Nonfiction books, novels, short story collections, scholarly graphic novels. **Considers these fiction areas:** action, adventure, cartoon, comic books, confession, family saga, feminist, gay, historical, humor, lesbian, literary, mainstream, regional, satire.

⚷ "LMQ focuses on bringing new voices in literary and commercial fiction to the market, as well as popularizing the ideas and arguments of scholars in the fields of history, psychology, sociology, political science, and current affairs. Actively seeking fiction writers who already have credits in magazines and quarterlies, as well as nonfiction writers who already have a media platform or some kind of a university affiliation." Does not want to receive romance, genre fiction, or children's material.

HOW TO CONTACT "We accepts electronic queries only. Only send additional materials if requested." Accepts simultaneous submissions. Responds in 1 week to queries. Responds in 1 month to mss. Obtains most new clients through recommendations from others, solicitations, conferences.

TERMS Agent receives 15% commission on domestic sales. Agent receives 20% commission on foreign sales. Offers written contract; 30-day notice must be given to terminate contract. Only charges for reasonable business expenses upon successful sale.

RECENT SALES Clients include: Peter Ho Davies, Kim Addonizio, Natasha Trethewey, Anne Carson, David Sirota, Katie Crouch, Uwen Akpan, Lydia Millet, Tom Perrotta, Jonathan Lopez, Chris Hayes, Caroline Weber.

● THE LITERARY GROUP INTERNATIONAL

14 Penn Plaza, Suite 925, New York NY 10122. (646)442-5896. **E-mail:** js@theliterarygroup.com. **Website:** www.theliterarygroup.com. **Contact:** Frank Weimann. 1900 Ave. of the Stars, 25 Fl., Los Angeles, CA 90067; Tel: (310)282-8961; **Fax:** (310)282-8903. 65% of clients are new/unpublished writers. Currently handles nonfiction books (50%), (50% fiction).

MEMBER AGENTS Frank Weimann.

REPRESENTS Nonfiction books, novels graphic novels. **Considers these fiction areas:** adventure, contemporary issues, detective, ethnic, experimental, family saga, fantasy, feminist, historical, horror, humor, literary, multicultural, mystery, psychic, romance, sports, thriller, young adult regional, graphic novels.

☞ This agency specializes in nonfiction (memoir, military, history, biography, sports, how-to).

HOW TO CONTACT Query with SASE. Prefers to read materials exclusively. Only responds if interested. Obtains most new clients through referrals, writers conferences, query letters.

TERMS Agent receives 15% commission on domestic sales. Agent receives 20% commission on foreign sales. Offers written contract; 30-day notice must be given to terminate contract.

RECENT SALES *One From the Hart*, by Stefanie Powers with Richard Buskin (Pocket Books); *Sacred Trust, Deadly Betrayal*, by Keith Anderson (Berkley); *Gotti Confidential*, by Victoria Gotti (Pocket Books); Anna Sui's illustrated memoir (Chronicle Books); *Mania*, by Craig Larsen (Kensington); *Everything Explained through Flowcharts*, by Doogie Horner (HarperCollins); *Bitch*, by Lisa Taddeo (TOR); film rights for *Falling Out of Fashion*, by Karen Yampolsky to Hilary Swank and Molly Smith for 2S Films.

WRITERS CONFERENCES San Diego State University Writers' Conference; Maui Writers' Conference; Agents and Editors Conference; NAHJ Convention in Puerto Rico, others.

● LITERARY MANAGEMENT GROUP, INC.

(615)812-4445. **E-mail:** brucebarbour@literarymanagementgroup.com; brb@brucebarbour.com. **Website:** http://literarymanagementgroup.com; www.brucebarbour.com. **Contact:** Bruce Barbour.

💬 Prior to becoming an agent, Mr. Barbour held executive positions at several publishing houses, including Revell, Barbour Books, Thomas Nelson, and Random House.

REPRESENTS Nonfiction books, novels.

☞ "Although we specialize in the area of Christian publishing from an Evangelical perspective, we have editorial contacts and experience in general interest books as well." Does not want to receive gift books, poetry, children's books, short stories, or juvenile/young adult fiction. No unsolicited mss or proposals from unpublished authors.

HOW TO CONTACT Query with SASE. E-mail proposal as an attachment.

TERMS Agent receives 15% commission on domestic sales.

● LOWENSTEIN ASSOCIATES INC.

121 W. 27th St., Suite 601, New York NY 10001. (212)206-1630. **Fax:** (212)727-0280. **E-mail:** assistant@bookhaven.com. **Website:** www.lowensteinassociates.com. **Contact:** Barbara Lowenstein. Member of AAR. Represents 150 clients. 20% of clients are new/unpublished writers. Currently handles nonfiction books (60%), novels (40%).

MEMBER AGENTS Barbara Lowenstein, president (nonfiction interests include narrative nonfiction, health, money, finance, travel, multicultural, popular culture, and memoir; fiction interests include literary fiction and women's fiction); Kathleen Ortiz, associate agent and foreign rights manager at Lowenstein Associates. She is seeking children's books (chapter, middle grade, and young adult) and young adult nonfiction.

REPRESENTS Nonfiction books, novels. **Considers these fiction areas:** crime, detective, erotica, ethnic, fantasy, feminist, historical, literary, mainstream, mystery, police, romance, suspense, thriller, young adult.

☞ "This agency specializes in health, business, creative nonfiction, literary fiction and commercial fiction—especially suspense, crime and women's issues. We are a full-service agency, handling domestic and foreign rights, film rights and audio rights to all of our books." Barbara Lowenstein is currently looking for writers who have a platform and are leading experts in their field, including business, women's issues, psychology, health, science and social issues, and is particularly interested in strong new voices in fiction and narrative nonfiction.

HOW TO CONTACT Please send us a one-page query letter, along with the first 10 pages pasted in the body of the message (if fiction; for nonfiction, please send only a query letter), by e-mail. Please put the word QUERY and the title of your project in the subject field of your e-mail and address it to the agent of your choice. Please do not send an attachment. We reply to all queries and generally send a response within 2-4 weeks. By mail: For Fiction: Mail a query letter, short synopsis, first chapter and a SASE For Nonfiction: Mail a query letter, proposal, if available, or else a project overview and a SASE. Responds in 4 weeks to queries. Obtains most new clients through recommendations from others, solicitations, conferences.

TERMS Agent receives 15% commission on domestic sales. Agent receives 20% commission on foreign sales. Offers written contract. Charges for large photocopy batches, messenger service, international postage.

WRITERS CONFERENCES Malice Domestic

TIPS "Know the genre you are working in and read! Also, please see our website for details on which agent to query for your project."

LYONS LITERARY, LLC

27 West 20th St., Suite 10003, New York NY 10011. (212)255-5472. **Fax:** (212)851-8405. **E-mail:** info@lyonsliterary.com. **Website:** www.lyonsliterary.com. **Contact:** Jonathan Lyons. Member of AAR. Other memberships include the Author's Guild, American Bar Association, New York State Bar Associaton, New York State Intellectual Property Law Section. Represents 37 clients. 15% of clients are new/unpublished writers. Currently handles nonfiction books (60%), novels (40%).

REPRESENTS Nonfiction books, novels. **Considers these fiction areas:** contemporary issues, crime, detective, fantasy, feminist, gay, historical, humor, lesbian, literary, mainstream, mystery, police, psychic, regional, satire, science fiction, sports, supernatural, suspense, thriller, women's chick lit.

"With my legal expertise and experience selling domestic and foreign language book rights, paperback reprint rights, audio rights, film/TV rights and permissions, I am able to provide substantive and personal guidance to my clients in all areas relating to their projects. In addition, with the advent of new publishing technology, Lyons Literary, LLC is situated to address the changing nature of the industry while concurrently handling authors' more traditional needs."

HOW TO CONTACT Only accepts queries through online submission form. Accepts simultaneous submissions. Responds in 8 weeks to queries. Responds in 12 weeks to mss. Obtains most new clients through recommendations from others.

TERMS Agent receives 15% commission on domestic sales. Agent receives 20% commission on foreign sales. Offers written contract.

WRITERS CONFERENCES Agents and Editors Conference.

TIPS "Please submit electronic queries through our website submission form."

DONALD MAASS LITERARY AGENCY

121 W. 27th St., Suite 801, New York NY 10001. (212)727-8383. **E-mail:** info@maassagency.com. **Website:** www.maassagency.com. Member of AAR. Other memberships include SFWA, MWA, RWA. Represents more than 100 clients. 5% of clients are new/unpublished writers. Currently handles novels (100%).

Prior to opening his agency, Mr. Maass served as an editor at Dell Publishing (New York) and as a reader at Gollancz (London). He also served as the president of AAR.

MEMBER AGENTS Donald Maass (mainstream, literary, mystery/suspense, science fiction, romance); Jennifer Jackson (commercial fiction, romance, science fiction, fantasy, mystery/suspense); Cameron McClure (literary, mystery/suspense, urban, fantasy, narrative nonfiction and projects with multicultural, international, and environmental themes, gay/lesbian); Stacia Decker (fiction, memoir, narrative nonfiction, pop-culture [cooking, fashion, style, music, art], smart humor, upscale erotica/erotic memoir and multicultural fiction/nonfiction); Amy Boggs (fantasy and science fiction, especially urban fantasy, paranormal romance, steampunk, YA/children's, and alternate history. historical fiction, multicultural fiction, westerns).

REPRESENTS Novels. **Considers these fiction areas:** crime, detective, fantasy, historical, horror, literary, mainstream, mystery, police, psychic, science fiction, supernatural, suspense, thriller, women's romance (historical, paranormal, and time travel).

This agency specializes in commercial fiction, especially science fiction, fantasy, mystery and suspense. Actively seeking to expand in literary fiction and women's fiction. We are fiction specialists. All genres are welcome. Does not want to receive nonfiction, picture books, prescriptive nonfiction, or poetry.

HOW TO CONTACT Query with SASE. Returns material only with SASE. Accepts simultaneous submissions. Responds in 2 weeks to queries. Responds in 3 months to mss.

TERMS Agent receives 15% commission on domestic sales. Agent receives 20% commission on foreign sales.

RECENT SALES *Codex Alera 5: Princep's Fury*, by Jim Butcher (Ace); *Fonseca 6: Bright Futures*, by Stuart Kaimsky (Forge): *Fathom*, by Cherie Priest (Tor); *Gospel Grrls 3: Be Strong and Curvaceous*, by Shelly Adina (Faith Words); *Ariane 1: Peacekeeper*, by Laura Reeve (Roc); *Execution Dock*, by Anne Perry (Random House).

WRITERS CONFERENCES Donald Maass: World Science Fiction Convention; Frankfurt Book Fair; Pacific Northwest Writers Conference; Bouchercon. Jennifer Jackson: World Science Fiction Convention; RWA National Conference.

TIPS We are fiction specialists, also noted for our innovative approach to career planning. Few new clients are accepted, but interested authors should query with a SASE. Works with subagents in all principle foreign countries and Hollywood. No prescriptive nonfiction, picture books, or poetry will be considered.

● MACGREGOR LITERARY INC.

2373 N.W. 185th Ave., Suite 165, Hillsboro OR 97124. (503)277-8308. **E-mail:** submissions@macgregorliterary.com. **Website:** www.macgregorliterary.com. **Contact:** Chip MacGregor. Signatory of WGA. Represents 40 clients. 10% of clients are new/unpublished writers. Currently handles nonfiction books (40%), novels (60%).

MEMBER AGENTS Chip MacGregor, Sandra Bishop, Amanda Luedeke.

REPRESENTS Nonfiction books, novels. **Considers these fiction areas:** crime, detective, historical, inspirational, mainstream, mystery, police, religious, romance, suspense, thriller, women's chick lit.

➤ "My specialty has been in career planning with authors—finding commercial ideas, then helping authors bring them to market, and in the midst of that assisting the authors as they get firmly established in their writing careers. I'm probably best known for my work with Christian books

over the years, but I've done a fair amount of general market projects as well." Actively seeking authors with a Christian worldview and a growing platform. Does not want to receive fantasy, sci-fi, children's books, poetry or screenplays.

HOW TO CONTACT Query with SASE. Accepts simultaneous submissions. Responds in 3 weeks to queries. Obtains most new clients through recommendations from others. Not looking to add unpublished authors except through referrals from current clients.

TERMS Agent receives 15% commission on domestic sales. Agent receives 15% commission on foreign sales. Offers written contract; 30-day notice must be given to terminate contract. Charges for exceptional fees after receiving authors' permission.

WRITERS CONFERENCES Blue Ridge Christian Writers' Conference; Write to Publish.

TIPS "Seriously consider attending a good writers' conference. It will give you the chance to be face-to-face with people in the industry. Also, if you're a novelist, consider joining one of the national writers' organizations. The American Christian Fiction Writers (ACFW) is a wonderful group for new as well as established writers. And if you're a Christian writer of any kind, check into The Writers View, an online writing group. All of these have proven helpful to writers."

● CAROL MANN AGENCY

55 Fifth Ave., New York NY 10003. (212)206-5635. **Fax:** (212)675-4809. **Website:** www.carolmannagency.com/. **Contact:** Eliza Dreier. Member of AAR. Represents roughly 200 clients. 15% of clients are new/unpublished writers. Currently handles nonfiction books (90%), novels (10%).

MEMBER AGENTS Carol Mann (health/medical, religion, spirituality, self-help, parenting, narrative nonfiction, current affairs); Laura Yorke; Gareth Esersky; Myrsini Stephanides (nonfiction areas of interest: pop culture and music, humor, narrative nonfiction and memoir, cookbooks; fiction areas of interest: offbeat literary fiction, graphic works, and edgy YA fiction). Joanne Wyckoff (nonfiction areas of interest: memoir, narrative nonfiction, personal narrative, psychology, women's issues, education, health and wellness, parenting, serious self-help, natural history); fiction.

REPRESENTS Nonfiction books, novels. **Considers these fiction areas:** commercial, literary.

➤ This agency specializes in current affairs, self-help, popular culture, psychology, parenting, and history. Does not want to receive genre fiction (romance, mystery, etc.).

HOW TO CONTACT Please see website for submission guidelines. Responds in 4 weeks to queries.

TERMS Agent receives 15% commission on domestic sales. Agent receives 20% commission on foreign sales. Offers written contract.

MANUS & ASSOCIATES LITERARY AGENCY, INC.

425 Sherman Ave., Suite 200, Palo Alto CA 94306. (650)470-5151. **Fax:** (650)470-5159. **E-mail:** manuslit@manuslit.com. **Website:** www.manuslit.com. **Contact:** Jillian Manus, Jandy Nelson, Penny Nelson. Member of AAR. Represents 75 clients. 30% of clients are new/unpublished writers. Currently handles nonfiction books (70%), novels (30%).

- Prior to becoming an agent, Ms. Manus was associate publisher of two national magazines and director of development at Warner Bros. and Universal Studios; she has been a literary agent for 20 years.

MEMBER AGENTS Jandy Nelson, jandy@manuslit.com (self-help, health, memoirs, narrative nonfiction, women's fiction, literary fiction, multicultural fiction, thrillers). Nelson is currently on sabbatical and not taking on new clients. Jillian Manus, jillian@manuslit.com (political, memoirs, self-help, history, sports, women's issues, Latin fiction and nonfiction, thrillers); Penny Nelson, penny@manuslit.com (memoirs, self-help, sports, nonfiction); Dena Fischer (literary fiction, mainstream/commercial fiction, chick lit, women's fiction, historical fiction, ethnic/cultural fiction, narrative nonfiction, parenting, relationships, pop culture, health, sociology, psychology); Janet Wilkens Manus (narrative fact-based crime books, religion, pop psychology, inspiration, memoirs, cookbooks); Stephanie Lee (not currently taking on new clients).

REPRESENTS Nonfiction books, novels. **Considers these fiction areas:** literary, mainstream, multicultural, mystery, suspense, thriller, women's quirky/edgy fiction.

- "Our agency is unique in the way that we not only sell the material, but we edit, develop concepts, and participate in the marketing effort. We specialize in large, conceptual fiction and nonfiction, and always value a project that can be sold in the TV/feature film market." Actively seeking high-concept thrillers, commercial literary fiction, women's fiction, celebrity biographies, memoirs, multicultural fiction, popular health, women's empowerment and mysteries. No horror, romance, science fiction, fantasy, western, young adult, children's, poetry, cookbooks, or magazine articles.

HOW TO CONTACT Query with SASE. If requested, submit outline, 2-3 sample chapters. All queries should be sent to the California office. Accepts simultaneous submissions. Responds in 3 months to queries. Responds in 3 months to mss. Obtains most new clients through recommendations from others, solicitations, conferences.

TERMS Agent receives 15% commission on domestic sales. Agent receives 20-25% commission on foreign sales. Offers written contract, binding for 2 years; 60-day notice must be given to terminate contract. Charges for photocopying and postage/UPS.

RECENT SALES *Nothing Down for the 2000s* and *Multiple Streams of Income for the 2000s*, by Robert Allen; *Missed Fortune 101*, by Doug Andrew; *Cracking the Millionaire Code*, by Mark Victor Hansen and Robert Allen; *Stress Free for Good*, by Dr. Fred Luskin and Dr. Ken Pelletier; *The Mercy of Thin Air*, by Ronlyn Domangue; *The Fine Art of Small Talk*, by Debra Fine; *Bone Men of Bonares*, by Terry Tamoff.

WRITERS CONFERENCES Maui Writers' Conference; San Diego State University Writers' Conference; Willamette Writers' Conference; BookExpo America; MEGA Book Marketing University.

TIPS "Research agents using a variety of sources."

THE EVAN MARSHALL AGENCY

6 Tristam Place, Pine Brook NJ 07058-9445. (973)882-1122. **Fax:** (973)882-3099. **E-mail:** evanmarshall@optonline.net. **Contact:** Evan Marshall. Member of AAR. Other memberships include MWA, Sisters in Crime. Currently handles novels (100%).

REPRESENTS Novels. **Considers these fiction areas:** action, adventure, erotica, ethnic, frontier, historical, horror, humor, inspirational, literary, mainstream, mystery, religious, satire, science fiction, suspense, western romance (contemporary, gothic, historical, regency).

HOW TO CONTACT Do not query. Currently accepting clients only by referal from editors and our own clients. Responds in 1 week to queries. Responds in 3 months to mss. Obtains most new clients through recommendations from others.

TERMS Agent receives 15% commission on domestic sales. Agent receives 20% commission on foreign sales. Offers written contract.

RECENT SALES *Watch Me Die,* by Erica Spindler (St. Martin's Press); *The First Day of the Rest of My Life,* by Cathy Lamb (Kensington); *Highland Protector,* by Hannah Howell (Zebra); *Devoured by Darkness,* by Alexandra Ivy (Kensington).

● THE MARTELL AGENCY

1350 Avenue of the Americas, Suite 1205, New York NY 10019. **Fax:** (212)317-2676. **E-mail:** afmartell@aol.com. **Contact:** Alice Martell.

REPRESENTS Considers these fiction areas: commercial Novels include mystery, thriller/suspense.

HOW TO CONTACT Query with SASE. Submit sample chapters. Submit via snail mail. No e-mail or fax queries.

RECENT SALES *Peddling Peril: The Secret Nuclear Arms Trade* by David Albright and Joel Wit (Five Press); *America's Women: Four Hundred Years of Dolls, Drudges, Helpmates, and Heroines,* by Gail Collins (William Morrow). Other clients include Serena Bass, Janice Erlbaum, David Cay Johnston, Mark Derr, Barbara Rolls, PhD.

● MAX AND CO., A LITERARY AGENCY AND SOCIAL CLUB

3929 Coliseum St., New Orleans LA 70115. (504)377-7745; (201)704-2483. **E-mail:** mmurphy@maxlit.com. **Website:** www.maxliterary.org. **Contact:** Michael Murphy.

MEMBER AGENTS Michael Murphy, Nettie Hartsock (literary and commercial fiction, business books and popular nonfiction, and the occasional Southern fiction book), Jack Perry (nonfiction books with a foundation in history, sports, business, politics, narrative nonfiction, math, and science).

REPRESENTS Considers these fiction areas: commercial, literary.

⌐ Seeking work in literary or eclectic fiction. In nonfiction, seeks narrative or creative nonfiction. Does not represent romance, science fiction, fantasy, tea-cozy or whodunnit mysteries. Does not represent self-help or prescriptive (how-to) nonfiction. Represents no children's or YA work.

HOW TO CONTACT Agency desires e-mailed submissions and will not accept nor respond to mailed submissions. There are four agents—two in New York, one in Austin, Texas, and Michael Murphy in New Orleans.

● MARGRET MCBRIDE LITERARY AGENCY

P.O. Box 9128, La Jolla CA 92038. (858)454-1550. **Fax:** (858)454-2156. **E-mail:** staff@mcbridelit.com. **Website:** www.mcbrideliterary.com. **Contact:** Michael Daley, submissions manager. Member of AAR. Other memberships include Authors Guild.

⌐ Prior to opening her agency, Ms. McBride worked at Random House, Ballantine Books, and Warner Books.

REPRESENTS Nonfiction books, novels. **Considers these fiction areas:** action, adventure, crime, detective, historical, humor, literary, mainstream, mystery, police, satire, suspense, thriller.

⌐ This agency specializes in mainstream fiction and nonfiction. PLEASE DO NOT SEND: screenplays, romance, poetry, or children's.

HOW TO CONTACT The agency is only accepting new clients by referral at this time. Query with synopsis, bio, SASE. Do not fax queries. Accepts simultaneous submissions. Responds in 4-6 weeks to queries. Responds in 6-8 weeks to mss.

TERMS Agent receives 15% commission on domestic sales. Agent receives 25% commission on foreign sales. Charges for overnight delivery and photocopying.

THE MCCARTHY AGENCY, LLC

7 Allen St., Rumson NJ 07660. Phone/**Fax:** (732)741-3065. **E-mail:** McCarthylit@aol.com; ntfrost@hotmail.com. **Contact:** Shawna McCarthy. Member of AAR. Currently handles nonfiction books (25%), novels (75%).

MEMBER AGENTS Shawna McCarthy, Nahvae Frost.

REPRESENTS Nonfiction books, novels. **Considers these fiction areas:** fantasy, juvenile, mystery, romance, science, womens.

HOW TO CONTACT Query via e-mail or regular mail to The McCarthy Agency, c/o Nahvae Frost, 101 Clinton Avenue, Apartment #2, Brooklyn, NY 11205 Accepts simultaneous submissions.

MCCARTHY CREATIVE SERVICES

625 Main St., Suite 834, New York NY 10044-0035. (212)832-3428. **Fax:** (212)829-9610. **E-mail:** paulmccarthy@mccarthycreative.com. **Website:** www.mccarthycreative.com. **Contact:** Paul D. McCarthy. Other memberships include the Authors Guild, American Society of Journalists & Authors, National Book Critics Circle, Authors League of America. Represents 5

clients. 0% of clients are new/unpublished writers. Currently handles nonfiction books (95%), novels (5%).

○ Prior to his current position, Mr. McCarthy was a professional writer, literary agent at the Scott Meredith Literary Agency, senior editor at publishing companies (Simon & Schuster, HarperCollins and Doubleday) and a public speaker. Learn much more about Mr. McCarthy by visiting his website.

MEMBER AGENTS Paul D. McCarthy.

REPRESENTS Nonfiction books, novels. **Considers these fiction areas:** glitz, adventure, confession, detective, erotica, ethnic, family, fantasy, feminist, gay, historical, horror, humor, literary, mainstream, mystery, regional, romance, science, sports, thriller, western, young, women's.

○━ "I deliberately founded my company to be unlimited in its range. That's what I offer, and the world has responded. My agency was founded so that I could maximize and build on the value of my combined experience for my authors and other clients, in all of my capacities and more. I think it's *very* important for authors to know that because I'm so exclusive as an agent, I may not be able to offer representation on the basis of the manuscript they submit. However, if they decide to invest in their book and lifetime career as authors, by engaging my professional, near-unique editorial services, there is the possibility that at the end of the process, when they've achieved the very best, most salable and competitive book they can write, I may see sufficient potential in the book and their next books, that I do offer to be their agent. Representation is never guaranteed." Established authors of serious and popular nonfiction, who want the value of being one of MCS's very exclusive authors who receive special attention, and of being represented by a literary agent who brings such a rich diversity and depth of publishing/creative/professorial experience, and distinguished reputation. No first novels. "Novels by established novelists will be considered very selectively."

HOW TO CONTACT Submit outline, one chapter (either first or best). Queries and submissions by e-mail only. Send as e-mail attachment. Responds in 3-4 weeks to queries. Obtains most new clients through recommendations from others.

TERMS Agent receives 15% commission on domestic sales. Agent receives 20% commission on foreign sales. Offers written contract; 30-day notice must be given to terminate contract. "All reading done in deciding whether or not to offer representation is free. Editorial services are available. Mailing and postage expenses that incurred on the author's behalf are always approved by them in advance."

TIPS "Always keep in mind that your query letter/proposal is only one of hundreds and thousands that are competing for the agent's attention. Therefore, your presentation of your book and yourself as author has to be immediate, intense, compelling, and concise. Make the query letter one-page, and after short, introductory paragraph, write a 150-word KEYNOTE description of your manuscript."

◐ **THE MCGILL AGENCY, INC.**
10000 N. Central Expressway, Suite 400, Dallas TX 75231. (214)390-5970. **E-mail:** info.mcgillagency@gmail.com. **Contact:** Jack Bollinger. Estab. 2009. Represents 10 clients. 50% of clients are new/unpublished writers.

MEMBER AGENTS Jack Bollinger (eclectic tastes in nonfiction and fiction); Amy Cohn (nonfiction interests include women's issues, gay/lesbian, ethnic/cultural, memoirs, true crime; fiction interests include mystery, suspense and thriller).

REPRESENTS **Considers these fiction areas:** historical, mainstream, mystery, romance, thriller.

HOW TO CONTACT Query via e-mail. Responds in 2 weeks to queries and 6 weeks to mss. Obtains new clients through conferences.

TERMS Agent receives 15% commission.

● **MENDEL MEDIA GROUP, LLC**
115 W. 30th St., Suite 800, New York NY 10001. (646)239-9896. **Fax:** (212)685-4717. **E-mail:** scott@mendelmedia.com. **Website:** www.mendelmedia.com. Member of AAR. Represents 40-60 clients.

REPRESENTS Nonfiction books, novels, scholarly, with potential for broad/popular appeal. **Considers these fiction areas:** action, adventure, contemporary issues, crime, detective, erotica, ethnic, feminist, gay, glitz, historical, humor, inspirational, juvenile, lesbian, literary, mainstream, mystery, picture books, police, religious, romance, satire, sports, thriller, young adult Jewish fiction.

○━ "I am interested in major works of history, current affairs, biography, business, politics, economics, science, major memoirs, narrative non-fiction, and other sorts of general nonfiction." Actively seeking new, major or definitive work on a subject of broad interest, or a controversial, but authoritative, new book on a subject that affects many people's lives. I also represent more light-hearted nonfiction projects, such as gift or novelty books, when they suit the market particularly well." Does not want "queries about projects written years ago that were unsuccessfully shopped to a long list of trade publishers by either the author or another agent. I am specifically not interested in reading short, category romances (regency, time travel, paranormal, etc.), horror novels, supernatural stories, poetry, original plays, or film scripts."

HOW TO CONTACT Query with SASE. Do not e-mail or fax queries. For nonfiction, include a complete, fully edited book proposal with sample chapters. For fiction, include a complete synopsis and no more than 20 pages of sample text. Responds in 2 weeks to queries. Responds in 4-6 weeks to mss. Obtains most new clients through recommendations from others.

TERMS Agent receives 15% commission on domestic sales. Agent receives 20% commission on foreign sales.

WRITERS CONFERENCES BookExpo America; Frankfurt Book Fair; London Book Fair; RWA National Conference; Modern Language Association Convention; Jerusalem Book Fair.

TIPS "While I am not interested in being flattered by a prospective client, it does matter to me that she knows why she is writing to me in the first place. Is one of my clients a colleague of hers? Has she read a book by one of my clients that led her to believe I might be interested in her work? Authors of descriptive nonfiction should have real credentials and expertise in their subject areas, either as academics, journalists, or policy experts, and authors of prescriptive nonfiction should have legitimate expertise and considerable experience communicating their ideas in seminars and workshops, in a successful business, through the media, etc."

⊘ MORTIMER LITERARY AGENCY

41769 Enterprise Circle N., Suite 107, Temecula CA 92590. (951)208-5674. **E-mail:** kmortimer@mortimerliterary.com. **E-mail:** queries@mortimerliterary.com. **Website:** www.mortimerliterary.com. **Contact:** Kelly Gottuso Mortimer. Romance Writers of

America. Represents 16 clients. 80% of clients are new/unpublished writers. Currently handles nonfiction books (40%), novels (40%), young adult books (20%).

REPRESENTS Nonfiction books, novels, young adult. **Considers these fiction areas:** Please refer to submissions page on website, as the list changes.

➤ "I keep a short client list to give my writers personal attention. I edit my clients' manuscripts as necessary. I send manuscripts out to preselected editors in a timely fashion and send my clients monthly reports. I only sign writers not yet published, or not published in the last 3 years. Those are the writers who need my help the most."

HOW TO CONTACT See website for submission guidelines. Accepts simultaneous submissions. Responds in 3 months to mss. Obtains most new clients through query letters.

TERMS Agent receives 15% commission on domestic sales. Agent receives 20% commission on foreign sales. Offers written contract. "I charge for postage-only the amount I pay and it comes out of the author's advance. The writer provides me with copies of their manuscripts if needed."

WRITERS CONFERENCES RWA, several conference. See schedule on website.

TIPS "Follow submission guidelines on the website, submit your best work, and don't query unless your manuscript is finished. Don't send material or manuscript that I haven't requested."

ⓘ DEE MURA LITERARY

269 West Shore Dr., Massapequa NY 11758-8225. (516)795-1616. **Fax:** (516)795-8797. **E-mail:** query@deemuraliterary.com. **Website:** http://deemuraliterary.com/. **Contact:** Dee Mura. Signatory of WGA. 50% of clients are new/unpublished writers.

MEMBER AGENTS Dee Mura, Karen Roberts, Bobbie Sokol, David Brozain.

REPRESENTS Considers these fiction areas: action, adventure, contemporary issues, crime, detective, ethnic, experimental, family saga, fantasy, feminist, gay, glitz, historical, humor, juvenile, lesbian, literary, mainstream, military, mystery, psychic, regional, romance, science fiction, sports, thriller, westerns, young adult political.

➤ "Some of us have special interests and some of us encourage you to share your passion and work with us." Does not want to receive "ideas for sitcoms, novels, films, etc., or queries without SASEs."

HOW TO CONTACT Query with SASE. Accepts e-mail queries (no attachments). If via e-mail, please include the type of query and your genre in the subject line. If via regular mail, you may include the first few chapters, outline, or proposal. Mark envelope "Attn: Query Dept. No fax queries. Accepts simultaneous submissions. Only responds if interested; responds as soon as possible. Obtains most new clients through recommendations from others, queries.

TERMS Agent receives 15% commission on domestic sales. Agent receives 20% commission on foreign sales. Offers written contract. Charges clients for photocopying, mailing expenses, overseas/long-distance phone calls/faxes.

RECENT SALES Sold more than 40 titles and 35 scripts in the last year.

TIPS "Please include a paragraph on your background, even if you have no literary background, and a brief synopsis of the project."

MUSE LITERARY MANAGEMENT

189 Waverly Place, #4, New York NY 10014-3135. (212)925-3721. **E-mail:** museliterarymgmt@aol.com. **Website:** www.museliterary.com/. **Contact:** Deborah Carter. Associations: NAWE, International Thriller Writers, Historical Novel Society, Associations of Booksellers for Children, The Authors Guild, Children's Literature Network, and American Folklore Society. Represents 10 clients. 90% of clients are new/unpublished writers.

REPRESENTS Novels, short story collections, poetry books. **Considers these fiction areas:** adventure, detective, juvenile, mystery, picture books, suspense, thriller, young adult espionage; middle-grade novels; literary short story collections, literary fiction with popular appeal.

Specializes in manuscript development, the sale and administration of print, performance, and foreign rights to literary works, and post-publication publicity and appearances. Actively seeking "writers with formal training who bring compelling voices and a unique outlook to their manuscripts. Those who submit should be receptive to editorial feedback and willing to revise during the submission process in order to remain competitive." Does not want "manuscripts that have been worked over

by book doctors (collaborative projects ok, but writers must have chops); category romance, chick lit, sci-fi, fantasy, horror, stories about cats and dogs, vampires or serial killers, fiction or nonfiction with religious or spiritual subject matter."

HOW TO CONTACT Query with SASE. Query via e-mail (no attachments). Discards unwanted queries. Responds in 1-2 weeks to queries; 2-3 weeks to mss. Obtains most new clients through recommendations from others, conferences.

TERMS Agent receives 15% commission on domestic sales. Agent receives 20% commission on foreign sales. One-year contract offered when writer and agent agree that the manuscript is ready for submission; manuscripts in development are not bound by contract. Sometimes charges for postage and photocopying. All expenses are preapproved by the client.

TIPS "I give editorial feedback and work on revisions on spec. Agency agreement is offered when the writer and I feel the manuscript is ready for submission to publishers. Writers should also be open to doing revisions with editors who express serious interest in their work, prior to any offer of a publishing contract. All aspects of career strategy are discussed with writers, and all decisions are ultimately theirs. I make multiple and simultaneous submissions when looking for rights opportunities, and share all correspondence. All agreements are signed by the writers. Reimbursement for expenses is subject to client's approval, limited to photocopying (usually press clips) and postage. I always submit fresh manuscripts to publishers printed in my office with no charge to the writer."

JEAN V. NAGGAR LITERARY AGENCY, INC.

216 E. 75th St., Suite 1E, New York NY 10021. (212)794-1082. **E-mail:** jweltz@jvnla.com; jvnla@jvnla.com. **E-mail:** jweltz@jvnla.com; jregel@jvnla.com; atasman@jvnla.com; atasman@jvnla.com. **Website:** www.jvnla.com. **Contact:** Jean Naggar. Member of AAR. Other memberships include PEN, Women's Media Group, Women's Forum, SCBWI. Represents 450 clients. 20% of clients are new/unpublished writers. Currently handles nonfiction books (35%), novels (45%), juvenile books (15%), scholarly books (5%).

Ms. Naggar has served as president of AAR.

MEMBER AGENTS Jennifer Weltz (subrights, children's, adults); Jessica Regel (young adult, adult, subrights); Jean Naggar (taking no new clients); Alice Tasman (adult, children's); Elizabeth Evans (adult nonfiction, some fiction and YA).

REPRESENTS Nonfiction books, novels. **Considers these fiction areas:** action, adventure, crime, detective, ethnic, family saga, feminist, historical, literary, mainstream, mystery, police, psychic, supernatural, suspense, thriller.

8—¬ This agency specializes in mainstream fiction and nonfiction and literary fiction with commercial potential.

HOW TO CONTACT Query via e-mail. Prefers to read materials exclusively. No fax queries. Responds in 1 day to queries. Responds in 2 months to mss. Obtains most new clients through recommendations from others.

TERMS Agent receives 15% commission on domestic sales. Agent receives 20% commission on foreign sales. Offers written contract. Charges for overseas mailing, messenger services, book purchases, long-distance telephone, photocopying—all deductible from royalties received.

RECENT SALES *Night Navigation*, by Ginnah Howard; *After Hours at the Almost Home*, by Tara Yelen; *An Entirely Synthetic Fish: A Biography of Rainbow Trout*, by Anders Halverson; *The Patron Saint of Butterflies*, by Cecilia Galante; *Wondrous Strange*, by Lesley Livingston; *6 Sick Hipsters*, by Rayo Casablanca; *The Last Bridge*, by Teri Coyne; *Gypsy Goodbye*, by Nancy Springer; *Commuters*, by Emily Tedrowe; *The Language of Secrets*, by Dianne Dixon; *Smiling to Freedom*, by Martin Benoit Stiles; *The Tale of Halcyon Crane*, by Wendy Webb; *Fugitive*, by Phillip Margolin; *BlackBerry Girl*, by Aidan Donnelley Rowley; *Wild Girls*, by Pat Murphy.

WRITERS CONFERENCES Willamette Writers Conference; Pacific Northwest Writers Conference; Bread Loaf Writers Conference; Marymount Manhattan Writers Conference; SEAK Medical & Legal Fiction Writing Conference.

TIPS "Use a professional presentation. Because of the avalanche of unsolicited queries that flood the agency every week, we have had to modify our policy. We will now only guarantee to read and respond to queries from writers who come recommended by someone we know. Our areas are general fiction and nonfiction—no children's books by unpublished writers, no multimedia, no screenplays, no formula fiction, and no mysteries by unpublished writers. We recommend patience and fortitude: the courage to be true to your own vision, the fortitude to finish a novel and polish it again and again before sending it out, and the patience to accept rejection gracefully and wait for the stars to align themselves appropriately for success."

◐ NELSON LITERARY AGENCY

1732 Wazee St., Suite 207, Denver CO 80202. (303)292-2805. **E-mail:** query@nelsonagency.com. **Website:** www.nelsonagency.com. **Contact:** Kristin Nelson, president and senior literary agent; Sara Megibow, associate literary agent. Member of AAR. RWA, SCBWI, SFWA.

REPRESENTS Novels, select nonfiction. **Considers these fiction areas:** commercial, literary, mainstream, women's chick lit (includes mysteries), romance (includes fantasy with romantic elements, science fiction, fantasy, young adult).

8—¬ NLA specializes in representing commercial fiction and high-caliber literary fiction. Actively seeking Latina writers who tackle contemporary issues in a modern voice (think *Dirty Girls Social Club*). Does not want short story collections, mysteries (except chick lit), thrillers, Christian, horror, or children's picture books.

HOW TO CONTACT Query by e-mail only.

RECENT SALES *New York Times* Best-selling author of *I'd Tell You I Love You, but Then I'd Have to Kill You*, Ally Carter's fourth novel in the Gallagher Girls series; *Hester* (historical fiction), by Paula Reed; *Proof by Seduction* (debut romance), by Courtney Milan; *Soulless* (fantasy debut), by Gail Carriger; *The Shifter* (debut children's fantasy), by Janice Hardy; *Real Life & Liars* (debut women's fiction), by Kristina Riggle; *Hotel on the Corner of Bitter and Sweet* (debut literary fiction), by Jamie Ford.

◐ NORTHERN LIGHTS LITERARY SERVICES, LLC

2323 State Rd. 252, Martinsville IN 46151. (888)558-4354. **Fax:** (208)265-1948. **E-mail:** queries@northernlightsls.com. **Website:** www.northernlightsls.com. **Contact:** Sammie Justesen. Represents 25 clients. 35% of clients are new/unpublished writers. Currently handles nonfiction books (90%), novels (10%).

MEMBER AGENTS Sammie Justesen (fiction and nonfiction); Vorris Dee Justesen (business and current affairs).

REPRESENTS Nonfiction books, novels. **Considers these fiction areas:** action, adventure, crime, detective, ethnic, family saga, feminist, glitz, historical, inspirational, mainstream, mystery, police, psychic, regional, religious, romance, supernatural, suspense, thriller, women's.

⚷━⊶ "Our goal is to provide personalized service to clients and create a bond that will endure throughout the writer's career. We seriously consider each query we receive and will accept hardworking new authors who are willing to develop their talents and skills. We enjoy working with healthcare professionals and writers who clearly understand their market and have a platform." Actively seeking general nonfiction—especially if the writer has a platform. Does not want to receive fantasy, horror, erotica, children's books, screenplays, poetry, or short stories.

HOW TO CONTACT Query with SASE. Submit outline/proposal, synopsis, 3 sample chapters, author bio. E-queries preferred. No phone queries. All queries considered, but the agency only replies if interested. If you've completed and polished a novel, send a query letter, a one-or-two page synopsis of the plot, and the first chapter. Also include your biography as it relates to your writing experience. Do not send an entire mss unless requested. If you'd like to submit a nonfiction book, send a query letter, along with the book proposal. Include a bio showing the background that will enable you to write the book. Accepts simultaneous submissions. Responds in 2 months to queries. Responds in 2 months to mss. Obtains most new clients through solicitations, conferences.

TERMS Agent receives 15% commission on domestic sales. Agent receives 20% commission on foreign sales. Offers written contract; 30-day notice must be given to terminate contract.

RECENT SALES *Intuitive Parenting*, by Debra Snyder, PhD (Beyond Words); *The Confidence Trap* by Russ Harris (Penguin); *The Never Cold Call Again Toolkit* by Frank Rumbauskas Jr. (Wiley); *Thank You for Firing Me*, by Candace Reed and Kitty Martini (Sterling); *The Wal-Mart Cure: Ten Lifesaving Supplements for Under $10* (Sourcebooks).

TIPS "If you're fortunate enough to find an agent who answers your query and asks for a printed manuscript, always include a letter and cover page containing your name, physical address, e-mail address and phone number. Be professional!"

● KATHI J. PATON LITERARY AGENCY

P.O. Box 2236 Radio City Station, New York NY 10101. (212)265-6586. **E-mail:** KJPLitBiz@optonline.net.

Website: www.PatonLiterary.com. **Contact:** Kathi Paton. Currently handles nonfiction books (85%), novels (15%).

REPRESENTS Nonfiction books, novels, short story collections book-based film rights. **Considers these fiction areas:** literary, mainstream, multicultural short stories.

⚷━⊶ This agency specializes in adult nonfiction.

HOW TO CONTACT Accepts e-mail queries only. Accepts simultaneous submissions. Accepts new clients through recommendations from current clients.

TERMS Agent receives 15% commission on domestic sales. Agent receives 20% commission on foreign sales. Offers written contract. Charges clients for photocopying.

WRITERS CONFERENCES Attends major regional panels, seminars, and conferences.

ALISON J. PICARD, LITERARY AGENT

P.O. Box 2000, Cotuit MA 02635. Phone/**Fax:** (508)477-7192. **E-mail:** ajpicard@aol.com. **Contact:** Alison Picard. Represents 48 clients. 30% of clients are new/unpublished writers. Currently handles nonfiction books (40%), novels (40%), juvenile books (20%).

REPRESENTS Nonfiction books, novels, juvenile. **Considers these fiction areas:** action, adventure, contemporary issues, crime, detective, erotica, ethnic, family saga, feminist, gay, glitz, historical, horror, humor, juvenile, lesbian, literary, mainstream, multicultural, mystery, New Age, picture books, police, psychic, romance, sports, supernatural, thriller, young adult.

⚷━⊶ "Many of my clients have come to me from big agencies, where they felt overlooked or ignored. I communicate freely with my clients and offer a lot of career advice, suggestions for revising manuscripts, etc. If I believe in a project, I will submit it to a dozen or more publishers, unlike some agents who give up after four or five rejections." No science fiction/fantasy, westerns, poetry, plays or articles.

HOW TO CONTACT Query with SASE. Accepts simultaneous submissions. Responds in 2 weeks to queries. Responds in 4 months to mss. Obtains most new clients through recommendations from others, solicitations.

TERMS Agent receives 15% commission on domestic sales. Agent receives 20% commission on foreign sales. Offers written contract, binding for 1 year; 1-week notice must be given to terminate contract.

RECENT SALES *Zitface*, by Emily Ormand (Marshall Cavendish); *Totally Together*, by Stephanie O'Dea (Running Press); *The Ultimate Slow Cooker Cookbook*, by Stephanie O'Dea (Hyperion); Two Untitled Cookingbooks, by Erin Chase (St. Martin's Press); *A Journal of the Flood Year*, by David Ely (Portobello Books-United Kingdom, L'Ancora, — Italy); *A Mighty Wall*, by John Foley (Llewellyn/Flux); *Jelly's Gold*, by David Housewright (St. Martin's Press).

TIPS "Please don't send material without sending a query first via mail or e-mail. I don't accept phone or fax queries. Always enclose an SASE with a query."

LINN PRENTIS LITERARY

155 East 116th St., #2F, New York NY 10029. **Fax:** (212)875-5565. **E-mail:** ahayden@linnprentis.com; linn@linnprentis.com. **Website:** www.linnprentis.com. **Contact:** Amy Hayden, acquisitions director; Linn Prentis, agent; Jordana Frankel assistant. Represents 18-20 clients. 25% of clients are new/unpublished writers. Currently handles nonfiction books (5%), novels (65%), story collections (7%), novella (10%), juvenile books (10%), scholarly books (3%).

REPRESENTS Nonfiction books, novels, short story collections, novellas (from authors whose novels I already represent), juvenile (for older juveniles), scholarly anthology. **Considers these fiction areas:** adventure, ethnic, fantasy, feminist, gay, glitz, historical, horror, humor, juvenile, lesbian, literary, mainstream, mystery, thriller.

⊶ "Because of the Virginia Kidd connection and the clients I brought with me at the start, I have a special interest in sci-fi and fantasy, but, really, fiction is what interests me. As for my nonfiction projects, they are books I just couldn't resist." Actively seeking hard science fiction, family saga, mystery, memoir, mainstream, literary, women's. Does not want to "receive books for little kids."

HOW TO CONTACT Query with SASE. Submit synopsis. No phone or fax queries. No snail mail. E-mail queries to ahayden@linnprentis.com. Include first ten pages and synopsis as either attachment or as text in the e-mail. Accepts simultaneous submissions. Obtains most new clients through recommendations from others, solicitations.

TERMS Agent receives 15% commission on domestic sales. Agent receives 20% commission on foreign sales. Offers written contract; 60-day notice must be given to terminate contract.

RECENT SALES Sold 15 titles in the last year. *The Sons of Heaven*, *The Empress of Mars*, and *The House of the Stag*, by Kage Baker (Tor); the last has also been sold to Dabel Brothers to be published as a comic book/graphic novel; *Indigo Springs* and a sequel, by A.M. Dellamonica (Tor); Wayne Arthurson's debut mystery plus a second series book; *Bone Crossed* and *Cry Wolf* for *New York Times* #1 best-selling author Patricia Briggs (Ace/Penguin). "The latter is the start of a new series."

TIPS "Consider query letters and synopses as writing assignments. Spell names correctly."

ⓓ QUICKSILVER BOOKS: LITERARY AGENTS

508 Central Park Ave., #5101, Scarsdale NY 10583. **Phone/Fax:** (914)722-4664. **E-mail:** quicksilverbooks@hotmail.com. **Website:** www.quicksilverbooks.com. **Contact:** Bob Silverstein. Represents 50 clients. 50% of clients are new/unpublished writers. Currently handles nonfiction books (75%), novels (25%).

◯ Prior to opening his agency, Mr. Silverstein served as senior editor at Bantam Books and managing editor at Dell Books/Delacorte Press.

REPRESENTS Nonfiction books, novels. **Considers these fiction areas:** action, adventure, glitz, mystery, suspense, thriller.

⊶ This agency specializes in literary and commercial mainstream fiction and nonfiction, especially psychology, New Age, holistic healing, consciousness, ecology, environment, spirituality, reference, self-help, cookbooks, and narrative nonfiction. Does not want to receive science fiction, pornography, poetry, or single-spaced mss.

HOW TO CONTACT Query with SASE. Authors are expected to supply SASE for return of ms and for query letter responses. Accepts simultaneous submissions. Responds in 2 weeks to queries. Responds in 1 month to mss. Obtains most new clients through recommendations, listings in sourcebooks, solicitations, workshop participation.

TERMS Agent receives 15% commission on domestic sales. Agent receives 20% commission on foreign sales. Offers written contract.

RECENT SALES *Simply Mexican*, by Lourdes Castro (Ten Speed Press); *Indian Vegan Cooking*, by Madhu

Gadia (Perigee/Penguin); *Selling Luxury*, by Robin Lent & Genevieve Tour (Wiley); *Get the Job You Want, Even When No One's Hiring*, by Ford R. Myers (Wiley); *Matrix Meditations*, by Victor & Kooch Daniels (Inner Traditions Bear & Co.); *Macrobiotics for Dummies* (Wiley); *The Power of Receiving* (Tarcher); *Eat, Drink, Think in Spanish* (Ten Speed Press); *Nice Girls Don't Win at Life* (Broadway).

WRITERS CONFERENCES National Writers Union.

TIPS "Write what you know. Write from the heart. Publishers print, authors sell."

RAINES & RAINES

103 Kenyon Rd., Medusa NY 12120. (518)239-8311. **Fax:** (518)239-6029. **Contact:** Theron Raines (member of AAR); Joan Raines; Keith Korman. Member of AAR. Represents 100 clients.

REPRESENTS Nonfiction books, novels. **Considers these fiction areas:** action, adventure, crime, detective, fantasy, frontier, historical, mystery, picture books, police, science fiction, suspense, thriller, Westerns, whimsical.

HOW TO CONTACT Query with SASE. Responds in 2 weeks to queries.

TERMS Agent receives 15% commission on domestic sales. Agent receives 20% commission on foreign sales. Charges for photocopying.

HELEN REES LITERARY AGENCY

14 Beacon St., Suite 710, Boston MA 02108. (617)227-9014. **Fax:** (617)227-8762. **E-mail:** reesagency@reesagency.com. **Website:** http://reesagency.com. **Contact:** Joan Mazmanian, Ann Collette, Helen Rees, Lorin Rees. Estab. 1983. Member of AAR. Other memberships include PEN. Represents more than 100 clients. 50% of clients are new/unpublished writers. Currently handles nonfiction books (60%), novels (40%).

MEMBER AGENTS Ann Collette (literary, mystery, thrillers, suspense, vampire, and women's fiction; in nonfiction, she prefers true crime, narrative nonfiction, military and war, work to do with race and class, and work set in or about Southeast Asia. Ann can be reached at: Agent10702@aol.com). Lorin Rees (literary fiction, memoirs, business books, self-help, science, history, psychology, and narrative nonfiction. lorin@reesagency.com).

REPRESENTS Nonfiction books, novels. **Considers these fiction areas:** historical, literary, mainstream, mystery, suspense, thriller.

HOW TO CONTACT Query with SASE, outline, 2 sample chapters. No unsolicited e-mail submissions. No multiple submissions. Responds in 3-4 weeks to queries. Obtains most new clients through recommendations from others, conferences, submissions.

TERMS Agent receives 15% commission on domestic sales. Agent receives 20% commission on foreign sales.

RECENT SALES Sold more than 35 titles in the last year. *Get Your Ship Together*, by Capt. D. Michael Abrashoff; *Overpromise and Overdeliver*, by Rick Berrara; *Opacity*, by Joel Kurtzman; *America the Broke*, by Gerald Swanson; *Murder at the B-School*, by Jeffrey Cruikshank; *Bone Factory*, by Steven Sidor; *Father Said*, by Hal Sirowitz; *Winning*, by Jack Welch; *The Case for Israel*, by Alan Dershowitz; *As the Future Catches You*, by Juan Enriquez; *Blood Makes the Grass Grow Green*, by Johnny Rico; *DVD Movie Guide*, by Mick Martin and Marsha Porter; *Words That Work*, by Frank Luntz; *Stirring It Up*, by Gary Hirshberg; *Hot Spots*, by Martin Fletcher; *Andy Grove: The Life and Times of an American*, by Richard Tedlow; *Girls Most Likely To*, by Poonam Sharma.

JODIE RHODES LITERARY AGENCY

8840 Villa La Jolla Dr., Suite 315, La Jolla CA 92037-1957. **Website:** jodierhodesliterary.com. **Contact:** Jodie Rhodes, president. Member of AAR. Represents 74 clients. 60% of clients are new/unpublished writers. Currently handles nonfiction books (45%), novels (35%), juvenile books (20%).

MEMBER AGENTS Jodie Rhodes; Clark McCutcheon (fiction); Bob McCarter (nonfiction).

REPRESENTS Nonfiction books, novels. **Considers these fiction areas:** ethnic, family saga, historical, literary, mainstream, mystery, suspense, thriller, women's, young adult.

➤ "Actively seeking witty, sophisticated women's books about career ambitions and relationships; edgy/trendy young adult and teen books; narrative nonfiction on groundbreaking scientific discoveries, politics, economics, military; and important current affairs by prominent scientists and academic professors." Does not want to receive erotica, horror, fantasy, romance, science fiction, religious/inspirational, or children's books (does accept young adult/teen).

HOW TO CONTACT Query with brief synopsis, first 30-50 pages, SASE. Do not call. Do not send complete ms unless requested. This agency does not return unrequested material weighing a pound or more that requires special postage. Include e-mail address with query. Accepts simultaneous submissions. Responds in 3 weeks to queries. Obtains most new clients through recommendations from others, agent sourcebooks.

TERMS Agent receives 15% commission on domestic sales. Agent receives 20% commission on foreign sales. Offers written contract; 1-month notice must be given to terminate contract. Charges clients for fax, photocopying, phone calls, postage. Charges are itemized and approved by writers upfront.

RECENT SALES Sold 42 titles in the last year. *The Ring*, by Kavita Daswani (HarperCollins); *Train to Trieste*, by Domnica Radulescu (Knopf); *A Year with Cats and Dogs*, by Margaret Hawkins (Permanent Press); *Silence and Silhouettes*, by Ryan Smithson (HarperCollins); *Internal Affairs*, by Constance Dial (Permanent Press); *How Math Rules the World*, by James Stein (HarperCollins); *Diagnosis of Love*, by Maggie Martin (Bantam); *Lies, Damn Lies, and Science*, by Sherry Seethaler (Prentice Hall); *Freaked*, by Jeanne Dutton (HarperCollins); *The Five Second Rule*, by Anne Maczulak (Perseus Books); *The Intelligence Wars*, by Stephen O'Hern (Prometheus); *Seducing the Spirits*, by Louise Young (the Permanent Press), and more.

TIPS "Think your book out before you write it. Do your research, know your subject matter intimately, and write vivid specifics, not bland generalities. Care deeply about your book. Don't imitate other writers. Find your own voice. We never take on a book we don't believe in, and we go the extra mile for our writers. We welcome talented, new writers."

● ANN RITTENBERG LITERARY AGENCY, INC.

15 Maiden Lane, Suite 206, New York NY 10038. **Website:** www.rittlit.com. **Contact:** Ann Rittenberg, president; Penn Whaling, associate. Member of AAR. Currently handles fiction 75%, nonfiction (25%).

REPRESENTS **Considers these fiction areas:** literary, thriller upmarket fiction.

⊶ This agent specializes in literary fiction and literary nonfiction. Does not want to receive screenplays, straight genre fiction, poetry, self-help.

HOW TO CONTACT Query with SASE. Submit outline, 3 sample chapters, SASE. Query via postal mail only. Accepts simultaneous submissions. Responds in 6 weeks to queries. Responds in 2 months to mss. Obtains most new clients through referrals from established writers and editors.

TERMS Agent receives 15% commission on domestic sales. Agent receives 20% commission on foreign sales. Offers written contract. This agency charges clients for photocopying only.

RECENT SALES *The Given Day*, by Dennis Lehane; *My Cat Hates You*, by Jim Edgar; *Never Wave Goodbye*, by Doug Magee; *House and Home*, by Kathleen McCleary; *Nowhere to Run*, by C.J. Box; and *Daughter of Kura*, by Debra Austin.

❶ RLR ASSOCIATES, LTD.

Literary Department, 7 W. 51st St., New York NY 10019. (212)541-8641. **Fax:** (212)262-7084. **E-mail:** sgould@rlrassociates.net. **Website:** www.rlrassociates.net. **Contact:** Scott Gould. Member of AAR. Represents 50 clients. 25% of clients are new/unpublished writers. Currently handles nonfiction books (70%), novels (25%), story collections (5%).

REPRESENTS Nonfiction books, novels, short-story collections, scholarly. **Considers these fiction areas:** action, adventure, cartoon, comic books, crime, detective, ethnic, experimental, family saga, feminist, gay, historical, horror, humor, lesbian, literary, mainstream, multicultural, mystery, police, satire, sports, suspense.

⊶ "We provide a lot of editorial assistance to our clients and have connections." Actively seeking fiction, current affairs, history, art, popular culture, health and business. Does not want to receive screenplays.

HOW TO CONTACT Query by either e-mail or mail. Accepts simultaneous submissions. Responds in 4-8 weeks to queries. Obtains most new clients through recommendations from others.

TERMS Agent receives 15% commission on domestic sales. Agent receives 20% commission on foreign sales. Offers written contract.

RECENT SALES Clients include Shelby Foote, The Grief Recovery Institute, Don Wade, Don Zimmer, The Knot.com, David Plowden, PGA of America, Danny Peary, George Kalinsky, Peter Hyman, Daniel Parker, Lee Miller, Elise Miller, Nina Planck, Karyn Bosnak, Christopher Pike, Gerald Carbone, Jason Lethcoe, Andy Crouch.

TIPS "Please check out our website for more details on our agency."

B.J. ROBBINS LITERARY AGENCY

5130 Bellaire Ave., North Hollywood CA 91607-2908. **E-mail:** Robbinsliterary@gmail.com. **E-mail:** amy.bjrobbinsliterary@gmail.com. **Contact:** (Ms.) B.J. Robbins, or Amy Maldonado. Member of AAR. Represents 40 clients. 50% of clients are new/unpublished writers. Currently handles nonfiction books (50%), novels (50%).

REPRESENTS Nonfiction books, novels. **Considers these fiction areas:** crime, detective, ethnic, literary, mainstream, mystery, police, sports, suspense, thriller.

HOW TO CONTACT Query with SASE. Submit outline/proposal, 3 sample chapters, SASE. Accepts e-mail queries (no attachments). Accepts simultaneous submissions. Responds in 2-6 weeks to queries. Responds in 6-8 weeks to mss. Obtains most new clients through conferences, referrals.

TERMS Agent receives 15% commission on domestic sales. Agent receives 20% commission on foreign sales. Offers written contract; 3-month notice must be given to terminate contract. This agency charges clients for postage and photocopying (only after sale of ms).

RECENT SALES Sold 15 titles in the last year. *The Sweetness of Tears*, by Nafisa Haji (William Morrow); *Paper Dollhouse: A Memoir*, by Dr. Lisa M. Masterson; *The Sinatra Club*, by Sal Polisi and Steve Dougherty (Gallery Books); *Getting Stoned with Savages*, by J. Maarten Troost (Broadway); *Hot Water*, by Kathryn Jordan (Berkley); *Between the Bridge and the River*, by Craig Ferguson (Chronicle); *I'm Proud of You* by Tim Madigan (Gotham); *Man of the House*, by Chris Erskine (Rodale); *Bird of Another Heaven*, by James D. Houston (Knopf); *Tomorrow They Will Kiss*, by Eduardo Santiago (Little, Brown); *A Terrible Glory*, by James Donovan (Little, Brown); *The Writing on My Forehead*, by Nafisa Haji (Morrow); *Seen the Glory*, by John Hough Jr. (Simon & Schuster); *Lost on Planet China*, by J. Maarten Troost (Broadway).

WRITERS CONFERENCES Squaw Valley Writers Workshop; San Diego State University Writers' Conference.

THE ROSENBERG GROUP

23 Lincoln Ave., Marblehead MA 01945. (781)990-1341. **Fax:** (781)990-1344. **Website:** www.rosenberggroup.com. **Contact:** Barbara Collins Rosenberg. Estab. 1998. Member of AAR. Recognized agent of the RWA. Represents 25 clients. 15% of clients are new/unpublished writers. Currently handles nonfiction books (30%), novels (30%), scholarly books (10%), (30% college textbooks).

Prior to becoming an agent, Ms. Rosenberg was a senior editor for Harcourt.

REPRESENTS Nonfiction books, novels, textbooks, college textbooks only. **Considers these fiction areas:** romance, women's.

Ms. Rosenberg is well-versed in the romance market (both category and single title). She is a frequent speaker at romance conferences. Actively seeking romance category or single title in contemporary romantic suspense, and the historical subgenres. Does not want to receive inspirational, time travel, futuristic or paranormal.

HOW TO CONTACT Query with SASE. No e-mail or fax queries; will not respond. See guidelines on website. Responds in 2 weeks to queries. Responds in 4-6 weeks to mss. Obtains most new clients through recommendations from others, solicitations, conferences.

TERMS Agent receives 15% commission on domestic sales. Agent receives 15% commission on foreign sales. Offers written contract; 1-month notice must be given to terminate contract. Charges maximum of $350/year for postage and photocopying.

RECENT SALES Sold 27 titles in the last year.

WRITERS CONFERENCES RWA National Conference; BookExpo America.

JANE ROTROSEN AGENCY LLC

318 E. 51st St., New York NY 10022. (212)593-4330. **Fax:** (212)935-6985. **Website:** www.janerotrosen.com. Estab. 1974. Member of AAR. Other memberships include Authors Guild. Represents more than 100 clients. Currently handles nonfiction books (30%), novels (70%).

MEMBER AGENTS Jane R. Berkey; Andrea Cirillo; Annelise Robey; Meg Ruley; Christina Hogrebe; Peggy Gordijn, director of rights.

REPRESENTS Nonfiction books, novels. **Considers these fiction areas:** crime, family saga, historical, mystery, police, romance, suspense, thriller, women's.

HOW TO CONTACT Query with SASE to the attention of "Submissions." Find appropriate agent contact/e-mail on website. Responds in 2 weeks to writers who have been referred by a client or colleague. Responds in 2 months to mss. Obtains most new clients through recommendations from others.

TERMS Agent receives 15% commission on domestic sales. Agent receives 20% commission on foreign sales. Offers written contract, binding for 3 years; 2-month notice must be given to terminate contract. Charges clients for photocopying, express mail, overseas postage, book purchase.

RUSSELL & VOLKENING

50 W. 29th St., Suite 7E, New York NY 10001. (212)684-6050. **Fax:** (212)889-3026. **Website:** www.randvinc.com. **Contact:** Jesseca Salky (adult, general fiction and nonfiction, memoirs: jesseca@randvinc.com); Carrie Hannigan (children's and young adult), Josh Getzler (mysteries, thrillers, literary and commercial fiction, young adult and middle grade, particularly adventures and mysteries for boys; e-mail queries only with cover letter and first 5 pages: josh@randvinc.com); Joy Azmitia (chick-lit, multicultural fiction, romance, humor, and nonfiction in the areas of travel, pop culture, and philosophy: joy@randvinc.com). Member of AAR. Represents 140 clients. 20% of clients are new/unpublished writers. Currently handles nonfiction books (45%), novels (50%), story collections (3%), novella (2%).

REPRESENTS Nonfiction books, novels, short story collections. **Considers these fiction areas:** action, adventure, crime, detective, ethnic, literary, mainstream, mystery, picture books, police, sports, suspense, thriller.

This agency specializes in literary fiction and narrative nonfiction. Actively seeking novels.

HOW TO CONTACT Query only with SASE to appropriate person. Responds in 4 weeks to queries.

TERMS Agent receives 15% commission on domestic sales. Agent receives 20% commission on foreign sales. Charges clients for standard office expenses relating to the submission of materials.

TIPS "If the query is cogent, well written, well presented, and is the type of book we'd represent, we'll ask to see the manuscript. From there, it depends purely on the quality of the work."

VICTORIA SANDERS & ASSOCIATES

241 Avenue of the Americas, Suite 11 H, New York NY 10014. (212)633-8811. **Fax:** (212)633-0525. **E-mail:** queriesvsa@gmail.com. **Website:** www.victoriasanders.com. **Contact:** Victoria Sanders, Diane Dickensheid. Estab. 1992. Member of AAR. Signatory of WGA. Represents 135 clients. 25% of clients are new/unpublished writers. Currently handles nonfiction books (30%), novels (70%).

MEMBER AGENTS Tanya McKinnon, Victoria Sanders, Chris Kepner (open to all types of books as long as the writing is exceptional. Include the first three chapters in the body of the e-mail. At the moment, he is especially on the lookout for quality nonfiction).

REPRESENTS Nonfiction books, novels. **Considers these fiction areas:** action, adventure, contemporary issues, ethnic, family saga, feminist, gay, lesbian, literary, thriller.

HOW TO CONTACT Query by e-mail only.

TERMS Agent receives 15% commission on domestic sales. Agent receives 20% commission on foreign sales. Offers written contract. Charges for photocopying, messenger, express mail. If in excess of $100, client approval is required.

RECENT SALES Sold 20+ titles in the last year.

TIPS "Limit query to letter (no calls) and give it your best shot. A good query is going to get a good response."

SCHIAVONE LITERARY AGENCY, INC.

236 Trails End, West Palm Beach FL 33413-2135. (561)966-9294. **Fax:** (561)966-9294. **E-mail:** profschia@aol.com. **Website:** www.publishersmarketplace.com/members/profschia; blog site: www.schiavoneliteraryagencyinc.blogspot.com. **Contact:** Dr. James Schiavone, CEO, corporate offices in Florida; Jennifer DuVall, president, New York office. New York office: 3671 Hudson Manor Terrace, No. 11H, Bronx, NY, 10463-1139, phone: (718)548-5332; fax: (718)548-5332; e-mail: jendu77@aol.com Other memberships include National Education Association. Represents 60+ clients. 2% of clients are new/unpublished writers. Currently handles nonfiction books (50%), novels (49%), textbooks (1%).

REPRESENTS Nonfiction books, novels, juvenile, scholarly, textbooks. **Considers these fiction areas:** ethnic, family saga, historical, horror, humor, juvenile, literary, mainstream, science fiction, young adult.

This agency specializes in celebrity biography and autobiography and memoirs. Does not want to receive poetry.

HOW TO CONTACT Query with SASE. Do not send unsolicited materials or parcels requiring a signature. Send no e-attachments. Accepts simultaneous submissions. Responds in 2 weeks to queries. Responds in

6 weeks to mss. Obtains most new clients through recommendations from others, solicitations, conferences.

TERMS Agent receives 15% commission on domestic sales. Agent receives 20% commission on foreign sales. Offers written contract. Charges clients for postage only.

WRITERS CONFERENCES Key West Literary Seminar; South Florida Writers' Conference; Tallahassee Writers' Conference, Million Dollar Writers' Conference; Alaska Writers Conference.

TIPS "We prefer to work with established authors published by major houses in New York. We will consider marketable proposals from new/previously unpublished writers."

⬤◎ SUSAN SCHULMAN LITERARY AGENCY

454 W. 44th St., New York NY 10036. (212)713-1633. **Fax:** (212)581-8830. **E-mail:** schulmanqueries@yahoo.com. **Contact:** Susan Schulman. Estab. 1980. Member of AAR. Signatory of WGA. Other memberships include Dramatists Guild. 10% of clients are new/unpublished writers. Currently handles nonfiction books (50%), novels (25%), juvenile books (15%), stage plays (10%).

MEMBER AGENTS Linda Kiss, director of foreign rights; Katherine Stones, theater; Emily Uhry, submissions editor.

REPRESENTS Considers these fiction areas: action, adventure, crime, detective, feminist, historical, humor, inspirational, juvenile, literary, mainstream, mystery, picture books, police, religious, suspense, women's, young adult.

⚱➝ "We specialize in books for, by and about women and women's issues including nonfiction self-help books, fiction and theater projects. We also handle the film, television and allied rights for several agencies as well as foreign rights for several publishing houses." Actively seeking new nonfiction. Considers plays. Does not want to receive poetry, television scripts or concepts for television.

HOW TO CONTACT Query with SASE. Submit outline, synopsis, author bio, 3 sample chapters. Accepts simultaneous submissions. Responds in 6 weeks to queries/mss. Obtains most new clients through recommendations from others, solicitations, conferences.

TERMS Agent receives 15% commission on domestic sales. Agent receives 20% commission on foreign sales.

Offers written contract; 30-day notice must be given to terminate contract.

RECENT SALES Sold 50 titles in the last year; hundred of subsidiary rights deals.

WRITERS CONFERENCES Geneva Writers' Conference (Switzerland); Columbus Writers' Conference; Skidmore Conference of the Independent Women's Writers Group.

TIPS "Keep writing!" Schulman describes her agency as "professional boutique, long-standing, eclectic."

⬤ SCRIBBLERS HOUSE, LLC LITERARY AGENCY

P.O. Box 1007, Cooper Station, New York NY 10276-1007. (212)714-7744. **E-mail:** query@scribblershouse.net. **Website:** www.scribblershouse.net. **Contact:** Stedman Mays, Garrett Gambino. 25% of clients are new/unpublished writers.

MEMBER AGENTS Stedman Mays, Garrett Gambino.

REPRESENTS Nonfiction books, occasionally novels. **Considers these fiction areas:** crime, historical, literary, suspense, thriller, women's.

HOW TO CONTACT "Query via e-mail. Put 'nonfiction query' or 'fiction query' in the subject line followed by the title of your project (send to our submissions e-mail on our website). Do not send attachments or downloadable materials of any kind with query. We will request more materials if we are interested. Usually respond in 2 weeks to 2 months to e-mail queries if we are interested (if we are not interested, we will not respond due to the overwhelming amount of queries we receive). We are only accepting e-mail queries at the present time." Accepts simultaneous submissions.

TERMS Agent receives 15% commission on domestic sales. Charges clients for postage, shipping and copying.

TIPS "If you must send by snail mail, we will return material or respond to a U.S. Postal Service-accepted SASE. (No international coupons or outdated mail strips, please.) Presentation means a lot. A well-written query letter with a brief author bio and your credentials is important. For query letter models, go to the bookstore or online and look at the cover copy and flap copy on other books in your general area of interest. Emulate what's best. Have an idea of other notable books that will be perceived as being in the same vein as yours. Know what's fresh about your project and articulate it in as few words as possible. Consult our website for the most up-to-date information on submitting."

○ SCRIBE AGENCY, LLC

5508 Joylynne Dr., Madison WI 53716. **E-mail:** whattheshizzle@scribeagency.com. **E-mail:** submissions@scribeagency.com. **Website:** www.scribeagency.com. **Contact:** Kristopher O'Higgins. Represents 11 clients. 18% of clients are new/unpublished writers. Currently handles novels (98%), story collections (2%).

MEMBER AGENTS Kristophor O'Higgins; Jesse Vogel.
REPRESENTS Nonfiction books, novels, short story collections, novellas anthologies. **Considers these fiction areas:** detective, erotica, experimental, fantasy, feminist, gay, horror, humor, lesbian, literary, mainstream, mystery, psychic, science fiction, thriller.

⊶ Actively seeking excellent writers with ideas and stories to tell.

HOW TO CONTACT E-queries only: submissions@scribeagency.com. See the website for submission info, as it may change. Responds in 3-4 weeks to queries. Responds in 5 months to mss.
TERMS Agent receives 15% commission on domestic sales. Agent receives 20% commission on foreign sales. Offers written contract. Charges for postage and photocopying.
RECENT SALES Sold 3 titles in the last year.
WRITERS CONFERENCES BookExpo America; The Writer's Institute; Spring Writer's Festival; WisCon; Wisconsin Book Festival; World Fantasy Convention.

SECRET AGENT MAN

P.O. Box 1078, Lake Forest CA 92609-1078. (949)698-6987. **E-mail:** scott@secretagentman.net. **E-mail:** query@secretagentman.net. **Website:** www.secretagentman.net. **Contact:** Scott Mortenson.
REPRESENTS Novels. **Considers these fiction areas:** detective, mystery, religious, suspense, thriller, Westerns.

⊶ Actively seeking selective mystery, thriller, suspense and detective fiction. Does not want to receive scripts or screenplays.

HOW TO CONTACT Query with SASE. Query via e-mail or snail mail; include sample chapter(s), synopsis and/or outline. Prefers to read the real thing rather than a description of it. Obtains most new clients through recommendations from others, solicitations.

LYNN SELIGMAN, LITERARY AGENT

400 Highland Ave., Upper Montclair NJ 07043. (973)783-3631. **Contact:** Lynn Seligman. Other memberships include Women's Media Group. Represents 32 clients. 15% of clients are new/unpublished writers. Currently handles nonfiction books (60%), novels (40%).

○ Prior to opening her agency, Ms. Seligman worked in the subsidiary rights department of Doubleday and Simon & Schuster, and served as an agent with Julian Bach Literary Agency (which became IMG Literary Agency). Foreign rights are represented by Books Crossing Borders, Inc.

REPRESENTS Nonfiction books, novels. **Considers these fiction areas:** detective, ethnic, fantasy, feminist, historical, horror, humor, literary, mainstream, mystery, romance, contemporary, gothic, historical, regency, science fiction.

⊶ "This agency specializes in general nonfiction and fiction. I also do illustrated and photography books and have represented several photographers for books."

HOW TO CONTACT Query with SASE. Prefers to read materials exclusively. Accepts simultaneous submissions. Responds in 2 weeks to queries. Responds in 2 months to mss. Obtains most new clients through referrals from other writers and editors.
TERMS Agent receives 15% commission on domestic sales. Agent receives 25% commission on foreign sales. Charges clients for photocopying, unusual postage, express mail, telephone expenses (checks with author first).
RECENT SALES Sold 15 titles in the last year. Lords of Vice series, by Barbara Pierce; Untitled series, by Deborah Leblanc.

◑ THE SEYMOUR AGENCY

475 Miner St., Canton NY 13617. (315)386-1831. **E-mail:** marysue@twcny.rr.com; nicole@theseymouragency.com. **Website:** www.theseymouragency.com. **Contact:** Mary Sue Seymour, Nicole Resciniti. Member of AAR. Signatory of WGA. Other memberships include RWA, Authors Guild. Represents 50 clients. 5% of clients are new/unpublished writers. Currently handles nonfiction books (50%), other (50% fiction).

○ Ms. Seymour is a retired New York State certified teacher.

MEMBER AGENTS Mary Sue Seymour (accepts queries in Christian, inspirational, romance, and nonfiction; Nicole Resciniti (accepts queries in same categories as Ms. Seymour in addition to action/suspense/thriller, mystery, sci-fi, fantasy, and YA/children's).

REPRESENTS Nonfiction books, novels. **Considers these fiction areas:** action, fantasy, mystery, religious, romance, science fiction, suspense, thriller, young adult.

HOW TO CONTACT Query with SASE, synopsis, first 50 pages for romance. Accepts e-mail queries. Accepts simultaneous submissions. Responds in 1 month to queries. Responds in 3 months to mss.

TERMS Agent receives 12-15% commission on domestic sales.

RECENT SALES Dinah Bucholz's *The Harry Potter Cookbook* to Adams Media.com; Vannetta Chapman's *A Simple Amish Christmas* to Abingdon Press; Shelley Shepard Gray's current book deal to Harper Collins; Shelley Galloway's multibook deal to Zondervan; Beth Wiseman's Christmas two novellas and multibook deal to Thomas Nelson; Mary Ellis's multibook deal to Harvest House, Barbara Cameron's novellas to Thomas Nelson and multibook deal to Abingdon Press.

WENDY SHERMAN ASSOCIATES, INC.

27 W. 24th St., New York NY 10010. (212)279-9027. **E-mail:** wendy@wsherman.com. **E-mail:** submissions@wsherman.com. **Website:** www.wsherman.com. **Contact:** Wendy Sherman. Member of AAR. Represents 50 clients. 30% of clients are new/unpublished writers.

MEMBER AGENTS Wendy Sherman (board member of AAR), Kim Perel.

REPRESENTS Considers these fiction areas: mainstream Mainstream fiction that hits the sweet spot between literary and commercial.

8—■ "We specialize in developing new writers, as well as working with more established writers. My experience as a publisher has proven to be a great asset to my clients."

HOW TO CONTACT Query via e-mail Accepts simultaneous submissions. Responds in 1 month to queries. Obtains most new clients through recommendations from others.

TERMS Agent receives 15% commission on domestic sales; 20% commission on foreign and film sales. Offers written contract.

RECENT SALES *Exposure*, by Therese Fowler, *It's All Relative*, by Wade Rouse. *In Stitches*, by Dr. Tony Youn, *Daughters of the Witching Hill*, by Mary Sharratt; *The Sweet By and By*, by Todd Johnson; *Supergirls Speak Out*, by Liz Funk; *Love in 90 Days* and *Sealing the Deal*, by Dr. Diana Kirschner; *A Long Time Ago* and *Essentially*, by Brigid Pasulka; *Changing Shoes*, by Tina Sloan.

TIPS "The bottom line is: Do your homework. Be as well prepared as possible. Read the books that will help you present yourself and your work with polish. You want your submission to stand out."

●❶ JEFFREY SIMMONS LITERARY AGENCY

15 Penn House, Mallory St., London NW8 8SX England. (44)(207)224-8917. **E-mail:** jasimmons@unicombox.co.uk. **Contact:** Jeffrey Simmons. Represents 43 clients. 40% of clients are new/unpublished writers. Currently handles nonfiction books (65%), novels (35%).

REPRESENTS Nonfiction books, novels. **Considers these fiction areas:** action, adventure, confession, crime, detective, family saga, literary, mainstream, mystery, police, suspense, thriller.

8—■ "This agency seeks to handle good books and promising young writers. My long experience in publishing and as an author and ghostwriter means I can offer an excellent service all around, especially in terms of editorial experience where appropriate." Actively seeking quality fiction, biography, autobiography, showbiz, personality books, law, crime, politics, and world affairs. Does not want to receive science fiction, horror, fantasy, juvenile, academic books, or specialist subjects (e.g., cooking, gardening, religious).

HOW TO CONTACT Submit sample chapter, outline/proposal, SASE (IRCs if necessary).Prefers to read materials exclusively. Responds in one week to queries. Responds in one month to mss. Obtains most new clients through recommendations from others, solicitations.

TERMS Agent receives 10-15% commission on domestic sales. Agent receives 15% commission on foreign sales. Offers written contract, binding for lifetime of book in question or until it becomes out of print.

TIPS "When contacting us with an outline/proposal, include a brief biographical note (listing any previous publications, with publishers and dates). Preferably tell us if the book has already been offered elsewhere."

● BEVERLEY SLOPEN LITERARY AGENCY

131 Bloor St. W., Suite 711, Toronto ON M5S 1S3 Canada. (416)964-9598. **Fax:** (416)921-7726. **E-mail:** beverly@slopenagency.ca. **Website:** www.slopenagency.ca. **Contact:** Beverley Slopen. Represents 70 clients.

20% of clients are new/unpublished writers. Currently handles nonfiction books (60%), novels (40%).

REPRESENTS Nonfiction books, novels, scholarly, textbooks, college. **Considers these fiction areas:** literary, mystery, suspense.

8—➤ "This agency has a strong bent toward Canadian writers." Actively seeking serious nonfiction that is accessible and appealing to the general reader. Does not want to receive fantasy, science fiction, or children's books.

HOW TO CONTACT Query with SAE and IRCs. Returns materials only with SASE (Canadian postage only). Accepts simultaneous submissions. Responds in 2 months to queries.

TERMS Agent receives 15% commission on domestic sales. Agent receives 10% commission on foreign sales. Offers written contract, binding for 2 years; 3-month notice must be given to terminate contract.

RECENT SALES *Solar Dance*, by Modris Eksteins (Knopf Canada); *God's Brain*, by Lionel Tiger & Michael McGuire (Prometheus Books); *What They Wanted*, by Donna Morrissey (Penguin Canada, Premium/DTV Germany); *The Age of Persuasion*, by Terry O'Reilly & Mike Tennant (Knopf Canada, Counterpoint US); *Prisoner of Tehran*, by Marina Nemat (Penguin Canada, Free Press US, John Murray UK); *Race to the Polar Sea*, by Ken McGoogan (HarperCollins Canada, Counterpoint US); *Transgression*, by James Nichol (HarperCollins US, McArthur Canada, Goldmann Germany); *Vermeer's Hat*, by Timothy Brook (HarperCollins Canada, Bloomsbury US); *Distantly Related to Freud*, by Ann Charney (Cormorant).

TIPS "Please, no unsolicited manuscripts."

VALERIE SMITH, LITERARY AGENT

1746 Route 44-55, Box 160, Modena NY 12548. **Contact:** Valerie Smith. Represents 17 clients. Currently handles nonfiction books (2%), novels (75%), story collections (1%), juvenile books (20%), scholarly books (1%), textbooks (1%).

REPRESENTS Nonfiction books, novels, juvenile, textbooks. **Considers these fiction areas:** fantasy, historical, juvenile, literary, mainstream, mystery, science, young women's/chick lit.

8—➤ "This is a small, personalized agency with a strong long-term commitment to clients interested in building careers. I have strong ties to science fiction, fantasy and young adult projects. I look for serious, productive writers

whose work I can be passionate about." Does not want to receive unsolicited mss.

HOW TO CONTACT Query with synopsis, bio, 3 sample chapters, SASE. Contact by snail mail only. Obtains most new clients through recommendations from others.

TERMS Agent receives 15% commission on domestic sales. Agent receives 20% commission on foreign sales. Offers written contract; 6-week notice must be given to terminate contract.

❶ SPECTRUM LITERARY AGENCY

320 Central Park W., Suite 1-D, New York NY 10025. **Fax:** (212)362-4562. **Website:** www.spectrumliterary-agency.com. **Contact:** Eleanor Wood, president. Estab. 1976. SFWA Represents 90 clients. Currently handles nonfiction books (10%), novels (90%).

MEMBER AGENTS Eleanor Wood, Justin Bell.

REPRESENTS Nonfiction books, novels. **Considers these fiction areas:** fantasy, historical, mainstream, mystery, romance, science fiction, suspense.

8—➤ Mr. Bell is actively seeking submissions in mysteries and a select amount of nonfiction

HOW TO CONTACT Query with SASE. Submit author bio, publishing credits. No unsolicited mss will be read. Queries and submissions by snail mail only. Ms. Wood and other agents have different addresses—see the website for full info. Responds in 1-3 months to queries. Obtains most new clients through recommendations from authors.

TERMS Agent receives 15% commission on domestic sales. Deducts for photocopying and book orders.

TIPS "Spectrum's policy is to read only book-length manuscripts that we have specifically asked to see. Unsolicited manuscripts are not accepted. The letter should describe your book briefly and include publishing credits and background information or qualifications relating to your work, if any."

❶ SPENCERHILL ASSOCIATES

P.O. Box 374, Chatham NY 12037. (518)392-9293. **Fax:** (518)392-9554. **E-mail:** submissions@spencerhillassociates.com. **Website:** www.spencerhillassociates.com. **Contact:** Karen Solem or Jennifer Schober (please refer to their website for the latest information). Member of AAR. Represents 96 clients. 10% of clients are new/unpublished writers.

○ Prior to becoming an agent, Ms. Solem was editor-in-chief at HarperCollins and an associate publisher.

MEMBER AGENTS Karen Solem; Jennifer Schober.
REPRESENTS Novels. **Considers these fiction areas:** crime, detective, historical, inspirational, literary, mainstream, police, religious, romance, thriller, young adult.

☛ "We handle mostly commercial women's fiction, historical novels, romance (historical, contemporary, paranormal, urban fantasy), thrillers, and mysteries. We also represent Christian fiction only—no nonfiction." No nonfiction, poetry, science fiction, children's picture books, or scripts.

HOW TO CONTACT Query submissions@spencer-hillassociates.com with synopsis and first three chapters attached as a .doc or .rtf file. "Please note: We no longer accept queries via the mail." Responds in 6-8 weeks to queries "if we are interested in pursuing."

TERMS Agent receives 15% commission on domestic sales. Agent receives 20% commission on foreign sales. Offers written contract; 3-month notice must be given to terminate contract.

● THE SPIELER AGENCY

27 W. 20 St., Suite 305, New York NY 10011. **E-mail:** thespieleragency@gmail.com. **Contact:** Katya Balter, acquisitions. Represents 160 clients. 2% of clients are new/unpublished writers.

Prior to opening his agency, Mr. Spieler was a magazine editor.

MEMBER AGENTS Joe Spieler, Eric Myers.
REPRESENTS Nonfiction books, novels, children's books. **Considers these fiction areas:** feminist, gay, lesbian, literary, mystery children's books, middle grade and young adult novels.

HOW TO CONTACT Accepts electronic submissions, or send query letter and sample chapters. Returns materials only with SASE; otherwise materials are discarded when rejected. Accepts simultaneous submissions. Cannot guarantee a personal response to all queries. Obtains most new clients through recommendations, listing in *Guide to Literary Agents*.

TERMS Agent receives 15% commission on domestic sales. Charges clients for messenger bills, photocopying, postage.

WRITERS CONFERENCES London Book Fair.

TIPS "Check http://www.publishersmarketplace.com/members/spielerlit/."

● NANCY STAUFFER ASSOCIATES

1540 Boston Post Rd., P.O. Box 1203, Darien CT 06820. (203)202-2500. **Fax:** (203)655-3704. **E-mail:** StaufferAssoc@optonline.net. **Website:** publishersmarketplace.com/members/nstauffer. **Contact:** Nancy Stauffer Cahoon. Other memberships include Authors Guild. 5% of clients are new/unpublished writers. Currently handles nonfiction books (15%), novels (85%).

REPRESENTS **Considers these fiction areas:** contemporary, literary, regional.

HOW TO CONTACT Obtains most new clients through referrals from existing clients.

TERMS Agent receives 15% commission on domestic sales. Agent receives 20% commission on foreign sales. Agent receives 15% commission on film sales.

RECENT SALES *The Magic and Tragic Year of My Broken Thumb*, by Sherman Alexie; *Bone Fire*, by Mark Spragg; *Claiming Ground*, by Laura Bell; *The Best Camera Is the One That's with You*, by Chase Jarvis.

● STEELE-PERKINS LITERARY AGENCY

26 Island Ln., Canandaigua NY 14424. (585)396-9290. **Fax:** (585)396-3579. **E-mail:** pattiesp@aol.com. **Contact:** Pattie Steele-Perkins. Member of AAR. Other memberships include RWA. Currently handles novels (100%).

REPRESENTS Novels. **Considers these fiction areas:** romance, women's category romance, romantic suspense, historical, contemporary, multi-cultural, and inspirational.

HOW TO CONTACT Submit synopsis and one chapter via e-mail (no attachments) or snail mail. Snail mail submissions require SASE. Accepts simultaneous submissions. Responds in 6 weeks to queries. Obtains most new clients through recommendations from others, queries/solicitations.

TERMS Agent receives 15% commission on domestic sales. Offers written contract, binding for 1 year; 1-month notice must be given to terminate contract.

RECENT SALES Sold 130 titles last year. This agency prefers not to share specific sales information.

WRITERS CONFERENCES RWA National Conference; BookExpo America; CBA Convention; Romance Slam Jam, Romantic Times.

TIPS "Be patient. E-mail rather than call. Make sure what you are sending is the best it can be."

● STERNIG & BYRNE LITERARY AGENCY

2370 S. 107th St., Apt. #4, Milwaukee WI 53227-2036. (414)328-8034. **Fax:** (414)328-8034. **E-mail:** jackbyrne@hotmail.com. **Website:** www.sff.net/people/jackbyrne. **Contact:** Jack Byrne. Other memberships include SFWA, MWA. Represents 30 clients. 10% of clients are new/unpublished writers. Currently handles nonfiction books (5%), novels (90%), juvenile books (5%).

REPRESENTS Nonfiction books, novels, juvenile. **Considers these fiction areas:** fantasy, horror, mystery, science fiction, suspense.

☛ "Our client list is comfortably full, and our current needs are therefore quite limited." Actively seeking science fiction/fantasy and mystery by established writers. Does not want to receive romance, poetry, textbooks, or highly specialized nonfiction.

HOW TO CONTACT Query with SASE. Prefers e-mail queries (no attachments); hard copy queries also acceptable. Responds in 3 weeks to queries. Responds in 3 months to mss.

TERMS Agent receives 15% commission on domestic sales. Agent receives 20% commission on foreign sales. Offers written contract; 2-month notice must be given to terminate contract.

TIPS "Don't send first drafts, have a professional presentation (including cover letter), and know your field. Read what's been done—good and bad."

● **THE STROTHMAN AGENCY, LLC**

197 Eighth St., Flagship Wharf - 611, Charlestown MA 02129. (617)742-2011. **Fax:** (617)742-2014. **E-mail:** strothmanagency@gmail.com. **Website:** www.strothmanagency.com. **Contact:** Wendy Strothman, Lauren MacLeod. Member of AAR. Other memberships include Authors' Guild. Represents 50 clients. Currently handles nonfiction books (70%), novels (10%), scholarly books (20%).

◗ Prior to becoming an agent, Ms. Strothman was head of Beacon Press (1983-1995) and executive vice president of Houghton Mifflin's Trade & Reference Division (1996-2002).

MEMBER AGENTS Wendy Strothman; Lauren MacLeod.

REPRESENTS Nonfiction books, novels, scholarly young adult and middle grade. **Considers these fiction areas:** literary, young adult middle grade.

☛ "Because we are highly selective in the clients we represent, we increase the value publishers place on our properties. We specialize in narrative nonfiction, memoir, history, science and nature, arts and culture, literary travel, current affairs, and some business. We have a highly se-lective practice in literary fiction, young adult and middle grade fiction, and nonfiction. We are now opening our doors to more commercial fiction but from authors who have a platform. If you have a platform, please mention it in your query letter. The Strothman Agency seeks out scholars, journalists, and other acknowledged and emerging experts in their fields. We are now actively looking for authors of well-written young-adult fiction and nonfiction. Browse the Latest News to get an idea of the types of books that we represent. For more about what we're looking for, read Pitching an Agent: The Strothman Agency on the publishing website www.strothmanagency.com." Does not want to receive commercial fiction, romance, science fiction or self-help.

HOW TO CONTACT Accepts queries only via e-mail at strothmanagency@gmail.com. See submission guidelines online. Accepts simultaneous submissions. Responds in 4 weeks to queries. Responds in 6 weeks to mss. Obtains most new clients through recommendations from others.

TERMS Agent receives 15% commission on domestic sales. Agent receives 20% commission on foreign sales. Offers written contract; 30-day notice must be given to terminate contract.

◐ **EMMA SWEENEY AGENCY, LLC**

245 E 80th St., Suite 7E, New York NY 10075. **E-mail:** queries@emmasweeneyagency.com. **Website:** www.emmasweeneyagency.com. Member of AAR. Other memberships include Women's Media Group. Represents 80 clients. 5% of clients are new/unpublished writers. Currently handles nonfiction books (50%), novels (50%).

MEMBER AGENTS Emma Sweeney, president; Eva Talmadge, rights manager and agent (represents literary fiction, young adult novel, and narrative nonfiction. Considers these nonfiction areas: popular science, pop culture and music history, biography, memoirs, cooking, and anything relating to animals. Considers these fiction areas: literary [of the highest writing quality possible], young adult; eva@emmasweeneyagency.com); Justine Wenger, junior agent/assistant (justine@emmasweeneyagency.com).

REPRESENTS Nonfiction books, novels.

☛ "We specialize in quality fiction and nonfiction. Our primary areas of interest include literary and women's fiction, mysteries and thrillers, science, history, biography, memoir, religious studies and the natural sciences." Does not want to receive romance, Westerns or screenplays.

HOW TO CONTACT Send query letter and first 10 pages in body of e-mail (no attachments) to queries@emmasweeneyagency.com. No snail mail queries.

TERMS Agent receives 15% commission on domestic sales. Agent receives 10% commission on foreign sales.

WRITERS CONFERENCES Nebraska Writers' Conference; Words and Music Festival in New Orleans.

◑ TALCOTT NOTCH LITERARY

2 Broad St., Second Floor, Suite 10, Milford CT 06460. (203)876-4959. **Fax:** (203)876-9517. **E-mail:** editorial@talcottnotch.net. **Website:** www.talcottnotch.net. **Contact:** Gina Panettieri, President. Represents 35 clients. 25% of clients are new/unpublished writers. Currently handles nonfiction books (50%), novels (20%), story collections (5%), juvenile books (20%), scholarly books (10%).

○ Prior to becoming an agent, Ms. Panettieri was a freelance writer and editor.

MEMBER AGENTS Gina Panettieri (nonfiction, mystery); Rachel Dowen (children's fiction, mystery).

REPRESENTS Nonfiction books, novels, juvenile, scholarly, textbooks. **Considers these fiction areas:** action, adventure, crime, detective, fantasy, juvenile, mystery, police, romance, suspense, thriller, young adult.

HOW TO CONTACT Query via e-mail (preferred) with first 10 pages of the ms within the body of the e-mail, not as an attachment, or with SASE. Accepts simultaneous submissions. Responds in 1 week to queries. Responds in 4-6 weeks to mss.

TERMS Agent receives 15% commission on domestic sales. Agent receives 20% commission on foreign sales. Offers written contract, binding for 1 year.

RECENT SALES Sold 36 titles in the last year. *Delivered From Evil*, by Ron Franscell (Fairwinds) and *Sourtoe* (Globe Pequot Press); *Hellforged*, by Nancy Holzner (Berkley Ace Science Fiction); *Welcoming Kitchen; 200 Allergen- and Gluten-Free Vegan Recipes*, by Kim Lutz and Megan Hart (Sterling); *Dr. Seteh's Love Prescription*, by Dr. Seth Meyers (Adams Media); *The Book of Ancient Bastards,* by Brian Thornton (Adams Media); *Hope in Courage*, by Beth Fehlbaum (Westside Books) and more.

TIPS "Know your market and how to reach them. A strong platform is essential in your book proposal. Can you effectively use social media/Are you a strong networker: Are you familiar with the book bloggers in your genre? Are you involved with the interest-specific groups that can help you? What can you do to break through the 'noise' and help present your book to your readers? Check our website for more tips and information on this topic."

● PATRICIA TEAL LITERARY AGENCY

2036 Vista Del Rosa, Fullerton CA 92831-1336. Phone/Fax: (714)738-8333. **Contact:** Patricia Teal. Member of AAR. Other memberships include RWA, Authors Guild. Represents 20 clients. Currently handles nonfiction books (10%), (90% fiction).

REPRESENTS Nonfiction books, novels. **Considers these fiction areas:** glitz, mainstream, mystery, romance, suspense.

⌐ This agency specializes in women's fiction, commercial how-to, and self-help nonfiction. Does not want to receive poetry, short stories, articles, science fiction, fantasy, or regency romance.

HOW TO CONTACT Published authors only may query with SASE. Accepts simultaneous submissions. Responds in 10 days to queries. Responds in 6 weeks to mss. Obtains most new clients through conferences, recommendations from authors and editors.

TERMS Agent receives 10-15% commission on domestic sales. Agent receives 20% commission on foreign sales. Offers written contract, binding for 1 year. Charges clients for ms copies.

RECENT SALES Sold 30 titles in the last year. *Texas Rose*, by Marie Ferrarella (Silhouette); *Watch Your Language*, by Sterling Johnson (St. Martin's Press); *The Black Sheep's Baby*, by Kathleen Creighton (Silhouette); *Man With a Message*, by Muriel Jensen (Harlequin).

WRITERS CONFERENCES RWA Conferences; Asilomar; BookExpo America; Bouchercon; Maui Writers Conference.

TIPS "Include SASE with all correspondence. I am taking on published authors only."

◎ ANN TOBIAS: A LITERARY AGENCY FOR CHILDREN'S BOOKS

520 E. 84th St., Apt. 4L, New York NY 10028. **E-mail:** AnnTobias84@hotmail.com. **Contact:** Ann Tobias. Estab. 1988. Represents 25 clients. 10% of clients are new/unpublished writers. Currently handles juvenile books (100%).

REPRESENTS Juvenile and young adult. **Considers these fiction areas:** picture books, poetry, poetry in translation, young adult illustrated mss; mid-level novels.

☞ This agency specializes in books for children.

HOW TO CONTACT For all age groups and genres: Send a one-page letter of inquiry accompanied by a one-page writing sample, double-spaced. No attachments will be opened. Other Responds in 2 months to mss. Obtains most new clients through recommendations from editors.

TERMS Agent receives 15% commission on domestic sales. Agent receives 20% commission on foreign sales. This agency charges clients for photocopying, overnight mail, foreign postage, foreign telephone.

WRITERS CONFERENCES 3LiteraryAgents.com. For questions, contact info@3literaryagents.com.

TIPS "Read at least 200 children's books in the age group and genre in which you hope to be published. Follow this by reading another 100 children's books in other age groups and genres so you will have a feel for the field as a whole."

◎● TRANSATLANTIC LITERARY AGENCY

2 Bloor St., Suite 3500, Toronto ON M4W 1A8 Canada. **E-mail:** info@tla1.com. **Website:** www.tla1.com. Represents 250 clients. 10% of clients are new/unpublished writers. Currently handles nonfiction books (30%), novels (15%), juvenile books (50%), textbooks (5%).

MEMBER AGENTS Lynn Bennett, Lynn@tla1.com, (juvenile and young adult fiction); Shaun Bradley, Shaun@tla1.com (literary fiction and narrative nonfiction); Marie Campbell, Marie@tla1.com (literary juvenile and young adult fiction); Andrea Cascardi, Andrea@tla1.com (literary juvenile and young adult fiction); Samantha Haywood, Sam@tla1.com (literary fiction, narrative nonfiction and graphic novels); Don Sedgwick, Don@tla1.com (literary fiction and narrative nonfiction).

REPRESENTS Nonfiction books, novels, juvenile. **Considers these fiction areas:** juvenile, literary, mainstream, mystery, suspense, young adult.

☞ "In both children's and adult literature, we market directly into the United States, the United Kingdom and Canada." Actively seeking literary children's and adult fiction, nonfiction. Does not want to receive picture books, poetry, screenplays or stage plays.

HOW TO CONTACT Submit e-query with synopsis, 2 sample chapters, bio. Always refer to the website, as guidelines will change. Also refer to website for appropriate agent contact info to send e-query. Responds in 2 weeks to queries. Obtains most new clients through recommendations from others.

TERMS Agent receives 15% commission on domestic sales. Agent receives 20% commission on foreign sales. Offers written contract; 45-day notice must be given to terminate contract. This agency charges for photocopying and postage when it exceeds $100.

RECENT SALES Sold 250 titles in the last year.

◐● TRIADA U.S. LITERARY AGENCY, INC.

P.O. Box 561, Sewickley PA 15143. (412)401-3376. **E-mail:** uwe@triadaus.com. **Website:** www.triadaus.com. **Contact:** Dr. Uwe Stender. Member of AAR. Represents 65 clients. 20% of clients are new/unpublished writers.

REPRESENTS Fiction, nonfiction. **Considers these fiction areas:** action, adventure, crime, detective, ethnic, historical, horror, juvenile, literary, mainstream, mystery, occult, police, romance, women's especially young adult, women's fiction, and mysteries.

☞ "We are looking for great writing and story platforms. Our response time is fairly unique. We recognize that neither we nor the authors have time to waste, so we guarantee a 5-day response time. We usually respond within 24 hours. " Actively looking for both fiction and nonfiction in all areas.

HOW TO CONTACT E-mail queries preferred; otherwise query with SASE. Accepts simultaneous submissions. Responds in 1-5 weeks to queries. Responds in 2-6 weeks to mss. Obtains most new clients through recommendations from others, conferences.

TERMS Agent receives 15% commission on domestic sales. Agent receives 20% commission on foreign sales. Offers written contract; 30-day notice must be given to terminate contract.

RECENT SALES *The Man Whisperer,* by Samantha Brett and Donna Sozio (Adams Media); *Whatever Happened to Pudding Pops*, by Gael Fashingbauer Cooper and Brian Bellmont (Penguin/Perigee); *86'd*, by Dan Fante (Harper Perennial); *Hating Olivia*, by Mark SaFranko (Harper Perennial); *Everything I'm Not Made Me Everything I Am*, by Jeff Johnson (Smiley Books).

TIPS "I comment on all requested manuscripts that I reject."

✚ THE UNTER AGENCY

23 W. 73rd St., Suite 100, New York NY 10023. (212)401-4068. **E-mail:** Jennifer@theunteragency.com. **Website:** www.theunteragency.com. **Contact:** Jennifer Unter. Estab. 2008.

REPRESENTS Considers these fiction areas: commercial, mainstream, picture books, young adult.

☞ This agency specializes in children's and nonfiction, but does take quality fiction.

HOW TO CONTACT Send an e-query.

✚🌓 UPSTART CROW LITERARY

P.O. Box 25404, Brooklyn NY 11202. **E-mail:** info@upstartcrowliterary.com. **E-mail:** chris.submission@gmail.com. **Website:** www.upstartcrowliterary.com. **Contact:** Chris Richman. Estab. 2009.

MEMBER AGENTS Michael Stearns; Chris Richman (special interest in books for boys, books with unforgettable characters, and fantasy that doesn't take itself too seriously); Danielle Chiotti (books ranging from contemporary women's fiction to narrative nonfiction, from romance to relationship stories, humorous tales and young adult fiction); Ted Malawer (accepting queries only through conference submissions and client referrals).

REPRESENTS Considers these fiction areas: women's, young adult middle grade.

HOW TO CONTACT This agency likes submissions sent via e-mails to Chris Richman or Danielle Chiotti.

🌓 VENTURE LITERARY

2683 Via de la Valle, G-714, Del Mar CA 92014. (619)807-1887. **Fax:** (772)365-8321. **E-mail:** submissions@ventureliterary.com. **Website:** www.ventureliterary.com. **Contact:** Frank R. Scatoni. Represents 50 clients. 40% of clients are new/unpublished writers. Currently handles nonfiction books (80%), novels (20%).

💬 Prior to becoming an agent, Mr. Scatoni worked as an editor at Simon & Schuster.

MEMBER AGENTS Frank R. Scatoni (general nonfiction, biography, memoir, narrative nonfiction, sports, serious nonfiction, graphic novels, narratives).

REPRESENTS Nonfiction books, novels graphic novels, narratives. **Considers these fiction areas:** action, adventure, crime, detective, literary, mainstream, mystery, police, sports, suspense, thriller, women's.

☞ Specializes in nonfiction, sports, biography, gambling, and nonfiction narratives. Actively seeking nonfiction, graphic novels and narra-

tives. Does not want fantasy, sci-fi, romance, children's picture books, or Westerns.

HOW TO CONTACT Considers e-mail queries only. *No unsolicited mss* and no snail mail whatsoever. See website for complete submission guidelines. Obtains most new clients through recommendations from others.

TERMS Agent receives 15% commission on domestic sales. Agent receives 20% commission on foreign sales. Offers written contract.

RECENT SALES *The 9/11 Report: A Graphic Adaptation*, by Sid Jacobson and Ernie Colon (FSG); *Having a Baby* by Cindy Margolis (Perigee/Penguin); *Phil Gordon's Little Blue Book*, by Phil Gordon (Simon & Schuster); *Atomic America*, by Todd Tucker (Free Press); *War as They Knew It*, by Michael Rosenberg (Grand Central); *Game Day*, by Craig James (Wiley); *The Blueprint* by Christopher Price (Thomas Dunne Books).

🌓 BETH VESEL LITERARY AGENCY

80 Fifth Ave., Suite 1101, New York NY 10011. (212)924-4252. **E-mail:** kezia@bvlit.com. **Contact:** Kezia Toth, assistant. Represents 65 clients. 10% of clients are new/unpublished writers. Currently handles nonfiction books (75%), novels (10%), story collections (5%), scholarly books (10%).

REPRESENTS Nonfiction books, novels. **Considers these fiction areas:** crime, detective, literary, police Francophone novels.

☞ "My specialties include serious nonfiction, psychology, cultural criticism, memoir, and women's issues." Actively seeking cultural criticism, literary psychological thrillers, and sophisticated memoirs. No uninspired psychology or run-of-the-mill first novels.

HOW TO CONTACT Query with SASE. Accepts simultaneous submissions. Responds in 2 weeks to queries. Responds in 1 month to mss. Obtains most new clients through referrals, reading good magazines, contacting professionals with ideas.

TERMS Agent receives 15% commission on domestic sales. Agent receives 20% commission on foreign sales. Offers written contract.

RECENT SALES Steve Silberman, *Neurotribes* to Penguin; Vicki Robin, *Blessing the Hands That Feed Us*, Viking; Christina Baker Kline, *Phantom Street*, William Morrowl Greg Tate, *James Browns' Body*, FSG; Lawrence Diller, *Remembering Ritalin*, Perigee Publishers; Marjorie Garber, *The Use and Abuse of Literature*, Pantheon.

WRITERS CONFERENCES Squaw Valley Writers Workshop, Iowa Summer Writing Festival.

TIPS "Try to find out if you fit on a particular agent's list by looking at his/her books and comparing yours. You can almost always find who represents a book by looking at the acknowledgements."

⦿ JOHN A. WARE LITERARY AGENCY

392 Central Park W., New York NY 10025. (212)866-4733. **Fax:** (212)866-4734. **Contact:** John Ware. Represents 60 clients. 40%% of clients are new/unpublished writers. Currently handles nonfiction books (75%), novels (25%).

REPRESENTS Nonfiction books, novels. **Considers these fiction areas:** detective, mystery, thriller accessible literary noncategory fiction.

⟞ Does not want personal memoirs.

HOW TO CONTACT Query with SASE. Send a letter only. Accepts simultaneous submissions. Responds in 2 weeks to queries.

TERMS Agent receives 15% commission on domestic sales, 20% commission on foreign sales, film.

RECENT SALES *One Shot at Forever*, by Chris Ballard (Hyperion); *Knights of The Sea*, by David Hanna (New American Library); *Becoming Clementine*, by Jennifer Niven (Plume); *Kosher USA*, by Roger Horowitz (Columbia); *The River's Own*, by Travis Hugh Culley (Random House).

TIPS "Writers must have appropriate credentials for authorship of proposal (nonfiction); no publishing track record required. I am open to good writing and interesting ideas by new or veteran writers."

⦿ IRENE WEBB LITERARY

551 W. Cordova Rd. #238, Santa Fe NM 87505. (505)988-1817. **E-mail:** webblit@gmail.com. **Website:** www.irenewebb.com. **Contact:** Irene Webb.

REPRESENTS Nonfiction books, novels. **Considers these fiction areas:** commercial, crime, horror, mystery, suspense, thriller, women's, young adult middle grade, literary and commercial fiction.

⟞ "Irene Webb Literary is known as one of the top boutique agencies selling books to film and TV. We have close relationships with top film producers and talent in Hollywood." Does not want to receive unsolicited manuscripts or screenplays.

HOW TO CONTACT Query via e-mail only. Obtains most new clients through recommendations from others, solicitations.

RECENT SALES *Secrets of a Soap Opera Diva*, by Victoria Rowell (Atria); *Now I Can See the Moon*, by Elaine Hall (Harper Studio); *Dead Write*, by Sheila Low (NAL); *East to the Dawn*, by Susan Butler (Fox Studio for the Amelia Earhart Story starring Hilary Swank).

⦿ THE WEINGEL-FIDEL AGENCY

310 E. 46th St., 21E, New York NY 10017. (212)599-2959. **Contact:** Loretta Weingel-Fidel. Currently handles nonfiction books (75%), novels (25%).

REPRESENTS Nonfiction books, novels. **Considers these fiction areas:** literary, mainstream.

⟞ This agency specializes in commercial and literary fiction and nonfiction. Actively seeking investigative journalism. Does not want to receive genre fiction, self-help, science fiction, or fantasy.

HOW TO CONTACT Accepts writers by referral only. *No unsolicited mss.*

TERMS Agent receives 15% commission on domestic sales. Agent receives 20% commission on foreign sales. Offers written contract, binding for 1 year with automatic renewal. Bills sent back to clients are all reasonable expenses, such as UPS, express mail, photocopying, etc.

TIPS "A very small, selective list enables me to work very closely with my clients to develop and nurture talent. I only take on projects and writers about which I am extremely enthusiastic."

⦿ LARRY WEISSMAN LITERARY, LLC

526 8th St., #2R, Brooklyn NY 11215. **E-mail:** lwsubmissions@gmail.com. **Contact:** Larry Weissman. Represents 35 clients. Currently handles nonfiction books (80%), novels (10%), story collections (10%).

REPRESENTS Nonfiction books, novels, short story collections. **Considers these fiction areas:** literary.

⟞ "Very interested in established journalists with bold voices. Interested in anything to do with food. Fiction has to feel 'vital' and short stories are accepted, but only if you can sell us on an idea for a novel as well." Nonfiction, including food and lifestyle, politics, pop culture, narrative, cultural/social issues, journalism. No genre fiction, poetry or children's.

HOW TO CONTACT "Send e-queries only. If you don't hear back, your project was not right for our list."

TERMS Agent receives 15% commission on domestic sales. Agent receives 20% commission on foreign sales.

● WM CLARK ASSOCIATES

186 Fifth Ave., Second Floor, New York NY 10010. (212)675-2784. **Fax:** (347)-649-9262. **E-mail:** general@wmclark.com. **Website:** www.wmclark.com. Estab. 1997. Member of AAR. 50% of clients are new/unpublished writers. Currently handles nonfiction books (50%), novels (50%).

REPRESENTS Nonfiction books, novels. **Considers these fiction areas:** contemporary issues, ethnic, historical, literary, mainstream Southern fiction.

&—★ William Clark represents a wide range of titles across all formats to the publishing, motion picture, television, and new media fields on behalf of authors of first fiction and award-winning, best-selling narrative nonfiction, international authors in translation, chefs, musicians, and artists. Offering individual focus and a global presence, the agency undertakes to discover, develop, and market today's most interesting content and the talent that create it, and forge sophisticated and innovative plans for self-promotion, reliable revenue streams, and an enduring creative career. Referral partners are available to provide services including editorial consultation, media training, lecture booking, marketing support, and public relations. Agency does not respond to screenplays or screenplay pitches. It is advised that before querying you become familiar with the kinds of books we handle by browsing our Book List, which is available on our website.

HOW TO CONTACT Accepts queries via online form only at www.wmclark.com/queryguidelines.html. We respond to all queries submitted via this form. Responds in 1-2 months to queries.

TERMS Agent receives 15% commission on domestic sales. Agent receives 20% commission on foreign sales. Offers written contract.

TIPS "WCA works on a reciprocal basis with Ed Victor Ltd. (UK) in representing select properties to the US market and vice versa. Translation rights are sold directly in the German, Italian, Spanish, Portuguese, Latin American, French, Dutch, and Scandinavian territories in association with Andrew Nurnberg Associates Ltd. (UK); through offices in China, Bulgaria, Czech Republic, Latvia, Poland, Hungary, and Russia; and through corresponding agents in Japan, Greece, Israel, Turkey, Korea, Taiwan, and Thailand."

○ WOLFSON LITERARY AGENCY

P.O. Box 266, New York NY 10276. **E-mail:** query@wolfsonliterary.com. **Website:** www.wolfsonliterary.com/. **Contact:** Michelle Wolfson. Adheres to AAR canon of ethics. Currently handles nonfiction books (70%), novels (30%).

REPRESENTS Nonfiction books, novels. **Considers these fiction areas:** mainstream, mystery, romance, suspense, thriller, women's, young adult.

&—★ Actively seeking commercial fiction, mainstream, mysteries, thrillers, suspense, women's fiction, romance, YA, practical nonfiction (particularly of interest to women), advice, medical, pop culture, humor, business.

HOW TO CONTACT E-queries only! Accepts simultaneous submissions. Responds only if interested. Positive response is generally given within 2-4 weeks. Responds in 3 months to mss. Obtains most new clients through recommendations from others, solicitations.

TERMS Agent receives 15% commission on domestic sales. Agent receives 25% commission on foreign sales. Offers written contract; 30-day notice must be given to terminate contract.

WRITERS CONFERENCES SDSU Writers' Conference; New Jersey Romance Writers of America Writers' Conference; American Independent Writers Conference in Washington DC.

TIPS "Be persistent."

● WRITERS' REPRESENTATIVES, LLC

116 W. 14th St., 11th Floor, New York NY 10011-7305. **Fax:** (212)620-0023. **E-mail:** transom@writersreps.com. **Website:** www.writersreps.com. Represents 130 clients. 10% of clients are new/unpublished writers. Currently handles nonfiction books (90%), novels (10%).

MEMBER AGENTS Lynn Chu, Glen Hartley, Christine Hsu.

REPRESENTS Nonfiction books, novels. **Considers these fiction areas:** literary.

&—★ Serious nonfiction and quality fiction. No motion picture or television screenplays.

HOW TO CONTACT Query with SASE. Prefers to read materials exclusively. Considers simultaneous queries, but must be informed at time of submission.

TERMS Agent receives 15% commission on domestic sales. Agent receives 20% commission on foreign sales.

TIPS "Always include a SASE; it will ensure a response from the agent and the return of your submitted material."

⬤ HELEN ZIMMERMANN LITERARY AGENCY

3 Emmy Lane, New Paltz NY 12561. (845)256-0977. **Fax:** (845)256-0979. **E-mail:** Helen@ZimmAgency.com. **Website:** www.zimmermannliterary.com. **Contact:** Helen Zimmermann. Estab. 2003. Represents 25 clients. 50% of clients are new/unpublished writers. Currently handles nonfiction books (80%), other (20% fiction).

REPRESENTS Nonfiction books, novels. **Considers these fiction areas:** family saga, historical, literary, mystery, suspense.

8—⚷ "As an agent who has experience at both a publishing house and a bookstore, I have a keen insight for viable projects. This experience also helps me ensure every client gets published well, through the whole process." Actively seeking memoirs, pop culture, women's issues, and accessible literary fiction. Does not want to receive horror, science fiction, poetry or romance.

HOW TO CONTACT Accepts e-mail queries only. E-mail should include a short description of project and bio, whether it be fiction or nonfiction. Accepts simultaneous submissions. Responds in 2 weeks to queries. Responds in 1 month to mss. Obtains most new clients through recommendations from others, solicitations.

TERMS Agent receives 15% commission on domestic sales. Offers written contract; 30-day notice must be given to terminate contract. Charges for photocopying and postage (reimbursed if project is sold).

RECENT SALES *She Bets Her Life: Women and Gambling*, by Mary Sojourner (Seal Press); *Seeds: One Man's Quest to Preserve the Trees of America's Most Famous People*, by Rick Horan (HarperCollins); *Saddled*, by Susan Richards (Houghton Mifflin Harcourt); *Final Target*, by Steven Gore (HarperPerennial); *Liberated Body, Captive Mind: A WWII POW Memoir*, by Normal Bussel (Pegasus Books).

WRITERS CONFERENCES BEA/Writer's Digest Books Writers' Conference; Portland, ME Writers Conference; Berkshire Writers and Readers Conference.

LITERARY MAGAZINES

//

This section contains markets for your literary short fiction. Although definitions of what constitutes "literary" writing vary, editors of literary journals agree they want to publish the best fiction they can acquire. Qualities they look for in fiction include fully developed characters, strong and unique narrative voice, flawless mechanics, and careful attention to detail in content and manuscript preparation. Most of the authors writing such fiction are well read and well educated, and many are students and graduates of university creative writing programs.

Please also review our Online Markets section for electronic literary magazines. At a time when paper and publishing costs rise while funding to small and university presses continues to be cut or eliminated, electronic literary magazines are helping generate a publishing renaissance for experimental as well as more traditional literary fiction. These electronic outlets for literary fiction also benefit writers by eliminating copying and postage costs, and providing the opportunity for much quicker responses to submissions. Also notice that some magazines with websites give specific information about what they offer online, including updated writer's guidelines and sample fiction from their publications.

STEPPING STONES TO RECOGNITION

Some well-established literary journals pay several hundred or even several thousand dollars for a short story. Most, though, can only pay with contributor's copies or a subscription to their publication. However, being published in literary journals offers the important benefits of experience, exposure and prestige. Agents and major book publishers regularly read literary magazines in search of new writers. Work from these journals is also selected for inclusion in annual prize anthologies.

You'll find most of the well-known prestigious literary journals listed here. Many, including *The Southern Review* and *Ploughshares*, are associated with universities, while others like *The Paris Review* are independently published.

SELECTING THE RIGHT LITERARY JOURNAL

Once you have browsed through this section and have a list of journals you might like to submit to, read those listings again carefully. Remember this is information editors provide to help you submit work that fits their needs. "You've Got a Story" will guide you through the process of finding markets for your fiction.

Note that you will find some magazines that do not read submissions all year long. Whether limited reading periods are tied to a university schedule or meant to accommodate the capabilities of a very small staff, those periods are noted within listings (when the editors notify us). The staffs of university journals are usually made up of student editors and a managing editor who is also a faculty member. These staffs often change every year. Whenever possible, we indicate this in listings and give the name of the current editor and the length of that editor's term. Also be aware that the schedule of a university journal usually coincides with that university's academic year, meaning that the editors of most university publications are difficult or impossible to reach during the summer.

FURTHERING YOUR SEARCH

It cannot be stressed enough that reading the listings for literary journals is only the first part of developing your marketing plan. The second part, equally important, is to obtain fiction guidelines and to read with great care the actual journal you'd like to submit to. Reading copies of these journals helps you determine the fine points of each magazine's publishing style and sensibility. There is no substitute for this type of hands-on research.

Unlike commercial periodicals available at most newsstands and bookstores, it requires a little more effort to obtain some of the magazines listed here. The super-chain bookstores are doing a better job these days of stocking literaries, and you can find some in independent and college bookstores, especially those published in your area. The Internet is an invaluable resource for submission guidelines, as more and more journals establish an online presence. You may, however, need to send for a sample copy. We include sample copy prices in the listings whenever possible. In addition to reading your sample copies, pay close attention to the **Tips** section of each listing. There you'll often find a very specific description of the style of fiction the editors at that publication prefer.

Another way to find out more about literary magazines is to check out the various prize anthologies and take note of journals whose fiction is being selected for publication in them. Studying prize anthologies not only lets you know which magazines are publishing award-winning work, but it also provides a valuable overview of what is considered to be the best fiction published today. Those anthologies include:

- *Best American Short Stories*, published by Houghton Mifflin.
- *New Stories from the South: The Year's Best*, published by Algonquin Books of Chapel Hill.
- *The O. Henry Prize Stories*, published by Doubleday/Anchor.
- *Pushcart Prize: Best of the Small Presses*, published by Pushcart Press.

At the beginnings of listings, we include symbols to help you narrow your search. Keys to those symbols can be found on the inside covers of this book.

❶ ACM (ANOTHER CHICAGO MAGAZINE)

P.O. Box 408439, Chicago IL 60640. **Website:** www.anotherchicagomagazine.net. **Contact:** Jacob S. Knabb, editor-in-chief. Estab. 1977. Magazine: 512×812; 200-220 pages; "art folio each issue." Biannual. Estab. 1977. Circ. 2,000. "*Another Chicago Magazine* is a literary magazine that publishes work by both new and established writers. We look for work that goes beyond the artistic and academic to include and address the larger world. The editors read submissions in Fiction, Poetry, Creative Nonfiction, and Et Al. year round. We often publish special theme issues and sections. We will post upcoming themes on our website. Fiction: Short stories and novel excerpts of 15-20 pages or less. Poetry: Usually no more than 4 pages. Creative Nonfiction: Usually no more than 20 pages. Et Al.: Work that doesn't quite fit into the other genres such as Word & Image Texts, Satire, and Interviews."

NEEDS Ethnic/multicultural, experimental, feminist, gay, lesbian, literary, translations, contemporary, prose poem. No religious, strictly genre or editorial. Receives 300 unsolicited mss/month. Reads mss from February 1 to August 31. Publishes ms 6-12 months after acceptance. **Publishes 10 new writers/year.** Recently published work by Stuart Dybek and Steve Almond. Short stories and novel excerpts of 15-20 pages or less.

HOW TO CONTACT "Please include the following contact information in your cover letter and on your ms: Byline (name as you want it to appear if published), mailing address, phone number, and e-mail. Include a self-addressed stamped envelope (SASE). If a SASE is not enclosed, you will only hear from us if we are interested in your work. Include the genre (e.g., fiction, et al.) of your work in the address." Responds in 3 months to queries; 6 months to mss. Accepts simultaneous, multiple submissions. Sample copy for $8 ppd. Writer's guidelines online.

PAYMENT/TERMS Pays small honorarium when possible, contributor's copies and 1 year subscription. Acquires first North American serial rights.

❶❸ ALASKA QUARTERLY REVIEW

ESB 208, University of Alaska-Anchorage, 3211 Providence Dr., Anchorage AK 99508. (907)786-6916. **E-mail:** aqr@uaa.alaska.edu. **Website:** www.uaa.alaska.edu/aqr. **Contact:** Ronald Spatz. Estab. 1982. Magazine: 6×9; 232-300 pages; 60 lb. Glatfelter paper; 12 pt. C15 black ink or 4-color; varnish cover stock; photos on cover and photo essays. AQR "publishes fiction, poetry, literary nonfiction and short plays in traditional and experimental styles." Semiannual. Circ. 2,700. "*AQR* publishes fiction, poetry, literary nonfiction and short plays in traditional and experimental styles."

NEEDS Experimental, literary, translations, contemporary, prose poem. "If the works in *Alaska Quarterly Review* have certain characteristics, they are these: freshness, honesty and a compelling subject. We look for the demonstration of craft, making the situation palpable and putting it in a form where it becomes emotionally and intellectually complex. Many of the pieces published in the *Alaska Quarterly Review* concern everyday life. We're not asking our writers to go outside themselves and their experiences to the absolute exotic to catch our interest. We look for the experiential and revelatory qualities of the work. We will, without hesitation, champion a piece that may be less polished or stylistically sophisticated, if it engages, surprises, and resonates. The joy in reading such a work is in discovering something true. Moreover, in keeping with our mission to publish new writers, we are looking for voices our readers do not know, and that, in all instances, have something important to convey." Receives 500 unsolicited mss/month. Accepts 7-18 mss/issue; 15-30 mss/year. Does not read mss May 10-August 25. Publishes ms 6 months after acceptance. **Publishes 6 new writers/year.** Recently published work by Linda LeGarde Grover, Scott Bear Don't Walk, Don Lago, Mark Wisniewski, Bojan Louis, Kirstin Allio, Aurelie Sheehan, Victoria Patterson, Amy Hempel, Lily Tuck, Christopher Kennedy, Julia Salvin, Bernard Cooper, Edith Pearlman. Publishes short shorts. Responds in 4 months to queries; responds in 4 months to mss. Simultaneous submissions "undesirable, but will accept if indicated." Sample copy for $6. Writer's guidelines online. No romance, children's, or inspirational/religious. not exceeding 100 pages

PAYMENT/TERMS Pays $50-200 subject to funding; pays in contributor's copies and subscriptions when funding is limited. Honorariums on publication when funding permits. Acquires first North American serial rights. Upon request, rights will be transferred back to author after publication. Pays $50-200 subject to funding; pays in contributor's copies and subscriptions when funding is limited.

❶ AMERICAN LITERARY REVIEW

University of North Texas, P.O. Box 311307, Denton TX 76203-1307. (940)565-2755. **E-mail:** americanliteraryreview@gmail.com; bond@unt.edu. **Website:** www.engl.unt.edu/alr. Estab. 1990. Magazine: 6×9; 128 pages; 70 lb. Mohawk paper; 67 lb. Wausau Vellum cover. "Publishes quality, contemporary poems and stories." Semi-annual. Circ. 1,200. "The *American Literary Review* welcomes submissions of previously unpublished poems, short stories, and creative non-fiction. We also accept submissions for cover art. Please include an SASE and cover letter with your submission. Also include enough postage to return your work. Please mark envelopes and cover letters 'Fiction', 'Poetry', or 'Nonfiction'. Simultaneous submissions are acceptable if noted in your cover letter. For any questions not covered in this section, please refer to our 'Frequently Asked Questions' page. Our reading period extends from October 1 to May 1. Unsolicited manuscripts received outside this reading period will be returned unread. Currently, we do not accept submissions via email. Submissions should be directed to the appropriate editor (Fiction, Poetry, Nonfiction, or Art)."

NEEDS Literary, mainstream. "No genre works." Receives 150-200 unsolicited mss/month. Accepts 5-6 mss/issue; 12-16 mss/year. Reading period: October 1-May 1. Publishes ms within 2 years after acceptance. Recently published work by Marylee MacDonald, Michael Isaac Shokrian, Arthur Brown, Roy Bentley, Julie Marie Wade, and Karin Forfota Poklen. Also publishes creative nonfiction, poetry. Critiques or comments on rejected mss. "We would like to see more short shorts and stylistically innovative and risk-taking fiction. We like to see stories that illuminate the various layers of characters and their situations with great artistry. Give us distinctive character-driven stories that explore the complexities of human existence." Looks for "the small moments that contain more than at first possible, that surprise us with more truth than we thought we had a right to expect." Length: 8,000 words or less.

HOW TO CONTACT Send complete ms with cover letter. Responds in 2-4 months to mss. Accepts simultaneous submissions. Sample copy for $8. Writer's guidelines for #10 SASE. "Submit only one story at a time. *American Literary Review* seeks distinctive, character-driven stories. Please mark envelopes and cover letters "Fiction". We have no set maximum for length, but stories under 8,000 words have the best chance of publication. We generally avoid novel excerpts unless they can stand alone as stories."

PAYMENT/TERMS Pays in contributor's copies. Acquires one time rights.

❶❸ AMERICAN SHORT FICTION

Badgerdog Literary Publishing, P.O. Box 301209, Austin TX 78703. (512) 538-1305. **Fax:** (512) 538-1306. **E-mail:** editors@americanshortfiction.org. **E-mail:** submissions@americanshortfiction.org. **Website:** www.americanshortfiction.org. **Contact:** Jill Myers, editor. Estab. 1991. Badgerdog launches and sustains young writers through its writers in the schools program, and supports emerging professional writers with its award-winning publication, *American Short Fiction*.

NEEDS "Open to publishing mystery or speculative fiction if we feel it has literary value." Does not want young adult or genre fiction. Length: 2,000-15,000 words. Average length: 6,000 words. Publishes short shorts. Average length of short shorts: 500 words.

HOW TO CONTACT Regular submissions are open. "We have recently switched to online submissions. Submitters should visit our publisher's online store to pay the submission fee. When the transaction is complete, submitters will be directed to our Submission Manager, where they can upload their stories. Our **Submission Manager requires that uploaded files be less than 500 KB.** Send complete ms."

PAYMENT/TERMS Writers receive $250-500, 2 contributor's copies, free subscription to the magazine. Additional copies $5.

❶ AMOSKEAG, THE JOURNAL OF SOUTHERN NEW HAMPSHIRE UNIVERSITY

2500 N. River Rd., Manchester NH 03106. **E-mail:** m.brien@snhu.edu. **Website:** www.amoskeagjournal.com. **Contact:** Michael J. Brien, editor. Estab. 1983; literary journal since 2005. Magazine has revolving editor and occasional themes (see website). Editorial term: 3 yrs. Literary magazine/journal. 6×9, 105-130 pages. Contains photographs. "We select fiction, creative nonfiction and poetry that appeals to general readers, writers, and academics alike. We accept work from writers nationwide, but also try to include New England writers. We tend not to accept much experimental work, but the language of poetry or prose must nevertheless be dense, careful and surprising." Annual.

NEEDS Ethnic/multicultural (general), experimental, feminist, gay, humor/satire, literary. Does not want genre fiction. Receives 200 mss/month. Accepts 10 prose mss and 20-25 poems/issue. Does not read December-July. Reading period is Aug-Dec. Ms published in late April. Published Ann Hood, Donald Hall, Craig Childs, Diane Les Becquets, Maxine Kumin, Jonathan Blake, Philip Dacey, Charles Harper Webb. Fiction and Creative Nonfiction. Publishes short shorts. Also publishes poetry. Sometimes comments on/critiques rejected mss. Does not want genre fiction.

HOW TO CONTACT Send complete ms with cover letter. Include brief bio, list of publications. Responds to queries in 1 month. Responds to mss in 4-5 months. Send either SASE (or IRC) for return of ms or disposable copy of ms and #10 SASE or email address for reply only. Considers simultaneous submissions, multiple submissions. Sample copy available for $6. Guidelines on website.

PAYMENT/TERMS Writers aren't paid, but receive 2 contributor's copies. Additional copies $7. Acquires one-time rights. Publication is copyrighted.

APALACHEE REVIEW

Apalachee Press, P.O. Box 10469, Tallahassee FL 32302. (850)644-9114. **E-mail:** arsubmissions@hotmail.com (for queries outside of the U.S.). **Website:** http://apalacheereview.org/index.html. **Contact:** Michael Trammell, editor; Mary Jane Ryals, fiction editor. Estab. 1976. Literary magazine/journal: trade paperback size, 100-140 pages. Includes photographs. "At *Apalachee Review*, we are interested in outstanding literary fiction, but we especially like poetry, fiction, and nonfiction that addresses intercultural issues in a domestic or international setting/context." Annual. Circ. 500. Member CLMP.

NEEDS Ethnic/multicultural, edgy, experimental, fantasy/sci-fi (with a literary bent), feminist, historical, humor/satire, literary, mainstream, mystery/suspense, New Age with a literary bent, translations. Does not want cliché-filled genre-oriented fiction. Receives 60-100 mss/month. Accepts 5-10 mss/issue. Manuscript published 1 yr after acceptance. Agented fiction 0.5%. **Publishes 1-2 new writers/year.** Recently published Lu Vickers, Joe Clark, Joe Taylor, Jane Arrowsmith Edwards, Vivian Lawry, Linda Frysh, Charles Harper Webb, Reno Raymond Gwaltney. Length: 600 words (min)-5,500 words (max). Average length: 3,500 words. Publishes short shorts. Average length of short shorts: 250 words. Also publishes literary essays, book reviews, poetry. Send review copies

to Michael Trammell, editor. Sometimes comments on/critiques rejected mss.

HOW TO CONTACT Send complete ms with cover letter. Include brief bio, list of publications. Responds to queries in 4-6 weeks. Responds to mss in 3-14 months. Send either SASE (international authors should see website for "international" guidelines, no IRCs, please) for return of ms or disposable copy of ms and #10 SASE for reply only. Considers simultaneous submissions. Sample copy available for $8 (current issue), $5 (back issue). Guidelines available for SASE, or check the website.

PAYMENT/TERMS Writers receive 2 contributors copies. Additional copies $5/each. Pays on publication. Acquires one time rights, electronic rights. Publication is copyrighted.

APPALACHIAN HERITAGE

CPO 2166, Berea KY 40404. (859)985-3699. **Fax:** (859)985-3903. **E-mail:** george_brosi@berea.edu; appalachianheritage@berea.edu. **Website:** http://community.berea.edu/appalachianheritage. **Contact:** George Brosi. Estab. 1973. Magazine: 6×9; 104 pages; 60 lb. stock; 10 pt. Warrenflo cover; drawings; b&w photos. "*Appalachian Heritage* is a Southern Appalachian literary magazine. We try to keep a balance of fiction, poetry, essays, scholarly works, etc., for a general audience and/or those interested in the Appalachian mountains." Quarterly.

NEEDS Historical, literary, regional. "We do not want to see fiction that has no ties to Southern Appalachia." Receives 60-80 unsolicited mss/month. Accepts 2-3 mss/issue; 12-15 mss/year. Publishes ms 3-6 months after acceptance. **Publishes 8 new writers/year.** Recently published work by Wendell Berry, Sharyn Mcrumb, Jayne Anne Phillips, Silas House, Ron Rash, and Jim Wayne Miller. Publishes short shorts. Occasionally comments on rejected mss.

HOW TO CONTACT Send complete ms. Send SASE for reply, return of ms or send a disposable copy of ms. Responds in 1 month to queries; 6 weeks to mss. Sample copy for $8. Writer's guidelines online.

PAYMENT/TERMS Pays 3 contributor's copies; $8 charge for extras. Acquires first North American serial rights.

ARKANSAS REVIEW

A Journal of Delta Studies, Department of English and Philosophy, P.O. Box 1890, Office: Wilson Hall, State University AR 72467-1890. (870) 972-3043; (870)972-

3674. **Fax:** (870)972-3045. **E-mail:** arkansasreview@astate.edu;. **E-mail:** jcollins@astate.edu; arkansasreview@astate.edu. **Website:** http://altweb.astate.edu/arkreview/. **Contact:** Dr. Janelle Collins, general editor/associate professor of English. Estab. 1998. Triannual magazine: 8¼×11; 64-100 pages; coated, matte paper; matte, 4-color cover stock; illustrations; photos. Publishes articles, fiction, poetry, essays, interviews, reviews, visual art evocative of or responsive to the Mississippi River Delta. Circ. 700. Accepts submissions by e-mail, fax. Send SASE for reply, return of ms or send a disposable copy of ms. Responds in 1 week to queries; 4 months to mss. Sample copy for $7.50. Writer's guidelines for #10 SASE. Pays 3 contributor's copies; additional copies for $5. Acquires first North American serial rights. "All material, creative and scholarly, published in the *Arkansas Review*, must evoke or respond to the natural and/or cultural experience of the Mississippi River Delta region."

NEEDS Literary (essays and criticism), regional (short stories). "No genre fiction. Must have a Delta focus." Receives 30-50 unsolicited mss/month. Accepts 2-3 mss/issue; 5-7 mss/year. Publishes ms 6-12 months after acceptance. Agented fiction 1%. **Publishes 3-4 new writers/year.** Recently published work by Susan Henderson, George Singleton, Scott Ely and Pia Erhart. Also publishes literary essays, poetry. Sometimes comments on rejected mss. 10,000 words maximum

HOW TO CONTACT Send complete ms.

TIPS Submit via mail. E-mails are more likely to be overlooked or lost. Submit a cover letter, but don't try to impress us with credentials or explanations of the submission. Immerse yourself in the literature of the Delta, but provide us with a fresh and original take on its land, its people, its culture. Surprise us. Amuse us. Recognize what makes this region particular as well as universal, and take risks. Help us shape a new Delta literature.

❶ THE AVALON LITERARY REVIEW

CCI Publishing, P.O. Box 780696, Orlando FL 32878. (407)574-7355. **E-mail:** submissions@avalonliteraryreview.com. **Website:** www.avalonliteraryreview.com. **Contact:** Valerie Rubino, managing editor. Estab. 2011. Quarterly magazine. "*The Avalon Literary Review* welcomes work from both published and unpublished writers and poets. We accept submissions of poetry, short fiction, and personal essays. The author's voice and point of view should be unique and clear. We seek pieces which spring from the author's life and experiences. Submissions which explore both the sweet and bitter of life, with a touch of humor, are a good fit for our *Review*. While we appreciate the genres of fantasy, science fiction and horror, our magazine is not the forum for such work."

NEEDS No erotica, science fiction, or horror. Length: 250-5,000.

HOW TO CONTACT Submit complete ms.

PAYMENT/TERMS Pays 5 contributor's copies.

❶ THE BALTIMORE REVIEW

P.O. Box 36418, Towson MD 21286. **Website:** www.baltimorereview.org. **Contact:** Susan Muaddi Darraj, managing editor. Estab. 1996. Semiannual magazine: 6×9; 150 pages; 60 lb. paper; 10 pt. CS1 gloss film cover. Showcase for the best short stories, creative nonfiction and poetry by writers in the Baltimore area and beyond. Accepts 20 mss/issue; approx. 40 mss/year. Publishes ms 1-9 months after acceptance. **Publishes "at least a few" new writers/year.** Average length: 3,000 words. Publishes short shorts. Also publishes poetry. Sample copy: $10, which included postage/handling. "The Baltimore Review publishes poetry, fiction, and creative nonfiction from Baltimore and beyond."

> ○ "We publish work of high literary quality from established and new writers. No specific preferences regarding theme or style, and all are considered."

NEEDS Ethnic/multicultural, literary, mainstream. "No science fiction, westerns, children's, romance, etc." No genre fiction. Length: 100-6,000 words.

HOW TO CONTACT Accepts submissions via online system only. Please visit website. Responds in 4-6 months to mss. Send complete ms.

PAYMENT/TERMS Pays 2 contributor's copies. Acquires first North American serial rights.

❶ BARBARIC YAWP

BoneWorld Publishing, 3700 County Rt. 24, Russell NY 13684-3198. (315)347-2609. **Website:** www.boneworldpublishing.com.

HOW TO CONTACT Send SASE for reply, return of ms or send a disposable copy of ms. Accepts simultaneous, multiple submissions and reprints.

PAYMENT/TERMS Pays 1 contributor's copy; additional copies $3.

TIPS "Don't give up. Read much, write much, submit much. Observe closely the world around you. Don't borrow ideas from TV or films. Revision is often necessary—grit your teeth and do it. Never fear rejection."

○⊙ BELLEVUE LITERARY REVIEW

NYU Langone Medical Center, Department of Medicine, 550 First Ave., OBV-A612, New York NY 10016. (212)263-3973. **E-mail:** info@BLReview.org. **E-mail:** stacy.bodziak@nyumc.org. **Website:** www.blreview. org. **Contact:** Stacy Bodziak, managing editor. Estab. 2001. A Journal of Humanity and Human Experience. Magazine: 6×9; 160 pages. "The *BLR* is a literary journal that examines human existence through the prism of health and healing, illness and disease. We encourage creative interpretations of these themes." Semiannual. Member CLMP.Literary. No genre fiction. Publishes ms 3-6 months after acceptance. Agented fiction 1%. **Publishes 3-6 new writers/year.** Recently published work by Amy Hempel, Sheila Kohler, Martha Cooley. Sample copy for $7. Writer's guidelines for SASE, e-mail or on website.

○ Work published in *Bellevue Literary Review* has appeared in *The Pushcart Prize*.

NEEDS Publishes short shorts. Also publishes literary essays, poetry. Sometimes comments on rejected mss Length: 5,000 words; average length: 2,500 words.
HOW TO CONTACT Submit online at www.blreview. org (preferred). Also accepts mss via regular mail. Send complete ms. Send SASE (or IRC) for return of ms or disposable copy of the ms and #10 SASE for reply only. Responds in 3-6 months to mss. Accepts simultaneous submissions.
PAYMENT/TERMS Pays 2 contributor's copies, 1-year subscription and 1 year gift subscription; additional copies $6. Pays on publication for first North American serial rights. Sends galleys to author.

○○⊙ BELOIT FICTION JOURNAL

Box 11, Beloit, 700 College St., Beloit WI 53511. (608)363-2079. **E-mail:** bfj@beloit.edu. **Website:** www. beloit.edu/english/fictionjournal. **Contact:** Chris Fink, editor-in-chief. Estab. 1985. Literary magazine: 6×9; 250 pages; 60 lb. paper; 10 pt. C1S cover stock; illustrations; photos on cover; ad-free. "We are interested in publishing the best contemporary fiction and are open to all themes except those involving pornographic, religiously dogmatic or politically propagandistic representations. Our magazine is for general readership, though most of our readers will probably have a specific interest in literary magazines." Annual.

○ Work first appearing in *Beloit Fiction Journal* has been reprinted in award-winning collections, including the Flannery O'Connor and the Milkweed Fiction Prize collections, and has won the Iowa Short Fiction award.

NEEDS Literary, mainstream, contemporary. Wants more experimental and short shorts. Would like to see more "stories with a focus on both language and plot, unusual metaphors and vivid characters. No pornography, religious dogma, science fiction, horror, political propaganda or genre fiction." Receives 200 unsolicited mss/month. Accepts 20 mss/year. Publishes ms 9 months after acceptance. **Publishes 3 new writers/year.** Recently published work by Dennis Lehane, Silas House and David Harris Ebenbach. Length: 250-10,000 words; average length: 5,000 words. Sometimes comments on rejected mss.
HOW TO CONTACT "Our reading period is from August 1-December 1 only. " No fax, e-mail, or disk submissions. Responds in 2 weeks to queries; 2 months to mss. Accepts simultaneous submissions if identified as such. Please send one story at a time. Always include SASE. Sample copy for $ 10 (new issue), $8 (back issue, double issue), $ 6 (back issue, single issue). Writer's guidelines for #10 SASE or on website. Literary magazine: 6×9; 250 pages; 60 lb. paper; 10 pt. C1S cover stock; illustrations; photos on cover; ad-free.
PAYMENT/TERMS Buys first North American serial rights only. Payment in copies.
TIPS "Many of our contributors are writers whose work we had previously rejected. Don't let one rejection slip turn you away from our—or any—magazine."

◑ BERKELEY FICTION REVIEW

10B Eshleman Hall, University of California, Berkeley CA 94720. (510)642-2892. **E-mail:** bfictionreview@ yahoo.com. **Website:** www.ocf.berkeley.edu/~bfr. **Contact:** Caitlin McGuire, editor. Estab. 1981. Magazine: 512×812; 180 pages; perfect-bound; glossy cover; some b&w art; photographs. "The mission of Berkeley Fiction Review is to provide a forum for new and emerging writers as well as writers already established. We publish a wide variety of contemporary short fiction for a literary audience." Annual. Circ. 1,000.
NEEDS Experimental, literary, mainstream. "Quality, inventive short fiction. No poetry or formula fiction." Receives 100 unsolicited mss/month. Accepts 10-15 mss/issue. **Publishes 10-15 new writers/year.**

Publishes short shorts. Occasionally comments on rejected mss.

HOW TO CONTACT Responds in 2-4 months to mss. Accepts simultaneous, multiple submissions. Sample copy for $10. Writer's guidelines for SASE and online. Accepts e-mail submissions in PDF or Word attachments.

PAYMENT/TERMS Pays one contributor's copy. Acquires first rights. Sponsors awards/contests.

ⓘ🎧 BIG MUDDY: A JOURNAL OF THE MISSISSIPPI RIVER VALLEY

MS2650 English Dept., Southeast MO State Universit, Cape Girardeau MO 63701. **Website:** www6.semo.edu/universitypress/bigmuddy. **Contact:** Susan Swartwout, publisher/editor. Estab. 2001. Magazine: 812×512 perfect-bound; 150 pages; acid-free paper; color cover stock; layflat lamination; illustrations; photos. "Big Muddy explores multidisciplinary, multicultural issues, people, and events mainly concerning, but not limited to, the 10-state area that borders the Mississippi River. We publish fiction, poetry, historical essays, creative nonfiction, environmental essays, biography, regional events, photography, art, etc." Semiannual. Circ. 500.

NEEDS Adventure, ethnic/multicultural, experimental, family saga, feminist, historical, humor/satire, literary, mainstream, military/war, fiction, nonfiction, poetry, mystery/suspense, regional (Mississippi River Valley; Midwest), translations. "No romance, fantasy or children's." Receives 50 unsolicited mss/month. Accepts 20-25 mss/issue. Publishes ms 6-12 months after acceptance.

HOW TO CONTACT Send SASE for return of ms or send a disposable copy of ms and #10 SASE for reply only. Responds in 12 weeks to mss. Accepts multiple submissions. Sample copy for $6. Writer's guidelines for SASE, e-mail, fax or on website. Reviews fiction, poetry, nonfiction.

PAYMENT/TERMS Pays 2 contributor's copies; additional copies $5. Acquires first North American serial rights.

THE BITTER OLEANDER

4983 Tall Oaks Dr., Fayetteville NY 13066. **Fax:** (315)637-5056. **E-mail:** info@bitteroleander.com. **Website:** www.bitteroleander.com. **Contact:** Paul B. Roth, editor and publisher.

NEEDS Zine specializing in poetry and short fiction: 6×9; 128 pages; 55 lb. paper; 12 pt. CIS cover stock; photos. "We're interested in the surreal; deep image particularization of natural experiences." Bi-annual. Receives 200 unsolicited mss/month. Accepts 4-5 mss/issue; 8-10 mss/year. Does not read in July. Recently published work by Mark Joseph Kiewlak, Judith Taylor Gold, Edwin García Lopez, Eros Alegra Clarke, Norberto Luis Romero (Spain), and Samanta Schweblin (Argentina). Max length: 2,500 words. Publishes short shorts. Also publishes literary essays, poetry. Always comments on rejected mss. Does not want family stories with moralistic plots, and no fantasy that involves hyper-reality of any sort. Length: 300-2,500 words.

HOW TO CONTACT Query. Send mss by mail with SASE for response. Whether you live in the U.S. or outside, we accept e-mail submissions or regular mail submissions if SASE is enclosed.

PAYMENT/TERMS Pays contributor's copies.

ⓘ🎧💲 BLACK WARRIOR REVIEW

P.O. Box 862936, Tuscaloosa AL 35486. (205)348-4518. **E-mail:** bwr@ua.edu; blackwarriorreview@gmail.com. **Website:** www.bwr.ua.edu. **Contact:** Jenny Gropp Hess, editor. Estab. 1974. Magazine: 6×9; 160 pages; color artwork. "We publish contemporary fiction, poetry, reviews, essays and art for a literary audience. We publish the freshest work we can find." Semiannual. Circ. 2,000.

> 🅞 Work that appeared in the *Black Warrior Review* has been included in the *Pushcart Prize* anthology, *Harper's Magazine, Best American Short Stories, Best American Poetry* and *New Stories from the South.*

NEEDS Literary, contemporary, short and short-short fiction. Wants "work that is conscious of form and well crafted. We are open to good experimental writing and short-short fiction. No genre fiction, please." Receives 300 unsolicited mss/month. Accepts 5 mss/issue; 10 mss/year. Unsolicited novel excerpts are not considered unless the novel is already contracted for publication. Publishes ms 6 months after acceptance. **Publishes 5 new writers/year.** Recently published work by Lily Hoang, Brian Evenson, Peter Markus, Aimee Bender, Lance Olson, Laird Hunt, Pamela Ryder, Michael C. Boyko, James Grinwis. Length: 7,500 words; average length: 2,000-5,000 words. Occasionally comments on rejected mss.

HOW TO CONTACT Now takes online submissions exclusively. Responds in 4 months to mss. Accepts simultaneous submissions if noted. Sample copy for $10. Writer's guidelines online. One story/chapter per envelope. Wants work that is conscious of form and well-crafted.

PAYMENT/TERMS Pays up to $100, copies, and a 1-year subscription. Pays on publication for first rights. True

◑ BLUELINE

120 Morey Hall, Dept. of English and Communication, Postdam NY 13676. (315)267-2043. **E-mail:** blueline@potsdam.edu. **Website:** www2.potsdam.edu/blueline. **Contact:** Donald McNutt, editor; Caroline Downing, art editor. Estab. 1979. Magazine: 6×9; 200 pages; 70 lb. white stock paper; 65 lb. smooth cover stock; illustrations; photos. "*Blueline* is interested in quality writing about the Adirondacks or other places similar in geography and spirit. We publish fiction, poetry, personal essays, book reviews and oral history for those interested in Adirondacks, nature in general, and well-crafted writing." Annual. Payment in copies. Submission period is July through November. *Blueline* welcomes electronic submissions, either in the body of an e-mail message or in Word or html formatted files. Please avoid using compression software."

> ◒ Proofread all submissions. It is difficult for our editors to get excited about work containing typographical and syntactic errors.

NEEDS Adventure, humor/satire, literary, regional, contemporary, prose poem, reminiscences, oral history, nature/outdoors. We also welcome short essays or creative nonfiction that interpret the literature or culture of the region, including New York State, New England, and eastern Canada. No urban stories or erotica. Receives 8-10 unsolicited mss/month. Accepts 6-8 mss/issue. Does not read January-August. Publishes ms 3-6 months after acceptance. **Publishes 2 new writers/year.** Recently published work by Joan Connor, Laura Rodley and Ann Mohin. Length: 500-3,000 words; average length: 2,500 words. Also publishes literary essays, poetry. Occasionally comments on rejected mss.

HOW TO CONTACT Accepts simultaneous submissions. Sample copy for $7.

PAYMENT/TERMS Pays 1 contributor's copy; charges $7 each for 3 or more copies. Acquires first rights.

BLUE MESA REVIEW

E-mail: bmreditr@unm.edu. **Website:** www.unm.edu/~bluemesa/index.htm. **Contact:** Suzanne Richar-

son, editor; Bonnie Arning, managing editor. "Originally founded by Rudolfo Anaya, Gene Frumkin, David Johnson, Patricia Clark Smith, and Lee Bartlette in 1989, the Blue Mesa Review emerged as a source of innovative writing produced in the Southwest. Over the years the magazine's nuance has changed, sometimes shifting towards more craft-oriented work, other times re-aligning with its original roots."

> ◒ Open for submissions from September 1 to May 31. Only accepts submissions through online submissions manager.

HOW TO CONTACT Submit up to 30 pages.
TIPS "Always write to us before sending any mss."

◑◒⑤ BOULEVARD

Opojaz, Inc., 6614 Clayton Rd., Box 325, Richmond Heights MO 63117. (314)862-2643. **Fax:** (314)862-2982. **E-mail:** kellyleavitt@boulevardmagazine.org; richardburgin@att.net; richardburgin@netzero.net. **E-mail:** http://boulevard.submishmash.com/submit. **Website:** www.boulevardmagazine.org. **Contact:** Richard Burgin, editor. Estab. 1985. Magazine: 512×812; 150-250 pages; excellent paper; high-quality cover stock; illustrations; photos. "*Boulevard* is a diverse literary magazine presenting original creative work by well-known authors, as well as by writers of exciting promise." Triannual. Receives over 600 unsolicited mss/month. Accepts about 10 mss/issue. Does not accept manuscripts between May 1 and October 1. Publishes ms 9 months after acceptance. **Publishes 10 new writers/year.** Recently published work by Joyce Carol Oates, Floyd Skloot, Alice Hoffman, Stephen Dixon, and Frederick Busch. Length: 9,000 words maximum; average length: 5,000 words. Publishes short shorts. Also publishes literary essays, literary criticism, poetry. Sometimes comments on rejected mss. Send complete ms. Accepts submissions on disk. SASE for reply. Responds in 2 weeks to queries; 3-4 months to mss. Accepts multiple submissions. No simultaneous submissions. Sample copy for $9. Writer's guidelines online.

> ◒ "*Boulevard* has been called 'one of the half-dozen best literary journals' by Poet Laureate Daniel Hoffman in *The Philadelphia Inquirer*. We strive to publish the finest in poetry, fiction and non-fiction."

NEEDS Confessions, experimental, literary, mainstream, novel excerpts. "We do not want erotica, sci-

ence fiction, romance, western or children's stories."
Also sponsors the Short Fiction Contest for Emerging
Writers. $1,500 and publication in Boulevard awarded
to the winning story by a writer who has not yet published a book of fiction, poetry, or creative non-fiction
with a nationally distributed press. All entries must be
postmarked by December 31, 2010. Entry fee is $15 for
each individual story, with no limit per author. Entry
fee includes a one-year subscription to Boulevard (one
per author). Make check payable to Boulevard. 8,000
words maximum.

HOW TO CONTACT Send complete ms. Now takes
online submissions: pdf, doc, docx, txt, rtf, jpg, gif,
mp3, mp4, m4a, zip, tiff, png

PAYMENT/TERMS Pays $50-500. Pays on publica-
tion for first North American serial rights. $50-$500
(sometimes higher) for accepted work

◐◯ THE BRIAR CLIFF REVIEW

3303 Rebecca St., Sioux City IA 51104-0100. (712)279-
5477. **E-mail:** tricia.currans-sheehan@briarcliff.edu
(editor); jeanne.emmons@briarcliff.edu (poetry).
Website: www.briarcliff.edu/bcreview. **Contact:** Tricia Currans-Sheehan, Jeanne Emmons, Phil Hey, Paul
Weber, editors. Estab. 1989. *The Briar Cliff Review*,
published annually in April, is "an attractive, eclectic
literary/art magazine." The *Briar Cliff Review* focuses
on (but is not limited to) "Siouxland writers and subjects. We are happy to proclaim ourselves a regional
publication. It doesn't diminish us; it enhances us."

NEEDS Accepts 5 mss/year. Reads mss only between
August 1 and November 1. **Publishes 10-14 new writ-
ers/year.** Publishes ms 3-4 months after acceptance.
Recently published work by Leslie Barnard, Daryl Murphy, Patrick Hicks, Siobhan Fallon, Shelley
Scaletta, Jenna Blum, Brian Bedard, Rebecca Tuch,
Scott H. Andrews, and Josip Novakovich. "No romance, horror, or alien stories." Length: 2,500-5,000
words; average length: 3,000 words.

HOW TO CONTACT Send SASE for return of ms.
Does not accept electronic submissions (unless from
overseas). Responds in 4-5 months to mss. Seldom
comments on rejected mss. Accepts simultaneous
submissions.

PAYMENT/TERMS Pays 2 contributor's copies; additional copies available for $12.

◐ BRILLANT CORNERS

Lycoming College, Williamsport PA 17701. Estab.
1996. Journal: 6×9; 90 pages; 70 lb. Cougar opaque,

vellum, natural paper; photographs. "We publish jazz-
related literature—fiction, poetry and nonfiction."
Semiannual. Receives 10-15 unsolicited mss/month.
Accepts 1-2 mss/issue; 2-3 mss/year. Publishes ms
4-12 months after acceptance. Publishes short shorts.
Also publishes literary essays, literary criticism, poetry. Rarely comments on rejected mss.

◯ Does not read mss May 15-September 1.

HOW TO CONTACT Submit with SASE for return
of ms or send disposable copy of ms. Accepts unpublished work only.

TIPS "We look for clear, moving prose that dem-
ostrates a love of both writing and jazz. We primarily
publish established writers, but we read all submissions carefully and welcome work by outstanding
young writers."

THE BROADKILL REVIEW

Broadkill Publishing Associates c/o John Milton &
Company, 104 Federal St., Milton DE 19968. **E-mail:**
the_broadkill_review@earthlink.net. **Website:** www.
thebroadkillreview.blogspot.com. **Contact:** Jamie
Brown, editor. Estab. 2005. PDF Literary magazine/
journal. Bimonthly. Contains illustrations, photographs. "Quality is the most important factor. Your
stories and poems should not rely on the unusual cir-
cumstance in place of actually having work which is
finely crafted, insightful of the human condition, or
which manages to make the reader continue to think
about it after they have finished reading it. We are
fans of John Gardner's *On Becoming a Novelist*, and
firmly believe in establishing 'the waking dream' as
the responsibility of the author." Member CLMP, Delaware Press Assn. Does not want anything gratuitous;
no theme issues. Receives 8-20 mss/month. Accepts
1-4 mss/issue; 16-20 mss/year. Manuscript published
1-3 months after acceptance. **Publishes 30 new writ-
ers/year.** Published Thom Wade Myers, Chad Clifton,
Tina Hession, Joshua D. Isard, Maryanne Khan, Richard Myers Peabody, H. A. Maxson, Bob Yearick, Gay-
lene Carbis, Louise D'Arcy, and Andee Jones. Length:
6,000 words (max). Average length: 3,300 words. Publishes short shorts. Also publishes literary essays, literary criticism, book reviews, poetry. Send two review
copies to Editor, The Broadkill Review, 104 Federal
Street, Milton, DE 19968.

◯ "*The Broadkill Review* accepts the best fiction, poetry and nonfiction by new and estab-

lished writers. We have published Pushcart nominated fiction and poetry."

NEEDS No erotica, fantasy, sci-fi 6,000 words/max.

HOW TO CONTACT Send complete ms with cover letter—preferably by e-mail. Include estimated word count, brief bio, list of publications. Responds to queries in 1 week. Responds to mss in 4-26 weeks. Send either SASE (or IRC) for return of ms or disposable copy of ms and #10 SASE for reply only. Considers simultaneous submissions, multiple submissions. Sample copy delivered electronically free upon request. Guidelines available via e-mail. Query

PAYMENT/TERMS Sometimes comments on/critiques rejected mss, if requested by the author. Writers receive contributor's copy. Pays on publication. Acquires first rights. Publication is copyrighted.

CAIRN: THE ST. ANDREWS REVIEW

1700 Dogwood Mile, Laurinburg NC 28352. (910)277-5310. **Fax:** (910)277-5020. **E-mail:** pressemail@sapc.edu. **Website:** www.sapc.edu/sapress.html. Estab. 1969. Magazine: 50-60 lb. paper. "*CAIRN* is a non-profit, national/international literary magazine which publishes established as well as emerging writers." Member CLMP and AWP.

NEEDS Poetry, essays, literary, short stories and short-short fiction. "We're looking for original, well-crafted work with style and insight." **Publishes 10-15 new writers/year.**

HOW TO CONTACT Send a recyclable copy of ms. by postal mail. Include SASE for reply only. Submissions are accepted September through December only. Accepts simultaneous submissions with notice. Responds in 3-4 months.

PAYMENT/TERMS Pays 2 contributor copy.

CALLALOO: A JOURNAL OF AFRICAN DIASPORA ARTS & LETTERS

Department of English, Texas A&M University, 4212 TAMU, College Station TX 77843-4227. (979)458-3108. **Fax:** (979)458-3275. **E-mail:** callaloo@tamu.edu. **Website:** http://callaloo.tamu.edu. Estab. 1976. *Callaloo: A Journal of African Diaspora Arts & Letters*, published quarterly, is devoted to poetry dealing with the African Diaspora, including North America, Europe, Africa, Latin and Central America, South America, and the Caribbean. Has published poetry by Aimeé Ceésaire, Lucille Clifton, Rita Dove, Yusef Komunyakaa, Natasha Tretheway, and Carl Phillips. Features about 15-20 poems (all forms and styles) in

each issue along with short fiction, interviews, literary criticism, and concise critical book reviews. Circulation is 1,600 subscribers of which half are libraries. Subscription: $39, $107 for institutions.

NEEDS Ethnic/multicultural (black culture), feminist, historical, humor/satire, literary, regional, science fiction, serialized novels, translations, contemporary, prose poem. "No romance, confessional. Would like to see more experimental fiction, science fiction and well-crafted literary fiction particularly dealing with the black middle class, immigrant communities and/or the black South." Accepts 3-5 mss/issue; 10-20 mss/year. **Publishes 5-10 new writers/year.** Recently published work by Charles Johnson, Edwidge Danticat, Thomas Glave, Nallo Hopkinson, John Edgar Wideman, Jamaica Kincaid, Percival Everett and Patricia Powell.

TIPS "We look for freshness of both writing and plot, strength of characterization, plausibilty of plot. Read what's being written and published, especially in journals such as *Callaloo*."

CALYX

Calyx, Inc., P.O. Box B, Corvallis OR 97339. (541)753-9384. **Fax:** (541)753-0515. **E-mail:** editor@calyxpress.org. **Website:** www.calyxpress.org. **Contact:** Editor. Estab. 1976. Magazine: 6×8; 128 pages per single issue; 60 lb. coated matte stock paper; 10 pt. chrome coat cover; original art. "*Calyx* exists to publish fine literature and art by women and is committed to publishing the work of all women, including women of color, older women, working class women and other voices that need to be heard. We are committed to discovering and nurturing beginning writers." Biannual. Receives approximately 1,000 unsolicited prose and poetry mss when open. Accepts 4-8 prose mss/issue; 9-15 mss/year. Publishes ms 4-12 months after acceptance. **Publishes 10-20 new writers/year.** Recently published work by M. Evelina Galang, Chitrita Banerji, Diana Ma, Catherine Brady. Responds in 4-12 months to mss. Accepts simultaneous submissions.

NEEDS Prose, poetry, visual art, short fiction, literary essays and literary criticism, interviews and review articles. Length: 5,000 words.

HOW TO CONTACT Reads mss October 1-December 31; submit only during this period. Include SASE. Mss received when not reading will be returned. All submissions (prose, poetry, art, reviews) should include author's name on each page and be accompanied by a brief (50-word or less) biographical statement, a SASE with forever stamp, phone number, and e-mail address. Even if you indicate that it is unnecessary to return your submission(s), please enclose a SASE for your notification. Prose and poetry should be submitted separately with separate SASEs for each submission category.

PAYMENT/TERMS Sample copy for $10 plus $4 postage. "Combination of free issues and 1 volume subscription." Payment dependent upon grant support. Also receive free issues and 1 volume subscription.

○ CC&D, CHILDREN, CHURCHES & DADDIES MAGAZINE: THE UNRELIGIOUS, NONFAMILY-ORIENTED LITERARY AND ART MAGAZINE

Scars Publications and Design, 829 Brian Court, Gurnee IL 60031. (847)281-9070. **E-mail:** ccandd96@scars.tv. **Website:** http://scars.tv/ccd. **Contact:** Janet Kuypers. Estab. 1993. "Our biases are works that relate to issues such as politics, sexism, society, and the like, but are definitely not limited to such. We publish good work that makes you think, that makes you feel like you've lived through a scene instead of merely reading it. If it relates to how the world fits into a person's life (political story, a day in the life, coping with issues people face), it will probably win us over faster. We have received comments from readers and other editors saying that they thought some of our stories really happened. They didn't, but it was nice to know they were so concrete, so believable people thought they were nonfiction. Do that to our readers." Interested in many topics including adventure, ethnic/multicultural, experimental, feminist, gay, historical, lesbian, literary, mystery/suspense, new age, psychic/supernatural/occult, science fiction. Does not want religious or rhyming or family-oriented material. Manuscript published 1 yr after acceptance. Published Mel Waldman, Kenneth DiMaggio, Pat Dixon, Robert William Meyers, Troy Davis, G.A. Scheinoha, Ken Dean. Average length: 1,000 words. "Contact us if you are interested in submitting very long stories, or parts of a novel (if you are accepted, it would appear in parts in multiple issues)." Publishes short shorts, essays and stories. Also publishes poetry. Always comments on/critiques rejected mss if asked.

NEEDS Literary magazine/journal: 5.5x8.5 perfect-bound, 84-page book. Contains illustrations and photographs as well as short stories, essays, and poetry. Monthly.

HOW TO CONTACT Send complete ms with cover letter or query with clips of published work. Prefers submissions by e-mail. "If you have e-mail and send us a snail-mail submission, we will accept writing only if you e-mail it to us." Responds to queries in 2 weeks; mss in 2 weeks. "Responds much faster to e-mail submissions and queries." Send either SASE (or IRC) for return of ms or disposable copy of ms and #10 SASE for reply only, but if you have e-mail PLEASE send us an electronic submission instead. (If we accept your writing, we'll only ask for you to e-mail it to us anyway.) Considers simultaneous submissions, previously published submissions, multiple submissions. Sample copy available of issues before 2010 for $6. Guidelines available for SASE, via e-mail, on website. Reviews fiction, essays, journals, editorials, short fiction.

◐ CENTER

202 Tate Hall, University of Missouri-Columbia, Columbia MO 65211-1500. (573)884-7773. **E-mail:** cla@missouri.edu. **Website:** center.missouri.edu. **Contact:** Managing editor. Estab. 2000. Magazine: 6×9; 150-250 pages; perfect bound, with 4-color card cover. "*Center* publishes poetry, fiction, creative nonfiction, and occasionally, translations. We publish work from a broad range of aesthetic categories and privilege work that is deliberately crafted, engaging, and accessible." Annual. Circ. 500.

NEEDS Ethnic/multicultural, experimental, humor/satire, literary. Receives 40-60 unsolicited mss/month. Accepts 2-4 mss/year. Reads mss from July 1-December 1 only. Publishes ms 6 months after acceptance. **Publishes 35% new writers/year.** Recently published work by Kim Chinquee, William Eisner, and April Ayers Lawson. Publishes short shorts. Also publishes literary essays, poetry. Sometimes comments on rejected mss. **Send submissions July 1-December 1.**

HOW TO CONTACT Send SASE (or IRC) for return of ms or send a disposable copy of ms and #10 SASE for reply only. Responds in 1 month to queries; 3-4 months to mss. Accepts simultaneous, multiple submissions. Sample copy for $3.50, current copy $7. Writer's guidelines online.

PAYMENT/TERMS Pays 2 contributor's copies; additional copies $3.50. Pays on publication for one-time rights.

◑ CHAFFIN JOURNAL

English Department, Eastern Kentucky University, C, Richmond KY 40475-3102. (859)622-3080. **E-mail:**

robert.witt@eku.edu. **Website:** www.english.edu/
chaffin_journal. **Contact:** Robert Witt, editor. Estab.
1998. Magazine: 8×512; 120-130 pages; 70 lb. paper; 80
lb. cover. "We publish fiction on any subject; our only
consideration is the quality." Annual. Circ. 150. Recently published work by Meridith Sue Willis, Marie Ma-
nilla, Raymond Abbott, Marjorie Bixler, Chris Helvey.
NEEDS Ethnic/multicultural, historical, humor/sat-
ire, literary, mainstream, regional (Appalachia). "No
erotica, fantasy." Receives 20 unsolicited mss/month.
Accepts 6-8 mss/year. Does not read mss October
1 through May 31. Publishes ms 6 months after acceptance. **Publishes 2-3 new writers/year.** Length:
10,000 words per submission period; average length:
5,000 words.
HOW TO CONTACT Send SASE for return of ms.
Responds in 1 week to queries; 3 months to mss. Accepts simultaneous, multiple submissions. Sample
copy for $6.
PAYMENT/TERMS Pays 1 contributor's copy; additional copies $6. Pays on publication for one-time rights.
TIPS "All manuscripts submitted are considered."

ⓞⓢ THE CHATTAHOOCHEE REVIEW

The Chattahoochee Review, 555 N. Indian Creek Dr.,
Clarkston GA 30021. **Website:** www.chattahoochee-
review.org. **Contact:** Lydia Ship, managing editor. Estab. 1980. *The Chattahoochee Review*, published quarterly, prints poetry, short fiction, essays, reviews, and
interviews. "We publish a number of Southern writers, but *The Chattahoochee Review* is not by design
a regional magazine. All themes, forms, and styles
are considered as long as they impact the whole person: heart, mind, intuition, and imagination." Has recently published work by George Garrett, Jim Daniels,
Jack Pendarvis, Ignacio Padilla, and Kevin Canty. *The
Chattahoochee Review* is 160 pages, digest-sized, professionally printed, flat-spined, with four-color silk-
matte card cover. Press run is 1,250; 300 are complimentary copies sent to editors and "miscellaneous
VIPs." Subscription: $20/year. Sample: $6.
PAYMENT/TERMS Pays $25/page for fiction and 2
contributor's copies.

ⓞ CHICAGO QUARTERLY REVIEW

517 Sherman Ave., Evanston IL 60202. **Website:** www.
chicagoquarterlyreview.com. **Contact:** Syed Afzal
Haider and Elizabeth McKenzie, editors. Estab. 1994.
Magazine: 6×9; 125 pages; illustrations; photos. Annual. Estab. 1994. Circ. 300.

NEEDS Literary. Receives 60-80 unsolicited mss/
month. Accepts 8-10 mss/issue; 16-20 mss/year. Publishes ms 6 months-1 year after acceptance. Agented
fiction 5%. **Publishes 8-10 new writers/year.** Length:
5,000 words; average length: 2,500 words. Publishes
short shorts. Also publishes literary essays, poetry.
Sometimes comments on rejected mss.
HOW TO CONTACT Send a disposable copy of ms
and #10 SASE for reply only. Responds in 2 months to
queries; 6 months to mss. Accepts simultaneous submissions. Up to 5 poems in a single submission; does
not accept multiple short story submissions. Sample
copy for $9.
PAYMENT/TERMS Pays 2 contributor's copies; additional copies $9. Pays on publication for one-time
rights.

ⓞ CHICAGO REVIEW

5801 S. Kenwood Ave., Chicago IL 60637. **E-mail:**
chicago-review@uchicago.edu. **Website:** humani-
ties.uchicago.edu/orgs/review. **Contact:** P. Genesius
Durica. Estab. 1946. Magazine for a highly literate
general audience: 6×9; 128 pages; offset white 60 lb.
paper; illustrations; photos. Quarterly. Circ. 3,500.
NEEDS Experimental, literary, contemporary. Receives 200 unsolicited mss/month. Accepts 2 mss/is-
sue; 8 mss/year. Recently published work by Harry
Mathews, Tom House, Viet Dinh and Doris Doör-
rie. Also publishes literary essays, literary criticism,
poetry. Does not generally publish pieces more than
5,000 words.
HOW TO CONTACT Submit ms with SASE. Does
not accept e-mail or fax submissions. Responds in
3-6 months to mss. No simultaneous submissions.
Sample copy for $15. Guidelines via website or SASE.
PAYMENT/TERMS Pays 3 contributor's copies and
subscription.
TIPS "We look for innovative fiction that avoids cli-
cheé."

ⓞⓞ☺ⓢ CHROMA

P.O. Box 44655, London N16 0WQ England. (44)
(0)20-3287-6335. **E-mail:** submissions@chroma-
journal.co.uk. **Website:** www.chromajournal.co.uk.
Contact: Shaun Levin, founding editor. Literary
magazine/journal. 52 pages. Contains illustrations.
Includes photographs. "*Chroma* is the only international queer literary and arts journal based in Europe.
We publish poetry, short prose and artwork by lesbian,
gay, bisexual and transgendered writers and artists.

We are always looking for new work and encourage work in translation. Each issue is themed, so please check the website for details. Past themes have included: Foreigners, Beauty, Islands, and Tormented." Semiannual. Estab. 2004. Circ. 1,000.

NEEDS Comics/graphic novels, erotica, ethnic/multicultural, experimental, feminist, gay, lesbian, literary. Receives 100 mss/month. Accepts 12 mss/issue; 24 mss/year. Ms published 3 months after acceptance. **Publishes 20 new writers/year.** Length: 2,000 words (min)-5,000 words (max). Average length: 3,000 words. Publishes short shorts. Average length of short shorts: 1,000 words. Also publishes book reviews, poetry. Send review copies to Eric Anderson, books editor. Sometimes comments on/critiques rejected mss.

HOW TO CONTACT Send complete ms with cover letter to submissions@chromajournal.co.uk. Include brief bio. Responds to queries in 1 month via e-mail. Considers simultaneous submissions, multiple submissions. Guidelines available on website.

PAYMENT/TERMS Writers receive up to $150. Additional copies $7. Pays on publication. Acquires first rights. Publication is copyrighted. "The *Chroma* International Queer Writing Competition runs every two years. The first was in 2006. Check guidelines on our website."

CIMARRON REVIEW

English Dept., Oklahoma State Univ., 205 Morrill Hall, Stillwater OK 74078. **E-mail:** cimarronreview@okstate.edu. **Website:** http://cimarronreview.okstate.edu. **Contact:** Toni Graham, fiction editor. Estab. 1967. Magazine: 6×9; 110 pages. "Poetry and fiction on contemporary themes; personal essays on contemporary issues that cope with life in the 21st century. We are eager to receive manuscripts from both established and less experienced writers who intrigue us with their unusual perspective, language, imagery and character." Quarterly. Recently published work by Molly Giles, Gary Fincke, David Galef, Nona Caspers, Robin Beeman, Edward J. Delaney. Also publishes literary essays, literary criticism, poetry. Reviews fiction. "We want strong literary writing. We are partial to fiction in the modern realist tradition and distinctive poetry—lyrical, narrative, etc."

NEEDS Literary-quality short stories and novel excerpts. No juvenile or genre fiction. Accepts 3-5 mss/issue; 12-15 mss/year. Publishes ms 2-6 months after acceptance. **Publishes 2-4 new writers/year.**

HOW TO CONTACT Send complete ms with SASE. Responds in 2-6 months to mss. Accepts simultaneous submissions. Sample copy for $7.

PAYMENT/TERMS Pays 2 contributor's copies. Acquires first North American serial rights.

COAL CITY REVIEW

Coal City Press, University of Kansas, Lawrence KS 66045. **E-mail:** coalcity@sunflower.com. **E-mail:** briandal@ku.edu. **Website:** www.coalcityreview.com. **Contact:** Mary Wharff, fiction editor. Literary magazine/journal: 812 X 512, 124-150 pages, heavy cover. Includes b&w photographs. Annual.

NEEDS Experimental, literary, contemporary. Does not want erotica, horror, romance, mystery. Receives 20-30 mss/month. Accepts 8-12 mss/issue. Reads year-round. Manuscript published up to 1 year after acceptance. Agented fiction 0%. **Publishes new writers every year.** Published Catherine Bell, Tasha Haas, Bill Church, Aimee Parkison, Thomas Zurwellen, John Talbird. Length: 50 words (min)—4,000 words (max). Average length: 2,000 words. Also publishes literary criticism, poetry. Sometimes comments on/critiques rejected manuscripts.

HOW TO CONTACT Submit via e-mail to coalcity@sunflower.com. Attach Word file. Include estimated word count, brief bio, list of publications. Responds to mss in 4 months. Send disposable copy of ms and #10 SASE for reply only. Considers simultaneous submissions. Guidelines available via e-mail.

PAYMENT/TERMS Writers receive 2 contributor's copies. Additional copies $5. Pays on publication. Acquires one time rights. Publication is copyrighted.

TIPS "We are looking for artful stories—with great language and great heart. Please do not send work that has not been thoughtfully and carefully revised or edited."

COLORADO REVIEW

Center for Literary Publishing, Colorado State University, 9105 Campus Delivery, Fort Collins CO 80523. (970)491-5449. **E-mail:** creview@colostate.edu. **Website:** http://coloradoreview.colostate.edu. **Contact:** Stephanie G'Schwind, editor-in-chief and nonfiction editor. Literary magazine published 3 times/year.

Work published in *Colorado Review* has been included in *Best American Poetry, Best New American Voices, Best Travel Writing, Best Food Writing,* and the *Pushcart Prize Anthology.*

NEEDS No genre fiction. Length: under 30 ms pages.

HOW TO CONTACT Send complete ms. Mss are read from August 1 to April 30. Mss received between May 1 and July 31 will be returned unread.S end no more than 1 story at a time.

PAYMENT/TERMS Pays $5/page.

CONFRONTATION

English Department, C.W. Post Campus Long Island University, Brookville NY 11548. (516)299-2720. **Fax:** (516)299-2735. **E-mail:** confrontationmag@gmail.com. **Website:** confrontationmagazine.org. **Contact:** Jonna Semeiks, editor-in-chief. Estab. 1968. "We are eclectic in our taste. Excellence of style is our dominant concern. We bring new talent to light. We are open to all submissions, each issue contains original work by famous and lesser-known writers and also contains a thematic supplement that 'confront' a topic; the ensuing confrontation is an attempt to see the many sides of an issue rather than a formed conclusion." - Martin Tucker, director Confrontation Publications

○ *Confrontation* has garnered a long list of awards and honors, including the Editor's Award for Distinguished Achievement from CCLP (to Martin Tucker) and NEA grants. Work from the magazine has appeared in numerous anthologies including the *Pushcart Prize, Best Short Stories* and *The O. Henry Prize Stories. Confrontation* does not read mss during June, July, or August and will be returned unread unless commissioned or requested.

NEEDS We judge on quality, so genre is open. No 'proselytizing' literature or genre fiction. 6,000 words.

HOW TO CONTACT Send complete ms.

PAYMENT/TERMS Pays $25-250.

TIPS Most open to fiction and poetry. Prizes are offered for the Sarah Tucker Award for fiction and the John V. Gurry Drama Award. "We look for literary merit. Keep trying."

✚❶◐◌ CONNECTICUT REVIEW

Connecticut State University, 39 Woodland St., Hartford CT 06105-2337. **E-mail:** ctreview@southernct. edu. **Website:** www.ctstateu.edu/ctreview/index.html. **Contact:** Vivian Shipley, editor. Estab. 1967. Magazine: 6x9; 208 pages; white/heavy paper; glossy/heavy cover; color and b&w illustrations and photos; artwork. *Connecticut Review* presents a wide range of cultural interests that cross disciplinary lines. Annual.

Circ. 2,500. Member CLMP. Literary. Receives 250 unsolicited mss/month. Accepts 40 mss/issue; 80 mss/year. Does not accept mss to read May 15-September 1. Publishes ms 1-2 years after acceptance. **Publishes 15-20 new writers/year.** Has published work by John Searles, Michael Schiavone, Norman German, Tom Williams, Paul Ruffin, Dick Allen. "*Connecticut Review* is a high-quality literary magazine. We take both traditional literary pieces and those on the cutting edge of their genres. ."

○ Poetry published in *Connecticut Review* has been included in *The Best American Poetry* and *The Pushcart Prize* anthologies; has received special recognition for Literary Excellence from Public Radio's series *The Poet and the Poem*; and has won the Phoenix Award for Significant Editorial Achievement from the Council of Editors of Learned Journals (CELJ).

NEEDS "We're looking for the best in literary writing in a variety of genres. Some issues contain sections devoted to announced themes. The editors invite the submission of academic articles of general interest, creative essays, translations, short stories, short-shorts, plays, poems and interviews." "No 'entertainment' fiction, though we don't mind if you entertain us while you plumb for the truth." Length: 50-4,000 words.

HOW TO CONTACT Send two disposable copies of ms and #10 SASE for reply only. Content must be under 4,000 words and suitable for circulation to libraries and high schools. Responds in 6 months to queries. Considers simultaneous submissions. Sample copy for $12. Writer's guidelines for SASE, but forms for submissions and guidelines available on website. Send complete ms.

PAYMENT/TERMS Pays 2 contributor's copies; additional copies $10. Pays on publication for first rights. Rights revert to author on publication. Sends galleys to author.

◐ COTTONWOOD

1301 Jayhawk Blvd. Room 400, Kansas Union, University of Kansas, Lawrence KS 66045. **E-mail:** tlorenz@ ku.edu. **Website:** www.cottonwoodmagazine.org/read. **Contact:** Tom Lorenz, fiction editor. Estab. 1965. Magazine: 6×9; 100 pages; illustrations; photos. "*Cottonwood* publishes high quality prose, poetry and artwork and is aimed at an audience that appreciates the same.

We have a national scope and reputation while maintaining a strong regional flavor." Semiannual. Circ. 500. **NEEDS** "We publish literary prose and poetry." Receives 25-50 unsolicited mss/month. Accepts 5-6 mss/issue; 10-12 mss/year. Publishes ms 6-18 months after acceptance. Agented fiction 10%. **Publishes 1-3 new writers/year.** Recently published work by Connie May Fowler, Oakley Hall, Cris Mazza. Length: 1,000-8,000 words; average length: 2,000-5,000 words. Publishes short shorts. Also publishes literary essays, literary criticism, poetry.

HOW TO CONTACT SASE for return of ms. Responds in 6 months to mss. Accepts simultaneous submissions. Sample copy for $8.50, 9×12 SAE and $1.90. Reviews fiction.

PAYMENT/TERMS Acquires one time rights.

CRAB ORCHARD REVIEW

Department of English, Mail Code 4503, Faner Hall 2380, Southern Illinois University at Carbondale, Carbondale IL 62901. (618)453-6833. **Fax:** (618)453-8224. **Website:** www.craborchardreview.siuc.edu/. Estab. 1995. Magazine: 512×812; 275 pages; 55 lb. recycled paper, card cover; photo on cover. "We are a general interest literary journal published twice/year. We strive to be a journal that writers admire and readers enjoy. We publish fiction, poetry, creative nonfiction, fiction translations, interviews and reviews."

NEEDS Ethnic/multicultural, literary, excerpted novel. No science fiction, romance, western, horror, gothic or children's. Wants more novel excerpts that also stand alone as pieces. List of upcoming themes available on website. Receives 900 unsolicited mss/month. Accepts 15-20 mss/issue; 20-40 mss/year. Reads February-April and August-October. Publishes ms 9-12 months after acceptance. Agented fiction 1%. **Publishes 4 new writers/year.** Recently published work by Francisco Aragón, Kerry Neville Bakken, Timothy Crandle, Amina Gautier, Jodee Stanley, Alia Yunis. Length: 1,000-6,500 words; average length: 2,500 words. Also publishes literary essays, poetry. Rarely comments on rejected mss. No science fiction, romance, western, horror, gothic or children's. Wants more novel excerpts that also stand alone as pieces. Length: 1,000-6,500 words.

HOW TO CONTACT Send SASE for reply, return of ms. Responds in 3 weeks to queries; 9 months to mss. Accepts simultaneous submissions. Sample copy for $12. Writer's guidelines for #10 SASE.

PAYMENT/TERMS Pays $100 minimum; $25/page maximum, 2 contributor's copies and a year subscription. Acquires first North American serial rights. Pays $100 minimum; $20/page maximum, 2 contributor's copies and a year subscription.

TIPS "We publish 2 issues per volume—1 has a theme (we read from May to November for the theme issue); the other doesn't (we read from January through April for the non-thematic issue). Consult our website for information about our upcoming themes."

CRAZYHORSE

College of Charleston, Dept. of English, 66 George St., Charleston SC 29424. (843)953-7740. **E-mail:** crazyhorse@cofc.edu. **Website:** www.crazyhorsejournal.org. Estab. 2,000. Semiannual literary magazine: 834×814; 150 pages; illustrations; photos. Submit up to two manuscripts per year between August 1 and May 31. The journal's mission is to publish the entire spectrum of today's fiction, essays, and poetry—from the mainstream to the avant-garde, from the established to the undiscovered writer. The editors are especially interested in original writing that engages in the work of honest communication. *Crazyhorse* publishes writing of fine quality regardless of style, predilection, subject. Raymond Carver called *Crazyhorse* "an indispensable literary magazine of the first order." We like to print a mix of writing regardless of its form, genre, school, or politics. We're especially on the lookout for original writing that doesn't fit the categories and that engages in the work of honest communication.

NEEDS Receives 200 unsolicited mss/month. Accepts 8-10 mss/issue; 16-20 mss/year. Publishes ms 6-12 months after acceptance. Recently published work by Luke Blanchard, Karen Brown, E. V. Slate, Melanie Rae Thon, Lia Purpura, Carolyn Walker. Length: 25 pages; average length: 15 pages. Publishes short shorts. Pays $20-35 per page of layout, depending on annual budget and grants received. Accepts all fiction of fine quality, including short shorts and literary essays.

HOW TO CONTACT No longer accepts submissions by mail. Responds in 1 week to queries; 3 months to mss. Accepts simultaneous submissions. Sample copy for $5; year subscription for $16. Writer's guidelines for SASE or by e-mail. Acquires first North American serial rights. Sends galleys to author. Click online to use our Submission Manager.

PAYMENT/TERMS Pays 2 contributor's copies and $20 per page.

TIPS Write to explore subjects you care about. The subject should be one in which something is at stake. Before sending, ask, "What's reckoned with that's important for other people to read?"

⊙ CUTTHROAT, A JOURNAL OF THE ARTS

P.O. Box 2414, Durango CO 81302. (970) 903-7914. **E-mail:** cutthroatmag@gmail.com. **Website:** www.cutthroatmag.com. **Contact:** William Luvaas, fiction editor. Literary magazine/journal and "one separate online edition of poetry, translations, short fiction, and book reviews yearly. 6×9, 180+ pages, fine cream paper, slick cover. Includes photographs. "We publish only high quality fiction and poetry. We are looking for the cutting edge, the endangered word, fiction with wit, heart, soul and meaning." Annual. Estab. 2005. Member CCLMP.

NEEDS Ethnic/multicultural, experimental, feminist, humor/satire, literary, mainstream. Does not want romance, horror, historical, fantasy, religious, teen, juvenile. List of upcoming themes available on website. Receives 100+ mss/month. Accepts 6 mss/issue; 10-12 mss/year. Does not read from October 1st-March 1st and from June 1st-July 15th. **Publishes 5-8 new writers/year.** Published Michael Schiavone, Rusty Harris, Timothy Rien, Summer Wood, Peter Christopher, Jamey Genna, Doug Frelke, Sally Bellerose, Marc Levy. Length: 500 words (min)-5,000 words (max). Publishes short shorts. Also publishes book reviews. Send review copies to Pamela Uschuk. Sometimes comments on/critiques rejected mss.

HOW TO CONTACT Send complete ms with cover letter. Accepts submissions by e-mail for online edition and from authors living overseas only. Include estimated word count, brief bio. Responds to queries in 1-2 weeks. Responds to mss in 6-8 months. Send either SASE (or IRC) for return of ms or disposable copy of ms and #10 SASE for reply only. Considers simultaneous submissions, multiple submissions. Sample copy available for $10. Guidelines available for SASE, on website.

PAYMENT/TERMS Writers receive contributor's copies. Additional copies $10. Pays on publication. Acquires first North American serial rights. Sends galleys to author. Publication is copyrighted. "Sponsors the Rick DeMarinis Short Fiction Prize ($1250 first prize). See separate listing and website for more information."

TIPS "Read our magazine and see what types of stories we've published. The piece must have heart and soul, excellence in craft. "

⊙⊙ DESCANT

TCU Box 297270, Ft. Worth TX 76129. (817)257-6537. **Fax:** (817)257-6239. **E-mail:** descant@tcu.edu. **Website:** www.descant.tcu.edu. **Contact:** David Kuhne, editor. Estab. 1956. Magazine: 6×9; 120-150 pages; acid-free paper; paper cover. "*Descant* seeks high quality poems and stories in both traditional and innovative form." Member CLMP. Offers 4 cash awards: The $500 Frank O'Connor Award for the best story in an issue; the $250 Gary Wilson Award for an outstanding story in an issue; the $500 Betsy Colquitt Award for the best poem in an issue; the $250 Baskerville Publishers Award for outstanding poem in an issue. Several stories first published by *Descant* have appeared in *Best American Short Stories*.

NEEDS Receives 20-30 unsolicited mss/month. Accepts 25-35 mss/year. Publishes ms 1 year after acceptance. Publishes 50% new writers/year. Recently published work by William Harrison, Annette Sanford, Miller Williams, Patricia Chao, Vonesca Stroud, and Walt McDonald. "No horror, romance, fantasy, erotica." Length: 1,000-5,000 words; average length: 2,500 words.

HOW TO CONTACT Send complete ms with cover letter. Include estimated word count and brief bio.

TIPS "We look for character and quality of prose. Send your best short work."

⊙ DISLOCATE

University of Minnesota English Department, the Edelstein-Keller Endowment, and Adam Lerner of the Lerner Publishing Group., Dept. of English, University of Minnesota, 1 Lind Hall, 207 Church St. SE, Minneapolis MN 55455. **Website:** http://dislocate.umn.edu. **E-mail:** dislocate.magazine@gmail.com. **Contact:** Shantha Susman. Magazine has revolving editor. Literary magazine/journal: 512 x 812, 128 pages. Annual. Estab. 2005. Circ. 2,000. The print journal covers literary writing that bends genres and otherwise pushes the envelope; the submission period for issue 7 is July 15 to November 15. See print journal submission guidelines. The online magazine publishes content of interest to writers and readers: Writing-related content may include articles, essays, interviews, and book reviews. Our culture-related content encompasses everything from arts to entertainment to fashion to "lifestyle" pieces. See online content submission guidelines. dislocate.umn.edu also runs a monthly Short Forms Contest; winners are published on the website and awarded prizes that vary from month to month. See contest submission guidelines and prize details. *dislocate* is a print and online literary journal dedicated to publishing the literature that pushes the traditional boundaries of form and genre. We like work that operates in the gray areas, that resists categorization, that ignores the limits; we like work that plays with the relationship between form and content. We publish fiction, nonfiction, and poetry, but we don't mind if we can't tell which one we're dealing with. In addition to our more "literary" content, dislocate also publishes articles and columns of interest to readers, writers, and other aesthetically curious individuals.

NEEDS Literary fiction. Receives 25-50 mss/month. Accepts 2-3 mss/year. Publishes short shorts. Also publishes literary essays, poetry. Send up to 6,000 words, double-spaced. Number your pages.

HOW TO CONTACT We are now using Submishmash for all submissions. (Submissions will become available when the reading period begins.) We will not consider or respond to submissions or by post or email. Send complete ms with cover letter. Considers simultaneous submissions, multiple submissions. Guidelines available on website. "We are now using Submishmash for all submissions. (Submissions will become available when the reading period begins.) We will not consider or respond to submissions or by post or email."

PAYMENT/TERMS Pays on publication.

TIPS "Looking for excellent writing that rearranges the world."

◑ ECLIPSE

Glendale College, 1500 N. Verdugo Rd., Glendale CA 91208. (818)240-1000. **Fax:** (818)549-9436. **E-mail:** eclipse@glendale.edu. Magazine: 812×512; 150-200 pages; 60 lb. paper. "*Eclipse* is committed to publishing outstanding fiction and poetry. We look for compelling characters and stories executed in ways that provoke our readers and allow them to understand the world in new ways." Annual. Circ. 1,800. CLMP.

NEEDS Ethnic/multicultural, experimental, literary. "Does not want horror, religious, science fiction or thriller mss." Receives 50-100 unsolicited mss/month. Accepts 10 mss/year. Publishes ms 6-12 months after

acceptance. **Publishes 8 new writers/year.** Recently published work by Amy Sage Webb, Ira Sukrungruang, Richard Schmitt, George Rabasa. Length: 6,000 words; average length: 4,000 words. Publishes short shorts. Also publishes poetry. Sometimes comments on rejected mss. Does not want horror, religious, science fiction, or thriller mss. Length: 6,000 words.

HOW TO CONTACT Send complete ms. Responds in 2 weeks to queries; 4-6 weeks to mss. Accepts simultaneous submissions. Sample copy for $8. Writer's guidelines for #10 SASE or by e-mail. Send complete ms

PAYMENT/TERMS Pays 2 contributor's copies; additional copies $7. Pays on publication for first North American serial rights.

◑⑤ ELLIPSIS MAGAZINE

Westminster College of Salt Lake City, 1840 S. 1300 E., Salt Lake City UT 84105. (801)832-2321. **E-mail:** ellipsis@westminstercollege.edu. **Website:** www.westminstercollege.edu/ellipsis. Estab. 1967. **Contact:** Stephanie Peterson (revolving editor; changes every year). Magazine: 6×9; 110-120 pages; 60 lb. paper; 15 pt. cover stock; illustrations; photos. *Ellipsis Magazine* needs good literary poetry, fiction, essays, plays and visual art. Annual. Estab. 1967. Circ. 2,000.

⚲ Reads submissions August 1 to November 1.

NEEDS Receives 110 unsolicited mss/month. Accepts 4 mss/issue. Does not read mss November 1-July 31. Publishes ms 3 months after acceptance. **Publishes 2 new writers/year.** Length: 6,000 words; average length: 4,000 words. Also publishes poetry. Rarely comments on rejected mss. Needs good literary fiction and plays.

HOW TO CONTACT Send complete ms. Send SASE (or IRC) for return of ms or send disposable copy of the ms and #10 SASE for reply only. Responds in 6 months to mss. Accepts simultaneous submissions. Sample copy for $7.50. Writer's guidelines online. Send complete ms.

PAYMENT/TERMS Pays $50 per story and one contributor's copy; additional copies $3.50. Pays on publication for first North American serial rights. Not copyrighted. Pays $50 per story and 1 contributor's copy; additional copies $3.50

EPOCH

Cornell University, 251 Goldwin Smith Hall, Cornell University, Ithaca NY 14853. (607)255-3385. **Fax:** (607)255-6661. Estab. 1947. Magazine: 6×9; 128 pages;

good quality paper; good cover stock. "Well-written literary fiction, poetry, personal essays. Newcomers always welcome. Open to mainstream and avant-garde writing." Circ. 1,000. "Well-written literary fiction, poetry, personal essays. Newcomers always welcome. Open to mainstream and avant-garde writing." **NEEDS** ethnic/multicultural, experimental, literary, mainstream, novel excerpts, literary short stories. "No genre fiction. Would like to see more Southern fiction (Southern US)." Receives 500 unsolicited mss/month. Accepts 15-20 mss/issue. Does not read in summer (April 15-September 15). Publishes ms an average of 6 months after acceptance. **Publishes 3-4 new writers/year.** Recently published work by Antonya Nelson, Doris Betts, Heidi Jon Schmidt. Also publishes poetry. Sometimes comments on rejected mss. No genre fiction. Would like to see more Southern fiction (Southern US).

HOW TO CONTACT Send complete ms. Responds in 2 weeks to queries; 6 weeks to mss. No simultaneous submissions. Sample copy for $5. Writer's guidelines for #10 SASE. Send complete ms.

PAYMENT/TERMS Pays $5 and up/printed page. Pays on publication for first North American serial rights. Pays $5 and up/printed page.

TIPS "Tell your story, speak your poem, straight from the heart. We are attracted to language and to good writing, but we are most interested in what the good writing leads us to, or where."

EUREKA LITERARY MAGAZINE

300 E. College Ave., Eureka College, Eureka IL 61530. **E-mail:** elm@eureka.edu. **Website:** www.eureka.edu/arts/literary/literary.htm. Estab. 1992. **Contact:** Zeke Jarvis, editor. Magazine: 6×9; 120 pages; 70 lb. white offset paper; 80 lb. gloss cover; photographs (occasionally). "We seek to be open to the best stories that are submitted to us. Our audience is a combination of professors/writers, students of writing and literature, and general readers." Semiannual. Estab. 1992. Circ. 500.

NEEDS Ethnic/multicultural, experimental, fantasy (science), feminist, historical, humor/satire, literary, mainstream, mystery/suspense (private eye/hard-boiled, romantic), science fiction (soft/sociological), translations. Would like to see more "good literary fiction stories, good magical realism, historical fiction. We try to achieve a balance between the traditional and the experimental. We look for the well-crafted story, but essentially any type of story that has depth and substance to it is welcome." Receives 100 unsolicited mss/month. Accepts 10-12 mss/issue; 20-30 mss/year. Does not accept mss in summer (May-August). **Publishes 5-6 new writers/year.** Recently published work by Jane Guill, Sarah Strickley, Ray Bradbury, Patrick Madden, Virgil Suarez, Cynthia Gallaher, Wendell Mayo, Tom Noyes, and Brian Doyle. Length: 4,000-6,000 words; average length: 5,000 words. Also publishes short shorts, flash fiction and poetry.

HOW TO CONTACT Accepts submissions by e-mail. Send SASE for reply, return of ms or send disposable copy of ms. Responds in 2 weeks to electronic queries; 4 months to mss. Accepts simultaneous submissions. Sample copy for $7.50.

EVANSVILLE REVIEW

University of Evansville English Dept., 1800 Lincoln Ave., Evansville IN 47722. (812)488-1402. **E-mail:** evansvillereview@evansville.edu. **Website:** http://evansvillereview.evansville.edu. **Contact:** Editor. Estab. 1990. **Contact:** Fiction editor. Magazine: 6×9; 180 pages; 70 lb. white paper; glossy full-color cover; perfect bound. Annual. Circ. 1,000.

NEEDS Does not want erotica, fantasy, experimental or children's fiction. "We're open to all creativity. No discrimination. All fiction, screenplays, nonfiction, poetry, interviews, and anything in between." Receives 70 unsolicited mss/month. Does not read mss December-August. Agented fiction 2%. **Publishes 20 new writers/year.** Recently published work by John Updike, Arthur Miller, X.J. Kennedy, Jim Barnes, Rita Dove. Also publishes literary essays, poetry.

HOW TO CONTACT Send SASE for reply, or send a disposable copy of ms. Responds in 1 month to queries; 3 months to mss. Accepts simultaneous, multiple submissions and reprints. Sample copy for $5. Writer's guidelines free.

PAYMENT/TERMS Pays 2 contributor's copies. Pays on publication for one time rights. Not copyrighted.

TIPS "Because editorial staff rolls over every 1-2 years, the journal always has a new flavor."

FAULTLINE

Dept. of English and Comparative Literature, University of California at Irvine, Irvine CA 92697-2650. **E-mail:** faultline@uci.edu. **Website:** www.humanities.uci.edu/faultline. Estab. 1992. **Contact:** Editors change in September each year. Literary magazine: 6×9; 200 pages; illustrations; photos. "We publish the very best of what we receive. Our interest is quality and literary merit." Annual. Estab. 1992.

NEEDS Translations, literary fiction, nonfiction up to 20 pages. Receives 150 unsolicited mss/month. Accepts 6-9 mss/year. Does not read mss April-September. Publishes ms 9 months after acceptance. Agented fiction 10-20%. **Publishes 30-40% new writers/year.** Recently published work by Maile Meloy, Aimee Bender, David Benioff, Steve Almond, Helen Maria Viramontes, Thomas Keneally. Publishes short shorts. Also publishes literary essays, poetry. Maximum 5,000 words.

HOW TO CONTACT Send SASE for reply, return of ms or send a disposable copy of ms. Responds in 2 weeks to queries; 4 months to mss. Accepts simultaneous submissions. Sample copy for $5. Writer's guidelines for business-size envelope. Send complete ms. "While simultaneous submissions are accepted, multiple submissions are not accepted. Please restrict your submissions to one story at a time, regardless of length."

PAYMENT/TERMS Pays 2 contributor's copies. Pays on publication for one-time rights. Pays in contributor copies.

FEMINIST STUDIES

0103 Taliaferro, University of Maryland, College Park MD 20742. **Website:** www.feministstudies.org. **Contact:** Ashwini Tambe, editorial director. Estab. 1974. "Over the years, Feminist Studies has been a reliable source of significant writings on issues that are important to all classes and races of women. Those familiar with the literature on women's studies are well aware of the importance and vitality of the journal and the frequency with which articles first published in Feminist Studies are cited and/or reprinted elsewhere. Indeed, no less than four anthologies have been created from articles originally published in Feminist Studies: Clio's Consciousness Raised: New Perspectives on the History of Women; Sex and Class in Women's History; U.S. Women in Struggle: A Feminist Studies Anthology; and Lesbian Subjects: A Feminist Studies Reader."

FICTION

c/o Dept. of English, City College, 138th St. & Covenant Ave., New York NY 10031. **Website:** www.fictioninc.com. Estab. 1972. Magazine: 6×9; 150-250 pages; illustrations; occasionally photos. "As the name implies, we publish only fiction; we are looking for the best new writing available, leaning toward the unconventional. *Fiction* has traditionally attempted

to make accessible the unaccessible, to bring the experimental to a broader audience." Semiannual. Estab. 1972. "As the name implies, we publish only fiction; we are looking for the best new writing available, leaning toward the unconventional.

NEEDS Experimental, humor/satire (satire), literary, translations, contemporary. No romance, science fiction, etc. Receives 250 unsolicited mss/month. Accepts 12-20 mss/issue; 24-40 mss/year. Reads mss September 15-April 15. Publishes ms 1 year after acceptance. Agented fiction 10-20%. Recently published work by Joyce Carol Oates, John Barth, Robert Musil, Romulus Linney. Publishes short shorts. Sometimes comments on rejected mss. No romance, science fiction, etc. Length: 5,000 words.

HOW TO CONTACT To submit, please send a complete manuscript with cover letter and SASE. No e-mail submissions. Responds in 3 months to mss. Accepts simultaneous submissions. Sample copy for $5. Writer's guidelines online.

PAYMENT/TERMS Pays $75 plus subscription. Acquires first rights. Pays $114.

✪◐✸ THE FIDDLEHEAD

University of New Brunswick, Campus House, 11 Garland Court, Box 4400, Fredericton NB E3B 5A3 Canada. (506)453-3501. **Fax:** (506) 453-5069. **E-mail:** fiddlehd@unb.ca; scl@unb.ca. **Website:** www.thefiddlehead.ca. **Contact:** Kathryn Taglia, Managing Editor. Estab. 1945. Magazine: 6×9; 128-180 pages; ink illustrations; photos. "No criteria for publication except quality. For a general audience, including many poets and writers." Quarterly. "Canada's longest living literary journal, *The Fiddlehead* is published four times a year at the University of New Brunswick, with the generous assistance of the University of New Brunswick, the Canada Council for the Arts, and the Province of New Brunswick. It is experienced; wise enough to recognize excellence; always looking for freshness and surprise. *The Fiddlehead* publishes short stories, poems, book reviews, and a small number of personal essays. Our full-colour covers have become collectors' items, and feature work by New Brunswick artists and from New Brunswick museums and art galleries. *The Fiddlehead* also sponsors an annual writing contest."

NEEDS Literary. Receives 100-150 unsolicited mss/month. Accepts 4-5 mss/issue; 20-40 mss/year. Publishes ms within 1 year after acceptance. Agented fiction: small percentage. **Publishes high percentage of**

new writers/year. Recently published work by Marjorie Celona, Wasela Hiyate, Alexander MacLeod, and Erika Van Winden. Average length: 3,000-6,000 words. Publishes short shorts. Occasionally comments on rejected mss.

HOW TO CONTACT Send SASE and *Canadian* stamps or IRCs for return of mss. Responds in 6 months to mss. No e-mail submissions. Simultaneous submissions only if stated on cover letter; must contact immediately if accepted elsewhere. Sample copy for $15 (US).

PAYMENT/TERMS Pays up to $40 (Canadian)/published page and 2 contributor's copies. Pays on publication for first or one time serial rights. True

ⓘ FIRST CLASS

P.O. Box 86, Friendship IN 47021. **E-mail:** christopherm@four-sep.com. **Website:** www.four-sep.com. **Contact:** Christopher M, editor. Estab. 1995. Magazine: 414×11; 48-60+ pages; 24 lb./60 lb. offset paper; craft cover; illustrations; photos. "First Class features short fiction and poetics from the cream of the small press and killer unknowns—mingling before your very hungry eyes. I publish plays, too." Biannual. Circ. 200-400.

NEEDS Erotica, literary, science fiction (soft/sociological), satire, drama. "No religious or traditional poetry, or 'boomer angst'—therapy-driven self loathing." Receives 50-70 unsolicited mss/month. Accepts 12-17 mss/issue; 20-30 mss/year. Publishes ms 1 month after acceptance. **Publishes 10-15 new writers/year.** Recently published work by Alan Catlin, Gary Every, John Bennet, B.Z. Niditch. Length: 5,000-8,000; average length: 2,000-3,000 words. Publishes short shorts. Also publishes poetry. Sometimes comments on rejected mss.

HOW TO CONTACT Send SASE or send a disposable copy of ms and #10 SASE for reply only. Responds in 4-8 week to queries. Accepts simultaneous submissions and reprints. Sample copy for $6. Writer's guidelines for #10 SASE. Reviews fiction.

PAYMENT/TERMS Pays 1 contributor's copy; additional copies $5. Acquires one time rights.

TIPS "Don't bore me with puppy dogs and the morose/sappy feeling you have about death. Belt out a good, short, thought-provoking, graphic, uncommon piece."

FIVE POINTS

Georgia State University, P.O. Box 3999, Atlanta GA 30302-3999. **E-mail:** info@langate.gsu.edu. **Website:** www.webdelsol.com/Five_Points. Estab. 1996. Magazine: 6×9; 200 pages; cotton paper; glossy cover; photos. *Five Points* is "committed to publishing work that compels the imagination through the use of fresh and convincing language." Triannual. Circ. 2,000.

NEEDS List of upcoming themes available for SASE. Receives 250 unsolicited mss/month. Accepts 4 mss/issue; 15-20 mss/year. Does not read mss April 30-September 1. Publishes ms 6 months after acceptance. **Publishes 1 new writer/year.** Recently published work by Frederick Busch, Ursula Hegi, Melanie Rae Thon. Average length: 7,500 words. Publishes short shorts. Also publishes literary essays, poetry. Sometimes comments on rejected mss.

HOW TO CONTACT Use online submission manager. Sample copy for $7.

PAYMENT/TERMS Pays $15/page minimum ($250 maximum), free subscription to magazine and 2 contributor's copies; additional copies $4. Acquires first North American serial rights. Sends galleys to author. Sponsors awards/contests. Pays $15/page minimum; $250 maximum, free subscription to magazine and 2 contributor's copies; additional copies $4.

ⓘ FLINT HILLS REVIEW

Dept. of English, Box 4019, Emporia State University, Emporia KS 66801-5087. **Website:** www.emporia.edu/fhr/. Estab. 1996. *Flint Hills Review*, published annually in late summer, is "a regionally focused journal presenting writers of national distinction alongside new authors." Magazine: 9×6; 115 pages; 60 lb. paper; glossy cover; illustrations; photos. "FHR seeks work informed by a strong sense of place or region, especially Kansas and the Great Plains region. We seek to provide a publishing venue for writers of the Great Plains and Kansas while also publishing authors whose work evidences a strong sense of place, writing of literary quality, and accomplished use of language and depth of character development." Annual. Circ. 300. CLMP.

NEEDS Ethnic/multicultural, gay, historical, regional (Plains), translations. "No religious, inspirational, children's." Want to see more "writing of literary quality with a strong sense of place." List of upcoming themes online. Receives 5-15 unsolicited mss/month. Accepts 2-5 mss/issue; 2-5 mss/year. Does not read mss April-December. **Publishes 4 new writers/year.** Recently published work by Kim Stafford, Elizabeth Dodd, Bart Edelman, and Jennifer Henderson.

Length: 1 page-5,000; average length: 3,000 words. Publishes short shorts. Also publishes literary essays, literary criticism, poetry.

HOW TO CONTACT Send a disposable copy of ms and #10 SASE for reply only.

PAYMENT/TERMS Pays 2 contributor's copies; additional copies $5.50.

THE FLORIDA REVIEW

Dept. of English, University of Central Florida, Suite P, P.O. Box 161346, Orlando FL 32816-1346. (407)823-5329. **E-mail:** flreview@mail.ucf.edu. **Website:** http://floridareview.cah.ucf.edu/. **Contact:** Jocelyn Bartkevicius, editor. Estab. 1972. Magazine: 6×9; 185 pages; semi-gloss full color cover, perfect bound. "We publish fiction of high 'literary' quality—stories that delight, instruct and take risks. Our audience consists of avid readers of fiction, poetry and creative nonfiction." Semiannual. Estab. 1972. Needs Experimental, literary. "We aren't particularly interested in genre fiction (sci-fi, romance, adventure, etc.) but a good story can transcend any genre." Receives over 500 unsolicited mss/month. Accepts 5-7 mss/issue; 10-14 mss/year. Publishes 3-5 new writers/year. Recently published work by Gerald Vizenor, Billy Collins, Sherwin Bitsui, Kelly Clancy, Denise Duhamel, Tony Hoagland, Baron Wormser, Marcia Aldrich, and Patricia Foster. Length: 2,000-8,000 words; average length: 5,000 words. Publishes short shorts. Also publishes creative nonfiction, poetry, and graphic narrative. Rarely comments on rejected mss. Accepts simultaneous submissions if notified promptly when accepted elsewhere.

NEEDS Publishes short shorts. Also publishes creative nonfiction, poetry, and graphic narrative. Length: 2,000-8,000 words; average length: 5,000 words. Publishes short shorts.

HOW TO CONTACT Send complete ms. Send SASE (or IRC) for return of the ms or send disposable copy of the ms and #10 SASE for reply only. Responds in 2 weeks to queries; 3 months to mss. Accepts simultaneous submissions. Sample copy for $8. Writer's guidelines for #10 SASE or online. Send complete ms. Send SASE (or IRC) for return of the ms or send disposable copy of the ms and #10 SASE for reply only.

PAYMENT/TERMS Rights held by UCF, revert to author after publication.

TIPS "We're looking for writers with fresh voices and original stories. We like risk."

FLYWAY

Iowa State University, 206 Ross Hall, Ames IA 50011. **E-mail:** flyway@iastate.edu. **Website:** www.flyway. org. Estab. 1995. **Contact:** Stephen Pett, editor. Estab. 1995 Literary magazine: 6×9; 120 pages; quality paper; cover stock; some illustrations; photos. "We publish quality fiction, creative nonfiction, and poetry with a particular interest in place as a component of 'story,' or with an 'environmental' sensibility. Accepted works are accompanied by brief commentaries by their authors, the sort of thing a writer might say introducing a piece at a reading." Biannual. Circ. 500. *Flyway, A Journal of Writing and Environment*, published 3 times/year, "is one of the best literary magazines for the money. It's packed with some of the most readable poems being published today—all styles, forms, lengths, and subjects."

NEEDS Literary. Receives 50 unsolicited mss/month. Accepts 2-5 short story and creative nonfiction mss/issue; 10-12 poetry mss/issue. Reads mss September 1-May 1. Publishes ms 6-8 months after acceptance. **Publishes 7-10 new writers/year.** Recently published work by Linda Hasselstrom, Ann Pancake, Ted Kooser, Michael Martone. Length: 5,000; average length: 3,500 words. Publishes short shorts. Often comments on rejected mss.

HOW TO CONTACT Send SASE. Sample copy for $8. Writer's guidelines with SASE.

PAYMENT/TERMS Pays 2 contributor's copies; additional copies $8. Acquires one time rights.

TIPS "Quality, originality, voice, drama, tension. Make it as strong as you can."

FOGGED CLARITY

Fogged Clarity and Nicotine Heart Press, P.O. Box 1016, Muskegon MI 49443-1016. (231)670-7033. **E-mail:** editor@foggedclarity.com. **E-mail:** submissions@foggedclarity.com. **Website:** www.foggedclarity.com. **Contact:** Ben Evans, executive editor/managing editor. Estab. 2008. "*Fogged Clarity* is an arts review that accepts submissions of poetry, fiction, non-fiction, music, visual art and reviews of work in all mediums. We seek art that is stabbingly eloquent. Our print edition will be released once every year, while new issues of our online journal will come out the beginning of every month. Artists maintain the copyrights to their work until they are monetarily compensated for said work. If your work is selected for our print edition and you consent to its publication, you will be compensated."

NEEDS Does not want genre, experimental, religious, etc. "We tend to only publish literary fiction."
HOW TO CONTACT Send complete ms.

😊 FOLIATE OAK LITERARY MAGAZINE

University of Arkansas-Monticello, Arts & Humanities, 562 University Dr., Monticello AR 71656. (870)460-1247. **E-mail:** foliateoak@uamont.edu. **Website:** www.foliateoak.uamont.edu. **Contact:** Diane Payne. Estab. 1973. "We are a general literary magazine for adults." Monthly magazine covering fiction, creative nonfiction, poetry, and art." Circ.: 500. "We are always interested in publishing intriguing photography, artwork, and graphic (you know, comics) literature. If you are sending a one-page comics or excerpts from a graphic novel, use PDF or. JPG format. Send all artwork as jpg or gif. We like to have at least 3 images. Remember to include your brief third person bio.

NEEDS Adventure, ethnic, experimental, mainstream, slice-of-life vignettes. Does not want horror or confession, or pornographic, racist, or homophobic content. Length: 200-2,500 words. Does not want horror or confession, or pornographic, racist, or homophobic content. Length: 200-2,500 words.

TIPS "Please submit all material via our online submission manager." Read our guidelines before submitting. http://www.foliateoak.uamont.edu/submission-guidelines.

🌓 FOLIO

Department of Literature, American University, Washington DC 20016. **E-mail:** folio.editors@gmail.com. **Website:** www.american.edu/cas/literature/folio/. **Contact:** Greta Schuler. Estab. 1984. Magazine: about 70 pages; illustrations; photos. "*Folio* is a nationally recognized literary journal sponsored by the College of Arts and Sciences at American University in Washington, D. C. Since 1984, we have published original creative work by both new and established authors. Past issues have included work by Michael Reid Busk, Billy Collins, William Stafford, and Bruce Weigl, and interviews with Michael Cunningham, Charles Baxter, Amy Bloom, Ann Beattie, and Walter Kirn. We look for well-crafted poetry and prose that is bold and memorable." Does not read submissions May-July. Publishes 2-3 new writers/year. Length: 5,000 words; average length: 2,500 words. Publishes short shorts. How to submit. Send a SASE for reply only. Responds in 3-4 months to submission. Accepts simultaneous submissions. Sample copy for $6. "Visit

our website and read the journal for more information." We look for work that ignites and endures, is artful and natural, daring and elegant." Semiannual.

NEEDS Literary. Does not want anything that is sexually offensive. Receives 50-60 unsolicited mss/month.

HOW TO CONTACT Send complete ms. Send a SASE (or IRC) for reply only.

PAYMENT/TERMS Pays 2 contributor's copies. Pays on publication for first North American serial rights.

🌓 FREEFALL MAGAZINE

Freefall Literary Society of Calgary, 922 Ninth Ave. SE, Calgary AB T2G 0S4 Canada. **E-mail:** freefallmagazine@yahoo.com. **Website:** www.freefallmagazine.ca. **Contact:** Lynn S. Fraser, managing editor. Estab. 1990. 812×534; 100 pages; bond paper; bond stock; b&w illustrations; photos. "*FreeFall* features the best of new, emerging writers and gives them the chance to get into print along with established writers. Magazine published biannually containing fiction, poetry, creative nonfiction, essays on writing, interviews, and reviews. Submit up to 5 poems at once. We are looking for exquisite writing with a strong narrative." Circ. 1,000. Buys first North American serial rights (ownership reverts to author after one time publication). Pays on publication. 100% freelance. Pays $25 per poem and one copy of the issue poems appeaer in. Wants prose of all types, up to 3,000 words; pays $10/page to a maximum of $100 per piece and one copy of issue piece appears in. We are looking for exquisite writing with a strong narrative."

PAYMENT/TERMS Pays $25 per poem and one copy of the issue poems appear in. Wants prose of all types, up to 3,000 words; pays $10/page to a maximum of $100 per piece and one copy of issue piece appears in.

TIPS "We look for thoughtful word usage, craftmanship, strong voice and unique expression coupled with clarity and narrative structure. Professional, clean presentation of work is essential. Carefully read *FreeFall* guidelines before submitting. Do not fold manuscript, and submit 9×11 envelope. Include SASE/IRC for reply and/or return of manuscript. You may contact us by e-mail after initial hardcopy submission. For accepted pieces a request is made for disk or e-mail copy. Strong Web presence attracts submissions from writers all over the world."

🌓 FRONT & CENTRE

573 Gainsborough Ave., Ottawa ON K2A 2Y6 Canada. (613)729-8973. **E-mail:** firth@istar.ca. **Website:** www.

blackbilepress.com. **Contact:** Matthew Firth, editor. Estab. 1998.

NEEDS Literary ("contemporary realism/gritty urban"). "No science fiction, horror, mainstream, romance or religious." Receives 20 unsolicited mss/month. Accepts 6-7 mss/issue; 10-20 mss/year. Publishes ms 6 months after acceptance. Agented fiction 10%. **Publishes 8-9 new writers/year.** Recently published work by Len Gasparini, Katharine Coldiron, Salvatore Difalco, Gerald Locklin, Amanda Earl, Tom Johns. Publishes short shorts. Always comments on rejected mss. Magazine: half letter-size; 40-50 pages; illustrations; photos. "We look for new fiction from Canadian and international writers—bold, aggressive work that does not compromise quality." Three issues per year. Circ. 500. Length: 50-4,000 words; average length: 2,500 words.

HOW TO CONTACT Send SASE (from Canada) (or IRCs from USA) for return of ms or send a disposable copy of ms with #10 SASE for reply only. Responds in 2 weeks to queries; 4 months to mss. Accepts multiple submissions. Sample copy for $5. Writer's guidelines for SASE or by e-mail. Reviews fiction.

PAYMENT/TERMS Acquires first rights. Not copyrighted.

TIPS "We look for attention to detail, unique voice, not overtly derivative, bold writing, not pretentious. We should like to see more realism. Read the magazine first—simple as that!"

◐◑❸ FUGUE LITERARY MAGAZINE

200 Brink Hall, University of Idaho P.O. Box 44110, Moscow ID 83844-1102. **E-mail:** fugue@uidaho.edu. **Website:** http://www.uiweb.uidaho.edu/fugue/. **Contact:** Jennifer Yeatts, Managing Editor. Estab. 1990. Magazine: 6×9; 175 pages; 70 lb. stock paper. By allowing the voices of established writers to lend their authority to new and emerging writers, *Fugue* strives to provide its readers with the most compelling stories, poems, essays, interviews and literary criticism possible. Biannual literary magazine. See website for details. Submissions of poetry, essays, and short stories are accepted Sept. 1 through May 1 (online submissions only). All material received outside of this period will be unread. See website for submission instructions. at: www.uiweb.uidho.edu/fugure/submit.html.

> ◗ Work published in *Fugue* has won the Pushcart Prize and has been cited in *Best American Essays*.

NEEDS Ethnic/multicultural, experimental, humor/satire, literary. Receives 80 unsolicited mss/month. Accepts 6-8 mss/issue; 12-15 mss/year. Does not read mss May 1-August 31. Publishes ms 6 months after acceptance. **Publishes 4-6 new writers/year.** Recently published work by Kent Nelson, Marilyn Krysl, Cary Holladay, Padgett Powell, Dean Young, W.S. Merwin, Matthew Vollmer. Publishes short shorts. Also publishes literary essays, literary criticism, poetry. Sometimes comments on rejected mss.

HOW TO CONTACT Send complete ms. Send SASE (or IRC) for return of the ms or disposable copy of the ms and #10 SASE for reply only. Responds in 3-4 months to mss. Accepts simultaneous submissions. Sample copy for $8. Writer's guidelines for SASE or on website. Please send no more than 5 poems, 2 short-shorts, one story, or one essay at a time. Submissions in more than one genre should be submitted separately. We will consider simultaneous submissions (submissions that have been sent concurrently to another journal), but we will not consider multiple submissions. All multiple submissions will be returned unread. Once you have submitted a piece to us, wait for a response on this piece before submitting again.

PAYMENT/TERMS All contributors receive payment and 2 complimentary copies of the journal. Pays on publication for first North American serial, electronic rights.

◐ GARGOYLE

Paycock Press, 3819 N. 13th St., Arlington VA 22201. (703)525-9296. **E-mail:** hedgehog2@erols.com. **Website:** www.gargoylemagazine.com. **Contact:** Richard Peabody, co-editor, Lucinda Ebersole, co-editor. Estab. 1976. Literary magazine: 512×812; 200 pages; illustrations; photos. "Gargoyle Magazine has always been a scallywag magazine, a maverick magazine, a bit too academic for the underground and way too underground for the academics. We are a writer's magazine in that we are read by other writers and have never worried about reaching the masses." Annual. Circ. 2,000.

NEEDS Erotica, ethnic/multicultural, experimental, gay, lesbian, literary, mainstream, translations. "No romance, horror, science fiction." Wants "edgy realism or experimental works. We run both." Wants to see more Canadian, British, Australian and Third World fiction. Receives 50-200 unsolicited mss/month. Accepts 10-15 mss/issue. Accepts submissions during June, July, and Aug. Publishes ms 6-12 months after acceptance. Agented fiction 5%. **Publishes 2-3 new writers/year.** Recently published work by Stephanie Allen, Tom Carson, Susaan Cokal, Ramola D., Janice Eidus, James Grady, Susan Smith Nash, Zena Polin, Wena Poon, Elisabeth Sheffield, and Daniel Stola. Length: 30 pages maximum; average length: 5-10 pages. Publishes short shorts. Also publishes literary essays, literary criticism, poetry. Sometimes comments on rejected mss. No romance, horror, science fiction Length: 1,000-4,500 words.

HOW TO CONTACT "We prefer electronic submissions. Please use submission engine online." For snail mail, send SASE for reply, return of ms or send a disposable copy of ms. Responds in 2 weeks to queries; 3 months to mss. Accepts simultaneous submissions. Sample copy for $12.95. Query in an email. Reviews artwork.

PAYMENT/TERMS Pays 10% of print run and so-so split (after/if) we break even. Acquires first North American serial, and first British rights. Sends galleys to author.

TIPS "We have to fall in love with a particular fiction."

GEORGETOWN REVIEW

Box 227, 400 East College St., Georgetown KY 40324. (502)863-8308. **Fax:** (502)868-8888. **E-mail:** gtownreview@georgetowncollege.edu. **Website:** http://georgetownreview.georgetowncollege.edu. **Contact:** Steven Carter, editor. Estab. 1993. *Georgetown Review,* published annually in May, is a literary journal of poetry, fiction, and creative nonfiction. " Does not want "work that is merely sentimental, political, or inspirational." *Georgetown Review* is 192 pages, digest-sized, offset-printed, perfect-bound, with 60 lb. glossy 4-color cover with art/graphics, includes ads. Press run is 1,000. Single copy: $7. Make checks payable to *Georgetown Review.*

NEEDS "We publish the best fiction we receive, regardless of theme or genre." Annual. Member CLMP. Receives 100-125 mss/month. Accepts 8-10 mss/issue; 15-20/year. Does not read January 1-August 31. Manuscript published 1 month-2 years after acceptance. No agented fiction. **Publishes 3-4 new writers/year.** Published Andrew Plattner, Sallie Bingham, Alison Stine. Also publishes literary essays, poetry, short-shorts. Sometimes comments on/critiques rejected mss. "Sponsors annual contest with $1,000 prize. Check website for guidelines." Does not want adventure, children's, fantasy, romance. Average

length: 4,000 words. Average length of short shorts: 500-1,500 words.

HOW TO CONTACT Send complete ms with cover letter. Include brief bio, list of publications.

PAYMENT/TERMS Writers receive 2 contributor's copies, free subscription to the magazine. Additional copies $5

TIPS "We look for fiction that is well written and that has a story line that keeps our interest. Don't send a first draft, and even if we don't take your first, second, or third submission, keep trying."

GERTRUDE

P.O. Box 83948, Portland OR 97283. **E-mail:** editor@gertrudepress.org. **Website:** www.gertrudepress.org. **Contact:** Eric Delehoy, editor. Magazine: 5×812; 64-72 pages; perfect bound; 60 lb. paper; glossy card cover; illustrations; photos. *Gertrude* is a "annual publication featuring the voices and visions of the gay, lesbian, bisexual, transgender and supportive community." Circ. 400.

NEEDS Ethnic/multicultural, feminist, gay, humor/satire, lesbian, literary, mainstream. "No romance, pornography or mystery." Wants more multicultural fiction. "We'd like to publish more humor and positive portrayals of gays—steer away from victim roles, pity." Receives 15-20 unsolicited mss/month. Accepts 4-8 mss/issue; 4-8 mss/year. Publishes ms 1-2 months after acceptance. **Publishes 4-5 new writers/year.** Recently published work by Carol Guess, Demrie Alonzo, Henry Alley and Scott Pomfret. Length: 200-3,000 words; average length: 1,800 words. Publishes short shorts. Also publishes poetry.

HOW TO CONTACT Send SASE for reply to query and a disposable copy of ms. Responds in 6-9 months to mss. Accepts multiple submissions Simultaneous submissions okay. Sample copy for $5, 6×9 SAE and 4 first class stamps. Writer's guidelines for #10 SASE. Also can submit via online subission form on website.

PAYMENT/TERMS Pays 1-2 contributor's copies; additional copies $4. Pays on publication. Author retains rights upon publication. Not copyrighted.

TIPS "We look for strong characterization, imagery and new, unique ways of writing about universal experiences. Follow the construction of your work until the ending. Many stories start out with zest, then flipper and die. Show us, don't tell us."

THE GEORGIA REVIEW

The University of Georgia, Athens GA 30602. (706)542-3481. **Fax:** (706)542-0047. **E-mail:** garev@uga.edu.

Website: www.uga.edu/garev. **Contact:** Stephen Corey, editor. Estab. 1947. Our readers are educated, inquisitive people who read a lot of work in the areas we feature, so they expect only the best in our pages. All work submitted should show evidence that the writer is at least as well-educated and well-read as our readers. Essays should be authoritative but accessible to a range of readers. No simultaneous or electronic submissions. **NEEDS** We seek original, excellent writing not bound by type. Ordinarily we do not publish novel excerpts or works translated into English, and we strongly discourage authors from submitting these.

HOW TO CONTACT Send complete ms.

PAYMENT/TERMS Pays $50/published page.

THE GETTYSBURG REVIEW

Gettysburg College, Gettysburg PA 17325. (717)337-6770. **Fax:** (717)337-6775. **Website:** www.gettysburgreview.com. Estab. 1988. Magazine: 614×10; 170 pages; acid free paper; full color illustrations. "Our concern is quality. Manuscripts submitted here should be extremely well written." Reading period September-May. Quarterly. Estab. 1988. Circ. 4,000. "Our concern is quality. Manuscripts submitted here should be extremely well written. Reading period September-May."

NEEDS Experimental, historical, humor/satire, literary, mainstream, novel excerpts, regional, serialized novels, contemporary. "We require that fiction be intelligent and esthetically written." Receives 350 unsolicited mss/month. Accepts 15-20 mss/issue; 60-80 mss/year. Publishes ms within 1 year after acceptance. **Publishes 1-5 new writers/year.** Recently published work by Nicholas Montemarano, Victoria Lancelotta, Leslie Pietrzyk, Kyle Minor, Kerry Neville-Bakken, Margot Singer. Length: 2,000-7,000 words; average length: 3,000 words. Publishes short shorts. Also publishes literary essays, literary criticism, poetry. Sometimes comments on rejected mss. High quality, literary. "We require that fiction be intelligent and esthetically written." Length: 2,000-7,000 words.

HOW TO CONTACT Send complete ms with SASE. Responds in 1 month to queries; 3-6 months to mss. Accepts simultaneous submissions. Sample copy for $10. Writer's guidelines online. Send complete ms.

PAYMENT/TERMS Pays $30/page. Pays on publication for first North American serial rights. Pays $30/page.

GINOSKO

P.O. Box 246, Fairfax CA 94978. **E-mail:** ginoskoeditor@aol.com. **Website:** www.ginoskoliteraryjournal.com. **Contact:** Robert Paul Cesaretti, editor. Estab. 2003. "*Ginosko* (ghin-océ-koe): To perceive, understand, realize, come to know; knowledge that has an inception, a progress, an attainment. The recognition of truth by experience." Accepting short fiction and poetry, creative nonfiction, interviews, social justice concerns, and spiritual insights for www.GinoskoLiteraryJournal.com. Member CLMP. Reads year round. Length of articles flexible; accepts excerpts. Publishing as semiannual ezine. Check downloadable issues on website for tone and style. Downloads free; accepts donations. Also looking for books, art, and music to post on website, and links to exchange.

NEEDS *Ginosko* Short Fiction Contest: Deadline is May 1; $12 entry fee; $500 prize.

GLIMMER TRAIN STORIES

Glimmer Train Press, Inc., 1211 NW Glisan St., Suite 207, Portland OR 97209. **Fax:** (503)221-0837. **E-mail:** eds@glimmertrain.org. **Website:** www.glimmertrain.org. Estab. 1991. Magazine: 225 pages; recycled; acid-free paper; 12 photographs. "We are interested in literary short stories published by new and established writers." Quarterly. Estab. 1991. Circ. 16,000. "We are interested in literary short stories, particularly by new and lightly published writers."

NEEDS literary. Receives 4,000 unsolicited mss/month. Accepts 10 mss/issue; 40 mss/year. Publishes ms up to 18 months after acceptance. Agented fiction 5%. **Publishes 20 new writers/year.** Recently published work by Charles Baxter, Thisbe Nissen, Herman Carrillo, Andre Dubus III, William Trevor, Patricia Henley, Alberto Rios, Ann Beattie. Sometimes comments on rejected mss. up to 12,000

HOW TO CONTACT Submit work online at www.glimmertrain.org. Different submission categories are open each month of the year. Accepted work published in *Glimmer Train Stories*. Responds in 2 months to mss. Accepts simultaneous submissions. Sample copy for $12 on website. Writer's guidelines online. Submit via the website. In a pinch, send paper.

PAYMENT/TERMS Pays $700 for standard submissions, up to $2,000 for contest winning stories. Pays on acceptance for first rights.

ⓞ GRASSLIMB

P.O. Box 420816, San Diego CA 92142. **E-mail:** editor@grasslimb.com. **Website:** www.grasslimb.com. **Contact:** Valerie Polichar, editor. Estab. 2002. Magazine: 14×20; 8 pages; 60 lb. white paper; illustrations.

"*Grasslimb* publishes literary prose, poetry and art. Fiction is best when it is short and avant-garde or otherwise experimental." Semiannual. Circ. 200.

NEEDS Experimental, literary, mystery/suspense (crime), regional, thriller/espionage, translations. Does not want romance or religious writings. Accepts 2-4 mss/issue; 4-8 mss/year. Publishes ms 3-6 months after acceptance. **Publishes 4 new writers/year.** Recently published work by Kuzhali Manickavel, Amanda Lyell. Length: 500-2,000 words; average length: 1,500 words. Publishes short shorts. Also publishes poetry. Rarely comments on rejected mss.

HOW TO CONTACT Send complete ms. Send SASE for return of ms or disposable copy of ms and #10 SASE for reply only. Responds in 4 months to mss. Accepts simultaneous and reprints, multiple submissions. Sample copy for $2.50. Writer's guidelines for SASE, e-mail or on website. Reviews fiction.

PAYMENT/TERMS Writers receive $10 minimum; $70 maximum, and 2 contributor's copies; additional copies $3. Pays on acceptance for first print publication serial rights.

TIPS "We publish brief fiction work that can be read in a single sitting over a cup of coffee. Work is generally 'literary' in nature, rather than mainstream. Experimental work welcome. Remember to have your work proofread and to send short work. We cannot read over 2,500 and prefer under 2,000 words. Include word count."

GREEN MOUNTAINS REVIEW

Johnson State College, 337 College Hill, Johnson VT 05656. (802)635.1350. **E-mail:** gmr@jsc.vsc.edu. **Website:** http://greenmountainsreview.com/. **Contact:** Elizabeth Powell, poetry editor. The editors are open to a wide rang of styles and subject matter.

NEEDS Adventure, experimental, humor/satire, literary, mainstream, serialized novels, translations. Recently published work by Tracy Daugherty, Terese Svoboda, Walter Wetherell, T.M. McNally, J. Robert Lennon, Louis B. Jones, and Tom Whalen. Publishes short shorts. Also publishes literary criticism, poetry. Sometimes comments on rejected mss. Length: 1,000-7,500 words.

PAYMENT/TERMS Pays contributor's copies, 1-year subscription and small honorarium, depending on grants.

TIPS We encourage you to order some of our back issues to acquaint yourself with what has been accepted in the past. Unsolicited mss. are read from Sept. 1 - Mar. 1.

THE GREENSBORO REVIEW

MFA Writing Program, 3302 HHRA Building, UNC Greensboro, Greensboro NC 27402-6170. (336)334-5459. **E-mail:** jlclark@uncg.edu. **Website:** www.greensbororeview.org. **Contact:** Jim Clark, editor. Magazine: 6×9; approximately 128 pages; 60 lb. paper; 80 lb. cover. Literary magazine featuring fiction and poetry for readers interested in contemporary literature. Semiannual. Circ. 1,000.

> Stories for *the Greensboro Review* have been included in *Best American Short Stories, The O. Henry Awards Prize Stories, New Stories from The South* and *Pushcart Prize.*

NEEDS Accepts 6-8 mss/issue; 12-16 mss/year. Unsolicited manuscripts must arrive by September 15 to be considered for the spring issue and by February 15 to be considered for the fall issue. Manuscripts arriving after those dates may be held for the next consideration. **Publishes 10% new writers/year.** Has published work by Renee Ashley, Michael Cadnum, Carl Dennis, Jack Gilbert, Chard diNiord, Curtis Smith, and Kevin Wilson.

HOW TO CONTACT Responds in 4 months to mss. Accepts simultaneous submissions. No e-mail submissions. Submit manuscripts by regular or by submission form on website. Sample copy for $8.

PAYMENT/TERMS Pays in contributor's copies. Acquires first North American serial rights.

TIPS "We want to see the best being written regardless of theme, subject or style."

GUD MAGAZINE

Greatest Uncommon Denominator Publishing, P.O. Box 1537, Laconia NH 03247. **E-mail:** editor@gud-magazine.com. **Website:** www.gudmagazine.com. Estab. 2006. Literary magazine/journal. "*GUD Magazine* transcends and encompasses the audiences of both genre and literary fiction. We're selling content, not media. If people want to buy just one story, they'll get it. If they want a PDF magazine, they'll get the whole issue. If they want a beautifully bound paper mag, they'll pay a little extra, but they'll get it. *GUD* features fiction (from flash to 15,000 word stories), art, poetry, essays, comics, reports and short drama. See website for more."

NEEDS Adventure, erotica, ethnic/multicultural, experimental, fantasy, horror, humor/satire, literary, science fiction, alternate history, mystery, why. Accepts 40 mss/year. Manuscript published 6 months after acceptance. Length: 15,000 words (max). Length: 1-15,000 words.

HOW TO CONTACT Submit via online form only. Responds to mss in up to 6 months. Considers simultaneous submissions, previously published submissions, and multiple submissions (art and poetry only). Guidelines available on website.

PAYMENT/TERMS Pays $450.

◉ GULF COAST: A JOURNAL OF LITERATURE AND FINE ARTS

University of Houston, Dept. of English, University of Houston, Houston TX 77204-3013. (713)743-3223. **E-mail:** editors@gulfcoastmag.org. **Website:** www.gulfcoastmag.org. **Contact:** The Editors. Estab. 1986. Magazine: 7×9; approx. 300 pages; stock paper, gloss cover; illustrations; photos. "Innovative fiction for the literary-minded." Estab. 1987. Buys 5-10 ms/year. Receives 300 unsolicited mss/month. Accepts 4-8 mss/issue; 12-16 mss/year. Agented fiction 5%. **Publishes 2-8 new writers/year.** Recently published work by Matt Bell, Megan Mayhew Bergman, Sarah Shun-Lien Bynum, Jenine Capot Crucet, Benjamin Percy, John Weir. Publishes short shorts. Sometimes comments on rejected mss.

NEEDS Ethnic/multicultural, experimental, literary, regional, translations, contemporary. "No children's, genre, religious/inspirational." Wants more "cutting-edge, experimental" fiction.

HOW TO CONTACT Gulf Coast reads general submissions, submitted by post or through the online submissions manager, from September 1 through March 1. Submissions e-mailed directly to the editors, or postmarked between March 1 and Sept. 1, will not be read or responded to. Please visit our contest page for contest submission guidelines. Responds in 4-6 months to mss. Accepts simultaneous submissions.

PAYMENT/TERMS Payment for accepted work varies depending on availability of funds, but is a minimum of $30 per poem, $20 per page of prose up to $150, $50 per review, and $100 per interview.

◑ GULF STREAM MAGAZINE

Florida International Univ., English Dept., N. Miami FL 33181-3000. **E-mail:** gulfstreamfiu@yahoo.com. **Website:** www.gulfstreamlitmag.com. Estab. 1989. **Contact:** fiction editor. Magazine: 512×812; 124 pages; recycled paper; 80 lb. glossy cover; cover illustrations. "We publish good quality fiction, nonfiction and poetry for a predominately literary market." Semiannual. Estab. 1989. Circ. 300.

○ "Submit online only. Please read guidelines on website in full. Submissions that do not conform to our guidelines will be discarded. We do not accept emailed or mailed submissions. We read from Sept 15- Dec 15; Jan 15 - Mar 15." Does not pay writers' expenses.

NEEDS Literary, mainstream, contemporary. Does not want romance, historical, juvenile, or religious work. Receives 250 unsolicited mss/month. Accepts 5 mss/issue; 10 mss/year. Does not read mss during the summer. Publishes ms 3-6 months after acceptance. **Publishes 2-5 new writers/year.** Past contributors include Sherman Alexie, Steve Almond, Jan Beatty, Lee Martin, Robert Wrigley, Dennis Lehane, Liz Robbins, Stuart Dybek, David Kirby, Ann Hood, Ha Jin, B.H. Fairchild, Naomi Shihab Nye, F. Daniel Rzicznek, and Connie May Fowler. Length: 7,500 words; average length: 5,000 words. Publishes short shorts. Also publishes poetry.

HOW TO CONTACT Responds in 6 months to mss. Accepts simultaneous submissions "if noted." Sample copy for $5. Writer's guidelines for #10 SASE.

PAYMENT/TERMS Pays in gift subscriptions and contributor's copies. Acquires first North American serial rights.

THE G.W. REVIEW

The George Washington University, 800 21st St. NW, Marvin Center Box 20, Washington DC 20052. (202)994-7779. **E-mail:** gwreview@gwu.edu. **Website:** http://thegwreview.weebly.com. Estab. 1980. "*The G.W. Review* seeks to expose readers to new and emerging writers from both the United States and abroad. New, innovative writing—both in style and subject—is valued above the author's previous publishing history."

NEEDS "We do not publish genre fiction (i.e., romance, mystery, crime, etc.)." Length: 1,000-6,000 words.

HOW TO CONTACT Send complete ms. Publishes 6 mss a year.

TIPS "We enjoy work that is thought-provoking and challenging in its subject matter and style."

HARPUR PALATE

English Department, P.O. Box 6000, Binghamton University, Binghamton NY 13902-6000. **E-mail:** harpur.palate@gmail.com. **Website:** http://harpurpalate.blogspot.com. **Contact:** Barrett Bowlin, managing editor. Estab. 2000. Magazine: 6×9; 180-200 pages;

coated or uncoated paper; 100 lb. coated cover; 4-color art portfolio insert. "We have no restrictions on subject matter or form. Quite simply, send us your highest-quality prose or poetry." Semiannual. Circ. 800.

NEEDS Adventure, ethnic/multicultural, experimental, historical, humor/satire, mainstream, mystery/suspense, novel excerpts, literary, fabulism, magical realism, metafiction, slipstream. Receives 400 unsolicited mss/month. Accepts 5-10 mss/issue; 12-20 mss/year. Publishes ms 1-2 months after acceptance. **Publishes 5 new writers/year.** Recently published work by Darryl Crawford and Tim Hedges, Jesse Goolsby, Ivan Faute, and Keith Meatto. Length: 250-8,000 words; average length: 2,000-4,000 words. Publishes short shorts. Also publishes poetry. Sometimes comments on rejected mss. No more than 1 submission per envelope. Length: 250-8,000 words.

HOW TO CONTACT Send complete ms with a cover letter. Fiction and flash fiction should be 250-8,000 words. Include e-mail address on cover. Include estimated word count, brief bio, list of publications. Send a disposable copy of ms and #10 SASE for reply only. Submission periods are: July 15-November 15 for the winter issue, and December 15-April 15 for summer. Responds in 1-3 week to queries; 4- 8 months to mss. Accepts simultaneous submissions if stated in the cover letter. Sample copy for $10. Writer's guidelines online.

PAYMENT/TERMS Pays 2 copies. Pays on publication for first North American serial, electronic rights. Sponsors awards/contests.

TIPS "*Harpur Palate* now accepts submissions all year; deadline for Winter issue is November 15, for Summer issue is April 15. We also sponsor a fiction contest for the Summer issue and a poetry contest for the Winter issue. We do not accept submissions via e-mail. We are interested in high quality writing of all genres, but especially literary poetry and fiction."

HARVARD REVIEW

Houghton Library of the Harvard College Library, Lamont Library, Harvard University, Cambridge MA 02138. (617)495-9775. **Fax:** (617)496-3692. **E-mail:** harvard_review@harvard.edu. **Website:** www.hcl.harvard.edu/harvardreview/. Estab. 1992. Magazine: 6×9; 256-272 pages; b&w illustrations; photographs. Semiannual. Circ. 2,000.

NEEDS Literary. Receives 200 unsolicited mss/month. Accepts 4 mss/issue; 8 mss/year. Publishes ms 3-6 months after acceptance. **Publishes 3-4 new writers/year.** Recently published work by Joyce Carol Oates, Alice Hoffman, William Lychack, Jim Crace, and Karen Bender. Length: 1,000-7,000 words; average length: 3,000-5,000 words. Publishes short shorts. Also publishes literary essays, literary criticism, poetry, and plays. Sometimes comments on rejected mss. Length: 7,000 words.

HOW TO CONTACT Send SASE for return of ms or disposable copy of ms and SASE for reply only. Responds within 6 months to queries. Accepts simultaneous submissions. Writer's guidelines online.

PAYMENT/TERMS Pays 2 contributor's copies; additional copies $7. Pays on publication for first North American serial rights. Sends galleys to author.

TIPS "There is no reading period. Include a cover letter citing recent publications or awards and SASE. Mss must be paginated and labeled with author's name on every page. Do not submit more than 2X/yr. We accept email submissions through http://www.tellitslant.com."

◖ HAWAI'I PACIFIC REVIEW

1060 Bishop St., Honolulu HI 96813. (808)544-1108. **Fax:** (808)544-0862. **E-mail:** pwilson@hpu.edu. **E-mail:** hpr-submissions@hpu.edu. **Website:** www.hpu.edu/hpr. **Contact:** Dr. Patrice M. Wilson, editor. Magazine: 6×9; 100 pages; glossy coated cover. "*Hawai'i Pacific Review* is looking for poetry, short fiction and personal essays that speak with a powerful and unique voice. We encourage experimental narrative techniques and poetic styles, and we welcome works in translation." Annual.

NEEDS Ethnic/multicultural (general), experimental, fantasy, feminist, historical (general), humor/satire, literary, mainstream, regional (Pacific), translations. "Open to all types as long as they're well done. Our audience is adults, so nothing for children/teens." Receives 30-50 unsolicited mss/month. Accepts 5-10 mss/year. Reads mss September- December each year. Publishes ms 10 months after acceptance. **Publishes 2-4 new writers/year.** Recently published work by Wendell Mayo, Elizabeth Crowell, Janet Flora, Mary Ann Cain, and Jean Giovanetti. Publishes short shorts. Also publishes literary essays, poetry. Sometimes comments on rejected mss.

HOW TO CONTACT Send SASE for return of ms or send a disposable copy of ms and SASE for reply only. Responds in 2 weeks to queries; 15 weeks to mss. Accepts simultaneous submissions but must be cited in the cover letter. Sample copy for $5.

PAYMENT/TERMS Pays 2 contributor's copies; additional copies $5. Pays on publication for first North American serial rights.

TIPS "We look for the unusual or original plot; prose with the texture and nuance of poetry. Character development or portrayal must be unusual/original; humanity shown in an original insightful way (or characters); sense of humor where applicable. Be sure it's a draft that has gone through substantial changes, with supervision from a more experienced writer, if you're a beginner. Write about intense emotion and feeling, not just about someone's divorce or shaky relationship. No soap-opera-like fiction."

HAWAII REVIEW

University of Hawaii Board of Publications, 2445 Campus Rd., Hemenway Hall 107, Honolulu HI 96822. (808)956-3030. **Fax:** (808)956-3083. **E-mail:** hawaiireview@gmail.com. **Website:** www.kaleo.org/hawaii_review. Estab. 1973.

HOW TO CONTACT Send complete ms.

TIPS "Make it new. Offers yearly award with $500 prizes in poetry and fiction."

HAYDEN'S FERRY REVIEW

c/o Virginia G. Piper Center for Creative Writing, Arizona State University, P.O. Box 875002, Tempe AZ 85287-5002. (480)965-1337. **E-mail:** HFR@asu.edu. **Website:** www.haydensferryreview.org. **Contact:** Beth Staples, managing editor. Estab. 1986. Editors change every 1-2 years. Magazine: 634×934; 150 pages; fine paper; illustrations; photos. "*Hayden's Ferry Review* publishes best quality fiction, poetry, translations, and creative nonfiction from new, emerging and established writers." Semiannual. Circ. 1,300.

> Work from *Hayden's Ferry Review* has been selected for inclusion in *Pushcart Prize* anthologies and *Best Creative Nonfiction*.

NEEDS Ethnic/multicultural, experimental, humor/satire, literary, regional, slice-of-life vignettes, contemporary, prose poem. Possible special issue. Receives 250 unsolicited mss/month. Accepts 5 mss/issue; 10 mss/year. Publishes ms 6 months after acceptance. Recently published work by Joseph Heller, Ron Carlson, Norman Dubie, John Updike, Richard Ford, Yusef Komunyakaa, Joel-Peter Witkin, Ai, David St. John, Gloria Naylor, Tess Gallagher, Ken Kesey, Naomi Shihab Nye, Allen Ginsberg, T.C. Boyle, Raymond Carver, Rita Dove, Chuck Rosenthal, Rick Bass, Charles Baxter, Pam Houston, Mary Ruefle, and Denise Duhamel. Publishes short shorts. Word length open.

HOW TO CONTACT Accepts submissions online. Responds in 2-3 days to queries; 2-4 months to mss. Accepts simultaneous submissions. Sample copy for $7.50. Writer's guidelines online. Send complete ms.

PAYMENT/TERMS Pays $50-100, 2 copies, and 1-year subscription. Pays on publication for first North American serial rights. Sends galleys to author.

THE HELIX

Central Connecticut State University English Dept., **E-mail:** helixmagazine@gmail.com. **Website:** helixmagazine.org. **Contact:** Collin Q. Glasow, editor-in-chief; Ashley Gravel, managing editor. **The Helix Magazine** is a Central Connecticut State University student run biannual publication. The magazine accepts submission from all over the globe, as it went national in 2007 and global in 2009. The magazine features CCSU student writing, writing from the Hartford County community and an array of submissions from all over the world. The magazine contains multiple genres of literature and art submissions including: poetry, short fiction, playwright, creative non-fiction paintings, photography, watercolor, collage, stencil and computer generated artwork. It is a student run and funded publication.

NEEDS "Published once each semester, The Helix is the longest running literary magazine of Central Connecticut State University. We accept submissions of poetry, short fiction pieces, short pieces of drama, creative nonfiction, and art (which includes anything that can be e-mailed in a .jpg format). Our Spring 2011 deadline is March 15. Contributions are invited from all members of the campus community, as well as the literary community at large. Payment for all accepted submissions is a copy of The Helix. Products: Each year we release a spring issue and a fall issue of our literary magazine, The Helix.

HOBART

P.O. Box 1658, Ann Arbor MI 48103. **E-mail:** aaron@hobartpulp.com. **Website:** www.hobartpulp.com. **Contact:** Aaron Burch, Editor. Literary magazine/journal. 6×9, 200 pages. Contains illustrations. Includes photographs. "We publish non-stuffy, unpretentious, high quality fiction that never takes itself too serious and always entertains." Semiannual. Estab. 2002. Circ. 1,000. Member CLMP. "We tend to like quirky stories like truck driving, mathematics and vagabonding. We like stories with humor (humorous but engaging, literary but not stuffy). We want to get excited about your story and hope you'll send your best work."

Send submissions to: websubmissions@hobartpulp.com. Query first if you'd like to interview someone for Hobart.

NEEDS Literary. Receives 200 mss/month. Accepts 20 mss/issue; 40 mss/year. Ms published 2-8 months after acceptance. **Publishes 2-5 new writers/year.** Published Benjamin Percy, Tod Goldberg, Chris Bachelder, Sheila Heti, Stephany Aulenback, Catherine Zeidler, and Ryan Call. Length: 1,000 words (min)-7,000 words (max). Average length: 3,000 words. Publishes short shorts. Also publishes literary essays. Sometimes comments on/critiques rejected mss. (for print)

HOW TO CONTACT Send complete ms with cover letter. Accepts submissions by e-mail. Responds to queries in 2 weeks. Responds to mss in 1-4 months. Send disposable copy of ms and #10 SASE for reply only. Considers simultaneous submissions. Sample copy available for $2. Guidelines available for SASE, via e-mail, on website.

PAYMENT/TERMS Writers receive $50-150, 2 contributor's copies, free subscription to the magazine. Additional copies $5. Pays on publication. Acquires first rights. Publication is copyrighted.

TIPS "The subject line must say, "print submission" and include your name, story title. Attach it as either a Word or .rtf document. For website submissions, we want stories shorter than 2,000 words, though 1,000 is better."

HOME PLANET NEWS

P.O. Box 455, High Falls NY 12440. (845)687-4084. **E-mail:** homeplanetnews@yahoo.com. **Website:** www.homeplanetnews.org. **Contact:** Donald Lev, editor. Estab. 1979. Tabloid; 1112×16; 24 pages; newsprint; illustrations; photos. "*Home Planet News* publishes mainly poetry along with some fiction, as well as reviews (books, theater and art) and articles of literary interest. We see *HPN* as a quality literary journal in an eminently readable format and with content that is urban, urbane and politically aware." Triannual. Circ. 1,000.

NEEDS Ethnic/multicultural, experimental, feminist, gay, historical, lesbian, literary, mainstream, science fiction (soft/sociological). No "children's or genre sto-

ries (except rarely some science fiction)." Publishes special fiction issue or anthology. Receives 12 unsolicited mss/month. Accepts 1 mss/issue; 3 mss/year. Publishes ms 1 year after acceptance. Recently published work by Hugh Fox, Walter Jackman, Jim Story. Length: 500-2,500 words; average length: 2,000 words. Publishes short shorts. Also publishes literary criticism.

HOW TO CONTACT Send complete ms. Send SASE for reply, return of ms or send a disposable copy of the ms. Responds in 6 months to mss. Sample copy for $4. Writer's guidelines for SASE.

PAYMENT/TERMS Pays 3 contributor's copies; additional copies $1. Acquires one-time rights.

HUNGER MOUNTAIN

Vermont College of Fine Arts, 36 College St., Montpelier VT 05602. (802)828-8517. **E-mail:** hungermtn@vermontcollege.edu. **Website:** www.hungermtn.org. Estab. 2002. Accepts high quality work from unknown, emerging, or successful writers. No genre fiction, drama, or academic articles, please.

NEEDS No genre fiction, meaning science fiction, fantasy, horror, erotic, etc.

HOW TO CONTACT Query with published clips.

PAYMENT/TERMS Pays $25-100.

TIPS "Mss must be typed, prose double-spaced. Poets submit at least 3 poems. No multiple genre submissions. Fresh viewpoints and human interest are very important, as is originality. We are committed to publishing an outstanding journal of the arts. Do not send entire novels, mss, or short story collections. Do not send previously published work."

THE IDAHO REVIEW

1910 University Dr., Boise ID 83725. (208)426-1002. **Fax:** (208)426-4373. **E-mail:** mwieland@boisestate. edu. Estab. 1998. **Contact:** Mitch Wieland, editor. Estab. 1998. Magazine: 6×9; 180-200 pages; acid-free accent opaque paper; coated cover stock; photos. "A literary journal for anyone who enjoys good fiction." Annual. Circ. 1,000. Member CLMP.

Recent stories reprinted in *The Best American Short Stories, The O. Henry Prize Stories, The Pushcart Prize,* and *New Stories from The South.*

NEEDS Experimental, literary. "No genre fiction of any type." Receives 150 unsolicited mss/month. Accepts 5-7 mss/issue; 5-7 mss/year. "We do not read from May 1-August 31." Publishes ms 1 year after acceptance. Agented fiction 5%. **Publishes 3 new writers/year.** Recently published work by Ann Beattie, Pam Houston, Rick Bass, Edith Pearlman, Joy Williams, Richard Bausch. Length: open; average length: 7,000 words. Publishes short shorts. Also publishes literary essays, poetry. Sometimes comments on rejected mss.

HOW TO CONTACT Send SASE for return of ms or send a disposable copy of ms and #10 SASE for reply only. Responds in 3-5 months to mss. Accepts simultaneous, multiple submissions. Sample copy for $8.95. Writer's guidelines for SASE. Reviews fiction.

PAYMENT/TERMS Pays $100 when funds are available plus 2 contributor's copies; additional copies $5. Pays on publication for first North American serial rights. Sends galleys to author.

TIPS "We look for strongly crafted work that tells a story that needs to be told. We demand vision and intlligence and mystery in the fiction we publish."

◐ ILLUMINATIONS

Dept. of English, College of Charleston, 66 George St., Charleston SC 29424-0001. (843)953-1920. **Fax:** (843)953-3180. **E-mail:** lewiss@cofc.edu. **Website:** www.cofc.edu/illuminations. **Contact:** Simon Lewis, editor. Estab. 1982. Magazine: 5×8; 80 pages; illustrations. "*Illuminations* is one of the most challengingly eclectic little literary magazines around, having featured writers from the United States, Britain and Romania, as well as Southern Africa." Annual. Circ. 500.

NEEDS Literary. Receives 5 unsolicited mss/month. Accepts 1 mss/year. **Publishes 1 new writer/year.** Recently published work by John Michael Cummings. Also publishes poetry. Sometimes comments on rejected mss.

HOW TO CONTACT Send SASE for reply, return of ms or send a disposable copy of ms. Responds in 2 weeks to queries; 2 months to mss. No simultaneous submissions. Sample copy for $10 and 6×9 envelope. Writer's guidelines free.

PAYMENT/TERMS Pays 2 contributor's copies of current issue; 1 of subsequent issue. Acquires one-time rights.

◐ ⑤ IMAGE

3307 Third Ave. W., Seattle WA 98119. (206)281-2988. **Fax:** (206)281-2979. **E-mail:** gwolfe@imagejournal. org. **Website:** www.imagejournal.org. **Contact:** Gregory Wolfe, publisher/editor. Estab. 1989. Magazine: 7×10; 136 pages; glossy cover stock; illustrations; photos. "*Image* is a showcase for the encounter between religious faith and world-class contemporary art. Each issue features fiction, poetry, essays, memoirs, reviews, an in-depth interview and articles about visual artists, film, music, etc. and glossy 4-color plates of contemporary visual art." Quarterly. Circ. 4,500. Member CLMP.

NEEDS Literary, essays. Receives 100 unsolicited mss/month. Accepts 2 mss/issue; 8 mss/year. Publishes ms 1 year after acceptance. Agented fiction 5%. Has published work by Annie Dillard, David James Duncan, Robert Olen Butler, Bret Lott, Melanie Rae Thon. Length: 4,000-6,000 words; average length: 5,000 words. "No sentimental, preachy, moralistic, obvious stories, or genre stories (unless they manage to transcend their genre)." Length: 4,000-6,000 words.

HOW TO CONTACT Send SASE for reply, return of ms or send disposable copy of ms. Responds in 1 month to queries; 3 months to mss. Sample copy for $16. Reviews fiction. Send complete ms. Does not accept e-mail submissions.

PAYMENT/TERMS Pays $10/page and 4 contributor's copies; additional copies for $6. Pays on acceptance. Sends galleys to author. Pays $10/page; $150 maximum.

◐ ⊙ ⑤ INDIANA REVIEW

Ballantine Hall 465, 1020 E. Kirkwood, Indiana University, Bloomington IN 47405-7103. (812)855-3439. **E-mail:** inreview@indiana.edu. **Website:** www.indiana.edu/~inreview. Estab. 1976. Magazine: 6×9; 160 pages; 50 lb. paper; Glatfelter cover stock. "*Indiana Review*, a nonprofit organization run by IU graduate students, is a journal of previously unpublished poetry and fiction. Literary interviews and essays also considered. We publish innovative fiction and poetry. We're interested in energy, originality and careful attention to craft. While we publish many well-known writers, we also welcome new and emerging poets and fiction writers." Semiannual.

> ⛢ Work published in *Indiana Review* received a Pushcart Prize (2001) and was included in *Best New American Voices* (2001). *IR* also received an Indiana Arts Council Grant and a NEA grant.

NEEDS Ethnic/multicultural, experimental, literary, mainstream, novel excerpts, regional, translations. No genre fiction. Receives 300 unsolicited mss/month. Accepts 7-9 mss/issue. Reads year-round, but

refer to web-site for closed submission periods. Publishes ms an average of 3-6 months after acceptance. **Publishes 6-8 new writers/year.** Recently published work by Kim Addonizio, Stuart Dybek, Marilyn Chin, Ray Gonzalez, Michael Martone, Melanie Rae Thon. Also publishes literary essays, poetry. "We look for daring stories which integrate theme, language, character, and form. We like polished writing, humor, and fiction which has consequence beyond the world of its narrator." No genre fiction. Length: 250-10,000 words. **HOW TO CONTACT** Send complete ms. Accepts online submissions. Cover letters should be *brief* and demonstrate specific familiarity with the content of a recent issue of *Indiana Review*. Include SASE. Responds in 4 months to mss. Accepts simultaneous submissions if notified *immediately* of other publication. Sample copy for $9. Writer's guidelines online. Send complete ms.
PAYMENT/TERMS Pays $5/page, plus 2 contributor's copies. Pays on publication for first North American serial rights. Sponsors awards/contests.

○ INKWELL MAGAZINE

Manhattanville College, 2900 Purchase St., Purchase NY 10577. (914)323-7239. **Fax:** (914)323-3122. **E-mail:** inkwell@mville.edu. **Website:** www.inkwelljournal. org. Estab. 1995. Literary Journal: 512×712; 120-170 pages; 60 lb. paper; 10 pt C1S, 4/c cover; illustrations; photos. "*Inkwell Magazine* is committed to presenting top quality poetry, prose and artwork in a high quality publication. *Inkwell* is dedicated to discovering new talent and to encouraging and bringing talents of working writers and artists to a wider audience. We encourage diverse voices and have an open submission policy for both art and literature." Annual. Circ. 1,000. Member CLMP. Receives 120 unsolicited mss/month. Accepts 45 mss/issue. Does not read mss December-July. Publishes ms 2 months after acceptance. **Publishes 3-5 new writers/year.** Recently published work by Alice Quinn, Margaret Gibson, Benjamin Cheever, Paul Muldoon, Pablo Medina, Carol Muske-Dukes. Length: 5,000 words; average length: 3,000 words. Publishes short shorts. Also publishes poetry. Send a disposable copy of ms and #10 SASE for reply only. Responds in 1 month to queries; 4-6 months to mss. Sample copy for $6. Writer's guidelines for SASE.

○ *Inkwell* is produced in affiliation with the Master of Arts in Writing program at Man-

hattanville College, and is staffed by faculty and graduate students of the program.
NEEDS Experimental, humor/satire, literary. "No erotica, children's literature, romance, religious." Does not want children's literature, erotica, pulp adventure, or science fiction. 5,000 words maximum
HOW TO CONTACT Send complete ms.
PAYMENT/TERMS Pays $10/page and 2 contributor's copies; additional copies $8. Acquires first North American serial, first rights. Sponsors awards/contests. Pays $75-150.
TIPS "We cannot accept electronic submissions."

○ $ THE IOWA REVIEW

308 EPB, The University of Iowa, Iowa City IA 52242. (319)335-0462. **Website:** iowareview.org. **Contact:** Russell Scott Valentino, editor. Estab. 1970. *The Iowa Review*, published 3 times/year, prints fiction, poetry, essays, reviews, and, occasionally, interviews. *The Iowa Review* is 512×812, approximately 200 pages, professionally printed, flat-spined, first-grade offset paper, Carolina CS1 10-point cover stock. Receives about 5,000 submissions/year, accepts up to 100. Press run is 2,900; 1,500 distributed to stores. Subscription: $25. Stories, essays, and poems for a general readership interested in contemporary literature.
NEEDS "We are open to a range of styles and voices and always hope to be surprised by work we then feel we need." Receives 600 unsolicited mss/month. Accepts 4-6 mss/issue; 12-18 mss/year. Does not read mss January-August. Publishes ms an average of 12-18 months after acceptance. Agented fiction less than 2%. **Publishes some new writers/year.** Recently published work by Bradley Bazzle, Chris Offutt, Alison Ruch.
HOW TO CONTACT Send complete ms with cover letter. "Don't bother with queries." SASE for return of ms. SASE required. Responds in 4 months to mss. Simultaneous submissions accepted.
PAYMENT/TERMS Pays $.08 per word ($100 minimum), plus 2 contributor's copies.
TIPS "We publish essays, reviews, novel excerpts, stories, poems, and photography. We have no set guidelines as to content or length, but strongly recommend that writers read a sample issue before submitting. Buys 65-80 unsolicited ms/year. Submit complete ms with SASE."

○ JABBERWOCK REVIEW

Department of English, Mississippi State University, Drawer E, Mississippi State MS 39762. **E-mail:** jabberwockreview@english.msstate.edu. **Website:** www.ms-state.edu/org/jabberwock. **Contact:** Michael Kardos, editor. Estab. 1979. Literary magazine/journal: 6x9; 120 pages; 60 lb paper; 80 lb cover.

NEEDS Ethnic/multicultural, experimental, feminist, gay, literary, mainstream, regional, translations. "No science fiction, romance." Receives 150 unsolicited mss/month. Accepts 7-8 mss/issue; 15 mss/year. "We do not read March 15 to September 1." Publishes ms 4-6 months after acceptance. **Publishes 1-5 new writers/year.** Recently published work by Robert Morgan, Charles Harper Webb, Ted Kooser, Alison Baker, Alyce Miller, Lorraine Lopez, J.D. Chapman. Length: 250-5,000 words; average length: 4,000 words. Publishes short shorts. Also publishes literary essays, poetry. Sometimes comments on rejected mss.

HOW TO CONTACT Send SASE (or IRC) for return of ms. Does not accept e-mail submissions. Responds in 5 months to mss. Accepts simultaneous submissions "with notification of such." Sample copy for $6. Writer's guidelines for SASE.

PAYMENT/TERMS Pays 2 contributor's copies. Sponsors awards/contests.

❶ J JOURNAL: NEW WRITING ON JUSTICE

619 West 54th St., 7th Fl, New York NY 10019. (212) 327-8697. **E-mail:** jjournal@jjay.cuny.edu. **Website:** www.jjournal.org. **Contact:** Adam Berlin and Jeffrey Heiman, editors. Estab. 2008. Literary magazine/journal: 6x9; 120 pages; 60 lb paper; 80 lb cover. "*J Journal* publishes literary fiction, creative nonfiction and poetry on the subjects of crime, criminal justice, law and law enforcement. While the themes are specific, they need not dominate the work. We're interested in questions of justice from all perspectives." Semiannual. Estab. 2008.

NEEDS Experimental, gay, historical (general), literary, military/war, regional. Receives 100 mss/month. Accepts 5 mss/issue; 10 mss/year. Ms. published 6 months after acceptance. Length: 750-6,000 words (max). Average length: 4,000 words. Also publishes poetry. Sometimes comments on/critiques rejected mss.

HOW TO CONTACT Send complete ms with cover letter. Include estimated word count, brief bio, list of publications. Responds to queries in 4 weeks; mss in 12 weeks. Send recyclable copy of ms and #10 SASE or email for reply only. Considers simultaneous submissions. Sample copy available for $10.

PAYMENT/TERMS Writers receive 2 contributor's copies. Additional copies $10. Pays on publication. Acquires first rights. Publication is copyrighted.

TIPS "We're looking for literary fiction/memoir/personal narrative poetry with a connection, direct or tangential, to the theme of justice."

❶❸ THE JOURNAL

The Ohio State University, 164 W. 17th Ave., Columbus OH 43210. (614)292-4076. **Fax:** (614)292-7816. **E-mail:** thejournal@osu.edu; thejournalmag@gmail.com. **Website:** english.osu.edu/research/journals/thejournal/. Estab. 1972. Magazine: 6x9; 150 pages. "We're open to all forms; we tend to favor work that gives evidence of a mature and sophisticated sense of the language." Semiannual.

NEEDS Novel excerpts, literary short stories. No romance, science fiction or religious/devotional. Receives 100 unsolicited mss/month. Accepts 2 mss/issue. Publishes ms 1 year after acceptance. Agented fiction 10%. **Publishes some new writers/year.** Recently published work by Michael Martone, Gregory Spatz, and Stephen Graham Jones. Sometimes comments on rejected mss. No romance, science fiction or religious/devotional.

HOW TO CONTACT Send complete ms with cover letter and SASE. Responds in 2 weeks to queries; 2 months to mss. Accepts simultaneous submissions. No electronic submissions. Sample copy for $7 or online. Writer's guidelines online.

PAYMENT/TERMS Pays $20. Pays on publication for first North American serial rights. Sends galleys to author. Pays $20.

TIPS "Manuscripts are rejected because of lack of understanding of the short story form, shallow plots, undeveloped characters. Cure: Read as much well-written fiction as possible. Our readers prefer 'psychological' fiction rather than stories with intricate plots. Take care to present a clean, well-typed submission."

❶❷❸ THE KENYON REVIEW

Finn House, 102 W. Wiggin, Gambier OH 43022. (740)427-5208. **Fax:** (740)427-5417. **E-mail:** kenyonreview@kenyon.edu. **Website:** KenyonReview.org. **Contact:** Marlene Landefeld. Estab. 1939. An international journal of literature, culture and the arts dedicated to an inclusive representation of the best in new writing (fiction, poetry, essays, interviews, criticism) from established and emerging writers.

NEEDS Excerpts from novels, condensed novels, ethnic/multicultural, experimental, feminist, gay, historical, humor/satire, lesbian, literary, mainstream, translations, contemporary. Receives 900 unsolicited mss/month. Unsolicited mss read September 15-January 15 only. Publishes ms 1 year after acceptance. Recently published work by Alice Hoffman, Beth Ann Fennelly, Romulus Linney, John Koethe, Albert Goldbarth, Erin McGraw. 3-15 typeset pages preferred **HOW TO CONTACT** Only accepting mss via online submissions program. Please visit website for instructions. Do not submit via e-mail or snail mail. No simultaneous submissions. Sample copy $12 single issue, includes postage and handling. Please call or e-mail to order. Writer's guidelines online. **PAYMENT/TERMS** Pays $15-40/page. Pays on publication for first rights.

○ KEREM

Jewish Study Center Press, 3035 Porter St. NW, Washington DC 20008. (202)364-3006. **E-mail:** langner@erols.com; kerem@simpatico.ca. **Website:** www.kerem.org. **Contact:** Gilah Langner, co-editor. Estab. 1992. Magazine: 6×9; 128 pages; 60 lb. offset paper; glossy cover; illustrations; photos. "Kerem publishes Jewish religious, creative, literary material—short stories, poetry, personal reflections, text study, prayers, rituals, etc." Estab. 1992.

NEEDS Jewish: feminist, humor/satire, literary, religious/inspirational. Receives 10-12 unsolicited mss/month. Accepts 1-2 mss/issue. Publishes ms 2-10 months after acceptance. **Publishes 2 new writers/year.** Also publishes literary essays, poetry.

HOW TO CONTACT Prefers submissions by e-mail. Send SASE for reply, return of ms or send disposable copy of ms. Responds in 2 months to queries; 5 months to mss. Accepts simultaneous, multiple submissions. Sample copy for $8.50. Writer's guidelines online.

PAYMENT/TERMS Pays free subscription and 2-10 contributor's copies. Acquires one time rights.

TIPS "Should have a strong Jewish content. We want to be moved by reading the manuscript!"

○ THE KIT-CAT REVIEW

244 Halstead Ave., Harrison NY 10528. (914)835-4833. **E-mail:** kitcatreview@gmail.com. **Contact:** Claudia Fletcher, editor. Estab. 1998. Magazine: 812×512; 75 pages; laser paper; colored card cover stock; illustrations. "The Kit-Cat Review is named after the 18th Century Kit-Cat Club, whose members included Addison, Steele, Congreve, Vanbrugh and Garth. Its purpose is to promote/discover excellence and originality." The Kit-Cat Review is part of the collections of the University of Wisconsin (Madison) and State University of New York (Buffalo). Quarterly.

NEEDS Ethnic/multicultural, experimental, literary, novel excerpts, slice-of-life vignettes. No stories with "O. Henry-type formula endings. Shorter pieces stand a better chance of publication." No science fiction, fantasy, romance, horror or new age. Receives 40 unsolicited mss/month. Accepts 6 mss/issue; 24 mss/year. Time between acceptance and publication is 6 months. **Publishes 14 new writers/year.** Recently published work by Chayym Zeldis, Michael Fedo, Louis Phillips, Elisha Porat. Length: 5,000 words maximum; average length: 2,000 words. Publishes short shorts. Also publishes literary essays, literary criticism, poetry. No stories with O. Henry-type formula endings. Shorter pieces stand a better chance of publication. 5,000 words maximum

HOW TO CONTACT Send complete ms. Accepts submissions by disk. Send SASE (or IRC) for return of ms, or send disposable copy of ms and #10 SASE for reply only. Responds in 1 week to queries; 2 months to mss. Accepts simultaneous, multiple submissions. Sample copy for $7 (payable to Claudia Fletcher). Writer's guidelines not available. Send complete ms.

PAYMENT/TERMS Pays $25-200 and 2 contributor's copies; additional copies $5. Pays on publication for first rights.

TIPS "Obtaining a sample copy is strongly suggested. Include a short bio, SASE, and word count for fiction and nonfiction submissions."

○ LA KANCERKLINIKO

162 rue Paradis, P.O. Box 174, 13444 Marseille Cantini Cedex France. (33)2-48-61-81-98. **Fax:** (33)2-48-61-81-98. **E-mail:** lseptier@hotmail.com. **Contact:** Laurent Septier. "An Esperanto magazine which appears 4 times annually. Each issue contains 32 pages. La Kancerkliniko is a political and cultural magazine." Quarterly. Circ. 300. Science fiction, short stories or very short novels. "The short story (or the very short novel) must be written only in Esperanto, either original or translation from any other language." Wants more science fiction. **Publishes 2-3 new writers/year.** Recently published work by

Mao Zifu, Manuel de Seabra, Peter Brown and Aldo de'Giorgi. Accepts disk submissions. Accepts multiple submissions.

NEEDS Science fiction, short stories, or very short novels. "The short story (or the very short novel) must be written only in Esperanto, either original or translation from any other language." Wants more science fiction. **Publishes 2-3 new writers/year.**

HOW TO CONTACT Accepts submissions by e-mail, fax. Accepts disk submissions. Accepts multiple submissions. Sample copy for 3 IRCs from Universal Postal Union.

PAYMENT/TERMS Pays in contributor's copies.

🄳 LAKE EFFECT

4951 College Dr., Erie PA 16563-1501. (814)898-6281. **Fax:** (814)898-6032. **E-mail:** goL1@psu.edu. **Website:** www.pserie.psu.edu/lakeeffect. **Contact:** George Looney, editor-in-chief. Estab. 1978. Magazine: 512×812; 180-200 pages; 55 lb. natural paper; 12 pt. C1S cover. "In addition to seeking strong, traditional stories, *Lake Effect* is open to more experimental, language-centered fiction as well." Annual. Estab. as *Lake Effect*, 2001; as Tempest, 1978. Member CLMP.

NEEDS Experimental, literary, mainstream. "No children's/juvenile, fantasy, science fiction, romance or young adult/teen." Receives 120 unsolicited mss/month. Accepts 5-9 mss/issue. Publishes ms 1 year after acceptance. **Publishes 6 new writers/year.** Recently published work by Edith Pearlman, Francois Camoin, Cris Mazza, Joan Connor, Aimee Parkison, Joanna Howard. Length: 4,500-5,000 words; average length: 2,600-3,900 words. Publishes short shorts. Also publishes literary essays, poetry.

HOW TO CONTACT Send SASE for return of ms or send a disposable copy of ms and #10 SASE for reply only. Responds in 3 weeks to queries; 2-6 months to mss. Accepts simultaneous submissions. Sample copy for $6. Writer's guidelines for SASE.

PAYMENT/TERMS Pays 2 contributor's copies; additional copies $2. Acquires first, onetime rights. Not copyrighted.

🄳 LANDFALL/OTAGO UNIVERSITY PRESS

P.O. Box 56, Dunedin New Zealand. **Fax:** (643)479-8385. **E-mail:** landfall@otago.ac.nz. **Contact:** Landfall Editor.

NEEDS Publishes fiction, poetry, commentary and reviews of New Zealand books.

HOW TO CONTACT Email your submission to landfall@otago.ac.nz. Submission guidelines are at www.otago.ac.nz/press/landfall.

TIPS "We concentrate on publishing work by New Zealand writers, but occasionally accept work from elsewhere."

🄳 THE LEDGE MAGAZINE

40 Maple Ave., Bellport NY 11713-2011. (631)286-5252. **E-mail:** info@theledgemagazine.com. **Website:** www.theledgemagazine.com. **Contact:** Tim Monaghan, Editor-in-Chief. Estab. 1988. Literary magazine/journal: 6 x 9, 300 pages, offset paper, glossy stock cover. "The Ledge Magazine publishes cutting-edge contemporary fiction by emerging and established writers." Annual. Receives 120 mss/month. Accepts 9 mss/issue. Manuscript published 6 months after acceptance. Also publishes poetry. Rarely comments on/critiques rejected mss. Send complete ms with cover letter. Include estimated word count, brief bio. Send SASE (or IRC) for return of ms.

NEEDS Erotica, ethnic/multicultural (general), literary. Receives 120 mss/month. Accepts 9 mss/issue. Manuscript published 6 months after acceptance. Published Pia Chatterjee, Xujun Eberlein, Clifford Garstang, Richard Jespers, William Luvaas, Michael Thompson. Length: 2,500 words (min)-7,500 words (max). Average length: 6,000 words. Also publishes poetry. Rarely comments on/critiques rejected mss. Length: 2,500 words (min)-7,500 words (max). Average length: 6,000 words.

HOW TO CONTACT Send complete ms with cover letter. Include estimated word count, brief bio. Responds to queries in 6 weeks. Responds to mss in 8 months. Send SASE (or IRC) for return of ms. Considers simultaneous submissions. Sample copy available for $10. Subscription: $20 (2 issues), $36 (4 issues). Guidelines available for SASE.

PAYMENT/TERMS Writers receive 1 contributor's copy. Additional copies $6. Pays on publication. Acquires first North American serial rights. Sends galleys to author. Publication is copyrighted.

🄳 LE FORUM

University of Maine, Franco American Center, Orono ME 04469-5719. (207)581-3764. **Fax:** (207)581-1455. **E-mail:** lisa_michaud@umit.maine.edu. **Website:** Francoamericanarchives.org. **Contact:** Lisa Michaud, managing editor. Estab. 1972. "We will consider any type of short fiction, poetry and critical essays having to do with Franco-American experience. They must be of good quality in French or English. We are also looking for Canadian writers with French-North American experiences." Receives 10 unsolicited mss/month. Accepts 2-4 mss/issue. **Publishes some new writers/year.** Length: 750-2,500 words; average length: 1,000 words. Occasionally comments on rejected mss. Include SASE. Accepts simultaneous submissions and reprints. Sample copy not available. Pays 3 copies."

HOW TO CONTACT Include SASE.

PAYMENT/TERMS Pays 3 contributor's copies.

◑ THE LISTENING EYE

Kent State University Geauga Campus, 14111 Claridon-Troy Rd., Burton OH 44021. (440)286-3840. **E-mail:** grace_butcher@msn.com. **Website:** http://reocities.com/Athens/3716/eye.htm. **Contact:** Grace Butcher, editor. Estab. 1970. Magazine: 512×812; 60 pages; photographs. "We publish the occasional very short stories (750 words/3 pages double spaced) in any subject and any style, but the language must be strong, unusual, free from cliché and vagueness. We are a shoestring operation from a small campus but we publish high-quality work." Annual. Estab. 1970. Circ. 250.

NEEDS Literary. "Pretty much anything will be considered except porn." Reads mss January 1-April 15 only. Publishes ms 3-4 months after acceptance. Recently published work by Elizabeth Scott, Sam Ruddick, H.E. Wright. Publishes short shorts. Also publishes poetry. Sometimes comments on rejected mss.

HOW TO CONTACT Send SASE for return of ms or disposable copy of ms with SASE for reply only. Responds in 4 weeks to queries; 4 months to mss. Accepts reprint submissions. Sample copy for $3 and $1 postage. Writer's guidelines for SASE.

PAYMENT/TERMS Pays 2 contributor's copies; additional copies $3 with $1 postage. Pays on publication for onetime rights.

TIPS "We look for powerful, unusual imagery, content and plot in our short stories. In poetry, we look for tight lines that don't sound like prose; unexpected images or juxtapositions; the unusual use of language; noticeable relationships of sounds; a twist in viewpoint; an ordinary idea in extraordinary language; an amazing and complex idea simply stated; play on words and with words; an obvious love of language. Poets need to read the 'Big 3'—Cummings, Thomas,

Hopkins—to see the limits to which language can be taken. Then read the 'Big 2'—Dickinson to see how simultaneously tight, terse, and universal a poem can be, and Whitman to see how sprawling, cosmic, and personal. Then read everything you can find that's being published in literary magazines today, and see how your work compares to all of the above."

◐◔ THE LITERARY REVIEW

285 Madison Ave., Madison NJ 07940. (973)443-8564. **Fax:** (973)443-8364. **E-mail:** tlr@fdu.edu. **Website:** www.theliteraryreview.org. **Contact:** Minna Proctor, Editor-In-Chief. Estab. 1957. Magazine: 6×9; 200 pages; professionally printed on textpaper; semigloss card cover; perfect-bound. "Literary magazine specializing in fiction, poetry and essays with an international focus. Our audience is general with a leaning toward scholars, libraries and schools." Quarterly. Estab. 1957. Circ. 2,000.

◔ Work published in *the Literary Review* has been included in *Editor's Choice, Best American Short Stories* and *Pushcart Prize* anthologies.

NEEDS Works of high literary quality only. Does not want to see "overused subject matter or pat resolutions to conflicts." Receives 90-100 unsolicited mss/month. Submit on line only; No paper mss. Accepts 20-25 mss/year. Does not read submissions June 1-September 1. Publishes ms 1-2 years after acceptance. Agented fiction 1-2%. **Publishes 80% new writers/year.** Recently published work by Irvin Faust, Todd James Pierce, Joshua Shapiro, Susan Schwartz Senstadt. Also publishes literary essays, literary criticism, poetry. Occasionally comments on rejected mss.

HOW TO CONTACT Responds in 6-12 months to mss. Submit online at www.theliteraryreview.org/submit.html only. Accepts multiple submissions. Sample copy for $8. Writer's guidelines for SASE. Reviews fiction.

PAYMENT/TERMS Pays 2 contributor's copies; $4 discount for extras. Acquires first rights.

◐ THE LONG STORY

18 Eaton St., Lawrence MA 01843. (978)686-7638. **E-mail:** rpburnham@mac.com. **Website:** web.me.com/rpburnham/Site/LongStory.html. **Contact:** R.P. Burnham. Estab. 1983. Magazine: 512×812; 160 pages; 60 lb. cover stock; illustrations (b&w graphics). For serious, educated, literary people. Annual. Circ. 600.

NEEDS Ethnic/multicultural, feminist, literary, contemporary. "No science fiction, adventure, romance, etc. We publish high literary quality of any kind but especially look for stories that have difficulty getting published elsewhere—committed fiction, working class settings, left-wing themes, etc." Receives 30-50 unsolicited mss/month. Accepts 6-7 mss/issue. Publishes ms 3 months to 1 year after acceptance. **Publishes 90% new writers/year.** Length: 8,000-20,000 words; average length: 8,000-12,000 words.

HOW TO CONTACT Include SASE. Responds in 2 months to mss. Accepts simultaneous submissions "but not wild about it." Sample copy for $7.

PAYMENT/TERMS Pays 2 contributor's copies; $5 charge for extras. Acquires first rights.

◑ LOUISIANA LITERATURE

SLU Box 10792, Southeastern Louisiana University, Hammond LA 70402. **E-mail:** lalit@selu.edu; ngerman@selu.edu. **Website:** www.louisianaliterature.org. **Contact:** Jack B. Bedell, editor. Estab. 1984. Magazine: 6×9; 150 pages; 70 lb. paper; card cover; illustrations. "Essays should be about Louisiana material; preference is given to fiction and poetry with Louisiana and Southern themes, but creative work can be set anywhere." Semiannual. Circ. 600 paid; 750-1,000 printed.

NEEDS Literary, mainstream, regional. "No sloppy, ungrammatical manuscripts." Receives 100 unsolicited mss/month. May not read mss June-July. Publishes ms 6-12 after acceptance. **Publishes 4 new writers/year.** Recently published work by Anthony Bukowski, Aaron Gwyn, Robert Phillips, R.T. Smith. Length: 1,000-6,000 words; average length: 3,500 words. Sometimes comments on rejected mss.

HOW TO CONTACT Include SASE. Responds in 3 months to mss. Sample copy for $8. Reviews fiction.

PAYMENT/TERMS Pays usually in contributor's copies. Acquires onetime rights.

TIPS "Cut out everything that is not a functioning part of the story. Make sure your manuscript is professionally presented. Use relevant specific detail in every scene. We love detail, local color, voice and craft. Any professional manuscript stands out."

● THE LOUISIANA REVIEW

Division of Liberal Arts, Louisiana State University at Eunice, P.O. Box 1129, Eunice LA 70535. (337)550-1315. **E-mail:** bfonteno@lsue.edu. **Website:** web.lsue.edu/la-review. **Contact:** Dr. Billy Fontenot, editor. Es-

tab. 1999. Magazine: 812x512 bound; 100-200 pages; b&w illustrations. "We are looking for excellent work by Louisiana writers as well as those outside the state who tell us their connection to it. Non-Louisiana material is considered, but Louisiana/Gulf Coast themed work gets priority." Annual. Circ. 300-600.

NEEDS Ethnic/multicultural (Cajun or Louisiana culture), historical (Louisiana-related or setting), regional (Louisiana, Gulf Coast). Receives 25 unsolicited mss/month. Accepts 5-7 mss/issue. Reads year-round. Publishes ms 6-12 months after acceptance. Recently published work by Ronald Frame, Tom Bonner, Laura Cario, Sheryl St. Germaine. Length: up to 9,000 words; average length: 2,000 words. Publishes short shorts. Also publishes poetry and b&w artwork. Sometimes comments on rejected mss.

HOW TO CONTACT Send SASE for return of ms. Responds in 5 weeks to queries; 10 weeks to mss. Accepts multiple submissions. Sample copy for $5.

PAYMENT/TERMS Pays 1 contributor's copy. Pays on publication for onetime rights. Not copyrighted but has an ISSN number.

TIPS "We do like to have fiction play out visually as a film would rather than static and undramatized. Louisiana or Gulf Coast settings and themes preferred."

◑ THE MACGUFFIN

18600 Haggerty Rd., Livonia MI 48152-2696. (734)462-4400, ext 5327. **E-mail:** macguffin@schoolcraft.edu. **Website:** www.macguffin.org. **Contact:** Steven A. Dolgin, editor; Nicholle Cormier, managing editor; Elizabeth Kircos, fiction editor. Estab. 1984. Magazine: 6×9; 160 pages; 60 lb. paper; 110 lb. cover; b&w illustrations, photos. "*The MacGuffin* is a literary magazine which publishes a range of material including poetry, creative nonfiction, fiction, and art. Material ranges from traditional to experimental. Our periodical attracts a variety of people with many different interests." Triannual. Circ. 500. "Our purpose is to encourage, support and enhance the literary arts in the Schoolcraft College community, the region, the state, and the nation. We also sponsor annual literary events and give voice to deserving new writers as well as established writers."

NEEDS Adventure, ethnic/multicultural, experimental, historical (general), humor/satire, literary, mainstream, translations, contemporary, prose poem. "No religious, inspirational, juvenile, romance, horror, pornography." Receives 80-100 unsolicited mss/

month. Accepts 14-18 mss/issue; 42-54 mss/year. Publishes ms 6 months to 1.5 years after acceptance. Agented fiction 10-15%. **Publishes 30 new writers/ year.** Recently published work by Thomas Lynch, Linda Nemec Foster, Jim Daniels, M. E. Parker, and Daniel Pearlman. Length: 100-5,000 words; average length: 2,000-2,500 words. Publishes short shorts. Also publishes literary essays. Occasionally comments on rejected mss. Does not want "obvious pornographic material." Length: 5,000 words.

HOW TO CONTACT Send SASE or e-mail. Responds in 4-6 months to mss. Sample copy for $6; current issue for $9. Writer's guidelines free on website or with SASE. Pays 2 contributor's copies. Acquires onetime rights. Submit 2 stories, maximum. Prose should be typed and double-spaced. Include word count. One submission/envelope/e-mail.

◑ THE MADISON REVIEW

University of Wisconsin, 600 N, Park St., 6193 Helen C. White Hall, Madison WI 53706. **E-mail:** madisonreview@gmail.com. **Website:** wwww.english.wisc.edu/madisonreview/madisonReviewHome.htm. **Contact:** Joe Malone and Anna Wehrwein, fiction editors; Joyce Edwards and Alex Konrad, poetry editors. Estab. 1972. *The Madison Review* is a student-run literary magazine that looks to publish the best available fiction and poetry.

◯ "We do not publish unsolicited interviews or genre ficion."

NEEDS "Well-crafted, compelling fiction featuring a wide range of styles and subjects." Receives 300 unsolicited mss/period. Accepts 6 mss/issue. Does not read May-September. Publishes ms 4 months after acceptance. **Publishes 4 new writers/year.** Recently published work by Lori Rader Day and Ian Williams. Average length: 4,000 words. Also publishes poetry. No genre—horror, fantasy, erotica, etc. Length: 500-30,000 words.

HOW TO CONTACT Send complete ms.

PAYMENT/TERMS Pays 2 contributor's copies, $5 charge for extras.

TIPS "Our editors have very ecclectic tastes, so don't specifically try to cater to us. Above all, we look for original, high quality work."

◯◑◒ THE MALAHAT REVIEW

The University of Victoria, P.O. Box 1700, STN CSC, Victoria BC V8W 2Y2 Canada. (250)721-8524. E-

mail: malahat@uvic.ca (for queries only). **Website:** www.malahatreview.ca. **Contact:** John Barton, editor. Estab. 1967. "We try to achieve a balance of views and styles in each issue. We strive for a mix of the best writing by both established and new writers." Quarterly.

NEEDS "General fiction, poetry, and creative nonfiction." Accepts 3-4 fiction mss/issue and 1 creative nonfiction ms/issue. Publishes ms within 6 months after acceptance. **Publishes 4-5 new writers/year.** Recently published work by Bill Gaston, Daryl Hine, Jan Zwicky, Steven Heighton. 8,000 words max.

HOW TO CONTACT Send complete ms. "Enclose proper Canadian postage on the SASE (or send IRC)." Responds in 2 weeks to queries; approx. 3 months to mss. No simultaneous submissions. Sample copy for $16.95 (US). Writer's guidelines online. Send complete ms.

PAYMENT/TERMS Pays $30 CAD/magazine page. Pays on acceptance for first world rights. Pays $30/magazine page

TIPS "Please do not send more than 1 submission at a time: 4-8 poems, 1 piece of creative non-fiction, or 1 short story (do not mix poetry and prose in the same submission). See *The Malahat Review*'s Open Season Awards for poetry and short fiction, creative non-fiction, long poem, and novella contests in the Awards section of our website."

◐◐◉ MANOA

English Dept., University of Hawaii, Honolulu HI 96822. (808)956-3070. **Fax:** (808)956-3083. **E-mail:** mjournal-l@listserv.hawaii.edu. **Website:** manoajournal.hawaii.edu. **Contact:** Frank Stewart, Poetry Editor. Estab. 1989. Magazine: 7×10; 240 pages. Most of each issue devoted to new work from Pacific and Asian nations, including high quality literary fiction, poetry, essays, personal narrative. Please see website for current projects. Authors should query before sending submissions. Semiannual. "High quality literary fiction, poetry, essays, personal narrative. In general, each issue is devoted to new work from Pacific and Asian nations. Our audience is international. US writing need not be confined to Pacific settings or subjects. Please note that we seldom publish unsolicited work."

NEEDS Query first and/or see website. No Pacific exotica. Length: 1,000-7,500 words.

HOW TO CONTACT Please query first before sending in mss. Include SASE. Does not accept submissions by e-mail. Sample copy for $20 (U.S.). Writer's guidelines online. Send complete ms.

PAYMENT/TERMS Pays $100-500 normally ($25/printed page). Pays on publication for first North American serial, non-exclusive, one time print rights. Sends galleys to author. Pays $100-500 normally ($25/printed page).

● MARGINALIA

Communication Arts, Language and Literature Department of Western State College of Colorado, P.O. Box 258, Pitkin CO 81241. (970) 642-0393. **E-mail:** marginaliajournal@gmail.com. **Website:** www.marginaliajournal.com. **Contact:** Alicita Rodriguez, editor. Estab. 2005. Annual literary magazine/journal. 6×9, 150 pages, 100 lb paper. "We like writing that pays close attention to the sentence. Language is not a means to an end. It should not be something that gets used solely to establish plot. We want gorgeous diction, unusual and striking imagery, reversed and playful syntax. We don't want to remember what the story or poem is about; we want to remember how it's told. We welcome any hybrid or unidentifiable genres, though we shun experimentation for experimentation's sake. We don't want work that depends on clever jokes or conceits. We like the odd but well-written traditional story, though we don't see too many of these. No gratuitous violence (especially against women and animals)."

NEEDS Experimental, literary. Does not want mainstream or genre fiction. List of upcoming themes available on Web site. Receives 40 mss/month. Accepts 20 mss/issue; 20 mss/year. Ms published 6-9 months after acceptance. Publishes 15% new writers/year. Published Brian Evenson, Laird Hunt, Mark Irwin, Steve Katz, Alex Lemon, Harry Matthews, Gina Ochsner, Lance Olsen, George Singleton, Abdelkrim Tabal, Wendy Walker, and Tom Whalen. Average length: 2,000 words. Publishes short shorts. Also publishes literary essays, book reviews, poetry, visual art. Send review copies to P.O. Box 258, Pitkin CO 81241. Sometimes comments on/critiques rejected mss.

HOW TO CONTACT Submit full ms via e-mail to marginaliajournal@gmail.com or by mail to P.O. Box 258, Pitkin CO 81241. Include estimated word count, brief bio, list of publications. Responds to mss in 6-9 months. Considers simultaneous submissions, multiple submissions. Sample copy available for $9. Sample copy, guidelines available on Web Site: www.margi-

naliajournal.com. Payment/Terms: Writers receive 3 contributor's copies. Additional copies $5. Pays on acceptance. Acquires first rights. Sends galleys to author. Publication is copyrighted. No contests at this time.

●● THE MARLBORO REVIEW

P.O. Box 243, Marlboro VT 05344. (802)254-4938. **E-mail:** editor@marlbororeview.org. **Website:** www.marlbororeview.org. **Contact:** Ellen Dudley. Estab. 1996. Magazine: 6×9; 80-120 pages; 60 lb. paper; photos. Wants material approached from a writer's sensibility. "Our only criterion for publication is strength of work." Semiannual. Estab. 1996. Circ. 1,000. Receives 400-500 unsolicited mss/month. "Accepts manuscripts September through May." Recently published work by Stephen Dobyns, Jean Valentine, Joseph Shuster, Chana Bloch, William Matthews and Alberto Rios. Length: 500-12,000 words; average length: 7,000 words. Publishes short shorts. Also publishes literary essays, literary criticism, poetry. Accepts 2-3 mss/issue; 4-6 mss/year. Accepts simultaneous, multiple submissions. Sample copy for $20. Writer's guidelines for SASE or on website. Reviews fiction. All rights revert to author on publication. Member CLMP, AWP. Recent contributors include Stephen Dobyns, Joan Aleshire, Jean Valentine, Robert Hill Long, Carol Frost.

> ○ Open to short fiction and poetry submissions. Include SASE with proper postage, otherwise your work will be discarded unread. Submissions received during the summer break will be returned unread.

NEEDS Cultural, philosophical, scientific and literary issues material Length: 1,000-7,500 words.

HOW TO CONTACT Send SASE for return of ms or send a disposable copy of ms and #10 SASE for reply only. No summer or e-mail submissions.

PAYMENT/TERMS Pays 2 contributor's copies; additional copies $8.

TIPS "Check Guidelines for details and restrictions. Open to most themes. We are particularly interested in translation, as well as cultural, scientific, and philosophical issues approached from a writer's sensibility. If you are overseas and must submit electronically, consult with Ellen Dudley before sending any files."

●●● THE MASSACHUSETTS REVIEW

South College, University of Massachusetts, Amherst MA 01003-9934. (413)545-2689. **Fax:** (413)577-0740. **E-mail:** massrev@external.umass.edu. **Website:** www.

massreview.org. Estab. 1959. Magazine: 6×9; 172 pages; 52 lb. paper; 65 lb. vellum cover; illustrations; photos. Quarterly.

○ Does not respond to mss without SASE.

NEEDS Short stories. Wants more prose less than 30 pages. Does not read fiction mss May 2 - September 30. Publishes ms 18 months after acceptance. Agented fiction Approximately 5%. **Publishes 3-5 new writers/ year.** Recently published work by Ahdaf Soueif, Elizabeth Denton, Nicholas Montemarano. Also publishes poetry. Sometimes comments on rejected mss. short stories. Wants more prose less than 30 pages. 25-30 pages maximum.

HOW TO CONTACT Send complete ms electronically or by mail. **If submitting online, there is a $3 submission fee.** No returned ms without SASE. Responds in 3 months to mss. Accepts simultaneous, multiple submissions. Sample copy for $8. Writer's guidelines online. Send complete ms.

PAYMENT/TERMS Pays $50. Pays on publication for first North American serial rights.

TIPS "No manuscripts are considered May-September. Electronic submission process on website. No fax or e-mail submissions. No simultaneous submissions. Shorter rather than longer stories preferred (up to 28-30 pages)." Looks for works that "stop us in our tracks." Manuscripts that stand out use "unexpected language, idiosyncrasy of outlook and are the opposite of ordinary."

● ○ ⊕ **MICHIGAN QUARTERLY REVIEW**

0576 Rackham Bldg., 915 E. Washington, University of Michigan, Ann Arbor MI 48109-1070. (734)764-9265. **E-mail:** mqr@umich.edu. **Website:** www.umich.edu/~mqr. **Contact:** Jonathan Freedman, editor; Vicki Lawrence, managing editor. Estab. 1962. Quarterly. "MQR is an eclectic interdisciplinary journal of arts and culture that seeks to combine the best of poetry, fiction, and creative nonfiction with outstanding critical essays on literary, cultural, social, and political matters. The flagship journal of the University of Michigan, MQR draws on lively minds here and elsewhere, seeking to present accessible work of all varieties for sophisticated readers from within and without the academy."

○ "The Laurence Goldstein Award is a $1,000 annual award to the best poem published in the *Michigan Quarterly Review* during the previous year. The Lawrence Foundation Award is a $1,000 annual award to the best short story published in the *Michigan Quarterly Review* during the previous year."

NEEDS Literary. "No genre fiction written for a market. Would like to see more fiction about social, political, cultural matters, not just centered on a love relationship or dysfunctional family." Receives 200 unsolicited mss/month. Accepts 2 mss/issue; 8 mss/ year. Publishes ms 1 year after acceptance. **Publishes 1-2 new writers/year.** Recently published work by Robert Boyers, Laura Kasischke, Herbert Gold, Alice Mattison, Joyce Carol Oates, Vu Tran. Length: 1,500-7,000 words; average length: 5,000 words. Also publishes literary essays, poetry. "No restrictions on subject matter or language. We are very selective. We like stories which are unusual in tone and structure, and innovative in language. No genre fiction written for a market. Would like to see more fiction about social, political, cultural matters, not just centered on a love relationship or dysfunctional family." Length: 1,500-7,000 words.

HOW TO CONTACT Send complete ms. "I like to know if a writer is at the beginning, or further along, in his or her career. Don't offer plot summaries of the story, though a background comment is welcome." Include SASE. Responds in 2 months to queries; 6 weeks to mss. No simultaneous submissions. Sample copy for $4. Writer's guidelines online. Send complete ms.

PAYMENT/TERMS Pays $10/published page. Pays on publication. Buys first serial rights. Sponsors awards/ contests.

● ○ **MID-AMERICAN REVIEW**

Bowling Green State University, Department of English, Box W, Bowling Green OH 43403. (419)372-2725. **E-mail:** mikeczy@bgsu.edu. **Website:** www.bgsu.edu/midamericanreview. **Contact:** Michael Czyzniejewski. Estab. 1981. Magazine: 6×9; 232 pages; 60 lb. bond paper; coated cover stock. Semi annual. "We try to put the best possible work in front of the biggest possible audience. We publish serious fiction and poetry, as well as critical studies in contemporary literature, translations and book reviews."

NEEDS Experimental, literary, translations, memoir, prose poem, traditional. "No genre fiction. Would like to see more short shorts." Receives 700 unsolicited mss/ month. Accepts 4-8 mss/issue. Publishes ms 6 months after acceptance. Agented fiction 5%. Publishes 4-8 new writers/year. Recently published work by Matthew Eck,

Becky Hagentson, and Kevin Wilson. Occasionally comments on rejected mss. Character-oriented, literary, experimental, short short. No genre fiction. Would like to see more short shorts. 6,000 words

HOW TO CONTACT Send complete ms with SASE. Responds in 4 months to mss. Sample copy for $9 (current issue), $5 (back issue); rare back issues $10. Writer's guidelines online. Reviews fiction.

PAYMENT/TERMS Pays $10/page up to $50, pending funding. Pays on publication when funding is available. Acquires first North American serial, one-time rights. Sponsors awards/contests. Pays $10/page up to $50, pending funding.

◑ MINNETONKA REVIEW

Minnetonka Review Press, LLC, P.O. Box 386, Spring Park MN 55384. **E-mail:** query@minnetonkareview. com. **Website:** www.minnetonkareview.com. **Contact:** Troy Ehlers, editor-in-chief. Literary magazine/journal. 6x9, 200 pages, recycled natural paper, glossy cover. Contains illustrations. Includes photographs. "We publish work of literary excellence. We are particularly attracted to fiction with careful prose, engaging and tension filled stories, and new perspectives, forms and styles." Semiannual. Estab. 2007. Circ. 1,000.

NEEDS Literary, mainstream. Receives 100 mss/month. Accepts 7 mss/issue; 15 mss/year. Does not read during the summer between May 15th and October 15th. Ms published 6-8 months after acceptance. **Publishes 6 new writers/year.** Published Bev Jafek, Daniel DiStasio, Nathan Leslie, Robin Lippincott, Megan Cass, Arthur Saltzman, Gary Amdahl, and Arthur Winfield Knight. Length: 1,200 words (min)-6,000 words (best). Will accept up to 10,00 words but must be outstanding. Average length: 4,000 words. Publishes short shorts. Average length of short shorts: 1,200 words. Also publishes literary essays, poetry. Rarely comments on/critiques rejected mss.

HOW TO CONTACT Send complete ms with cover letter. Accepts submissions by mail or by submission manager online. Include brief bio. Responds to queries in 2 weeks. Responds to mss in 4 months. Send either SASE (or IRC) for return of ms or disposable copy of ms and #10 SASE for reply only. Considers simultaneous submissions. Sample copy available for $9. Guidelines available for SASE, via e-mail, on website.

PAYMENT/TERMS Writers receive 3 contributor's copies. Additional copies $7. Pays on publication. Acquires first North American serial rights. Publication

is copyrighted. "Two authors from each issue receive a $150 Editor's Prize. Other contests with $1,000 prize are held from time to time. Details are available on our website."

TIPS "The trick seems to be holding our attention, whether via novelty, language, style, story, good descriptions or tension. Always be honing your craft, reading and writing. And when you read, it helps to be familiar with what we publish, but in general, you should be reading a number of literary journals and anthologies. Think of your work as a contribution to a greater literary dialogue."

● MISSISSIPPI REVIEW

Univ. of Southern Mississippi, 118 College Dr., #5144, Hattiesburg MS 39406-0001. (601)266-4321. **Fax:** (601)266-5757. **E-mail:** elizabeth@mississippireview. com. **Website:** www.mississippireview.com. Estab. 1972. "Literary publication for those interested in contemporary literature—writers, editors who read to be in touch with current modes."

 ◒ "We do not accept unsolicited manuscripts except under the rules and guidelines of the *Mississippi Review* Prize Competition. See website for guidelines."

NEEDS Annual fiction and poetry competition. $1,000 awarded in each category plus publication of all winners and finalists. Fiction entries 5,000 words or less. Poetry entry equals 1-3 poems; page limit is 10. $15 entry fee includes copy of prize issue. No limit on number of entries. Deadline October 1. No mss returned. **Publishes 25-30 new writers/year.** No juvenile or genre fiction. 30 pages maximum.

HOW TO CONTACT Sample copy for $8. Writer's guidelines online.

PAYMENT/TERMS Acquires first North American serial rights.

◐◔◔ THE MISSOURI REVIEW

357 McReynolds Hall, University of Missouri, Columbia MO 65211. (573)882-4474. **Fax:** (573)884-4671. **E-mail:** tmr@missourireview.com. **Website:** www.missourireview.com. Estab. 1978. Magazine: 634×10; 200 pages.

 ◒ "We publish contemporary fiction, poetry, interviews, personal essays, cartoons, special features—such as History as Literature series and Found Text series—for the literary and the general reader interested in a wide range of subjects."

NEEDS Literary fiction on all subjects, novel excerpts. Word count is best if between 2,000 and 30,000 words; shorter or longer must be truly exceptional to be published. No genre fiction. Receives 500 unsolicited mss/month. Accepts 5-7 mss/issue; 16-20 mss/year. **Publishes 6-10 new writers/year.** Recently published work by Nat Akin, Jennifer Bryan, Bruce Ducker, William Lychack, Cynthia Morrison Phoel. Also publishes literary essays, poetry. Often comments on rejected mss. No genre or flash fiction. no preference.

HOW TO CONTACT Send complete ms. May include brief bio and list of publications. Send SASE for reply, return of ms or send disposable copy of ms. **Online submissions via website with a $3 charge.** Responds in 2 weeks to queries; 12 weeks to mss. Writer's guidelines online. Send complete ms.

PAYMENT/TERMS Pays $30/printed page up to $750. Offers signed contract. Sponsors awards/contests.

TIPS "Send your best work." *The Missouri Review* holds two annual contests, the **Jeffrey E. Smith Editors' Prize** in Fiction, Essay and Poetry, and our recently instituted **Audio Competition**.

❶ THE MOCHILA REVIEW

Missouri Western State University, 4525 Downs Dr., St. Joseph MO 64507. **E-mail:** church@missouriwestern.edu. **Website:** www.missouriwestern.edu/orgs/mochila/homepage.htm. **Contact:** Bill Church, editor. Estab. 2000. "Good readership, no theme." Annual. Estab. 2000. "We are looking for writing that has a respect for the sound of language. We value poems that have to be read aloud so your mouth can feel the shape of the words. Send us writing that conveys a sense of urgency, writing that the writer can't *not* write. We crave fresh and daring work."

NEEDS Literary. Does not accept genre work, erotica. Receives 25 unsolicited mss/month. Accepts 5-10 mss/issue. Does not read mss December-July. Publishes ms 6 months after acceptance. **Publishes 2-3 new writers/year.** Length: 5,000 words (max); average length: 3,000 words. Publishes short shorts; average 500 words. Also publishes literary essays, poetry. Rarely comments on rejected mss. Length: 5,000 words.

HOW TO CONTACT Send complete disposable copy of ms with cover letter and #10 SASE for reply only. Include estimated word count, brief bio, and list of publications. Responds in 3-5 months to mss. Accepts simultaneous submissions. Sample copy for $7. Writer's guidelines for SASE or on website.

PAYMENT/TERMS Pays 2 contributor's copies; additional copies $5. Acquires first rights. Publication not copyrighted.

TIPS "Manuscripts with fresh language, energy, passion and intelligence stand out. Study the craft and be entertaining and engaging."

❶ NASSAU REVIEW

Nassau Community College, State University of New York, English Dept. Y9, 1 Education Dr., Garden City NY 11530-6793. (516)572-7792. **E-mail:** christina.rau@ncc.edu. **Contact:** Christina Rau, editor. Estab. 1964. *The Nassau Review*, published annually, welcomes submissions of many genres, preferring work that is innovative, captivating, well-crafted, and unique, work that crosses boundaries of genres and tradition. New and seasoned writers are both welcome. All work must be in English. Simultaneous submission accepted. No children's lit, fan fiction, or previously published work (online included). Full guidelines will be available at www.ncc.edu. E-mail submissions in the body of the e-mail only with the subject line indicating genre and your full name. No attachments. No hard copies. *Nassau Review* is about 190 pages, digest-sized, flat-spined. Press run is 1,100. Sample: free. Submit 3-5 poems with 50 lines max each or 1 prose piece with 3,000 words max. Reading period: September 1—February 1. Responds in up to 4 months. Pays 2 contributor's copies. Sponsors an annual aitjprs awards contest with two $250 awards. Check the website for announcements."

TIPS "We look for narrative drive, perceptive characterization and professional competence. Write concretely. Does not want over-elaborate details, and avoid digressions."

❶ NATURAL BRIDGE

Dept. of English, University of Missouri-St. Louis, One University Blvd., St. Louis MO 63121. (314)516-7327. **E-mail:** natural@umsl.edu. **Website:** www.umsl.edu/~natural. Estab. 1999. *Natural Bridge*, published biannually, seeks "fresh, innovative poetry, both free and formal, on any subject. We want poems that work on first and subsequent readings—poems that entertain and resonate and challenge our readers. *Natural Bridge* also publishes fiction, essays, and translations." Has published poetry by Ross Gay, Beckian Fritz Goldberg, Joy Harjo, Bob Hicok, Sandra Kohler, and Timothy Liu. *Natural Bridge* is 150-200 pages, digest-sized, printed on 60 lb. opaque recycled, acid-free paper, true binding, with 12 pt. coated glossy or matte cover. Receives about 1,200 poems/year, accepts about 1%. Press run is 1,000 (200 subscribers, 50 libraries). Single copy: $10; subscription: $15/year, $25/2 years. Make checks payable to *Natural Bridge*. Member: CLMP.

NEEDS Literary. List of upcoming themes available for SASE or online. Receives 900 unsolicited mss/submission period. Accepts 35 mss/issue; 70 mss/year. Submit only July 1-August 31 and November 1-December 31. Publishes ms 9 months after acceptance. **Publishes 12 new writers/year.** Recently published work by Tayari Jones, Steve Stern, Jamie Wriston Colbert, Lex Williford, and Mark Jay Mirsky. Also publishes literary essays, poetry. Sometimes comments on rejected mss.

HOW TO CONTACT Send SASE for return of ms or send a disposable copy of ms and #10 SASE for reply only. Responds in 6 months to mss. Accepts simultaneous submissions. Sample copy for $8. Writer's guidelines for SASE, e-mail, or on website. **Does not accept electronic submissions.**

PAYMENT/TERMS Pays 2 contributor's copies and a one-year subscription; additional copies $5. Acquires first North American serial rights.

① NERVE COWBOY

Liquid Paper Press, P.O. Box 4973, Austin TX 78765. **Website:** www.jwhagins.com/nervecowboy.html. **Contact:** Joseph Shields or Jerry Hagins. Estab. 1996. Magazine: 7×812; 64 pages; 20 lb. paper; card stock cover; illustrations. "Nerve Cowboy publishes adventurous, comical, disturbing, thought-provoking, accessible poetry and fiction. We like to see work sensitive enough to make the hardest hard-ass cry, funny enough to make the most helpless brooder laugh and disturbing enough to make us all glad we're not the author of the piece." Semiannual.

NEEDS Literary. No "racist, sexist or overly offensive work. Wants more unusual stories with rich description and enough twists and turns that leave the reader thinking." Receives 40 unsolicited mss/month. Accepts 2-3 mss/issue; 4-6 mss/year. Publishes ms 6-12 months after acceptance. **Publishes 5-10 new writers/year.** Recently published work by Lori Jakiela, Michele Anne Jaquays, Tom Schmidt, David Elsey, Michael A. Flanagan. Length: 1,500 words; average length: 750-1,000 words. Publishes short shorts. Also publishes poetry. "No racist, sexist or overly offensive

work. Wants more unusual stories with rich description and enough twists and turns that leave the reader thinking." Length: 1,500 words.

HOW TO CONTACT Send SASE for reply, return of ms or send a disposable copy of ms. Responds in 6 weeks to queries; 3 months to mss. Accepts reprint submissions. No simultaneous submissions. Sample copy for $6. Writer's guidelines for #10 SASE or online.

PAYMENT/TERMS Pays 1 contributor's copy. Acquires one time rights.

TIPS "We look for writing which is very direct and elicits a visceral reaction in the reader. Read magazines you submit to in order to get a feel for what the editors are looking for. Write simply and from the gut."

① ① ⊙ NEW DELTA REVIEW

Department of English, 15 Allen Hall, Louisiana State University, Baton Rouge LA 70803-5001. **E-mail:** new-delta@lsu.edu. **Website:** http://ndrmag.org. Estab. 1984. "We seek vivid and exciting work from new and established writers. We have published fiction from writers such as Stacy Richter, Mark Poirier, and George Singleton."

> ⊙ *Semiannual. Editors change every year. Check website. Magazine: 6x9; 75-125 pages; high quality paper; glossy card cover; color artwork. New Delta Review also sponsors the Matt Clark Prizes for fiction and poetry. Work from the magazine has been included in the Pushcart Prize anthology.*

NEEDS Publishes short shorts. Receives 150 unsolicited mss/month. Accepts 3-4 mss/issue; 6-8 mss/year. Reads from August 15-April 15. **Publishes 1-3 new writers/year.** Also publishes poetry. "No Elvis stories, overwrought 'Southern' fiction, or cancer stories." Average length: 15 ms pages.

PAYMENT/TERMS Pays in contributor's copies. Charge for extras.

TIPS "Our staff is open-minded and youthful. We base decisions on merit, not reputation. The ms that's most enjoyable to read gets the nod. Be bold, take risks, surprise us."

① ⊙ NEW ENGLAND REVIEW

Middlebury College, Middlebury VT 05753. (802)443-5075. **E-mail:** nereview@middlebury.edu. **Website:** go.middlebury.edu/nereview; www.nereview.com. Estab. 1978. Literary only. Reads September 1-May 31 (postmarked dates).

⚫ No e-mail submissions.

NEEDS Literary. Receives 550 unsolicited mss/month. Accepts 6 mss/issue; 24 fiction mss/year. Does not accept mss June-August. Publishes ms approx 2-6 months after acceptance. Agented fiction less than 5%. **Publishes approx. 10 new writers/year.** Recently published work by Steve Almond, Christine Sneed, Roy Kesey, Thomas Gough, Norman Lock, Brock Clarke. Publishes short shorts and translations. Sometimes comments on rejected mss. Send 1 story at a time, unless it is very short. Serious literary only, novel excerpts. Prose length: not strict on word count

HOW TO CONTACT "Send complete mss with cover letter, hard copy only. Will consider simultaneous submissions, but must be stated as such and you must notify us immediately if the manuscript is accepted for publication elsewhere." No poetry simultaneous submissions please. SASE. Responds in 2 weeks to queries; 3 months to mss. Sample copy for $10, add $3 CAN or $5 for overseas. Writer's guidelines online. No electronic submissions. Send complete ms.

PAYMENT/TERMS Pays $10/page ($20 minimum), and 2 copies. Pays on publication for first North American serial, first, second serial (reprint) rights. Sends galleys to author. Pays $10/page ($20 minimum), and 2 copies

TIPS "We consider short fiction, including short-shorts, novellas, and self-contained extracts from novels in both traditional and experimental forms. In nonfiction, we consider a variety of general and literary, but not narrowly scholarly essays; we also publish long and short poems; screenplays; graphics; translations; critical reassessments; statements by artists working in various media; testimonies; and letters from abroad. We are committed to exploration of all forms of contemporary cultural expression in the US and abroad. With few exceptions, we print only work not published previously elsewhere."

⚫⚫⑤ NEW LETTERS

University of Missouri-Kansas City, 5101 Rockhill Rd., Kansas City MO 64110. (816)235-1168. **Fax:** (816)235-2611. **E-mail:** newletters@umkc.edu. **Website:** www.newletters.org. Estab. 1934.

⚫ Submissions are not read between May 1 and October 1.

NEEDS No genre fiction. 5,000 words maximum.

HOW TO CONTACT Send complete ms.

PAYMENT/TERMS Pays $30-75.

TIPS "We aren't interested in essays that are footnoted, or essays usually described as scholarly or critical. Our preference is for creative nonfiction or personal essays. We prefer shorter stories and essays to longer ones (an average length is 3,500-4,000 words). We have no rigid preferences as to subject, style, or genre, although commercial efforts tend to put us off. Even so, our only fixed requirement is on good writing."

⚫ NEW MADRID

Murray State University, Department of English and Philosophy, 7C Faculty Hall, Murray KY 42071-3341. (270)809-4730. **E-mail:** msu.newmadrid@murraystate.edu. **Website:** http://newmadridjournal.org. **Contact:** Ann Neelon, editor. Literary magazine/journal: 160 pages. "*New Madrid* is the national journal of the low-residency MFA program at Murray State University. It takes its name from the New Madrid seismic zone, which falls within the central Mississippi Valley and extends through western Kentucky." Semiannual. Circ. 1,000.

NEEDS Literary. See website for guidelines and upcoming themes. "We have two reading periods, one from August 15-October 15, and one from January 15-March 15." Also publishes poetry and creative nonfiction. Rarely comments on/critiques rejected mss.

HOW TO CONTACT Accepts submissions by Online Submissions Manager only. Include brief bio, list of publications. Considers multiple submissions. Guidelines available on website.

PAYMENT/TERMS Pays 2 contributor's copies on publication. Acquires first North American serial rights. Publication is copyrighted.

⚫⑤ NEW MILLENNIUM WRITINGS

New Messenger Writing and Publishing, P.O. Box 2463, Knoxville TN 37901. (865)428-0389. **E-mail:** donwilliams7@charter.net. **Website:** http://newmillenniumwritings.com. **Contact:** Don Williams, editor. Estab. 1996. "While we only accept general submissions January-March, we hold 4 contests twice each year for all types of fiction, nonfiction, short-short fiction, and poetry."

⚫ Annual anthology. 6x9, 204 pages, 50 lb. white paper, glossy 4-color cover. Contains illustrations. Includes photographs. "Superior writing is the sole criterion." Received Golden Presscard Award from Sigma Delta Chi (1997).

NEEDS Receives average of 200 mss/month. Accepts 60 mss/year. Agented fiction 0%. Publishes 10 new writers/year. Rarely comments on/critiques rejected mss. Has published work by Charles Wright, Ted Kooser, Pamela Uschuk, William Pitt Root, Allen Wier, Lucille Clifton, John Updike, and Don Williams. Length: 200 -6,000 words. Average length: 4,000 words for fiction. Short-short fiction length: no more than 1,000 words.

HOW TO CONTACT Accepts mss through biannual *New Millennium Writing* Awards for Fiction, Poetry, and Nonfiction; also accepts general submissions January-March. Visit website for more information, or see listing for *New Millennium Writing* Awards in Contests & Awards section.

◐ NEW OHIO REVIEW

English Department, 360 Ellis Hall, Ohio University, Athens OH 45701. (740)597-1360. **E-mail:** noreditors@ohio.edu. **Website:** www.ohiou.edu/nor. **Contact:** Jill Allyn Rosser, editor. Estab. 2007. *NOR*, published biannually in spring and fall, publishes fiction, nonfiction, and poetry.

NEEDS *NOR*, published biannually in spring and fall, publishes fiction, nonfiction, and poetry. Wants "literary submissions in any genre. Translations are welcome if permission has been granted." Has published work by Billy Collins, Stephen Dunn, Stuart Dybek, Eleanor Wilner, Yusef Komunyakaa, Kim Addonizio, William Olson. Single: $9; Subscription: $16. Member: CLMP.

HOW TO CONTACT Send complete ms online at www.newohioreview.com. "We accept literary submissions in any genre, however we do not accept unsolicited translations. Please do not send more than 6 poems in a single submission." Reading period is September 1-May 1, "but we will consider work year-round from subscribers. Please do not submit more than once every 6 months." Send complete ms.

PAYMENT/TERMS Pays $20/page, $50 minimum honorarium.

◐◔⑤ NEW ORLEANS REVIEW

Box 195, Loyola University, New Orleans LA 70118. (504)865-2295. **E-mail:** noreview@loyno.edu. **Website:** http://neworleansreview.org. **Contact:** Christopher Chambers, editor; Amberly Fox, managing editor. Estab. 1968. Biannual magazine publishing poetry, fiction, translations, photographs, and nonfiction on literature, art and film. Readership: those interested in contemporary literature and culture. New Orleans Review is a journal of contemporary literature and culture, publishing new poetry, fiction, nonfiction, art, photography, film and book reviews. The journal was founded in 1968 and has since published an eclectic variety of work by established and emerging writers including Walker Percy, Pablo Neruda, Ellen Gilchrist, Nelson Algren, Hunter S. Thompson, John Kennedy Toole, Richard Brautigan, Barry Spacks, James Sallis, Jack Gilbert, Paul Hoover, Rodney Jones, Annie Dillard, Everette Maddox, Julio Cortazar, Gordon Lish, Robert Walser, Mark Halliday, Jack Butler, Robert Olen Butler, Michael Harper, Angela Ball, Joyce Carol Oates, Diane Wakoski, Dermot Bolger, Roddy Doyle, William Kotzwinkle, Alain Robbe-Grillet, Arnost Lustig, Raymond Queneau, Yusef Komunyakaa, Michael Martone, Tess Gallagher, Matthea Harvey, D. A. Powell, Rikki Ducornet, and Ed Skoog.

NEEDS Good writing, from conventional to experimental. Length: up to 6,500 words.

HOW TO CONTACT We are now using an online submission system and require a $3 fee. See website for details.

PAYMENT/TERMS Pays $25-50 and 2 copies.

TIPS "We're looking for dynamic writing that demonstrates attention to the language, and a sense of the medium, writing that engages, surprises, moves us. We're not looking for genre fiction, or academic articles. We subscribe to the belief that in order to truly write well, one must first master the rudiments: grammar and syntax, punctuation, the sentence, the paragraph, the line, the stanza. We receive about 3,000 manuscripts a year, and publish about 3% of them. Check out a recent issue, send us your best, proofread your work, be patient, be persistent."

◐◔◐ THE NEW ORPHIC REVIEW

706 Mill St., Nelson BC V1L 4S5 Canada. (250)354-0494. **Fax:** (250)354-0494. **E-mail:** dreamhorsepress@yahoo.com. **Website:** www.dreamhorsepress.com; www3.telus.net/neworphicpublishers-hekkanen. Estab. 1998. **Contact:** Ernest Hekkanen, editor-in-chief. Magazine; 512×812; 120 pages; common paper; 100 lb. color cover. "In the traditional Orphic fashion, our magazine accepts a wide range of styles and approaches—from naturalism to the surreal, but, please, get to the essence of the narrative, emotion, conflict, state of being, whatever." Semiannual. Estab. 1998. Circ. 300.

NEEDS Ethnic/multicultural, experimental, fantasy, historical (general), literary, mainstream. "No detective or sword and sorcery stories." List of upcoming themes available for SASE. Receives 20 unsolicited mss/month. Accepts 10 mss/issue; 22 mss/year. Publishes ms 1 year after acceptance. **Publishes 6-8 new writers/year.** Recently published work by Eveline Hasler (Swiss), Leena Krohn (Finnish), Pekka Salmi. Length: 2,000-10,000 words; average length: 3,500 words. Publishes short shorts. Also publishes literary essays, literary criticism, poetry. Sometimes comments on rejected mss.

HOW TO CONTACT Send SASE (or IRC) for return of ms or send a disposable copy of ms and #10 SASE for reply only. Responds in 1 month to queries; 4 months to mss. Accepts simultaneous, multiple submissions. Sample copy for $17.50. Writer's guidelines for SASE. Reviews fiction.

PAYMENT/TERMS Pays 1 contributor's copy; additional copies $14. Pays on publication for first North American serial rights.

TIPS "I like fiction that deals with issues, accounts for every motive, has conflict, is well written and tackles something that is substantive. Don't be mundane; try for more, not less."

◑ NEW SOUTH

Campus Box 1894, Georgia State Univ., MSC 8R0322 Unit 8, Atlanta GA 30303-3083. (404)651-4804. **Fax:** (404)651-1710. **E-mail:** new_south@langate.gsu.edu. **Website:** www.review.gsu.edu. Estab. 1980. Literary journal. *"New South* is a biannual literary magazine publishing poetry, fiction, creative nonfiction, and visual art. We're looking for original voices and well-written manuscripts. No subject or form biases." Biannual. After more than 30 years *GSU Review* has become *New South.* Our role as George State University's journal of art & literature has not changed; however, it was time for a revision, a chance for a clearer mission.

NEEDS Literary fiction and creative nonfiction. Receives 200 unsolicited mss/month. Publishes and welcomes short shorts. Length: 7,500 words.

HOW TO CONTACT Include SASE for notification. Responds in 3-5 months. Sample copy for $5. Writer's guidelines for SASE or on website. Send complete ms.

PAYMENT/TERMS Pays in contributor's copy. Acquires one-time rights.

◑ NIMROD

800 S. Tucker Dr., Tulsa OK 74104-3189. (918)631-3080. **Fax:** (918)631-3033. **E-mail:** nimrod@utulsa.edu. **Web-**site: www.utulsa.edu/nimrod/. **Contact:** Susan Mase, fiction editor. Estab. 1956. Magazine: 6×9; 192 pages; 60 lb. white paper; illustrations; photos. "We publish one thematic issue and one awards issue each year. A recent theme was 'Crossing Borders,' a compilation of poetry and prose from all over the world. We seek vigorous, imaginative, quality writing. Our mission is to discover new writers and publish experimental writers who have not yet found a 'home' for their work." Semiannual. "We accept contemporary poetry and/or prose. May submit adventure, ethnic, experimental, prose poem or translations. No science fiction or romance." Receives 120 unsolicited mss/month. **Publishes 5-10 new writers/year.** Recently published work by Shannon Robinson, Sue Pace, Emil Draitser and Margaret Kaufman. Also publishes poetry. SASE for return of ms. Accepts queries by e-mail. Does not accept submissions by e-mail unless the writer is living outside the U.S. Responds in 5 months to mss. Accepts multiple submissions. Pays 2 contributor's copies.

TIPS "We have not changed our fiction needs: quality, vigor, distinctive voice. We have, however, increased the number of stories we print. See current issues. We look for fiction that is fresh, vigorous, distinctive, serious and humorous, unflinchingly serious, ironic—whatever. Just so it is quality. Strongly encourage writers to send #10 SASE for brochure for annual literary contest with prizes of $1,000 and $2,000."

◑ ◔ NORTH AMERICAN REVIEW

University of Northern Iowa, 1222 W. 27th St., Cedar Falls IA 50614. (319)273-6455. **Fax:** (319)273-4326. **E-mail:** nar@uni.edu. **Website:** northamericanreview. org. **Contact:** Kim Groninga, nonfiction editor. Estab. 1815. "The *NAR* is the oldest literary magazine in America and one of the most respected; though we have no prejudices about the subject matter of material sent to us, our first concern is quality."

> ◑ "This is the oldest literary magazine in the country and one of the most prestigious. Also one of the most entertaining—and a tough market for the young writer."

NEEDS Open (literary). "No flat narrative stories where the inferiority of the character is the paramount concern." Wants to see more "well-crafted literary stories that emphasize family concerns. We'd also like to see more stories engaged with environmental concerns." Reads fiction mss all year. Publishes ms an average of 1 year after acceptance. **Publishes**

2 new writers/year. Recently published work by Lee Ann Roripaugh, Dick Allen, Rita Welty Bourke. No flat narrative stories where the inferiority of the character is the paramount concern.

HOW TO CONTACT Accepts submissions by USPS mail only. Send complete ms with SASE. Responds in 3 months to queries; 4 months to mss. No simultaneous submissions. Sample copy for $7. Writer's guidelines online.

PAYMENT/TERMS Pays $5/350 words; $20 minimum, $100 maximum.

💲 NORTH CAROLINA LITERARY REVIEW

East Carolina University, ECU Mailstop 555 English, Greenville NC 27858-4353. (252)328-1537. **Fax:** (252)328-4889. **E-mail:** nclrsubmissions@ecu.edu; bauerm@ecu.edu; rodmand@ecu.edu. **Website:** http://www.nclr.ecu.edu/submissions/artists-and-photographers.html. **Contact:** Diane Rodman, art acquisitions editor. Estab. 1992. "Articles should have a North Carolina slant. First consideration is always for quality of work. Although we treat academic and scholarly subjects, we do not wish to see jargon-laden prose; our readers, we hope, are found as often in bookstores and libraries as in academia. We seek to combine the best elements of magazine for serious readers with best of scholarly journal."

NEEDS Regional (North Carolina). Must be North Carolina related — either a North Carolina connected writer or set in North Carolina. Publishes ms 1 year after acceptance. "Fiction submissions accepted during Doris Betts Prize Competition; see our submission guidelines for detail." 5,000 words maximum.

HOW TO CONTACT Accepts submissions via online submissions manager. Responds in 1 month to queries; within 6 months to mss. Sample copy for $10-25. Writer's guidelines online. Query.

PAYMENT/TERMS Pays on publication for first North American serial rights. Rights returned to writer on request. $50-100 honorarium, extra copies, back issues or subscription (negotiable).

TIPS "By far the easiest way to break in is with special issue sections. We are especially interested in reports on conferences, readings, meetings that involve North Carolina writers, and personal essays or short narratives with a strong sense of place. See back issues for other departments. Interviews are probably the other easiest place to break in; no discussions of poetics/theory, etc., except in reader-friendly (accessible) language; interviews should be personal, more like conversations, that explore connections between a writer's life and his/her work."

◐ ⊕ NORTH DAKOTA QUARTERLY

Merrifeild Hall Room 110, 276 Centennial Drive Stop 7209, Grand Forks ND 58202-7209. (701)777-3322. **E-mail:** ndq@und.edu. **Website:** www.und.nodak.edu/org/ndq. Estab. 1911. **Contact:** Robert Lewis, editor. Magazine: 6×9; 200 pages; bond paper; illustrations; photos. "*North Dakota Quarterly* is a literary journal publishing essays in the humanities; some short stories, some poetry. Occasional special topic issues." General audience. Quarterly.

> 💬 Work published in *North Dakota Quarterly* was selected for inclusion in *The O. Henry Prize Stories, The Pushcart Prize Series* and *Best American Essays.*

NEEDS Ethnic/multicultural, experimental, feminist, historical, literary, Native American. Receives 125-150 unsolicited mss/month. Accepts 4 mss/issue; 16 mss/year. Publishes ms 2 years after acceptance. **Publishes 4-5 new writers/year.** Recently published work by Louise Erdrich, Robert Day, Maxine Kumin and Fred Arroyo. Average length: 3,000-4,000 words. Also publishes literary essays and criticism. Sometimes comments on rejected mss.

HOW TO CONTACT SASE. Responds in 3 months to mss. Sample copy for $10. Reviews fiction.

PAYMENT/TERMS Pays 2-4 contributor's copies; 30% discount for extras. Acquires onetime rights. Sends galleys to author.

◑ NORTHWEST REVIEW

5243 University of Oregon, Eugene OR 97403-5243. (541)346-3957. **Fax:** (541)346-0537. **E-mail:** nweditor@uoregon.edu. **Website:** http://nwr.uoregon.edu. **Contact:** Geri Doran, general editor. Estab. 1957. **Contact:** Geri Doran, general editor. Magazine: 6×9; 140-160 pages; high quality cover stock; illustrations; photos. "A general literary review featuring poems, stories, essays and reviews, circulated nationally and internationally. For a literate audience in avant-garde as well as traditional literary forms; interested in the important writers who have not yet achieved their readership." Triannual. Circ. 1,200.

> 💬 Poetry published by *Northwest Review* has been included in *The Best American Poetry, Poetry Daily*, and *Verse Daily.*

NEEDS Experimental, feminist, literary, translations, contemporary. Receives 150 unsolicited mss/month. Accepts 4-5 mss/issue; 12-15 mss/year. **Publishes some new writers/year.** Recently published work by Diana Abu-Jaber, Madison Smartt Bell, Maria Flook, Charles Marvin. Also publishes literary essays, literary criticism, poetry. Comments on rejected mss "when there is time."

HOW TO CONTACT Responds in 4 months to mss. No simultaneous submissions. Sample copy for $4. Reviews fiction.

PAYMENT/TERMS Pays 3 contributor's copies and 1-year subscription; 40% discount on extras. Acquires first rights.

TIPS "Our advice is to persist."

⊕ NORTHWIND

Chain Bridge Press, LLC., 4201 Wilson Blvd., #110-321, Arlington VA 22203. **Website:** www.northwind-magazine.com. **Contact:** Tom Howard, managing editor. Estab. 2011. "Our focus is originality and provocative, compulsively readable prose and poetry, in any style or genre. We look for smart, lyrical writing that will appeal to an intelligent and culturally sophisticated audience."

NEEDS Does not want to see short-shorts, allegories or fables, overtly religious or polemic narratives, hard science fiction, occult. Length: 1,500-10,000 words.

HOW TO CONTACT Submit complete ms.

PAYMENT/TERMS Pays up to $150.

TIPS "For fiction and nonfiction, make the first paragraph the strongest one. Love your characters and make us love them (or hate them) too. Respect your reader; we love subtlety. Don't be afraid to be light-hearted or playful—not all great stories are tragic or depressing. Show us that you care about your craft by editing carefully before you send it in to us."

⑩❂⑤ NOTRE DAME REVIEW

University of Notre Dame, 840 Flanner Hall, Notre Dame IN 46556. (574)631-6952. **Fax:** (574)631-4795. **E-mail:** english.ndreview.1@nd.edu. **Website:** www. nd.edu/~ndr/review.htm. Estab. 1995. Literary magazine: 6×9; 200 pages; 50 lb. smooth paper; illustrations; photos. "*The Notre Dame Review* is an independent, noncommercial magazine of contemporary American and international fiction, poetry, criticism and art. We are especially interested in work that takes on big issues by making the invisible seen, that gives voice to the voiceless. In addition to showcasing celebrated authors like Seamus Heaney and Czelaw Milosz, the *Notre Dame Review* introduces readers to authors they may have never encountered before, but who are doing innovative and important work. In conjunction with the *Notre Dame Review*, the online companion to the printed magazine engages readers as a community centered in literary rather than commercial concerns, a community we reach out to through critique and commentary as well as aesthetic experience." Semiannual.

NEEDS No genre fiction. Upcoming theme issues planned. Receives 75 unsolicited mss/month. Accepts 4-5 mss/issue; 10 mss/year. Does not read mss November-January or April-August. Publishes ms 6 months after acceptance. **Publishes 1 new writer/year.** Recently published work by Ed Falco, Jarda Cerverka, David Green. Publishes short shorts. Also publishes literary criticism, poetry. "We're eclectic. Upcoming theme issues planned. List of upcoming themes or editorial calendar available for SASE. Does not read mss May-August." No genre fiction. Length: 3,000 words.

HOW TO CONTACT Send complete ms with cover letter. Include 4-sentence bio. Send SASE for response, return of ms, or send a disposable copy of ms. Responds in 6 months to mss. Accepts simultaneous submissions. Sample copy for $6. Writer's guidelines online. Mss sent during summer months will be returned unread.

PAYMENT/TERMS Pays $5-25. Pays on publication for first North American serial rights.

TIPS "We're looking for high quality work that takes on big issues in a literary way. Please read our back issues before submitting."

OBSIDIAN III

North Carolina State University, Department of English, Box 8105, Raleigh NC 27695-8105. (919)515-4153. **E-mail:** obsidian@gw.ncsu.edu. **Website:** www.ncsu. edu/chass/obsidian/. **Contact:** Sheila Smith McKoy, editor. Estab. 1975. Magazine: 130 pages. "Creative works in English by black writers, scholarly critical studies by all writers on black literature in English." Published 2 times/year (spring/summer, fall/winter). Estab. 1975.

NEEDS Ethnic/multicultural (Pan-African), feminist, literary. Accepts 7-9 mss/year. Publishes ms 4-6 months after acceptance. **Publishes 20 new writers/year.** Recently published work by R. Flowers Rivera, Terrance Hayes, Eugene Kraft, Arlene McKanic, Pearl

Bothe Williams, Kwane Dawes, Jay Wright, and Octavia E. Butler.

HOW TO CONTACT Accepts submissions by e-mail. Responds in 4 months to mss. Sample copy for $10.

PAYMENT/TERMS Pays in contributor's copies. Acquires onetime rights. Sponsors awards/contests.

◑ OHIO TEACHERS WRITE

644 Overlook Dr., Columbus OH 45601. **E-mail:** rmcclain@bright.net; ohioteacherswrite@gmail.com. **Website:** www.octela.org/OTW.html. Estab. 1995. Editors change every 3 years. Magazine: 8½×11; 50 pages; 60 lb. white offset paper; 65 lb. blue cover stock; illustrations; photos. "The purpose of the magazine is three fold: (1) to provide a collection of fine literature for the reading pleasure of teachers and other adult readers; (2) to encourage teachers to compose literary works along with their students; (3) to provide the literate citizens of Ohio a window into the world of educators not often seen by those outside the teaching profession." Annual. Circ. 1,000. Submissions are limited to Ohio Educators.

NEEDS Adventure, ethnic/multicultural, experimental, fantasy (science fantasy), feminist, gay, historical, humor/satire, lesbian, literary, mainstream, regional, religious/inspirational, romance (contemporary), science fiction (hard science, soft/sociological), western (frontier, traditional), senior citizen/retirement, sports, teaching. Receives 2 unsolicited mss/month. Accepts 7 mss/issue. "We read only in May when editorial board meets." Recently published work by Lois Spencer, Harry R. Noden, Linda J. Rice, June Langford Berkley. Publishes short shorts. Also publishes poetry. Often comments on rejected mss.

HOW TO CONTACT Send SASE with postage clipped for return of ms or send a disposable copy of ms. Accepts multiple submissions. Sample copy for $6.

PAYMENT/TERMS Pays 2 contributor's copies; additional copies $6. Acquires first rights.

◔◑ OPEN WIDE MAGAZINE

40 Wingfield Road, Lakenheath, Brandon SK Ip27 9HR UK. **E-mail:** contact@openwidemagazine.co.uk. **Website:** www.openwidemagazine.co.uk. **Contact:** Liz Roberts. Estab. 2001. Online literary magazine/journal: Quarterly. Open Wide Magazine has been publishing poetry, fiction, reviews and interviews. With our Feel Free Press imprint we published two print anthologies 'Poems Written Whilst Staring Death In The Face' and 'Destination Anywhere', 32 broadsides, a paperback poetry collection by K.M Dersley and chapbooks by Debbie Kirk, Luke Buckham, Shane Allison and Dan Provost. Also as Open Wide Books we published online chapbook collections from Ben Myers, Melissa Mann, Ben Barton, James D Quinton and Emily McPhillips. Receives 100 mss/month. Accepts 25 mss/issue. Publishes 30 new writers/year. Length: 500-4,000. Average length: 2,500. Publishes short shorts. Also publishes poetry, reviews (music, film, art) and interviews. Rarely comments on/critiques rejected mss. Include estimated word count, brief bio. Send either SASE (or IRC) for return of ms or disposable copy of ms and #10 SASE for reply only.

NEEDS Short fiction and poetry journal enjoys adventure, ethnic/multicultural, experimental, feminist, humor/satire, mainstream, mystery/suspense, principle beat. Receives 100 mss/month. Accepts 25 mss/issue. Manuscript published 3 months after acceptance. Publishes 30 new writers/year. Length: 500-4,000. Average length: 2,500. Publishes short shorts. Also publishes poetry, reviews (music, film, art) and interviews. Rarely comments on/critiques rejected mss.

HOW TO CONTACT Accepts submissions by e-mail and online. Include estimated word count, brief bio. Send either SASE (or IRC) for return of ms or disposable copy of ms and #10 SASE for reply only. The magazine costs just £1.00 for a PDF copy that is mailed to you at the e-mail address you provide us with via your Paypal account, unless you specify otherwise.

PAYMENT/TERMS Acquires one-time rights. Publication is copyrighted.

◑ OYEZ REVIEW

Roosevelt University, Dept. of Literature & Languages, 430 S. Michigan Ave., Chicago IL 60605-1394. (312)341-3500. **E-mail:** oyezreview@roosevelt.edu. **Website:** legacy.roosevelt.edu/roosevelt.edu/oyezreview. Estab. 1965. Literary magazine/journal. "*Oyez Review* publishes fiction, creative nonfiction, poetry and art. There are no restrictions on style, theme, or subject matter."

> Reading period is August 1-October 1. Responds by mid-December.

NEEDS Publishes short stories and flash fiction from established authors and newcomers. Literary excellence is our goal and our primary criterion. Send us your best work, and you will receive a thoughtful, thorough reading. Recently published J. Weintraub, Lori Rader Day, Joyce Goldenstern, Norman Lock, Peter Obourn, Jotham Burrello. We publish short stories and flash fiction on their merit as contemporary literature rather than the category within the genre. 5,500 words maximum.

HOW TO CONTACT Accepts art and international submissions by e-mail. Sample copy available for $5. Guidelines available on website. Send complete ms.

PAYMENT/TERMS Writers receive 2 contributors copies. Acquires first North American serial rights.

OYSTER BOY REVIEW

P.O. Box 1483, Pacifica CA 94044. **E-mail:** email_2010@oysterboyreview.com. **Website:** www.oysterboyreview.com. **Contact:** Damon Suave, editor/publisher. Estab. 1993. Electronic and print magazine. "We publish kick-ass, teeth-cracking stories." Published 4 times a year.

NEEDS No genre fiction. "Fiction that revolves around characters in conflict with themselves or each other; a plot that has a beginning, a middle, and an end; a narrative with a strong moral center (not necessarily 'moralistic'); a story with a satisfying resolution to the conflict; and an ethereal something that contributes to the mystery of a question, but does not necessarily seek or contrive to answer it." Submissions closed for 2009. **Publishes 4 new writers/year.** Recently published work by Todd Goldberg, Ken Wainio, Elisha Porat, Kevin McGowan.

HOW TO CONTACT Accepts multiple submissions. Sample copy not available.

TIPS "Keep writing, keep submitting, keep revising."

PACIFIC REVIEW

Dept. of English and Comparative Literature, San Diego State University, 5500 Campanile Dr., MC6020, San Diego CA 92182-6020. **E-mail:** pacificreview_sdsu@yahoo.com. **Website:** http://pacificREVIEW.sdsu.edu. **Contact:** Lester O'Connor, fiction editor. "We welcome submissions of previously published poems, short stories, translations, and creative nonfiction, including essays and reviews." For information on theme issues see website. **Publishes 15 new writers/year.** Recently published work by Ai, Alurista, Susan Daitch, Lawrence Ferlinghetti, William T. Vollmann.

PAYMENT/TERMS Pays 2 contributor's copies.

TIPS "We welcome all submissions, especially those created in or in the context of the West Coast/California and the space of our borders."

PACKINGTOWN REVIEW

The University of Illinois at Chicago, English Department, UH 2027 MC 162, University of Illinois at Chi-

cago, 601 S. Morgan, Chicago IL 60607. (908)745-1547. **E-mail:** editors@packingtownreview.com. **Website:** www.packingtownreview.com. **Contact:** Editor. Estab. 2008. Magazine has revolving editor. Editorial term: 2 years. Next term: 2013. Literary magazine/journal. 812x11, 250 pages. "*Packingtown Review* publishes imaginative and critical prose by emerging and established writers. We welcome submissions of poetry, scholarly articles, drama, creative nonfiction, fiction, and literary translation, as well as genre-bending pieces." Annual.

NEEDS Comics/graphic novels, ethnic/multicultural (general), experimental, feminist, gay, glitz, historical (general), literary, mainstream, military/war, translations. Does not want to see uninspired or unrevised work. "We also would like to avoid fantasy, science fiction, overtly religious, or romantic pieces." Ms published max of one year after acceptance. Length: 3,000 words (min)-8,000 words (max). Publishes short shorts. Also publishes literary essays, literary criticism, book reviews, poetry. Send review copies to Jennifer Moore and Matthew Corey Editor. Sometimes comments on/critiques rejected mss.

HOW TO CONTACT Send complete ms with cover letter. Include estimated word count, brief bio. Responds to queries in 3 weeks. Responds to mss in 3 months. Considers simultaneous submissions. See website for price guidelines. Guidelines available for SASE, via e-mail.

PAYMENT/TERMS Writers receive 2 contributor's copies. Pays on publication. Acquires first North American serial rights. Sends galleys to author. Publication is copyrighted.

PADDLEFISH

1105 W. 8th St., Yankton SD 57078. (605) 688-1362. **E-mail:** james.reese@mtmc.edu. **Website:** www.mmcpaddlefish.com. **Contact:** Dr. Jim Reese, Editor. Estab. 2007. Literary magazine/journal. 6x9, 200 pages. Includes photographs. "We publish unique and creative pieces." Annual. Send complete ms with cover letter. Include estimated word count, brief bio, list of publications. Send disposable copy of ms and #10 SASE for reply only. Writers receive 1 contributor's copy. Additional copies $8. Sends galleys to author. Publication is copyrighted. "Cash prizes are award to Mount Marty students."

NEEDS Adventure, comics/graphic novels, erotica, ethnic/multicultural, experimental, family saga, fantasy, feminist, gay, glitz, historical, horror, humor/satire, lesbian, literary, mainstream, military/war, mystery, new age, psychic/supernatural/occult, religious, romance, science fiction, thriller/espionage, translations, western, young adult/teen. Does not want excessive or gratuitous language, sex or violence. Receives 300 mss/month. Accepts 30 mss/year. Submission period is Nov 1-Feb 28. Ms published 3-9 months after acceptance. **Publishes 5-10 new writers/year.** Published David Lee, William Kloefkorn, David Allen Evans, Jack Anderson and Maria Mazziotti Gillan. Length: 2,500 words (max). Publishes short shorts. Also publishes literary essays, poetry. Rarely comments on/critiques rejected mss. Does not want excessive or gratuitous language, sex or violence. Length: 2,500 words.

HOW TO CONTACT Send complete ms with cover letter. Include estimated word count, brief bio, list of publications. Send disposable copy of ms and #10 SASE for reply only. Guidelines available for SASE.

PAYMENT/TERMS Writers receive 1 contributor's copy. Additional copies $8. Acquires onetime rights. Sends galleys to author. Publication is copyrighted. "Cash prizes are award to Mount Marty students."

🅞🅢 PAINTED BRIDE QUARTERLY

Drexel University, Dept. of English and Philosophy, 3141 Chestnut St., Philadelphia PA 19104. **E-mail:** pbq@drexel.edu. **Website:** http://webdelsol.com/pbq. Estab. 1973. "PBQ seeks literary fiction, experimental and traditional." Publishes online each quarter and a print annual each spring. Estab. 1973. *Painted Bride Quarterly* seeks literary fiction, experimental and traditional.

NEEDS Ethnic/multicultural, experimental, feminist, gay, lesbian, literary, translations. "No genre fiction." "Publishes theme-related work, check website; holds annual fiction contests. **Publishes 24 new writers/year.** Length: 5,000 words; average length: 3,000 words. Publishes short shorts. Also publishes literary essays, literary criticism, poetry. Occasionally comments on rejected mss. Publishes theme-related work, check website; holds annual fiction contests. No genre ficiton. Up to 5,000 words.

HOW TO CONTACT Send complete ms. No electronic submissions. Responds in 6 months to mss. Sample copy online. Writer's guidelines online. Reviews fiction. Send complete ms.

PAYMENT/TERMS Acquires first North American serial rights. Pays contributor's copy.

⊕ PANK

PANK, Department of Humanities, 1400 Townsend Dr., Houghton MI 49931-1200. **Website:** www.pank-magazine.com. **Contact:** M. Bartley Seigel, Editor. Estab. 2007. "PANK comes from the end of the road, the edge of things, a north shore, up country, a place of amagamation, and unplumbed depths, where things are made and unmade, and unimagined futures are born. An ultima Thule, PANK—no soft hands here. We bear old scar and fresh scab, callous, blood and dirt. PANK is serene melancholy, spiritual longing, quirk and anomaly. PANK is progressive, experimental and improvisational. PANK inhabits its contradictions—your work should, too.

> 🅠 To read PANK is to know PANK. Or, read a lot within the literary magazine and small press universe—there's plenty to choose from. Unfortunately, we see a lot of submissions from writers who have clearly read neither PANK nor much else. Serious writers are serious readers. Read. Seriously."

🅞🅖 THE PARIS REVIEW

62 White St., New York NY 10013. (212)343-1333. **E-mail:** queries@theparisreview.org. **Website:** www.theparisreview.org. **Contact:** Lorin Stein, editor. "Fiction and poetry of superlative quality, whatever the genre, style or mode. Our contributors include prominent, as well as less well-known and previously unpublished writers. Writers at Work interview series includes important contemporary writers discussing their own work and the craft of writing."

> 🅠 Address submissions to proper department. Do not make submissions via e-mail.

NEEDS Study the publication. Annual Aga Khan Fiction Contest award of $1,000. Recently published work by Karl Taro Greenfeld, J. Robert Lennon, and Belle Boggs. no limit

HOW TO CONTACT Send complete ms.

PAYMENT/TERMS Pays $500-1,000.

🅢🅞 PASSION

Crescent Moon Publishing, P.O. Box 393, Maidstone Kent ME14 5XU United Kingdom. (44)(162)272-9593. **E-mail:** cresmopub@yahoo.co.uk. **Website:** www.crescentmoon.org.uk. Estab. 1988. **Contact:** Jeremy Robinson, editor. *Passion*, published quarterly, features poetry, fiction, reviews, and essays on feminism, art, philosophy, and the media. Wants "thought-provoking, incisive, polemical, ironic, lyric, sensual, and hilarious work." Does not want "rubbish, trivia, party politics, sport, etc." Has published poetry by Jeremy Reed, Penelope Shuttle, Alan Bold, D.J. Enright, and Peter Redgrove. Single copy: £2.50 ($4 USD); subscription: £10 ($17 USD). Make checks payable to Crescent Moon Publishing.

NEEDS Does not want "rubbish, trivia, party politics, sport, etc."

ⓓⓖ THE PATERSON LITERARY REVIEW

Passaic County Community College, Cultural Affairs Dept., One College Blvd., Paterson NJ 07505-1179. (973)684-6555. **Fax:** (973)523-6085. **E-mail:** mGillan@pccc.edu. **Website:** www.pccc.edu/poetry. **Contact:** Maria Mazziotti Gillan, editor/executive director. Magazine: 6×9; 400 pages; 60 lb. paper; 70 lb. cover; illustrations; photos. Annual.

> Work for *PLR* has been included in the *Pushcart Prize* anthology and *Best American Poetry*.

NEEDS Ethnic/multicultural, literary, contemporary. "We are interested in quality short stories, with no taboos on subject matter." Receives 60 unsolicited mss/month. Publishes ms 6-12 months after acceptance. **Publishes 5% new writers/year.** Recently published work by Robert Mooney and Abigail Stone. Also publishes literary essays, literary criticism, poetry.

HOW TO CONTACT Send SASE for reply or return of ms. "Indicate whether you want story returned." Accepts simultaneous submissions. Sample copy for $13 plus $1.50 postage. Reviews fiction.

PAYMENT/TERMS Pays in contributor's copies. Acquires first North American serial rights.

TIPS Looks for "clear, moving and specific work."

ⓞ PENNSYLVANIA ENGLISH

Penn State DuBois, College Place, DuBois PA 15801-3199. (814)375-4785. **Fax:** (814)375-4785. **E-mail:** ajv2@psu.edu. **Website:** www.english.iup.edu/pcea. **Contact:** Antonio Vallone, editor. Estab. 1985. Magazine: 514×814; up to 200 pages; perfect bound; full-color cover featuring the artwork of a Pennsylvania artist. "Our philosophy is quality. We publish literary fiction (and poetry and nonfiction). Our intended audience is literate, college-educated people." Annual. Circ. 300.

NEEDS Literary, mainstream, contemporary. "No genre fiction or romance." Reads mss during the summer. Publishes ms up tp 12 months after acceptance. **Publishes 4-6 new writers/year.** Recently published

work by Dave Kress, Dan Leone and Paul West. Publishes short shorts. Also publishes literary essays, literary criticism, poetry. Sometimes comments on rejected mss.

HOW TO CONTACT SASE. Does not accept electronic submissions. "We are creating Pennsylvania English Online—www.pennsylvaniaenglish.com—for electronic submissions and expanded publishing opportunities." Responds in up to 12 months to mss. Accepts simultaneous submissions. Does not accept previously published work. Sample copy for $10.

PAYMENT/TERMS Pays in 2 contributor's copies. Acquires first North American serial rights.

ⓓ PEREGRINE

Amherst Writers & Artists Press, P.O. Box 1076, Amherst MA 01004. (413)253-3307. **Fax:** (413)253-7764. **E-mail:** peregrine@amherstwriters.com. **Website:** www.amherstwriters.com. **Contact:** Nancy Rose, editor. Estab. 1983. Magazine: 6×9; 100 pages; 60 lb. white offset paper; glossy cover. "Peregrine has provided a forum for national and international writers since 1983, and is committed to finding excellent work by emerging as well as established writers. We welcome work reflecting diversity of voice. We like to be surprised. We look for writing that is honest, unpretentious, and memorable. We like to be surprised. All decisions are made by the editors." Annual. Member CLMP.

NEEDS Poetry and prose. "No previously published work. No children's stories." Short pieces have a better chance of publication. No electronic submissions. Accepts 6-12 mss/issue. Reads January-April. Publishes ms 4 months after acceptance. **Publishes 8-10 new writers/year.** Recently published work by Douglas Andrew, Brad Buchanan, Krikor N. Der Hohanesian, Myron Ernst, Laura Hogan, Lucy Honig, Dana Kroos, M.K. Meder, Pat Schneider, John Surowiecki, Edwina Trentham, Sacha Webley, Fred Yannantuono. Publishes short shorts.

HOW TO CONTACT Enclose sufficiently stamped SASE for return of ms; if disposable copy, enclose #10 SASE (use Forever stamp) for response. Accepts manuscripts postmarked March 15-May 15. Accepts simultaneous submissions. Sample copy for $12. Writer's guidelines for #10 SASE or website.

PAYMENT/TERMS Pays contributor's copies. All rights return to writer upon publication.

ⓓ PHILADELPHIA STORIES

Fiction/Art/Poetry of the Delaware Valley, 93 Old York Road, Suite 1/#1-753, Jenkintown PA 19046.

(215) 551-5889. **Fax:** (215) 635-0195. **E-mail:** christine@philadelphiastories.org; info@philadelphiastories.org. **Website:** www.philadelphiastories.org. **Contact:** Christine Weiser, co-publisher/managing editor. Carla Spataro, fiction editor/co-publisher. Estab. 2004. Literary magazine/journal. 812×11; 24 pages; 70# matte text, all four-color paper; 70# Matte Text cover. Contains illustrations., photographs. "*Philadelphia Stories* magazine publishes fiction, poetry, essays and art written by authors living in, or originally from, Pennsylvania, Delaware, or New Jersey." Estab. 2004. Quarterly. Circ. 10,000. Member CLMP.

NEEDS Experimental, literary, mainstream. "We will consider anything that is well written but are most inclined to publish literary or mainstream fiction. We are NOT particularly interested in most genres (sci fi/fantasy, romance, etc.)." List of upcoming themes available for SASE, on website. Receives 45-80 mss/month. Accepts 3-4 mss/issue for print, additional 1-2 online; 12-16 mss/year for print, 4-8 online. Ms published 1-2 months after acceptance. **Publishes 50% new writers/year.** Published katherine Hill, Jenny Lentz, Tom Larsen, Liz-Abrams-Morley, and Mitchell Sommers. Length: 5,000 words (max). Average length: 4,000 words. Publishes short shorts. Average length of short shorts: 800 words. Also publishes literary essays, book reviews, poetry. Send review queries to: info@philadelphiastories.org. Rarely comments on/critiques rejected mss.

HOW TO CONTACT Send complete ms with cover letter via online submission form only. Include estimated word count, list of publications, affiliation to the Philadelphia area. Responds to mss in 12 weeks. Considers simultaneous submissions. Sample copy available for $5, on website. Guidelines available on website.

PAYMENT/TERMS Writers receive 2+ contributor's copies. Pays on publication. Acquires onetime rights. Publication is copyrighted. "Launched First National Fiction contest in 2009 with $1,000 prize and plans another one for 2010. Visit our website for opportunities."

PHOEBE: A JOURNAL OF LITERATURE AND ART

George Mason Univ., 4400 University Dr., Fairfax VA 22030. **E-mail:** phoebe@gmu.edu. **Website:** www.phoebejournal.com. Estab. 1972. Phoebe. **Contact:** Editors change every year. Recently published work by Blake Butler, Kim Chinquee, Beth Staples, and more. Accepts simultaneous submissions. Sample copy for $6. Phoebe Magazine: 9×6; 112-120 pages; 80 lb. paper; 0-5 illustrations; 0-10 photos. "We publish mainly fiction and poetry with some visual art." Biannual. "*Phoebe* prides itself on supporting up-and-coming writers, whose style, form, voice, and subject matter demostrate a vigorous appeal to the senses, intellect, and emotions of our readers. No romance, western, juvenile, or erotica." Receives 300 unsolicited mss/month. Accepts 3-7 mss/issue. Does not read mss in summer. Publishes ms 3-6 months after acceptance. **Publishes 8-10 new writers/year.**

PAYMENT/TERMS Pays 2 contributor's copies or one-year subscription. Acquires onetime rights. All rights revert to author on publication.

THE PINCH

Dept. of English, The University of Memphis, Memphis TN 38152. (901)678-4591. **E-mail:** editor@thepinchjournal.com. **Website:** www.thepinchjournal.com. **Contact:** Kristen Iverson, editor-in-chief. Estab. 1980. (Formerly *River City*) Magazine: 7×10; 168 pages. Semiannual. "Semiannual literary magazine. We publish fiction, creative nonfiction, poetry, and art of literary quality by both established and emerging artists." Give 2 copies of journal in which work appears on publication.

NEEDS Short stories, poetry, creative nonfiction, essays, memoir, travel, nature writing, photography, art. **Publishes some new writers every year.** Recently published work by Chris Fink, George Singleton, Stephen Dunn, Denise Duhamel, Floyd Skloot, and Beth Ann Fennelly. "Character-based, fresh use of language." No genre fiction. Length: 7,000 words/max.

HOW TO CONTACT Send complete ms. Responds in 2 months to mss. Sample copy for $12.

PAYMENT/TERMS Pays 2 contributor's copies. Acquires first North American serial rights.

TIPS "We have a new look and a new edge. We're soliciting work from writers with a national or international reputation as well as strong, interesting work from emerging writers. The Pinch Literary Award (previously River City Writing Award) in Fiction offers a $1,500 prize and publication. Check our website for details."

PISGAH REVIEW

Division of Humanities, Brevard College, 400 N. Broad St., Brevard NC 28712. (828)884-8349. **E-mail:** tinerjj@brevard.edu. **Website:** www.pisgahreview.

com. **Contact:** Jubal Tiner, editor. Estab. 2005. Literary magazine/journal: 512 x 812, 120 pages. Includes cover artwork. "*Pisgah Review* publishes primarily literary short fiction, creative nonfiction and poetry. Our only criteria is quality of work; we look for the best." Semiannual. Circ. 200.

NEEDS Ethnic/multicultural, experimental, literary, mainstream. Special interests: stories rooted in the theme of place—physical, psychological, or spiritual. Does not want genre fiction or inspirational stories. Receives 85 mss/month. Accepts 6-8 mss/issue; 12-15 mss/year. Manuscript published 6 months after acceptance. **Publishes 5 new writers/year.** Published Ron Rash, Thomas Rain Crowe, Joan Conner, Gary Fincke, and Steve Almond. Length: 2,000 words (min)-7,500 words (max). Average length: 4,000 words. Publishes short shorts. Average length of short shorts: 1,000 words. Also publishes poetry and creative nonfiction. Sometimes comments on/critiques rejected mss.

HOW TO CONTACT Send complete ms with cover letter. Accepts submissions by e-mail and online submission form on website. Responds to mss in 4-6 months. Send either SASE (or IRC) for return of ms or disposable copy of ms and #10 SASE for reply only. Considers simultaneous submissions. Sample copy available for $7. Guidelines available on website.

PAYMENT/TERMS Writers receive 2 contributor's copies. Additional copies $7. Pays on publication. Acquires first North American serial rights. Sends galleys to author. Publication is copyrighted.

PLAIN SPOKE

Amsterdam Press, 6199 Steubenville Road SE, Amsterdam OH 43903. (740) 543-4333. **E-mail:** plainspoke@gmail.com. **Website:** www.plainspoke.net. **Contact:** Cindy Kelly, editor. Estab. 2007. Shaun M. Barcalow, fiction editor. Estab. 2007. Magazine: digest-sized; 36-52 pages; heavy paper; card cover. "We publish work that has a sense of word economy, strong voice, Americana appeal, tightness, and shies away from the esoteric and expositional. We like to be surprised." Quarterly.

NEEDS Comics, experimental, folksy, humor/satire, literary, mainstream, western (frontier saga), Americana, flash fiction, metafiction. Does not want science fiction, furry, cliché, plot-driven, formulaic. Receives 80 mss/month. Accepts 2-3 mss/issue; 10-12 mss/year. Length: 1,500-3,000 words. Average length: 1,750 words. Publishes short shorts. Average length of short

shorts: fewer than 1,000 words. Also publishes literary essays, literary criticism, book reviews, poetry. Send review copies with cover letter to reviews editor. Often comments on/critiques rejected manuscripts.

HOW TO CONTACT Send complete ms with cover letter. Accepts submissions by e-mail and on disk. Include estimated word count, brief bio in third person, list of publications. "Limit publication credits to 6." Responds to mss in 1-4 months. Send disposable copy of ms and #10 SASE for reply only. Considers simultaneous submissions, multiple submissions. Guidelines available for SASE, via e-mail, on website.

PAYMENT/TERMS Writers receive 1 contributor copy; additional copies $4. Pays on publication. Acquires first North American serial rights. Publication is copyrighted.

PLEIADES

Pleiades Press, Department of English, University of Central Missouri, Martin 336, Warrensburg MO 64093. (660)543-4425. **Fax:** (660)543-8544. **E-mail:** pleiades@ucmo.edu. **Website:** www.ucmo.edu/englphil/pleiades. **Contact:** G.B. Crump, Matthew Eck and Phong Nguyen, prose editors. Estab. 1991. Magazine: 512×812; 250 pages; 60 lb. paper; perfect-bound; 8 pt. color cover. "We publish contemporary fiction, poetry, interviews, literary essays, special-interest personal essays, reviews for a general and literary audience." Semiannual.

> "Also sponsors the Lena-Miles Wever Todd Poetry Series competition, a contest for the best book ms by an American poet. The winner receives $1,000, publication by Pleiades Press, and distribution by Louisiana State University Press. Deadline September 30. Send SASE for guidelines."

NEEDS Ethnic/multicultural, experimental, feminist, gay, humor/satire, literary, mainstream, novel excerpts, regional, translations, magical realism. No science fiction, fantasy, confession, erotica. Receives 100 unsolicited mss/month. Accepts 8 mss/issue; 16 mss/year. "We're slower at reading manuscripts in the summer." Publishes ms 9 months after acceptance. **Publishes 4-5 new writers/year.** Recently published work by Sherman Alexie, Edith Pearlman, Joyce Carol Oates, James Tate. Length: 2,000-6,000 words; average length: 3,000-6,000 words. Also publishes literary essays, literary criticism, poetry. Sometimes comments on rejected mss. We read fiction year-round. No science fiction, fantasy, confession, erotica. Length: 2,000-6,000 words.

HOW TO CONTACT Send complete ms. Include 75-100 word bio and list of publications. Send SASE for reply, return of ms or send a disposable copy of ms. Responds in 2 months to queries; 2 months to mss. Accepts simultaneous submissions. Sample copy for $6 (back issue), $8 (current issue). Writer's guidelines for #10 SASE. Send complete ms.

PAYMENT/TERMS Pays 2 contributor copies. Pays on publication for first North American serial, second serial (reprint) rights. Occasionally requests rights for TV, radio reading, website. Pays $10.

TIPS "Submit only 1 genre at a time to appropriate editors. Show care for your material and your readers—submit quality work in a professional format. Include cover letter with brief bio and list of publications. Include SASE. Cover art is solicited directly from artists. We accept queries for book reviews. For summer submissions, the poetry and nonfiction editors will no longer accept mss sent between June 1 & August 31. Any sent after May 31 will be held until the end of summer. Please do not send your only copy of anything."

🌐🎧💲 PLOUGHSHARES

Emerson College, Ploughshares, 120 Boylston St., Boston MA 02116. **Website:** www.pshares.org. **Contact:** Ladette Randolph, editor. Estab. 1971. *Ploughshares*, published 3 times/year, is "a journal of new writing guest-edited by prominent poets and writers to reflect different and contrasting points of view. Translations are welcome if permission has been granted. Our mission is to present dynamic, contrasting views on what is valid and important in contemporary literature and to discover and advance significant literary talent. Each issue is guest-edited by a different writer. We no longer structure issues around preconceived themes." Editors have included Carolyn Forché, Gerald Stern, Rita Dove, Chase Twichell, and Marilyn Hacker. Has published poetry by Donald Hall, Li-Young Lee, Robert Pinsky, Brenda Hillman, and Thylias Moss. Ploughshares is 200 pages, digest-sized. Receives about 11,000 poetry, fiction, and essay submissions/year. Press run is 6,000. Subscription: $30 domestic, $30 plus shipping (see website) foreign. Sample: $14 current issue, $7 back issue, please inquire for shipping rates.

> 🔇 A competitive and highly prestigious market. Rotating and guest editors make cracking

the line-up even tougher, since it's difficult to know what is appropriate to send. Reads submissions June 1-January 15 (postmark); mss submitted January 16-May 31 will be returned unread. "We do accept electronic submissions — there is a $3 fee per submission, which is waived if you are a subscriber."

NEEDS Recently published work by ZZ Packer, Antonya Nelson, Stuart Dybek. "No genre (science fiction, detective, gothic, adventure, etc.), popular formula or commerical fiction whose purpose is to entertain rather than to illuminate."

TIPS "We no longer structure issues around preconceived themes. If you believe your work is in keeping with our general standards of literary quality and value, submit at any time during our reading period."

🌐😈 PMS

University of Alabama at Birmingham, HB 217, 1530 3rd Ave. South, Birmingham AL 35294-1260. (205)934-8578. **E-mail:** kmadden@uab.edu. **Website:** www.pms-journal.org/submissions-guidelines. **Contact:** Kerry Madden, Editor-in-Chief. Literary magazine/journal: 6x9; 120 pages; recycled white; matte paper; cover photos. "We print one issue a year, our cover price is $7, and our journal publishes fine creative work by women writers from across the nation (and beyond) in the three genres listed in the title." Circ. 1,500. Member Council of Literary Magazines and Presses and the Council of Editors of Learned Journals." Receives 30 mss/month. Accepts 4-6 mss/issue. As of 2009, reading period is January 1 through March 30. Ms published within 6 months after acceptance. Publishes 5 new writers/year. Published Vicki Covington, Kim Aubrey, Patricia Brieschke, Gaines Marsh. Length: 4,500 words (max). Average length: 3,500-4,000 words. Publishes short shorts. Average length of short shorts: 300-350 words. Also publishes literary essays, poetry. Rarely comments on/critiques rejected mss. "This is an all women's literary journal. The subject field is wide open."

NEEDS Comics/graphic novels, ethnic/multicultural (general), experimental, feminist, literary, translations. "We don't do erotic, mystery work, and most popular forms. We publish short stories and essays including memoirs and other brands of creative nonfiction. Length: 4,300 words.

HOW TO CONTACT Send complete ms with cover letter. Include list of publications. Responds to queries in 1 month. Responds to mss in 1-4 months. Send disposable copy of ms and #10 SASE for reply only. Considers simultaneous submissions, multiple submissions. Sample copy available for $7. Guidelines available for SASE, on website.

PAYMENT/TERMS Writers receive 2 contributor's copies. Additional copies $7. Pays on publication. Acquires one-time rights. Publication is copyrighted.

TIPS "We seek unpublished original work that we can recycle. Include cover letter, brief bio with SASE. All mss should be typed on 1-side of 8 x 11 white paper with author's name, address, phone no. and email address on front of each submission." Reading period runs Jan. 1-Mar. 31. Submissions received at other times of the year will be returned unread. Best way to make contact is through e-mail.

POINTED CIRCLE

Portland Community College—Cascade, 705 N. Killing, Portland OR 97217. **E-mail:** lutgarda.cowan@pcc.edu. **Contact:** Lutgarda Cowan, English instructor, faculty advisor. Estab. 1980. Magazine: 80 pages; b&w illustrations; photos. "Anything of interest to educationally/culturally mixed audience." Annual. Ethnic/multicultural, literary, regional, contemporary, prose poem. "We will read whatever is sent, but encourage writers to remember we are a quality literary/arts magazine intended to promote the arts in the community. No pornography, nothing trite. Be mindful of deadlines and length limits." Accepts submissions only October 1-March 1, for July 1 issue. Accepts submissions by e-mail, mail. Prose up to 3,000 words; poetry up to 6 pages; artwork in high-resolution digital form. Submitted materials will not be returned; SASE for notification only. Accepts multiple submissions.

NEEDS Ethnic/multicultural, literary, regional, contemporary, prose poem. "We will read whatever is sent, but encourage writers to remember we are a quality literary/arts magazine intended to promote the arts in the community. No pornography, nothing trite. Be mindful of deadlines and length limits." Accepts submissions only October 1-March 1, for July 1 issue.

HOW TO CONTACT Accepts submissions by e-mail, mail. Prose up to 3,000 words; poetry up to 6 pages; artwork in high-resolution digital form. Submitted materials will not be returned; SASE for notification only. Accepts multiple submissions.

PAYMENT/TERMS Pays 2 copies. Acquires one-time rights.

POLYPHONY H.S.

Polyphony High School, 1514 Elmwood Ave., Suite 2, Evanston IL 60201. (847)910-3221. **E-mail:** polyphonyhs@gmail.com. **Website:** www.polyphonyhs.com. Estab. 2005. "Our mission is to create a high-quality literary magazine written, edited, and published by high school students. We strive to build respectful, mutually beneficial, writer-editor relationships that form a community devoted to improving students' literary skills in the areas of poetry, fiction, and creative nonfiction."

HOW TO CONTACT Submit with online submission process.

PAYMENT/TERMS Pays 2 contributor's copies.

THE PORTLAND REVIEW

Portland State University, P.O. Box 347, Portland OR 97207-0347. (503)725-4533. **E-mail:** theportlandreview@gmail.com. **Website:** portlandreview.tumblr.com. **Contact:** Jacqueline Treiber, editor. Estab. 1956.

NEEDS unpublished poetry and prose. Fiction/nonfiction prose of up to 5,000 words or 5 poems per submission. Receives 200 unsolicited mss/week. Accepts up to 24 mss/issue. No fantasy, detective, or western. 5,000 words maximum.

HOW TO CONTACT Ms and SASE for submissions. Review queries via e-mail. Submission guidelines online. All ms submissions not following guidelines are immediately rejected. Send complete ms.

PAYMENT/TERMS Pays contributor's copies. Acquires first North American serial rights. Pays contributor's copies.

TIPS "View website for current samples and guidelines."

POST ROAD

P.O. Box 600725, Newtown MA 02460. **E-mail:** postroad@bc.edu; ricco@postroadmag.com. **Website:** www.postroadmag.com. **Contact:** Ricco Siasoco, managing editor. Literary magazine/journal. 812 x 1112, 240 pages, 60 lb. opaque paper, gloss cover. "*Post Road* is a nationally distributed literary magazine based out of New York and Boston that publishes work in the following genres: art, criticism, fiction, nonfiction, and poetry. *Post Road* also features two innovations: the Recommendations section, where established writers write 500-1,000 words on a favorite book(s) or author(s); and the Etcetera section, where we publish interviews, profiles, translations, letters, classic reprints, documents, topical essays, travelogues, etc." Estab. 2000. Circ. 2,000.

NEEDS Literary. Receives 100 mss/month. Accepts 4-6 mss/issue; 8-12 mss/year. See website for reading periods. Manuscript published 6 months after acceptance. Published Brian Booker, Louis E. Bourgeois, Becky Bradway, Adam Braver, Ashley Capps, Susan Choi, Lisa Selin Davis, Rebecca Dickson, Rick Moody. Average length: 5,000 words. Average length of short shorts: 1,500 words. Also publishes literary essays, literary criticism, poetry. Sometimes comments on/critiques rejected manuscripts.

HOW TO CONTACT Accepts submissions by online submissions manager only. Include brief bio. Responds to mss in 1 months. Send SASE (or IRC) for return of ms. Considers simultaneous submissions. Guidelines available on website.

PAYMENT/TERMS Writers receive 2 contributor's copies. Pays on publication. Acquires first North American serial rights. Sends galleys to author. Publication is not copyrighted.

TIPS "Looking for interesting narrative, sharp dialogue, deft use of imagery and metaphor. Be persistent and be open to criticism."

POTOMAC REVIEW

Montgomery College, 51 Mannakee St., MT/212, Rockville MD 20850. (301)251-7417. **Fax:** (301)738-1745. **E-mail:** zachary.benavidez@montgomerycollege.edu. **Website:** www.montgomerycollege.edu/potomacreview. **Contact:** Zachary Benavidez, editor. Estab. 1994. Magazine: 512×812; 175 pages; 50 lb. paper; 65 lb. color cover. Potomac Review "reflects a view of our region looking out to the world, and in turn, seeks how the world views the region." Biannual.

NEEDS "Stories and poems with a vivid, individual quality that get at 'the concealed side' of life." Flash fiction accepted. Essays and creative non-fiction pieces welcome. No themes. Receives 300+ unsolicited mss/month. Accepts 40-50 mss/issue. Publishes ms within 1 year after acceptance. Recently published work by Jennine Capo Crucet, T.J. Forrester, Irene Keliher, Myfanwy Collins, Tiger D. Quinn, and Julee Newberger. Length: 5,000 words; average length: 2,000 words.

HOW TO CONTACT Send SASE with adequate postage for reply and/or return of ms. Responds in 3 -6 months to mss. Accepts simultaneous submissions. Sample copy for $10. Writer's guidelines on website.

PAYMENT/TERMS Pays 2 or more contributor's copies; additional copies for a 40% discount.

TIPS "Send us interesting, well crafted stories. Have something to say in an original, provocative voice. Read recent issue to get a sense of the journal's new direction."

THE PRAIRIE JOURNAL

P.O. Box 68073, 28 Crowfoot Terrace NW, Calgary AB Y3G 3N8 Canada. **E-mail:** editor@prairiejournal.org (queries only); prairiejournal@yahoo.com. **Website:** prairiejournal.org. **Contact:** A.E. Burke, literary editor. Estab. 1983. Journal: 7×812; 50-60 pages; white bond paper; Cadillac cover stock; cover illustrations. "The audience is literary, university, library, scholarly and creative readers/writers."

> "Use our mailing address for submissions and queries with samples sor clippings."

NEEDS Literary, regional. No genre (romance, horror, western—sagebrush or cowboys—erotic, science fiction, or mystery). Receives 100 unsolicited mss/month. Accepts 10-15 mss/issue; 20-30 mss/year. Suggested deadlines: April 1 for spring/summer issue; October 1 for fall/winter. Publishes ms 4-6 months after acceptance. Publishes 60 new writers/year. Recently published work by Robert Clark, Sandy Campbell, Darcie Hasack, Christopher Blais. Length: 100-3,000 words; average length: 2,500 words. Also publishes literary essays, literary criticism, poetry. Sometimes comments on rejected mss. No genre (romance, horror, western—sagebrush or cowboys), erotic, science fiction, or mystery. Length: 100-3,000 words.

HOW TO CONTACT Send complete ms with SASE (IRC). Include cover letter of past credits, if any. Reply to queries for SAE with 55¢ for postage or IRC. No American stamps. Responds in 2 weeks to queries; 6 months to mss. No simultaneous submissions. No e-mail submissions. Sample copy for $6. Writer's guidelines online. Reviews fiction. Send complete ms.

PAYMENT/TERMS Pays $10-75. Pays on publication for first North American serial rights. In Canada, author retains copyright with acknowledgement appreciated.

TIPS "We publish many, many new writers and are always open to unsolicited submissions because we are 100% freelance. Do not send US stamps, always use IRCs. We have poems and reviews online (query first)."

PRAIRIE SCHOONER

The University of Nebraska Press, Prairie Schooner, 123 Andrews Hall, University of Nebraska, Lincoln

NE 68588-0334. (402)472-7211, 1-800-715-2387. **E-mail:** jengelhardt2@unlnotes.unl.edu. **Website:** http://prairieschooner.unl.edu. Estab. 1926. Magazine: 6×9; 200 pages; good stock paper; heavy cover stock. "A fine literary quarterly of stories, poems, essays and reviews for a general audience that reads for pleasure."

○ Submissions must be received between September 1 and May 1.

NEEDS Good fiction (literary). Receives 500 unsolicited mss/month. Accepts 4-5 mss/issue. Mss are read September through May only. **Publishes 5-10 new writers/year.** Recently published work by Robert Olen Butler, Janet Burroway, Aimee Phan, Valerie Sayers, Daniel Stern. Also publishes poetry. "We try to remain open to a variety of styles, themes, and subject matter. We look for high-quality writing, 3-D characters, well-wrought plots, setting, etc. We are open to realistic and/or experimental fiction."

HOW TO CONTACT Send complete ms with SASE and cover letter listing previous publications—where, when. Responds in 4 months to mss. Sample copy for $6. Writer's guidelines and excerpts online. Reviews fiction. Send complete ms.

PAYMENT/TERMS Pays in contributor's copies and prize money awarded. Will reassign rights upon request after publication. Sponsors awards/contests. Pays 3 copies of the issue in which the writer's work is published.

TIPS "Send us your best, most carefully crafted work and be persistent. Submit again and again. Constantly work on improving your writing. Read widely in literary fiction, nonfiction, and poetry. Read *Prairie Schooner* to know what we publish."

⊕ PRAIRIE WINDS

Dakota Wesleyan University English Department, 1200 University Ave., Mitchell SD 57301. (605)995-2633. **E-mail:** prairiewinds@dwu.edu. **Website:** www.dwu.edu/prairiewinds. **Contact:** Joe Ditta, faculty advisor. Estab. 1946. *Prairie Winds* is a literary annual interested in poetry, fiction, creative nonfiction, and essays of general interest. Selection of mss takes place in February, magazine goes to press in March, and is distributed in April of each year.

NEEDS No pornography. Length: 3,000 words maximum.

HOW TO CONTACT Submit complete ms.

PAYMENT/TERMS Pays contributor's copies.

○①①⑤ PRISM INTERNATIONAL

Department of Creative Writing, Buch E462, 1866 Main Mall, University of British Columbia, Vancouver BC V6T 1Z1 Canada. (604)822-2514. **Fax:** (604)822-3616. **Website:** www.prismmagazine.ca. Estab. 1959. Magazine: 6×9; 80 pages; Zephyr book paper; Cornwall, coated one-side cover; artwork on cover. "An international journal of contemporary writing—fiction, poetry, drama, creative nonfiction and translation." Readership: "public and university libraries, individual subscriptions, bookstores—a worldwide audience concerned with the contemporary in literature." Quarterly.

NEEDS Experimental, traditional. New writing that is contemporary and literary. Short stories and self-contained novel excerpts (up to 25 double-spaced pages). Works of translation are eagerly sought and should be accompanied by a copy of the original. Would like to see more translations. "No gothic, confession, religious, romance, pornography, or sci-fi." Also looking for creative nonfiction that is literary, not journalistic, in scope and tone. Receives over 100 unsolicited mss/month. Accepts 70 mss/year. "PRISM publishes both new and established writers; our contributors have included Franz Kafka, Gabriel Garcíía Maárquez, Michael Ondaatje, Margaret Laurence, Mark Anthony Jarman, Gail Anderson-Dargatz and Eden Robinson." Publishes ms 4 months after acceptance. **Publishes 7 new writers/year.** Recently published work by Ibi Kaslik, Melanie Little, Mark Anthony Jarman. Publishes short shorts. Also publishes poetry. For Drama: one-acts/excerpts of no more than 1500 words preferred. Also interested in seeing dramatic monologues.

HOW TO CONTACT Send complete ms by mail. "Keep it simple. U.S. contributors take note: Do not send SASEs with U.S. stamps, they are not valid in Canada. Send International Reply Coupons instead." Responds in 4 months to queries; 3-6 months to mss. Sample copy for $11 or on website. Writer's guidelines online. Send complete ms.

PAYMENT/TERMS Pays $20/printed page of prose, $40/printed page of poetry, and 1-year subscription. Pays on publication for first North American serial rights. Selected authors are paid an additional $10/page for digital rights. Cover art pays $300 and 4 copies of issue. Sponsors awards/contests, including annual short fiction, poetry, and nonfiction contests.

TIPS "We are looking for new and exciting fiction. Excellence is still our No. 1 criterion. As well as poetry, imaginative nonfiction and fiction, we are especially open to translations of all kinds, very short fiction pieces and drama which work well on the page. Translations must come with a copy of the original language work. We pay an additional $10/printed page to selected authors whose work we place on our online version of *Prism*."

⭘ PUERTO DEL SOL

New Mexico State University, English Department, P.O.Box 30001, MSC 3E, Las Cruces NM 88003. (505)646-3931. **E-mail:** contact@puertodelsol.org. **Website:** www.puertodelsol.org. **Contact:** Carmen Giménez Smith, editor-in-chief. Estab. 1964. Magazine: 7×9; 200 pages; 60 lb. paper; 70 lb. cover stock. www.puertodelsol.org. Email: contact@puertodelsol.org. "We publish innovative work from emerging and established writers and artists. Poetry, fiction, nonfiction, drama, theory, artwork, interviews, reviews, and interesting combinations thereof." Semiannual. Circ. 1,500.

NEEDS Literary, experimental, theory, drama, work in translation. Accepts 8-12 mss/issue; 16-24 mss/year. Does not accept mss April 1-September 14. **Publishes 8-10 new writers/year.** Recently accepted and published work by Kim Chinquee, Grace Krilanovich, Robert Lopez, Peter Markus, Shya Scanlon. Responds in 3-6 months to mss. Accepts simultaneous submissions. Sample copy for $10.

HOW TO CONTACT Submit 1 short story, 2-4 short short stories, or 5 poems at a time through online submission manager. Responds in 3-6 months to mss. Accepts simultaneous submissions. Sample copy for $8. Email: contact@puertodelsol.org. Send complete ms

PAYMENT/TERMS Pays 2 contributor's copies. Acquires one-time print and electronic rights and anthology rights. Rights revert to author after publication.

TIPS "We are especially pleased to publish emerging writers who work to push their art form or field of study in new directions."

⭘⭘⭘ QUARTERLY WEST

University of Utah, 255 S. Central Campus Dr., Room 3500, Salt Lake City UT 84112. **E-mail:** quarterlywest@gmail.com. **Website:** www.utah.edu/quarterlywest. **Contact:** Matt Kirkpatrick & Cami Nelson, editors. Estab. 1976. Magazine: 7×10; 50 lb. paper; 4-color cover stock. "We publish fiction, poetry, and nonfic-

tion in long and short formats, and will consider experimental as well as traditional works." Semiannual.

> ⭘ *Quarterly West* was awarded first place for Editorial Content from the American Literary Magazine Awards. Work published in the magazine has been selected for inclusion in the *Pushcart Prize* anthology and *The Best American Short Stories* anthology.

NEEDS Ethnic/multicultural, experimental, humor/satire, literary, mainstream, novel excerpts, slice-of-life vignettes, translations, short shorts, translations. No detective, science fiction or romance. Receives 300 unsolicited mss/month. Accepts 6-10 mss/issue; 12-20 mss/year. Reads mss between September 1 and May 1 only. "Submissions received between May 2 and August 31 will be returned unread." Publishes ms 6 months after acceptance. **Publishes 3 new writers/year.** Recently published work by Steve Almond, Linh Dinh. No preferred lengths; interested in longer, fuller short stories and short shorts. No detective, science fiction or romance.

HOW TO CONTACT Send complete ms. Brief cover letters welcome. Send SASE for reply or return of ms. Responds in 6 months to mss. Accepts simultaneous submissions if notified. Sample copy for $7.50. Writer's guidelines online.

PAYMENT/TERMS Pays $15-50, and 2 contributor's copies. Pays on publication for first North American serial rights..

TIPS We publish a special section of short shorts every issue, and we also sponsor a biennial novella contest. We are open to experimental work—potential contributors should read the magazine! Don't send more than 1 story/submission. Biennial novella competition guidelines available upon request with SASE. We prefer work with interesting language and detail—plot or narrative are less important. We don't do Western themes or religious work.

⊕ THE RAG

11901 SW 34th Ave., Portland OR 97219. **E-mail:** raglitmag@gmail.com. **Website:** http://raglitmag.com. **Contact:** Seth Porter, editor; Dan Reilly, editor. Estab. 2011. "The Rag focuses on the grittier genres that tend to fall by the wayside at more traditional literary magazines. The Rag's ultimate goal is to put the literary magazine magazine back into the entertainment market while rekindling the social and cultural value short fiction once held in North American literature."

NEEDS "We accept all styles and themes." Length: 2,000-10,000 words.

HOW TO CONTACT Send complete ms.

PAYMENT/TERMS Pays $50-300+.

❶ ⑤ RATTAPALLAX

Rattapallax Press, 217 Thompson St., Suite 353, New York NY 10012. (212)560-7459. **E-mail:** info@rattapallax.com. **Website:** www.rattapallax.com. **Contact:** Alan Cheuse, fiction editor. Estab. 1999. Literary magazine: 9×12; 128 pages; bound; some illustrations; photos. "General readership. Our stories must be character driven with strong conflict. All accepted stories are edited by our staff and the writer before publication to ensure a well-crafted and written work." Semiannual. *Rattapallax* is a literary magazine that focuses on issues dealing with globalization.

NEEDS Literary. Receives 15 unsolicited mss/month. Accepts 3 mss/issue; 6 mss/year. Publishes ms 3-6 months after acceptance. Agented fiction 15%. **Publishes 3 new writers/year.** Recently published work by Stuart Dybek, Howard Norman, Molly Giles, Rick Moody. Length: 1,000-10,000 words; average length: 5,000 words. Publishes short shorts. Also publishes poetry. Often comments on rejected mss.

HOW TO CONTACT Send SASE for return of ms. Responds in 3 months to queries; 3 months to mss. Sample copy for $7.95. Writer's guidelines for SASE or on website.

PAYMENT/TERMS Pays 2 contributor's copies; additional copies for $7.95. Pays on publication for first North American serial rights. Sends galleys to author.

❶ ⑤ THE RAVEN CHRONICLES

A Journal of Art, Literature, & the Spoken Word, 12346 Sand Point Way N.E., Seattle WA 98125. (206)941-2955. **E-mail:** editors@ravenchronicles.org. **Website:** www.ravenchronicles.org. Estab. 1991. Magazine: 812×11; 88-100 pages; 50 lb. book; glossy cover; b&w illustrations; photos. "*The Raven Chronicles* is designed to promote transcultural art, literature and the spoken word." Biannual. Circ. 2,500-5,000.

NEEDS Ethnic/multicultural, literary, regional, political, cultural essays. "No romance, fantasy, mystery or detective." Receives 300-400 unsolicited mss/month. Accepts 35-60 mss/issue; 105-150 mss/year. Publishes ms 12 months after acceptance. **Publishes 50-100 new writers/year.** Recently published work by David Romtvedt, Sherman Alexie, D.L. Birchfield, Nancy Redwine, Diane Glancy, Greg Hischak, Sha-

ron Hashimoto. Length: 2,500 words (but negotiable); average length: 2,000 words. Publishes short shorts. Also publishes literary essays, literary criticism, poetry. Sometimes comments on rejected mss.

HOW TO CONTACT Send complete ms with SASE. Does not accept unsolicited submissions by e-mail (except foreign submissions). Responds in 3 months to mss. Does not accept simultaneous submissions. Sample copy for $5.19-10.19. Writer's guidelines for #10 SASE.

PAYMENT/TERMS Pays $10-40 and 2 contributor's copies; additional copies at half cover cost. Pays on publication for first North American serial rights. Sends galleys to author. See website for submission deadlines.

TIPS Looks for "clean, direct language, written from the heart, and experimental writing. Read sample copy, or look at *Before Columbus* anthologies and *Greywolf Annual* anthologies."

❾ ⓪ THE READER

19 Abercromby Square, Liverpool, Merseyside LG9 7ZG United Kingdom. **E-mail:** magazine@thereader.org.uk; info@thereader.org.uk. **Website:** www.thereader.org.uk. **Contact:** Philip Davis, editor. Estab. 1997. Literary magazine/journal: 216 x 138 mm, 130 pages, 80 gsm (Silver Offset) paper. Includes photographs. "*The Reader* is a quarterly literary magazine aimed at the intelligent 'common reader'—from those just beginning to explore serious literary reading to professional teachers, academics and writers. As well as publishing short fiction and poetry by new writers and established names, the magazine features articles on all aspects of literature, language, and reading; regular features, including a literary quiz and 'Our Spy in NY', a bird's-eye view of literary goings-on in New York; reviews; and readers' recommendations of books that have made a difference to them. *The Reader* is unique among literary magazines in its focus on reading as a creative, important and pleasurable activity, and in its combination of high-quality material and presentation with a genuine commitment to ordinary but dedicated readers." Quarterly. Estab. 1997.

NEEDS Literary. Receives 10 mss/month. Accepts 1-2 mss/issue; 8 mss/year. Manuscript published 16 months after acceptance. Publishes 4 new writers/year. Published Karen King Arbisala, Ray Tallis, Sasha Dugdale, Vicki Seal, David Constantine, Jonathan Meades, Ramesh Avadhani. Length: 1,000 words (min)-3,000 words (max). Average length: 2,300 words. Publishes short shorts. Average length of short shorts: 1,500 words. Also publishes literary essays, literary criticism, poetry. Sometimes comments on/critiques rejected mss.

HOW TO CONTACT No e-mail submissions. Send complete ms with cover letter. Include estimated word count, brief bio, list of publications. Responds to queries in 2 months; mss in 2 months. Send SASE (or IRC) for return of ms. Considers simultaneous submissions, multiple submissions. Guidelines available for SASE.

PAYMENT/TERMS Additional copies $14. Pays on publication. Sends galleys to author.

TIPS "The style or polish of the writing is less important than the deep structure of the story (though of course, it matters that it's well written). The main persuasive element is whether the story moves us—and that's quite hard to quantify—it's something to do with the force of the idea and the genuine nature of enquiry within the story. When fiction is the writer's natural means of thinking things through, that'll get us. "

THE RED CLAY REVIEW

Dr. Jim Elledge, Director, M. A. in Professional Writing Program, Department of English, Kennesaw State University, 1000 Chastain Rd., #2701, Kennesaw GA 30144-5591. **E-mail:** redclayreview@gmail.com. **Website:** http://redclayreview.com. **Contact:** Dr. Jim Elledge, director, M. A. in Professional Writing Program. Magazine has revolving editor. Editorial term: 1 year. Literary magazine/journal. 812×512; 80-120 pages, 60# white paper, 10-pt matte lam. cover. "*The Red Clay Review* is dedicated to publishing only the most outstanding graduate literary pieces. It has been established by members of the Graduate Writers Association at Kennesaw State University. It is unique because it only includes the work of graduate writing students. We publish poems (must be limited to 300 words, double spaced, 12 pt. font, 3-5 poems per submission), fiction/non-fiction pieces (must not exceed 10 pages, double spaced, 12 pt. font), and 10 minute plays/scenes (should be limited to 11 total pages since the first page will usually be mostly taken up by character listing/setting description.)" Annual. Estab. 2008.

NEEDS "We do not have any specific themes or topics, but keep in mind that we are a literary publication. We will read whatever is sent in. We will publish whatever we deem to be great literary writing. So in essence, every topic is open to submission, and we are all interested in a wide variety of subjects. We do not prohibit any topic or subject matter from being submitted. As long as submissions adhere to our guidelines, we are open to reading them. However, subject matter in any area that is too extreme may be less likely to be published because we want to include a broad collection of literary graduate work, but on the other hand, we cannot morally reject great writing." Receives 12 mss/month. Does not read November 1- June 1. Ms published 6 months after acceptance. Length: 2,500 words (min)-8,000 words (max). Publishes short shorts. Also publishes literary essays, poetry. Never comments on/critiques rejected mss.

HOW TO CONTACT Send complete ms with cover letter. Include brief bio, list of publications, and an e-mail address must be supplied for the student, as well as the student's advisor's contact information (to verify student status). Responds to mss in 12-16 weeks. Considers simultaneous submissions, multiple submissions. Guidelines available on website.

PAYMENT/TERMS Writers receive 2 contributor's copies. Pays on publication. Acquires first rights. Publication is copyrighted.

REDIVIDER

Department of Writing, Literature, and Publishing, Emerson College, 120 Boylston St., Boston MA 02116. **E-mail:** fiction@redividerjournal.com; poetry@redividerjournal.com. **Website:** www.redividerjournal.org. Estab. 1986. Editors change each year. Magazine: 512×812; 160 pages; 60 lb. paper. *Redivider*, a journal of literature and art, is published twice a year by students in the graduate writing, literature and publishing department of Emerson College. Biannual.

NEEDS Literary. Receives 100 unsolicited mss/month. Accepts 6-8 mss/issue; 10-12 mss/year. Publishes ms 3-6 months after acceptance. Publishes short shorts. Also publishes poetry. Sometimes comments on rejected mss.

HOW TO CONTACT "We are taking electronic submissions solely through our online submissions manager. Hard copy submissions and inquiries may be sent to the appropriate genre editor through postal mail. Send disposable copy of ms." Accepts simultaneous submissions with notification. Sample copy for $6 with a #10 SASE. Writer's guidelines for SASE or online.

PAYMENT/TERMS Pays 2 contributor's copies; additional copies $6. Pays on publication for onetime rights. Sponsors awards/contests.

TIPS "Our deadlines are July 1 for the Fall issue, and December 1 for the Spring issue."

● RED ROCK REVIEW

College of Southern Nevada, CSN Department of English, J2A, 3200 E. Cheyenne Ave., North Las Vegas NV 89030. (702)651-4094. **Fax:** (702)651-4639. **E-mail:** redrockreview@csn.edu. **Website:** sites.csn.edu/english/redrockreview/. **Contact:** Rich Logsdon, Senior Editor. Estab. 1994. Magazine: 5×8; 125 pages. "We're looking for the very best literature. Stories need to be tightly crafted, strong in character development, built around conflict. Poems need to be tightly crafted, characterised by expert use of language." "We are dedicated to the publication of fine contemporary literature."

NEEDS Experimental, literary, mainstream. Receives 350 unsolicited mss/month. Accepts 40-60 mss/issue; 80-120 mss/year. Does not read mss during summer. Publishes ms 3-5 after acceptance. **Publishes 5-10 new writers/year.** Recently published work by Charles Harper Webb, Mary Sojourner, Mark Irwin. Length: less than 7,500 words. Publishes short shorts. Also publishes literary essays, literary criticism, poetry. Sometimes comments on rejected mss. Length: 7,500 words.

HOW TO CONTACT Send SASE (or IRC) for return of ms. Responds in 2 weeks to queries; 3 months to mss. Does not accept general submissions June-August, or in December. Accepts simultaneous, multiple submissions. Sample copy for $5.50. Writer's guidelines for SASE, by e-mail or on website.

PAYMENT/TERMS Pays 2 contributor's copies. Pays on acceptance for first rights.

TIPS "Open to short fiction and poetry submissions from Sept. 1-May 31. Include SASE and include brief bio. No general submissions between June 1st and August 31st. See guidelines online."

● REED MAGAZINE

San Jose State University, Dept. of English, One Washington Square, San Jose CA 95192-0090. (408) 927-4458. **E-mail:** reed@email.sjsu.edu. **Website:** http://www.reedmag.org/drupal/. **Contact:** Nick Taylor, editor. Estab. 1944. Literary magazine/journal. 9×5.75, 200 pages, semi-gloss paper, card cover. Contains illustrations. Includes photographs. "Reed Magazine is one of the oldest student-run literary journals west of the Mississippi. We publish outstanding fiction, poetry, nonfiction and art as a service to the South Bay literary community." Annual. Circ. 3500. Member CLMP.

NEEDS Ethnic/multicultural (general), experimental, feminist, gay, historical (general), humor/satire, lesbian, literary, mainstream, regional (northern California). Does not want children's, young adult, fantasy, or erotic. Receives 30 mss/month. Accepts 5-7 mss/issue. Does not read Nov 2-May 31. Ms published 6 months after acceptance. Publishes 3-4 new writers/year. Published Tommy Mouton, Alan Soldofsky, Gwen Goodkin and Al Young. Length: 2,000 words (min)-6,000 words (max). Average length: 3,500 words. Also publishes literary essays, book reviews, poetry. Send review copies to Nick Taylor, Editor. Never comments on/critiques rejected mss.

HOW TO CONTACT Submit online. Include estimated word count, brief bio. Responds to mss in 6 months. Considers simultaneous submissions, multiple submissions. Sample copy available for $8. Guidelines available on website.

PAYMENT/TERMS Writers receive free subscription to the magazine. Additional copies $5. Pays on publication. Acquires first North American serial rights. Sends galleys to author. Publication is copyrighted. "Sponsors the Steinbeck Award, given annually for the best short story. The prize is $1,000 and there's a $15 entry fee."

TIPS "Well-written, original, clean grammatical prose is essential. Keep submitting! The readers are students and change every year."

● ⑤ THE REJECTED QUARTERLY

P.O. Box 1351, Cobb CA 95426. **E-mail:** bplankton@yahoo.com. **Website:** www.rejectedq.com. **Contact:** Daniel Weiss and Jeff Ludeke, fiction editors. Estab. 1998. Magazine: 812×11; 36-44 pages; 60 lb. paper; 10-pt. coated cover stock; illustrations. "We want the best literature possible, regardless of genre. We do, however, have a bias toward the unusual and toward speculative fiction. We aim for a literate, educated audience. *The Rejected Quarterly* believes in publishing the highest quality rejected fiction and other writing that doesn't fit anywhere else. We strive to be different, but will go for quality every time, whether conventional or not." Semiannual.

NEEDS Length: 8,000 words.

HOW TO CONTACT Send SASE for reply, return of ms or send a disposable copy of ms. No longer accepting e-mail submissions. Responds in 2-4 weeks to queries; 1-9 months to mss. Accepts reprint submissions. Sample copy for $7.50 (IRCs for foreign requests). Reviews fiction.

PAYMENT/TERMS Pays $20 and 1 contributor's copy; additional copies $5.

TIPS "We read mss from June through August only. We are looking for high-quality writing that tells a story or expresses a coherent idea. We want unique stories, original viewpoints, and unusual slants. We are getting far too many inappropriate submissions. Please be familiar with the magazine. Be sure to include your rejection slips! Send out quality rather than quantity."

RIVER OAK REVIEW

Elmhurst College, 190 Prospect Ave., Elmhurst IL 60126-3296. (630) 617-3137. **Fax:** (630) 617-3609. **E-mail:** riveroak@elmhurst.edu. **Website:** www.riveroakreview.org. **Contact:** Ron Wiginton, fiction editor, ronw@elmhurst.edu. Literary magazine/journal: 6×9, 195 pages; perfect bound paper; glossy, 4 color cover. "We try with each issue to showcase many voices of America, loud and soft, radical and sublime. Each piece we publish, prose or poetry, is an attempt to capture a part of 'us', with the notion that it is through our art that we are defined as a culture." Estab. 1993. Circ. 500.

NEEDS ethnic/multicultural (general), experimental, literary, mainstream, translations. Does not want genre fiction or "lessons of morality; 'idea' driven stories usually do not work." Receives 50-75 mss/month. Accepts 7-8 mss/issue; 14-16 mss/year. Ms published 3 months after acceptance. Agented fiction 1%. **Publishes 2-3 new writers/year.** Published Adam Lichtenstein, Robert Moulthrop, J. Malcom Garcia and Laura Hope-Gill. Length: 250 words (min)-7,000 words (max). Average length: 3,000 words. Publishes short shorts. Average length of short shorts: 750 words. Also publishes literary essays, book reviews, poetry. Send review copies to Ron Wiginton, Editor. Sometimes comments on/critiques rejected mss.

HOW TO CONTACT Send complete ms with cover letter. Accepts submissions by e-mail. Include list of publications. Responds to mss in 6 months. Send disposable copy of ms and #10 SASE for reply only. Considers simultaneous submissions. Sample copy available for $5. Guidelines available for SASE, via e-mail, on website, via fax.

PAYMENT/TERMS Writers receive 2 contributor's copies. Additional copies $10. Pays on publication. Acquires first North American serial rights. Publication is copyrighted.

RIVER STYX MAGAZINE

Big River Association, 3547 Olive St., Suite 107, St. Louis MO 63103. (314)533-4541. **E-mail:** bigriver@riverstyx.org. **Website:** www.riverstyx.org. **Contact:** Richard Newman, Editor. Estab. 1975. Magazine: 6×9; 100 pages; color card cover; perfect-bound; b&w visual art. "*River Styx* publishes the highest quality fiction, poetry, interviews, essays, and visual art. We are an internationally distributed multicultural literary magazine." Mss read May-November.

> Work published in *River Styx* has been selected for inclusion in past volumes of *New Stories From the South*, *The Best American Poetry*, *Beacon's Best*, *Best New Poets* and *The Pushcart Prize Anthology*

NEEDS Ethnic/multicultural, experimental, feminist, gay, lesbian, literary, mainstream, novel excerpts, translations, short stories, literary. "No genre fiction, less thinly veiled autobiography." Receives 350 unsolicited mss/month. Accepts 2-6 mss/issue; 6-12 mss/year. Reads only May through November. Publishes ms 1 year after acceptance. **Publishes 20 new writers/year.** Recently published work by George Singleton, Philip Graham, Katherine Min, Richard Burgin, Nancy Zafris, Jacob Appel, and Eric Shade. Publishes short shorts. Also publishes poetry. Sometimes comments on rejected mss. No genre fiction, less thinly veiled autobiography. no more than 23-30 manuscript pages.

HOW TO CONTACT Send complete ms. SASE required. Responds in 4 months to mss. Accepts simultaneous submissions "if a note is enclosed with your work and if we are notified immediately upon acceptance elsewhere." Sample copy for $8. Writer's guidelines online. Send complete ms.

PAYMENT/TERMS Pays 2 contributor copies, plus 1-year subscription; cash payment as funds permit. Pays on publication for first North American serial, onetime rights.

RIVERWIND

3301 Hocking Park Way, Nelsonville OH 45764. (740)753-3591. **E-mail:** williams_k@hocking.edu. Estab. 1976. Magazine: 7×7; 125-150 pages; 60 lb. offset paper; illustrations; photos. *Riverwind* is an established magazine that prints fiction, poetry, black-and-white photos and prints, drawings, creative nonfiction, book reviews and plays. Special consideration is given to writers from the Appalachian region. Annual. Estab. 1976. Circ. 200-400.

NEEDS Adventure, ethnic/multicultural (Appalachian), humor/satire, literary, mainstream, regional. DOES NOT WANT erotica, fantasy, horror, experimental, religious, children's/juvenile. Receives 25 unsolicited mss/month. Does not read mss June-September. Publishes ms 6-9 months after acceptance. **Publishes many new writers/year.** Recently published work by Gerald Wheeler, Wendy McVicker, Roy Bentley, Perry A. White, Tom Montag, Beau Beadreaux. Length: 500-2,500 words; average length: 1,750 words. Publishes short shorts. Also publishes literary essays, literary criticism, poetry. Rarely comments on rejected mss.

HOW TO CONTACT Send complete ms. Accepts submissions by e-mail, disk. Send disposable copy of ms and #10 SASE for reply only. Responds in 4 weeks to queries; 8-16 weeks to mss. Accepts simultaneous, multiple submissions. Sample copy for $5. Writer's guidelines for #10 SASE or by e-mail.

PAYMENT/TERMS Pays 2 contributor's copies. Pays on publication for first North American serial rights.

TIPS "Avoid stereotypical plots and characters. We tend to favor realism but not sentimentality."

ROANOKE REVIEW

Roanoke College, 221 College Lane, Salem VA 24153-3794. **E-mail:** review@roanoke.edu. **Website:** http://roanokereview.wordpress.com. Estab. 1967. **Contact:** Paul Hanstedt, editor. Magazine: 6×9; 200 pages; 60 lb. paper; 70 lb. cover. "We're looking for fresh, thoughtful material that will appeal to a broader as well as literary audience. Humor encouraged." Annual. Estab. 1967. Circ. 500.

NEEDS Feminist, gay, humor/satire, lesbian, literary, mainstream, regional. Receives 150 unsolicited mss/month. Accepts 5-10 mss/year. Does not read mss February 1-September 1. Publishes ms 6 months after acceptance. **Publishes 1-5 new writers/year.** Has published work by Siobhan Fallon, Jacob M. Appel, and JoeAnn Hart. Length: 1,000-5,000 words; average length: 3,000 words. Publishes short shorts. Also publishes poetry. Sometimes comments on rejected mss.

HOW TO CONTACT Send SASE for return of ms or send a disposable copy of ms and #10 SASE for reply only. Responds in 1 month to queries; 6 months to mss. Sample copy for 8×11 SAE with $2 postage. Writer's guidelines for SASE.

PAYMENT/TERMS Pays $10-50/story (when budget allows) and 2 contributor's copies; additional copies $5. Pays on publication for one-time rights.

TIPS "Pay attention to sentence-level writing—verbs, metaphors, concrete images. Don't forget, though, that plot and character keep us reading. We're looking for stuff that breaks the MFA story style." "Be real. Know rhythm. Concentrate on strong images."

THE ROCKFORD REVIEW

The Rockford Writers Guild, P.O. Box 858, Rockford IL 61105. **E-mail:** editors@rockfordwritersguild.com. **Website:** www.rockfordwritersguild.com. **Contact:** Connie Kluntz, Managing Editor. Estab. 1947. Magazine: 100 pages; perfect bound; color illustrations; b&w photos. Rockford Writers' Guild is a nonprofit corporation established in 1947 with the mission to promote the literary arts in Rockford, IL and beyond. Monthly meetings, interaction with other writers, writers groups, editorial support, current information and useful resources through the website, discounts on book production, and other benefits are just part of what RWG offers to its members. Semiannual. "Published twice/year. Members only edition in summer-fall and winter-spring edition which is open to all writers. Open season to submit for the winter-spring edition of the Rock Review is August. If pubished in the winter-spring edition of the Rockford Review, payment is one copy of magazine and $5 per published piece. Credit line given. Check website for frequent updates. We are also on Facebook under Rockford Writers' Guild."

NEEDS Ethnic/multicultural, experimental, fantasy, humor/satire, literary, regional, science fiction (hard science, soft/sociological). "No graphic sex, translations or overly academic work." Recently published work by James Bellarosa, Sean Michael Rice, John P. Kristofco, L.S. Sedishiro. Also publishes literary essays.

HOW TO CONTACT Please go online and follow the rules for submission: www.rockfordwritersguild.com/submit.html. Please note that submissions rules may change from time to time and for each edition there is a different theme to write about. So, check the website regularly. Be sure your mss conform to the rules, or they may not be considered. Pays 1 contributor's copy and pays two editor's choice awards of $25 each: one for prose and one for poetry. 1,300 words or less for prose.

PAYMENT/TERMS If published in the winter-spring edition of the *Rockford Review*, payment is one copy of magazine and $5 per published piece. Pays on publication.

TIPS "We're wide open to new and established writers alike—particularly short satire."

○①⑤ ROOM

P.O. Box 46160, Station D, Vancouver BC V6J 5G5 Canada. **E-mail:** contactus@roommagazine.com. **Website:** www.roommagazine.com. **Contact:** Growing Room Collective. Estab. 1975. Magazine: 112 pages; illustrations; photos. *ROOM* is Canada's oldest literary journal by and for women. Since 1975, *ROOM* has been a forum in which women can share their unique perspectives on the world, each other and themselves."

NEEDS Accepts literature that illustrates the female experience—short stories, creative nonfiction, poetry—by, for and about women. Receives 100-120 unsolicited mss/month. Accepts 18-20 mss/issue; 75-80 mss/year. Publishes ms 1 year after acceptance. **Publishes 15-20 new writers/year.**

HOW TO CONTACT We accept e-mail submissions with some guidelines—see our full guidelines at our website. Or, send complete ms with a cover letter. Include estimated word count and brief bio. Do not send a SASE. Responds in 6 months to mss. Sample copy for $13 or online. Writer's guidelines online. Reviews fiction.

PAYMENT/TERMS Pays $50 (Canadian), 2 contributor's copies, and a 1-year subscription. Pays on publication for first North American serial rights.

①① SALMAGUNDI

Skidmore College, 815 North Broadway, Saratoga Springs NY 12866. (518)580-5000 ext. 4495. **Fax:** (518)580-5188. **E-mail:** salmagun@skidmore.edu. **Website:** cms.skidmore.edu/salmagundi/index.cfm. Estab. 1965. Magazine: 8×5; 200-300 pages; illustrations; photos. "*Salmagundi* publishes an eclectic variety of materials, ranging from short-short fiction to novellas from the surreal to the realistic. Authors include Nadine Gordimer, Russell Banks, Steven Millhauser, Gordon Lish, Clark Blaise, Mary Gordon, Joyce Carol Oates and Cynthia Ozick. Our audience is a generally literate population of people who read for pleasure." Quarterly. Circ. 4,800. Member CLMP.

○ *Salmagundi* authors are regularly represented in *Pushcart* collections and *Best American Short Story* collections.

NEEDS Ethnic/multicultural (multicultural), experimental, family saga, gay, historical (general), literary, poetry. Receives 300-500 unsolicited mss/month. Accepts 2 mss/year. Read unsolicited mss October 1-May 1 "but from time to time close the doors even during this period because the backlog tends to grow out of control." Publishes ms up to 2 years after acceptance. Agented fiction 10%. Also publishes literary essays, literary criticism, poetry. Magazine: 8×5; 200-300 pages; illustrations; photos.

HOW TO CONTACT *Currently not accepting unsolicited mss.* Send complete ms by e-mail (pboyes@skidmore.edu). Responds in 6 months to mss. Sample copy for $5. Writer's guidelines for #10 SASE.

PAYMENT/TERMS Pays 6-10 contributor's copies and subscription to magazine. Acquires first, electronic rights.

● SANDY RIVER REVIEW

University of Maine at Farmington, 238 Main St., Farmington ME 04938. **E-mail:** srreview@gmail.com. **Website:** studentorgs.umf.maine.edu/~srreview. **Contact:** Kelsey Moore, editor. "*The Sandy River Review* seeks prose, poetry and art submissions twice a year for our Spring and Fall issues. Prose submissions may be either Fiction or Creative Non-Fiction and should be 15 pages or fewer in length, 12 pt., Times Roman font, double-spaced. Most of our art is published in black & white, and must be submitted as 300 dpi quaity, CMYK color mode, and saved as a .TIF file. We publish a wide variety of work from students as well as professional, established writers. Your submission should be polished and imaginative with strongly drawn characters and an interesting, original narrative. The review is the face of the University of Maine at Farmington's venerable BFA Creative Writing program, and we strive for the highest quality prose and poetry standard."

NEEDS The review is a literary journal—please, no horror, science fiction, romance. Length: 4,500-5,000 words.

HOW TO CONTACT Send complete ms.

① SANTA MONICA REVIEW

1900 Pico Blvd., Santa Monica CA 90405. **Website:** www.smc.edu/sm_review/. Estab. 1989. Magazine: 250 pages. "The editors are committed to fostering new talent as well as presenting new work by established writers. There is also a special emphasis on presenting and promoting writers who make their home in Southern California." Circ. 4,000.

NEEDS Experimental, literary, memoirs. "No crime and detective, mysogyny, footnotes, TV, dog stories. We want more self-conscious, smart, political, humorous, digressive, meta-fiction." Receives 250 unsolicited mss/month. Accepts 10 mss/issue; 20 mss/year. Agented fiction 10%. **Publishes 5 new writers/year.** Recently published work by Charles Baxter, Greg Bills, John Cage, Bernard Cooper, Mary Jeselnik-Koral, Amy Gerstler, Judith Grossman, Peter Handke, Jim Krusoe, Michelle Latiolais, and Deena Metzger. Also publishes literary essays.

HOW TO CONTACT Send complete ms. Send disposable copy of ms. Responds in 3 months to mss. Accepts simultaneous, multiple submissions. Sample copy for $7.

PAYMENT/TERMS Pays 5 contributor's copies. Acquires first North American serial rights. Sends galleys to author.

◐ THE SARANAC REVIEW

CVH, Department of English, SUNY Plattsburgh, 101 Broad St., Plattsburgh NY 12901. (518)564-2414. **Fax:** (518)564-2140. **E-mail:** saranacreview@plattsburgh.edu. **Website:** http://research.plattsburgh.edu/saranacreview. **Contact:** Fiction Editor. Estab. 2004. Magazine: 512×812; 180 pages; 80 lb. cover/70 lb. paper; glossy cover stock; illustrations; photos. "*The Saranac Review* is committed to dissolving boundaries of all kinds, seeking to publish a diverse array of emerging and established writers from Canada and the U.S. *The Saranac Review* aims to be a textual clearing in which a space is opened for cross-pollination between American and Canadian writers. In this way the magazine reflects the expansive bright spirit of the etymology of its name, Saranac, meaning 'cluster of stars.'" Annual.

NEEDS Ethnic/multicultural, historical, literary, flash fiction. Publishes ms 8 months after acceptance. Also publishes poetry and literary/creative nonfiction. Sometimes comments on rejected mss.

HOW TO CONTACT Send complete ms. Send SASE (or IRC) for return of ms or send disposable copy of the ms and #10 SASE for reply only. Responds in 4 months to mss. Accepts simultaneous submissions. Sample copy for $6. Writer's guidelines online, or by e-mail. "Please send one story at a time." Maximum length: 7,000 words.

PAYMENT/TERMS Pays 2 contributor's copies; discount on extras. Pays on publication for first North American serial, first rights.

THE SEATTLE REVIEW

Box 354330, University of Washington, Seattle WA 98195. (206)543-2302. **E-mail:** seaview@u.washington.edu. **Website:** www.seattlereview.org. Estab. 1978. **Contact:** Andrew Feld, editor-in-chief. Magazine: 6×9; 150 pages; illustrations; photos. "Includes fiction, nonfiction, poetry and one interview per issue with an established writer." Semiannual. Estab. 1978. Circ. 1,000. Receives 200 unsolicited mss/month. Accepts 2-4 mss/issue; 4-8 mss/year. Does not read mss May 31-October 1. Publishes ms 1-212 years after acceptance. **Publishes 3-4 new writers/year.** Recently published work by Rick Bass, Lauren Whitehurst, Martha Hurwitz. Length: 4,000 words; average length: 3,000 words. Includes general fiction, poetry, craft essays on writing, and one interview per issue with a Northwest writer.

◑   Editors accept submissions only from October 1 through May 31.

NEEDS Literary. Nothing in "bad taste (porn, racist, etc.)." Wants more creative nonfiction. "We also publish a series called Writers and their Craft, which deals with aspects of writing fiction (also poetry)—point of view, characterization, etc, rather than literary criticism, each issue." "Nothing in bad taste (porn, racist, etc.). No genre fiction or science fiction." Length: 500-10,000 words.

HOW TO CONTACT Mail submissions with SASE, Attention: Guest Fiction Editor. Submissions must be typed on white, 8 1/2x11 paper. The title page must include the word count (no more than 4,000 words), as well as the author's name and address. Send complete ms. Send SASE (or IRC) for return of ms or send disposable copy of ms and #10 SASE for reply only. Responds in 4-6 months to mss. No simultaneous submissions, accepts multiple submissions. Sample copy for $8. Writer's guidelines for #10 SASE, online or by e-mail. Send complete ms.

PAYMENT/TERMS Pays 2 contributor's copies. Acquires first North American serial rights. Pays $0-100.

TIPS "Know what we publish: no genre fiction; look at our magazine and decide if your work might be appreciated. Beginners do well in our magazine if they send clean, well-written manuscripts. We've published a lot of 'first stories' from all over the country and take pleasure in discovery."

THE SEWANEE REVIEW

University of the South, 735 University Ave., Sewanee TN 37383-1000. (931)598-1000. **Website:** www.sewanee.edu/sewanee_review. Estab. 1892. "A literary quarterly, publishing original fiction, poetry, essays on literary and related subjects, and book reviews for well-educated readers who appreciate good American and English literature." Quarterly. Estab. 1892. "A literary quarterly, publishing original fiction, poetry, essays on literary and related subjects, and book reviews for well-educated readers who appreciate good American and English literature."

NEEDS Literary, contemporary. No erotica, science fiction, fantasy or excessively violent or profane material. Send query letter for reviews. Send complete ms for fiction. Length: 3,500-7,500 words.

PAYMENT/TERMS Pays $10-12/printed page of prose; $2.50/line of poetry. 2 contributor copies. Pays on publication for first North American serial, second serial (reprint) rights.

SHENANDOAH

Washington and Lee University, Mattingly House, 2 Lee Ave., Lexington VA 24450-2116. (540)458-8765. **Fax:** (540)458-8461. **E-mail:** shenandoah@wlu.edu. **Website:** shenandoah.wlu.edu/faq.html. **Contact:** R. T. Smith, editor. Estab. 1950. Triannual. Estab. 1950. Circ. 2,000. "Unsolicited manuscripts will not be read between January 1 and October 1, 2010. All manuscripts received during this period will be recycled unread."

NEEDS Mainstream, novel excerpts. No sloppy, hasty, slight fiction. Publishes ms 10 months after acceptance. No sloppy, hasty, slight fiction.

HOW TO CONTACT Send complete ms. Responds in 2 months to mss. Sample copy for $10. Writer's guidelines online. Send complete ms.

PAYMENT/TERMS Pays $25/page (cap $250). Pays on publication for first North American serial, one-time rights.

➊ SHORT STORY AMERICA

Short Story America, LLC, 66 Thomas Sumter St., Beaufort SC 29907. (843)597-3220. **E-mail:** tim@shortstoryamerica.com;sarah@shortstoryamerica.com. **Website:** www.shortstoryamerica.com. **Contact:** Tim Johnston or Sarah Turocy, Acquisitions. Estab. 2010. "Our readers are fans of the short story. Our audience simply wants to enjoy reading great stories."

NEEDS No erotica. 500-12,000/words.

HOW TO CONTACT Send complete ms.

PAYMENT/TERMS "Pays $100 per story ($50 for flash), new or reprint, and authors also share in anthology and audio royalties as well."

TIPS "We want stories which readers will remember and want to read again. If your story entertains from the first page forward, and the pacing and conflict engages the reader's interest from plot, character and thematic standpoints, then please submit your story today! If the reader genuinely wants to know what eventually happens in your story, and is still thinking about it 10 minutes after finishing, then your story works."

➊➌ SNOWY EGRET

The Fair Press, P.O. Box 9265, Terre Haute IN 47808. **Website:** www.snowyegret.net. Estab. 1922. **Contact:** Editors. Magazine: 8½×11; 60 pages; text paper; heavier cover; illustrations. "We publish works which celebrate the abundance and beauty of nature and examine the variety of ways in which human beings interact with landscapes and living things. Nature writing from literary, artistic, psychological, philosophical and historical perspectives." Semiannual. Estab. 1922. Circ. 400. *Snowy Egret*, published in spring and autumn, specializes in work that is "nature-oriented: poetry that celebrates the abundance and beauty of nature or explores the interconnections between nature and the human psyche." Has published poetry by Conrad Hilberry, Lyn Lifshin, Gayle Eleanor, James Armstrong, and Patricia Hooper. *Snowy Egret* is 60 pages, magazine-sized, offset-printed, saddle-stapled. Receives about 500 poems/year, accepts about 30. Press run is 400. Sample: $8; subscription: $15/year, $25 for 2 years.

NEEDS "No genre fiction, e.g., horror, western, romance, etc." Receives 25 unsolicited mss/month. Accepts up to 6 mss/issue; up to 12 mss/year. Publishes ms 6 months after acceptance. **Publishes 20 new writers/year.** Recently published work by James Hinton, Ron Gielgun, Tom Noyes, Alice Cross, Maeve Mullin Ellis. Length: 500-10,000 words; average length: 1,000-3,000 words. Publishes short shorts. Sometimes comments on rejected mss.

HOW TO CONTACT Send complete ms with SASE. Cover letter optional: do not query. Responds in 2 months to mss. Accepts simultaneous submissions if noted. Sample copy for 9×12 SASE and $8. Writer's guidelines for #10 SASE.

PAYMENT/TERMS Pays $2/page plus 2 contributor's copies. Pays on publication for first North American serial, one-time anthology rights, or reprint rights. Sends galleys to author. True

SO TO SPEAK

George Mason University, 4400 University Dr., MSN 2C5, Fairfax VA 22030-4444. **E-mail:** sts@gmu.edu (inquiries only). **Website:** http://sotospeakjournal. org. **Contact:** Jen Daniels, editor-in-chief. Estab. 1993. **Contact:** Lisa Hill-Corley, fiction editor; Jen Daniels, editor-in-chief. Magazine: 512×812; approximately 100 pages. "We are a feminist journal of language and art." Semiannual. Circ. 1,000.

NEEDS Ethnic/multicultural, experimental, feminist, lesbian, literary, mainstream, regional, translations. "No science fiction, mystery, genre romance." Receives 100 unsolicited mss/month. Accepts 3-5 mss/issue; 6-10 mss/year. Publishes ms 6 months after acceptance. **Publishes 7 new writers/year.** Length: For fiction, up to 5,000 words; for poetry, 3-5 pages per submission; average length: for fiction, up to 5,000 words; for poetry, 3-5 pages per submission. Publishes flash and short fiction, creative nonfiction, poetry, and visual art.

HOW TO CONTACT Accepts submissions only via submissions manager on website. Does not accept paper or e-mail submissions. "Fiction submitted during the August 1–October 15 reading period will be considered for our Spring Issue and requires no reading fee. Fiction submitted during the January 1–March 15 reading period will be considered for our Fall annual fiction contest and must be accompanied by a $15 reading fee. See contest guidelines. Contest entries will not be returned." Responds in 6 months to mss. Accepts simultaneous submissions. Sample copy for $7. Reviews fiction.

PAYMENT/TERMS Pays contributor copies. Acquires first North American serial rights. Sponsors awards/contests.

TIPS "We do not read between March 15 and August 15. Every writer has something they do exceptionally well; do that and it will shine through in the work. We look for quality prose with a definite appeal to a feminist audience. We are trying to move away from strict genre lines. We want high quality fiction, nonfiction, poetry, art, innovative and risk-taking work."

SOUTH CAROLINA REVIEW

Clemson University, Strode Tower Room 611, Box 340522, Clemson SC 29634-0522. (864)656-5399.

Fax: (864)656-1345. **E-mail:** cwayne@clemson.edu. **Website:** www.clemson.edu/cedp/cudp/scr/scrintro. htm. **Contact:** Wayne Chapman, editor. Magazine: 6×9; 200 pages; 60 lb. cream white vellum paper; 65 lb. color cover stock. Semiannual. Estab. 1967. Circ. 500.

NEEDS Literary, mainstream, poetry, essays, reviews. Does not read mss June-August or December. Receives 50-60 unsolicited mss/month. Recently published work by Ronald Frame, Dennis McFadden, Dulane Upshaw Ponder, and Stephen Jones. Rarely comments on rejected mss.

HOW TO CONTACT Send complete ms. Requires text on disk upon acceptance in WordPerfect or Microsoft Word in PC format. Responds in 2 months to mss. Sample copy for $16 includes postage inside the U.S. Reviews fiction.

PAYMENT/TERMS Pays in contributor's copies.

THE SOUTHEAST REVIEW

Florida State University, Tallahassee FL 32306-1036. **Website:** southeastreview.org. **Contact:** Katie Cortese, editor. Estab. 1979. Magazine: 6×9; 160 pages; 70 lb. paper; 10 pt. Krome Kote cover; photos. *The Southeast Review* publishes literary fiction, poetry, and nonfiction. Biannual. Circ. 1,000.

NEEDS "*SER* is now accepting submissions of fiction, poetry, nonfiction, and book reviews. We try to respond to submissions within 2-4 months. If, after four months, you have not heard back regarding your submission, you may query the appropriate section editor. SER accepts simultaneous submissions, but we request that you withdraw the submission by way of our online Submission Manager if your piece is accepted elsewhere. All submissions must be typed (poetry single-spaced and prose doubled-spaced) and properly formatted then uploaded to our online Submission Manager as a .doc or .rtf file only. Submission Manager restricts you from sending us your work more than twice per year. Please wait until you receive a reply regarding a submission before you upload the next."

HOW TO CONTACT Submit complete ms through online manager only up to 7,500 words. Does not accept e-mail or paper. No previously published submissions. Accepts submissions year-round, though please be advised that the response time is slower during the summer months. Response time is usually between 2-4 months.

PAYMENT/TERMS Pays 2 contributor's copies. Acquires first North American serial rights, which then revert to author.

TIPS *The Southeast Review* accepts regular submissions for publication consideration year-round exclusively through the **online Submission Manager**. Any breaks, hiatuses, or interruptions to the reading period will be announced online, and are more likely to occur during the summer months. *SER* does not, under any circumstances, accept work via e-mail. **Except during contest season, paper submissions sent through regular postal mail will not be read or returned.** Please note that, during contest season, entries to our World's Best Short Short Story, Poetry, and Creative Nonfiction competitions must still be sent through regular postal mail. "Avoid trendy experimentation for its own sake (present-tense narration, observation that isn't also revelation). Fresh stories, moving, interesting characters and a sensitivity to language are still fiction mainstays. We also publish the winner and runners-up of the World's Best Short Story Contest, Poetry Contest, and Creative Nonfiction Contest."

● SOUTHERN CALIFORNIA REVIEW

3501 Trousdale Pkwy., Mark Taper Hall, THH 355J, University of Southern California, Los Angeles CA 90089-0355. **E-mail:** scr@college.usc.edu. **Website:** http://usc.edu/scr. **Contact:** Fiction Editor. Estab. 1982. Magazine: 150 pages; semiglosss cover stock. "Formerly known as the *Southern California Anthology,* *Southern California Review (SCR)* is the literary journal of the Master of Professional Writing program at the University of Southern California. It has been publishing fiction and poetry since 1982 and now also accepts submissions of creative nonfiction, plays, and screenplays. Printed every fall and spring with original cover artwork, every issue contains new, emerging, and established authors." Semiannual. Circ. 1,000. **NEEDS** "We accept short shorts but rarely use stories more than 8,000 words. Novel excerpts are acceptable if they can stand alone. We do consider genre work (horror, mystery, romance, sci-fi) if it transcends the boundaries of the genre." Receives 120 unsolicited mss/month. Accepts 10-15 mss/issue. Publishes ms 4 months after acceptance. **Publishes 20-30 new writers/year.** Has published work by Judith Freeman, Gary Fincke David Francis, Gerald Locklin, Seth Greenland, and interviews with Nathan Englander, Steve Almond, Danzy Senna. Publishes short shorts. **HOW TO CONTACT** Send complete, typed, double-spaced ms. Cover letter should include list of previous publications. Address to the proper editor (Fiction, Poetry, etc.). Please include a cover letter. Be sure your full name and contact information (address, phone, and email) appear on the first page of the manuscript. Response time for submissions is 3 to 6 months. No electronic or e-mail submissions are accepted. Every submission must include a self-addressed stamped envelope (SASE). Sample copy for $10. Writer's guidelines for SASE and on website.

PAYMENT/TERMS Pays in 2 contributor copies. Acquires first rights.

SOUTHERN HUMANITIES REVIEW

Auburn University, 9088 Haley Center, Auburn University AL 36849. (334)844-9088. **E-mail:** shrengl@auburn.edu. **E-mail:** shrsubmissions@auburn.edu. **Website:** www.auburn.edu/english/shr/home.htm. **Contact:** Karen Beckwith. Estab. 1967. Magazine: 6×9; 100 pages; 60 lb neutral pH, natural paper; 65 lb. neutral pH medium coated cover stock; occasional illustration; photos. "We publish essays, poetry, fiction and reviews. Our fiction has ranged from very traditional in form and content to very experimental. Literate, college-educated audience. We hope they read our journal for both enlightenment and pleasure." Quarterly. Circ. 800. *Southern Humanities Review* publishes fiction, poetry, and critical essays on the arts, literature, philosophy, religion, and history for a well-read, scholarly audience.

NEEDS Feminist, humor/satire, regional. Slower reading time in summer. Receives 25 unsolicited mss/month. Accepts 1-2 mss/issue; 4-6 mss/year. Recently published work by Chris Arthur, Andrea Deagon, Sheryl St. Germain, Patricia Foster, Janette Turner Hospital, Paula Koöhlmeier, David Wagner, Yves Bonnefoy, Neil Grimmett, and Wayne Flynt. Also publishes literary essays, literary criticism, poetry. Sometimes comments on rejected mss. Length: 15,000 words.

HOW TO CONTACT Send complete ms, cover letter with an explanation of the topic chosen—special, certain book, etc., a little about the author if he/she has never submitted." No e-mail submissions. No simultaneous submissions. Responds in 3 months to mss. Send complete ms.

PAYMENT/TERMS Pays in contributor copies. Rights revert to author on publication. Pays 2 contributor copies

TIPS "Send us the ms with SASE. If we like it, we'll take it or we'll recommend changes. If we don't like it, we'll send it back as promptly as possible. Read the journal. Send typewritten, clean copy, carefully proofread. We also award the annual Hoepfner Prize of $100 for the best published essay or short story of the year. Let someone whose opinion you respect read your story and give you an honest appraisal. Rewrite, if necessary, to get the most from your story."

THE SOUTHERN REVIEW

Louisiana State University, Old President's House, Baton Rouge LA 70803-5001. (225)578-5108. **Fax:** (225)578-5098. **E-mail:** southernreview@lsu.edu. **Website:** www.lsu.edu/tsr. **Contact:** Cara Blue Adams, Editor. Estab. 1935. Magazine: 240 pages; 50 lb. Glatfelter paper; 65 lb. #1 grade cover stock. Quarterly. Circ. 3,000. Reading period: September1-June 1. All mss submitted during summer months will be recycled.

NEEDS Literary. "We select fiction that conveys a unique and compelling voice and vision." Receives approximately 300 unsolicited mss/month. Accepts 4-6 mss/issue. Reading period: September-May. Publishes ms 6 months after acceptance. Agented fiction 1%. **Publishes 10-12 new writers/year.** Recently published work by Jack Driscoll, Don Lee, Peter Levine, and Debbie Urbanski. Also publishes literary essays, literary criticism, poetry, and book reviews. Short stories of lasting literary merit, with emphasis on style and technique; novel excerpts. "We emphasize style and substantial content. No mystery, fantasy or religious mss." Length: 4,000-8,000 words.

HOW TO CONTACT Mail hard copy of ms with cover letter and SASE. No queries. "Prefer brief letters giving author's prefessional information, including recent or notable publcations. Biographical info not necessary." Responds within 10 weeks to mss. Sample copy for $8. Writer's guidelines online. Reviews fiction, poetry. Submit one ms. in any genre at a time. "We rarely publish work that is longer than 8,000 words. We consider novel excerpts if they stand alone."

PAYMENT/TERMS Pays $30/page. Pays on publication for first North American serial rights. Sends page proof to author via e-mail. Sponsors awards/contests.

TIPS "Careful attention to craftsmanship and technique combined with a developed sense of the creation of story will always make us pay attention."

❶ SOUTHWESTERN AMERICAN LITERATURE

Center for the Study of the Southwest, Brazos Hall, Texas State University-San Marcos, San Marcos TX 78666-4616. (512)245-2224. **Fax:** (512)245-7462. **E-mail:** swpublications@txstate.edu. **Website:** http://swrhc.txstate.edu/cssw/. **Contact:** Twister Marquiss, assistant editor; Mark Busby, co-editor; Dick Maurice Heaberlin, co-editor. Estab. 1971. Magazine: 6x9; 125 pages; 80 lb. cover stock. "We publish fiction, non-fiction, poetry, literary criticism and book reviews. Generally speaking, we want material covering the Greater Southwest or material written by Southwest writers." Biannual.

NEEDS ethnic/multicultural, literary, mainstream, regional. "No science fiction or romance." Receives 10-15 unsolicited mss/month. Accepts 1-2 mss/issue; 4-5 mss/year. Publishes ms 6 months after acceptance. **Publishes 1-2 new writers/year.** Recently published work by Sherwin Bitsui, Alison Hawthorne Deming, Keith Ekiss, Sara Marie Ortiz, Karla K. Morton, Lowell Mick White, John Blanchard, Jeffrey C. Alfier, Carol Hamilton, and Larry D. Thomas. Length: 6,250 words; average length: 4,000 words. Also publishes literary essays, literary criticism, poetry. Sometimes comments on rejected mss.

HOW TO CONTACT Send complete ms. Include cover letter, estimated word count, 2-5 line bio and list of publications. Accepts e-mail submissions: swpublications@txstate.edu. Include bio and list of publications in e-mail. Responds in 3-6 months to mss. Sample copy for $10. Writer's guidelines free.

PAYMENT/TERMS Pays 2 contributor copies. Acquires first rights.

TIPS "We look for crisp language, an interesting approach to material; a regional approach is desired but not required. Read widely, write often, revise carefully. We are looking for stories that probe the relationship between the tradition of Southwestern American literature and the writer's own imagination in creative ways. We seek stories that move beyond stereotype and approach the larger defining elements and also ones that, as William Faulkner noted in his Nobel Prize acceptance speech, treat subjects central to good literature—the old verities of the human heart, such as honor and courage and pity and suffering, fear and humor, love and sorrow."

❶ SOUTHWEST REVIEW

P.O. Box 750374, Dallas TX 75275-0374. (214)768-1037. **Fax:** (214)768-1408. **E-mail:** swr@smu.edu. **Website:** www.smu.edu/southwestreview. **Contact:** Jennifer Cranfill, senior editor. Estab. 1915. Magazine: 6×9;

150 pages. "The majority of our readers are well read adults who wish to stay abreast of the latest and best in contemporary fiction, poetry, and essays in all but the most specialized disciplines." Quarterly. Estab. 1915. Circ. 1,600.

NEEDS "High literary quality; no specific requirements as to subject matter, but cannot use sentimental, religious, western, poor science fiction, pornographic, true confession, mystery, juvenile or serialized or condensed novels." Receives 200 unsolicited mss/month. Publishes ms 6-12 months after acceptance. Recently published work by Alice Hoffman, Sabina Murray, Alix Ohlin. Also publishes literary essays, poetry. Occasionally comments on rejected mss.

HOW TO CONTACT Mail complete ms to P.O. Box or submit online. Please note that online submissions require a $2.00 administrative fee. Responds in 1-4 months to mss. Accepts multiple submissions. Sample copy for $6. Writer's guidelines for #10 SASE or on website.

PAYMENT/TERMS Pays negotiable rate and 3 contributor copies. Acquires first North American serial rights. Sends galleys to author.

STAND MAGAZINE

School of English, University of Leeds, Leeds LS2 9JT United Kingdom. (44)(113)343-4794. **E-mail:** stand@leeds.ac.uk. **Website:** www.standmagazine.org. Estab. 1952. North American Office: Department of English, VCU, Richmond VA 23284-2005. (804) 828-1331. **E-mail:** dlatane@vcu.edu. **Website:** www.standmagazine.org. "*Stand Magazine* is concerned with what happens when cultures and literatures meet, with translation in its many guises, with the mechanics of language, with the processes by which the policy receives or disables its cultural makers. *Stand* promotes debate of issues that are of radical concern to the intellectual community worldwide." Quarterly. Estab. 1952 in Leeds UK. Circ. 3,000 worldwide. "Quarterly literary magazine."

○ "U.S. submissions can be made through the Virginia office (see separate listing)."

NEEDS "No genre fiction." Publishes ms 12 months after acceptance.

HOW TO CONTACT Send complete ms. Responds in 6 weeks to queries; 3 months to mss. Sample copy for $12. Writer's guidelines for #10 SASE with sufficient number of IRCs or online.

PAYMENT/TERMS Payment varies. Pays on publication. Acquires first world rights.

STORIE

Via Suor Celestina Donati 13/E, Rome 00167 Italy. (+39) 06 614 8777. **Fax:** (+39) 06 614 8777. **E-mail:** storie@tiscali.it. **Website:** www.storie.it. Estab. 1989. **Contact:** Gianluca Bassi, editor; Barbara Pezzopane, assistant editor; George Lerner, foreign editor. Magazine: 186 pages; illustrations; photographs. "*Storie* is one of Italy's leading literary magazines. Committed to a truly crossover vision of writing, the bilingual (Italian/English) review publishes high quality fiction and poetry, interspersed with the work of alternative wordsmiths such as filmmakers and musicians. Through writings bordering on narratives and interviews with important contemporary writers, it explores the culture and craft of writing." Bimonthly. Estab. 1989. Circ. 20,000.

NEEDS Literary. Receives 150 unsolicited mss/month. Accepts 6-10 mss/issue; 30-50 mss/year. Does not read mss in August. Publishes ms 2 months after acceptance. Publishes 20 new writers/year. Recently published work by Joyce Carol Oates, Haruki Murakami, Paul Auster, Robert Coover, Raymond Carver, T.C. Boyle, Ariel Dorfman, Tess Gallagher. Length: 2,000-6,000 words; average length: 1,500 words. Publishes short shorts. Also publishes literary essays, literary criticism, poetry. Sometimes comments on rejected mss.

HOW TO CONTACT Accepts submissions by e-mail or on disk. Include brief bio. Send complete ms with cover letter. "Manuscripts may be submitted directly by regular post without querying first; however, we do not accept unsolicited manuscripts via e-mail. Please query via e-mail first. We only contact writers if their work has been accepted. We also arrange for and oversee a high-quality, professional translation of the piece." Responds in 1 month to queries; 6 months to mss. Accepts multiple submissions. Sample copy for $ 10. Writer's guidelines online.

PAYMENT/TERMS Pays $30-600 and 2 contributor's copies. Pays on publication for first (in English and Italian) rights.

STRAYLIGHT

UW-Parkside, English Dept., 900 Wood Rd., P.O. Box 2000, Kenosha WI 53141. (262)595-2139. **Fax:** (262)595-2271. **E-mail:** straylight@litspot.net. **Website:** www.straylightmag.com. **Contact:** Fiction Editor. Magazine has revolving editor. Editorial term: 1 years. Literary magazine/journal: 6x9 115 pages, quality paper, uncoated index stock cover. Contains illustrations. Includes photographs. "*Straylight* publishes high quality, character-based fiction of any style. We tend not to publish strict genre pieces, though we may query them for future special issues. We do not publish erotica." Biannual with special issues. Estab. 2005.

NEEDS Ethnic/multicultural (general), experimental, gay, lesbian, literary, mainstream, regional. Special interests: genre fiction in special theme issues. Accepts 3-5 mss/issue; 6-10 mss/year. Does not read May-August. Manuscript published 6 months after acceptance. Agented fiction 10%. Length: 2,500 words (min)-6,000 words (max). Average length: 2,500 words. Publishes short shorts. Also publishes poetry. Rarely comments on/critiques rejected mss.

HOW TO CONTACT Send complete ms with cover letter. Accepts submissions by e-mail. Include brief bio, list of publications. Responds to queries in 2 weeks. Responds to mss in 2 months. Send either SASE (or IRC) for return of ms or disposable copy of ms and #10 SASE for reply only. Sample copy available for $10. Guidelines available for SASE, on website.

PAYMENT/TERMS Writers receive 2 contributor's copies. Additional copies $3. Pays on publication. Acquires first North American serial rights. Publication is copyrighted.

TIPS "We tend to publish character-based and inventive fiction with cutting-edge prose. We are unimpressed with works based on strict plot twists or novelties. Read a sample copy to get a feel for what we publish."

⊙ STRUGGLE:

P.O. Box 28536, Detroit MI 48228. (313)273-9039. **E-mail:** timhall11@yahoo.com. **Website:** www.strugglemagazine.net. **Contact:** Tim Hall, Editor. Estab. 1985. Magazine: 512×812; 36-72 pages; 20 lb. white bond paper; colored cover; illustrations; occasional photos. Publishes short shorts. Normally comments on rejected mss. Recently published work by Billie Louise Jones, Stephen Graf, Juan H. Rodriguez, Paris Smith, Gregory Alan Norton. Publishes material related to "the struggle of the working class and all progressive people against the rule of the rich—including their war policies, repression, racism, exploitation of the workers, oppression of women and immigrants and general culture, etc." Quarterly. Recently published work by Billie Louise Jones, Tyler Plosia, Margaret Dimacou. Accepts multiple submissions. Magazine: 512×812; 36-72 pages; 20

lb. white bond paper; colored cover; illustrations; occasional photos.

NEEDS "Readers would like fiction about anti-globalization, the fight against racism, prison conditions, neo-conservatism and the Iraq and Afghanistan wars, the struggle of immigrants, and the disillusionment with the Obama Administration as it reveals it craven service to the rich billionaires. Would also like to see more fiction that depicts life, work and struggle of the working class of every background; also the struggles of the 1930s and '60s illustrated and brought to life." Length: 4,000 words; average length: 1,000-3,000 words.

HOW TO CONTACT Email. Accepts submissions by e-mail, mail.

PAYMENT/TERMS Pays 1 contributor's copy. No rights acquired. Not copyrighted.

⊙⊙⊙⊙ SUBTERRAIN

Strong Words for a Polite Nation, P.O. Box 3008, MPO, Vancouver BC V6B 3X5 Canada. (604)876-8710. **Fax:** (604)879-2667. **E-mail:** subter@portal.ca. **Website:** www.subterrain.ca. **Contact:** Brian Kaufman, editor-in-chief. Magazine: 814×10⅞; 56 pages; gloss stock paper; color gloss cover stock; illustrations; photos. *subTerrain* magazine is published 3 times a year from modest offices just off of Main Street in Vancouver, BC. We strive to produce a stimulating fusion of fiction, poetry, photography, and graphic illustration from uprising Canadian, U.S. and International writers and artists. "Looking for unique work and perspectives from Canada and beyond." Triannual. Estab. 1988. Circ. 3,000. "*subTerrain* magazine is published 3 times a year from modest offices just off of Main Street in Vancouver, BC. We strive to produce a stimulating fusion of fiction, poetry, photography and graphic illustration from uprising Canadian, U.S. & International writers and artists."

NEEDS Literary. Does not want genre fiction or children's fiction. Receives 100 unsolicited mss/month. Accepts 4 mss/issue; 10-15 mss/year. Publishes ms 4 months after acceptance. Recently published work by John Moore. Also publishes literary essays, literary criticism. Rarely comments on rejected mss.

HOW TO CONTACT Send complete ms. Include disposable copy of the ms and #10 SASE for reply only. Responds in 2-4 months to mss. Accepts multiple submissions. Sample copy for $5. Writer's guidelines online.

PAYMENT/TERMS Pays $25 per page for prose. Pays on publication for first North American serial rights.

SUBTROPICS

University of Florida, P.O. Box 112075, 4008 Turlington Hall, Gainesville FL 32611-2075. **E-mail:** dleavitt@ufl.edu; subtropics@english.ufl.edu. **Website:** www.english.ufl.edu/subtropics. **Contact:** David Leavitt. Estab. 2005. Literary magazine/journal: 9x6, 160 pages. Includes photographs. "*Subtropics* — headed by fiction editor David Leavitt, poetry editor Sidney Wade, and managing editor Mark Mitchell—is committed to publishing the best new fiction, poetry, literary nonfiction, and translation by emerging and established writers. In addition to new work, *Subtropics* also, from time to time, republishes important and compelling stories, essays, and poems that have lapsed out of print." Triannual. Circ. 3,500. Member CLMP. "Magazine published 3 times/year through the University of Florida's English department. *Subtropics* seeks to publish the best literary fiction, essays, and poetry being written today, both by established and emerging authors. We will consider works of fiction of any length, from short shorts to novellas and self-contained novel excerpts. We give the same latitude to essays. We appreciate work in translation and, from time to time, republish important and compelling stories, essays, and poems that have lapsed out of print by writers no longer living."

NEEDS Literary. Does not want genre fiction. Receives 1,000 mss/month. Accepts 5-6 mss/issue; 15-18 mss/year. Does not read May 1-August 31. Ms published 3-6 months after acceptance. Agented fiction 33%. **Publishes 1-2 new writers/year.** Published John Barth, Ariel Dorfman, Tony D'Souza, Allan Gurganus, Frances Hwang, Kuzhali Manickavel, Eileen Pollack, Padgett Powell, Nancy Reisman, Jarret Rosenblatt, Joanna Scott, and Olga Slavnikova. Average length: 5,000 words. Publishes short shorts. Average length of short shorts: 400 words. Also publishes literary essays, poetry. Rarely comments on/critiques rejected mss. Literary fiction only, including short-shorts. No genre fiction.

HOW TO CONTACT Send complete ms with cover letter. Responds to mss in 2-6 weeks. Send disposable copy of ms. Replies via e-mail only. Do not include SASE. Considers simultaneous submissions. Sample copy available for $12.95. Guidelines available on website. Send complete ms.

PAYMENT/TERMS Writers receive $500-1,000, 2 contributor's copies. Additional copies $12.95. Pays on acceptance. Acquires first North American serial rights. Publication is copyrighted. Pays $500 for short-shorts; $1,000 for full stories.

TIPS "We publish longer works of fiction, including novellas and excerpts from forthcoming novels. Each issue will include a short-short story of about 250 words on the back cover. We are also interested in publishing works in translation for the magazine's English-speaking audience."

THE SUN

107 N. Roberson St., Chapel Hill NC 27516. (919)942-5282. **Fax:** (919)932-3101. **Website:** www.thesunmagazine.org. **Contact:** Luc Sanders, assistant editor. Estab. 1974. Magazine: 812×11; 48 pages; offset paper; glossy cover stock; photos. Monthly. "We are open to all kinds of writing, though we favor work of a personal nature."

NEEDS Literary. Open to all fiction. Receives 800 unsolicited mss/month. Accepts 20 short stories/year. Publishes ms 6-12 months after acceptance. Recently published work by Tony Hoagland, David James Duncan, Poe Ballantine, Linda McCullough Moore, Brenda Miller. Also publishes poetry and nonfiction. No science fiction, horror, fantasy, or other genre fiction. "We avoid stereotypical genre pieces like science fiction, romance, western, and horror. Read an issue before submitting." 7,000 words maximum.

HOW TO CONTACT Send complete ms. Accepts reprint submissions. Sample copy for $5. Writer's guidelines online. Send complete ms.

PAYMENT/TERMS Pays $300-1,500. Pays on publication for first, one-time rights.

TIPS "Do not send queries except for interviews. We're looking for artful and sensitive photographs that aren't overly sentimental. We're open to unusual work. Read the magazine to get a sense of what we're about. Send the best possible prints of your work. Our submission rate is extremely high. Please be patient after sending us your work. Send return postage and secure return packaging."

SYCAMORE REVIEW

Purdue University Dept. of English, 500 Oval Dr., West Lafayette IN 47907. (765) 494-3783. **Fax:** (765) 494-3780. **E-mail:** sycamore@purdue.edu. **Website:** www.sycamorereview.com. **Contact:** Anthony Cook. Magazine: 8×8; 130-180 pages; heavy, textured, uncoated paper; heavy laminated cover. "Journal devoted to contemporary literature. We publish both traditional and experimental fiction, personal essay, poetry, interviews, drama and graphic art. Novel excerpts welcome if they stand alone as a story." Semiannual. Estab. 1989. Circ. 1,000. "Strives to publish the best writing by new and established writers. Looks for well crafted and engaging work, works that illuminate our lives in the collective human search for meaning. We would like to publish more work that takes a reflective look at our national identity and how we are perceived by the world. We look for diversity of voice, pluralistic worldviews, and political and social context."

○ *Sycamore Review* is Purdue University's internationally acclaimed literary journal, affiliated with Purdue's College of Liberal Arts and the Dept. of English. Art should present politics in a language that can be felt.

NEEDS Experimental, humor/satire, literary, mainstream, regional, translations. "We generally avoid genre literature but maintain no formal restrictions on style or subject matter. No romance, children's." Would like to see more experimental fiction. Publishes ms 11 months after acceptance. Recently published work by Lucia Perillo, Sherman Alexie, G.C. Waldrep, June Armstrong, W.P. Osborn, William Giraldi. Also publishes poetry. Sometimes comments on rejected mss.

HOW TO CONTACT Send complete ms with SASE, cover letter with previous publications and address. Responds in 3-4 months to mss. Accepts simultaneous submissions. Sample copy for $5. Writer's guidelines for #10 SASE or online.

PAYMENT/TERMS Copies of journal/acquires one-time rights.

TIPS "We look for originality, brevity, significance, strong dialogue, and vivid detail. We sponsor the Wabash Prize for Poetry (deadline: mid-October) and Fiction (deadline: March 1). $1,000 award for each. All contest submissions will be considered for regular inclusion in the *Sycamore Review*. No e-mail submissions—no exception. Include SASE.

◑◉ TAKAHE

P.O. Box 13-335, Christchurch 8001 New Zealand. (03)359-8133. **E-mail:** admin@takahe.org.nz. **Website:** www.takahe.org.nz/index.php. **Contact:** Fiction Editor. "*Takahe* is a hardcopy literary magazine which appears three times a year and publishes short stories, poetry, and artwork by both established and emerging writers. The publisher is Takahe Collective Trust, a non-profit organization formed by established writers to help new writers get into print."

NEEDS "We are particularly losing interest in stories offer a new perspective; something a little different." **Publishes 20 new writers/year.** Recently published work by Raewyn Alexander, Simon Minto, Claire Baylis, Hayden Williams, Sarah Penwarden, Michael Botur, Doc Drumheller, Andrew McIntyre.

HOW TO CONTACT Send complete ms by e-mail (poetry in hard copy). Include e-mail address, mailing address, 40 word bio and SASE (IRC for overseas submissions). See website for formatting. No simultaneous submissions. Copyright reverts to author on publication.

PAYMENT/TERMS NZ residents receive $30 (amount subject to change) and all contributors receive two hard copies of the issue in which their work appears. Overseas contributors receive a one-year subscription to *Takahe* in lieu of payment.

TIPS "We pay a flat rate to each writer/poet appearing in a particular issue regardless of the number/length of items. Editorials and literary commentaries are by invitation only."

◐ TALKING RIVER

Division of Literature and Languages, 500 8th Ave., Lewiston ID 83501. (208)792-2189. **Fax:** (208)792-2324. **E-mail:** talkingriver@lcmail.lcsc.edu. **Website:** www.lcsc.edu/talkingriverreview. **Contact:** Kevin Goodan, editorial advisor. Estab. 1994. Magazine: 6×9; 150-200 pages; 60 lb. paper; coated, color cover; illustrations; photos. "We look for new voices with something to say to a discerning general audience." Semiannual. Circ. 250.

NEEDS Ethnic/multicultural, feminist, humor/satire, literary, regional. "Wants more well-written, character-driven stories that surprise and delight the reader with fresh, arresting yet unselfconscious language, imagery, metaphor, revelation." No stories that are sexist, racist, homophobic, erotic for shock value; no genre fiction.

HOW TO CONTACT Send complete manuscript with cover letter. Include estimated word count, 2-sentence bio and list of publications. Send SASE for reply, return of ms or send disposable copy of ms. Responds in 3 months to mss. Does not accept simultaneous submissions. Sample copy for $6. Writer's guidelines for #10 SASE. Send complete manuscript with cover letter. Include estimated word count, 2-sentence bio and list of publications.

PAYMENT/TERMS Pays contributor's copies; additional copies $4. Acquires one-time rights.

TAMPA REVIEW

University of Tampa Press, 401 W. Kennedy Blvd., Tampa FL 33606. (813)253-6266. **Fax:** (813)258-7593. **Website:** tampareview.ut.edu. **Contact:** Richard Mathews, editor. Estab. 1988. An international literary journal publishing art and literature from Florida and Tampa Bay as well as new work and translations from throughout the world.

NEEDS "We are far more interested in quality than in genre. Nothing sentimental as opposed to genuinely moving, nor self-conscious style at the expense of human truth." Length: 200-5,000 words.

HOW TO CONTACT Send complete ms. Include brief bio.

PAYMENT/TERMS Pays $10/printed page.

TIPS "Send a clear cover letter stating previous experience or background. Our editorial staff considers submissions between September and December for publication in the following year."

TAPROOT LITERARY REVIEW

Box 204, Ambridge PA 15003. (724)266-8476. **E-mail:** taproot10@aol.com. **Contact:** Tikvah Feinstein, editor. Estab. 1987. Magazine: 512×812; 93 pages; 20 lb. paper; hardcover; attractively printed; saddlestitched. "We select on quality, not topic. Variety and quality are our appealing features." Annual. Circ. 500.

NEEDS Literary. "No pornography, religious, popular, romance fiction. Wants more stories with multicultural themes, showing intensity, reality and human emotions that readers can relate to, learn from, and most importantly—be interesting." The majority of ms published are received through annual contest. Receives 20 unsolicited mss/month. Accepts 6 mss/issue. **Publishes 2-4 new writers/year.** Recently published work by Bruce Mikkiff, Derrick Harrison Hurd, Faith Romeo Cataffa, B.Z. Niditch, Alicia Stakay, Alena Horowitz, Shirley Barasch, and Tikvah Feinstein. Publishes short shorts. Also publishes poetry. Sometimes comments on rejected mss.

HOW TO CONTACT Accepts submissions by e-mail. Send for guidelines first. Send complete ms with a cover letter. Include estimated word count and bio. Responds in 6 months to mss. No simultaneous submissions. "The best way for fiction writers to break into *Taproot* is through the annual contest. Send a SASE for guidelines. Sample copy for $5, 6×12 SAE with 5 first-class stamps. Writer's guidelines for #10 SASE.

PAYMENT/TERMS Awards $25 in prize money for first place fiction and poetry winners each issue; certificate for 2nd and 3rd place; 1 contributor's copy.

TIPS "*Taproot* is getting more fiction submissions, and every one is read entirely. This takes time, so response can be delayed at busy times of year. Our contest is a good way to start publishing. Send for a sample copy and read it through. Ask for a critique and follow suggestions. Don't be offended by any suggestions—just take them or leave them and keep writing. Looks for a story that speaks in its unique voice, told in a well-crafted and complete, memorable style, a style of signature to the author. Follow writer's guidelines. Research markets. Send cover letter. Don't give up."

TEXAS REVIEW

Texas Review Press, Department of English, Sam Houston State University, Box 2146, Huntsville TX 77341-2146. (936)294-1992. **Fax:** (936)294-3070. **E-mail:** eng_pdr@shsu.edu; cww006@shsu.edu. **Website:** www.shsu.edu/~www_trp. **Contact:** Dr. Paul Ruffin, editor/director. Estab. 1976. Claude Wolley, assistant to director. Magazine: 6×9; 148-190 pages; best quality paper; 70 lb. cover stock; illustrations; photos. "We publish top quality poetry, fiction, articles, interviews and reviews for a general audience." Estab. 1976. Semiannual. Circ. 1,200. A member of the Texas A&M University Press consortium.

NEEDS Humor/satire, literary, mainstream, contemporary fiction. "We are eager enough to consider fiction of quality, no matter what its theme or subject matter. No juvenile fiction." Receives 40-60 unsolicited mss/month. Accepts 4 mss/issue; 6 mss/year. Does not read mss May-September. Publishes ms 6-12 months after acceptance. **Publishes some new writers/year.** Recently published work by George Garrett, Ellen Gilchrist, Fred Chappell. Also publishes literary essays, literary criticism, poetry. Sometimes comments on rejected mss.

HOW TO CONTACT Send complete ms. No mss accepted via fax. Send disposable copy of ms and #10 SASE for reply only. Responds in 2 weeks to queries; 3-6 months to mss. Accepts multiple submissions. Sample copy for $5. Writer's guidelines for SASE and on website.

PAYMENT/TERMS Pays contributor's copies and one-year subscription. Pays on publication for first North American serial, onetime rights. Sends galleys to author.

⊘ THEMA

Thema Literary Society, P.O. Box 8747, Metairie LA 70011-8747. **E-mail:** thema@cox.net. **Website:** http://themaliterarysociety.com. Estab. 1988. Magazine: 512×812; 150 pages; Grandee Strathmore cover stock; b&w illustrations. Circ. 350.

NEEDS Adventure, ethnic/multicultural, experimental, fantasy, historical, humor/satire, literary, mainstream, mystery/suspense, novel excerpts, psychic/supernatural/occult, regional, religious/inspirational, science fiction, slice-of-life vignettes, western, contemporary, sports, prose poem. "No erotica." Themes with deadlines for submission in 2011 (publication in 2012): "Your Reality or Mine?" (March 1); "Wisecracks & Poems" (July 1); "Who Keeps Them Tidy?" (November 1). For more information, visit *THEMA*'s website. Publishes ms within 6 months after acceptance. **Publishes 9 new writers/year.** Recently published work by Michael Fontana, Sky Andrews Gerspacher, Malaika Favorite, and Mark Krieger. Publishes short shorts. Also publishes poetry. Sometimes comments on rejected mss. No erotica. fewer than 6,000 words preferred

HOW TO CONTACT Send complete ms with SASE, cover letter, include "name and address, brief introduction, specifying the intended target issue for the mss." SASE. Responds in 1 week to queries; 5 months to mss. Accepts simultaneous, multiple submissions and reprints. Does not accept e-mailed submissions. Sample copy for $10. Writer's guidelines for #10 SASE.

PAYMENT/TERMS Pays $10-25. Pays on acceptance for one-time rights.

TIPS "Be familiar with the themes. Don't submit unless you have an upcoming theme in mind. Specify the target theme on the first page of your manuscript or in a cover letter. Put your name on first page of manuscript only. (All submissions are judged in blind review after the deadline for a specified issue.) Most open to fiction and poetry. Don't be hasty when you consider a theme—mull it over and let it ferment in your mind. We appreciate interpretations that are carefully constructed, clever, subtle, and well thought out."

⊙⊜ THIRD WEDNESDAY: A LITERARY ARTS MAGAZINE

174 Greenside Up, Ypsilanti MI 48197. (734) 434-2409. **E-mail:** submissions@thirdwednesday.org; Laurence-

WT@aol.com. **Website:** http://thirdwednesday.org. **Contact:** Laurence Thomas, editor. Estab. 2007.

NEEDS Does not want "purely anecdotal accounts of incidents, sentimentality, pointless conclusions, or stories without some characterization or plot development." Length: 1,500 words (max). Average length: 1,000 words.

HOW TO CONTACT Send complete ms with cover letter. Include estimated word count, brief bio.

TIPS "Of course, originality is important, along with skill in writing, deft handling of language, and meaning, which goes hand in hand with beauty—whatever that is. Short fiction is specialized and difficult, so the writer should read extensively in the field."

⊙⊙ TICKLED BY THUNDER

14076-86A Ave., Surrey BC V3W 0V9 Canada. (604)591-6095. **E-mail:** info@tickledbythunder.com. **Website:** www.tickledbythunder.com. **Contact:** Larry Lindner, publisher. Estab. 1990. Magazine: digest-sized; 24 pages; bond paper; bond cover stock; illustrations; photos. "*Tickled By Thunder* is designed to encourage beginning writers of fiction, poetry and nonfiction." Quarterly. Estab. 1990.

NEEDS Fantasy, humor/satire, literary, mainstream, mystery/suspense, science fiction, western. "No overly indulgent horror, sex, profanity or religious material." Receives 25 unsolicited mss/month. Accepts 3 mss/issue; 12 mss/year. Publishes ms 3-9 months after acceptance. **Publishes 5 new writers/year.** Recently published work by John Connors and J-Ann Godfrey. Length: 2,000 words; average length: 1,500 words. Also publishes literary essays, literary criticism, poetry.

HOW TO CONTACT Send complete ms. Include estimated word count and brief bio. Send SASE or IRC for return of ms; or send disposable copy of ms and #10 SASE for reply only. Only subscribers may send e-mail submissions online. Responds in 3 months to queries; 6 months to mss. Accepts simultaneous, multiple submissions and reprints. Writer's guidelines online.

PAYMENT/TERMS Pays on publication for first, second serial (reprint) rights.

TIN HOUSE

McCormack Communications, P.O. Box 10500, Portland OR 97210. (503)274-4393. **Fax:** (503)222-1154. **E-mail:** info@tinhouse.com. **Website:** www.tinhouse.com. **Contact:** Cheston Knapp, managing editor; Holly Macarthur, founding editor. Estab. 1998. "We are a general interest literary quarterly. Our watchword is quality. Our audience includes people interested in literature in all its aspects, from the mundane to the exalted."

NEEDS 5,000 words maximum.

HOW TO CONTACT Send complete ms September 1-May 31 via regular mail or online submission form. No fax or e-mail submissions.

PAYMENT/TERMS Pays $200-800.

⊕ TOAD SUCK REVIEW

Univ. of Central Arkansas, Dept. of Writing, Univ. of Central Arkansas, Dept. of Writing, Conway AR 72035. **E-mail:** toadsuckreview@gmail.com. **Website:** http://toadsuckreview.org. **Contact:** Mark Spitzer, Editor. Estab. 2011. 6 x 11 magazine, 150 pages, 70 lb. white. Illustrations and photographs. Accepts outstanding work by beginning and established writers. Born from the legendary *Exquisite Corpse Annual*, the innovative *Toad Suck Review* is a cutting-edge mixture of poetry, fiction, creative nonfiction, translations, reviews, and artwork with a provocative sense of humor and an interest in diverse cultures and politics. Publishes short shorts; average length: 500 words. No themes planned for 2012 issues. Reads mss in the fall. Published Kevin Brockmeie, Teresa Bergen, Daniel Grandbois, William Lychack. Publishes 5 unpublished writers each year. Rarely comments on rejected mss. Responds to ms in 1 week to 9 months. Acquires one time rights.

NEEDS No religious, straight-up realism, odes to dead dogs. Length: 200-10,000 words; average length: 5,000 words.

HOW TO CONTACT Send cover letter with complete disposable copy of ms, brief bio, and list of publications. Send reviews of novels and short story collections to Review Editor. Include cover letter with disposable copy of complete mss.

PAYMENT/TERMS Pays contributor's copies. Pays contributor's copies. Charges $10 for each additional copy.

◑ TORCH: POETRY, PROSE AND SHORT STORIES BY AFRICAN AMERICAN WOMEN

3720 Gattis School Rd., Suite 800, Round Rock TX 78664. **E-mail:** info@torchpoetry.org (inquiries), poetry@torchpoetry.org (submissions). **Website:** www.torchpoetry.org. **Contact:** Amanda Johnston, editor. Estab. 2006. *TORCH: Poetry, Prose, and Short Stories by African American Women*, published semiannually online, provides "a place to publish contemporary poetry, prose, and short stories by experienced and emerging writers alike. We prefer our contributors to take risks, and offer a diverse body of work that examines and challenges preconceived notions regarding race, ethnicity, gender roles, and identity." Has published poetry by Sharon Bridgforth, Patricia Smith, Crystal Wilkinson, Tayari Jones, and Natasha Trethewey. Receives about 250+ submissions/year, accepts about 20. Number of unique visitors: 600+/month. Submit 3 poems at a time. No previously published poems or simultaneous submissions. Accepts e-mail submissions only (as one MS Word attachment). Send to poetry@torchpoetry.org with "Poetry Submission" in subject line. Cover letter is preferred (in the body of the e-mail). Reads submissions April 15-August 31 only. Time between acceptance and publication is 2-7 months. Sometimes comments on rejected poems. Guidelines available on website. Always sends prepublication galleys. No payment. Acquires rights to publish accepted work in online issue and in archives. Rights revert to authors upon publication. "Within *TORCH*, we offer a special section called Flame that features an interview, biography, and work sample by an established writer as well as an introduction to their Spark—an emerging writer who inspires them and adds to the boundless voice of creative writing by Black women." A free online newsletter is available; see website.

◑◒ TRANSITION: AN INTERNATIONAL REVIEW

104 Mount Auburn St., 3R, Cambridge MA 02138. (617)496-2845. **Fax:** (617)496-2877. **E-mail:** transition@fas.harvard.edu. **Website:** www.transitionmagazine.com. **Contact:** Sara Bruya, managing editor. Estab. 1961. Magazine: 912×612; 150-175 pages; 70 lb. Finch Opaque paper; 100 lb. White Warren Lustro dull cover; illustrations; photos. "Transition Magazine is a trimestrial international review known for compelling and controversial writing from and about Africa and the Diaspora. This prestigious magazine is edited at the W.E.B. Du Bois Institute of Harvard Univ. by Tommie Shelby, Vincent Brown, and Glenda Carpio. The magazine attracts famous contributors such as Wole Soyinka, Jamaica Kincaid, and Carlos Fuentes, but is also committed to providing space for new voices; Transition recently made a capsule collection of Cape Verde's finest fiction available for the

first time in English. In the words of our publisher, Henry Louis Gates, Jr., Transition seeks to publish fiction, poetry, and criticism that wrestles with "the freshest, most compelling, most curious ideas about race—indeed, about what it means to be human—today." Quarterly. Circ. 3,000.

NEEDS Publishes fiction, poetry, creative nonfiction, and cultural and political criticism. Sometimes comments on rejected mss.

HOW TO CONTACT E-mail us to request the Transition Style Guide. Email submissions are preferred. If submitting by mail, please include a SASE to receive a response from Transition. Mss will not be returned. You will receive confirmation of receipt and notification of editorial decision after review of your work. We are not able to respond to requests for status updates. If your piece is longer than 20 pages, please also send a hard copy (in Times New Roman, font size 12, double spaced). For all submissions, please include the following information in your email or cover letter and in the top left corner of the first page of all documents: name, address, e-mail address, word count, date of submission. Please also include a title with each work. Sara Bruya, Managing Editor.

PAYMENT/TERMS 1 contributor's copy.

TIPS "We look for a non-white, alternative perspective, dealing with issues of race, ethnicity and identity in an unpredictable, provocative way."

VIRGINIA QUARTERLY REVIEW

University of Virginia, One West Range, P.O. Box 400223, Charlottesville VA 22904-4223. (434)924-3124. **Fax:** (434)924-1397. **E-mail:** editors@vqronline.org. **Website:** www.vqronline.org. Estab. 1925. "A national journal of literature and discussion, featuring nonfiction, fiction, and poetry for educated general readers." Quarterly. Circ. 6,000. **Needs** Ethnic/multicultural, feminist, historical, humor/satire, literary, mainstream, mystery/suspense, novel excerpts, translations. Accepts 3 mss/issue; 20 mss/year. Publishes ms 3-6 months after acceptance. A national journal of literature and thought. A lay, intellectual audience; people who are not out-and-out scholars but who are interested in ideas and literature.

NEEDS Length: 3,000-7,000 words.

HOW TO CONTACT Submit complete ms. online. No queries. Word count: 2,000-8,000 words. Submissions are limited to one prose piece and three poems every six months. Responds in 3-4 months to mss.

Sample copy for $14. Writer's guidelines online. Occasionally closes submissions to catch up on backlog; check website to find when submissions are open. Send complete ms.

PAYMENT/TERMS Pays $.20/word; $5 per line for poetry. Pays on publication for first North American rights and nonexclusive online rights. Submissions only accepted online. Pays $100/page maximum.

TIPS "Submissions only accepted online."

WEST BRANCH

Stadler Center for Poetry, Bucknell University, Lewisburg PA 17837-2029. (570)577-1853. **Fax:** (570)577-1885. **E-mail:** westbranch@bucknell.edu. **Website:** www.bucknell.edu/westbranch. *West Branch* publishes poetry, fiction, and nonfiction in both traditional and innovative styles.

NEEDS No genre fiction.

HOW TO CONTACT Send complete ms.

PAYMENT/TERMS Pays $20-100 ($10/page).

TIPS "All submissions must be sent via our online submission manager. Please see website for guidelines. We recommend that you acquaint yourself with the magazine before submitting."

WESTERN HUMANITIES REVIEW

University of Utah, English Department, 255 S. Central Campus Dr., Room 3500, Salt Lake City UT 84112-0494. (801)581-6070. **Fax:** (801)585-5167. **E-mail:** whr@mail.hum.utah.edu. **Website:** www.hum.utah.edu/whr. **Contact:** Dawn Lonsinger, Managing Editor. Estab. 1947. Circ. 1,300.

Reads mss September 1-April 1. Mss sent outside these dates will be returned unread.

NEEDS "Looking for work that continues to resonate after reading is over. Especially interested in experimental and innovative fiction." Does not want genre (romance, sci-fi, etc.). Receives 100 mss/month. Accepts 5-6 mss/issue; 6-8 mss/year. Does not read April-September. Publishes ms up to 1 year after acceptance. **Publishes 3-5 new writers/year.** Recently published work by Michael Martone, Steve Almond, Craig Dworkin, Benjamin Percy, Francois Camoin, Kate Bernheimer, Lidia Yuknavitch. Publishes short shorts. Also innovative literary criticism and poetry. Rarely comments on rejected mss. Does not want genre (romance, sci-fi, etc.). Length: 5,000 words.

HOW TO CONTACT Send one story per reading period. No e-mail submissions or queries. Sample copy for $10. Writer's guidelines online. Send complete ms.

PAYMENT/TERMS Pays in contributor's copies on publication. Additional Information Runs Utah Writers' Contest every fall. Pays $5/published page (when funds available).

TIPS "Because of changes in our editorial staff, we urge familiarity with recent issues of the magazine. We do not publish writer's guidelines because we think that the magazine itself conveys an accurate picture of our requirements. Please, no e-mail submissions."

WHISKEY ISLAND MAGAZINE

Rhodes Tower 1636, Cleveland OH 44115. (216)687-2000. **E-mail:** whiskeyisland@csuohio.edu. **Website:** www.csuohio.edu/class/english/whiskeyisland. Editors change each year. Magazine of fiction, creative nonfiction, theater writing, poetry and art. "We provide a forum for new writers, for themes and points of view that are both traditional and experimental." Semiannual. Press run: 1,000. "This is a nonprofit literary magazine that has been published (in one form or another) by students of Cleveland State University for over 30 years. Also features the Annual Student Creative Writing Contest."

"We accept original poetry, prose, and art submissions from August 15 through May 1 of each year. We accept simultaneous submissions and ask that you identify them as such in your cover letter. No multiple submissions, please, and no previously published work either. Reporting time is about 3 months."

NEEDS "From flash fiction to 5,000 words." Receives 100 unsolicited mss/month. Accepts 46 mss/issue. Recently published work by Carolyn Furnish, Carl Peterson, and Shannon Robinson. "Most recent issue features three writers' first publications. We nominate for *Pushcart Prize*."

HOW TO CONTACT Send complete ms. Accepts submissions by mail and e-mail. Accepts simultaneous submissions. Responds in 6 months. Sample copy for $6. Subscription $12.

PAYMENT/TERMS Pays 2 contributor copies and 1-year subscription. Acquires one-time rights. Sponsors annual fiction contest with $500 prize and publication. $10 per entry.

TIPS "See submissions page. Include SASE. Wait at least a year before submitting again."

WHITE FUNGUS: AN EXPERIMENTAL ARTS MAGAZINE

Website: www.whitefungus.com. P.O Box 6173, Wellington, Aotearoa, New Zealand. (64) 4 382 9113. **E-mail:** whitefungusmail@yahoo.com. **Website:** www.whitefungus.com. **Contact:** Ron Hanson, Editor. Literary magazine/journal. Oversize A5, 104 pages, matte paper, matte card cover. Contains illustrations, photographs. "*White Fungus* covers a range of experimental arts including literature, poetry, visual arts, comics and music. We are interested in material that is bold, innovative and well-researched. Independence of thought and meaningful surprises are a high priority." Semiannual. Estab. 2004. Circ. 2,000.

NEEDS Comics/graphic novels, ethnic/multicultural, experimental, feminist, gay, historical (general), humor/satire, lesbian, literary, science fiction. "*White Fungus* considers submissions on the basis of quality rather than genre." Receives 20 mss/month. Accepts 3 mss/issue; 6 mss/year. Ms published 1-12 months after acceptance. **Publishes 2 new writers/year.** Published Hamish Low, Cyril Wong, Aaron Coyes, Hamish Wyn, Tim Bollinger, Kate Montgomery, Tessa Laird, and Tobias Fischer. Average length: 1,200 words. Publishes short shorts. Average length of short shorts: 1,000 words. Also publishes literary criticism, poetry. Sometimes comments on/critiques rejected mss.

HOW TO CONTACT Query with clips of published work. Accepts submissions by e-mail, on disk. Include brief bio, list of publications. Responds to queries in 1 week. Responds to mss in 1 week. Send either SASE (or IRC) for return of ms or disposable copy of ms and #10 SASE for reply only. Considers simultaneous submissions, multiple submissions. Sample copy available for $10. Guidelines available via e-mail.

PAYMENT/TERMS Writers receive 10 contributor's copies, free subscription to the magazine. Additional copies $6. Pays on publication. Acquires first rights. Publication is copyrighted.

WILLARD & MAPLE

163 S. Willard Street, Freeman 302, Box 34, Burlington VT 05401. (802)860-2700 ext.2462. **E-mail:** willardandmaple@champlain.edu. Estab. 1996. **Contact:** Fiction Editor. Magazine: perfect bound; 125 pages; illustrations; photos. "*Willard & Maple* is a student-run literary magazine from Champlain College that publishes a wide array of poems, short stories, cre-

ative essays, short plays, pen and ink drawings, black and white photos, and computer graphics. We now accept color." Annual. Estab. 1996.

NEEDS "We accept all types of mss." Receives 20 unsolicited mss/month. Accepts 1 mss/year. Does not read mss March 31-September 1. Publishes ms within 1 year after acceptance. **Publishes 10 new writers/ year.** Has published work by Ian Frisch, Mark Belair, Rachel Chalmers, Robin Gaines, W.J. Everts, and Shirley O. Length: 5,000 words; average length: 2,500 words. Publishes short shorts. Also publishes literary essays, poetry. Sometimes comments on rejected mss.

HOW TO CONTACT Send complete mss. Send SASE for return of ms or send disposable copy of mss and #10 SASE for reply only. Responds in 6 months to queries; 6 months to mss. Accepts simultaneous, multiple submissions. Sample copy for $10. Writer's guidelines for SASE or send e-mail. Reviews fiction.

PAYMENT/TERMS Pays 2 contributor's copies; additional copies $12. Pays on publication for one-time rights.

TIPS "The power of imagination makes us infinite."

WILLOW REVIEW

College of Lake County Publications, College of Lake County, 19351 W. Washington St., Grayslake IL 60030-1198. (847)543-2956. **E-mail:** com426@clcillinois.edu. **Website:** www.clcillinois.edu/community/willowreview.asp. **Contact:** Michael Latza, editor. Estab. 1969. Circ. 800. *Willow Review*, published annually, is interested in poetry, creative nonfiction, and fiction of high quality. "We have no preferences as to form, style, or subject, as long as each poem stands on its own as art and communicates ideas." Has published poetry by Lisel Mueller, Lucien Stryk, David Ray, Louis Rodriguez, John Dickson, and Patricia Smith. *Willow Review* is 88-96 pages, digest-sized, professionally printed, flat-spined, with a 4-color cover featuring work by an Illinois artist. Press run is 1,000. Subscription: $18 for 3 issues, $30 for 6 issues. Sample: $5 (back issue). The editors award prizes for best poetry and prose in the issue. Prize awards vary contingent on the current year's budget but normally ranges from $100-400. There is no reading fee or separate application for these prizes. All accepted mss. are eligible.

NEEDS Accepts short fiction. Send complete ms with cover letter. Include estimated word count, brief bio, list of publications. Responds to mss in 3-4 months. Send either SASE (or IRC) for return of ms or dispos-

able copy of ms and #10 SASE for reply only. Considers simultaneous submissions, multiple submissions. Sample copy available for $5. Guidelines available for SASE, via e-mail.Writers receive 2 contributors copies. Additional copies $7. Pays on publication. All rights revert to author upon publication.

TIPS Include SASE. No email submissions, please.

WILLOW SPRINGS

501 N. Riverpoint Blvd., Suite 425, Spokane WA 99202. (509)359-7435. **E-mail:** willowspringsewu@gmail.com. **Website:** http://willowsprings.ewu.edu. Estab. 1977. Willow Springs is published twice a year, in spring and fall. Submissions in all genres are closed between June 1st and August 31st.

NEEDS We accept any good piece of literary fiction. Buy a sample copy. Does not want to see genre fiction that does not transcend its subject matter.

HOW TO CONTACT Send complete ms.

TIPS Please submit all manuscripts with a cover letter and a brief bio. While we have no specific length restrictions, we generally publish fiction and nonfiction no longer than 10,000 words and poetry no longer than 120 lines, though those are not strict rules. *Willow Springs* values poems and essays that transcend the merely autobiographical and fiction that conveys a concern for language as well as story.

☺ WINDSOR REVIEW

Dept. of English, University of Windsor, Windsor ON N9B 3P4 Canada. (519)253-3000; (519) 253-4232 ext. 2290. **Fax:** (519)971-3676. **E-mail:** uwrevu@uwindsor. ca. **Website:** www.uwindsor.ca. **Contact:** Marty Gervais, art editor. Estab. 1965. Biannual 4-color literary magazine featuring poetry, short fiction and art. Circ. 400. Guidelines free for #10 SASE with first-class postage. "We try to offer a balance of fiction and poetry distinguished by excellence."

NEEDS No genre fiction (science fiction, romance), but would consider if writing is good enough. No genre fiction (science fiction, romance), but would consider if writing is good enough. Length: 1,000-5,000 words.

HOW TO CONTACT Send complete ms. Length: 1,000-5,000 words Send complete ms.

PAYMENT/TERMS Pays $25, 1 contributor's copy and a free subscription.

◐ WISCONSIN REVIEW

University of Wisconsin Oshkosh, 800 Algoma Blvd., Oshkosh WI 54901. (920)424-2267. **E-**

mail: wisconsinreview@uwosh.edu. **Website:** www.uwosh.edu/wisconsinreview. Estab. 1966. **E-mail:**wisconsinreview@uwosh.edu. **Website:** www. uwosh.edu/wisconsinreview. *Wisconsin Review*, published annually, is a "contemporary poetry, prose, and art magazine run by students at the University of Wisconsin Oshkosh." *Wisconsin Review* is 250 pages, digest-sized, perfect-bound, with 4-color glossy cover stock. Receives about 400 poetry submissions/year, accepts about 50; Press run is 2,000. Single copy: $10; subscription: $10 plus $3 extra per issue for shipments outside the U.S.

NEEDS Send complete ms with cover letter and SASE. Sample copy and yearly subscription $10/year. Pays with 2 contributor copies. Acquires first rights. Simultaneous submissions are not accepted.

HOW TO CONTACT Send complete ms with cover letter and SASE. Sample copy and yearly subscription $10/year. Pays with 2 contributor copies. Acquires first rights. Simultaneous submissions are not accepted.

TIPS "We are open to any poetic form and style, and look for outstanding imagery, new themes, and fresh voices - poetry that induces emotions."

❶ ❸ WITHERSIN MAGAZINE, DARK, DIFFERENT; PLEASANTLY SINISTER

Temecula CA 92591. (951) 795-5498. **E-mail:** withersin@hotmail.com. **Website:** withersin.com. **Contact:** Misty Gersley, editor-in-chief. Literary magazine/journal. 6×9, 100 pages. Contains illustrations. Includes photographs. "A literary chimera, Withersin explores the bittersweet stain of the human condition. Comprised of an impressive array of original razor wire fiction, oddments and incongruities, obscure historical footnotes, unconventional research articles, delectable interviews, highlights, reviews and releases in film, music and print; all sewn together with threads of deviant art." Triannual. Circ. 600.

NEEDS Comics/graphic novels, experimental, historical (general), horror, literary, psychic/supernatural/occult, regional (specific and unique places; legends and lore). Does not want romance, erotica (read: pornography), or politically charged pieces. List of upcoming themes available for SASE, on website. Receives 100-300 mss/month. Accepts 3-5 mss/issue; 9-15 mss/year. Does not read July-March. Ms published 9-18 months after acceptance. **Publishes 5 new writers/year.** Published David Bain, Robert Heinze,

Edward Morris, Michael Pignatella, M.W. Anderson, Sunil Sadanand, David Sackmyster, Mark Allan Gunnells and Chet Gottfried. Length: 500 words (min)-3,000 words (max). Average length: 2,000 words. Publishes short shorts. Average length of short shorts: 500 words. Also publishes literary essays, literary criticism, book reviews, poetry. Often comments on/critiques rejected mss.

HOW TO CONTACT Send complete ms with cover letter. Accepts submissions by e-mail, on disk. Include estimated word count, brief bio. Responds to queries in 2-3 weeks. Responds to mss in 4-6 weeks. Send either SASE (or IRC) for return of ms or disposable copy of ms and #10 SASE for reply only. Considers previously published submissions (reprints have different pay scale), multiple submissions. Sample copy available for $7.25, on website. Guidelines available for SASE, via e-mail, on website.

PAYMENT/TERMS Writers receive 1-5¢ per word, 3000 word payment cap, 1 contributor's copy. Additional copies $7.25. Pays on publication. Acquires first North American serial rights, onetime rights. Publication is copyrighted. Occasionally sponsors contests, check website for details. "We also sponsor videography contests on www.youtube.com/withersin."

❶ THE WORCESTER REVIEW

1 Ekman St., Worcester MA 01607. (508)797-4770. **E-mail:** rodgerwriter@myfairpoint.net. **Website:** wreview.homestead.com. **Contact:** Rodger Martin, managing editor. Estab. 1972. Magazine: 6×9; 100 pages; 60 lb. white offset paper; 10 pt. CS1 cover stock; illustrations; photos. "We like high quality, creative poetry, artwork and fiction. Critical articles should be connected to New England." Annual. Circ. 1,000.

NEEDS Literary, prose poem. "We encourage New England writers in the hopes we will publish at least 30% New England but want the other 70% to show the best of writing from across the U.S." Receives 20-30 unsolicited mss/month. Accepts 2-4 mss/issue. Publishes ms 11 months after acceptance. Agented fiction less than 10%. Recently published work by Robert Pinsky, Marge Piercy, Wes McNair, Ed Hirsch. Length: 1,000-4,000 words; average length: 2,000 words. Publishes short shorts. Also publishes literary essays, literary criticism, poetry. Sometimes comments on rejected mss.

HOW TO CONTACT Send complete ms. Responds in 1 year to mss. Accepts simultaneous submissions only if other markets are clearly identified. Sample copy for $8. Writer's guidelines free.

PAYMENT/TERMS Pays 2 contributor copies and honorarium if possible. Acquires onetime rights. Doesn't pay for fiction.

TIPS "Send only one short story—reading editors do not like to read two by the same author at the same time. We will use only one. We generally look for creative work with a blend of craftsmanship, insight and empathy. This does not exclude humor. We won't print work that is shoddy in any of these areas."

ⓘ XAVIER REVIEW

Xavier University, 1 Drexel Dr., New Orleans LA 70125-1098. **Website:** www.xula.edu/review/. **Contact:** Dr. Nicole P. Green, editor. Estab. 1980. Magazine: 6×9; 75 pages; 50 lb. paper; 12 pt. CS1 cover; photographs. Magazine of "poetry/fiction/nonfiction/reviews (contemporary literature) for professional writers, libraries, colleges and universities." Semiannual.

NEEDS Recently published work by Andrei Codrescu, Terrance Hayes, Naton Leslie, Patricia Smith. Also publishes literary essays, literary criticism.

HOW TO CONTACT Send complete ms. Include 2-3 sentence bio.

PAYMENT/TERMS Pays 2 contributor's copies.

THE YALE REVIEW

Yale University, P.O. Box 208243, New Haven CT 06520-8243. (203)432-0499. **Fax:** (203)432-0510. **Website:** www.yale.edu/yalereview. **Contact:** J.D. McClatchy, editor. Estab. 1911.

NEEDS Buys quality fiction. Length: 3,000-5,000 words.

HOW TO CONTACT Submit complete ms with SASE. All submissions should be sent to the editorial office.

PAYMENT/TERMS Pays $400-500.

THE YALOBUSHA REVIEW

University of Mississippi, P.O. Box 1848, Dept. of English, University MS 38677. (662)915-3175. **E-mail:** yreditor@yahoo.com. **Website:** www.olemiss.edu/yalobusha. Estab. 1995. Magazine: 5×10; 125 pages; illustrations; photos. Annual. "Literary journal seeking quality submissions from around the world." Circ. 500.

NEEDS Experimental, historical, humorous, literary, novel excerpts, short shorts. Does not want sappy confessional or insights into parenthood. Receives 100 unsolicited mss/month. Accepts 3-6 mss/issue. Reading period: July 15-November 15. Publishes ms 4 months after acceptance. **Publishes 2-4 new writers/year.** Recently published work by John Brandon, Steve Almond, Shay Youngblood, Dan Chaon. Length: 10,000 words; average length: 4,000 words. Publishes short shorts. Also publishes nonfiction, poetry. Length: 10,000 words.

HOW TO CONTACT Send complete ms. Include a brief bio. and #10 SASE for reply only. Does not accept electronic submissions unless from outside the U.S. Accepts simultaneous submissions; no previously published work. Send disposable copy of ms and #10 SASE for reply only. Responds in 2-4 months to mss. Reading period is July 15-November 15. Sample copy for $10. Writer's guidelines for #10 SASE. Send complete ms with cover letter and SASE.

PAYMENT/TERMS Pays 2 contributor's copies. Pays honorarium when funding available. Acquires first North American serial rights.

ⓘⓒ YEMASSEE

University of South Carolina, Department of English, Columbia SC 29208. (803)777-2085. **Fax:** (803)777-9064. **E-mail:** editor@yemasseejournalonline.org; manager@yemasseejournalonline.org. **Website:** http://yemasseejournalonline.org. **Contact:** Zack O'Neill and Bhavin Tailor, co-editors. Estab. 1993. Magazine: 512×812; 70-90 pages; 60 lb. natural paper; 65 lb. cover; cover illustration. "We are open to a variety of subjects and writing styles. We publish primarily fiction and poetry, but we are also interested in one-act plays, brief excerpts of novels, and interviews with literary figures. Our essential consideration for acceptance is the quality of the work." Semiannual. Estab. 1993. Circ. 750. Condensed novels, ethnic/multicultural, experimental, feminist, gay, historical, humor/satire, lesbian, literary, regional. "No romance, religious/inspirational, young adult/teen, children's/juvenile, erotica. Wants more experimental work." Receives 30 unsolicited mss/month. Accepts 1-3 mss/issue; 2-6 mss/year. "We read from August-May and hold ms over to the next year if they arrive in the summer." **Publishes 6 new writers/year.** Recently published work by Robert Coover, Chris Railey, Virgil Suárez, Susan Ludvigson, Kwame Dawes. Publishes short shorts. Also publishes literary essays, poetry. Send complete ms. Include estimated word count, brief bio, list of publications. Send SASE for reply, return of ms, or send disposable copy of ms. Responds in 2 weeks to queries; 4 months to mss. Accepts simultaneous submissions. William Richey Short

Fiction Contest submission deadline: November 15, 2010. See separate listing. *"Yemassee* is the University of South Carolina's literary journal. Our readers are interested in high quality fiction, poetry, drama, and creative nonfiction. We have no editorial slant; quality of work is our only concern." "We publish in the fall and spring, printing three to five stories and 12-15 poems per issue. We tend to solicit reviews, essays, and interviews but welcome unsolicited queries. We do not favor any particular aesthetic or school of writing. Please limit any submission to 7,500 words. Simultaneous submissions are accepted, given that you identify them as such on your cover letter and immediately notify us if the submission is accepted elsewhere. We do not consider any work that has been previously published in any form, print or electronic. We do not accept electronic submissions (exceptions are made for overseas submissions and submissions from incarcerated persons). Address your manuscripts to the appropriate genre editor. Include a cover letter with your contact information (including email address) and a SASE with sufficient postage. NO MANUSCRIPTS WILL BE RETURNED. Response time generally ranges from one to four months. Contributors receive 3 copies of the issue in which their work appears."

◯ Stories from *Yemassee* have been published in *New Stories From the South.*

NEEDS Length: 250-7,500 words.
HOW TO CONTACT Sample copy for $5. Writer's guidelines for #10 SASE. Acquires first rights. Send complete ms.
PAYMENT/TERMS Pays 3 contributor's copies. Pays in contributor copies.

ZAHIR

Zahir Publishing, 315 South Coast Hwy. 101, Suite U8, Encinitas CA 92024. **E-mail:** zahirtales@gmail.com. **Website:** www.zahirtales.com. **Contact:** Sheryl Tempchin, editor. Estab. 2003. Online magazine. "We publish literary speculative fiction." Quarterly. "We publish literary speculative fiction."
NEEDS fantasy, literary, psychic/supernatural/occult, science fiction, surrealism, magical realism. No children's stories, excessive violence or pornography. Accepts 5-8 mss/issue; 20-25 mss/year. Publishes ms 2-12 months after acceptance. **Publishes 6 new writers/year.** Sometimes comments on rejected mss. No children's stories or stories that deal with exces-

sive violence or anything pornographic. 6,000 words maximum.
HOW TO CONTACT Send complete ms. Send SASE (or IRC) for return of ms, or send disposable copy of the ms and #10 SASE or e-mail address for reply only. E-mail queries okay. E-mail submissions okay through online submission form on our website. Responds in 1-2 weeks to queries; 1-3 months to mss. Accepts reprints submissions. Accepts simultaneous submissions. No multiple submissions. Writer's guidelines for #10 SASE, by e-mail, or online. Send complete ms. or submit through online submission form.
PAYMENT/TERMS Pays $10 and one copy of annual print anthology. Pays on publication for electronic rights and first, second serial (reprint) rights.

ZOETROPE: ALL-STORY

The Sentinel Bldg., 916 Kearny St., San Francisco CA 94133. (415)788-7500. **Website:** www.all-story.com. Estab. 1997. **Contact:** Michael Ray, editor. Magazine specializing in the best of contemporary short fiction. *"Zoetrope: All Story* presents a new generation of classic stories." Quarterly. Estab. 1997. Circ. 20,000. *Zoetrope: All Story* presents a new generation of classic stories.

◯ Does not accept submissions September 1 - December 31 (with the exception of stories entered in the annual Short Fiction Contest, which are considered for publication in the magazine).

NEEDS Literary short stories, one-act plays. Accepts 25-35 mss/year. Publishes ms 5 months after acceptance. Length: 7,000 words (max).
HOW TO CONTACT Send complete ms. Does not accept mss June 1-August 1, or via e-mail. Responds in 5 months (if SASE included) to mss. Accepts simultaneous submissions. Sample copy for $6.95. Writer's guidelines online. Send stories to: *Zoetrope:All-Story* Attn: Fiction Editor. "Writers should submit only one story at a time and no more than two stories a year. Before submitting, non-subscribers should read several issues of the magazine to determine if their works fit with *All-Story.* Electronic versions of the magazine are available to read, in part, at the website; and print versions are available for purchase by single-issue order and subscription. We consider unsolicited submissions of short stories and one-act plays no longer than 7,000 words. Excerpts from larger works, screenplays, treatments, and poetry will be returned unread. We do not accept artwork or design submissions. We do

not accept unsolicited revisions nor respond to writers who don't include an SASE." Send complete ms by mail to: *Zoetrope:All-Story* Attn: Fiction Editor.

PAYMENT/TERMS Pays $1,000. Acquires first serial rights.

ZYZZYVA

466 Geary Street, Suite 401, San Francisco CA 94102. (415)440-1510. **E-mail:** editor@zyzzyva.org. **Website:** www.zyzzyva.org. **Contact:** Howard Junker. Estab. 1985. "We feature work by writers currently living on the West Coast or in Alaska and Hawaii only. We are essentially a literary magazine, but of wide-ranging interests and a strong commitment to nonfiction." Circ. 2,500.

NEEDS Ethnic/multicultural, experimental, humor/satire, mainstream. Receives 300 unsolicited mss/month. Accepts 15 mss/issue; 45 mss/year. Publishes ms 3 months after acceptance. Agented fiction 1%. **Publishes 15 new writers/year.** Recently published work by Rick Barot, Jackson Bliss, Dust Wells. Publishes short shorts. Also publishes literary essays, poetry. Length: 100-7,500 words.

HOW TO CONTACT Send complete ms. Responds in 1 week to queries; 1 month to mss. Sample copy for $7 or online. Writer's guidelines online. Send complete ms.

PAYMENT/TERMS Pays $50. Pays on acceptance for first North American serial and one time anthology rights.

TIPS "West Coast writers means those currently living in California, Alaska, Washington, Oregon, or Hawaii."

SMALL CIRCULATION MAGAZINES

//

This section of *Novel & Short Story Writer's Market* contains general interest, special interest, regional and genre magazines with circulations under 10,000. Although these magazines vary greatly in size, theme, format and management, the editors are all looking for short stories. Their specific fiction needs present writers of all degrees of expertise and interests with an abundance of publishing opportunities. Among the diverse publications in this section are magazines devoted to almost every topic, every level of writing, and every type of writer. Some of the markets listed here publish fiction about a particular geographic area or by authors who live in that locale.

Although not as high-paying as the large-circulation consumer magazines, you'll find some of the publications listed here do pay writers 1-5¢/word or more. Also, unlike the big consumer magazines, these markets are very open to new writers and relatively easy to break into. Their only criterion is that your story be well written, well presented and suitable for their particular readership.

In this section you will also find listings for zines. Zines vary greatly in appearance as well as content. Some paper zines are photocopies published whenever the editor has material and money, while others feature offset printing and regular distribution schedules. A few have evolved into very slick four-color, commercial-looking publications.

SELECTING THE RIGHT MARKET

First, zero in on those markets most likely to be interested in your work. Begin by looking at the Category Index. If your work is more general—or conversely, very specialized—you may wish to browse through the listings, perhaps looking up those magazines published in your state or region. Also check the Online Markets section for other specialized and genre publications.

In addition to browsing through the listings and using the Category Index, check the openness icons at the beginning of listings to find those most likely to be receptive to your work. This is especially true for beginning writers, who should look for magazines that say they are especially open to new writers O and for those giving equal weight to both new and established writers ◑. For more explanation about these icons, see the inside covers of this book.

Once you have a list of magazines you might like to try, read their listings carefully. Much of the material within each listing carries clues that tell you more about the magazine. "How to Use NSSWM" describes in detail the listing information common to all the markets in our book.

The physical description appearing near the beginning of the listings can give you clues about the size and financial commitment to the publication. This is not always an indication of quality, but chances are a publication with expensive paper and four-color artwork on the cover has more prestige than a photocopied publication featuring a clip-art cover. For more information on some of the paper, binding and printing terms used in these descriptions, see Printing and Production Terms Defined.

FURTHERING YOUR SEARCH

It cannot be stressed enough that reading the listing is only the first part of developing your marketing plan. The second part, equally important, is to obtain fiction guidelines and read the actual magazine. Reading copies of a magazine helps you determine the fine points of the magazine's publishing style and philosophy. There is no substitute for this type of hands-on research.

Unlike commercial magazines available at most newsstands and bookstores, it requires a little more effort to obtain some of the magazines listed here. You may need to send for a sample copy. We include sample copy prices in the listings whenever possible. See "The Business of Fiction Writing" for the specific mechanics of manuscript submission. Above all, editors appreciate a professional presentation. Include a brief cover letter and send a self-addressed, stamped envelope for a reply. Be sure the envelope is large enough to accommodate your manuscript, if you would like it returned, and include enough stamps or International Reply Coupons (for replies from countries other than your own) to cover your manuscript's return. Many publishers today appreciate receiving a disposable manuscript, eliminating the cost to writers of return postage and saving editors the effort of repackaging manuscripts for return.

Most of the magazines listed here are published in the U.S. You will also find some English-speaking markets from around the world. These foreign publications are denoted with a ◕ symbol at the beginning of listings. To make it easier to find Canadian markets, we include a ◌ symbol at the start of those listings.

◗●◗⑤ ALBEDO ONE

2 Post Rd., Lusk, Co Dublin Ireland. (353)1 8730 177. **E-mail:** bobn@yellowbrickroad.ie. **Website:** www.albedo.com. **Contact:** Editor. Estab. 1993. Magazine: A4; 64 pages. "We hope to publish interesting and unusual fiction by new and established writers. We will consider anything, as long as it is well written and entertaining, though our definitions of both may not be exactly mainstream. We like stories with plot and characters that live on the page. Most of our audience are probably committed genre fans, but we try to appeal to a broad spectrum of readers." Triannual. Circ. 900.

NEEDS Experimental, fantasy, horror, literary, science fiction. Receives more than 80 unsolicited mss/month. Accepts 15-18 mss/year. Publishes ms 1 year after acceptance. Publishes 6-8 new writers/year. Length: 2,000-9,000 words; average length: 4,000 words. Also publishes literary criticism. Sometimes comments on rejected mss.

HOW TO CONTACT Responds in 3 months to mss. PDF—electronic—sample copies are available for download at a reduced price. Guidelines available by e-mail or on website. Reviews fiction.

PAYMENT/TERMS Pays €3 per 1,000 words, and 1 contributor's copy. Pays on publication for first rights.

◗ ANY DREAM WILL DO REVIEW

250 Jeanell Dr., Carson City NV 89703. (775)786-0345. **E-mail:** cassjmb@intercomm.com. **Website:** www.willigocrazy.org/Ch08.htm. **Contact:** Dr. Jean M. Bradt, editor and publisher. Estab. 2001. Magazine: 512×812; 52 pages; 20 lb. bond paper; 12 pt. Carolina cover stock. "The *Any Dream Will Do Review* showcases a new literary genre, Fiction In The Raw, which attempts to fight the prejudice against consumers of mental-health services by touching hearts, that is, by exposing the consumers' deepest thoughts and emotions. In the Review's stories, accomplished authors honestly reveal their most intimate secrets. See website for detailed instructions on how to write Fiction In The Raw." Published every 4 or 5 years. The 52-page Does not accept queries. Annual magazine written by, for, and about persons living with mental illness.

NEEDS Adapted ethnic/multicultural, mainstream, psychic/supernatural/occult, romance (contemporary), science fiction (soft/sociological), all of which must follow the guidelines at website. Accepts 10 mss/issue; 5 mss/year. Publishes ms 12 months after acceptance. **Publishes 2 new writers/year.** Publishes short-shorts. No pornography, true-life stories, black humor, political material, testimonials, experimental fiction, or depressing accounts of hopeless or perverted people. Length: 400-4,000 words.

HOW TO CONTACT Send complete ms. Accepts submissions by e-mail (cassjmb@intercomm.com). Please submit by e-mail. If you must submit by hard copy, please send disposable copies. No queries, please. Responds in 8 weeks to mss. Sample copy for $4 plus postage. Writer's guidelines online. Not accepting stories. Send complete ms. Often comments on rejected mss.

PAYMENT/TERMS Pays in contributor's copies; additional copies $4 plus postage. Acquires first North American serial rights.

◗⊜⑤ THE APUTAMKON REVIEW

the WordShed, LLC, P.O. Box 190, Jonesboro ME 04648. **E-mail:** thewordshed@tds.net. **Website:** http://thewordshed.com. **Contact:** Les Simon, Publisher. Magazine. Approx. 190 pages. Contains b&w illustrations. Includes photographs. "All age groups living in downeast Maine and the Canadian Maritimes, or thereabouts, are invited to participate. "*The Aputamkon Review* will present a mishmash of truths, half truths and outright lies, including but not limited to short fiction, tall tales, creative non-fiction, essays, (some) poetry, haiku, b&w visual arts, interviews, lyrics and music, quips, quirks, quotes that should be famous, witticisms, follies, comic strips, cartoons, jokes, riddles, recipes, puzzles, games. Stretch your imagination. Practically anything goes." Annual. Estab. 2006. Circ. 500. Member Maine Writers and Publishers Alliance.

NEEDS Adventure, children's/juvenile, comics/graphic novels, ethnic/multicultural, experimental, family saga, fantasy, glitz, historical, horror, humor/satire, literary, mainstream, military/war, mystery, psychic/supernatural/occult, religious, romance, science fiction, thriller/espionage, translations, western, young adult/teen. Does not want mss which are heavy with sex or religion. Receives 1-20 mss/month. Accepts 30-40 mss/year. Ms published max of 12 months after acceptance. Length: 50 words (min)-3,000 words (max). Average length: 500 words. Publishes short shorts. Also publishes literary essays, literary criticism, poetry. Rarely comments on/critiques rejected mss.

HOW TO CONTACT Send complete ms with cover letter. Accepts submissions in the body of an e-mail, on disk via USPS. Submission period is 12 months a year; reading January 1 through March 31. Responds only between Jan. 31 and April 30. Include age if under 18, and a bio will be requested upon acceptance of work. Responds to queries or submissions in 2-8 weeks. Send SASE (or IRC) for return of ms or a disposable copy of ms and #10 SASE for reply only. Considers simultaneous submissions, multiple submissions. Sample copy available for $12.85 US plus $2.75 US s/h. Guidelines available for SASE, via e-mail, via fax..

PAYMENT/TERMS Submissions receive $10-35 depending on medium, plus one copy. Pays on acceptance. Acquires first North American serial rights. Publication is copyrighted. All rights revert back to the contributors upon publication.

○⑤ BLACK LACE

P.O. Box 83912, Los Angeles CA 90083-0912. (310)410-0808. **Fax:** (310)410-9250. **E-mail:** newsroom@blk.com. **Website:** www.blacklace.org. **Contact:** Editor. Estab. 1991. Magazine: 8 1/8×10 5/8; 48 pages; book stock; color glossy cover; illustrations; photos. "*Black Lace* is a lifestyle magazine for African-American lesbians. Its content ranges from erotic imagery to political commentary." Quarterly.

NEEDS "*Black Lace* seeks erotic material of the highest quality, but it need not be written by professional writers. The most important thing is that the work be erotic and that it feature black men in the life or ITL themes. We are not interested in stories that demean black women or place them in stereotypical situations." Ethnic/multicultural, lesbian. Wants "full-length erotic fiction of 2,000-4,000 words detailing the exploits of black women in the life. Avoid interracial stories of idealized pornography." Accepts 4 mss/year. Recently published work by Nicole King, Wanda Thompson, Lynn K. Pannell, Sheree Ann Slaughter, Lyn Lifshin, JoJo and Drew Alise Timmens. Publishes short shorts. Also publishes literary essays, literary criticism, poetry.

HOW TO CONTACT Query with published clips or send complete ms by mail, e-mail, or fax. Send a disposable copy of ms. No simultaneous submissions. Accepts electronic submissions. Sample copy for $7. Writer's guidelines free.

PAYMENT/TERMS Pays $50 and 2 contributor's copies. Acquires first North American serial rights. Right to anthologize.

○⑤ CONCEIT MAGAZINE

P.O. Box 884223, San Francisco CA 94188-4223. **E-mail:** conceitmagazine2007@yahoo.com. **Website:** www.myspace.com/conceitmagazine; www.sites.google.com/site/conceitmagazine/home. **Contact:** Perry Terrell, Editor. Also on Facebook, Twitter, LinkedIn, Goodreads and Grouply. Magazine. 812×512, 44 pages, copy paper paper. Contains illustrations, photographs. "If it's on your mind, write it down and send it to Perry Terrell at *Conceit Magazine*. Writing is good therapy." Monthly. Estab. 2007. Circ. 900+. Needs adventure, children's/juvenile, ethnic/multicultural, experimental, family saga, fantasy, feminist, gay, historical, horror (futuristic, psychological, supernatural), humor/satire, lesbian, literary, mainstream, military/war, mystery, new age, psychic/supernatural/occult, religious, romance (contemporary, futuristic/time travel, historical, regency, suspense), science fiction (soft/sociological), thriller/espionage, translations, western, young adult/teen (adventure, easy-to-read, fantasy/science fiction, historical, mystery/suspense, problem novels, romance, series, sports, western). Does not want profanity, porn, gruesomeness. List of upcoming themes available for SASE and on website. Receives 40-50 mss/month. Accepts 20-22 mss/issue; up to 264 mss/year. Ms published 3-10 months after acceptance. **Publishes 150 new writers/year.** Published D. Neil Simmers, Tamara Fey Turner, Eve J. Blohm, Barbara Hantman, David Body. Length: 100 words (min)-3,000 words (max). Average length: 1,500-2,000 words. Publishes short shorts. Average length of short shorts: 50-500 words. Also publishes literary essays, literary criticism, book reviews, poetry. Send review copies to Perry Terrell. Sometimes comments on/critiques rejected mss.

HOW TO CONTACT Query first or send complete ms with cover letter. Accepts submissions by e-mail, by fax and snail mail. Include estimated word count, brief bio, list of publications. Responds to queries in 2-3 weeks. Responds to mss in 4-6 months. Send either SASE (or IRC) for return of ms or disposable copy of ms and #10 SASE for reply only. Considers simultaneous submissions, previously published submissions, multiple submissions. Sample copy free with SASE. Guidelines available for SASE, via e-mail, on website, via fax.

PAYMENT/TERMS Writers receive 1 contributor copy. Additional copies $4.50. PayPal to conceitmagazine@yahoo.com. Pays writers through contests. Pays on publication. Acquires one time rights. Publication is copyrighted. "Occasionally sponsors contests. Send SASE or check blog on website for details."

CREATIVE WITH WORDS PUBLICATIONS

P.O. Box 223226, Carmel CA 93922. **Fax:** (831)655-8627. **E-mail:** geltrich@mbay.net. **Website:** creative-withwords.tripod.com. **Contact:** Brigitta Geltrich, publisher/editor. Estab. 1975.

NEEDS Ethnic/multicultural, humor/satire, mystery/suspense (amateur sleuth, private eye), regional (folklore), young adult/teen (adventure, historical). "Do not submit essays." No violence or erotica, overly religious fiction, or sensationalism. "Twice a year we publish *the Eclectics* written by adults only (20 and older); throughout the year we publish thematic anthologies written by all ages." List of upcoming themes available for SASE. Limit poetry to 20 lines or less, 46 characters per line or less. Receives 50-200 unsolicited mss/month. Accepts 50-80 mss/anthology. Publishes ms 1-2 months after acceptance. Recently published work by Najwa Salam Brax, Sirock Brighton, Roger D. Coleman, Antoinette Garrick, and Maria Dickerhof. Sometimes comments on rejected mss.

HOW TO CONTACT Send complete ms with a cover letter with SASE. Include estimated word count. Responds in 2 weeks to queries; 1-2 months after a specific theme's due date to mss. Please request a list of themes with SASE before sending manuscript. Sample copy for $7. Make checks payable to Brigitta Ludgate. Writer's guidelines for #10 SASE.

PAYMENT/TERMS 20% reduction cost on 1-9 copies ordered, 30% reduction on 10 to 19 copies, 40% reduction on each copy on order of 20 or more. Acquires one time rights. Does not accept previously published mss.

DARK TALES

7 Offley Street, Worcester WR3 8BH United Kingdom. **E-mail:** sean@darktales.co.uk. **Website:** www.darktales.co.uk. **Contact:** Sean Jeffery, editor. Estab. 2003. Magazine: Contains illustrations. "We publish horror and speculative short fiction from anybody, anywhere, and the publication is professionally illustrated throughout." Circ. 350+.

NEEDS Horror (dark fantasy, futuristic, psychological, supernatural), science fiction (soft/sociological). Receives 25+ mss/month. Accepts 10-15 mss/issue; 25-40 mss/year. Ms published 6 months after accep-

tance. **Publishes 20 new writers/year.** Published Davin Ireland, Niall McMahon, David Robertson, Valerie Robson, K.S. Dearsley, and Mark Cowley. Length: 500-3,500 words. Average length: 2,500 words. Publishes short shorts. Average length of short shorts: 500 words. Sometimes comments on/critiques rejected mss. Has occasional contests; see website for details.

HOW TO CONTACT Send complete ms with cover letter. Include estimated word count, list of publications. Responds to queries in 1 week. Responds to mss in 12 weeks. Send disposable copy of ms and #10 SASE for reply only. Sample copy available for $3. Guidelines available on website.

PAYMENT/TERMS Writers receive $5 per thousand words. Additional copies $7.10. Pays on publication. Acquires first British serial rights. Sends galleys to author. Publication is copyrighted.

DOWN IN THE DIRT

829 Brian Court, Gurnee IL 60031-3155. (847)281-9070. **E-mail:** alexrand@scars.tv. **Website:** scars.tv. **Contact:** Alexandria Rand, editor. Estab. 2000. Magazine: 512×812; perfect-bound 84-page book. Monthly.

NEEDS Adventure, ethnic/multicultural, experimental, fantasy, feminist, gay, historical, horror, lesbian, literary, mystery/suspense, New Age, psychic/supernatural/occult, science fiction. No religious or rhyming or family-oriented material. Publishes ms within 1 year after acceptance. Recently published work by Pat Dixon, Mel Waldman, Ken Dean Aeon Logan, Helena Wolfe. Average length: 1,000 words. Publishes short shorts. Also publishes poetry. "Contact us if you are interested in submitting very long stories, or parts of a novel (if accepted, it would appear in parts in multiple issues)." Always, if asked, comments on rejected mss.

HOW TO CONTACT Query editor with e-mail submission. "99.5% of all submissions are via e-mail only, so if you do not have electronic access, there is a strong chance you will not be considered. We recommend you e-mail submissions to us, either as an attachment or by placing it directly in the letter). For samples of what we've printed in the past, visit our website: http://scars.tv/dirt. Responds in 1 month to queries; 1 month to mss. Accepts simultaneous, multiple submissions and reprints. Sample copy for $6. Writer's guidelines for SASE, e-mail or on the website.

FLOYD COUNTY MOONSHINE

720 Christiansburg Pike, Floyd VA 24091. (540)745-5150. **E-mail:** floydshine@gmail.com. **Contact:** Aar-

on Moore, editor-in-chief. Estab. 2008. *Floyd County Moonshine*, published biannually, is a "literary and arts magazine in Floyd, Virginia, and the New River Valley. We accept poetry, short stories, and essays addressing all manner of themes; however, preference is given to those works of a rural or Southern/Appalachian nature. We welcome cutting-edge and innovative fiction and poetry in particular."

○ Wants "rustic innovation." Has published poetry by Steve Kistulentz, Louis Gallo, Ernie Wormwood, R.T. Smith, Chelsea Adams, and Justin Askins. Single copy: $8; subscription: $20/1 year, $38/2 years.

○⑤ IRREANTUM

The Association for Mormon Letters, P.O. Box 1315, Salt Lake City UT 84110-1315. **E-mail:** editor@aml-pubs.org. **Website:** www.irreantum.org. Estab. 1999. Magazine or zine: 812×712; 100-120 pages; 20 lb. paper; 20 lb. color cover; illustrations; photos. "While focused on Mormonism, *Irreantum* is a cultural, humanities-oriented magazine, not a religious magazine. Our guiding principle is that Mormonism is grounded in a sufficiently unusual, cohesive, and extended historical and cultural experience that it has become like a nation, an ethnic culture. We can speak of Mormon literature at least as surely as we can of a Jewish or Southern literature. *Irreantum* publishes stories, one-act dramas, stand-alone novel and drama excerpts, and poetry by, for, or about Mormons (as well as author interviews, essays, and reviews). The magazine's audience includes readers of any or no religious faith who are interested in literary exploration of the Mormon culture, mindset, and worldview through Mormon themes and characters. *Irreantum* is currently the only magazine devoted to Mormon literature." Biannual. Circ. 300.

NEEDS "High quality work that explores the Mormon experience, directly or by implication, through literature. We acknowledge a broad range of experience with Mormonism, both as a faith and as a culture—on the part of devoted multi-generation Mormons, ethnic Mormons, new converts, and people outside the faith and culture who interact with Mormons and Mormon culture. We are committed to respectful exploration of Mormonism through literature. Receives 5 unsolicited mss/month. Accepts 3 mss/issue; 6 mss/year. Publishes ms 3-12 months after acceptance. **Publishes 3 or more new writers/ year.** Recently published work by Orson Scott Card,

Terryl Givens, Jack Harrell, Eric Samuelsen, Michael Collins, Phyllis Barber, Paul Swenson. Length: 1,000-5,000 words; average length: 5,000 words. Publishes short shorts. Also publishes literary essays, literary criticism, poetry. Sometimes comments on rejected mss. Annual fiction contest and annual personal essay contest with cash prizes. Length: 1,000-5,000 words.

HOW TO CONTACT Accepts submissions by e-mail only in Microsoft Word or rich text files only. Accepts critical essays to criticalessaysubmissions@ mormonletter.org. "The fiction and personal essay/ creative nonfiction we publish is selected from the contest entries for the annual fiction contest and annual personal essay contest with offer cash prizes. There is a submission window—January 1-May 31st— for fiction and creative nonfiction submissions. All unsolicited fiction and creative nonfiction must be submitted according to contest rules which can be found on the website." Winner will receive a copy of the *Irreantum* issue in which his or her work appears. Send complete ms. with cover letter. Include a brief bio and list of publications. Responds in 2 weeks to queries, 2 months to mss. Accepts simultaneous and reprints, multiple submissions. Sample copy $15. Writer's guidelines on website. Reviews fiction.

PAYMENT/TERMS Pays $0-100. Pays on publication for one time rights.

○ ITALIAN AMERICANA

80 Washington St., Providence RI 02903-1803. **E-mail:** itamericana@yahoo.com. **Website:** www.italianamericana.com. **Contact:** C.B. Albright, editor-in-chief. Estab. 1974. Magazine: 6×9; 240 pages; varnished cover; perfect bound; photos. "*Italian Americana* contains historical articles, fiction, poetry and memoirs, all concerning the Italian experience in the Americas." Semiannual. Circ. 1,200.

NEEDS Literary, Italian American. No nostalgia. Wants to see more fiction featuring "individualized characters." Receives 10 unsolicited mss/month. Accepts 3 mss/issue; 6-7 mss/year. Publishes ms up to 1 year after acceptance. Agented fiction 5%. **Publishes 2-4 new writers/year.** Publishing 2 issues a year of historical articles, fiction, memoir, poetry and reviews. Seeking historical articles. Award-winning authors in all categories, such as Mary Caponegro, Sal La Puma, Dana Gioia (past poetry editor).

HOW TO CONTACT Send complete ms (in duplicate) with a cover letter. Include 3-5 line bio, list of publications. Responds in 1 month to queries; 2 months to mss. No simultaneous submissions. Subscription: $20/year; $35/2 years. Sample copy for $7. Writer's guidelines for #10 SASE. Reviews fiction.

PAYMENT/TERMS 1 contributor's copy; additional copies $7. Acquires first North American serial rights.

●◉ KELSEY REVIEW

P.O. Box B, Liberal Arts Division, Trenton NJ 08690. **E-mail:** kelsey.review@mccc.edu. **Website:** www. mccc.edu/community_kelsey-review.shtml. **Contact:** Holly-Katharine Matthews. Estab. 1988. Magazine: 7×14; 98 pages; glossy paper; soft cover. "Must live or work in Mercer County, NJ." Annual. *Kelsey Review,* published annually in September by Mercer County Community College, serves as "an outlet for literary talent of people living and working in Mercer County, New Jersey only." Has no specifications as to form, length, subject matter, or style. Fiction: 4,000 word limit. Poetry: Not more than 6 pages. Non-Fiction: 2,500 word limit. Black and White art. Does not want to see poetry "about kittens and puppies." Has published poetry by Vida Chu, Carolyn Foote Edelmann, and Mary Mallery. *Kelsey Review* is about 90 glossy pages, 7x11, with paper cover. Receives 100+ submissions/year, accepts 10. Press run is 2,000; all distributed free to contributors, area libraries, bookstores, and schools.

NEEDS Regional (Mercer County, NJ only), open. Receives 10 unsolicited mss/month. Accepts 24 mss/issue. Reads mss only in May. **Publishes 10 new writers/ year.** Recently published work by Thom Beachamps, Janet Kirk, Bruce Petronio. Publishes short shorts. Also publishes literary essays, poetry.

HOW TO CONTACT The deadline for all submissions is May 15. Submissions are limited to people who live, work, or give literary readings in Mercer County, NJ. Decisions on which material will be published are made by the four-person editorial board in June and July. Contributors will be notified of submission acceptance determination(s) by the second week of August. SASE for return of ms. Responds no later than September 1 to mss. Accepts multiple submissions. Sample copy free.

PAYMENT/TERMS 3 contributor's copies. Rights revert to author on publication.

◐ KRAX MAGAZINE

63 Dixon Lane, Leeds Yorkshire Br LS12 4RR United Kingdom. **Contact:** A. Robson, co-editor. "Krax pub-

lishes lighthearted, humorous and whimsical writing. It is for anyone seeking light relief at a gentle pace. Our audience has grown middle-aged along with us, especially now that we're annual and not able to provide the instant fix demanded by teens and twenties." "Contemporary light-hearted poetry from Britain, America and elsewhere. Currently over 68 pages of anything but stodgy poetry, short fiction and glowingly brilliant graphics. Usually there is and interview with a writer of interest and a sizeable review section covering a vast range of related books, magazines, pamphlets, audio tape and CD's."

NEEDS "No war stories, horror, space bandits, boy-girl soap opera. We publish mostly poetry of a light-hearted nature but use comic or spoof fiction, witty and humorous essays. Would like to see more whimsical items, trivia ramblings or anything daft." Accepts 1 mss/issue. **Publishes 1 new writer/year.** Recently published work by Aaron Dabrowski, Rovert L. Voss.

HOW TO CONTACT No specific guidelines but cover letter appreciated. Sample copy for $2.

❶❷❸ LADY CHURCHILL'S ROSEBUD WRISTLET

150 Pleasant St., #306, Easthampton MA 01027. **E-mail:** smallbeerpress@gmail.com. **Website:** www. smallbeerpress.com/lcrw. **Contact:** Gavin Grant, editor. Estab. 1996. Zine: half legal size; 60 pages; 60 lb. paper; glossy cover; illustrations; photos. Semiannual. Circ. 1,000. "We accept fiction, non-fiction, poetry, and black and white art. The fiction we publish most of tends toward but is not limited to the speculative. This does not mean only quietly desperate stories. We will consider items that fall out with regular categories. We do not accept multiple submissions. We read everything, sometimes slow, sometimes fast. Our apologies for reading so slowly. At the moment we are only reading paper submissions. If six months has passed and you contact us we will try and reply with our decision. We occasionally solicit work but most of what we publish is work that comes in over the transom and we are very happy that we have generally published a couple of new writers in each issue. We recommend you read *Lady Churchill's Rosebud Wristlet* before submitting. You can procure a copy from us or from assorted book shops."

NEEDS Comics/graphic novels, experimental, fantasy, feminist, literary, science fiction, translations, short story collections. Receives 100 unsolicited mss/

month. Accepts 4-6 mss/issue; 8-12 mss/year. Publishes ms 6-12 months after acceptance. **Publishes 2-4 new writers/year.** Recently published work by Ted Chiang, Gwenda Bond, Alissa Nutting, Charlie Anders. Length: 200-7,000 words; average length: 3,500 words. Also publishes literary essays, poetry. Sometimes comments on rejected mss. "We do not publish gore, sword and sorcery or pornography. We can discuss these terms if you like. There are places for them all, this is not one of them."

HOW TO CONTACT Send complete ms with a cover letter. Include estimated word count. Send SASE (or IRC) for return of ms, or send a disposable copy of ms and #10 SASE for reply only. Responds in 4 weeks to queries; 3-6 months to mss. Sample copy for $5. Writer's guidelines online. Reviews fiction.

PAYMENT/TERMS Pays 1¢/word, $20 minimum and 2 contributor's copies; additional copies contributor's discount 40%. Pays on publication for first serial, non-exclusive anthology, and electronic rights.

⊙ LEFT CURVE

P.O. Box 472, Oakland CA 94604-0472. (510)763-7193. **E-mail:** editor@leftcurve.org. **Website:** www.leftcurve.org. **Contact:** Csaba Polony, editor. Estab. 1974. Magazine: 8½×11; 144 pages; 60 lb. paper; 100 pt. C1S gloss layflat lamination cover; illustrations; photos. "*Left Curve* is an artist-produced journal addressing the problem(s) of cultural forms emerging from the crises of modernity that strive to be independent from the control of dominant institutions, based on the recognition of the destructiveness of commodity (capitalist) systems to all life." Published irregularly. Circ. 2,000.

NEEDS Ethnic/multicultural, experimental, historical, literary, regional, science fiction, translations, contemporary, prose poem, political. "No topical satire, religion-based pieces, melodrama. We publish critical, open, social/political-conscious writing." Receives 50 unsolicited mss/month. Accepts 3-4 mss/issue. Publishes ms 6-12 months after acceptance. Recently published work by Mike Standaert, Ilan Pappe, Terrence Cannon, John Gist. Length: 500-5,000 words; average length: 1,200 words. Publishes short shorts. Sometimes comments on rejected mss.

HOW TO CONTACT Send complete ms. Accepts submissions by e-mail (editor@leftcurve.org). Send complete ms with cover letter. Include "statement of writer's intent, brief bio and reason for submitting

to *Left Curve*." Accepts electronic submissions and hard copy, though for accepted work we request e-mail copy, either in body of text or as attachments." For accepted longer work we prefer submission of final draft in digital form via disk or e-mail. Responds in 6 months to mss. Sample copy for $12; backcopies $10. Writer's guidelines available with SASE.

PAYMENT/TERMS Contributor's copies. Rights revert to author.

⊙⊙ THE LONDON MAGAZINE

11 Queen's Gate, London En SW7 5ELU UK. +44 (0)20 7584 5977. **E-mail:** admin@thelondonmagazine.net; editorial@thelondonmagazine.net. **Website:** www.thelondonmagazine.net. **Contact:** Editor. Estab. 1732. Unpublished poetry, short fiction, features on literary/artistic themes, reviews. Can take approx. 1 month to respond. Publications currently unpaid. Bimonthly. We look for poetry and short fiction that startles and entertains us. We are obviously interested in writing that has a London focus, but not exclusively so, since London is a world city with international concerns. Reviews, essays, memoir pieces and features should be erudite, lucid and incisive. Please look at *The London Magazine* before you submit work, so that you can see the type of material we publish. Non-fiction pieces should be between 800 and 2,000 words. Short fiction should address mature and sophisticated themes. Moreover, it should have an elegance of style, structure and characterisation. We do not normally publish science fiction or fantasy writing, or erotica. We will consider short stories of up to 4,000 words in length. Abstraction is the enemy of good poetry. Poetry should display a commitment to the ultra specificities of language, and show a refined sense of simile and metaphor. The structure should be tight and exact. We do not normally publish long, loose poems.

NEEDS 6,000 words maximum.

HOW TO CONTACT Send complete ms.

PAYMENT/TERMS Pays minimum £20; average £30-50; maximum £150 for a major contribution.

⊙⊙⊙ MAMAZINA

Mom Writer's Productions, LLC., Mamazina Magazine, PO Box 210, Hastings on Hudson NY 10706. (877)771-6667. **E-mail:** managingeditor@mamazina.com. **E-mail:** mamazinamagazine@gmail.com. **Website:** http://mamazina.wordpress.com. **Contact:** Kris Underwood, Managing Editor. Estab. 2005.

Online and print literary magazine. Print: 8x10, 84 pages. Contains illustrations. Includes photographs. "*Mamazina*—formerly *Mom Writer's Literary Magazine*—is a publication written by moms for moms across the globe who come together to share their stories. We publish creative nonfiction essays, fiction, columns, book reviews, profiles about mom writers and visual art. *Mamazina* seeks writing that is vivid, complex and practical. We are not looking for 'sugarcoated' material. We believe the art of Motherhood is deserving of literary attention. We are a literary magazine for mothers with something to say. We're proud to have published essays that are emotionally moving, smart, raw and, sometimes, humorous. *Mamazina* honors the fulfilling and tedious work that women do by making their stories visible through print." Semi-annual. Estab. 2005-Online, 2007- Print. Circ. 6,000. Member Mom Writers Publishing Cooperative. "Send all submissions to mamazinamagazine@gmail.com with poetry, fiction, etc., along with "Submission" in the subject line. Please include a short cover letter with contact information and bio. We strongly prefer email submissions, but if you must send via snail mail: PO Box 210 Hastings On Hudson, NY 10706. A submission fee of $12 must accompany all pieces. Online payments: JoinMama.net or include a check made out to MAMAPALOOZA. We prefer previously unpublished pieces. We do consider reprints, if you have the rights and the work is not currently available online. The author retains rights. Please credit us if your work is republished. Simultaneous submissions are OK, but please notify us if accepted elsewhere. We will review your work and get back to you within 3-4 weeks. For all essay and poetry submissions — we read submissions in Dec./January and June/July."

NEEDS Adventure, ethnic/multicultural, family saga, feminist, literary, mainstream, romance (contemporary, suspense). Special interests: motherhood. Does not want children/juvenile, religious, horror, or western. Receives 20-30 mss/month. Accepts 2 mss/issue; 4 mss/year. Ms published 1-4 months after acceptance. **Publishes 2 new writers/year.** Length: 800-1,500 words. Average length: 1,400 words. Publishes short shorts. Average length of short shorts: 1,200 words. Also publishes literary essays, book reviews, poetry. Send review copies to Kathy Schlaeger, Reviews Editor, Mom Writer's Literary Magazine, 6224 Deer Run Road Liberty Township, OH 45044. Rarely comments on/critiques rejected mss.

HOW TO CONTACT *MAMAZINA* does not accept any submissions by snail mail. Please send all submissions via e-mail. Please *do not* send attachments. Send complete ms with cover letter. Include estimated word count, brief bio. For all essay and poetry submissions—we read submissions in January and July. All submissions carry a $12 reading fee, payable by using the PayPal on our website. Please read our letter explaining the new submission procedure. Responds to mss in 1-3 months. Considers simultaneous submissions. Guidelines available on website.

PAYMENT/TERMS Writers receive $100 max., 1 contributor's copy. Additional copies $10. Pays on publication. Acquires one time rights. Publication is copyrighted.

TIPS "May be any genre. Story must flow smoothly and really get our attention (all editors). Must be within the word limits and submitted correctly. Also, please have a title for your story."

THE NOCTURNAL LYRIC

P.O. Box 542, Astoria OR 97103. **E-mail:** thenocturnallyric@rocketmail.com. **Website:** www.angelfire.com/ca/nocturnallyric. **Contact:** Susan Moon, editor. Estab. 1987. "Annual magazine. Magazine: 812×11; 40 pages; illustrations. Fiction and poetry submitted should have a bizarre horror theme. Our audience encompasses people who stand proudly outside of the mainstream society."

NEEDS Horror (dark fantasy, futuristic, psychological, supernatural, satirical). "No sexually graphic material—it's too overdone in the horror genre lately." Receives 25-30 unsolicited mss/month. Accepts 10-11 mss/issue; 10-11 mss/year. Publishes ms 1 year after acceptance. Publishes 20 new writers/year. Recently published work by Murphy Edwards, Tim Scott, Richard Grebe, Melissa S. Mutlu, and Jessica Brown. Length: 2,000 words maximum; average length: 1,500 words. Publishes short shorts. Also publishes literary essays, poetry. Rarely comments on rejected mss.

HOW TO CONTACT Send complete ms with cover letter. Include estimated word count. Responds in 3 month to queries; 8 months to mss. Accepts simultaneous, multiple submissions and reprints. Sample copy for $2 (back issue); $3 (current issue). Writer's guidelines online. Pays with discounts on subscriptions and discounts on copies of issue. Pays on acceptance. Not copyrighted. Any stories submitted now won't be read until Feb 2012. If you submit a story now,

#72 is the soonest you will be printed if accepted. #72 will be out in the Fall of 2012. Any poetry sent after March 2011 won't be read until March 2012. If you submit a poem now, #72 is the soonest you will be printed if accepted. #72 will be out in the Fall of 2012. **TIPS** "A manuscript stands out when the story has a very original theme and the ending is not predictable. Don't be afraid to be adventurous with your story. Mainstream horror can be boring. Surreal, satirical horror is what true nightmares are all about."

NOVA SCIENCE FICTION MAGAZINE

17983 Paseo Del Sol, Chino Hills CA 91709-3947. **Contact:** Wesley Kawato. Estab. 1999. Zine specializing in evangelical Christian science fiction: 812×512; 64 pages; cardstock cover. "We publish religious science fiction short stories, no fantasy or horror. One story slot per issue will be reserved for a story written from an evangelical Christian viewpoint." Biannual. Estab. 1999. Circ. 25.

"NOVA doesn't accept unsolicited manuscripts; writers must first query and in the query must indicate you've been published, attended Clarion Workshop or meet other requirements. **Pay:** Half a penny per word . **Word count (maximum):** 7,000 words. Does not **want:** Stories showing that man will one day outgrow his need for religion; in fact, makes a point of saying magazine isn con-trolled by Libertarians or the Secular Humanist. **Mail query to:** NOVA Science Fiction, C/O: Wesley Kawato, 17983 Paseo Del Sol, Chino Hills, CA 91709-3947."

NEEDS Science fiction (hard science/technological, soft/sociological, religious). "No stories where the villain is a religious fanatic and stories that assume the truth of evolution." Accepts 6 mss/issue; 12 mss/year. Publishes ms 3 months after acceptance. **Publishes 7 new writers/year.** Recently published work by Jonathan Cooper, Lawrence Dagstine, Don Kerr, Gary Carter, Wesley Lambert, Susan Taylor, Erik Leinhart, David Baumann, Francis Alexander, Mark Galbert, Howard Bowman. Length: 250-7,000 words; average length: 4,000 words. Publishes short shorts. Sometimes comments on rejected mss.

HOW TO CONTACT Query first. Include estimated word count and list of publications. Responds in 3 months to queries and mss. Send SASE (or IRC) for return of ms. Accepts reprints, multiple submissions. Sample copy for $6. Guidelines free for SASE.

PAYMENT/TERMS Pays $1.25-35. Pays on publication for first North American serial rights. Not copyrighted.

OPIUM MAGAZINE

Literary Humor for the Deliriously Captivated, 166 Albion St., San Francisco CA 94110. **E-mail:** opiumforthearts@gmail.com. **Website:** http://opiummagazine.com. **Contact:** Todd Zuniga, editor. Biannual magazine. Contains black-and-white cartoons, illustrations, and photographs. "*Opium Magazine* displays an eclectic mix of stories, poetry, reviews, cartoons, interviews and much more. It features 'estimated reading times' that precede each piece. While the focus is often humorous literature, we love to publish heartbreaking, serious work. Our rule is that all work must be well written and engaging from the very first sentence. While we publish traditional pieces, we're primarily engaged by writers who take risks." Updated daily. Estab. 2001. Circ. 25,000 hits/month. Member CLMP.

NEEDS Comics/graphic novels, experimental, humor/satire, literary, mainstream. "Vignettes and first-person 'look at what a whacky time I had going to Spain' stories aren't going to get past first base with us." Receives 200 mss/month. Accepts 60 mss/year. Manuscript published 4 months after acceptance. Agented fiction 10%. **Publishes 10-12 new writers/year.** Published Etgar Keret, Art Spiegelman, Jack Handey, Terese Svoboda. Length: 50-1,200 words. Average length: 700 words. Publishes short shorts. Average length of short shorts: 400 words. Also publishes literary essays, literary criticism, poetry. Sometimes comments on/critiques rejected mss.

HOW TO CONTACT Send complete ms with cover letter by e-mail only at: opiumforthearts@gmail.com. Ms received via snail mail will not be read. Include estimated word count, brief bio, list of publications, and your favorite book. Responds to queries in 2 weeks. Responds to mss in 15 weeks. Considers simultaneous submissions. Guidelines available via e-mail or on website.

PAYMENT/TERMS Acquires first North American serial rights. Publication is copyrighted.

ORACLE STORY & LETTERS

7510 Lake Glen Drive, Glen Dale MD 20769. (301)352-2533. **Fax:** (301)352-2529. **E-mail:** hekwonna@aol.

com. **Contact:** Obi H. Ekwonna, publisher. Estab. 1989. Magazine: 512×812; 60 lb. white bound paper. Quarterly. Estab. 1989. Circ. 1,000.

NEEDS Adventure, children's/juvenile (adventure, fantasy, historical, mystery, series), comics/graphic novels, ethnic/multicultural, family saga, fantasy (sword and sorcery), historical, literary, mainstream, military/war, romance (contemporary, historical, suspense), thriller/espionage, western (frontier saga), young adult/teen (adventure, historical). Does not want gay/lesbian or erotica works. Receives 10 unsolicited mss/month. Accepts 7 mss/issue. Publishes ms 4 months after acceptance. **Publishes 5 new writers/year.** Recently published work by Joseph Manco, I.B.S. Sesay. Publishes short shorts. Also publishes literary essays, literary criticism, poetry. Rarely comments on rejected mss.

HOW TO CONTACT Send complete ms. Accepts submissions by disk. Send SASE (or IRC) for return of the ms, or send a disposable copy of the ms and #10 SASE for reply only. Responds in 1 month to mss. Accepts multiple submissions. Sample copy for $10. Writer's guidelines for #10 SASE, or by e-mail.

PAYMENT/TERMS Pays 1 contributor's copy. Pays on publication for first North American serial rights.

PARADOXISM

200 College Rd., Gallup NM 87301. **Fax:** (503)863-7532. **E-mail:** smarand@unm.edu. **Website:** www.gallup.unm.edu/~smarandache/a/paradoxism.htm. **Contact:** Dr. Florentin Smarandache. Estab. 1993. Magazine: 812×11; 100 pages; illustrations. "*Paradoxism* is an avant-garde movement based on excessive use of antinomies, antitheses, contradictions, paradoxes in the literary creations set up by the editor in the 1980s as an anti-totalitarian protest." Annual. Circ. 500.

NEEDS Experimental, literary. "Contradictory, uncommon, experimental, avant garde." Plans specific themes in the next year. Publishes annual special fiction issue or anthology. Receives 5 unsolicited mss/month. Accepts 10 mss/issue. Recently published work by Mircea Monu, Doru Motoc and Patrick Pinard. Publishes short shorts. Also publishes literary essays, literary criticism, poetry. Sometimes comments on rejected mss. "Please send: a) paradoxist essays, criticism, poetry, short dramas, short prose, or b) outer-art essays, criticism, outer-paintings, outer-collages, outer-photos, respectively to: "*Paradoxism*" journal (or Outer-Art journal)."

HOW TO CONTACT Send a disposable copy of ms. Responds in 2 months to mss. Accepts simultaneous submissions. Sample copy for $19.95 and 812×11 SASE. Writer's guidelines online.

PAYMENT/TERMS Pays subscription. Pays on publication. Not copyrighted.

TIPS "We look for work that refers to the paradoxism or is written in the paradoxist style. The Basic Thesis of the paradoxism: everything has a meaning and a non-meaning in a harmony with each other. The Essence of the paradoxism: a) the sense has a non-sense, and reciprocally b) the non-sense has a sense. The Motto of the paradoxism: 'All is possible, the impossible too!' The Symbol of the paradoxism: a spiral—optic illusion, or vicious circle."

PASSAGES NORTH

English Department, Northern Michigan University, 1401 Presque Isle Ave., Marquette MI 49855. (906)227-1203. **E-mail:** passages@nmu.edu. **Website:** www.passagesnorth.com. Estab. 1979. *Passages North*, published annually in spring, prints poetry, short fiction, creative nonfiction, essays, and interviews. Magazine: 7×10; 200-300 pgs; 60 lb. paper. Publishes work by established and emerging writers. Has published poetry by Moira Egan, Frannie Lindsay, Ben Lerner, Bob Hicok, Gabe Gudding, John McNally, Steve Almond, Tracy Winn, and Midege Raymond. *Passages North* is 250 pages. Single copy: $13; subscription: $13/year, $23 for 2 years.

NEEDS Receives 200 unsolicited mss/month. Accepts 12-15 mss/year. Reads mss September-May. **Publishes 10% new writers/year.** Also publishes literary essays, poetry. Comments on rejected mss when there is time. Send complete ms with cover letter. Responds in 2-4 months to mss. Accepts simultaneous submissions. Pays 2 contributor's copies. Rights revert to author upon publication. Publication is copyrighted. Occasionally sponsors contests; check website for details. No genre fiction, science fiction, "typical commercial press work." Length: 7,000 words (max). Average length 3,000 words. Publishes short shorts; average length: 1,000 words.

THE PUCKERBRUSH REVIEW

English Dept., University of Maine, 413 Neville Hall, Orono ME 04469. **E-mail:** sanphip@aol.com. **Website:** http://puckerbrushreview.com. **Contact:** Sanford Phippen, Editor. Estab. 1971. Magazine: 9×12; 80-100 pages; illustrations. "We publish interviews, fiction, reviews, poetry for a literary audience." Semi-annual. Estab. 1979. Circ. 500. "Wants to see more original, quirky and well-written fiction. No genre fiction. Nothing cliché, nothing overly sensational except in its human interest." Receives 30 unsolicited mss/month. Accepts 6 mss/issue; 12 mss/year. Publishes ms 1 year after acceptance. Recently published work by John Sullivan, Beth Thorpe, Chenoweth Hall, Merle Hillman, Wayne Burke. Publishes short shorts. Also publishes literary essays, literary criticism, poetry. Sometimes comments on rejected mss. Include SASE. Responds in 2 months to mss. Accepts simultaneous, multiple submissions. Sample copy for $3. Writer's guidelines for SASE. Reviews fiction and poetry. Pays in contributor's copies. *The Puckerbrush Review*, a print-only journal published twice/year, looks for "freshness and simplicity." Has published poetry by Wolly Swist and Muska Nagel. Submit 5 poems at a time. Guidelines available for SASE. Pays 2 contributor's copies.

> "Please submit your poetry, short stories, literary essays and reviews through our website link. Hard-copy submissions will no longer be accepted."

SLATE & STYLE

2861 S. 93 Plaza APT 8, Omaha NE 68124. (402)350-1735. **E-mail:** bpollpeter@hotmail.com. **Website:** www.nfb-writers-division.org. **Contact:** Bridgit Pollpeter, editor. Estab. 1982. Quarterly magazine: 28-32 print/40 Braille pages; available by e-mail, cassette and in large print. "Accepts articles of interest to writers, and resources for blind writers." Needs adventure, fantasy, humor/satire, contemporary, blindness. No erotica. "Avoid theme of death." Does not read mss in June or July. Publishes 2 new writers/year. Recently published work by Bruce Adkins, Patricia Hubschman, Kristen Diaz, and Amy Krout-horn. Accepts short stories up to 2,000 words. Publishes short shorts. Also publishes literary criticism, poetry. Sometimes comments on rejected mss. Accepts submissions by e-mail: bpollpeter@hotmail.com. Responds in 3-6 weeks to queries; 3-6 weeks to mss. Sample copy for $3. Pays in contributor's copies. Acquires one time rights. Sponsors awards/contests.

SPACE AND TIME

458 Elizabeth Ave., Somerset NJ 08873. **E-mail:** nytebird45@aol.com. **Website:** www.spaceandtimemag-azine.com. **Contact:** Linda D. Addison. Estab. 1966. Magazine. 8½x11, 48 pages, matte paper, glossy cover. Contains illustrations. "We love stories that blend elements—horror and science fiction, fantasy with SF elements, etc. We challenge writers to try something new and send us their unclassifiable works—what other publications reject because the work doesn't fit in their 'pigeonholes.'" Quarterly. Circ. 2,000. Receives 250 mss/reading period. Accepts 8 mss/issue; 32 mss/year. Only open during announced reading periods. Check website to see if submissions are open. Ms published 3-6 months after acceptance. **Publishes 2-4 new writers/year.** Published PD Cacek, AR Morlan, Jeffrey Ford, Charles De Lint and Jack Ketchum. Also publishes poetry, occasional book reviews. Sample copy available for $6.50. Guidelines available only on website. Additional copies $5. Acquires first North American serial rights, one-time rights. Publication is copyrighted.

NEEDS Fantasy (high, sword and sorcery, modern), horror (dark fantasy, futuristic, psychological, supernatural), romance (futuristic/time travel), science fiction (hard science/technological, soft/sociological). Does not want anything without some sort of speculative element. Length: 1,000-10,000/words. Average length: 6,500 words. Average length of short shorts: 1,000.

HOW TO CONTACT Send review copies to Publisher Hildy Silverman, hildy@spaceandtimemagazine.com. Sometimes comments on/critiques rejected mss. Send complete ms with cover letter. Accepts submissions by e-mail only. Include estimated word count, brief bio, list of publications. Responds to queries in 4-6 weeks. Responds to mss in 4-6 weeks. Send disposable query letter and #10 SASE for reply only if unable to email submission.

PAYMENT/TERMS Payment made upon publication and is a flat $5.00 per poem plus 2 contributor's copies.

STEAMPUNK MAGAZINE

Strangers in a Tangled Wilderness, Wales. **E-mail:** readers@steampunkmagazine.com. **Website:** steampunkmagazine.com. **Contact:** Allegra Hawksmoor. "**We are currently not accepting submissions.** Please keep in mind before submitting that we publish under Creative Commons licensing, which means that people will be free to reproduce and alter your work for noncommercial purposes. We also, regretfully, are no longer able to offer payment to our contributors."

Magazine/Online magazine. 8 1/2×7", 80 pages, recycled paper. Contains illustrations. "*SteamPunk Magazine* is involved in supporting the SteamPunk subculture, a subculture that offers a competing vision of humanity's interaction with technology, a subculture that wears too many goggles." Quarterly. Estab. 2007. Circ. 1,000 print; 60,000 online.

NEEDS Adventure, comics/graphic novels, ethnic/multicultural, experimental, fantasy (space fantasy), feminist, horror (dark fantasy, supernatural), humor/satire, literary, military/war, mystery, romance (gothic, historical), science fiction, western. Special interests: steampunk. "We are not interested in promoting misogynist, nationalistic, pro-colonial, monarchical, homophobic, or otherwise useless text." List of upcoming themes available on website. Receives 5-12 mss/month. Accepts 1-2 mss/issue; 3-6 mss/year. Manuscript published 2 months after acceptance. **Publishes 6-10 new writers/year.** Published John Reppion, Margaret Killjoy, GD Falksen, Will Strop, Catastraphone Orchestra, and Olga Izakson. Length: 500-6,000 words. Average length: 3,500 words. Publishes short shorts. Average length of short shorts: 800 words. Also publishes literary essays, literary criticism, book reviews. Send review copies to Magpie Killjoy. Sometimes comments on/critiques rejected mss.

HOW TO CONTACT Send complete ms with cover letter. Accepts submissions by e-mail only. Include brief bio, list of publications. Responds to queries in 2 weeks. Responds to mss in 2 months. Considers simultaneous submissions, previously published submissions, multiple submissions. Sample copy available for $3, on website. Guidelines available on website.

PAYMENT/TERMS Pays in contributor copies.

○ TRAIL OF INDISCRETION

Fortress Publishing, Inc., 3704 Hartzdale Dr., Camp Hill PA 17011. (717) 350-8760. **E-mail:** fortresspublishinginc@yahoo.com; cosmicshark@comcast.net. **Website:** www.fortresspublishinginc.com. **Contact:** Brian Koscienski, editor in chief. Zine specializing in genre fiction: digest (512×812), 48 pages, 24 lb. paper, glossy cover. "We publish genre fiction—sci-fi, fantasy, horror, etc. We'd rather have a solid story containing great characters than a weak story with a surprise 'trick' ending." Quarterly. Estab. 2006. Circ. 100.

NEEDS Trail of Indiscretion accepts horror, sci fi, and fantasy short fiction (5000 words or less). No graphic sex or violence/no profanity. Submit story as a .doc to: fortresspublishinginc@yahoo.com. Adventure, fantasy (space fantasy, sword and sorcery), horror (dark fantasy, futuristic, psychological, supernatural), humor/satire, psychic/supernatural/occult, science fiction (hard science/technological, soft/sociological). Does not want "touchy-feely 'coming of age' stories or stories where the protagonist mopes about contemplating his/her own mortality." Accepts 5-7 mss/issue. Manuscript published 3-9 months after acceptance. **Publishes 2-10 new writers/year.** Published Cliff Ackman (debut), Roger Arnold, Susan Kerr (debut), Kristine Ong Muslim, Tala Bar, CJ Henderson, Danielle Ackley-McPhail. Length: 5,000 words (max). Average length: 3,000 words. Publishes short shorts. Sometimes comments on/critiques rejected mss.

HOW TO CONTACT Send complete ms with cover letter. Accepts submissions by e-mail. Include estimated word count, brief bio, list of publications. Responds to queries in 1-2 weeks. Responds to mss in 1-10 weeks. Send either SASE (or IRC) for return of ms or disposable copy of ms and #10 SASE for reply only. Considers simultaneous submissions, previously published submissions. Sample copy available for $4 or on website. Guidelines available for SASE, via e-mail, on website.

PAYMENT/TERMS Writers receive 1 contributor copy. Additional copies $2.50. Pays on publication. Acquires one time rights. Publication is copyrighted.

○◐ TRANSITION: AN INTERNATIONAL REVIEW

104 Mount Auburn St., 3R, Cambridge MA 02138. (617)496-2845. **Fax:** (617)496-2877. **E-mail:** transition@fas.harvard.edu. **Website:** www.transitionmagazine.com. **Contact:** Sara Bruya, managing editor. Estab. 1961. Magazine: 912×612; 150-175 pages; 70 lb. Finch Opaque paper; 100 lb. White Warren Lustro dull cover; illustrations; photos. "Transition Magazine is a trimestrial international review known for compelling and controversial writing from and about Africa and the Diaspora. This prestigious magazine is edited at the W.E.B. Du Bois Institute of Harvard Univ. by Tommie Shelby, Vincent Brown, and Glenda Carpio. The magazine attracts famous contributors such as Wole Soyinka, Jamaica Kincaid, and Carlos Fuentes, but is also committed to providing space for new voices; Transition recently made a capsule collection of Cape Verde's finest fiction available for the first time in English. In the words of our publisher, Henry Louis Gates, Jr., Transi-

tion seeks to publish fiction, poetry, and criticism that wrestles with "the freshest, most compelling, most curious ideas about race—indeed, about what it means to be human—today." Quarterly. Circ. 3,000.

NEEDS Publishes fiction, poetry, creative nonfiction, and cultural and political criticism. Sometimes comments on rejected mss.

HOW TO CONTACT E-mail us to request the Transition Style Guide. Email submissions are preferred. If submitting by mail, please include a SASE to receive a response from Transition. Mss will not be returned. You will receive confirmation of receipt and notification of editorial decision after review of your work. We are not able to respond to requests for status updates. If your piece is longer than 20 pages, please also send a hard copy (in Times New Roman, font size 12, double spaced). For all submissions, please include the following information in your email or cover letter and in the top left corner of the first page of all documents: name, address, e-mail address, word count, date of submission. Please also include a title with each work. Sara Bruya, Managing Editor.

PAYMENT/TERMS 1 contributor's copy.

⃠Ⓢ WEIRD TALES

P.O. Box 38190, Tallahassee FL 32315. **E-mail:** weirdtales@gmail.com. **Website:** www.weirdtales.

net. **Contact:** Marvin Kaye, editor-in-chief. Estab. 1923. "We publish fantastic fiction, supernatural horror for an adult audience." Published 6 times a year. fantasy (sword and sorcery), horror, psychic/supernatural/occult, translations. No hard science fiction or non-fantasy. Agented fiction 10%. **Publishes 8 new writers/year.** Recently published work by Michael Moorcock, Tanith Lee, Thomas Ligotti, Darrell Schweitzer, Sarah Monette and Michael Boatman. Length: up to 10,000 words, but very few longer than 8,000; average length: 4,000 words. Publishes short shorts. Send complete ms via submissions manager online. No multiple submissions. Also accepts e-mail submissions to weirdtales@gmail.com. For hardcopy submissions through the mail: provide an SASE with proper postage to ensure a response. If the postage is not enough to return the manuscript, it will be considered disposable. *Weird Tales* is not responsible for loss or damage to any unsolicited work Sample copy for $6. Writer's guidelines for #10 SASE or by e-mail. Reviews books of fantasy fiction. Pays 3-4¢/word and 2 contributor's copies on acceptance.

NEEDS "Looking for darkly fantastical fiction, work that is unique and unusual. Stories that are recognized as weird tales for the 21st Century."

ONLINE MARKETS

As production and distribution costs go up and the number of subscribers falls, more and more magazines are giving up print publication and moving online. Relatively inexpensive to maintain and quicker to accept and post submissions, online fiction sites are growing fast in numbers and legitimacy. The benefit for writers is that your stories can get more attention in online journals than in small literary journals. Small journals have small print runs—500-1,000 copies—so there's a limit on how many people will read your work. There is no limit when your work appears online.

There is also no limit to the types of online journals being published, offering outlets for a rich and diverse community of voices. These include genre sites, particular those for science fiction/fantasy and horror, and mainstream short fiction markets. Online literary journals range from the traditional to those with a decidedly more quirky bent. Writers will also find online outlets for more highly experimental and multimedia work.

While the medium of online publication is different, the traditional rules of publishing apply to submissions. Writers should research the site and archives carefully, looking for a match in sensibility for their work. Follow submission guidelines exactly and submit courteously. True, these sites aren't bound by traditional print schedules, so your work theoretically may be published more quickly. But that doesn't mean online journals have larger staffs, so exercise patience with editors considering your manuscript.

Also, while reviewing the listings in this market section, notice they are grouped differently from other market listings. In our Literary Magazines section, for example, you'll find primarily publications searching for only literary short fiction. But Online Markets are grouped by medium, so you'll find publishers of mystery short stories listed next to those looking for horror next to those specializing in flash fiction, so review with care. In addition, online markets with print counterparts can be found listed in the print markets sections.

A final note about online publication: Like literary journals, the majority of these markets are either nonpaying or very low paying. In addition, writers will not receive print copies of the publications because of the medium. So in most cases, do not expect to be paid for your exposure.

5-TROPE

E-mail: editor.5trope@gmail.com. **Website:** www.5trope.com. **Contact:** Gunnar Benediktsson, editor. Online literary journal. "We aim to publish the new and original in fiction, poetry and new media. We are seeking writers with a playful seriousness about language and form." Quarterly. Estab. 1999. Circ. 5,000.

NEEDS Avant-garde prose, experimental, literary. "No religious, horror, fantasy, espionage." Receives 75 unsolicited mss/month. Accepts 6 mss/issue; 18 mss/year. Publishes ms 6-12 months after acceptance. **Publishes 5 new writers/year.** Recently published work by Cole Swensen, Carol Novack, Christopher Kennedy, Mike Topp, Norman Lock, Jeff Johnson, Peter Markus, Mandee Wright, and Jane Unrue. Length: 25-5,000 words; average length: 1,000 words. Publishes short shorts. Also publishes poetry. Sometimes comments on rejected mss.

HOW TO CONTACT Accepts submissions by e-mail. Send complete mss electronically. Sample copy online.

PAYMENT/TERMS Acquires first rights. Sends galleys to author.

TIPS "Before submitting, please visit our site, read an issue, and consult our guidelines for submission. Include your story within the body of an e-mail, not as an attachment. Include a descriptive subject line to get around spam filters. Experimental work should have a clarity about it, and should never be sentimental. Our stories are about the moment of rupture, not the moment of closure."

THE 13TH WARRIOR REVIEW

P.O. Box 5122, Seabrook NJ 08302-3511. **E-mail:** the-editor@asteriusonline.com. **Website:** www.asteriusonline.com/13thWR/. **Contact:** John C. Erianne, editor. Estab. 1997. *The 13th Warrior Review*, published 2-3 times annually online, seeks "excellent literary-quality poetry as well as fiction, essays, and reviews. All excellent poetry will be given serious consideration." Has published poetry by P.Q. Perron, Cindy Rosmus, B.Z Niditch, Genine Hanns, John Sweet, and Corey Ginsberg.

NEEDS Literary/mainstream, erotica, experimental, magical realism, meta-fiction. Receives 500 unsolicited mss/month. Accepts 4-8 mss/issue; 10-15 mss/year. **Publishes 1-2 new writers/year.** Recently published work by Cindy Rosmus, Jeff Blechle, Elizabeth Farren, and Andrew Hellem. Length: 500-6,000 words; aver-

age length: 1,800 words. Publishes short shorts. Also publishes literary essays, literary criticism, poetry, and book reviews. Sometimes comments on rejected mss.

HOW TO CONTACT Reviews fiction. Send complete ms. Include estimated word count, brief bio and address/e-mail. Send SASE or IRC for return of ms or send a disposable copy of ms and #10 SASE for reply only. Accepts submissions by e-mail (no attachments).

THE ADIRONDACK REVIEW

Black Lawrence Press, 8405 Bay Parkway, Apt C8, Brooklyn NY 11214. **E-mail:** editors@theadirondack-review.com; angela@blacklawrencepress.com. **Website:** www.adirondackreview.homestead.com. **Contact:** Angela Leroux-Lindsey, Kara Christenson, Diane Goettel, editor. Estab. 2000. *The Adirondack Review*, published quarterly online, is a literary journal dedicated to quality free verse poetry and short fiction as well as book and film reviews, art, photography, and interviews. "We are open to both new and established writers. Our only requirement is excellence. We would like to publish more French and German poetry translations as well as original poems in these languages. We publish an eclectic mix of voices and styles, but all poems should show attention to craft. We are open to beginners who demonstrate talent, as well as established voices. The work should speak for itself."

NEEDS Adventure, experimental, family saga, gay, historical (general), psychological, translations. Does not want sci-fi, fantasy. Receives over 200 mss/month. Accepts 5-10 mss/issue; 20-30 mss/year. Manuscript published 1-5 months after acceptance. Agented fiction 5%. **Publishes 15% new writers/year.** Published Frank Haberle, Steve Gillis, Melinda Misrala, Kate Swoboda. Length: 700-8,000 words. Average length: 2,000 words. Publishes short shorts. Average length of short shorts: 800 words. Also publishes literary essays, literary criticism, book reviews, poetry. Rarely comments on/critiques rejected mss.

HOW TO CONTACT Send complete ms with cover letter. Accepts submissions by e-mail. Include estimated word count, brief bio, list of publications, and "how they learned about the magazine." Send either SASE (or IRC) for return of ms or disposable copy of ms and #10 SASE for reply only. Considers simultaneous submissions, multiple submissions.

ALLEGORY

1225 Liberty Bell Dr., Cherry Hill NJ 08003. **E-mail:** submissions@allegoryezine.com. **Website:** www.allegoryezine.com. **Contact:** Ty Drago, editor. Estab. 1998. Online magazine specializing in science fiction, fantasy and horror. "We are an e-zine by writers for writers. Our articles focus on the art, craft and business of writing. Our links and editorial policy all focus on the needs of fiction authors." Triannual.

NEEDS Fantasy (space fantasy, sword and sorcery, sociological), horror (dark fantasy, futuristic, supernatural), science fiction (hard science/technological, soft/sociological). "No media tie-ins (*Star Trek*, *Star Wars*, etc., or space opera, vampires)." Receives 150 unsolicited mss/month. Accepts 8 mss/issue; 24 mss/year. Publishes ms 1-2 months after acceptance. Agented fiction 5%. **Publishes 10 new writers/year.** Length: 1,500-7,500 words; average length: 4,500 words. Also publishes literary essays, literary criticism. Often comments on rejected mss.

HOW TO CONTACT All submissions should be sent by e-mail (no letters or telephone calls please) in either text or RTF format. Please place "Submission [Title]-[first and last name] in the subject line. Include the following in both the body of the e-mail and the attachment: your name, name to use on the story (byline), if different, your preferred e-mail address, your mailing address, the story's title and the story's word count. Responds in 8 weeks to mss. Accepts simultaneous submissions and reprints. Writer's guidelines online.

PAYMENT/TERMS $15/story-article. Pays on publication for one time, electronic rights.

TIPS "Give us something original, preferably with a twist. Avoid gratuitous sex or violence. Funny always scores points. Be clever, imaginative, but be able to tell a story with proper mood and characterization. Put your name and e-mail address in the body of the story. Read the site and get a feel for it before submitting."

ANDERBO.COM

Anderbo Publishing, 270 Lafayette St., Suite 1412, New York NY 10012-3364. **E-mail:** editors@anderbo.com. **Website:** www.anderbo.com. **Contact:** Rick Rofihe, editor-in-chief. Online literary magazine/journal. "Quality fiction, poetry, 'fact' and photography on a website with 'print-feel' design." Member CLMP.

> Received the Best New Online Magazine or Journal, *storySouth* Million Writers Award in 2005.

NEEDS Literary. Does not want any genre literature. "We're interested only in literary fiction, poetry, and literary 'fact.'" Receives 200 mss/month. Accepts 20

mss/year. Ms published one month after acceptance. **Publishes 6 new writers/year.** Published Lisa Margonelli, Margot Berwin, Jeffrey Lent, and Susan Breen. Length: 3,500. Average length: 1,750 words. Publishes short shorts. Average length of short shorts: 1,400 words. Also publishes literary essays, poetry. Rarely comments on/critiques rejected mss.

HOW TO CONTACT Send complete ms with cover letter. Accepts submissions by e-mail. Include brief bio, list of publications. Responds to queries in 2 weeks. Responds to mss in 1-4 weeks. Considers simultaneous submissions. Guidelines available on website.

PAYMENT/TERMS Acquires first rights, first North American serial rights, one time rights, electronic rights. Publication is copyrighted.

TIPS "We are looking for fiction that is unique, urgent, accessible and involving. Look at our site and read what we've already published."

BABEL: THE MULTILINGUAL, MULTICULTURAL ONLINE JOURNAL AND COMMUNITY OF ARTS AND IDEAS

E-mail: submissions@towerofbabel.com. **Website:** http://towerofbabel.com. **Contact:** Malcolm Lawrence, Editor-in-Chief. Estab. 1995. Publishes regional reports from international stringers all over the planet, as well as features, round table discussions, fiction, columns, poetry, erotica, travelogues, and reviews of all the arts and editorials. We're interested in fiction, non-fiction and poetry from all over the world, including multicultural or multilingual work. Cover letter is required. Reviews books/chapbooks of poetry and other magazines, single- and multi-book format. Open to unsolicited reviews. Send materials for review consideration.

> *Babel* is recognized by the UN as one of the most important social and human sciences online periodicals.

NEEDS We are currently looking for WordPress bloggers in the following languages: Arabic, Bulgarian, Bengali, Catalan, Czech, Welsh, Danish, German, English, Esperanto, Spanish, Persian, Finnish, Faroese, French, Hebrew, Croatian, Indonesian, Italian, Japanese, Korean, Latvian, Malay, Dutch, Polish, Portuguese, Russian, Albanian, Serbian, Swedish, Tamil, Thai, Ukrainian, Urdu, Uzbek, Vietnamese and Chinese.

HOW TO CONTACT Send queries/mss by email. "Please send submissions with a resumé/cover letter or biography attached to the email." Reviews novels and short story collections.

PAYMENT/TERMS does not pay.

TIPS "We would like to see more fiction with first-person male characters written by female authors, as well as more fiction first-person female characters written by male authors. We would also like to see that dynamic in action when it comes to other languages, cultures, races, classes, sexual orientations and ages. Know what you are writing about and write passionately about it."

◑◐◯ THE BARCELONA REVIEW

Correu Vell 12-2, Barcelona 08002 Spain. **E-mail:** editor@barcelonareview.com. **Website:** www.barcelonareview.com. **Contact:** Jill Adams, editor. "*TBR* is an international review of contemporary, cutting-edge fiction published in English, Spanish and Catalan. Our aim is to bring both new and established writers to the attention of a larger audience. Well-known writers such as Alicia Erian in the U.S., Michel Faber in the U.K., Carlos Gardini in Argentina, and Nuria Amat in Spain, for example, were not known outside their countries until appearing in *TBR*. Our multilingual format increases the audience all the more. Internationally known writers, such as Irvine Welsh and Douglas Coupland, have contributed stories that ran in small press anthologies available only in one country. We try to keep abreast of what's happening internationally and to present the best finds every two months. Our intended audience is anyone interested in high-quality contemporary fiction that often (but not always) veers from the mainstream; we assume that our readers are well read and familiar with contemporary fiction in general."

NEEDS Short fiction. "Our bias is towards potent and powerful cutting-edge material; given that general criteria, we are open to all styles and techniques and all genres. No slice-of-life stories, vignettes or reworked fables, and nothing that does not measure up, in your opinion, to the quality of work in our review, which we expect submitters to be familiar with." **Publishes 20 new writers/year.** Recently published work by Niall Griffiths, Adam Haslett, G.K. Wuori, Adam Johnson, Mary Wornov, Emily Carter, Jesse Shepard, and Julie Orringer.

HOW TO CONTACT Send submissions by e-mail as an attached file. Hard copies accepted but cannot be returned. No simultaneous submissions. Reply takes 8 weeks.

PAYMENT/TERMS "In lieu of pay we sometimes offer a highly professional Spanish translation to English language writers and vice versa to Spanish writers. Work is showcased along with two or more known authors in a high quality literary review with an international readership. Author retains all rights although for the Internet only we ask for exclusive rights for the time period agreed upon."

TIPS "Send top drawer material that has been drafted two, three, four times—whatever it takes. Then sit on it for a while and look at it afresh. Keep the text tight. Grab the reader in the first paragraph and don't let go. Keep in mind that a perfectly crafted story that lacks a punch of some sort won't cut it. Make it new, make it different. Surprise the reader in some way. Read the best of the short fiction available in your area of writing to see how yours measures up. Don't send anything off until you feel it's ready and then familiarize yourself with the content of the review/magazine to which you are submitting."

◑ BLACKBIRD

Virginia Commonwealth University Department of English, P.O. Box 843082, Richmond VA 23284. (804)827-4729. **E-mail:** blackbird@vcu.edu. **Website:** www.blackbird.vcu.edu. **Contact:** Mary Flinn, Gregory Donovan, senior editors. Estab. 2001. Online journal: 80+ pages if printed; illustrations; photos. "We strive to maintain the highest quality of writing and design, bringing the best things about a print magazine to the outside world. We publish fiction that is carefully crafted, thoughtful and surprising." Semi-annual. Estab. 2001. Circ. 30,000 readers per month.

NEEDS Literary, novel excerpts. Does not want science fiction, religious/inspirational, condensed novels, horror, romance, children's. Receives 400-600 unsolicited mss/month. Accepts 4-5 mss/issue; 8-10 mss/year. Does not read from April 15-November 1. Publishes ms 3-6 months after acceptance. **Publishes 1-2 new writers/year.** Length: 5,000-10,000 words; average length: 5,000-6,500 words. Also publishes literary essays, literary criticism, poetry. Sometimes comments on rejected mss.

HOW TO CONTACT Send complete ms online at www.blackbirdsubmissions.vcu.edu. Include cover letter, name, address, telephone number, brief biographical comment. Responds in 6 months to mss. Accepts simultaneous submissions. Sample copy online. Writer's guidelines online.

PAYMENT/TERMS Pays $200 for fiction, $40 for poetry. Pays on publication for first North American serial rights.

TIPS "We like a story that invites us into its world, that engages our senses, soul and mind."

🌓🔗💲 THE CAFE IRREAL

E-mail: editors@cafeirreal.com. **Website:** www.cafeirreal.com. **Contact:** G.S. Evans, Alice Whittenburg, coeditors. Estab. 1998. E-zine: illustrations. *"The Cafe Irreal* is a webzine focusing on short stories and short shorts of an irreal nature." Quarterly. "Our audience is composed of people who read or write literary fiction with fantastic themes, similar to the work of Franz Kafka, Kobo Abe, or Clarice Lispector. This is a type of fiction (irreal) that has difficulty finding its way into print in the English-speaking world and defies many of the conventions of American literature especially. As a result ours is a fairly specialized literary publication, and we would strongly recommend that prospective writers look at our current issue and guidelines carefully."Quarterly.

NEEDS Experimental, fantasy (literary), science fiction (literary), translations. "No horror or 'slice-of-life' stories; no genre or mainstream science fiction or fantasy." Accepts 8-10 mss/issue; 30-40 mss/year. Recently published work by Ignacio Padilla, Peter Cherches, Michal Ajvaz, Marianne Villanueva, and Bruce Holland Rogers. Length: 2,000 words (max). Publishes short shorts. Also publishes literary essays, literary criticism. Sometimes comments on rejected mss.

HOW TO CONTACT Accepts submissions by e-mail. "No attachments, include submission in body of e-mail. Include estimated word count." Responds in 2-4 months to mss. No simultaneous submissions. Sample copy online. Writer's guidelines online.

PAYMENT/TERMS Pays 1¢/word, $2 minimum. Pays on publication for first-time electronic rights. Sends galleys to author. True

TIPS "Forget formulas. Write about what you don't know, take me places I couldn't possibly go, don't try to make me care about the characters. Read short fiction by writers such as Franz Kafka, Jorge Luis Borges, Donald Barthelme, Magnus Mills, Ana Maria Shua and Stanislaw Lem. Also read our website and guidelines."

🌓💲 ORSON SCOTT CARD'S INTERGALACTIC MEDICINE SHOW

Hatrack River Publications, P.O. Box 18184, Greensboro NC 27419. **Website:** InterGalacticMedicineShow.

com; oscIGMS.com. **Contact:** Edmund R. Schubert, editor. Estab. 2005. E-zine specializing in science fiction and fantasy. Contains illustrations. "We like to see well-developed milieus and believeable, engaging characters. We also look for clear, unaffected writing. Asimov, Niven, Tolkien, Yolen and Hobb are more likely to be our literary exemplars than James Joyce." Bimonthly.

NEEDS Fantasy (space fantasy, sword and sorcery), horror (dark fantasy, futuristic), science fiction (hard science/technological, soft/sociological), young adult/teen (fantasy/science fiction). Receives 300-400 mss/month. Accepts 7 mss/issue; 30+ mss/year. Ms published 4-9 months after acceptance. Agented fiction 5%. **Publishes 4-6 new writers/year.** Published Peter S. Beagle, Tim Pratt, Eugie Foster, James Maxey, Eric James Stone, Alethea Kontis, Steven Savile and Cat Rambo. Length: 1,000 words (min)-10,000 words (max). Average length: 4,000-7,000 words. Publishes short shorts. Average length of short shorts: 750 words. Also publishes book reviews. Sometimes comments on/critiques rejected mss.

HOW TO CONTACT Submit ms via submission form on website. Include estimated word count, e-mail address. Responds to queries in 2 weeks. Responds to mss in 3-6 months. Considers simultaneous submissions, previously published submissions (if obscure publication). Guidelines available on website.

PAYMENT/TERMS Writers receive 6¢ per word for first 7,500 words, 5¢ per word beyond 7,500, contributor's copy. Pays on publication. Acquires first North American serial rights, electronic rights. Publication is copyrighted.

TIPS "Plain and simple, we want to see plots that go somewhere, filled with people we care about. Stories that show the author has a real undersanding of the subtleties of human nature. Proper manuscript formatting and up-to-date contact information are overlooked by more writers than you could imagine. Also, please bear in mind that all stories must be PG-13 suitable. Gratuitous sex, violence or language will get you rejected right away."

🌓 CEZANNE'S CARROT

Spiritual, Transformational & Visionary Art, Inc., P.O. Box 6037, Santa Fe NM 87502-6037. **E-mail:** query@cezannescarrot.org. **Website:** www.cezannescarrot.org. **Contact:** Barbara Jacksha and Joan Kremer, editors. Online magazine. *"Cezanne's Carrot* publishes "high quality literary fiction and creative nonfiction that explores spiritual, metaphysical, transformational, visionary, or mind-expanding themes. We are most interested in stories that push us into a transcendent realm, that give us a higher understanding of our expanding, multi-dimensional selves."

○ **Publishes 1-5 new writers/year.** Published Bruce Holland Rogers, Tamara Kaye Sellman, Tantra Bensko, R. Virgil Ellis, Rebecca Hodgkins, Cheryl Wood Ruggiero, Corey Mesler, Christine Boyka Kluge, and Charles P. Ries. Length: 100 words (min)-3,000 words (max). Average length: 1,800 words. Publishes short shorts. Send complete ms with cover letter. Include estimated word count, brief bio, list of publications. Pays $10 per story upon publication.

NEEDS Experimental, fantasy (speculative), literary, new age, psychic/supernatural/occult, science fiction (soft/sociological), magical realism, irrealism, visionary, surrealism, metaphysical, spiritual, "and other genres, as long as the work is literary and embraces the journal's metaphysical mission and theme. Does not want horror, gore, murder, serial-killers, abuse stories, drug stories, vampires or other monsters, political stories, war stories, stories written for children, stories that primarily promote an agenda or a particular religion. We're not interested in dogma in any form." Receives 100-200 mss/month. Accepts 24-36 mss/issue; 40-60 mss/year. Manuscript published 1-9 months after acceptance. Does not want horror, gore, murder, serial-killers, abuse stories, drug stories, vampires or other monsters, political stories, war stories, stories written for children, stories that primarily promote an agenda or a particular religion. Not interested in dogma in any form.

HOW TO CONTACT Send complete ms with cover letter. Accepts submissions by e-mail only. Include estimated word count, brief bio, list of publications. Responds to mss in 1-6 months. Considers simultaneous submissions, previously published submissions. Guidelines available on website.

PAYMENT/TERMS Pays $10 per story upon publication. Acquires one time rights, reprint rights.

○○○○○ CHIZINE: TREATMENT OF LIGHT AND SHADE IN WORDS

Canada. Estab. 1997. **E-mail:** savory@rogers.com. **Contact:** Brett Alexander Savory, editor-in-chief. E-zine. "Subtle, sophisticated dark fiction with a literary bent." Quarterly. Estab. 1997. "Subtle, sophisticated dark fiction with a literary bent." Quarterly.

○ Received Bram Stoker Award for Other Media in 2000.

NEEDS Experimental, fantasy, horror (dark fantasy, futuristic, psychological, supernatural), literary, mystery, science fiction (soft/sociological), Does not want "tropes of vampires, werewolves, mummies, monsters, or anything that's been done to death." Receives 100 mss/month. Accepts 3-4 mss/issue; 12-16 mss/year. Does not read June, July, and August due to Chizine Short Story Contest. Length: 4,000 words (max). Publishes short shorts. Average length of short shorts: 500 words. Also publishes poetry. Send to savory@rogers.com to query. Always comments on/critiques rejected mss.

HOW TO CONTACT Send complete ms with cover letter. Accepts only submissions by e-mail. Include estimated word count, brief bio. Responds to queries in 1 week. Responds to mss within 3 months. Considers simultaneous submissions so long as we're told it is simultaneous. Guidelines available on website.

PAYMENT/TERMS Writers receive 7¢/word, with a $280 max. Pays on publication. Acquires all rights for 90 days, then archival rights for one year. Sends any edits to author. Publication is copyrighted. Sponsors the Chizine Short Story contest. Guidelines posted on website around May. See entry in Contests & Awards section.

○⑤ CONTRARY

3133 S. Emerald Ave., Chicago IL 60616-3299. **E-mail:** chicago@contrarymagazine.com (no submissions). **Website:** www.contrarymagazine.com. **Contact:** Jeff McMahon, editor. Estab. 2003. Online literary magazine/journal. Contains illustrations. "*Contrary* publishes fiction, poetry, literary commentary, and prefers work that combines the virtues of all those categories. Founded at the University of Chicago, it now operates independently and not-for-profit on the South Side of Chicago. We like work that is not only contrary in content, but contrary in its evasion of the expectations established by its genre. Our fiction defies traditional story form. For example, a story may bring us to closure without ever delivering an ending. We don't insist on the ending, but we do insist on the closure. And we value fiction as poetic as any poem." Quarterly. Circ. 38,000 unique readers. Member CLMP.

NEEDS Literary. Receives 650 mss/month. Accepts 6 mss/issue; 24 mss/year. Ms published no more than

21 days after acceptance. **Publishes 1 new writer/year.** Published Sherman Alexie, Andrew Coburn, Amy Reed, Clare Kirwan, Stephanie Johnson, Laurence Davies, and Edward McWhinney. Length: 2,000 words (max). Average length: 750 words. Publishes short shorts. Average length of short shorts: 750 words. Also publishes literary essays, poetry. Rarely comments on/critiques rejected mss.

HOW TO CONTACT Accepts submissions through website only. www.contrarymagazine.com/Contrary/Submissions.html. Include estimated word count, brief bio, list of publications. Responds to queries in 2 weeks. Responds to mss in 3 months. Considers simultaneous submissions. Guidelines available on website.

PAYMENT/TERMS Pays $20-60. Pays on publication. Acquires first rights and perpetual archive and anthology rights. Publication is copyrighted. True

TIPS "Beautiful writing catches our eye first. If we realize we're in the presence of unanticipated meaning, that's what clinches the deal. Also, we're not fond of expository fiction. We prefer to be seduced by beauty, profundity and mystery than to be presented with the obvious. We look for fiction that entrances, that stays the reader's finger above the mouse button. That is, in part, why we favor microfiction, flash fiction and short-shorts. Also, we hope writers will remember that most editors are looking for very particular species of work. We try to describe our particular species in our mission statement and our submission guidelines, but those descriptions don't always convey nuance. That's why many editors urge writers to read the publication itself; in the hope that they will intuit an understanding of its particularities. If you happen to write that particular species of work we favor, your submission may find a happy home with us. If you don't, it does not necessarily reflect on your quality or your ability. It usually just means that your work has a happier home somewhere else."

THE COPPERFIELD REVIEW

E-mail: info@copperfieldreview.com. **Website:** www.copperfieldreview.com. **Contact:** Meredith Allard, executive editor. Estab. 2000. "We are an online literary journal that publishes historical fiction and articles, reviews and interviews related to historical fiction. We believe that by understanding the lessons of the past through historical fiction we can gain better insight into the nature of our society today, as well as a better understanding of ourselves." Quarterly.

NEEDS Historical (general), romance (historical), western (frontier saga, traditional). "We will consider submissions in most fiction categories, but the setting must be historical in nature. We don't want to see anything not related to historical fiction." Receives 30 unsolicited mss/month. Accepts 7-10 mss/issue; 28-40 mss/year. Responds to mss during the months of January, April, July, and October. **Publishes "between 30 and 40 percent" new writers/year.** Publishes short shorts. Also publishes literary essays, literary criticism, poetry. Seldom comments on rejected mss. We will consider submissions in most fiction categories, but the setting must be historical in nature. We don't want to see anything not related to historical fiction. Length: 500-3,000 words.

HOW TO CONTACT Send complete ms. Accepts submissions by e-mail. Responds in 6 weeks to queries. Accepts simultaneous, multiple submissions and reprints. Sample copy online. Writer's guidelines online. Reviews fiction. Name and e-mail address should appear on the first page of the submission.

PAYMENT/TERMS Acquires one time rights.

TIPS "We wish to showcase the very best in literary historical fiction. Stories that use historical periods and details to illuminate universal truths will immediately stand out. We are thrilled to receive thoughtful work that is polished, poised and written from the heart. Be professional, and only submit your very best work. Be certain to adhere to a publication's submission guidelines, and always treat your e-mail submissions with the same care you would use with a traditional publisher. Above all, be strong and true to your calling as a writer. It is a difficult, frustrating but wonderful journey. It is important for writers to review our online submission guidelines prior to submitting."

⊘ DARGONZINE

E-mail: dargon@dargonzine.org. **Website:** dargonzine.org. **Contact:** Jon Evans, editor. E-zine specializing in fantasy fiction. "*DargonZine* is an E-zine that prints original fantasy fiction by aspiring fantasy writers. The Dargon Project is a shared world anthology whose goal is to provide a way for aspiring fantasy writers to meet and improve their writing skills through mutual contact and collaboration as well as contact with a live readership via the Internet."

NEEDS Fantasy. "Our goal is to write fantasy fiction that is mature, emotionally compelling, and professional. Membership in the Dargon Project is a requirement for publication." **Publishes 1-3 new writers/year.** Guidelines available on website. Sample copy online. "As a strictly noncommercial magazine, our writers' only compensation is their growth and membership in a lively writing community. Authors retain all rights to their stories."

TIPS "The Readers and Writers FAQs on our website provide much more detailed information about our mission, writing philosophy and the value of writing for *DargonZine*."

DIAGRAM

Dept. of English, Univ. of Arizona, P.O. Box 210067, Tucson AZ 85721-0067. **E-mail:** editor@thediagram. com. **Website:** www.thediagram.com. "We specialize in work that pushes the boundaries of traditional genre or work that is in some way schematic. We do publish traditional fiction and poetry, too, but hybrid forms (short stories, prose poems, indexes, tables of contents, etc.) are particularly welcome! We also publish diagrams and schematics (original and found). Bimonthly. Circ. 300,000 + hits/month. Member CLMP. "*Diagram* is an electronic journal of text and art, found and created. We're interested in representations, naming, indicating, schematics, labelling and taxonomy of things; in poems that masquerade as stories; in stories that disguise themselves as indices or obituaries."

⚪ "We sponsor yearly contests for unpublished hybrid essays and innovative fiction. Guidelines on website."

NEEDS Experimental, literary. "We don't publish genre fiction, unless it's exceptional and transcends the genre boundaries." Receives 100 unsolicited mss/month. Accepts 2-3 mss/issue; 15 mss/year. **Publishes 6 new writers/year.** Average length: 250-2,000 words. Publishes short shorts. Also publishes literary essays, poetry. Often comments on rejected mss.

HOW TO CONTACT Send complete ms. Accepts submissions by Web submissions manager; no e-mail, please. If sending by post, send SASE for return of the ms, or send disposable copy of the ms and #10 SASE for reply only. Responds in 2 weeks to queries; 1-2 months to mss. Accepts simultaneous submissions. Sample copy for $12 for print version. Writer's guidelines online.

PAYMENT/TERMS Acquires first, serial, electronic rights.

TIPS "Submit interesting text, images, sound and new media. We value the insides of things, vivisec-tion, urgency, risk, elegance, flamboyance, work that moves us, language that does something new, or does something old—well. We like iteration and reiteration. Ruins and ghosts. Mechanical, moving parts, balloons, and frenzy. We want art and writing that demonstrates/interaction; the processes of things; how functions are accomplished; how things become or expire, move or stand. We'll consider anything. We do not consider e-mail submissions, but encourage electronic submissions via our submissions manager software. Look at the journal and submissions guidelines before submitting."

⚫ DUCTS

P.O. Box 3203, Grand Central Station, New York NY 10163. **E-mail:** fiction@ducts.org; essays@ducts.org. **Website:** www.ducts.org/content. **Contact:** Jonathan Kravetz. Estab. 1999. Semi-annual. Estab. 1999. DUCTS is a webzine of personal stories, fiction, essays, memoirs, poetry, humor, profiles, reviews and art. "DUCTS was founded in 1999 with the intent of giving emerging writers a venue to regularly publish their compelling, personal stories. The site has been expanded to include art and creative works of all genres. We believe that these genres must and do overlap. DUCTS publishes the best, most compelling stories and we hope to attract readers who are drawn to work that rises above."

NEEDS Ethnic/multicultural, humor/satire, literary, mainstream. "Please do not send us genre work, unless it is extraordinarily unique." Receives 50 unsolicited mss/month. Accepts 40 mss/issue; 80 mss/year. Publishes ms 1-6 months after acceptance. Publishes 10-12 new writers/year. Recently published work by Charles Salzberg, Mark Goldblatt, Richard Kostelanz, and Helen Zelon. Publishes short shorts. Also publishes literary essays, literary criticism, poetry. Sometimes comments on rejected mss.

HOW TO CONTACT Reading period is January 1 - August 31. Send complete ms. Accepts submissions by e-mail to appropriate departments. Responds in 1-4 weeks to queries; 1-6 months to mss. Accepts simultaneous and reprints submissions. Writer's guidelines on ducts.org.

PAYMENT/TERMS $15. Acquires one time rights.

TIPS "We prefer writing that tells a compelling story with a strong narrative drive."

ECLECTICA

E-mail: editors@eclectica.org. **E-mail:** submissions@ eclectica.org. **Website:** www.eclectica.org. Estab.

1996. Online magazine. "*Eclectica* is a quarterly World Wide Web journal devoted to showcasing the best writing on the Web, regardless of genre. 'Literary' and 'genre' work appear side-by-side in each issue, along with pieces that blur the distinctions between such categories. Pushcart Prize, National Poetry Series, and Pulitzer Prize winners, as well as Nebula Award nominees, have shared issues with previously unpublished authors." "A sterling quality literary magazine on the World Wide Web. Not bound by formula or genre, harnessing technology to further the reading experience and dynamic and interesting in content."

NEEDS High quality work in any genre. Also publishes poetry.

HOW TO CONTACT Accepts submissions by e-mail. "While we will consider simultaneous submissions, please be sure to let us know that they are simultaneous and keep us updated on their publication status." Guidelines available on website.

PAYMENT/TERMS Acquires first North American serial rights, electronic rights.

TIPS "Works which cross genres—or create new ones—are encouraged. This includes prose poems, 'heavy' opinion, works combining visual art and writing, electronic multimedia, hypertext/html, and types we have yet to imagine. No length restrictions. We will consider long stories and novel excerpts, and serialization of long pieces. Include short cover letter."

EPIPHANY

E-mail: contact@epiphmag.com. **E-mail:** submissions@epiphmag.com. **Website:** http://epiphmag.com. **Contact:** JW Smith, editor. Estab. 2010. Epiphany was started in 2010, solely to be an online venue in which writers and artists can display their works. "Epiphany's dynamic formatting sets our publication apart from other online magazines. We strive to bring poetry, prose, fiction, nonfiction, artwork, and photography together to form a visually and creatively stimulating experience for our readers." Six issues/year in February, April, June, August, October, and December.

○ "Epiphany is a non-paying market at this time."

NEEDS Fiction should be a minimum of 500 words and a maximum of 4,000 words.

HOW TO CONTACT Accepts 40-50 mss/year. Send complete ms.

TIPS "We are open to a variety of writing styles and content subject matter. Our audience includes writers, artists, students, teachers, and all who enjoy reading short fiction, poetry, and creative nonfiction. We will not publish any works which we feel have a derogatory nature. Please visit our submission guidelines page at www.epiphmag.com/guide.html for more details."

➕ ◑ ESSAYS & FICTIONS

526 S. Albany St. Apt. 1N, Ithaca NY 14850. (914)572-7351. **E-mail:** essaysandfictions@gmail.com. **Website:** http://essaysandfictions.com. **Contact:** David Pollock and Danielle Winterton, co-founding editors. Estab. 2007. Essays & Fictions is an online journal of literature and criticism.

NEEDS "Essays & Fictions publishes fictional essay, reflective essay, academic rhetorical essay, literary narrative essay, lyric essay, linear fiction, non-linear fiction, essayistic fiction, fictionalized memoir, questionable histories, false historical accounts, botched accounts, cultural analysis, criticism or commentary, compositional analysis, criticism or commentary, or any blend thereof. We do not differentiate between essay and fiction in the table of contents because we consciously challenge the validity of genre boundaries and definitions. We believe language is not fixed and neither is truth. As art, forms of literature have varying degrees of truth value. Many writers have recently chosen to compose works that blend or subvert the genres of short fiction and essay. We are particularly interested in publishing these kinds of writers. We encourage writers to experiment with hybrid forms that lead to literary transcendence." Semiannual. Receives 10-20 mss/month, accepts approx 3/month, 6/year. Reading periods are February 1-May 31 for October issue, and September 1-December 31 for May issue. **Publishes 3-4 new writers each year.** Authors published: John Taylor, Philippe Jaccottet, Myronn Hardy, Veroniki Dalakoura, Margot Berwin, William Luvaas, Greg Sanders, Danielle Winterton, David Pollock, Joshua Land, Melita Schaum, Karl Parker, Stephen Poleskie. Does not want "genre writing, American Realism, or straight, formulaic reflective memoir." Length: up to 10,000 words. Average length: 3,000 words.

HOW TO CONTACT Send complete ms with cover letter.

PAYMENT/TERMS Contributors get one free copy and 15% off additional copies of the issue in which they are published.

TIPS "We look for confident work that uses form/structure and voice in interesting ways without sounding overly self-conscious or deliberate. We encourage rigorous excellence of complex craft in our submissions and discourage bland reproductions of reality. Read the journal. Be familiar with the *Essays & Fictions* aesthetic. We are particularly interested in writers who read theory and/or have multiple intellectual and artistic interests, and who set high intellectual standards for themselves and their work."

◐ THE EXTERNALIST: A JOURNAL OF PERSPECTIVES

c/o Larina Warnock, P.O. Box 2052, Corvallis OR 97339. **E-mail:** editor@theexternalist.com; fiction@theexternalist.com; poetry@theexternalist.com. **Website:** www.theexternalist.com. **Contact:** Larina Warnock. Online magazine, PDF format, 45-60 pages. "*The Externalist* embraces the balance between craft, entertainment and substance with a focus on subjects that are meaningful in human context. The externalist writer is the writer who is driven by a desire to write well while also writing in such a way that others can understand their perspective (even if they disagree or can't relate), and in this way, keeps an eye on the world outside of self. Externalism values craft and content equally. It recognizes there are still important lessons to be learned, there is still a need to understand and relate to the world around us, and differences are as important as similarities, and vice versa. The externalist believes there are significant human concerns across the globe and here in the United States, and that good literature has the power to create discussion around these concerns. The externalist also believes the multiplicity of perspectives found in today's quickly changing world can (and should) be valued as a means to comprehension—a way to change the things that do not work and give force to the things that do." Bimonthly. Estab. 2007. Circ. approx.1,000 unique visitors a month.

◯ Work published in *The Externalist* has received awards from "Best of the Web."

NEEDS Adventure, ethnic/multicultural, family saga, fantasy, feminist, gay, historical, horror, humor/satire, lesbian, literary, mainstream, military/war, mystery, new age, psychic/supernatural/occult, religious, science fiction, thriller/espionage, and western, but "all fiction must have an externalist focus regardless of genre." Does not want children's or young adult literature, erotica or pornography, or standard romance. "We do not publish any work that is designed to in-

spire hate or violence against any population. Highly experimental work is strongly discouraged. Slice-of-life fiction that does not deal with a significant social issue will not be accepted." List of upcoming themes available on website. Receives 20-25 mss/month. Accepts 2-3 mss/issue; 12-18 mss/year. Ms published 4 months after acceptance. Publishes 10-15 new writers/year. Published Simon Perchik, Lois Shapley Bassen, and Shaul Hendel. Length: 500-5,000 words. Average length: 3,500 words. Publishes short shorts. Average length of short shorts: 750 words. Also publishes literary essays, literary criticism, poetry. Often comments on/critiques rejected mss.

HOW TO CONTACT E-mail submissions only. Include estimated word count, brief bio. Responds to queries in 2-3 weeks. Responds to mss in 3 months. Considers simultaneous submissions, previously published submissions. Guidelines available on website.
PAYMENT/TERMS Contributor's link on Web page (see website for details). Acquires first North American serial rights. Sends galleys to author. Publication is copyrighted. "All work published in *The Externalist* is eligible for Editor's Choice (each issue) and our annual Best of *The Externalist* anthology."
TIPS "The fiction that appears in *The Externalist* is well-crafted and speaks subtly about significant social issues in our world today. The more thought-provoking the story, the more likely we will accept it for publication. The editor has a soft spot for well written satire. However, read the work we publish before submitting. Familiarize yourself with externalism. This information is on our website free of charge, and even a brief look at the material we publish will improve your chances. Follow the guidelines! We do not open unsolicated attachments, and manuscripts that do not follow our e-mail formatting guidelines stand a good chance of hitting our junk mail folder and not being seen."

◐◯ FAILBETTER.COM

2022 Grove Ave., Richmond VA 23221. **E-mail:** tdidato@failbetter.com; submissions@failbetter.com. **Website:** www.failbtetter.com. **Contact:** Thom Didato, publisher. Estab. 2000. "We are a quarterly online magazine published in the spirit of a traditional literary journal—dedicated to publishing quality fiction, poetry, and artwork. While the Web plays host to hundreds, if not thousands, of genre-related sites (many of which have merit), we are not one of them." Quarterly. Member CLMP.

NEEDS Literary, short stories, novel excerpts. "No genre fiction—romance, fantasy or science fiction." Always would like to see more "character-driven literary fiction where something happens!" Receives 175-200 unsolicited mss/month. Accepts 3-5 mss/issue; 12-20 mss/year. Publishes ms 4-8 months after acceptance. **Publishes 4-6 new writers/year.** Recently published work by Michael Martone, Daniel Alarcon, Pascal Mercier, Jeffrey Lent, and Elizabeth Crane. Publishes short shorts. Often comments on rejected mss. Accepts submissions by e-mail. Include the word "submission" in the subject line. Responds in 3-4 months to email submissions; 4-6 month s to snail mail mss. Accepts simultaneous submissions. All issues are available online. Acquires one-time rights.

TIPS "Read an issue. Read our guidelines! We place a high degree of importance on originality, believing that even in this age of trends it is still possible. We are not looking for what is current or momentary. We are not concerned with length: One good sentence may find a home here, as the bulk of mediocrity will not. Most importantly, know that what you are saying could only come from you. When you are sure of this, please feel free to submit."

FICKLE MUSES

315 Terrace Street SE, Albuquerque NM 87106. E-mail: fiction2@ficklemuses.com. **Website:** www.ficklemuses.com. Estab. *Fickle Muses* is an online journal of poetry and fiction engaged with myth and legend.. Online magazine. Contains illustrations. Includes photographs. "We feature poetry and short stories that re-imagine old myths or reexamine mythic themes contemporarily." Weekly.

NEEDS Literary. "Stories may cross over into any genre as long as the story is based in a myth or legend. Does not want stories that treat myth as a false belief or stereotype (e.g. the myth of beauty). No pure genre (romance, horror, mystery, etc.)." Receives 13-15 mss/month. Accepts 12-24 mss/year. Ms published up to 3 months after acceptance. **Publishes approx 10% new writers/year.** Published Neil de la Flor, Maureen Seaton, Virginia Mohlere, and M.M. De Voe. Length: 1,000-5,000 words. Average length: 2,000 words. Publishes short shorts. Average length of short shorts: 500 words. Also publishes literary essays, literary criticism, book reviews, poetry. Send review query to fiction@ficklemuses.com. Rarely comments on/critiques rejected mss.

HOW TO CONTACT Send complete ms with cover letter. Accepts submissions by e-mail only. Include estimated word count and "a brief description of the myth or legend your story is based on if it is not standard knowledge." Responds to queries in 3 weeks. Responds to mss in 3 weeks. Considers simultaneous submissions, previously published submissions. Guidelines available on website.

PAYMENT/TERMS Acquires one time rights. Publication is not copyrighted.

TIPS "Originality. An innovative look at an old story. I'm looking to be swept away. Get a feel for our website."

FLASHQUAKE

P.O. Box 2154, Albany NY 12220-0154. **E-mail:** cbell@flashquake.org. **Website:** www.flashquake.org. **Contact:** Cindy Bell, publisher/editor-in-chief. E-zine specializing in flash literature. "*Flashquake* is a quarterly online literary journal featuring flash literature—flash fiction, flash nonfiction, and short poetry. Send us works that will leave readers thinking. We define flash as works less than 1,000 words, shorter pieces will impress us. Poetry can be up to 35 lines; prose poetry up to 300 lines. We want the best story you can tell us in the fewest words you need to do it! Move us, engage us, give us a complete story with characters, plot, and a beginning, middle and end."

NEEDS Ethnic/multicultural (general), experimental, literary, flash literature of all types: fiction, memoir, creative nonfiction, poetry, and artwork. "Not interested in romance, graphic sex, graphic violence, gore, jokey humor, vampires, or work of a religious nature." Receives 200-250 unsolicited mss/month. Accepts 30 mss/issue. Publishes ms 1-3 months after acceptance. Publishes only short shorts. Comments on most rejected mss.

HOW TO CONTACT Accepts submissions online at http://flashquake.submishmash.com/Submit only. No land mail. Include brief bio, mailing address, and e-mail address. Guidelines and submission instructions on website.

PAYMENT/TERMS Pays $5-25 plus CD copy of site. Pays within two weeks of publication for electronic rights. Sponsors occasional awards/contests.

TIPS "Read our submission guidelines before submitting. Proofread your work thoroughly! We will instantly reject your work for spelling and grammar errors. Save your document as plain text and paste it into an e-mail message. We do not open attachments. We like experimental work, but that is not a license to forget narrative clarity, plot, character development or reader satisfaction."

FULLOSIA PRESS

P.O. Box 280, Ronkonkoma NY 11779. **E-mail:** deanofrpps@aol.com. **Website:** rpps_fullosia_press.tripod. com. **Contact:** J.D. Collins, editor; Geoff Jackson, associate editor. Estab. 1999. E-zine. "Part-time publisher of fiction and non-fiction. Our publication is right wing and conservative, leaning to views of Patrick Buchanan but amenable to the opposition's point of view. We promote an independent America. We are anti-global, anti-UN. Collects unusual news from former British or American provinces. Fiction interests include military, police, private detective, courthouse stories." Monthly. Circ. 175.

NEEDS Historical (American), military/war, mystery/suspense, thriller/espionage. Christmas, St. Patrick's Day, Fourth of July. Publishes ms 1 week after acceptance. **Publishes 10 new writers/year.** Recently published work by Geoff Jasckson, "Awesome" Dave Lawrence, John Grey, James Davies, Andy Martin, and Michael Levy. Length: 500-2,000 words; average length: 750 words. Publishes short shorts. Also publishes literary essays. Always comments on rejected mss.

HOW TO CONTACT Query with or without published clips. Accepts submissions by e-mail. Include brief bio and list of publications. Responds in 1 month to mss. Please avoid mass mailings. Sample copy online. Reviews fiction.

PAYMENT/TERMS Acquires electronic rights.

TIPS "Make your point quickly. If you haven't done so, after five pages, everybody hates you and your characters."

THE FURNACE REVIEW

16909 N. Bay Rd. #305, Sunny Isles FL 33160. **E-mail:** editor@thefurnacereview.com. **E-mail:** submissions@thefurnacereview.com. **Website:** http://thefurnacereview.com. **Contact:** Ciara LaVelle, editor. Estab. 2004. "We reach out to a young, well-educated audience, bringing them new, unique, fresh work they won't find elsewhere." Quarterly. Estab. 2004.

NEEDS Experimental, literary, mainstream. Does not want children's, science fiction, or religious submissions. Receives 50-60 unsolicited mss/month. Accepts 1-5 mss/issue; 5-8 mss/year. **Publishes 10-20 new writers/year.** Recently published work by Amy

Greene, Dominic Preziosi, and Sandra Soson. Length: 7,000 words; average length: 4,000 words. Publishes short shorts. Also publishes poetry.

HOW TO CONTACT Send complete ms. Accepts submissions only by e-mail at submissions@thefurnacereview.com or online at http://thefurnacereview.com/submit/. Responds in 4 month to queries. Accepts simultaneous submissions.

PAYMENT/TERMS Acquires first North American serial rights.

GREEN HILLS LITERARY LANTERN

McClain Hall, Truman State University, Kirksville MO 63501. (660)785-4513. **E-mail:** jbeneven@truman. edu. **Website:** http://ll.truman.edu/ghllweb/. **Contact:** Joe Benevento, poetry editor. Estab. 1990. "The mission of GHLL is to provide a literary market for quality fiction writers, both established and beginners, and to provide quality literature for readers from diverse backgrounds. We also see ourselves as a cultural resource for North Missouri. Our publication works to publish the highest quality fiction—dense, layered, subtle—and, at the same time, fiction which grabs the ordinary reader. We tend to publish traditional short stories, but we are open to experimental forms." Annual. The GHLL is now an online, open-access journal.

NEEDS Ethnic/multicultural, experimental, feminist, humor/satire,literary, mainstream, regional. "Our main requirement is literary merit. Wants more quality fiction about rural culture. No adventure, crime,erotica, horror, inspirational, mystery/suspense, romance." Receives 40 unsolicited mss/month. Length: 7,000 words; average length: 3,000 words. Publishes shortshorts. Also publishes poetry.

GUERNICA

165 Bennett Ave., 4C, New York NY 10040. **E-mail:** editors@guernicamag.com; art@guernicamag.com; publisher@guernicamag.com. **Website:** www.guernicamag.com. **Contact:** Erica Wright, poetry; Dan Eckstein, art/photography. Estab. 2005. "*Guernica*, published biweekly, is one of the web's most acclaimed new magazines. 2009: *Guernica* is called a "great online literary magazine" by *Esquire*. *Guernica* contributors come from dozens of countries and write in nearly as many languages."

 Received Caine Prize for African Writing, Best of the Net, cited by *Esquire* as a "great literary magazine."

NEEDS Literary, preferably with an international approach. No genre fiction. Length: 700-2500 words.

HOW TO CONTACT Submit complete ms with cover letter, attn: Meakin Armstrong to fiction@guernicamag.com. In subject line (please follow this format exactly): "fiction submission." Submit complete ms with cover letter, attn: Meakin Armstrong to fiction@guernicamag.com. In subject line (please follow this format exactly): "fiction submission." Include bio and list of previous publications. Accepts 26 mss/year. Has published Jesse Ball, Elizabeth Crane, Josh Weil, Justo Arroyo, Sergio Ramírez Mercado, Matthew Derby, E.C. Osondu (Winner of the 2009 Caine Prize for African Writing).

TIPS "Please read the magazine first before submitting. Most stories that are rejected simply do not fit our approach. Submission guidelines available online."

◐◉ IDEOMANCER

Wales. **E-mail:** publisher@ideomancer.com. **Website:** www.ideomancer.com. **Contact:** Leah Bobet, publisher. Estab. 2001. Online magazine. Contains illustrations. "*Ideomancer* publishes speculative fiction and poetry that explores the edges of ideas; stories that subvert, refute and push the limits. We want unique pieces from authors willing to explore non-traditional narratives and take chances with tone, structure and execution, balance ideas and character, emotion and ruthlessness. We also have an eye for more traditional tales told with excellence." Quarterly.

NEEDS Fantasy (mythic, urban, historical, low, literary), horror (dark fantasy, futuristic, psychological, supernatural), science fiction (hard science/technological, soft/sociological). Special interests: slipstream, hyperfiction and poetry. Does not want fiction without a speculative element. Receives 160 mss/month. Accepts 3 mss/issue; 9-12 mss/year. Does not read February, May, August, and November. Ms published within 12 months of acceptance. **Publishes 1-2 new writers/year.** Published Sarah Monette, Ruth Nestvold, Christopher Barzak, Nicole Kornher-Stace, Tobias Buckell, Yoon Ha Lee, and David Kopaska-Merkel. Length: 7,000 words (max). Average length: 4,000 words. Publishes short shorts. Average length of short shorts: 1,000 words. Also publishes book reviews, poetry. *Requests only* to have a novel or collection reviewed should be sent to the publisher. Often comments on/critiques rejected mss.

HOW TO CONTACT Send complete ms with cover letter. Accepts submissions by e-mail only. Include estimated word count. Responds to queries in 1 week. Responds to mss in 4 weeks. Guidelines available on website.

PAYMENT/TERMS Writers receive 3¢ per word, max of $40. Pays on acceptance. Acquires electronic rights. Publication is copyrighted.

TIPS "Beyond the basics of formatting the fiction as per our guidelines, good writing and intriguing characters and plot, where the writer brings depth to the tale, make a manuscript stand out. We receive a number of submissions which showcase good writing, but lack the details that make them spring to life for us. Visit our website and read some of our fiction to see if we're a good fit. Read our submission guidelines carefully and use rtf formatting as requested. We're far more interested in your story than your cover letter, so spend your time polishing that."

◐ LITERAL LATTE

200 E. 10th St., Suite 240, New York NY 10003. (212)260-5532. **E-mail:** litlatte@aol.com. **Website:** www.literal-latte.com. Estab. 1994. **Contact:** Jenine Gordon Bockman. "Publishes great writing in many flavors and styles. *Literal Latte* expanded the readership for literary magazines by offering free copies in New York coffeehouses and bookstores. Now online only and free to the world." CLMP. Bimonthly online publication with an annual print anthology featuring the best of the website. "We want great writing in all styles and subjects. A feast is made of a variety of flavors."

NEEDS Experimental, fantasy, literary, science fiction. Receives 4,000 unsolicited mss/month. Accepts 5-8 mss/issue; 40 mss/year. Agented fiction 1%. **Publishes 6 new writers/year.** Length: 500-8,000 words; average length: 4,000 words. Publishes short shorts. Often comments on rejected mss. Maximum 6,000 words.

HOW TO CONTACT Send SASE for return of mss or send a disposable copy of ms and e-mail for reply only. Responds in 6 months to mss. Accepts simultaneous, multiple submissions. Sample copy for $3. Writer's guidelines for SASE, e-mail or check website. Reviews fiction. Send complete ms.

PAYMENT/TERMS Pays annual anthology. First rights. May request additional rights to put piece in annual anthology. Pays on publication for first, one-time rights. Sponsors awards/contests. Pays minimum of anthology copies and maximum of $1,000.

TIPS "Keeping free thought free and challenging entertainment are not mutually exclusive. Words make a manuscript stand out, words beautifully woven together in striking and memorable patterns."

⊕ LITERARY JUICE

Mishawaka IN 46545. **E-mail:** info@literaryjuice.com. **E-mail:** srajan@literaryjuice.com. **Website:** www.literaryjuice.com. **Contact:** Sara Rajan, editor-in-chief; Andrea O'Connor and Dinesh Rajan, managing editors. Bimonthly online literary magazine. "*Literary Juice* publishes original works of short fiction, flash fiction, and poetry. We do not publish non-fiction material, essays, or interviews, nor do we accept previously published works."

NEEDS We do NOT publish works with intense sexual content. Length: 100-2,500 words.

HOW TO CONTACT Submit complete ms.

TIPS "It is crucial that writers read our submission guidelines, which can be found on our website. Most importantly, send us your very best writing. We are looking for works that are not only thought-provoking, but venture into unconventional territory as well. For instance, avoid sending mainstream stories and poems (stories about wizards or vampires fall into this category). Instead, take the reader to a new realm that has yet to be explored."

MCSWEENEY'S

849 Valencia St., San Francisco CA 94110. **E-mail:** printsubmissions@mcsweeneys.net; websubmissions@mcsweeneys.net. **Website:** www.mcsweeneys.net. Online literary journal. "Timothy McSweeney's Internet Tendency is an offshoot of Timothy McSweeney's Quarterly Concern, a journal created by nervous people in relative obscurity, and published four times a year." Daily. Online literary journal.

NEEDS Literate humor. Sometimes comments on rejected mss. Sometimes comments on rejected mss.

HOW TO CONTACT Accepts submissions by e-mail. "For submissions to the website, paste the entire piece into the body of an e-mail. Absolute length limit of 1,500 words, with a preference for pieces significantly shorter (700-1,000 words)." Sample copy online. Writer's guidelines online. "For submissions to the website, paste the entire piece into the body of an e-mail."

TIPS "Please read the writer's guidelines before submitting and send your submissions to the appropriate address." "Do not submit your work to both the print submissions address and the Web submissions address, as seemingly hundreds of writers have been doing lately. If you submit a piece of writing intended for the magazine to the Web submissions address, you will confuse us, and if you confuse us, we will accidentally delete your work without reading it."

⊙ MICROHORROR: SHORT STORIES. ENDLESS NIGHTMARES

P.O. Box 32259, Pikesville MD 21282-2259. (443) 670-6133. **E-mail:** microhorror@gmail.com. **Website:** www.microhorror.com. **Contact:** Nathan Rosen, editor. Estab. 2006. Online magazine. "*MicroHorror* is not a magazine in the traditional sense. Instead, it is a free online archive for short-short horror fiction. With a strict limit of 666 words, *MicroHorror* showcases the power of the short-short horror to convey great emotional impact in only a few brief paragraphs." Estab. 2006.

> Golden Horror Award from Horrorfind.com in 2007.

NEEDS Horror (dark fantasy, futuristic, psychological, supernatural), young adult/teen (horror). Receives 25 mss/month. Accepts 300 mss/year. Ms published 1-3 days after acceptance. **Publishes 50 new writers/year.** Published Chris Allinotte, Kevin G. Bufton, Santiago Eximeno, Oonah V Joslin, Brian Laing, Caroline Robinson, and Chris Yodice. Length: 666 words (max). Publishes short shorts. Average length of short shorts: 500 words. Often comments on/critiques rejected mss.

HOW TO CONTACT Send complete ms with cover letter. Accepts submissions by e-mail. Include estimated word count, brief bio. Responds to queries in 1 week. Responds to mss in 1 week. Send either SASE (or IRC) for return of ms or disposable copy of ms and #10 SASE for reply only. Considers simultaneous submissions, previously published submissions, multiple submissions. Guidelines available on website.

PAYMENT/TERMS Acquires one time rights. Publication is copyrighted.

TIPS "This is horror. Scare me. Make shivers run down my spine. Make me afraid to look behind the shower curtain. Pack the biggest punch you can into a few well chosen sentences. Read all the horror you can, and figure out what makes it scary. Trim away all the excess trappngs until you get right to the core, and use what you find."

⊙ MIDWAY JOURNAL

P.O. Box 14499, St. Paul MN 55114. (612) 825-4811. **E-mail:** editors@midwayjournal.com. **Website:** www.midwayjournal.com. **Contact:** Ralph Pennel, fiction editor. Estab. 2006. Online magazine. "*Midway Journal* accepts submissions of aesthetically ambitious work that occupies the realms between the experimental and transitional. *Midway*, or its position is midway, is a place of boundary crossing, where work complicates and even questions the boundaries between forms, binaries and genres." Bimonthly. Member CLMP.

NEEDS Comics/graphic novels, ethnic/multicultural (general), experimental, feminist, gay, historical (general), humor/satire, lesbian, literary, science fiction (soft/sociological), translations. Does not want new age, young adult/teen, children/juvenile or erotica. "Writers should visit current and back issues to see what we have or have not published in the past." Receives 30 mss/month. Accepts 3-4 mss/issue; 18-24 mss/year. Does not read June 1-Nov 30. Ms published 4-12 months after acceptance. Agented fiction 1%. **Publishes 2-5 new writers/year.** Published Steve Almond, Alden Jones, Scott T. Hutchinson, and Marjorie Maddox. Length: 250-25,000 words. Average length: 3,000 words. Publishes short shorts. Average length of short shorts: 600 words. Also publishes literary essays, poetry, and drama. Sometimes comments on/critiques rejected mss.

HOW TO CONTACT Send complete ms with cover letter. Accepts international submissions by e-mail. Include estimated word count, brief bio, list of publications. Responds to queries in 1-2 weeks. Please see website for submission guidelines. Send either SASE (or IRC) for return of ms or disposable copy of ms and #10 SASE for reply only. Considers simultaneous submissions, previously published submissions. Guidelines available on website.

PAYMENT/TERMS Acquires one time rights. Publication is copyrighted.

TIPS "An interesting story with engaging writing, both in terms of style and voice, make a manuscript stand out. Round characters are a must. Writers who take chances either with content or with form grab an editor's immediate attention. Spend time with the words on the page. Spend time with the language. The language and voice are not vehicles, they, too, are tools."

⬤ MOBIUS

505 Christianson, Madison WI 53714. (608)242-1009. **E-mail:** fmschep@charter.net. **Website:** www.mobiusmagazine.com. **Contact:** Fred Schepartz, editor. Es-

tab. 1989. No longer a print magazine. Strictly a web-based magazine, but with the same quarterly publication schedule. "Looking for fiction which uses social change as either a primary or secondary theme. This is broader than most people think. Need social relevance in one way or another. For an artistically and politically aware and curious audience." Quarterly.

NEEDS Ethnic/multicultural, experimental, fantasy, feminist, gay, historical, horror, humor/satire, lesbian, literary, mainstream, science fiction, contemporary, prose poem. "No porn, no racist, sexist or any other kind of -ist. No Christian or spirituality proselytizing fiction." Wants to see more science fiction, erotica "assuming it relates to social change." Receives 15 unsolicited mss/month. Accepts 3-5 mss/issue. Publishes ms 3-9 months after acceptance. **Publishes 10 new writers/year.** Recently published work by Margaret Karmazin, Benjamin Reed, John Tuschen, Ken Byrnes. Length: 500-5,000 words; average length: 3,500 words. Publishes short shorts. Always comments on rejected mss.

HOW TO CONTACT Include SASE. Responds in 4 weeks to mss. Accepts reprints, but no multiple or simultaneous submissions." Sample copy for $2, 9×12 SAE and 3 first class stamps. Writer's guidelines for SASE.

PAYMENT/TERMS Acquires one time electronic rights as well as archival rights. All rights revert back to author after publication.

TIPS "Note that fiction and poetry may be simultaneously published in e-version of Mobius. Due to space constraints of print version, some works may be accepted in e-version, but not print version. We like high impact, we like plot and character-driven stories that function like theater of the mind. Looks for first and foremost, good writing. Prose must be crisp and polished; the story must pique my interest and make me care due to a certain intellectual, emotional aspect. Second, *Mobius* is about social change. We want stories that make some statement about the society we live in, either on a macro or micro level. Not that your story needs to preach from a soapbox (actually, we prefer that it doesn't), but your story needs to have *something* to say."

◯ NECROLOGY SHORTS: TALES OF MACABRE AND HORROR

Isis International, P.O. Box 510232, St. Louis MO 63151. **E-mail:** editor@necrologyshorts.com; submit@necrologyshorts.com. **Website:** www.necrologyshorts.com. **Contact:** John Ferguson, editor. Estab. 2009. Consumer publication published online daily and through Amazon Kindle. "*Necrology Shorts* is an online publication which publishes fiction, articles, cartoons, artwork, and poetry daily. Embracing the Internet, e-book readers, and new technology, we aim to go beyond the long time standard of a regular publication to bringing our readers a daily flow of entertainment. We will also be publishing an annual collection for each year in print, e-book reader, and Adobe PDF format. Our main genre is suspense horror similar to H.P. Lovecraft and/or Robert E. Howard. We also publish science fiction and fantasy. We would love to see work continuing the Cthulhu Mythos, but we accept all horror. We also hold contests, judged by our readers, to select the top stories and artwork. Winners of contests receive various prizes, including cash."

HOW TO CONTACT Submit complete ms. by e-mail to submit@necrologyshorts.com. Buys 1,000 mss/year. Responds in 1 month. Guidelines on website. We review submissions in the order we receive them. Please allow 1-2 weeks for us to review your work. If your submission passes review, it will be added to *Necrology Shorts* within 72 hours. You will be notified when your submission is posted. If your submission does not pass review we will notify you of any problems and reasons. Submission can be resubmitted once it is corrected. Send complete ms.

TIPS "*Necrology Shorts* is looking to break out of the traditional publication types to use the Internet, e-book readers, and other technology. We not only publish works of authors and artists, we let them use their published works to brand themselves and further their profits of their hard work. We love to see traditional short fiction and artwork, but we also look forward to those that go beyond that to create multimedia works. The best way to get to us is to let your creative side run wild and not send us the typical fare. Don't forget that we publish horror, sci-fi, and fantasy. We expect deranged, warped, twisted, strange, sadistic, and things that question sanity and reality."

NITE-WRITER'S INTERNATIONAL LITERARY ARTS JOURNAL

158 Spencer Ave., Suite 100, Pittsburgh PA 15227. (412)668-0691. **E-mail:** nitewritersliteraryarts@gmail. com. **Website:** http://nitewritersinternational.webs. com. **Contact:** John Thompson. Estab. 1994. An on-

line literary arts journal. "*Nite-Writer's International Literary Arts Journal* is dedicated to the emotional intellectual with a creative perception of life." Quarterly.

NEEDS Literary mainstream, historical, adventure, erotica, humor/satire, inspirational, senior citizen/retirement, sports. Average length: 2,500 words. Also publishes literary essays, literary criticism, photography, poetry, nonfiction, and haiku/senryu.

HOW TO CONTACT "If submitting by snail mail, enclose SASE for return of mss. Responds within 6 months to mss. Accepts simultaneous submissions and previously published work (let us know when & where). Send SASE for writer's guidelines or go to our website for guidelines. Does not pay at this time. Will offer a print on demand service quarterly. Copyright reverts to author upon publication. Retains First North American Serial rights."

TIPS "Read a lot of what you write — study the market. Don't fear rejection, but use it as learning tool to strengthen your work before resubmitting."

NORTHWIND

Chain Bridge Press, LLC., 4201 Wilson Blvd., #110-321, Arlington VA 22203. **Website:** www.northwind-magazine.com. **Contact:** Tom Howard, managing editor. Estab. 2011. "Our focus is originality and provocative, compulsively readable prose and poetry, in any style or genre. We look for smart, lyrical writing that will appeal to an intelligent and culturally sophisticated audience."

NEEDS Does not want to see short-shorts, allegories or fables, overtly religious or polemic narratives, hard science fiction, occult. Length: 1,500-10,000 words.

HOW TO CONTACT Submit complete ms.

PAYMENT/TERMS Pays up to $150.

TIPS "For fiction and nonfiction, make the first paragraph the strongest one. Love your characters and make us love them (or hate them) too. Respect your reader; we love subtlety. Don't be afraid to be lighthearted or playful—not all great stories are tragic or depressing. Show us that you care about your craft by editing carefully before you send it in to us."

NUVEIN ONLINE

(626)401-3466. **E-mail:** editor@nuvein.com. **Website:** http://nuvein.net; www.nuvein.org. Online magazine published by the Nuvein Foundation for Literature and the Arts. "We are open to short fiction, poetry and essays that explore topics divergent from the mainstream.

Our vision is to provide a forum for new and experienced voices rarely heard in our global community."

⊙ *Nuvein Online* has received the Visionary Media Award.

NEEDS Fiction, poetry, plays, movie/theatre reviews/articles and art. Wants more "experimental fiction, ethnic works, and pieces dealing with the exploration of gender and sexuality, as well as works dealing with the clash of cultures." **Publishes 20 new writers/year.** Recently published work by J. Knight, Paul A. Toth, Rick Austin, Robert Levin and Scott Essman, as well as interviews with film directors Guillermo Del Toro, Alejandro Gonzalez Iññarritu and Frank Darabont.

HOW TO CONTACT Query. Accepts submissions by e-mail. Send work as attachment. Sample copy online.

TIPS "Read over each submission before sending it, and if you, as the writer, find the piece irresistable, e-mail it to us immediately!"

O⑤ ON THE PREMISES

On The Premises, LLC, 4323 Gingham Court, Alexandria VA 22310. **E-mail:** questions@onthepremises. com; tarlrk@cox.net. **Website:** www.OnThePremises.com. Estab. 2006. **Contact:** Tarl Roger Kudrick or Bethany Granger, Co-Publishers. E-zine. "Stories published in *On the Premises* are winning entries in contests that are held every four months. Each contest challenges writers to produce a great story based on a broad premise that our editors supply as part of the contest. *On the Premises* aims to promote newer and/or relatively unknown writers who can write what we feel are creative, compelling stories told in effective, uncluttered and evocative prose. Entrants pay no fees, and winners receive cash prizes in addition to publication." Triannual. Estab. 2006. Member Small Press Promotions. "We are a contest-based fiction magazine publishing the best submitted stories based on each issue's specific premise." Published every 4 months covering fiction by newer and/or relatively unknown writers.

NEEDS Adventure, ethnic/multicultural (general), experimental, family saga, fantasy, feminist, historical (general), horror, humor/satire, literary, mainstream, military/war, mystery, new age, psychic/supernatural/occult, romance, science fiction, thriller/espionage, western. Does not want young adult fiction, children's fiction, X-rated fiction. "In general, we don't like stories that were written solely to make a social or political point, especially if the story seems to assume that no intelligent person could possibly disagree with the author. Save the ideology for editorial and opinion pieces, please. But above all, we NEVER EVER want to see stories that do not use the contest premise! Use the premise, and make it 'clear' and 'obvious' that you are using the premise." Themes are announced the day each contest is launched. List of past and current premises available on website. Receives 20-100 mss/month. Accepts 3-6 mss/issue; 9-18 mss/year. Does not read February, June, and October. Ms published a month or less after acceptance. **Publishes 3-6 new writers/year.** Published A'llyn Ettien, Cory Cramer, Mark Tullius, Michael Van Ornum, Ken Liu and K. Stodard Hayes. Length: 1,000-5,000 words. Average length: 3,500 words. Sometimes comments on/critiques rejected mss. "All genres considered. All stories must be based on the broad premise supplied as part of the contest. Sample premise, taken from the first issue: One or more characters are traveling in a vehicle, and never reach their intended destination. Why not? What happens instead?" No young adult or children's fiction. Does not want stories unrelated to the contest premise; no preachy fiction.

HOW TO CONTACT Send complete ms with cover letter. "We are a contest-based magazine and we strive to judge all entries 'blindly.' We request that an author's name and contact information be in the body of the email." Accepts submissions by e-mail only. Responds to mss in 2 weeks after contest deadline. Guidelines available on website. Send complete ms

PAYMENT/TERMS Writers receive $40-180. Pays on acceptance. Acquires electronic rights. Sends galleys to author. Publication is copyrighted.

TIPS "Make sure you use the premise, not just interpret it. If the premise is 'must contain a real live dog,' then think of a creative, compelling way to use a real dog. Revise you draft, then revise again and again. Remember, we judge blindly, so craftmanship and creativity matter, not how well known you are."

○○ THE ORACULAR TREE

29 Hillyard St., Chatham ON N7L 3E1 Canada. **Website:** www.oraculartree.com. Estab. 1977. **Contact:** Jeff Beardwood, editor. E-zine specializing in practical ideas for transforming our lives. "The stories we tell ourselves and each other predict the outcome of our lives. We can affect gradual social change by transforming our deeply rooted cultural stories. The genre is not as important as the message and the high qual-

ity of the writing. We accept stories, poems, articles and essays which will reach well-educated, open-minded readers around the world. We offer a forum for those who see a need for change, who want to add their voices to a growing search for positive alternatives." Monthly. Estab. 1997. Circ. 250,000 hits/month.

NEEDS Serial fiction, poetry, essays, novels and novel excerpts, visual art, short fiction, news. "We'll look at any genre that is well written and can examine a new cultural paradigm. No tired dogma, no greeting card poetry, please." Receives 20-30 unsolicited mss/month. Accepts 80-100 mss/year. Publishes ms 3 months after acceptance. **Publishes 20-30 new writers/year.** Recently published work by Elisha Porat, Lyn Lyfshin, Rattan Mann, and Dr. Elaine Hatfield. Publishes short shorts. Also publishes literary essays, poetry. Often comments on rejected mss.

HOW TO CONTACT Send complete ms. Accepts submissions by e-mail. Responds in 2 weeks to queries; 2 months to mss. Accepts simultaneous, multiple submissions and reprints. Sample copy online. Writer's guidelines online.

PAYMENT/TERMS Author retains copyright; one-time archive posting.

TIPS "The underlying idea must be clearly expressed. The language should be appropriate to the tale, using creative license and an awareness of rhythm. We look for a juxtaposition of ideas that creates resonance in the mind and heart of the reader. Write from your honest voice. Trust your writing to unfold."

OUTER ART

The University of New Mexico, 200 College Road, Gallup NM 87301. **Website:** www.gallup.unm. edu/~smarandache/a/outer-art.htm.. Estab. 2000.

NEEDS Experimental, literary, outer-art. Publishes ms 1 month after acceptance. Publishes short shorts. Also publishes literary essays, literary criticism.

HOW TO CONTACT Accepts submissions by e-mail. Send SASE (or IRC) for return of the ms. Responds in 1 month to mss. Accepts simultaneous submissions and reprints. Writer's guidelines online.

◐◑ PAPERPLATES

19 Kenwood Ave., Toronto ON M6C 2R8 Canada. (416)651-2551. **E-mail:** magazine@paperplates.org. **Website:** www.paperplates.org. **Contact:** Karl Buchner, fiction editor. Estab. 1990. Electronic magazine. Quarterly. Estab. 1990.

NEEDS Condensed novels, ethnic/multicultural, feminist, gay, lesbian, literary, mainstream, translations. "No science fiction, fantasy or horror." Receives 12 unsolicited mss/month. Accepts 2-3 mss/issue; 6-9 mss/year. Publishes ms 6-8 months after acceptance. Recently published work by Lyn Fox, David Bezmozgis, Fraser Sutherland, and Tim Conley. Length: 1,500-3,500 words; average length: 3,000 words. Publishes short shorts. Also publishes literary essays, literary criticism, poetry.

HOW TO CONTACT Accepts submissions by e-mail and land mail. Responds in 6 weeks to queries; 6 months to mss. Accepts simultaneous submissions. Sample copy online. Writer's guidelines online.

PAYMENT/TERMS No payment. Acquires first North American serial rights.

◑ THE PAUMANOK REVIEW

Website: www.paumanokreview.com. Estab. 2000. **Contact:** Katherine Arline, editor. Online literary magazine. "TPR is dedicated to publishing and promoting the best in world art and literature." Quarterly. Estab. 2000.

> J.P. Maney's *Western Exposures* was selected for inclusion in the *E2INK Best of the Web Anthology.*

NEEDS Mainstream, narrative, experimental, historical, mystery, horror, western, science fiction, slice-of-life vignette, serial, novel excerpt. Receives 100 unsolicited mss/month. Accepts 6-8 mss/issue; 24-32 mss/year. Publishes ms 6 weeks after acceptance. **Publishes 4 new writers/year.** Recently published work by Patty Friedman, Elisha Porat, Barry Spacks and Walt McDonald. Length: 1,000-6,000 words; average length: 3,000 words. Publishes short shorts. Also publishes literary essays, poetry. Usually comments on rejected mss.

HOW TO CONTACT Send complete ms as attachment (Word, RTF, HTML, TXT) or pasted in body of e-mail. Include estimated word count, brief bio, two ways to contact you, list of publications, and how you discovered *TPR*. Responds in 1 week to queries; 1 month to mss. Accepts simultaneous submissions and reprints. No multiple submissions. Sample copy online. Writer's guidelines online.

PAYMENT/TERMS Acquires one time, anthology rights. Galleys offered in HTML or PDF format.

TIPS "Though this is an English-language publication, it is not US-or UK-centric. Please submit accordingly.

TPR is a publication of Wind River Press, which also publishes *Critique* magazine and select print and electronic books."

◑ PBW

513 N. Central Ave., Fairborn OH 45324. (937)878-5184. **E-mail:** rianca@aol.com. Estab. 1988. Electronic disk zine; 700 pages, specializing in avant-garde fiction and poetry. "*PBW* is an experimental floppy disk (CD-Rom) that prints strange and 'unpublishable' in an above-ground-sense writing." Twice per year.

HOW TO CONTACT "Manuscripts are only taken if they are submitted on disk or by e-mail." Send SASE for reply, return of ms. Sample copy not available.

PAYMENT/TERMS All rights revert back to author. Not copyrighted.

◑◉ THE PEDESTAL MAGAZINE

6815 Honors Court, Charlotte NC 28210. (704)643-0244. **E-mail:** pedmagazine@carolina.rr.com. **Website:** www.thepedestalmagazine.com. **Contact:** Nathan Leslie, fiction editor; John Amen, editor-in-chief. Estab. 2000. Online literary magazine/journal. "We publish poetry, fiction, reviews and interviews. We are committed to the individual voice and publish an eclectic mix of high-quality work." Bimonthly. Member CLMP. "We are committed to promoting diversity and celebrating the voice of the individual."

  ◒ *Pedestal 56* is now online.

NEEDS Adventure, ethnic/multicultural, experimental, family saga, fantasy, feminist, gay, glitz, historical, horror, humor/satire, lesbian, literary, mainstream, military/war, mystery, new age, psychic/supernatural/occult, romance, science fiction, thriller/espionage. Receives 100-150 mss/month. Accepts 3-5 mss/issue; 18-24 mss/year. Closed to submissions at the following times: January, March, May, July, September, November: from the 12th-19th; February, April, June, August, October, December: from the 14th-28th. Ms published 1-3 weeks after acceptance. **Publishes 1-2 new writers/year.** Published Grant Tracy, Mary Grabar, Karen Heuler, James Scott Iredell, Don Shea, Mary Carroll-Hackett, R.T. Smith, and Richard Peabody. Publishes short shorts. Also publishes book reviews, poetry. Send review query to pedmagazine@carolina.rr.com. Rarely comments on/critiques rejected mss. "We are receptive to all sorts of high-quality literary fiction. Genre fiction is encouraged as long as it crosses or comments upon its genre and is both character-driven and psychologically acute. We encourage submissions of short fiction, no more than 3 flash fiction pieces at a time. There is no need to query prior to submitting; please submit via the submission form—no email to the editor." Length: 4,000 words.

HOW TO CONTACT Submit via the online form provided on the website. Include brief bio, list of publications. Responds to queries in 2-3 days. Responds to mss in 4-6 weeks. Considers simultaneous submissions, multiple submissions. Guidelines available on website. For the December issue (reading cycle October 28-December 14), Bruce Boston and Marge Simon will be jointly guest-editing a special speculative fiction issue. Speculative includes science fiction, fantasy, horror, slipstream, surreal, and experimental. All fiction submitted between October 28 and December 14 should be speculative and not exceed 1,500 words.

PAYMENT/TERMS Writers receive 8¢/word. Pays on publication. Acquires first rights. Sends galleys to author. Publication is copyrighted.

TIPS "If you send us your work, please wait for a response to your first submission before you submit again."

◑ PERSIMMON TREE: MAGAZINE OF THE ARTS BY WOMEN OVER SIXTY

1534 Campus Drive, Berkeley CA 94708. **E-mail:** editor@persimmontree.org; Submissions@persimmontree.org. **Website:** www.persimmontree.org. **Contact:** Nan Gefen, editor. Online magazine. "*Persimmon Tree* is a showcase for the talent and creativity of women over sixty, but the magazine appeals to readers of all ages." Quarterly. Estab. 2007. Member Council of Literary Magazines.

NEEDS Ethnic/multicultural (general), experimental, family saga, feminist, gay, historical (general), humor/satire, lesbian, literary, mainstream. Receives 80-100 mss/month. Accepts 2-3 mss/issue; 8-12 mss/year. Ms published 3-6 months after acceptance. **Publishes 2-3 new writers/year.** Published Grace Paley, Paula Gunn Allen, Daphne Muse, Carole Rosenthal and Sandy Boucher. Length: 1,200 words (min)-3,000 words (max). Average length: 2,000 words. Publishes short shorts. Also publishes literary essays, literary criticism, book reviews, poetry.

HOW TO CONTACT Send complete ms with cover letter. Accepts submissions by e-mail only at Submissions@persimmontree.org. Include estimated word count, brief bio, list of publications. Responds to mss in 3-6 months. Considers simultaneous submissions, multiple submissions. Guidelines available on website.

PAYMENT/TERMS Acquires one time rights. Sends galleys to author. Publication is copyrighted.

TIPS "High quality of writing, an interesting or unique point of view, make a manuscript stand out. Make it clear that you're familiar with the magazine. Tell us why the piece would work for our audience."

THE PINK CHAMELEON

E-mail: dpfreda@juno.com. **Website:** www.thepinkchameleon.com. **Contact:** Mrs. Dorothy Paula Freda, editor/publisher. Estab. 2000. Reading period from January-April 30 and September-October 31. Needs fiction and nonfiction.

NEEDS Fiction and nonfiction short stories, adventure, family saga, fantasy, humor/satire, literary, mainstream, mystery/suspense, religious/inspirational, romance, science fiction, western, young adult/teen, psychic/supernatural. "No violence for the sake of violence." Receives 20 unsolicited mss/month. Publishes ms within 1 year after acceptance. **Publishes 50% new writers/year.** Recently published work by Deanne F. Purcell, Martin Green, Albert J. Manachino, James W. Collins, Ron Arnold, Sally Kosmalski, Susan Marie Davniero and Glen D. Hayes. Publishes short shorts. No novels or novel excerpts. Also publishes essays, poetry. Sometimes comments on rejected mss. Length: 500-2,500 words; average length: 2,000 words. .

HOW TO CONTACT Send complete ms in the body of the e-mail. No attachments. Responds in 1 month to mss. Accepts reprints. No simultaneous submissions. Sample copy online. Writer's guidelines online.

PAYMENT/TERMS "Non-profit. Acquires one time rights for one year but will return rights earlier on request."

TIPS "Simple, honest, evocative emotion, upbeat fiction and nonfiction submissions that give hope for the future; well-paced plots; stories, poetry, articles, essays that speak from the heart. Read guidelines carefully. Use a good, but not ostentatious, opening hook. Stories should have a beginning, middle and end that make the reader feel the story was worth his or her time. This also applies to articles and essays. In the latter two, wrap your comments and conclusions in a neatly packaged final paragraph. Turnoffs include violence, bad language. Simple, genuine and sensitive work does not need to shock with vulgarity to be interesting and enjoyable."

⚙ ○ PREMONITIONS

13 Hazely Combe, Arrenton Isle of Wight PO30 3AJ United Kingdom. **Website:** www.pigasuspress.co.uk. Pigasus Press, 13 Hazely Combe, Arreton Isle of Wight PO30 3AJ United Kingdom. **Website:** www.pigasuspress.co.uk. **E-mail:** mail@pigasuspress.co.uk. **Contact:** Tony Lee, editor. "A magazine of science fiction, horror stories, genre poetry and fantastic artwork." Biannual.

NEEDS Science fiction (hard, contemporary science fiction/fantasy). "No sword and sorcery, supernatural horror." Accepts 12 mss/issue.

HOW TO CONTACT "Unsolicited submissions are always welcome, but writers must enclose SAE/IRC for reply, plus adequate postage to return ms if unsuitable. No fiction or poetry submissions accepted via e-mail." Sample copy online.

TIPS "Potential contributors are advised to study recent issues of the magazine."

⚙⚙⚙ PSEUDOPOD

Escape Artists, Inc., P.O. Box 965609, Marietta GA 30066. **Fax:** (866)373-8739. **E-mail:** editor@pseudopod.org. **E-mail:** submit@pseudopod.org. **Website:** pseudopod.org. **Contact:** Shawn M. Garrett, editor. Online audio magazine. 25-40 min weekly episode, 5-10 min for sporadic specials like flash fiction or movie/book reviews. "*Pseudopod* is a genre magazine in audio form. We're looking for horror: dark, weird fiction. We run the spectrum from grim realism or crime drama, to magic-realism, to blatantly supernatural dark fantasy. We publish highly literary stories reminiscent of Poe or Lovecraft as well as vulgar shock-value pulp fiction. We don't split hairs about genre definitions, and we do not observe any taboos about what kind of content can appear in our stories. Originality demands that you're better off avoiding vampires, zombies, and other recognizable horror tropes unless you have put a very unique spin on them. What matters most is that the stories are dark and compelling."

NEEDS Horror (dark fantasy, futuristic, psychological, supernatural, sentimental, literary, erotic, splatterpunk, romantic, humorous). Does not want archetypical vampire, zombie, or werewolf fiction. Receives 100 mss/month. Accepts 1 mss/issue; 70 mss/year. Manuscript published 1 month after acceptance. **Publishes 20 new writers/year.** Published Joel Arnold, Kevin J. Anderson, Richard Dansky, Scott Sigler,

Paul Jessup, Nicholas Ozment, and Stephen Gaskell. Length: 2,000-6,000 words. Average length: 3,000 words. Publishes short shorts. Average length of short shorts: 800 words. Often comments on/critiques rejected manuscripts. "We want short stories between about 2,000 and 6,000 words; we are quite hesitant to produce stories any longer than that. The longer the story is, the more brilliant it needs to be to sustain audience interest. We currently pay $100 for short fiction at this length. Flash Fiction: We sometimes podcast short five-to-ten minute bonus pieces between our weekly main episodes. For this we're looking at fiction under1,500 words, with a sweet spot between 500 and 1000 words. Yes, that's really short. That's the point. Our flash pieces are frequently quirkier and more experimental than our weekly features. We pay $20 for flash fiction."

HOW TO CONTACT Send complete ms with cover letter. Accepts submissions by e-mail. Include estimated word count, brief bio, brief list of publications. Responds to queries in 2 weeks. Responds to mss in 2 months. Considers simultaneous submissions, previously published submissions. Sample copy, guidelines available on website. Does not want multiple submissions. Paste submission in body of an email you will use for correspondence.

PAYMENT/TERMS Writers receive $20 over 2,000 words, $100 over 2,000 words. Pays on acceptance.

TIPS "Let the writing be guided by a strong sense of who the (hopefully somewhat interesting) protagonist is, even if zero time is spent developing any other characters. Preferably, tell the story using standard past tense, third person, active voice."

❶❸ RAVING DOVE

P.O. Box 28, West Linn OR 97068. **E-mail:** editor@ravingdove.org. **E-mail:** ravingdog@gmail.com. **Website:** www.ravingdove.org/. **Contact:** Jo-Ann Moss, editor. Estab. 2004. Online literary magazine. "*Raving Dove* publishes writing, poetry, and art with universal, anti-violence, anti-hate, human rights, and social justice themes. We share sentiments that oppose physical and psychological violence in all its forms, including war, discrimination against sexual orientation, and every shade of bigotry." Quarterly. Online literary journal published 4 times/year. "Our mission is to share thought-provoking poetry and prose that champions human rights and social justice, and opposes physical and psychological violence in all its forms, including war, discrimination against sexual orientation, and every shade of bigotry."

NEEDS Literary, mainstream. "*Raving Dove* is not a political publication. Material for or against one specific person or entity will not be considered, fictitious or otherwise." Ms published up to 3 months after acceptance. Length: 2,000 words (max). Also publishes poetry. 3,000 words maximum

HOW TO CONTACT Accepts submissions by e-mail only. Include brief bio, submission genre, i.e., fiction, nonfiction, poetry, etc., in the e-mail subject line. Responds to mss in 3 months. Considers simultaneous submissions. Guidelines available on website. Send complete ms.

PAYMENT/TERMS Not currently a paying market. (Check website for current information.) Acquires one time North American and Internet serial rights, exclusive for the duration of the edition in which the work appears (3 months). True

❶ REALPOETIK

Athens GA **E-mail:** realpoetikblog@gmail.com. **Website:** realpoetik.org. Estab. 1993.

NEEDS "We do not want to see anything that fits neatly into categories. We subvert categories." Publishes ms 2-4 months after acceptance. **Publishes 20-30 new writers/year.** Average length: 250-500 words. Publishes short shorts. Also publishes literary essays, literary criticism, poetry. Sometimes comments on rejected mss. Query with or without published clips or send complete ms. Accepts submissions by e-mail. Responds in 1 month to queries. Sample copy online.

TIPS "Be different but interesting. Complexity and consciousness are always helpful. Write short. We're a post-modern e-zine. Query us before submitting at RealPoetikblog@gmail.com."

❶ RESIDENTIAL ALIENS

ResAliens Press, 7412 E Brookview Cir., Wichita KS 67226. **E-mail:** resaliens@gmail.com. **Website:** www.resaliens.com; residentialaliens.blogspot.com. **Contact:** Lyn Perry, founding editor. Estab. 2007. Online magazine/E-zine. "Because reading and writing speculative fiction is a strong interest of mine, I thought I'd contribute to the genre of faith-informed speculative fiction by offering other writers and readers of science fiction, fantasy, spiritual and supernatural thrillers a quality venue in which to share their passion. You could say *ResAliens* is speculative fiction with a spiritual thread." Monthly.

NEEDS Fantasy (space fantasy, sword and sorcery), horror (supernatural), science fiction (soft/sociological), thriller. Does not want straight horror, gore, erotica. Will publish another sci-fi/Fantasy anthology. List of upcoming themes available for SASE, on website. Receives 50 mss/month. Accepts 5-6 mss/issue; 65-75 mss/year. Ms published 1-2 months after acceptance. **Publishes 25 new writers/year.** Published George L. Duncan (author of novel *A Cold and Distant Memory*), Patrick G. Cox (author of novel *Out of Time*), Merrie Destefano (editor of *Victorian Homes Magazine*), Brandon Barr and Mike Lynch (authors of the science fiction novel *When the Sky Fell*; Ben Loory, *Stories for Nighttime and Some for the Day* (Penguin Press). Length of short stories: 500-5,000 words. Average length: 3,500 words. Publishes short shorts. Average length of short shorts: 900 words. Will take serial novellas of 2-5 installments (up to 20,000 words). Also publishes book reviews. Send review copies to resaliens@gmail.com. Often comments on/critiques rejected mss.

HOW TO CONTACT Send complete ms with cover letter via e-mail. Include estimated word count, brief bio. Responds to queries in 2-5 days; to mss in 1-2 weeks. Considers simultaneous submissions, previously published submissions, multiple submissions. Sample copy and guidelines available on website.

PAYMENT/TERMS Writers receive PDF file as their contributor's copy. Acquires one time rights, electronic rights, 6-month archive rights. Sends galleys to author. Publication is copyrighted. "Occasionally sponsors contests."

TIPS "We want stories that read well and move quickly. We enjoy all sorts of speculative fiction, and 'tried and true' forms and themes are fine as long as the author has a slightly different take or a fresh perspective on a topic. For example, time machine stories are great—how is yours unique or interesting?"

❶ R-KV-R-Y, A QUARTERLY LITERARY JOURNAL

90 Meetings in 90 Days Press, 499 North Canon Dr., Suite 400, Beverly Hills CA 90210. **E-mail:** r.kv.r.y.editor@gmail.com. **Website:** www.rkvry.com. **Contact:** Mary Akers, editor-in-chief. Online magazine. 100 Web pages. Contains illustrations. Includes photographs. "*r.kv.r.y.* publishes three short stories of high literary quality every quarter. We publish fiction that varies widely in style. We prefer stories of character development, psychological penetration, and lyricism, without sentimentality or purple prose. We ask that all submissions address issues related to recovery from any type of physical, psychological, or cultural loss, dislocation or oppression. We include but do not limit ourselves to issues of substance abuse. We do not publish the standard 'what it was like, what happened and what it is like now' recovery narrative. Works published by *r.kv.r.y.* embrace almost every area of adult interest related to recovery: literary affairs, history, folklore, fiction, poetry, literary criticism, art, music, and the theatre. Material should be presented in a fashion suited to a quarterly that is neither journalistic nor academic. We welcome academic articles from varying fields. We encourage our academic contributors to free themselves from the contraints imposed by academic journals, letting their knowledge, wisdom, and experience rock and roll on these pages. Our intended audience is people of discriminating taste, original ideas, heart, and love of narrative and language." Quarterly. Estab. 2004. Circ. 15,000 quarterly readers.

NEEDS Literary. List of upcoming themes available on website. Receives 30 stories/month. Accepts 3 stories/issue; 12 stories/year. Manuscript published 2-3 months after acceptance. Agented fiction 10%. **Publishes 5-6 new writers/year.** Published TJ Forrester, Kim Chinquee, Alicia Gifford, Andrew Tibbets, Jason Schneiderman. Length: 3,000 words (max). Average length: 2,000 words. Publishes short shorts. Average length of short shorts: 1,000 words. Also publishes literary essays, book reviews, poetry. Sometimes comments on/critiques rejected manuscripts.

HOW TO CONTACT Submit complete manuscript with cover letter through our on-line submission system. Responds to mss in 1-3 months. Considers simultaneous submissions, previously published submissions. Guidelines available on website.

PAYMENT/TERMS Acquires electronic rights. Posts proof pages on site. Publication is copyrighted.

TIPS "Wants strong focus on character development and lively writing style with strong voice. Read our present and former issues (archived online) as well as fiction found in such journals and magazines as *Granta*, *The New Yorker*, *Tri-Quarterly*, *The Atlantic*, *Harper's*, *Story* and similar sources of the highest quality fiction."

❶❷❸ ROSE & THORN JOURNAL

Website: www.roseandthornjournal.com. **Contact:** Barbara Quinn. **E-mail:** editor@roseandthornjournal.com.

Website: www.roseandthornjournal.com. Online journal specializing in literary works of fiction, nonfiction, poetry, and essays. "We created this publication for readers and writers alike. We provide a forum for emerging and established voices. We blend contemporary writing with traditional prose and poetry in an effort to promote the literary arts." Quarterly. Circ. 120,000.

NEEDS Adventure, ethnic/multicultural, experimental, fantasy, historical, horror (dark fantasy, futuristic, psychological, supernatural), humor/satire, literary, mainstream, mystery/suspense, New Age, regional, religious/inspirational, romance (contemporary, futuristic/time travel, gothic, historical, regency, romantic suspense), science fiction, thriller/espionage, western. Receives "several hundred" unsolicited mss/month. Accepts 8-10 mss/issue; 40-50 mss/year. **Publishes many new writers/year.** Publishes short shorts. Also publishes literary essays, poetry. Sometimes comments on rejected mss. extreme erotica, political or social rants, gratuitous violence. Length: 3,000 max.

HOW TO CONTACT Query with or without published clips or send complete ms. Accepts submissions by e-mail. Include estimated word count, 150-word bio, list of publications and author's byline. Responds in 1 week to queries; 1 month to mss. Accepts simultaneous submissions and reprints. Sample copy free. Writer's guidelines online. Length: 3,000 word limit.

PAYMENT/TERMS Writer retains all rights. Sends galleys to author. Pays $5 for each piece published.

TIPS "Clarity, control of the language, evocative stories that tug at the heart and make their mark on the reader long after it's been read. We look for uniqueness in voice, style and characterization. New twists on old themes are always welcome. Use all aspects of good writing in your stories, including dynamic characters, strong narrative voice and a riveting original plot. We have eclectic tastes, so go ahead and give us a shot. Read the publication and other quality literary journals so you'll see what we look for. Always check your spelling and grammar before submitting. Reread your submission with a critical eye and ask yourself, 'Does it evoke an emotional response? Have I completely captured my reader?' Check your submission for 'it' and 'was' and see if you can come up with a better way to express yourself. Be unique."

SLOW TRAINS LITERARY JOURNAL

P.O. 4741, Denver CO 80155. **E-mail:** editor@slowtrains. com. **Website:** www.slowtrains.com. Estab. 2000. .

NEEDS Literary. No romance, sci-fi, or other specific genre-writing. Receives 100+ unsolicited mss/month. Accepts 10-15 mss/issue; 40-50 mss/year. Publishes ms 3 months after acceptance. **Publishes 20- 40 new writers/year.** Length: 1,000-5,000 words; average length: 3,500 words. Publishes short shorts. Also publishes literary essays, poetry. Rarely comments on rejected mss.

HOW TO CONTACT Accepts submissions by e-mail pasted into the body of the text. Responds in 2 months. Accepts simultaneous and reprints submissions. Sample copy online. Writer's guidelines online.

PAYMENT/TERMS Pays 2 contributor's copies. Acquires one time, electronic rights with optional archiving.

TIPS "The first page must be able to pull the reader in immediately. Use your own fresh, poetic, compelling voice. Center your story around some emotional truth, and be sure of what you're trying to say."

SNREVIEW

197 Fairchild Ave., Fairfield CT 06825-4856. (203)366-5991. **E-mail:** editor@snreview.org. **Website:** www. snreview.org. **Contact:** Joseph Conlin, editor. Estab. 1999. E-zine, Kindle and print edition specializing in literary short stories, essays and poetry. "We search for material that not only has strong characters and plot but also a devotion to imagery." Now available in a print edition. Quarterly.

NEEDS literary, mainstream. Receives 300 unsolicited mss/month. Accepts 40+ mss/issue; 150 mss/year. Publishes ms 3 months after acceptance. **Publishes 75 new writers/year.** Recently published work by Frank X. Walker, Adrian Louis, Barbara Burkhardt, E. Lindsey Balkan, Marie Griffin and Jonathan Lerner. Length: 1,000-7,000 words; average length: 4,000 words. Also publishes literary essays, literary criticism, poetry.

HOW TO CONTACT Accepts submissions by e-mail only. Copy and paste work into the body of the e-mail. Don't send attachments. Include 100 word bio and list of publications. Responds in 7 months to mss. Accepts simultaneous submissions. Sample copy online. Writer's guidelines online. A print edition and a Kindle edition of *SNReview* is now available from an on-demand printer.

PAYMENT/TERMS Acquires first electronic and print rights.

SPACEWESTERNS

P.O. Box 93, Parker Ford PA 19457. **Website:** www. spacewesterns.com. **E-mail:** submissions2018@spacewesterns.com. **Contact:** N.E. Lilly, editor-in-chief. E-zine. "Aside from strictly short stories we also like to see stage plays, screen plays, comics, audio files of stories, short form videos and animation." Weekly. Estab. 2007.

NEEDS adventure, comics/graphic novels, ethnic/multicultural, fantasy (space fantasy), horror (dark fantasy, futuristic, psychological, supernatural), humor/satire, mystery, science fiction (hard science/technological, soft/sociological), western (frontier saga, traditional), but it *must be space western*, science fiction western. List of upcoming themes available on website. Receives 12 mss/month. Accepts 52 mss/year. Ms published within 6 months after acceptance. **Publishes 12 new writers/year.** Published Camille Alexa, Vonnie Winslow Crist, Jens Rushing, Amanda Spikol, Donald Jacob Uitvlugt, John M. Whalen, A.R. Yngve, Filamena Young. Length: 2,500-7,500 words. Average length: 4,000-5,000 words. Also publishes literary essays, literary criticism, book reviews, poetry. Send review copies to N. E. Lilly. Often comments on/critiques rejected mss.

HOW TO CONTACT Send complete ms with cover letter. Accepts submissions by e-mail only. Include estimated word count. Responds to queries immediately. Responds to mss in 6 weeks. Considers previously published submissions, multiple submissions. Guidelines available on website.

PAYMENT/TERMS Writers receive 1¢ per word, $50 max. Pays on publication. Publication is copyrighted.

TIPS "First of all, have a well-crafted manuscript (no spelling or grammar errors). Secondly, a good idea—many errors will be forgiven for a solid concept and fresh idea. Be yourself. Write what you love. Familiarize yourself with the scope of the Universe and astronomical concepts."

⬤ STILL CRAZY

(614)746-0859. **E-mail:** editor@crazylitmag.com. **Website:** crazylitmag.com. **Contact:** Barbara Kussow, editor. "*Still Crazy* publishes writing by people over age 50 and writing by people of any age if the topic is about people over 50. The editor is particularly interested in material that challenges the stereotypes of older people and that portrays older people's inner lives as rich and rewarding." Semiannual.

○ Accepts 3-4 mss/issue; 6-8/year.

NEEDS Feminist. Special interests: seniors (over 50). "Does not want material that is too sentimental or in-

spirational, 'Geezer' humor, or anything too grim." Accepts 3-4 mss/issue; 6-8 mss/year. Manuscript published 6-12 months after acceptance. Length: 3,500 words (max) under 2,500 words more likely to be published. Publishes short shorts. Sometimes features a "First Story," a story by an author who has not been published before. Also publishes poetry and short nonfiction 1,500 words or less. Sometimes comments on/critiques rejected mss. Paper copies $10; subscriptions $18 (2 issues per year); downloads $4.

HOW TO CONTACT Upload submissions via submissions manager on website. Attach MS Word doc or cut and paste into text of e-mail. Include estimated word count, brief bio, age of writer or "Over 50." Responds to mss in 3-5 months. Considers simultaneous submissions, previously published submissions (please indicate when and where), multiple submissions. Guidelines available on website.

PAYMENT/TERMS Acquires one-time rights. Publication is not copyrighted. Pays one contributor copy.

TIPS Looking for "interesting characters and interesting situations that might interest readers of all ages. Humor and Lightness welcome."

⬤ STIRRING: A LITERARY COLLECTION

c/o Erin Elizabeth Smith, Department of English, 301 McClung Tower, University of Tennessee, Knoxville TN 37996-0430. **E-mail:** eesmith81@gmail.com. **Website:** www.sundresspublications.com/stirring/. **Contact:** Erin Elizabeth Smith, managing and poetry editor. Estab. 1999.

○ "*Stirring* is one of the oldest continually-published literary journals on the web. *Stirring* is a monthly literary magazine that publishes poetry, short fiction, creative nonfiction, and photography by established and emerging writers."

⬤ STORY BYTES

Website: www.storybytes.com. **E-mail:** editor@storybytes.com. **Website:** www.storybytes.com. **Contact:** M. Stanley Bubien, editor. Electronic zine. "We are strictly an electronic publication, appearing on the Internet in three forms. First, the stories are sent to an electronic mailing list of readers. They also get placed on our website, both in PDF and HTML format."

NEEDS "Stories must be very short—having a length that is the power of 2, specifically: 2, 4, 8, 16, 32, etc." No sexually explicit material. "Would like to see more material dealing with religion—not necessarily 'inspirational' stories, but those that show the struggles of living a life of faith in a realistic manner." **Publishes 33% new writers/year.** Recently published work by Richard K. Weems, Joseph Lerner, Lisa Cote, and Thomas Sennet.

HOW TO CONTACT Please query first. Query with or without published clips or send complete ms. Accepts submissions by e-mail. "I prefer plain text with story title, authorship and word count. Only accepts electronic submissions. See website for complete guidelines." Sample copy online. Writer's guidelines online.

TIPS "In *Story Bytes* the very short stories themselves range in topic. Many explore a brief event—a vignette of something unusual, unique and at times something even commonplace. Some stories can be bizarre, while others quite lucid. Some are based on actual events, while others are entirely fictional. Try to develop conflict early on (in the first sentence if possible!), and illustrate or resolve this conflict through action rather than description. I believe we'll find an audience for electronic published works primarily in the short story realm."

STORYSOUTH

5603B W. Friendly Ave., Suite 282, Greensboro NC 27410. **E-mail:** terry@storysouth.com. **Website:** www.storysouth.com. **Contact:** Terry Kennedy, editor. Estab. 2001. "*storySouth* is interested in fiction, creative nonfiction, and poetry by writers from the New South. The exact definition of New South varies from person to person and we leave it up to the writer to define their own connection to the southern United States." Quarterly.

NEEDS Experimental, literary, regional (South), translations. Receives 70 unsolicited mss/month. Accepts 5 mss/issue; 20 mss/year. Publishes ms 1 month after acceptance. **Publishes 5-10 new writers/year.** Average length: 4,000 words. Publishes short shorts. Also publishes literary essays, literary criticism, poetry. Often comments on rejected mss. Average length: 4,000 words.

HOW TO CONTACT Send complete ms. Accepts online submissions only. Responds in 4 months to mss. Accepts simultaneous submissions. Writer's guidelines online.

PAYMENT/TERMS Acquires one time rights.

TIPS "What really makes a story stand out is a strong voice and a sense of urgency—a need for the reader to keep reading the story and not put it down until it is finished."

STRANGE HORIZONS

Strange Horizons, Inc., P.O. Box 1693, Dubuque IA 52004-1693. **Website:** http://strangehorizons.com. **E-mail:** fiction@strangehorizons.com. Online magazine. "We're a science fiction magazine dedicated to showcasing new voices in the genre." Weekly. Estab. 2000.

NEEDS Fantasy (space fantasy, sword and sorcery), feminist, science fiction (hard science/technological, soft/sociological). Does not want horror; see website. Receives 300 mss/month. Accepts 48 or 50 mss/year. Does not read December. Ms published 2-4 months after acceptance. **Publishes 5-10 new writers/year.** Published Liz Williams, Charlie Anders, Elizabeth Bear, Carrie Vaughn, Benjamin Rosenbaum and Ruth Nestvold. Length: 2,000-8,000 words. Average length: 3,600 words. Publishes short shorts rarely. Also publishes literary essays, literary criticism, book reviews, poetry. Send review queries to reviews@strangehorizons.com. Rarely comments on/critiques rejected mss.

HOW TO CONTACT Accepts submissions by submission form online. Responds to queries in 1 week. Responds to mss in 3 months. Guidelines available on website.

PAYMENT/TERMS Writers receive 5¢ per word. Pays on acceptance. Acquires first rights.

THE SUMMERSET REVIEW

25 Summerset Dr., Smithtown NY 11787. **E-mail:** editor@summersetreview.org. **Website:** www.summersetreview.org. **Contact:** Joseph Levens, editor. Estab. 2002. Magazine: illustrations and photographs. "Our goal is simply to publish the highest quality literary fiction and essays intended for a general audience. This is a simple online literary journal of high quality material, so simple you can call it unique." Periodically releases print issues. Quarterly.

NEEDS Literary. No sci-fi, horror, or graphic erotica. Receives 150 unsolicited mss/month. Accepts 4 mss/issue; 18 mss/year. Publishes ms 2-3 months after acceptance. **Publishes 5-10 new writers/year.** Length: 8,000 words; average length: 3,000 words. Publishes short shorts. Also publishes literary essays. Usually critiques on mss that were almost accepted.

HOW TO CONTACT Send complete ms. Accepts submissions by e-mail. Responds in 1-2 weeks to queries; 4-12 weeks to mss. Accepts simultaneous and reprints submissions. Writer's guidelines online.

PAYMENT/TERMS Complimentary copy of back issue in print. Acquires no rights other than one-time publishing, although we request credit if first published in the *Summerset Review*. Sends galleys to author.

TIPS "Style counts. We prefer innovative or at least very smooth, convincing voices. Even the dullest of premises or the complete lack of conflict make for an interesting story if it is told in the right voice and style. We like to find little, interesting facts and/or connections subtly sprinkled throughout the piece. Harsh language should be used only if/when necessary. If we are choosing between light and dark subjects, the light will usually win."

⊙⊙ TERRAIN.ORG: A JOURNAL OF THE BUILT & NATURAL ENVIROMENTS

Terrain.org, P.O. Box 19161, Tucson AZ 19161. 520-241-7390. **Website:** www.terrain.org. **Contact:** Simmons Buntin, editor-in-chief. "Terrain.org is based on and thus welcomes quality submissions from new and experienced authors and artists alike. Our online journal accepts only the finest poetry, essays, fiction, articles, artwork, and other contributions' material that reaches deep into the earth's fiery core, or humanity's incalculable core, and brings forth new insights and wisdom. Sponsors *Terrain.org 2nd Annual Contest in Poetry, Fiction, and Nonfiction!* Submissions due by August 1. How to Submit: Go to Submission Manager Online Tool." Semiannual.

NEEDS Adventure, ethnic/multicultural, experimental, family saga, fantasy, feminist, historical, horror, humor/satire, literary, mainstream, military/war, mystery, psychic/supernatural/occult, science fiction, thriller/espionage, translations, western. Special interests: environmental. Does not want erotica. All issues are theme-based. List of upcoming themes available on website. Receives 25 mss/month. Accepts 3-5 mss/issue; 6-10 mss/year. Does not read August 1-September 30 and February 1-March 30. Manuscript published five weeks to 18 months after acceptance. Agented fiction 5%. **Publishes 1-3 new writers/year.** Published Al Sim, Jacob MacArthur Mooney, T.R. Healy, Deborah Fries, Andrew Wingfield, Braden Hepner, Chavawn Kelly, Tamara Kaye Sellman. Length: 1,000-8,000 words. Average length: 5,000 words. Publishes short shorts. Average length of short shorts: 750 words. Also publishes literary essays, literary criticism, book reviews, poetry, articles, and artwork. Send review copies to Simmon Buntin. Sometimes comments on/critiques rejected mss.

HOW TO CONTACT Send complete ms with cover letter. Accepts submissions online at http://sub.terrain.org. Include brief bio. Responds to queries in 2 weeks. Responds to mss in 8-12 weeks. Considers simultaneous submissions, previously published submissions. Guidelines available on website. Accepts submissions online@ http://sub.terrain.org. Include brief bio. Send complete ms with cover letter.

PAYMENT/TERMS Acquires one-time rights. Sends galleys to author. Publication is copyrighted.

TIPS "We have three primary criteria in reviewing fiction: 1) The story is compelling and well-crafted. 2) The story provides some element of surprise; i.e., whether in content, form or delivery we are unexpectedly delighted in what we've read. 3) The story meets an upcoming theme, even if only peripherally. Read fiction in the current issue and perhaps some archived work, and if you like what you read—and our overall enviromental slant—then send us your best work. Make sure you follow our submission guidelines (including cover note with bio), and that your manuscript is as error-free as possible."

⊙ TOASTED CHEESE

E-MAIL: editors@toasted-cheese.com. E-mail: submit@toasted-cheese.com. Website: www.toasted-cheese.com. Estab. 2001. E-zine specializing in fiction, creative nonfiction, poetry and flash fiction. "*Toasted Cheese* accepts submissions of previously unpublished fiction, flash fiction, creative nonfiction and poetry. Our focus is on quality of work, not quantity. Some issues will therefore contain fewer/more pieces than previous issues. We don't restrict publication based on subject matter. We encourage submissions from innovative writers in all genres." Quarterly.

NEEDS Adventure, children's/juvenile, ethnic/multicultural, fantasy, feminist, gay, historical, horror, humor/satire, lesbian, literary, mainstream, mystery/suspense, New Age, psychic/supernatural/occult, romance, science fiction, thriller/espionage, western. "No fan fiction. No chapters or excerpts unless they read as a stand-alone story. No first drafts." Receives 150 unsolicited mss/month. Accepts 1-10 mss/issue; 5-30 mss/year. **Publishes 15 new writers/year.** Publishes short shorts. Also publishes poetry.

HOW TO CONTACT Send complete ms in body of e-mail; no attachments. Accepts submissions by e-mail. Responds in 4 months to mss. No simultaneous submissions. Sample copy online. Follow online submission guidelines.

PAYMENT/TERMS Acquires electronic rights. Sponsors awards/contests.

TIPS "We are looking for clean, professional writing from writers of any level. Accepted stories will be concise and compelling. We are looking for writers who are serious about the craft: tomorrow's literary stars before they're famous. Take your submission seriously, yet remember that levity is appreciated. You are submitting not to traditional 'editors' but to fellow writers who appreciate the efforts of those in the trenches. Follow online submission guidelines."

TOWER OF LIGHT FANTASY FREE ONLINE

9701 Harford Road, Carney MD 21234. **E-mail:** msouth847@yahoo.com. **Website:** www.tolfantasy. net. **Contact:** Michael Southard, editor. Online magazine. "To publish great fantasy stories, especially the genre-blending kind such as dark fantasy, urban, science, and superhero fantasy. Romantic fantasy (not erotic, however) is also acceptable. And *Tower of Light* would very much like to showcase new work by beginning writers." Biannual. Estab. 2007.

NEEDS Fantasy (space fantasy, sword and sorcery), horror (dark fantasy, futuristic, supernatural), psychic/supernatural/occult, religious (fantasy), romance (fantasy). Does not want erotic fantasy, or anything that does not have a mystical or supernatural element. List of upcoming themes available on website. Receives 15-30 mss/month. Accepts 6 mss/issue; 12 mss/year. Reading period: Jan 1-Mar 31; July 1-Aug 31. Ms published 6-12 months after acceptance. Published Ian Whates, Christopher Heath, Tom Williams, Daniel Henderson, Alice M. Roelke, Matthew Baron, Eric S. Brown, Ryder Patzuk-Russell, and Mischell Lyne. Length: 500-4,000 words. Average length: 3,500 words. Publishes short shorts. Also publishes book reviews. Send review copies to Michael Southard. Sometimes comments on/critiques rejected mss.

HOW TO CONTACT Send ms in the body of e-mail. Unfortunately, artwork must be sent as an attachment. Responds to mss in 6-12 weeks. Considers previously published submissions, multiple submissions. Guidelines, sample copy available on website.

PAYMENT/TERMS Writers and artists receive $5. Pays on publication. Acquires one time rights, electronic rights. Occasionally sends galleys to author. Publication is not copyrighted.

TIPS "Strong, well-developed characters that really elicit an emotional response, good writing, original plots and world-building catch my attention. Send me a good story, and make sure to check your spelling and grammar. I don't mind a couple of errors, but when there's more than half a dozen, it gets really irritating. Make sure to study the guidelines thoroughly; I'm looking for character-driven stories, preferably in third person limited point-of-view."

VERBSAP.COM, CONCISE PROSE. ENOUGH SAID.

AL **Website:** www.verbsap.com. **E-mail:** editor@verbsap.com. **Contact:** Laurie Seider, editor. Online magazine. "Verbsap showcases an eclectic selection of the finest in concise prose by established and emerging writers." Published quarterly. Estab. 2005.

NEEDS Literary, mainstream. Does not want violent, racist or pornographic content. Accepts 200 mss/year. Ms published 2-4 weeks after acceptance. Length: 3,000 words (max). Average length: 2,000 words. Publishes short shorts. Average length of short shorts: 900 words. Also publishes literary essays, author and artist interviews, and book reviews. Always comments on/critiques rejected mss.

HOW TO CONTACT Follow online guidelines. Accepts submissions by e-mail. Responds to mss in 1-3 weeks. Considers simultaneous submissions. Guidelines available on website.

PAYMENT/TERMS Sends galleys to author. Publication is copyrighted.

TIPS "We're looking for stark, elegant prose. Make us weep or make us laugh, but move us. You might find our 'Editor's Notebook' essays helpful."

WEB DEL SOL

Wed del Sol Association, 2020 Pennsylvania Ave. NW, Suite 443, Washington D.C. 20006. **E-mail:** editor@webdelsol.com. **Website:** www.webdelsol.com. **Contact:** Michael Neff, editor-in-chief. Estab. 1994. Electronic magazine. "The goal of *Web Del Sol* is to use the medium of the Internet to bring the finest in contemporary literary arts to a larger audience. To that end, WDS not only web-publishes collections of work by accomplished writers and poets, but hosts over 25 literary arts publications on the WWW such as *Del Sol*

Review, North American Review, Global City Review, The Literary Review and *The Prose Poem*." Estab. 1994.

NEEDS Literary. "*WDS* publishes work considered to be literary in nature, i.e. non-genre fiction. *WDS* also publishes poetry, prose poetry, essays and experimental types of writing." **Publishes 100-200 new writers/year.**

HOW TO CONTACT "Submissions by e-mail from September through November and from January through March only. Submissions must contain some brief bio, list of prior publications (if any), and a short work or portion of that work, neither to exceed 1,000 words. Editors will contact if the balance of work is required." Sample copy online.

TIPS "*WDS* wants fiction that is absolutely cutting edge, unique and/or at a minimum, accomplished with a crisp style and concerning subjects not usually considered the objects of literary scrutiny. Read works in such publications as *Conjunctions* (www.conjunctions.com) and *North American Review* (webdelsol.com/NorthAmReview/NAR) to get an idea of what we are looking for."

WILD VIOLET

P.O. Box 39706, Philadelphia PA 19106-9706. **E-mail:** wildvioletmagazine@yahoo.com. **Website:** www.wildviolet.net. **Contact:** Alyce Wilson, editor. Estab. 2001. Online magazine: illustrations, photos. "Our goal is to make a place for the arts: to make the arts more accessible and to serve as a creative forum for writers and artists. Our audience includes English-speaking readers from all over the world, who are interested in both 'high art' and pop culture." Quarterly.

NEEDS Comics/graphic novels, ethnic/multicultural, experimental, fantasy (space fantasy, sword and sorcery), feminist, gay, horror (dark fantasy, futuristic, psychological, supernatural), humor/satire, lesbian, literary, New Age, psychic/supernatural/occult, science fiction. "No stories where sexual or violent content is just used to shock the reader. No racist writings." Receives 30 unsolicited mss/month. Accepts 5 mss/issue; 20 mss/year. **Publishes 30 new writers/year.** Recently published work by Rik Hunik, Wayne Scheer, Jane McDonald, Mark Joseph Kiewlak, T. Richard Williams, and Susan Snowden. Length: 500-6,000 words; average length: 3,000 words. Also publishes literary essays, literary criticism, poetry. Sometimes comments on rejected mss.

HOW TO CONTACT Send complete ms. Accepts submissions by e-mail. Include estimated word count

and brief bio. Send SASE for return of ms or send a disposable copy of ms and #10 SASE for reply only. Responds in 1 week to queries; 3-6 months to mss. Accepts simultaneous, multiple submissions. Sample copy online. Writer's guidelines by e-mail.

PAYMENT/TERMS Writers receive bio and links on contributor's page. Request limited electronic rights, for online publication and archival only. Sponsors awards/contests.

TIPS "We look for stories that are well-paced and show character and plot development. Even short shorts should do more than simply paint a picture. Manuscripts stand out when the author's voice is fresh and engaging. Avoid muddying your story with too many characters and don't attempt to shock the reader with an ending you have not earned. Experiment with styles and structures, but don't resort to experimentation for its own sake."

WORD RIOT

P.O. Box 414, Middletown NJ 07748-3143. (732)706-1272. **Fax:** (732)706-5856. **E-mail:** wr.submissions@gmail.com. **Website:** www.wordriot.org. **Contact:** Jackie Corley, publisher. Estab. 2002. Online magazine. Monthly. Member, CLMP.

NEEDS Humor/satire, literary, mainstream. "No fantasy, science fiction, romance." Accepts 20-25 mss/issue; 240-300 mss/year. Publishes ms 1-2 months after acceptance. Agented fiction 5%. Publishes 8-10 new writers/year. Length: 300-6,000 words; average length: 2,700 words. Publishes flash fiction, short stories, creative nonfiction and poetry. Also publishes literary essays, poetry. Often comments on rejected mss.

HOW TO CONTACT Accepts submissions by e-mail; also by online submission form at wordriot.submishmash.com/Submit. Do not send submissions by mail. Include estimated word count and brief bio. Responds in 4-6 weeks to mss. Accepts multiple submissions. Sample copy online. Writer's guidelines online.

PAYMENT/TERMS Acquires electronic rights. Not copyrighted. Sponsors awards/contests.

TIPS "We're always looking for something edgy or quirky. We like writers who take risks."

THE WRITE PLACE AT THE WRITE TIME

E-mail: submissions@thewriteplaceatthewritetime.org. **Website:** www.thewriteplaceatthewritetime.org. **Contact:** Nicole M. Bouchard, Editor-in-Chief. Estab. 2008.

NEEDS This online quarterly literary publication features fiction, poetry, "Our Stories" - nonfiction, a Writers' Craft Box of writing essays and resources from professionals in the field, an Exploration of Theme page, Archives of past issues, A Writers' Contest, fine artwork from artists whose backgrounds include having done work for *The New York Times*, and Best-Selling author interviews such as Janet Fitch (*White Oleander*), Frances Mayes (*Under the Tuscan Sun*) and Arthur Golden (*Memoirs of a Geisha*); all of whom have had their works adapted into major motion pictures. Encourages beginning or unpublished writers to submit work for consideration; publishes new writers. Accepts outstanding work by beginning and established writers. Email: editorialstaff@thewriteplaceatthewritetime.org. No erotica, explicit horror/gore/violence, political Length: 3,500 words/max; average length of stories: 3,000 words. Average length of short-shorts: 1,000 words.

HOW TO CONTACT Send complete ms with cover letter by e-mail. Include est. word count, brief bio. Accepts multiple submissions, up to 3 fiction/nonfiction stories or 5 poems at a time. Accepts 6-8 mss/year; receives 24-32 mss/year

PAYMENT/TERMS We are not currently offering monetary compensation.

TIPS "We sponsor writer's contests—visit the website for details." Our publication is copyrighted. Sends prepublication galleys to author depending on whether the story underwent significant edits. We like to work closely with our writers. If the material is only slightly edited, then we don't.

THE WRITING DISORDER

P.O. Box 93613, Los Angeles CA 90093. (323)336-5822. **E-mail:** submit@thewritingdisorder.com. **Website:** www.thewritingdisorder.com. **Contact:** C.E. Lukather, editor; Paul Garson, managing editor. Estab. 2009. Quarterly literary magazine featuring new and established writers. "*The Writing Disorder* is an online literary magazine devoted to literature, art, and culture. The mission of the magazine is to showcase new and emerging writers—particularly those in writing programs—as well as established ones. The magazine also features original artwork, photography, and comic art. Although it strives to publish original and experimental work, *The Writing Disorder* remains rooted in the classic art of storytelling."

NEEDS Does not want to see romance, religious, or fluff. 7,500 words maximum.

HOW TO CONTACT Query.

PAYMENT/TERMS Pays contributor's copies.

TIPS "We are looking for work from new writers, writers in writing programs, and students and faculty of all ages."

CONSUMER MAGAZINES

In this section of *Novel & Short Story Writer's Market* are consumer magazines that reach a broad readership. Many have circulations in the hundreds of thousands or millions. And among the oldest magazines listed here are ones not only familiar to us, but also to our parents, grandparents and even great-grandparents: *The Atlantic Monthly* (1857); *Esquire* (1933); and *Ellery Queen's Mystery Magazine* (1941).

Consumer periodicals make excellent markets for fiction in terms of exposure, prestige and payment. Because these magazines are well known, however, competition is great. Even the largest consumer publications buy only one or two stories an issue, yet thousands of writers submit to these popular magazines.

Despite the odds, it is possible for talented new writers to break into print in the magazines listed here. Your keys to breaking into these markets are careful research, professional presentation and, of course, top-quality fiction.

TYPES OF CONSUMER MAGAZINES

In this section you will find a number of popular publications, some for a broad-based, general-interest readership and others for large but select groups of readers—children, teenagers, women, men and seniors. There are also religious and church-affiliated magazines, publications devoted to the interests of particular cultures and outlooks, and top markets for genre fiction.

SELECTING THE RIGHT MARKET

Unlike smaller journals and publications, most of the magazines listed here are available at newsstands and bookstores. Many can also be found in the library, and guidelines and sample copies are almost always available by mail or online. Start your search by reviewing the listings, then familiarize yourself with the fiction included in the magazines that interest you.

Don't make the mistake of thinking that just because you are familiar with a magazine, their fiction is the same today as when you first saw it. Nothing could be further from the truth. Consumer magazines, no matter how well established, are constantly revising their fiction needs as they strive to expand their audience base.

In a magazine that uses only one or two stories an issue, take a look at the nonfiction articles and features as well. These can give you a better idea of the audience for the publication and clues to the type of fiction that might appeal to them.

If you write genre fiction, look in the Category Index. There you will find a list of markets that say they are looking for a particular subject.

FURTHERING YOUR SEARCH

See "How to Use NSSWM" for information about the material common to all listings in this book. In this section in particular, pay close attention to the number of submissions a magazine receives in a given period and how many they publish in the same period. This will give you a clear picture of how stiff your competition can be.

While many of the magazines listed here publish one or two pieces of fiction in each issue, some also publish special fiction issues once or twice a year. When possible, we have indicated this in the listing information. We also note if the magazine is open to novel excerpts as well as short fiction, and we advise novelists to query first before submitting long work.

The "Business of Fiction Writing" covers the basics of submitting your work. Professional presentation is a must for all markets listed. Editors at consumer magazines are especially busy, and anything you can do to make your manuscript easy to read and accessible will help your chances of being published. Most magazines want to see complete manuscripts, but watch for publications in this section that require a query first.

The maple leaf symbol ✪ identifies our Canadian listings. You will also find some English-speaking markets from around the world. These foreign magazines are denoted with ✪ at the beginning of the listings.

◐ ⑤ AFRICAN AMERICAN REVIEW

St. Louis University, 317 Adorjan Hall, 3800 Lindell Blvd., St. Louis MO 63108. (314)977-3688. **Fax:** (314)977-1514. **E-mail:** keenanam@slu.edu. **Website:** aar.slu.edu. Estab. 1967. Magazine: 7X10; 200 pages; 55 lb., acid-free paper; 100 lb. skid stock cover; illustrations; photos. "Essays on African-American literature, theater, film, art and culture generally; interviews; poetry and fiction; book reviews." Quarterly. Circ. 2,000.

NEEDS Ethnic/multicultural, experimental, feminist, literary, mainstream. "No children's/juvenile/young adult/teen." Receives 35 unsolicited mss/month. Accepts 10 mss/year. Publishes ms 1 year after acceptance. Agented fiction 0%. Recently published work by Solon Timothy Woodward, Eugenia Collier, Jeffery Renard Allen, Patrick Lohier, Raki Jones, Olympia Vernon. Length: 2,500-5,000 words; average length: 3,000 words. Also publishes literary essays, literary criticism, poetry. Sometimes comments on rejected mss. No children's/juvenile/young adult/teen. Length: No more than 1,500 words.

HOW TO CONTACT Submit complete ms only via online manuscript fasttrack at http://aar.expressacademic.org. Responds in 1 week to queries; 3 months to mss. Sample copy for $12. Writer's guidelines online. Reviews fiction.

PAYMENT/TERMS Pays 1 contributor's copy and 5 offprints. Provides first North American serial rights. Sends galleys to author.

◐ AFRICAN VOICES

African Voices Communications, Inc., 270 W. 96th St., New York NY 10025. (212)865-2982. **Fax:** (212)316-3335. **E-mail:** africanvoices@aol.com. **Website:** www.africanvoices.com. Estab. 1992. *African Voices*, published quarterly, is an "art and literary magazine that highlights the work of people of color. We publish ethnic literature and poetry on any subject. We also consider all themes and styles: avant-garde, free verse, haiku, light verse, and traditional. We do not wish to limit the reader or author."

◌ Considers poetry written by children. Has published poetry by Reg E. Gaines, Maya Angelou, Jessica Care Moore, Asha Bandele, Tony Medina, and Louis Reyes Rivera. *African Voices* is about 48 pages, magazine-sized, professionally printed, saddle-stapled, with paper cover. Receives about 100 submissions/year, accepts about 30%. Press run is 20,000. Single copy: $4; subscription: $12.

NEEDS Length: 500-2,500 words.

HOW TO CONTACT Send complete ms. Include short bio. Send SASE for return of ms. Responds in 3 months to queries. Accepts simultaneous and reprints submissions. Reviews fiction.

PAYMENT/TERMS Pays $25-50. Pays on publication for first North American serial rights.

◐ ⑤ AIM: AMERICA'S INTERCULTURAL MAGAZINE

P.O. Box 390, Milton WA 98354-0390. (253) 815-9030. **Fax:** (206) 543-2746. **E-mail:** apiladoone@aol.com. **Website:** www.aimmagazine.org. **Contact:** Ruth Apilado, associate editor. Estab. 1975. Publishes material "to purge racism from the human bloodstream through the written word—that is the purpose of Aim Magazine."

NEEDS Publishes short shorts. Has published work by Christina Touregny, Thomas Lee Harris, Michael Williams and Jake Halpern. Does not wanted "religious" work.

PAYMENT/TERMS Pays $25-35.

◐ ALIMENTUM, THE LITERATURE OF FOOD

P.O. Box 210028, Nashville TN 37221, Nashville TN 37221. **E-mail:** submissions@alimentumjournal.com. **Website:** www.alimentumjournal.com. **Contact:** Cortney Davis, Poetry Editor. Estab. 2005. Literary magazine/journal: 6×7.5, 128 pages, matte cover. Contains illustrations. "All of our stories, poems and essays have food or drink as a theme." Semiannual. "We're seeking fiction, creative nonfiction, and poetry all around the subject of food or drink. We do not read year-round. Check website for reading periods."

NEEDS Literary. Special interests: food related. Receives 100 mss/month. Accepts 20-24 mss/issue. Manuscript published one to two years after acceptance. **Publishes average of 2 new writers/year.** Published Mark Kurlansky, Oliver Sacks, Dick Allen, Ann Hood, Carly Sachs. Length: 3,000 words (max). Average length: 1,000-2,000 words. Publishes short shorts. Also publishes literary essays, poetry, spot illustrations. Rarely comments on/critiques rejected mss.

HOW TO CONTACT Send complete ms with cover letter. Snail mail only. No previously published work. 5-poem limit per submission. Simultaneous submissions okay. Responds to queries and mss in 1-3 months. Send either SASE (or IRC) for return of ms or disposable copy of ms and #10 SASE for reply only. Sample copy available for $10. Guidelines available on website. Check for submission reading periods as they vary from year to year. Send complete ms.

PAYMENT/TERMS Writers receive 1 contributor's copy. Additional contributor's copies $8. Pays on publication. Acquires first North American serial rights. Publication is copyrighted.

TIPS "No email submissions, only snail mail. Mark outside envelope to the attention of Poetry, Fiction, or Nonfiction Editor."

ⓘⓟⓢ ANALOG SCIENCE FICTION & FACT

Dell Magazine Fiction Group, Dell Magazines, Analog Science Fiction & Fact, 267 Broadway, 4th Floor, New York NY 10007-2352. (212)686-7188. **Fax:** (212)686-7414. **E-mail:** analog@dellmagazines.com. **Website:** www.analogsf.com. **Contact:** Dr. Stanley Schmidt, editor. Estab. 1930.

> ○ Fiction published in *Analog* has won numerous Nebula and Hugo Awards.

NEEDS "Basically, we publish science fiction stories. That is, stories in which some aspect of future science or technology is so integral to the plot that, if that aspect were removed, the story would collapse. The science can be physical, sociological, or psychological. The technology can be anything from electronic engineering to biogenetic engineering. But the stories must be strong and realistic, with believable people doing believable things—no matter how fantastic the background might be." No fantasy or stories in which the scientific background is implausible or plays no essential role. Prefers lengths between 2,000 and 7,000 words for shorts, 10,000-20,000 words for novelettes, and 40,000-80,000 for serials.

HOW TO CONTACT Submit via online submissions manager.

PAYMENT/TERMS Analog pays 6-8 cents per word for short stories up to 7,500 words, $450-600 for stories between 7,500 and 10,000 words, and 5-6 cents per word for longer material.

ⓘⓢ ANTIOCH REVIEW

P.O. Box 148, Yellow Springs OH 45387-0148. **E-mail:** mkeyes@antiochreview.org. **Website:** http://antiochcollege.org/antioch_review/. **Contact:** Muriel Keyes. Estab. 1941. Magazine: 6×9; 200 pages; 50 lb. book

offset paper; coated cover stock; illustrations "seldom." "Literary and cultural review of contemporary issues, and literature for general readership." Quarterly. Circ. 3,000. Receives 275 unsolicited mss/month. Accepts 5-6 mss/issue; 20-24 mss/year. No mss accepted June 1-September 1. Publishes ms 10 months after acceptance. Agented fiction 1-2%. **Publishes 1-2 new writers/year.** Recently published work by Edith Pearlman, Peter LaSalle, Rosellen Brown, Nathan Oates, Stephen O'Connor, and Susan Miller. Literary and cultural review of contemporary issues, and literature for general readership.

> ○ Work published in the *Antioch Review* has been included frequently in *The Best American Poetry*, *The Best New Poets* and *The Pushcart Prize*.

NEEDS Literary, experimental, contemporary, translations. No science fiction, fantasy or confessions. Quality fiction only, distinctive in style with fresh insights into the human condition. No science fiction, fantasy, or confessions. generally under 8,000.

HOW TO CONTACT Send complete ms with SASE, preferably mailed flat. Responds in 4-6 months to mss. Sample copy for $7. Writer's guidelines online.

PAYMENT/TERMS Pays $15/printed page. Pays on publication. Pays $15/printed page.

○ⓢ AOIFE'S KISS

The Speculative Fiction Foundation, P.O. Box 782, Cedar Rapids IA 52406-0782. **E-mail:** aoifeskiss@yahoo.com. **Website:** www.samsdotpublishing.com. **Contact:** Tyree Campbell, Managing Editor. Estab. 2002. *Aoife's Kiss* (print version) is 54 pages, magazine-sized, offset-printed, saddle-stapled, perfect-bound, with color paper cover, includes ads. Receives about 300 poems/year, accepts about 50 (17%). Press run is 150; 5 distributed free to reviewers. Single copy: $7; subscription: $22/year, $40 for 2 years. Make checks payable to Sam's Dot Publishing. "Aoife's Kiss is a print and online magazine of fantasy, science fiction, horror, sword & sorcery, and slipstream, published quarterly in March, June, September, and December. Aoife's Kiss publishes short stories, poems, illustrations, articles, and movie/book/chapbook reviews, and interviews with noted individuals in those genres."

NEEDS *Aoife's Kiss*, published quarterly, prints "fantasy, science fiction, sword and sorcery, alternate history, dark fantasy short stories, poems, illustrations, and movie and book reviews." Wants "fantasy, science fiction, spooky horror, and speculative poetry with minimal angst."

HOW TO CONTACT Accepts e-mail submissions (pasted into body of message); no disk submissions. "Submission should include snail mail address and a short (1-2 lines) bio." Reads submissions year round. Accepts e-mail submissions (pasted into body of message); no disk submissions. "Submission should include snail mail address and a short (1-2 lines) bio." Reads submissions year-round.

⬤⬤ ART TIMES

A Literary Journal and Resource for All the Arts, P.O. Box 730, Mount Marion NY 12456-0730. (845)246-6944. **Fax:** (845)246-6944. **E-mail:** info@ArtTimes-Journal.com. **Website:** www.arttimesjournal.com. **Contact:** Raymond J. Steiner. Estab. 1984. Magazine: 12×15; 24 pages; Jet paper and cover; illustrations; photos. "Art Times covers the art fields and is distributed in locations most frequented by those enjoying the arts. Our copies are distributed throughout the Northeast region as well as in most of the galleries of Soho, 57th Street and Madison Avenue in the metropolitan area; locations include theaters, galleries, museums, cultural centers and the like. Our readers are mostly over 40, affluent, art-conscious and sophisticated. Subscribers are located across U.S. and abroad (Italy, France, Germany, Greece, Russia, etc.)." Monthly. Circ. 28,000. Receives 30-50 unsolicited mss/month. Accepts 1 mss/issue; 10 mss/year. Publishes ms 3 years after acceptance. **Publishes 6 new writers/year.** Publishes short shorts.

NEEDS Adventure, ethnic/multicultural, fantasy, feminist, gay, historical, humor/satire, lesbian, literary, mainstream, science fiction, contemporary. "We seek literary pieces, nothing violent, sexist, erotic, juvenile, racist, romantic, political, etc." Looks for quality short fiction that aspires to be literary. Publishes 1 story each issue. "Nothing violent, sexist, erotic, juvenile, racist, romantic, political, off-beat, or related to sports or juvenile fiction." 1,500 words maximum.

HOW TO CONTACT Send complete ms with SASE. Responds in 6 months to mss. Accepts simultaneous, multiple submissions. Sample copy for 9×12 SAE and 6 first-class stamps. Writer's guidelines for #10 SASE or on website. Send complete ms.

PAYMENT/TERMS Pays $25 maximum (honorarium) and 1 year's free subscription. Pays on publication for first North American serial, first rights.

⬤⬤⬤ ASIMOV'S SCIENCE FICTION

Dell Magazine Fiction Group, 267 Broadway, 4th Floor, New York NY 10007. (212)686-7188. **Fax:** (212)686-7414. **E-mail:** asimovssf@dellmagazines.com. **Website:** www.asimovs.com. **Contact:** Brian Bieniowski, managing editor; Sheila Williams, editor; Victoria Green, senior art director; June Levine, associate art director. Estab. 1977. Magazine: 5' 7/8 x 8' 5/8 (trim size); 112 pages; 30 lb. newspaper; 70 lb. to 8 pt. C1S cover stock; illustrations; rarely photos. Magazine consists of science fiction and fantasy stories for adults and young adults. Publishes "the best short science fiction available." Receives approximately 800 unsolicited mss/month. Accepts 10 mss/issue. Publishes ms 6-12 months after acceptance. Agented fiction 10%. **Publishes 10 new writers/year.** Recently published work by Robert Silverberg and Larry Niven. Publishes short shorts. Sometimes comments on rejected mss. Reviews fiction. "Magazine consists of science fiction and fantasy stories for adults and young adults. Publishes the best short science fiction available."

> 💬 Named for a science fiction "legend," *Asimov's* regularly receives Hugo and Nebula Awards. Editor Gardner Dozois has received several awards for editing including Hugos and those from *Locus* magazine.

NEEDS Fantasy, science fiction (hard science, soft sociological). No horror or psychic/supernatural. Would like to see more hard science fiction. "Science fiction primarily. Some fantasy and humor but no sword and sorcery. No explicit sex or violence that isn't integral to the story. It is best to read a great deal of material in the genre to avoid the use of some very old ideas. Send complete ms and SASE with *all* submissions." No horror or psychic/supernatural. Would like to see more hard science fiction. Length: 750-15,000 words.

HOW TO CONTACT Send complete ms with SASE. Responds in 2 months to queries; 3 months to mss. No simultaneous or reprint submissions. Sample copy for $5. Writer's guidelines for #10 SASE or online.

PAYMENT/TERMS Pays 5-8¢/word. Pays on acceptance. Buys first North American serial, nonexclusive foreign serial rights; reprint rights occasionally. Sends galleys to author. Pays 5-8¢/word

⬤⬤ THE ATLANTIC MONTHLY

The Watergate, 600 New Hampshire Ave., NW, Washington DC 20037. (202)266-6000. **Website:** www.theatlantic.com. **Contact:** James Bennet, editor; C. Michael Curtis, fiction editor; David Barber, poetry editor. Estab. 1857. General monthly magazine for an educated readership with broad cultural interests. Literary and contemporary fiction. Receives 1,000 unsolicited mss/month. Accepts 7-8 mss/year. **Publishes 3-4 new writers/year.** Recently published work by Mary Gordon, Tobias Wolff. Accepts multiple submissions. Writer's guidelines online. General magazine for an educated readership with broad cultural and public-affairs interests. "The Atlantic considers unsolicited manuscripts, either fiction or nonfiction. A general familiarity with what we have published in the past is the best guide to our needs and preferences. Manuscripts must be typewritten and double-spaced. Receipt of manuscripts will be acknowledged if accompanied by a self-addressed stamped envelope. Manuscripts will not be returned. **At this time, the print magazine does not read submissions sent via fax or e-mail.** TheAtlantic.com no longer accepts unsolicited submissions."

NEEDS Seeks fiction that is clear, tightly written with strong sense of 'story' and well-defined characters. No longer publishes fiction in the regular magazine. Instead, it will appear in a special newsstand-only fiction issue. Preferred length: 2,00-6,000 words.

HOW TO CONTACT Send complete mss. Responds in 2 months. Send complete ms.

PAYMENT/TERMS Pays $3,000. Pays on acceptance for first North American serial rights.

TIPS "Writers should be aware that this is not a market for beginner's work (nonfiction and fiction), nor is it truly for intermediate work. Study this magazine before sending only your best, most professional work. When making first contact, cover letters are sometimes helpful, particularly if they cite prior publications or involvement in writing programs. Common mistakes: melodrama, inconclusiveness, lack of development, unpersuasive characters and/or dialogue."

BABYBUG

Carus Publishing, 70 East Lake St., Chicago IL 60601. **E-mail:** babybug@caruspub.com. **Website:** www.cricketmag.com. **Contact:** Marianne Carus, editor-in-chief; Suzanne Beck, managing art director. Estab. 1994. "A listening and looking magazine for infants and toddlers ages 6 to 24 months, *Babybug* is 6×7, 24 pages long, printed in large type on high-quality cardboard stock with rounded corners and no staples."

NEEDS "*Babybug* is 'the listening and looking boardbook magazine for infants and toddlers,' intended to be read aloud by a loving adult to foster a love of books and reading in young children ages 6 months-2 years." Looking for very simple and concrete stories. Length: 4-6 short sentences.

PAYMENT/TERMS $25 min.

BACKROADS

P.O. Box 317, Branchville NJ 07826. **Fax:** (973)948-0823. **E-mail:** editor@backroadsusa.com. **Website:** www.backroadsusa.com. Estab. 1995. "*Backroads* is a motorcycle tour magazine geared toward getting motorcyclists on the road and traveling. We provide interesting destinations, unique roadside attractions and eateries, plus Rip & Ride Route Sheets. We cater to all brands. Although Backroads is geared towards the motorcycling population, it is not by any means limited to just motorcycle riders. Non-motorcyclists enjoy great destinations too. As time has gone by, Backroads has developed more and more into a cutting edge touring publication. We like to see submissions that give the reader the distinct impression of being part of the ride they're reading. Words describing the feelings and emotions brought on by partaking in this great and exciting lifestyle are encouraged."

NEEDS Travel, motorcycle-related stories. Publishes ms 3 months after acceptance. Articles must be motorcycle-related and include images of motorcycles to accompany story. It helps if you actually ride a motorcycle.

HOW TO CONTACT Query. Accepts submissions by e-mail. Sample copy for $5. Writer's guidelines on website.

PAYMENT/TERMS Pays 5¢/word. Pays on publication for one-time rights.

THE BEAR DELUXE MAGAZINE

Orlo, 810 SE Belmont, Studio 5, Portland OR 97214. (503)242-1047. **E-mail:** bear@orlo.org. **Website:** www.orlo.org. **Contact:** Tom Webb, editor-in-chief; Kristin Rogers Brown, art director. Estab. 1993. Magazine: 9×12; 48 pages; newsprint paper; Kraft paper cover illustrations; photos. "*The Bear Deluxe Magazine* provides a fresh voice amid often strident and polarized environmental discourse. Street level, solution-oriented, and nondogmatic, *Bear Deluxe* presents lively creative discussion to a diverse readership." Semiannual. "*The Bear Deluxe Magazine* is a national independent environmental arts magazine publishing significant works of reporting, creative nonfiction, literature, visual art and design. Based in the Pacific Northwest, it reaches across cultural and political divides to engage readers on vital issues effecting the environment. Published twice per year, *The Bear Deluxe* includes a wider array and a higher-percentage of visual art work and design than many other publications. Artwork is included both as editorial support and as stand alone or independent art. It has included nationally recognized artists as well as emerging artists. As with any publication, artists are encouraged to review a sample copy for a clearer understanding of the magazine's approach. Unsolicited submissions and samples are accepted and encouraged. *The Bear Deluxe* has been recognized for both its editorial and design excellence. Over the years, awards and positive reviews have been handed down from *Print* magazine, *Utne Reader, Literary Arts, Adbusters*, the Bumbershoot Arts Festival, *Orion, Fact Sheet 5*, the Regional Arts and Culture Council, *The Oregonian*, and the *Library Journal*, among others."

NEEDS Adventure, condensed novels, historical, horror, humor/satire, mystery/suspense, novel excerpts, western. "No detective, children's or horror." Environmentally focused: humor/satire, literary, science fiction. "We would like to see more nontraditional forms." List of upcoming themes available for SASE. Receives 20-30 unsolicited mss/month. Accepts 2-3 mss/issue; 8-12 mss/year. Publishes ms 3 months after acceptance. Publishes 5-6 new writers/year. Recently published work by Peter Houlahan, John Reed and Karen Hueler. Length: 750-4,500 words; average length: 2,500 words. Publishes short shorts. Also publishes literary essays, literary criticism, poetry. Sometimes comments on rejected mss. Stories must have some environmental context, but we view that in a broad sense.

HOW TO CONTACT Query with or without published clips or send complete ms. Send disposable copy of mss. Responds in 3 months to queries; 6 months to mss. Accepts simultaneous submissions and reprints. Sample copy for $5. Writer's guidelines for #10 SASE or on website. Reviews fiction. Also send SASE for guides to new Doug Fir Fiction Award ($1,000 top prize).

PAYMENT/TERMS Pays free subscription to the magazine, contributor's copies and 5¢/word; additional copies for postage. Pays on publication for first, one time rights.

TIPS "Offer to be a stringer for future ideas. Get a copy of the magazine and guidelines, and query us with specific nonfiction ideas and clips. We're look-ing for original, magazine-style stories, not fluff or PR. Fiction, essay, and poetry writers should know we have an open and blind review policy and should keep sending their best work even if rejected once. Be as specific as possible in queries."

BELLINGHAM REVIEW

Mail Stop 9053, Western Washington University, Bellingham WA 98225. (360)650-4863. **E-mail:** bhreview@wwu.edu. **Website:** www.bhreview.org. **Contact:** Marilyn Bruce, managing editor. Estab. 1977. Annual nonprofit magazine published once a year in the Spring. Seeks "Literature of palpable quality: poems stories and essays so beguiling they invite us to touch their essence. The *Bellingham Review* hungers for a kind of writing that nudges the limits of form, or executes traditional forms exquisitely."

NEEDS Experimental, humor/satire, literary, regional (Northwest). Does not want anything nonliterary. 6,000 words maximum.

HOW TO CONTACT Send complete ms.

PAYMENT/TERMS Pays as funds allow.

TIPS "Open submission period is from Sept. 15-Dec. 1. Manuscripts arriving between December 2 and September 14 will be returned unread. The *Bellingham Review* holds 3 annual contests: the 49th Parallel Award for poetry, the Annie Dillard Award for Nonfiction, and the Tobias Wolff Award for Fiction. Submissions: December 1 - March 15. See the individual listings for these contests under Contests & Awards for full details."

THE BINNACLE

University of Maine at Machias, 116 O'Brien Ave., Machias ME 04654. **E-mail:** ummbinnacle@maine.edu. **Website:** www.umm.maine.edu/binnacle. Estab. 1957. "We are interested in fresh voices, not Raymond Carver's, and not the Iowa Workshop's. We want the peculiar, and the idiosyncratic. We want playful and experimental, but understandable. Please see our website (www.umm.maine.edu/binnacle) for details on our Annual Ultra-Short Competition." Semiannual, plus annual Ultra-Short Competition editon. Publishes ms 3 months after acceptance. Sample copy for $7. Writer's guidelines online at website or by e-mail. Acquires one-time rights. "We accept submissions for the Fall Edition from March 15 to October 15 and report to writers between October 15 and November 15. We accept submissions for the Spring Edition from September 15 to March 15 and report to writers between March 15 and April 15. We accept submissions for our Ultra-Short Competition between December 1 and February 15 and report to writers between May 15 and June 15."

NEEDS Ethnic/multicultural, experimental, humor/satire, mainstream, slice-of-life vignettes. No extreme erotica, fantasy, horror, or religious, but any genre attuned to a general audience can work. 2,500 words maximum.

HOW TO CONTACT Submissions by e-mail only. Responds in 1 month to queries; 3 months to mss. Accepts simultaneous submissions. Send complete ms.

PAYMENT/TERMS $300 in prizes for Ultra-Short. $50 per issue for one work of editor's choice.

◐ ⑤ BOMB MAGAZINE

New Arts Publications, 80 Hanson Place, Suite 703, Brooklyn NY 11217. (718)636-9100. **Fax:** (718)636-9200. **E-mail:** firstproof@bombsite.com; generalinquiries@bombsite.com. **Website:** www.bombsite.com. **Contact:** Monica de la Torre. Estab. 1981. Magazine: 9 x 11.5; 104 pages; 70 lb. glossy cover; illustrations; photos. Receives 200 unsolicited mss/month. Accepts 6 mss/issue; 24 mss/year. Publishes ms 3-6 months after acceptance. Agented fiction 70%. Publishes 2-3 new writers/year. Recently published work by Lynne Tillman, Dennis Cooper, Susan Wheeler, and Laurie Sheck. Annual Fiction Contest—Deadline April 16 (Postmarked by April 16th). The winner of our 2011 contest will receive a $500 prize and publication in *BOMB Magazine*'s literary supplement, First Proof. Reading Fee: $20; includes a free one-year subscription to *BOMB* (for Canadian addresses add $6, for addresses outside US and Canada, add $12); make all checks and money orders payable to *BOMB Magazine*. "Written, edited and produced by industry professionals and funded by those interested in the arts. Publishes work which is unconventional and contains an edge, whether it be in style or subject matter."

NEEDS Experimental, novel excerpts, contemporary. No genre: romance, science fiction, horror, western. Written, edited and produced by industry professionals and funded by those interested in the arts. Publishes writing which is unconventional and contains an edge, whether it be in style or subject matter. Quarterly.

HOW TO CONTACT Send completed ms with SASE. Emailed submissions will not be considered.

PAYMENT/TERMS Pays $100, and contributor's copies.

◑ ⑪ ⑤ BOSTON REVIEW

PO Box 425786, Cambridge MA 02142. (617)324-1360. **Fax:** (617)452-3356. **E-mail:** review@bostonreview.net. **Website:** www.bostonreview.net. **Contact:** Dept. Editor. Estab. 1975. Magazine: 1034×1434; 60 pages; newsprint. "The editors are committed to a society and culture that foster human diversity and a democracy in which we seek common grounds of principle amidst our many differences. In the hope of advancing these ideals, the *Review* acts as a forum that seeks to enrich the language of public debate." Bimonthly. Receives 150 unsolicited mss/month. Accepts 4-6 mss/year. Publishes ms 4 months after acceptance. Recently published work by Dagberto Gilb, Charles Johnson, Deb Olin Unferth, T.E. Holt, and Yvonne Woon. Occasionally comments on rejected mss. Sample copy for $5 or online. Writer's guidelines online. Reviews fiction. *Boston Review* reads fiction submissions between September 15 and June 15 each year. Acquires first North American serial, first rights. "The editors are committed to a society and culture that foster human diversity and a democracy in which we seek common grounds of principle amidst our many differences. In the hope of advancing these ideals, the *Review* acts as a forum that seeks to enrich the language of public debate."

   ○   *Boston Review* is a recipient of the Pushcart Prize in Poetry.

NEEDS Ethnic/multicultural, experimental, literary, regional, translations, contemporary, prose poem. "The editors are looking for fiction in which a heart struggles against itself, in which the messy unmanageable complexity of the world is revealed. Sentences that are so sharp they cut the eye." "I'm looking for stories that are emotionally and intellectually substantive and also interesting on the level of language. Things that are shocking, dark, lewd, comic, or even insane are fine so long as the fiction is *controlled* and purposeful in a masterly way. Subtlety, delicacy, and lyricism are attractive too." No romance, erotica, genre fiction. Length: 1,200-5,000 words. Average length: 2,000 words.

HOW TO CONTACT Send complete ms with SASE or submit through online submissions manager. Responds in 4 months to queries. Accepts simultaneous submissions if noted. Send complete ms.

PAYMENT/TERMS Pays $300, and 3 contributor's copies.

BOYS' LIFE

Boy Scouts of America, P.O. Box 152079, 1325 West Walnut Hills Ln., Irving TX 75015. (972)580-2366. **Fax:** (972)580-2079. **Website:** www.boyslife.org. **Contact:** J.D. Owen, editor-in-chief; Michael Goldman, managing editor; Aaron Derr, senior writer. Estab. 1911. *Boys' Life* is a monthly 4-color general interest magazine for boys 7-18, most of whom are Cub Scouts, Boy Scouts or Venturers.

TIPS "We strongly recommend reading at least 12 issues of the magazine before submitting queries. We are a good market for any writer willing to do the necessary homework. Write for a boy you know who is 12. Our readers demand punchy writing in relatively short, straightforward sentences. The editors demand well-reported articles that demonstrate high standards of journalism. We follow the *Associated Press* manual of style and usage. Learn and read our publications before submitting anything."

BRAIN, CHILD

March Press, P.O. Box 714, Lexington VA 24450. (540) 463-4817. **E-mail:** editor@brainchildmag.com. **Website:** www.brainchildmag.com. **Contact:** Jennifer Niesslein and Stephanie Wilkinson, co-editors. Estab. 2000. *"Brain, Child* reflects modern motherhood—the way it really is. We like to think of *Brain, Child* as a community, for and by mothers who like to think about what raising kids does for (and to) the mind and soul. *Brain, Child* isn't your typical parenting magazine. We couldn't cupcake-decorate our way out of a paper bag. We are more 'literary' than 'how-to,' more *New Yorker* than *Parents*. We shy away from expert advice on childrearing in favor of first-hand reflections by great writers (Jane Smiley, Barbara Ehrenreich, Anne Tyler) on life as a mother. Each quarterly issue is full of essays, features, humor, reviews, fiction, art, cartoons, and our readers' own stories. Our philosophy is pretty simple: Motherhood is worthy of literature. And there are a lot of ways to mother, all of them interesting. We're proud to be publishing articles and essays that are smart, down to earth, sometimes funny, and sometimes poignant."

NEEDS "We publish fiction that has a strong motherhood theme." No genre fiction. Length: 800-5,000 words.

HOW TO CONTACT Send complete ms.

PAYMENT/TERMS Payment varies.

TIPS Prefers e-mail submissions. No attachments.

BROKEN PENCIL

P.O. Box 203, Station P, Toronto ON M5S 2S7 Canada. **E-mail:** editor@brokenpencil.com. **E-mail:** fiction@brokenpencil.com. **Website:** www.brokenpencil.com. Estab. 1995. Magazine. "Founded in 1995 and based in Toronto, Canada, *Broken Pencil* is a website and print magazine published four times a year. It is one of the few magazines in the world devoted to underground culture and the independent arts. We are a great resource and a lively read. A cross between the *Utne Reader*, an underground *Reader's Digest*, and the now defunct *Factsheet15*, *Broken Pencil* reviews the best zines, books, Web sites, videos, and artworks from the underground and reprints the best articles from the alternative press. Also, ground-breaking interviews, original fiction, and commentary on all aspects of the independent arts. From the hilarious to the perverse, *Broken Pencil* challenges conformity and demands attention." Quarterly. Accepts 8 mss/year. Manuscript published 2-3 months after acceptance. Acquires first rights. *Broken Pencil* is one of the few magazines in the world devoted exclusively to underground culture and the independent arts. We are a great resource and a lively read! *Broken Pencil* reviews the best zines, books, Web sites, videos and artworks from the underground and reprints the best articles from the alternative press. From the hilarious to the perverse, *Broken Pencil* challenges conformity and demands attention.

NEEDS Adventure, erotica, ethnic/multicultural, experimental, fantasy, historical, horror, humor/satire, amateur sleuth, romance, science fiction We're particularly interested in work from emerging writers. Length: 500-3,000 words.

HOW TO CONTACT Accepts submissions by e-mail. The thing to do is to pitch us with specific ideas, and maybe include a few of your previous articles. Also a little background info about you would be nice. It will take us a while to get back to you, so be patient. Send complete ms.

PAYMENT/TERMS Our payments range from $30 to $300 depending on what kind of article you are writing.

TIPS Write in to receive a list of upcoming themes and then pitch us stories based around those themes. If you keep your ear to the ground in the alternative and underground arts communities, you will be able to find content appropriate for *Broken Pencil*.

◐☻○⑤ CADET QUEST MAGAZINE

P.O. Box 7259, Grand Rapids MI 49510-7259. (616)241-5616. **Fax:** (616)241-5558. **E-mail:** submissions@calvinistcadets.org. **Website:** www.calvinistcadets.org. **Contact:** G. Richard Broene, editor. Estab. 1958. "*Cadet Quest Magazine* shows boys 9-14 how God is at work in their lives and in the world around them."

> ○ Accepts submissions by mail, or by e-mail (must include ms in text of e-mail). Will not open attachments.

NEEDS Considerable fiction is used. Fast-moving stories that appeal to a boy's sense of adventure or sense of humor are welcome. Avoid preachiness. Avoid simplistic answers to complicated problems. Avoid long dialogue and little action. No fantasy, science fiction, fashion, horror or erotica. Length: 900-1,500 words.

HOW TO CONTACT Send complete ms.

PAYMENT/TERMS Pays 4-6¢/word, and 1 contributor's copy.

TIPS "Best time to submit stories/articles is early in the year (February-April). Also remember readers are boys ages 9-14. Stories must reflect or add to the theme of the issue and be from a Christian perspective."

⊕⑤ CALLIOPE

Cobblestone Publishing Co., 30 Grove St., Suite C, Peterborough NH 03458-1454. (603)924-7209. **Fax:** (603)924-7380. **E-mail:** cfbakeriii@meganet.net. **Website:** www.cobblestonepub.com. **Contact:** Rosalie Baker and Charles Baker, co-editors; Lou Waryncia, editorial director; Ann Dillon, art director. Estab. 1990. Articles must relate to the issue's theme. Lively, original approaches to the subject are the primary concerns of the editors in choosing material.

> ○ A query must consist of the following to be considered (please use nonerasable paper): a brief cover letter stating subject and word length of the proposed article; a detailed one-page outline explaining the information to be presented in the article; an bibliography of materials the author intends to use in preparing the article; a SASE. Writers new to *Calliope* should send a writing sample with query. In all correspondence, please include your complete address as well as a telephone number where you can be reached. A writer may send as many queries for one issue as he or she wishes, but each query must have a separate

cover letter, outline and bibliography as well as a SASE. Telephone and e-mail queries are not accepted. Handwritten queries will not be considered. Queries may be submitted at any time, but queries sent well in advance of deadline *may not be answered for several months.*

NEEDS Middle readers and young adults: adventure, folktales, plays, history, biographical fiction. Material must relate to forthcoming themes. Length: 1000 words maximum.

PAYMENT/TERMS Pays 20-25¢/word.

TIPS "Authors are urged to use primary resources and up-to-date scholarly resources in their bibliography. In all correspondence, please include your complete address and a telephone number where you can be reached."

◐⑤ CHRYSALIS READER

1745 Gravel Hill Rd., Dillwyn VA 23936. (434)983-3021. **E-mail:** editor@swedenborg.com; rlawson@sover.net. **E-mail:** chrysalis@hovac.com. **Website:** www.swedenborg.com/chrysalis. **Contact:** Robert F. Lawson, editor. Estab. 1985. Book series: 712×10; 192 pages; coated cover stock; illustrations; photos. "*The Chrysalis Reader* audience includes people from numerous faiths and backgrounds. Many of them work in psychology, education, religion, the arts, sciences, or one of the helping professions. The style of writing may be humorous, serious, or some combination of these approaches. Essays, poetry, and fiction that are not evangelical in tone but that are unique in addressing the *Chrysalis Reader* theme are more likely to be accepted. Our readers are interested in expanding, enriching, or challenging their intellects, hearts, and philosophies, and many also just want to enjoy a good read. For these reasons the editors attempt to publish a mix of writings. Articles and poetry must be related to the theme; however, you may have your own approach to the theme not written in our description." Query with SASE. Accepts submissions by e-mail and USPS. Responds in 1 month to queries; 4-6 months to mss. No previously published work. Sample copy for $10 and 812×11 SAE. Writer's guidelines and themes for issues for SASE or on website.Pays $25-100. Pays at page-proof stage. Acquires first rights, makes work-for-hire assignments. Sends galleys to author.

> ○ "This journal explores contemporary questions of spirituality from a Swedenborgian multifaith perspective."

NEEDS Adventure, experimental, historical, literary, mainstream, mystery/suspense, science fiction, fiction (leading to insight), contemporary, spiritual, sports. No religious works. See upcoming theme at website. Receives 50 unsolicited mss/month. Accepts 20-40 mss/year. Publishes ms 9 months after acceptance. **Publishes 10 new writers/year.** Recently published work by Robert Bly, William Kloefkorn, Raymond Moody, Virgil Suárez, Carol Lem, Alan Magee, John Hitchcock. Also publishes literary essays, literary criticism, poetry. Sometimes comments on rejected mss. Length: 1,500-3,000 words.

CICADA MAGAZINE

Cricket Magazine Group, 70 E. Lake St., Suite 300, Chicago IL 60601. (312)701-1720. **Fax:** (312)701-1728. **E-mail:** dvetter@caruspub.com. **Website:** www.cicadamag.com. **Contact:** Marianne Carus, editor-in-chief; Deborah Vetter, executive editor; John Sandford, art director. Estab. 1998. Bimonthly literary magazine for ages 14 and up. Publishes original short stories, poems, and first-person essays written for teens and young adults. *Cicada* publishes fiction and poetry with a genuine teen sensibility, aimed at the high school and college-age market. The editors are looking for stories and poems that are thought-provoking but entertaining.

NEEDS Young adults: adventure, contemporary, fantasy, historical, humor/satire, multicultural, nature/environment, romance, science fiction, sports, suspense/mystery. Buys up to 42 mss/year. The main protagonist should be at least 14 and preferably older. Stories should have a genuine teen sensibility and be aimed at readers in high school or college. 5,000 words maximum (up to 15,000 words/novellas).

PAYMENT/TERMS Pays up to 25¢/word.

TIPS "Quality writing, good literary style, genuine teen sensibility, depth, humor, good character development, avoidance of stereotypes. Read several issues to familarize yourself with our style."

COBBLESTONE

A Division of Carus Publishing, 30 Grove St., Suite C, Peterborough NH 03458. (800)821-0115. **Fax:** (603)924-7380. **E-mail:** customerservice@caruspub.com. **Website:** www.cobblestonepub.com. "We are interested in articles of historical accuracy and lively, original approaches to the subject at hand. Our magazine is aimed at youths from ages 9 to 14. Writers are encouraged to study recent COBBLESTONE back issues for content and style. (Sample issues are available for $6.95 plus $2.00 shipping and handling. Sample issues will not be sent without prepayment.) All material must relate to the theme of a specific upcoming issue in order to be considered. To be considered, a query must accompany each individual idea (however, you can mail them all together) and must include the following: a brief cover letter stating the subject and word length of the proposed article, a detailed one-page outline explaining the information to be presented in the article, an extensive bibliography of materials the author intends to use in preparing the article, a SASE. Authors are urged to use primary resources and up-to-date scholarly resources in their bibliography. Writers new to COBBLESTONE® should send a writing sample with the query. If you would like to know if your query has been received, please also include a stamped postcard that requests acknowledgment of receipt. In all correspondence, please include your complete address as well as a telephone number where you can be reached. A writer may send as many queries for one issue as he or she wishes, but each query must have a separate cover letter, outline, bibliography, and SASE. All queries must be typed. **Please do not send unsolicited manuscripts - queries only!** Prefers to work with published/established writers. Each issue presents a particular theme, making it exciting as well as informative. Half of all subscriptions are for schools. All material must relate to monthly theme."

NEEDS Length: 800 words maximum.

HOW TO CONTACT Query.

PAYMENT/TERMS Pays 20-25¢/word.

TIPS "Review theme lists and past issues to see what we're looking for."

COSMOS MAGAZINE

Luna Media Pty Ltd., Level 1, 49 Shepherd St., Chippendale, Sydney NSW 2008 Australia. (61)(2)9310-8500. **Fax:** (61)(2)9698-4899. **E-mail:** submissions@cosmosmagazine.com. **Website:** www.cosmosmagazine.com. Estab. 2005. "An Australian brand with a global outlook, COSMOS internationally respected for its literary writing, excellence in design and engaging breadth of content. Won the 2009 Magazine of the Year and twice Editor of the Year at the annual Bell Awards for Publishing Excellence; the American Institute of Physics Science Writing Award; the Reuters/IUCN Award for Excellence in Environmental

Journalism; the City of Sydney Lord Mayor's Sustainability Award and an Earth Journalism Award. COSMOS is the brainchild of Wilson da Silva, a former ABC TV science reporter and past president of the World Federation of Science Journalists. It is backed by an Editorial Advisory Board that includes Apollo 11 astronaut Buzz Aldrin, ABC Radio's Robyn Williams, and is chaired by Dr. Alan Finkel, the neuroscientist and philanthropist who is the Chancellor of Monash University in Melbourne."

NEEDS Science fiction No fantasy—science fiction only. Length: 2,000-4,000 words.

PAYMENT/TERMS Pays flat $300 per story.

CRICKET

Carus Publishing Co., 700 E. Lake St., Suite 300, Chicago IL 60601. (312)701-1720, ext. 10. **Website:** www.cricketmag.com. **Contact:** Marianne Carus, editor-in-chief; Lonnie Plecha, executive editor; Karen Kohn, senior art director. Estab. 1973. "*Cricket* is looking for more fiction and nonfiction for the older end of its 9-14 age range, as well as contemporary stories set in other countries. It also seeks humorous stories and mysteries (not detective spoofs), fantasy and original fairy tales, stand-alone excerpts from unpublished novels, and well-written/researched science articles."

NEEDS Middle readers, young adults/teens: contemporary, fantasy, folk and fairy tales, history, humorous, science fiction, suspense/mystery. Buys 70 mss/year. Recently published work by Aaron Shepard, Arnold Adoff, and Nancy Springer. No didactic, sex, religious, or horror stories. Length: 200-2,000 words.

HOW TO CONTACT Submit complete ms.

PAYMENT/TERMS Pays 25¢/word maximum, and 6 contributor's copies; $2.50 charge for extras.

EARTH ISLAND JOURNAL

Earth Island Institute, 300 Broadway, Suite 28, San Francisco CA 94133. **E-mail:** editor@earthisland.org. **Website:** www.earthislandjournal.org. Estab. 1985. We are looking for in-depth, vigorously reported stories that reveal the connections between the environment and other contemporary issues. Our audience, though modest, includes many of the leaders of the environmental movement. Article pitches should be geared toward this sophisticated audience.

○ ○ ⊖ ELLERY QUEEN'S MYSTERY MAGAZINE

Dell Magazines Fiction Group, 267 Broadway, 4th Floor, New York NY 10017. (212)686-7188. **Fax:** (212)686-7414. **E-mail:** elleryqueenmm@dellmagazines.com. **Website:** www.themysteryplace.com/eqmm. Estab. 1941. Magazine: 5⅞×8⅜, 112 pages with special 192-page combined March/April and September/October issues. "*Ellery Queen's Mystery Magazine* welcomes submissions from both new and established writers. We publish every kind of mystery short story: the psychological suspense tale, the deductive puzzle, the private eye case, the gamut of crime and detection from the realistic (including the policeman's lot and stories of police procedure) to the more imaginative (including locked rooms and impossible crimes). EQMM has been in continuous publication since 1941. From the beginning, three general criteria have been employed in evaluating submissions: We look for strong writing, an original and exciting plot, and professional craftsmanship. We encourage writers whose work meets these general criteria to read an issue of EQMM before making a submission." Magazine for lovers of mystery fiction.

○ "EQMM uses an online submission system (http://eqmm.magazinesubmissions.com) that has been designed to streamline our process and improve communication with authors. We ask that all submissions be made electronically, using this system, rather than on paper. All stories should be in standard manuscript format and submitted in .DOC format. We cannot accept .DOCX, .RTF, or .TXT files at this time. For detailed submission instructions, see http://eqmm.magazinesubmissions.com or our writers guidelines page (http://www.themysteryplace.com/eqmm/guidelines)."

NEEDS Mystery/suspense. No explicit sex or violence, no gore or horror. Seldom publishes parodies or pastiches. "We accept only mystery, crime, suspense and detective fiction." 2,500-8,000 words is the preferred range. Also publishes minute mysteries of 250 words; novellas up to 20,000 words from established authors. Publishes ms 6-12 months after acceptance. Agented fiction 50%. **Publishes 10 new writers/year.** Recently published work by Jeffery Deaver, Joyce Carol Oates, and Margaret Maron. Sometimes comments on rejected mss. "We always need detective stories. Special consideration given to anything timely and original." No explicit sex or violence, no gore or horror. Seldom publishes parodies or pastiches. "We do not want true detective or crime stories." Most stories 2,500-8,000 words. Accepts longer and shorter submissions—including minute mysteries of 250 words, and novellas of up to 20,000 words from established authors

HOW TO CONTACT Send complete ms with SASE for reply. No e-mail submissions. No query necessary. Responds in 3 months to mss. Accepts simultaneous, multiple submissions. Sample copy for $5.50. Writer's guidelines for SASE or online.

PAYMENT/TERMS Pays 5-8¢/ a word, occasionally higher for established authors. Pays on acceptance for first North American serial rights.

TIPS "We have a Department of First Stories to encourage writers whose fiction has never before been in print. We publish an average of 10 first stories every year. Mark subject line Attn: Dept. of First Stories."

ESQUIRE

300 W. 57th St., 21st Floor, New York NY 10019. (212)649-4020. **Website:** www.esquire.com. Estab. 1933. *Esquire* is geared toward smart, well-off men. General readership is college educated and sophisticated, between ages 30 and 45. Written mostly by contributing editors on contract. Rarely accepts unsolicited mss.

NEEDS "Literary excellence is our only criterion." No pornography, science fiction or 'true romance' stories.

HOW TO CONTACT Send complete ms. To submit a story, use online submission manager at http://esquiresubmissions.com.

TIPS "A writer has the best chance of breaking in at *Esquire* by querying with a specific idea that requires special contacts and expertise. Ideas must be timely and national in scope."

⦿⊛ EVANGEL

Free Methodist Publishing House, P.O. Box 535002, Indianapolis IN 46253-5002. (317)244-3660. **Contact:** Julie Innes, editor. Estab. 1897. *Evangel,* published quarterly, is an adult Sunday School paper. "Devotional in nature, it lifts up Christ as the source of salvation and hope. The mission of *Evangel* is to increase the reader's understanding of the nature and character of God and the nature of a life lived for Christ. Material that fits this mission and isn't longer than 1 page will be considered." *Evangel* is 8 pages, 5.5 x 8.5, printed in 4-color, unbound, color and b&w photos. Does not want rhyming work. Accepts about 5% of poetry received. Fiction involves people coping with everday crises, making decisions that show spiritual growth.

Weekly distribution. Recently published work by Kelli Wise and Hope Byler. Press run is about 10,000. Subscription: $2.59/quarter (13 weeks).

NEEDS Receives 300 unsolicited mss/month. Accepts 3-4 mss/issue; 156-200 mss/year. Publishes ms 18-36 months after acceptance. Responds in 4-6 weeks to queries. Accepts multiple submissions. Publishes 7 new writers/year. Send complete ms. Pays 4¢/word and 2 contributor's copies. "No fiction without any semblance of Christian message or where the message clobbers the reader. Looking for devotional style short pieces 500 words or less."

TIPS "Desire, concise, tight writing that supports a solid thesis and fits the mission expressed in the guidelines."

FLAUNT

1422 N. Highland Ave., Los Angeles CA 90028. (323)836-1000. **E-mail:** info@flauntmagazine.com. **Website:** www.flaunt.com. **Contact:** Lee Corbin, art director; Andrew Pogany, senior editor. Estab. 1998. Magazine. "10 times a year, *Flaunt* features the bold work of emerging photographers, writers, artists, and musicians. The quality of the content is mirrored in the sophisticated, interactive format of the magazine, using advanced printing techniques, fold-out articles, beautiful papers, and inserts to create a visually stimulating, surprisingly readable, and intelligent book that pushes the magazine into the realm of art-object. *Flaunt* magazine has for the last eight years made it a point to break new ground, earning itself a reputation as an engine and outlet for the culture of the cutting edge. *Flaunt* takes pride in reinventing itself each month, while consistently representing a hybrid of all that is interesting in entertainment, fashion, music, design, film, art, and literature." Estab. 1998. Circ. 110,000.

NEEDS Experimental, urban, academic. We publish 3 fiction pieces a year. Length: 500-5,000 words.

HOW TO CONTACT Guidelines available via e-mail.

PAYMENT/TERMS Acquires one time rights and first option to reprint. Pays one time flat rate to be determined upon correspondence. Pays up to $500.

◐⦿ FREEFALL MAGAZINE

Freefall Literary Society of Calgary, 922 Ninth Ave. SE, Calgary AB T2G 0S4 Canada. **E-mail:** freefallmagazine@yahoo.com. **Website:** www.freefallmagazine.ca. **Contact:** Lynn S. Fraser, managing editor. Estab. 1990. 812×534; 100 pages; bond paper; bond stock;

b&w illustrations; photos. "*FreeFall* features the best of new, emerging writers and gives them the chance to get into print along with established writers. Magazine published biannually containing fiction, poetry, creative nonfiction, essays on writing, interviews, and reviews. Submit up to 5 poems at once. We are looking for exquisite writing with a strong narrative." Circ. 1,000. Buys first North American serial rights (ownership reverts to author after one time publication). Pays on publication. 100% freelance.

PAYMENT/TERMS Pays $25 per poem and one copy of the issue poems appear in. Wants prose of all types, up to 3,000 words; pays $10/page to a maximum of $100 per piece and one copy of issue piece appears in.

TIPS "We look for thoughtful word usage, craftmanship, strong voice and unique expression coupled with clarity and narrative structure. Professional, clean presentation of work is essential. Carefully read *FreeFall* guidelines before submitting. Do not fold manuscript, and submit 9×11 envelope. Include SASE/IRC for reply and/or return of manuscript. You may contact us by e-mail after initial hardcopy submission. For accepted pieces a request is made for disk or e-mail copy. Strong Web presence attracts submissions from writers all over the world."

FUNNY TIMES

Funny Times, Inc., P.O. Box 18530, Cleveland Heights OH 44118. (216)371-8600. **Fax:** (216)371-8696. **E-mail:** info@funnytimes.com. **Website:** www.funnytimes.com. Estab. 1985. Zine specializing in humor: tabloid; 24 pages; newsprint; illustrations. "Funny Times is a monthly review of America's funniest cartoonists and writers. We are the Reader's Digest of modern American humor with a progressive/peace-oriented/environmental/politically activist slant." Monthly. Circ. 70,000. *Funny Times* is a monthly review of America's funniest cartoonists and writers. We are the *Reader's Digest* of modern American humor with a progressive/peace-oriented/environmental/politically activist slant.

NEEDS Humor/satire. "Anything funny." Receives hundreds unsolicited mss/month. Accepts 5 mss/issue; 60 mss/year. Publishes ms 3 months after acceptance. Agented fiction 10%. **Publishes 10 new writers/year.** Publishes short shorts. Anything funny. Length: 500-700 words.

HOW TO CONTACT Query with published clips. Include list of publications. Send SASE for return of ms

or disposable copy of ms. Responds in 3 months to mss. Accepts simultaneous and reprints submissions. Sample copy for $3 or 9×12 SAE with 4 first-class stamps ($1.22 postage). Writer's guidelines online.

PAYMENT/TERMS Pays $50-150. Pays on publication for one-time, second serial (reprint) rights.

TIPS Send us a small packet (1-3 items) of only your very funniest stuff. If this makes us laugh, we'll be glad to ask for more. We particularly welcome previously published material that has been well received elsewhere.

GOOD OLD DAYS

Dynamic Resource Group, 306 E. Parr Rd., Berne IN 46711. **Fax:** (260)589-8093. **E-mail:** editor@goodolddaysonline.com. **Website:** www.goodolddaysonline.com. **Contact:** Ken Tate, editor. "We look for strong narratives showing life as it was in the middle decades of the 20th century. Our readership is comprised of nostalgia buffs, history enthusiasts, and the people who actually lived and grew up in this era."

HARDBOILED

Gryphon Publications, P.O. Box 209, Brooklyn NY 11228. **Website:** www.gryphonbooks.com. Estab. 1988. "Hard-hitting crime fiction and private-eye stories—the newest and most cutting-edge work and classic reprints."

NEEDS "No pastiches, violence for the sake of violence." Length: 500-3,000 words.

HOW TO CONTACT Query or send complete ms.

PAYMENT/TERMS Pays $5-50.

TIPS "Your best bet for breaking in is short hard crime fiction filled with authenticity and brevity. Try a subscription to *Hardboiled* to get the perfect idea of what we are after."

HARPER'S MAGAZINE

666 Broadway, 11th Floor, New York NY 10012. (212)420-5720. **Fax:** (212)228-5889. **E-mail:** readings@harpers.org. **Website:** www.harpers.org. Estab. 1850. Magazine: 8×1034; 80 pages; illustrations. "*Harper's Magazine* encourages national discussion on current and significant issues in a format that offers arresting facts and intelligent opinions. By means of its several shorter journalistic forms—Harper's Index, Readings, Forum, and Annotation—as well as with its acclaimed essays, fiction, and reporting, *Harper's* continues the tradition begun with its first issue in 1850: to inform readers across the whole spectrum

of political, literary, cultural, and scientific affairs." Monthly. Estab. 1850. Circ. 230,000.

NEEDS Humor/satire. Stories on contemporary life and its problems. Receives 50 unsolicited mss/month. Accepts 12 mss/year. Publishes ms 3 months after acceptance. **Publishes some new writers/year.** Recently published work by Rebecca Curtis, George Saunders, Haruki Murakami, Margaret Atwood, Allan Gurganus, Evan Connell, and Dave Bezmosgis. Will consider unsolicited fiction. Length: 3,000-5,000 words.

HOW TO CONTACT Query by mail, except for submissions to the Readings section, which can be submitted via readings@harpers.org. Responds in 3 months to queries. Accepts reprints submissions. SASE required for all unsolicited material. Sample copy for $6.95. Query.

PAYMENT/TERMS Generally pays 50¢-$1/word. Pays on acceptance. Vary with author and material. Sends galleys to author.

TIPS Some readers expect their magazines to clothe them with opinions in the way that Bloomingdale's dresses them for the opera. The readers of *Harper's Magazine* belong to a different crowd. They strike me as the kind of people who would rather think in their own voices and come to their own conclusions.

HIGHLIGHTS FOR CHILDREN

803 Church St., Honesdale PA 18431. (570)253-1080. **Fax:** (570)251-7847. **Website:** www.highlights.com. **Contact:** Christine French Clark, editor-in-chief; Cindy Faber Smith, art director. Estab. 1946. "This book of wholesome fun is dedicated to helping children grow in basic skills and knowledge, in creativeness, in ability to think and reason, in sensitivity to others, in high ideals, and worthy ways of living—for children are the world's most important people. We publish stories for beginning and advanced readers. Up to 500 words for beginners (ages 3-7), up to 800 words for advanced (ages 8-12)."

NEEDS Meaningful stories appealing to both girls and boys, up to age 12. Vivid, full of action. Engaging plot, strong characterization, lively language. Prefers stories in which a child protagonist solves a dilemma through his or her own resources. Seeks stories that the child ages 8-12 will eagerly read, and the child ages 2-7 will like to hear when read aloud (500-800 words). Stories require interesting plots and a number of illustration possiblities. Also need rebuses (picture stories 120 words or under), stories with urban settings, stories for beginning readers (100-500 words), sports and humorous stories, adventures, holiday stories, and mysteries. We also would like to see more material of 1-page length (300 words), both fiction and factual. No war, crime or violence.

HOW TO CONTACT Send complete ms.

PAYMENT/TERMS Pays $150 minimum plus 2 contributor's copies.

TIPS "Know the magazine's style before submitting. Send for guidelines and sample issue if necessary." Writers: "At *Highlights* we're paying closer attention to acquiring more nonfiction for young readers than we have in the past." Illustrators: "Fresh, imaginative work encouraged. Flexibility in working relationships a plus. Illustrators presenting their work need not confine themselves to just children's illustrations as long as work can translate to our needs. We also use animal illustrations, real and imaginary. We need crafts, puzzles and any activity that will stimulate children mentally and creatively. We are always looking for imaginative cover subjects. Know our publication's standards and content by reading sample issues, not just the guidelines. Avoid tired themes, or put a fresh twist on an old theme so that its style is fun and lively. We'd like to see stories with subtle messages, but the fun of the story should come first. Write what inspires you, not what you think the market needs. We are pleased that many authors of children's literature report that their first published work was in the pages of *Highlights*. It is not our policy to consider fiction on the strength of the reputation of the author. We judge each submission on its own merits. With factual material, however, we do prefer that writers be authorities in their field or people with first-hand experience. In this manner we can avoid the encyclopedic article that merely restates information readily available elsewhere. We don't make assignments. Query with simple letter to establish whether the nonfiction subject is likely to be of interest. A beginning writer should first become familiar with the type of material that *Highlights* publishes. Include special qualifications, if any, of author. Write for the child, not the editor. Write in a voice that children understand and relate to. Speak to today's kids, avoiding didactic, overt messages. Even though our general principles haven't changed over the years, we are contemporary in our approach to issues. Avoid worn themes."

ALFRED HITCHCOCK'S MYSTERY MAGAZINE

Dell Magazines, 475 Park Ave. S., 11th Floor, New York NY 10016. (212)686-7188. **Website:** www.themysteryplace.com/ahmm. Estab. 1956.

NEEDS "Original and well-written mystery and crime fiction. Because this is a mystery magazine, the stories we buy must fall into that genre in some sense or another. We are interested in nearly every kind of mystery: stories of detection of the classic kind, police procedurals, private eye tales, suspense, courtroom dramas, stories of espionage, and so on. We ask only that the story be about crime (or the threat or fear of one). We sometimes accept ghost stories or supernatural tales, but those also should involve a crime." No sensationalism. Up to 12,000 words.

HOW TO CONTACT Send complete ms.

PAYMENT/TERMS Payment varies.

TIPS "No simultaneous submissions, please. Submissions sent to *Alfred Hitchcock's Mystery Magazine* are not considered for or read by *Ellery Queen's Mystery Magazine*, and vice versa."

HORIZONS

100 Witherspoon St., Louisville KY 40202-1396. (502)569-5897. **Fax:** (502)569-8085. **E-mail:** susan.jackson-dowd@pcusa.org. **Website:** www.pcusa.org/horizons/. **Contact:** Susan Jackson Dowd, communications coordinator. Estab. 1988. "We include fiction and nonfiction, memoirs, essays, historical, and informational articles, all of interest to the Orthodox Jewish Woman." Quarterly. Estab. 1994. "Magazine owned and operated by Presbyterian women offering information and inspiration for Presbyterian women by addressing current issues facing the church and the world."

NEEDS Historical, humor/satire, mainstream, slice-of-life vignettes. Nothing not suitable to Orthodox Jewish values. Receives 4-6 unsolicited mss/month. Accepts 2-3 mss/issue; 10-12 mss/year. Publishes ms 6 months after acceptance. **Publishes 15- 20 new writers/year.** Length: 1,000-3,000 words; average length: 1,500 words. Also publishes poetry. Length: 800-1,200 words.

HOW TO CONTACT Send complete ms. Accepts submissions by e-mail, fax. Responds in 1 week to queries; 2 months to mss. Accepts simultaneous submissions. Writer's guidelines available. Send complete ms.

PAYMENT/TERMS Pays 5¢/word. Pays 4-6 weeks after publication. Acquires one-time rights.

◐ ⊖ IRREANTUM

The Association for Mormon Letters, P.O. Box 1315, Salt Lake City UT 84110-1315. **E-mail:** editor@aml-pubs.org. **Website:** www.irreantum.org. Estab. 1999. Magazine or zine: 812×712; 100-120 pages; 20 lb. paper; 20 lb. color cover; illustrations; photos. "While focused on Mormonism, *Irreantum* is a cultural, humanities-oriented magazine, not a religious magazine. Our guiding principle is that Mormonism is grounded in a sufficiently unusual, cohesive, and extended historical and cultural experience that it has become like a nation, an ethnic culture. We can speak of Mormon literature at least as surely as we can of a Jewish or Southern literature. *Irreantum* publishes stories, one-act dramas, stand-alone novel and drama excerpts, and poetry by, for, or about Mormons (as well as author interviews, essays, and reviews). The magazine's audience includes readers of any or no religious faith who are interested in literary exploration of the Mormon culture, mindset, and worldview through Mormon themes and characters. *Irreantum* is currently the only magazine devoted to Mormon literature." Biannual. Circ. 300.

◖ Also publishes short shorts, literary essays, literary criticism, and poetry.

NEEDS "High quality work that explores the Mormon experience, directly or by implication, through literature. We acknowledge a broad range of experience with Mormonism, both as a faith and as a culture—on the part of devoted multi-generation Mormons, ethnic Mormons, new converts, and people outside the faith and culture who interact with Mormons and Mormon culture. We are committed to respectful exploration of Mormonism through literature. Receives 5 unsolicited mss/month. Accepts 3 mss/issue; 6 mss/year. Publishes ms 3-12 months after acceptance. **Publishes 3 or more new writers/ year.** Recently published work by Orson Scott Card, Terryl Givens, Jack Harrell, Eric Samuelsen, Michael Collins, Phyllis Barber, Paul Swenson. Length: 1,000-5,000 words; average length: 5,000 words. Publishes short shorts. Also publishes literary essays, literary criticism, poetry. Sometimes comments on rejected mss. Annual fiction contest and annual personal essay contest with cash prizes. Length: 1,000-5,000 words.

HOW TO CONTACT Accepts submissions by e-mail only in Microsoft Word or rich text files only. Accepts critical essays to criticalessaysubmissions@

mormonletter.org. "The fiction and personal essay/ creative nonfiction we publish is selected from the contest entries for the annual fiction contest and annual personal essay contest with offer cash prizes. There is a submission window—January 1-May 31st—for fiction and creative nonfiction submissions. All unsolicited fiction and creative nonfiction must be submitted according to contest rules which can be found on the website." Winner will receive a copy of the *Irreantum* issue in which his or her work appears. Send complete ms. with cover letter. Include a brief bio and list of publications. Responds in 2 weeks to queries, 2 months to mss. Accepts simultaneous and reprints, multiple submissions. Sample copy $15. Writer's guidelines on website. Reviews fiction.

PAYMENT/TERMS Pays $0-100. Pays on publication for one time rights.

TIPS *Irreantum* is not interested in didactic or polemnical fiction that primarily attempts to prove or disprove Mormon doctrine, history, or corporate policy. We encourage beginning writers to focus on human elements first, with Mormon elements introduced only as natural and organic to the story. Readers can tell if you are honestly trying to explore human experience or if you are writing with a propagandistic agenda either for or against Mormonism. For conservative, orthodox Mormon writers, beware of sentimentalism, simplistic resolutions, and foregone conclusions.

JACK AND JILL

Children's Better Health Institute, P.O. Box 567, Indianapolis IN 46206-0567. (317)636-8881. **E-mail:** j.goodman@cbhi.org. **Website:** www.jackandjillmag. org. Estab. 1938. "Write entertaining and imaginative stories for kids, not just about them. Writers should understand what is funny to kids, what's important to them, what excites them. Don't write from an adult 'kids are so cute' perspective. We're also looking for health and healthful lifestyle stories and articles, but don't be preachy."

NEEDS Young readers and middle readers: adventure, contemporary, folktales, health, history, humorous, nature, sports. Buys 30-35 mss/year. Length: 500 words.

HOW TO CONTACT Submit complete ms. Queries not accepted.

PAYMENT/TERMS Pays up to 25¢/word.

TIPS "We are constantly looking for new writers who can tell good stories with interesting slants—stories that are not full of out-dated and time-worn expressions. We like to see stories about kids who are smart and capable, but not sarcastic or smug. Problem-solving skills, personal responsibility, and integrity are good topics for us. Obtain current issues of the magazine and study them to determine our present needs and editorial style."

KALEIDOSCOPE

Kaleidoscope Press, 701 S. Main St., Akron OH 44311-1019. (330)762-9755. **Fax:** (330)762-0912. **E-mail:** mshiplett@udsakron.org. **Website:** www.udsakron. org/kaleidoscope.htm. **Contact:** Mildred Shiplett. Estab. 1979. Magazine: 8½×11; 64 pages; non-coated paper; coated cover stock; illustrations (all media); photos. Subscribers include individuals, agencies, and organizations that assist people with disabilities and many university and public libraries. Open to new writers but appreciates work by established writers as well. Especially interested in work by writers with a disability, but features writers both with and without disabilities. "Writers without a disability must limit themselves to our focus, while those with a disability may explore any topic (although we prefer original perspectives about experiences with disability)." Semiannual.

Kaleidoscope has received awards from the American Heart Association, the Great Lakes Awards Competition and Ohio Public Images.

NEEDS "We look for well-developed plots, engaging characters and realistic dialogue. We lean toward fiction that emphasizes character and emotions rather than action-oriented narratives. No fiction that is stereotypical, patronizing, sentimental, erotic, or maudlin. No romance, religious or dogmatic fiction; no children's literature." Receives 35-40 unsolicited mss/month. Accepts 20 mss/year. Agented fiction 1%. **Publishes 2 new writer/year.** Recently published work by Carole Hall, Deshae E. Lott, and James M. Bellarosa. Also publishes poetry. Short stories, novel excerpts. Traditional and experimental styles. Works should explore experiences with disability. Use people-first language. No fiction that is stereotypical, patronizing, sentimental, erotic, or maudlin. No romance, religious or dogmatic fiction; no children's literature. 5,000 words maximum.

HOW TO CONTACT Accepts submissions by fax and e-mail, double-spaced with full address. Query first or send complete ms and cover letter. Include author's education and writing background and, if author has a disability, how it influenced the writing. SASE.

Responds in 3 weeks to queries; 6 months to mss. Accepts simultaneous, multiple submissions and reprints. Sample copy for $6 prepaid. Writer's guidelines online. **PAYMENT/TERMS** Pays $10-25, and 2 contributor's copies. Pays on publication for first rights, reprints permitted with credit given to original publication. Rights revert to author upon publication.

TIPS "Articles and personal experiences should be creative rather than journalistic and with some depth. Writers should use more than just the simple facts and chronology of an experience with disability. Inquire about future themes of upcoming issues. Sample copy very helpful. Works should not use stereotyping, patronizing, or offending language about disability. We seek fresh imagery and thought-provoking language. Please double-space work, number pages & include full name and address."

LADYBUG

Carus Publishing Co., 700 E. Lake St., Suite 300, Chicago IL 60601. (312)701-1720. **Website:** www.cricketmag.com. **Contact:** Marianne Carus, editor-in-chief; Suzanne Beck, managing art director. Estab. 1990. "We look for quality literature and nonfiction." Subscription: $35.97/year (12 issues). sample: $5; sample pages available on website.

NEEDS Picture-oriented material: adventure, animal, fantasy, folktales, humorous, multicultural, nature/environment, problem-solving, science fiction, sports, suspense/mystery. "Open to any easy fiction stories." Buys 50 mss/year. Length: 800 words maximum.

HOW TO CONTACT Submit complete ms, include SASE.

PAYMENT/TERMS Pays 25¢/word ($25 minimum).

TIPS "Reread ms before sending. Keep within specified word limits. Study back issues before submitting to learn about the types of material we're looking for. Writing style is paramount. We look for rich, evocative language and a sense of joy or wonder. Remember that you're writing for preschoolers—be age-appropriate, but not condescending or preachy. A story must hold enjoyment for both parent and child through repeated read-aloud sessions. Remember that people come in all colors, sizes, physical conditions, and have special needs. Be inclusive!"

LEADING EDGE

4087 JKB, Provo UT 84602. **E-mail:** editor@leadingedgemagazine.com. **Website:** www.leadingedgemagazine.com. Estab. 1980. Twice yearly magazine. "We strive to encourage developing and established talent and provide high quality speculative fiction to our readers." Does not accept mss with sex, excessive violence, or profanity. "*Leading Edge* is a magazine dedicated to new and upcoming talent in the field of science fiction and fantasy." Has published work by Orson Scott Card, Brandon Sanderson, and Dave Wolverton. Has published poetry by Michael Collings, Tracy Ray, Susan Spilecki, and Bob Cook.

Accepts unsolicited submissions.

NEEDS Length: 15,000 words maximum.

HOW TO CONTACT Send complete ms with cover letter and SASE. Include estimated word count.

PAYMENT/TERMS Pays 1¢/word; $10 minimum.

TIPS "Buy a sample issue to know what is currently selling in our magazine. Also, make sure to follow the writer's guidelines when submitting."

LIGUORIAN

One Liguori Dr., Liguori MO 63057-9999. (636)464-2500. **Fax:** (636)464-8449; (636)464-2503. **E-mail:** liguorianeditor@liguori.org. **Website:** www.liguorian.org. **Contact:** Cheryl Plass, managing editor. Estab. 1913. Magazine: 40 pages; 4-color illustrations; photos. "Our purpose is to lead our readers to a fuller Christian life by helping them better understand the teachings of the gospel and the church and by illustrating how these teachings apply to life and the problems confronting them as members of families, the church, and society."

NEEDS Religious/inspirational, young adult/teen, senior citizen/retirement. "Stories submitted to *Liguorian* must have as their goal the lifting up of the reader to a higher Christian view of values and goals. We are not interested in contemporary works that lack purpose or are of questionable moral value." Receives 25 unsolicited mss/month. Accepts 10 mss/year. **Publishes 8-10 new writers/year.** 1,500-2,000 words preferred

HOW TO CONTACT Send complete mss of 400-2,000 words. Accepts submissions by e-mail, fax, disk. Responds in 3 months to mss. Sample copy for 9×12 SASE with 3 first-class stamps or online. Writer's guidelines for #10 SASE and on website. Send complete ms.

PAYMENT/TERMS Pays 12-15¢/word and 5 contributor's copies. Pays on acceptance. Buys first rights.

TIPS "First read several issues containing short stories. We look for originality and creative input in each story we read. Since most editors must wade through mounds of manuscripts each month, consideration for the editor requires that the market be studied, the manuscript be carefully presented and polished before submitting. Our publication uses only one story a month. Compare this with the 25 or more we receive over the transom each month. Also, many fiction mss are written without a specific goal or thrust, i.e., an interesting incident that goes nowhere is *not a story*. We believe fiction is a highly effective mode for transmitting the Christian message and also provides a good balance in an unusually heavy issue."

◐◎ LITERARY MAMA

SC 29843. **E-mail:** lminfo@literarymama.com. **Website:** www.literarymama.com. **Contact:** Caroline M. Grant, editor-in-chief. Estab. 2003. Departments include columns, creative nonfiction, fiction, Literary Reflections, poetry, Profiles & Reviews. We are interested in reading pieces that are long, complex, ambiguous, deep, raw, irreverent, ironic, body conscious. **TIPS** "We seek top-notch creative writing. We also look for quality literary criticism about mother-centric literature and profiles of mother writers. We publish writing with fresh voices, superior craft, vivid imagery. Please send submission (copied into e-mail) to appropriate departmental editors. Include a brief cover letter. We tend to like stark revelation (pathos, humor, and joy), clarity, concrete details, strong narrative development; ambiguity, thoughtfulness, delicacy, irreverence, lyricism, sincerity; the elegant. We need the submissions 3 months before the following months: October (Desiring Motherhood); May (Mother's Day Month); and June (Father's Day Month)."

◐◉ LIVE

Gospel Publishing House, 1445 N. Boonville Ave., Springfield MO 65802-1894. (417)862-1447. **Fax:** (417)862-6059. **E-mail:** rl-live@gph.org. **Website:** www.gospelpublishing.com. Estab. 1928. "*LIVE* is a take-home paper distributed weekly in young adult and adult Sunday school classes. We seek to encourage Christians to live for God through fiction and true stories which apply Biblical principles to everyday problems." Weekly.
NEEDS Religious/inspirational, inspirational, prose poem. No preachy fiction, fiction about Bible characters, or stories that refer to religious myths (e.g., Santa Claus, Easter Bunny, etc.). No science fiction or biblical fiction. No controversial stories about such subjects as feminism, war or capital punishment, "city, ethnic, racial settings." Accepts 2 mss/issue. Publishes ms 18

months after acceptance. **Publishes 50-70 new writers/year.** Recently published work by Tim Woodruff, Barbara Bryden, Katherine Crawford, Roy Borges. No preachy fiction, fiction about Bible characters, or stories that refer to religious myths (e.g., Santa Claus, Easter Bunny, etc.). No science or Bible fiction. No controversial stories about such subjects as feminism, war or capital punishment. Length: 800-1,200 words.
HOW TO CONTACT Send complete ms. Accepts submissions by e-mail or regular mail. Responds in 6 weeks to mss. Accepts simultaneous submissions. Sample copy for #10 SASE. Writer's guidelines for #10 SASE or by e-mail request. Send complete ms.
PAYMENT/TERMS Pays 7-10¢/word. Pays on acceptance for first, second serial (reprint) rights.
TIPS "Don't moralize or be preachy. Provide human interest articles with Biblical life application. Stories should consist of action, not just thought-life; interaction, not just insight. Heroes and heroines should rise above failures, take risks for God, prove that scriptural principles meet their needs. Conflict and suspense should increase to a climax! Avoid pious conclusions. Characters should be interesting, believable, and realistic. Avoid stereotypes. Characters should be active, not just pawns to move the plot along. They should confront conflict and change in believable ways. Describe the character's looks and reveal his personality through his actions to such an extent that the reader feels he has met that person. Readers should care about the character enough to finish the story. Feature racial, ethnic, and regional characters in rural and urban settings."

LULLWATER REVIEW

Emory University, P.O. Box 122036, Atlanta GA 30322. **Fax:** (404)727-7367. **E-mail:** lullwater@lullwaterreview. com. **E-mail:** emorylullwaterreview@gmail.com. **Contact:** Rachel Wisotsky, co-editor-in-chief. Estab. 1990. Magazine: 6×9; 100 pages; 60 lb. paper; photos. "*Lullwater Review* seeks submissions that are strong and original. We require no specific genre or subject." Semi annual. Member, Council of Literary Magazines and Presses. "We're a small, student-run literary magazine published out of Emory University in Atlanta, GA with two issues yearly—once in the fall and once in the spring. You can find us in the *Index of American Periodical Verse*, the *American Humanities Index* and as a member of the Council of Literary Magazines and Presses. We welcome work that brings a fresh perspective, whether through language or the visual arts."

NEEDS Adventure, condensed novels, ethnic/multicultural, experimental, fantasy, historical, humor/satire, mainstream, mystery/suspense, novel excerpts, religious/inspirational, science fiction, slice-of-life vignettes, suspense, western. Recently published work by Greg Jenkins, Thomas Juvik, Jimmy Gleacher, Carla Vissers, and Judith Sudnolt. No romance or science fiction, please. 5,000 words maximum.

HOW TO CONTACT Send complete ms. Accepts submissions by postal mail only. Responds in 1-3 months to queries; 3-6 months to mss. Accepts simultaneous submissions. Sample copy for $5. Writer's guidelines for #10 SASE. Send complete ms via e-mail. *Does not accept postal mail submissions.*

PAYMENT/TERMS Pays 3 contributor copies. Pays on publication for first North American serial rights. Sponsors awards/contests. Pays 3 contributor copies.

TIPS "We at the *Lullwater Review* look for clear cogent writing, strong character development and an engaging approach to the story in our fiction submissions. Stories with particularly strong voices and well-developed central themes are especially encouraged. Be sure that your manuscript is ready before mailing it off to us. Revise, revise, revise! Be original, honest, and of course, keep trying."

◐ ⦶ ☺ ⑤ THE MAGAZINE OF FANTASY & SCIENCE FICTION

P.O. Box 3447, Hoboken NJ 07030. (201) 876-2551. **E-mail:** fandsf@aol.com. **Website:** www.fandsf.com. **Contact:** Gordon Van Gelder, editor. Estab. 1949. Magazine: 5×8; 240 pages; groundwood paper; card stock cover; illustrations on cover only. "For more than 60 years, we have been one of the leading publishers of fantastic fiction (which includes fantasy stories, science fiction, and some horror fiction). Our vision has changed little over six decades—we remain committed to publishing great stories without regard for whether they're classified as sf or fantasy. *The Magazine of Fantasy and Science Fiction* publishes various types of science fiction and fantasy short stories and novellas, making up about 80% of each issue. The balance of each issue is devoted to articles about science fiction, a science column, book and film reviews, cartoons, and competitions." Circ. 30,000.

○ The *Magazine of Fantasy and Science Fiction* won a Nebula Award for Best Novelet for "The Merchant and the Alchemist's Gate" by Ted Chiang in in 2008. Also won the 2007 World Fantasy Award for Best Short Story for "Journey into the Kingdom" by M. Rickert. Editor Van Gelder won the Hugo Award for Best Editor (short form), 2007 and 2008.

NEEDS Adventure, fantasy (space fantasy, sword and sorcery), horror (dark fantasy, futuristic, psychological, supernatural), psychic/supernatural/occult, science fiction (hard science/technological, soft/sociological), young adult/teen (fantasy/science fiction, horror). "We're always looking for more science fiction." Receives 60-900 unsolicited mss/month. Accepts 5-10 mss/issue; 600-100 mss/year. Publishes ms 6-9 months after acceptance. **Publishes 3-6 new writers/year.** Agented fiction 5%. Recently published work by Peter S. Beagle, Ursula K. Le Guin, Alex Irvine, Pat Murphy, Joyce Carol Oates, Gene Wolfe, Ted Chiang, S.L. Gilbow, and Robert Silverberg. Length: Up to 25,000 words; average length: 7,500 words. Publishes short shorts. Send book review copies to Gordon Van Gelder. Sometimes comments on rejected mss. "Prefers character-oriented stories. We receive a lot of fantasy fiction, but never enough science fiction." Length: up to 25,000 words .

HOW TO CONTACT Send complete ms with SASE (or IRC). Include list of publications, estimated word count. No electronic submissions. Responds in 2 months to queries, 6-8 weeks to mss. Accepts reprint submissions. Sample copy for $6. Writer's guidelines for SASE or on website.

PAYMENT/TERMS Pays 6-9¢/word, 2 contributor's copies; additional copies $4.20. Pays on acceptance for first North American serial rights. Sends galleys to author. Publication is copyrighted.

TIPS "Good storytelling makes a submission stand out. Regarding manuscripts, a well-prepared manuscript (i.e., one that follows the traditional format, like that describted here: http://www.sfwa.org/writing/vonda/vonda.htm) stands out more than any gimmicks. Read an issue of the magazine before submitting. New writers should keep their submissions under 15,000 words—we rarely publish novellas by new writers."

○ METAL SCRATCHES

P.O. Box 685, Forest Lake MN 55025. **E-mail:** metalscratches@metalscratches.com. **Website:** www.metalscratches.com. **Contact:** Kim Mark, editor. Estab. 2003. "Semiannual publication looking for stories written about the darker side of humanity—fiction with an edge, a metal scratch."

NEEDS Experimental, horror (psychological), literary. "No poetry, science fiction, rape, murder or horror as in gore." Receives 20 unsolicited mss/month. Accepts 5-6 mss/issue; 20 mss/year. Publishes ms 6 months after acceptance. **Publishes 3 new writers/year.** Length: 3,500 words; average length: 3,000 words. Publishes short shorts. Sometimes comments on rejected mss. Magazine: 512×812; 35 pages; heavy cover-stock. "Metal Scratches focuses on literary fiction that examines the dark side of humanity. We are not looking for anything that is 'cute' or 'sweet'." Semiannual. Pays 2 contributor's copies and one year subscription; additional copies for $3. Pays on publication for one-time rights. Not copyrighted. Does not want horror, science fiction, children's, religion, or poetry.

HOW TO CONTACT Send complete ms. Accepts submissions by e-mail. (No attachments.) Send disposable copy of ms and #10 SASE for reply only. Responds in 1 month to mss. Accepts simultaneous, multiple submissions. Sample copy for $5. Writer's guidelines for SASE or by e-mail.

○⑤ MINDFLIGHTS

Double-Edged Publishing Inc., 9618 Misty Brook Cove, Cordova TN 38016. (901)213-3768. **E-mail:** editor@mindflights.com; MindFlightsEditors@gmail.com. **Website:** www.mindflights.com. **Contact:** Selena Thomason, managing editor. Estab. 2007. "Publishes science fiction, fantasy, and all genres of speculative fiction and poetry. We want work that is grounded in a Christian or Christian-friendly worldview, without being preachy. Please see our vision and guidelines page for details. *MindFlights* is the merging of two established magazines: *The Sword Review* and *Dragons, Knights, & Angels*." Monthly e-zine, annual print edition. "Paving new roads for Christ-reflected short fiction. Not preachy, but still a reflection of the truth and light. Examples of this are in the writings of C.S. Lewis and Tolkien. We strive to provide quality fiction and poetry, all in means that respect traditional values and Christian principles. Be uplifting, encouraging with something interesting to our audience—fans of sci-fi and fantasy who are comfortable with an environment committed to a Christian world view."

○ "No postal submissions accepted. See our portal entry and submission process online."

NEEDS Fantasy (space fantasy, sword and sorcery), science fiction (hard science/technological, soft/sociological), special interests: speculative fiction and poetry with Christian themes. Does not want to see work "that would be offensive to a Christian audience. Also, we are a family-friendly market and thus do not want to see explicit sex, illicit drug use, gratuitous violence or excessive gore." Receives 30 mss/month. Accepts 4 mss/issue; 48 mss/year. Ms published 2 months after acceptance. **Publishes 6-12 new writers/year.** Length: 500-5,000 words. Average length: 3,000 words. Publishes short shorts. Average length of short shorts: 700 words. Also publishes poetry. Always comments on/critiques rejected mss. "Illustrations are compensated with $10 gratuity payment." Does not want to see any work that would be offensive to a Christian audience. Length: 50-5,000 words.

HOW TO CONTACT Send complete ms via online form. Include estimated word count. Responds to queries in 2 weeks. Responds to mss in 4 weeks. Considers previously published submissions, multiple submissions. Guidelines available on website. "We only accept submissions via our online form. Send complete ms. after August 1, when we plan to resume taking submissions."

PAYMENT/TERMS Writers receive 1/2¢ per word, $5 min and $25 max, 1 contributor's copy if selected for print edition. Additional copies $7.50. Pays on acceptance. Acquires first rights, first North American serial rights, one time rights, electronic rights. Sends galleys to author. Publication is copyrighted. Occasional contests. "Details and entry process would be on our website when contest is announced." Pays $5-25

TIPS "Only a very small portion of the works accepted for *MindFlights* will appear in our annual print edition. Most will appear online only. Although our guidelines currently indicate that upon acceptance of a work we will ask for rights for either print, the web, or both, and our contracts clearly indicate which rights we are requesting, we are concerned that authors may be assuming that all works accepted will appear in the print edition. Thank you."

○⑤ NA'AMAT WOMAN

350 Fifth Ave., Suite 4700, New York NY 10118. (212)563-5222. **Fax:** (212)563-5710. **E-mail:** naamat@naamat.org; judith@naamat.org. **Website:** www.naamat.org. **Contact:** Judith Sokoloff, editor. Estab. 1926. "Magazine covering a wide variety of subjects of interest to the Jewish community—including political and social issues, arts, profiles; many articles about Israel and women's issues.

Fiction must have a Jewish theme. Readers are the American Jewish community." Circ. 15,000. "We cover issues and topics of interest to the Jewish community in the U.S., Israel, and the rest of the world with emphasis on Jewish women's issues."

NEEDS Ethnic/multicultural, historical, humor/satire, literary, novel excerpts, women-oriented. Receives 10 unsolicited mss/month. Accepts 3-5 mss/year. "We want serious fiction, with insight, reflection and consciousness." "We do not want fiction that is mostly dialogue. No corny Jewish humor. No Holocaust fiction." Length: 2,000-3,000 words.

HOW TO CONTACT Query with published clips or send complete mss. Responds in 6 months to queries; 6 months to mss. Sample copy for 9×1112 SAE and $1.20 postage. Sample copy for $2. Writer's guidelines for #10 SASE, or by e-mail.

PAYMENT/TERMS Pays 10¢/word and 2 contributor's copies. Pays on publication for first North American serial, first, one time, second serial (reprint) rights, makes work-for-hire assignments.

TIPS "No maudlin nostalgia or romance; no hackneyed Jewish humor."

◐◑ THE NEW WRITER

P.O. Box 60, Cranbrook Kent TN17 2ZR United Kingdom. (44)(158)021-2626. **E-mail:** editor@thenewwriter.com. **Website:** www.thenewwriter.com. **Contact:** Sarah Jackson, poetry editor. Estab. 1996. Magazine: A4; 56 pages; illustrations; photos. Contemporary writing magazine which publishes "the best in fact, fiction and poetry." Publishes 6 issues per annum. "Contemporary writing magazine which publishes the best in fact, fiction and poetry."

NEEDS "We will consider most categories apart from stories written for children. No horror, erotic or cosy fiction." Accepts 4 mss/issue; 24 mss/year. Publishes ms 1 year after acceptance. Agented fiction 5%. **Publishes 12 new writers/year.** Recently published work by Sally Zigmond, Lorna Dowell, Wes Lee, Amy Licence, Cathy Whitfield, Katy Darby, Clio Gray. Length: 2,000-5,000 words; average length: 3,500 words. Publishes short shorts. Also publishes literary essays, literary criticism, poetry. Often comments on rejected mss. *No unsolicited mss.* Accepts fiction from subscribers only. "We will consider most categories apart from stories written for children. No horror, erotic, or cosy fiction."

HOW TO CONTACT Query with published clips. Accepts submissions by e-mail, fax. Send SASE (or IRC) for return of ms or send a disposable copy of ms and #10 SASE for reply only. "We consider short stories from subscribers only but we may also commission guest writers." Responds in 2 months to queries; 4 months to mss. Accepts simultaneous submissions. Sample copy for SASE and A4 SAE with IRCs only. Writer's guidelines for SASE. Reviews fiction.

PAYMENT/TERMS Pays £10 per story by credit voucher; additional copies for £1.50. Pays on publication for one time rights. Sponsors awards/contests. Pays £10 per story by credit voucher; additional copies for £1.50.

TIPS "Hone it—always be prepared to improve the story. It's a competitive market."

●⑤ THE NEW YORKER

4 Times Square, New York NY 10036. (212) 286-5900. **E-mail:** beth_lusko@newyorker.com; toon@cartoonbank.com. **Website:** www.newyorker.com; www.cartoonbank.com. **Contact:** Bob Mankoff, cartoon; David Remnick, editor-in-chief. Estab. 1925. A quality magazine of interesting, well-written stories, articles, essays and poems for a literate audience. Weekly. A quality weekly magazine of distinct news stories, articles, essays, and poems for a literate audience.

> *The New Yorker* receives approximately 4,000 submissions per month.

NEEDS Accepts 1 mss/issue. Publishes 1 ms/issue.

HOW TO CONTACT Send complete ms as .pdf attachments via online e-mail manager. No more than 1 story or 6 poems should be submitted. No attachments. Responds in 3 months to mss. No simultaneous submissions. Writer's guidelines online. Send complete ms. Fiction, poetry, Shouts & Murmurs, and newsbreaks should be sent as pdf attachments. Do not paste them into the message field.

PAYMENT/TERMS Payment varies. Pays on acceptance. Payment varies.

TIPS "Be lively, original, not overly literary. Write what you want to write, not what you think the editor would like. Send poetry to Poetry Department."

⑤ ONE-STORY

One-Story, LLC, 232 3rd St., #A111, Brooklyn NY 11215. **Website:** www.one-story.com. **Contact:** Maribeth Batcha, publisher. Estab. 2002. "*One-Story* is a literary magazine that contains, simply, **one story**. It is a subscription-only magazine. Every 3 weeks subscribers are sent *One-Story* in the mail. *One Story* is artfully designed, lightweight, easy to carry, and ready to entertain on buses, in bed, in subways, in cars, in the park, in the bath, in the waiting rooms of doctor's, on the couch, or in line at the supermarket. Subscribers also have access to a website, www.one-story.com, where they can learn more about *One-Story* authors, and hear about readings and events. There is always time to read *One-Story*."

○ "Accepts submissions via website only (.rtf files). Receives 100 submissions a week. Submit between June & Sept. Publishes each writer one time only."

NEEDS Literary short stories. One Story only accepts short stories. Do not send excerpts. Do not send more than 1 story at a time. Publishes ms 3-6 months after acceptance. Recently published work by John Hodgman, Melanie Rae Thon, Daniel Wallace and Judy Budnitz. *One-Story* only accepts short stories. Do not send excerpts. Do not send more than 1 story at a time. Length: 3,000-8,000 words.

HOW TO CONTACT Send complete ms. Accepts online submissions only. Responds in 2-6 months to mss. Sample copy for $5. Writer's guidelines online. Send complete ms.

PAYMENT/TERMS Pays $100. Pays on publication for first North American serial rights. Buys the rights to publish excerpts on website and in promotional materials.

TIPS *"One-Story* is looking for stories that are strong enough to stand alone. Therefore they must be very good. We want the best you can give."

○○ ON SPEC

P.O. Box 4727, Station South, Edmonton AB T6E 5G6 Canada. (780)413-0215. **Fax:** (780)413-1538. **E-mail:** onspec@onspec.ca. **E-mail:** onspecmag@gmail.com. **Website:** www.onspec.ca. Estab. 1989. Magazine: 514×8; 112-120 pages; illustrations. "We publish speculative fiction by new and established writers, with a strong preference for Canadian authored works. We are moving towards offering a digital version of our issues in addition to our print circulation." Quarterly.

○ Submission deadlines are February 28, May 31, August 31, and November 30.

NEEDS Fantasy, horror, science fiction, magic realism. No media tie-in or shaggy-alien stories. No condensed or excerpted novels, Religious/inspirational stories, fairy tales. "We would like to see more horror, fantasy, science fiction—well-developed stories with complex characters and strong plots." Receives 100 unsolicited mss/month. Accepts 10 mss/issue; 40 mss/year. "We read manuscripts during the month after each deadline: February 28/May 31/August 31/November 30." Publishes ms 6-18 months after acceptance. **Publishes 10-15 new writers/year.** Recently published work by Mark Shainblum, Hugh Spencer, Kate Riedel, and Leah Bobet. Length: 1,000-6,000 words; average length: 4,000 words. Also publishes poetry. Often comments on rejected mss. No media tie-in or shaggy-alien stories. No condensed or excerpted novels, religious/inspirational stories, fairy tales.

HOW TO CONTACT Send complete ms. Accepts submissions by disk. SASE with Canadian postage for return of ms or send a disposable copy of ms plus #10 SASE for response. Include Canadian postage or IRCs. No e-mail or fax submissions. Responds in 2 weeks to queries; 4 months after deadline to mss. Accepts simultaneous submissions. Sample copy for $8. Writer's guidelines for #10 SASE or on website.

PAYMENT/TERMS Pays $50-200 for fiction. Short stories (under 1,000 words): $50 plus 1 contributor's copy. Pays on acceptance for first North American serial rights.

TIPS "We want to see stories with plausible characters, a well-constructed, consistent, and vividly described setting, a strong plot and believable emotions; characters must show us (not tell us) their emotional responses to each other and to the situation and/or challenge they face. Also: don't send us stories written for television. We don't like media tie-ins, so don't watch TV for inspiration! Read, instead! Absolutely no e-mailed or faxed submissions. Strong preference given to submissions by Canadians."

PORTLAND MONTHLY

165 State St., Portland ME 04101. (207)775-4339. **E-mail:** staff@portlandmonthly.com. **Website:** www.portlandmagazine.com. **Contact:** Colin Sargent, editor. Estab. 1985. Monthly city lifestyle magazine—fiction, style, business, real estate, controversy, fashion, cuisine, interviews and art relating to the Maine area.

NEEDS 700 words or less.

HOW TO CONTACT Send complete ms.

TIPS "Our target audience is our 100,000 readers, ages 18-90. We write for our readers alone, and while in many cases we're delighted when our interview subjects enjoy our stories once they're in print, we are not writing for them but only for our readers. Interview subjects may not ever read or hear any portion of our stories before the stories are printed, and in the interest of objective distance, interview subjects are never to be promised complimentary copies of the magazine. It is the writer's responsibility to return all materials such as photos or illustrations to the interview subjects providing them."

⟳ THE SAVAGE KICK LITERARY MAGAZINE

Murder Slim Press, 29 Alpha Rd., Gorleston Norfolk NR31 0EQ United Kingdom. **E-mail:** moonshine@murderslim.com. **Website:** www.murderslim.com. Estab. 2005. "*Savage Kick* primarily deals with viewpoints outside the mainstream...honest emotions told in a raw, simplistic way. It is recommended that you are very familiar with the *SK* style before submitting. We have only accepted 8 new writers in 4 years of the magazine. Ensure you have a distinctive voice and story to tell."

NEEDS "Real-life stories are preferred, unless the work is distinctively extreme within the crime genre. No Poetry of any kind, no mainstream fiction, Oprah-style fiction, Internet/chat language, teen issues, excessive Shakespearean language, surrealism, overworked irony, or genre fiction (horror, fantasy, science fiction, western, erotica, etc.)." Length: 500-6,000 words.

HOW TO CONTACT Send complete ms.

PAYMENT/TERMS Pays $35.

⦸ SHORT STUFF

Bowman Publications, Short Stuff Magazine, Bowman Publications, 2001 I St., #500, Fairbury NE 68352. (402)587-5003. **E-mail:** shortstf89@aol.com. Estab. 1989. Bowman Publications, 712 W. 10th St., Loveland CO 80537. (970)669-9139. "We are perhaps an enigma in that we publish only clean stories in any genre. We'll tackle any subject, but don't allow obscene language or pornographic description. Our magazine is for grown-ups, not X-rated 'adult' fare." Bimonthly. Estab. 1989. Circ. 10,400.

Ọ "We are now open to submissions."

NEEDS Adventure, historical, humor/satire, mainstream, mystery/suspense, romance, science fiction (seldom), western. "We want to see more humor—not essay format—real stories with humor; 1,000-word mysteries, historical pieces. The 1,000-word pieces have the best chance of publication. We are no longer accepting essays for publication in the magazine. In particular, we are absolutely, positively not accepting any Erma Bombeck-like essays, e.g. essys proclaiming how wonderful hubby is or bemoaning how your children are sticking pencils up their noses." No erotica; nothing morbid or pornographic. Issues are Valentine s (February/March); Easter (April/May); Mom's and Dad's (June/July); Americana (August/September); Halloween (October/November); and Holiday (December/January). Receives 500 unsolicited mss/month. Accepts 9-12 mss/issue; 76 mss/year. **Publishes 90% new writers/year.** Recently published work by Bill Hallstead, Dede Hammond, Skye Gibbons.

HOW TO CONTACT Send complete ms. Responds in 6 months to mss. Sample copy for $1.50 and 9×12 SAE with 5 first-class stamps. Writer's guidelines for #10 SASE.

PAYMENT/TERMS Payment varies. Payment and contract upon publication. Acquires first North American serial rights. Payment varies.

TIPS "Don't send floppy disks or cartridges. We are holiday oriented; mark on outside of envelope if story is for Easter, Mother's Day, etc. We receive 500 manuscripts each month. This is up about 200%. Because of this, I implore writers to send 1 manuscript at a time. I would not use stories from the same author more than once an issue and this means I might keep the others too long. Please don't e-mail your stories! If you have an e-mail address, please include that with cover letter so we can contact you. If no SASE, we destroy the manuscript."

SOFA INK QUARTERLY

Sofa Ink, P.O. Box 625, American Fork UT 84003. **E-mail:** publisher@sofaink.com. **E-mail:** acquisitions@sofaink.com. **Website:** www.sofaink.com; www.sofainkquarterly.com. **Contact:** David Cowsert. Estab. 2005. Literary magazine/journal. "The magazine is distributed primarily to waiting rooms and lobbies of medical facilities. All our stories and poetry have positive endings. We like to publish a variety of genres with a focus on good storytelling and word mastery that does not include swearing, profaning deity, gore, excessive violence or gratuitous sex." Quarterly. Estab. 2005. Circ. 650. "Sofa Ink Quarterly offers wonderful original stories, poetry, and nonfiction that is entertaining yet wholesome. Sofa Ink Quarterly showcases original writing and art that avoids sensationalism. There is no swearing, profaning deity, excessive gore, gratuitous violence or gratuitous sex. You will find exceptional storytelling, delightful poetry, and beautiful art."

NEEDS Adventure, ethnic/multicultural, experimental, fantasy, historical, humor/satire, mainstream, mystery/suspense, romance, science fiction, slice-of-life vignettes, western. Does not want erotic or religious. Accepts 12-20 mss/year. Manuscript published 3 months after acceptance. Length: 7,500 words (max). Also publishes poetry. Does not want erotic, religious.

HOW TO CONTACT Send complete ms with cover letter. Accepts submissions by e-mail. Responds to queries in 1-3 months. Responds to mss in 1-3 months. Considers simultaneous submissions. Sample copy available for $6. Guidelines available for SASE, on website.

PAYMENT/TERMS Writers receive $5 flat-rate payment. **Pays on acceptance.** Acquires first North American serial rights. Publication is copyrighted. Pays $5.

TIPS Follow the content guidelines. Electronic submissions should be in a Word attachment rather than in the body of the message.

SPIDER

Cricket Magazine Group, 70 East Lake St., Suite 300, Chicago IL 60601. (312)701-1720. **Fax:** (312)701-1728. **Website:** www.cricketmag.com. Estab. 1994. Monthly reading and activity magazine for children ages 6 to 9. *Spider* introduces children to the highest quality stories, poems, illustrations, articles, and activities. It was created to foster in beginning readers a love of reading and discovery that will last a lifetime. We're looking for writers who respect children's intelligence.

NEEDS Stories should be easy to read. Recently published work by Polly Horvath, Andrea Cheng, and Beth Wagner Brust. No romance, horror, religious. Length: 300-1,000 words.

HOW TO CONTACT Submit complete ms and SASE.

PAYMENT/TERMS Pays up to 25¢/word.

TIPS "We'd like to see more of the following: engaging nonfiction, fillers, and 'takeout page' activities; folktales, fairy tales, science fiction, and humorous stories. Most importantly, do not write down to children."

ST. ANTHONY MESSENGER

28 W. Liberty St., Cincinnati OH 45202-6498. (513)241-5615. **Fax:** (513)241-0399. **E-mail:** mageditors@americancatholic.org. **Website:** www.americancatholic.org. **Contact:** John Feister. Estab. 1893. **Contact:** John Feister, editor-in-chief. Magazine: 8×1034; 60 pages; illustrations; photos. "*St. Anthony Messenger* is a Catholic family magazine which aims to help its readers lead more fully human and Christian lives. We publish articles which report on a changing church and world, opinion pieces written from the perspective of Christian faith and values, personality profiles, and fiction which entertains and informs." Estab. 1893. Circ. 308,884.

NEEDS Mainstream, religious/inspirational, senior citizen/retirement. "We do not want mawkishly sentimental or preachy fiction. Stories are most often rejected for poor plotting and characterization; bad dialogue—listen to how people talk; inadequate motivation. Many stories say nothing, are 'happenings' rather than stories." No fetal journals, no rewritten Bible stories. Receives 60-70 unsolicited mss/month. Accepts 1 mss/issue; 12 mss/year. Publishes ms 1 year after acceptance. **Publishes 3 new writers/year.** Recently published work by Geraldine Marshall Gutfreund, John Salustri, Beth Dotson, Miriam Pollikatsikis and Joseph Pici. Sometimes requests revisions before acceptance. "We do not want mawkishly sentimental or preachy fiction. Stories are most often rejected for poor plotting and characterization; bad dialogue—listen to how people talk; inadequate motivation. Many stories say nothing, are 'happenings' rather than stories. No fetal journals, no rewritten Bible stories." Length: 2,000-2,500 words.

HOW TO CONTACT Send complete ms. Accepts submissions by e-mail, fax. "For quickest response send self-addressed stamped postcard with choices: 'Yes, we're interested in publishing; Maybe, we'd like to hold for future consideration; No, we've decided to pass on the publication.'" Responds in 3 weeks to queries; 2 months to mss. No simultaneous submissions. Sample copy for 9×12 SASE with 4 first-class stamps. Writer's guidelines online. Reviews fiction. Send complete ms.

PAYMENT/TERMS Pays 16¢/word maximum and 2 contributor's copies; $1 charge for extras.

TIPS "The freelancer should consider why his or her proposed article would be appropriate for us, rather than for *Redbook* or *Saturday Review*. We treat human problems of all kinds, but from a religious perspective. Articles should reflect Catholic theology, spirituality, and employ a Catholic terminology and vocabulary. We need more articles on prayer, scripture, Catholic worship. Get authoritative information (not merely library research); we want interviews with experts. Write in popular style; use lots of examples, stories, and personal quotes. Word length is an important consideration."

○ STONE SOUP

Children's Art Foundation, P.O. Box 83, Santa Cruz CA 95063-0083. (831)426-5557. **Fax:** (831)426-1161.

E-mail: editor@stonesoup.com. **Website:** www.stone-soup.com. **Contact:** Ms. Gerry Mandel, editor. Estab. 1973. *Stone Soup* is 48 pages, 7x10, professionally printed in color on heavy stock, saddle-stapled, with coated cover with full-color illustration. Receives 5,000 poetry submissions/year, accepts about 12. Press run is 15,000 (14,000 subscribers, 3,000 shelf sales, 500 other). Subscription: membership in the Children's Art Foundation includes a subscription, $37/year. *Stone Soup*, published 6 times/year, showcases writing and art by children ages 13 and under. "We have a preference for writing and art based on real-life experiences; no formula stories or poems. We only publish writing by children ages 8 to 13. We do not publish writing by adults."

○ "Stories and poems from past issues are available online."

NEEDS We do not like assignments or formula stories of any kind. Length: 150-2,500 words.

HOW TO CONTACT Send complete ms; no SASE.

PAYMENT/TERMS Pays $40 for stories. Authors also receive 2 copies, a certificate, and discounts on additional copies and on subscriptions.

TIPS "All writing we publish is by young people ages 13 and under. We do not publish any writing by adults. We can't emphasize enough how important it is to read a couple of issues of the magazine. You can read stories and poems from past issues online. We have a strong preference for writing on subjects that mean a lot to the author. If you feel strongly about something that happened to you or something you observed, use that feeling as the basis for your story or poem. Stories should have good descriptions, realistic dialogue, and a point to make. In a poem, each word must be chosen carefully. Your poem should present a view of your subject, and a way of using words that are special and all your own."

THE STORYTELLER

2441 Washington Rd., Maynard AR 72444. (870)647-2137. **E-mail:** storytellermag1@@yahoo.com. **Website:** www.thestorytellermagazine.com. Estab. 1996.

NEEDS Does not want anything graphic, religious or bashing—even in fiction. Length: 1,500 words.

HOW TO CONTACT Send complete ms with SASE.

TIPS *The Storyteller* is one of the best places you will find to submit your work, especially new writers. Our best advice, be professional. You have one chance to make a good impression. Don't blow it by being unprofessional.

THE STRAND MAGAZINE

P.O. Box 1418, Birmingham MI 48012-1418. (248)788-5948. **Fax:** (248)874-1046. **E-mail:** strandmag@strandmag.com. **Website:** www.strandmag.com. Estab. 1998. P After an absence of nearly half a century, the magazine known to millions for bringing Sir Arthur Conan Doyle's ingenious detective, Sherlock Holmes, to the world has once again appeared on the literary scene. First launched in 1891, *The Strand*, included in its pages the works of some of the greatest writers of the 20th century: Agatha Christie, Dorothy Sayers, Margery Allingham, W. Somerset Maugham, Graham Greene, P.G. Wodehouse, H.G. Wells, Aldous Huxley and many others. In 1950, economic difficulties in England caused a drop in circulation which forced the magazine to cease publication.

NEEDS We are not interested in submissions with any sexual content. Length: 2,000-6,000 words.

HOW TO CONTACT Query first. Include SASE.

PAYMENT/TERMS Pays $50-175.

TIPS No gratuitous violence, sexual content, or explicit language, please.

SUSPENSE MAGAZINE

JRSR Ventures, 26500 W. Agoura Rd., Suite 102-474, Calabasas CA 91302. **Fax:** (310)626-9670. **E-mail:** editor@suspensemagazine.com; john@suspensemagazine.com. **Website:** www.suspensemagazine.com. **Contact:** John Raab, publisher/CEO/editor-in-chief. Estab. 2007.

NEEDS No explicit scenes 500-5,000/words.

HOW TO CONTACT Query.

TIPS "Unpublished writers are welcome and encouraged to query. Our emphasis is on horror, suspense, thriller and mystery."

⊕○ TALENT DRIPS EROTIC PUBLISHINGS

Cleveland OH 44102. (216)799-9775. **E-mail:** talent_drips_eroticpublishing@lycos.com. **Website:** http://ashygirlforgirls.tripod.com/talentdripseroticpublishings. **Contact:** Kimberly Steele, founder. Estab. 2007. *Talent Drips*, published bimonthly online, focuses solely on showcasing new erotic fiction.

NEEDS Wants erotic short stories.

HOW TO CONTACT Submit short stories between 5,000 and 10,000 words by e-mail to talent_drips_eroticpublishing@lycos.com. Should be pasted into body of message. Reads submissions during publication months only. Time between acceptance and publication is 2 months. Guidelines available on website. Responds in 3 weeks. Pays $15 for each accepted short story. Acquires electronic rights only. Work archived on the site for one year.

TIPS "Does not want sci-fi/fantasy submissions; mythical creatures having pointless sex is not a turn-on; looking for more original plots than 'the beast takes the submissive maiden' stuff."

TALES OF THE TALISMAN

Hadrosaur Productions, P.O. Box 2194, Mesilla Park NM 88047-2194. **E-mail:** hadrosaur@zianet.com. **Website:** www.talesofthetalisman.com. **Contact:** David Lee Summers, editor. Estab. 1995. *"Tales of the Talisman* is a literary science fiction and fantasy magazine. We publish short stories, poetry, and articles with themes related to science fiction and fantasy. Above all, we are looking for thought-provoking ideas and good writing. Speculative fiction set in the past, present, and future is welcome. Likewise, contemporary or historical fiction is welcome as long as it has a mythic or science fictional element. Our target audience includes adult fans of the science fiction and fantasy genres along with anyone else who enjoys thought-provoking and entertaining writing."

❍ Fiction and poetry submissions are limited to reading periods of January 1-February 15 and July 1-August 15.

NEEDS "We do not want to see stories with graphic violence. Do not send 'mainstream' fiction with no science fictional or fantastic elements. Do not send stories with copyrighted characters, unless you're the copyright holder." Length: 1,000-6,000 words.

HOW TO CONTACT Send complete ms.

PAYMENT/TERMS Pays $6-10.

TIPS "Let your imagination soar to its greatest heights and write down the results. Above all, we are looking for thought-provoking ideas and good writing. Our emphasis is on character-oriented science fiction and fantasy. If we don't believe in the people living the story, we generally won't believe in the story itself."

TELLURIDE MAGAZINE

Big Earth Publishing, Inc., P.O. Box 964, Telluride CO 81435-0964. (970)728-4245. **Fax:** (970)728-4302. **E-mail:** duffy@telluridemagazine.com. **Website:** www. telluridemagazine.com. **Contact:** Mary Duffy, editor-in-chief. Estab. 1982. *"Telluride Magazine* speaks specifically to Telluride and the surrounding mountain environment. Telluride is a resort town supported by the ski industry in winter, festivals in summer, outdoor recreation year round and the unique lifestyle all of that affords. As a National Historic Landmark District with a colorful mining history, it weaves a tale that readers seek out. The local/visitor interaction is key to Telluride's success in making profiles an important part of the content. Telluriders are an environmentally minded and progressive bunch who appreciate efforts toward sustainability and protecting the natural landscape and wilderness that are the region's number one draw."

NEEDS "Please contact us; we are very specific about what we will accept." 800-1,200 words.

HOW TO CONTACT Query with published clips.

U.S. CATHOLIC

Claretian Publications, 205 W. Monroe St., Chicago IL 60606. (312)236-7782. **Fax:** (312)236-8207. **E-mail:** editors@uscatholic.org. **E-mail:** submissions@uscatholic. org. **Website:** www.uscatholic.org. Estab. 1935. *"U.S. Catholic* is dedicated to the belief that it makes a difference whether you're Catholic. We invite and help our readers explore the wisdom of their faith tradition and apply their faith to the challenges of the 21st century."

❍ Please include SASE with written ms.

NEEDS Accepts short stories. "Topics vary, but unpublished fiction should be no longer than 2,500 words and should include strong characters and cause readers to stop for a moment and consider their relationships with others, the world, and/or God. Specifically religious themes are not required; subject matter is not restricted. E-mail literaryeditor@uscatholic.org. Usually responds in 8-10 weeks. Minimum payment is $300." Length: 2,500-3,000 words.

HOW TO CONTACT literaryeditor@uscatholic.org. Send complete ms.

PAYMENT/TERMS Pays $300.

⑤ WHOLE LIFE TIMES

Whole Life Media, LLC, 23705 Vanowen St., #306, West Hills CA 91307. (877)807-2599. **Fax:** (310)933-1693. **E-mail:** editor@wholelifemagazine.com. **Website:** www. wholelifemagazine.com. Estab. 1979. Online market. *"WLT* accepts up to three longer stories (800-1,100 words) per issue, and payment ranges from $150-200 depending on topic, research required and writer experience. In addition, we have a number of regular departments that pay $75-150 depending on topic, research required and writer experience. City of Angels is our FOB section featuring short, newsy blurbs on our coverage topics, generally in the context of LA. These are generally 200-400 words and pay $25-35 depending on length and topic. This is a great section for writers who are new to us. BackWords is a 750-word personal essay that often highlights a seminal moment or event in the life of the writer and pays $100. *WLT* has editorial exchange relationships with local magazines in San Francisco and Chicago that occasionally co-assign (and increase the fee paid) or reprint at 50%. In the event that the magazine decides not to publish your assigned story, a kill fee of 50 percent of the original fee is offered. However, no kill fee is offered for unsolicited submissions or if this is your first assignment with us; you are free to publish the work elsewhere. If we do print your work, we customarily pay within 30-45 days of publication. We pay by invoice, so please be sure to submit one, and name the file with your name. We ask for one-time print rights and non-exclusive perpetual web publishing rights. Thank you for your interest in *Whole Life Times*, voice of the Los Angeles community for 33 years."

○ "We are a regional publication and favor material that somehow links to our area via topics, sources, similar.

HOW TO CONTACT We accept articles at any time by e-mail. If you would like your article to be considered for a specific issue, we should have it in hand 2-4 months before the issue of publication. Original photos and illustrations are welcome and may be submitted along with your article for consideration. If you are sending very large images, graphs, or other original art, please e-mail us for ftp submission guidelines. Please include a one-sentence credit line to accompany your story. If you do not include it, the story will run with your byline only.

TIPS Send complete ms. Submissions are accepted via email. Artwork should also be sent via email as hard copies will not be returned. "Queries should be professionally written and show an awareness of current topics of interest in our subject area. We welcome investigative reporting and are happy to see queries that address topics in a political context. We are especially looking for articles on health and nutrition. No regular columns sought." Submissions should be double-spaced in AP style as an attached unformatted MS Word file (.doc). If you do not have Microsoft Word and must email in another program, please also copy and paste your story in the message section of your email."

WOMAN'S WORLD

Bauer Publishing Co., 270 Sylvan Ave., Englewood Cliffs NJ 07632. (201)569-6699. **Fax:** (201)569-3584. **E-mail:** dearww@aol.com. **Website:** http://winit.womansworldmag.com. **Contact:** Stephanie Saible, editor-in-chief. Estab. 1980. "We publish short romances and mini-mysteries for all women, ages 18-68."

○ *Woman's World* is not looking for freelancers to take assigments generated by the staff, but it will assign stories to writers who have made a successful pitch.

NEEDS "Short story, romance, and mainstream of 800 words and mini-mysteries of 1,000 words. Each of our stories has a light romantic theme and can be written from either a masculine or feminine point of view. Women characters may be single, married, or divorced. Plots must be fast moving with vivid dialogue and action. The problems and dilemmas inherent in them should be contemporary and realistic, handled with warmth and feeling. The stories must have a positive resolution. Specify Fiction on envelope. Always enclose SASE. Responds in 4 months. No phone or fax queries. Pays $1,000 for romances on acceptance for North American serial rights for 6 months. The 1,000 word mini-mysteries may feature either a 'whodunnit' or 'howdunnit' theme. The mystery may revolve around anything from a theft to murder. However, we are not interested in sordid or grotesque crimes. Emphasis should be on intricacies of plot rather than gratuitous violence. The story must include a resolution that clearly states the villain is getting his or her come-uppance. Submit complete mss. Specify Mini-Mystery on envelope. Enclose SASE. No phone queries." Not interested in science fiction, fantasy, historical romance, or foreign locales. No explicit sex, graphic language, or seamy settings. Romances—800 words; mysteries—1,000 words.

HOW TO CONTACT Send complete ms.

PAYMENT/TERMS Pays $1,000/romances; $500/mysteries.

TIPS The whole story should be sent when submitting fiction. Stories slanted for a particular holiday should be sent at least 6 months in advance. "Familiarize yourself totally with our format and style. Read at least a year's worth of *Woman's World* fiction. Analyze and dissect it. Regarding romances, scrutinize them not only for content but tone, mood and sensibility."

BOOK PUBLISHERS

In this section, you will find many of the "big name'" book publishers. Many of these publishers remain tough markets for new writers or for those whose work might be considered literary or experimental. Indeed, some only accept work from established authors, and then often only through an author's agent. Although having your novel published by one of the big commercial publishers listed in this section is difficult, it is not impossible. The trade magazine *Publishers Weekly* regularly features interviews with writers whose first novels are being released by top publishers. Many editors at large publishing houses find great satisfaction in publishing a writer's first novel.

Find the publishing industry's "family tree," which maps out each of the large book publishing conglomerates' divisions, subsidiaries and imprints. Remember, most manuscripts are acquired by imprints, not their parent company, so avoid submitting to the conglomerates themselves.

Also listed here are "small presses" publishing four or more titles annually. Included among them are independent presses, university presses and other nonprofit publishers. Introducing new writers to the reading public has become an increasingly important role of these smaller presses at a time when the large conglomerates are taking fewer chances on unknown writers. Many of the successful small presses listed in this section have built their reputations and their businesses in this way and have become known for publishing prize-winning fiction.

These smaller presses also tend to keep books in print longer than larger houses. And, since small presses publish a smaller number of books, each title is equally important to the publisher, and each is promoted in much the same way and with the same commitment. Editors also stay at small presses longer because they have more of a stake in the business—

often they own the business. Many smaller book publishers are writers themselves and know firsthand the importance of a close editor-author or publisher-author relationship.

TYPES OF BOOK PUBLISHERS

Large or small, the publishers in this section publish books "for the trade." That is, unlike textbook, technical or scholarly publishers, trade publishers publish books to be sold to the general consumer through bookstores, chain stores or other retail outlets. Within the trade book field, however, there are a number of different types of books.

The easiest way to categorize books is by their physical appearance and the way they are marketed. Hardcover books are the more expensive editions of a book, sold through bookstores and carrying a price tag of around $20 and up. Trade paperbacks are soft-bound books, also sold mostly in bookstores, but they carry a more modest price tag of usually around $10 to $20. Today a lot of fiction is published in this form because it means a lower financial risk than hardcover.

Mass market paperbacks are another animal altogether. These are the smaller "pocket-size" books available at bookstores, grocery stores, drug stores, chain retail outlets, etc. Much genre or category fiction is published in this format. This area of the publishing industry is very open to the work of talented new writers who write in specific genres such as science fiction, romance and mystery.

At one time publishers could be easily identified and grouped by the type of books they produce. Today, however, the lines between hardcover and paperback books are blurred. Many publishers known for publishing hardcover books also publish trade paperbacks and have paperback imprints. This enables them to offer established authors (and a very few lucky newcomers) hard-soft deals in which their book comes out in both versions. Thanks to the mergers of the past decade, too, the same company may own several hardcover and paperback subsidiaries and imprints, even though their editorial focuses may remain separate.

CHOOSING A BOOK PUBLISHER

In addition to checking the bookstores and libraries for books by publishers that interest you, you may want to refer to the Category Index at the back of this book to find publishers divided by specific subject categories. The subjects listed in the Index are general. Read individual listings to find which subcategories interest a publisher. For example, you will find several romance publishers listed, but read the listings to find which type of romance is considered—gothic, contemporary, regency or futuristic. See "You've Got a Story" for more on how to refine your list of potential markets.

A NOTE ABOUT AGENTS

Some publishers are willing to look at unsolicited submissions, but most feel having an agent is in the writer's best interest. In this section more than any other, you'll find a number of publishers who prefer submissions from agents. That's why we've included a section of agents open to submissions from fiction writers. For even more agents along with a great deal of helpful articles about approaching and working with them, refer to *Guide to Literary Agents* (Writer's Digest Books).

If you use the Internet or another resource to find an agent not listed in this book, be wary of any agents who charge large sums of money for reading a manuscript. Reading fees do not guarantee representation. Think of an agent as a potential business partner and feel free to ask tough questions about his or her credentials, experience and business practices.

HARRY N. ABRAMS INC.

Subsidiary of La Martiniere Group, 115 West 18th St., 6th Floor, New York NY 10011. (212)206-7715. **Fax:** (212)519-1210. **E-mail:** abrams@abramsbooks.com. **Website:** www.abramsbooks.com. **Contact:** Managing editor. Estab. 1951. Publishes hardcover and "a few" paperback originals. Averages 150 total titles/year. Responds in 6 months to queries. No simultaneous submissions, electronic submissions.

IMPRINTS Stewart, Tabori & Chang; Abrams Books for Young Readers; Abrams Gifts & Stationery.

TERMS Pays royalty. Average advance: variable. Publishes ms 2 years after acceptance. Book catalog for $5. Responds in 6 months (if interested) to queries.

ABSEY & CO.

23011 Northcrest Dr., Spring TX 77389. (281)257-2340. **E-mail:** abseyandco@aol.com; info@absey.biz. **Website:** www.absey.biz. **Contact:** Edward Wilson, editor-in-chief. "We accept mainstream fiction and nonfiction, poetry, educational books, especially those dealing in language arts. We do not accept e-mail submissions of manuscripts. Submit: A brief cover letter; a chapter by chapter outline; an author's information sheet (please focus on relevantqualifications and previous publishing experience); two or three sample chapters; SASE."

TERMS Responds to mss in 6-9 months.

TIPS Absey publishes a few titles every year. We like the author and the illustrator working together to create something magical. Authors and illustrators have input into every phase of production."

Ⓐ ACE SCIENCE FICTION AND FANTASY

Imprint of the Berkley Publishing Group, Penguin Group (USA), Inc., 375 Hudson St., New York NY 10014. (212)366-2000. **Website:** www.penguin.com. **Contact:** Anne Sowards, editor; Jessica Webb, editorial assistant. Estab. 1953. Estab. 1953. Publishes hardcover, paperback, and trade paperback originals and reprints. Averages 75 total titles, 75 fiction titles/year. Ace publishes science fiction and fantasy exclusively. Publishes hardcover, paperback, and trade paperback originals and reprints Guidelines for #10 SASE.

NEEDS Fantasy, science fiction. No other genre accepted. No short stories. Published *Iron Sunrise*, by Charles Stross; *Neuromancer,* by William Gibson; *King Kelson's Bride*, by Katherine Kurtz. Does not accept unsolicited mss. No other genre accepted. No short stories.

HOW TO CONTACT Submit 1-2 sample chapter(s), synopsis. Send SASE or IRC. Responds in 2-3 months to queries. Due to the high volume of manuscripts received, most Penguin Group (USA) Inc. imprints do not normally accept unsolicited manuscripts. Query first with SASE.

TERMS Accepts simultaneous submissions. Pays royalty. Offers advance. Publishes ms 1-2 years after acceptance. Ms guidelines for #10 SASE. Pays royalty. Pays advance. Responds in 2 months to queries. Responds in 6 months to manuscripts.

ACME PRESS

P.O. Box 1702, Westminster MD 21158-1702. (410)848-7577. **Contact:** (Ms.) E.G. Johnston, man. ed. Estab. 1991. "We operate on a part-time basis." Publishes hardcover and trade paperback originals. **Published some debut authors within the last year.** Averages 1-2 total titles/year. Publishes hardcover and trade paperback originals. Book catalog and ms guidelines for #10 SASE. Does not accept electronic submissions.

NEEDS Humor. "We accept submissions on any subject as long as the material is humorous; prefer full-length novels. No cartoons or art (text only). No pornography, poetry, short stories or children's material." Published *She-Crab Soup* by Dawn Langley Simmons (fictional memoir); *Biting the Wall*, by J.M. Johnston (mystery); *SuperFan*, by Lyn A. Sherwood (football); and *Hearts of Gold*, by James Magorian (caper). "We accept submissions on any subject as long as the material is humorous; prefer full-length novels. No cartoons or art (text only)."

HOW TO CONTACT Accepts unsolicited mss. Agented fiction 25%. Responds in 2 weeks to queries; 2 months to mss. Accepts simultaneous submissions. Always comments on rejected mss. Please include the following contact information in your cover letter and on your manuscript: Byline (name as you want it to appear if published), mailing address, phone number, and e-mail. Include a self-addressed stamped envelope (SASE). If a SASE is not enclosed, you will only hear from us if we are interested in your work. Include the genre (e.g., fiction, et al.) of your work in the address. "Acme Press is "always looking for the great comic novel." Send for their submission guidelines or ask how to receive a book catalogue, by writing to them at P.O. Box 1702, Westminster MD 21158-1702." Submit first 3-5 chapters, synopsis.

TERMS Pays 25 author's copies and 50% of profits. Average advance: small. Publishes ms 1 year after acceptance. Book catalog and ms guidelines for #10 SASE. Pays 25 author's copies and 50% of profits. Pays small advance. Responds in 2 weeks to queries. Responds in 2 months to mss.

ALONDRA PRESS, LLC

4119 Wildacres Dr., Houston TX 77072. **E-mail:** lark@ alondrapress.com. **Website:** www.alondrapress.com. **Contact:** Pennelope Leight, fiction editor; Solomon Tager, nonfiction editor. Estab. 2007. Publishes trade paperback originals and reprints. Guidelines available online.

NEEDS "Just send us a few pages in an email attachment, or the entire manuscript. We will look at it quickly and tell you if it interests us."

TERMS Responds in 1 month to queries/proposals; 3 months to mss.

TIPS "Be sure to read our guidelines before sending a submission. We will not respond to authors who do not observe our simple guidelines. Send your submissions in an e-mail attachment only."

AMBASSADOR BOOKS, INC.

Paulist Press, 997 MacArthur Blvd., Mahwah NJ 07430. (201)825-7300; (800)218-1903. **Fax:** (800)836-3161. **E-mail:** info@paulistpress.com; ggoggins@paulistpress.com; jconlan@paulistpress.com. **Website:** www.ambassadorbooks.com. "We are a Christian publishing company seeking spirituality-focused books for children and adults." Publishes hardcover and trade paperback originals. Book catalog online for download, or write for paper catalog.

Preference is given to non-simultaneous submissions (responds in 1-2 months). Accepts simultaneous submissions.

NEEDS Not accepted except in adult or juvenile fables.
HOW TO CONTACT Query with SASE or submit complete ms.
TERMS Pays 8-10% royalty on net sales. Responds in up to 4 months to queries.

AMIRA PRESS

Wales. (704)858-7533. **E-mail:** yvette@amirapress. com. **Website:** www.amirapress. **Contact:** Yvette A. Lynn, CEO (any sub genre). Estab. 2007. "We are a small press which publishes sensual and erotic romance. Our slogan is "Erotic and Sensual Romance. Immerse Yourself." Our authors and stories are diverse. **Published 30 new writers last year.** Averages 50 fiction titles/year. Member EPIC. Distributes/promotes titles through Amazon, Mobipocket, Fictionwise, BarnesandNoble.com, Target.com, Amirapress. com, AllRomance Ebooks, and Ingrams. Format publishes in paperback originals, e-books. POD printing. Guidelines available online.

HOW TO CONTACT Submit complete ms with cover letter by e-mail. "No snail mail." Include estimated word count, heat level, brief bio, list of publishing credits. Accepts unsolicited mss. Sometimes critiques/comments on rejected mss.

TERMS Pays royalties, 8.5% of cover price (print)—30% of cover price (Ebooks). Responds in 3 months.

TIPS "Please read our submission guidelines thoroughly and follow them when submitting. We do not consider a work until we have all the requested information and the work is presented in the format we outline."

ANAPHORA LITERARY PRESS

104 Banff Dr., Apt. 101, Edinboro PA 16412. (814)273-0004. **E-mail:** pennsylvaniajournal@gmail.com. **Website:** www.anaphoraliterary.wordpress.com. **Contact:** Anna Faktorovich, editor-in-chief (general interest). Estab. 2007. "We are actively seeking submissions at this time. Single and multiple-author books in fiction (poetry, novels, and short story collections). The genre is not as important as the quality of work. You should have a completed full-length ms ready to be emailed or mailed upon request.In the Winter of 2010, Anaphora began accepting book-length single-author submissions. We are actively seeking single and multiple-author books in fiction (poetry, novels, and short story collections) and non-fiction (academic, legal, business, journals, edited and un-edited dissertations, biographies, and memoirs). Email submissions to pennsylvaniajournal@gmail.com. Profits are split 50/50% with single-author writers. There are no costs to have a book produced by Anaphora. We do not offer any free contributor copies." Format publishes in trade paperback originals and reprints; mass market paperback originals and reprints. Catalog and guidelines available online at website.

NEEDS Short stories can be included in *Pennsylvania Literary Journal.* Two novellas might be published in a single book. "We are actively seeking submissions at this time. The genre is not as important as the quality of work. You should have a completed full-length ms ready to be emailed or mailed upon request."

HOW TO CONTACT Query with SASE. Submit proposal package, including synopsis, 1 sample chapter, and completed ms. Looking for single and multiple-author books in fiction (poetry, novels, and short story collections).

TERMS Pays 10-30% royalty on retail price. "We currently publish journals, which are authored by several people. If we publish a novel or a critical book by a single author, we will share our profits with the author." Responds in 1 month on queries, proposals, and mss.

TIPS "Our audience is academics, college students and graduates, as well as anybody who loves literature. Regardless of profits, we love publishing great books and we enjoy reading submissions. So, if you are reading this book because you love writing and hope to publish as soon as possible, send a query letter or a submission to us. But, remember—proofread your work (most of our editors are English instructors)."

ANGOOR PRESS LLC

2734 Bruchez Pkwy., Unit 103, Denver CO 80234. **E-mail:** submissions@angoorpress.com. **Website:** www.angoorpress.com. **Contact:** Carolina Maine, Founder, Editor. Estab. 2010. No catalog available. Manuscript guidelines are free by request.

HOW TO CONTACT Submit proposal package, including market search, author bio and book marketing plan.

TERMS Pays 5%-20% on wholesale price in royalties. Responds 3 months to proposals and manuscripts.

TIPS "Christians."

⊘○ ANNICK PRESS, LTD.

15 Patricia Ave., Toronto ON M2M 1H9 Canada. (416)221-4802. **Fax:** (416)221-8400. **E-mail:** annickpress@annickpress.com. **Website:** www.annickpress.com. **Contact:** Rick Wilks, director; Colleen MacMillan, associate publisher; Sheryl Shapiro, creative director. "Annick Press maintains a commitment to high quality books that entertain and challenge. Our publications share fantasy and stimulate imagination, while encouraging children to trust their judgment and abilities." Publishes 5 picture books/year; 6 young readers/year; 8 middle readers/year; 9 young adult titles/year. Publishes picture books, juvenile and YA fiction and nonfiction; specializes in trade books. Book catalog and guidelines available online

💬 *Does not accept unsolicited mss.*

NEEDS Publisher of children's books. Publishes hardcover and trade paperback originals. Average print order: 9,000. First novel print order: 7,000. Plans 18 first novels this year. Averages 25 total titles/year. Distributes titles through Firefly Books Ltd. Juvenile, young adult. Recently published *The Apprentice's Masterpiece: A Story of Medieval Spain*, by Melanie Little, ages 12 and up; Chicken, Pig, Cow series, written and illustrated by Ruth Ohi, ages 2-5; Single Voices series, Melanie Little, Editor, ages 14 and up; *Crusades*, by Laura Scandiffio, illustrated by John Mantha, ages 9-11. Not accepting picture books at this time.

TERMS Pays authors royalty of 5-12% based on retail price. Offers advances (average amount: $3,000). Pays illustrators royalty of 5% minimum.

ANTARCTIC PRESS

7272 Wurzbach, Suite 204, San Antonio TX 78240. (210)614-0396. **E-mail:** davidjhutchison@yahoo.com; apcog1@gmail.com; rod_espinosa@antarctic-press.com. **Website:** www.antarctic-press.com. **Contact:** David Hutchison. Estab. 1985. "Antarctic Press is a Texas-based company that was started in 1984. Since then, we have grown to become one of the largest publishers of comics in the United States. Over the years we have produced over 850 titles with a total circulation of over 5 million. Among our titles are some of the most respected and longest-running independent series in comics today. Since our inception, our main goal has been to establish a series of titles that are unique, entertaining, and high in both quality and profitability. The titles we currently publish exhibit all these traits, and appeal to a wide audience. Antarctic Press is among the top 10 publishers of comics in the United States. However, the difference in market shares between the top five publishers and the next five publishers is dramatic. Most of the publishers ranked above us have a far greater share of the market place. That being the case, we are an independent publisher with a small staff, and many of our employees have multiple responsibilities. Bigger companies would spread these responsibilities out among a larger staff. Additionally, we don't have the same financial power as a larger company. We cannot afford to pay high page rates; instead, we work on an advance and royalty system which is determined by sales or potential sales of a particular book. We pride ourselves on being a company that gives new talent a chance to get published and take a shot at comic stardom."

NEEDS Comic books, graphic novels.

TERMS Pays royalty on net receipts; ms guidelines online.

☼ ANVIL PRESS

P.O. Box 3008 MPO, Vancouver BC V6B 3X5 Canada. (604)876-8710. **Fax:** (604)879-2667. **E-mail:** info@anvilpress.com. **E-mail:** christine@anvilpress.com. **Website:** www.anvilpress.com. **Contact:** Brian Kaufman. Estab. 1988. "Three-person operation with volunteer editorial board." Publishes trade paperback originals. Books: offset or web printing; perfect bound. **Published some debut authors within the last year.** Averages 8-10 total titles/year. Published *Stolen*, by Annette Lapointe (novel); *Suburban Pornography*, by Matthew Firth (stories); *Elysium and Other Stories*, by Pamela Stewart; *Dirtbags*, by Teresa McWhirter (novel); *Black Rabbit and Other Stories* by Salvatore DiFalco. Publishes ms 8 months after acceptance. Book catalog for 9×12 SAE with 2 first-class stamps. Ms guidelines online. "Anvil Press publishes contemporary adult fiction, poetry, and drama, giving voice to up-and-coming Canadian writers, exploring all literary genres, discovering, nurturing, and promoting new Canadian literary talent. Currently emphasizing urban/suburban themed fiction and poetry; de-emphasizing historical novels." Publishes trade paperback originals. Book catalog for 9×12 SAE with 2 first-class stamps Guidelines available online.

☐ Canadian authors only.

NEEDS Experimental, literary, short story collections. Contemporary, progressive, modern literature—no formulaic or genre. Contemporary, modern literature; no formulaic or genre.

HOW TO CONTACT Accepts unsolicited mss, or query with SASE. Include estimated word count, brief bio. Send SASE for return of ms or send a disposable ms and SASE for reply only. No e-mail submissions. Responds in 2 months to queries; 6 months to mss. Accepts simultaneous submissions. Submit to: Anvil Press P.O. Box 3008, Main Post Office, Vancouver, BC V6B 3X5. Query with SASE.

TERMS Pays 15% royalty on net receipts. Average advance: $500. Pays advance. Responds in 2 months to queries. Responds in 6 months to manuscripts

TIPS "Audience is young, informed, educated, aware, with an opinion, culturally active (films, books, the performing arts). No U.S. authors. Research the appropriate publisher for your work."

⊕☻ ARCHAIA

1680 Vine St., Suite 912, Los Angeles CA 90028. **E-mail:** editorial@archaia.com, submissions@archaia.com.

Website: www.archaia.com. **Contact:** Submissions Editor. "Archaia Entertainment, LLC is a multi-award-winning graphic novel publisher with more than 50 renowned publishing brands, including such domestic and international hits as *Artesia, Mouse Guard, The Killer, Gunnerkrigg Court, Awakening, Titanium Rain, Days Missing, Tumor, Syndrome, Okko, The Secret History,* and a line of Jim Henson graphic novels including *Fraggle Rock* and *The Dark Crystal.* Archaia has built an unparalleled reputation for producing meaningful content that perpetually transforms minds, building one of the industry's most visually stunning and eclectic slates of graphic novels. Archaia is the reigning 2010 Graphic Novel Publisher of the Year according to *Ain't It Cool News, Graphic Policy,* and *Comic Related.* Archaia has also successfully emerged as a prolific storyteller in all facets of the entertainment industry, extending its popular brands into film, television, gaming, and branded digital media."

NEEDS "Archaia publishes creator-owned comic books and graphic novels in the adventure, fantasy, horror, pulp noir, and science fiction genres that contain idiosyncratic and atypical writing and art. *Archaia does not generally hire freelancers or arrange for freelance work, so submissions should only be for completed book and series proposals.*"

HOW TO CONTACT Query with outline/synopsis and photocopies of completed pages. Prefers e-mail submissions with pdf attachments. Accepts queries by snail mail. Include info on estimated page count, intended formats, and other technical details.

TERMS Submissions guidelines on website.

⊕ ARKHAM BRIDGE PUBLISHING

P.O. Box 2346, Everett WA 98213. **E-mail:** arkhambridgepublishing@arkhambridgepublishing.com. **E-mail:** submissions@arkhambridgepublishing.com. **Website:** www.arkhambridgepublishing.com. **Contact:** James Davis, senior editor. Estab. 2009. "Arkham Bridge Publishing is a book and periodical publisher based in Washington State, aiming to bring works by new authors to the national market. We publish many genres, but especially aim to publish science-fiction, fantasy, and alternate history works." Catalog free on request or online at website: www.arkhambridge.com/bookstore. Guidelines free on request with SAE or online at website.

NEEDS "Arkham Bridge is looking to expand into more fiction markets with more titles, and will accept and review all fiction submissions."

HOW TO CONTACT Submit completed ms.

TERMS Responds in 1 month.

TIPS "Arkham Bridge Publishing is looking to expand and grow, having only one book title and two magazine titles at this time. We see no problem with receiving and reviewing a greater quantity of queries and manuscripts, and we intend to begin publishing between one and three titles each year."

ARSENAL PULP PRESS

#101-211 East Georgia St., Vancouver BC V6A 1Z6 Canada. (604)687-4233. **Fax:** (604)687-4283. **E-mail:** info@arsenalpulp.com. **Website:** www.arsenalpulp.com. **Contact:** Editorial Board. Estab. 1980. Literary press. Publishes hardcover and trade paperback originals, and trade paperback reprints. **Published some debut authors within the last year.** Plans 1,500 first novels this year. Plans 2 first novels this year. Averages 20 total titles/year. Distributes titles through Whitecap Books (Canada) and Consortium (U.S.). Promotes titles through reviews, excerpts, and print advertising. Accepts unsolicited mss. Accepts 10% agented fiction. Responds in 2 months to queries; 4 months to mss. Accepts simultaneous submissions. Sometimes comments on rejected mss. Publishes ms 1 year after acceptance. Book catalog and submission guidelines on website. Publishes trade paperback originals, and trade paperback reprints Book catalog for 9×12 SAE with IRCs or online Guidelines available online.

"We are interested in literature that traverses uncharted territories, publishing books that challenge and stimulate and ask probing questions about the world around us. With a staff of five, located in a second-floor office in the historic Vancouver district of Gastown, we publish between 14 and 20 new titles per year, as well as an average of 12 to 15 reprints."

IMPRINTS Tillacum Library, Advance Editions.

NEEDS Gay/lesbian, literary fiction and nonfiction, multicultural, regional (British Columbia), cultural studies, pop culture, political/sociological issues, cookbooks No children's books or genre fiction, i.e., westerns, romance, horror, mystery, etc.

HOW TO CONTACT Submit outline, 2-3 sample chapter(s), synopsis. Include list of publishing credits. Send copy of ms and SASE (or with International Reply Coupons if sent from outside Canada) OR include e-mail address if manuscript does not need to be returned.

TERMS Responds in 2 months to queries. Responds in 4 months to proposals and manuscripts.

ARTEMIS PRESS

236 W. Portal Avenue #525, San Francisco CA 94127. (866)216-7333. **E-mail:** artemispressdigital-info@yahoo.com; submissions@artemispress.com. **Website:** www.artemispress.com. **Contact:** Susan R. Skolnick, publisher and editor-in-chief. Estab. 2000. "Publisher of short fiction of interest to the worldwide women's community. We specialize in lesbian-related titles but are interested in all women-centered titles. We are open to working with new authors." Publishes electronic editions of original, previously published material. **Published no debut authors within the last year.** Titles distributed and promoted online to target market.

NEEDS "Artemis Press is currently looking to purchase novellas, flash fiction, short fiction works of interest to women of all backgrounds, sexual orientations and ethnicities. We are especially interested in purchasing lesbian romance and erotica, lesbian and female detective fiction, as well as lesbian erotica. We will consider short fiction featuring strong, dynamic women characters in other genres. We are also looking for authors who are interested in writing short fiction to spec. Our short fiction needs are as follows: Flash Fiction — 1000 to 1500 words; Short Short Fiction — 1501 to 3000 words; Short Fiction — 3001 — 15,000 words; Novellas — 15,001 to 40,000 words. Send us a query email for more information. Please note: we no longer accept unsolicited manuscripts! Please query first via email." Wants: Mystery/detective, suspense, romance, erotica, paranormal/ghost stories, and science fiction. Published *The Ladies Next Door*, by Jacqui Singleton (humor/satire); *Selects Her Own*, by Claire Garden (humor/satire); *Clicking Stones*, by Nancy Tyler Glenn (New Age/mystic; *Moon Madness and Other Stories*, by Liann Snow (short story collection); *Faith in Love*, by Liann Snow (humor/satire; *Luna Ascending: Stories of Love and Magic*, by Renee Brown (short story collection); *Windrow Garden*, by Janet McClellan (romance); *Never Letting Go*, by Suzanne Hollo (humor/satire; *Minding Therapy*, by Ros Johnson (humor/satire).

HOW TO CONTACT Does not accept unsolicited mss. Agented fiction 5%. Responds in 3 months to queries. Does not accept simultaneous submissions.

TERMS Buys all rights. Publishes ms 6 months after acceptance. Ms guidelines online.

TIPS "We like to see clean manuscripts and an indication that the author has proofed and self-edited before submitting. Query via e-mail only to artemispressdigital-editor@yahoo.com."

ARTE PUBLICO PRESS

University of Houston, 452 Cullen Performance Hall, Houston TX 77204-2004. **Fax:** (713)743-3080. **E-mail:** submapp@mail.uh.edu. **Website:** www.artepublicopress.com. **Contact:** Nicolas Kanellos, editor. Estab. 1979. "Small press devoted to the publication of contemporary U.S.-Hispanic literature." Publishes hardcover originals, trade paperback originals and reprints. Averages 36 total titles/year. Book catalog available free. Guidelines available online.

Arte Publico Press is the oldest and largest publisher of Hispanic literature for children and adults in the United States. "We are a showcase for **Hispanic** literary creativity, arts and culture. Our endeavor is to provide a national forum for U.S.-Hispanic literature."

IMPRINTS Piñata Books.

NEEDS Ethnic, literary, mainstream/contemporary, written by U.S.-Hispanic authors. Recent publications include *Women Who Live in Coffee Shops and Other Stories*, by Stella Pope Duarte; *The Name Partner*, by Carlos Cisneros; and *The Party for Papá Luis/La fiesta para Papá Luis*, by Diane Gonzales Bertrand.

HOW TO CONTACT Manuscripts must be submitted online at: www.artepublicopress.com. Agented fiction 1%. Responds in 2-4 months to queries; 3-6 months to mss. Accepts simultaneous submissions. Sometimes comments on rejected mss. Query with SASE. Submit outline/proposal, clips, 2 sample chapters. Submit complete ms.

TERMS Pays 10% royalty on wholesale price. Provides 20 author's copies; 40% discount on subsequent copies. Average advance: $1,000-3,000. Publishes ms 2 years after acceptance. Ms guidelines online. Pays 10% royalty on wholesale price. Provides 20 author's copies; 40% discount on subsequent copies. Pays $1,000-3,000 advance. Responds in 1 month to queries & to proposals. Responds in 4 months to manuscripts.

TIPS "Include cover letter in which you 'sell' your book—why should we publish the book, who will want to read it, why does it matter, etc.Use our ms submission online form. Format files accepted are: Word, plain/text, rich/text files. Other formats will not be accepted. Manuscript files cannot be larger than 5MB. Once editors review your ms, you will receive an email with the decision. Revision process could take up to four (4) months."

ASPEN MOUNTAIN PRESS

18121-C East Hampden Ave., Aurora CO 80013. **E-mail:** submissions@aspenmountainpress.com. **Website:** www.AspenMountainPress.com. **Contact:** Sandra Hicks, Editor-in-Chief. Estab. 2006. "We are a small electronic press that specializes in e-books. A few outstanding stories are considered for print. We currently encourage newer, outstanding writers to take their craft to the next level. The bulk of our stories are romantic with varying degrees of sensuality/sexuality. We encourage romances between consenting adults. We encourage discussion among our authors; we frequently discuss marketing, we take author input into covers seriously, we pay every month royalties are earned." Publishes e-books. Format: POD printing; perfect bound. Average print order: 250-500. Debut novel print order: 250. **Published 30 debut writers last year in e-book.** Plans 25-30 debut novels this year. Averages 65 fiction titles/year. Member RWA, CIPA. Distributes/promotes titles through Fictionwise, All Romance eBooks, Mobipocket, Amazon, 1Romance eBooks, Bookstrand.

IMPRINTS Aurora Regency.

NEEDS Erotica, fantasy (space fantasy, sword and sorcery), gay, historical (erotic regency), horror (dark fantasy, futuristic, psychological, supernatural), lesbian, mystery/suspense (amateur sleuth, cozy, police procedural, private eye/hardboiled), psychic/supernatural, romance (contemporary, futuristic/time travel, gothic, regency, romantic suspense), science fiction (hard science/technological, soft/sociological), western (frontier saga, traditional, gay). Special interests: "We want heroes the reader can identify with and science fiction romance—No first person!" Published *Cold Warriors*, by Clare Dargin (science fiction romance); *Del Fantasma: Texas Tea*, by Maura Anderson (erotic paranormal romance); and *Cover Me*, by L.B. Gregg (erotic gay thriller). "We are also opening a regency line late summer 2010. See our website for details regarding Aurora Regency."

HOW TO CONTACT Query with outline/synopsis and 4 sample chapters. Accepts queries by e-mail only; does not accept mail. Include estimated word count, brief bio, list of publishing credits, and indicate whether the ms is finished. Responds to queries in 3 months.

Accepts unsolicited mss. Often critiques/comments on rejected mss. Responds to mss in 3-4 months.

TERMS Sends pre-roduction galleys to author. Ms published 3-12 months after acceptance. Writer's guidelines on website. Pays royalties of 8% min for print, 35-40% max for e-books, 50% of net from resellers.

TIPS "Gay romances and erotica are very popular in e-books. Well-written science fiction and fantasy are also doing well. Eliminate dialogue tags when possible. Have someone outside your family read your submission and check for continuity errors, typing mistakes, and pacing. Follow the submission guidelines. Have a website and a blog. Have some idea on how you are going to market your book and let people know about it. Think outside the box. Traditional marketing, such as book marks, does not make sense in our industry."

Ⓐⓧⓖ ATHENEUM BOOKS FOR YOUNG READERS

Simon & Schuster, 1230 Avenue of the Americas, New York NY 10020. **Website:** http://imprints.simonand-schuster.biz/atheneum; www.simonsayskids.com. **Contact:** Caitlyn Dlouhy, editorial director; Justin Chanda, VP/publisher; Namrata Tripathi, executive editor; Emma Dryden, vice president. Estab. 1960. Atheneum Books for Young Readers is a hardcover imprint with a focus on literary fiction and fine picture books for preschoolers through young adults. Publishes special interest, first novels and new talent. Publishes 20+ picture books/year; 20+ middle readers/year; 20+ young adult titles/year.

NEEDS Middle grade and YA adventure, fantasy, humor, mainstream/contemporary, mystery, suspense, and picture books. All in juvenile versions. "We have few specific needs except for books that are fresh, interesting and well written. Fad topics are dangerous, as are works you haven't polished to the best of your ability. We also don't need safety pamphlets, ABC books, coloring books and board books. In writing picture book texts, avoid the coy and 'cutesy,' such as stories about characters with alliterative names. *Query only. No unsolicited mss.*" No paperback romance-type fiction.

HOW TO CONTACT *"We do not accept unsolicited queries, partial, or full manuscript submissions, unless from an agent."*

TERMS Pays royalty on hardcover retail price: 10% fiction; 5% author, 5% illustrator (picture book). Of-fers $5,000-$8,000 advance for new authors. Publishes ms up to 3 years after acceptance.

TIPS "Study our titles."

Ⓓ AUNT LUTE BOOKS

P.O. Box 410687, San Francisco CA 94141. (415)826-1300. **Fax:** (415)826-8300. **E-mail:** books@auntlute.com, submissions@auntlute.com. **Website:** www.auntlute.com. **Contact:** Acquisitions editor. Estab. 1982. Small feminist and women-of-color press. Publishes hardcover and paperback originals. Does not publish single-author collections of poetry. Averages 4 total titles/year.

NEEDS Ethnic, feminist, lesbian. We encourage you to consult our catalog to get a sense of the areas in which we publish and the audiences we currently serve.

HOW TO CONTACT Accepts unsolicited ms queries. Please include SASE. Please do not send manuscripts by certified mail or return receipt requested. We do not accept e-mailed submissions. Alternately, submit cover letter, two sample chapters (approx 50 pages), brief synopsis, and SASE to: Aunt Lute Books, Attn. Acquisitions Editor, P.O. Box 410687, San Francisco, CA 94141. Do not staple any pages, and make sure that each page is numbered and has your name at the top. Responds in 3 months.

TERMS Pays royalty.

TIPS "We seek manuscripts, both fiction and non-fiction, by women from a variety of cultures, ethnic backgrounds and subcultures; women who are self-aware and who, in the face of all contradictory evidence, are still hopeful that the world can reserve a place of respect for each woman in it. We seek work that explores the specificities of the worlds from which we come, and which examines the intersections between the borders which we all inhabit."

Ⓐ AVALON BOOKS

Thomas Bouregy & Sons, Inc., 160 Madison Ave., 5th Floor, New York NY 10016. (212)598-0222. **Fax:** (212)979-1862. **E-mail:** editorial@avalonbooks.com; avalon@avalonbooks.com; lbrown@avalonbooks.com. **Website:** www.avalonbooks.com. **Contact:** Lia Brown, editor. Estab. 1950. Publishes hardcover originals. Guidelines available online.

NEEDS "We publish contemporary romances, historical romances, mysteries and westerns. Time period and setting are the author's preference. The historical romances will maintain the high level of reading expected by our readers. The books shall be wholesome fiction, without graphic sex, violence or strong language."

HOW TO CONTACT "We do accept unagented material. We no longer accept e-mail queries. When submitting, include a query letter, a 2-3 page (and no longer) synopsis of the entire ms, and the first three chapters. All submissions must be typed and double spaced. If we think that your novel might be suitable for our list, we will contact you and request that you submit the entire manuscript. **Please note that any unsolicited full manuscripts will not be returned.** There is no need to send your partial to any specific editor at Avalon. The editors read all the genres that are listed above. Address your letter to: **The Editors.**"

TERMS Pays 10% royalty. Pays $1,000 advance. Responds in 2-3 months to queries.

TIPS "Avalon Books are geared and marketed for librarians to purchase and distribute."

AVON BOOKS

Harper Collins Publishers, 10 E. 53 Street, New York NY 10022. **Website:** www.harpercollins.com. **Contact:** Michael Morrison, publisher. Estab. 1941. "Avon has been publishing award-winning books since 1941. It is recognized for having pioneered the historical romance category and continues to bring the best of commercial literature to the broadest possible audience." Publishes hardcover and paperback originals and reprints.

◯ *Does not accept unsolicited mss.*

HOW TO CONTACT Query with SASE.

🅐🅞 B & H PUBLISHING

127 Ninth Ave. N., Nashville TN 37234. **Website:** www.bhpublishinggroup.com. Estab. 1934. Publishes hardcover and paperback originals. B & H is the book division of LifeWay, the world's largest publisher of Christian materials. Averages 90 total titles, 20 fiction titles/year. Member: ECPA.

NEEDS Religious/inspirational (contemporary women's fiction, suspense, romance, thriller, historical romance). Engaging stories told from a Christian worldview.

HOW TO CONTACT *At this time B&H only accepts manuscripts from literary agents.* For additional information, the agent may call us at 615-251-2438. Writer's Guidelines are available by sending a self-addressed stamped envelope to: Pat Carter: Writer's Guidelines, B&H Publishing Group, 127 9th Avenue North, MSN 115. Accepts simultaneous submissions.

TERMS Pays negotiable royalty. Publishes ms 10-12 months after acceptance. Ms guidelines for #10 SASE.

BAEN BOOKS

P.O. Box 1188, Wake Forest NC 27588. (919)570-1640. **E-mail:** artdirector@baen.com. **Website:** www.baen.com. Estab. 1983. "We publish only science fiction and fantasy. Writers familiar with what we have published in the past will know what sort of material we are most likely to publish in the future: powerful plots with solid scientific and philosophical underpinnings are the sine qua non for consideration for science fiction submissions. As for fantasy, any magical system must be both rigorously coherent and integral to the plot, and overall the work must at least strive for originality."

NEEDS "Style: Simple is generally better; in our opinion good style, like good breeding, never calls attention to itself. Length: 100,000 - 130,000 words Generally we are uncomfortable with manuscripts under 100,000 words, but if your novel is really wonderful send it along regardless of length."

HOW TO CONTACT "Query letters are not necessary. We prefer to see complete manuscripts accompanied by a synopsis. We prefer not to see simultaneous submissions. Electronic submissions are strongly preferred. *We no longer accept submissions by e-mail.* Send ms by using the submission form at: http://ftp.baen.com/Slush/submit.aspx. No disks unless requested. Attach ms as a Rich Text Format (.rtf) file. Any other format will not be considered."

TERMS Responds to mss within 12-18 months.

🅞 BAEN PUBLISHING ENTERPRISES

P.O. Box 1403, Riverdale NY 10471-0671. (718)548-3100. **E-mail:** info@baen.com; toni@baen.com; e-editors@baen.com. **Website:** www.baen.com. Estab. 1983. **Website:** www.baen.com. **Contact:** Toni Weisskopf, publisher. Estab. 1983. "We publish books at the heart of science fiction and fantasy." Publishes hardcover, trade paperback and mass market paperback originals and reprints. **Published some debut authors within the last year.** Plans 2-3 first novels this year. Averages 120 total titles, 120 fiction titles/year. Distributes titles through Simon & Schuster. Publishes hardcover, trade paperback and mass market paperback originals and reprints. Book catalog available free. Guidelines available online.

NEEDS Fantasy, science fiction. Interested in science fiction novels (based on real science) and fantasy novels "that at least strive for originality." Length: 110,00-150,000 words. Published *In Fury Born*, by David Weber; *Music to My Sorrow*, by Mercedes Lackey and Rosemary Edghill; *Ghost*, by John Ringo.

HOW TO CONTACT Submit synopsis and complete ms. "Electronic submissions are strongly preferred. Attach manuscript as a Rich Text Format (.rtf) file. Any other format will not be considered." Additional submission guidelines online. Include estimated word count, brief bio. Send SASE or IRC. Responds in 9-12 months. No simultaneous submissions. Sometimes comments on rejected mss.

TERMS Pays royalty on retail price. Offers advance. Ms guidelines online. Responds in 9-12 months to manuscripts.

TIPS "Keep an eye and a firm hand on the overall story you are telling. Style is important but less important than plot. Good style, like good breeding, never calls attention to itself. Read *Writing to the Point*, by Algis Budrys. We like to maintain long-term relationships with authors."

Ⓐⵁ BAKER BOOKS

6030 East Fulton Rd., Ada MI 49301. **Website:** www. bakerbooks.com. Estab. 1939. Baker Book House Company, P.O. Box 6287, Grand Rapids MI 49516-6287. (616)676-9185. **Fax:** (616)676-2315. **Contact:** Jeanette Thomason, special projects editor (mystery, literary, women's fiction); Lonnie Hull DuPont, editoral director (all genres); Vicki Crumpton, acquisitions editor (all genres). "Midsize publisher of work that interests Christians." Publishes hardcover and trade paperback originals and trade paperback reprints. Books: web offset print. Plans 5 first novels this year. Averages 200 total titles/year. Distributes titles through Ingram and Spring Arbor into both CBA and ABA markets worldwide. Publishes in hardcover and trade paperback originals, and trade paperback reprints. Book catalog for 9½×12½ envelope and 3 first-class stamps. Guidelines for #10 SASE and online.

NEEDS Literary, mainstream/contemporary, mystery, picture books, religious. "We are mainly seeking fiction of two genres: contemporary women's fiction and mystery." Published *Praise Jerusalem!* and *Resting in the Bosom of the Lamb*, by Augusta Trobaugh (contemporary women's fiction); *Touches the Sky*, by James Schaap (western, literary); and *Face to Face*, by Linda Dorrell (mystery); *Flabbergasted*, by Ray Blackston; *The Fisherman*, by Larry Huntsberger.

HOW TO CONTACT Does not accept unsolicited mss. We will consider unsolicited work only through one of the following avenues. Materials sent to our editorial staff through a professional literary agent will be considered. In addition, our staff attends various writers' conferences at which prospective authors can develop relationships with those in the publishing industry. You may also submit your work to one or more of the following manuscript submission services, which serve as a liaison between publishers and prospective authors: Authonomy.com, The Writer's Edge, and Christian Manuscript Submissions, an online service of the Evangelical Christian Publishers' Association.

TERMS Pays 14% royalty on net receipts. Offers advance. Publishes ms within 1 year after acceptance. Ms guidelines for #10 SASE.

TIPS "We are not interested in historical fiction, romances, science fiction, biblical narratives or spiritual warfare novels. Do not call to 'pass by' your idea."

Ⓐ BALLANTINE BOOKS

1745 Broadway, New York NY 10019. (212)782-9000. **Website:** www.randomhouse.com/BB. Estab. 1952. "Ballantine's list encompasses a large, diverse offering in a variety of formats." Publishes hardcover, trade paperback, mass market paperback originals.

NEEDS Confession, ethnic, fantasy, feminist, gay/lesbian, historical, humor, literary, mainstream/contemporary (women's), military/war, multicultural, mystery, romance, short story collections, spiritual, suspense, general fiction.

HOW TO CONTACT *Agented submissions only.*

TERMS Pays 8-15% royalty. Average advance: variable. Ms guidelines online.

ⒶⒹⓄⓈ BANCROFT PRESS

P.O. Box 65360, Baltimore MD 21209-9945. (410)358-0658. **Fax:** (410)764-1967. **E-mail:** bruceb@bancroftpress.com; HDemchick@bancroftpress.com (if bancrof account is down). **Website:** www.bancroftpress.com. **Contact:** Bruce Bortz, editor/publisher (health, investments, politics, history, humor, literary novels, mystery/thrillers, chick lit, young adult). "Small independent press publishing literary and commercial fiction." Publishes hardcover and trade paperback originals. Also packages books for other publishers (no fee to authors). **Published 5 debut authors within the last two years.** Averages 4-6 fiction titles/year. Published *The Re-Appearance of Sam Webber*, by Scott Fugua (literary); *Hume's Fork*, by Ron Cooper (literary); *The Case against My Brother*, by Libby Sternberg (historical/young adult); *Finn* by Matthew Olshan (young adult);

and *The Sinful Life of Lucy Burns* by Elizabeth Leikness (fantasy/women's). Accepts unsolicited mss. Agented fiction 100%. Responds in 6-12 months to mss. Accepts simultaneous submissions. Sometimes comments on rejected mss. Ms guidelines online. "Bancroft Press is a general trade publisher. We publish young adult fiction and adult fiction, as well as occasional nonfiction. Our only mandate is 'books that enlighten.'"

HOW TO CONTACT Query with SASE or submit outline, 2 sample chapter(s), synopsis, by mail or e-mail or submit complete ms. Accepts queries by e-mail, fax. Include brief bio, list of publishing credits. Send SASE for return of ms or send a disposable ms and SASE for reply only.

TERMS Pays various royalties on retail price. Average advance: $1500. Publishes ms up to 3 years after acceptance. Pays 6-8% royalty. Pays various royalties on retail price. Pays $750 advance. Responds in 6-12 months to queries, proposals and manuscripts

TIPS "We advise writers to visit our website and to be familiar with our previous work. Patience is the number one attribute contributors must have. It takes us a very long time to get through submitted material, because we are such a small company. Also, we only publish 4-6 books per year, so it may take a long time for your optioned book to be published. We like to be able to market our books to be used in schools and in libraries. We prefer fiction that bucks trends and moves in a new direction. We are especially interested in mysteries and humor (especially humorous mysteries)."

Ⓐ BANTAM DELL PUBLISHING GROUP
1745 Broadway, New York NY 10019. **E-mail:** bdpublicity@randomhouse.com. **Website:** www.bantamdell.com. Estab. 1945. "In addition to being the nation's largest mass market paperback publisher, Bantam publishes a select yet diverse hardcover list." Publishes hardcover, trade paperback, and mass market paperback originals; mass market paperback reprints. Averages 350 total titles/year.

NEEDS Adventure, fantasy, horror.

HOW TO CONTACT *Agented submissions only.*

TERMS Offers advance. Publishes ms 1 year after acceptance.

Ⓐ Ⓒ BANTAM DOUBLEDAY DELL BOOKS FOR YOUNG READERS
Random House Children's Publishing, 1745 Broadway, New York NY 10019. (212)782-9000. **Fax:** (212)782-8234. **Website:** www.randomhouse.com/kids. **Con-**

tact: Michelle Poplof, editorial director. Publishes hardcover, trade paperback, and mass market paperback series originals, trade paperback reprints. Averages 300 total titles/year.

NEEDS Adventure, fantasy, historical, humor, juvenile, mainstream/contemporary, mystery, picture books, suspense, chapter books, middle-grade. Published *Bud, Not Buddy*, by Christopher Paul Curtis; *The Sisterhood of the Traveling Pants*, by Ann Brashares.

HOW TO CONTACT Does not accept unsolicited mss. *Agented submissions only.*

TERMS Pays royalty. Average advance: varied. Publishes ms 2 years after acceptance. Book catalog for 9×12 SASE.

● BARBOUR PUBLISHING INC.
1800 Barbour Dr., P.O. Box 719, Urichsville OH 44683. (740)922-6045. **E-mail:** editors@barbourbooks.com; aschrock@barbourbooks.com; fictionsubmit@barbourbooks.com. **Website:** www.barbourbooks.com. **Contact:** Ashley Schrock, creative director. Estab. 1981. Publishes hardcover, trade paperback and mass market paperback originals and reprints. Published 40% debut authors within the last year. Averages 250 total titles/year.

IMPRINTS Heartsong Presents (contact Joanne Simmons, managing editor).

NEEDS Historical, contemporary, religious, romance, western, mystery. All submissions must be Christian mss. "Heartsong romance is 'sweet'—no sex, no bad language. Other genres may be 'grittier'—real-life stories. All must have Christian faith as an underlying basis. Common writer's mistakes are a sketchy proposal, an unbelievable story, and a story that doesn't fit our guidelines for inspirational romances."

HOW TO CONTACT Submit 3 sample chapter(s), synopsis by e-mail only. For submission of your manuscripts, please follow the link online to download the appropriate guidelines.

TERMS Pays 8-16% royalty on net price. Average advance: $1,000-8,000. Publishes ms 1-2 years after acceptance. Pays 0-16% royalty on net price or makes outright purchase of $500-6,000. Pays $500-10,000 advance. Purchaes one-time rights, according to project. Only if interested. Responds in 1 month to queries.

BARRON'S EDUCATIONAL SERIES, INC.
250 Wireless Blvd., Hauppauge NY 11788. **Website:** barronseduc.com. Estab. 1941. waynebarr@bar-

ronseduc.com. **Contact:** Wayne Barr, Acquisitions. Publishes hardcover, paperback, and mass market originals and software. Published 10% debut authors within the last year. Averages 400 total titles/year. Estab. 1941.

NEEDS Middle grade, YA.

HOW TO CONTACT Accepts simultaneous submissions. E-mail queries only, no attachments.

TERMS Pays 12-13% royalty on net receipts. Average advance: $3-4,000. Publishes ms 18 months after acceptance. Ms queries via e-mail, but no attached proposals.

TIPS "The writer has the best chance of selling us a book that will fit into one of our series. Children's books have less chance for acceptance because of the glut of submissions. SASE must be included for the return of all materials. Please be patient for replies."

BAYLOR UNIVERSITY PRESS

One Bear Place 97363, Waco TX 76798. (254)710-3164; 3522. **Fax:** (254)710-3440. **E-mail:** carey_newman@baylor.edu. **Website:** www.baylorpress.com. **Contact:** Dr. Carey C. Newman, director. "We publish contemporary and historical scholarly works about culture, religion, politics, science, and the arts." Publishes hardcover and trade paperback originals. Guidelines available online.

TERMS Pays 10% royalty on wholesale price. Responds in 2 months to proposals.

FREDERIC C. BEIL, PUBLISHER, INC.

609 Whitaker St., Savannah GA 31401. (912)233-2446. **Fax:** (912)233-6456. **E-mail:** books@beil.com. **Website:** www.beil.com. **Contact:** Mary Ann Bowman, editor. Estab. 1982. Publishes hardcover originals and reprints. Books: acid-free paper; offset printing; Smyth-sewn, hardcover binding; illustrations. Plans 3 first novels this year. Averages 10 total titles, 4 fiction titles/year. Frederic C. Beil publishes in the fields of history, literature, and biography. Publishes hardcover originals and reprints. Book catalog available free.

IMPRINTS The Sandstone Press; Hypermedia, Inc.

NEEDS History, biography, fiction. Published *Dancing by the River*, by Marlin Barton; *Joseph Jefferson*, by Arthur Bloom (biography); *The Invisible Country*, by H.E. Francis (fiction).

HOW TO CONTACT *Does not accept unsolicited mss.* We prefer postal mail queries. Query with SASE. Responds in 3 days to queries. Accepts simultaneous submissions. Query with SASE.

TERMS Pays 7.5% royalty on retail price. Publishes ms 20 months after acceptance. Pays 7 1/2% royalty on retail price. Responds in 1 week to queries.

TIPS "Our objectives are (1) to offer to the reading public carefully selected texts of lasting value; (2) to adhere to high standards in the choice of materials and in bookmaking craftsmanship; (3) to produce books that exemplify good taste in format and design; and (4) to maintain the lowest cost consistent with quality."

◑ BELLEVUE LITERARY PRESS

New York University School of Medicine, Dept. of Medicine, NYU School of Medicine, 550 First Avenue, OBV 612, New York NY 10016. (212) 263-7802. **E-mail:** BLPsubmissions@gmail.com. **Website:** http://blpress.org. **Contact:** Erika Goldman, editorial director (literary fiction); Leslie Hodgkins, editor (literary fiction). Estab. 2005. "We're a small literary press that publishes nonfiction and fiction that ranges the intersection of the sciences (or medicine) and the arts." Publishes hardcover originals, paperback originals. Debut novel print order: 3000. Plans 2 debut novels this year. Averages 8 total titles/year; 2 fiction titles/year. Member CLMP. Distributes/promotes titles through Consortium.

HOW TO CONTACT Send query letter or query with outline/synopsis and 3 sample chapters. Accepts queries by snail mail, e-mail. Include estimated word count, brief bio, list of publishing credits. Send disposable copy of ms and SASE for reply only. Agented fiction: 75%. Responds to queries in 2 weeks. Accepts unsolicited mss. Considers simultaneous submissions. Rarely critiques/comments on rejected mss. Responds to mss in 6 weeks.

TERMS Sends preproduction galleys to author. Manuscript published 8-12 months after acceptance. Writer's guidelines not available. Pays royalties 6-15%, advance $1,000. Book catalogs on website.

TIPS "We are a project of New York University's School of Medicine and while our standards reflect NYU's excellence in scholarship, humanistic medicine, and science, our authors need not be affiliated with NYU. We are not a university press and do not receive any funding from NYU. Our publishing operations are financed exclusively by foundation grants, private donors, and book sales revenue."

◮◯ THE BERKLEY PUBLISHING GROUP

Penguin Group (USA) Inc., 375 Hudson St., New York NY 10014. **Website:** http://us.penguingroup.com/.

Contact: Leslie Gelbman, president and publisher. Estab. 1955. The Berkley Publishing Group publishes a variety of general nonfiction and fiction including the traditional categories of romance, mystery and science fiction. Publishes paperback and mass market originals and reprints.

> "Due to the high volume of manuscripts received, most Penguin Group (USA) Inc. imprints do not normally accept unsolicited manuscripts. The preferred and standard method for having manuscripts considered for publication by a major publisher is to submit them through an established literary agent."

IMPRINTS Ace; Berkley; Jove.
NEEDS No occult fiction.
HOW TO CONTACT *Prefers agented submissions.*

BILINGUAL REVIEW PRESS

Hispanic Research Center, Arizona State University, P.O. Box 875303, Tempe AZ 85287-5303. (480)965-3867. **Fax:** (480)965-0315. **E-mail:** brp@asu.edu. **Website:** www.asu.edu/brp. **Contact:** Gary Keller, publisher. Estab. 1973. "University affiliated." Publishes hardcover and paperback originals and reprints. Books: 60 lb. acid-free paper; single sheet or web press printing; perfect-bound.
NEEDS Ethnic, literary, short story collections. Always seeking Chicano, Puerto Rican, Cuban-American, or other U.S. Hispanic themes with strong and serious literary qualities and distinctive and intellectually important themes. Does *not* publish children's literature or trade genres such as travelogues and adventure fiction. Novels set in a pre-Columbian past are not likely to be published. Published *Moving Target: A Memoir of Pursuit*, by Ron Arias; *Contemporary Chicano and Chicana Art: Artists, Works, Culture, and Education*, Gary Keller, et al; *Triumph of Our Communities: Four Decades of Mexican American Art*, Gary Keller et al; *Assumption and Other Stories*, by Daniel A. Olivas; *Renaming Ecstasy: Latino Writings on the Sacred*, edited by Orlando Ricardo Menes.
HOW TO CONTACT Accepts unsolicited mss. Query with SASE or submit 2-3 sample chapter(s). Accepts queries by e-mail, mail. Include brief bio, list of publishing credits. Send SASE or IRC. Responds in 3-4 weeks to queries; 3-4 months to mss.
TERMS Pays 10% royalty. Average advance: $500-1,000. Publishes ms 2 years after acceptance. Ms guidelines by e-mail.

TIPS "Writers should take the utmost care in assuring that their manuscripts are clean, grammatically impeccable, and have perfect spelling. This is true not only of the English but the Spanish as well. All accent marks need to be in place as well as other diacritical marks. When these are missing it's an immediate first indication that the author does not really know Hispanic culture and is not equipped to write about it. We are interested in publishing creative literature that treats the U.S Hispanic experience in a distinctive, creative, revealing way. The kind of books that we publish we keep in print for a very long time irrespective of sales. We are busy establishing and preserving a U.S. Hispanic canon of creative literature."

BIRCH BOOK PRESS

P.O. Box 81, Delhi NY 13753. **Fax:** (607)746-7453. **E-mail:** birchbrook@copper.net. **Website:** www.birchbrookpress.info. **Contact:** Tom Tolnay, editor/publisher; Barbara dela Cuesta, assoc. editor. Estab. 1982. Small publisher of popular culture and literary titles in mostly handcrafted letterpress editions. Specializes in fiction anthologies with specific theme, and an occasional novella. "Not a good market for full-length novels." Occasionally publishes hardcover and trade paperback originals. Books: 70 lb. vellum paper; letterpress printing; wood engraving illustrations. Averages 4 total titles, 2 fiction, 2 poetry titles/year. Member, Small Press Center, Publishers Marketing Association, Academy of American Poets.
IMPRINTS Birch Brook Press; Birch Brook Impressions. "Letterpress editions are printed in our own shop."
NEEDS Literary, regional (Adirondacks), popular culture, special interest (flyfishing, baseball, books about books, outdoors).
HOW TO CONTACT Query with SASE or submit sample chapter(s), synopsis. Responds in 2 months to queries. Accepts simultaneous submissions. Sometimes comments on rejected mss.
TERMS Modest flat fee on anthologies. Usually publishes ms 10-18 months after acceptance. Pays modest royalty on acceptance. Responds in 3 to 6 months to mss.
TIPS "Write well on subjects of interest to BBP, such as outdoors, flyfishing, baseball, music, literary stories and occasional novellas, books about books."

BKMK PRESS

University of Missouri - Kansas City, 5101 Rockhill Rd., Kansas City MO 64110-2499. (816)235-2558.

Fax: (816)235-2611. **E-mail:** bkmk@umkc.edu. **Website:** www.umkc.edu/bkmk. **Contact:** Ben Furnish, managing editor. Estab. 1971. Ms guidelines online. "BkMk Press publishes fine literature. Reading period January-June." Publishes trade paperback originals Guidelines available online

NEEDS Literary, short story collections. Not currently acquiring novels.

HOW TO CONTACT Query with SASE or submit 2-3 sample stories between January 1 and June 30. Responds in 8 months to mss. Accepts simultaneous submissions. Query with SASE.

TERMS Pays 10% royalty on wholesale price. Publishes ms 1 year after acceptance. Responds in 4-6 months to queries.

TIPS "We skew toward readers of literature, particularly contemporary writing. Because of our limited number of titles published per year, we discourage apprentice writers or `scattershot' submissions."

BLACK HERON PRESS

P.O. Box 13396, Mill Creek WA 98082. **Website:** www.blackheronpress.com. **Contact:** Jerry Gold, publisher. Estab. 1984. "Black Heron Press publishes primarily literary fiction." Publishes hardcover and trade paperback originals, trade paperback reprints. Catalog available online and for 6" x 9" SAE with 3 first-class stamps. Guidelines available for #10 SASE.

NEEDS "All of our fiction is character driven. We don't want to see fiction written for the mass market. If it sells to the mass market, fine, but we don't see ourselves as a commercial press."

HOW TO CONTACT Submit proposal package, including cover letter & first 40-50 pages pages of your completed novel.

TERMS Pays 8% royalty on retail price. Responds in 6 months to queries and mss.

TIPS "Our readers love good fiction—they are scattered among all social classes, ethnic groups, and zip code areas. If you can't read our books, at least check out our titles on our website."

○ BLACK LYON PUBLISHING, LLC

P.O. Box 567, Baker City OR 97814. **E-mail:** info@blacklyonpublishing.com. **E-mail:** queries@blacklyonpublishing.com. **Website:** www.blacklyonpublishing.com. **Contact:** The Editors (romance & general fiction love stories). Estab. 2007. "Black Lyon Publishing is a small, independent publisher. We produce 1-2 romance or general fiction novels each month in both 5x8 trade paperback and PDF e-books formats. We are very focused on giving new novelists a launching pad into the industry." Publishes paperback originals, e-books. **Published 4 new writers last year.** Plans 12 debut novels this year. Averages 15-20 fiction titles/year. Distributes/promotes titles through website, Ingram and Baker & Taylor, bookstores, and major online retailers. "Our novellas follow the guidelines of the full-length novels — only shorter! We are currently accepting contemporary and paranormal romances, as well as inspirational romances. (Note: We are especially interested in novellas with holiday settings and themes, i.e., Christmas, Halloween, Independence Day.) *20,000-40,000 words.*

○ "We are now seeking novella submissions for our upcoming Lyonettes imprint. Please see information online."

NEEDS Romance (contemporary, futuristic/time travel, gothic, historical, regency period, romantic suspense). Special interests: ancient times. Published *Cast in Stone*, by Kerry A. Jones (paranormal romance); *The Medallion of Solaus*, by Kimberly Adkins (paranormal romance); *Maya's Gold*, by Mary Vine (contemporary romance).

HOW TO CONTACT We prefer e-mail, but will accept snail mail queries. No unrequested manuscripts or file attachments please. We delete them. And please, no multiple submissions. Send query letter. Query with outline/synopsis and sample chapters. Include estimated word count, brief bio, list of publishing credits. Send SASE or IRC for return of ms or disposable copy of ms and SASE/IRC for reply only. Responds to queries in 8-12 weeks. No unsolicited mss. Considers simultaneous submissions, submissions on CD or disk. Often critiques/comments on rejected mss. Responds to mss in 1 week.

TERMS Sends preproduction galleys to author. Ms published within 6 months after acceptance. Writer's guidelines on website. Pays royalties and author's copies. Book catalogs on website.

TIPS "Write a good, solid romance with a setting, premise, character or voice just a little 'different' than what you might usually find on the market. We like unique books—but they still need to be romances."

○ ⑤ BLACK MOUNTAIN PRESS

109 Roberts, Asheville NC 28801. (828)273-3332. **E-mail:** jackmoe@theBlackMountainPress.com. **Website:** www.theBlackMountainPress.com. **Contact:**

Jack Moe, editor (how-to, poetry); James Robiningski (short story collections, novels). Estab. 1994. Publishes hardcover, trade paperback, and electronic originals. Book catalog and ms guidelines available online at website.

○ "Apathetic to zealots."

NEEDS "Creative literary fiction and poetry or collection of short stories are wanted for the next few years."

HOW TO CONTACT Submit complete ms.

TERMS Pays 5-10% royalty on retail price. Pays $100-500 advance. Responds in 4-6 months to mss.

TIPS "Don't be afraid of sending your anti-government, anti-religion, anti-art, anti-literature, experimental, avant-garde efforts here. But don't send your work before it's fully cooked, we do, however, enjoy fresh, natural, and sometimes even raw material, just don't send in anything that is "glowing" unless it was savaged from a FoxNews book-burning event."

⑨ BLACK ROSE WRITING

P.O. Box 1540, Castroville TX 78009. **E-mail:** creator@blackrosewriting.com. **Website:** www.blackrosewriting.com. **Contact:** Reagan Rothe. Estab. 2006. "

HOW TO CONTACT Query via e-mail. Submit synopsis and author bio. Please allow 3-4 weeks for response.

TERMS Responds in 1-2 months to mss.

TIPS "Please query via email first with synopsis and author information. Allow 3-4 weeks for response. Always spell-check and try and sent an edited manuscript. Do not forward your initial contact e-mails."

BLACK VELVET SEDUCTIONS PUBLISHING

1350-C W. Southport, Box 249, Indianapolis IN 46217. (888)556-2750. **E-mail:** lauriesanders@blackvelvetseductions.com. **Website:** www.blackvelvetseductions.com. **Contact:** Laurie Sanders, acquisitions editor. Estab. 2005. "We publish two types of material: 1) romance novels and short stories and 2) romantic stories involving spanking between consenting adults. We look for well-crafted stories with a high degree of emotional impact. No first person point of view. All material must be in third person point of view." Publishes trade paperback and electronic originals. "We have a high interest in republishing backlist titles in electronic and trade paperback formats once rights have reverted to the author." Catalog free or online. Guidelines online or by e-mail (guidelines@blackvelvetseductions.

com). Query with SASE. Submit complete ms. Only accepts electronic submissions. Recent Titles: *Her Cowboy's Way*, by Starla Kaye; *Spanked!* by Cara Bristol, Starla Kaye, and Richard Savage; *Night Angel*, by Renee Reeves; *Toy's Story: Acquisition of a Sex Toy*, by Robert Cloud, *His Perfect Submissive*, by Alyssa Aaron.

IMPRINTS Forbidden Experiences (erotic romance of all types); Tender Destinations (sweet romance of all types); Sensuous Journeys (sensuous romance of all types); Amorous Adventures (romantic suspense); Erotic relationship stories (erotic short stories, usually including spanking, with a romantic relationship at their core).

NEEDS Erotic romance, historical romance, multicultural romance, romance, short story collections, romantic stories, romantic suspense, western romance. All stories must have a strong romance element. "There are very few sexual taboos in our erotic line. We tend to give our authors the widest latitude. If it is safe, sane, and consensual we will allow our authors latitude to show us the eroticism. However, we will not consider manuscripts with any of the following: bestiality (sex with animals), necrophilia (sex with dead people), pedophillia (sex with children)."

HOW TO CONTACT Contact us electronically. Only accepts electronic submissions.

TERMS Pays 10% royalty for paperbacks; 50% royalty for electronic books. Reports in 6-12 months. Accepts simultaneous submissions: Yes. SASE returns. Responds in 6 months to queries. Accepts only complete mss. Only accepts electronic submissions. Pays 10% royalty for paperbacks; 50% royalty for electronic books. Responds in 6 months to queries. Responds in 8 months to proposals. Responds in 8-12 months to mss.

TIPS "We publish romance and erotic romance. We look for books written in very deep point of view."

BLIND EYE BOOKS

1141 Grant Street, Bellingham WA 98225. **E-mail:** editor@blindeyebooks.com. **Website:** www.blindeyebooks.com. **Contact:** Nicole Kimberling, editor. Estab. 2007. "Blind Eye Books publishes science fiction, fantasy and paranormal romance novels featuring gay or lesbian protagonists. We do not publish short story collections, poetry, erotica, horror or non-fiction. We would hesitate to publish any manuscript that is less than 70,000 or over 150,000 words."

NEEDS Science fiction, fantasy, and paranormal romance novels featuring gay or lesbian protagonists.

Published *The Archer's Heart* by Astrid Amara, *Tangle* (anthology), and *Wicked Gentlemen* by Ginn Hale. **HOW TO CONTACT** Submit complete ms with cover letter. Accepts queries by snail mail. Send disposable copy of ms and SASE for reply only. Does not return rejected mss. Authors living outside the U.S. can e-mail the editor for submission guidelines. **TERMS** Writer's guidelines on website.

😊 BLOODFIRE STUDIOS

P.O. Box 710451, San Diego CA 92171. **E-mail:** likewecare@bloodfire.com. **Website:** www.bloodfire.com. **Contact:** Dennis Greenhil, VP of Publishing. Estab. 1997. "Midsize Independent Publisher working mostly in Sci/Fi, Horror, and Manga. We pride ourselves on maintaining a high level of quality comparable to the big publishers. Art, Story, paper, etc meet or exceed Marvel and DC standards." Publishes paperback originals, paperpack reprints. Format: 60-80 lb gloss paper; saddle stitch, perfect bound binding; illustrations. **Publishes 4 debut writers/year.** Publishes 6-10 titles/year. Various distributors including Diamond Comics, direct sales, conventions, etc. Advertising and self-promotion through various channels.

💬 *"No longer able to accept unsolicited submissions."*

HOW TO CONTACT Prefers submissions from writers, artists, writer-artists, creative teams. BloodFire Studios is not actively looking for new stories or character ideas. Writing submissions should be submitted in a script format like a play or movie (novel and short story formats are usually passed over). Presentation is important, so make sure its easy to read. A 12 point font and double spaced lines are recommended. It also helps to make sure it's clean. Submission can be sent via e-mail but ONLY AS HYPERLINKS. Use the "Click here to email us" button online and enter "Writing submission" in the subject line. It will be forwarded to the appropriate editor. Follow guidelines posted on website closely or submissions will be trashed. "We attend major industry shows such as San Diego Comic Con, Wizard World LA and Wizard World Chicago." Responds to mss/art packets in a few weeks. Considers simultaneous submissions. Often comments on rejected mss. **TERMS** Payment and rights varies on contract terms for each book. Ms published about a year after acceptance. Writer's and artist's guidelines, book catalog on website.

TIPS "Make sure you follow the guidelines to the letter. Make sure the art, writing, etc fits within the genres published."

⊕ BOBO STRATEGY

2506 N. Clark, #301, Chicago IL 60614. **E-mail:** info@bobostrategy.com. **E-mail:** submissions@bobostrategy.com. **Website:** www.bobostrategy.com. **Contact:** Chris Cunliffe, editor-in-chief. Estab. 2008. "We seek writing that brings clarity and simplicity to the complex. If your idea is good, we may be willing to take a chance on you." Publishes trade paperback originals. Accepts simultaneous submissions. "We seek writing that brings clarity and simplicity to the complex. If your idea is good, we may be willing to take a chance on you." Trade paperback originals. Catalog online at website. Guidelines available by e-mail.

NEEDS Accepts poetry, regional, short story collections. Nonfiction: accepts architecture, art, chess, creative nonfiction, government, humanities, memoirs, politics, regional, travel, world affairs, general nonfiction, how-to, humor, technical, textbook.

HOW TO CONTACT "We are not currently seeking unsolicited mss." Query with SASE; submit proposal package, including: outline, 1 sample chapter. E-mail preferred..

TERMS Pays 0-10% royalty on retail price; outright purchase up to $2,500. Responds in 1 month on queries and proposals; responds in 2 months on mss. Catalog online at website. Guidelines available by e-mail. Reviews artwork; send photocopies. E-mail preferred. Pays 0-10% royalty on retail price; outright purchase up to $2,500. Responds in 1 month on queries and proposals; responds in 2 months on mss.

⬤ BOOKS FOR ALL TIMES, INC.

Box 202, Warrenton VA 20188. (540)428-3175. **E-mail:** staff@bfat.com. **Website:** www.bfat.com. **Contact:** Joe David, publisher & editor. Estab. 1981. One-man operation. Publishes paperback originals.

NEEDS Literary, mainstream/contemporary, short story collections. "No novels at the moment; hopeful, though, of publishing a collection of quality short stories. No popular fiction or material easily published by the major or minor houses specializing in mindless entertainment. Only interested in stories of the Victor Hugo or Sinclair Lewis quality."

HOW TO CONTACT Query with SASE. Responds in 1 month to queries. Sometimes comments on rejected mss. Joe David, publisher.

TERMS Pays negotiable advance. "Publishing/payment arrangement will depend on plans for the book."
TIPS Interested in "controversial, honest stories which satisfy the reader's curiosity to know. Read Victor Hugo, Fyodor Dostoyevsky and Sinclair Lewis for example."

BRANDEN PUBLISHING CO., INC.

P.O. Box 812094, Wellesley MA 02482. (781)235-3634. **Fax:** (781)235-3634. **E-mail:** branden@brandenbooks.com. **Website:** www.brandenbooks.com. **Contact:** Adolph Caso, editor. Estab. 1909. Publishes hardcover and trade paperback, plus Kindle and Nook editions. Reprints and software. Books: 55-60 lb. acid-free paper; case—or perfect-bound; illustrations. Averages 15 total titles, 5 fiction titles/year.
NEEDS Ethnic (histories, integration), historical, literary, military/war, religious (historical-reconstructive), short story collections. Looking for "contemporary, fast pace, modern society."
HOW TO CONTACT Does not accept unsolicited mss. Query with SASE. Responds in 1 month to queries.
TERMS Pays 5-10% royalty on net receipts. 10 author's copies. Average advance: $1,000 maximum. Publishes ms 10 months after acceptance.

BRIDGE WORKS PUBLISHING CO.

Box 1798, 221 Bridge Lane, Bridgehampton NY 11932. (631)537-3418. **Fax:** (631)537-5092. **Website:** www.bridgeworksbooks.com. **Contact:** Barbara Phillips, editorial director. Estab. 1992. Estab. 1992. "Bridge Works is very small, publishing only 1-6 titles a year." **Publishing some debut authors.** Distributes titles through National Book Network. "Our books are routinely reviewed in major publications, and we work closely with authors in both the editorial and marketing processes."
NEEDS Publishes mainstream quality fiction and nonfiction, also thrillers. "Query with SASE before submitting ms."
HOW TO CONTACT We now can only consider queries coming via literary agents. They may be accompanied by the first 50 pages of the manuscript. A SASE should be enclosed for reply and return of any enclosure. The query should be addressed to Barbara Phillips, Editorial Director and Co-Publisher. Write to address above, including synopsis and estimated word count, or query Barabara Phillips at: bap@hamptons.com. Responds in 1 month to query and 50 pages, 2 months to entire ms. Sometimes comments on rejected mss. Query with SASE before submitting ms. Does not read simultaneous submissions.
TERMS Pays 8% of net received from wholesalers and bookstores. Average advance: $1,000. Publishes ms 1 year after acceptance. Book catalog and ms guidelines for #10 SASE.

BROADWAY BOOKS

The Crown Publishing Group/Random House, 1745 Broadway, New York NY 10019. (212)782-9000. **Fax:** (212)782-9411. **Website:** www.broadwaybooks.com. **Contact:** William Thomas, editor-in-chief. Estab. 1995. Broadway publishes general interest nonfiction and fiction for adults. Publishes hardcover and trade paperback originals and reprints.

> "Broadway publishes high quality general interest nonfiction and fiction for adults."

IMPRINTS Broadway Books; Broadway Business; Doubleday; Doubleday Image; Doubleday Religious Publishing; Main Street Books; Nan A. Talese.
NEEDS Broadway Books publishes a variety of nonfiction books across several categories, including memoir, health & fitness, inspiration & spirituality, history, current affairs & politics, marriage & relationships, animals, travel & adventure narrative, pop culture, humor, and personal finance. Publishes a limited list of commercial literary fiction. Published *Freedomland*, by Richard Price.
HOW TO CONTACT *Agented submissions only.*
TERMS Pays royalty on retail price. Pays advance.

C&R PRESS

812 Westwood Ave., Chattanooga TN 37405. (423)645-5375. **Website:** www.crpress.org. **Contact:** Chad Prevost, editorial director and publisher; Ryan G. Van Cleave, executive director and publisher. Estab. 2006. Publishes hardcover, trade paperback, mass market paperback, and electronic originals. Catalog and guidelines available online at website.
IMPRINTS Illumis Books.
NEEDS "We want dynamic, exciting literary fiction and we want to work with authors (not merely books) who are engaged socially and driven to promote their work because of their belief in the product, and because it's energizing and exciting to do so and a vital part of the process."
HOW TO CONTACT Submit complete ms via e-mail.
TERMS Responds in up to 1 month on queries and proposals, 1-2 months on mss.

⊘ CALAMARI PRESS

Via Titta Scarpetta #28, Rome 00153 Italy. **E-mail:** derek@calamaripress.net. **Website:** www.calamaripress.com. "Calamari Press publishes book objects of literary text and art and experimental fiction." Publishes paperback originals. Format: 60 lb. natural finch opaque paper; digital printing; perfect or saddle-stitched bound. Average print order: 500-1,000. Debut novel print order: 300. Averages 2-3 total titles/year; 2 fiction titles/year.

NEEDS Adventure, comics/graphic novels, ethnic/multicultural, experimental, literary, short story collections.

HOW TO CONTACT Query with outline/synopsis and 3 sample chapters. Accepts queries by e-mail only. Include brief bio. Send SASE or IRC for return of ms. Query with outline/synopsis and 3 sample chapters. Accepts queries by e-mail only. Include brief bio. Send SASE or IRC for return of ms.

TERMS Pays in author's copies. Pays in author's copies. Responds to mss in 2 weeks.

⊘ CANDLEWICK PRESS

99 Dover St., Somerville MA 02144. (617)661-3330. **Fax:** (617)661-0565. **E-mail:** bigbear@candlewick.com. **Website:** www.candlewick.com. **Contact:** Deb Wayshak, executive editor (fiction); Joan Powers, editor-at-large (picture books); Liz Bicknell, editorial director/associate publisher (poetry, picture books, fiction); Mary Lee Donovan, executive editor (picture books, nonfiction/fiction); Hilary Van Dusen, senior editor (nonfiction/fiction); Sarah Ketchersid, senior editor (board, toddler); Joan Powers, editor-at-large. Estab. 1991. "Candlewick Press publishes high-quality, illustrated children's books for ages infant through young adult. We are a truly child-centered publisher."

NEEDS Picture books: animal, concept, contemporary, fantasy, history, humor, multicultural, nature/environment, poetry. Middle readers, young adults: contemporary, fantasy, history, humor, multicultural, poetry, science fiction, sports, suspense/mystery.

HOW TO CONTACT "We do not accept editorial queries or submissions online. If you are an author or illustrator and would like us to consider your work, please read our submissions policy (online) to learn more."

TERMS Pays authors royalty of 2½-10% based on retail price. Offers advance.

TIPS "*We no longer accept unsolicited mss.* See our website for further information about us."

CAVE HOLLOW PRESS

P.O. Drawer J, Warrensburg MO 64093. **E-mail:** gbcrump@cavehollowpress.com. **Website:** www.cavehollowpress.com. **Contact:** G.B. Crump, editor. Estab. 2001. "Our website is updated frequently to reflect the current type of fiction Cave Hollow Press is seeking." Publishes trade paperback originals. Book catalog for #10 SASE. Guidelines available free.

NEEDS "Our website is updated frequently to reflect the current type of fiction Cave Hollow Press is seeking."

HOW TO CONTACT Query with SASE.

TERMS Pays 7-12% royalty on wholesale price. Pays negotiable amount in advance. Responds in 1-2 months to queries and proposals. Responds in 3-6 months to manuscripts.

TIPS "Our audience varies based on the type of book we are publishing. We specialize in Missouri and Midwest regional fiction. We are interested in talented writers from Missouri and the surrounding Midwest. Check our submission guidelines on the website for what type of fiction we are interested in currently."

⊕ ◑ CHAMPAGNE ROSE PRESS

The Wild Rose Press, P.O. Box 708, Adam's Basin NY 14410. **E-mail:** queryus@thewildrosepress.com. **Website:** www.thewildrosepress.com. **Contact:** Roseann Armstrong, editor. Estab. 2006. "The Champagne Rose line is the contemporary romance line of the Wild Rose Press. Our contemporary stories are filled with sexual tension and passionate chemistry. The setting can take place anywhere in the world today. Champagne Rose couples explore their relationship both emotionally and physically. In each full-length novel, there must be one fully consummated love scene. In the case of short stories, if this isn't realistic for the plot of the story, then the physical encounters must be ripe with tension. The characters should leave us remembering them long after we turn the last page. We should feel their feelings, share their joys and their heartaches. And, as with all romances, we should close the book completely satisfied by the happy-ever-after ending." Publishes paperback originals, reprints, and e-books in a POD format. Publishes approximately 60 fiction titles/year. Member: EPIC, Romance Writers of America. Distributes/promotes titles through major distribution chains, including Ingrams, Baker & Taylor, Sony, Amazon.com, Kindle, as well as smaller and online distributors. Publishes paperback originals, reprints, and e-books in a POD format. Guidelines available on website.

NEEDS Contemporary, futuristic/time travel, gothic, historical, regency, romantic suspense, erotic, and paranormal romances. Plans several anthologies "in several lines of the company in the next year, including Cactus Rose, Yellow Rose, American Rose, Black Rose, and Scarlet Rose." Has published *Calendar of Love*, by Susan Lyons; *Seduction's Stakes*, by Claire Ashgrove; and *A Perfect Fit*, by Sheridon Smythe.

HOW TO CONTACT *Does not accept unsolicited mss.* Send query letter with outline and synopsis of up to 5 pages. Prefers queries by e-mail; accepts by mail. Include estimated word count, brief bio, and list of publishing credits. Send SASE or IRC for return of ms. Agented fiction less than 1%. Responds to queries in 4 weeks; to mss in 12 weeks. Does not consider simultaneous submissions. Always comments on rejected mss.

TERMS Pays royalty of 7% minimum; 35% maximum. Sends prepublication galleys to author. Time between acceptance and publication is approximately 1 year. Writer's guidelines available on website. Pays royalty of 7% minimum; 35% maximum. Responds to queries in 4 weeks; to mss in 12 weeks.

TIPS "Polish your manuscript, make it as error free as possible, and follow our submission guidelines."

CHANGELING PRESS LLC

P.O. Box 1046, Martinsburg WV 25402. **E-mail:** Submissions@changelingpress.com. **Website:** www. changelingpress.com. **Contact:** Sheri Ross Fogarty, editor-in-chief. Publishes print and e-books. Publishes print and e-books. Special interests: "We publish Sci-Fi, Futuristic, Paranormal, Fantasy, Suspense, Horror, and Humor, BDSM, and Fetish Love Stories. We publish Interludes and Novellas only, from 8,000 to 25,000 words total length—NO 100,000 word sagas, please! (Series and Serials welcome)." Responds to queries in 2 months. Accepts unsolicited mss. Considers e-mail submissions. Publishes in print and e-books.

NEEDS Special interests: "We publish Sci-Fi, Futuristic, Paranormal, Fantasy, Suspense, Horror, and Humor, BDSM, and Fetish Love Stories. We publish Interludes and Novellas only, from 8,000 to 25,000 words total length — NO 100,000 word sagas, please! (Series and Serials welcome)." Pays royalties of 35% gross paid monthly.

HOW TO CONTACT Submit complete ms with cover letter via e-mail only. Responds to queries in 2

months. Accepts unsolicited mss. Considers e-mail submissions.

TERMS Pays royalties of 35% gross paid monthly.

TIPS 'ePublishing' does not mean 'no editing.' 'Good enough' is never good enough. From editors to proofreaders to artists and marketing staff, our team of dedicated professionals is here for your support."

CHARLESBRIDGE PUBLISHING

85 Main St., Watertown MA 02472. (617)926-0329. **Fax:** (617)926-5720. **E-mail:** tradeart@charlesbridge. com. **Website:** www.charlesbridge.com. Estab. 1980. "Charlesbridge publishes high-quality books for children, with a goal of creating lifelong readers and lifelong learners. Our books encourage reading and discovery in the classroom, library, and home. We believe that books for children should offer accurate information, promote a positive worldview, and embrace a child's innate sense of wonder and fun. To this end, we continually strive to seek new voices, new visions, and new directions in children's literature." Publishes hardcover and trade paperback nonfiction and fiction, children's books for the trade and library markets. Guidelines available online.

> "We're always interested in innovative approaches to a difficult genre, the nonfiction picture book."

IMPRINTS Charlesbridge, Imagine Publishing.

NEEDS Strong stories with enduring themes. Charlesbridge publishes both picture books and transitional bridge books (books ranging from early readers to middle-grade chapter books). Our fiction titles include lively, plot-driven stories with strong, engaging characters. No alphabet books, board books, coloring books, activity books, or books with audiotapes or CD-ROMs.

HOW TO CONTACT *Exclusive submissions only.* "Charlesbridge accepts unsolicited manuscripts submitted exclusively to us for a period of three months. 'Exclusive Submission' should be written on all envelopes and cover letters. Please submit only one or two manuscript(s) at a time. For picture books and shorter bridge books, please send a complete manuscript. For fiction books longer than 30 manuscript pages, please send a detailed plot synopsis, a chapter outline, and three chapters of text. Manuscripts should be typed and double-spaced. Please do not submit material by email, by fax, or on a computer disk. Illustrations are not necessary. Please make a copy of your manuscript, as we cannot be responsible for submissions lost in the mail. Include your name and address on the first page of your manuscript and in your cover letter. Be sure to list any previously published work or relevant writing experience."

TERMS Pays royalty. Pays advance. Responds in 3 months. If you have not heard back from us after 3 months, you may assume we do not have a place for your project and submit it elsewhere.

TIPS "To become acquainted with our publishing program, we encourage you to review our books and visit our website (www.charlesbridge.com), where you will find our catalog. To request a printed catalog, please send a 9"×12" SASE with $2.50 in postage."

CHRONICLE BOOKS FOR CHILDREN

680 Second St., San Francisco CA 94107. (415)537-4200. **Fax:** (415)537-4460. **E-mail:** frontdesk@chroniclebooks.com. **Website:** www.chroniclekids.com. "Chronicle Books for Children publishes an eclectic mixture of traditional and innovative children's books. Our aim is to publish books that inspire young readers to learn and grow creatively while helping them discover the joy of reading. We're looking for quirky, bold artwork and subject matter. Currently emphasizing picture books. De-emphasizing young adult." Publishes hardcover and trade paperback originals. Book catalog for 9x12 envelope and 3 first-class stamps. Guidelines available online.

NEEDS We do not accept proposals by fax, via e-mail, or on disk. When submitting artwork, either as a part of a project or as samples for review, do not send original art.

● CITY LIGHTS BOOKS

261 Columbus Ave., San Francisco CA 94133. **Website:** www.citylights.com. Estab. 1953. (415)362-1901. **Fax:** (415)362-4921. **E-mail:** staff@citylights.com. **Website:** www.citylights.com. **Contact:** Editorial staff. Publishes paperback originals. Plans 1-2 first novels this year. Averages 12 total titles, 4-5 fiction titles/year.

NEEDS Fiction, essays, memoirs, translations, poetry and books on social and political issues.

HOW TO CONTACT Submit one-page description of the book and a sample chapter or two with SASE. Does not accept unsolicited mss. Does not accept queries by e-mail. See website for guidelines.

◔ CLARION BOOKS

Houghton Mifflin Co., 215 Park Ave. S., New York NY 10003. **Website:** www.houghtonmifflinbooks.com;

www.hmco.com. **Contact:** Dinah Stevenson, vice president and publisher; Jennifer B. Greene, senior editor (contemporary fiction, picture books for all ages, nonfiction); Jennifer Wingertzahn, editor (fiction, picture books); Lynne Polvino, editor (fiction, nonfiction, picture books); Christine Kettner, art director. Estab. 1965. Publishes hardcover originals for children. Guidelines for #10 SASE or online.

NEEDS Adventure, historical, humor, mystery, suspense, strong character studies. Clarion is highly selective in the areas of historical fiction, fantasy and science fiction. A novel must be superlatively written in order to find a place on the list. Accepts fiction translations.

HOW TO CONTACT Submit complete ms. No queries, please. Send to only *one* Clarion editor.

TERMS Pays 5-10% royalty on retail price. Average advance: start at $6,000. Publishes ms 2 years after acceptance. Ms guidelines available at website. Pays 5-10% royalty on retail price. Pays minimum of $4,000 advance. Responds in 2 months.

◔ CLEIS PRESS

Cleis Press & Viva Editions, 2246 Sixth St., Berkeley CA 94710. (510)845-8000 or (800)780-2279. **Fax:** (510)845-8001. **E-mail:** cleis@cleispress.com. **E-mail:** bknight@cleispress.com. **Website:** www.cleispress.com and www.vivaeditions.com. **Contact:** Brenda Knight, associate publisher. Estab. 1980. "Cleis Press publishes provocative works by women and men in the areas of gay and lesbian studies, sexual politics, fiction, feminism, self-help, erotica, gender studies, and human rights." Publishes trade paperback originals and reprints. Averages 50 total titles, 30 fiction titles/year. Accepts unsolicited mss.

IMPRINTS Viva Edition

NEEDS feminist, gay/lesbian, literary "We are looking for high quality fiction and nonfiction."

HOW TO CONTACT Submit complete ms. Accepts queries by e-mail. Include brief bio, list of publishing credits. Send SASE for return of ms or send a disposable ms and SASE for reply only. Agented fiction 10%. Responds in 1 month to queries.

TERMS Pays royalty on retail price. Publishes ms 1 year after acceptance. Pays royalty on retail price. Responds in 1 month to queries.

◑◔ COFFEE HOUSE PRESS

79 13th NE, Suite 110, Minneapolis MN 55413. (612)338-0125. **Fax:** (612)338-4004. **E-mail:** info@

coffeehousepress.org. **Website:** www.coffeehouse-press.org. **Contact:** Chris Fischbach, associate publisher. Estab. 1984. This successful nonprofit small press has received numerous grants from various organizations including the NEA, the McKnight Foundation and Target. Books published by Coffee House Press have won numerous honors and awards. Example: The Book of Medicines by Linda Hogan won the Colorado Book Award for Poetry and the Lannan Foundation Literary Fellowship. Publishes hardcover and trade paperback originals. Book catalog and ms guidelines online.

NEEDS Seeks literary novels, short story collections and poetry.

HOW TO CONTACT Query first with outline and samples (20-30 pages).

TERMS Responds in 4-6 weeks to queries; up to 6 months to mss.

TIPS Look for our books at stores and libraries to get a feel for what we like to publish. No phone calls, e-mails, or faxes.

ⒶⒼ CONSTABLE & ROBINSON, LTD.

3 The Lanchesters, 162 Fulham Palace Rd., London En WG 9ER United Kingdom. 0208-741-3663. **Fax:** 0208-748-7562. **E-mail:** enquiries@constablerobinson.com. **Website:** http://constablerobinson.co.uk/. **Contact:** Krystyna Green, editorial director (crime fiction). Constable & Robinson continues into the 21st century as a truly independent company. We publish a nonfiction list of current affairs, history and biography, military history, psychology and health, as well as literary novels and a constantly growing list of genre fiction in both hardback and paperback. Among our commercially successful series are the well-known Mammoth paperback anthologies, the bestselling and widely respected Overcoming list of CBT self-help titles, and the Brief History and Guide series. Our new fiction imprint, Corsair, launched in April 2010. Averages 160 total titles/year. Publishes hardcover and trade paperback originals Book catalog available free.

IMPRINTS Corsair, Constable Hardback; Robinson Paperback.

NEEDS Publishes "crime fiction (mysteries) and historical crime fiction." Length 80,000 words minimum; 130,000 words maximum. Recently published *Roma* and *The Judgement of Caesar*, by Steven Saylor; *The Yeane's Midnight*, by Ed O'Connor; *The More Deceived*, by David Roberts.

HOW TO CONTACT *Agented submissions only.* No e-mail submissions. Submit by post 3 sample chapter(s), synopsis, and cover letter. Responds in 1 month to queries; 3 months to mss. Accepts simultaneous submissions.

TERMS Pays royalty. Offers advance. Publishes ms 1 year after acceptance. Responds in 1 month to queries and proposals; 3 months to mss

TIPS Constable & Robinson Ltd. is looking for "crime novels with good, strong identities. Think about what it is that makes your book(s) stand out from the others. We do not publish thrillers."

☼ COTEAU BOOKS

Thunder Creek Publishing Co-operative Ltd., 2517 Victoria Ave., Regina SK S4P 0T2 Canada. (306)777-0170. **Fax:** (306)522-5152. **E-mail:** coteau@coteaubooks.com. **Website:** www.coteaubooks.com. **Contact:** Geoffrey Ursell, publisher. Estab. 1975. AKA Thunder Creek Publishing Co-operative Ltd. "Coteau Books publishes the finest Canadian fiction, poetry, drama and children's literature, with an emphasis on western writers." Publishes trade paperback originals and reprints. Books: offset printing; perfect bound; 4-color illustrations. Averages 16 total titles, 4-6 fiction titles/year. Distributes titles through Fitzhenry & Whiteside.

NEEDS Ethnic, fantasy, feminist, gay/lesbian, historical, humor, juvenile, literary, mainstream/contemporary, multicultural, multimedia, mystery, regional, short story collections, spiritual, sports, young adult. Canadian authors *only*. No science fiction. No children's picture books.

HOW TO CONTACT Accepts unsolicited mss. Fiction accepted January 1-April 30; children's/teen novels May 1-August 31; poetry September 1-December 31; nonfiction accepted year-round. Submit complete manuscript, or 3-4 sample chapter(s), author bio. Responds in 2-3 months to queries; 6 months to mss. No simultaneous submissions. Sometimes comments on rejected mss. Submit bio, complete ms, SASE.

TERMS Pays 10% royalty on retail price. "We're a co-operative and receive subsidies from the Canadian, provincial and local governments. We do not accept payments from authors to publish their works." Publishes ms 1-2 years after acceptance. Ms guidelines online.

COVENANT COMMUNICATIONS, INC.

920 E. State Rd., American Fork UT 84003. (801)756-9966. **Fax:** (801)756-1049. **E-mail:** info@covenant-lds; submissions@covenant-lds.com. **Website:** www.

covenant-lds.com. **Contact:** Kathryn Jenkins, managing editor. Estab. 1958. Averages 80+ total titles/year. "Currently emphasizing inspirational, doctrinal, historical, biography. Our fiction is also expanding, and we are looking for new approaches to LDS literature and storytelling." Guidelines available online.

NEEDS Historical fiction, suspense, mystery, romance, children's; all submissions must have strong LDS (Church of Jesus Christ of Latter-day Saints, or "Mormons") content. "We publish exclusively to the 'Mormon' (The Church of Jesus Christ of Latter-Day Saints) market. Fiction must feature characters who are members of that church, grappling with issues relevant to that religion."

HOW TO CONTACT E-mail your manuscript, along with a 1-page cover letter, a 1- to 2-page plot summary, and the Author Questionnaire. We request that all submissions be submitted via e-mail as Microsoft Word attachments. If you cannot e-mail your submission, please burn the Word document onto a CD and mail it. Follow submission guidelines on website. Requires electronic submission. Responds in 4 months to mss.

TERMS Pays 612-15% royalty on retail price. Generally publishes ms 6-12 months after acceptance. Ms guidelines online. Pays 6 1/2-15% royalty on retail price. Responds in 1 month on queries & proposals; 4 months on manuscripts.

TIPS "Our audience is exclusively LDS (Latter-Day Saints, 'Mormon')." We do not accept manuscripts that do not have a strong LDS theme or feature strong LDS characters.

⊕ CRIMSON ROMANCE

Adams Media, a division of F+W Media, Inc., 57 Littlefield St., Avon MA 02322. (508)427-7100. **E-mail:** editorcrimson@gmail.com. **Contact:** Jennifer Lawler, editor. "Direct to e-book imprint of Adams Media." Publishes electronic originals.

NEEDS "We're open to romance submissions in five popular subgenres: romantic suspense, contemporary, paranormal, historical, and erotic romance. Within those subgenres, we are flexible about what happens. It's romance, so there must be a happily-ever-after, but we're open to how your characters get there. You won't come up against preconceived ideas about what can or can't happen in romance or what kind of characters you can or can't have. Our only rule is everyone has to be a consenting adult. Other than that, we're looking for smart, savvy heroines, fresh voices, and new takes on old favorite themes. We're looking for full-length novels, and while we prefer to work on the shorter end of the spectrum (50,000 words, give or take), we're not going to rule you out because you go shorter or longer."

HOW TO CONTACT "If you have a finished novel you'd like for us to consider, please just drop editor Jennifer Lawler a line at editorcrimson@gmail.com with a brief description of your work–please, no attachments until I know you're not a spambot. That's it! I'll get back to you as quickly as I can–within a few days for queries and within a few weeks if I request a full."

⊘ CROSSQUARTER PUBLISHING GROUP

P.O. Box 23749, Santa Fe NM 87502. **E-mail:** info@crossquarter.com. **Website:** www.crossquarter.com. **Contact:** Anthony Ravenscroft, acquisitions. "We emphasize personal sovereignty, self responsibility and growth with pagan or pagan-friendly emphasis for young adults and adults." Publishes trade paperback originals and reprints. Book catalog for $1.75. Guidelines available online.

Query letters are required. *No unsolicited mss.*

HOW TO CONTACT Query with SASE.

TERMS Pays 8-10% royalty on wholesale or retail price. Responds in 3 months to queries.

TIPS "Our audience is earth-conscious people looking to grow into balance of body, mind, heart and spirit."

CROSSWAY BOOKS

A division of Good News Publishing, 1300 Crescent St., Wheaton IL 60174. (630)682-4300. **Fax:** (630)682-4785. **E-mail:** info@crossway.org. **E-mail:** submissions@crossway.org. **Website:** www.crosswaybooks.org. **Contact:** Jill Carter, editorial administrator. Estab. 1938. "'Making a difference in people's lives for Christ' as its maxim, Crossway Books lists titles written from an evangelical Christian perspective." Member ECPA. Distributes titles through Christian bookstores and catalogs. Promotes titles through magazine ads, catalogs.

Does not accept unsolicited mss.

TERMS Pays negotiable royalty.

CROWN BOOKS FOR YOUNG READERS

1540 Broadway, New York NY 10171. (212)572-2600 or (800)200-3552. **Website:** www.randomhouse.com/kids. See listing for Bantam, Doubleday, Dell/Delacorte, Knopf and Crown Books for Young Readers.

○ Random House Children's Publishing only accepts submissions through agents.

ⒶⓄ CROWN PUBLISHING GROUP

Imprint of Random House, Inc., 1745 Broadway, New York NY 10019. (212)782-9000. **E-mail:** CrownBiz@ randomhouse.com. **Website:** www.randomhouse. com/crown. Estab. 1933. "The group publishes a selection of popular fiction and nonfiction by both established and rising authors." Publishes popular fiction and nonfiction hardcover originals.

○ *Agented submissions only.* See website for more details.

IMPRINTS Bell Tower; Broadway Business; Clarkson Potter; Crown Business; Crown Forum; Harmony Books; Shaye Arehart Books; Three Rivers Press.
HOW TO CONTACT *Agented submissions only.*

☺ DARK HORSE COMICS, INC.

10956 SE Main St., Milwaukie OR 97222. (503)652-8815. **Fax:** (503)654-9440. **E-mail:** dhcomics@dark-horse.com. **Website:** www.darkhorse.com. "In addition to publishing comics from top talent like Frank Miller, Mike Mignola, Stan Sakai and internationally-renowned humorist Sergio Aragonés, Dark Horse is recognized as the world's leading publisher of licensed comics."
NEEDS Comic books, graphic novels. Published *Astro Boy Volume 10 TPB*, by Osamu Tezuka and Reid Fleming; *Flaming Carrot Crossover #1* by Bob Burden and David Boswell.
HOW TO CONTACT Submit synopsis to dhcomics@ darkhorse.com. See website (www.darkhorse.com) for detailed submission guidelines and submission agreement, which must be signed. Include a full script for any short story or single-issue submission, or the first eight pages of the first issue of any series. Submissions can no longer be mailed back to the sender.
TIPS "If you're looking for constructive criticism, show your work to industry professionals at conventions."

MAY DAVENPORT, PUBLISHERS

26313 Purissima Rd., Los Altos Hills CA 94022. (650)947-1275. **Fax:** (650)947-1373. **E-mail:** md-books@earthlink.net. **Website:** www.maydaven-portpublishers.com. **Contact:** May Davenport, editor/publisher. Estab. 1976. "We prefer books which can be used in high schools as supplementary readings in English or creative writing courses. Reading skills have to be taught, and novels by humourous authors can be more pleasant to read than Hawthorne's or Melville's novels, war novels, or novels about past generations. Humor has a place in literature." Publishes hardcover and paperback originals. Averages 4 total titles/year. Distributes titles through direct mail order.
IMPRINTS md Books (nonfiction and fiction).
NEEDS Humor, literary. "We want to focus on novels junior and senior high school teachers can share with the reluctant readers in their classrooms."
HOW TO CONTACT Query with SASE. Responds in 1 month to queries.
TERMS Pays 15% royalty on retail price. Publishes ms 1 year after acceptance. Ms guidelines for #10 SASE. Pays 15% royalty on retail price (if book sells). Pays no advance. Responds in 1 month to queries .

DAW BOOKS, INC.

Penguin Group (USA), 375 Hudson St., New York NY 10014-3658. (212)366-2096. **Fax:** (212)366-2090. **Website:** www.dawbooks.com. **Contact:** Peter Stampfel, submissions editor. Estab. 1971. Publishes hardcover and paperback originals and reprints. Averages 60 total titles/year. DAW Books publishes science fiction and fantasy. Publishes hardcover and paperback originals and reprints Guidelines available online

○ Simultaneous submissions not accepted, unless prior arrangements are made by agent.

NEEDS Fantasy, science fiction. "We are interested in science fiction and fantasy novels. We are also interested in paranormal romantic fantasy. We like character-driven books. We accept both agented and unagented manuscripts. Long books are not a problem. We are not seeking short stories, poetry, or ideas for anthologies. We do not want any nonfiction manuscripts."
HOW TO CONTACT Submit complete ms with SASE. Do not submit your only copy of anything. Responds within 3 months to mss. The average length of the novels we publish varies but is almost never less than 80,000 words.
TERMS Pays in royalties with an advance negotiable on a book-by-book basis. Ms guidelines online. Pays in royalties with an advance negotiable on a book-by-book basis. Responds in 3 months to manuscripts.

Ⓐ Ⓞ DELACORTE PRESS BOOKS FOR YOUNG READERS

Imprint of Random House Children's Books/Random House, Inc., 1745 Broadway, New York NY 10019. (212)782-9000. **Website:** www.randomhouse.com/

kids; www.randomhouse.com/teens. Distinguished literary fiction and commercial fiction for the middle grade and young adult categories.

○ Although not currently accepting unsolicited mss, mss are being sought for 2 contests: Delacorte Dell Yearling Contest for a First Middle-Grade Novel and Delacorte Press Contest for a First Young Adult Novel. Submission guidelines can be found online at www.randomhouse.com/kids/writingcontests.

Ⓐ DEL REY BOOKS

Imprint of Random House Publishing Group, 1745 Broadway, 18th Floor, New York NY 10019. (212)782-9000. **E-mail:** delrey@randomhouse.com. **Website:** www.randomhouse.com. Estab. 1977. "We are a long-established imprint with an eclectic frontlist. We're seeking interesting new voices to add to our best-selling backlist. Publishes hardcover, trade paperback, and mass market originals and mass market paperback reprints. Averages 120 total titles, 80 fiction titles/year. Del Rey publishes top level fantasy, alternate history, and science fiction. Publishes hardcover, trade paperback, and mass market originals and mass market paperback reprints

NEEDS Fantasy (should have the practice of magic as an essential element of the plot), science fiction (well-plotted novels with good characterizations and interesting extrapolations), alternate history. Published *Gentlemen of the Road*, by Michael Chabon; *Kraken*, by China Miéville; *His Majesty's Dragon*, by Naomi Novik; *The Man with the Iron Heart,* by Harry Turtledove; and *Star Wars: Order 66*, by Karen Traviss.

HOW TO CONTACT Does not accept unsolicited mss. *Agented submissions only.* Agented submissions only.

TERMS Pays royalty on retail price. Publishes ms 1 year after acceptance. Ms guidelines online. Pays competitive advance.

TIPS "Del Rey is a reader's house. Pay particular attention to plotting, strong characters, and dramatic, satisfactory conclusions. It must be/feel believable. That's what the readers like. In terms of mass market, we basically created the field of fantasy bestsellers. Not that it didn't exist before, but we put the mass into mass market."

Ⓐ DIAL BOOKS FOR YOUNG READERS

Imprint of Penguin Group USA, 345 Hudson St., New York NY 10014. (212)366-2000. **Website:** www.

penguin.com/youngreaders. **Contact:** Lauri Hornik, president/publisher; Kathy Dawson, associate publisher; Kate Harrison, senior editor; Liz Waniewski, editor; Alisha Niehaus, editor; Jessica Garrison, editor; Lily Malcom, art director. Estab. 1961. "Dial Books for Young Readers publishes quality picture books for ages 18 months-6 years; lively, believable novels for middle readers and young adults; and occasional nonfiction for middle readers and young adults." Publishes hardcover originals. Book catalog for 9×12 envelope and 4 first-class stamps.

NEEDS Especially looking for lively and well-written novels for middle grade and young adult children involving a convincing plot and believable characters. The subject matter or theme should not already be overworked in previously published books. The approach must not be demeaning to any minority group, nor should the roles of female characters (or others) be stereotyped, though we don't think books should be didactic, or in any way message-y. No topics inappropriate for the juvenile, young adult, and middle grade audiences. No plays.

HOW TO CONTACT Accepts unsolicited queries and up to 10 pages for longer works and unsolicited mss for picture books.

TERMS Pays royalty. Pays varies advance. Responds in 4-6 months to queries.

TIPS "Our readers are anywhere from preschool age to teenage. Picture books must have strong plots, lots of action, unusual premises, or universal themes treated with freshness and originality. Humor works well in these books. A very well-thought-out and intelligently presented book has the best chance of being taken on. Genre isn't as much of a factor as presentation."

Ⓐ DIAL PRESS

1745 Broadway, New York NY 10019. **Website:** www.randomhouse.com/bantamdell/. Estab. 1924. (212)782-9000. **Fax:** (212)782-9523. **Website:** www.randomhouse.com/bantamdell/. **Contact:** Susan Kamil, vice president, editorial director. Estab. 1924. Averages 6-12 total titles/year.

NEEDS Literary (general). Published *Mary and O'Neil* (short story collection); *Niagara Falls Over Again*, by Elizabeth Mccracken (fiction).

HOW TO CONTACT *Agented submissions only.* Accepts simultaneous submissions.

TERMS Pays royalty on retail price. Offers advance. Publishes ms 18 months after acceptance.

DIGITAL MANGA PUBLISHING

1487 West 178th St., Suite 300, Gardenia CA 90248. **Website:** www.emanga.com; http://www.dmpbooks. com. "We are currently accepting open submissions of completed works for inclusion on our Emanga.com storefront. Submissions must be original and not infringe on copyrighted works by other creators. Please note that we are a manga publisher; we do not distribute Western style comics or literary novels. Completed works must contain a minimum of 90 pages of content. We accept submissions for all genres of manga which comply to US law and we only accept submissions from persons aged 18 and over. Please do not send your original copies as we cannot return them to you. If your work is published online elsewhere, please feel free to include a link for us to further view your portfolio."

Ⓐ DOUBLEDAY

1745 Broadway, New York NY 10019. **E-mail:** ddaypub@randomhouse.com. **Website:** www.randomhouse.biz. Estab. 1897. Publishes hardcover originals. Averages 70 total titles/year.

NEEDS Adventure, confession, ethnic, experimental, feminist, gay/lesbian, historical, humor, literary, mainstream/contemporary, religious, short story collections.

HOW TO CONTACT *Agented submissions only.* Does not accept unsolicited mss by e-mail. No simultaneous submissions.

TERMS Pays royalty on retail price. Offers advance. Publishes ms 1 year after acceptance.

DOUBLEDAY BOOKS FOR YOUNG READERS

1540 Broadway, New York NY 10036. (212)782-9000. **Website:** www.randomhouse.com/kids.

　Ⓞ Only accepts mss submitted by an agent. Trade picture book list, from preschool to age 8.

◑◐ DRAGON MOON PRESS

3521 43A Ave., Red Deer AB T4N 3E9 Canada. **E-mail:** dmpsubmissions@gmail.com. **Website:** www.dragonmoonpress.com. **Contact:** Gwen Gaddes, publisher. Estab. 1994. "Dragon Moon Press is dedicated to new and exciting voices in science fiction and fantasy." Publishes trade paperback and electronic originals. Books: 60 lb. offset paper; short run printing and offset printing. Average print order: 250-3,000. Averages 4-6 total titles, 4-5 fiction titles/year. Distributed through Baker & Taylor. Promoted locally through authors and online at leading retail bookstores like Amazon, Barnes & Noble, Chapters, etc.

NEEDS "At present, we are only accepting solicited manuscripts via referral from our authors and partners. All manuscripts already under review will still be considered by our readers, and we will notify you of our decision." For solicited submissions: Market: "We prefer manuscripts targeted to the adult market or the upper border of YA. No middle grade or children's literature, please. Fantasy, science fiction (soft/sociological). No horror or children's fiction, short stories or poetry."

HOW TO CONTACT Please visit our website for submission guidelines. Accepts simultaneous submissions. No submissions on disk. "All submissions are requested electronically—do not mail submissions, as we will not respond. All mailed submissions are shredded and recycled. All queries should be emailed to dmpsubmissions@gmail.com with the words BOOK SUBMISSION: and your book title in the subject line."

TERMS Pays 8-15% royalty on retail price. Publishes ms 2 years after acceptance.

TIPS "First, be patient. Read our guidelines. Not following our submission guidelines can be grounds for automatic rejection. Second, be patient, we are small and sometimes very slow as a result, especially during book launch season. Third, we view publishing as a family affair. Be ready to participate in the process and show some enthusiasm and understanding in what we do. Remember also, this is a business and not about egos, so keep yours on a leash! Show us a great story with well-developed characters and plot lines, show us that you are interested in participating in marketing and developing as an author, and show us your desire to create a great book and you may just find yourself published by Dragon Moon Press."

◑◐ DREAMCATCHER BOOKS & PUBLISHING

55 Canterbury St. #8 & 9, Saint John NB E2L 2C6 Canada. (506)632-4008. **Fax:** (506)632-4009. **E-mail:** dreamcatcherpub@nb.aibn.com. **Website:** www.dreamcatcherpublishing.ca. **Contact:** Elizabeth Margaris, publisher. Estab. 1998. Publishes mainstream fiction, with first consideration to Atlantic Canadian writers. "Especially interested in green themes, hope & inspiration (including autobiographies) with a hu-

mourous twist." Imprints: Magi Press (vanity press). "DreamCatcher Publishing, Inc. is an independent book publisher located in downtown Saint John, New Brunswick that produces original high-quality Canadian fiction and non-fiction of general interest for adults and children. Our aim is to introduce the public to some of its best hidden talent, nurturing Canadian authors who deserve to be published in distinguished works of the highest literary and design standards. We wish to publish books that provoke and inform, as well as educate and entertain readers of all ages and walks of life."

HOW TO CONTACT Submission Guidelines: (a) A query letter introducing your manuscript; (b) 1 page synopsis; (c) a short author bio. A reply takes 6 to 8 weeks.

DUFOUR EDITIONS

P.O. Box 7, 124 Byers Road, Chester Springs PA 19425. (610)458-5005 or (800)869-5677. **Fax:** (610)458-7103. **E-mail:** orders@dufoureditions.com. **Website:** www. dufoureditions.com. Estab. 1948. **Contact:** Thomas Lavoie, associate publisher. Estab. 1948. Small, independent publisher, tending toward literary fiction. Publishes hardcover originals, trade paperback originals, and reprints. Averages 3-4 total titles, 1-2 fiction titles/year. Promotes titles through catalogs, reviews, direct mail, sales reps, Book Expo, and wholesalers. We publish literary fiction by good writers which is well received and achieves modest sales. De-emphsazing poetry and nonfiction. Publishes hardcover originals, trade paperback originals and reprints. Book catalog available free.

NEEDS Literary, short story collections. "We like books that are slightly off-beat, different and well-written." Published *Tideland*, by Mitch Cullin; *The Case of the Pederast's Wife*, by Clare Elfman; *Last Love in Constantinople*, by Milorad Pavic; *Night Sounds and Other Stories*, by Karen Shoemaker; *From the Place in the Valley Deep in the Forest*, by Mitch Cullen (short stories); and *Beyond Faith and Other Stories*, by Tom Noyes. We like books that are slightly off-beat, different and well-written.

HOW TO CONTACT Query with SASE. Accepts queries by e-mail, fax. Include estimated word count, brief bio, list of publishing credits. Responds in 3 months to queries; 6 months to mss. Accepts simultaneous submissions. Query with SASE.

TERMS Pays 6-10% royalty on net receipts. Average advance: $100-500. Publishes ms 18 months after acceptance. Pays $100-500 advance. Responds in 3 months to queries. Responds in 3 months to proposals. Responds in 6 months to manuscripts.

TIPS Audience is sophisticated, literate readers especially interested in foreign literature and translations, and a strong Irish-Celtic focus, as well as work from U.S. writers. Check to see if the publisher is really a good match for your subject matter.

Ⓐ⬤ DUTTON (ADULT TRADE)

Penguin Group, Inc., 375 Hudson St., New York NY 10014. (212)366-2000. **Website:** us.penguingroup. com. **Contact:** Brian Tart, publisher. Estab. 1852.

> "Query letters *only* (must include SASE). A query letter should be typed and, ideally, fit on one page. Please include a brief synopsis of your manuscript and your publishing credits, if any."

TERMS Pays royalty.

TIPS "Write the complete manuscript and submit it to an agent or agents. They will know exactly which editor will be interested in a project."

DUTTON CHILDREN'S BOOKS

Penguin Group (USA), Inc., 375 Hudson St., New York NY 10014. **E-mail:** duttonpublicity@ us.penguingroup.com. **Website:** www.penguin.com. **Contact:** Sara Reynolds, art director. Estab. 1852. Publishes hardcover originals as well as novelty formats. Averages 50 titles/year. 10% of books form first-time authors. Dutton Children's Books publishes high-quality fiction and nonfiction for readers ranging from preschoolers to young adults on a variety of subjects. Currently emphasizing middlegrade and young adult novels that offer a fresh perspective. De-emphasizing photographic nonfiction and picture books that teach a lesson. Approximately 80 new hardcover titles are published every year, fiction and nonfiction for babies through young adults. Publishes hardcover originals as well as novelty formats.

> "Cultivating the creative talents of authors and illustrators and publishing books with purpose and heart continue to be the mission and joy at Dutton."

NEEDS Dutton Children's Books has a diverse, general-interest list that includes picture books and fiction for all ages, from middle grade to young adult novels. Published *Big Chickens Fly the Coop*, by Leslie Helakoski, illustrated by Henry Cole (picture book); *Antsy*

Does Time, by Neal Shusterman (middle-grade novel); *Paper Towns*, by John Green (young adult novel). Dutton Children's Books has a diverse, general interest list that includes picture books; easy-to-read books; and fiction for all ages, from first chapter books to young adult readers.

HOW TO CONTACT Query letter only; include SASE Query with SASE.

TERMS Pays royalty on retail price. Offers advance Pays royalty on retail price. Pays advance.

○ DZANC BOOKS

Dzanc Books, Inc., 2702 Lillian, Ann Arbor MI 48104. **E-mail:** info@dzancbooks.org. **E-mail:** wickettd@yahoo.com; dan@dzancbooks.org. **Website:** www.dzancbooks.org. **Contact:** Steve Gillis, editor (literary fiction); Dan Wickett, editor (literary fiction); Keith Taylor, editor (literary fiction). "We're an independent non-profit publishing literary fiction. We also set up writer-in-residence programs and help literary journals develop their subscription bases." Publishes paperback originals. Averages 6 fiction titles/year, 20 titles/year when imprints are included, (1) If submitting a novel *(please, no young adult fiction)* or literary nonfiction, please submit the first one or two chapters (no more than 35 pages) using our submission manager. (2) If submitting a story collection, please see the Short Story Collection contest guidelines below. (3) Please note that due to an increased number of incoming manuscripts, it might take up to 5 or 6 months to respond. "Dzanc is currently holding its fourth annual contest for all authors wishing to submit a short story collection to Dzanc Books. The winning author will be published by Dzanc in late 2014, and will receive a $1000 advance. Entry to the Dzanc Short Story Collection Contest requires a $20 reading fee and a full manuscript, both submitted through our submission manager. The contest deadline is December 31, 2011."

NEEDS Literary. Plans anthology *The Best of the Web*, in which online journal editors nominate stories and poems — series and press editors select from that list and selected reading. Published Roy Kesey, Yannick Murphy, Peter Markus, Hesh Kestin, Kyle Minor.

HOW TO CONTACT Query with outline/synopsis and 35 sample pages. Accepts queries by e-mail. Include brief bio. Agented fiction: 3%. Accepts unsolicited mss. Considers simultaneous submissions, submissions on CD or disk. Rarely critiques/comments on rejected mss. Responds to mss in 5 months.

TERMS Sends preproduction galleys to author. Manuscript published 12-36 months after acceptance. Writer's guidelines on website.

TIPS "Every word counts—it's amazing how many submissions have poor first sentences or paragraphs and that first impression is hard to shake when it's a bad one."

○○ THE ECCO PRESS

10 E. 53rd St., New York NY 10022. (212)207-7000. **Fax:** (212)702-2460. **Website:** www.harpercollins.com. **Contact:** Daniel Halpern, editor-in-chief. Estab. 1970. Publishes hardcover and trade paperback originals and reprints.

NEEDS Literary, short story collections. "We can publish possibly one or two original novels a year." Published *Blonde*, by Joyce Carrol Oates; *Pitching Around Fidel*, by S.L. Price.

HOW TO CONTACT *Does not accept unsolicited mss.* Query with SASE.

TERMS Pays royalty. Pays negotiable advance.

TIPS "We are always interested in first novels and feel it's important that they be brought to the attention of the reading public."

○ EDGE SCIENCE FICTION AND FANTASY PUBLISHING/TESSERACT BOOKS

Hades Publications, Box 1714, Calgary AB T2P 2L7 Canada. (403)254-0160. **Fax:** (403)254-0456. **E-mail:** publisher@hadespublications.com. **Website:** www.edgewebsite.com. **Contact:** Editorial Manager. Estab. 1996. "We are an independent publisher of science fiction and fantasy novels in hard cover or trade paperback format. We produce high-quality books with lots of attention to detail and lots of marketing effort. We want to encourage, produce and promote thought-provoking and fun-to-read science fiction and fantasy literature by 'bringing the magic alive: one world at a time' (as our motto says) with each new book released." Publishes hardcover and trade paperback originals. Books: natural offset paper; offset/web printing; HC/perfect binding; b&w illustration only. Average print order: 2,000-3,000. Plans 20 first novels this year. Averages 16-20 total titles/year. Member of Book Publishers Association of Alberta (BPAA), Independent Publishers Association of Canada (IPAC), Publisher's Marketing Association (PMA), Small Press Center.

NEEDS Fantasy (space fantasy, sword and sorcery), science fiction (hard science/technological, soft/sociological). "We are looking for all types of fantasy and science fiction, horror except juvenile/young adlut, erotica, religious fiction, short stories, dark/gruesome fantasy, or poetry." Length: 75,000-100,000/words. Published *Stealing Magic*, by Tanya Huff; *Forbidden Cargo*, by Rebecca K. Rowe, *The Hounds of Ash and Other Tales of Fool Wolf* by Greg Keyes.

HOW TO CONTACT Accepts unsolicited mss. Submit first 3 chapters and synopsis, Check website for guidelines or send SAE & IRCs for same. Include estimated word count. Responds in 4-5 months to mss. No simultaneous submissions, electronic submissions. Rarely comments on rejected mss.

TERMS Pays 10% royalty on wholesale price. Average advance: negotiable. Publishes ms 18-20 months after acceptance. Ms guidelines online.

TIPS "Send us your best, polished, completed manuscript. Use proper manuscript format. Take the time before you submit to get a critique from people who can offer you useful advice. When in doubt, visit our website for helpful resources, FAQs and other tips."

⊕ ELIXIRIST

P.O. Box 17132, Sugar Land TX 77496. **E-mail:** support@elixirist.com; submissions@elixirist.com. **Website:** www.elixirist.com. **Contact:** Juanita Samborski, Acquisitions Editor (romance, comedy, chicklit, urban fantasy); Sean Samborski, Publisher (speculative, comedy, horror, literary). Estab. 2010. Small, commercial publisher dealing primarily in the print market in multiple genre formats. A small, commercial publisher dealing primarily in the print market in multiple genre formats. Format publishes in trade paperback, mass market paperback, and electronic originals. Catalog and guidelines available for SASE.

NEEDS Adventure, comic books, contemporary, experimental, fantasy, gothic, historical, horror, humor, juvenile, literary, mainstream, mystery, occult, religious, romance, science fiction, sports, suspense, western, young adult, speculative subgenres.

HOW TO CONTACT Query with SASE; submit synopsis and 3 sample chapters.

TERMS Pays 6-12% royalty on retail price. Responds in 12 months on queries, proposals, and mss.

TIPS "We publish novels in genres ranging from young adult to literary, multi-genres appealing to both male and female readers."

⊕ ⊙ ELOHI GADUGI / THE HABIT OF RAINY NIGHTS PRESS

900 NE 81st Ave., #209, Portland OR 97213. **E-mail:** editors@elohigadugi.org. **Website:** http://rainynightspress.org. **Contact:** Patricia McLean, nonfiction editor (narrative nonfiction); Duane Poncy, fiction editor (general fiction, native American); Ger Killeen, poetry editor. Estab. 2003. Format publishes in electronic originals Catalog and guidelines available online at website.

IMPRINTS The Habit of Rainy Nights Press (Patricia McLean or Duane Poncy, Editors); Elohi Gadugi Books / Elohi Gadugi Digital (Duane Poncy, Editor).

NEEDS "We publish emerging writers whose fiction explores the important concerns of the contemporary world with depth and compassion. Have a strong narrative voice and character-driven story. We don't particularly care for the current trend of books about 'me.' We are not adverse to magical realism, poetic language, and books that take a chance." Romance, Christian, new age, vampires, zombies, superheros

HOW TO CONTACT Submit using submission manager on website.

TERMS Pays 20-25% royalty on retail price (60-70% of wholesale for e-books). Responds in 1-2 months on queries; 2-3 months on mss.

TIPS "Respect your work. Make sure it is ready for publication. Polish, polish, polish. We cannot consider books that need a lot of basic cleaning up. Have something to say—we are not interested in using up vital resources to publish fluff."

⊕ ENETE ENTERPRISES

3600 Mission #10, San Diego CA 92109. **E-mail:** EneteEnterprises@gmail.com. **Website:** www.EneteEnterprises.com. **Contact:** Shannon Enete, editor. Estab. 2011. Publishes hardcover originals, trade paperback originals, mass market paperback originals, electronic originals. Guidelines available on website.

NEEDS "We are looking for new fiction that could grow into a series of books."

HOW TO CONTACT Submit query, proposal, or ms by e-mail.

TERMS Pays royalties of 1-15%. Responds to queries/proposals in 1 month; mss in 1-3 months.

TIPS "Send me your best work. Do not rush a draft."

ENGLISH TEA ROSE PRESS

The Wild Rose Press, P.O. Box 708, Adams Basin NY 14410-0708. (585)752-8770. **E-mail:** queryus@thewildrosepress.com. **Website:** www.thewildrosepress.com.

Contact: Nicole D'Arienzo, editor. Estab. 2006. "In the English Tea Rose line we have conquering heroes, high seas adventure, and scandalous gossip. The love stories that will take you back in time. From the windswept moors of Scotland, to the Emerald Isle, to the elegant ballrooms of Regency England, the men and women of this time are larger than life and willing to risk it all for the love of a lifetime. English Tea Rose stories encompass historical romances set before 1900 which are not set on American soil. Send us your medieval knights, Vikings, Scottish highlanders, marauding pirates, and ladies and gentlemen of the Ton. English Tea Rose romances should have strong conflict and be emotionally driven; and, whether the story is medieval, Regency, set during the renaissance, or any other pre-1900 time, they must stay true to their period in historical accuracy and flavor. English Tea Roses can range from sweet to spicy, but should not contain overly explicit language." Publishes paperback originals, reprints, and e-books in a POD format. Published 5 debut authors last year. Publishes approximately 10 fiction titles/year. Member: EPIC, Romance Writers of America. Distributes/promotes titles through major distribution chains, including Ingrams, Baker & Taylor, Sony, Amazon.com, Kindle, as well as smaller and online distributors. Format publishes in paperback originals, reprints, and e-books in a POD format. Writer's guidelines available on website.

○ *Does not accept unsolicited mss.* Agented fiction less than 1%. Always comments on rejected mss. Sends prepublication galleys to author.

NEEDS Contemporary, futuristic/time travel, gothic, historical, regency, romantic suspense, erotic, and paranormal romances. Plans several anthologies "in several lines of the company in the next year, including Cactus Rose, Yellow Rose, American Rose, Black Rose, and Scarlet Rose." Has published *Nothing to Commend Her*, by Jo Barrett; *The Dragon & The Rose*, by Gini Rifkin; and *Wish for the Moon*, by Sandra Jones.

HOW TO CONTACT *Does not accept unsolicited mss.* Send query letter with outline and a list of publishing credits. Include estimated word count, brief bio, and list of publishing credits. Agented fiction less than 1%. Responds to queries in 4 weeks; to mss in 12 weeks. Does not consider simultaneous submissions. Always comments on rejected mss. Send query letter with outline and a list of publishing credits. Include estimated word count, brief bio, and list of publishing credits.

TERMS Pays royalty of 7% minimum; 35% maximum. Sends prepublication galleys to author. Time between acceptance and publication is approximately 1 year. Writer's guidelines available on website. **Advice** "Polish your manuscript, make it as error free as possible, and follow our submission guidelines." Pays royalty of 7% minimum; 35% maximum. Responds to queries in 4 weeks; to mss in 12 weeks.

TIPS "Polish your manuscript, make it as error free as possible, and follow our submission guidelines."

Ⓐ⊘ EOS

Imprint of HarperCollins General Books Group, 10 E. 53rd St., New York NY 10022. (212)207-7000. **Website:** www.eosbooks.com. Estab. 1998. **Contact:** Diana Gill, senior editor. Estab. 1998. Publishes hardcover originals, trade and mass market paperback originals, and reprints. Averages 40-46 total titles, 40 fiction titles/year. Eos publishes quality science fiction/fantasy with broad appeal. Publishes hardcover originals, trade and mass market paperback originals, and reprints Guidelines for #10 SASE.

NEEDS Fantasy, science fiction. Published *The Isle of Battle*, by Sean Russell (fantasy); *Trapped*, by James Alan Gardner. No horror or juvenile.

HOW TO CONTACT *Agented submissions only.* Include list of publishing credits, brief synopsis. Agented fiction 99%. Responds in 6 months to queries. Never comments on rejected mss. *All unsolicited mss returned.*

TERMS Pays royalty on retail price. Average advance: variable. Publishes ms 18-24 months after acceptance. Ms guidelines for #10 SASE. Pays royalty on retail price. Pays variable advance.

TIPS "Query via e-mail. Your query should be brief—no more than a 2-page description of your book. Do not send chapters or full synopsis at this time. You will receive a response—either a decline or a request for more material—in approximately 1-2 months."

ESCAPE COLLECTIVE PUBLISHING

P.O. Box 8821, Olympia WA 98509. **E-mail:** admin@escapecollective.com. **E-mail:** longfic@escapecollective.com; anthology@escapecollective.com. **Website:** www.escapecollective.com. **Contact:** Alexandra J. Ash, editor; Patrick Jennings-Mapp, editor. Estab. 2010. "Escape Collective Publishing is on the cutting edge of technology and business. We are a cooperative, which means that our company is run by writers, for writers. In our quest to publish the best in digital genre fiction, we incorporate the most important elements of traditional publishing (precise editing, comprehensive marketing, working with great cover artists) with the accessibility and ease of downloadable prose. Because we only produce work for e-readers and, therefore, have very little overhead, our authors receive a huge percentage of the profit from their own work and our customers receive great fiction at an affordable price. Everybody wins!" Publishes electronic originals. Catalog available online at website. Guidelines available online at website.

NEEDS No fan fiction, realist (mainstream/literary) fiction, nonfiction, erotica, Christian/religious themes, poetry, children's stories, art, graphic novels, previously published work, unedited mss.

HOW TO CONTACT Submit proposal package, including 2-5 page synopsis and 1 sample chapter. "In the email subject line, put Submission: The Title-Your Last Name-The Genre-Length."

TERMS Responds in 1 month to queries; 3 months to mss.

TIPS "Be professional and courteous and we will return the favor! Read our submission guidelines and blog and review our published works for an idea of what we like."

⊕☺◑ ETERNAL PRESS

Canada. **E-mail:** submissionseternalpress@gmail.com. **Website:** www.eternalpress.biz. **Contact:** Ally Robertson. Estab. 2007. Publishes ebooks. Although we will always primarily function as an eBook publisher, we also offer many of our titles in print." Eternal Press clearly distinguishes between romance, erotic romance, and erotica. GLBT romance may be any flame level depending on language, theme, the development of the romantic relationship, and sexual frequency and intensity.

NEEDS "We are currently accepting: Novellas, and full-length manuscripts from 20,000-140,000 words. Genres: Romance, Erotica, GBLT and BDSM, Paranormal, Fantasy, Mystery, Sci-Fi, Suspense, Thriller, Historical, Young Adult. **We are particularly interested in:** Erotica Paranormal (vampire/shapeshifter/witch) GBLT Romance BDSM Young Adult Longer length novellas and novels. **We are currently NOT seeking:** Short stories, short story collections or anthologies, Poetry, Nonfiction, Religious genre fiction. Thematic elements of spiritual beliefs are welcome, but we are not currently publishing stories that fall into the religious category."

HOW TO CONTACT Query with cover letter in the body of the e-mail (submissionseternalpress@gmail.com) that contains the outline/synopsis, bio, word count, genre; with a subject line: SUBMISSIONS_your name_book title.

TERMS Writer's guidelines on website. Eternal Press pays 40% royalties on net revenue to the author for eBooks and 25% net on revenue for print. We hold all rights for five (5) years from date of publication. Open to new writers but please follow our guidelines. "If we accept your manuscript for publication, we will supply you with specific formatting guidelines. You must be able to do edits in MS Word's track changes."

⑤ FAERY ROSE

The Wild Rose Press, P.O. Box 708, Adams Basin NY 14410-0708. (585)752-8770. **E-mail:** queryus@thewildrosepress.com. **Website:** www.thewildrosepress.com. **Contact:** Amanda Barnett, editor. Estab. 2006. "Our Fairy Tales are not for children. The Faery line is a fantasy world where you can allow your imagination free rein, a place to enjoy romance with mystical or mythical characters. We are looking for a sensual hero who knows what he wants and who goes after his leading lady. The heroine should always be a female we can identify with, 'someone we want to see achieve her dreams with strength she draws from inside.' Dragons don't just frolic in the mist but turn into mortal men and women with love and lust on their minds. Elves have minds and hearts, looking for love with a bit of mischief thrown in. Ghosts who come back to life for the love of their life and wizards, warlocks, and witches who crank up the romance like they spit out a spell. Futuristic worlds, filled with science fiction warriors who can wield a sword as well as a laser and not afraid, be they woman or man, to go after what their heart desires. Time travels moving through centuries with the hero and heroine seeking not the secrets of the ages but love." Publishes paperback originals, reprints, and e-books in a POD format. Published 25 debut authors last year. Publishes approximately 60 fiction titles/year. Member: EPIC, Romance Writers of America. Distributes/promotes titles through major distribution chains, including Ingrams, Baker & Taylor, Sony, Amazon.com, Kindle, as well as smaller and online distributors. Publishes paperback originals, reprints, and e-books in a POD format. Guidelines online.

NEEDS Contemporary, futuristic/time travel, gothic, historical, regency, romantic suspense, erotic, and paranormal romances. Plans several anthologies "in several lines of the company in the next year, including Cactus Rose, Yellow Rose, American Rose, Black Rose, and Scarlet Rose." Has published *It Takes Two*, by Sheridon Smythe; *Ties That Bind*, by Keena Kincaid; and *Human Touch*, by J.L. Wilson. *Does not accept unsolicited mss.*

HOW TO CONTACT *Does not accept unsolicited mss.* Send query letter with outline and synopsis of up to 5 pages. Accepts all queries by e-mail. Include estimated word count, brief bio, and list of publishing credits. Agented fiction less than 1%. Always comments on rejected mss.

TERMS Pays royalty of 7% minimum; 35% maximum. Sends prepublication galleys to author. Responds to queries in 4 weeks; mss in 12 weeks.

TIPS "Polish your manuscript, make it as error free as possible, and follow our submission guidelines."

Ⓐ⊘Ⓢ FARRAR, STRAUS & GIROUX/ BOOKS FOR YOUNG READERS

Books for Young Readers, 175 Fifth Ave., New York NY 10010. (646)307-5151. **Website:** www.fsgkidsbooks.com. **Contact:** Children's Editorial Department. Estab. 1946. Averages 75 total titles/year. "We publish original and well-written material for all ages." Publishes hardcover originals and trade paperback reprints For catalog fax request or email to: childrens. publicity@fsgbooks.com Guidelines available online

IMPRINTS Frances Foster Books.

NEEDS Children's/juvenile, picture books, middle grade, young adult, narrative nonfiction. "Do not query picture books; just send manuscript. Do not fax queries or manuscripts." Published *Adele and Simon*, by Barbara McClintock; *The Cabinet of Wonders*, by Marie Rutkoski. True Do not query picture books; just send manuscript. Do not fax or e-mail queries or manuscripts.

HOW TO CONTACT For novels and other longer mss, query with SASE and three sample chapters. Do not query picture books, just send ms with cover letter. Include brief bio, list of publishing credits. Agented fiction 50%. Responds in 2 months to queries; 4 months to mss. Accepts simultaneous submissions. No electronic submissions or submissions on disk. Query with SASE. Hard copy submissions only.

TERMS Pays 2-6% royalty on retail price for paperbacks, 3-10% for hardcovers. Average advance: $3,000-25,000. Publishes ms 18 months after accep-

tance. Book catalog for 9×12 SAE with $2.00 postage. Ms guidelines for #10 SASE. Tips:"Study our list to avoid sending something inappropriate. Send query letters for long manuscripts; don't ask for editorial advice (just not possible, unfortunately); and send SASEs!" Pays 2-6% royalty on retail price for paperbacks, 3-10% for hardcovers. Pays $3,000-25,000 advance. Responds in 2 months to queries. Responds in 3 months to manuscripts

TIPS Audience is full age range, preschool to young adult. Specializes in literary fiction.

Ⓐ FARRAR, STRAUS & GIROUX PAPERBACKS

18 West 18th St., New York NY 10011. (212)741-6900. **E-mail:** fsg.publicity@fsgbooks.com; fsg.editorial@fsgbooks.com. **Website:** http://www.fsgbooks.com/. FSG Paperbacks emphasizes literary nonfiction and fiction, as well as poetry. Publishes hardcover and trade paperback originals and reprints. Averages 180 total titles/year.

NEEDS Literary. Published *The Corrections*, by Jonathan Franzen; *The Haunting of L.*, by Howard Norman.

HOW TO CONTACT Unsolicited submissions are accepted at Farrar, Straus & Giroux. All submissions must be submitted through the mail—we do not accept electronic submissions, or submissions delivered in person. Please include a cover letter describing your submission, along with the first 50 pages of the manuscript. If you are submitting poems, please include 3-4 poems.

FC2

Center for Publications, School of Arts and Sciences-UHV, 3007 N. Ben Wilson, Victoria TX 77901. **E-mail:** fc2.cmu@gmail.com. **Website:** http://fc2.org. **Contact:** Carmen Edington, managing editor. Estab. 1974. Publisher of innovative fiction. Publishes hardcover and paperback originals. Books: perfect/Smyth binding; illustrations. Average print order: 2,200. Averages 6 total titles, 6 fiction titles/year. Titles distributed through University of Alabama Press. No open submissions except through Ronald Sukenick Innovative Fiction Prize. Does not accept unsolicited mss. See website for contest info. Agented fiction 5%. Publishes hardcover and paperback originals. Ms guidelines online.

NEEDS Experimental, feminist, gay/lesbian, innovative; modernist/postmodern; avant-garde; anarchist; minority; cyberpunk. Published *Book of Lazarus*, by Richard Grossman; *Is It Sexual Harassment Yet?* by

Cris Mazza; *Liberty's Excess*, by Lidia Yuknavitch; *The Wavering Knife*, by Brian Evenson.

HOW TO CONTACT Does not accept unsolicited mss. See website for contest info. Agented fiction 5%. Responds in 3 weeks to queries; 9-6 months to mss. Accepts simultaneous submissions.

TERMS Pays 10% royalty. Publishes ms 1-3 years after acceptance. Ms guidelines online. Pays 10% royalty. Responds in 3 weeks to queries; 9-6 months to mss.

TIPS "Be familiar with our list."

FLORIDA ACADEMIC PRESS

P.O. Box 540, Gainesville FL 32602. (352)332-5104. **Fax:** (352)331-6003. **E-mail:** fapress@gmail.com. **Website:** www.floridaacademicpress.com. Estab. 1997. Publishes hardcover and trade paperback originals. . Averages 10 total titles/year. Hardcover and trade paperback originals. Catalog available online.

NEEDS Serious fiction and scholarly social science manuscripts. Does not want "children's books, poetry, science fiction, religious tracts, anthologies, or booklets."

HOW TO CONTACT Responds in 4-12 weeks to mss. Submit completed ms by hard copy only.

TERMS Pays 5-8% royalty on retail price, depending if paperback or hardcover. Publishes ms 3-5 months after acceptance. 5-8% royalty on retail price and higher on sales of 2,500+ copies a year. Responds in 2 months on mss if rejected; 3-4 months if sent for external review

TIPS Considers complete mss only. "Manuscripts we decide to publish must be re-submitted by the author in ready-to-print PDF files. Match our needs—do not send blindly. Books we accept for publication must be submitted in camera-ready format. The Press covers all publication/promotional expenditures."

ⓞⓞ FORGE AND TOR BOOKS

175 Fifth Ave. 14th Floor, New York NY 10010. **Website:** www.tor.com; us.macmillan.com/TorForge. aspx. Estab. 1980. "Tor Books are science fiction, fantasy and horror, and occasionally, related nonfiction. Forge books are everything else—general fiction, historical fiction, mysteries and suspense, women's fiction and nonfiction. Orb titles are trade paperback reprint editions of science fiction, fantasy and horror books." Publishes hardcover, trade paperback and mass market paperback originals, trade and mass market paperback reprints.

NEEDS Historical, horror, mainstream/contemporary, mystery (amateur sleuth, police procedural, private eye/hard-boiled), science fiction, suspense, thriller/espionage, western (frontier saga, traditional), thriller; general fiction and fantasy.

HOW TO CONTACT Accepts unsolicited mss. Do not query; "submit only the first 3 chapters of your book and a synopsis of the entire book. Your cover letter should state the genre of the submission and previous sales or publications if relevant." Include estimated word count, brief bio, list of publishing credits. Agented fiction 95%. Sometimes comments on rejected mss. Responds in 6-8 months. No simultaneous submissions. Additional guidelines on website. Tor. com welcomes original speculative fiction short stories and poetry. We define speculative fiction broadly, including SF, fantasy, horror, alternate history, and related genres. We're particularly interested in stories under 12,000 words, and may even be slightly more likely to take a chance on shorter stories from new writers. We will consider stories that are slightly longer than 12k—we will not read anything over 17,500 words. You can send your novel to our corporate cousins at Tor Books, as long as you follow their submissions guidelines. E-mail: tor.comsubs@gmail.com.

TERMS "We pay 25 cents a word for the first 5,000 words, 15 cents a word for the next 5,000, and 10 cents a word after that." Paperback: Pays 6-8% royalty for first-time authors, 8-10% royalty for established authors. Hardcover: Pays 10% first 5,000; 1212% second 5,000; 15% thereafter. Offers advance. Publishes ms 12-18 months after acceptance.

TIPS "The writing must be outstanding for a new author to break into today's market."

ⓞ FORT ROSS INC.—INTERNATIONAL RIGHTS

26 Arthur Pl, Yonkers NY 10701. (914)375-6448. **E-mail:** fortross@optonline.net. **Website:** www.fortrossinc.com. **Contact:** Dr. Kartsev, executive director. Estab. 1992. "We welcome Russia-related manuscripts as well as books from well-established fantasy and romance novel writers who would like to have their novels translated in Russia by our publishing house in cooperation with the local publishers." Publishes hardcover and paperback originals. Published 2 debut authors within the last year. Averages 20 total titles/year. "Generally, we publish Russia-related books in English or Russian. Sometimes we publish various fiction and nonfiction books in collaboration with the east European publishers in translation. We are looking mainly for

well-established authors." Publishes paperback originals. 100 queries received/year; 100 mss received/year. Pays 6-8% royalty on wholesale price or makes outright purchase of $500-1,500; negotiable advance. Publishes in hardcover and paperback originals.

HOW TO CONTACT Does not accept unsolicited mss. Query with SASE. Include estimated word count, brief bio, list of publishing credits. Send SASE for return of ms or send a disposable ms and SASE for reply only. Responds in 1 month to queries; 3 months to mss. Accepts simultaneous submissions. Pays 5-10% royalty on wholesale price or makes outright purchase of $500-1,500. Average advance: $500-1,000; negotiable.

TERMS Responds in 1 month to queries and proposals; 3 months to mss.

◑ FREYA'S BOWER

Wild Child Publishing, P.O. Box 4897, Culver City CA 90231-4897. **E-mail:** mbaun@freyasbower.com. **Website:** http://www.freyasbower.com. **Contact:** Marci Baun, publisher. Estab. 2006. Closed to submissions from authors not already signed with either Freya's Bower or Wild Child Publishing from March 15, 2011 to September 15, 2011. "Freya's Bower is a small, independent press that started out in March 2006. We are known for working with newer/unpublished authors and editing to the standards of NYC publishers. We respond promptly to submissions." Publishes paperback originals, e-books. Average print order: 50-200. Debut novel print order: 50. Averages 75 total titles/year; 75 fiction titles/year. Member EPIC. Distributes/promotes titles through Ingram, All Romance eBooks, Fictionwise, Mobipocket, Amazon, Omnilit, and website.

NEEDS Erotica and romance of all genres. Has published *Love Bites Back*, by Christopher C. Newman (vampire/paranormal novella); *Dark Succession*, by Teresa D'Amario (a shapeshifter/paranormal novel); *The Art of Losing*, by Lisa Troy (a contemporary erotica novel); *Two Hearts and a Crow*, by Jane Toombs (a contemporary romance novella).

HOW TO CONTACT Query with outline/synopsis and one sample chapter. Accepts queries by e-mail only. Include estimated word count, brief bio. Writers submit material per submissions guidelines. See website for details. Responds to queries in 2-4 weeks. Accepts unsolicited mss. Often critiques/comments on rejected mss. Responds to mss in 6-8 weeks. Does not accept simultaneous submissions. To contact us:

Click on the contact link that appears at the bottom of every page on the website and complete the form.

TERMS Sends preproduction galleys to author. Ms published 2-5 months after acceptance. Writer's guidelines on website. Pays royalties 10-40%. Book catalogs on website.

TIPS "We look for good stories. While we accept material that is popular, we are more focused on quality. Do your homework. Read our submission guidelines thoroughly. Read a few of our books. Study your craft. While we are willing to work with newer authors, we expect them to be willing to revise and eager to learn. A good attitude goes a long way . . . on both sides."

FRONT STREET

Boyds Mills Press, 815 Church St., Honesdale PA 18431. **Website:** www.frontstreetbooks.com. **Contact:** Acquisitions Editor. Estab. 1994. "We are an independent publisher of books for children and young adults." Publishes hardcover originals and trade paperback reprints. Book catalog available online. Guidelines available online.

NEEDS Adventure, ethnic, historical, humor, juvenile, literary, picture books, young adult (adventure, fantasy/science fiction, historical, mystery/suspense, problem novels, sports). "We look for fresh voices for children and young adults. Titles on our list entertain, challenge, or enlighten, always employing novel characters whose considered voices resonate." Published *The Bear Makers* by Andrea Cheng; *Drive* by Nathan Clement; *The Adventurous Deeds of Deadwood Jones* by Helen Hemphill.

HOW TO CONTACT Accepts unsolicited and international mss. Query with outline/synopsis, first 3 chapters, and SASE and label the package "Manuscript Submission." Agented fiction 30%. Responds in 3 months to mss. Accepts simultaneous submissions. Query with SASE. Submit complete ms, if under 100 pages, with SASE. Keeps illustration samples on file. Reviews artwork/photos w/ms. Send photocopies. "High-quality fiction for children and young adults." Publishes hardcover originals and trade paperback reprints. Books: coated paper; offset printing; case binding; 4-color illustrations. Averages 15 fiction titles/year. Distributes titles through independent sales reps, wholesalers, and via order line directly from Front Street. Promotes titles through sales and professional conferences, sales reps, reviews, catalogs, website, and direct marketing.

TERMS Pays royalty on retail price. Pays advance. Responds in 3 months.

TIPS "Read through our recently published titles and review our website. Check to see what's on the market and in our catalog before submitting your story. Feel free to query us if you're not sure."

GASLIGHT PUBLICATIONS

P.O. Box 1344, Studio City CA 91614. **Website:** http://playerspress.home.att.net/gaslight_catalogue.htm. **Contact: Contact:** Simon Waters, fiction editor (Sherlock Holmes only). Estab. 1960. Publishes hardcover and paperback originals and reprints. Books: paper varies; offset printing; binding varies; illustrations. Average print order: 5,000. Averages 4-12 total titles, 2-4 fiction titles/year. Promotes titles through sales reps, trade, library, etc.

NEEDS Sherlock Holmes only.

HOW TO CONTACT Accepts unsolicited mss. Query with SASE. Include estimated word count, brief bio, list of publishing credits. Send SASE for return of ms or send a disposable ms and SASE for reply only. Agented fiction 10%. Responds in 2 weeks to queries; 1 year to mss.

TERMS Pays 8-10% royalty. Royalty and advance dependent on the material. Publishes ms 1-6 months after acceptance.

TIPS "Please send only Sherlock Holmes material. Other stuff just wastes time and money."

GAUTHIER PUBLICATIONS, INC.

Frog Legs Ink, P.O. Box 806241, Saint Clair Shores MI 48080. **Fax:** (586)279-1515. **E-mail:** info@gauthier-publications.com; submissions@gauthierpublications.com. **Website:** www.eatabook.com. **Contact:** Elizabeth Gauthier, creative director (children's/fiction). Hardcover originals and trade paperback originals. Guidelines available for #10 SASE, or online at website http://gauthierpublications.com, or by email at: submissions@gauthierpublications.com.

> Frog Legs Ink (imprint) is always looking for new writers and illustrators. We are currently looking for horror/thriller short stories for an upcoming collection.

IMPRINTS Frog Legs Ink, Hungry Goat Press, Dragon-Fish Comics.

NEEDS "We are particularly interested in mystery, thriller, graphic novels, horror and Young Adult areas for the upcoming year. We do, however, consider most subjects if they are intriguing and well written."

HOW TO CONTACT Query with SASE. "Please do not send full ms unless we ask for it If we are interested we will request a few sample chapters and outline. Since we do take the time to read and consider each piece, response can take up to 8 weeks. Mailed submissions without SASE included are destroyed if we are not interested."

TERMS Pays 5-10% royalty on retail price.

✛ ☺ GEMSTONE PUBLISHING

Diamond Comic Distributors, 3679 Concord Road, P.O. Box 12001, York PA 17402. (888) 375-9800 ext. 1617. **E-mail:** wheather@gemstonepub.com. **Website:** www.gemstonepub.com. **Contact:** Heather Winter. "Best known as the home of *The Overstreet Comic Book Price Guide*, Gemstone Publishing, a division of Geppi's Entertainment Publishing & Auctions, was formed by Diamond Comic Distributors President and Chief Executive Officer Stephen A. Geppi as a conduit for his efforts in preserving and promoting the history of the comics medium."

GENESIS PRESS, INC.

P.O. Box 101, Columbus MS 39701. (888)463-4461. **Fax:** (662)329-9399. **E-mail:** customerservice@genesis-press.com. **Website:** www.genesis-press.com. Estab. 1993. Publishes hardcover and trade paperback originals and reprints. Genesis Press is the largest privately owned African-American book publisher in the country. Genesis has steadily increased its reach, and now brings its readers everything from suspense and science fiction to Christian-oriented romance and non-fiction. Publishes hardcover and trade paperback originals and reprints. Guidelines available online.

IMPRINTS Indigo (romance); Black Coral (fiction); Indigo Love Spectrum (interracial romance); Indigo after Dark (erotica); Obsidian (thriller/myster); Indigo Glitz (love stories for young adults); Indigo Vibe (for stylish audience under 35 years old); Mount Blue (Christian); Inca Books (teens); Sage (self-help/inspirational).

NEEDS Averages 30 total titles/year.Erotica, ethnic, literary, multicultural, romance, women's. Published *Cherish the Flame*, by Beverly Clark; *No Apologies*, by Seressia Glass.

HOW TO CONTACT Query with SASE or submit 3 sample chapter(s), synopsis. Responds in 2 months to queries; 4 months to mss.

TERMS Pays 6-12% royalty on invoice price. Average advance: $750-5,000. Publishes ms 1 year after acceptance. Ms guidelines online. Responds in 2 months to queries. Responds in 4 months to manuscripts.

TIPS Be professional. Always include a cover letter and SASE. Follow the submission guidelines posted on our website or send SASE for a copy.

GHOST ROAD PRESS

820 S. Monaco Pkwy, #288, Denver CO 80224. (303)758-7623. **E-mail:** matt.grp@gmail.com. **Website:** ghostroadpress.com.

NEEDS "Genre-based mss in literary, science fiction, young adult, fantasy, mystery, and crime fiction."

HOW TO CONTACT *Not currently accepting submissions.* "Send an attachment (word or.rtf only) that includes a complete synopsis, a description of your marketing plan and platform, and the first three chapters. To view a complete list of our titles and changing submission guidelines, please visit website." Responds in 2-3 months. Accepts simultaneous submissions.

GIVAL PRESS

Gival Press, LLC, P.O. Box 3812, Arlington VA 22203. (703)351-0079. **E-mail:** givalpress@yahoo.com. **Website:** www.givalpress.com. **Contact:** Robert L. Giron, editor-in-chief (area of interest: literary). Estab. 1998. A small, award-winning independent publisher that publishes quality works by a variety of authors from an array of walks of life. Works are in English, Spanish, and French and have a philosophical or social message. Publishes paperback originals and reprints and e-books. Books: perfect-bound. Average print order: 500. **Publishes established and debut authors.** Publishes 2 novels/year. Member AAP, PMA, Literary Council of Small Presses and Magazines. Distributes books through Ingram and BookMasters, Inc. Publishes trade paperback, electronic originals, and reprints. Book catalog available online, free on request/for #10 SASE. Guidelines available online, by email, free on request/for #10 SASE.

NEEDS Literary, multicultural, GLBT. "Looking for French books with English translation." The Annual Gival Press Novel Award contest deadline is May 30. The Annual Gival Press Short Story Award contest deadline is August 8. Guidelines on website. Recently published *That Demon Life*, by Lowell Mick White; *Twelve Rivers of the Body*, by Elizabeth Oness; and *A Tomb of the Periphery*, by John Domini.

HOW TO CONTACT Does not accept unsolicited mss. Query by e-mail first. Include description of project, estimated word count, brief bio, list of pub-

lishing credits. Agented fiction 5%. Responds by e-mail within 2-3 weeks. Rarely comments on rejected mss. Always query first via email; provide description, author's bio, and supportive material.

TERMS Pays 20 contributor's copies. Offers advance. Publishes ms 1 year after acceptance. For book catalog send SASE and on website. Ms guidelines by SASE or on website. Royalties (% varies). Responds in 1 month to queries, 3 months to proposals & mss.

TIPS "Our audience is those who read literary works with depth to the work. Visit our website—there is much to be read/learned from the numerous pages."

⊕ GLASS PAGE BOOKS

P.O. Box 333, Signal Mountain TN 37377. **E-mail:** glasspage@comcast.net. **Website:** www.glasspage-books.com. **Contact:** Pamela Alexander, owner/publisher. Estab. 2010. Publishes hardcover originals, trade paperback originals, mass market paperback originals, electronic originals. Book catalogue available online at website. Ms guidelines available online at website.

HOW TO CONTACT Query with SASE.

TERMS Pays 15-20% royalty on net gains. Responds in 1 month to proposals; 2 months to mss.

TIPS "Please include information about the author when sending us a query."

○ THE GLENCANNON PRESS

P.O. Box 1428, El Cerrito CA 94530. (510)528-4216. **Fax:** (510)528-3194. **E-mail:** merships@yahoo.com. **Website:** www.glencannon.com. **Contact:** Bill Harris (maritime, maritime children's). Estab. 1993. "We publish quality books about ships and the sea." Average print order: 1,000. First novel print order: 750. Member PMA, BAIPA. Distributes titles through Baker & Taylor. Promotes titles through direct mail, magazine advertising and word of mouth. Accepts unsolicited mss. Often comments on rejected mss. Publishes hardcover and paperback originals and hardcover reprints.

IMPRINTS Smyth: perfect binding; illustrations.

NEEDS "We publish quality books about ships and the sea." Publishes hardcover and paperback originals and hardcover reprints. Books: Smyth: perfect binding; illustrations. Average print order: 1,000. First novel print order: 750. Averages 4-5 total titles, 1 fiction titles/year. Member PMA, BAIPA. Distributes titles through Baker & Taylor. Promotes titles through direct mail, magazine advertising and word of mouth.

HOW TO CONTACT Submit complete ms. Include brief bio, list of publishing credits. Send SASE for return of ms or send a disposable ms and SASE for reply only.
TERMS Pays 10-20% royalty. Responds in 1 month to queries; 2 months to mss.
TIPS "Write a good story in a compelling style."

☯ GOOSE LANE EDITIONS

500 Beaverbrook Ct., Suite 330, Fredericton, New Brunswick E3B 5X4 Canada. (506)450-4251. **Fax:** (506)459-4991. **Website:** www.gooselane.com/submissions.php. **Contact:** Angela Williams, publishing assistant. Estab. 1954. Publishes hardcover and paperback originals and occasional reprints. Books: some illustrations. Average print order: 3,000. First novel print order: 1,500. Averages 16-18 total titles, 6-8 fiction titles/year. Distributes titles through University of Toronto Press (UTP). "Goose Lane publishes literary fiction and nonfiction from well-read and highly skilled Canadian authors." Publishes hardcover and paperback originals and occasional reprints.
NEEDS Literary (novels), mainstream/contemporary, short story collections. "Our needs in fiction never change: substantial, character-centered literary fiction." Published *Reading by Lightning* by Joan Thomas. No children's, YA, mainstream, mass market, genre, mystery, thriller, confessional or science fiction.
HOW TO CONTACT Accepts unsolicited mss. Query with SASE. Responds in 6-8 months to mss. No simultaneous submissions. Query with SAE with Canadian stamps or IRCs. No U.S. stamps.
TERMS Pays 8-10% royalty on retail price. Average advance: $200-1,000, negotiable. Ms guidelines online. **Tips:** "Specializes in high quality Canadian literary fiction, poetry, and nonfiction. We consider submissions from outside Canada only when the author is Canadian and the book is of extraordinary interest to Canadian readers. We do not publish books for children or for the young adult market." Pays 8-10% royalty on retail price. Pays $500-3,000, negotiable advance. Responds in 6 months to queries.
TIPS "Writers should send us outlines and samples of books that show a very well-read author with highly developed literary skills. Our books are almost all by Canadians living in Canada; we seldom consider submissions from outside Canada. If I were a writer trying to market a book today, I would contact the targeted publisher with a query letter and synopsis, and request manuscript guidelines. Purchase a recent book from the publisher in a relevant area, if possible. Always send an SASE with IRCs or suffient return postage in Canadian stamps for reply to your query and for any material you'd like returned should it not suit our needs. Specializes in high quality Canadian literary fiction, poetry, and nonfiction. We consider submissions from outside Canada only when the author is Canadian and the book is of extraordinary interest to Canadian readers. We do not publish books for children or for the young adult market."

GOTHIC CHAPBOOK SERIES

2272 Quail Oak, Baton Rouge LA 70808. **E-mail:** gothicpt12@aol.com. **Website:** www.gwcgothicpress. com. Estab. 1979. "One person operation on a part-time basis." Publishes paperback originals. Books: printing or photocopying. Average print order: 150-200. Distributes titles through direct mail and book dealers.
NEEDS Horror (dark fantasy, psychological, supernatural). Need novellas and short stories.
HOW TO CONTACT *Submissions are sought by invitation only.* Include estimated word count, brief bio, list of publishing credits. Send SASE for return of ms or send a disposable ms and SASE for reply only. Responds in 2 weeks to queries; 2 months to mss. Sometimes comments on rejected mss.
TERMS Pays 10% royalty. Ms guidelines for #10 SASE.
TIPS "Know gothic and horror literature well."

GRAYWOLF PRESS

250 Third Ave. N., Suite 600, Minneapolis MN 55401. **E-mail:** wolves@graywolfpress.org. **Website:** www. graywolfpress.org. **Contact:** Katie Dublinski, editorial manager (nonfiction, fiction). Estab. 1974. Growing independent literary press, nonprofit corporation. Publishes trade cloth and paperback originals. Books: acid-free quality paper; offset printing; hardcover and soft binding. Average print order: 3,000-10,000. First novel print order: 3,000-7,500. Averages 27 total titles, 8-10 fiction titles/year. Distributes titles nationally through Farrar, Straus and Giroux. "Graywolf Press is an independent, nonprofit publisher dedicated to the creation and promotion of thoughtful and imaginative contemporary literature essential to a vital and diverse culture." Publishes trade cloth and paperback originals. Book catalog available free. Guidelines available online.
NEEDS Literary novels, short story collections. "Familiarize yourself with our list before submitting your

work." Published *The Adderall Diaries*, by Stephen El-liot; *Castle*, by J. Robert Lennon; *The Heyday of the Insensitive Bastards*, by Robert Boswell; *I Am Not Sidney Poitier*, by Percival Everett. "Familiarize yourself with our list first." No genre books (romance, western, science fiction, suspense).

HOW TO CONTACT Send full ms during open submission period including SASE/IRC, estimated word count, brief bio, list of publishing credits. Agented fiction 90%. Does not accept unsolicited queries, book proposals, or sample chapters. Responds in 3-6 months to submissions. Accepts simultaneous submissions. Query with SASE. Please do not fax or e-mail.

TERMS Pays royalty on retail price, author's copies. Average advance: $2,500-15,000. Publishes ms 18-24 months after acceptance. Ms guidelines online. Pays royalty on retail price. Pays $1,000-25,000 advance. Responds in 3 months to queries.

GREENE BARK PRESS

P.O. Box 1108, Bridgeport CT 06601. (610)434-2802. **Fax:** (610)434-2803. **E-mail:** service@greenebarkpress. com. **Website:** www.greenebarkpress.com. **Contact:** Thomas J. Greene, publisher; Tara Maroney, associate publisher. Estab. 1991. "We only publish children's fiction—all subjects, but usually reading picture book format appealing to ages 3-9 or all ages." Publishes hardcover originals. Averages 1-6 total titles/year. Distributes titles through Baker & Taylor and Quality Books. Promotes titles through ads, trade shows (national and regional), direct mail campaigns. "Greene Bark Press only publishes books for children and young adults, mainly picture and read-to books. All of our titles appeal to the imagination and encourage children to read and explore the world through books. We only publish children's fiction-all subjects-but in reading picture book format appealing to ages 3-9 or all ages." Publishes hardcover originals Guidelines for SASE.

NEEDS Juvenile. Published *Edith Ellen Eddy*, by Julee Granger.

HOW TO CONTACT Submit complete ms. Responds in 3 months to queries; 6 months to mss. Accepts simultaneous submissions. No electronic submissions. Submit complete ms. No queries or ms by e-mail.

TERMS Pays 10-15% royalty on wholesale price. Publishes ms 1 year after acceptance. Ms guidelines for SASE or e-mail request. Pays 10-15% royalty on wholesale price. Responds in 2 months to queries. Responds in 6 months to manuscripts.

TIPS "Audience is children who read to themselves and others. Mothers, fathers, grandparents, godparents who read to their respective children, grandchildren. Include SASE, be prepared to wait, do not inquire by telephone."

➊ ➌ GREY GECKO PRESS

565 S. Mason Rd., Suite 154, Katy TX 77450. **E-mail:** info@greygeckopress.com. **E-mail:** submissions@ greygeckopress.com. **Website:** www.greygeckopress. com. **Contact:** Hilary Comfort, editor-in-chief; Jason Aydelotte, executive director. Estab. 2011. Publishes hardcover, trade paperback, and electronic originals. Book catalog and ms guidelines for #10 SASE, by e-mail or online.

NEEDS "We do not publish extreme horror (e.g., "Hostel," "Saw," etc.). New and interesting stories by unpublished authors will always get our attention. Innovation is a core value of our company."

HOW TO CONTACT "We prefer electronic submissions but will accept: Query with SASE. Submit proposal package including synopsis and 3 sample chapters."

TERMS Pays 50-85% royalties on wholesale price. Responds in 2 weeks to queries and proposals; 1 months to mss.

TIPS "Be willing to be a part of the Grey Gecko Family. Publishing with us is a partnership, not indentured servitude."

➊ GRIT CITY PUBLICATIONS

309 Hill St., Pittsburgh PA 15140. (412)607-4592. **E-mail:** GritCityPublications@gmail.com. **Website:** www.GritCityPublications.com. **Contact:** Ron Gavalik, publisher. Estab. 2011. Publishes electronic originals. Book catalog and guidelines available online at website.

NEEDS "Please keep in mind we seek genre fiction for transformation into our unique fiction medium that's not published anywhere else. That's what makes EmotoBooks a hit with our fans. GCP publishes EmotoBooks. We seek shorter works of 6,000-10,000 words for EmotoSingles. We also seek works over 15,000 words for EmotoSerials. EmotoSerials are either short-term (novella length) or long-term (novel length). Writers are also required to read our "How To Create EmotoBooks handbook." This is a free download from the Write Emotobooks page on the website.

HOW TO CONTACT Query EmotoSerials through e-mail; submit completed EmotoSingles only by e-mail.

TERMS Pays 11.7-18.4% royalty on retail price. Does not offer advance. Responds to queries in 1 month; mss in 3.

TIPS "We ask writers to experience already published EmotoBooks to discover the new medium and learn our style."

GUERNICA EDITIONS

Box 117, Station P, Toronto ON M5S 2S6 Canada. (416)658-9888. **Fax:** (416)657-8885. **E-mail:** antoniodalfonso@sympatico.ca. **Website:** www.guernicaeditions.com. **Contact:** Antonio D'Alfonso, editor/publisher (poetry, nonfiction, novels). Estab. 1978. "Guernica Editions is a small press that produces works of fiction and nonfiction on the viability of pluriculturalism." Publishes trade paperback originals, reprints, and software. Books: various paper; offset printing; perfect binding. Average print order: 1,000. Averages 25 total titles, 18-20 fiction titles/year. Distributes titles through professional distributors. "Guernica Editions is an independent press dedicated to the bridging of cultures. We do original and translations of fine works. We are seeking essays on authors and translations with less emphasis on poetry." Publishes trade paperback originals, reprints, and software. Book catalog available online.

NEEDS Literary, multicultural. "We wish to open up into the fiction world and focus less on poetry. We specialize in European, especially Italian, translations." Publishes anthology of Arab women/Italian women writers. Published *At the Copa*, by Marisa Labozzetta; *In the Claws of the Cat*, by Claude Forand; *Unholy Stories*, by Carole David; *Girls Closed In* by France Theoret. "We wish to open up into the fiction world and focus less on poetry. We specialize in European, especially Italian, translations."

HOW TO CONTACT Query with SASE. Must have Canadian postage. Include estimated word count, brief bio, list of publishing credits. Responds in 1 month to queries; 1 year to mss. No simultaneous submissions. Guernica prefers to receive manuscript queries by e-mail. However, we also accept such queries by snail mail at our postal address. Before inquiring, however, please check our website to determine the type of material that best fits our publishing house.

TERMS Pays 8-10% royalty on retail price. Or makes outright purchase of $200-5,000. Average advance: $200-2,000. Publishes ms 15 months after acceptance. Pays 8-10% royalty on retail price, or makes outright purchase of $200-5,000. Pays $200-2,000 advance. Responds in 1 month to queries. Responds in 6 months to proposals. Responds in 1 year to manuscripts

H&S PUBLISHING, LLC

Best Places On Earth, 4330 Kauai Beach Dr., Suite G21, Lihue HI 96766. (808)822-7449. **Fax:** (808)822-2312. **E-mail:** sales@hshawaii.com. **Website:** www.bestplaceshawaii.com. **Contact:** Rob Sanford, editor. Estab. 1985. "Small independent publishing house founded and run by published authors." Publishes hardcover and paperback orginals and reprints. Books: recycled paper; digital printing; perfect binding; illustrations.

NEEDS Adventure, humor, literary, mainstream/contemporary, new age/mystic, regional (Hawaii), inspirational, religious mystery/suspense, religious thriller, thriller/espionage.

HOW TO CONTACT Send 1st chapter and synopsis. Include estimated word count, why author wrote book, and marketing plan. Send SASE for return of ms or send a disposable ms and SASE for reply only. Responds in 1 month to queries; 3 months to mss. Accepts simultaneous submissions. Sometimes comments on rejected mss. Send 1st chapter and synopsis. Include estimated word count, why author wrote book, and marketing plan. Send SASE for return of ms or send a disposable ms and SASE for reply only.

TERMS Pays 15-35% royalty. Pays 15-35% royalty. Responds in 1 month to queries; 3 months to mss. Sometimes comments on rejected mss.

TIPS "Do what you do best and enjoy most. Your writing is an outcome of the above."

HADLEY RILLE BOOKS

P.O. Box 25466, Overland Park KS 66225. **E-mail:** subs@hadleyrillebooks.com. **Website:** www.hadleyrillebooks.com. **Contact:** Eric T. Reynolds, editor/publisher. Estab. 2005. "Small publisher, one to two person operation. The first 9 titles are anthologies, mostly science fiction, with a little fantasy (in two titles). We've published new works by well-known authors (for example, new works by Sir Arthur C. Clarke, Mike Resnick, Stephen Baxter, Jay Lake, G. David Nordley, Robert Sheckley, Terry Bisson) as well as up-and-coming and new authors. At present time, about half of our anthologies are by invitation only, the other half are open to unsolicited submissions. We publish the kind of innovative anthologies that are generally not considered by larger publishers (somewhat common in the SF genre).

Some of our anthologies are experimental, for example, the first title (*Golden Age SF*) had well-known authors write 'Golden Age' SF stories as if they were living during that time. The second title, *Visual Journeys*, asked each contributing author to choose a work of space art and write a story based on it. We included color plates of the art with each story. We're currently in the middle of a Ruins anthology series with stories that are set in or are about ruins. An anthology in 2009 will feature stories that deal with the consequences of global warming. Well-known futurists and SF writers are writing for this." Publishes hardcover originals, paperback originals. Format: Offset and POD printing. Published 50 new writers last year. Averages 6 fiction titles/year. Distributes/promotes titles via distrubtors, promotes at conventions, online advertising and by reviews.

NEEDS Science fiction, fantasy, short story collections. Check website for current needs. Some anthologies are and will be open to unsolicited submissions, and will be announced on website. Published *Golden Age SF: Tales of a Bygone Future* (science fiction), *Visual Journeys: A Tribute to Space* (science fiction), *Ruins Terra* (SF/fantasy/horror). We currently don't have any anthologies open for submissions, but we will in the future. Please check back periodically.

HOW TO CONTACT Send query letter. Accepts queries by e-mail. Include estimated word count, brief bio. Agented fiction: less than 5%. Accepts unsolicited mss. Often critiques/comments on rejected mss. We only accept email queries and submissions and for 2010 only during the months of January, February, June, July, November, December.

TERMS Sends preproduction galleys to author. Ms published generally 6 months after acceptance. Writer's guidelines on website. Pays royalties of 12 of the ratio of 1 to the number of stories in the book, advance of $30 for unsolicated work. Book catalogs on website.

HAMPTON ROADS PUBLISHING CO., INC.

665 Third Street, Suite 400, San Francisco CA 94107. **E-mail:** submissions@hrpub.com; submissions@redwheelweiser.com. **Website:** www.hrpub.com. **Contact:** Ms. Pat Bryce, Acquisitions Editor. Estab. 1989. 1125 Stoney Ridge Rd., Charlottesville VA 22902. (434)296-2772. **Fax:** (434)296-5096. **E-mail:** editorial@hrpub.com. **Website:** www.hamptonroadspub.com **Contact:** Frank Demarco, chief editor. Estab. 1989. "We work as a team to produce the best books we are capable of producing which will impact, uplift and contribute to positive change in the world. We publish what defies or doesn't quite fit the usual genres. We are noted for visionary fiction." Publishes hardcover and trade paperback originals. Publishes and distributes hardcover and paperback originals on subjects including metaphysics, health, complementary medicine, visionary fiction and other related topics. Average print order: 3,000-5,000. Averages 24-30 total titles, 4 fiction titles/year. Distributes titles through distributors. Promotes titles through advertising, representatives, author signings, and radio-TV interviews with authors. "Our reason for being is to impact, uplift, and contribute to positive change in the world. We publish books that will enrich and empower the evolving consciousness of mankind. Though we are not necessarily limited in scope, we are most interested in manuscripts on the following subjects: Body/Mind/Spirit, Health and Healing, Self-Help. Please be advised that at the moment we are not accepting: Fiction or Novelized material that does not pertain to body/mind/spirit, Channeled writing. Publishes and distributes hardcover and trade paperback originals on subjects including metaphysics, health, complementary medicine, visionary fiction, and other related topics Guidelines available online.

"Please know that we only publish a handful of books every year, and that we pass on many well written, important works, simply because we cannot publish them all. We review each and every proposal very carefully. However, due to the volume of inquiries, we cannot respond to them all individually. Please give us 30 days to review your proposal. If you do not hear back from us within that time, this means we have decided to pursue other book ideas that we feel fit better within our plan."

NEEDS Literary, new age/mystic, psychic/supernatural, spiritual, visionary fiction, past-life fiction, based on actual memories. "Fiction should have one or more of the following themes: spiritual, inspirational, metaphysical, i.e., past life recall, out-of-body experiences, near death experience, paranormal." Published *Rogue Messiahs*, by Colin Wilson; *Spirit Matters*, by Michael Lerner; and *The Authenticator*, by William M. Valtos. Fiction should have 1 or more of the following themes: spiritual, inspirational, metaphysical, i.e., past-life recall, out-of-body experiences, near-death experience, paranormal.

HOW TO CONTACT Accepts unsolicited mss. Submit outline, 2 sample chapter(s), synopsis. Accepts queries by e-mail, fax. Send SASE for return of ms or send a disposable ms and SASE for reply only. Agented fiction 5%. Responds in 1-2 months to queries; 1-6 months to mss. Accepts simultaneous submissions.
TERMS Pays royalty. Average advance: less than $10,000. Publishes ms 1 year after acceptance. Ms guidelines online. Pays royalty. Pays $1,000-50,000 advance. Responds in 2-4 months to queries. Responds in 1 month to proposals. Responds in 6-12 months to manuscripts.

HARLEQUIN AMERICAN ROMANCE
233 Broadway, Suite 1001, New York NY 10279. **Website:** www.eharlequin.com. A Harlequin book line. "Upbeat and lively, fast paced and well plotted, American Romance celebrates the pursuit of love in the backyards, big cities and wide-open spaces of America." Publishes paperback originals and reprints. Books: newspaper print paper; web printing; perfect bound. Length: 55,000-60,000 words. Senior Editor: Kathleen Scheibling; Editor: Johanna Raisanen; Assistant Editor: Laura Barth. Editorial Office: Toronto, Canada. "American Romance features heartwarming romances with strong family elements. These are stories about the pursuit of love, marriage and family in America today."
NEEDS Romance (contemporary, American). Needs "all-American stories with a range of emotional and sensual content that are supported by a sense of community within the plot's framework. In the confident and caring heroine, the tough but tender hero, and their dynamic relationship that is at the center of this series, real-life love is showcased as the best fantasy of all!"
HOW TO CONTACT Query with SASE. No simultaneous submissions, electronic submissions, or submissions on disk.
TERMS Pays royalty. Offers advance. Ms guidelines online.

HARLEQUIN BLAZE
225 Duncan Mill Road, Don Mills ON M3B 3K9 Canada. (416)445-5860. **Website:** www.eharlequin.com. **Contact:** Brenda Chin, associate editor. "Harlequin Blaze is a red-hot series. It is a vehicle to build and promote new authors who have a strong sexual edge to their stories. It is also the place to be for seasoned authors who want to create a sexy, sizzling, longer contemporary story." Publishes paperback originals. Books: newspaper print; web printing; perfect bound.
NEEDS Romance (contemporary). "Sensuous, highly romantic, innovative plots that are sexy in premise and execution. The tone of the books can run from fun and flirtatious to dark and sensual. Submissions should have a very contemporary feel—what it's like to be young and single today. We are looking for heroes and heroines in their early 20s and up. There should be a a strong emphasis on the physical relationship between the couples. Fully described love scenes along with a high level of fantasy and playfulness." Length: 55,000-60,000 words.
HOW TO CONTACT No simultaneous submissions, electronic submissions, submissions on disk.
TERMS Pays royalty. Offers advance. Ms guidelines online.
TIPS "Are you a *Cosmo* girl at heart? A fan of *Sex and the City*? Or maybe you have a sexually adventurous spirit. If so, then Blaze is the series for you!"

HARLEQUIN DESIRE
233 Broadway, Suite 1001, New York NY 10279. (212)553-4200. **Website:** www.eharlequin.com. **Contact:** Krista Stroever. Always powerful, passionate, and provocative. Starting with April titles, Silhouette Desire books will be published as Harlequin Desire. "Desire novels are sensual reads and a love scene or scenes are still needed. But there is no set number of pages that needs to be fulfilled. Rather, the level of sensuality must be appropriate to the storyline. Above all, every Silhouette Desire novel must fulfill the promise of a powerful, passionate and provocative read." Publishes paperback originals and reprints. Books: newspaper print; web printing; perfect bound.
NEEDS Romance. Looking for novels in which "the conflict is an emotional one, springing naturally from the unique characters you've chosen. The focus is on the developing relationship, set in a believable plot. Sensuality is key, but lovemaking is never taken lightly. Secondary characters and subplots need to blend with the core story. Innovative new directions in storytelling and fresh approaches to classic romantic plots are welcome." Manuscripts must be 50,000-55,000 words.
HOW TO CONTACT Does not accept unsolicited mss. Query with word count, brief bio, publishing history, synopsis (no more than 2 single-spaced pages), SASE/IRC. No simultaneous submissions. www.eharlequin.com.
TERMS Pays royalty. Offers advance. Detailed ms guidelines for SASE or on website.

⊕○ HARLEQUIN HISTORICALS

Eton House, 18-24 Paradise Road, Richmond Surrey TW9 1SR United Kingdom. **Website:** www.eharlequin. com. **Contact:** Linda Fildew, senior editor. "The primary element of a Harlequin Historical novel is romance. The story should focus on the heroine and how her love for one man changes her life forever. For this reason, it is very important that you have an appealing hero and heroine, and that their relationship is a compelling one. The conflicts they must overcome—and the situations they face—can be as varied as the setting you have chosen, but there must be romantic tension, some spark between your hero and heroine that keeps your reader interested." Publishes paperback originals and reprints. Books: newsprint paper; perfect bound.

NEEDS Romance (historical). "We will not accept books set after 1900. We're looking primarily for books set in North America, England or France between 1100 and 1900 A.D. We do not buy many novels set during the American Civil War. We are, however, flexible and will consider most periods and settings. We are not looking for gothics or family sagas, nor are we interested in the kind of comedy of manners typified by straight Regencies. Historical romances set during the Regency period, however, will definitely be considered." Length: 70,000-75,000/words.

HOW TO CONTACT Submit the first three chapters along with a 1-2 page synopsis of your novel.

TERMS Pays royalty. Offers advance. Ms guidelines online.

○○ HARLEQUIN SUPERROMANCE

225 Duncan Mill Road, Don Mills ON M3B 3K9 Canada. **Website:** www.eharlequin.com. **Contact:** Victoria Curran, editor. "The Harlequin Superromance line focuses on believable characters triumphing over true-to-life drama and conflict. At the heart of these contemporary stories should be a compelling romance that brings the reader along with the hero and heroine on their journey of overcoming the obstacles in their way and falling in love. Because of the longer length relevant subplots and secondary characters are welcome but not required. This series publishes a variety of story types—family sagas, romantic suspense, Westerns, to name a few—and tones from light to dramatic, emotional to suspenseful. Settings also vary from vibrant urban neighborhoods to charming small towns. The unifying element of Harlequin Superromance stories is the realistic treatment of character and plot. The characters should seem familiar to readers—similar to people they know in their own lives—and the circumstances within the realm of possibility. The stories should be layered and complex in that the conflicts should not be easily resolved. The best way to get an idea of we're looking for is to read what we're currently publishing. The aim of Superromance novels is to produce a contemporary, involving read with a mainstream tone in its situations and characters, using romance as the major theme. To achieve this, emphasis should be placed on individual writing styles and unique and topical ideas." Publishes paperback originals. Books: newspaper print; perfect bound.

NEEDS Romance (contemporary). "The criteria for Superromance books are flexible. Aside from length (70,000-75,000 words), the determining factor for publication will always be quality. Authors should strive to break free of stereotypes, clichés and worn-out plot devices to create strong, believable stories with depth and emotional intensity. Superromance novels are intended to appeal to a wide range of romance readers."

HOW TO CONTACT Accepts unsolicited submissions. Submit 3 sample chapter(s) and synopsis. Send SASE for return of ms or send a disposable ms and SASE for reply only. No simultaneous submissions, electronic submissions, submissions on disk.

TERMS Pays royalty. Offers advance. Ms guidelines online.

TIPS "A general familiarity with current Superromance books is advisable to keep abreast of ever-changing trends and overall scope, but we don't want imitations. We look for sincere, heartfelt writing based on true-to-life experiences the reader can identify with. We are interested in innovation."

⊘○ HARPERCOLLINS CANADA, LTD.

2 Bloor St. E., 20th Floor, Toronto ON M4W 1A8 Canada. (416)975-9334. **Fax:** (416)975-5223. **Website:** www.harpercollins.ca. Estab. 1989. 2 Bloor St. East, 20th Floor, Toronto ON M4W 1A8 Canada. (416)975-9334. **Fax:** (416)975-5223. **Website:** www.harpercanada.com. Harpercollins is not accepting unsolicited material at this time.

○ HarperCollins Canada is not accepting unsolicited material at this time.

IMPRINTS HarperCollinsPublishers; HarperPerennialCanada (trade paperbacks); HarperTrophyCanada (children's); Phyllis Bruce Books.

HARPERCOLLINS CHILDREN'S BOOKS/ HARPERCOLLINS PUBLISHERS

10 East 53rd, New York NY 10022. (212)207-6901. E-mail: Dana.fritts@Harpercollins.com; Mischa.Rosenberg@Harpercollins.com. **Website:** www.harpercollins.com. **Contact:** Mischa Rosenberg, assistant designer; Dana Fritts, designer. Imprints: HarperTrophy, HarperTeen, EOS, HarperFestival, Greenwillow Books, Joanna Cotler Books, Laura Geringer Books, Katherine Tegen Books.; Art samples may be sent to Martha Rago or Stephanie Bart-Horvath. *Please do not send original art.* Works with over 100 illustrators/year. Responds only if interested. Samples returned with SASE; samples filed only if interested. HarperCollins, one of the largest English language publishers in the world, is a broad-based publisher with strengths in academic, business and professional, children's, educational, general interest, and religious and spiritual books, as well as multimedia titles. Publishes hardcover and paperback originals and paperback reprints. Available online.

IMPRINTS HarperCollins Australia/New Zealand: Angus & Robertson, Fourth Estate, HarperBusiness, HarperCollins, HarperPerenniel, HarperReligious, HarperSports, Voyager; **HarperCollins Canada**: HarperFlamingoCanada, PerennialCanada; **HarperCollins Children's Books Group:** Amistad, Julie Andrews Collection, Avon, Joanna Cotler Books, Eos, Laura Geringer Books, Greenwillow Books, HarperAudio, HarperCollins Children's Books, HarperFestival, HarperTempest, HarperTrophy, Rayo, Katherine Tegen Books; **HarperCollins General Books Group:** Access, Amistad, Avon, Caedmon, Ecco, Eos, Fourth Estate, HarperAudio, HarperBusiness, HarperCollins, HarperEntertainment, HarperLargePrint, HarperResource, HarperSanFrancisco, HarperTorch, Harper Design International, Perennial, PerfectBound, Quill, Rayo, ReganBooks, William Morrow, William Morrow Cookbooks; **HarperCollins UK:** Collins Bartholomew, Collins, HarperCollins Crime & Thrillers, Collins Freedom to Teach, HarperCollins Children's Books, Thorsons/Element, Voyager Books; **Zondervan:** Inspirio, Vida, Zonderkidz, Zondervan.

NEEDS "We look for a strong story line and exceptional literary talent."

HOW TO CONTACT Only accepts agented mss. Agented submissions only. *All unsolicited mss returned.*

TERMS Art guidelines available with SASE. Negotiate a flat fee upon acceptance. 1 month, will contact if interested.

TIPS "We do not accept any unsolicited material."

HAWK PUBLISHING GROUP

7107 S. Yale Ave., #345, Tulsa OK 74136. (918)492-3677. **Fax:** (918)492-2120. **Website:** www.hawkpublishing.com. Estab. 1999. Independent publisher of general trade/commercial books, fiction and nonfiction. Publishes hardcover and trade paperback originals. Averages 6-8 total titles, 3 fiction titles/year. Member PMA. Titles are distributed by NBN/Biblio Distribution. "Please visit our website and read the submission guidelines before sending anything to us. The best way to learn what might interest us is to visit the website, read the information there, look at the books, and perhaps even read a few of them." Publishes hardcover and trade paperback originals. Guidelines available online.

"Hawk Publishing is a royalty paying small press publisher of non-fiction instructional pamphlets, guides, cards, books and fine art photographic posters by some of today's most critically acclaimed artists, craftsmen, experts and hobbyists. We'll have three main imprints to start. We will print various lengths from pamphlet or booklet form to actual books. We may also offer some manuscripts in ebook formats, where appropriate. Currently, manuscripts with a large number of graphics do not readily lend themselves to ebook formats, so we will make decisions on ebook offerings on a case by case basis."

IMPRINTS Art Works, Earth Works, Paper Works.

NEEDS Looking for good books of all kinds. Not interested in juvenile, poetry, or short story collections. Published *I Survived Cancer,* by Jim Chastain; *Everlasting*, by Carol Johnson; *Ghost Band*, by John Wooley. Looking for good books of all kinds. Not interested in juvenile, poetry, or short story collections. Does not want childrens or young adult books.

HOW TO CONTACT Accepts unsolicited mss. Submit first 20 pages of your book, synopsis, author bio. Include list of publishing credits. Accepts simultaneous submissions. "Submissions will not be returned, so send only copies. No SASE. No submissions by e-mail or by 'cerified mail' or any other service that requires a signature." Replies only if interested. If you have not heard from us within 3 months after the receipt of your submission, you may safely assume that we were not able to find a place for it in our list."

TERMS Pays royalty. Publishes ms 1-2 years after acceptance. Ms guidelines online. Pays royalty.

TIPS "Prepare a professional submission and follow the guidelines. The simple things really do count; use 12 pt. pitch with 1-inch margins and only send what is requested."

HELICON NINE EDITIONS

P.O. Box 22412, Kansas City MO 64113. **Website:** www.heliconnine.com. **Contact:** Gloria Vando Hickok. Estab. 1990. Subsidiary of Midwest Center for the Literary Arts, Inc. Small not-for-profit press publishing poetry, fiction, creative nonfiction and anthologies. Publishes paperback originals. Also publishes one-story chapbooks called *feuillets*, which come with envelope, 250 print run. Books: 60 lb. paper; offset printing; perfect bound; 4-color cover. Average print order: 1,000-5,000. Distributes titles through Baker & Taylor, Brodart, Ingrams, Follet (library acquisitions), and booksellers. Promotes titles through reviews, readings, radio, and television interviews.

HOW TO CONTACT Does not accept unsolicited mss.

TERMS Pays royalty. Author's copies. Offers advance. Publishes ms 12-18 months after acceptance.

TIPS "We accept short story collections, welcome new writers and first books. Submit a clean, readable copy in a folder or box—paginated with title and name on each page. Also, do not pre-design book, i.e., no illustrations, unless they are an integral part of the book. We'd like to see books that will be read 50-100 years from now."

HENDRICK-LONG PUBLISHING CO., INC.

10635 Tower Oaks, Suite D, Houston TX 77070. 832-912-READ. **Fax:** (832)912-7353. **E-mail:** hendricklong@att.net. **Website:** hendricklongpublishing.com. **Contact:** Vilma Long. Estab. 1969. Only considers manuscripts with Texas theme. Publishes hardcover and trade paperback originals and hardcover reprints. Averages 4 total titles/year. "Hendrick-Long publishes historical fiction and nonfiction about Texas and the Southwest for children and young adults." Publishes hardcover and trade paperback originals and hardcover reprints Book catalog for 8½×11 or 9×12 SASE with 4 first-class stamps Guidelines available online

NEEDS Juvenile, young adult.

HOW TO CONTACT Submit outline, 2 sample chapter(s), synopsis. Responds in 3 months to queries. No simultaneous submissions. Please, no e-mail submissions. Query with SASE.

TERMS Pays royalty on selling price. Offers advance. Publishes ms 18 months after acceptance. Book catalog for 812×11 or 9×12 SASE with 4 first-class stamps. Ms guidelines online. Pays royalty on selling price. Pays advance. Responds in 3 months to queries.

Ⓐ☺ HESPERUS PRESS

19 Bulstrode St., London W1U 2JN UK. +44 (0) 20 7486 5005. **E-mail:** info@hesperuspress.com. **Website:** www.hesperuspress.com. Estab. 2001. Hesperus is a small, independent publisher mainly of classic literary fiction translated fiction, and biographies of literary figures. Publishes paperback originals. Books: munken paper; traditional printing; sewn binding. Average print order: 2,000. Distributes titles through Trafalgar Square in the US, Grantham Book Services in the UK.

🗩 Does not accept unsolicited mss. *Agented submissions only.* Query with SASE. Accepts queries by mail. Include estimated word count, brief bio, list of publishing credits. Agented fiction 100%. No submissions on disk.

NEEDS Literary. Published *Carlyle's House*, by Virginia Woolf (rediscovered modern classic); *No Man's Land*, by Graham Greene (rediscovered modern classic); *The Princess of Mantua*, by Marie Ferranti (award-winning fiction in translation); *The Maytrees*, by Annie Dillard (new fiction).

HOW TO CONTACT Does not accept unsolicited mss. *Agented submissions only.* Query with SASE. Accepts queries by mail. Include estimated word count, brief bio, list of publishing credits. Agented fiction 100%. Responds in 8-10 weeks to queries; 8-10 weeks to mss. Accepts simultaneous submissions. No submissions on disk.

TERMS Responds in 8-10 weeks to queries; 8-10 weeks to mss.

TIPS Find an agent to represent you.

ⓞ☺ HIGHLAND PRESS PUBLISHING

P.O. Box 2292, High Springs FL 32655. (386) 454-3927. **Fax:** (386) 454-3927. **E-mail:** The.Highland.Press@gmail.com; Submissions.hp@gmail.com. **Website:** www.highlandpress.org. **Contact:** Leanne Burroughs, CEO (fiction); she will forward all mss to appropriate editor. Estab. 2005. Publishes paperback originals, paperback reprints. Format: off set printing; perfect bound. Average print order: 1,000. Debut novel print order: 1,000. Averages 30 total titles/year; 30 fiction titles/year. Distributes/promotes titles through Ingrams, Baker & Taylor, Nielsen, Powells. "With our focus on historical romances, Highland Press Publishing is known as your 'Passport to Romance.' We focus on historical romances and our award-winning anthologies. Our short stories/novellas are heart warming. As for our historicals, we publish historical novels like many of us grew up with and loved. History is a big part of the story and is tactfully woven throughout the romance." We have recently opened oursubmissions up to all genres, with the exception of erotica. Our newest lines are inspirational, regency, and young adult. Paperback originals. Catalog and guidelines available online at website.

NEEDS Children's/juvenile (adventure, animal, easy-to-read, fantasy, historical, mystery, preschool/picture book, series), comedy (romance/suspense), contemporary (romance/mystery/suspense); family saga, fantasy (space fantasy), historical, horror (dark fantasy, futuristic, supernatural), mainstream, military/war, mystery/suspense (amateur/sleuth, cozy, police, private eye/hardboiled), religious (children's, general, family, inspirational, fantasy, mystery/suspense, thriller, romance), romance (contemporary, futuristic/time travel, gothic, historical, regency period, suspense), short story collections, thriller/espionage, western (frontier saga, traditional), young adult/teen (adventure, paranormal, fantasy/science fiction, historical, horror, mystery/suspense, romance, series, western, chapter books).

HOW TO CONTACT Send query letter. Query with outline/synopsis and sample chapters. Accepts queries by snail mail, e-mail. Include estimated word count, target market. Send disposable copy of ms and SASE for reply only. Agented fiction: 10%. Responds to queries in 8 weeks. Accepts unsolicited mss. Considers simultaneous submissions, e-mail submissions. Sometimes critiques/comments on rejected mss. Responds to mss in 3-12 months. Send query letter. Query with outline/synopsis and sample chapters. Accepts queries by snail mail, e-mail. Include estimated word count, target market.

TERMS Sends preproduction galleys to author. Ms published within 12 months after acceptance. Pays royalties 7.5-8% Responds in 8 weeks to queries; responds in 3-12 months to mss

HOLIDAY HOUSE, INC.

425 Madison Ave., New York NY 10017. (212)688-0085. **Fax:** (212)421-6134. **E-mail:** info@holidayhouse.com. **Website:** holidayhouse.com. **Contact:** Mary Cash, editor-in-chief. Estab. 1935. Publishes 35 picture books/year; 3 young readers/year; 15 middle readers/year; 8 young adult titles/year. 20% of books by first-time authors; 10% from agented writers. Mission Statement: "To publish high-quality books for children.Holiday House publishes children's and young adult books for the school and library markets. We have a commitment to publishing first-time authors and illustrators. We specialize in quality hardcovers from picture books to young adult, both fiction and nonfiction, primarily for the school and library market." Publishes hardcover originals and paperback reprints. Guidelines for #10 SASE.

"Holiday House is an independent publisher of children's books only. We specialize in quality hardcovers, from picture books to young adult, both fiction and nonfiction. We publish children's books for ages four and up. We do not publish mass-market books, including, but not limited to, pop-ups, activity books, sticker books, coloring books, or licensed books."

NEEDS All levels of young readers: adventure, contemporary, fantasy, folktales, ghost, historical, humor, literary, multicultural, school, suspense/mystery, sports. Recently published *Anansi's Party Time*, by Eric Kimmel, illustrated by Janet Stevens; *The Blossom Family* series, by Betsy Byars; *Washington at Valley Forge*, by Russell Freedman. Children's books only.

HOW TO CONTACT Send queries only to editor. Responds to queries in 3 months; mss in 4 months. "If we find your book idea suits our present needs, we will notify you by mail." Once a ms has been requested, the writers should send in the exclusive submission. Please send the entire manuscript, whether submitting a picture book or novel. We do not accept certified or registered mail. There is no need to include a SASE. We do not consider submissions by e-mail or fax. Please note that you do not have to supply illustrations. However, if you have illustrations you would like to include with your submission, you may send detailed sketches or photocopies of the original art.

Do not send original art. Query with SASE. No phone calls, please.

TERMS Pays authors and illustrators an advance against royalties. Originals returned at job's completion. Book catalog, ms guidelines available for a SASE. Pays royalty on list price, range varies. Agent's royalty. Responds in 4 months.

TIPS "We need manuscripts with strong stories and writing."

ⓐⓞ HENRY HOLT

175 Fifth Avenue, New York NY 10011. **Website:** www. henryholt.com. Publishes hardcover and paperback originals and reprints.

HOW TO CONTACT Closed to submissions. *Agented submissions only.*

HOMA & SEKEY BOOKS

P.O. Box 103, Dumont NJ 07628. (201)384-6692. **Fax:** (201)384-6055. **E-mail:** info@homabooks.com. **E-mail:** submission@homabooks.com. **Website:** www. homabooks.com. **Contact:** Shawn Ye, editor (fiction and nonfiction). Estab. 1997. Estab. 1997. "We focus on publishing East Asia-related titles. Both translations and original English manuscripts are welcome." Publishes hardcover and paperback originals. Books: natural paper; web press; perfect bound; illustrations. Averages 7 total titles, 3 fiction titles/year. Member PMA. Distributes titles through Ingram, Baker & Taylor, etc. Publishes hardcover originals and trade paperback originals and reprints. Book catalog available online. Guidelines available online.

NEEDS Ethnic (Asian), literary, mystery, young adult (adventure, historical, mystery/suspense, romance). Wants China-related titles. Published *Willow Leaf, Maple Leaf: A Novel of Immigration Blue*, by David Ke; *The Curse of Kim's Daughter* by Park Kyong-Ni (translation); *A Floating City on The Water* (translation). We publish books on Asian topics. Books should be Asia-related.

HOW TO CONTACT Accepts unsolicited mss. Query with SASE or submit outline, 2 sample chapter(s). Accepts queries by e-mail (as attachments), mail. Include estimated word count, brief bio, list of publishing credits and marketing analysis. Send SASE for return of ms or send a disposable ms and SASE for reply only. Responds in 8 weeks to queries; 8-10 weeks to proposals; 20 weeks to mss. Accepts simultaneous submissions, electronic submissions. Sometimes comments on rejected mss. Submit proposal package, clips, 2 sample chapters. Submit complete ms.

TERMS Pays 5-10% royalty. Publishes ms 1 year after acceptance. Book catalog for 9×12 SASE. Ms guidelines online. Pays 5-10% royalty on retail price. Responds in 2 months to queries. Responds in 3 months to proposals. Responds in 4 months to manuscripts.

ⓘ HOUGHTON MIFFLIN HARCOURT BOOKS FOR CHILDREN

222 Berkeley St., Boston MA 02116. (617)351-5000. **E-mail:** children's_books@hmco.com. **Website:** www. houghtonmifflinbooks.com. **Contact:** Submissions coordinator. "Houghton Mifflin gives shape to ideas that educate, inform and, above all, delight." Publishes hardcover originals and trade paperback originals and reprints. Averages 100 total titles/year. Promotes titles through author visits, advertising, reviews.

NEEDS Adventure, ethnic, historical, humor, juvenile (early readers), literary, mystery, picture books, suspense, young adult, board books. Published *Trainstop* by Barbara Lehman; *The Willowbys* by Lois Lowry; *Just Grace Walker the Dog* by Cherise Mericle Harper.

HOW TO CONTACT Accepts unsolicited mss. Responds only if interested. Do not send SASE. Accepts simultaneous submissions. No electronic submissions.

TERMS Pays 5-10% royalty on retail price. Average advance: variable. Publishes ms 18-24 months after acceptance. Book catalog for 9×12 SASE with 3 first-class stamps. Ms guidelines online.

TIPS "The Children's Book Division will read unsolicited manuscripts. Please send them to us by conventional mail only. We do not accept e-mailed or faxed manuscripts. Because confirmation postcards are easily separated from the ms or hidden, we do not encourage you to include them with your submission."

ⓐ HOUGHTON MIFFLIN HARCOURT CO.

222 Berkeley St., Boston MA 02116. (617)351-5000. **Website:** www.hmhco.com; www.hmhbooks.com. Estab. 1832. Publishes hardcover originals and trade paperback originals and reprints. Averages 250 total titles/year. Publishes hardcover originals and trade paperback originals and reprints.

> "Houghton Mifflin Harcourt gives shape to ideas that educate, inform and delight. In a new era of publishing, our legacy of quality thrives as we combine imagination with technology, bringing you new ways to know."

IMPRINTS American Heritage Dictionaries; Clarion Books; Great Source Education Group; Houghton Mifflin; Houghton Mifflin Books for Children; Houghton Mifflin Paperbacks; Mariner Books; Mc-Dougal Littell; Peterson Field Guides; Riverside Publishing; Sunburst Technology; Taylor's Gardening Guides; Edusoft; Promissor; Walter Lorraine Books; Kingfisher.

NEEDS Literary. "We are not a mass market publisher. Study the current list." Published *Extremely Loud and Incredibly Close*, by Jonathan Safran Foer; *The Plot against America*, by Philip Roth; *Heir to the Glimmering World*, by Cynthia Ozick.

HOW TO CONTACT Does not accept unsolicited mss. *Agented submissions only.* Accepts simultaneous submissions.

TERMS Hardcover: pays 10-15% royalty on retail price, sliding scale, or flat rate based on sales; paperback: 712% flat rate, but negotiable. Average advance: variable. Publishes ms 3 years after acceptance.

☺ IMAGE COMICS

Submissions, 2134 Allston Way, 2nd Floor, Berkeley CA 94704. **E-mail:** submissions@imagecomics.com. **Website:** www.imagecomics.com. **Contact:** Eric Stephenson, publisher. Estab. 1992. "We are looking for good, well-told stories and exceptional artwork that run the gamut in terms of both style and genre. Image is a comics and graphic novels publisher formed by seven of Marvel Comics' best-selling artists: Erik Larsen, Jim Lee, Rob Liefeld, Todd McFarlane, Whilce Portacio, Marc Silvestri, and Jim Valentino. Since that time, Image has gone on to become the third largest comics publisher in the United States." Publishes comic books, graphic novels. See this company's website for detailed guidelines.

NEEDS "We are not looking for any specific genre or type of comic book. We are looking for comics that are well written and well drawn, by people who are dedicated and can meet deadlines."

HOW TO CONTACT Query with 1 page synopsis and 5 pages or more of samples. "We do not accept writing (that is plots, scripts, whatever) samples! If you're an established pro, we might be able to find somebody willing to work with you but it would be nearly impossible for us to read through every script that might find its way our direction. Do not send your script or your plot unaccompanied by art—it will be discarded, unread." Accepts queries by snail mail, e-mail. Sometimes critiques/comments on rejected mss.

TERMS Writer's guidelines on website.

① IMAJINN BOOKS

P.O. Box 74274, Phoenix AZ 85087-4274. (623)236-3361. **E-mail:** editors@imajinnbooks.com. **Website:** www.imajinnbooks.com. **Contact:** Linda J. Kichline, editor. Estab. 1998. "ImaJinn Books, Inc. is a small independent print-on-demand publishing house that specializes in Regency Romance, Urban Fantasy, and paranormal romances with story lines involving psychics or psychic phenomena, witches, vampires, werewolves, space travel, the future." Publishes trade paperback originals. Books: print-on-demand; perfect binding; no illustrations. **Publishes 3-4 debut authors per year.** Distributes titles through Ingram Books and imajinnbooks.com. Promotes titles through advertising and review magazines.

NEEDS Fantasy (romance), horror (romance), psychic/supernatural (romance), all Urban Fantasy story lines, and all Regency romance story lines. "We look for specific story lines based on what the readers are asking for and what story lines in which we're short. We post our current needs on our website." Published *Half Past Hell* by Jaye Roycraft (horror romance); *Grave Illusions*, by Lina Gardiner (urban fantasy), and *The Hermitage*, by Sharon Sobel (Regency romance).

HOW TO CONTACT Query by e-mail only. Include estimated word count, brief bio, list of publishing credits. Agented fiction 20%. Responds in 3 months to queries; 9-12 months to mss. Often comments on rejected mss.

TERMS Pays 6-10% royalty on retail price. Average advance: 100-200. Publishes ms 1-3 years after acceptance. Book catalog and ms guidelines online.

TIPS "Carefully read the author guidelines, and read books published by ImaJinn Books. Do not submit manuscript without querying first."

① INGALLS PUBLISHING GROUP, INC

P.O. Box 2500, Banner Elk NC 28604. (828)297-6884. **Fax:** (828)297-6880. **E-mail:** editor@ingallspublishinggroup.com; sales@ingallspublishinggroup.com. **Website:** www.ingallspublishinggroup.com. **Contact:** Rebecca Owen. Estab. 2001. Estab. 2001. Publishes hardcover originals, paperback originals and paperback reprints. Exploring digital technologies for printing and e-books. Member IBPA, MWA, SIBA. "We are a small regional house focusing on popular fiction and memoir. At present, we are most interested in regional fiction, historical fiction and mystery fiction." Accepts unsolicited mss. Query first. Will specifically request if interested in reading synopsis and 3 sample chapters. Accepts queries by e-mail. Include estimated word count, brief bio, list of publishing credits. Agented fiction 10%. Accepts electronic submissions. No submissions on disk. Often comments on rejected mss. Publishes hardcover originals, paperback originals and paperback reprints. Guidelines available online.

NEEDS Regional (southeast US), mystery (amateur sleuth, cozy, police procedural, private eye/hard-boiled), regional (southern Appalachian), romance (contemporary, historical, romantic suspense adventure).

HOW TO CONTACT Accepts unsolicited mss. Query first. Will specifically request if interested in reading synopsis and 3 sample chapters. Accepts queries by e-mail. Include estimated word count, brief bio, list of publishing credits. Agented fiction 10%. Responds in 6 weeks to queries or mss. Accepts simultaneous submissions, electronic submissions. No submissions on disk. Often comments on rejected mss. Query first. Will specifically request if interested in reading synopsis and 3 sample chapters. Accepts queries by e-mail. Include estimated word count, brief bio, list of publishing credits. No submissions on disk.

TERMS Pays 10% royalty. Publishes ms 6 months-2 years after acceptance. Ms guidelines online. Pays 10% royalty. Responds in 6 weeks to queries or mss.

☺ INSOMNIAC PRESS

520 Princess Ave., London ON N6B 2B8 Canada. (416)504-6270. **E-mail:** mike@insomniacpress.com. **Website:** www.insomniacpress.com. **Contact:** Mike O'Connor, publisher. Estab. 1992. "Midsize independent publisher with a mandate to produce edgy experimental fiction." Publishes trade paperback originals and reprints, mass market paperback originals, and electronic originals and reprints. First novel print order: 3,000. Averages 20 total titles, 5 fiction titles/year. We publish a mix of commercial (mysteries) and literary fiction. Published *Pray for Us Sinners*, by Patrick Taylor (novel). Agented fiction 5%. Responds in 1 week to queries; 2 months to mss. Accepts simultaneous submissions. Sometimes comments on rejected mss. Ms guidelines online. Publishes trade paperback originals and reprints, mass market paperback originals, and electronic originals and reprints. Guidelines available online.

NEEDS Comic books, ethnic, experimental, gay/lesbian, humor, literary, mainstream/contemporary, multicultural, mystery, suspense. "We publish a mix of commercial (mysteries) and literary fiction."

HOW TO CONTACT Accepts unsolicited mss. Accepts queries by e-mail. Include estimated word count, brief bio, list of publishing credits. Send SASE for return of ms or send a disposable ms and SASE for reply only. Query via e-mail, submit proposal.

TERMS Pays 10-15% royalty on retail price. Average advance: $500-1,000. Publishes ms 6 months after acceptance.

TIPS "We envision a mixed readership that appreciates up-and-coming literary fiction and poetry as well as solidly researched and provocative nonfiction. Peruse our website and familiarize yourself with what we've published in the past."

◉ INTERLINK PUBLISHING GROUP, INC.

46 Crosby St., Northampton MA 01060. (413)582-7054. **Fax:** (413)582-7057. **E-mail:** info@interlinkbooks.com; editor@interlinkbooks.com. **Website:** www.interlinkbooks.com. **Contact:** Michel Moushabeck, publisher; Pam Thompson, editor. Estab. 1987. "Midsize independent publisher specializing in world travel, world literature, world history and politics." Publishes hardcover and trade paperback originals. Books: 55 lb. Warren Sebago Cream white paper; web offset printing; perfect binding. Average print order: 5,000. Averages 50 total titles, 2-4 fiction titles/year. Distributes titles through Baker & Taylor. Promotes titles through book mailings to extensive, specialized lists of editors and reviews; authors read at bookstores and special events across the country. Interlink is a independent publisher of a general trade list of adult fiction and nonfiction with an emphasis on books that have a wide appeal while also meeting high intellectual and literary standards. Publishes hardcover and trade paperback originals. Book catalog and guidelines available free online.

IMPRINTS Crocodile Books, USA; Codagan Guides, USA; Interlink Books; Olive Branch Press; Clockroot Books.

NEEDS Ethnic, international. "Adult—We are looking for translated works relating to the Middle East, Africa or Latin America." Recently published *Everything Good Will Come*, by Sefi Atta (first novel); *The Gardens of Light*, by Amin Maalouf (novel translated from French); *War in the Land of Egypt*, by Yusef Al-Qaid (novel translated from Arabic). "We are looking for translated works relating to the Middle East, Africa or Latin America." No science fiction, romance, plays, erotica, fantasy, horror.

HOW TO CONTACT "Become familiar with the kinds of books we publish. Request a catalog or read them at your local library, If you believe your ms might fit our list, please send a query letter to the attention of Pam Thompson. The query letter may (but doesn't have to) include any of the following: a writing sample (preferably the opening of the book) of no more than 10 pages, a brief synopsis and bio. Send an SASE as well. The only fiction we publish falls into our 'Interlink WorldFiction' series. Most of these books, as you can see in our catalog, are translated fiction from around the world. The idea behind the series is to bring fiction from other countries to a North American audience. So unless you were born outside the United States, your novel will not fit into the series. All of our children's books are picture books designed for ages 3-8. We publish very few of them, and most are co-published with overseas publishing houses. We do not consider unsolicited manuscripts of children's books." Query with SASE and a brief sample. Responds in 3 months to queries. Accepts simultaneous submissions. No electronic submissions.

TERMS Pays 6-8% royalty on retail price. Average advance: small. Publishes ms 18 months after acceptance. Ms guidelines online. Pays 6-8% royalty on retail price. Pays small advance. Responds in 3-6 months to queries

TIPS "Any submissions that fit well in our publishing program will receive careful attention. A visit to our website, your local bookstore, or library to look at some of our books before you send in your submission is recommended."

INVERTED-A

P.O. Box 267, Licking MO 65542. **E-mail:** amnfn@well.com. **Contact:** Aya Katz, chief editor (poetry, novels, political); Nets Katz, science editor (scientific, academic). Estab. 1985. Publishes paperback originals. Books: offset printing. Average print order: 1,000. Average first novel print order: 500. Distributes through Baker & Taylor, Amazon, Bowker.

NEEDS Utopian, political. Needs poetry submission for our newsletter, *Inverted-A Horn*.

HOW TO CONTACT Does not accept unsolicited mss. Query with SASE. Reading period open from January 2 to March 15. Accepts queries by e-mail. Include estimated word count. Responds in 1 month to queries; 3 months to mss. Accepts simultaneous submissions. Sometimes comments on rejected mss.

TERMS Pays in 10 author's copies. Publishes ms 1 year after acceptance. Ms guidelines for SASE.

TIPS "Read our books. Read the *Inverted-A Horn*. We are different. We do not follow industry trends."

ION IMAGINATION PUBLISHING

A division of Ion Imagination Entertainment, Inc., P.O. Box 210943, Nashville TN 37221-0943. **Fax:** (615)646-6276. **E-mail:** ionimagin@aol.com. **Website:** www.flumpa.com. **Contact:** Keith Frickey, editor. Estab. 1994. Small, independent publisher of science-related children's fiction, multimedia and audio products. Publishes hardcover and paperback originals. Average first novel print order: 10,000. Member SPAN and PMA.

⚫ Received the Parents' Choice, National Parenting Centers Seal of Approval, Dr. Toy, Parent Council.

NEEDS Children's/juvenile (adventure, animal, preschool/picture book, science).

HOW TO CONTACT Does not accept unsolicited mss. Query with SASE. Include brief bio, list of publishing credits. Responds in 1 month to queries. Accepts simultaneous submissions. Sometimes comments on rejected queries.

TERMS Pays royalty.

ITALICA PRESS

595 Main St., Suite 605, New York NY 10044-0047. (212)935-4230. **Fax:** (212)838-7812. **E-mail:** inquiries@italicapress.com. **Website:** www.italicapress.com. **Contact:** Ronald G. Musto and Eileen Gardiner, publishers. Estab. 1985. Small, independent publisher of Italian fiction in translation. "First-time translators published. We would like to see translations of Italian writers who are well-known in Italy who are not yet translated for an American audience." Publishes trade paperback originals. Books: 50-60 lb. natural paper; offset printing; illustrations. Average print order: 1,500. Averages 6 total titles, 2 fiction titles/year. Distributes/promotes titles through website. "Italica Press publishes English translations of modern Italian fiction and medieval and Renaissance nonfiction." Publishes trade paperback originals Book catalog and guidelines available online.

NEEDS Translations of 20th, century Italian fiction. Published *Game Plan for a Novel*, by Gianna Manzini; *The Great Bear*, by Ginevra Bompianai; *Sparrow*, by Giovanni Verga.

HOW TO CONTACT Accepts unsolicited mss. Query with SASE. Accepts queries by e-mail, fax. Responds in 1 month to queries; 2 months to mss. Accepts simultaneous submissions, electronic submissions, submissions on disk.

TERMS Pays 7-15% royalty on wholesale price. Pays author's copies. Publishes ms 1 year after acceptance. Responds in 1 month to queries. Responds in 4 months to manuscripts.

TIPS "We are interested in considering a wide variety of medieval and Renaissance topics (not historical fiction), and for modern works we are only interested in translations from Italian fiction by well-known Italian authors." *Only* fiction that has been previously published in Italian. A *brief* call saves a lot of postage. 90% of proposals we receive are completely off base— but we are very interested in things that are right on target. Please send return postage if you want your *only* fiction that has been previously published in Italian. A *brief* call saves a lot of postage.

JOURNEYFORTH

Imprint of BJU Press, 1700 Wade Hampton Blvd., Greenville SC 29614. (864)242-5100, ext. 4350. **Fax:** (864)298-0268. **E-mail:** jb@bju.edu. **Website:** www.journeyforth.com. **Contact:** Nancy Lohr. Estab. 1974. "Small independent publisher of trustworthy novels and biographies for readers pre-school through high school from a conservative Christian perspective, Christian living books, and Bible studies for adults." Publishes paperback originals. Book catalog available free Guidelines available online at www.bjupress.com/books/freelance.php.

NEEDS Adventure (children's/juvenile, young adult), historical (children's/juvenile, young adult), juvenile (animal, easy-to-read, series), mystery (children's/juvenile, young adult), sports (children's/juvenile, young adult), suspense (young adult), western (young adult), young adult (series). "Our fiction is all based on a moral and Christian worldview." Does not want short stories.

HOW TO CONTACT Accepts unsolicited mss. Query with SASE or submit outline, 5 sample chapters or submit complete ms. Include estimated word count, brief bio, list of publishing credits. Send SASE for return of ms or send a disposable ms and SASE for reply only. Responds 3 months to mss. Submit 5 sample chapters, synopsis, SASE.

TERMS Pays royalty. Publishes ms 12-18 months after acceptance. Ms guidelines online. Guidelines at www.

bjupress.com/books/freelance.php. Pays royalty. Responds in 1 month to queries. Responds in 3 months to manuscripts.

TIPS "Study the publisher's guidelines. No picture books and no submissions by e-mail."

✚ ⑤ JUPITER GARDENS PRESS

Jupiter Gardens, LLC, P.O. Box 191, Grimes IA 50111-0191. **E-mail:** submissions@jupitergardens.com. **Website:** www.jupitergardens.com. **Contact:** Mary Wilson, publisher (romance, sf/f, new age). Estab. 2007. Format publishes in trade paperback originals and reprints; electronic originals and reprints Catalog available online at website. Guidelines available online at website.

IMPRINTS Pink Petal Books, Mary Wilson, publisher; Jupiter Storm, Sasha Vivelo, senior editor.

NEEDS "We only publish romance (all sub-genres), science fiction & fantasy & metaphysical fiction. Our science fiction and fantasy covers a wide variety of topics, such as feminist fantasy, or more hard science fiction and fantasy which looks at the human condition. Our young adult imprint, Jupiter Storm, with thought provoking reads that explore the full range of speculative fiction, includes science fiction or fantasy and metaphysical fiction. These readers would enjoy edgy contemporary works. Our romance readers love seeing a couple, no matter the gender, overcome obstacles and grow in order to find true love. Like our readers, we believe that love can come in many forms."

HOW TO CONTACT "To submit your work for consideration, please email submissions@jupitergardens.com with a cover letter detailing your writing experience (if any, we do welcome new authors), and attach in DOC or RTF format, a 2-4 page synopsis, and the first 3 chapters. Our current response time is 2-4 weeks. We accept simultaneous submissions, but ask that you be prepared to allow us our regular response times." Submit proposal package, including synopsis, 3 sample chapters, and promotional plan/market analysis.

TERMS 40% royalty on retail price. Responds in 1 months on proposals, 2 months on mss.

◐ JUST US BOOKS, INC.

356 Glenwood Ave, 3rd Floor, East Orange NJ 07017. (973)672-7701. **Fax:** (973)677-7570. **E-mail:** katura_hudson@justusbooks.com; cheryl_hudson@justusbooks.com. **Website:** www.facebook.com/JustUsBooks. **Contact:** Wade and Cheryl Hudson. Estab. 1988. Small, independent publisher of children's

books that focus on Black history, culture, and experiences (fiction and nonfiction). Publishes hardcover originals, paperback originals, hardcover reprints, and paperback reprints (under its Sankofa Books imprint for previously published titles). Averages 4-8 total titles, 2-4 fiction titles/year. Member, Small Press Association; Children Book Council.

NEEDS Ethnic (African American), young adult (adventure, easy-to-read, historical, mystery/suspense, problem novels, series, sports). Published *Path to my African Eyes*, by Ermila Moodley; *12 Brown Boys*, by Omar Tyree.

HOW TO CONTACT Currently accepting queries for young adult titles only. "We are not considering picture books, poetry, activity books or any other manuscripts at this time." Query with SASE, ms synopsis and pitch letter by mail only. Include brief bio, list of publishing credits. Send SASE for reply. Responds to queries in 10-12 weeks. Accepts simultaneous submissions.

TERMS Pays royalty. Ms guidelines for SASE or on website.

TIPS "We are looking for realistic, contemporary characters; stories and interesting plots that introduce both conflict and resolution. We will consider various themes and story-lines, but before an author submits a query we urge them to become familiar with our books."

KEARNEY STREET BOOKS

P.O. Box 2021, Bellingham WA 98227. (360)738-1355. **E-mail:** garyrmc@mac.com. **Website:** http://kearneystreetbooks.com.

NEEDS Only publishes books about music or musicians. Published *Such a Killing Crime*, Robert Lopresti (mystery); *Tribute to Orpheus* (short story collection).

HOW TO CONTACT Send query letter first. Accepts queries by e-mail. Send disposable copy of ms and SASE for reply only. Responds to queries in 1 week. Accepts unsolicited mss. Responds to mss in 6-10 months. Considers simultaneous submissions, submissions on CD or disk. Never critiques/comments on rejected mss. Does not return rejected mss.

TERMS Sends preproduction galleys to author. Manuscript published 18 months after acceptance. Pays "after expenses, profits split 50/50."

TIPS "We publish very few titles. Nobody makes any money. This is all about the love of good fiction shunned by the corporations."

Ⓐ KENSINGTON PUBLISHING CORP.

119 West 40th St., New York NY 10018. (800)221-2647; (212)407-1500. **E-mail:** kensingtonmarketing@kensingtonbooks.com; jscognamiglio@kensingtonbooks.com. **Website:** www.kensingtonbooks.com. **Contact:** John Scognamiglio, editor-in-chief. Estab. 1975. Full-service trade commercial publisher, all formats. Publishes hardcover and trade paperback originals, mass market paperback originals and reprints. Averages over 500 total titles/year.

NEEDS Book-length fiction and nonfiction for popular audiences. Adult and YA.

HOW TO CONTACT Accepts unsolicited and unagented mss. You may **QUERY ONLY** by e-mail. Do not attach manuscripts or proposals to e-mail queries. An editor will respond if he or she is interested in seeing your material based on your query. Submit to one editor only. Responds in 1 month to queries; 4 months to mss. Accepts simultaneous submissions. John Scognamiglio, Editor-in-Chief of Kensington, Fiction (historical romance, women's contemporary fiction, historical fiction, paranormal romance, urban fantasy, gay fiction and non-fiction, mysteries, suspense, mainstream fiction, young adult fiction, memoirs, erotica); jscognamiglio@kensingtonbooks.com. Michaela Hamilton, Editor-in-Chief of Citadel, Executive Editor of Kensington (nonfiction including popular culture, current events, narrative nonfiction, true crime, business, biography, memoir, law enforcement, military; selected fiction including thrillers, mainstream novels); mhamilton@kensingtonbooks.com. Alicia Condon, Editorial Director of Brava (paranormal and fantasy romance, romantic suspense, historical and contemporary romance, young adult paranormal romance of 80,000—100,000 words); acondon@kensingtonbooks.com. Selena James, executive editor (African American fiction, Dafina Books); Audrey LaFehr, editorial director (women's fiction); Michaela Hamilton, executive editor. See more online at website. See all the editors' and e-mails online at website.

TERMS Advance against royalties based on net sales. Publishes ms 12-24 months after acceptance.

ALLEN A. KNOLL, PUBLISHERS

200 W. Victoria Street, Santa Barbara CA 93101. (805)564-3377. **E-mail:** bookinfo@knollpublishers.com. **Website:** www.knollpublishers.com. **Contact:** Submissions. Estab. 1990. Small independent publisher, publishes a few titles a year. Specializes in "books

for intelligent people who read for fun." Publishes hardcover originals. Books: offset printing; sewn binding. Titles distributed through Ingram, Baker & Taylor. Format publishes in hardcover originals.

NEEDS Fiction published: *They Fall Hard*, by Alistair Boyle (mystery); Bomber Hanson series, by David Champion (mystery); *The Duchess to the Rescue*, by Alexandra Eden (children's fiction); *The Real Sleeper*, by T.R. Gardner II (a love story). Nonfiction. Published: *Lotusland: A Photographic Odyssey* (garden book); *To Die For*, by David Champion (mystery).

HOW TO CONTACT *Does not accept unsolicited mss.*

TERMS Varies.

Ⓐ● ALFRED A. KNOPF

1745 Broadway, 21st Floor, New York NY 10019. **Website:** knopf.knopfdoubleday.com. Estab. 1915. Publishes hardcover and paperback originals.

NEEDS Publishes book-length fiction of literary merit by known or unknown writers. Length: 40,000-150,000 words. Published *Gertrude and Claudius*, by John Updike; *The Emperor of Ocean Park*, by Stephen Carter; *Balzac and the Little Chinese Seamstress*, by Dai Sijie.

HOW TO CONTACT *Agented submissions only.* Query with SASE or submit sample chapter(s).

TERMS Royalties vary. Offers advance. Responds in 2-6 months to queries.

KNOPF PUBLISHING GROUP

Imprint of Random House, 1745 Broadway, New York NY 10019. (212)751-2600. **Website:** www.randomhouse.com/knopf. **Contact:** Senior Editor. Estab. 1915. Division of Random House, Inc. "Throughout history, Knopf has been dedicated to publishing distinguished fiction and nonfiction." Publishes hardcover and paperback originals. "We usually only accept work through an agent, but you may still send a query to our slush pile." Publishes hardcover and paperback originals.

> 🗩 Knopf is a general publisher of quality nonfiction and fiction. "We usually only accept work through an agent, but you may still send a query to our slush pile."

IMPRINTS Alfred A. Knopf; Everyman's Library; Pantheon Books; Schocken Books; Vintage Anchor Publishing (Vintage Books, Anchor Books).

NEEDS Publishes book-length fiction of literary merit by known or unknown writers. Length: 40,000-150,000 words.

HOW TO CONTACT Submit query, 25-page sample, SASE.

Ⓓ L&L DREAMSPELL

P.O. Box 1984, Friendswood TX 77546. **E-mail:** Administrator@lldreamspell.com. **Website:** www.lldreamspell.com. **Contact:** Lisa René Smith, editor (fiction). "L&L Dreamspell is a micro publishing company based in the Houston, Texas area, publishing both fiction and nonfiction. Run by two gusty women, Linda Houle and Lisa René Smith, we believe in making new author's dreams come true! We are a standard royalty paying publisher, and accept submissions for consideration through our website. We want to read outstanding mysteries, romance novels, and anything paranormal. New genres include thriller, horror, and young adult. Check our website for more information. We're still a young company—our nonfiction line was added in 2008. Linda and Lisa encourage all authors to follow their dreams…" Publishes paperback originals, e-books. Debut novel print order: 150. Averages at least 24- to 36 books per year. Member PMA, SPAN. Distributes/promotes titles via Lightningsource, in addition to using a local printer (we also distribute our titles).

NEEDS Adventure, erotica, fantasy, horror, mainstream, mystery/suspense, new age/mystic, romance. "We still have anthologies open for submission. Writers may submit stories per our website's guidelines." Published *The Key*, by Pauline Baird Jones (mainstream romance/sci fi); *Cold Tears*, by John Foxjohn (mystery), voted best mystery in 2007 by preditors and editors readers poll; *Dance on His Grave*, by Sylvia Dickey Smith (mystery); *Murder New York* - style mystery anthology featuring an Agatha Award winning story by Elizabeth Zelvin.

HOW TO CONTACT Query with outline/synopsis and 1 sample chapter. Accepts queries, submissions by e-mail only. Include estimated word count, list of publishing credits. Responds to queries in 2 weeks. Accepts unsolicited mss. Considers simultaneous submissions. Often critiques/comments on rejected mss. Responds to mss in 3 months. Address: L&L Dreamspell 376 West Quarry Road, London, Texas 76854.

TERMS Sends preproduction galleys to author. Ms published 1 year after acceptance. Writer's guidelines on website. Pays royalties min 15%. Book catalogs not available.

TIPS "We do pay attention to trends, but a great manuscript will always find an audience. Please follow our website submission guidelines if you want us to read your work."

ⒶⓄ LAUREL-LEAF

Imprint of Random House Children's Books/Random House, Inc., 1745 Broadway, New York NY 10019. (212)782-9000. **Website:** www.randomhouse.com/teens.

> ⓠ Quality reprint paperback imprint for young adult paperback books. *Does not accept unsolicited mss.*

Ⓓ LEAPFROG PRESS

Box 2110, Teaticket MA 02536. (508)349-1925. **Fax:** (508)349-1180. **E-mail:** leapfrog@leapfrogpress.com; acquisitions@leapfrogpress.com. **Website:** www.leapfrogpress.com. **Contact:** Sarah Murphy, acquisitions editor. Estab. 1996. "We search for beautifully written literary titles and market them aggressively to national trade and library accounts. We also sell film, translation, foreign, and book club rights." Publishes paperback originals. Books: acid-free paper; sewn binding. Average print order: 3,000. First novel print order: 2,000 (average). Member, Publishers Marketing Association, PEN. Distributes titles through Consortium Book Sales and Distribution, St. Paul, MN. Promotes titles through all national review media, bookstore readings, author tours, website, radio shows, chain store promotions, advertisements, book fairs.

> ⓠ *The Devil and Daniel Silverman* by Theodore Rosak was nominated for the American Library Association Stonewall Award and was a San Francisco Chronicle best seller. *The German Money* by Lev Raphael was a Booksense 76 pick.

NEEDS "Genres often blur; look for good writing. We are most interested in works that are quirky, that fall outside of any known genre, and of course well written and finely crafted. We are most interested in literary fiction." Published *The War at Home*, by Nora Eisenberg; *Junebug*, by Maureen McCoy; *Paradise Dance*, by Michael Lee; *The Ghost Trap*, by K. Stephens; and *Billie Girl*, by Vickie Weaver. See website for more recent titles.

HOW TO CONTACT Query by e-mail only. Send letter and first 5 to 10 ms pages within e-mail message. No attachments. Responds in 2-3 weeks to queries by e-mail; 6 months to mss. May consider simultaneous submissions.

TERMS Pays 4-8% royalty on net receipts. Average advance: negotiable. Publishes ms 1-2 years after acceptance.

TIPS "We like anything that is superbly written and genuinely original. We like the idiosyncratic and the peculiar. We rarely publish nonfiction. Send only your best work, and send only completed work that is ready. That means the completed ms has already been through extensive editing and is ready to be judged. We consider submissions from both previously published and unpublished writers. We are uninterested in an impressive author bio if the work is poor; if the work is excellent, the author bio is equally unimportant."

LEAPING DOG PRESS AND ASYLUM ARTS PUBLISHING

P.O. Box 90473, Raleigh NC 27675-0473. (877)570-6873. **Fax:** (877)570-6873. **E-mail:** editor@leapingdogpress.com. **Website:** www.leapingdogpress.com. **Contact:** Jordan Jones, editor & publisher. Member: CLMP, SPAN, and PMA. "Leaping Dog Press and Asylum Arts Press publish accessible, edgy, witty, and challenging contemporary poetry, fiction, and works in translation, with Asylum Arts Press having an additional focus on surrealism and the avant garde."

NEEDS "Please bear in mind that we are a small press that publishes only 4-6 titles a year." Does not want "genre fiction, self help, dog books, etc."

HOW TO CONTACT Query by mail with a cover letter "containing your reasons for considering LPD or AA and your ideas for marketing your title; a proposed table of contents; a bio or CV and a list of publications; two chapters or 20 pages of fiction." Does not accept e-mail or electronic submissions or queries. Include SASE.

Ⓓ LEE & LOW BOOKS

95 Madison Ave., #1205, New York NY 10016. (212)779-4400. **E-mail:** general@leeandlow.com. **Website:** www.leeandlow.com. **Contact:** Louise May, editor-in-chief (multicultural children's fiction/nonfiction). Estab. 1991. "Our goals are to meet a growing need for books that address children of color, and to present literature that all children can identify with. We only consider multicultural children's books. Currently emphasizing material for 5-12 year olds. Sponsors a yearly New Voices Award for first-time picture book authors of color. Contest rules online at website or for SASE." Publishes hardcover originals and trade paperback reprints.

Book catalog available online. Guidelines available online or by written request with SASE.

NEEDS Picture books, young readers: anthology, contemporary, history, multicultural, poetry. Picture book, middle reader: contemporary, history, multicultural, nature/environment, poetry, sports. Average word length: picture books—1,000-1,500 words. Recently published *Gracias~Thanks*, by Pat Mora; *Balarama*, by Ted and Betsy Lewin; *Yasmin's Hammer*, by Ann Malaspina; *Only One Year*, by Andrea Cheng (chapter book). "We do not publish folklore or animal stories."

HOW TO CONTACT Submit complete ms.

TERMS Pays net royalty. Pays authors advances against royalty. Pays illustrators advance against royalty. Photographers paid advance against royalty. Responds in 6 months to mss if interested.

TIPS "Check our website to see the kinds of books we publish. Do not send mss that don't fit our mission."

⊘ LETHE PRESS

118 Heritage Ave., Maple Shade NJ 08052. (609)410-7391. **E-mail:** editor@lethepressbooks.com. **Website:** www.lethepressbooks.com. **Contact:** Steve Berman, publisher. Estab. 2001. "Named after the Greek river of memory and forgetfulness (and pronounced Lee-Thee), Lethe Press is a small press devoted to ideas that are often neglected or forgotten by mainstream, profit-oriented publishers." Distributes/promotes titles. Lethe Books are distributed by Ingram Publications and Bookazine, and are available at all major bookstores, as well as the major online retailers.

NEEDS *Rarely accepts unsolicited mss.* Primarily interested in gay fiction, poetry and nonfiction titles. Has imprint for gay spirituality titles. Also releases work of occult and supernatural, sci-fi, and east asian interests.

HOW TO CONTACT Send query letter. Accepts queries by e-mail.

🌑🌑 ARTHUR A. LEVINE BOOKS

Scholastic, Inc., 557 Broadway, New York NY 10012. (212)343-4436. **Fax:** (212)343-4890. **E-mail:** alevine@scholastic.com; eclement@scholastic.com. **Website:** www.arthuralevinebooks.com. **Contact:** Arthur A. Levine, editorial director; Cheryl Klein, senior editor. Estab. 1996. Imprint of Scholastic, Inc. Publishes hardback and soft cover prints and reprints.

NEEDS "Arthur A. Levine is looking for distinctive literature, for children and young adults, for whatever's extraordinary." Averages 18-20 total titles/year.

TERMS Responds in 1 month to queries; 5 months to mss.

LIQUID SILVER BOOKS

Indianapolis IN **E-mail:** tracey@liquidsilverbooks.com. **Website:** www.liquidsilverbooks.com. **Contact:** Tracey West, acquisitions editor; Terri Schaefer, editorial director. Estab. 1999. Liquid Silver Books is an imprint of Atlantic Bridge Publishing, a royalty paying, full-service ePublisher. Atlantic Bridge has been in business since June 1999. Liquid Silver Books is dedicated to bringing high quality erotic romance to our readers. Liquid Silver Books, Romance's Silver Lining.

> 💬 "We are foremost an ePublisher. We believe the market will continue to grow for eBooks. It is our prime focus. At this time our print publishing is on hiatus. We will update the submission guidelines if we reinstate this aspect of our publishing."

NEEDS NEEDS Contemporary, gay and lesbian, paranormal, supernatural, sci-fi, fantasy, historical, suspense, and western romances. We do not accept literary Erotica submissions.

HOW TO CONTACT E-mail entire ms as an attachment in .RTF format in Arial 12pt. "Include in the body of the email: author bio, your thoughts on ePublishing, a blurb of your book, including title and series title if applicable. Ms must include Pen name, real name, snail mail and email contact information on the first page, top left corner." More writer's guidelines available online at website.

TERMS Responds to mss in 4-6 weeks.

🅐⊘ LITTLE, BROWN AND CO.

Hachette Book Group USA, 237 Park Ave., New York NY 10017. (212)364-1100. **Website:** www.hachettebookgroup.com. Estab. 1837. "One of the country's oldest and most distinguished publishing houses, Little, Brown is committed to publishing fiction of the highest quality and non-fiction of lasting significance, by many of America's finest writers." Publishes hardcover originals and paperback originals and reprints.

> 💬 "Unsolicited manuscripts, submissions, and queries will not be answered. If you are interested in having a manuscript considered for publication, we recommend that you first enlist the services of an established literary agent."

Ⓐ LITTLE, BROWN AND CO. ADULT TRADE BOOKS

237 Park Ave., New York NY 10017. **E-mail:** publicity@littlebrown.com. **Website:** www.hachettebookgroup.com. **Contact:** Michael Pietsch, publisher. Estab. 1837. "The general editorial philosophy for all divisions continues to be broad and flexible, with high quality and the promise of commercial success as always the first considerations." Publishes hardcover originals and paperback originals and reprints. Guidelines available online.

NEEDS Literary, mainstream/contemporary. Published *Cross Country*, by James Patterson; *Outliers*, by Malcolm Gladwell; *The Historian*, by Elizabeth Kostova; *When You Are Engulfed in Flames*, by David Sedaris. Literary, mainstream/contemporary. Published *Cross Country*, by James Patterson; *Outliers*, by Malcolm Gladwell; *The Historian*, by Elizabeth Kostova; *When You Are Engulfed in Flames*, by David Sedaris.

HOW TO CONTACT *Agented submissions only.*

TERMS Pays royalty. Offer advance.

Ⓐ LITTLE, BROWN AND CO. BOOKS FOR YOUNG READERS

Hachette Book Group USA, 237 Park Ave., New York NY 10017. (212)364-1100. **Fax:** (212)364-0925. **E-mail:** pamela.gruber@hbgusa.com. **Website:** www.lb-kids.com; www.lb-teens.com. Estab. 1837. "Little, Brown and Co. Children's Publishing publishes all formats including board books, picture books, middle grade fiction, and nonfiction YA titles. We are looking for strong writing and presentation, but no predetermined topics." *Only interested in solicited agented material.* Fiction: Submit complete ms. Nonfiction: Submit cover letter, previous publications, a proposal, outline and 3 sample chapters. Do not send originals.

NEEDS Picture books: humor, adventure, animal, contemporary, history, multicultural, folktales. Young adults: contemporary, humor, multicultural, suspense/mystery, chick lit. Multicultural needs include "any material by, for and about minorities." Average word length: picture books—1,000; young readers—6,000; middle readers—15,000- 50,000; young adults—50,000 and up.

HOW TO CONTACT *Agented submissions only.*

TERMS Pays authors royalties based on retail price. Pays illustrators and photographers by the project or royalty based on retail price. Sends galleys to authors; dummies to illustrators. Pays negotiable advance. Re-

sponds in 1 month to queries; 2 months to proposals and mss.

TIPS "In order to break into the field, authors and illustrators should research their competition and try to come up with something outstandingly different."

Ⓞ LIVINGSTON PRESS

University of West Alabama, Station 22, Livingston AL 35470. **E-mail:** jwt@uwa.edu. **Website:** www.livingstonpress.uwa.edu. **Contact:** Joe Taylor, director. Estab. 1974. "Small university press specializing in offbeat and/or Southern literature." Publishes hardcover and trade paperback originals. Books: acid free; offset; some illustrations. Average print order: 2,500. First novel print order: 2,500. Plans 5 first novels this year. Averages 10 fiction titles/year. "Livingston Press, as do all literary presses, looks for authorial excellence in style. Currently emphasizing novels. Other than Tartts Contest, we read in June only." Our standing policy is to read over-the-transom, open submission, ONLY in June of every year. We have committed to books until Fall 2011, and we will be reading only Tartts entries until June 2010. Our next Tartts Story Collection Contest closes on December 31, 2010. See Tartts Fiction Award on our website. When we are reading over the transom, we accept only fiction—either story collections or novels. Publishes hardcover and trade paperback originals Book catalog for SASE. Guidelines available online.

Ⓞ Reads mss in March only.

IMPRINTS Swallow's Tale Press.

NEEDS Experimental, literary, short story collections, off-beat or Southern. "We are interested in form and, of course style." Published *The Gin Girl*, by River Jordan (novel); *Pulpwood*, by Scott Ely (stories); *Live Cargo*, by Paul Toutonghi (stories). "We are interested in form and, of course, style."

HOW TO CONTACT Query with SASE. Include estimated word count, brief bio, list of publishing credits. Send SASE for return of ms or send a disposable ms and SASE for reply only. Responds in 1 month to queries; 1 year to mss. Accepts simultaneous submissions. Send only in June and July. We are especially interested in novels and story collections that intertwine in one way or another.

TERMS Pays 10% of 1,500 print run, 150 copies; thereafter pays a mix of royalties and books. Publishes ms 18 months after acceptance. Book catalog for SASE. Ms guidelines online. Pays 150 contributor's copies, after sales of 1,500, standard royalty. Responds in 1 month to queries. Responds in 6 mos. - 1 year to manuscripts.

TIPS "Our readers are interested in literature, often quirky literature that emphasizes form and style. Please visit our website for current needs."

LOOSE ID

P.O. Box 425690, San Francisco CA 94142-5960. **E-mail:** submissions@loose-id.com. **Website:** www.loose-id.com. **Contact:** Treva Harte, editor-in-chief. Estab. 2004. "*Loose Id* is love unleashed. We're taking romance to the edge." Publishes e-books. Distributes/promotes titles. "The company promotes itself through web and print advertising wherever readers of erotic romance may be found, creating a recognizable brand identity as the place to let your id run free and the people who unleash your fantasies. It is currently pursuing licensing agreements for foreign translations, and has a print program of 2 to 5 titles per month."

NEEDS Wants nontraditional erotic romance stories, including gay, lesbian, heroes and heroines, multiculturalism, cross-genre, fantasy, and science fiction, straight contemporary or historical romances.

HOW TO CONTACT Query with outline/synopsis and three sample chapters. Accepts queries by e-mail. Include estimated word count, list of publishing credits, and why your submission is "Love Unleashed." Responds to queries in 1 months. Considers e-mail submissions. "Loose Id is actively acquiring stories from both aspiring and established authors. Before submitting a query or proposal, please read the guidelines on our website. Please don't hesitate to contact us at submissions@ loose-id.com for any information you don't see there."

TERMS Manuscript published within 1 year after acceptance. Writer's guidelines on website. Pays e-book royalties 35%.

◑ LOST HORSE PRESS

105 Lost Horse Lane, Sandpoint ID 83864. (208)255-4410. **Fax:** (208)255-1560. **E-mail:** losthorsepress@mindspring.com. **Website:** www.losthorsepress.org. **Contact:** Christine Holbert, editor. Estab. 1998. Publishes hardcover and paperback originals. Books: 60-70 lb. natural paper; offset printing; b&w illustration. Average print order: 500-2,500. First novel print order: 500. Averages 4 total titles/year. Distributed by Eastern Washington University Press. Publishes hardcover and paperback originals.

NEEDS Literary, regional (Pacific NW), short story collections, poetry.

HOW TO CONTACT "Regrettably, Lost Horse Press is *no longer accepting unsolicited manuscripts for review.* However, we welcome submissions for The Idaho Prize for Poetry, a national competition offering $1,000 prize money plus publication for a book-length manuscript. Please check The Idaho Prize for Poetry submission guidelines for more information."

TERMS Publishes ms 6 months-1 year after acceptance. Please check submission guidelines on website before submitting ms.

◑ LOVE SPELL

Dorchester Publishing, 200 Madison Ave., Suite 2000, New York NY 10016. (212)725-8811. **Fax:** (212)532-1054. **E-mail:** adavis@dorchesterpub.com; submissions@dorchesterpub.com. **Website:** www.dorchesterpub.com. **Contact:** Alissa Davis, editorial assistant. Publishes mass market paperback originals. Book catalog for free online or by calling (800)481-9191. Guidelines available online.

> "Love Spell publishes the many sub-genres of romance: time-travel, paranormal, fantasy, futuristic, romantic suspense, and African-American. Despite the exotic settings, we are still interested in character-driven plots."

NEEDS "Books industry-wide are getting shorter; we're interested in 70,000 - 90,000 words."

HOW TO CONTACT "We are currently acquiring only the following: romance, horror, Westerns, and thrillers. Authors should attach their full ms in a Word or .rtf document, along with a 3- to 7-page synopsis. The body of the e-mail should contain the material of a normal cover letter: contact information, including physical address and phone number; word count (70,000-90,000 words); the genre of the novel; and a brief, tantalizing description of the plot. If by mail: Query with SASE. Submit clips. No material will be returned without SASE."

TERMS Pays royalty on retail price. Pays variable advance. Responds in 6-8 months to mss.

TIPS "The best way to learn to write a Love Spell Romance is by reading several of our recent releases. The best-written stories are usually ones writers feel passionate about—so write from your heart! Also, the market is very tight these days so more than ever we are looking for refreshing, standout original fiction."

$ MARTIN SISTERS PUBLISHING, LLC

P.O. Box 1749, Barbourville KY 40906-1499. **E-mail:** publisher@martinsisterspublishing.com. **Website:** www.martinsisterspublishing.com. **Contact:** Denise Melton, Publisher/Editor (Fiction/non-Fiction); Melissa Newman, Publisher/Editor (Fiction/non-Fiction). Estab. 2011. Firm/imprint publishes trade and mass market paperback originals; electronic originals. Catalog and guidelines available online.

IMPRINTS Ivy House Books — literary/mainstream fiction; rainshower books — christian fiction and non-fiction; Skyvine Books — science fiction/fantasy/paranormal; romance; Martin Sisters Books — non-fiction/short story collections/coffee table books/ cookbooks; Barefoot Books — young adult. Query Ms. Newman or Ms. Melton for all imprints listed at submissions@martinsisterspublishing.com.

NEEDS Adventure, confession, fantasy, historical, humor, juvenile, literary, mainstream, military, mystery, poetry in translation, regional, religious, romance, science fiction, short story collections, spiritual, sports, suspense, war, western, young adult.

HOW TO CONTACT Send query letter only to submissions@martinsisterspublishing.com; publisher@martinsisterspublishing.com.

TERMS Pays 7.5% royalty/max on retail price. No advance offered. Time between acceptance of ms and publication is 6 months. Accepts simultaneous submissions. No SASE returns. Responds in 1 month on queries, 2 months on proposals, 3-6 months on mss. Catalog and guidelines available online.

○😀 MARVEL COMICS

417 5th Ave., New York NY 10016. (212)576-4000. **Fax:** (212)576-8547. **Website:** marvel.com. Publishes hardcover originals and reprints, trade paperback reprints, mass market comic book originals, electronic reprints. Averages 650 total titles/year.

NEEDS Adventure, comic books, fantasy, horror, humor, science fiction, young adult. "Our shared universe needs new heroes and villains; books for younger readers and teens needed."

HOW TO CONTACT "If you are an aspiring comic book artist or writer, we suggest you publish or publicly post your material, continue to create, and if you have the right stuff . . . we'll find you." Please note: Unsolicited writing samples will not be read. *Any unsolicited or solicited writing sample received without a signed Marvel Idea Submission Form will be destroyed unread.*" (Download Marvel Idea Submission Form from website.) Responds only if interested in 3-5 weeks.

TERMS Pays on a per-page work-for-hire basis, which is contracted. Ms guidelines online.

💬 MAVERICK MUSICALS AND PLAYS

89 Bergann Rd., Maleny QLD 4552 Australia. Phone/ **Fax:** (61)(7)5494-4007. **E-mail:** helen@mavmuse.com. **Website:** www.mavmuse.com. Estab. 1978. Guidelines available online.

NEEDS "Looking for two-act musicals and one- and two-act plays. See website for more details."

⊘ MCBOOKS PRESS

ID Booth Building, 520 N. Meadow St., Ithaca NY 14850. (607)272-2114. **Fax:** (607)273-6068. **E-mail:** jackie@mcbooks.com. **Website:** www.mcbooks.com. **Contact:** Jackie Swift, editorial director. Estab. 1979. Small independent publisher. Publishes Julian Stockwin, John Biggins, Colin Sargent, and Douglas W. Jacobson. Publishes trade paperback and hardcover originals and reprints. Averages 8 fiction titles/ year. Distributes titles through Independent Publishers Group. Publishes trade paperback and hardcover originals and reprints. Guidelines available online.

NEEDS "We are looking for a few good novels and are open to almost any genre or style, except romance, inspirational, science fiction, fantasy, and children's. Our main criteria is an exceptionally strong story combined with an author who can show he/she has a good grasp on self-promotion through networking, personal appearances, and tireless internet presence."

HOW TO CONTACT Does not accept unsolicited mss. Submission guidelines available on website. Query with SASE or via e-mail. Include list of publishing credits and a well thought-out marketing plan. Responds in 3 months to queries. Accepts simultaneous submissions. E-mail queries prefered. If querying by mail, include SASE. Send excerpt as RTF file attachment.

TERMS Pays 5-10% royalty on retail price. Average advance: $1,000-5,000. Pays 5-10% royalty on retail price. Responds in 3 months to queries and proposals

TIPS "In the current tough book market, the author's ability to use the internet for self promotion is almost as important as his/her ability to tell a great story really well. Unfortunately, writing ability alone is not enough. Show that you're savvy with personal web sites, blogs, and social networking. And show you nkow who your audience is and how to generate word-of-mouth."

⊘ ⌂ MARGARET K. MCELDERRY BOOKS

Imprint of Simon & Schuster Children's Publishing Division, Simon & Schuster, 1230 Sixth Ave., New York NY 10020. (212)698-7200. **Website:** www.simonsayskids.com. **Contact:** Justin Chanda, vice president; Karen Wojtyla, editorial director; Gretchen Hirsch, associate editor; Emily Fabre, assistant editor. Ann Bobco, executive art director. Estab. 1971. "Margaret K. McElderry Books publishes hardcover and paperback trade books for children from pre-school age through young adult. This list includes picture books, middle grade and teen fiction, poetry, and fantasy. The style and subject matter of the books we publish is almost unlimited. We do not publish textbooks, coloring and activity books, greeting cards, magazines, pamphlets, or religious publications." Guidelines for #10 SASE.

NEEDS We will consider any category. Results depend on the quality of the imagination, the artwork, and the writing. Average word length: picture books—500; young readers—2,000; middle readers—10,000-20,000; young adults—45,000-50,000. *No unsolicited mss.*

HOW TO CONTACT Send query letter with SASE.

TERMS Pays authors royalty based on retail price. Pays illustrator royalty of by the project. Pays photographers by the project. Original artwork returned at job's completion. Offers $5,000-8,000 advance for new authors.

TIPS "Read! The children's book field is competitive. See what's been done and what's out there before submitting. We look for high quality: an originality of ideas, clarity and felicity of expression, a well organized plot, and strong character-driven stories. We're looking for strong, original fiction, especially mysteries and middle grade humor. We are always interested in picture books for the youngest age reader. Study our titles."

◑ MEDALLION PRESS, INC.

1020 N. Cedar Ave., #216, St. Charles IL 60174. 630-513-8316. **E-mail:** submissions@medallionpress.com. **Website:** www.medallionpress.com. **Contact:** Emily Steele, editorial director, emily@medallionpress.com. Estab. 2003. "We are an independent publisher looking for books that are outside of the box. " Publishes trade paperback, hardcover, and e-book originals. Average print order: 5,000.

NEEDS nonfiction, mainstream fiction, historical fiction, mystery, thriller, suspense, romance (historical, time travel, paranormal, hard-boiled mystery), horror (paranormal, survival, serial killer, sci-fi, general), science fiction, fantasy (steampunk, contemporary, epic, historical, paranormal, urban life), literary fiction, young adult fiction, Christian, young adults writing for young adults. Published *Motiv8n' U*, by Staci Boyer (nonfiction, self-help); *The Clockwork Man*, by William Jablonsky (steampunk); *Plum Blossoms in Paris,* by Sarah Hina (mainstream fiction); *The Frenzy Way,* by Greg Lamberson (horror).

HOW TO CONTACT "Minimum word count 80K for adult fiction, 60K for YA, no exceptions." No poetry, anthologies, erotica. Submit first 3 consecutive chapters and a synopsis. Accepts queries only by e-mail to submissions@medallionpress.com. Include estimated word count, brief bio, list of publishing credits. Responds in 4-6 months to mss. Accepts simultaneous submissions. Sometimes comments on rejected mss.

TERMS Offers advance. Publishes ms 1-2 years after acceptance. Ms guidelines online.

TIPS "We are not affected by trends. We are simply looking for well crafted, original, grammatically correct works of fiction. Please visit our website at http://medallionpress.com/guidlines/index.html for the most current guidelines prior to submitting anything to us."

MERIWETHER PUBLISHING LTD.

885 Elkton Dr., Colorado Springs CO 80907. (719)594-9916. **Fax:** (719)594-9916. **E-mail:** editor@meriwether.com. **Website:** www.meriwetherpublishing.com. **Contact:** Ted Zapel; Rhonda Wray. Estab. 1969. "Our niche is drama. Our books cover a wide variety of theatre subjects from play anthologies to theatrecraft. We publish books of monologs, duologs, short one-act plays, scenes for students, acting textbooks, how-to speech and theatre textbooks, improvisation and theatre games. Our Christian books cover worship on such topics as clown ministry, storytelling, banner-making, drama ministry, children's worship and more. We also publish anthologies of Christian sketches. We do not publish works of fiction or devotionals."

NEEDS Middle readers, young adults: anthology, contemporary, humor, religion. "We publish plays, not prose-fiction. Our emphasis is comedy plays instead of educational themes."

TERMS Pays authors royalty of 10% based on retail or wholesale price. Responds to queries in 3 weeks, mss in 2 months or less.

TIPS "We are currently interested in finding unique treatments for theater arts subjects: scene books, how-to books, musical comedy scripts, monologs and short comedy plays for teens."

◯ MID-LIST PRESS

6524 Brownlee Drive, Nashville TN 37205. (612)822-3733. **Fax:** (612)823-8387. **E-mail:** guide@midlist.org. **Website:** www.midlist.org. **Contact:** Acquisitions director. Estab. 1989. Estab. 1989. "We are a nonprofit literary press dedicated to the survival of the mid-list, those quality titles that are being neglected by the larger commercial houses. Our focus is on new and emerging writers." Publishes hardcover and trade paperback originals. Mid-List publishes only book-length works. Fiction and nonfiction manuscripts must be at least 50,000 words in length. Poetry collections must be at least 60 pages in length (single-spaced, each poem beginning a new page). Mid-List Press does not publish children's books. Books: acid-free paper; offset printing; perfect or Smyth-sewn binding. Average print order: 2,000. Averages 4 total titles, 1 fiction titles/year. Distributes titles through Baker & Taylor, Midwest Library Service, Brodart, Follett and Emery Pratt. Promotes titles through publicity, direct mail, catalogs, author's events and review and awards.

NEEDS General fiction. Published *The Woman Who Never Cooked*, by Mary L. Tabor; *The Echo of Sand*, by Gail Chehab (first novel).

HOW TO CONTACT Accepts unsolicited mss. Agented fiction less than10%. Do not include SASE. No email or fax queries. Responds only if interested by telephone or e-mail. Accepts simultaneous submissions. Ms guidelines online.

TERMS Pays 40-50% royalty on net receipts. Average advance: $1,000. Publishes ms 12-18 months after acceptance.

TIPS "Write first for guidelines or visit our website before submitting. And take the time to read some of the titles we've published."

◑ MILKWEED EDITIONS

1011 Washington Ave. S., Suite 300, Minneapolis MN 55415. (612)332-3192. **Fax:** (612)215-2550. **E-mail:** submissions@milkweed.org. **Website:** www.milk-weed.org. Estab. 1979. "Milkweed Editions publishes with the intention of making a humane impact on society, in the belief that literature is a transformative art uniquely able to convey the essential experiences of the human heart and spirit. To that end, Milkweed Editions publishes distinctive voices of literary merit in handsomely designed, visually dynamic books, exploring the ethical, cultural, and esthetic issues that free societies need continually to address." Publishes hardcover, trade paperback, and electronic originals; trade paperback and electronic reprints. Book catalog available online at website. Guidelines available online at website http://www.milkweed.org/content/blogcategory/.

◗ "Please consider our previous publications when considering submissions."

NEEDS Novels for adults and for readers 8-13. High literary quality. For adult readers: literary fiction, nonfiction, poetry, essays. Middle readers: adventure, contemporary, fantasy, multicultural, nature/environment, suspense/mystery. Does not want to see folktales, health, hi-lo, picture books, poetry, religion, romance, sports. Average length: middle readers—90-200 pages. Recently published *Perfect*, by Natasha Friend (contemporary); *The Linden Tree*, by Ellie Mathews (contemporary); *The Cat*, by Jutta Richter (contemporary/translation). No romance, mysteries, science fiction.

HOW TO CONTACT Query with SASE, submit completed ms.

TERMS Pays authors variable royalty based on retail price. Offers advance against royalties. Pays varied advance from $500-10,000. Responds in 6 months to queries, proposals, and mss.

TIPS "We are looking for excellent writing with the intent of making a humane impact on society. Please read submission guidelines before submitting and acquaint yourself with our books in terms of style and quality before submitting. Many factors influence our selection process, so don't get discouraged. Nonfiction is focused on literary writing about the natural world, including living well in urban environments."

MILKWEED FOR YOUNG READERS

1011 Washington Ave. S, Open Book, Suite 300, Minneapolis MN 55415. **Website:** www.milkweed.org. **Contact:** Daniel Slager, publisher. Estab. 1984. "Milkweed for Young Readers are works that embody humane values and contribute to cultural understanding." Publishes hardcover and trade paperback originals. Averages 1-2 total titles/year. Distributes titles through Publishers Group West. Promotes titles individually through print advertising, website and author tours.

HOW TO CONTACT Authors can now submit and manage their submissions through Milkweed's Submission Manager. If you have any problems, contact us through e-mail. If you send by postal mail, please address submissions to: Fiction Reader (or Nonfiction, Poetry, Children's, as appropriate).

○$ MONDIAL

203 W. 107th St., Suite 6C, New York NY 10025. (212)851-3252. **Fax:** (208)361-2863. **E-mail:** contact@mondialbooks.com. **Website:** www.mondialbooks.com; www.librejo.com. **Contact:** Andrew Moore, editor. Estab. 1996. Publishes trade paperback originals and reprints Guidelines available online

NEEDS Adventure, erotica, ethnic, gay, historical, literary, mainstream, multicultural, mystery, poetry, romance, short, translation. Published *Two People*, by David Windham; *Bitterness*, by Malama Katulwende; *Winter Ridge: A Love Story*, by Bruce Kellner.

HOW TO CONTACT Query through online submission form. Responds to queries in 3 months.

TERMS Pays 10% royalty of the selling price of each book copy sold. Pays 10% royalty on wholesale price.

○◐ MONSOON BOOKS

52 Telok Blangah Road, 098829, 139527 Singapore. **E-mail:** submissions@monsoonbooks.com.sg. **Website:** www.monsoonbooks.com.sg. **Contact:** Philip Tathum, publisher (fiction). Estab. 2002. "Monsoon Books is an independent publisher of fiction and nonfiction with Asian themes, based in Singapore with worldwide distribution." Unsolicited manuscripts are welcomed from published and unpublished authors alike. Publishes paperback originals, paperback reprints. Books: Mungken 80 gram paper; offset printing; threadsewn binding. Average print order: 3,000. First novel print order: 3,000. **Published 7 new writers last year.** Plans 10 first novels this year. Averages 20 total titles/year; 12 fiction titles/year. Distributes titles through Worldwide Distribution and promotes through Freelance Publicists for USA and Asia.

NEEDS Erotica, ethnic/multicultural, family saga, gay, historical, horror (supernatural), humor satire, literary, mainstream, military/war, mystery/suspense (police procedural, private eye/hard-boiled), regional (Asia), thriller/espionage, translations, young adult (romance). Special interests: Southeast Asia. Published *Rouge Raider*, by Nigel Barley (historical fiction); *Straights and Narrow*, by Grace McClurg (thriller); *Private Dancer*, by Stephen Leather (general fiction/international relationships). Not accepting any poetry.

HOW TO CONTACT Query with outline/synopsis and submit complete ms with cover letter. Accepts queries by snail mail, fax, and e-mail (submissions@monsoonbooks.com.sg. Please include estimated word count, brief bio, list of publishing credits, and list of three comparative titles. Send hard copy submissions to: Monsoon Books Pte Ltd, 71 Ayer Rajah Crescent #01-01, Mediapolis Phase, Singapore 139951. We are not able to return hard copy manuscripts. We do not encourage hand deliveries. Agented fiction 20%. Responds in 8 weeks to your submissions. If you do not hear from us by then, e-mail us. Accepts simultaneous submissions, submissions on CD or disk. Rarely comments on rejected manuscripts. Monsoon Books regularly works with literary agents from the UK and Australia (such as David Higham Associates in London and Cameron's Management in Sydney) and we are particularly keen to hear from agents with manuscripts set in Southeast or North Asia as well as manuscripts written by authors from this region.

TERMS Pays 7-10% royalty. Advance is negotiable. Publishes ms 6-12 months after acceptance. Guidelines online.

TIPS "Due to the difficulty of getting published in New York and London, Monsoon represents a more viable option and is attracting new writers from USA, UK and Australia."

○◐ MOODY PUBLISHERS

820 N. LaSalle Blvd., Chicago IL 60610. **E-mail:** pressinfo@moody.edu. **E-mail:** acquisitions@moody.edu. **Website:** www.moodypublishers.org. Estab. 1894. Guidelines for SASE or on website.

○ Moody Publishers does not accept unsolicited mss in any category unless submitted via:— a professional literary agent— an author who has published with us— an associate from a Moody Bible Institute ministry— personal contact at a writers conference.

NEEDS Small, evangelical Christian publisher. "We publish fiction that reflects and supports our evangelical worldview and mission." Publishes hardcover, trade and mass market paperback originals. Averages 70 total titles, 10-12 fiction titles/year. Member, CBA. Distributes and promotes titles through sales reps, print advertising, promotional events, Internet, etc. NEEDS Contemporary, historical, literary, mystery, suspense, science fiction. Recently published *My Hands Came Away Red*, by Lisa McKay (suspense novel); *Feeling for Bones*, by Bethany Pierce (contemporary/literary).

TERMS Pays variable royalty. Average advance: $1,000-10,000.

TIPS "Get to know Moody Publishers and understand what kinds of books we publish. We will decline all submissions that do not support our evangelical Christian beliefs and mission."

✚ ● MOON SHADOW PRESS

Wakestone Press, 200 Brook Hollow Rd., Nashville TN 37205. (615)739-6428. **Website:** http://www.wakestonepress.com. **Contact:** Frank Daniels III, editor (youth fiction). Estab. 2010. "Moon Shadow Press, an imprint of Wakestone Press, was founded on the belief that neither authors nor stories get proper attention. Wakestone looks for authors who, with the right team and support, can break out of the crowded, chaotic catalog of books to get their stories widely read. We love the current confusing pace of the publishing business with its challenges in distirbution, technology, marketing and consumption. We think that these market challenges are an exciting time to bring both new and old stories to readers in a way of forms and formats. Our experience in a wide range of publishing ventures has led us to understand that the media world is an either/and world, where readers want to have both short- and long-form stories, in print and digital formats, in multi-media and one-dimensional media. Our goal is to enable authors to tell and sell their stories and make them a part of our culture. Currently Moon Shadow Press is working on publishing youth titles. Format publishes in hardcover and paperback originals; e-books. Catalogs available online at website. Send SASE for writer's guidelines.

TERMS Pays 7.5-15% royalty. Pays $2,000 advance (negotiable) Responds to queries in 4 weeks; mss in 2 months.

TIPS "Be honest, be creative, be interesting."

☺ NBM PUBLISHING

40 Exchange Pl., Suite 1308, New York NY 10005. **E-mail:** nbmgn@nbmpub.com. **Website:** nbmpub.com. **Contact:** Terry Nantier, editor/art director. Es-

tab. 1976. "One of the best regarded quality graphic novel publishers. Our catalog is determined by what will appeal to a wide audience of readers." Publishes hardcover originals, paperback originals. Format: offset printing; perfect binding. Average print order: 3,000-4,000; average debut writer's print order: 2,000. Publishes 1-2 debut writers/year. Publishes 30 titles/year. Member: PMA, CBC. Distributed/promoted "ourselves." Imprints: ComicsLit (literary comics), Eurotica (erotic comics). Publishes graphic novels for an audience of 18-34 year olds. Types of books include fiction, fantasy, mystery, science fiction, horror and social parodies. Circ. 5,000-10,000.

NEEDS Literary fiction mostly, children's/juvenile (especially fairy tales, classics), creative nonfiction (especially true crime), erotica, ethnic/multicultural, humor (satire), manga, mystery/suspense, translations, young adult/teen. Does not want superhero or overly violent comics.

HOW TO CONTACT Prefers submissions from writer-artists, creative teams. Send a 1-page synopsis of story along with a few pages of comics (copies, NOT originals) and a SASE. Attends San Diego Comicon. Agented submissions: 2%. Responds to queries in 1 week; to ms/art packages in 3-4 weeks. Sometimes comments on rejected manuscripts.

TERMS Royalties and advance negotiable. Publishes ms 6 months to 1 year after acceptance. Writer's guidelines on website. Artist's guidelines on website. Book catalog free upon request.

✚ NEW ISSUES POETRY & PROSE

Western Michigan University, 1903 W. Michigan Ave., Kalamazoo MI 49008-5463. (269)387-8185. **Fax:** (269)387-2562. **E-mail:** new-issues@wmich.edu. **Website:** wmich.edu/newissues. **Contact:** Managing Editor. Estab. 1996. Publishes hardcover originals and trade paperback originals. Averages 8 titles/year. Has recently published*Vivisect*, by Lisa Lewis; *Pima Road Notebook*, by Keith Ekiss; and *Tocqueville*, by Khaled Mattawa. Guidelines available online, by e-mail, or by SASE.

NEEDS Literary, poetry, translations.

HOW TO CONTACT Query first. All unsolicited mss returned unopened. 50% of books published are by first time authors. Agented submissions: less than 5%. Responds to mss in 6 months.

TERMS Manuscript published 18 months after acceptance. Accepts simultaneous submissions. Writer's guidelines by SASE, e-mail, or online.

⊕⊜⑤ NEW LIBRI PRESS

4230 95th Ave. SE, Mercer Island WA 98040. **E-mail:** stasa@newlibri.com. **E-mail:** query@newlibri.com. **Website:** http://www.newlibri.com. **Contact:** Michael Muller, editor (nonfiction and foreign writers); Stanislav Fritz (literary). Estab. 2011. Publishes hardcover, trade paperback, mass market paperback, electronic original, electronic reprints. Catalog not available yet.

NEEDS "Open to most ideas right now; this will change as we mature as a press." As a new press, we are more open than most and time will probably shape the direction. That said, trite as it is, we want good writing that is fun to read. While we currently are not looking for some sub-genres, if it is well writeen and a bit off the beaten path, submit to us. We are ebook friendly, which means some fiction may be less likely to currently sell(e.g. picture books would work only on an iPad or Color Nook as of this writing)."

HOW TO CONTACT Submit proposal package, including snyopsis, 5 sample chapters; submit completed ms.

TERMS Pays 20-35% royalty on wholesale price. No advance. Responds in 1 month on queries and mss; 2 months on proposals.

TIPS "Our audience is someone who is comfortable reading an ebook,or someone who is tired of the recycled authors of mainstream publishing, but still wants a good, relatively fast, reading experience. The industry is changing, while we accept for the traditional model, we are searching for writings who are interested in sharing the risk and controlling their own destiny. We embrace writers with no agent."

◐◑ NEW VICTORIA PUBLISHERS

P.O. Box 13173, Chicago IL 60613. (773)793-2244. **E-mail:** newvictoriapub@att.net. **E-mail:** queries@newvictoria.com. **Website:** www.newvictoria.com. **Contact:** Patricia Feuerhaken, president. Estab. 1976. "Publishes mostly lesbian fiction—strong female protagonists. Most well known for Stoner McTavish mystery series." Distributes titles through Amazon Books, Bella books, Bulldog Books (Sydney, Australia), and Women and Children First Books (Chicago). Promotes titles "mostly through lesbian feminist media." Publishes trade paperback originals. Catalog free on request; for #10 SASE; or online at website. Guidelines free on request; for #10 SASE; or online.

○ *Mommy Deadest*, by Jean Marcy, won the Lambda Literary Award for Mystery. *Mom-*

my Deadest, by Jean Marcy, won the Lambda Literary Award for Mystery.

NEEDS Lesbian, feminist fiction including adventure, erotica, fantasy, historical, humor, mystery (amateur sleuth), or science fiction. "Looking for strong feminist, well drawn characters, with a strong plot and action. We will consider any original, well written piece that appeals to the lesbian/feminist audience." Publishes anthologies or special editions. We advise you to look through our catalog or visit our website to see our past editorial decisions as well as what we are currently marketing. Our books average 80-100,000 words, or 200-220 single-spaced pages.

HOW TO CONTACT Accepts unsolicited mss, but prefers query first. Submit outline, synopsis, and sample chapters (50 pages). No queries by e-mail or fax; please send SASE or IRC. No simultaneous submissions.

TERMS Pays 10% royalty.

◐⊙ NORTIA PRESS

27525 Puerta Real, Ste. 100-467, Mission Viejo CA 92701. **E-mail:** acquisitions@nortiapress.com. **Website:** www.NortiaPress.com. Estab. 2009. Publishes trade paperback and electronic originals. Catalog and guidelines available for SASE with first-class stamps

NEEDS "We focus mainly on literary and historical fiction, but are open to other genres. No vampire stories, science fiction, or erotica, please."

HOW TO CONTACT "Submit a brief e-mail query. Please include a short bio, approximate word count of book, and expected date of completion (fiction titles should be completed before sending a query). All unsolicited snail mail will be discarded without review. We specialize in working with experienced authors who seek a more collaborative and fulfilling relationship with their publisher. As such, we are less likely to accept pitches form first-time authors, no matter how good the idea. As with any pitch, please make your e-mail very brief and to the point, so the reader is not forced to skim it. Always include some biographic information. Your life is interesting."

TERMS Pays negotiable royalties on wholesale price. Responds in 1 month to queries; months to proposals.

⊘ W.W. NORTON CO., INC.

500 Fifth Ave., New York NY 10110. **Fax:** (212)869-0856. **E-mail:** manuscripts@wwnorton.com. **Website:** www.wwnorton.com. Estab. 1923. Ms guidelines online.

NEEDS Literary, poetry, poetry in translation, religious. High-qulity literary fiction. Published *Ship*

Fever, by Andrea Barrett; *Oyster* by Jannette Turner Hospital; *Power* by Linda Hogan.

HOW TO CONTACT *Does not accept unagented submissions or unsolicited mss.* If you would like to submit your proposal (6 pages or less) by e-mail, paste the text of your query letter and/or sample chapter into the body of the e-mail message. Do not send attachments.

TERMS Pays royalty. Pays advance. Responds to queries in 2 months.

OAK TREE PRESS

140 E. Palmer, Taylorville IL 62568. (217)824-6500. **E-mail:** oaktreepub@aol.com. **E-mail:** queryotp@aol.com. **Website:** www.oaktreebooks.com. **Contact:** Billie Johnson, publisher (mysteries, romance, nonfiction); Sarah Wasson, acquisitions editor (all); Barbara Hoffman, senior editor (children's, young adult, educational). Estab. 1998. "Oak Tree Press is an independent publisher that celebrates writers, and is dedicated to the many great unknowns who are just waiting for the opportunity to break into print. We're looking for mainstream, genre fiction, narrative nonfiction, how-to. Sponsors 3 contests annually: Dark Oak Mystery, Timeless Love Romance and CopTales for true crime and other stories of law enforcement professionals." Publishes trade paperback and hardcover books. Catalog and guidelines available online.

"I am always on the lookout for good mysteries, ones that engage quickly. I definitely want to add to our Timeless Love list. I am also looking at a lot of nonfiction, especially in the "how-to" category. We are one of a few publishers who will consider memoirs, especially memoirs of folks who are not famous, and this is because I enjoy reading them myself. In addition, plans are in progress to launch a political/current affairs imprint, and I am actively looking for titles to build this list. Then, of course, there is always that "special something" book that you can't quite describe, but you know it when you see it."

NEEDS Adventure, confession, ethnic, fantasy (romance), feminist, humor, mainstream/contemporary, mystery (amateur sleuth, cozy, police procedural, private eye/hard-boiled), new age/mystic, picture books, romance (contemporary, futuristic/time travel, romantic suspense), suspense, thriller/espionage, young adult (adventure, mystery/suspense, romance). Em-

phasis on mystery and romance novels. "No science fiction or fantasy novels, or stories set far into the future. Next, novels substantially longer than our stated word count are not considered, regardless of genre. We look for manuscripts of 70-90,000 words. If the story really charms us, we will bend some on either end of the range. No right-wing political or racist agenda, gratuitous sex or violence, especially against women, or depict harm of animals."

HOW TO CONTACT Does not accept or return unsolicited mss. Query with SASE. Accepts queries by e-mail. Include estimated word count, brief bio, list of publishing credits, brief description of ms. Send SASE for return of ms or send a disposable ms and SASE for reply only.

TERMS Royalties based on sales. No advance. Responds in 4-6 weeks.

OBRAKE BOOKS

Obrake Canada, Inc., 3401 Dufferin Street, P.O. Box 27538, Toronto, ON M6A3B8 Canada. **E-mail:** editors@obrake.com. **Website:** www.obrake.com. **Contact:** Echez Godoy, acquisitions editor (fiction-suspense, thriller, multicultural, science fiction, literary, romance, short story collection, mystery, ethnic, African based novels, African American characters and interest). Estab. 2006. "We're a small independent publisher. We publish mainly thriller, suspense, romance, mystery, multicutural, and ethnic novels and short story collections." Average print order: 1,500. Debut novel print order: 1,500. **Published 1 new writer(s) last year.** Plans 3 debut novels this year. Averages 10 total titles/year; 7 fiction titles/year. Member Independent Publishers Association PMA (USA), Canadian Booksellers Association (CBA), Book Promoters Association of Canada (BPAC). Publishes hardcover and paperback originals, paperback reprints.

NEEDS Looking for adventure, children's/juvenile (adventure, fantasy, historical, mystery), comics/graphic novels, erotica, ethnic/multicultural, feminist, gay, historical (general), horror (psychological, supernatural), lesbian, literary, mainstream, mystery/suspense, psychic/supernatural, regional, religious (mystery/suspense, thriller, romance), romance (contemporary, historical, romantic suspense), short story collections, thriller/espionage, young adult/teen (adventure, fantasy/science fiction, historical, horror, romance).

HOW TO CONTACT Send query letter. Query with outline/synopsis and 3 sample chapters, 50 pages max. Accepts queries by snail mail, e-mail. Include estimated word count, brief bio. Send SASE or IRC for return of ms or disposable copy of ms and SASE/IRC for reply only. Agented fiction: 5%. Responds to queries in 3-6 weeks. Accepts unsolicited mss. Considers simultaneous submissions, submissions on CD or disk. Rarely critiques/comments on rejected mss. Responds to mss in 3-6 months.

TIPS "Visit our website and follow our submission guidelines."

OCEANVIEW PUBLISHING

595 Bay Isles Rd., Suite 120-G, Longboat Key FL 34228. **E-mail:** submissions@oceanviewpub.com. **Website:** www.oceanviewpub.com. **Contact:** Robert Gussin, CEO. Estab. 2006. "Independent publisher of nonfiction and fiction, with primary interest in original mystery, thriller and suspense titles. Accepts new and established writers." Publishes hardcover and electronic originals. Catalog and guidelines available online.

NEEDS Accepting adult mss with a primary interest in the mystery, thriller and suspense genres—from new & established writers. No children's or YA literature, poetry, cookbooks, technical manuals or short stories.

HOW TO CONTACT Within body of e-mail only, include author's name and brief bio (Indicate if this is an agent submission), ms title and word count, author's mailing address, phone number and e-mail address. Attached to the e-mail should be the following: A synopsis of 750 words or fewer. The first 30 pages of the ms. Please note that we accept only Word documents as attachments to the submission e-mail. Do not send query letters or proposals.

TERMS Responds in 3 months on mss.

ONSTAGE PUBLISHING

190 Lime Quarry Rd., Suite 106-J, Madison AL 35758-8962. (256)461-0661. **E-mail:** onstage123@knology.net. **Website:** www.onstagepublishing.com. **Contact:** Dianne Hamilton, senior editor. Estab. 1999. At this time, we only produce fiction books for ages 8-18. We will not do anthologies of any kind. Query first for nonfiction projects as nonfiction projects must spark our interest. Now accepting e-mail queries and submissions. For submissions: Put the first 3 chapters in the body of the e-mail. Do not use attachments! We will no longer return any mss. Only an SASE envelope is needed. Send complete ms if under 20,000 words, otherwise send synopsis and first 3 chapters.

To everyone who has submitted a ms, we are currently about 6 months behind. We should get back on track eventually. Please feel free to submit your ms to other houses. OnStage Publishing understands that authors work very hard to produce the finished ms and we do not have to have exclusive submission rights. Please let us know if you sell your ms. Meanwhile, keep writing and we'll keep reading for our next acquisitions.

NEEDS Middle readers: adventure, contemporary, fantasy, history, nature/environment, science fiction, suspense/mystery. Young adults: adventure, contemporary, fantasy, history, humor, science fiction, suspense/mystery. Average word length: chapter books—4,000-6,000 words; middle readers—5,000 words and up; young adults—25,000 and up. Recently published *China Clipper* by Jamie Dodson (an adventure for boys ages 12+); *Huntsville, 1892: Clara* (a chapter book for grades 3-5). "We do not produce picture books."

TERMS Pays authors/illustrators/photographers advance plus royalties.

TIPS "Study our titles and get a sense of the kind of books we publish, so that you know whether your project is likely to be right for us."

ORCA BOOK PUBLISHERS

P.O. Box 5626, Stn. B, Victoria BC V8R 6S4 Canada. **Fax:** (877)408-1551. **E-mail:** orca@orcabook.com. **Website:** www.orcabook.com. **Contact:** Christi Howes, editor (picture books); Sarah Harvey, editor (young readers); Andrew Wooldridge, editor (juvenile and teen fiction); Bob Tyrrell, publisher (YA, teen). Estab. 1984. Publishes hardcover and trade paperback originals, and mass market paperback originals and reprints. Book catalog for 8½x11 SASE. Guidelines available online.

Only publishes Canadian authors.

NEEDS Picture books: animals, contemporary, history, nature/environment. Middle readers: contemporary, history, fantasy, nature/environment, problem novels, graphic novels. Young adults: adventure, contemporary, hi-lo (Orca Soundings), history, multicultural, nature/environment, problem novels, suspense/mystery, graphic novels. Average word length: picture books—500-1,500; middle readers—20,000-35,000; young adult—25,000-45,000; Orca Soundings—13,000-15,000; Orca Currents—13,000-15,000. Published *Tall in the Saddle*, by Anne Carter, illustrated by David McPhail (ages 4-8, picture book); *Me and Mr. Mah*, by Andrea Spalding, illustrated by Janet Wilson (ages 5 and up, picture book); *Alone at Ninety Foot*, by Katherine Holubitsky (young adult). No romance, science fiction.

HOW TO CONTACT Query with SASE. Submit proposal package, outline, clips, 2-5 sample chapters, SASE.

TERMS Pays 10% royalty. Responds in 1 month to queries; 2 months to proposals and mss.

TIPS "Our audience is students in grades K-12. Know our books, and know the market."

ORCHARD BOOKS

557 Broadway, New York NY 10012. **E-mail:** mcroland@scholastic.com. **Website:** www.scholastic.com. **Contact:** Ken Geist, vice president/editorial director; David Saylor, vice president/creative director.

> *Orchard is not accepting unsolicited manuscripts.*

NEEDS All levels: animal, contemporary, history, humor, multicultural, poetry. Recently published *Bulldog's Big Day*, by Kate McMullan and Pascal Lemaitre; *Story County: Here We Come!*, by Derek Anderson; *Robin Hood and the Golden Arrow*, by Robert San Souci and E.B. Lewis; *Eight Days*, by Edwidge Danticat and Alix Delinois; *If You're a Monster and You Know It*, by Rebecca Emberley and Ed Emberley; *One Drowsy Dragon*, by Ethan Long; *Max Spaniel: Funny Lunch*, by David Catrow; *Firehouse!*, by Mark Teague; *Farm*, by Elisha Cooper, *Princess Pigtoria and the Pea*, by Pamela Duncan Edwards and Henry Cole; *While the World Is Sleeping*, by Pamela Duncan Edwards and Daniel Kirk; *One More Hug for Madison*, by Caroline Jayne Church.

TERMS Most commonly offers an advance against list royalties.

TIPS "Read some of our books to determine first whether your manuscript is suited to our list."

OUTRIDER PRESS, INC.

2036 North Winds Dr., Dyer IN 46311. (219)322-7270. **Fax:** (219)322-7085. **E-mail:** outriderpress@sbcglobal.net. **Website:** www.outriderpress.com. **Contact:** Whitney Scott, editor. Estab. 1988. Publishes trade paperback originals. Guidelines available online.

> Accepts unsolicited mss. Query with SASE. Accepts queries by mail. Include estimat-

ed word count, brief bio, list of publishing credits. Accepts simultaneous submissions, electronic submissions, submissions on disk. Sometimes comments on rejected mss. In affiliation with Tallgrass Writers Guild, publishes an annual anthology with cash prizes. Anthology theme for 2012 is: "'Deep waters: rivers, lakes and seas.' As always, broadly interpreted with a variety of historic/geographic/psychological settings welcomed." Pays honorarium. Ms guidelines for SASE. Was a *Small Press Review* "Pick" for 2000. Sponsors an anthology competition for short stories, poetry, and creative nonfiction.

NEEDS Ethnic, experimental, family saga, fantasy (space fantasy, sword and sorcery), feminist, gay/lesbian, historical, horror (psychological, supernatural), humor, lesbian, literary, mainstream/contemporary, mystery (amateur sleuth, cozy, police procedural, private eye/hard-boiled), new age/mystic, psychic/supernatural, romance (contemporary, futuristic/time travel, gothic, historical, regency period, romantic suspense), science fiction (soft/sociological), short story collections, thriller/espionage, western (frontier saga, traditional). Published *Telling Time*, by Cherie Caswell Dost; *If Ever I Cease to Love*, by Robert Klein Engler; *62000 Reasons*, by Paul Miller; *Aquarium Octopus*, by Claudia Van Gerven; and *Heat*, by Deborah Thompson.

HOW TO CONTACT Query with SASE.

TERMS Pays honorarium. Responds in 6 weeks to queries; 4 months to proposals and mss.

TIPS "It's always best to familiarize yourself with our publications. We're especially fond of humor/irony."

PANTHEON BOOKS

Random House, Inc., 1745 Broadway, 3rd Floor, New York NY 10019. **E-mail:** pantheonpublicity@randomhouse.com. **Website:** www.pantheonbooks.com. Estab. 1942. Publishes hardcover and trade paperback originals and trade paperback reprints.

> Pantheon Books publishes both Western and non-Western authors of literary fiction and important nonfiction. "We only accept mss submitted by an agent. You may still send a 20-50 page sample and a SASE to our slushpile. Allow 2-6 months for a response."

HOW TO CONTACT *Does not accept unsolicited mss.* Send SASE or IRC. No simultaneous submissions.

PAYCOCK PRESS

3819 N. 13th St., Arlington VA 22201. (703)525-9296. **E-mail:** hedgehog2@erols.com. **Website:** www.gargoylemagazine.com. **Contact:** Lucinda Ebersole and Richard Peabody. Estab. 1976. "Too academic for underground, too outlaw for the academic world. We tend to be edgy and look for ultra-literary work." Publishes paperback originals. Books: POD printing. Average print order: 500. Averages 1 total title/year. Member CLMP. Distributes through Amazon and website.

NEEDS Wants: experimental, literary, short story collections.

HOW TO CONTACT Accepts unsolicited mss. Accepts queries by e-mail. Include brief bio. Send SASE for return of ms or send a disposable ms and SASE for reply only.

TERMS Responds to queries in 1 month; mss in 4 months.

TIPS "Check out our website. Two of our favorite writers are Paul Bowles and Jeanette Winterson."

PEACHTREE CHILDREN'S BOOKS

Peachtree Publishers, Ltd., 1700 Chattahoochee Ave., Atlanta GA 30318-2112. (404)876-8761. **Fax:** (404)875-2578. **E-mail:** hello@peachtree-online.com. **Website:** www.peachtree-online.com. **Contact:** Helen Harriss, submissions editor. "We publish a broad range of subjects and perspectives, with emphasis on innovative plots and strong writing." Publishes hardcover and trade paperback originals. Book catalog for 6 first-class stamps. Guidelines available online.

IMPRINTS Freestone; Peachtree Jr.

NEEDS Looking for very well-written middle grade and young adult novels. Juvenile, picture books, young adult. Looking for very well written middle grade and young adult novels. No adult fiction. No short stories. Published *Martina the Beautiful Cockroach, Night of the Spadefoot Toads, The Boy Who Was Raised by Librarians.* No collections of poetry or short stories; no romance or science fiction.

HOW TO CONTACT Submit complete ms with SASE.

TERMS Pays royalty on retail price. Responds in 6 months and mss.

PEACHTREE PUBLISHERS, LTD.

1700 Chattahoochee Ave., Atlanta GA 30318. (404)876-8761. **Fax:** (404)875-2578. **E-mail:** hello@peachtree-online.com; jackson@peachtree-online.com. **Website:** www.peachtree-online.com. **Contact:** Helen Harriss, acquisitions editor; Loraine Joyner, art

director; Melanie McMahon Ives, production manager. Estab. 1977.

NEEDS Picture books, young readers: adventure, animal, concept, history, nature/environment. Middle readers: adventure, animal, history, nature/environment, sports. Young adults: fiction, mystery, adventure. Does not want to see science fiction, romance.

HOW TO CONTACT Submit complete ms or 3 sample chapters by postal mail only.

TERMS Responds to queries and mss in 6-7 months.

PEDLAR PRESS

P.O. Box 26, Station P, Toronto ON M5S 2S6 Canada. (416)534-2011. **E-mail:** feralgrl@interlog.com. **Website:** www.pedlarpress.com. **Contact:** Beth Follett, owner/editor. Distributes in Canada through LitDist-Co.; in the US distributes directly through publisher.

NEEDS Experimental, feminist, gay/lesbian, literary, picture books, short story collections. Canadian writers only. Published *Black Stars in a White Night Sky,* by Jonarno Lawson, illustrated by Sherwin Tjia.

HOW TO CONTACT Query with SASE, sample chapter(s), synopsis.

TERMS Pays 10% royalty on retail price. Average advance: $200-400.

TIPS "I select manuscripts according to my taste, which fluctuates. Be familiar with some if not most of Pedlar's recent titles."

PELICAN PUBLISHING COMPANY

1000 Burmaster St., Gretna LA 70053. (504)368-1175. **Fax:** (504)368-1195. **E-mail:** editorial@pelicanpub.com. **Website:** www.pelicanpub.com. **Contact:** Nina Kooij, editor-in-chief. Estab. 1926. "We believe ideas have consequences. One of the consequences is that they lead to a best-selling book. We publish books to improve and uplift the reader. Currently emphasizing business and history titles." Publishes 20 young readers/year; 3 middle readers/year. "Our children's books (illustrated and otherwise) include history, biography, holiday, and regional. Pelican's mission is to publish books of quality and permanence that enrich the lives of those who read them." Publishes hardcover, trade paperback and mass market paperback originals and reprints. Book catalog and ms guidelines online.

NEEDS We publish maybe 1 novel a year, usually by an author we already have. Almost all proposals are returned. Young readers: history, holiday, science, multicultural and regional. Middle readers: Louisiana History. Multicultural needs include stories about African-

Americans, Irish-Americans, Jews, Asian-Americans, and Hispanics. Does not want animal stories, general Christmas stories, "day at school" or "accept yourself" stories. Maximum word length: young readers—1,100; middle readers—40,000. Recently published *The Oklahoma Land Run* by Una Belle Townsend (ages 5-8, historical/regional). No young adult, romance, science fiction, fantasy, gothic, mystery, erotica, confession, horror, sex, or violence. Also no psychological novels.

HOW TO CONTACT Query with SASE. Submit outline, clips, 2 sample chapters, SASE.

TERMS Pays authors in royalties; buys ms outright "rarely." Illustrators paid by "various arrangements." Advance considered. Responds in 1 month to queries; 3 months to mss.

PEMMICAN PUBLICATIONS, INC.

150 Henry Ave., Winnipeg MB R3B 0J7 Canada. (204)589-6346. **Fax:** (204)589-2063. **E-mail:** pemmican@pemmican.mb.ca. **Website:** www.pemmican.mb.ca. **Contact:** Randal McILroy, managing editor (Metis culture & heritage). Estab. 1980. "Pemmican Publications is a Metis publishing house, with a mandate to publish books by Metis authors and illustrators and with an emphasis on culturally relevant stories. We encourage writers to learn a little about Pemmican before sending samples. Pemmican publishes titles in the following genres: Adult Fiction, which includes novels, story collections and anthologies; Non-Fiction, with an emphasis on social history and biography reflecting Metis experience; Children's and Young Adult titles; Aboriginal languages, including Michif and Cree." Publishes trade paperback originals and reprints. Book catalog available free with SASE. Guidelines available online.

NEEDS All manuscripts must be Metis culture and heritage related.

HOW TO CONTACT Submit proposal package including outline and 3 sample chapters.

TERMS Pays 10% royalty on retail price. Responds to queries, proposals, and mss in 3 months.

TIPS "Our mandate is to promote Metis authors, illustrators and stories. No agent is necessary."

PENGUIN GROUP USA

375 Hudson St., New York NY 10014. (212)366-2000. **Website:** www.penguin.com. **Contact:** Peter Stampfel, submission editor (DAW Books). General interest publisher of both fiction and nonfiction. Guidelines available online at website.

No unsolicited mss. Submit work through a literary agent.

IMPRINTS Exceptions are DAW Books and G.P. Putnam's Sons Books for Young Readers, which are accepting submissions. See individual listings for more information. **Penguin Adult Division**: Ace Books, Alpha Books, Avery, Berkley Books, Dutton, Gotham Books, HPBooks, Hudson Street Press, Jove, New American Library, Penguin, The Penguin Press, Perigee, Plume, Portfolio, G.P. Putnam's Sons, Riverhead, Sentinel, Jeremy P. Tarcher, Viking; **Penguin Children's Division:** Dial Books for Young Readers, Dutton Children's Books, Firebird, Grosset & Dunlap, Philomel, Price Stern Sloan, Puffin Books, G.P. Putnam's Sons, Speak, Viking Children's Books, Frederick Warne.

NEEDS "We publish first novels if they are of professional quality. A literary agent is not required for submission. We will not consider mss that are currently on submission to another publisher unless prior arrangements have been made with a literary agent. Please enclose a SASE with your submission for our correspondence. We ask that you only send us disposable copies of your ms, which will be recycled in the event they are not found suitable for publication. We regret that we are no longer able to return submitted ms copies, as the process resulted in too many difficulties with the postal service and unnecessary expense for the prospective authors. It may require up to three months or more for our editors to review a submission and come to a decision. If you want to be sure we have received your manuscript, please enclose a stamped, self-addressed postcard that we will return when your ms. It is not necessary for you to register or copyright your work before publication—it is protected by law as long as it has not been published. When published, we will copyright the book in the author's name and register that copyright with the Library of Congress. DAW Books is currently accepting manuscripts in the science fiction/fantasy genre. We publish science fiction and fantasy novels. The average length of the novels we publish varies but is almost never less than 80,000 words. Do not submit handwritten material." We do not want short stories, short story collections, novellas, or poetry.

HOW TO CONTACT "Due to the high volume of mss we receive, Penguin Group (USA) Inc. imprints do not normally accept unsolicited mss. On rare occasion, however, a particular imprint may be open to reading such. The Penguin Group (USA) web site features a listing of which imprints (if any) are currently accepting unsolicited manuscripts." Continue to check website for updates to the list.

TERMS Responds in 3 months generally.

● THE PERMANENT PRESS

Attn: Judith Shepard, 4170 Noyac Rd., Sag Harbor NY 11963. (631)725-1101. **Fax:** (631)725-8215. **E-mail:** judith@thepermanentpress.com; shepard@thepermanentpress.com. **Website:** www.thepermanentpress.com. **Contact:** Judith and Martin Shepard, acquisitions/co-publishers. Estab. 1978. Mid-size, independent publisher of literary fiction. "We keep titles in print and are active in selling subsidiary rights." Average print order: 1,500. Averages 14 total titles. Accepts unsolicited mss. Pays 10-15% royalty on wholesale price. Offers $1,000 advance. Publishes in hardcover originals.

NEEDS Promotes titles through reviews. Literary, mainstream/contemporary, mystery. Especially looking for high-line literary fiction, "artful, original and arresting." Accepts any fiction category as long as it is a "well-written, original full-length novel." Published *Black Swan* and five other thrllers by Chris Knopf; *All Cry Chaos* by Leonard Rosen; *The Double Life of Alfred Buber* by Davis Schmahmann; *The Singular Exploits of Wonder Mom & Party Girl* by Marc Schuster; *The Ringer* by Jenny Shank; and multiple novels by Michael Stein, Larry Duberstein, Howard Owen, Berry Fleming, and K.C. Frederick.

HOW TO CONTACT Accepts unsolicited mss. Send SASE for return of ms or send a disposable ms and SASE for reply only. Responds in weeks or months to queries and submissions. "We don't accept simultaneous submissions."

TERMS Pays 10-15% royalty on wholesale price. Offers $1,000 advance. Publishes ms within 18 months after acceptance. Responds in weeks or months to queries and submissions.

TIPS "We are looking for good books—be they 10th novels or first ones, it makes little difference. The fiction is more important than the track record. Send us the first 25 pages; it's impossible to judge something that begins on page 302. Also, no outlines—let the writing present itself."

● DAVID PHILIP PUBLISHERS

New Africa Books, P.O. Box 46962, Glosderry 7702 South Africa. **Fax:** (21)6743358. **E-mail:** info@newafricabooks.co.za. **Website:** www.newafricabooks.co.za.

NEEDS "Fiction with southern African concern or focus. Progressive, often suitable for school or university prescription, literary, serious but with commercial potential."

HOW TO CONTACT Submit 1 sample chapter(s), detailed synopsis and letter of motivation.

TERMS Pays royalty. Write for guidelines.

TIPS "Familiarize yourself with list of publishers to which you wish to submit work."

◐ PHILOMEL BOOKS

Imprint of Penguin Group (USA), Inc., 375 Hudson St., New York NY 10014. (212)414-3610. **Website:** www.us.penguingroup.com. **Contact:** Michael Green, president/publisher; Annie Ericsson, junior designer. Estab. 1980. "We look for beautifully written, engaging manuscripts for children and young adults." Publishes hardcover originals. Book catalog for 9×12 envelope and 4 first-class stamps. Guidelines for #10 SASE.

NEEDS All levels: adventure, animal, boys, contemporary, fantasy, folktales, historical fiction, humor, sports, multicultural. Middle readers, young adults: problem novels, science fiction, suspense/mystery. No concept picture books, mass-market "character" books, or series. Average word length: picture books—1,000; young readers—1,500; middle readers—14,000; young adult—20,000. No series or activity books. No generic, mass-market oriented fiction.

HOW TO CONTACT *No unsolicited mss.*

TERMS Pays authors in royalties. Average advance payment "varies." Illustrators paid by advance and in royalties. Pays negotiable advance.

TIPS Wants "unique fiction or nonfiction with a strong voice and lasting quality. Discover your own voice and own story and persevere." Looks for "something unusual, original, well written. Fine art or illustrative art that feels unique. The genre (fantasy, contemporary, or historical fiction) is not so important as the story itself and the spirited life the story allows its main character."

PIANO PRESS

P.O. Box 85, Del Mar CA 92014. (619)884-1401. **Fax:** (858)755-1104. **E-mail:** pianopress@pianopress.com. **Website:** www.pianopress.com. **Contact:** Elizabeth C. Axford, editor. Estab. 1998. "We publish music-related books, either fiction or nonfiction, coloring books, songbooks, and poetry." Book catalog available for #10 SASE and 2 first-class stamps.

NEEDS Picture books, young readers, middle readers, young adults: folktales, multicultural, poetry, music. Average word length: picture books—1,500-2,000. Recently published *Strum a Song of Angels*, by Linda Oatman High and Elizabeth C. Axford; *Music and Me*, by Kimberly White and Elizabeth C. Axford.

TERMS Pays authors, illustrators, and photographers royalty of 5-10% based on retail price. Responds to queries in 3 months; mss in 6 months.

TIPS "We are looking for music-related material only for any juvenile market. Please do not send non-music-related materials. Query first before submitting anything."

●○ PIATKUS BOOKS

Little, Brown Book Group, 100 Victoria Embankment, London WA EC4Y 0DY United Kingdom. 0207 911 8000. **Fax:** 0207 911 8100. **E-mail:** info@littlebrown. co.uk. **Website:** piatkus.co.uk. **Contact:** Emma Beswetherick, senior editor. Estab. 1979. "Until 2007, Piatkus operated as an independent publishing house. Now it exists as a commercial imprint of Hachette-owned Little, Brown Book Group." Publishes hardcover originals, paperback originals, and paperback reprints. Guidelines available online.

○ Piatkus no longer accepts fiction proposals.

NEEDS Quality family saga, historical, literary. Best-selling authors include: Nora Roberts, JD Robb, Christina Jones, Julia Quinn, Nick Brownlee.

TERMS Responds in 3 months to mss.

TIPS "Study our list before submitting your work."

●❶❷ PICADOR USA

MacMillan, 175 Fifth Ave., New York NY 10010. (212)674-5151. **E-mail:** david.saint@picadorusa.com; pressinquiries@macmillanusa.com. **Website:** www. picadorusa.com. **Contact:** Frances Coady, publisher (literary fiction). Estab. 1994. Picador publishes high-quality literary fiction and nonfiction. "We are open to a broad range of subjects, well written by authoritative authors." Publishes hardcover and trade paperback originals and reprints. Averages 70-80 total titles/year. Titles distributed through Von Holtzbrinck Publishers. Titles promoted through national print advertising and bookstore co-op. Book catalog for 9×12 SASE and $2.60 postage. Ms guidelines for #10 SASE or online.

○ Does not accept unsolicited mss. *Agented submissions only.*

TERMS Pays 7-15% on royalty. Advance varies. Responds to queries in 2 months.

❶ PINEAPPLE PRESS, INC.

P.O. Box 3889, Sarasota FL 34230. (941)739-2219. **Fax:** (941)739-2296. **E-mail:** info@pineapplepress.com. **Website:** www.pineapplepress.com. **Contact:** June Cussen, executive editor. Estab. 1982. "We are seeking quality nonfiction on diverse topics for the library and book trade markets. Our mission is to publish good books about Florida." Publishes hardcover and trade paperback originals. Book catalog for 9×12 SAE with $1.25 postage. Guidelines available online.

NEEDS Picture books, young readers, middle readers, young adults: animal, folktales, history, nature/environment. Recently published *The Treasure of Amelia Island*, by M.C. Finotti (ages 8-12).

HOW TO CONTACT Query or submit outline/synopsis and 3 sample chapters.

TERMS Pays authors royalty of 10-15%. Responds to queries/samples/mss in 2 months.

TIPS "Quality first novels will be published, though we usually only do one or two novels per year and they must be set in Florida. We regard the author/editor relationship as a trusting relationship with communication open both ways. Learn all you can about the publishing process and about how to promote your book once it is published. A query on a novel without a brief sample seems useless."

❷ PLAN B PRESS

P.O. Box 4067, Alexandria VA 22303. (215)732-2663. **E-mail:** planbpress@gmail.com. **Website:** www.planbpress.com. **Contact:** Steven Allen May, president. Estab. 1999. Plan B Press is a "small publishing company with an international feel. Our intention is to have Plan B Press be part of the conversation about the direction and depth of literary movements and genres. Plan B Press's new direction is to seek out authors rarely-to-never published, sharing new voices that might not otherwise be heard. Plan B Press is determined to merge text with image, writing with art." Publishes poetry and short fiction. Wants "experimental poetry, concrete/visual work." Has published poetry by Lamont B. Steptoe, Michele Belluomini, Jim Mancinelli, Lyn Lifshin, Robert Miltner, and Steven Allen May. Publishes 1 poetry book/year and 5-10 chapbooks/year. Manuscripts are selected through open submission and through competition (see below). Books/chapbooks are 24-48 pages, with covers with art/graphics.

TERMS Pays author's copies. Responds to queries in 1 month; mss in 3 months.

PLEXUS PUBLISHING, INC.

143 Old Marlton Pike, Medford NJ 08055. (609)654-6500. **Fax:** (609)654-4309. **E-mail:** jbryans@plexuspublishing.com. **Website:** www.plexuspublishing.com. **Contact:** John B. Bryans, editor-in-chief/publisher. Estab. 1977. Plexus publishes regional-interest (southern New Jersey and the greater Philadelphia area) fiction and nonfiction including mysteries, field guides, nature, travel and history. Also a limited number of titles in health/medicine, biology, ecology, botany, astronomy. Publishes hardcover and paperback originals. Book catalog and book proposal guidelines for 10x13 SASE.

NEEDS Mysteries and literary novels with a strong regional (southern New Jersey) angle.

HOW TO CONTACT Query with SASE.

TERMS Pays $500-1,000 advance. Responds in 3 months to proposals.

A● PLUME

375 Hudson St., New York NY 10014. **Website:** www.penguinputnam.com. Estab. 1948. Division of Penguin Putnam Inc., 375 Hudson St., New York NY 10014. (212)366-2000. **Website:** www.penguinputnam.com. **Contact:** Trena Keating, editor-in-chief/associate publisher (literary fiction). Estab. 1948. Publishes paperback originals and reprints. **Published some debut authors within the last year.**

NEEDS "All kinds of commercial and litearary fiction, including mainstream, historical, New Age, western, thriller, gay. Full length novels and collections." Published *Girl with a Pearl Earring*, by Tracy Chevalier; *Liar's Moon*, by Phillip Kimball; *The True History of Paradise*, by Margaret Cezain-Thompson.

HOW TO CONTACT *Agented submissions only.* Accepts simultaneous submissions.

TERMS Pays in royalties and author's copies. Offers advance. Publishes ms 12-18 months after acceptance. Book catalog for SASE.

TIPS "Write the complete manuscript and submit it to an agent or agents."

O POCOL PRESS

Box 411, Clifton VA 20124. (703)830-5862. **Website:** www.pocolpress.com. **Contact:** J. Thomas Hetrick, editor. Estab. 1999. "Pocol Press is dedicated to producing high-quality books from first-time, non-agented authors. However, all submissions are welcome. We're dedicated to good storytellers and to the written word, specializing in short fiction and baseball. Several of our books have been used as literary texts at universities and in book group discussions around the nation. Pocol Press does not publish children's books, romance novels, or graphic novels." Publishes trade paperback originals. Book catalog and guidelines available online.

◘ "Our authors are comprised of veteran writers and emerging talents."

NEEDS "We specialize in thematic short fiction collections by a single author and baseball fiction. Expert storytellers welcome." Horror (psychological, supernatural), literary, mainstream/contemporary, short story collections, baseball. Published *Gulf*, by Brock Adams (short fiction); *The Last of One* by Stephan Solberg (novel); *A Good Death* by David E. Lawrence.

HOW TO CONTACT Does not accept or return unsolicited mss. Query with SASE or submit 1 sample chapter(s).

TERMS Pays 10-12% royalty on wholesale price. Responds in 1 month to queries; 2 months too mss.

TIPS "Our audience is aged 18 and over. Pocol Press is unique; we publish good writing and great storytelling. Write the best stories you can. Read them to you friends/peers. Note their reaction. Publishes some of the finest fiction by a small press."

O◘ POISONED PEN PRESS

6962 E. 1st Ave., #103, Scottsdale AZ 85251. (480)945-3375. **Fax:** (480)949-1707. **E-mail:** editor@poisonedpenpress.com; info@poisonedpenpress.com. **E-mail:** submissions@poisonedpenpress.com. **Website:** www.poisonedpenpress.com. **Contact:** Jessica Tribble. Estab. 1996. "Our publishing goal is to offer well-written mystery novels of crime and/or detection where the puzzle and its resolution are the main forces that move the story forward." Publishes hardcover originals, and hardcover and trade paperback reprints. Book catalog and guidelines available online at website.

NEEDS Mss should generally be longer than 65,000 words and shorter than 100,000 words. Member Publishers Marketing Associations, Arizona Book Publishers Associations, Publishers Association of West. Distributes through Ingram, Baker & Taylor, Brodart. Does not want novels centered on serial killers, spousal or child abuse, drugs, or extremist groups, although we do not entirely rule such works out.

HOW TO CONTACT Accepts unsolicited mss. Electronic queries only. "Query with SASE. Submit clips, first 3 pages. We must receive both the synopsis and ms pages electronically as separate attachments to an e-mail message or as a disk or CD which we will not return."

TERMS Pays 9-15% royalty on retail price. Responds in 2-3 months to queries and proposals; 6 months to mss.

TIPS "Audience is adult readers of mystery fiction."

PRAIRIE JOURNAL PRESS

P.O. Box 68073, Calgary AB T3G 3N8 Canada. **E-mail:** prairiejournal@yahoo.com. **Website:** www.geocities.com/prairiejournal/. **Contact:** Anne Burke, literary editor. Estab. 1983.

Prairie Journal Press authors have been nominees for The Journey Prize in fiction and finalists and honorable mention for the National Magazine awards. Prairie Journal Press authors have been nominees for The Journey Prize in fiction and finalists and honorable mention for the National Magazine awards.

NEEDS Literary, short story collections. Published *Prairie Journal Fiction, Prairie Journal Fiction II* (anthologies of short stories); *Solstice* (short fiction on the theme of aging); and *Prairie Journal Prose.*

HOW TO CONTACT Submit with SAE with IRC for individuals. No U.S. stamps please. Accepts unsolicited mss. Sometimes comments on rejected mss.

TERMS Pays 1 author's copy; honorarium depends on grant/award provided by the government or private/corporate donations.

TIPS "We wish we had the means to promote more new writers. We look for something different each time and try not to repeat types of stories if possible. We receive fiction of very high quality. Short fiction is preferable although excerpts from novels are considered if they stand alone on their own merit."

PS BOOKS

Philadelphia Stories, Inc., 2021 S. 11th St., Philadelphia PA 19148. (215)551-5889. **Fax:** (215)635-0195. **E-mail:** info@psbookspublishing.org. **E-mail:** marc@psbookspublishing.org. **Website:** www.psbookspublishing.org. **Contact:** Marc Schuster, acquisitions editor. Estab. 2008. Due to an overwhelming number of submissions, **PS Books is no longer accepting unsolic-**

ited manuscripts. If, in the future, we return to reading unsolicited manuscripts, the following guidelines will apply. "In 2008, the publishers of Philadelphia Stories magazine launched a books division called PS Books. The needs of PS Books closely mirror those of the magazine; we are looking for novel-length fiction and narrative nonfiction manuscripts featuring polished prose, a controlled voice, strong characters, and interesting subjects. Please read our current titles to get a sense of what we publish. For information on submitting a query package, please visit our website." Publishes paperback originals. Format: cougar smooth paper; offset commercial printing; perfect-bound. Average print order: 500-1,000. Debut novel print order: 500-1,000. Plans 1 debut novel this year. Averages 2 total titles/year; 1-2 fiction titles/year. Member CLMP. Distributes/promotes titles Baker & Taylor, direct marketing.

NEEDS Humor, Literary, Mainstream, Regional (Delaware valley, greater Philadelphia). Anthologies planned include *The Best of Philadelphia Stories, vol. 2*; *By Any Other Name*. Published *Broad Street*, by Christine Weiser (upmarket commercial fiction); *The Singular Exploits of Wonder Mom and Party Girl*, by Marc Schuster (literary fiction).

HOW TO CONTACT Query with outline/synopsis and first 20 pages. Accepts queries by e-mail only. Include estimated word count, brief bio, list of publishing credits. Send disposable copy of ms and SASE for reply only. Responds to queries in 2 months. Considers simultaneous submissions, e-mail submissions. Rarely critiques/comments on rejected mss. Responds to mss in 3 months.

TIPS "We are looking for well written literary or upmarket commercial fiction and non-fiction. We prefer novels to be under 300 pages (100,000 words) and expect authors to submit a marketing plan. Only send us polished work that fits our guidelines. We encourage authors to read our current titles and to read work published on the *Philadelphia Stories* website."

PUCKERBRUSH PRESS

413 Neville Hall, Orono ME 04469. (207)581-3832. **Website:** http://puckerbrushreview.com. **Contact:** Sanford Phippen, editor. Estab. 1971. Publishes trade paperback originals and reprints of literary fiction and poetry. Book catalog for large SASE and 34¢. Guidelines for SASE.

NEEDS Literary, short story collections. Published *Cora's Seduction*, by Mary Gray Hughes (short stories); *When Soft Was the Sun*, by Merle Hillman (fiction); *The Crow on the Spruce*, by C. Hall (Maine fiction); *Night-Sea Journey*, by M. Alpert (poetry).

HOW TO CONTACT Submit complete ms. Accepts queries by phone. Include brief bio, list of publishing credits.

TERMS Pays 10-15% royalty on wholesale price. Responds in 1 month to queries; 2 months to proposals; 3 months to mss.

TIPS "Be true to your vision, not to fashion. For sophisticated readers who retain love of literature. Maine writers continue to be featured."

ⓞⓒ PUFFIN BOOKS

Imprint of Penguin Group (USA), Inc., 345 Hudson St., New York NY 10014. (212)366-2000. **Website:** www.penguinputnam.com. **Contact:** Kristin Gilson, editorial director. "Puffin Books publishes high-end trade paperbacks and paperback reprints for preschool children, beginning and middle readers, and young adults." Publishes trade paperback originals and reprints. Book catalog for 9×12 SAE with 7 first-class stamps.

IMPRINTS Speak, Firebird, Sleuth.

NEEDS Picture books, young adult novels, middle grade and easy-to-read grades 1-3: fantasy and science fiction, graphic novels, classics. Recently Published *Three Cups of Tea* young readers edition, by Greg Mortenson and David Oliver Relin, adapted for young readers by Sarah Thomson; *The Big Field*, by Mike Lupica; *Geek Charming*, by Robin Palmer.

HOW TO CONTACT *No unsolicited mss.* Submit 3 sample chapters with SASE.

TERMS Royalty varies. Pays varies advance. Responds in 5 months.

TIPS "Our audience ranges from little children 'first books' to young adult (ages 14-16). An original idea has the best luck."

ⓞⓒ PUREPLAY PRESS

350 Judah St., Suite 302, San Francisco CA 94122. **E-mail:** info@pureplaypress.com; editor@pureplaypress.com. **Website:** www.pureplaypress.com. **Contact:** David Landau, editor/publisher. Estab. 2001. "Founded in 2001 by writers and editors who felt the need to publish works about Cuba's history and culture. At present we have 12 books in print, all with Cuban themes, and we are beginning to publish on other subjects. Our byword is freedom from the status quo. The qualities we prize in the written word are sincerity, simplicity, elegance and clarity of expression. We are convinced that culture is infinite, and creativity general. We strive to be considerate to readers and encouraging to writers.Our books are closely edited, carefully designed, printed with high-quality materials and then marketed by all plausible means, including the World Wide Web. We are interested in fiction, history, poetry, politics and culture."

HOW TO CONTACT "While we cannot receive unsolicited manuscripts, we will consider proposals of up to 250 words in length. The most effective proposal is a statement about the work that might serve as copy for a book-jacket or a back cover."

ⓐⓒ G.P. PUTNAM'S SONS

Penguin Putnam, Inc., 345 Hudson St., New York NY 10014. (212)414-3610. **Fax:** (212)366-2664. **E-mail:** susan.kochan@us.penguingroup.com. **Website:** www.penguinputnam.com; www.us.penguingroup.com. **Contact:** Susan Kochan, associate editorial director.

NEEDS Juvenile picture books: animal, concept, contemporary, humor, multicultural. Young readers: adventure, contemporary, history, humor, multicultural, special needs, suspense/mystery. Middle readers: adventure, contemporary, history, humor, fantasy, multicultural, problem novels, sports, suspense/mystery. Young adults: contemporary, history, fantasy, problem novels, special needs. Does not want to see series. Average word length: picture books—200-1,000; middle readers—10,000-30,000; young adults—40,000-50,000. Recently published *Good Night, Goon: A Parody* by Michael Rex (ages 4-8); *Geek Magnet*, by Kieran Scott (ages 12 and up).

HOW TO CONTACT Accepts unsolicited mss. No SASE required, as will only respond if interested. Picture books: send full mss. Fiction: Query with outline/synopsis and 10 ms pages. When submitting a portion of a longer work, please provide an accompanying cove letter that briefly describes your ms's plot, genre, the intended age group, and your publishing credits, if any. Do not send art unless requested.

TERMS Pays authors royalty based on retail price. Sends prepublication galleys to authors. Pays author royalty based on retail price. Responds in 4 months if interested.

TIPS "Study our catalogs and get a sense of the kind of books we publish, so that you know whether your project is likely to be right for us."

ⓞ QUIXOTE PRESS

3544 Blakslee St., Wever IA 52658. (800)571-2665. **Fax:** (319)372-7485. **Website:** www.heartsntummies.

com. **Contact:** Bruce Carlson. Quixote Press specializes in humorous and/or regional folklore and special-interest cookbooks. Publishes trade paperback originals and reprints. **Published many debut authors within the last year.**

○ Quixote Press specializes in humorous and/or regional folklore and special-interest cookbooks. Publishes trade paperback originals and reprints. Published many debut authors within the last year. Needs humor, short story collections. Query with SASE. Accepts simultaneous submissions. Pays 10% royalty on wholesale price. Publishes ms 1 year after acceptance.

NEEDS Humor, short story collections. Published *Eating Ohio*, by Rus Pishnery (short stories about Ohio); *Lil' Red Book of Fishing Tips*, by Tom Whitecloud (fishing tales); *How to Talk Hoosier*, by Netha Bell (humor); *Cow Whisperer*, by Skip Holmes (humor); *Flour Sack Bloomers*, by Lucy Fetterhoff (history).

HOW TO CONTACT Query with SASE. Accepts simultaneous submissions. www.heartsntummies.com. Contact: Bruce Carlson.

TERMS Pays 10% royalty on wholesale price. Publishes ms 1 year after acceptance.

TIPS "Carefully consider marketing considerations. Audience is women in gift shops, on farm sites, direct retail outlets, wineries, outdoor sport shops, etc. Contact us at *you idea* stage, not complete ms stage. Be receptive to design input by us."

Ⓐ⊘ RANDOM HOUSE, INC.

1745 Broadway, New York NY 10013. **Website:** www.randomhouse.com. Estab. 1925. "Random House has long been committed to publishing the best literature by writers both in the United States and abroad."

HOW TO CONTACT *Agented submissions only.*

TERMS Pays royalty. Offers advance. Ms guidelines online.

Ⓐ⊘ RANDOM HOUSE CHILDREN'S BOOKS

Random House, Inc., 1745 Broadway, New York NY 10019. (212)782-9000. **Website:** www.randomhouse.com. Estab. 1925. "Producing books for preschool children through young adult readers, in all formats from board to activity books to picture books and novels, Random House Children's Books brings together world-famous franchise characters, multi-

million-copy series and top-flight, award-winning authors, and illustrators."

○ Submit mss through a literary agent.

IMPRINTS BooksReportsNow.com, GoldenBooks.com, Junie B. Jones, Kids@Random, Seusville, Teachers@Random, Teens@Random; **Knopf/Delacorte/Dell Young Readers Group:** Bantam, Crown, David Fickling Books, Delacorte Press, Dell Dragonfly, Dell Laurel-Leaf, Dell Yearling, Doubleday, Alfred A. Knopf, Wendy Lamb Books; **Random House Young Readers Group:** Akiko, Arthur, Barbie, Beginner Books, The Berenstain Bears, Bob the Builder, Disney, Dragon Tales, First Time Books, Golden Books, Landmark Books, Little Golden Books, Lucas Books, Mercer Mayer, Nickelodeon, Nick, Jr., pat the bunny, Picturebacks, Precious Moments, Richard Scarry, Sesame Street Books, Step Into Reading, Stepping Stones, Star Wars, Thomas the Tank Engine and Friends.

NEEDS "Random House publishes a select list of first chapter books and novels, with an emphasis on fantasy and historical fiction." Chapter books, middle-grade readers, young adult.

HOW TO CONTACT *Does not accept unsolicited mss.*

TIPS "We look for original, unique stories. Do something that hasn't been done before."

●○ RANSOM PUBLISHING

Radley House, 8 St. Cross Road, Winchester Hampshire SO23 9HXUK United Kingdom. +44 (0) 01962 862307. **Fax:** +44 (0) 05601 148881. **E-mail:** ransom@ransom.co.uk. **Website:** www.ransom.co.uk. **Contact:** Jenny Ertle, editor. Estab. 1995. Independent UK publisher with distribution in English speaking markets throughout the world. Specializes in books for reluctant and struggling readers. Our high quality, visually stimulating, age appropriate material has achieved wide acclaim for its ability to engage and motivate those who either can't or won't read. One of the few English language publishers to publish books with very high interest age and very low reading age. Has a developing list of children's books for home and school use. Specializes in phonics and general reading programs. Publishes paperback originals. Ms guidelines by e-mail.

NEEDS Easy reading for young adults. Books for reluctant and struggling readers.

HOW TO CONTACT Accepts unsolicited mss. Query with SASE or submit outline/proposal. Prefers queries by e-mail. Include estimated word count, brief bio, list of publishing credits.

TERMS Pays 10% royalty on net receipts. Responds to mss in 3-4 weeks.

☯☮☊ RED DEER PRESS

195 Allstate Pkwy., Markham ON L3R 4TB Canada. (905)477-9700. **Fax:** (905)477-9179. **E-mail:** rdp@reddeerpress.com; dionne@reddeerpress.com; val@reddeerpress.com. **Website:** www.reddeerpress.com. **Contact:** Richard Dionne, publisher. Estab. 1975. Book catalog for 9 x 12 SASE.

○ Red Deer Press has received numerous honors and awards from the Book Publishers Association of Alberta, Canadian Children's Book Centre, the Governor General of Canada and the Writers Guild of Alberta.

NEEDS Publishes young adult, adult non-fiction, science fiction, fantasy, and paperback originals "focusing on books by, about, or of interest to Canadians." Books: offset paper; offset printing; hardcover/perfect-bound. Average print order: 5,000. First novel print order: 2,500. Distributes titles in Canada and the US, the UK, Australia and New Zealand. Young adult (juvenile and early reader), contemporary. No romance or horror.

HOW TO CONTACT Accepts unsolicited mss. Query with SASE. No submissions on disk.

TERMS Pays 8-10% royalty. Responds to queries in 6 months.

TIPS "We're very interested in young adult and children's fiction from Canadian writers with a proven track record (either published books or widely published in established magazines or journals) and for manuscripts with regional themes and/or a distinctive voice. We publish Canadian authors exclusively."

⊘ RED HEN PRESS

P.O. Box 3537, Granada Hills CA 91394. (818)831-0649. **Fax:** (818)831-6659. **E-mail:** redhenpressbooks.com. **Website:** www.redhen.org. **Contact:** Mark E. Cull, publisher/editor (fiction). Estab. 1993. "*Red Hen Press is not currently accepting unsolicited material.* At this time, the best opportunity to be published by Red Hen is by entering one of our contests. Please find more information in our award submission guidelines." Publishes trade paperback originals. Book catalog available free. Guidelines available online.

○ The mission of Red Hen Press is to discover, publish, and promote works of literary excellence that have been overlooked by mainstream presses, and to build audiences for literature in two ways: by fostering the literacy of youth and by bringing distinguished and emerging writers to the public stage.

NEEDS Ethnic, experimental, feminist, gay/lesbian, historical, literary, mainstream/contemporary, short story collections. "We prefer high-quality literary fiction." Published *The Misread City: New Literary Los Angeles*, edited by Dana Gioia and Scott Timberg; *Rebel*, by Tom Hayden

HOW TO CONTACT Query with SASE.

TERMS Responds in 1 month to queries; 2 months to proposals; months to mss.

TIPS "Audience reads poetry, literary fiction, intelligent nonfiction. If you have an agent, we may be too small since we don't pay advances. Write well. Send queries first. Be willing to help promote your own book."

RED SAGE PUBLISHING, INC.

P.O. Box 4844, Seminole FL 33775. (727)391-3847. **E-mail:** submissions@eredsage.com. **Website:** www.eredsage.com. **Contact:** Alexandria Kendall, publisher; Theresa Stevens, managing editor. Estab. 1995. Publishes books of romance fiction, written for the adventurous woman. Guidelines available online.

HOW TO CONTACT Submission guidelines online at http://www.eredsage.com/store/RedSageSubmissionGuidelines_HowToSendSubmission.html.

TERMS Pays advance.

☯☊ RED TUQUE BOOKS, INC.

477 Martin St., Unit #6, Penticton BC V2A 5L2 Canada. (778)476-5750. **Fax:** (778)476-5651. **Website:** www.redtuquebooks.ca. **Contact:** David Korinetz, executive editor.

NEEDS Adventure, short story collections, young adult and teen (specifically adventure and science fiction), graphic novels, and fantasy (space fantasy, sword and sorcery).

HOW TO CONTACT Submit a query letter and first five pages. Include total word count. A one-page synopsis is optional. Accepts queries by e-mail and mail. SASE for reply only.

TERMS Pays 5-7% royalties on net sales. Pays $250 advance. Responds in 3 weeks.

TIPS "Well-plotted, character-driven stories, preferably with happy endings, will have the best chance of being accepted. Keep in mind that authors who like to begin sentences with "and, or, and but" are less likely to be considered. Don't send anything gruesome or overly explicit; tell us a good story, but think PG."

RENAISSANCE HOUSE

465 Westview Ave., Englewood NJ 07631. (800)547-5113. **E-mail:** raquel@renaissancehouse.net. **Website:** www.renaissancehouse.net. Publishes biographies, folktales, coffee table books, instructional, textbooks, adventure, picture books, juvenile and young adult. Specializes in multicultural and bilingual titles, Spanish-English. Submit outline/synopsis. Will consider e-mail submissions. Children's, educational, multicultural, and textbooks, advertising rep. Represents 80 illustrators. 95% of artwork handled is children's book illustration. Currently open to illustrators and photographers seeking representation. Open to both new and established illustrators.

NEEDS Picture books: animal, folktales, multicultural. Young readers: animal, anthology, folktales, multicultural. Middle readers, young adult/teens: anthology, folktales, multicultural, nature/environment.

TERMS Responds to queries/mss in 2 months.

RIVER CITY PUBLISHING

1719 Mulberry St., Montgomery AL 36106. **E-mail:** jgilbert@rivercitypublishing.com. **Website:** www.rivercitypublishing.com. **Contact:** Jim Gilbert, editor. Estab. 1989. Midsize independent publisher (8-10 books per year). River City primarily publishes narrative nonfiction that reflects the South. "We are looking for mainly for narrative histories, sociological accounts, and travel. Only biographies and memoirs from noted persons will be considered; we are closed to all personal memoir submissions." Publishes hardcover and trade paperback originals.

NEEDS Literary fiction, narrative nonfiction, regional (southern), short story collections. No poetry, memoir, or children's books. Published *Murder Creek*, by Joe Formichella (true crime); *Breathing Out the Ghost*, by Kirk Curnutt (novel); *The Bear Bryant Funeral Train*, by Brad Vice (short story collection).

HOW TO CONTACT See nonfiction submission guidelines.

TERMS Pays 10-15% royalty on retail price. Pays $500-5,000 advance. Responds to mss in 9 months.

TIPS "Only send your best work after you have received outside opinions. From approximately 1,000 submissions each year, we publish no more than 8 books and few of those come from unsolicited material. Competition is fierce, so follow the guidelines

exactly. All first-time novelists should submit their work to the Fred Bonnie Award contest."

RIVERHEAD BOOKS

Penguin Putnam, 375 Hudson Street, Office #4079, New York NY 10014. **E-mail:** ecommerce@us.penguingroup.com. **E-mail:** riverhead.web@us.penguingroup.com. **Website:** www.riverheadbooks.com. **Contact:** Megan Lynch, senior editor.

NEEDS Literary, mainstream, contemporary. Among the award-winning writers whose careers Riverhead has launched so far are Pearl Abraham (*The Romance Reader*; *Giving Up America*), Jennifer Belle (*Going Down*; *High Maintenance*), Adam Davies (*The Frog King*), Junot Díiaz (*Drown*), Alex Garland (*The Beach*; *The Tesseract*), Nick Hornby (*High Fidelity*; *About a Boy*; *How to Be Good*), Khaled Hosseini (*The Kite Runner*), ZZ Packer (*Drinking Coffee Elsewhere*), Iain Pears (*The Dream of Scipio*; *Instance of the Fingerpost*), Danzy Senna (*Caucasia*), Gary Shteyngart (*The Russian Debutante's Handbook*), Aryeh Lev Stollman (*The Far Euphrates*; *The Illuminated Soul*; *The Dialogues of Time and Entropy*), Sarah Waters (*Tipping the Velvet*; *Affinity*; *Fingersmith*).

HOW TO CONTACT *Submit through agent only. No unsolicited mss.*

RONSDALE PRESS

3350 W. 21st Ave., Vancouver BC V6S 1G7 Canada. (604)738-4688. **Fax:** (604)731-4548. **E-mail:** ronsdale@shaw.ca. **Website:** http://ronsdalepress.com. **Contact:** Ronald B. Hatch, director (fiction, poetry, social commentary); Veronica Hatch, managing director (children's literature). Estab. 1988. "Ronsdale Press is a Canadian literary publishing house that publishes 12 books each year, three of which are children's titles. Of particular interest are books involving children exploring and discovering new aspects of Canadian history." Publishes trade paperback originals. Book catalog for #10 SASE. Guidelines available online.

Canadian authors only.

NEEDS Young adults: Canadian novels. Average word length: middle readers and young adults—50,000. Recently published *Red Goodwin*, by John Wilson (ages 10-14); *Tragic Links*, by Cathy Beveridge (ages 10-14); *Dark Times*, edited by Ann Walsh (anthology of short stories, ages 10 and up); *Submarine Outlaw*, by Phillip Roy; *The Way Lies North*, by Jean Rae Baxter (ages 10-14).

HOW TO CONTACT Submit complete ms.

TERMS Pays 10% royalty on retail price. Responds to queries in 2 weeks; mss in 2 months.

SALVO PRESS

E-mail: schmidt@salvopress.com. **E-mail:** query@salvopress.com. **Website:** www.salvopress.com. **Contact:** Scott Schmidt, publisher. Estab. 1998. Book catalog and ms guidelines online.

NEEDS "We are a small press specializing in mystery, suspense, espionage and thriller fiction. Our press publishes in trade paperback and most e-book formats." Publishes hardcover, trade paperback originals and e-books in most formats. Books: 512×812; or 6×9 printing; perfect binding. Averages 6-12 fiction total titles/year, mostly fiction. "Our needs change, check our website."

HOW TO CONTACT Query by e-mail only. Please place the word "Query" as the subject. Include estimated word count, brief bio, list of publishing credits, "and something to intrigue me so I ask for more."

TERMS Pays 10% royalty. Responds in 5 minutes to 1 month to queries; 2 months to mss.

SAMHAIN PUBLISHING, LTD

577 Mulberry St., Suite 1520, Macon GA 31201. (478)314-5144. **Fax:** (478)314-5148. **E-mail:** editor@samhainpublishing.com. **Website:** samhainpublishing.com. **Contact:** Laurie M. Rauch, executive editor. Estab. 2005. "A small, independent publisher, Samhain's motto is 'It's all about the story.' We look for fresh, unique voices who have a story to share with the world. We encourage our authors to let their muse have its way and to create tales that don't always adhere to current trends. One never knows what the next hot genre will be or when it will start, so write what's in your soul. These are the books that, whether the story is based on formula or is an original, when written from the heart will earn you a life-time readership." Publishes e-books and paperback originals. POD/offset printing; line illustrations. Guidelines available online.

Preditor and Editors Best Publisher 2006.

NEEDS NEEDS Erotica and all genres and all heat levels of romance (contemporary, futuristic/time travel, gothic, historical, paranormal, regency period, romantic suspense, fantasy, action/adventure, etc.), as well as fantasy, urban fantasy or science fiction with strong romantic elements, with word counts between 12,000 and 120,000 words. "Samhain is now accepting submissions for our line of horror novels. We are actively seeking talented writers who can tell an exciting, dramatic and frightening story, and who are eager to promote their work and build their community of readers. We are looking for novels 'either supernatural or non-supernatural, contemporary or historical' that are original and compelling. Authors can be previously unpublished or established, agented or un-agented. Content can range from subtle and unsettling to gory and shocking. The writing is what counts."

HOW TO CONTACT Accepts unsolicited mss. Query with outline/synopsis and either 3 sample chapters or the full ms. Accepts queries by e-mail only. Include estimated word count, brief bio, list of publishing credits, and "how the author is working to improve craft: association, critique groups, etc."

TERMS Pays royalties 30-40% for e-books, average of 8% for trade paper, and author's copies (quantity varies). Responds in 4 months to queries and mss.

TIPS "Because we are an e-publisher first, we do not have to be as concerned with industry trends and can publish less popular genres of fiction if we believe the story and voice are good and will appeal to our customers. Please follow submission guidelines located on our website, include all requested information and proof your query/manuscript for errors prior to submission."

SARABANDE BOOKS, INC.

2234 Dundee Rd., Suite 200, Louisville KY 40205. (502)458-4028. **Fax:** (502)458-4065. **E-mail:** info@sarabandebooks.org. **Website:** www.sarabandebooks.org. **Contact:** Sarah Gorham, editor-in-chief. Estab. 1994. "Sarabande Books was founded to publish poetry, short fiction, and creative nonfiction. We look for works of lasting literary value. Please see our titles to get an idea of our taste. Accepts submissions through contests and open submissions." Publishes trade paperback originals. Book catalog available free. Contest guidelines for #10 SASE or on website.

Charges $10 handling fee with alternative option of purchase of book from website (email confirmation of sale must be included with submission).

NEEDS Literary, novellas, short novels, 250 pages maximum, 150 pages minimum. We consider novels and non-fiction in a wide variety of genres and subject matters with a special emphasis on mysteries and crime fiction. We do not consider science fiction, fantasy, or horror. Our target length is 70,000-90,000 words. Queries can be sent via email, fax or regular post. Submissions to Mary McCarthy Prize in Short Fiction accepted January through February. Published *Other Electricities*, by Ander Monson; *More Like Not Running Away*, by Paul Shepherd, and *Water: Nine Stories*, by Alyce Miller.

TERMS Pays royalty. 10% on actual income received. Also pays in author's copies. Pays $500-1,000 advance.

TIPS "Sarabande publishes for a general literary audience. Know your market. Read-and buy-books of literature. Sponsors contests for poetry and fiction."

Ⓐ SCHOLASTIC PRESS

Imprint of Scholastic, Inc., 557 Broadway, New York NY 10012. (212)343-6100. **Fax:** (212)343-4713. **Website:** www.scholastic.com. **Contact:** David Saylor, editorial director, Scholastic Press, creative director and associate publisher for all Scholastic hardcover imprints. Scholastic Press publishes fresh, literary picture book fiction and nonfiction; fresh, literary nonseries or nongenre-oriented middle grade and young adult fiction. Currently emphasizing subtly handled treatments of key relationships in children's lives; unusual approaches to commonly dry subjects, such as biography, math, history, or science. De-emphasizing fairy tales (or retellings), board books, genre, or series fiction (mystery, fantasy, etc.). Publishes hardcover originals.

NEEDS Looking for strong picture books, young chapter books, appealing middle grade novels (ages 8-11) and interesting and well-written young adult novels. Wants fresh, exciting picture books and novels—inspiring, new talent. Published *Chasing Vermeer*, by Blue Balliet; *Here Today*, by Ann M. Martin; *Detective LaRue*, by Mark Teague.

HOW TO CONTACT *Agented submissions and previously published authors only.*

TERMS Pays royalty on retail price. Pays variable advance. Responds in 3 months to queries; 6-8 months to mss.

TIPS Read *currently* published children's books. Revise, rewrite, rework and find your own voice, style and subject. We are looking for authors with a strong and unique voice who can tell a great story and have the ability to evoke genuine emotion. Children's publishers are becoming more selective, looking for irresistible talent and fairly broad appeal, yet still very willing to take risks, just to keep the game interesting."

Ⓩ SCIENCE & HUMANITIES PRESS

P.O. Box 7151, Chesterfield MO 63006. (636)394-4950. **E-mail:** banis@sciencehumanitiespress.com. **Website:** www.sciencehumanitiespress.com. **Contact:** Dr. Bud Banis, publisher. Publishes trade paperback originals and reprints, and electronic originals and reprints. Book catalog available online. Guidelines available online.

IMPRINTS Science & Humanities Press, BeachHouse Books, MacroPrintBooks (large print editions), Heuristic Books, Early Editions Books.

NEEDS Adventure, historical, humor, literary, mainstream/contemporary, military/war, mystery, regional, romance, science fiction, short story collections, spiritual, sports, suspense, western, young adult. "We prefer books with a theme that gives a market focus."

HOW TO CONTACT *Does not accept unsolicited mss without a SASE. We prefer books with a theme that gives a market focus. Brief description by e-mail.*

TERMS Pays 8% royalty on retail price. Responds in 2 months to queries and proposals; 3 months to mss.

TIPS "Our expertise is electronic publishing for continuous short-run-in-house production."

Ⓒ SECOND STORY PRESS

20 Maud St., Suite 401, Toronto ON M5V 2M5 Canada. (416)537-7850. **Fax:** (416)537-0588. **E-mail:** info@secondstorypress.ca; marketing@secondstorypress.com. **Website:** www.secondstorypress.ca.

NEEDS Considers non-sexist, non-racist, and non-violent stories, as well as historical fiction, chapter books, picture books. Recently published *Lilly and the Paper Man*, by Rebecca Upjohn; *Mom and Mum Are Getting Married!*, by Ken Setterington.

HOW TO CONTACT *Accepts appropriate material from residents of Canada only.* Submit complete ms or submit outline and sample chapters by postal mail only. No electronic submissions or queries.

Ⓞ SERIOUSLY GOOD BOOKS

999 Vanderbilt Beach Rd., Naples FL 34119. **E-mail:** seriouslygoodbks@aol.com. **Website:** www.seriouslygoodbks.net. Estab. 2010. Publishes historial fiction only. Publishes trade paperback and electronic originals. Book catalog and writers guidelines online at website.

HOW TO CONTACT Query by e-mail.

TERMS Pays 15% minimum royalties. Respons in 1 month to queries.

TIPS "Looking for historial fiction with substance. We seek well-researched historical fiction in the vein of Rutherfurd, Mary Renault, Maggie Anton, Robert Harris, etc. Please don't query with historical fiction mixed with other genres (romance, time travel, vampires, etc.)."

⊘ SEVEN STORIES PRESS

140 Watts St., New York NY 10013. (212)226-8760. **Fax:** (212)226-1411. **E-mail:** anna@sevenstories.com. **Website:** www.sevenstories.com. **Contact:** Daniel Simon; Anna Lui. Estab. 1995. Founded in 1995 in New York City, and named for the seven authors who committed to a home with a fiercely independent spirit, Seven Stories Press publishes works of the imagination and political titles by voices of conscience. While most widely known for its books on politics, human rights, and social and economic justice, Seven Stories continues to champion literature, with a list encompassing both innovative debut novels and National Book Award–winning poetry collections, as well as prose and poetry translations from the French, Spanish, German, Swedish, Italian, Greek, Polish, Korean, Vietnamese, Russian, and Arabic. Publishes hardcover and trade paperback originals. Book catalog and ms guidelines free.

HOW TO CONTACT "We are currently unable to accept any unsolicited full manuscripts. We do accept query letters and sample chapters. Please send no more than a cover letter and two sample chapters, along with a 44-cent SASE or postcard for reply. (If you would like your submission materials returned to you, please include sufficient postage.)"

TERMS Pays 7-15% royalty on retail price. Pays advance. Responds in 1 month to queries and mss.

TIPS "Each year we also publish an annual compilation of censored news stories by Project Censored. Features of this series include the Top 25 Censored News Stories of the year—which has a history of identifying important neglected news stories and which is widely disseminated in the alternative press—as well as the "Junk Food News" chapter and chapters on hot-button topics for the year. Seven Stories also maintains a publishing partnership with Human Rights Watch through the yearly publication of the World Report, a preeminent account of human rights abuse around the world—a report card on the progress of the world's nations towards the protection of human rights for people everywhere."

Ⓐ☺ SEVERN HOUSE PUBLISHERS

9-15 High St., Sutton, Surrey SM1 1DF United Kingdom. (44)(208)770-3930. **Fax:** (44)(208)770-3850. **Website:** www.severnhouse.com. **Contact:** Amanda Stewart, editorial director. Severn House is currently emphasizing suspense, romance, mystery. Large print imprint from existing authors. Publishes hardcover and trade paperback originals and reprints. Book catalog available free.

IMPRINTS Creme de la Crime.

NEEDS Adventure, fantasy, historical, horror, mainstream/contemporary, mystery, romance, short story collections, suspense. Recently published *Future Scrolls*, by Fern Michaels (historical romance); *Weekend Warrios*, by Fern Michaels; *The Hampton Passion*, by Julie Ellis (romance); *Looking Glass Justice*, by Jeffrey Ashford (crime and mystery); and *Cold Tactics*, by Ted Allbeury (thriller).

HOW TO CONTACT *Agented submissions only.*

TERMS Pays 7 1/2-15% royalty on retail price. Pays $750-5,000 advance. Responds in 3 months to proposals.

Ⓞ SILVER LEAF BOOKS, LLC

P.O. Box 6460, Holliston MA 01746. **E-mail:** editor@silverleafbooks.com. **Website:** www.silverleafbooks.com. **Contact:** Brett Fried, editor. "Silver Leaf Books is a small press featuring primarily new and upcoming talent in the fantasy, science fiction, mystery, thrillers, suspense, and horror genres. Our editors work closely with our authors to establish a lasting and mutually beneficial relationship, helping both the authors and company continue to grow and thrive." Publishes hardcover originals, trade paperback originals, paperback originals, electronic/digital books. Average print order: 3,000. Debut novel print order: 3,000. **Published 1 new writer last year**. Plans 4 debut novels this year. Averages 6 total titles/year; 6 fiction titles/year. Distributes/promotes titles through Baker & Taylor Books and Ingram. Guidelines available online at website.

NEEDS Fantasy (space fantasy, sword and sorcery), horror (dark fantasy, futuristic, psychological, supernatural), mystery/suspense (amateur sleuth, cozy, police procedural, private eye/hard-boiled), science fiction (hard science/technological, soft/sociological), young adult (adventure, fantasy/science fiction, horror, mystery/suspense). Published *The Apprentice of Zoldex* and *The Darkness Within*, by Clifford B. Bowyer; *When the Sky Fell,* by Mike Lynch and Brandon Barr.

HOW TO CONTACT Query with outline/synopsis and 3 sample chapters. Accepts queries by snail mail. Include estimated word count, brief bio and marketing plan. Send SASE or IRC for return of ms or disposable copy of ms and SASE/IRC for reply only.

TERMS Pays royalties, and provides author's copies. Responds to queries in 6 months; mss in 4 months.
TIPS "Follow the online guidelines, be thorough and professional."

SIMON & SCHUSTER

1230 Avenue of the Americas, New York NY 10020. (212)698-7000. **Website:** www.simonsays.com.

Accepts agented submissions only.

SIMON & SCHUSTER ADULT PUBLISHING GROUP

1230 Avenue of the Americas, New York NY 10020. **E-mail:** ssonline@simonsays.com; Lydia.Frost@simonandschuster.com. **Website:** www.simonsays.com. Estab. 1924. (formerly Simon & Schuster Trade Division, Division of Simon & Schuster) , The Simon & Schuster Adult Publishing Group includes a number of publishing units that offer books in several formats. Each unit has its own publisher, editorial group and publicity department. Common sales and business departments support all the units. The managing editorial, art, production, marketing, and subsidiary rights departments have staff members dedicated to the individual imprints.
HOW TO CONTACT *Agented submissions only.*

SMALL BEER PRESS

150 Pleasant St., #306, Easthampton MA 01027. (413) 203-1636. **Fax:** (413) 203-1636. **E-mail:** info@smallbeerpress.com. **Website:** www.smallbeerpress.com. **Contact:** Gavin J. Grant, acquisitions. Estab. 2000.

Small Beer Press also publishes the zine *Lady Churchill's Rosebud Wristlet*. "SBP's books have recently received the Tiptree and Crawford Awards and have been Indiebound."

NEEDS Literary, experimental, speculative, story collections. Recently published *The Monkey's Wedding and Other Stories*, by Joan Aiken; *Meeks*, by Julia Holmes; *What I Didn't See and Other Stories*, by Karen Joy Fowler.
HOW TO CONTACT "We do not accept unsolicited novel or short story collection manuscripts. Queries are welcome. Please send queries with an SASE by mail."
TIPS "Please be familiar with our books first to avoid wasting your time and ours, thank you."

SOFT SKULL PRESS INC.

Counterpoint, 1919 Fifth St., Berkeley CA 94710. (510)704-0230. **Fax:** (510)704-0268. **E-mail:** info@softskull.com. **Website:** www.softskull.com. Publishes hardcover and trade paperback originals. Book catalog and guidelines on website.
NEEDS Confession, experimental, pop culture, gay/lesbian, erotica, graphic novels and comics, literary, mainstream/contemporary, multicultural, short story collections. Agented submissions encouraged. Soft Skull Press accepts unsolicited submissions. E-mail with a subject heading of "SUBMISSION OF Fiction/Nonfiction/Graphic Novel" (whichever is appropriate). Include contact information on your attachment/s, be that a sample chapter or the whole manuscript. Attachments should be no bigger than 2 megabytes. For graphic novels, send a minimum of five fully inked pages of art, along with a synopsis of your storyline.
TERMS Pays 7-10% royalty. Average advance: $100-15,000. Responds in 2 months to proposals; 3 months to mss.
TIPS "See our website for updated submission guidelines. Submit electronically."

SOHO PRESS, INC.

853 Broadway, New York NY 10003. **E-mail:** soho@sohopress.com. **Website:** www.sohopress.com. **Contact:** Bronwen Hruska, publisher; Katie Herman, editor. Estab. 1986. Soho Press publishes primarily fiction, as well as some narrative literary nonfiction and mysteries set abroad. No electronic submissions, only queries by e-mail. Publishes hardcover and trade paperback originals; trade paperback reprints. Guidelines available online.
NEEDS Adventure, ethnic, feminist, historical, literary, mainstream/contemporary, mystery (police procedural), suspense, multicultural. Published *Thirty-Three Teeth*, by Colin Cotterill; *When Red is Black*, by Qiu Xiaolong; *Murder on the Ile Saint-Louis*, by Cara Black; *The Farming of Bones*, by Edwidge Danticat; *The Darkest Child*, by Delores Phillips; *The First Wave*, by James R. Benn.
HOW TO CONTACT Submit 3 sample chapters and cover letter with synopsis, author bio, SASE. *No e-mailed submissions.*
TERMS Pays 10-15% royalty on retail price (varies under certain circumstances). Responds in 3 months to queries and mss.
TIPS "Soho Press publishes discerning authors for discriminating readers, finding the strongest possible writers and publishing them. Before submitting,

look at our website for an idea of the types of books we publish, and read our submission guidelines."

ⒶⒶ SOURCEBOOKS LANDMARK

Sourcebooks, Inc., P.O. Box 4410, Naperville IL 60567. **E-mail:** info@sourcebooks.com. **E-mail:** romance@sourcebooks.com. **Website:** www.sourcebooks.com. **Contact:** Todd Stocke. "Our fiction imprint, Sourcebooks Landmark, publishes a variety of commercial fiction, including specialties in historical fiction and Austenalia. We are interested first and foremost in books that have a story to tell."

> "We publish a variety of titles. We are currently only reviewing agented fiction manuscripts with the exception of Romance fiction. Find out more information about our Romance fiction submission guidelines online at our website."

NEEDS "We are actively acquiring single-title and single-title series Romance fiction (90,000 to 120,000 actual digital words) for our Casablanca imprint. We are looking for strong writers who are excited about marketing their books and building their community of readers, and whose books have something fresh to offer in the genre of Romance." Receipt of email submissions will be acknowledged within 21 days via email. **HOW TO CONTACT** Responds to queries in 6-8 weeks. Email: romance@sourcebooks.com. Or mail hard copy to: Leah Hulltenschmidt, Sourcebooks, Inc., 390 Fifth Ave., Suite 907, New York, NY 10018. If you have any questions about our guidelines, please don't hesitate to email deb.werksman@sourcebooks. com. Please allow 21 days for response.

SOUTHERN METHODIST UNIVERSITY PRESS

P.O. Box 750415, Dallas TX 75275. (214)768-1436. **Fax:** (214)768-1428. **E-mail:** d-vance@tamu.edu. **Website:** www.tamupress.com. **Contact:** Diana Vance. Estab. 1937. " Known nationally as a publisher of the highest quality scholarly works and books for the "educated general reader," SMU Press publishes in the areas of ethics and human values, literary fiction, medical humanities, performing arts, Southwestern studies, and sport. Publishes hardcover and trade paperback originals and reprints. Book catalog available free. Guidelines available online. **NEEDS** "We are willing to look at 'serious' or 'literary' fiction. No mass market, science fiction, formula, thriller, romance."

HOW TO CONTACT Accepts unsolicited mss. Query with SASE. No simultaneous submissions. Sometimes comments on rejected mss. Proposals may be submitted in hard copy or as attachments to emails addressed to the appropriate acquisitions editor. To determine who that is, send a brief description of your manuscript to the acquisitions assistant, Diana Vance, at d-vance@tamu.edu. If one of our editors has invited your manuscript, please use this downloadable proposal form. Because of the volume of proposals received, the Press cannot normally return material to authors. Please do not send original art or other irreplaceable materials.

TERMS Pays 10% royalty on wholesale price, 10 author's copies. Pays $500 advance. Responds in 2 weeks to queries; 1 month to proposals; up to 1 year to mss.

Ⓞ SPEAK UP PRESS

P.O. Box 100506, Denver CO 80250. (303)715-0837. **Fax:** (303)715-0793. **E-mail:** info@speakuppress.org. **E-mail:** submit@speakuppress.org. **Website:** www.speakuppress.org. Estab. 1999. As a 501(c)3 nonprofit organization, Speak Up Press is supported by individuals, corporations, and foundations from across the country. Speak Up Press publishes *Speak Up Online* quarterly, featuring the original fiction, nonfiction, and poetry of teens (13-19 years old).

> *Only accepts submissions via e-mail.*

TIPS "Follow submission guidelines."

Ⓓ SPOUT PRESS

P.O. Box 581067, Minneapolis MN 55458. (612) 782-9629. **E-mail:** spoutpress@hotmail.com; editors@spoutpress.org. **Website:** www.spoutpress.org. **Contact:** Carrie Eidem, fiction editor. Estab. 1989. Ms guidelines for SASE or on website. "Small independent publisher with a permanent staff of five—interested in experimental fiction for our magazine and books." Publishes paperback originals. Books: perfect bound; illustrations. Average print order: 1,000. Distibutes and promotes books through the website, events and large Web-based stores such as Amazon. com. Runs annual. Accepts submissions all year around fall through spring. See website for specific dates and details. Does not accept unsolicited mss. Query with SASE. Accepts queries by mail. Include estimated word count, brief bio, list of publishing credits. Send SASE for return of ms or send a disposable ms and SASE for reply only. Rarely comments on rejected mss. Individual arrangement with author depending on the book.

NEEDS Ethnic, experimental, literary, short story collections. Published *Northern Oracle,* by Kirsten Dierking, *Hotel Sterno,* by Jeffrey Little, and other single author collections. Runs annual. Accepts submissions all year around fall through spring. See website for specific dates and details.

HOW TO CONTACT Does not accept unsolicited mss. Query with SASE. Accepts queries by mail. Include estimated word count, brief bio, list of publishing credits. Send SASE for return of ms or send a disposable ms and SASE for reply only.

TERMS Responds in 1 month to queries; 3-5 months to mss.

TIPS "We tend to publish writers after we know their work via publication in our journal, *Spout Magazine.*"

STARCHERONE BOOKS

Dzanc Books, P.O. Box 303, Buffalo NY 14201. (716)885-2726. **E-mail:** starcherone@gmail.com; publisher@starcherone.com. **Website:** www.starcherone.com. **Contact:** Ted Pelton, publisher; Carra Stratton, acquisitions editor. Estab. 2000. Non-profit publisher of literary and experimental fiction. Publishes paperback originals and reprints. Books: acid-free paper; perfect bound; occasional illustrations. Average print order: 1,000. Average first novel print order: 1,000. **Published 2 debut authors within the last year.** Member CLMP. Titles distributed through website, Small Press Distribution, Amazon, independent bookstores. Catalog and guidelines available online at website.

HOW TO CONTACT Accepts queries by mail or e-mail during August and September of each year. Submissions of unsolicited mss will risk being returned or discarded, unread. Include brief bio, list of publishing credits. Always query before sending ms.

TERMS Pays 10-12.5% royalty. Responds in 2 months to queries; 6-10 months to mss.

TIPS During the late summer/early fall each year, after our contest has concluded, we have an OPEN CONSIDERATION PERIOD of approximately six weeks. During this time, we read queries from authors who already have established their credentials in some way, generally through prior publication, awards, and the like. We ask for queries from writers describing their projects and their writing credentials. From these, we invite submissions. Our next period for receiving queries will be in the late summer/early fall. In October of each year, we begin our ANNUAL CONTEST. "Become familiar with our interests in fiction. We are interested in new strategies for creating stories and fictive texts. Do not send genre fiction unless it is unconventional in approach."

STEEPLE HILL BOOKS

Imprint of Harlequin Enterprises, 233 Broadway, Suite 1001, New York NY 10279. (212)553-4200. **Fax:** (212)227-8969. **Website:** www.eharlequin.com. **Contact:** Joan Marlow Golan, executive editor; Melissa Endlich, senior editor (inspirational contemporary romance, historical romance, romantic suspense); Tina James, senior editor (inspirational romantic suspense and historical romance); Emily Rodmell, associate editor. Estab. 1997. Publishes mass market paperback originals. "This series of contemporary, inspirational love stories portrays Christian characters facing the many challenges of life, faith, and love in today's world." Publishes mass market paperback originals and reprints Guidelines available online, free on request, for #10 SASE

IMPRINTS Love Inspired; Love Inspired Suspense; Love Inspired Historical.

NEEDS Romance (Christian, 70,000-75,000 words). Wants all genres of inspirational woman's fiction including contemporary and historical romance, chick/mom-lit, relationship novels, romantic suspense, mysteries, family sagas, and thrillers. Published *A Mother at Heart,* by Carolyne Aarsen. "We are looking for authors writing from a Christian worldview and conveying their personal faith and ministry values in entertaining fiction that will touch the hearts of believers and seekers everywhere."

HOW TO CONTACT No unsolicited mss. Query with SASE, synopsis. No simultaneous submissions. Query with SASE, submit completed ms.

TERMS Pays royalty. Offers advance. Detailed ms guidelines online. Pays royalty on retail price. Pays advance. 3 months on proposals and mss

Ⓐ ST. MARTIN'S PRESS

175 Fifth Ave., New York NY 10010. (212)677-7456. **Website:** www.stmartins.com. Estab. 1952. General interest publisher of both fiction and nonfiction. Publishes hardcover, trade paperback and mass market originals. Averages 1,500 total titles/year.

NEEDS Fantasy, historical, horror, literary, mainstream/contemporary, mystery, science fiction, suspense, western (contemporary), general fiction; thriller.

HOW TO CONTACT *Agented submissions only.*
TERMS Pays royalty. Offers advance. Ms guidelines online.

SYNERGEBOOKS

205 S. Dixie Dr., Haines City FL 33844. (863)956-3015. **Fax:** (863)588-2198. **E-mail:** synergebooks@aol.com. **Website:** www.synergebooks.com. **Contact:** Debra Staples, publisher/acquisitions editor. Estab. 1999. "SynergEbooks is first and foremost a digital publisher, so most of our marketing budget goes to those formats. Authors are required to direct-sell a minimum of 100 digital copies of a title before it's accepted for print." Publishes trade paperback and electronic originals. Book catalog available online at www.synergebooks.com/paperbacks.html. Guidelines available online at www.synergebooks.com/subguide.html.
NEEDS SynergEbooks publishes at least 40 new titles a year, and only 1-5 of those are put into print in any given year. "SynergEbooks is first and foremost a digital publisher, so most of our marketing budget goes to those formats. Authors are required to direct-sell a minimum of 100 digital copies of a title before it's accepted for print."
HOW TO CONTACT Submit proposal package, including synopsis, 1-3 sample chapters, and marketing plans.
TERMS Pays 15-40% royalty; makes outright purchase.
TIPS "At SynergEbooks, we work with the author to promote their work."

Ⓐ NAN A. TALESE

Imprint of Doubleday, Random House, Inco, 1745 Broadway, New York NY 10019. (212)782-8918. **Fax:** (212)782-8448. **Website:** www.nanatalese.com. **Contact:** Nan A. Talese, publisher and editorial director; Ronit Feldman, assistant editor. "Nan A. Talese publishes nonfiction with a powerful guiding narrative and relevance to larger cultural trends and interests, and literary fiction of the highest quality." Publishes hardcover originals. Averages 15 total titles/year. Nan A. Talese publishes nonfiction with a powerful guiding narrative and relevance to larger cultural interests, and literary fiction of the highest quality. Publishes hardcover originals *Agented submissions only.*
NEEDS Literary. "We want well-written narratives with a compelling story line, good characterization and use of language. We like stories with an edge." *Agented submissions only.* Published *The Blind Assassin*, by Margaret Atwood; *Atonement*, by Ian McEwan;

Great Shame, Thomas Keneally. Well-written narratives with a compelling story line, good characterization and use of language. We like stories with an edge.
HOW TO CONTACT Responds in 1 week to queries; 2 weeks to mss. Accepts simultaneous submissions.
TERMS Pays variable royalty on retail price. Average advance: varying. Publishes ms 1 year after acceptance. Agented submissions only. Pays variable royalty on retail price. Pays varying advance.
TIPS "Audience is highly literate people interested in story, information and insight. We want well-written material submitted by agents only. See our website."

TANGLEWOOD BOOKS

P.O. Box 3009, Terre Haute IN 47803. **E-mail:** ptierney@tanglewoodbooks.com. **Website:** www.tanglewoodbooks.com. **Contact:** Kairi Hamlin, acquisitions editor; Peggy Tierney, publisher. Estab. 2003. "Tanglewood Press strives to publish entertaining, kid-centric books."
NEEDS Picture books: adventure, animal, concept, contemporary, fantasy, humor. Average word length: picture books—800. Recently published *68 Knots*, by Micheal Robert Evans (young adult); *The Mice of Bistrot des Sept Freres*, written and illustrated by Marie Letourneau; *Chester Raccoon and the Acorn Full of Memories*, by Audrey Penn and Barbara Gibson.
HOW TO CONTACT Query with 3-5 sample chapters.
TERMS Responds to mss in up to 18 months.
TIPS "Please see lengthy 'Submissions' page on our website."

TAYLOR TRADE PUBLISHING

The Rowman & Littlefield Publishing Group, 5360 Manhattan Circle, #101, Boulder CO 80303. (303)543-7835. **Fax:** (303)543-0043. **E-mail:** rrinehart@rowman.com. **E-mail:** tradeeditorial@rowman.com. **Website:** www.rlpgtrade.com. **Contact:** Acquisitions Editor. Publishes hardcover originals, trade paperback originals and reprints See catalog online at website. Submission guidelines available on website under "Author Resources."
TERMS Responds in 2 months to queries.

THIRD WORLD PRESS

P.O. Box 19730, Chicago IL 60619. (773)651-0700. **Fax:** (773)651-7286. **E-mail:** twpress3@aol.com; GWENMTWP@aol.com. **Website:** www.thirdworldpressinc.com. **Contact:** Bennett J. Johnson. Estab. 1967. "We look for the maximum effect of creative expression and cultural enlightenment in all of the written genres, including fiction, nonfiction, poetry, drama, young adult, and children's books that may not have an outlet otherwise. Third World Press welcomes the opportunity to review solicited and unsolicited manuscripts that explore African-centered life and thought through the genres listed. Publishes hardcover and trade paperback originals and reprints. Guidelines for #10 SASE.

◯ Third World Press is open to submissions in July only.

NEEDS "We primarily publish nonfiction, but will consider fiction by and about Blacks."

HOW TO CONTACT Query with SASE. Submit outline, clips, 5 sample chapters.

TERMS Compensation based upon royalties. Individual arrangement with author depending on the book, etc. Responds in 6 months to queries. Responds in 5 months to mss.

ⒶⓄ TIN HOUSE BOOKS

2617 NW Thurman St., Portland OR 97210. (503)473-8663. **Fax:** (503)473-8957. **E-mail:** meg@tinhouse.com. **Website:** www.tinhouse.com. **Contact:** Lee Montgomery, editorial director; Meg Storey, editor; Tony Perez, associate editor. "We are a small independent publisher dedicated to nurturing new, promising talent as well as showcasing the work of established writers. Our Tin House New Voice series features work by authors who have not previously published a book." Distributes/promotes titles through Publishers Group West. Publishes hardcover originals, paperback originals, paperback reprints. Guidelines available on website.

HOW TO CONTACT *Agented mss only.* We no longer read unsolicited submissions by authors with no representation. We will continue to accept submissions from agents.

TERMS Responds to queries in 2-3 weeks; mss in 2-3 months.

Ⓞ TITAN PRESS

PMB 17897, Encino CA 91416. **E-mail:** titan91416@yahoo.com. **Website:** www.calwriterssfv.com. **Contact:** Stefanya Wilson, editor. Estab. 1981. Publishes hardcover and paperback originals. Ms guidelines for #10 SASE.

NEEDS Literary, mainstream/contemporary, short story collections. Published *Orange Messiahs*, by Scott Alixander Sonders (fiction).

HOW TO CONTACT Does not accept unsolicited mss. Query with SASE. Include brief bio, social security number, list of publishing credits.

TERMS Pays 20-40% royalty. Responds to queries in 3 months.

TIPS "Look, act, sound, and *be* professional."

TO BE READ ALOUD PUBLISHING, INC.

P.O. Box 632426, Nacogdoches TX 75963. **E-mail:** michael@tobereadaloud.org. **E-mail:** submissions@tobereadaloud.org. **Website:** www.tobereadaloud.org. **Contact:** Michael Powell, president (short stories); Stephen Powell, editor (poetry). Estab. 2006. Publishes trade paperback originals and reprints. Guidelines available via e-mail.

NEEDS All submissions should be written by authors born in one of the following states: Alabama, Arkansas, Florida, Georgia, Louisiana, Kentucky, Mississippi, North Carolina, South Carolina, Tennessee, Virginia, or West Virginia.

HOW TO CONTACT Submit complete ms. Attach as a Word .doc.

TERMS Makes outright purchase of $100-200. Responds in 3 months to queries, proposals, and mss.

TIPS "Our audience is high school drama students. Read your selection aloud before submitting. We service the UIL of Texas mostly; check their annual categories and write accordingly to match them."

Ⓞ TOP COW PRODUCTIONS

10390 Santa Monica Blvd., Suite 340, Los Angeles CA **Website:** http://www.topcow.com/Site/.

HOW TO CONTACT *No unsolicited submissions.* Prefers submissions from artists. See website for details and advice on how to break into the market.

TORQUERE PRESS

P.O. Box 2545, Round Rock TX 78680. (512)586-3553. **Fax:** (866)287-2968. **E-mail:** editor@torquerepress.com. **E-mail:** submissions@torquerepress.com. **Website:** www.torquerepress.com. **Contact:** Shawn Clements, submissions editor (homoerotica, suspense, gay/lesbian); Lorna Hinson, senior editor (gay/lesbian romance, historicals). Estab. 2003. "We are a gay and lesbian press focusing on romance and genres of romance. We particularly like paranormal and western romance." Publishes trade paperback originals and electronic originals and reprints Book catalog available online. Guidelines available online.

IMPRINTS Top Shelf (Shawn Clements, editor); Single Shots (Kil Kenny, editor); Screwdrivers (M. Rode, editor); High Balls (Vincent Diamond, editor).

NEEDS All categories gay and lesbian themed. Adventure, erotica, historical, horror, mainstream, multicultural, mystery, occult, romance, science fiction, short story collections, suspense, western. Published *Broken Road*, by Sean Michael (romance); *Soul Mates: Bound by Blood*, by Jourdan Lane (paranormal romance). Imprints accepting submissions.

HOW TO CONTACT Submit proposal package, 3 sample chapters, clips.

TERMS Pays 8-40% royalty. Pays $35-75 for anthology stories. Responds in 1 month to queries and proposals; 2-4 months to mss.

TIPS "Our audience is primarily people looking for a familiar romance setting featuring gay or lesbian protagonists. Please read guidelines carefully and familiarize yourself with our lines."

☁ TRADEWIND BOOKS

202-1807 Maritime Mews, Granville Island, Vancouver BC V6H 3W7 Canada. (604)662-4405. **E-mail:** tradewindbooks@mail.lycos.com. **Website:** www.tradewindbooks.com. **Contact:** Michael Katz, publisher; Carol Frank, art director; R. David Stephens, senior editor. "Tradewind Books publishes juvenile picture books and young adult novels. Requires that submissions include evidence that author has read at least 3 titles published by Tradewind Books." Publishes hardcover and trade paperback originals. Book catalog and ms guidelines online.

NEEDS Picture books: adventure, multicultural, folktales. Average word length: 900 words. Recently published *City Kids*, by X.J. Kennedy and illustrated by Phillpe Beha; *Roxy* by PJ Reece; *Viva Zapata!* by Emilie Smith and illustrated by Stefan Czernecki.

HOW TO CONTACT Send complete ms for picture books. *YA novels by Canadian authors only. Chapter books by US authors considered.*

TERMS Pays 7% royalty on retail price. Pays variable advance. Responds to mss in 2 months.

TRAVIS LAKE PUBLISHING LLC

P.O. Box 410, City College Station TX 77841. **E-mail:** contact@travislakepublishing.com. **E-mail:** submissions@travislakepublishing.com. **Website:** www.travislakepublishing.com. **Contact:** Sandra J. Smith, partner/editor-in-chief (mystery, thriller, science fiction, fantasy); Stephen D. Dealer, partner/publisher (history, civil rights, law, business). Estab. 2011. Publishes electronic originals, electronic reprints, trade paperback originals. Catalog available for #10 SASE or online at website. Guidelines available for #10 SASE or online at website.

NEEDS "We are looking primarily for novel length manuscripts of between 35,000 and 125,000 words. Optimal length is around 82,000 words, approximately the length of a 328 page novel. At this time we do NOT publish romance or erotica. Depictions of sex should be no more explicit than what can be found in an R rated movie."

HOW TO CONTACT Submit proposal package including synopsis, 3 sample chapters, a "professinal query letter which includes the title of your novel, word count, genre, short bio, whether or not proposed work has been previously published in any format, and your contact information."

TERMS Advance range up to $200. Royalties run from 8% (trades) to %50 (electronic). Responds in 1 month on queries and proposals.

☁ ◐ ☁ TURNSTONE PRESS

206-100 Arthur St., Winnipeg MB R3B 1H3 Canada. (204)947-1555. **Fax:** (204)942-1555. **E-mail:** info@turnstonepress.com. **E-mail:** editor@turnstonepress.com. **Website:** www.turnstonepress.com. Estab. 1976. "Turnstone Press is a literary publisher, not a general publisher, and therefore we are only interested in literary fiction, literary non-fiction—including literary criticism—and poetry. We do publish literary mysteries, thrillers, and noir under our Ravenstone imprint. We publish only Canadian authors or landed immigrants, we strive to publish a significant number of new writers, to publish in a variety of genres, and to have 50% of each year's list be Manitoba writers and/or books with Manitoba content." Guidelines available online at website.

HOW TO CONTACT "Samples must be 40 to 60 pages, typed/printed in a minimum 12 point serif typeface such as Times, Book Antiqua, or Garamond."

TERMS Responds in 4-7 months.

TIPS "As a Canadian literary press, we have a mandate to publish Canadian writers only. Do some homework before submitting works to make sure your subject matter/genre/writing style falls within the publishers area of interest."

◐ TWILIGHT TIMES BOOKS

P.O. Box 3340, Kingsport TN 37664. **Website:** www.twilighttimesbooks.com. **Contact:** Andy M. Scott, managing editor. Estab. 1999. "We publish compelling literary fiction by authors with a distinctive voice." Guidelines available online.

HOW TO CONTACT Accepts unsolicited mss. Do not send complete mss. Queries via e-mail only. Include estimated word count, brief bio, list of publishing credits, marketing plan.

TERMS Pays 8-15% royalty. Responds in 4 weeks to queries; 2 months to mss.

TIPS "The only requirement for consideration at Twilight Times Books is that your novel must be entertaining and professionally written."

⦿ UNBRIDLED BOOKS

200 N. Ninth Street, Suite A, Columbia MO 65201. **Website:** http://unbridledbooks.com. Estab. 2004. "Unbridled Books is a premier publisher of works of rich literary quality that appeal to a broad audience."

HOW TO CONTACT Please query first by e-mail. Due to the heavy volume of submissions, we regret that at this time we are not able to consider uninvited mss. Please query either Fred Ramey or Greg Michalson, but NOT BOTH.

TIPS "We try to read each ms that arrives, so please be patient."

UNIVERSITY OF GEORGIA PRESS

330 Research Dr., Athens GA 30602. (706)369-6130. **Fax:** (706)369-6131. **E-mail:** books@ugapress.uga.edu. **Website:** www.ugapress.org. Estab. 1938. University of Georgia Press is a midsized press that publishes fiction only through the Flannery O'Connor Award for Short Fiction competition. Publishes hardcover originals, trade paperback originals, and reprints. Book catalog and ms guidelines for #10 SASE or online.

NEEDS Short story collections published in Flannery O'Connor Award Competition.

HOW TO CONTACT Mss for Flannery O'Connor Award for Short Fiction accepted in April and May.

TERMS Pays 7-10% royalty on net receipts. Pays rare, varying advance. Responds in 2 months to queries.

TIPS "Please visit our website to view our book catalogs and for all manuscript submission guidelines."

UNIVERSITY OF IOWA PRESS

100 Kuhl House, 119 W. Park Rd., Iowa City IA 52242. (319)335-2000. **Fax:** (319)335-2055. **E-mail:** uipress@uiowa.edu. **Website:** www.uiowapress.org. **Contact:** Holly Carver, director; Joseph Parsons, acquisitions editor. Estab. 1969. "We publish authoritative, original nonfiction that we market mostly by direct mail to groups with special interests in our titles, and by advertising in trade and scholarly publications." Publishes hardcover and paperback originals. Book catalog available free. Guidelines available online.

NEEDS Currently publishes the Iowa Short Fiction Award selections.

TERMS Pays 7-10% royalty on net receipts.

UNIVERSITY OF NEVADA PRESS

Morrill Hall, Mail Stop 0166, Reno NV 89557. (775)784-6573. **Fax:** (775)784-6200. **Website:** www.unpress.nevada.edu. **Contact:** Joanne O'Hare, director. Estab. 1961. "Small university press. Publishes fiction that primarily focuses on the American West." Member: AAUP Publishes hardcover and paperback originals and reprints. Guidelines available online.

NEEDS "We publish in Basque Studies, Gambling Studies, Western literature, Western history, Natural science, Environmental Studies, Travel and Outdoor books, Archeology, Anthropology, and Political Studies, all focusing on the West". The Press also publishes creative nonfiction and books on regional topics for a general audience. Has published *The Mechanics of Falling and Other Stories*, by Catherine Brady; *Little Lost River*, by Pamela Johnston; *Moon Lily*, by Susan Lang.

HOW TO CONTACT Submit proposal package, outline, clips, 2-4 sample chapters. Include estimated word count, brief bio, list of publishing credits. Send SASE or IRC. No e-mail submissions.

TERMS Responds in 2 months.

⑤ UNIVERSITY OF NEW MEXICO PRESS

1 University of New Mexico, MSC05 3185, Albuquerque NM 87131. (505)277-3324 or (800)249-7737. **Fax:** (505)277-3343. **E-mail:** clark@unm.edu. **E-mail:** wcwhiteh@unm.edu. **Website:** www.unmpress.com. **Contact:** W. Clark Whitehorn, editor-in-chief. Estab. 1929. "The Press is well known as a publisher in the fields of anthropology, archeology, Latin American studies, art and photography, architecture and the history and culture of the American West, fiction, some poetry, Chicano/a studies and works by and about American Indians. We focus on American West, Southwest and Latin American regions." Publishes hardcover originals and trade paperback originals and reprints. Book catalog available for free. Please read and follow the submission query guidelines on the Author Information page online. Do not send your entire ms or additional materials until requested. If your book is accepted for publication, you will be notified.

TERMS Pays variable royalty. Pays variable royalty. Pays advance.

ⓘ UNIVERSITY OF WISCONSIN PRESS

1930 Monroe St., 3rd Floor, Madison WI 53711. (608)263-1110. **Fax:** (608)263-1132. **E-mail:** uwiscpress@uwpress.wisc.edu. **E-mail:** kadushin@wisc.edu. **Website:** www.wisc.edu/wisconsinpress. **Contact:** Raphael Kadushin, senior acquisitions editor. Estab. 1937. Publishes hardcover originals, paperback originals, and paperback reprints. Averages 98 total titles, 15 fiction titles/year. Member, AAUP. Distributes titles through ads, reviews, catalog, sales reps, etc. Publishes hardcoveroriginals, paperback originals, and paperback reprints.

○ **Published 5-8 debut authors within the last year.** Member, AAUP. Distributes titles through ads, reviews, catalog, sales reps, etc.

NEEDS Gay/lesbian, historical, lesbian, mystery, regional (Wisconsin), short story collections. Recently published *A Friend of Kissinger*, by David Milofsky; *Beijing*, by Philip Gambone; *Latin Moon in Manhattan*, by Jaime Manrique. Gay/lesbian, historical,lesbian, mystery, regional (Wisconsin), short story collections. Recentlypublished *A Friend of Kissinger*, by David Milofsky; *Beijing*, by Philip Gambone; <i>*Latin Moon in Manhattan*, by Jaime Manrique.

HOW TO CONTACT Does not accept unsolicited mss. Query with SASE or submit outline, 1-2 sample chapter(s), synopsis. Accepts queries by e-mail, mail, fax. Include estimated word count, brief bio. Send copy of ms and SASE. Direct your inquiries in the areas of autobiography/memoir, biography, classical studies, dance and performance studies, film, food, gender studies, GLBT studies, Jewish studies, Latino/a memoirs, and travel to Raphael Kadushin, kadushin@wisc.edu. Agented fiction: 40%. Direct non-fiction inquiries in the areas of African studies, anthropology, environmental studies, human rights, Irish studies, Latin American studies, Slavic studies, Southeast Asian studies, and U.S. History to Gwen Walker, gcwalker@uwpress.wisc.edu. See website for more contact info. Responds in 2 weeks to queries; 8 weeks to mss. Rarely comments on rejected mss.

TERMS Pays royalty. Publishes ms 9-18 months after acceptance. Ms guidelines online. Pays royalty. Responds in 2 weeks toqueries; 8 weeks to mss. Rarely comments on rejected mss.

TIPS "Make sure the query letter and sample text are well-written, and read guidelines carefully to make sure we accept the genre you are submitting."

⊕ UNTREED READS PUBLISHING

506 Kansas St., San Francisco CA 94107. (415)621-0465. **Fax:** (415)621-0465. **E-mail:** general@untreedreads.com. **E-mail:** submissions@untreedreads.com. **Website:** www.untreedreads.com. **Contact:** Jay A. Hartman, editor-in-chief (fiction-all genres). Estab. 2009. Publishes electronic originals and reprints. Catalog and guidelines available online at website.

NEEDS "We look forward to long-terms relationships with our authors. We encourage works that are either already a series or could develop into a series. We are one of the few publishers publishing short stories and are happy to be a resource for these good works. We welcome short story collections. Also, we look forward to publishing children's books, cookbooks, and other works that have been known for illustrations in print as the technology in the multiple ereaders improves. We hope to be a large platform for diverse content and authors. We seek mainstream content, but if you're an author or have content that doesn't seem to always 'fit' into traditional market we'd like to hear from you." No erotica, picture books, poetry, poetry in translation, or romance.

HOW TO CONTACT Submit porposal package with 3 sample chapters. Submit completed ms.

TERMS Pays 50-60% royalty on retail price. Responds in ½ month on queries, 1 month on proposals, and 1 ½ months on mss.

TIPS "For our fiction titles we lean toward a literary audience. For nonfiction titles, we want to be a platform for business people, entrepreneurs, and speakers to become well known in their fields of expertise. However, for both fiction and nonfiction we want to appeal to many audiences."

⊕ VANHOOK HOUSE

925 Orchard St., Charleston WV 25302. **E-mail:** editor@vanhookhouse.com. **E-mail:** acquisitions@vanhookhouse.com. **Website:** www.vanhookhouse.com. **Contact:** Jim Whyte, acquisitions, all fiction/true crime/military/war. Estab. 2009. "VanHook House is a small press focused on the talents of new, unpublished authors. We are looking for works of fiction and non-fiction to add to our catalog. No erotica or sci-fi, please. Query via email. Queries accepted ONLY during submissions periods." Hardcover and trade

paperback originals; trade paperback reprints. Book catalog and guidelines free on request and available online at website.

○ "We employ the expertise of individuals qualified to review works falling within their field of study. Be sure of all sources and facts, as VanHook House *will* confirm any and all information. All editing is done in a way to ensure the author's voice remains unchanged."

TERMS Pays authors 8-10% royalty on wholesale price. Advance negotiable. Responds in 1 month on queries; 2 months on proposals; 3 months on mss.
TIPS "Visit our website."

○ VÉHICULE PRESS

Box 125, Place du Parc Station, Montreal QC H2X 4A3 Canada. (514)844-6073. **Fax:** (514)844-7543. **E-mail:** vp@vehiculepress.com. **Website:** www.vehiculepress.com. **Contact:** Simon Dardick, president/ publisher. Estab. 1973. "Montreal's Véhicule Press has published the best of Canadian and Quebec literature-fiction, poetry, essays, translations, and social history." Publishes trade paperback originals by Canadian authors mostly. Book catalog for 9 x 12 SAE with IRCs.

○ Mostly Canadian authors.

IMPRINTS Signal Editions (poetry); Dossier Quebec (history, memoirs); Esplanade Editions (fiction).
NEEDS Contact Andrew Steinmetz. Literary, regional, short story collections. Published *Optique*, by Clayton Bailey; *Seventeen Tomatoes: Tales from Kashmir*, by Jaspreet Singh; *A Short Journey by Car*, by Liam Durcan. No romance or formula writing.
HOW TO CONTACT Query with SASE.
TERMS Pays 10-15% royalty on retail price. Pays $200-500 advance. Responds in 4 months to queries.
TIPS "Quality in almost any style is acceptable. We believe in the editing process."

○☺ VERTIGO

DC Universe, Vertigo-DC Comics, 1700 Broadway, New York NY 10019. **Website:** www.dccomics.com.
NEEDS "The DC TALENT SEARCH program is designed to offer aspiring artists the chance to present artwork samples directly to the DC Editors and Art Directors. The process is simple: during your convention visit, drop off photocopied samples of your work and enjoy the show! No lines, no waiting. If the DC folks like what they see, a time is scheduled for you the following day to meet a DC representative person-

ally and discuss your artistic interests and portfolio. At this time, DC Comics does not accept unsolicited writing submissions by mail. See submission guidelines online. "We're seeking artists for all our imprints, including the DC Universe, Vertigo, WildStorm, Mad magazine, Minx, kids comics and more!"

ⒶVIKING

Imprint of Penguin Group (USA), Inc., 375 Hudson St., New York NY 10014. (212)366-2000. **Website:** us.penguingroup.com/static/pages/publishers/adult/viking.html. Estab. 1925. Viking publishes a mix of academic and popular fiction and nonfiction. Publishes hardcover and originals.
NEEDS Literary, mainstream/contemporary, mystery, suspense. Published *Lake Wobegon Summer 1956*, by Garrison Keillor; *A Day Late and A Dollar Short*, by Terry McMillian; *A Common Life*, by Jan Karon; *In the Heart of the Sea*, by Nathaniel Philbrick.
HOW TO CONTACT Agented submissions only.
TERMS Pays 10-15% royalty on retail price.

ⒶⒹ VIKING CHILDREN'S BOOKS

345 Hudson St., New York NY 10014. **E-mail:** averystudiopublicity@us.penguingroup.com. **Website:** www.penguingroup.com. **Contact:** Catherine Frank, executive editor. "Viking Children's Books is known for humorous, quirky picture books, in addition to more traditional fiction. We publish the highest quality fiction, nonfiction, and picture books for pre-schoolers through young adults." Publishes hardcover originals.

○ *Does not accept unsolicited submissions.*

NEEDS All levels: adventure, animal, contemporary, fantasy, history, humor, multicultural, nature/environment, poetry, problem novels, romance, science fiction, sports, suspense/mystery. Recently published *Llama Llama Misses Mama*, by Anna Dewdney (ages 2 up, picture book); *Wintergirls*, by Laurie Halse Anderson (ages 12 and up); *Good Luck Bear*, by Greg Foley (ages 2 up); *Along for the Ride*, by Sarah Dessen (ages 12 up).
HOW TO CONTACT *Accepts agented mss only.*
TERMS Pays 2-10% royalty on retail price or flat fee. Pays negotiable advance. Responds to queries/mss in 6 months.
TIPS No "cartoony" or mass-market submissions for picture books.

ⒶVILLARD BOOKS

Imprint of Random House Publishing Group, 1745 Broadway, New York NY 10019. (212)572-2600. **Web-**

site: www.atrandom.com. Estab. 1983. Publishes hardcover and trade paperback originals. Averages 40-50 total titles/year. "Villard Books is the publisher of savvy and sometimes quirky, best-selling hardcovers and trade paperbacks." Publishes hardcover and trade paperback originals

NEEDS Commercial fiction. Commercial fiction.

HOW TO CONTACT *Agented submissions only.* Agented fiction 95%. Accepts simultaneous submissions. Agented submissions only.

TERMS Pays negotiable royalty. Average advance: negotiable.

Ⓐ VINTAGE ANCHOR PUBLISHING

1745 Broadway, New York NY 10019. **E-mail:** vintageanchorpublicity@randomhouse.com. **Website:** www.randomhouse.com. **Contact:** Furaha Norton, editor.

NEEDS Literary, mainstream/contemporary, short story collections. Published *Snow Falling on Cedars*, by Guterson (contemporary); *Martin Dressler*, by Millhauser (literary).

HOW TO CONTACT *Agented submissions only.* Accepts simultaneous submissions. No electronic submissions.

TERMS Pays 4-8% royalty on retail price. Average advance: $2,500 and up.

VIZ MEDIA LLC

P.O. Box 77010, 295 Bay St., San Francisco CA 94133. (415)546-7073. **E-mail:** evelyn.dubocq@viz.com. **Website:** www.viz.com. "VIZ Media, LLC is one of the most comprehensive and innovative companies in the field of manga (graphic novel) publishing, animation and entertainment licensing of Japanese content. Owned by three of Japan's largest creators and licensors of manga and animation, Shueisha Inc., Shogakukan Inc., and Shogakukan-Shueisha Productions, Co., Ltd., VIZ Media is a leader in the publishing and distribution of Japanese manga for English speaking audiences in North America, the United Kingdom, Ireland, and South Africa and is a global ex-Asia licensor of Japanese manga and animation. The company offers an integrated product line including magazines such as SHONEN JUMP and SHOJO BEAT, graphic novels, and DVDs, and develops, markets, licenses, and distributes animated entertainment for audiences and consumers of all ages."

HOW TO CONTACT VIZ Media is currently accepting submissions and pitches for original comics. Keep in mind that all submissions must be accompanied by a signed release form.

WAKESTONE PRESS

200 Brook Hollow Rd., Nashville TN 37205. (615)739-6428. **E-mail:** submissions@wakestonepress.com. **Website:** www.wakestonepress.com. **Contact:** Frank Daniels III, editor. Estab. 2010. Publishes hardcover, trade paperback and electronic originals. Catalog free by request. Guidelines free by request.

IMPRINTS Wakestone Press LLC; Moonshadow Press (subsidiary): Fiction imprint targeting young adults (10 - up).

HOW TO CONTACT Submit in Microsoft Word file(s) a proposal package, including: book outline several (2-3) sample chapter(s) and author bio(s).

TERMS Pays 7.5%-20% on wholesale price. Outright purchases $10,000-$20,000 maximum. Pays $2,000-$5,000 advance. Responds 1 month to queries and proposals; 2 months to mss.

WALKER AND CO.

Walker Publishing Co., 175 Fifth Ave., 7th Floor, New York NY 10010. (212)727-8300. **Fax:** (212)727-0984. **E-mail:** rebecca.mancini@bloomsburyusa.com. **Website:** www.walkeryoungreaders.com. **Contact:** Emily Easton, publisher (picture books, middle grade & young adult novels); Stacy Cantor, associate editor (picture books, middle grade, and young adult novels); Mary Kate Castellani, assistant editor (picture books, middle grade, and young adult novels). Estab. 1959. "Walker publishes general nonfiction on a variety of subjects, as well as children's books." Publishes hardcover trade originals. Book catalog for 9×12 envelope and 3 first-class stamps.

NEEDS Accepts unsolicited mss. Query with SASE. Include "a concise description of the story line, including its outcome, word length of story, writing experience, publishing credits, particular expertise on this subject and in this genre. Common mistake: not researching our publishing program and forgetting SASE."

HOW TO CONTACT Query with SASE. Send complete ms for picture books.

TERMS Pays 5-10% royalty.

Ⓐ WATERBROOK MULTNOMAH PUBLISHING GROUP

Random House, 12265 Oracle Blvd., Suite 200, Colorado Springs CO 80921. (719)590-4999. **Fax:** (719)590-8977. **Website:** www.waterbrookmultnomah.com. Estab. 1996. Publishes hardcover and trade paperback originals. Book catalog available online.

NEEDS Adventure, historical, literary, mainstream/ contemporary, mystery, religious (inspirational, religious mystery/suspense, religious thriller, religious romance), romance (contemporary, historical), science fiction, spiritual, suspense. Published *A Name of Her Own*, by Jane Kirkpatrick (historical); *Women's Intuition*, by Lisa Samson (contemporary); *Thorn in My Heart*, by Liz Curtis Higgs (historical).

HOW TO CONTACT Agented submissions only.

TERMS Pays royalty. Responds in 2-3 months to queries/proposals/mss.

WHITE MANE PUBLISHING COMPANY INC.

73 W. Burd St., P.O. Box 708, Shippensburg PA 17257. (717)532-2237; (888)948-6263. **Fax:** (717)532-6110. **E-mail:** marketing@whitemane.com. **Website:** www. whitemane.com. Estab. 1987.

IMPRINTS White Mane Books, Burd Street Press, White Mane Kids

HOW TO CONTACT "Download and print out the Proposal Guidelines form. Fill out the form and mail it along with the title of the manuscript, statement of purpose, marketing ideas, a sample dust jacket paragraph, general manuscript information, and how you were referred to White Mane."

WILD CHILD PUBLISHING

P.O. Box 4897, Culver City CA 90231. (310) 721-4461. **E-mail:** admin@wildchildpublishing.com. **Website:** www.wildchildpublishing.com. **Contact:** Marci Baun, editor-in-chief (genres not covered by other editors); Faith Bicknell-Brown, managing editor (horror and romance); S.R. Howen, editor (science fiction and nonfiction). Estab. 1999. Wild Child Publishing is a small, independent press that started out as a magazine in September 1999. We are known for working with newer/unpublished authors and editing to the standards of NYC publishers. Publishes paperback originals, e-books. Format: POD printing; perfect bound. Average print order: 50-200. Member EPIC. Distributes/promotes titles through Ingrams and own website, Mobipocket Kindle, Amazon, and soon with Fictionwise. Freya's Bower already distributes through Fictionwise. Book catalogs on website.

NEEDS Adventure, children's/juvenile, erotica for Freya's Bower only, ethnic/multicultural, experimental, fantasy, feminist, gay, historical, horror, humor/satire, lesbian, literary, mainstream, military/ war, mystery/suspense, New Age/mystic, psychic/ supernatural, romance, science fiction, short story collections, thriller/espionage, western, young adult/ teen (fantasy/science fiction). Multiple anthologies planned.

HOW TO CONTACT Query with outline/synopsis and 1 sample chapter. Accepts queries by e-mail only. Include estimated word count, brief bio. Often critiques/comments on rejected mss. Published *Weirdly: A Collection of Strange Tales*, by Variety(horror/psychological thriller); *Quits: Book 2: Devils*, by M.E. Ellis (horror, psychological thriller, paranormal).

TERMS Pays royalties 10-40%. Responds in 1 month to queries and mss.

TIPS "Read our submission guidelines thoroughly. Send in entertaining, well-written stories. Be easy to work with and upbeat."

WILDE PUBLISHING

P.O. Box 4581, Alburquerque NM 87196. **Fax:** (419)715-1430. **E-mail:** wilde@unm.edu. **Contact:** Josiah Simon, Dusty, McGowan, and David Wilde. Estab. 1989. Publishes hardcover and paperback originals. Ms guidelines for #10 SASE.

NEEDS Children's/juvenile, fantasy (sword and sorcery), historical, literary, military/war, mystery, psychic/supernatural, romance, short story collections, thriller/espionage, western, young adult. Published *Scuttlebut*, by David Wilde (military) and *Harry The Magician*, byt Dusty McGowan (children).

HOW TO CONTACT Does not accept unsolicited mss. Query with SASE. Accepts queries by e-mail, fax, mail. Include cover letter, brief bio, list of publishing credits. Send SASE for return of ms or send a disposable ms and SASE for reply only. Accepts submissions on disk. No simultaneous submissions.

TERMS Pay depends on grants and awards.

TIPS "Check spelling, write frequently, avoid excuses!"

THE WILD ROSE PRESS

P.O. Box 708, Adams Basin NY 14410. (585) 752-8770. **E-mail:** queryus@thewildrosepress.com; rpenders@ thewildrosepress.com. **Website:** www.thewildrosepress.com. **Contact:** Nicole D'Arienzo, editor. Estab. 2006. Publishes paperback originals, reprints, and e-books in a POD format. Guidelines available on website.

"The American Rose line publishes stories about the French and Indian wars; Colonial America; the Revolutionary War; the war of 1812; the War Between the States; the Reconstruction era; the dawn of the new century. These are the struggles at the heart of the American Rose story. The central romantic relationship is the key driving force, set against historically accurate backdrop. These stories are for those who long for the courageous heroes and heroines who fought for their freedom and settled the new world; for gentle southern belles with spines of steel and the gallant gentlemen who sweep them away. This line is wide open for writers with a love of American history." Published 5 debut authors last year. Member: EPIC, Romance Writers of America. Has received two Eppie Awards (2007) for First Place, and the New Jersey Golden Leaf Award for 2006 and 2007.

NEEDS "The American Rose line publishes stories about the French and Indian wars; Colonial America; the Revolutionary War; the war of 1812; the War Between the States; the Reconstruction era; the dawn of the new century. These are the struggles at the heart of the American Rose story. The central romantic relationship is the key driving force, set against historically accurate backdrop. These stories are for those who long for the courageous heroes and heroines who fought for their freedom and settled the new world; for gentle southern belles with spines of steel and the gallant gentlemen who sweep them away. This line is wide open for writers with a love of American history." Publishes paperback originals, reprints, and e-books in a POD format. Published 5 debut authors last year. Publishes approximately 10 fiction titles/year. Member: EPIC, Romance Writers of America. Distributes/promotes titles through major distribution chains, including Ingrams, Baker & Taylor, Sony, Kindle, Amazon.com, as well as smaller and online distributors. Please do not submit women's fiction, poetry, science fiction, fanfiction, or any type of nonfiction. *Does not accept unsolicited mss.* Send query letter with outline and synopsis of up to 5 pages. Accepts all queries by e-mail. Include estimated word count, brief bio, and list of publishing credits.

HOW TO CONTACT *Does not accept unsolicited mss.* Send query letter with outline and synopsis of up to 5 pages. Accepts all queries by e-mail. Include estimated word count, brief bio, and list of publishing credits. Agented fiction less than 1%. Always comments on rejected mss. Sends prepublication galleys to author. Only our full length (over 65K words) will go to print. For information on distribution visit our FAQ section. We only publish **ROMANCE**. Please do not submit women's fiction, poetry, science fiction, fanfiction, or any type of nonfiction. For more information on how we define **ROMANCE,** please read the articles listed in the FAQ section . We may or may not respond to a query for something that is NOT a romance.

TERMS Pays royalty of 7% minimum; 35% maximum. Responds in 1 month to queries; 3 months to mss.

TIPS "Polish your manuscript, make it as error free as possible, and follow our submission guidelines."

⊘ WILDSTORM

DC Universe, 1700 Broadway, New York NY 10019. **Website:** http://www.dccomics.com/wildstorm/. DC Universe, 1700 Broadway, New York NY 10019. (212)636-5400. **Website:** http://www.dccomics.com/wildstorm/. Wildstorm is part of the DC Universe.

○ *Does not accept unsolicited mss.*

HOW TO CONTACT "At this time, DC Comics does not accept unsolicited artwork or writing submissions."

Ⓐ⊘ WILLIAM MORROW

HarperCollins, 10 E. 53rd St., New York NY 10022. (212)207-7000. **Fax:** (212)207-7145. **Website:** www.harpercollins.com. Estab. 1926. "William Morrow publishes a wide range of titles that receive much recognition and prestige—a most selective house." Book catalog available free.

NEEDS Publishes adult fiction. Morrow accepts only the highest quality submissions in adult fiction. *No unsolicited mss or proposals.*

HOW TO CONTACT Agented submissions only.

TERMS Pays standard royalty on retail price. Pays varying advance.

Ⓓ WILSHIRE BOOK COMPANY

9731 Variel Ave., Chatsworth CA 91311. (818)700-1522. **Fax:** (818)700-1527. **E-mail:** mpowers@mpowers.com. **Website:** www.mpowers.com. **Contact:** Rights Department. Estab. 1947. Publishes trade paperback originals and reprints. Ms guidelines online.

NEEDS "You are not only what you are today, but also what you choose to become tomorrow." Looking for adult fables that teach principles of psychological growth. Distributes titles through wholesalers, bookstores and mail order. Promotes titles through author interviews on radio and television.Wants adult allegories that teach principles of psychological growth or offer guidance in living. Minimum 30,000 words. No standard fiction.

HOW TO CONTACT Submit 3 sample chapters. Submit complete ms. Include outline, author bio, analysis of book's, competition and SASE.

TERMS Pays standard royalty. Pays advance. Responds in 2 months.

TIPS "We are vitally interested in all new material we receive. Just as you are hopeful when submitting your manuscript for publication, we are hopeful as we read each one submitted, searching for those we believe could be successful in the marketplace. Writing and publishing must be a team effort. We need you to write what we can sell. We suggest you read the successful books similar to the one you want to write. Analyze them to discover what elements make them winners. Duplicate those elements in your own style, using a creative new approach and fresh material, and you will have written a book we can catapult onto the bestseller list. You are welcome to telephone or e-mail us for immediate feedback on any book concept you may have. To learn more about us and what we publish, and for complete manuscript guidelines, visit our website."

WINDRIVER PUBLISHING, INC.

72 N. WindRiver Rd., Silverton ID 83867. (208)752-1836. **Fax:** (208)752-1876. **E-mail:** info@windriverpublishing.com. **Website:** www.windriverpublishing.com. **Contact:** E. Keith Howick, Jr., president; Gail Howick, vice president/editor-in-chief. Estab. 2003. "Authors who wish to submit book proposals for review must do so according to our Submissions Guidelines, which can be found on our website, along with an on-line submission form, which is our preferred submission method. *We do not accept submissions of any kind by e-mail.*" Publishes hardcover originals and reprints, trade paperback originals, and mass market originals. Book catalog available online. Guidelines available online.

HOW TO CONTACT *Does not accept unsolicited mss.*

TERMS Responds in 1-2 months to queries; 4-6 months to proposals/mss.

TIPS "We do not accept manuscripts containing graphic or gratuitous profanity, sex, or violence. See online instructions for details."

WIZARDS OF THE COAST BOOKS FOR YOUNG READERS

P.O. Box 707, Renton WA 98057. (425)254-2287. **E-mail:** nina.hess@wizards.com. **Website:** www.wizards.com. **Contact:** Nina Hess. Estab. 2003. Wizards of the Coast publishes only science fiction and fantasy shared-world titles. Currently emphasizing solid fantasy writers. De-emphasizing gothic fiction. Dragonlance; Forgotten Realms; Magic: The Gathering; Eberron. Wizard of the Coast publishes games as well, including Dungeons & Dragons® role-playing game. Publishes hardcover and trade paperback originals and trade paperback reprints. Catalog available on website. Ms guidelines available on website.

NEEDS Young readers, middle readers, young adults: fantasy only. Average word length: middle readers—30,000-40,000; young adults—60,000-75,000. Recently published *A Practical Guide to Dragon-Riding*, by Lisa Trumbauer (ages 6 and up); *The Stowaway*, by R.A. Salvatore and Geno Salvatore (10 and up), *Red Dragon Codex*, by R. Henham (ages 8-12).

HOW TO CONTACT Query with samples.

TERMS Pays authors 4-6% based on retail price. Pays illustrators by project. Offers advances (average amount: $4,000).

TIPS Editorial staff attended or plans to attend ALA conference.

WOODLEY MEMORIAL PRESS

English Dept., Washburn University, Topeka KS 66621. **E-mail:** karen.barron@washburn.edu. **Website:** www.washburn.edu/reference/woodley-press. **Contact:** Kevin Rabas, acquisitions editor. Estab. 1980. "Woodley Memorial Press is a small, nonprofit press which publishes novels and fiction collections by Kansas writers only; by 'Kansas writers' we mean writers who reside in Kansas or have a Kansas connection." Publishes paperback originals. Guidelines available on website.

NEEDS Literary, mainstream/contemporary, short story collections. Published KS Notable Book winner *Great Blues*, by Steve Semken; *The Trouble With Campus Security*, by G.W. Clift; and *Loading The Stone*, by Harley Elliot. "We prefer to work with authors of first books, for whom the book is an important step in a writing career. We rely heavily on the author's enthusiasm for the book, because almost all sales are generated by the author's promotion of the book through mailings (we'll pay), readings and book signings."

HOW TO CONTACT Accepts unsolicited mss. Accepts queries by e-mail.

TERMS Responds in 2 weeks to queries; 6 months to mss.

TIPS "We only publish one to three works of fiction a year, on average, and those will definitely have a Kansas connection. We seek authors who are dedicated to promoting their works."

YELLOW SHOE FICTION SERIES

P.O. Box 25053, Baton Rouge LA 70894. **Website:** www.lsu.edu/lsupress. **Contact:** Michael Griffith, editor. Estab. 2004.

> "Looking first and foremost for literary excellence, especially good manuscripts that have fallen through the cracks at the big commercial presses. I'll cast a wide net."

HOW TO CONTACT Does not accept unsolicited mss. Accepts queries by mail, Attn: Rand Dotson. No electronic submissions.

TERMS Pays royalty. Offers advance.

ZEBRA BOOKS

Kensington, 850 Third Ave., 16th Floor, New York NY 10022. (212)407-1500. **E-mail:** mrecords@kensingtonbooks.com. **Website:** www.kensingtonbooks.com. **Contact:** Megan Records, associate editor. Zebra Books is dedicated to women's fiction, which includes, but is not limited to romance. Publishes hardcover originals, trade paperback and mass market paperback originals and reprints. Book catalog available online.

NEEDS Mostly historical romance. Some contemporary romance, westerns, horror, and humor.

HOW TO CONTACT Agented submissions only. You may QUERY ONLY by e-mail. Do not attach manuscripts or proposals to e-mail queries. An editor will respond if he or she is interested in seeing your material based on your query. SUBMIT TO ONE EDITOR ONLY. For fiction, send cover letter, first three chapters, and synopsis (no more than five pages). Note that we do not publish science fiction or fantasy. We do not publish poetry.

ZONDERVAN

Division of HarperCollins Publishers, 5300 Patterson Ave. SE, Grand Rapids MI 49530. (616)698-6900. **Fax:** (616)698-3454. **E-mail:** submissions@zondervan.com. **E-mail:** christianmanuscriptsubmissions.com. **Website:** www.zondervan.com. Estab. 1931. "Our mission is to be the leading Christian communications company meeting the needs of people with resources that glorify Jesus Christ and promote biblical principles." Publishes hardcover and trade paperback originals and reprints. Guidelines available online.

IMPRINTS Zondervan, Zonderkidz, Youth Specialties, Editorial Vida.

NEEDS Refer to nonfiction. Inklings-style fiction of high literary quality. Christian relevance in all cases. Will not consider collections of short stories or poetry.

HOW TO CONTACT Submit TOC, curriculum vitae, chapter outline, intended audience.

TERMS Pays 14% royalty on net amount received on sales of cloth and softcover trade editions; 12% royalty on net amount received on sales of mass market paperbacks. Pays variable advance. Responds in 2 months to queries; 3 months to proposals; 4 months to mss.

CONTESTS & AWARDS

In addition to honors and, quite often, cash prizes, contests and awards programs offer writers the opportunity to be judged on the basis of quality alone without the outside factors that sometimes influence publishing decisions. New writers who win contests may be published for the first time, while more experienced writers may gain public recognition of an entire body of work.

Listed here are contests for almost every type of fiction writing. Some focus on form, such as short stories, novels or novellas, while others feature writing on particular themes or topics. Still others are prestigious prizes or awards for work that must be nominated, such as the Pulitzer Prize in Fiction. Chances are, no matter what type of fiction you write, there is a contest or award program that may interest you.

SELECTING & SUBMITTING TO A CONTEST

Use the same care in submitting to contests as you would sending your manuscript to a publication or book publisher. Deadlines are very important, and where possible, we've included this information. At times contest deadlines were only approximate at our press deadline, so be sure to write, call or look online for complete information.

Follow the rules to the letter. If, for instance, contest rules require your name on a cover sheet only, you will be disqualified if you ignore this and put your name on every page. Find out how many copies to send. If you don't send the correct amount, by the time you are contacted to send more, it may be past the submission deadline. An increasing number of contests invite writers to query by e-mail, and many post contest information on their websites. Check listings for e-mail and website addresses.

One note of caution: Beware of contests that charge entry fees that are disproportionate to the amount of the prize. Contests offering a $10 prize, but charging $7 in entry fees, are a waste of your time and money.

If you are interested in a contest or award that requires your publisher to nominate your work, it's acceptable to make your interest known. Be sure to leave the publisher plenty of time, however, to make the nomination deadline.

24-HOUR SHORT STORY CONTEST

WritersWeekly.com, 13435 S. McCall Rd., #394, Port Charlotte FL 33981. **E-mail:** writersweekly@writersweekly.com. **Website:** www.writersweekly.com/misc/contest.php. **Contact:** Angela Hoy. "Quarterly contest in which registered entrants receive a topic at start time (usually noon Central Time) and have 24 hours to write a story on that topic. All submissions must be returned via e-mail. Each contest is limited to 500 people. Guidelines via e-mail or online." Deadline: Quarterly—see website for dates. 1st Place: $300; 2nd Place: $250; 3rd Place: $200. There are also 20 honorable mentions and 60 door prizes. The top 3 winners' entries are posted on WritersWeekly.com (non-exclusive electronic rights only). Writers retain all rights to their work. Angela Hoy (publisher of WritersWeekly.com and Booklocker.com).

AEON AWARD

Albedo One/Aeon Press, Aeon Award, 8 Bachelor's Walk, Dublin 1 Ireland. +353 1 8730177. **E-mail:** fraslaw@yahoo.co.uk. **Website:** www.albedo1.com. **Contact:** Frank Ludlow, event coordinator. "We aim to encourage new writers into the genre and to encourage existing writers to push at their boundaries" Annual. Competition/award for short stories. Categories: any speculative genre, "i.e. fantasy, SF horror or anything in between or unlcassifiable (like slipstream)." A short list is drawn up by the Albedo One editorial team and the final decision is made by renowned author Ian Watson. Entry Fee: € 7. Pay via website. Guidelines available in December. Accepts inquiries by fax, e-mail. The best stories of each submission period are shortlisted for the grand prize. **The competition is run in four quarterly periods with probable deadlines of the end of March, June, September and November.** Check the website for definite dates. Entries should be unpublished. Award open to "anyone with € 7 and a burning desire to be the best." Length: under 8,000 words. Cover letter should include name, address, e-mail, word count, novel/story title. It is essential the story is marked so it can be identified with its author. Writers may submit own work. "As the contest is initially judged by the editorial staff of Albedo One, I think it is fair to say that choices will be influenced by the individual tastes of these people. You can see what they like in Albedo One on a regular basis. I wish I could say there is a certain formula, but we pick the best stories submitted to us and although there can of-

ten be little evidence of genre influence visible on the page, we always feel that the stories are informed by the author's genre sensibilities. In other words, we like stories by authors who used to like/write science fiction. Confused? Pick up an issue of the magazine and check it out." Results announced within two months of the final deadline. Winners notified by e-mail, and at event/banquet. rize: First prize €1,000, second €200, and third €100. The top three stories are guaranteed publication in Albedo One.

AHWA FLASH & SHORT STORY COMPETITION

AHWA (Australian Horror Writers Association), **E-mail:** ahwacomps@australianhorror.com. **Website:** http://australianhorror.com. **Contact:** David Carroll, competitions officer. Competition/award for short stories and flash fiction. The writers of the winning story in each category will receive paid publication in Midnight Echo, the magazine of the Australian Horror Writers Association, and an engraved plaque. "We're after horror stories, tales that frighten, yarns that unsettle us in our comfortable homes. All themes in this genre will be accepted, from the well-used (zombies, vampires, ghosts etc) to the highly original, so long as the story is professional and well written. No previously published entries will be accepted— all tales must be an original work by the author. Stories can be as violent or as bloody as the storyline dictates, but those containing gratuitous sex or violence will not be considered. Please check your entries for spelling and grammar mistakes and follow standard submission guidelines (eg, 12 point font, Ariel, Times New Roman, or Courier New, one and a half spacing between lines, with title and page number on each page)." There are 2 categories: short stories (1,001 to 8,000 words) and flash fiction (less than 1,000 words). Writers may submit to one or both categories, but entry is limited to 1 story per author per category. Please send your submission as an attached rtf or doc to competitions@australianhorror.com. Alternatively, contact us to arrange postal submissions. Entry free for AHWA members; for non-members, $5 for flash, $10 for short story. Payment can be made via our secure Paypal option using ahwa@australianhorror.com. Alternatively, contact us and we can arrange other payment methods (eg, direct debit). Cheques will not be accepted due to the cost associated with banking them. Full guidelines available from on website. Accepts inquiries by e-mail. Entry deadline each year is May 31. Results announced July/August.

AIM MAGAZINE SHORT STORY CONTEST

P.O. Box 390, Milton WA 98354. (253)815-9030. E-mail: editor@aimmagazine.org; information@aim-magazine.org. **Website:** www.aimmagazine.org. **Contact:** Ruth Apilado, associate editor. Estab. 1974. "$100 prize offered to contest winner for best unpublished short story (4,000 words maximum) 'promoting brotherhood among people and cultures.'" Deadline: August 15 Judges by staff members.

AKC GAZETTE ANNUAL FICTION CONTEST

260 Madison Ave., New York NY 10016. (212)696-8333. Annual contest for short stories under 2,000 words. The *Gazette* sponsors an annual fiction contest for short short stories on some subject relating to purebred or mixed breed dogs. Fiction for our magazine needs a slant toward the serious fancier with real insight into the human/dog bond and breed-specific purebred behavior. Deadline: Begins April 15. until January 31 (postmark). $500, $250 and $100 for top 3 entries. Top entry published in AKC magazines. Judges by panel.

ALABAMA STATE COUNCIL ON THE ARTS INDIVIDUAL ARTIST FELLOWSHIP

201 Monroe St., Montgomery AL 36130-1800. (334)242-4076, ext. 236. **Fax:** (334)240-3269. **E-mail:** anne.kimzey@arts.alabama.gov. **Website:** www.arts.state.al.us. **Contact:** Anne Kimzey, literature program manager. Purpose: To recognize the achievements and potential of Alabama writers. Deadline: March 1. Applications must be submitted online by eGRANT. Judged by independent peer panel. Winners notified by mail and announced on website in June.

AMERICAN ASSOCIATION OF UNIVERSITY WOMEN AWARD IN JUVENILE LITERATURE

4610 Mail Service Center, Raleigh NC 27699-4610. (919)733-9375. **E-mail:** michael.hill@ncdcr.gov. **Contact:** Michael Hill, awards coordinator. Annual award. Book must be published during the year ending June 30. Submissions made by author, author's agent or publisher. Deadline for entries: July 15. SASE for contest rules. Awards a cup to the winner and winner's name inscribed on a plaque displayed within the North Carolina Office of Archives and History. Purpose of award: to recognize the year's best work of ju-

venile literature by a North Carolina resident. Judged by three-judge panel.

Competition receives 10-15 submissions per category.

AMERICAN LITERARY REVIEW SHORT FICTION AWARD

P.O. Box 311307, University of North Texas, Denton TX 76203-1307. (940)565-2755. **E-mail:** american-literaryreview@gmail.com. **Website:** www.engl.unt.edu/alr. "To award excellence in short fiction." Three prizes of $1,000 each and publication in the *American Literary Review* will be given for a poem, a short story, and an essay. 2010 **Poetry Judge: Claire Bateman**; **Fiction Judge: Donald Hays**; **Creative Nonfiction Judge: Debra Monroe**. Judged by rotating outside writer. Entry fee: $15. For guidelines, send SASE or visit website. Accepts inquiries by email and phone. Deadline: November 1. Entries must be unpublished. Contest open to anyone not affiliated with the University of North Texas. "Only solidly crafted, character-driven stories will have the best chance for success." Winners announced and notified by mail and phone in February. List of winners available for SASE.

AMERICAN MARKETS NEWSLETTER SHORT STORY COMPETITION

1974 46th Ave., San Francisco CA 94116. **E-mail:** sheila.oconnor@juno.com. Award is "to give short story writers more exposure." Accepts fiction and nonfiction up to 2,000 words. Entries are eligible for cash prizes, and all entries are eligible for worldwide syndication whether they win or not. "Send double-spaced mss with your story/article title, byline, word count, and address on the first page above your article/story's first paragraph (no need for separate cover page). There is no limit to the number of entries you may send." Prize: 1st Place: $300; 2nd Place: $100; 3rd Place: $50. Judged by a panel of independent judges. **Entry fee:** $12 per entry; $20 for 2; $25 for 3; $30 for 4; $5 each entry thereafter. For guidelines, send SASE, fax or e-mail. Deadline: June 30 and December 31. Contest offered biannually. Published and unpublished stories are actively encouraged. Add a note of where and when previously published. Open to any writer. "All kinds of fiction are considered. We especially want women's pieces—romance, with a twist in the tale—but all will be considered." Results announced within 3 months of deadlines. Winners notified by mail if they include SASE. Award is "to give short story writers more exposure." Contest offered biannually. Open to any writer. "All kinds of fiction are considered. We especially want women's pieces—romance, with a twist in the tale—but all will be considered." Results announced within 3 months of deadlines. Winners notified by mail if they include SASE. Deadline: June 30 and December 31. 1st Place: $300; 2nd Place: $100; 3rd Place: $50. Judged by a panel of independent judges.

AMERICAN SCANDINAVIAN FOUNDATION TRANSLATION PRIZE

58 Park Ave., New York NY 10016. (212)879-9779. **Fax:** (212)686-2115. **E-mail:** info@amscan.org. **Website:** www.amscan.org. **Contact:** Valerie Hymas. American Scandinavian Foundation. Cover letter should include name, address, phone, e-mail and title. Entries must be unpublished. Length: no more than 50 pages for drama, fiction; no more than 35 pages for poetry. Open to any writer. Accepts inquiries by fax, e-mail, phone. Results announced in November. Winners notified by mail. Results available for SASE or by fax, e-mail, website. Guidelines available in January for SASE, by fax, phone, e-mail or on website. Award to recognize excellence in fiction, poetry and drama translations of Scandinavian writers born after 1800. Deadline: June 1. $2,000 grand prize; $1,000 prize.

AMERICAN SHORT STORY CONTEST

American Short Fiction, P.O. Box 301209, Austin TX 78703. (512)538-1305. **Fax:** (512)538-1306. **Website:** www.americanshortfiction.org. **Contact:** Jill Meyers, editor. "Contest offered annually to reward and recognize short stories under 1,000 words." 1st Place: $500 and publication; 2nd Place: $250 and publication. Submissions accepted between February 15 and May 1. 1st Place: $500 & publication; 2nd Place: $250 & publication.

A MIDSUMMER TALE

E-mail: editors@toasted-cheese.com. **Website:** www. toasted-cheese.com. **Contact:** Theryn Fleming, editor. A Midsummer Tale is a contest open to non-genre fiction, creative non-fiction, and hybrids thereof. Theme changes each year. Ideally, stories will take place during a warm time of the year, and this element will be an integral part of the story. The word range is 1,000-5,000 words. Check website for current focus and contest address. First prize: $20 Amazon gift certificate, publication; Second prize: $15 Amazon gift certificate, publication; Third prize: $10 Amazon gift certificate, publication. Categories: non-genre fiction, creative nonfiction.

Judged by two Toasted Cheese editors who blind-judge each contest. Each judge has her own criteria for selecting winners. No entry fee. Guidelines, including the e-mail address to which you should send your entry and instructions for what to include and how to format, are available April 1 on website. Accepts inquiries by e-mail. **Deadline: June 21.** Entries must be unpublished. Open to any writer. Results announced July 31 on website. Winners notified by e-mail.

● THE SHERWOOD ANDERSON FOUNDATION FICTION AWARD

264 Tobacco Rd., Madison NC 27025. (336)427-4450. **E-mail:** dspear003@gmail.com. **Website:** sherwood-andersonfoundation.org. **Contact:** David M. Spear, foundation co-president. Contest is to honor, preserve and celebrate the memory and literary work of Sherwood Anderson, American realist for the first half of the 20th century. Annual award supports developing writers of short stories and novels. Entrants must have published at least one book of fiction or have had several short stories published in major literary and/or commercial publication. Self-published stories do not qualify. Send a detailed resumé that includes a bibliography of your publications. Include a cover letter that provides a history of your writing experience and your plans for writing projects. Also, submit 2 or 3 examples of what you consider to be your best work. Do not send manuscripts by e-mail. Only mss in English will be accepted. Open to any writer who meets the qualifications listed above. Accepts inquiries by e-mail. Mail your application to the above address. No mss or publications will be returned. Deadline: April 1. $15,000 grant award.

ANNUAL BOOK COMPETITION

Washington Writers' Publishing House, P.O. Box 15271, Washington DC 20003. **E-mail:** wwphpress@gmail.com. **Website:** www.washingtonwriters.org. **Fiction:** Fiction writers living within 60 driving miles of the Capitol (Baltimore area included) are invited to submit TWO copies of a FICTION manuscript, novel or a collection of short stories (no more than 350 pages, double or 1-1/2 spaced), each copy with an acknowledgments page for stories or excerpts previously published in journals or anthologies, a reading fee of $25.00, and a stamped, self-addressed reply envelope. Manuscripts will only be returned with appropriate return packaging and postage. Literary fiction only, please. **General Info:** Author's name should not appear on the manuscript. The title page of each copy should contain the title only. Provide name, address, telephone number, e-mail address, and title on a separate cover sheet accompanying the submission. A separate page for acknowledgments may be included for stories or excerpts previously published in journals and anthologies. The winner will receive $500 and 50 copies of the book.

ARROWHEAD REGIONAL ARTS COUNCIL INDIVIDUAL ARTIST SUPPORT GRANT

Arrowhead Regional Arts Council, 1301 Rice Lake Rd., Suite 120, Duluth MN 55811. (218)722-0952 or (800)569-8134. **E-mail:** info@aracouncil.org. **Website:** www.aracouncil.org. Award is to provide financial support to regional artists wishing to take advantage of impending, concrete opportunities that will advance their work or careers. Deadline: August, November, March. Prize: up to $2,500. Judged by the ARAC Board.

ART AFFAIR SHORT STORY AND WESTERN SHORT STORY CONTESTS

P.O. Box 54302, Oklahoma City OK 73154. **E-mail:** artaffair@aol.com. **Website:** www.shadetreecreations.com. **Contact:** Barbara Shepherd. The annual Art Affair Writing Contests include (General) Short Story and Western Short Story categories and offer 1st Prize: $50 and certificate; 2nd Prize: $25 and certificate; and 3rd Prize: $15 and certificate in both categories. Honorable Mention certificates will be awarded at the discretion of the judges. Open to any writer. All short stories must be unpublished. Multiple entries accepted in both categories with separate entry fees for each. Submit original stories on any subject and timeframe for general Short Story category, and submit original western stories for Western Short Story - word limit for all entries is 5,000 words. (Put word count in the upper right-hand corner of first page; mark "Western" on western short stories. All ms. must be double-spaced on 8.5x11 white paper. Type title of short story on first page and headers on following pages. Include cover page with writer's name, address, phone number, and ms title. Do not include SASE; mss will not be returned. Guidelines available on website. **Entry Fee:** $5 per story. Make check payable to Art Affair. Winners' list will be published on the Art Affair website in December.

◐☺ ARTIST TRUST FELLOWSHIP AWARD

1835 12th Ave., Seattle WA 98122. (209)467-8734 ext. 9. **Fax:** (206)467-9633. **E-mail:** miguel@artist-trust.org. **Website:** artisttrust.org. **Contact:** Miguel Guillen, Program Manager. "Artist Trust Fellowship awards practicing professional Washington State artists of exceptional talent and demonstrated ability." Annual. Prize: $7,500. "The Fellowship awards are multidisciplinary awards. The categories for 2012 are Emerging Fields & Cross-disciplinary, Folk & Traditional, Visual and Performing Art; for 2012 are Literary, Music, Media and Craft. Accepted genres for Literary are: poetry, fiction, graphic novels, experimental works, creative non-fiction, screen plays, film scripts and teleplays." Receives about 175 entries per category. Entries are judged by work samples as specified in the guidelines. Winners are selected by a multidisciplinary panel of artists and arts professionals. No entry fee. Guidelines available around December, please check website. Accepts inquiries by e-mail, phone. Submission period is December-February. Website should be consulted for the exact date. Entries can be unpublished or previously published. Washington State residents only. Length: up to 15 pages for poetry, fiction, graphic novels, experimental works and creative non-fiction, and up to 20 pages for screen plays, film scripts and teleplays. All mss must be typed with a 12-pnt font size or larger and cannot be single spaced (except for poetry). Include artist statement and resume with name, address, phone, e-mail, and novel/story title. "The Fellowship awards are highly competitive. Please follow guidelines with care." Results announced in the spring. Winners notified by mail. Results made available to entrants on website. "The fellowship is a merit-based award of $7,500 to practicing professional Washington State artists of exceptional talent and demonstrated ability. Literature fellowships are offered every other year. The award is made on the basis of work of the past 5 years. Applicants must be individual artists; Washington State residents; not matriculated students; and generative artists. Offered every 2 years in even years. Guidelines and application online." Deadline: February 26. Prize: $7,500.

THE ART OF MUSIC ANNUAL WRITING CONTEST

P.O. Box 85, Del Mar CA 92014-0085. (619)884-1401. **Fax:** (858)755-1104. **E-mail:** info@theartofmusicinc.org. **E-mail:** eaxford@aol.com. **Website:** www.theartofmusicinc.org; www.pianopress.com. **Contact:** Elizabeth C. Axford. Offered biannually. Categories are: Essay, short story, poetry, song lyrics, and illustrations for cover art. Acquires one-time rights. All entries must be accompanied by an entry form indicating category and age; parent signature is required of all writers under age 18. Poems may be of any length and in any style; essays and short stories should not exceed 5 double-spaced, typewritten pages. All entries shall be previously unpublished (except poems and song lyrics) and the original work of the author. Inquiries accepted by e-mail, phone. Short stories should be no longer than 5 pages typed and double spaced. Open to any writer. "Make sure all work is fresh and original. Music-related topics only." Results announced October 31. Winners notified by mail. For contest results, send SASE or visit website. "The purpose of the contest is to promote the art of music through writing." Deadline: June 30. Prize: Cash, medal, certificate, publication in the anthology *The Art of Music: A Collection of Writings*, and copies of the book. Judged by a panel of published poets, authors and songwriters.

◐ THE ATHENAEUM LITERARY AWARD

219 S. Sixth St., Philadelphia PA 19106-3794. **Website:** www.PhilaAthenaeum.org. **Contact:** Jill LeMin Lee. Annual award to recognize and encourage outstanding literary achievement in Philadelphia and its vicinity. Prize: A certificate bearing the name of the award, the seal of the Athenaeum, the title of the book, the name of the author and the year. Categories: The Athenaeum Literary Award is granted for a work of general literature, not exclusively for fiction. Judged by a committee appointed by the Board of Directors. No entry fee. Deadline: December 31 of the year of publication. Entries must be previously published. Nominations shall be made in writing to the Literary Award Committee by the author, the publisher, or a member of the Athenaeum, accompanied by a copy of the book. Open to work by residents of Philadelphia and its vicinity. Guidelines available for SASE, by fax, by e-mail and on website. Accepts inquiries by fax, e-mail and phone. Juvenile fiction is not included. Results announced in Spring. Winners notified by mail. For contest results, see website.

◑ ATLANTIC WRITING COMPETITION FOR UNPUBLISHED MANUSCRIPTS

Writers' Federation of Nova Scotia, 1113 Marginal Rd., Halifax NS B3H 4P7. (902)423-8116. **Fax:** (902)422-0881. **E-mail:** director@writers.ns.ca; talk@writers.ns.ca. **Website:** www.writers.ns.ca. **Contact:** Nate Crawford, program coordinator. Estab. 1975. "Annual contest for beginners to try their hand in a number of categories: novel, short story, poetry, writing for younger children, writing for juvenile/young adult. Only 1 entry/category is allowed. Established writers are also eligible, but must work in an area that's new to them. Because our aim is to help Atlantic Canadian writers grow, judges return written comments when the competition is concluded. Anyone residing in the Atlantic Provinces for at least 6 months prior to the contest deadline is eligible to enter."$35 fee for novel ($30 for WFNS members); $25 fee for all other categories ($20 for WFNS members). Needs poetry, essays, juvenile, novels, articles, short stories. "Annual contest for beginners to try their hand in a number of categories: novel, short story, poetry, writing for younger children, writing for juvenile/young adult. Only 1 entry/category is allowed. Established writers are also eligible, but must work in an area that's new to them. Because our aim is to help Atlantic Canadian writers grow, judges return written comments when the competition is concluded. Anyone residing in the Atlantic Provinces for at least 6 months prior to the contest deadline is eligible to enter." Deadline: First Friday in December. **Novel**—1st Place: $200; 2nd Place: $150; 3rd Place: $75. **Writing for Younger Children and Juvenile/Young Adult**—1st Place: $150; 2nd Place: $75; 3rd Place: $50. **Poetry and Short Story**—1st Place: $150; 2nd Place: $75; 3rd Place: $50. a team of 2-3 professional writers, editors, booksellers, librarians, or teachers.

AUTUMN HOUSE FICTION PRIZE

Autumn House Press, 87 ½ Westwood St., Pittsburgh PA 15211. **E-mail:** info@autumnhouse.org. **Website:** http://autumnhouse.org. "We ask that all submissions from authors new to Autumn House come through one of our annual contests. All finalists will be considered for publication. The final judge for the Fiction Prize is Stewart O'Nan. Fiction submissions should be approximately 200-300 pages. All fiction sub-genres (short stories, short-shorts, novellas, or novels) or any combination of sub-genres are eligible. If you wish to be informed of the results of the competition, please include SASE. Autumn House Press assumes no responsibility for lost or damaged manuscripts. All entries must be clearly marked "Fiction Prize" on the outside envelope. Thirty dollar handling fee (check or money order) must be enclosed. Send manuscript and $30.00 fee to:Autumn House Press: P.O. Box 60100, Pittsburgh PA 15211. Deadline: June 30. Winners will receive book publication, $1,000 advance against royalties, and a $1,500 travel grant to participate in the 2013 Autumn House Master Authors Series in Pittsburgh

ⓘ AWP AWARD SERIES

Mail Stop 1E3, George Mason University, Fairfax VA 22030. **E-mail:** awp@awpwriter.org. **Website:** www. awpwriter.org. **Contact:** Supriya Bhatnagar, director of publications. The AWP Award Series was established in cooperation with several university presses in order to publish and make fine fiction and nonfiction available to a wide audience. Offered annually to foster new literary talent. Guidelines for SASE and on website. Entries must be unpublished. "This information should appear in cover letter only." Open to any writer. Guidelines available on website in November. No phone calls, please. Mss published previously in their entirety, including self-publishing, are not eligible. No mss returned. Results announced in August. Winners notified by mail or phone. For contest results send SASE, or visit website. No phone calls, please. Cover letter should include name, address, phone number, e-mail and title. "This information should appear in cover letter only." Mss must be postmarked between Jan. 1 - Feb. 28 novel ($2,000), Donald Hall Prize in Poetry ($5,000), Grace Paley Prize in Short Fiction ($5,000), and creative nonfiction ($2,000).

BAKELESS PRIZE

Bread Loaf Writers' Conference/ Middlebury College and Houghton Mifflin, Bakeless Prize, Bread Loaf Writers' Conference, Middlebury College, Middlebury VT 05753. **Website:** www.bakelessprize.org. "To promote first books of the highest caliber." Annual. Prize: Publication by Graywolf Press and fellowship to attend Bread Loaf Writers'Conference. Categories: One award each for Fiction (average 500 entries), Poetry (average 700 entries) and Creative Nonfiction (average 100 entries). Judges and guidelines announced on web site in June. Entry fee: $10. Make checks payable to Middlebury College. Accepts inquiries by e-mail. **Submission period is September 15 to November 1.** Entries should be unpublished. Anyone writing in English may enter contest. Cover letter should include name, address, phone, e-mail, novel/ story title. No identifying information on ms. Writers may submit own work. "Make sure your manuscript is ready." Results announced May. Winners notified by phone in April. Results made available to entrants with SASE, on website.

BARD FICTION PRIZE

Bard College, P.O. Box 5000, Annandale-on-Hudson NY 12504-5000. (845)758-7087. **E-mail:** bfp@bard. edu. **Website:** www.bard.edu/bfp. **Contact:** Irene Zedlacher. Estab. 2001. The Bard Fiction Prize is intended to encourage and support young writers of fiction to pursue their creative goals and to provide an opportunity to work in a fertile and intellectual environment. Prize: $30,000 cash award and appointment as writer-in-residence at Bard College for 1 semester. Judged by committee of 5 judges (authors associated with Bard College). No entry fee. Cover letter should include name, address, phone, e-mail and name of publisher where book was previously published. Guidelines available by SASE, fax, phone, e-mail, or on website. Deadline: July 15. Entries must be previously published. Open to U.S. citizens aged 39 and below. Results announced by October 15. Winners notified by phone. For contest results, e-mail, or visit website. Open to younger American writers.

ⓘ MILDRED L. BATCHELDER AWARD

50 E. Huron St., Chicago IL 60611. **Website:** www.ala. org/alsc. Judged by Batchelder Award selection committee. No entry fee. Deadline: December 31. Books should be US trade publications for which children, up to and including age 14, are the potential audience. Previously published translations only. Accepts inquiries by fax, e-mail and phone. Guidelines available in February for SASE, by fax, phone, e-mail or on website. Results announced at ALA Midwinter Meeting. Winners notified by phone. Contest results by phone, fax, for SASE or visit website. The Batchelder Award is given to the most outstanding children's book originally published in a language other than English in a country other than the United States, and subsequently translated into English for publication in the United States.

⊕ BELLEVUE LITERARY REVIEW GOLDENBERG PRIZE FOR FICTION

Bellevue Literary Review, NYU Dept of Medicine, 550 First Ave., OBV-A612, New York NY 10016. (212)263-3973. **Fax:** (212)263-3206. **E-mail:** info@blreview. org; stacy@blreview.org. **Website:** www.blreview. org. **Contact:** Stacy Bodziak, managing editor. The BLR prizes award outstanding writing related to themes of health, healing, illness, the mind and the body. Annual. Competition/award for short stories. Prize: $1,000 and publication in *The Bellevue Literary Review*. Receives about 200-300 entries per category.

BLR editors select semi-finalists to be read by an independent judge who chooses the winner. Previous judges include Amy Hempel, Rick Moody, Rosellen Brown, and Andre Dubus III. **Entry fee:** $15, or $20 to include 1-year subscription to *The Bellevue Literary Review*. Send credit card information or make checks payable to Bellevue Literary Review. Guidelines available in February. Accepts inquiries by e-mail, phone, mail. Submissions open in February. **Entry deadline:** July 1. Entries should be unpublished. Anyone may enter contest. Length: No minimum; maximum of 5,000 words. Cover letter should include name, address, phone, e-mail, story title. Title and word count should appear on ms. Writers may submit own work. Results announced in December and made available to entrants with SASE, by e-mail, on website. Winners notified by mail, by e-mail. The BLR prizes award outstanding writing related to themes of health, healing, illness, the mind and the body. Annual. Competition/award for short stories. Receives about 200-300 entries per category. Results announced in December and made available to entrants with SASE, by e-mail, on website. Winners notified by mail, by e-mail. Deadline: July 1. $1,000 and publication in *The Bellevue Literary Review*. BLR editors select semi-finalists to be read by an independent judge who chooses the winner. Previous judges include Amy Hempel, Rick Moody, Rosellen Brown, and Andre Dubus III.

GEORGE BENNETT FELLOWSHIP

Phillips Exeter Academy, 20 Main St., Exeter NH 03833-2460. **E-mail:** teaching_opportunities@exeter.edu. **Website:** www.exeter.edu. Annual award for fellow and family "to provide time and freedom from material considerations to a person seriously contemplating or pursuing a career as a writer. Applicants should have a ms in progress which they intend to complete during the fellowship period." Duties: To be in residency for the academic year; and to make oneself available informally to students interested in writing. The committee favors writers who have not yet published a book with a major publisher. Residence at the Academy during the fellowship period required. Deadline for application: December 1. Prize: Cash stipend, room and board. Judged by committee of the English department.

BEST LESBIAN EROTICA

BLE 2013, 31-64 21st St., #319, Long Island City NY 11106. **E-mail:** kwarnockble@gmail.com. **Contact:** Kathleen Warnock, series editor. Categories: Novel excerpts, short stories; "poetry will be considered but is not encouraged." No entry fee. Include cover page with author's name/pen name if using one, title of submission(s), address, phone, e-mail. "All submissions must be typed and double-spaced. You may submit double-sided copies. Length: 5,000 words. You may submit 2 different pieces of work. Submit 2 hard copies of each submission. Will only accept e-mail copies if the following conditions apply: You live outside of North America or Europe; the cost of postage would be prohibitive from your home country; the post office system in your country is dreadful (US does not count); the content of your submission may be illegal to send via postal mail in your home country." Accepts both previously published and unpublished material; will accept submissions that have appeared in other themed anthologies. Open to any writer. All submissions must include an e-mail address for response. "No mss will be returned, so please do not include SASE." Payment: $100 for each published story, plus 2 copies of the anthology. Categories: Novel excerpts, short stories; "poetry will be considered but is not encouraged." No entry fee. Include cover page with author's name/pen name if using one, title of submission(s), address, phone, e-mail. "All submissions must be typed and double-spaced. You may submit double-sided copies. Length: 5,000 words. You may submit 2 different pieces of work.

BINGHAMTON UNIVERSITY JOHN GARDNER FICTION BOOK AWARD

Creative Writing Program, Binghamton University, Department of English, General LIterature, and Rhetoric, P.O. Box 6000, Binghamton NY 13902-6000. (607)777-2713. **E-mail:** cwpro@binghamton.edu. **Website:** http://english.binghamton.edu/cw-pro. **Contact:** Maria Mazziotti Gillan, director. Estab. 2001. Contest offered annually for a novel or collection of fiction published in previous year. Offered annually for a novel or collection of short stories published that year in a press run of 500 copies or more. Each book submitted must be accompanied by an application form. Publisher may submit more than 1 book for prize consideration. Send 3 copies of each book. Guidelines available on website. Award's purpose is "to serve the literary community by calling attention to outstanding books of fiction." Deadline: March 1. Prize: $1,000. Judged by a professional writer not on Binghamton University faculty.

IRMA S. AND JAMES H. BLACK AWARD

610 W. 112th St., New York NY 10025. (212)875-4450. **Fax:** (212)875-4558. **E-mail:** kfreda@bankstreet.edu. **Website:** http://bankstreet.edu/childrenslibrary/irmasimontonblackhome.html. **Contact:** Kristin Freda, award director. Offered annually for a book for young children, for excellence of both text and illustrations. Entries must have been published during the previous calendar year. Prize: press function and scroll and seals by Maurice Sendak for attaching to award winner's book run. Judged by adult children's literature experts and children 6-10 years old. No entry fee. Guidelines for SASE, fax, e-mail or on website. Accepts inquiries by phone, fax, e-mail. Deadline: December 15. Entries must be previously published. "Write to address above. Usually publishers submit books they want considered, but individuals can too. No entries are returned." Winners notified by phone in April and announced in May. A list of winners will be available on website.

JAMES TAIT BLACK MEMORIAL PRIZES

University of Edinburgh, David Hume Tower, George, Edinburgh EH8 9JX Scotland. **Website:** www.englit.ed.ac.uk/jtbinf.htm. "Two prizes each of £10,000 are awarded: one for the best work of fiction, one for the best biography or work of that nature, published during the calendar year January 1 to December 31." Judged by professors of English Literature with the assistance of teams of postgraduate readers. No entry fee. Accepts inquiries by fax, e-mail, phone. **Deadline: December 1.** Entries must be previously published. "Eligible works are those written in English and first published or co-published in Britain in the year of the award. Works should be submitted by publishers." Open to any writer. Winners notified by phone, via publisher. Contact department of English Literature for list of winners or check website.

THE BOARDMAN TASKER AWARD FOR MOUNTAIN LITERATURE

The Boardman Tasker Charitable Trust, 8 Bank View Rd., Darley Abbey Derby DE22 1EJ UK. Phone/fax: UK 01332342246. **E-mail:** steve@people-matter.co.uk. **Website:** www.boardmantasker.com. **Contact:** Steve Dean. Offered annually to reward a work of nonfiction or fiction, in English or in translation, which has made an outstanding contribution to mountain literature, in English or in translation, which has made

an outstanding contribution to mountain literature. May be fiction, nonfiction, poetry or drama. Not an anthology. Subject must be concerned with a mountain environment. Previous winners have been books on expeditions, climbing experiences, a biography of a mountaineer, novels." Guidelines available in January by e-mail or on website. Entries must be previously published. Open to any writer. Results announced in November. Winners notified by phone or e-mail. For contest results, e-mail or visit website. "The winning book needs to be well written to reflect a knowledge of and a respect and appreciation for the mountain environment." "The award is to honor Peter Boardman and Joe Tasker, who disappeared on Everest in 1982." Deadline: Midnight of August 17. Prize: £3,000 Judged by a panel of 3 judges elected by trustees.

BOSTON GLOBE-HORN BOOK AWARDS

The Boston Globe, Horn Book, Inc., 56 Roland St., Suite 200, Boston MA 02129. (617)628-0225. **Fax:** (617)628-0882. **E-mail:** info@hbook.com; khedeen@hbook.com. **Website:** hbook.com/bghb/. **Contact:** Katrina Hedeen. Estab. 1967. Offered annually for excellence in literature for children and young adults (published June 1-May 31). Categories: picture book, fiction and poetry, nonfiction. Judges may also name several honor books in each category. Books must be published in the US, but may be written or illustrated by citizens of any country. The Horn Book Magazine publishes speeches given at awards ceremonies. Guidelines for SASE or online. Deadline for entries: May 15. Winners receive $500 and an engraved silver bowl; honor book recipients receive an engraved silver plate. Judged by a panel of 3 judges selected each year.

THE BRIAR CLIFF REVIEW FICTION, POETRY, AND CREATIVE NONFICTION COMPETITION

The Briar Cliff Review, Briar Cliff University, 3303 Rebecca St., Sioux City IA 51104-0100. **E-mail:** tricia.currans-sheehan@briarcliff.edu (editor); jeanne.emmons@briarcliff.edu (poetry). **Website:** www.briarcliff.edu/bcreview. **Contact:** Tricia Currans-Sheehan, editor. Purpose of Award: "to reward good writers and showcase quality writing." Offered annually for unpublished poem, story, and essay. Prize: $1,000, and publication in spring issue of *The Briar Cliff Review*. All entrants receive a copy of the magazine with winning entries. Judged by editors. "We guarantee a considerate reading." **Entry fee:** $20. Guidelines available in August for SASE. Inquiries accepted by e-mail. Deadline: Submissions between August 1 and November 1. No mss returned. Entries must be unpublished. Length: 6,000 words maximum. Open to any writer. Results announced in December or January. Winners notified by phone or letter around December 20. "Send us your best. We want stories with a plot." Offered annually for unpublished poetry, fiction and essay. Award to reward good writers and showcase quality writing. Deadline: August 1-November 1. $1,000 and publication in spring issue of *The Briar Cliff Review*. Entrants receive copy of the magazine (a $15 value) with winning entries. Judged by editors of *The Briar Cliff Review*. "We guarantee a considerate reading."

◑◯ THE BRIDPORT PRIZE

P.O. Box 6910, Dorset DT6 9QB United Kingdom. +44 (0)1308 428 333. **E-mail:** frances@bridportprize.org.uk. **Website:** www.bridportprize.org.uk. **Contact:** Frances Everitt, administrator. Award to "promote literary excellence, discover new talent." Categories: Short stories, poetry, flash fiction. 2010 introduced a new category for flash fiction: £1,000 sterling 1st Prize for the best short, short story of under 250 words. Deadline: May 31. Prize: £5,000 sterling; £1,000 sterling; £500 sterling; various runners-up prizes and publication of approximately 13 best stories and 13 best poems in anthology; plus 6 best flash fiction stories. Judged by 1 judge for fiction (in 2012, Patrick Gale) and 1 judge for poetry (in 2012, Gwyneth Lewis).

◔ BURNABY WRITERS' SOCIETY CONTEST

E-mail: info@bws.bc.ca. **Website:** www.bws.bc.ca; http:burnabywritersnews.blogspot.com. **Contact:** Eileen Kernaghan. "Offered annually for unpublished work. Open to all residents of British Columbia. Categories vary from year to year. Send SASE for current rules. For complete guidelines see website or burnabywritersnews.blogspot.com." Purpose is to encourage talented writers in all genres. Deadline: May 31. 1st Place: $200; 2nd Place: $100; 3rd Place: $50; and public reading.

◑◯ THE CAINE PRIZE FOR AFRICAN WRITING

51a Southwark St., London SE1 1RU United Kingdom. **E-mail:** info@caineprize.com. **Website:** www.caineprize.com. **Contact:** Nick Elam, administrator. Annual award for a short story (3,000-10,000 words) by an African writer. "An 'African writer' is normally taken to mean someone who was born in Africa, who is a national of an African country, or whose parents are African, and whose work has reflected African sensibilities." Entries must have appeared for the first time in the 5 years prior to the closing date for submissions, which is January 31 each year. Publishers should submit 6 copies of the published original with a brief cover note (no pro forma application). "Please indicate nationality or passport held." Prize: £10,000. Judged by a panel of judges appointed each year. No entry fee. Cover letter should include name, address, phone, e-mail, title and publication where story was previously published. Deadline: January 31. Entries must be previously published. Word length: 3,000-10,000 words. Manuscripts not accepted. Entries must be submitted by publishers not authors. Results announced in mid-July. Winners notified at event/banquet. For contest results, send fax, e-mail or visit our website.

● JOHN W. CAMPBELL MEMORIAL AWARD FOR BEST SCIENCE FICTION NOVEL OF THE YEAR

English Department, University of Kansas, Lawrence KS 66045. (785)864-3380. **Fax:** (785)864-1159. **E-mail:** jgunn@ku.edu. **Website:** www.ku.edu/~sfcenter. **Contact:** James Gunn, professor and director. Award to "honor the best science fiction novel of the year." Prize: Trophy. Winners receive an expense-paid trip to the university to receive their award. Their names are also engraved on a permanent trophy. Categories: novels. Judged by a jury. No entry fee. Deadline: see website. Entries must be previously published. Open to any writer. Accepts inquiries by e-mail and fax. "Ordinarily publishers should submit work, but authors have done so when publishers would not. Send for list of jurors." Results announced in July. For contest results, send SASE.

◔ CANADIAN AUTHORS ASSOCIATION MOSAID TECHNOLOGY INC. AWARD FOR FICTION

Box 419, 320 South Shores Rd., Campbellford ON K0L 1L0 Canada. **Website:** www.canauthors.org. **Contact:** Anita Purcell. Deadline: December 15. Prize: $2,500 and a silver medal.

KAY CATTARULLA AWARD FOR BEST SHORT STORY

Texas Institute of Letters, P.O. Box 609, Round Rock TX 78680. **E-mail:** tilsecretary@yahoo.com. **Website:** http://texasinstituteofletters.org. Offered annually for work published January 1-December 31 of previous year to recognize the best short story. The story submitted must have appeared in print for the first time to be eligible. Writers must have been born in Texas, must have lived in Texas for at least 2 consecutive years, or the subject matter of the work must be associated with Texas. See website for guidelines and deadline date. Prize: $1,000. Offered annually for work published January 1-December 31 of previous year to recognize the best short story. The story submitted must have appeared in print for the first time to be eligible. Writers must have been born in Texas, must have lived in Texas for at least 2 consecutive years, or the subject matter of the work must be associated with Texas. See website for guidelines. Deadline: See website for exact date. $1,000.

THE CHARITON REVIEW SHORT FICTION PRIZE

Truman State University Press, 100 East Normal Ave., Kirksville MO 63501-4221. **Website:** http://tsup.truman.edu. An annual award for the best unpublished short fiction on any theme up to 5,000 words in English. Prize: $1,000 and publication in *The Chariton Review* for the winner. Three finalists will also be published in the Spring issue. The final judge will be announced after the finalists have been selected in January.

COLORADO BOOK AWARDS

Colorado Center for the Book, 1490 Lafayette St., Suite 101, Denver CO 80218. (303)894-7951, ext. 21. **Fax:** (303)864-9361. **E-mail:** long@coloradohumanities.org. **Website:** www.coloradocenterforthebook.org. **Contact:** Margaret Coval, executive director; Jennifer Long, program adjudicator. Offered annually for work published by December of previous year. "The purpose is to champion all Colorado authors, editors, illustrators, and photographers, and in particular, to honor the award winners raising the profiles of both their work and Colorado as a state whose people promote and support reading, writing, and literacy through books. The categories are generally: children's literature, young adult and juvenile literature, fiction, genre fiction (romance, mystery/thriller, science fiction/fantasy, historical), biography, history, anthology, poetry, pictorial, graphic novel/comic, creative nonfiction, and general nonfiction, as well as other categories as determined each year. Open to authors who reside or have resided in Colorado."

○ CRAZYHORSE FICTION PRIZE

College of Charleston, Dept. of English, 66 George St., Charleston SC 29424. (843)953-7740. **Fax:** (843)953-7740. **E-mail:** crazyhorse@cofc.edu. **Website:** www.crazyhorsejournal.org. The journal's mission is to publish the entire spectrum of today's fiction, essays, and poetry—from the mainstream to the avant-garde, from the established to the undiscovered writer. The editors are especially interested in original writing that engages in the work of honest communication. *Crazyhorse* publishes writing of fine quality regardless of style, predilection, subject. Contest open to any writer. **Deadline: January 15th of each year**; see website. $2,000 and publication in *Crazyhorse*. Judged by anonymous writer whose identity is disclosed when the winners are announced in April. Past judges: Diana Abu-Jaber (2004), T.M. McNally (2005), Dan Chaon (2006), Antonya Nelson (2007), Ha Jin (2008); Ann Pratchett (2009).

○ CROSSTIME SHORT SCIENCE FICTION CONTEST

P.O. Box 23749, Santa Fe NM 87502. (505)690-3923. **Fax:** (214)975-9715. **Website:** www.crossquarter.com. Annual contest for short science fiction (up to 7,500 words) showcasing the best of the human spirit. No horror or dystopia. Deadline: March 15. Prizes: 1st place: $250; 2nd place: $125; 3rd place: $75; 4th place: $50; Winners are also combined into an anthology. Costs $15; $10 for each additional submission. Guidelines and entry form available online.

THE CRUCIBLE POETRY AND FICTION COMPETITION

Crucible, Barton College, College Station, Wilson NC 27893. (252)399-6344. **E-mail:** crucible@barton.edu. **Website:** www.barton.edu/SchoolofArts&Sciences/English/Crucible.htm. **Contact:** Terrence L. Grimes, editor. "Offered annually for unpublished mss. Fiction is limited to 8,000 words; poetry is limited to 5 poems. Guidelines online or by email or for SASE. All submissions should be electronic." Deadline: May. 1st Place: $150; 2nd Place: $100 (for both poetry and fiction. Winners are also published in *Crucible*. Judged by in-house editorial board.

○ DEAD OF WINTER

E-mail: editors@toasted-cheese.com. **Website:** www.toasted-cheese.com. **Contact:** Stephanie Lenz, editor. The contest is a winter-themed horror fiction contest with a new topic each year. Topic and word limit announced October 1. The topic is usually geared toward a supernatural theme. Categories: Short stories. No entry fee. Results announced January 31. Winners notified by e-mail. List of winners on website. Deadline: December 21. Prize: Amazon gift certificates in the amount of at least $20, $15 and $10; publication in *Toasted Cheese*. Also offers honorable mention. Judged by 2 *Toasted Cheese* editors who blind judge each contest. Each judge uses her own criteria to rate entries.

●●⑤ THE DEBUT DAGGER

Crime Writers' Association, New Writing Competition, P.O. Box 273, Borehamwood Herts WD6 2XA England. **Website:** www.thecwa.co.uk. **Contact:** L. Evans, chair. "An annual competition for unpublished crime writers. Submit the opening 3,000 words of a crime novel, plus a 500-1,000 word synopsis of its continuance. Open to any writer who has not had a novel commercially published in any genre." First prize is £700. See website for details and for prize information.

DELAWARE DIVISION OF THE ARTS

820 N. French St., Wilmington DE 19801. (302)577-8278. **Fax:** (302)577-6561. **E-mail:** kristin.pleasanton@state.de.us. **Website:** www.artsdel.org. **Contact:** Kristin Pleasanton, coordinator. Award "to help further careers of emerging and established professional artists." For Delaware residents only. Prize: $10,000 for masters; $6,000 for established professionals; $3,000 for emerging professionals. Judged by out-of-state, nationally recognized professionals in each artistic discipline. No entry fee. Guidelines available after May 1 on website. Accepts inquiries by e-mail, phone. Expects to receive 25 fiction entries. Deadline: August 1. Open to any Delaware writer. Results announced in December. Winners notified by mail. Results available on website.

DOBIE PAISANO FELLOWSHIPS

University Station (G0400), Austin TX 78712-0531. (512)471-7620. **E-mail:** adameve@mail.utexas.edu. **Website:** www.utexas.edu/ogs/Paisano.. The annual Dobie Paisano fellowships provide an opportunity for creative or nonfiction writers to live and write for an extended period in an environment that offers isolation and tranquility. At the time of application, the applicant must: be a native Texan, have lived in Texas at some time for at least three years, or have published significant work with a Texas subject. The Ralph A. Johnston Memorial Fellowship, aimed at writers who have demonstrated some publishing and critical success, offers a $20,000 stipend over four months. The Jesse H. Jones Writing Fellowship offers an $18,000 stipend over five and a half months. Criteria for making the awards include quality of work, character of the proposed project, and suitability of the applicant for life at Paisano, the late J. Frank Dobie's ranch near Austin, TX. Annual deadline in January; awards announced in May. Application fee: $20/one fellowship, $30 both fellowships. Applications and detailed information are available on the website.

JACK DYER FICTION PRIZE

Crab Orchard Review, Department of English, Mail Code 4503, Faner Hall 2380, Southern Illinois University at Carbondale, Carbondale IL 62901. **E-mail:** jtribble@siu.edu. **Website:** www.craborchardreview.siu.edu. **Contact:** Jon C. Tribble, man. editor. Offered annually for unpublished short fiction. *Crab Orchard Review* acquires first North American serial rights to all submitted work. Open to any writer; US citizens only. Deadline: March 1-May 4. Prize: $2,000 and publication and 1-year subscription to *Crab Orchard Review*. Judged by editorial staff (pre-screening); winner chosen by genre editor.

DZANC PRIZE

Dzanc Books, 2702 Lillian, Ann Arbor MI 48104. (734) 722-3761. **E-mail:** info@dzancbooks.org. **Website:** www.dzancbooks.org. "Our goal is to help authors find means of producing their work and doing community service." Annual. Prize: $5,000. Single category of a combination of work in progress and literary community service. Entries are judged by Dzanc editors (Steve Gillis, and Dan Wickett). No entry fee. Accepts inquiries by e-mail (prize@dzancbooks.org). Entry deadline is Nov. 1, 2011. Entries should be unpublished. Any author with a work of literary fiction in progress, and literary community service that is based in the United States, may enter contest. Writers may submit own work. "Have a good idea of what we're looking for in terms of literary community service (see website)" Results announced in January. Winners notified by e-mail. Results made available to entrants via email, and on website.

MARY KENNEDY EASTHAM FLASH FICTION PRIZE

Category in the Soul Making Keats Literary Competition, The Webhallow House, 1544 Sweetwood Dr., Broadmoor Village CA 94015-2029. **E-mail:** pennobhill@aol.com. **Website:** www.soulmakingcontest.us. **Contact:** Eileen Malone. "Three flash fiction (short-short) stories per entry, under 500 words. Previously published material is accepted. Indicate category on each story. Identify only with 3x5 card. Open annually to any writer." Deadline: November 30 (annually) 1st Place: $100; 2nd Place: $50; 3rd Place: $25.

EATON LITERARY AGENCY'S ANNUAL AWARDS PROGRAM

Eaton Literary Agency, P.O. Box 49795, Sarasota FL 34230. (941)366-6589. **Fax:** (941)365-4679. **E-mail:** eatonlit@aol.com. **Website:** www.eatonliterary.com. **Contact:** Richard Lawrence, V.P.. Offered biannually for unpublished mss. Prize: $2,500 (over 10,000 words); $500 (under 10,000 words). Judged by an independent agency in conjunction with some members of Eaton's staff. No entry fee. Guidelines available for SASE, by fax, e-mail, or on website. Accepts inquiries by fax, phone and e-mail. Deadline: **March 31** (mss under 10,000 words); **August 31** (mss over 10,000 words). Entries must be unpublished. Open to any writer. Results announced in April and September. Winners notified by mail. For contest results, send SASE, fax, e-mail, or visit website. Offered biannually for unpublished mss. Entries must be unpublished.

THE EMILY CONTEST

18207 Heaton Dr., Houston TX 77084. **E-mail:** emily@whrwa.com. **Website:** www.whrwa.com. The mission of The Emily is to professionally support writers and guide them toward a path to publication. Prize: first place entry in each category receives an Emily brooch and are entered into the Best of the Best Contest; all finalists receive certificates. First round judging is by two judges, at least one is a published author. All judges are experienced critiquers or trained. Each entry has two final round judges and include both editors at major romance publishing houses and agents from major literary agencies." Categories include: Comtemporary Single Title, Contemporary Series, Paranormal, and Historical. Entry fee: $20 for WHRWA members; $30 for non-members. Deadline: October 6, 2009. Entries submitted via e-mail, length: first 35 pages of an unpublished novel. Open to all "unpublished romance writers not contracted by the contest deadline and published authors entering a category they're not published in." Guidelines available on the website. Inquiries can be made by e-mail. "We look for dynamic, interesting romance stories with a hero and heroine readers can relate to and love. Hook us from the beginning and keep the level of excitement high." Results announced the second Saturday in February. Winners notified by e-mail or phone. For contest results, visit website.

⊕ ☾ THE FAR HORIZONS AWARD FOR SHORT FICTION

The Malahat Review, University of Victoria, P.O. Box 1700, Stn CSC, Victoria BC V8W 2Y2 Canada. (250)721-8524. **Fax:** (250)472-5051. **E-mail:** malahat@uvic.ca. **Website:** www.malahatreview.ca. **Contact:** John Barton, editor. Open to "emerging short fiction writers from Canada, the US, and elsewhere" who have not yet published their fiction in a full-length book (48 pages or more). Winner and finalists contacted by e-mail. Deadline: May 1 of odd-numbered years Offers $1,000 CAD, publication in fall issue of *The Malahat Review* (see separate listing in Magazines/Journals). Announced in fall on website, Facebook page, and in quarterly e-newsletter, *Malahat Lite*.

THE VIRGINIA FAULKNER AWARD FOR EXCELLENCE IN WRITING

Prairie Schooner, 123 Andrews Hall, University of Nebraska-Lincoln, Lincoln NE 68588-0334. (402)472-0911. **Fax:** (402)472-9771. **E-mail:** PrairieSchooner@unl.edu. **Website:** www.prairieschooner.unl.edu. **Contact:** Kwame Dawes. Offered annually for work published in *Prairie Schooner* in the previous year. Categories: short stories, essays, novel excerpts and translations. Guidelines for SASE or on website. Prize: $1,000. Judged by Editorial Board.

☾ FIRST BOOK AWARD

Saskatchewan Book Awards, Inc., 100-2400 College Ave., Regina SK S4P 0K1 Canada. (306)569-1585. **Fax:** (306)569-4187. **E-mail:** director@bookawards.sk.ca. **Website:** www.bookawards.sk.ca. **Contact:** Executive director, book submissions. Estab. 1993. Offered annually. "This award is presented to a Saskatchewan author for the best first book, judged on the quality of writing." Books from the following categories will be considered: Children's; drama; fiction (short fiction by a single author, novellas, novels); nonfiction (all categories of nonfiction writing except cookbooks, directories, how-to books, or bibliographies of minimal critical content); and poetry. Deadline: November 1. Prize: $2,000 (CAD).

FIRSTWRITER.COM INTERNATIONAL SHORT STORY CONTEST

firstwriter.com, United Kingdom. **Website:** www.firstwriter.com. **Contact:** J. Paul Dyson, managing editor. "Accepts short stories up to 3,000 words on any subject and in any style." Deadline: April 1 Prize total about $300. Ten special commendations will also be awarded and all the winners will be published in *firstwriter* magazine and receive a $36 subscription voucher, allowing an annual subscription to be taken out for free. All submissions are automatically considered for publication in *firstwriter* magazine and may be published there online. Judged by *firstwriter* magazine editors.

◐◯ FISH ONE-PAGE PRIZE (FLASH FICTION)

Durrus, Bantry, County Cork Ireland. **E-mail:** info@fishpublishing.com. **Website:** www.fishpublishing.com. Fish One-Page Prize (Flash Fiction). Guidelines on website or by e-mail. Stories with a word limit of 300. First Prize €1,000. Deadline March 20. Results 30 April. Entry €14. First Prize €1,000. Chris Stewart will judge the 2011 prize.

◐◯ FISH SHORT STORY PRIZE

Durrus, Bantry Co. Cork Ireland. **E-mail:** info@fishpublishing.com. **Website:** www.fishpublishing.com. First prize of 3,000 Euro and the best 10 stories published in the Fish Anthology. Overall prize fund 5,000 Euro. Second Prize is one week at Anam Cara Writers Retreat in West Cork plus 300 Euro. Third Prize 300 Euro. Closing date 30th November. Winners announced 17 March. Online entry fee 20 Euro story. Postal entry €25. The best 10 will be published in the 2011 Fish Anthology, launched in July at the West Cork Literary Festival. Entries must not have been published before. Entry on-line or by post. Geographical area covered: Worldwide. See our website for full details of competitions, and information on the Fish Editorial and Critique Services, and the Fish Online Writing Courses." Established in 1994, Hon. Patrons Roddy Doyle, Colum McCann, Frank McCourt, Dermot Healy.

◯ FLORIDA FIRST COAST WRITERS' FESTIVAL NOVEL, SHORT FICTION, PLAYWRITING & POETRY AWARDS

FCCJ North Campus, 4501 Capper Rd., Jacksonville FL 32218-4499. (904)766-6760. **Fax:** (904)766-6654. **Website:** opencampus.fccj.org/WF/. Conference and contest "to create a healthy writing environment, honor writers of merit and find a novel manuscript to recommend to New York publishers for 'serious consideration.'" Judged by university faculty and freelance and professional writers. Entry fee: $7 for poetry or $18 for 3 poems. **Deadline: December 1 for poetry.** Entries

must be unpublished. Word length: 30 lines for poetry. Open to any writer. Guidelines available on the website or in the fall for SASE. Accepts inquiries by fax and e-mail. "For stories and novels, make the opening pages sparkle. For plays, make them at least two acts and captivating. For poems, blow us over with imagery and insight and avoid clichés and wordiness." Results announced on the website and at FCCJ's Florida First Coast Writers' Festival held in the spring.

H.E. FRANCIS SHORT STORY AWARD

University of Alabama in Huntsville, Department of English, Huntsville AL 35899. **Website:** www.uah.edu/colleges/liberal/english/whatnewcontest.html. "Offered annually for unpublished work, not to exceed 5,000 words. Acquires first-time publication rights." Deadline: December 31. $1,000. Judged by a panel of nationally recognized, award-winning authors, directors of creative writing programs, and editors of literary journals.

SOEURETTE DIEHL FRASER AWARD FOR BEST TRANSLATION OF A BOOK

P.O. Box 609, Round Rock TX 78680. **E-mail:** tilsecretary@yahoo.com. **Website:** http://texasinstituteofletters.org. Offered every 2 years to recognize the best translation of a literary book into English. Translator must have been born in Texas or have lived in the state for at least 2 consecutive years at some time. Deadline: Early January; see website for exact date. $1,000.

GIVAL PRESS NOVEL AWARD

Gival Press, LLC, P.O. Box 3812, Arlington VA 22203. (703)351-0079. **E-mail:** givalpress@yahoo.com. **Website:** www.givalpress.com. **Contact:** Robert L. Giron. Offered annually for a previously unpublished original novel (not a translation). Guidelines by phone, on website, via e-mail, or by mail with SASE. Results announced late fall of same year. Winners notified by phone. Results made available to entrants with SASE, by e-mail, on website. "To award the best literary novel." Deadline: May 30. $3,000, plus publication of book with a standard contract and author's copies. Final judge is announced after winner is chosen. Entries read anonymously.

◯ GIVAL PRESS SHORT STORY AWARD

Gival Press, P.O. Box 3812, Arlington VA 22203. (703)351-0079. **E-mail:** givalpress@yahoo.com. **Website:** www.givalpress.com. **Contact:** Robert L. Giron, publisher. "To award the best literary short story." Annual. Prize: $1,000 and publication on website. Category: Literary short story. Receives about 100-150 entries per category. Entries are judged anonymously. **Entry fee:** $25. Make checks payable to Gival Press, LLC. Guidelines available online, via e-mail, or by mail. **Deadline:** August 8. Entries must be unpublished. Open to anyone who writes original short stories in English. Length: 5,000-15,000 words. Include name, address, phone, e-mail, word count, title on cover letter; include short bio. Only the title and word count should be found on ms. Writers may submit their own ficiton. "We publish literary works." Results announced in the fall of the same year. Winners notified by phone. Results available with SASE, by e-mail, on website. Annual. Category: Literary short story. Receives about 100-150 entries per category. Guidelines available online, via e-mail, or by mail. Results announced in the fall of the same year. Winners notified by phone. Results available with SASE, by e-mail, and on website. "To award the best literary short story." Deadline: August 8. $1,000 and publication on website. Entries are judged anonymously.

GLIMMER TRAIN'S FAMILY MATTERS

Glimmer Train, 4763 SW Maplewood Rd., P.O. Box 80430, Portland OR 97280. (503)221-0836. **Fax:** (503)221-0837. **E-mail:** eds@glimmertrain.org. **Website:** www.glimmertrain.org. **Contact:** Linda Swanson-Davies. "Offered for stories about family. Submissions to this category generally range from 1,500-6,000 words, but up to 12,000 is fine. Open in the months of April and October. Submit online at www.glimmertrain.org. Winners will be called 2 months after the close of the contest." 1st Place: $1,500, publicationin *Glimmer Train Stories*, and 20 copies of that issue; 2nd Place: $500; 3rd Place: $300.

GLIMMER TRAIN'S FICTION OPEN

Glimmer Train, Inc., Glimmer Train Press, Inc., 4763 SW Maplewood Rd., P.O. Box 80430, Portland OR 97280. (503)221-0836. **Fax:** (503)221-0837. **E-mail:** eds@glimmertrain.org. **Website:** www.glimmertrain.org. **Contact:** Linda Swanson-Davies. "Submissions to this category generally range from 2,000-8,000 words, but up to 20,000 is fine. Open in the months of March, June, September, and December. Submit online at www.glimmertrain.org. Winners will be called 2 months after the close of the contest." 1st Place $2,500, publication in *Glimmer Train Stories*, and 20 copies of that issue; 2nd Place $1,000; 3rd Place: $600.

GLIMMER TRAIN'S SHORT-STORY AWARD FOR NEW WRITERS

Glimmer Train Press, Inc., 1211 NW Glisan St., Suite 207, Portland OR 97209. (503)221-0836. **Fax:** (503)221-0837. **E-mail:** eds@glimmertrain.org. **Website:** www.glimmertrain.org. **Contact:** Linda Swanson-Davies. "Offered for any writer whose fiction hasn't appeared in a nationally distributed print publication with a circulation over 5,000. Submissions to this category generally range from 1,500-6,000 words, but up to 12,000 is fine. Open in the months of February, May, August, and November. Submit online at www.glimmertrain.org. Winners will be called 2 months after the close of the contest." 1st Place: $1,500, publication in *Glimmer Train Stories*, and 20 copies of that issue; 2nd Place: $500; 3rd Place: $300.

GLIMMER TRAIN'S VERY SHORT FICTION AWARD (JANUARY)

Glimmer Train Press, Inc., 4763 SW Maplewood Rd., P.O. Box 80430, Portland OR 97280. (503)221-0836. **Fax:** (503)221-0837. **E-mail:** eds@glimmertrain.org. **Website:** www.glimmertrain.org. **Contact:** Linda Swanson-Davies. eds@glimmertrain.org; www.glimmertrain.org; **Contact:** Linda Swanson-Davies. Award to encourage the art of the very short story. "We want to read your original, unpublished, very short story—word count not to exceed 3,000 words." Prize: $1,200 and publication in Glimmer Train Stories and 20 author's copies (1st place); First/Second runners-up: $500/$300 respectively and possible publication. Entry fee: $15/story. **Contest open in the months of January and July.** Open to all writers. Make your submissions online at www.glimmertrain. org. Winners will be called and results announced two months after the close of each contest. "Offered to encouragethe art of the very short story. Word count: 3,000 maximum. Open January 1-31. Submit online at www.glimmertrain.org. Winners will be called on March 31." 1st Place: $1,500, publication in *Glimmer Train Stories*, and 20 copies of that issue; 2nd Place: $500; 3rd Place: $300.

GLIMMER TRAIN'S VERY SHORT FICTION CONTEST (JULY)

Glimmer Train Press, Inc., 4763 SW Maplewood Rd., P.O. Box 80430, Portland OR 97280. (503)221-0836. **Fax:** (503)221-0837. **E-mail:** eds@glimmertrain.org. **Website:** www.glimmertrain.org. **Contact:** Linda Swanson-Davies. "Offered to encourage the artof the very short story. Word count: 3,000 maximum. Open July 1-31. Submit online at www.glimmertrain.org. Winners will be called on October 1." 1st Place: $1,500, publication in *Glimmer Train Stories*, and 20 copies of that issue; 2nd Place: $500; 3rd Place: $300.

THE GOODHEART PRIZE FOR FICTION

Mattingly House, 2 Lee Ave., Lexington VA 24450-0303. **Website:** http://shenandoah.wlu.edu. Awarded to best story published in Shenandoah during a volume year. Prize: $1,000. Judged by writer whose identity is revealed after the prize winner has been selected. No entry fee. All stories published in the review are automatically considered for the prize. Winners are notified by mail or e-mail each Spring. Results are available on website. "Read Shenandoah to familiarize yourself with the work we publish."

☯ GOVERNOR GENERAL'S LITERARY AWARD FOR FICTION

Canada Council for the Arts, 350 Albert St., P.O. Box 1047, Ottawa ON K1P 5V8 Canada. (613)566-4414, ext. 5573. **Fax:** (613)566-4410. **Website:** www.canadacouncil.ca/prizes/ggla. Offered annually for the best English-language and the best French-language work of fiction by a Canadian. Publishers submit titles for consideration. Deadline depends on the book's publication date. Books in English: March 15, June 1 or August 7. Books in French: March 15 or July 15. Each laureate receives $25,000; non-winning finalists receive $1,000.

● GRANTS FOR ARTIST'S PROJECTS

Artist Trust, 1835 12th Ave., Seattle WA 98122. (206) 467-8734, ext. 11. **Fax:** (206) 467-9633. **E-mail:** miguel@artisttrust.org. **Website:** www.artisttrust.org. **Contact:** Monica Miller, director of programs. "The GAP Program provides support for artist-generated projects, which can include (but are not limited to) the development, completion or presentation of new work." Annual. Prize: maximum of $1,500 for projects. Accepted are poetry, fiction, graphic novels, experimental works, creative non-fiction, screen plays, film scripts and teleplays. Entries are judged by work sample as specified in the guidelines. Winners are selected by a discipline-specific panel of artists and artist professionals. No entry fee. Guidelines available in March. Accepts inquiries by mail, phone. Submission period is March-May. **Deadline: May 2013**; check website for specific date. Website should be consulted for exact date. Entries can be unpublished or previously published. Washington state residents only.

Length: 8 pages max for poetry, fiction, graphic novels, experimental work and creative nonfiction; up to 12 pages for screen plays, film scripts and teleplays. All mss must be typed with a 12-point font size or larger and cannot be single-spaced (except for poetry). Include application with project proposal and budget, as well as resume with name, address, phone, e-mail, and novel/story title. "GAP awards are highly competitive. Please follow guidelines with care." Results announced in the fall. Winners notified by email. Results made available to entrants by e-mail and on website. "The GAP grant is awarded annually to 60 artists of all disciplines including writers. The award is meant to help finance a specific project, which can be in very early stages or near completion. Full-time students are not eligible. Open to Washington state residents only. Up to $1,500 for artist-generated projects." Deadline: May 2013. Check website for specific date.

◐ GREAT LAKES COLLEGES ASSOCIATION NEW WRITERS AWARD

535 W. William, Suite 301, Ann Arbor MI 48103. (734)661-2350. **Fax:** (734)661-2349. **E-mail:** wegner@glca.org. **Website:** www.glca.org. **Contact:** Gregory R. Wegner. The New Writers Award is given for an author's first published volume, 1 in each category of fiction, creative nonfiction, and poetry. Writer must be nominated by publisher, and a publisher can submit only 1 entry for a given genre. The writer can submit a work directly if it is self-published. Prize: Winners are invited to tour the GLCA colleges. An honorarium of $500 will be guaranteed the author by each GLCA member college they visit. Judges are professors of literature and creative writing at GLCA's member colleges. No entry fee. Submitted volumes must be written in English and published in the US or Canada. Submit 4 copies of the book to Gregory R. Wegner, director of program development, at the GLCA mailing address listed above. Guidelines are published in February for a given year's award. Accepts inquiries by e-mail. Results announced in January of each year. The New Writers Award is given for an author's first published volume, 1 in each category of fiction, creative nonfiction, and poetry. Guidelines available for SASE, by e-mail, or on the GLCA website. Additional details as well as a listing of winning writers are also available on the GLCA website. Deadline: July 25. Winners are invited to tour the GLCA colleges; tours are scheduled during the academic year.

An honorarium of $500 will be guaranteed the author by each GLCA member college they visit, as well as travel expenses, hotel accommodations, and hospitality. Judges are professors of literature and creative writing at GLCA's member colleges.

THE GRUB STREET BOOK PRIZE IN FICTION

Grub Street, 160 Boylston Street, Boston MA 02116. (617) 695-0075. **Fax:** (617) 695-0075. **E-mail:** info@grubstreet.org. **Website:** http://grubstreet.org. **Contact:** Christopher Castellani, artistic director. "Supports writers who are publishing beyond their first or second, third, fourth (or beyond…) book, and who live outside of New England." Annual. Competition/award for short story collections, novels. Prize: Each winner receives a $1,000 honorarium and a Friday night reading/book party at Grub Street's event space in downtown Boston. The reading and party are co-sponsored by a local independent bookstore, which will sell books at the event. Winners will lead a two-hour informal craft class on a topic of their choice for a small group of aspiring Grub Street writers. Winners also invited as guest authors to *Muse and the Marketplace* literary conference. Grub Street provides accommodations for all time in Boston and covers all travel and meal expenses. Categories: Fiction, Poetry, and Non-fiction. Different deadlines apply for each category. Entries are judged by a guest judge and committee of readers drawn from the Grub Street staff. Committee members negotiate their top picks at a meeting facilitated by the guest judge. **Entry fee: $10.** Send credit card information or make checks payable to Grub Street. Guidelines available in June. Accepts inquiries by fax, e-mail, phone. **Entry deadline is October 15th.** Entries should be previously published or under contract.

HAMMETT PRIZE

328 Eighth Ave., #114, New York NY 10001. **Fax:** (815)361-1477. **E-mail:** mfrisque@igc.org. **Website:** www.crimewritersna.org.. **Contact:** Mary A. Frisque, executive director, North American Branch. Award established "to honor a work of literary excellence in the field of crime writing by a U.S. or Canadian author." Award for novels, story collections, nonfiction by one author. Prize: trophy. Judged by committee. "Our reading committee seeks suggestions from publishers and they also ask the membership for recommendations. Eligible books are read by a committee of members of the organization. The committee chooses 5 nominated books, which are then sent to 3 outside judges for a final selection. Judges are outside the crime writing field." No entry fee. For guidelines, send SASE or e-mail. Accepts inquiries by e-mail. **Deadline: December 1.** Entries must be previously published. To be eligible "the book must have been published in the US or Canada during the calendar year." The author must be a US or Canadian citizen or permanent resident. Nominations announced in January; winners announced in fall. Winners notified by mail, phone, and recognized at awards ceremony. For contest results, send SASE or e-mail.

WILDA HEARNE FLASH FICTION CONTEST

Big Muddy: A Journal of the Mississippi River Valley, WHFF Contest, Southeast Missouri State University Press, One University Plaza, MS 2650, Cape Girardeau MO 63701. **Website:** www6.semo.edu/universitypress/hearne.htm. "We're searching for the best short-short story of any theme." Annual. Prize: $200 and publication in Big Muddy. Semi-finalists will be chosen by a regional team of published writers. The final ms will be chosen by Susan Swartwout, publisher of Southeast Missouri State University Press. Entry fee: $15 (includes a copy of Big Muddy in which the winning story appears). Make checks payable to SEMO UP - WHFF. Guidelines available in January. Accepts inquiries by e-mail, phone. **Submission period is Jan 1-Sept 1.** Entries should be unpublished. Anyone may enter contest. Length: 500 words max. Cover letter should include name, address, phone, e-mail, story title. The title and page numbers should appear on each page of the ms. Writers may submit own work. Results announced fall. Winners notified by mail, by phone, by e-mail. Results made available to entrants with SASE.

DRUE HEINZ LITERATURE PRIZE

University of Pittsburgh Press, Eureka Building, 5th Floor, 3400 Forbes Ave., Eureka Bldg., 5th Floor, Pittsburgh PA 15260. (412)383-2492. **Fax:** (412)383-2466. **Website:** www.upress.pitt.edu. Estab. 1981. Offered annually to writers who have published a book-length collection of fiction or a minimum of 3 short stories or novellas in commercial magazines or literary journals of national distribution. Does not return mss. Deadline: Submit May 1- June 30 only. Prize: $15,000. Judged by anonymous nationally known writers such as Robert Penn Warren, Joyce Carol Oates, and Margaret Atwood.

LORIAN HEMINGWAY SHORT STORY COMPETITION

Hemingway Days Festival, P.O. Box 993, Key West FL 33041-0993. **E-mail:** shortstorykw@gmail.com. **Website:** www.shortstorycompetition.com. **Contact:** Eva Eliot, editorial assistant; Joanne Denning, contest development director. Estab. 1981. Award to "encourage literary excellence and the efforts of writers whose voices have yet to be heard." Offered annually for unpublished short stories up to 3,500 words. Guidelines available via mail, e-mail, or online. Deadline: May 15. 1st Place: $1,500, plus publication of his or her winning story in *Cutthroat: A Journal of the Arts*; 2nd-3rd Place: $500; honorable mentions will also be awarded. Judged by a panel of writers, editors, and literary scholars selected by author Lorian Hemingway. (Lorian Hemingway is the competition's final judge.) Results announced at the end of July during Hemingway Days festival. Winners notified by phone prior to announcement. For contest results, send e-mail or visit website.

○ HIGHLIGHTS FOR CHILDREN FICTION CONTEST

803 Church St., Honesdale PA 18431-1824. (570)253-1080. **Fax:** (570)251-7847. **E-mail:** eds@highlights-corp.com. **Website:** www.Highlights.com. **Contact:** Christine French Cully, fiction contest editor. Purpose of the contest: to stimulate interest in writing for children and reward and recognize excellence. Unpublished submissions only. Deadline for entries: January 31; entries accepted after January 1 only. SASE for contest rules and return of entries. No entry fee. Awards 3 prizes of $1,000 each in cash and a pewter bowl (or, at the winner's election, attendance at the Highlights Foundation Writers Workshop at Chautauqua) and a pewter bowl. Judging by a panel of Highlights editors and outside judges. Winning pieces are purchased for the cash prize of $1,000 and published in Highlights; other entries are considered for purchase at regular rates. Requirements for entrants: open to any writer 16 years of age or older. Winners announced in May. Length up to 800 words. Stories for beginning readers should not exceed 500 words. Stories should be consistent with Highlights editorial requirements. No violence, crime or derogatory

humor. Send SASE or visit website for guidelines and current theme.

THE HILLERMAN MYSTERY NOVEL COMPETITION

Wordharvest & St. Martins Press, 304 Calle Oso, Santa Fe NM 87501. (505)471-1565. **E-mail:** wordharvest@wordharvest.com. **Website:** www.hillermanconference.com. **Contact:** Anne Hillerman and Jean Schaumberg, co-organizers. Purpose: "To honor the contributions made by Tony Hillerman to the art and craft of the mystery." Annual competition/award for novels. Prize: $10,000 advance and publication by Thomas Dunne Books/St. Martin's Minotaur imprint. Categories: unpublished mystery novels set in the American southwest, written by a first-time author in the mystery genre. One entry per author. Nominees will be selected by judges chosen by the editorial staff of St. Martin's Press, with the assistance of independent judges selected by organizers of the Tony Hillerman Writers Conference (Wordharvest), and the winner will be chosen by St. Martin's editors. No entry fee. Accepts inquiries by e-mail, phone. **Deadline:** June 1. Entries should be unpublished; self-published work is generally accepted. Length: no less than 220 typewritten pages, or approximately 60,000 words. Cover letter should include name, address, phone, e-mail, list of publishing credits. Please include SASE for response. Writers may submit their own work. "Make sure murder or another serious crime or crimes is at the heart of the story, and emphasis is on the solution rather than the details of the crime. The story's primary setting should be the southwest US, which includes CA, AZ, CO, NV, NM, OK, TX, and UT." Results announced at the Tony Hillerman Writers Conference. St. Martin's Press notifies the winner by phone or by e-mail 2-3 weeks prior to the conference. Results made available to entrants on website. Annual competition/award for novels. Categories: Unpublished mystery novels set in the American southwest, written by a first-time author in the mystery genre. All entries must be mailed to St. Martin's Press at the address below. Entry form is online at the website. For additional copies of the rules and to request an entry form, please send a SASE to: **St. Martin's Press/ Hillerman Mystery Competition Thomas Dunne Books/St. Martin's Press, 175 Fifth Ave., New York, NY 10010.** "To honor the contributions made by Tony Hillerman to the art and craft of the mystery." Deadline: June 1. Prize: $10,000 advance and publication by

Thomas Dunne Books/St. Martin's Minotaur imprint. Nominees will be selected by judges chosen by the editorial staff of St. Martin's Press, with the assistance of independent judges selected by organizers of the Tony Hillerman Writers Conference (Wordharvest), and the winner will be chosen by St. Martin's editors.

⊕ TONY HILLERMAN MYSTERY SHORT STORY CONTEST

Sponsored by Wordharvest Writers Workshops and *New Mexico Magazine*, (505) 471-1565. **E-mail:** wordharvest@wordharvest.com. **E-mail:** www.wordharvest.com. **Website:** www.wordharvest.com.. **Contact:** Anne Hillerman and Jean Schaumberg, co-organizers. Annual competition/award for mystery short stories. "What we are looking for: Your best mystery short story, set primarily in New Mexico. We're seeking compelling, original, well-written stories that have not been previously published." "To honor the contributions made by Tony Hillerman to the art and craft of the mystery." All entries must be postmarked no later than August 15. Prize: The winning story will be published in an issue of *New Mexico Magazine*, probably the February issue which is devoted to books and reading. The winner will receive publication in the magazine, two tickets to the awards ceremony at the Tony Hillerman Writers Conference and other prizes.

◯ TOM HOWARD/JOHN H. REID SHORT STORY CONTEST

c/o Winning Writers, 351 Pleasant St., PMB 222, Northampton MA 01060-3961. (866)946-9748. **E-mail:** johnreid@mail.qango.com. **Website:** www.winningwriters.com. **Contact:** John Reid. Estab. 1993. Now in its 20th year. Open to all writers. Prizes of $3,000, $1,000, $400 and $250 will be awarded, plus 6 Most Highly Commended Awards of $150 each. Submit any type of short story, essay or other work of prose. "You may submit work that has been published or won prizes elsewhere, as long as you own the online publication rights." **Entry fee:** $15. Make checks payable to Winning Writers ("US funds only, please"). Submit online or by mail. Early submission encouraged. Contest is sponsored by Tom Howard Books and assisted by Winning Writers. Judges: John H. Reid and Dee C. Konrad. See the complete guidelines and past winners. Guidelines available in July on website. Prefers inquiries by e-mail. **Deadline:** March 31. "Both published and unpublished works are ac-cepted. In the case of published work, the contestant must own the online publication rights." Length: 5,000 words max per entry. Cover letter should include name, address, phone, e-mail, story title, and place(s) where story was previously published (if any). Only the title should be on the actual ms. Writers may submit own work. Read past winning entries at www.winningwriters.com/contests/tomstory/ts_pastwinners.php. Winners notified by e-mail. Results made available to entrants on website. Now in its 20th year. Open to all writers. Submit any type of short story, essay or other work of prose. "You may submit work that has been published or won prizes elsewhere, as long as you own the online publication rights. Both published and unpublished works are accepted. In the case of published work, the contestant must own the online publication rights." Contest is sponsored by Tom Howard Books and assisted by Winning Writers. See the complete guidelines and past winners. Guidelines available in July on website. Read past winning entries at www.winningwriters.com/contests/tomstory/ts_pastwinners.php. Winners notified by e-mail. Results made available to entrants on website. Deadline: March 31 1st Place: $3,000; 2nd Place: $1,000; 3rd Place: $400; 4th Place: $250; and 6 Most Highly Commended Awards of $150 each. The winners will be published on the Winning Writers website. Judged by John H. Reid; assisted by Dee C. Konrad.

THE JULIA WARD HOWE/BOSTON AUTHORS AWARD

The Boston Authors Club, 33 Brayton Rd., Brighton MA 02135. (617)783-1357. **E-mail:** bostonauthors@aol.com; lawson@bc.edu. **Website:** www.bostonauthorsclub.org. **Contact:** Alan Lawson. Estab. 1900. This annual award honors Julia Ward Howe and her literary friends who founded the Boston Authors Club in 1900. It also honors the membership over 110 years, consisting of novelists, biographers, historians, governors, senators, philosophers, poets, playwrights, and other luminaries. There are 2 categories: trade books and books for young readers (beginning with chapter books through young adult books). Works of fiction, nonfiction, memoir, poetry, and biography published in 2010 are eligible. Authors must live or have lived (college counts) within a 100-mile radius of Boston within the last 5 years. Subsidized books, cook books and picture books are not eligible. Fee is $25 per title.

⊙⊙ HENRY HOYNS & POE/FAULKNER FELLOWSHIPS

Creative Writing Program, 219 Bryan Hall, P.O. Box 400121, University of Virginia, Charlottesville VA 22904-4121. (434)924-6675. **Fax:** (434)924-1478. **E-mail:** creativewriting@virginia.edu. **Website:** www.creativewriting.virginia.edu. **Contact:** Jeb Livingood, associate director. Two-year MFA program in poetry and fiction; all students receive first-year fellowships of $16,000. Sample poems/prose required with application. **Deadline:** December 15. In 2010, 800 applicants for 10 fellowships. Two-year MFA program in poetry and fiction; all students receive first-year fellowships of $16,000. Sample poems/prose required with application. In 2010, 800 applicants for 10 fellowships. Deadline: December 15.

⊙ L. RON HUBBARD'S WRITERS OF THE FUTURE CONTEST

P.O. Box 1630, Los Angeles CA 90078. (323)466-3310. **Fax:** (323)466-6474. **E-mail:** contests@authorservicesinc.com. **Website:** www.writersofthefuture.com. **Contact:** Joni Labaqui, contest director. Estab. 1983. Foremost competition for new and amateur writers of unpublished science fiction or fantasy short stories or novelettes. Offered "to find, reward and publicize new speculative fiction writers so they may more easily attain professional writing careers." Open to writers who have not professionally published a novel or short novel, more than 1 novelette, or more than 3 short stories. Eligible entries are previously unpublished short stories or novelettes (under 17,000 words) of science fiction or fantasy. Guidelines for SASE or on website. Accepts inquiries by fax, e-mail, phone. Prize (awards quarterly): 1st Place: $1,000; 2nd Place: $750; and 3rd Place: $500. Annual grand prize: $5,000. "Contest has 4 quarters. There shall be 3 cash prizes in each quarter. In addition, at the end of the year, the 4 first-place, quarterly winners will have their entries rejudged, and a grand prize winner shall be determined." Judged by K.D. Wentworth (initial judge), then by a panel of 4 professional authors. **Deadline:** December 31, March 31, June 30, September 30. Entries must be unpublished. Limit 1 entry per quarter. No entry fee; entrants retain all rights to their stories. Open to any writer. Mss: White paper, black ink; double-spaced; typed; each page appropriately numbered with title, no author name. Include cover page with author's name, address, phone number, e-mail address (if available), as well as estimated word count and the title of the work. Results announced quarterly in e-newsletter. Winners notified by phone. Foremost competition for new and amateur writers of unpublished science fiction or fantasy short stories or novelettes. Offered "to find, reward and publicize new speculative fiction writers so they may more easily attain professional writing careers." Open to writers who have not professionally published a novel or short novel, more than 1 novelette, or more than 3 short stories. Entries must be unpublished. Limit 1 entry per quarter. Open to any writer. Results announced quarterly in e-newsletter. Winners notified by phone. Deadline: December 31, March 31, June 30, September 30. Prize (awards quarterly): 1st Place: $1,000; 2nd Place: $750; and 3rd Place: $500. Annual grand prize: $5,000. "Contest has 4 quarters. There shall be 3 cash prizes in each quarter. In addition, at the end of the year, the 4 first-place, quarterly winners will have their entries rejudged, and a grand prize winner shall be determined." Judged by K.D. Wentworth (initial judge), then by a panel of 4 professional authors.

INDEPENDENT PUBLISHER BOOK AWARDS

Jenkins Group/Independent Publisher Online, 1129 Woodmere Ave., Ste. B, Traverse City MI 49686. (231)933-4954, ext. 1011. **Fax:** (231)933-0448. **E-mail:** jimb@bookpublishing.com. **Website:** www.independentpublisher.com. **Contact:** Jim Barnes. "The Independent Publisher Book Awards were conceived as a broad-based, unaffiliated awards program open to all members of the independent publishing industry. The staff at *Independent Publisher* magazine saw the need to bring increased recognition to the thousands of exemplary independent, university, and self-published titles produced each year. The IPPY Awards reward those who exhibit the courage, innovation, and creativity to bring about change in the world of publishing. Independent spirit and expertise comes from publishers of all areas and budgets, and we judge books with that in mind. Entries will be accepted in 67 categories. Open to any published writer." Offered annually for books published between January 1 and December 31. Deadline: March 20. Gold, silver and bronze medals for each category; foil seals available to all. Judged by a panel of experts representing the fields of design, writing, bookselling, library, and reviewing.

INDIANA REVIEW (SHORT-SHORT/ PROSE-POEM) CONTEST

Indiana Review, Ballantine Hall 465, 1020 E. Kirkwood Ave., Indiana University, Bloomington IN 47405-7103. (812)855-3439. **Fax:** (812)855-9535. **E-mail:** inreview@indiana.edu. **Website:** http://indianareview.org. **Contact:** Alessandra Simmons, editor. Offered annually for unpublished work. Maximum story/poem length is 500 words. Guidelines available in March for SASE, by phone, e-mail, on website, or in publication. Deadline: June. Prize: $1,000, plus publication, contributor's copies, and a year's subscription to *Indiana Review.* Guest judge for 2011 was Ander Monson.

◯ INDIANA REVIEW FICTION CONTEST

BH 465/Indiana University, 1020 E. Kirkwood Ave., Bloomington IN 47405-7103. (812)855-3439. **Fax:** (812)855-4253. **E-mail:** inreview@indiana.edu. **Website:** http://indianareview.org. **Contact:** Deborah Kim, editor. Contest for fiction in any style and on any subject. Mss will not be returned. No works forthcoming elsewhere, are eligible. Simultaneous submissions accepted, but in the event of entrant withdrawal, contest fee will not be refunded. Length: 35 pages maximum, double spaced. Open to any writer. Cover letter must include name, address, phone number and title of story. Entrant's name should appear only in the cover letter, as all entries will be considered anonymously. Results announced January. Winners notified by mail. For contest results, send SASE. "We look for a command of language and structure, as well as a facility with compelling and unusual subject matter. It's a good idea to obtain copies of issues featuring past winners to get a more concrete idea of what we are looking for." See website for updates to guidelines. Deadline: Mid-October. Prize: $1,000, publication in the Indiana Review and contributor's copies. Judged by guest judges. 2010 prize judged by Dan Chaon.

INDIVIDUAL EXCELLENCE AWARDS

Ohio Arts Council, 727 E. Main St., Columbus OH 43205-1796. (614)466-2613. **E-mail:** ken.emerick@oac.state.oh.us. **Website:** www.oac.state.oh.us. **Contact:** Ken Emerick. "An award of excellence for completed work for Ohio residents who are not students." Annual. Competition/award for short stories, novels, story collections. Prize: $5,000 or $10,000, determined by review panel. Categories: fiction/nonfiction, poetry, criticism, playwriting/screenplays. Receives about 125 poetry, 125 fiction/nonfiction, 10-15 criticism, 25-30 playwriting entries per year. Judged by three-person panel of out-of-state panelists, anonymous review. No entry fee. Guidelines available in June on website. A cepts inquiries by e-mail, phone. Deadline: September 1. Open to Ohio residents living and working in the state for at least one year prior to the deadline who are also not students. Length: 20-30 pages fiction/nonfiction, 10-15 pages poetry, 30-50 pages criticism, 1 play or 2 short 1-act plays. Cover letter should include name, address, title of work. None of this information should appear on the actual manuscript. Writers may submit own work. "Submit concise bodies of work or sections, not a sampling of styles." Results announced Jan. Winners notified by mail. Results made available to entrants on website.

INKWELL SHORT FICTION CONTEST

Inkwell Literary Magazine, Manhattanville College, 2900 Purchase St., Purchase NY 10577. (914) 323-7239. **Fax:** (914) 323-3122. **E-mail:** inkwell@mville.edu. **Website:** www.inkwelljournal.org. Annual. Competition/award for short stories. Entry fee: $15. Make checks payable to Inkwell-Manhattanville College. Guidelines available in June. Accepts inquiries by fax, e-mail, phone. Entries must be unpublished. Anyone may enter contest. Length: 5,000 words max. Cover letter should include name, address, phone, e-mail, word count, novel/story title. Only title on ms. Writers may submit own work. "Follow the guidelines. Proofread your work. Don't write for editors, teachers, or critics; write for you, and for your readers." Winners notified by phone, by e-mail. Results made available to entrants with SASE, by e-mail. Deadline for entry: October 30 $1,500. Entries judged by editorial staff. Finalists are picked by a celebrity judge.

INTERNATIONAL READING ASSOCIATION CHILDREN'S BOOK AWARDS

P.O. Box 8139, 800 Barksdale Rd., Newark DE 19714-8139. (302)731-1600, ext. 221. **E-mail:** exec@reading.org. "This award is for newly published authors of children's books who show unusual promise in the children's book field." Offered annually for an author's first or second published book in fiction and nonfiction in 3 categories: primary (preschool-age 8), intermediate (ages 9-13), and young adult (ages 14-17). Guidelines and deadlines for SASE. Prize: 6 awards of $1,000 each, and a medal for each category. Categories: fiction and nonfiction. No entry fee. The book will be considered one time during the year of first copyright in English. **Deadline: November 1**. For guidelines with specific information write to Executive Office, International Reading Association.

◐ ⦿ THE IOWA REVIEW AWARD IN POETRY, FICTION, AND NONFICTION

308 EPB, University of Iowa, Iowa City IA 52242. **E-mail:** iowa-review@uiowa.edu. **Website:** www.iowareview.org. **Contact:** Contest Coordinator. *The Iowa Review* Award in Poetry, Fiction, and Nonfiction presents $1,500 to each winner in each genre, $750 to runners-up. Winners and runners-up published in *The Iowa Review* (see separate listing in Magazines/Journals). 2011 winners were Emily Van Kley, John Van Kirk, and Helen Phillips. Deadline: Submit January 1-31 (postmark). 2012 Judges: Timothy Donnelly, Ron Currie, Jr., and Meghan Daum.

THE IOWA SHORT FICTION AWARD

Iowa Writers' Workshop, 507 N. Clinton St., 102 Dey House,, Iowa City IA 52242-1000. **Website:** www.uiowapress.org. **Contact:** Jim McCoy, director. Annual award "to give exposure to promising writers who have not yet published a book of prose." Open to any writer. Current University of Iowa students are not eligible. No application forms are necessary. Announcement of winners made early in year following competition. Winners notified by phone. No application forms are necessary. Do not send original ms. Include SASE for return of ms. Deadline: September 30. Submission period: August 1-September 30. Prize: publication by University of Iowa Press Judged by senior Iowa Writers' Workshop members who screen mss; published fiction author of note makes final selections.

JAMES JONES FIRST NOVEL FELLOWSHIP

Wilkes University, Creative Writing Department, 245 S. River St., Wilkes-Barre PA 18766. (570)408-4547. **Fax:** (570)408-3333. **E-mail:** Jamesjonesfirstnovel@wilkes.edu. **Website:** www.wilkes.edu/pages/1159.asp. Offered annually for unpublished novels, novellas, and closely-linked short stories (all works in progress). "The award is intended to honor the spirit of unblinking honesty, determination, and insight into modern culture exemplified by the late James Jones." The competition is open to all American writers who have not previously published novels. Deadline: March 1. Prize: $10,000; 2 runners-up get $750 honorarium.

JUST DESERTS SHORT-SHORT FICTION PRIZE

Passages North, NMU 1401 Presque Isle Ave., Marquette MI 49855. **E-mail:** passages@nmu.edu. **Website:** www.passagesnorth.com. Offered every other year—check website for details. Prize: $1,000 1st Prize and 2 honorable mentions. **Entry fee:** $15 for up to 2 stories; includes contest issue. Make checks payable to Northern Michigan University. **Deadline:** Submission period is October 15-February 15. Entries should be unpublished. Anyone may enter contest. Length: Max of 1,000 words. Cover letter should include name, address, phone, e-mail; may also be submitted online at www.passagesnorth.com. Writers may submit own work. Winners notified by e-mail. Results made available to entrants with SASE. Offered every other year—check website for details. Deadline: Submission period is October 15-February 15. $1,000 1st Prize and 2 honorable mentions.

⦿ E.M. KOEPPEL SHORT FICTION AWARD

P.O. Box 140310, Gainesville FL 32614-0310. **Website:** www.writecorner.com. **Contact:** Mary Sue Koeppel, editor. Award for short stories. Prize: $1,100 first prize, and $100 for Editors' Choices. Judged by award-winning writers. Entry fee: $15 first story, $10 each additional story. Make checks payable to Writecorner Press. Send 2 title pages: One with title only and one with title, name, address, phone, e-mail, short bio. Place no other identification of the author on the ms that will be used in the judging. Guidelines available for SASE or on website. Accepts inquiries by e-mail and phone. Expects 300+ entries. **Deadline: October 1-April 30**. Entries must be unpublished. Open to any writer. Winning stories published on website. Winners notified by mail, phone in July (or earlier). For results, send SASE or see website.

⦿ THE LAWRENCE FOUNDATION AWARD

123 Andrews Hall, P.O. Box 880334, Lincoln NE 68588-0334. **Website:** www.unl.edu/schooner/psmain.htm.. Offered annually for the best short story published in Prairie Schooner in the previous year. Prize: $1,000. Judged by editorial staff of Praire Schooner. No entry fee. Only work published in Prairie Schooner in the previous year is considered. Work is nominated by editorial staff. Results announced in the Spring issue. Winners notified by mail in February or March.

LAWRENCE FOUNDATION PRIZE

0576 Rackham Building, Ann Arbor MI 48109-1070. (734)764-9265. **E-mail:** mqr@umich.edu. **Website:** www.umich.edu/~mqr. **Contact:** Vicki Lawrence, managing editor. Competition for short stories. Prize: $1,000. Judged by editorial board. No entry fee. No deadline. "An annual cash prize awarded to the author of the best short story published in Michigan Quarterly Review each year. Stories must be already published in Michigan Quarterly Review. This is not a competition in which manuscripts are read outside of the normal submission process." Guidelines available for SASE or on website. Accepts inquires by e-mail and phone. Results announced in December. Winners notified by phone or mail.

LET'S WRITE LITERARY CONTEST

The Gulf Coast Writers Association, P.O. Box 10294, Gulfport MS 39505. **E-mail:** writerpllevin@gmail.com. **Website:** www.gcwriters.org. **Contact:** Philip Levin. "The Gulf Coast Writers Association sponsors this nationally recognized contest, which accepts unpublished poems and short stories from authors all around the US. This is an annual event which has been held for over 20 years." Deadline: April 15 1st Prize: $80; 2nd Prize: $50; 3rd Prize: $20.

LITERAL LATTÉ FICTION AWARD

Literal Latté, 200 E. 10th St., Suite 240, New York NY 10003. (212)260-5532. **E-mail:** litlatte@aol.com. **Website:** www.literal-latte.com. **Contact:** Edward Estlin, contributing editor. "Award to provide talented writers with 3 essential tools for continued success: money, publication, and recognition. Offered annually for unpublished fiction (maximum 10,000 words). Guidelines online. Open to any writer." Deadline: January 15. 1st Place: $1,000 and publication in *Literal Latté*; 2nd Place: $300; 3rd Place: $200; also up to 7 honorable mentions.

LITERAL LATTÉ SHORT SHORTS CONTEST

Literal Latte, 200 E. 10th St., Suite 240, New York NY 10003. (212)260-5532. **E-mail:** litlatte@aol.com. **Website:** www.literal-latte.com. **Contact:** Jenine Gordon Bockman, editor. Estab. Annual contest. Send unpublished shorts. 2,000 words max. All styles welcome. Postmark by June 30th. Name, address, phone number, email address (optional) on cover page only. Include SASE or email address for reply. All entries considered for publication. Postmarked by June 30th. Prize: $500. The Editors.

⭕ THE LONG STORY CONTEST, INTERNATIONAL

A. E. Coppard Prize for Fiction, White Eagle Coffee Store Press, P.O. Box 383, Fox River Grove IL 60021. (847)639-9200. **E-mail:** wecspress@aol.com. **Website:** whiteeaglecoffeestorepress.com. **Contact:** Frank E. Smith, publisher. Estab. 1993. Offered annually since 1993 for unpublished work to recognize and promote long short stories of 8,000-14,000 words (about 30-50 pages, double-spaced, 12-point font). Sample of previous winner: $6.95, including postage. Open to any writer, no restrictions on materials. Prize: A.E. Coppard Prize of $1,000 and publication, plus 25 copies of chapbook and 10 press kits. Categories: "No limits on style or subject matter." Entry fee: $15 fee; $10 for second story in same envelope. Guidelines available in April by SASE, e-mail, or on website. Accepts inquiries by e-mail. Length: 8,000-14,000 words (30-50 pages double-spaced, 12-point font) single story; may have multi-parts or be a self-contained novel segment. Deadline: December 15. Accepts previously unpublished submissions, but previous publication of small parts with acknowledgment is okay. Simultaneous submissions OK. Send cover with name, address, phone; second title page with title only. Submissions are not returned; they are recycled. "SASE for most current information." Results announced in late spring. Winners notified by phone. For contest results, send SASE or visit website in late spring. "Write with richness and depth. This has become the premiere competition in the world for long stories, giving many winners and finalists the opportunity to move to the next level of publishing success." Offered annually for unpublished work to recognize and promote long short stories of 8,000-14,000 words (about 30-50 pages, double-spaced, 12-point font). Sample of previous winner: $6.95, including postage. Open to any writer; no restrictions on materials." December 15 A.E. Coppard Prize of $1,000, publication, plus 25 copies of chapbook and 10 press kits.

THE HUGH J. LUKE AWARD

Prairie Schooner, 123 Andrews Hall, P.O. Box 880334, Lincoln NE 68588-0334. (402)472-0911. **Fax:** (402)472-9771. **E-mail:** jengelhardt2@unl.edu. **Website:** www.prairieschooner.unl.edu. **Contact:** Kwame Dawes. "Offered annually for work published in *Prairie Schooner* in the previous year. Guidelines for SASE or on website. Results announced in the

Spring issue. Winners notified by mail in February or March." Prize: $250. Judged by editorial staff of Prairie Schooner.

LUMINA

Sarah Lawrence College, Sarah Lawrence College Slonim House 1 Mead Way, Bronxville NY 10708. **Website:** http://pages.slc.edu/~lumina/contest.html. Sarah Lawrence College's graduate literary journal of poetry, fiction, and nonfiction accepts submissions every year from September 1st - November 15th. We also feature an annual contest. For more information, visit our website or email us at lumina@gm.slc.edu.

THE MARY MACKEY SHORT STORY PRIZE

Category in the Soul Making Keats Literary Competition, The Webhallow House, 1544 Sweetwood Dr., Broadmoor Village CA 94015-2029. **E-mail:** pennobhill@aol.com. **Website:** www.soulmakingcontest. us. **Contact:** Eileen Malone. Open annually to any writer. "One story/entry, up to 5,000 words. All prose works must be typed, page numbered, and double-spaced. Identify only with 3x5 card." $5/entry (make checks payable to NLAPW). Needs fiction, short stories. **Deadline:** November 30 (annually). **Prizes:** 1st Place: $100; 2nd Place: $50; 3rd Place: $25. Open annually to any writer. Deadline: November 30 (annually) 1st Place: $100; 2nd Place: $50; 3rd Place: $25.

◑○ THE MALAHAT REVIEW NOVELLA PRIZE

The Malahat Review, University of Victoria, P.O. Box 1700 STN CSC, Victoria BC V8W 2Y2 Canada. (250)721-8524. **E-mail:** malahat@uvic.ca. **Website:** malahatreview.ca. **Contact:** John Barton, editor. "Held in alternate years with the Long Poem Prize. Offered to promote unpublished novellas. Obtains first world rights. After publication rights revert to the author. Open to any writer." Submit novellas between 10,000 and 20,000 words in length. Include separate page with author's name, address, e-mail, and novella title; no identifying information on mss. pages. No e-mail submissions. Do not include SASE for results; mss will not be returned. Guidelines available on website. Deadline: February 1 (even years). $1,500 CAD and one year's subscription. 2010 winner was Tony Tulathimutte. Winner and finalists contacted by e-mail. Winner published in summer issue of *The Malahat Review* and announced on website, Facebook page, and in quarterly e-newsletter, *Malahat Lite*.

MARY MCCARTHY PRIZE IN SHORT FICTION

Sarabande Books, P.O. Box 4456, Louisville KY 40204. (502)458-4028. **Fax:** (502)458-4065. **E-mail:** info@sarabandebooks.org. **Website:** www.sarabandebooks.org. **Contact:** Kirby Gann, managing editor. Offered annually to publish an outstanding collection of stories, novellas, or a short novel (less than 250 pages). All finalists considered for publication. Deadline: January 1-February 15. $2,000 and publication (standard royalty contract).

THE MCGINNIS-RITCHIE MEMORIAL AWARD

Southwest Review, P.O. Box 750374, Dallas TX 75275-0374. (214)768-1037. **Fax:** (214)768-1408. **E-mail:** swr@mail.smu.edu. **Website:** www.smu.edu/southwestreview. **Contact:** Jennifer Cranfill, senior editor, and Willard Spiegelman, editor-in-chief. "The McGinnis-Ritchie Memorial Award is given annually to the best works of fiction and nonfiction that appeared in the magazine in the previous year. Mss are submitted for publication, not for the prizes themselves. Guidelines for SASE or online." Prize: 2 cash prizes of $500 each. Judged by Jennifer Cranfill and Willard Spiegelman.

MEMPHIS MAGAZINE FICTION AWARDS

Memphis Magazine, Davis-Kidd Booksellers, Burke's Books, Midtown Books, 460 Tennessee St., Memphis TN 38103. **E-mail:** sadler@memphismagazine.com. **Website:** www.memphismagazine.com. **Contact:** Marilyn Sadler. Competition/award for short stories. Prize: $1,000 grand prize and publication in Memphis; two $500 honorable mention awards. Judged by a panel of five, all with fiction writing experience and publications. Entry fee: $10/story. Guidelines available in April by phone, on website, in publication. Accepts inquiries by fax, e-mail, phone. Deadline: Aug. 1. Entries should be unpublished. "Manuscripts may be previously published as long as previous publication was not in a national magazine with over 20,000 circulation or in a regional publication within Shelby County." Open to all authors who live within 150 miles of Memphis. Length: 3,000-4,500 words. Cover letter should include name, address, phone, story title. Do not put your name anywhere on the ms itself. Writers may submit own work. "Each story should be typed, double-spaced, with unstapled, numbered pages. Stories are not required to have a Memphis or

Southern theme, but we do want a compelling story and first-rate writing." Winners contacted in late September.

DAVID NATHAN MEYERSON PRIZE FOR FICTION

Southwest Review, P.O. Box 750374, Dallas TX 75275-0374. (214) 768-1037. **Fax:** (214) 768-1408. **E-mail:** swr@smu.edu. **Website:** www.smu.edu/southwestreview. **Contact:** Jennifer Cranfill, senior editor. Annual award given to awriter who has not published a first book of fiction, either a novel or collection of stories. Postmarked deadline for entry is May 1. $1,000 and publication in the *Southwest Review*.

MICRO AWARD

c/o Alan Presley, PSC 817 Box 23, FPO AE 09622-0023. **E-mail:** admin@microaward.org. **Website:** www.microaward.org. **Contact:** Alan Presley. Annual contest. The Micro Award was established to recognize outstanding flash fiction from both print and electronic media. It is open to all genres. Self-published stories are eligible. An author may submit one story of his or her own; the senior editor of a magazine or anthology, or any staff member designated by him or her, may submit two stories if both are from his or her own publication and neither is self-written. The Micro Award was established to recognize outstanding flash fiction (in English) from both print and electronic media. Mailed submissions must be postmarked from Oct. 1 to Dec. 31, 2011 and received by Jan. 15, 2012. Emailed submissions should be sent to admin@microaward.org from Oct. 1 to Dec. 31, 2011. The text of the story must be inserted in the body of the email or attached as a Rich Text file. It is also permissible to include the URL information for a story or stories accessible online. The author of the winning story will receive $500 (US). A panel of 3 judges.

MIDLAND AUTHORS AWARD

Society of Midland Authors, P.O. Box 10419, Chicago IL 60610-0419. **E-mail:** writercc@aol.com. **Website:** www.midlandauthors.com. **Contact:** Carol Jean Carlson. "Established in 1915, the Society of Midland Authors Award (SMA) is presented to one title in each of six categories 'to stimulate creative effort,' one of SMA's goals, to be honored at the group's annual awards banquet in May." Annual. Competition/award for novels, story collections (by single author). Prize: cash prize of at least $300 and a plaque that is awarded at the SMA banquet. Categories: children's nonfiction and fiction, adult nonfiction and fiction, adult biography, and poetry. Judging is done by a panel of three judges for each category that includes a mix of experienced authors, reviewers, book sellers, university faculty and librarians. No entry fee. Guidelines available in September-November with SASE, on website, in publication. Accepts inquiries by e-mail, phone. **Deadline: Feb. 1.** Entries must be published in the prior calendar year, e.g. 2007 for 2008 award. "The contest is open to any title with a recognized publisher that has been published within the year prior to the contest year." Open to authors or poets who reside in, were born in, or have strong ties to a Midland state, which includes Illinois, Indiana, Iowa, Kansas, Michigan, Minnesota, Missouri, Nebraska, North Dakota, South Dakota, Ohio and Wisconsin. SMA only accepts published work accompanied by a completed award form. Writers may submit own work. Entries can also be submitted by the publisher's rep. "Write a great story and be sure to follow contest rules by sending a copy of the book to each of the three judges for the given category who are listed on SMA's website." Results announced at the SMA Awards Banquet each May. Other announcements follow in the media. Winners notified by mail, by phone. Results made available to entrants on website, in our monthly membership newsletter. Results will also go to local media in the form of press releases.

MIGHTY RIVER SHORT STORY CONTEST

Big Muddy: A Journal of the Mississippi River Valley, MRSS Contest, Southeast Missouri State University Press, One University Plaza, MS 2650, Cape Girardeau MO 63701. **Website:** www6.semo.edu/universitypress/mrss.htm. "We're searching for the best short story relating in some way to the Mississippi River or a sister River: its landscape, people, culture, history, current events, or future." Annual. Competition/award for short stories. Prize: $500 and publication in Big Muddy. Semi-finalists will be chosen by a regional team of published writers. The final ms will be chosen by Susan Swartwout, publisher of Southeast Missouri State University Press. Entry fee: $15 (includes a copy of Big Muddy in which the winning story appears). Make checks payable to SEMO UP - MRSS. Guidelines available in January. Accepts inquiries by phone andy by e-mail. **Submission period is Jan 1- Aug 1.** Entries should be unpublished. Anyone may enter contest. Length: up to 30 pages, double-spaced. Cover letter should include name, address, phone, e-mail, story title. The title and page numbers should appear on each page of the ms. Writers may submit own work. Results announced Fall. Winners notified by mail, by phone, by e-mail. Results made available to entrants with SASE.

● MILKWEED EDITIONS NATIONAL FICTION PRIZE

1011 Washington Ave. S., Suite 300, Minneapolis MN 55415. (612)332-3192. **Fax:** (612)215-2550. **E-mail:** editor@milkweed.org. **Website:** www.milkweed.org. **Contact:** Patrick Thoman, editor and program manager. Annual award for unpublished works. "Looking for a novel, novella, or a collection of short stories. Manuscripts should be of high literary quality and must be double-spaced and between 150-400 pages in length. Milkweed Editions prefers submissions through its online submissions manager." Winner will be chosen from the mss Milkweed accepts for publication each year. All mss submitted to Milkweed will automatically be considered for the prize. Submission directly to the contest is no longer necessary. Must be written in English." Catalog available on request for $1.50. Guidelines for SASE or online. Prize: Publication by Milkweed Editions, and a cash advance of $5,000 against royalties agreed upon in the contractual arrangement negotiated at the time of acceptance. Judged by Milkweed Editions. No entry fee. Deadline: rolling. Entries must be unpublished. Previous winners: The Father Shore, by Matthew Eck; Visigoth, by Gary Amdahl; Crossing Bully Creek, by Margaret Erhart; Ordinary Wolves, by Seth Kantner; Roofwalker, by Susan Power—this is the caliber of fiction we are searching for." Winners are notified by phone.

MILLION WRITERS AWARD

5603B W. Friendly Ave., Suite 282, Greensboro NC 27410. **E-mail:** editors@storysouth.com. **Website:** www.storysouth.com. **Contact:** Jason Sanford, editor emeritus. Contest "to honor and promote the best fiction published annually in online journals and magazines. The reason for the Million Writers Award is that most of the major literary prizes for short fiction (such as the O. Henry Awards) ignore Web-published fiction. This award aims to show that world-class fiction is being published online and to promote this fiction to the larger reading and literary community." Prize: Cash prize and publicity for the author and story. Categories: short stories. Judged by StorySouth judges.

No entry fee. Cover letter should include e-mail address, word count, title and publication where story was previously published. Guidelines available in winter on website. Deadline: varies. Entries must be previously published. All stories must be 1,000 words or longer. Open to any writer. Results announced in spring on website. Winners notified by e-mail.

THE MILTON CENTER POSTGRADUATE FELLOWSHIP

3307 Third Ave. W, Seattle WA 98119. **Website:** www.imagejournal.org/milton. **Contact:** Anna Johnson, program director. Award "to bring emerging writers of Christian commitment to the Center, where their primary goal is to complete their first book-length manuscript in fiction, poetry or creative nonfiction." A $16,000 stipend is offered. $25 application fee. Guidelines on website. **Deadline: March 15**. Open to any writer.

●$ MISSISSIPPI REVIEW PRIZE

Mississippi Review, 118 College Dr., #5144, Hattiesburg MS 39406-0001. (601)266-4321. **Fax:** (601)266-5757. **E-mail:** editors@mississippireview.com; rief@mississippireview.com. **Website:** www.mississippireview.com. "Our annual contest awards prizes of $1,000 in fiction and in poetry. Winners and finalists will make up next winter's print issue of the national literary magazine *Mississippi Review*. Contest is open to all writers in English except current or former students or employees of The University of Southern Mississippi. Fiction entries should be 1000-5000 words, poetry entries should be three poems totaling 10 pages or less. There is no limit on the number of entries you may submit. Entry fee is $15 per entry, payable to the *Mississippi Review*. Each entrant will receive a copy of the prize issue. No manuscripts will be returned. Previously published work is ineligible. Contest opens April 2. Deadline is October 1. Winners will be announced in late January and publication is scheduled for May next year. Entries should have "MR Prize," author name, address, phone, e-mail and title of work on page one."

MONTANA PRIZE IN FICTION

Cutbank Literary Magazine, English Dept., LA 133, UMT, Missoula MT 59812. **Website:** www.cutbankonline.org. **Contact:** Josh Foman, editor-in-chief; fiction editors: Dana Fitz Gale, Andrew Gray, Kevin Kalinowski, Carl Corder. "Since CutBank was founded in 1973, we have watched as the landscape for literary and small magazines has broadened considerably, resulting in more quality short stories, essays, and poems finding their way to an audience each year. Occasionally, we come across a submission that seems to stand above the already impressive work being published in its genre, the sort of piece that serves to credit the wide field of literary publications generally. The goal of CutBank 's annual contests it to provoke, identify, and reward work of that caliber." Annual. Competition/award for short stories. Prize: $500 and publication in the summer issue of CutBank. Entries are narrowed down to a pool of five to ten submissions which are then submitted to a guest judge for selection of the winner. The judge of the 2010-2011 Montana Prize in Fiction is Eileen Myles. Entry fee: $18 (includes a one-year, two-issue subscription to CutBank). Limit of one work of fiction per submitter (though writers may also submit work to our contests in other genres). Make checks payable to Cutbank Literary Magazine. Entries are accepted online only.Guidelines available in November. Accepts inquiries by e-mail. Entries should be unpublished. Anyone may enter contest. Please submit no more than 40 double-spaced pages. Cover letter should include name, address, phone, e-mail, novel/story title. Only name and title on ms. Writers may submit own work. "Read the magazine and get a sense of our style. We are seeking work that showcases an authentic voice, a boldness of form, and a rejection of functional fixedness." Results announced June. Winners notified by e-mail. Results made available to entrants on website.

✚ⓢ THE HOWARD FRANK MOSHER SHORT FICTION PRIZE

Vermont College, 36 College St., Montpelier VT 05602. (802)828-8517. **E-mail:** hungermtn@vcfa.edu. **Website:** www.hungermtn.org. **Contact:** Miciah Bay Gault, editor. Estab. 2002. The annual Howard Frank Mosher Short Fiction Prize offers $1,000 and publication in *Hunger Mountain* (see separate listing in Magazines/Journals); 2 runners-up receive $100 and are considered for publication. Submit story under 10,000 words. Guidelines available on website. Deadline: June 30.

●ⓢ NATIONAL BOOK AWARDS

The National Book Foundation, 90 Broad St., Suite 609, New York NY 10004. (212)685-0261. **E-mail:** nationalbook@nationalbook.org. **Website:** www.nationalbook.org. Presents $10,000 in each of 4 categories (fiction, nonfiction, poetry, and young people's literature), plus 16 short-list prizes of $1,000 each to finalists.

Submissions must be previously published and **must be entered by the publisher**. General guidelines available on website; interested publishers should phone or e-mail the Foundation. Deadline: See website for current year's deadline.

NATIONAL READERS' CHOICE AWARDS

Oklahoma Romance Writers of America (OKRWA), **E-mail:** nrca@okrwa.com. **Website:** www.okrwa.com. Contest "to provide writers of romance fiction with a competition where their published novels are judged by readers." Prize: "There is no monetary award; plaques and finalist certificates awarded at the awards banquet hosted at the Annual National Romance Writers Convention." Categories: See the website for categories and descriptions. Additional award for best first book. Entry fee: $25; PayPal accepted or make checks payable to OKRWA Treasurer. See website for entry address and contact information. All entries must have an original copyright date during the current contest year. (See website for details.) Entries will be accepted from authors, editors, publishers, agents, readers, whoever wants to fill out the entry form, pay the fee and supply the books. **Deadline:** December 1; book deadline: 15 January. (See website for exact dates.) No limit to the number of entries, but each title may be entered only in one category. Open to any writer published by an RWA approved non-vanity/non-subsidy press. For guidelines, send e-mail or visit website. Entry form required— available on website. Deadline for entry forms is 1 December. Five copies of each entry must be mailed to the category coordinator; contact information for coordinator will be provided by December 15. Finalists announced in April. Winners notified by phone, if not at the awards ceremony, in July. Winners listed in RWA's Romance Writers Report. List of winners will be mailed; also available by e-mail in August.

○ NATIONAL WRITERS ASSOCIATION NOVEL WRITING CONTEST

The National Writers Association, 10940 S. Parker Rd. #508, Parker CO 80134. (303)841-0246. **E-mail:** natlwritersassn@hotmail.com. **Website:** www.nationalwriters.com. **Contact:** Sandy Whelchel, director. Categories: Open to any genre or category. Entry fee: $35. Opens December 1. Open to any writer. Annual contest to help develop creative skills, to recognize and reward outstanding ability, and to increase the opportunity for the marketing and subsequent publication of novel mss. Deadline: April 1 1st Place: $500; 2nd Place: $250; 3rd Place: $150. Judged by editors and agents.

NATIONAL WRITERS ASSOCIATION SHORT STORY CONTEST

The National Writers Association, 10940 S. Parker Rd. #508, Parker CO 80134. (303)841-0246. **Fax:** (303)841-2607. **E-mail:** natlwritersassn@hotmail.com. **Website:** www.nationalwriters.com. **Contact:** Sandy Whelchel, director. Annual contest to encourage writers in this creative form, and to recognize those who excel in fiction writing. Deadline: July 1 1st Place: $200; 2nd Place: $100; 3rd Place: $50.

THE NELLIGAN PRIZE FOR SHORT FICTION

Colorado Review/Center for Literary Publishing, 9105 Campus Delivery, Dept. of English, Colorado State University, Ft. Collins CO 80523-9105. (970)491-5449. **E-mail:** creview@colostate.edu. **Website:** http://nelliganprize.colostate.edu. **Contact:** Stephanie G'Schwind, editor. "The Nelligan Prize for Short Fiction was established in memory of Liza Nelligan, a writer, editor, and friend of many in Colorado State University's English Department, where she received her master's degree in literature in 1992. By giving an award to the author of an outstanding short story each year, we hope to honor Liza Nelligan's life, her passion for writing, and her love of fiction." Annual. Competition/award for short stories. Prize: $1,500 plus publication in Colorado Review. Receives approximately 900 stories. All entries are read blind by Colorado Review's editorial staff. 15 entries are selected to be sent on to a final judge. Entry fee: $15. Send credit card information or make checks payable to Colorado Review. Payment also accepted via our online submission manager link from website. Deadline: March 12 $1,500 and publication of story in *Colorado Review.*

O NEW LETTERS LITERARY AWARDS

New Letters, UMKC, University House, Room 105, 5101 Rockhill Rd., Kansas City MO 64110-2499. (816)235-1168. **Fax:** (816)235-2611. **Website:** www. newletters.org. Award has 3 categories (fiction, poetry, and creative nonfiction) with 1 winner in each. Offered annually for previously unpublished work. "For guidelines, send an SASE to *New Letters*, or visit www.newletters.org." Deadline: May 18 "1st place: $1,500, plus publication; first runners-up: a copy of a recent book of poetry or fiction courtesy of our affiliate BkMk Press. Preliminary judges are regional writers of prominence and experience. All judging is done anonymously. Winners picked by a final judge of national repute. Previous judges include Maxine Kumin, Albert Goldbarth, Charles Simic, Janet Burroway."

NEW MILLENNIUM AWARDS FOR FICTION, POETRY, AND NONFICTION

P.O. Box 2463, Room M2, Knoxville TN 37901. (423)428-0389. **Website:** www.newmillenniumwritings.com/awards; www.writingawards.com. "No restrictions as to style, content or number of submissions. Previously published pieces OK if online or under 5,000 print circulation. Send any time between now and midnight, June 17, for the Summer Awards program, January 31 for the Winter Awards. Simultaneous and multiple submissions welcome. Each fiction or nonfiction piece is a separate entry and should total no more than 6,000 words, except for the Short-Short Fiction Award, which should total no more than 1,000 words. (Nonfiction includes essays, profiles, memoirs, interviews, creative nonfiction, travel, humor, etc.) Each poetry entry may include up to 3 poems, not to exceed 5 pages total. All 20 poetry finalists will be published. Include name, phone, address, e-mail, and category on cover page only." Entries should be postmarked on or before June 17 or January 31. Prize: $1,000 for Best Poem; $1,000 for Best Fiction; $1,000 for Best Nonfiction; $1,000 for Best Short-Short Fiction.

NEW SOUTH WRITING CONTEST

Georgia State University, Campus Box 1894, MSC 8R0322, Unit 8, Atlanta GA 30303-3083. **E-mail:** newsouth@gsu.edu. **Website:** www.review.gsu.edu. **Contact:** Editor. Offered annually to publish the most promising work of up-and-coming writers of poetry (up to 3 poems) and fiction (9,000 word limit). Rights revert to writer upon publication. Guidelines online. Deadline: March 5 1st Place: $1,000 in each category; 2nd Place: $250; and publication to winners.

NORTH CAROLINA ARTS COUNCIL REGIONAL ARTIST PROJECT GRANTS

North Carolina Arts Council, Dept. of Cultural Resources, MSC #4632, Raleigh NC 27699-4634. (919)807-6500. **Fax:** (919)807-6532. **E-mail:** david.potorti@ncdcr.gov. **Website:** www.ncarts.org. **Contact:** David Potorti, literature director. Open to any writer living in North Carolina. See website for contact information for the local arts councils that distribute these grants. $500-3,000 awarded to writers to pursue projects that further their artistic development. Deadline: Generally late summer/early fall $500-3,000 awarded to writers to pursue projects that further their artistic development. Open to any writer living in North Carolina. See website for contact information for the local arts councils that distribute these grants.

❸ NORTH CAROLINA WRITERS' FELLOWSHIPS

North Carolina Arts Council, Dept. of Cultural Resources, Raleigh NC 27699-4632. (919)807-6500. **Fax:** (919)807-6532. **E-mail:** davidpotorti@ncdcr.gov. **Website:** www.ncarts.org. **Contact:** David Potorti, literature director. Offered every even year to support writers of fiction, poetry, literary nonfiction, literary translation, and spoken word. See website for guidelines and other eligibility requirements. Writers must be current residents of North Carolina for at least 1 year, must remain in residence in North Carolina during the grant year, and may not pursue academic or professional degrees while receiving grant. Fellowships offered to support writers in the development and creation of their work. See website for details. $10,000 grant. Reviewed by a panel of literature professionals (writers and editors).

NORTHERN CALIFORNIA BOOK AWARDS

Northern California Book Reviewers Association, c/o Poetry Flash, 1450 Fourth St. #4, Berkeley CA 94710. (510)525-5476. **E-mail:** editor@poetryflash.org. **Website:** www.poetryflash.org. **Contact:** Joyce Jenkins, executive director. Estab. 1981. Annual Northern California Book Award for outstanding book in literature, open to books published in the current calendar year by Northern California authors. Annual award. NCBR presents annual awards to Bay Area (northern California) authors annually in fiction, nonfiction, poetry and children's literature. Purpose is to encourage writers and stimulate interest in books and reading." Previously published books only. Must be published the calendar year prior to spring awards ceremony. Submissions nominated by publishers; author or agent could also nominate published work. Deadline for entries: December. No entry forms. Send 3 copies of the book to attention: NCBR. No entry fee. Awards $100 honorarium and award certificate. Judging by voting members of the Northern California Book Reviewers. Books that reach the "finals" (usually 3-5 per category) displayed at annual award ceremonies (spring). Nominated books are displayed and sold at the Northern California Book Awards in the spring of each year; the winner is asked to read at the San Francisco Public Library's Main Branch.

FRANK O'CONNOR AWARD FOR SHORT FICTION

descant, Texas Christian University's literary journal, TCU Box 297270, Fort Worth TX 76129. (817)257-6537. **Fax:** (817)257-6239. **E-mail:** descant@tcu.edu. **Website:** www.descant.tcu.edu. **Contact:** Dan Williams and Alex Lemon, editors. Offered annually for unpublished short stories. Publication retains copyright but will transfer it to the author upon request. fiction, short stories. **Deadline:** September-March. **Prize:** $500. Offered annually for unpublished short stories. Publication retains copyright but will transfer it to the author upon request. Deadline: September-March Prize: $500.

❸ SEAN O'FAOLAIN SHORT STORY PRIZE

The Munster Literature Centre, Frank O'Connor House, 84 Douglas Street, Cork Ireland. +353-214319255. **E-mail:** munsterlit@eircom.net. **Website:** www.munsterlit.ie. **Contact:** Patrick Cotter, artistic director. "To reward writers of outstanding short stories" Annual. Prize: 1st prize €1500 (approx US $2,200); 2nd prize €500 (approx $730). Four runners-up prizes of €100 (approx $146). All six stories to be published in Southword Literary Journal. Receives about 700 entries. Guest judge reads each and every story anonymously. Judge in 20098 was Philip O Ceallaigh. Entry fee: $20. Make checks payable to Munster Literature Centre. Guidelines available in November. Accepts inquiries by e-mail, phone. **Entry deadline is July 31.** Entries should be unpublished. Anyone may enter contest. Length: 3,000 words max. Cover letter should include name, address, phone, e-mail, word count, novel/story title. No identifying information on ms. "Read previous winners in Southword Journal. " Results announced last day of Frank O'Connor International Short Story Festival in third weekend of September. Winners notified by mail or by e-mail. Results made available to entrants on website.

OHIOANA BOOK AWARDS

Ohioana Library Association, 274 E. First Ave., Suite 300, Columbus OH 43201-3673. (614)466-3831. **Fax:** (614)728-6974. **E-mail:** ohioana@ohioana.org. **Website:** www.ohioana.org. **Contact:** Linda Hengst, executive director. Offered annually to bring national attention to Ohio authors and their books, published in the last 2 years. (Books can only be considered once.) Categories: Fiction, nonfiction, juvenile, poetry, and books about Ohio or an Ohioan. Writers must have been born in Ohio or lived in Ohio for at least 5 years, but books about Ohio or an Ohioan need not be written by an Ohioan. Prize: certificate and glass sculpture. Judged by a jury selected by librarians, book reviewers, writers and other knowledgeable people. Each winter the jury considers all books received since the previous jury. No entry fee. **Deadline: December 31.** A copy of the book must be received by the Ohioana Library by December 31 prior to the year the award is given; literary quality of the book must be outstanding. No entry forms are needed, but they are available July 1 of each year. Specific questions should be sent to Ohioana. Results announced in August or September. Winners notified by mail in May.

OHIOANA WALTER RUMSEY MARVIN GRANT

Ohioana Library Association, 274 E. First Ave., Suite 300, Columbus OH 43201. (614)466-3831. **Fax:** (614)728-6974. **E-mail:** ohioana@ohioana.org. **Website:** www.ohioana.org. **Contact:** Linda Hengst. Award "to encourage young, unpublished writers 30 years of age or younger." Competition for short stories or novels in progress. Prize: $1,000. **No entry fee.** Up to 6 pieces of prose may be submitted; maximum 60 pages, minimum 10 pages double-spaced, 12-point type. **Deadline:** January 31. Entries must be unpublished. Open to unpublished authors born in Ohio or who have lived in Ohio for a minimum of 5 years. Must be 30 years of age or younger. Guidelines for SASE or on website. Winner notified in May or June. Award given in October. Award "to encourage young, unpublished writers 30 years of age or younger." Competition for short stories or novels in progress. Open to unpublished authors born in Ohio or who have lived in Ohio for a minimum of 5 years. Must be 30 years of age or younger. Guidelines for SASE or on website. Winner notified in May or June. Award given in October. Deadline: January 31. Prize: $1,000.

ON THE PREMISES CONTEST

On The Premises, LLC, 4323 Gingham Court, Alexandria VA 22310. (202) 262-2168. **E-mail:** questions@onthepremises.com. **Website:** www.onthepremises.com. **Contact:** Tarl Roger Kudrick or Bethany Granger, co-publishers. "*On the Premises* aims to promote newer and/or relatively unknown writers who can write what we feel are creative, compelling stories told in effective, uncluttered and evocative prose. Each contest challenges writers to produce a great story based on a broad premise that our editors supply as part of the contest." Competition/award for short stories. 1st Prize: $180; 2nd Prize: $140; 3rd Prize: $100; Honorable Mentions recieve $40. All prize winners are published in *On the Premises* magazine in HTML and PDF format. Entries are judged blindly by a panel of judges with professional editing and writing experience. Open to everyone. No entry fee. Contests held every 4 months. Check website for exact dates. Submissions are accepted by e-mail only. Entries should be unpublished. Length: minimum 1,000 words; maximum 5,000. E-mail should include name, address, e-mail, and novel/story title, with ms attached. No name or contact info should be in ms. Writers may submit own work. "Write something compelling, creative, and well-crafted. Above all, clearly use the contest premise." Results announced within 2 weeks of contest deadline. Winners notified via newsletter and with publication of *On the Premises*. Results made available to entrants on website and in publication.

OPEN SEASON AWARDS

The Malahat Review, University of Victoria, P.O. Box 1700, Stn CSC, Victoria BC V8V 2Y2 Canada. **Fax:** (250)472-5051. **E-mail:** malahat@uvic.ca. **Website:** www.malahatreview.ca. **Contact:** John Barton, editor. The annual Open Season Awards offer prizes in 3 categories: Poetry, fiction, and creative nonfiction. 2011 winner in Poetry category: Cynthia Woodman Kerkham; Fiction: Philip Huynh; Creative Nonfiction: Jessica Hiemstra-van der Horst. Winner and finalists contacted by e-mail. Winners published in spring issue of *Malahat Review* announced in winter on website, Facebook page, and in quarterly e-newsletter, *Malahat lite*. Deadline: November 1 (postmark) every year. Offers $1,000 CAD and publication in *The Malahat Review* in each category.

OREGON BOOK AWARDS

224 NW 13th Ave., Suite 306, #219, Portland OR 97209. (503)227-2583. **E-mail:** susan@literary-arts.org. **Website:** www.literary-arts.org. **Contact:** Susan Denning. The annual Oregon Book Awards celebrate Oregon authors in the areas of poetry, fiction, nonfiction, drama and young readers' literature published between August 1, 2010 and July 31, 2011. Prize: Finalists are invited on a statewide reading tour and are promoted

in bookstores and libraries across the state. Judged by writers who are selected from outside Oregon for their expertise in a genre. Past judges include Mark Doty, Colson Whitehead and Kim Barnes. Entry fee determined by initial print run; see website for details. Deadline: last Friday in August. Entries must be previously published. Oregon residents only. Accepts inquiries by phone and e-mail. Finalists announced in January. Winners announced at an awards ceremony in November. List of winners available in April.

● OREGON LITERARY FELLOWSHIPS

224 NW 13th Ave., Suite 306, Portland OR 97209. **E-mail:** susan@literary-arts.org. **Website:** www.literary-arts.org. Annual fellowships for writers of fiction, poetry, literary nonfiction, young readers and drama. Prize: $2500 minimum award, for approximately 12 writers. Judged by out-of-state writers. No entry fee. Guidelines available in February for SASE. Accepts inquiries by e-mail, phone. **Deadline: last Friday in June.** Oregon residents only. Recipients announced in January.

⊕ KENNETH PATCHEN AWARD FOR THE INNOVATIVE NOVEL

Eckhard Gerdes Publishing, Civil Coping Mechanisms, 12 Simpson Street, Apt. D, Geneva IL 60134. **E-mail:** egerdes@experimentalfiction.com. **Website:** www.experimentalfiction.com; www.copingmechanisms.net. **Contact:** Eckhard Gerdes. "This award will honor the most innovative novel submitted during the previous calendar year. Kenneth Patchen is celebrated for being among the greatest innovators of American fiction, incorporating strategies of concretism, asemic writing, digression, and verbal juxtaposition into his writing long before such strategies were popularized during the height of American postmodernist experimentation in the 1970s." Deadline for entry: All submissions must be postmarked between January 1 and July 31, 2011. Prize: $1,000, 20 complimentary copies. Judged by novelist Yuriy Tarnawsky.

○ PEARL SHORT STORY PRIZE

3030 E. Second St., Long Beach CA 90803-5163. (562)434-4523. **E-mail:** Pearlmag@aol.com. **Website:** www.pearlmag.com. **Contact:** Marilyn Johnson, fiction editor. Award to "provide a larger forum and help widen publishing opportunities for fiction writers in the small press and to help support the continuing publication of Pearl." Prize: $250, publication in Pearl and 10 copies of the journal. Judged by the editors of Pearl: Marilyn Johnson, Joan Jobe Smith, Barbara Hauk. En-

try fee: $10/story. Include a brief bio and SASE for reply or return of mss. Accepts simultaneous submissions, but asks to be notified if story is accepted elsewhere. **Submission period: April 1-May 31(postmark).** Entries must be unpublished. "Although we are open to all types of fiction, we look most favorably on coherent, well-crafted narratives containing interesting, believable characters in meaningful situations." Length: 4,000 words maximum. Open to any writer. Guidelines for SASE or on website. Accepts queries by e-mail or fax. Results announced in September. Winners notified by mail. For contest results, send SASE, e-mail, or visit website. Award to "provide a larger forum and help widen publishing opportunities for fiction writers in the small press and to help support the continuing publication of *Pearl*." Prize: $250, publication in *Pearl* and 10 copies of the journal. Judged by the editors of *Pearl*: Marilyn Johnson, Joan Jobe Smith, Barbara Hauk. Entry fee: $10/story. Include a brief bio and SASE for reply or return of mss. Accepts simultaneous submissions, but asks to be notified if story is accepted elsewhere. **Submission period: April 1-May 31(postmark).** Entries must be unpublished. "Although we are open to all types of fiction, we look most favorably on coherent, well-crafted narratives containing interesting, believable characters in meaningful situations." Length: 4,000 words maximum. Open to any writer. Guidelines for SASE or on website. Accepts queries by e-mail or fax. Results announced in September. Winners notified by mail. For contest results, send SASE, e-mail, or visit website.

PEN CENTER USA LITERARY AWARDS

PEN Center USA, P.O. Box 6037, Beverly Hills CA 90212. (424)258-1180. **E-mail:** awards@penusa.org. **Website:** www.penusa.org. Offered for work published or produced in the previous calendar year. Open to writers living west of the Mississippi River. Award categories: fiction, poetry, research nonfiction, creative nonfiction, translation, children's/young adult, drama, screenplay, teleplay, journalism. Guidelines and submission form available on website. for SASE or download from website. Deadline for book categories: 4 copies must be received by December 31. Deadline for non-book categories: 4 copies must be received by January 31.

PEN/FAULKNER AWARDS FOR FICTION

PEN/Faulkner Foundation, 201 E. Capitol St., Washington DC 20003. (202)675-0345. **Fax:** (202)675-0360.

E-mail: jneely@penfaulkner.org. **Website:** www.penfaulkner.org. **Contact:** Jessica Neely, executive director. Offered annually for best book-length work of fiction by an American citizen published in a calendar year. Deadline: October 31. $15,000 (one Winner); $5,000 (4 Finalists).

THE PINCH LITERARY AWARD IN FICTION AND POETRY

The University of Memphis/Hohenberg Foundation, Department of English, 435 Patterson Hall, Memphis TN 38152. (901)678-4591. **E-mail:** editor@thepinchjournal.com. **Website:** www.thepinchjournal.com. Offered annually for unpublished short stories of 5,000 words maximum or up to three poems. Guidelines on website. Cost: $20, which is put toward one issue of *The Pinch*. Deadline: March 15. Prize: 1st place Fiction: $1,500 and publication; 1st place Poetry: $1,000 and publication. Offered annually for unpublished short stories of 5,000 words maximum or up to three poems. Guidelines on website. Deadline: March 15 1st place Fiction: $1,500 and publication; 1st place Poetry: $1,000 and publication.

PNWA LITERARY CONTEST

Pacific Northwest Writers Association, PMB 2717-1420 NW Gilman Blvd, Suite 2, Issaquah WA 98027. (425)673-2665. **Fax:** (206)824-4559. **E-mail:** staff@pnwa.org. **Website:** www.pnwa.org. **Contact:** Kelli Liddane. **Open to students.** Annual contest. Purpose of contest: "Valuable tool for writers as contest submissions are critiqued (2 critiques)." Unpublished submissions only. Submissions made by author. Deadline for entries: February 18, 2011. Entry fee is $35/entry for members, $50/entry for nonmembers. Awards $700-1st; $300-2nd. Awards in all 12 categories.

POCKETS FICTION-WRITING CONTEST

P.O. Box 340004, Nashville TN 37203-0004. (615)340-7333. **Fax:** (615)340-7267. **E-mail:** pockets@upperroom.org; theupperroommagazine@upperroom.org. **Website:** www.pockets.upperroom.org. **Contact:** Lynn W. Gilliam, senior editor. *Pockets* is a devotional magazine for children between the ages of 6 and 11. Contest offered annually for unpublished work to discover new children's writers. Prize: $1,000 and publication in *Pockets*. Categories: short stories. Judged by *Pockets* staff and staff of other Upper Room Publications. No entry fee. Guidelines available on website or send #10 SASE. **Deadline: Must be postmarked** between March 1-August 15. Entries must be unpublished. Because the purpose of the contest is to discover new writers, previous winners are not eligible. No violence, science fiction, romance, fantasy or talking animal stories. Word length 1,000-1,600 words. Open to any writer. Winner announced November 1 and notified by U.S. mail. Contest submissions accompanied by SASE will be returned Nov. 1. "Send SASE with 4 first-class stamps to request guidelines and a past issue, or go to: http://pockets.upperroom.org."

"We do not accept mss sent by Fax or e-mail."

EDGAR ALLAN POE AWARD

1140 Broadway, Suite 1507, New York NY 10001. (212)888-8171. **Fax:** (212)888-8107. **E-mail:** mwa@mysterywriters.org. **Website:** www.mysterywriters.org. Estab. 1945. Mystery Writers of America is the leading association for professional crime writers in the United States. Members of MWA include most major writers of crime fiction and non-fiction, as well as screenwriters, dramatists, editors, publishers, and other professionals in the field. We welcome everyone who is interested in mysteries and crime writing to join MWA. Purpose of the award: to honor authors of distinguished works in the mystery field. Previously published submissions only. Submissions made by the author, author's agent; "normally by the publisher." Work must be published/produced the year of the contest. Deadline for entries: Must be received by November 30. Submission information can be found at: www.mysterywriters.org. No entry fee. Awards ceramic bust of "Edgar" for winner; scrolls for all nominees. Judging by professional members of Mystery Writers of America (writers). Nominee press release sent in mid January. Winner announced at the Edgar® Awards Banquet, held in late April/early May.

THE KATHERINE ANNE PORTER PRIZE FOR FICTION

Nimrod International Journal, The University of Tulsa, 800 S. Tucker Dr., Tulsa OK 74104. (918)631-3080. **Fax:** (918)631-3033. **E-mail:** nimrod@utulsa.edu. **Website:** www.utulsa.edu/nimrod. **Contact:** Francine Ringold. "This annual award was established to discover new, unpublished writers of vigor and talent. Open to US residents only." Deadline: April 30. Prizes: 1st Place: $2,000 and publication; 2nd Place: $1,000 and publication. *Nimrod* retains the right to publish any submission. The *Nimrod* editors select the finalists and a recognized author selects the winners.

○ KATHERINE ANNE PORTER PRIZE IN SHORT FICTION

The University of North Texas Press, 1155 Union Cir., #311336, Denton TX 76203-5017. (940)565-2142. **Fax:** (940)565-4590. **Website:** web3.unt.edu/untpress. **Contact:** Laura Kopchick, editor, University of Texas at Arlington. Contest is offered annually. Prize is awarded to a collection of short fiction. The University of North Texas Press announces the 2012 Katherine Anne Porter Prize in Short Fiction. Entries will be judged by an eminent writer. Entries can be a combination of short-shorts, short stories, and novellas, from 100 to 200 book pages in length (word count between 27,500 and 50,000). Material should be previously unpublished in book form. Once a winner is declared and contracted for publication, UNT Press will hold the rights to the stories in the winning collection. They may no longer be under consideration for serial publication elsewhere and must be withdrawn by the author from consideration. Please include two cover sheets: one with title only, and one with title, your name, address, e-mail, phone, and acknowledgment of any previously published material. Your name should not appear anywhere on the ms except on the one cover page. The winning manuscript will be announced in January 2012. Manuscripts cannot be returned and must be accompanied by a $25 entry fee (payable to UNT Press) and a letter-sized SASE for notification. Entry must be postmarked between May 1 and June 30. $1000 and publication by University of North Texas Press (standard author contract).

PRAIRIE SCHOONER BOOK PRIZE

Prairie Schooner and the University of Nebraska Press, 123 Andrews Hall, University of Nebraska, Lincoln NE 68588-0334. (402)472-0911. **E-mail:** jengelhardt2@unlnotes.unl.edu; jengelhardt2@unl.edu. **Website:** prairieschooner.unl.edu. **Contact:** Kwame Dawes, editor. Annual. Competition/award for story collections. Prize: $3,000 and publication through the University of Nebraska Press for one book of short fiction and one book of poetry. Entry fee: $25. Make checks payable to Prairie Schooner. Deadline: Submissions are accepted between January 15 and March 15; check website for updates. Entries should be unpublished. Send full manuscript (the author's name should not appear anywhere on the ms). Send two cover pages: one listing only the title of the ms, and the other listing the title, author's name, address, telephone number, and e-mail address. Send SASE for notification of results. All mss will be recycled. You may also send an optional SAS postcard for confirmation of receipt of ms. Winners notified by phone, by e-mail. Results made available to entrants on website, in publication. $3,000 and publication through the University of Nebraska Press (1 award in fiction and 1 award in poetry). Kwame Dawes, editor of *Prairie Schooner*, and members of the Book Series Literary Board.

PRAIRIE SCHOONER GLENNA LUSCHEI AWARDS

201 Andrews Hall, P.O. Box 880334, Lincoln NE 68588-0334. (402)472-0911. **Fax:** (402)472-9771. **E-mail:** jengelhardt2@unl.edu. **Contact:** Hilda Raz, editor-in-chief. Awards to honor work published the previous year in Prairie Schooner, including poetry, essays and fiction. Prize: $250 in each category. Judged by editorial staff of Prairie Schooner. No entry fee. For guidelines, send SASE or visit website. "Only work published in Prairie Schooner in the previous year is considered." Work nominated by the editorial staff. Results announced in the Spring issue. Winners notified by mail in February or March.

PUSHCART PRIZE

Pushcart Press, P.O. Box 380, Wainscott NY 11975. (631)324-9300. **Website:** www.pushcartprize.com. **Contact:** Bill Henderson. Estab. 1976. "Little magazine and small book press editors (print or online) may make up to six nominations from their year's publications by our December 1, (postmark) deadline. The nominations may be any combination of poetry, short fiction, essays or literary whatnot. Editors may nominate self-contained portions of books — for instance, a chapter from a novel. We welcome translations, reprints and both traditional and experimental writing. One copy of each selection should be sent. No nominations can be returned. There is no entry fee and no forms to fill out. We also accept nominations from our staff of distinguished Contributing Editors." Deadline: December 1.

�‍○ QUEBEC WRITERS' FEDERATION BOOK AWARDS

1200 Atwater, Westmount QC H3Z 1X4 Canada. (514)933-0878. **Website:** www.Qwf.org. Award "to honor excellence in writing in English in Quebec." Prize: $2,000 (Canadian) in each category. Categories: fiction, poetry, nonfiction, first book, translation, and children's and young adult. Each prize judged by panel of 3 jurors, different each year. $20 entry fee. Guidelines for submissions sent to Canadian publishers and posted on website in March. Accepts inquiries by e-mail. Deadline: May 31, August 15. Entries must be previously published. Length: must be more than 48 pages. "Writer must have resided in Quebec for 3 of the previous 5 years." Books may be published anywhere. Winners announced in November at Annual Awards Gala and posted on website.

THE RED HOUSE CHILDREN'S BOOK AWARD

2 Bridge Wood View, Horsforth, Leeds, West Yorkshire LS18 5PE United Kingdom. **E-mail:** info@rhcba. co.uk. **Website:** www.redhousechildrensbookaward. co.uk. **Contact:** Sinead Kromer, national co-ordinator. (formerly The Children's Book Award), Owned and co-ordinated by the Federation of Children's Book Groups (Reg. Charity No. 268289). Purpose of the award is to enable children choose the best works of fiction published in the UK. Prize: trophy and silver bookmarks, portfolio of children's letters and pictures. Categories: Books for Younger Children, Books for Younger Readers, Books for Older Readers. No entry fee. **Closing Date is December 31.** Either author or publisher may nominate title. Guidelines available on website. Accepts enquiries by email and phone. Shortlist announced in February and winners announced in May. Winners notified at award ceremony and dinner at the Birmingham Botanical Gardens and via the publisher. For contest results, visit the website.

RHODE ISLAND ARTIST FELLOWSHIPS AND INDIVIDUAL PROJECT GRANTS

Rhode Island State Council on the Arts, One Capitol Hill, 3rd Floor, Providence RI 02908. (401)222-3880. **Fax:** (401)222-3018. **E-mail:** Cristina.DiChiera@arts. ri.gov. **Website:** www.arts.ri.gov. **Contact:** Cristina DiChiera, director of individual artist programs. Annual fellowship competition is based upon panel review of mss for poetry, fiction, and playwriting/screenwriting. Project grants provide funds for community-based arts projects. Rhode Island artists may apply without a nonprofit sponsor. Applicants for all RSCA grant and award programs must be at least 18 years old and not currently enrolled in an arts-related degree program. Online application and guidelines can be found at www.arts.ri.gov/grants/guidelines/. Deadline: April 1 and October 1. Fellowship awards:

$5,000 and $1,000. Grants range from $500-10,000, with an average of around $3,000.

THE ROGERS WRITERS' TRUST FICTION PRIZE

The Writers' Trust of Canada, 90 Richmond St. E., Suite 200, Toronto ON M5C 1P1 Canada. (416)504-8222. **Fax:** (416)504-9090. **E-mail:** info@writerstrust. com. **Website:** www.writerstrust.com. **Contact:** Amanda Hopkins. "Awarded annually for a distinguished work of fiction—either a novel or short story collection—published within the previous year. Presented at the Writers' Trust Awards event held in Toronto each fall. Open to Canadian citizens and permanent residents only." Deadline: August 1. $25,000 and $2,500 to 4 finalists.

RROFIHE TROPHY

Anderbo.com, 270 Lafayette St., #705, New York NY 10012. **E-mail:** rrofihe@yahoo.com. **Website:** www. anderbo.com/anderbo1/anderrrofihetrophy2011. html. **Contact:** Rick Rofihe, editor. "Ninth annual contest for an unpublished short story (up to 5,000 words). Stories should be typed, double-spaced, on 8 1/2 x 11 paper with the author's name and contact information on the first page, and name and story title on the upper right corner of remaining pages. Limit 1 submission/author. Author must not have been previously published in *Open City*. Enclose SASE to receive names of winner and honorable mentions. All mss are nonreturnable and will be recycled. Acquires first North American serial rights (from winner only)." Deadline: October 15 (postmarked). $500, a trophy, and publication on Anderbo.com. Judge: Rick Rofihe

SASKATCHEWAN FICTION AWARD

Saskatchewan Book Awards, Inc., 100-2400 College Ave., Regina SK S4P 0K1 Canada. (306)569-1585. **Fax:** (306)569-4187. **E-mail:** director@bookawards.sk.ca. **Website:** www.bookawards.sk.ca. **Contact:** Executive director, book submissions. Estab. 1995. Offered annually. "This award is presented to a Saskatchewan author for the best book of fiction (novel or short fiction), judged on the quality of writing." Deadline: November 1. Prize: $2,000 (CAD).

SASKATOON BOOK AWARD

Saskatchewan Book Awards, Inc., 100-2400 College Ave., Regina SK S4P 0K1 Canada. (306)569-1585. **Fax:** (306)569-4187. **E-mail:** director@bookawards.sk.ca. **Website:** www.bookawards.sk.ca. **Contact:** Executive director, book submissions. Estab. 1998. Offered annually. "This award is presented to a Saskatoon author (or pair of authors) for the best book, judged on the quality of writing." Books from the following categories will be considered: Children's; drama; fiction (short fiction by a single author, novellas, novels); nonfiction (all categories of nonfiction writing except cookbooks, directories, how-to books, or bibliographies of minimal critical content); poetry. Deadline: November 1. Prize: $2,000 (CAD).

⊕ THE SATURDAY EVENING POST GREAT AMERICAN FICTION CONTEST

The Saturday Evening Post Society, 1100 Waterway Blvd., Indianapolis IN 46202. **E-mail:** fictioncontest@saturdayeveningpost.com. **Website:** www.saturdayeveningpost.com/fiction-contest. "In its nearly 3 centuries of publication, *The Saturday Evening Post* has included fiction by a who's who of American authors, including F. Scott Fitzgerald, William Faulkner, Kurt Vonnegut, Ray Bradbury, Louis L'Amour, Sinclair Lewis, Jack London, and Edgar Allan Poe. The *Post*'s fiction has not just entertained us; it has played a vital role in defining who we are as Americans. In launching this contest, we are seeking America's next great, unpublished voices." Deadline: July 1. The winning story will receive $500 and publication in the magazine and online. Five runners-up will be published online and receive $100 each.

○ THE SCARS EDITOR'S CHOICE AWARDS

829 Brian Court, Gurnee IL 60031-3155. **E-mail:** editor@scars.tv. **Website:** http://scars.tv. **Contact:** Janet Kuypers, editor/publisher (whom all reading fee checks need to be made out to). Award "to showcase good writing in an annual book." Categories: short stories, poetry. Entry fee: $19/short story, and $15/poem. Deadline: Revolves for appearing in different upcoming books as winners. Prize: Publication of story/essay and 1 copy of the book. Entries may be unpublished or previously published, "as long as you retain the rights to your work." Open to any writer. For guidelines, visit website. Accepts inquiries by e-mail. "E-mail is always preferred for inquiries and submissions. (If you have access to e-mail, we will request that you e-mail your contest submission, and we will hold it until we receive the reading fee payment for the submission.)" Length: "We appreciate shorter works. Shorter stories, more vivid and more real storylines in writing have a good chance." Results

announced at book publication, online. Winners notified by mail when book is printed. For contest results, send SASE or e-mail or look at the contest page at website. " Award "to showcase good writing in an annual book." Categories: short stories, poetry. Entries may be unpublished or previously published, "as long as you retain the rights to your work." Open to any writer. For guidelines, visit website. Accepts inquiries by e-mail."

A. DAVID SCHWARTZ FICTION PRIZE

Dept. of English; University of Wisconsin-Milwauke, Milwaukee WI 53201. (414) 229-4708. **E-mail:** info@creamcityreview.org. **Website:** www.creamcityreview.org. **Contact:** Ann Stewart McBee, editor-in-chief. "To recognize what the judge determines to be the most original, well-crafted work of previously unpublished short fiction. We are devoted to publishing memorable and energetic fiction, poetry, and creative non-fiction by new and established writers. Cream city review is particularly interested in publishing new voices; our reputation and long publishing history attracts well-known writers, often leading to unpublished writers appearing next to poet laureates. Our contest is open to all writers in all places, so long as the work is in English, original and previously unpublished." Annual. Competition/award for short stories. Prize: $1,000 plus publication in cream city review. Receives about 50-250 entries. Entries are judged by guest-judges; 2009 was Kelly Link; 2010: David Treuer. Entry fee: $15. Fee includes the award-winners issue. Make checks payable to cream city review. **Deadline: early December.** Guidelines available on website. Anyone may enter contest. Length: A work of more than 30 pages would have to be particularly impressive. Cover letter should include name, address, phone, e-mail, novel/story title. Also include on first page of ms. Writers may submit own work. "See aesthetic statement; read previous issues of cream city review to gain an understanding of the work we are interested in publishing; familiarize yourself with the work of the judge." Results announced at time of publication (April/May). Winners notified by e-mail. Winners announced February/March. Results made available to entrants with SASE, on website.

SCRIPTAPALOOZA TELEVISION WRITING COMPETITION

7775 Sunset Blvd., Suite #200, Hollywood CA 90046. (323)654-5809. **E-mail:** info@scriptapalooza.com. **Website:** www.scriptapaloozatv.com. "Seeking talented writers who have an interest in American television writing." Prize: $500, $200, and $100 in each category (total $3,200); production company consideration. Categories: Sitcoms, pilots, 1-hour dramas, and reality shows. Entry fee: $40; accepts PayPal credit card, or make checks payable to Scriptapalooza. Deadline: April 15 and October 1 each year. Length: Standard television format whether 1 hour, 1-half hour, or pilot. Open to any writer 18 or older. Guidelines available now for SASE or on website. Accepts inquiries by e-mail, phone. "Pilots should be fresh and new and easy to visualize. Spec scripts should stay current with the shows, up-to-date story lines, characters, etc." Winners announced February 15 and August 30. For contest results, visit website. "Biannual competition accepting entries in 4 categories: Reality shows, sitcoms, original pilots, and 1-hour dramas. There are more than 25 producers, agents, and managers reading the winning scripts. Two past winners won Emmys because of Scriptapalooza and 1 past entrant now writes for Comedy Central." Winners announced February 15 and August 30. For contest results, visit website. Deadline: October 1 and April 15 1st Place: $500; 2nd Place: $200; 3rd Place: $100 (in each category); production company consideration.

MICHAEL SHAARA AWARD FOR EXCELLENCE IN CIVIL WAR FICTION

Civil War Institute at Gettysburg College, 300 N. Washington St., Campus Box 435, Gettysburg PA 17325. (717)337-6590. **Fax:** (717)337-6596. **E-mail:** civilwar@gettysburg.edu. **Website:** www.gettysburg.edu/cwi. **Contact:** Diane Brennan. Estab. 1997. Offered annually for fiction published January 1-December 31. Contest "to encourage examination of the Civil War from unique perspectives or by taking an unusual approach." All Civil War novels are eligible. Publishers should make nominations, but authors and critics can nominate as well. Prize: $5,000, which includes travel stipend. No entry fee. **Deadline: December 31.** Entries must be previously published. Judged for presentation of unique perspective, use of unusual approach, effective writing, contribution to existing body of Civil War literature. Competition open to authors of Civil War novels published for the first time in the year designated by the award (i.e. for 2008 award, only novels published in 2008 are eligible). Guidelines available on website. Accepts inquiries by fax, e-mail, and phone. Cover letter should include name, address, phone, e-mail, and title. Need

4 copies of novel. "Enter well before deadline. Results announced in July. Winners notified by phone. For contest results, visit website." "Offered annually for fiction published for the first time in January 1-December 31 of the year of the award to encourage examination of the Civil War from unique perspectives or by taking an unusual approach. All Civil War novels are eligible. To nominate a novel, send 4 copies of the novel to the address above with a cover letter. Nominations should be made by publishers, but authors and critics can nominate as well." Deadline: December 31 $5,000

🎧 SKIPPING STONES HONOR (BOOK) AWARDS

P.O. Box 3939, Eugene OR 97403-0939. Phone/fax: (541)342-4956. **E-mail:** editor@skippingstones.org. **Website:** www.skippingstones.org. **Contact:** Arun N. Toké. Estab. 1994. Annual awards since 1994 to "promote multicultural and/or nature awareness through creative writings for children and teens and their educators." Prize: Honor certificates; gold seals; reviews; press release/publicity. Categories: Short stories, novels, story collections, poetry, nonfiction, and teaching resources, including DVDs. Judged by "a multicultural committee of teachers, librarians, parents, students and editors." Entry fee: $50. **Deadline: February 1** post mark/ship date each year. Entries must be previously published. Open to published books and teaching resources that appeared in print during a two year period prior to the deadline date. Guidelines for SASE or e-mail and on website. Accepts inquiries by e-mail, fax, phone. "We seek authentic, exceptional, child/youth friendly books that promote intercultural, international, intergenerational harmony, and understanding through creative ways. Writings that come out of your own experiences and cultural understanding seem to have an edge." Results announced in May each year. Winners notified through personal notifications, press release and by publishing reviews of winning titles in the summer issue and on website. Reviews are often reprinted in several other educational publications and reported in others. Attractive gold honor seals available for winners. For contest results, send SASE, e-mail, or visit website. Annual awards to "promote multicultural and/or nature awareness through creative writings for children and teens and their educators." Categories: Short stories, novels, story collections, poetry, nonfiction, and teaching resources, including

DVDs. "We seek authentic, exceptional, child/youth friendly books that promote intercultural, international, intergenerational harmony, and understanding through creative ways. Writings that come out of your own experiences and cultural understanding seem to have an edge." Results announced in May each year. Winners notified through personal notifications, press release and by publishing reviews of winning titles in the summer issue and on website. Reviews are often reprinted in several other educational publications and reported in others. Attractive gold honor seals available for winners. For contest results, send SASE, e-mail, or visit website. Deadline: February 1 post mark/ship date each year. Honor certificates; gold seals; reviews; press release/publicity. Judged by "a multicultural committee of teachers, librarians, parents, students and editors."

THE BERNICE SLOTE AWARD

Prairie Schooner, 123 Andrews Hall, PO Box 880334, Lincoln NE 68588-0334. (402)472-0911. **Fax:** (402)472-9771. **E-mail:** jengelhardt2@unl.edu. **Website:** www.prairieschooner.unl.edu. **Contact:** Kwame Dawes. Offered annually for the best work by a beginning writer published in Prairie Schooner in the previous year. Categories: short stories, essays and poetry. Judged by editorial staff of Prairie Schooner. No entry fee. For guidelines, send SASE or visit website. "Only work published in the journal during the previous year will be considered." Work is nominated by the editorial staff. Results announced in the Spring issue. Winners notified by mail in February or March. Prize is $500.

●❸ KAY SNOW WRITERS' CONTEST

9045 SW Barbur Blvd. #5A, Portland OR 97219-4027. (503)452-1592. **Fax:** (503)452-0372. **E-mail:** wilwrite@teleport.com. **Website:** www.willamettewriters.com. **Contact:** Lizzy Shannon, contest director. Annual contest. **Open to students.** Purpose of contest: "to encourage beginning and established writers to continue the craft." Unpublished, original submissions only. Submissions made by the author. Deadline for entries: April 23rd. SASE for contest rules and entry forms. Entry fee is $10, Williamette Writers' members; $15, non-members; free for student writers grades 1-12. Awards cash prize of $300 per category (fiction, nonfiction, juvenile, poetry, script writing), $50 for students in three divisions: 1-5, 6-8, 9-12. Judges are anonymous.

SOUTH DAKOTA ARTS COUNCIL

711 E. Wells Ave., Pierre SD 57501. (605)773-3131. **Fax:** (605)773-5977. **E-mail:** sdac@state.sd.us. **Website:** www.artscouncil.sd.gov. **Contact:** Michael Pangburn, executive director. "Artist Fellowships ($5,000), Artist Project Grants ($1,000- 2,000), and Artist Collaboration Grants (up to $6,000) are planned for fiscal 2012." No entry fee. Deadline: March 1. Open to South Dakota residents only. Students pursuing an undergraduate or graduate degree are ineligible. Guidelines and application available on website only. Applicants must submit signature page through the mail. All other materials are submitted online through an e-grant system. Application materials include current résumé no longer than 5 pages; appropriate samples of artistic work (see guidelines); up to 5 pages additional documentation; SASE with adequate postage for return of ms (if desired).

SPUR AWARDS

1080 Mesa Vista Hall MSC06 3770, 1 University of New Mexico, Alberquerque NM 87131. (615)791-1444. **E-mail:** wwa@unm.edu. **Website:** www.westernwriters.org. Purpose of award is "to reward quality in the fields of western fiction and nonfiction." Prize: Trophy. Categories: short stories, novels, poetry, songs, scripts and nonfiction. No entry fee. **Deadline: January 10.** Entries must be published during the contest year. Open to any writer. Guidelines available in Sept./Oct. for SASE, on website or by phone. Inquiries accepted by e-mail or phone. Results announced annually in Summer. Winners notified by mail. For contest results, send SASE.

JOHN STEINBECK FICTION AWARD

Reed Magazine. San Jose State University, Dept. of English, One Washington Square, San Jose CA 95192. **E-mail:** reed@email.sjsu.edu. **Website:** www.reedmag.org/drupal/. **Contact:** Nick Taylor, editor. "Award for an unpublished short story of up to 6,000 words." Annual. Competition/award for short stories. Prize: $1,000 prize and publication in Reed Magazine. Receives several hundred entries per category. Entries are judged by a prominent fiction writer; 2007 judge was Tobias Wolff. Entry fee: $15 (includes issue of Reed). **Submission period is June 1 - November 1.** Anyone may enter contest. "Do not submit any pornographic material, science fiction, fantasy, or children's literature. The work must be your own, (no translations)." Results announced in April.

STEVEN TURNER AWARD FOR BEST FIRST WORK OF FICTION

6335 W. Northwest Hwy., #618, Dallas TX 75225. **Website:** www.texasinstituteofletters.org. Deadline:

normally first week in January; see website for specific date. Prize: $1,000.

STONY BROOK SHORT FICTION PRIZE

State University of New York, Stony Brook NY 11794-5350. **Website:** www.stonybrook.edu/fictionprize. **Contact:** John Westermann. Award "to recognize excellent undergraduate fiction." Prize: $1,000 and publication on website. Categories: Short stories. Judged by faculty of the Department of English & Creative Writing Program. No entry fee. Guidelines available on website. Inquiries accepted by e-mail. Expects 300 entries. Word length: 7,500 words or less. "Only undergraduates enrolled full time in American or Canadian colleges and universities for the 2006-2007 academic year are eligible. Proof required. Students of all races and backgrounds are encouraged to enter. Guidelines for SASE or on website. Ms should include name, permanent address, phone, e-mail, word count and title. Winners notified by phone; results posted on website by June.

● THEODORE STURGEON MEMORIAL AWARD FOR BEST SHORT SF OF THE YEAR

English Department, University of Kansas, Lawrence KS 66045. (785)864-3380. **Fax:** (785)864-1159. **E-mail:** jgunn@ku.edu. **Website:** www.ku.edu/~sfcenter.. **Contact:** James Gunn, professor and director. Award to "honor the best science fiction short story of the year." Prize: Trophy. Winners receive expense-paid trip to the University and have their names engraved on permanent trophy. Categories: short stories. Judged by jury. No entry fee. Entries must be previously published. Guidelines available in December by phone, e-mail or on website. Accepts inquiries by e-mail and fax. Entrants for the Sturgeon Award are by nomination only. Results announced in July. For contest results, send SASE.

◐○ SUBTERRAIN ANNUAL LITERARY AWARDS COMPETITION: THE LUSH TRIUMPHANT

P.O. Box 3008 MPO, Vancouver BC V6B 3X5 Canada. (604)876-8710. **Fax:** (604)879-2667. **E-mail:** subter@portal.ca. **Website:** www.subterrain.ca. Entrants may submit as many entries in as many categories as they like. Fiction: Max of 3,000 words. Poetry: A suite of 5 related poems (max of 15 pages). Creative Nonfiction based on fact, adorned with fiction): Max of 4,000 words. Deadline: May 15. Winners in each category will receive $750 cash (plus payment for publication)

and publication in the Winter issue. First runner-up in each category will received a $250 cash prize and be published in the Spring issue of *subTerrain*. All entrants receive a complimentary 1-year subscription to *subTerrain*.

SYDNEY TAYLOR MANUSCRIPT COMPETITION

Association of Jewish Libraries, Sydney Taylor Manuscript Award Competition, 204 Park St., Montclair NJ 07042. **E-mail:** stmacajl@aol.com. **Contact:** Aileen Grossberg. **Open to students** and to any unpublished writer of fiction. Annual contest. Estab. 1985. Purpose of the contest: "This competition is for unpublished writers of fiction. Material should be for readers ages 8-11, with universal appeal that will serve to deepen the understanding of Judaism for all children, revealing positive aspects of Jewish life." Unpublished submissions only. Deadline for entries: December 15. Download rules and forms from website. No entry fee. Awards $1,000. Award winner will be notified in April, and the award will be presented at the convention in June. Judging by qualified judges from within the Association of Jewish Libraries. Requirements for entrants: must be an unpublished fiction writer; also, books must range from 64-200 pages in length. "AJL assumes no responsibility for publication, but hopes this cash incentive will serve to encourage new writers of children's stories with Jewish themes for all children."

○ THREE CHEERS AND A TIGER

E-mail: editors@toasted-cheese.com. **Website:** www.toasted-cheese.com. **Contact:** Stephanie Lenz, editor. Purpose of contest is to write a short story (following a specific theme) within 48 hours. Contests are held first weekend in spring (mystery) and first weekend in fall (sf/f). Prize: Amazon gift certificates and publication. Categories: Short stories. Blind-judged by 2 *Toasted Cheese* editors. Each judge uses his or her own criteria to choose entries. No entry fee. Entries must be unpublished. Word limit announced at the start of the contest. Contest-specific information is announced 48 hours before the contest submission deadline. Open to any writer. Accepts inquiries by e-mail. "Follow the theme, word count and other contest rules. We have more suggestions at our website." Results announced in April and October. Winners notified by e-mail. List of winners on website. Purpose of contest is to write a short story (following a specific theme) within 48 hours. Contests are held first weekend in spring (mystery) and first weekend in fall (sf/f).

● THE THURBER PRIZE FOR AMERICAN HUMOR

77 Jefferson Ave., Columbus OH 43215. **Website:** www.thurberhouse.org. "The Award recognizes the art of humor writing." Prize: $5,000 for the finalist, non-cash prizes awarded to two runners-up. Judged by well-known members of the national arts community. Entry fee: $65 per title. Deadline: April. Published submissions or accepted for publication in U.S. for the first time. Primarily pictorial works such as cartoon collections are not considered. Word length: no requirement. See website for application form and guidelines. Results announced in October. Winners notified in person at the Algonquin Hotel in New York City. For contest results, visit website.

◐◯ TICKLED BY THUNDER FICTION CONTEST

Tickled by Thunder fiction magazine, 14076 86A Ave., Surrey BC V3W 0V9 Canada. **E-mail:** info@tickledbythunder.com. **Website:** www.tickledbythunder.com. **Contact:** Larry Lindner. Annual contest to encourage unpublished fiction writers. Deadline: February 15. $150, subscription, publication, and 2 copies of the magazine. Judged by the publisher and other various writers he knows who have not entered the contest.

◐ TORONTO BOOK AWARDS

City of Toronto c/o Toronto Protocol, 100 Queen St. W., City Clerk's Office, 2nd floor, West Tower, Toronto ON M5H 2N2 Canada. (416)392-7805. **Fax:** (416)392-1247. **E-mail:** bkurmey@toronto.ca. **Website:** www.toronto.ca/book_awards. **Contact:** Bev Kurmey, protocol officer. The Toronto Book Awards honor authors of books of literary or artistic merit that are evocative of Toronto. Annual award for short stories, novels, poetry or short story collections. Prize: $15,000. Each short-listed author (usually 4-6) receives $1,000 and the winner receives the remainder. Categories: No separate categories—novels, short story collections, books of poetry, biographies, history, books about sports, children's books—all are judged together. Judged by jury of five who have demonstrated interest and/or experience in literature, literacy, books and book publishing. No entry fee. Cover letter should include name, address, phone, e-mail and title of entry. Six copies of the entry book are also required. **Deadline: last week of March.** Entries must be previously

published. Guidelines available in September on website. Accepts inquires by fax, e-mail, phone. Finalists announced in June; winners notified in September at a gala reception. Guidelines and results available on website.

WAASMODE SHORT FICTION PRIZE

Passages North, Department of English, Northern Michigan University, 1401 Presque Isle Ave., Marquette MI 49855. (906)227-1203. **Fax:** (906)227-1096. **E-mail:** passages@nmu.edu. **Website:** www.passagesnorth.com. **Contact:** Kate Myers Hanson. Offered every 2 years to publish new voices in literary fiction (maximum 5,000 words). Guidelines for SASE or online. "In association with the Just Desserts Contest, we have our Waasmode Short Fiction Prize, which is also $1,000 1st Place prize and publication. It is a 7,500 word maximum word count. It is also given every other year. When we are not having our fiction contest, we are having our poetry and nonfiction contests. Elinor Benedict Poetry Prize: $1,000 1st Place prize and publication; $15 for up to 3 poems entry fee ($3 for each additional poem after that). Thomas J. Hruska Memorial Prize in Nonfiction: $1,000 1st Place prize and publication; $15 per essay entry fee. Submissions accepted at www.passagesnorth.com. Deadline: Submit October 15-February 15. $1,000 and publication for winner; 2 honorable mentions are also published; all entrants receive a copy of *Passages North*.

WABASH PRIZE FOR FICTION

Sycamore Review, Department of English, 500 Oval Dr., Purdue University, West Lafayette IN 47907. **E-mail:** sycamore@purdue.edu. **Website:** www.sycamorereview.com. **Contact:** Mehdi Okasi, editor-in-chief.

○ Submit one short story (not to exceed 10,000 words). No identifying information should appear on the manuscript. Include cover letter with all identifying information along with a word count. Include SASE to receive notification of the winner and check made payable to Sycamore Review for entry.

○ THE ROBERT WATSON LITERARY PRIZE IN FICTION AND POETRY

3302 Hall for Humanities, UNCG, P.O. Box 26170, Greensboro NC 27402-6170. (336)334-5459. **E-mail:** jlclark@uncg.edu. **Website:** www.greensbororeview.org. **Contact:** Jim Clark, editor. Offered annually for fiction (7,500 word limit) and poetry(3-5 poems).

Sample issue for $8. Prize: $1,000 each for best short story and poem. Judged by editors of *The Greensboro Review*. Guidelines for SASE or on website. **Deadline: September 15**. **Fee:** $14. Entries must be unpublished. No submissions by e-mail. Open to any writer. Winners notified by mail, phone or e-mail. List of winners published in Spring issue. "All manuscripts meeting literary award guidelines will be considered for cash award as well as for publication in the Spring issue of The Greensboro Review."

WILLA LITERARY AWARD

Women Writing the West, 8547 East Arapaho Rd., #J-541, Greenwood Village CO 80112-1436. **E-mail:** slyon.www@gmail.com. **Website:** www.womenwritingthewest.org. **Contact:** Alice D. Trego, contest director; Suzanne Lyon, WILLA chair. The WILLA Literary Award honors the best in literature featuring women's or girls' stories set in the West published each year. Women Writing the West (WWW), a nonprofit association of writers and other professionals writing and promoting the Women's West, underwrites and presents the nationally recognized award annually (for work published between January 1 and December 31). The award is named in honor of Pulitzer Prize winner Willa Cather, one of the country's foremost novelists. The award is given in 7 categories: Historical fiction, contemporary fiction, original softcover fiction, creative nonfiction, scholarly nonfiction, poetry, and children's/young adult fiction/nonfiction. Deadline: February 1 Winner receives $100 and a trophy. Finalist receives a plaque. Award announcement is in early August, and awards are presented to the winners and finalists at the annual WWW Fall Conference. Judged by professional librarians not affiliated with WWW.

○ WISCONSIN INSTITUTE FOR CREATIVE WRITING FELLOWSHIP

6195B H.C. White Hall, 600 N. Park St., Madison WI 53706. **E-mail:** rfkuka@wisc.edu. **Website:** www.wisc.edu/english/cw. **Contact:** Ron Kuka, program coordinator. Fellowship provides time, space and an intellectual community for writers working on first books. Receives approximately 300 applicants a year for each genre. Judged by English Department faculty and current fellows. "Candidates must not yet have published, or had accepted for publication, a book by application deadline." Open to any writer with either an M.F.A. or Ph.D. in creative writing. Please enclose

a SASE for notification of results. Results announced by May 1. "Send your best work. Stories seem to have a small advantage over novel excerpts." Applicants should submit up to 10 pages of poetry or one story of up to 30 pages and a résumé or vita directly to the program during the month of February. An applicant's name must not appear on the writing sample (which must be in ms form) but rather on a separate sheet along with address, social security number, phone number, e-mail address and title(s) of submission(s). Candidates should also supply the names and phone numbers of two references. Accepts inquiries by e-mail and phone. Deadline: February. Prize: $27,000 for a 9-month appointment.

TOBIAS WOLFF AWARD IN FICTION

Bellingham Review, Mail Stop 9053, Western Washington University, Bellingham WA 98225. (360)650-4863. **E-mail:** bhreview@wwu.edu. **Website:** www.bhreview.org. **Contact:** Brenda Miller. Offered annually for unpublished work. Prize: $1,000, plus publication and subscription. Categories: Novel excerpts and short stories. Entry fee: $18 for 1st entry; $10 each additional entry. Guidelines available in September for SASE or on website. **Deadline:** Contest runs December 1-March 15. Entries must be unpublished. Length: 6,000 words or less per story or chapter. Open to any writer. *"Bellingham Review* accepts electronic and mailed submissions. Enter electronic submissions through Submittable, a link to which is available on the website." Winner announced in August and notified by mail or e-mail. For contest results, send SASE with mailed submissions. Offered annually for unpublished work. Guidelines available in September for SASE or online. Deadline: December 1-March 15. $1,000, plus publication and subscription. All finalists considered for publication. All entrants receive subscription.

WORLD FANTASY AWARDS

P.O. Box 43, Mukilteo WA 98275-0043. **E-mail:** sfexecsec@gmail.com. **Website:** www.worldfantasy.org. **Contact:** Peter Dennis Pautz, president. Awards "to recognize excellence in fantasy literature worldwide." Offered annually for previously published work in several categories, including life achievement, novel, novella, short story, anthology, collection, artist, special award-pro and special award-nonpro. Works are recommended by attendees of current and previous 2 years' conventions and a panel of judges. Prize: Bust of HP Lovecraft. Judged by panel. No entry fee. Guidelines available in

December for SASE or on website. **Deadline: June 1.** Entries must be previously published. Published submissions from previous calendar year. Word length: 10,000-40,000 for novella, 10,000 for short story. "All fantasy is eligible, from supernatural horror to Tolkienesque to sword and sorcery to the occult, and beyond." Cover letter should include name, address, phone, e-mail, word count, title, and publications where submission was previously published, submitted to the address above and the panel of judges when they appear on the website. Results announced November 1 at annual convention. For contest results, visit website. Awards "to recognize excellence in fantasy literature worldwide." Offered annually for previously published work in several categories, including life achievement, novel, novella, short story, anthology, collection, artist, special award-pro and special award-nonpro. Works are recommended by attendees of current and previous 2 years' conventions and a panel of judges. Judged by panel. No entry fee. Guidelines available in December for SASE or on website. Deadline: June 1.

WORLD'S BEST SHORT-SHORT STORY FICTION CONTEST, NARRATIVE NONFICTION CONTEST & SOUTHEAST REVIEW POETRY CONTEST

English Department, Florida State University, Tallahassee FL 32306. **E-mail:** southeastreview@gmail.com. **Website:** www.southeastreview.org. **Contact:** Katie Cortese, acquisitions editor. Estab. 1979. Annual award for unpublished short-short stories (500 words or less), poetry, and narrative nonfiction (6,000 words or less). Deadline: March 15. $500 per category. Winners and finalists will be published in *The Southeast Review.*

WRITER'S DIGEST ANNUAL WRITING COMPETITION

Writer's Digest, a publication of F+W Media, Inc., 700 E. State St., Iola WI 54990. (513)531-2690, ext. 1328. **E-mail:** writing-competition@fwmedia.com; nicole. florence@fwmedia.com. **Website:** www.writersdigest.com. **Contact:** Nicki Florence. Writing contest with 10 categories: Inspirational Writing (spiritual/religious, maximum 2,500 words); Memoir/Personal Essay (maximum 2,000 words); Magazine Feature Article (maximum 2,000 words); Short Story (genre, maximum 4,000 words); Short Story (mainstream/literary, maximum 4,000 words); Rhyming Poetry (maximum 32 lines); Nonrhyming Poetry (maximum 32 lines); Stage Play (first 15 pages and 1-page synop-

sis); TV/Movie Script (first 15 pages and 1-page synopsis). Entries must be original, in English, unpublished*/unproduced (except for Magazine Feature Articles), and not accepted by another publisher/producer at the time of submission. *Writer's Digest* retains one-time publication rights to the winning entries in each category. Deadline: May. Grand Prize: $3,000 and a trip to New York City to meet with editors and agents; *Writer's Digest* will fly you and a guest to The Big Apple for the conference. While you're there, a *Writer's Digest* editor will arrange for you to meet and share your work with four editors or agents! 1st Place: $1,000, ms critique and marketing advice from a *Writer's Digest* editor, commentary from an agent, and $100 of Writer's Digest Books; 2nd Place: $500 and $100 of Writer's Digest Books; 3rd Place: $250 and $100 of Writer's Digest Books; 4th Place: $100 and $50 of *Writer's Digest* Books; 5th Place: $50 and $50 of *Writer's Digest* Books; 6th-10th place $25.

WRITER'S DIGEST INTERNATIONAL SELF-PUBLISHED BOOK AWARDS

Writer's Digest, 10151 Carver Rd., Suite 200, Blue Ash OH 45242. (715)445-4612, ext. 13430. **E-mail:** writing-competition@fwmedia.com. **Website:** www.writersdigest.com. **Contact:** Nicole Florence. Contest open to all English-language self-published books for which the authors have paid the full cost of publication, or the cost of printing has been paid for by a grant or as part of a prize. Categories include: Mainstream/Literary Fiction, Nonfiction, Inspirational (spiritual/new age), Life Stories (biographies/autobiographies/family histories/memoirs), Children's Books, Reference Books (directories/encyclopedias/guide books), Poetry, Middle-Grade/Young Adult Books. Deadline: April 20 Grand Prize: $3,000, promotion in *Writer's Digest* and *Publisher's Weekly*, and 10 copies of the book will be sent to major review houses with a guaranteed review in *Midwest Book Review*; 1st Place (9 winners): $1,000, promotion in *Writer's Digest*; Honorable Mentions: promotion in *Writer's Digest*, $50 of Writer's Digest Books, and a certificate.

WRITERS-EDITORS NETWORK ANNUAL INTERNATIONAL WRITING COMPETITION

Florida Freelance Writers Association, P.O. Box A, North Stratford NH 03590-0167. **E-mail:** contest@writers-editors.com. **Website:** www.writers-editors. com. **Contact:** Dana K. Cassell, executive director.

"Annual award to recognize publishable talent. Categories: Nonfiction (previously published article/essay/column/nonfiction book chapter; unpublished or self-published article/essay/column/nonfiction book chapter); fiction (unpublished or self-published short story or novel chapter); children's literature (unpublished or self-published short story/nonfiction article/book chapter/poem); poetry (unpublished or self-published free verse/traditional)." Guidelines available online. Deadline: March 15 1st Place: $100; 2nd Place: $75; 3rd Place: $50. All winners and Honorable Mentions will receive certificates as warranted. Judged by editors, librarians, and writers.

WRITERS' FELLOWSHIP

Department of Cultural Resources, Raleigh NC 27699-4632. **Website:** www.ncarts.org. NC Arts Council, Department of Cultural Resources, Raleigh NC 27699-4632. (919) 807-6512. **Fax:** (919) 807-6532. **E-mail:** debbie.mcgill@ncdcr.gov. **Website:** www.ncarts.org. **Contact:** Deborah McGill, literature director. Fellowships are awarded to support the creative development of NC writers and to stimulate the creation of new work. Prize: $10,000. Categories: short stories, novels, literary nonfiction, literary translation, spoken word. Work for children also invited. Judged by a panel of literary professionals appointed by the NC Arts Council, a state agency. No entry fee. Mss must not be in published form. We receive approximately 300 applications. Word length: 20 double-spaced pages (max). The work must have been written within the past 5 years. Only writers who have been full-time residents of NC for at least 1 year as of the application deadline and who plan to remain in the state during the grant year may apply. Guidelines available in late August on website. Accepts inquiries by fax, e-mail, phone. Results announced in late summer. All applicants notified by mail. Fellowships are awarded to support the creative development of NC writers and to stimulate the creation of new work. Prize: $10,000. Categories: short stories, novels, literary nonfiction, literary translation, spoken word. Work for children also invited. Judged by a panel of literary professionals appointed by the NC Arts Council, a state agency. No entry fee. Mss must not be in published form. We receive approximately 300 applications. Word length: 20 double-spaced pages (max). The work must have been written within the past 5 years. Only writers who have been full-time residents of NC for at least 1 year as of the application deadline and who plan to remain in the state during the grant year may apply. Guidelines available in late August on website. Accepts inquiries by fax, e-mail, phone. Results announced in late summer. All applicants notified by mail.

WRITERS GUILD OF ALBERTA AWARDS

Writers Guild of Alberta, Percy Page Centre, 11759 Groat Rd., Edmonton AB T5M 3K6 Canada. (780)422-8174. **Fax:** (780)422-2663. **E-mail:** mail@writersguild.ab.ca. **Website:** www.writersguild.ab.ca. **Contact:** Executive Director. Offers the following awards: Wilfrid Eggleston Award for Nonfiction; Georges Bugnet Award for Fiction; Howard O'Hagan Award for Short Story; Stephan G. Stephansson Award for Poetry; R. Ross Annett Award for Children's Literature; Gwen Pharis Ringwood Award for Drama; Jon Whyte Memorial Essay Prize; James H. Gray Award for Short Nonfiction; Amber Bowerman Memorial Travel Writing Award. Eligible entries will have been published anywhere in the world between January 1 and December 31 of the current year; the authors must have been residents of Alberta for at least 12 of the 18 months prior to December 31. Unpublished mss, except in the drama, essay, and short nonfiction categories, are not eligible. Anthologies are not eligible. Works may be submitted by authors, publishers, or any interested parties. Deadline: December 31. Winning authors receive $1,500; essay prize winners receive $700. Other awards: Isabel Miller Young Writers Award; authors must be 12-18 years of age and a resident of Alberta.

ZOETROPE SHORT STORY CONTEST

916 Kearny St., San Francisco CA 94133. (415)788-7500. **E-mail:** contests@all-story.com. **Website:** www.all-story.com. Annual contest for unpublished short stories. Prize: 1st place: $1,000; 2nd place: $500, 3rd place: $250; plus 7 honorable mentions. Entry fee: $15. Guidelines for SASE, by e-mail, in publication, or on website. Entries must be unpublished. Word length: 5,000 words maximum. Open to any writer. "Please mark envelope clearly 'short fiction contest'." For details, please visit the website this summer, or email us. Winners notified by phone or e-mail December 1. Results announced December 1. A list of winners will be posted on website and published in spring issue. The winning story will be published at the website as a special supplement to the spring issue.

CONFERENCES & WORKSHOPS

///

Why are conferences so popular? Writers and conference directors alike tell us it's because writing can be such a lonely business—at conferences writers have the opportunity to meet (and commiserate) with fellow writers, as well as meet and network with publishers, editors and agents. Conferences and workshops provide some of the best opportunities for writers to make publishing contacts and pick up valuable information on the business, as well as the craft, of writing.

The bulk of the listings in this section are for conferences. Most conferences last from one day to one week and offer a combination of workshop-type writing sessions, panel discussions and a variety of guest speakers. Topics may include all aspects of writing from fiction to poetry to scriptwriting, or they may focus on a specific type of writing, such as those conferences sponsored by the Romance Writers of America (RWA) for writers of romance or by the Society of Children's Book Writers and Illustrators (SCBWI) for writers of children's books.

Workshops, however, tend to run longer—usually one to two weeks. Designed to operate like writing classes, most require writers to be prepared to work on and discuss their fiction while attending. An important benefit of workshops is the opportunity they provide writers for an intensive critique of their work, often by professional writing teachers and established writers.

Each of the listings here includes information on the specific focus of an event as well as planned panels, guest speakers and workshop topics. It is important to note, however, some conference directors were still in the planning stages for 2013 when we contacted them. If it was not possible to include 2013 dates, fees or topics, we have provided information from 2012 so you can get an idea of what to expect. For the most current information, it's best to check the conference website or send a self-addressed, stamped envelope to the director in question about three months before the date(s) listed.

FINDING A CONFERENCE

Many writers try to make it to at least one conference a year, but cost and location count as much as subject matter or other considerations when determining which conference to attend. There are conferences in almost every state and province and even some in Europe open to North Americans.

To make it easier for you to find a conference close to home—or to find one in an exotic locale to fit into your vacation plans—we've divided this section into geographic regions. The conferences appear in alphabetical order under the appropriate regional heading.

Note that conferences appear under the regional heading according to where they will be held, which is sometimes different from the address given as the place to register or send for information. The regions are as follows:

Northeast: Connecticut, Maine, Massachusetts, New Hampshire, New York, Rhode Island, Vermont

Midatlantic: Washington DC, Delaware, Maryland, New Jersey, Pennsylvania

Midsouth: North Carolina, South Carolina, Tennessee, Virginia, West Virginia

Southeast: Alabama, Arkansas, Florida, Georgia, Louisiana, Mississippi, Puerto Rico

Midwest: Illinois, Indiana, Kentucky, Michigan, Ohio

North Central: Iowa, Minnesota, Nebraska, North Dakota, South Dakota, Wisconsin

South Central: Colorado, Kansas, Missouri, New Mexico, Oklahoma, Texas

West: Arizona, California, Hawaii, Nevada, Utah

Northwest: Alaska, Idaho, Montana, Oregon, Washington, Wyoming

Canada

International

LEARNING & NETWORKING

Besides learning from workshop leaders and panelists in formal sessions, writers at conferences also benefit from conversations with other attendees. Writers on all levels enjoy sharing insights. Often, a conversation over lunch can reveal a new market for your work or let you know which editors are most receptive to the work of new writers. You can find out about recent editor changes and about specific agents. A casual chat could lead to a new contact or resource in your area.

Many editors and agents make visiting conferences a part of their regular search for new writers. A cover letter or query that starts with "I met you at the Green Mountain Writers Conference," or "I found your talk on your company's new romance line at the Moonlight and Magnolias Writer's Conference most interesting . . ." may give you a small leg up on the competition.

While a few writers have been successful in selling their manuscripts at a conference, the availability of editors and agents does not usually mean these folks will have the time there to read your novel or six best short stories (unless, of course, you've scheduled an individual meeting with them ahead of time). While editors and agents are glad to meet writers and discuss work in general terms, usually they don't have the time (or energy) to give an extensive critique during a conference. In other words, use the conference as a way to make a first, brief contact.

SELECTING A CONFERENCE

Besides the obvious considerations of time, place and cost, choose your conference based on your writing goals. If, for example, your goal is to improve the quality of your writing, it will be more helpful to you to choose a hands-on craft workshop rather than a conference offering a series of panels on marketing and promotion. If, on the other hand, you are a science fiction novelist who would like to meet your fans, try one of the many science fiction conferences or "cons" held throughout the country and the world.

Look for panelists and workshop instructors whose work you admire and who seem to be writing in your general area. Check for specific panels or discussions of topics relevant to what you are writing now. Think about the size—would you feel more comfortable with a small workshop of eight people or a large group of 100 or more attendees?

If your funds are limited, start by looking for conferences close to home, but you may want to explore those that offer contests with cash prizes—and a chance to recoup your expenses. A few conferences and workshops also offer scholarships, but the competition is stiff and writers interested in these should find out the requirements early. Finally, students may want to look for conferences and workshops that offer college credit. You will find these options included in the listings here. Again, send a SASE for the most current details.

NORTHEAST

ASJA WRITERS CONFERENCE

American Society of Journalists and Authors, 1501 Broadway, Suite 403, New York NY 10036. (212)997-0947. **Fax:** (212)937-2315. **E-mail:** asjaoffice@asja.org; director@asja.org. **Website:** www.asja.org/wc. **Contact:** Alexandra Owens, executive director. Estab. 1971.
COSTS $200+, depending on when you sign up (includes lunch). Check website for updates.
ACCOMMODATIONS The hotel holding our conference always blocks out discounted rooms for attendees.
ADDITIONAL INFORMATION Brochures available in February. Registration form is on the website. Inquire by e-mail or fax. Sign up for conference updates on website.

BREAD LOAF WRITERS' CONFERENCE

Middlebury College, Middlebury VT 05753. (802)443-5286. **Fax:** (802)443-2087. **E-mail:** ncargill@middlebury.edu. **Website:** www.middlebury.edu/blwc. Estab. 1926.
COSTS $2,345 (includes tuition, housing).
ACCOMMODATIONS Bread Loaf Campus in Ripton, Vermont.
ADDITIONAL INFORMATION 2011 Conference Dates: August 10-20. Location: mountain campus of Middlebury College. Average attendance: 230.

✪ COD WRITERS' CONFERENCE

P.O. Box 408, Osterville MA 02655. **E-mail:** writers@capecodwriterscenter.org. **Website:** www.capecodwriterscenter.org. **Contact:** Nancy Rubin Stuart, artistic director.
COSTS Vary, average for one 5-day class and registration: $200.

GOTHAM WRITERS' WORKSHOP

WritingClasses.com, 555 Eighth Ave., Suite 1402, New York NY 10018. (212)974-8377. **Fax:** (212)307-6325. **E-mail:** dana@write.org. **Website:** www.writingclasses.com. **Contact:** Dana Miller, director of student relations. Estab. 1993.
COSTS $395/10-week workshops; $125 for the four-week online selling seminars and 1-day intensive courses; $295 for 6-week creative writing and business writing classes.
ADDITIONAL INFORMATION "Participants do not need to submit workshop material prior to their first class." Sponsors a contest for a free 10-week online creative writing course (value=$420) offered each term. Students should fill out a form online at www.writingclasses.com to participate in the contest. The winner is randomly selected. For brochure send e-mail, visit website, call or fax. Accepts inquiries by e-mail, phone, fax. Agents and editors participate in some workshops.

GREEN MOUNTAIN WRITERS CONFERENCE

47 Hazel St., Rutland VT 05701. (802)236-6133. **E-mail:** ydaley@sbcglobal.net. **Website:** www.vermontwriters.com. **Contact:** Yvonne Daley, director. Estab. 1999.
COSTS $500 before July 1; $525 after July 1. Partial scholarships are available.
ACCOMMODATIONS "We have made arrangements with a major hotel in nearby Rutland and 3 area bed and breakfast inns for special accommodations and rates for conference participants. You must make your own reservations."
ADDITIONAL INFORMATION Participants' mss can be read and commented on at a cost. Sponsors contests. Conference publishes a literary magazine featuring work of participants. Brochures available in January on website or for SASE, e-mail. Accepts inquiries by SASE, e-mail, phone. "We offer the opportunity to learn from some of the nation's best writers at a small, supportive conference in a lakeside setting that allows one-to-one feedback. Participants often continue to correspond and share work after conferences." Further information available on website, by e-mail or by phone.

IWWG ANNUAL SUMMER CONFERENCE

International Women's Writing Guild "Remember the Magic" Annual Summer Conference, International Women's Writing Guild, P.O. Box 810, Gracie Station, New York NY 10028. (212)737-7536. **Fax:** (212)737-9469. **E-mail:** iwwg@iwwg.org. **Website:** www.iwwg.org. **Contact:** Hannelore Hahn, executive director.

IWWG EARLY SPRING IN CALIFORNIA CONFERENCE

International Women's Writing Guild, P.O. Box 810, Gracie Station, New York NY 10028-0082. (212)737-7536. **Fax:** (212)737-9469. **E-mail:** iwwg@iwwg.org. **Website:** www.iwwg.org. **Contact:** Hannelore Hahn, executive director. Estab. 1976.
COSTS $350/members; $380/nonmembers for weekend program with room and board; $125 for weekend program without room and board.

ACCOMMODATIONS All participants stay at the conference site or may commute.

ADDITIONAL INFORMATION Brochures/guidelines are available online or for a SASE. Inquire via e-mail or fax.

IWWG MEET THE AGENTS/MEET THE AUTHORS PLUS ONE DAY WRITING WORKSHOP

c/o International Women's Writing Guild, P.O. Box 810, Gracie Station, New York NY 10028-0082. (212)737-7536. **Fax:** (212)737-9469. **E-mail:** dirhahn@aol.com. **Website:** www.iwwg.org. Estab. 1980.

COSTS $190/members for the weekend/ $220/nonmembers for the weekend (includes lunch); $125 members/$135 nonmembers for Saturday (includes lunch); $125 members/$135 nonmembers for all day Sunday (includes lunch); $85 members/$95 nonmembers for Sunday afternoon.

JOURNEY INTO THE IMAGINATION: A WEEKEND WRITING WORKSHOP

995 Chapman Rd., Yorktown NY 10598. (914)962-4432. **E-mail:** emily@emilyhanlon.com. **Website:** www.creativesoulworks.com. **Contact:** Emily Hanlon. Estab. 2004.

COSTS 2012: 3 nights—$625-825, dependent on choice of room. Early Registration extended to March 1.

ADDITIONAL INFORMATION For brochure, visit website.

THE MACDOWELL COLONY

100 High St., Peterborough NH 03458. (603)924-3886. **Fax:** (603)924-9142. **E-mail:** admissions@macdowellcolony.org. **Website:** www.macdowellcolony.org. Estab. 1907.

COSTS Travel reimbursement and stipends are available for participants of the residency, based on need. There are no residency fees.

MANHATTANVILLE SUMMER WRITERS' WEEK

2900 Purchase St., Purchase NY 10577. (914)323-5239. **Fax:** (914)323-3122. **E-mail:** sirabiank@mville.edu. **Website:** www.manhattanville.edu. **Contact:** Karen Sirabian, program director.

THE MANUSCRIPT WORKSHOP IN VERMONT

P.O. Box 529, Londonderry VA 05148. **E-mail:** aplbrk2@earthlink.net. **Website:** www.barbaraseuling.com. **Contact:** Barbara Seuling, director.

NEW YORK COMIC BOOK MARKETPLACE

(formerly known as Big Apple Con), 401 Seventh Ave. 33rd St., New York NY 10001-2062. (347)581-6166. **E-mail:** mikecarbo@gmail.com. **Website:** www.nycbm.com. **Contact:** Michael Carbonaro, director.

◯ Formerly known as Big Apple Con.

◉ ODYSSEY FANTASY WRITING WORKSHOP

P.O. Box 75, Mont Vernon NH 03057. **E-mail:** jcavelos@sff.net. **Website:** www.odysseyworkshop.org. Estab. 1996.

COSTS In 2010: $1,900 tuition, $775 housing (double room), $1,550 (single room); $35 application fee, $400-600 food (approximate), $450 processing fee to receive college credit.

ADDITIONAL INFORMATION Students must apply and include a writing sample. Application deadline April 10. Students' works are critiqued throughout the 6 weeks. Workshop information available in October. For brochure/guidelines send SASE, e-mail, visit website, call or fax. Accepts inquiries by SASE, e-mail, fax, phone.

THE PUBLISHING GAME

Peanut Butter & Jelly Press, P.O. Box 590239, Newton MA 02459. **E-mail:** alyza@publishinggame.com. **Website:** www.publishinggame.com. **Contact:** Alyza Harris, manager. Estab. 1998.

COSTS $195.

ACCOMMODATIONS "All locations are well-known hotels easily accessible by public transportation." Offers discounted conference rates for participants who choose to arrive early. Offers list of area lodging.

ADDITIONAL INFORMATION Brochures available for SASE. Accepts inquiries by SASE, e-mail, phone, fax, but e-mail preferred. Agents and editors attend conference. "If you're considering finding a literary agent, self-publishing your book or just want to sell more copies of your book, this conference will teach you everything you need to know to successfully publish and promote your work."

ROBERT QUACKENBUSH'S CHILDREN'S BOOK WRITING AND ILLUSTRATING WORKSHOP

460 E. 79th St., New York NY 10075. (212)861-2761. **E-mail:** rqstudios@aol.com. **Website:** www.rquackenbush.com.

ACCOMMODATIONS A list of recommended hotels and restaurants is sent upon receipt of deposit to applicants living out of the area of New York City.

ADDITIONAL INFORMATION Class is for beginners and professionals. Critiques during workshop. Private consultations also available at an hourly rate. "Programs suited to your needs; individualized schedules can be designed. Write or phone to discuss your goals and you will receive a prompt reply." Conference information available 1 year prior to conference. For brochure, send SASE, e-mail, visit website, call or fax. Accepts inquiries by fax, e-mail, phone, SASE.

WRITERS OMI AT LEDIG HOUSE
55 Fifth Ave., 15th Floor, New York NY 10003. (212)206-6114. **E-mail:** writers@artomi.org. **Website:** www.artomi.org.

ACCOMMODATIONS Residents provide their own transportation. Offers overnight accommodations.

ADDITIONAL INFORMATION "Agents and editors from the New York publishing community are invited for dinner and discussion. Bicycles, a swimming pool, and nearby tennis court are available for use."

YADDO
The Corporation of Yaddo Residencies, Box 395, 312 Union Ave., Saratoga Springs NY 12866-0395. (518)584-0746. **Fax:** (518)584-1312. **E-mail:** chwait@yaddo.org; Lleduc@yaddo.org. **Website:** www.yaddo.org. **Contact:** Candace Wait, program director. Estab. 1900. Two seasons: large season is May-August; small season is October-May (stays from 2 weeks to 2 months; average stay is 5 weeks). Accepts 230 artists/year. Accommodates approximately 35 artists in large season. Those qualified for invitations to Yaddo are highly qualified writers, visual artists (including photographers), composers, choreographers, performance artists and film and video artists who are working at the professional level in their fields. Artists who wish to work collaboratively are encouraged to apply. An abiding principle at Yaddo is that applications for residencies are judged on the quality of the artists' work and professional promise. Site includes four small lakes, a rose garden, woodland, swimming pool, tennis courts. Yaddo's non-refundable application fee is $30, to which is added a fee for media uploads ranging from $5-10 depending on the discipline. Application fees must be paid by credit card. Two letters of recommendation are requested. Applications are considered by the Admissions Committee and in-

vitations are issued by March 15 (deadline: January 1) and October 1 (deadline: August 1). Information available on website.

COSTS No fee is charged; residency includes room, board and studio space. Limited travel expenses are available to artists accepted for residencies at Yaddo.

ACCOMMODATIONS No stipends are offered.

MIDATLANTIC

ALGONKIAN FIVE DAY NOVEL CAMP
2020 Pennsylvania Ave. NW, Suite 443, Washington DC 20006. **E-mail:** algonkian@webdelsol.com. **Website:** fwwriters.algonkianconferences.com.

ALTERNATIVE PRESS EXPO (APE)
Comic-Con International, P.O. Box 128458, San Diego CA 92112-8458. (619)491-2475. **Fax:** (619)414-1022. **E-mail:** cci-info@comic-con.org. **Website:** www.comic-con.org/ape/. **Contact:** Eddie Ibrahim, director of programming.

AMERICAN INDEPENDENT WRITERS (AIW) AMERICAN WRITERS CONFERENCE
1001 Connecticut Ave. NW, Suite 701, Washington D.C. 20036. (202) 775-5150. **Fax:** (202) 775-5810. **E-mail:** info@amerindywriters.org. **E-mail:** donald@amerindywriters.org. **Website:** www.amerindywriters.org. **Contact:** Donald O. Graul Jr., executive director. Estab. 1975.

AMERICAN INDEPENDENT WRITERS (AIW) SPRING WRITERS CONFERENCE
1001 Connecticut Ave. NW, Suite 701, Washington D.C. 20036. (202)775-5150. **Fax:** (202)775-5810. **E-mail:** info@amerindywriters.org; donald@amerindywriters.org. **Website:** www.amerindywriters.org. **Contact:** Donald O. Graul, Jr., executive director. Estab. 1975.

ADDITIONAL INFORMATION See the website or send a SASE in mid-February for brochures/guidelines and fees information.

BALTIMORE COMIC-CON
Baltimore Convention Center, One West Pratt St., Baltimore MD 21201. (410)526-7410. **E-mail:** press@baltimorecomiccon.com. **Website:** www.baltimorecomiccon.com. **Contact:** Marc Nathan. Estab. 1999.

ACCOMMODATIONS Does not offer overnight accommodations. Provides list of area hotels or lodging options.

ADDITIONAL INFORMATION For brochure, visit website.

BALTIMORE WRITERS' CONFERENCE

PRWR Program, Linthicum Hall 218K, Towson University, 8000 York Rd., Towson MD 21252. (410)704-5196. **E-mail:** prwr@towson.edu. **Website:** www.towson.edu/writersconference. Estab. 1994.

COSTS $75-95 (includes all-day conference, lunch and reception). Student special rate of $35 before mid-October, $50 thereafter.

ACCOMMODATIONS Hotels are close by, if required.

ADDITIONAL INFORMATION Writers may register through the BWA website. Send inquiries via e-mail.

GREATER LEHIGH VALLEY WRITERS GROUP 'THE WRITE STUFF' WRITERS CONFERENCE

3650 Nazareth Pike, PMB #136, Bethlehem PA 18020-1115. **E-mail:** writestuffchair@glvwg.org. **Website:** http://www.glvwg.org/. **Contact:** Donna Brennan, chair. Estab. 1993.

COSTS Members, $100 (includes Friday evening session and all Saturday workshops, 2 meals, and a chance to pitch to an editor or agent); non-members, $120. Late registration, $135. Pre-conference workshops require an additional fee.

ADDITIONAL INFORMATION "The Writer's Flash contest is judged by conference participants. Write 100 words or less in fiction, creative nonfiction, or poetry. Brochures available in January by SASE, or by phone, e-mail, or on website. Accepts inquiries by SASE, e-mail or phone. Agents and editors attend conference. For updated info refer to the website. Greater Lehigh Valley Writer's Group hosts a friendly conference has remained one of the most friendly conferences and gives you the most for your money. Breakout rooms offer craft topics, business of publishing, editor and agent panels. Book fair with book signing by published authors and presenters."

HIGHLIGHTS FOUNDATION FOUNDERS WORKSHOPS

814 Court St., Honesdale PA 18437. (570)253-1172. **Fax:** (570)253-0179. **E-mail:** contact@highlightsfoundation.org. **Website:** www.highlightsfoundation.org/pages/current/FWsched_preview.html. **Contact:** Kent L. Brown, Jr. Estab. 2000.

ACCOMMODATIONS Coordinates pickup at local airport. Offers overnight accommodations. Participants stay in guest cabins on the wooded grounds surrounding Highlights Founders' home adjacent to the house/conference center.

ADDITIONAL INFORMATION Some workshops require pre-workshop assignment. Brochure available for SASE, by e-mail, on website, by phone, by fax. Accepts inquiries by phone, fax, e-mail, SASE. Editors attend conference. "Applications will be reviewed and accepted on a first-come, first-served basis, applicants must demonstrate specific experience in writing area of workshop they are applying for—writing samples are required for many of the workshops."

HIGHLIGHTS FOUNDATION WRITERS WORKSHOP AT CHAUTAUQUA

814 Court St., Honesdale PA 18431. (570)253-1192. **Fax:** (570)253-0179. **E-mail:** contact@highlightsfoundation.org. **Website:** www.highlightsfoundation.org. Estab. 1985.

ACCOMMODATIONS We coordinate ground transportation to and from airports, trains, and bus stations in the Erie, Pennsylvania and Jamestown/Buffalo, NY area. We also coordinate accommodations for conference attendees.

ADDITIONAL INFORMATION "We offer the opportunity for attendees to submit a ms for review at the conference. Workshop brochures/guidelines are available upon request."

MONTROSE CHRISTIAN WRITERS' CONFERENCE

218 Locust St., Montrose PA 18801. (570)278-1001 or (800)598-5030. **Fax:** (570)278-3061. **E-mail:** info@montrosebible.org. **Website:** www.montrosebible.org. Estab. 1990.

COSTS In 2009 registration (tuition) was $155.

ACCOMMODATIONS Will meet planes in Binghamton, NY and Scranton, PA. On-site accomodations: room and board $285-330/conference; $60-70/day including food (2009 rates). RV court available.

ADDITIONAL INFORMATION "Writers can send work ahead of time and have it critiqued for a small fee." The attendees are usually church related. The writing has a Christian emphasis. Conference information available in April. For brochure send SASE, visit website, e-mail, call or fax. Accepts inquiries by SASE, e-mail, fax, phone.

JENNY MCKEAN MOORE COMMUNITY WORKSHOPS

English Department, George Washingtion University, 801 22nd St. NW, Rome Hall, Suite 760, Washington DC 20052. (202) 994-6180. **Fax:** (202) 994-7915. **E-mail:** tvmallon@gwu.edu. **Website:** www.gwu.

edu/~english/creative_jennymckeanmoore.html.
Contact: Thomas Mallon, director of creative writing. Estab. 1976.
ADDITIONAL INFORMATION Admission is competitive and by ms.

WILLIAM PATERSON UNIVERSITY SPRING WRITER'S CONFERENCE

English Department, Atrium 232, 300 Pompton Rd., Wayne NJ 07470. (973)720-3067. **Fax:** (973)720-2189. **E-mail:** parrasj@wpunj.edu. **Website:** http://euphrates.wpunj.edu/writersconference.
COSTS $55 (includes lunch).

PHILADELPHIA WRITERS' CONFERENCE

P.O. Box 7171, Elkins Park PA 19027-0171. (215) 619-7422. **E-mail:** dresente@mc3.edu. **Website:** www.pwcwriters.org. **Contact:** Dana Resente. Estab. 1949.
COSTS Advance registration postmarked by April 15 is $205; after April 8 and walk-in registration is $225. The banquet and buffet are $40 each. Master classes are $50.
ACCOMMODATIONS Holiday Inn, Independence Mall, Fourth and Arch Streets, Philadelphia, PA 19106-2170. "Hotel offers discount for early registration."
ADDITIONAL INFORMATION Sponsors contest. "Length is generally 2,500 words for fiction or nonfiction. 1st Prize, in addition to cash and certificate, gets free tuition for following year." Also offers ms critique. Accepts inquiries by e-mail and SASE. Agents and editors attend conference. Visit us on the web for further agent and speaker details."

⊕○ SCBWI–NEW JERSEY; ANNUAL SUMMER CONFERENCE

SCBWI-New Jersey: Society of Children's Book Writers & Illustrators, New Jersey NJ **Website:** www.newjerseyscbwi.com. **Contact:** Kathy Temean, regional advisor.

MIDSOUTH

AEC CONFERENCE ON SOUTHERN LITERATURE

Arts & Education Council (AEC), 3069 S. Broad St., Suite 2, Chattanooga TN 37408-3056. (423)267-1218 or (800)267-4232. **Fax:** (423)267-1018. **E-mail:** srobinson@artsedcouncil.org. **Website:** http://artsedcouncil.org; http://southernlitconference.org. **Contact:** Susan Robinson.

AMERICAN CHRISTIAN WRITERS CONFERENCES

P.O. Box 110390, Nashville TN 37222-0390. (800)219-7483. **Fax:** (615)834-7736. **E-mail:** acwriters@aol.com. **Website:** www.acwriters.com. **Contact:** Reg Forder, director. Estab. 1981.
COSTS $150 for one day, $250 for two days, plus meals and accommodations.
ACCOMMODATIONS Special rates are available at the host hotel (usually a major chain like Holiday Inn).
ADDITIONAL INFORMATION Send a SASE for conference brochures/guidelines.

AWP ANNUAL CONFERENCE AND BOOKFAIR

MS 1E3, George Mason Univ., Fairfax VA 22030. (703)993-4317. **E-mail:** conference@awpwriter.org. **Website:** www.awpwriter.org/conference. **Contact:** Anne Le, conference coordinator. Estab. 1967.
COSTS Early registration fees: $40 student; $140 AWP member; $160 non-member.
ACCOMMODATIONS Provide airline discounts and rental-car discounts. Special rate at Hilton Chicago & Palmer House Hilton Hotels.
ADDITIONAL INFORMATION AWP Annual Conference & Bookfair, Chicago IL. Annual. Conference duration: 4 days. AWP holds its Annual Conference in a different region of North America in order to celebrate the outstanding authors, teachers, writing programs, literary centers, and small press publishers of that region. The Annual Conference typically features 350 presentations: readings, lectures, panel discussions, and forums plus hundreds of book signings, receptions, dances, and informal gatherings. The conference attracts more than 8,000 attendees and more than 500 publishers. All genres are represented. "We will offer 175 panels on everything from writing to teaching to critical analysis." In 2009, Art Spiegelman was the keynote speaker. Others readers were Charles Baxter, Isaiah Sheffer, Z.Z. Packer, Nareem Murr, Marilynne Robinson; 2008: John Irving, Joyce Carol Oates, among others.

⤵ BLUE RIDGE "AUTUMN IN THE MOUNTAINS" NOVEL RETREAT

(800)588-7222. **E-mail:** ylehman@bellsouth.net. **Website:** www.lifeway.com/novelretreat. **Contact:** Yvonne Lehman, director. Estab. 2007.
COSTS Retreat Tuition: $315; Room: $69-89; Meals: $124.

ACCOMMODATIONS Mountain Laurel Hotel on campus.

BLUE RIDGE "SUMMER IN THE MOUNTAINS" NOVEL RETREAT

(800)588-7222. **E-mail:** ylehman@bellsouth.net. **Website:** www.gideonfilmfestival.com. **Contact:** Yvonne Lehman, director.

COSTS Tuition $315, Room $69-89, Meals $159.

⊙ KILLER NASHVILLE

P.O. Box 680686, Franklin TN 37068-0686. (615)599-4032. **E-mail:** contact@killernashville.com. **Website:** www.killernashville.com. **Contact:** Clay Stafford. Estab. 2006.

COSTS Signings events are free; current prices for events available on website.

ADDITIONAL INFORMATION "Additional information about registration is provided at www.KillerNashville.com."

VIRGINIA FESTIVAL OF THE BOOK

Virginia Festival of the Book Foundation for the Humanities, 145 Ednam Dr., Charlottesville VA 22903-4629. (434)982-2983. **Fax:** (434)296-4714. **E-mail:** vabook@virginia.edu; spcoleman@virginia.edu. **Website:** www.vabook.org. **Contact:** Nancy Damon, program director. Estab. 1995.

COSTS Most events are free and open to the public. Two luncheons, a breakfast, and a reception require tickets.

ACCOMMODATIONS Overnight accommodations available.

ADDITIONAL INFORMATION "The festival is a 5-day event featuring authors, illustrators, and publishing professionals. Authors must apply to the festival to be included on a panel. Applications accepted only online.

THE WRITERS WORKSHOP

445 Ridge Springs Dr., Chapel Hill NC 27516. **E-mail:** bob@bobmayer.org. **Website:** www.bobmayer.org. **Contact:** Bob Mayer. Estab. 2002.

COSTS Varies; depends on venue

ADDITIONAL INFORMATION Limited to 8 participants and focused on their novel and marketability.

SOUTHEAST

HOW TO BE PUBLISHED WORKSHOPS

P.O. Box 100031, Irondale AL 35210-3006. **E-mail:** mike@writing2sell.com. **Website:** www.writing2sell.com. **Contact:** Michael Garrett. Estab. 1986.

COSTS $79-99.

⊙ WRITE IT OUT

P.O. Box 704, Sarasota FL 34230-0704. (941)359-3824. **E-mail:** rmillerwio@aol.com. **Website:** www.writeitout.com. **Contact:** Ronni Miller, director. Estab. 1997.

COSTS 2012 fees: Italy, $1,450; Cape Cod, $675. Price includes tution, private conferences and salons. Room, board, and airfare not included.

ADDITIONAL INFORMATION "Critiques on work are given at the workshops." Conference information available year round. For brochures/guidelines e-mail, call, or visit website. Accepts inquiries by phone, e-mail. Workshops have "small groups, option to spend time writing and not attend classes, with personal appointments with instructors."

WRITERS IN PARADISE

Eckerd College, 4200 54th Ave. South, St. Petersburg FL 33711. (727) 864-7994. **Fax:** (727) 864-7575. **E-mail:** cayacr@eckerd.edu. **Website:** www.writersinparadise.com. **Contact:** Christine Caya, conference coordinator. Estab. 2005.

COSTS 2010 tuition fee: 700

ACCOMMODATIONS Does not offer overnight accommodations. Provides list of preferred conference hotels and lodging options.

ADDITIONAL INFORMATION Application materials are required of all attendees. Acceptance is based on a writing sample and a letter detailing your writing background. Submit 1 short story (25 page max) or the opening 25 pages of a novel-in-progress, plus a 2-page synopsis of the book. Deadline for application materials is December 1. "Writers in Paradise is a conference for writers of various styles and approaches. While admission is selective, the admissions committee accepts writers with early potential as well as those with strong backgrounds in writing." Sponsors contest. "At the final Evening Reading Series Event, co-directors Dennis Lehane and Sterling Watson will announce 'The Best of' nominees of the Writers in Paradise Conference. Winners will be published in *Sabal—A Review Featuring the Best Writing of the Writers in Paradise Conference at Eckerd College*. One winner and 1 honorable mention will be selected from each workshop based on the material brought into the workshop for discussion. Selection will be made by the faculty member leading the workshop. There are no additional fees or entry forms needed." Information available in October. For brochure, send SASE, call, e-mail. Agents participate in conference. Editors participate in conference. "The tranquil seaside landscape sets the tone for this informal gathering of writers, teachers, editors and literary agents. After 8 days of workshopping and engagemnt with peers and professionals in your field, you will leave this unique opportunity with solid ideas about how to find an agent and get published, along with a new and better understanding of your craft."

MIDWEST

BACKSPACE AGENT-AUTHOR SEMINAR

P.O. Box 454, Washington MI 48094-0454. (732)267-6449. **Fax:** (586)532-9652. **E-mail:** chrisg@bksp.org. **Website:** www.bksp.org. Estab. 2006.
COSTS All 3 days: May 26-28; includes Agent-Author Seminar, Conference Program, Book Signing & Cocktail Reception, Donald Maass workshop—$700. **Backspace Members Receive a $120 discount on a 3-day registration! First 2 days**: May 26-27; includes Agent-Author Seminar, Conference Program, Book Signing & Cocktail Reception—$550. **Day, 1 only**: May 26; Agent-Author Seminar, small-group workshops and agent panels—$325. **Day 2 only**: May 27; Conference Program, Book Signing & Cocktail Reception—$250. **Day 3 only:** May 28; Donald Maass workshop—$150. Tickets for the Friday evening cocktail reception may be purchased for $85 each. One reception ticket is included with the 3-day, 2-day and Friday only (May 27) registrations. **EXTRA EVENING WORKSHOP:** Jeff Kleinman from Folio Literary Management, assisted by Andrea Walker, Vice President and Editorial Director of Reagan Arthur Books, an imprint of Little, Brown, will hold his always-popular Buy This Book! role-playing workshop from 7-9 p.m. on Thursday, May 26. **Cost for the 2-hour workshop is $45** .
ADDITIONAL INFORMATION The Backspace Agent-Author Seminar offers plenty of face time with attending agents. This casual, no-pressure seminar is a terrific opportunity to network, ask questions, talk about your work informally and listen from the people who make their lives selling books.

BACKSPACE WRITERS CONFERENCE & AGENT AUTHOR SEMINAR

P.O. Box 454, Washington MI 48094. (732)267-6449. **E-mail:** karendionne@bksp.org. **Website:** www.backspacewritersconference.com. **Contact:** Christopher Graham or Karen Dionne, co-founders.

COSTS $200-700; offers member, group, and student discounts along with additional workshops that are priced separately.
ACCOMMODATIONS "We offer a special conference rate at the Radisson Martinique for conference attendees. Average price of $199-279/night, must be booked 30 days in advance." The Radisson Martinique in Manhattan NY, is located in Mid-town, Manhattan, just a few blocks from Madison Square Garden/NY Penn Station.
ADDITIONAL INFORMATION 2012 dates: May 24-26. Dates for the November 2012 Agent-Author Seminar: Noveber 1-2. Conference duration: 3 days. Average attendance: 150-200. Conference. "We focus on all genres, from nonfiction to literary fiction and everything in between, covering all popular genres from mysteries, and thrillers to young adult and romance. Formal pitch sessions are a staple at most writers'conferences. However, in planning our Backspace events, we discovered that agents hate conducting pitch sessions almost as much as authors dread doing them. In fact, many of the agents we've talked to are happy to sit on a panel or conduct a workshop, but decline to participate in formal pitch sessions. The goal of the Backspace Agent-Author Seminars is to help authors connect with agents - lots of agents - thereby giving authors the opportunity to ask questions specific to their interests and concerns. We facilitate this through small group workshops of usually no more than 10 writers and 2 agents. Workshops concentrate on query letters and opening pages. That's why we've built so much free time into the program. The full 15 minutes between panels also allows plenty of opportunity for seminar registrants to talk to agents. Many of the agents will also be available during the noon hour. Remember, agents attend conferences because they want to help authors. They're looking for new talent, and welcome the chance to hear about your work. Instead of a tense, angst-filled pitch session where it's difficult for all but the most confident authors to put their best foot forward, an interesting, relaxed, enjoyable conversation leaves a much more positive impression. And even if authors don't get the chance to mention their project, the pleasant conversation gives the author a point of reference when sending a formal query letter to the agent's office after the seminar is over." 20112 agents in attendance: Donald Maass, Kristin Nelson, Janet Reid, Jeff Kleinman, and many more. Keynote speaker: Lauren Baratz-Logsted. Workshop conduc-

tor: David L. Robbins. Also attending: *New York Times* bestselling authors Darcie Chan and Lorenzo Carcaterra. See website for more information. Brochures available in January. Accepts inquiries by e-mail and phone. Agents and editors attend conference.

FESTIVAL OF FAITH AND WRITING

Department of English, Calvin College, 1795 Knollcrest Circle SE, Grand Rapids MI 49546. (616)526-6770. **E-mail:** ffw@calvin.edu. **Website:** www.calvin.edu/festival. Estab. 1990.

COSTS Consult festival website.

ACCOMMODATIONS Shuttles are available to and from local hotels. Shuttles are also available for overflow parking lots. A list of hotels with special rates for conference attendees is available on the festival website. High school and college students can arrange on-campus lodging by e-mail.

ADDITIONAL INFORMATION Online registration opens in October. Accepts inquiries by e-mail and phone

KENTUCKY WOMEN WRITERS CONFERENCE

232 E. Maxwell St., Lexington KY 40506. (859)257-2874. **E-mail:** kentuckywomenwriters@gmail.com. **Website:** www.uky.edu/wwc/. **Contact:** Julie Wrinn, director. Estab. 1979.

COSTS $150 for 2 days, $80 for 1 day, $30 for students. Some snacks included. Meals and accommodations are not included.

ADDITIONAL INFORMATION Sponsors prizes in poetry ($200), fiction ($200), nonfiction ($200), playwriting ($500), and spoken word ($500). Winners also invited to read during the conference. Pre-registration opens May 1.

KENYON REVIEW WRITERS WORKSHOP

Kenyon College, Gambier OH 43022. (740)427-5207. **Fax:** (740)427-5417. **E-mail:** kenyonreview@kenyon.edu; writers@kenyonreview.org. **Website:** www.kenyonreview.org. **Contact:** Anna Duke Reach, director. Estab. 1990. T

COSTS $1,995 includes tuition, room and board.

ACCOMMODATIONS The workshop operates a shuttle to and from Gambier and the airport in Columbus, Ohio. Offers overnight accommodations. Participants are housed in Kenyon College student housing. The cost is covered in the tuition.

ADDITIONAL INFORMATION Application includes a writing sample. Admission decisions are made on a rolling basis. Workshop information is available online at www.kenyonreview.org/workshops in November. For brochure send e-mail, visit website, call, fax. Accepts inquiries by SASE, e-mail, phone, fax.

◉ MAGNA CUM MURDER

Magna Cum Murder Crime Writing Festival, The E.B. and Bertha C. Ball Center, Ball State University, Muncie IN 47306. (765)285-8975. **Fax:** (765)747-9566. **E-mail:** magnacummurder@yahoo.com; kennisonk@aol.com. **Website:** www.magnacummurder.com. Estab. 1994.

COSTS Check website for updates.

MIDWEST WRITERS WORKSHOP

Ball State University, Department of Journalism, Muncie IN 47306. (765)282-1055. **E-mail:** midwestwriters@yahoo.com. **Website:** www.midwestwriters.org. **Contact:** Jama Kehoe Bigger, director.

OHIO KENTUCKY INDIANA CHILDREN'S LITERATURE CONFERENCE

Northern Kentucky University, 405 Steely Library, Highland Heights KY 41099. (859)572-6620. **Fax:** (859) 572-5390. **E-mail:** smithjen@nku.edu. **Website:** http://oki.nku.edu. **Contact:** Jennifer Smith, staff development coordinator.

☺ SPACE (SMALL PRESS AND ALTERNATIVE COMICS EXPO)

Back Porch Comics, P.O. Box 20550, Columbus OH 43220. **E-mail:** bpc13@earthlink.net. **Website:** www.backporchcomics.com/space.htm.

COSTS Admission: $5 per day or $8 for weekend.

ADDITIONAL INFORMATION For brochure, visit website. Editors participate in conference.

WESTERN RESERVE WRITERS & FREELANCE CONFERENCE

7700 Clocktower Dr., Kirtland OH 44094. (440) 525-7812. **E-mail:** deencr@aol.com. **Website:** www.deannaadams.com. **Contact:** Deanna Adams, director/conference coordinator. Estab. 1983.

COSTS Fall all-day conference includes lunch: $95. Spring half-day conference, no lunch: $69.

ADDITIONAL INFORMATION Brochures for the conferences are available by January (for spring conference) and July (for fall). Also accepts inquiries by e-mail and phone, or see website. Editors and agents often attend the conferences.

⊕ WOMEN WRITERS WINTER RETREAT

Homestead House B&B, 38111 West Spaulding, Willoughby OH 44094. (440)946-1902. **E-mail:** deencr@aol.com. **Website:** www.deannaadams.com. Estab. 2007.

COSTS Single room: $299. Shared Room: $225 (includes complete weekend package, with B&B stay and all meals and workshops); weekend commute: $150; Saturday only: $125 (prices include lunch and dinner). **ADDITIONAL INFORMATION** Brochures for the writers retreat are available by December. Accepts inquiries and reservations by e-mail or phone. See website for additional information.

NORTH CENTRAL

GREAT LAKES WRITERS FESTIVAL

Lakeland College, P.O. Box 359, Sheboygan WI 53082-0359. **E-mail:** elderk@lakeland.edu. **Website:** www.greatlakeswritersfestival.org. Estab. 1991.

COSTS Free and open to the public. Participants may purchase meals and must arrange for their own lodging.

ACCOMMODATIONS Does not offer overnight accommodations. Provides list of area hotels or lodging options.

ADDITIONAL INFORMATION All participants who would like to have their writing considered as an object for discussion during the festival workshops should submit it to Karl Elder electronically by October 15. Participants may submit material for workshops in 1 genre only (poetry, fiction, or creative nonfiction). Sponsors contest. Contest entries must contain the writer's name and address on a separate title page, typed, and be submitted as clear, hard copy on Friday at the festival registration table. Entries may be in each of 3 genres per participant, yet only 1 poem, 1 story, and/or 1 nonfiction piece may be entered. There are 2 categories—high school students on 1 hand, all others on the other—of cash awards for first place in each of the 3 genres. The judges reserve the right to decline to award a prize in 1 or more of the genres. Judges will be the editorial staff of *Seems* (a.k.a. Word of Mouth Books), excluding the festival coordinator, Karl Elder. Information available in September. For brochure, visit website.

GREEN LAKE CHRISTIAN WRITERS CONFERENCE

W2511 State Road 23, Green Lake Conference Center, Green Lake WI 54941-9599. (920)294-3323. **E-mail:** program@glcc.org. **Website:** www.glcc.org. Estab. 1948.

ACCOMMODATIONS Hotels, lodges and all meeting rooms are a/c. Affordable rates, excellent meals.

ADDITIONAL INFORMATION Brochure and scholarship info from website or contact Jan White (920-294-7327). To register, call 920-294-3323.

INTERNATIONAL MUSIC CAMP CREATIVE WRITING WORKSHOP

111-11th Ave. SW, Minot ND 58701. (701)838-8472. **Fax:** (701)838-1351. **E-mail:** info@internationalmusiccamp.com. **Website:** www.internationalmusiccamp.com. **Contact:** Dr. Timothy Wollenzien, camp director. Estab. 1956.

COSTS $385, includes tuition, room and board. Early bird registration (postmarked by May 1) $370.

ACCOMMODATIONS Airline and depot shuttles are available upon request. Housing is included in the $370 fee.

ADDITIONAL INFORMATION Conference information is available in September. For brochure, visit website, e-mail, call, or fax. Accepts inquiries by e-mail, phone and fax.

IOWA SUMMER WRITING FESTIVAL

C215 Seashore Hall, University of Iowa, Iowa City IA 52242. (319)335-4160. **Fax:** (319)335-4743. **E-mail:** iswfestival@uiowa.edu. **Website:** www.uiowa.edu/~iswfest. Estab. 1987.

COSTS $560 for full week; $280 for weekend workshop. Housing and meals are separate.

ACCOMMODATIONS Accommodations available at area hotels. Information on overnight accommodations available by phone or on website.

ADDITIONAL INFORMATION Brochures are available in February. Inquire via e-mail or on website.

WRITERS' INSTITUTE

21 North Park St., Room 7331, Madison WI 53715. (608)265-3972. **Fax:** (608)265-2475. **E-mail:** lscheer@dcs.wisc.edu. **Website:** www.uwwritersinstitute.org. **Contact:** Laurie Scheer. Estab. 1989.

COSTS $245 includes materials, breaks.

ACCOMMODATIONS Provides a list of area hotels or lodging options.

ADDITIONAL INFORMATION Sponsors contest. Submit 1-page writing sample and $10 entry fee.

SOUTH CENTRAL

ASPEN SUMMER WORDS LITERARY FESTIVAL & WRITING RETREAT

Aspen Writers' Foundation, 110 E. Hallam St., #116, Aspen CO 81611. (970)925-3122. **Fax:** (970)925-5700.

E-mail: info@aspenwriters.org. **Website:** www.aspenwriters.org. **Contact:** Natalie Lacy, programs coordinator. Estab. 1976.

COSTS Check website each year for updates.

ACCOMMODATIONS Discount lodging at the conference site will be available. 2011 rates to be announced. Free shuttle around town.

ADDITIONAL INFORMATION Workshops admission deadline is April 15. Manuscripts for juried workshops must be submitted by April 15 for review and selection. 10 page limit for workshop application manuscript. A limited number of partial-tuition scholarships are available. Deadline for agent/editor meeting registration is May 27th. Brochures available for SASE, by e-mail and phone request, and on website.

CRESTED BUTTE WRITERS CONFERENCE

P.O. Box 1361, Crested Butte CO 81224. **Website:** www.crestedbuttewriters.org/conf.php. **Contact:** Barbara Crawford or Theresa Rizzo, co-coordinators. Estab. 2006.

COSTS $330 Nonmembers, $300 members, $297 Early Bird, The Sandy Writing Contest Finalist $280, and groups of 5 or more $280.

ACCOMMODATIONS The conference is held at The Elevation Hotel, located at the Crested Butte Mountain Resort at the base of the ski mountain (Mt. Crested Butte, CO). The quaint historic town lies nestled in a stunning mountain valley 3 short miles from the resort area of Mt. Crested Butte. A free bus runs frequently between the 2 towns. The closest airport is 10 miles away, in Gunnison CO. Our website lists 3 lodging options besides rooms at the Event Facility. All condos, motels and hotel options offer special conference rates. No special travel arrangements are made through the conference; however, information for car rental from Gunnison airport or the Alpine Express shuttle is listed on the conference FAQ page.

ADDITIONAL INFORMATION Our conference workshops address a wide variety of writing craft and business. Our most popular workshop is Our First Pages Readings—with a twist. Agents and editors read opening pages volunteered by attendees-with a few best selling authors' openings mixed in. Think the A/E can identify the bestsellers? Not so much. Each year one of our attendees has been mistaken for a best seller and obviously garnered requests from some on the panel. Agents attending: Stephen Barr—Writers house, Marisa Corvisiero—L. Perkins Agency, and Helen Breitwieser—Cornerstone Literary. The agents will be speaking and available for meetings with attendees through our Pitch and Pages system. Editors attending: Holly Blanck—St. Martin's Press and Mike Braff-Del Rey/Spectra. Award-winning authors: Robin D. Owens, Sophie Littlefield, Juliet Blackwell and Kaki Warner. Writers may request additional information by e-mail.

EAST TEXAS CHRISTIAN WRITERS CONFERENCE

The School of Humanities, Dr. Jerry L. Summers, Dean, Scarborough Hall, East Texas Baptist Univ., 1209 N. Grove, Marshall TX 75670. (903)923-2269. **E-mail:** jhopkins@etbu.edu; contest@etbu.edu. **Website:** www.etbu.edu/News/CWC. **Contact:** Joy Cornish. Estab. 2002. **Humanities Secretary:** Joy Cornish. Annual Conference held the second weekend in April, Friday and Saturday, April 9-10, 2010. Conference duration: 2 days (Friday & Saturday). Average attendance: 190. "Primarily we are interested in promoting quality Christian writing that would be accepted in mainstream publishing." Site: We use the classrooms, cafeterias, etc. of East Texas Baptist University. Past conference themes were Back to Basics, Getting Started in Fiction, Writers & Agents, Writing Short Stories, Writing for Newspapers, The Significance of Style, Writing Fillers and Articles, Writing Devotionals, Blogging for Writers, Christian Non-Fiction, Inspirational Writing, E-Publishing, Publishing on Demand, and Editor and Author Relations. Past conference speakers/workshop leaders were David Jenkins, Bill Keith, Pete Litterski, Joe Early, Jr., Mary Lou Redding, Marie Chapian, Denny Boultinghouse, Vickie Phelps, Michael Farris, Susan Farris, Pamela Dowd, Donn Taylor, Terry Burns, Donna Walker-Nixon, Lexie Smith, Marv Knox, D.D. Turner, Jim Pence, Andrea Chevalier, Marie Bagnull, and Leonard Goss.

ACCOMMODATIONS Visit website for a list of local hotels offering a discounted rate.

TONY HILLERMAN WRITERS CONFERENCE

1063 Willow Way, Santa Fe NM 87505. (505)471-1565. **E-mail:** wordharvest@wordharvest.com. **Website:** www.wordharvest.com. **Contact:** Jean Schaumberg, co-director. Estab. 2004.

COSTS Previous year's costs: $395 per-registration.

ACCOMMODATIONS Hotel Santa Fe; offers $115 single or double occupancy. Book online with the hotel.

ADDITIONAL INFORMATION Sponsors a $10,000 first mystery novel contest with St. Marttin's Press and a mystery short story contest with *New Mexico Magazine*.Brochures available in July for SASE, by phone, e-mail, and on website. Accepts inquiries by SASE, phone, e-mail. Deadline for the Hillerman Mystery Competition is June 1; August 15 for the Hillerman Short Story contest.

NATIONAL WRITERS ASSOCIATION FOUNDATION CONFERENCE

P.O. Box 4187, Parker CO 80134. (303)841-0246. **Fax:** (303)841-2607. **E-mail:** natlwritersassn@hotmail.com. **Website:** www.nationalwriters.com. **Contact:** Sandy Whelchel, executive director. Estab. 1926.

COSTS Approximately $100.

ADDITIONAL INFORMATION Awards for previous contests will be presented at the conference. Brochures/guidelines are online, or send a SASE.

NIMROD ANNUAL WRITERS' WORKSHOP

800 S. Tucker Dr., Tulsa OK 74104. (918)631-3080. **E-mail:** nimrod@utulsa.edu. **Website:** www.utulsa.edu/nimrod. **Contact:** Eilis O'Neal, managing editor. Estab. 1978.

COSTS Approximately $50. Lunch provided. Scholarships available for students.

ADDITIONAL INFORMATION *Nimrod International Journal* sponsors *Nimrod* Literary Awards: The Katherine Anne Porter Prize for fiction and The Pablo Neruda Prize for poetry. Poetry and fiction prizes: $2,000 each and publication (1st prize); $1,000 each and publication (2nd prize). Deadline: must be postmarked no later than April 30.

SCIENCE FICTION WRITERS WORKSHOP

English Department/University of Kansas, Wesoce Hall, 1445 Jayhawk Blvd., Room 3001, Lawrence KS 66045-7590. (785)864-2508. **E-mail:** cmckit@ku.edu. **Website:** www.sfcenter.ku.edu/SFworkshop.htm. Estab. 1985.

COSTS See website for tuition rates, dormitory housing costs, and deadlines.

ACCOMMODATIONS Housing information is available. Several airport shuttle services offer reasonable transportation from the Kansas City International Airport to Lawrence.

ADDITIONAL INFORMATION Admission to the workshop is bysubmission of an acceptable story, usually by May. Two additional stories are submitted by the middle of June. These 3 stories are distributed to other participants for critiquing and are the basis for the first week of the workshop. One story is rewritten for the second week, when students also work with guest authors. See website for guidelines. This workshop is intended for writers who have just started to sell their work or need that extra bit of understanding or skill to become a published writer.

STEAMBOAT SPRINGS WRITERS GROUP

P.O. Box 774284, Steamboat Springs CO 80477. (970)879-8079. **E-mail:** susan@steamboatwriters.com. **Website:** www.steamboatwriters.com. **Contact:** Susan de Wardt, director. Estab. 1982. Group meets year-round on Thursdays, 12-2 p.m. at Arts Depot; guests welcome. Annual conference held in July. Conference duration: 1 day. Average attendance: 35. "Our conference emphasizes instruction within the seminar format. Novices and polished professionals benefit from the individual attention and camaraderie which can be established within small groups. A pleasurable and memorable learning experience is guaranteed by the relaxed and friendly atmosphere of the old train depot. Registration is limited." Site: Restored train depot.

COSTS $50 before May 25, $60 after. Fee covers all seminars and luncheon.

ACCOMMODATIONS Lodging available at Steamboat Resorts.

ADDITIONAL INFORMATION Optional dinner and activities during evening preceding conference. Accepts inquiries by e-mail, phone, mail.

⊕ STORY WEAVERS CONFERENCE

Oklahoma Writer's Federation, (405)682-6000. **E-mail:** president@owfi.org. **Website:** www.OWFI.org. **Contact:** Linda Apple, president.

The theme of our conference is to create good stories with strong bones. We will be exploring cultural writing and cultural sensitivity in writing. This year we will also be looking at the cutting edge of publishing and the options it is producing.

COSTS Cost is $150 before April. $175 after April. Cost includes awards banquet and famous author banquet. Three extra sessions are available for an extra fee: How to Self-Publish Your Novel on Kindle, Nook, and iPad (and make more money than being published by New York), with Dan Case; When Polar Bear Wishes Came True: Understanding and Creat-

ing Meaningful Stories, with Jack Dalton; How to Create Three-Dimensional Characters, with Steven James.
ACCOMMODATIONS The site is at the Embassy Suite using their meeting halls. There are very few stairs and the rooms are close together for easy access.
ADDITIONAL INFORMATION We have 20 speakers, five agents, and nine publisher/editors for a full list and bios, please see website.

SUMMER WRITING PROGRAM

Naropa University, 2130 Arapahoe Ave., Boulder CO 80302. (303)245-4600. **Fax:** (303)546-5287. **E-mail:** swpr@naropa.edu. **Website:** www.naropa.edu/swp. **Contact:** Julie Kazimer, registration manager. Estab. 1974.
COSTS In 2012: $475/week, $1,800 for all 4 weeks (non-credit students)
ACCOMMODATIONS Offers overnight accommodations. Housing is available at Snow Lion Apartments. Single room is $45/night or $315/week; single bedroom apartment is $64/night or $448/week.
ADDITIONAL INFORMATION If students would like to take the Summer Writing Program for academic credit, they must submit a non-degree seeking academic credit student application, transcripts, a letter of intent, and 5-10 pages of their creative work. Information available in January. For catalog of upcoming program, fill out catalog request form on website. Accepts inquiries by e-mail, phone.

MARK TWAIN CREATIVE WRITERS WORKSHOPS

5101 Rockhill Rd., Kansas City MO 64110-2499. (816)235-1168. **Fax:** (816)235-2611. **E-mail:** BeasleyM@umkc.edu. **Website:** www.newletters.org/writingConferences.asp. **Contact:** Betsy Beasley, administrative associate. Estab. 1990.

○ Held first 3 weeks of June, from 9:30 to 12:30 each weekday morning. Conference duration: 3 weeks. Average attendance: 40. Focus is on fiction, poetry and literary nonfiction. University of Missouri-Kansas City Campus Panels planned for next conference include the full range of craft essentials. Staff includes Robert Stewart, editor-in-chief of newsletters and BkMk Press. Submit for workshop 6 poems/one short story prior to arrival. Conference information is available in March by SASE, e-mail or on website. Editors participate in conference.

COSTS Fees for regular and noncredit courses.

ACCOMMODATIONS Offers list of area hotels or lodging options.
ADDITIONAL INFORMATION Submit for workshop 6 poems/one short story prior to arrival. Conference information is available in March by SASE, e-mail or on website. Editors participate in conference.

WEST

ABROAD WRITERS CONFERENCES

17363 Sutter Creek Rd., Sutter Creek CA 95685. (209)296-4050. **E-mail:** abroadwriters@yahoo.com. **Website:** www.abroad-crwf.com/index.html.

○ "Abroad Writers' Conference is proud to be holding Kolkata, India's first major literary conference in their historic City of Joy. This large literary conference and workshop will take place at the Victoria Memorial Museum and the Oberoi Hotel. We will have 40 authors including two Nobel Prize winners and literary agents. Workshops will be held in fiction, non-fiction, memoir, playwriting and poetry."

COSTS Prices start at $2,750. Discounts and upgrades may apply. Particpants must apply to program no later than 3 months before departure. To secure a place you must send in a deposit of $700. Balance must be paid in full twelve weeks before departure. See website for pricing details.
ADDITIONAL INFORMATION Agents participate in conference. Application is online at website.

BLOCKBUSTER PLOT INTENSIVE WRITING WORKSHOPS (SANTA CRUZ)

Santa Cruz CA **E-mail:** contact@blockbusterplots. com. **Website:** www.blockbusterplots.com. **Contact:** Martha Alderson M.A., instructor. Estab. 2000.
COSTS $95 per day.
ACCOMMODATIONS Provides list of area hotels and lodging options.
ADDITIONAL INFORMATION Brochures available by e-mail or on website. Accepts inquiries by e-mail.

JAMES BONNET'S STORYMAKING: THE MASTER CLASS

P.O. Box 7484, Santa Monica CA 90406. (310)451-5418. **E-mail:** bonnet@storymaking.com. **Website:** www.storymaking.com. **Contact:** James Bonnet. Estab. 1990.
COSTS $375 for weekend seminar; $1,650 for 7-day workshop/retreat.

ACCOMMODATIONS Provides a list of area hotels or lodging options.

ADDITIONAL INFORMATION For brochure, e-mail, visit website, or call. Accepts inquiries by SASE, e-mail, phone, and fax. James Bonnet is the author of *Stealing Fire From the Gods: The Complete Guide to Story for Writers and Filmmakers.*

CALIFORNIA CRIME WRITERS CONFERENCE

Co-sponsored by Sisters in Crime/Los Angeles and the Southern California Chapter of Mystery Writers of America, **E-mail:** sistersincrimela@gmail.com. **Website:** www.ccwconference.org. Estab. 1995.

ADDITIONAL INFORMATION Conference information is available on the website.

CLARION SCIENCE FICTION AND FANTASY WRITERS' WORKSHOP

UC San Diego, 9500 Gilman Dr., #0410, La Jolla CA 92093-0410. (858) 534-2115. **E-mail:** clarion@ucsd. edu. **Website:** http://clarion.ucsd.edu. **Contact:** Program coordinator. Estab. 1968.

COSTS The fees for 2013 (application, tuition, room and board) are approximately $4,900. Scholarships are available.

ACCOMMODATIONS Participants make their own travel arrangements to and from the campus. Campus residency is required. Participants are housed in semi-private accommodations (private bedroom, shared bathroom) in student apartments. The room and board fee includes 3 meals a day at a campus dining facility. Room and board are included in the workshop fee.

ADDITIONAL INFORMATION "Workshop participants are selected on the basis of their potential for highly successful writing careers. Applications are judged by a review panel composed of the workshop instructors. Applicants submit an application ($50 fee) and 2 complete short stories, each between 2,500 words and 6,000 words in length. The application deadline (typically, March 1) is posted on the Clarion website." Information available in September. For additional information, visit website.

LAS VEGAS WRITERS CONFERENCE

Henderson Writers' Group, 614 Mosswood Dr., Henderson NV 89015. (702)564-2488; or, toll-free, (866)869-7842. **E-mail:** marga614@mysticpublishers. com. **Website:** www.lasvegaswritersconference.com. **COSTS** $400 before December 31, $450 until conference, and $500 at the door. One day registration is $275.

ADDITIONAL INFORMATION Sponsors contest. Agents and editors participate in conference.

LEAGUE OF UTAH WRITERS' ANNUAL ROUNDUP

P.O. Box 18430, Kearns UT 84118. **E-mail:** writerscache435@gmail.com. **Website:** www.luwriters. org/index.html. **Contact:** Tim Keller, president; Irene Hastings, president-elect; Dorothy Crofts, secretary.

MENDOCINO COAST WRITERS CONFERENCE

1211 Del Mar Dr., Fort Bragg CA 95437. (707)937-9983. **E-mail:** info@mcwc.org. **Website:** www.mcwc. org. Estab. 1988.

COSTS $525+ (includes panels, meals, 2 socials with guest readers, 4 public events, 3 morning intensive workshops in 1 of 6 subjects, and a variety of afternoon panels and lectures)

ACCOMMODATIONS Information on overnight accommodations is made available.

ADDITIONAL INFORMATION Emphasis is on writers who are also good teachers. Brochures are online after in mid-February. Send inquiries via e-mail.

⊙ MOUNT HERMON CHRISTIAN WRITERS CONFERENCE

37 Conference Drive, Mount Hermon CA 95041. **E-mail:** info@mounthermon.org. **Website:** www.mounthermon.org/writers. Estab. 1970.

COSTS Registration fees include tuition, all major morning sessions, keynote sessions, and refreshment breaks. Room and board varies depending on choice of housing options. See website for current costs.

ACCOMMODATIONS Registrants stay in hotel-style accommodations. Meals are buffet style, with faculty joining registrants. See website Nov. 1 for cost updates.

ADDITIONAL INFORMATION "The residential nature of our conference makes this a unique setting for one-on-one interaction with faculty/staff. There is also a decided inspirational flavor to the conference, and general sessions with well-known speakers are a highlight. Registrants may submit 2 works for critique in advance of the conference, then have personal interviews with critiquers during the conference. All conference information is online by December 1 of each year. Send inquiries via e-mail. Tapes of past conferences are also available online."

PIMA WRITERS' WORKSHOP

Pima College, 2202 W. Anklam Rd., Tucson AZ 85709. (520)206-6084. **Fax:** (520)206-6020. **E-mail:** mfiles@pima.edu. **Contact:** Meg Files, director.

SANTA BARBARA WRITERS CONFERENCE

27 W. Anapamu St., Suite 305, Santa Barbara CA 93101. (805)568-1516. **E-mail:** info@sbwriters.com. **Website:** www.sbwriters.com. Estab. 1972.

◯ Speakers have included Ray Bradbury, William Styron, Eudora Welty, James Michener, Sue Grafton, Charles M. Schulz, Clive Cussler, Fannie Flagg, Elmore Leonard, and T.C. Boyle. Agents will appear on a panel, plus there will be an agents and editors day that allows writers to pitch their projects in one-on-one meetings.

ACCOMMODATIONS Hyatt Santa Barbara.

ADDITIONAL INFORMATION Register online or contact for brochure and registration forms.

SCBWI–VENTURA/SANTA BARBARA; FALL CONFERENCE

Simi Valley CA 93094-1389. **E-mail:** alexisinca@aol.com. **Website:** www.scbwisocal-org/calendar. **Contact:** Alexis O'Neill, regional advisor. Estab. 1971.

SQUAW VALLEY COMMUNITY OF WRITERS

P.O. Box 1416, Nevada City CA 95959-1416. (530)470-8440. **E-mail:** info@squawvalleywriters.org. **Website:** www.squawvalleywriters.org. **Contact:** Brett Hall Jones, executive director. Estab. 1969.

◯ Annual conference held in July. Conference duration: 7 days. Average attendance: 124. "Writers workshops in fiction, nonfiction, and memoir assist talented writers by exploring the art and craft as well as the business of writing." Offerings include daily morning workshops led by writer-teachers, editors, or agents of the staff, limited to 12-13 participants; seminars; panel discussions of editing and publishing; craft colloquies; lectures; and staff readings. Past themes and panels included "Personal History in Fiction, Narrative Structure, Promise and Premise: Recognizing Subject"; "The Nation of Narrative Prose: Telling the Truth in Memoir and Personal Essay"; and "Anatomy of a Short Story." The workshops are held in a ski lodge at the foot of this ski area. Literary agent speakers have recently included Michael Carlisle, Henry Dunow, Susan Golomb, Joy Harris, B.J. Robbins, Janet Silver, and Peter Steinberg. Agents will be speaking and available for meetings with attendees.

COSTS Tuition is $840, which includes 6 dinners.

ACCOMMODATIONS The Community of Writers rents houses and condominiums in the Valley for participants to live in during the week of the conference. Single room (1 participant): $725/week. Double room (twin beds, room shared by conference participant of the same sex): $350/week. Multiple room (bunk beds, room shared with 2 or more participants of the same sex): $210/week. All rooms subject to availability; early requests are recommended. Can arrange airport shuttle pick-ups for a fee.

ADDITIONAL INFORMATION Admissions are based on submitted ms (unpublished fiction, 1 or 2 stories or novel chapters); requires $35 reading fee. Submit ms to Brett Hall Jones, Squaw Valley Community of Writers, P.O. Box 1416, Nevada City, CA 95959. Brochures are available online or for a SASE in February. Send inquiries viae-mail. Accepts inquiries by SASE, e-mail, phone. Agents and editors attend/participate in conferences.

THRILLERFEST

P.O. Box 311, Eureka CA 95502. **E-mail:** infocentral@thrillerwriters.org. **Website:** www.thrillerfest.com. **Contact:** Kimberley Howe, executive director. Estab. 2006.

COSTS Price will vary from $300-1,100, depending on which events are selected. Various package deals are available offering savings, and Early Bird pricing is offered beginning August of each year.

ACCOMMODATIONS Grand Hyatt in New York City.

TMCC WRITERS' CONFERENCE

5270 Neil Rd., Reno NV 89502. (775)829-9010. **Fax:** (775)829-9032. **E-mail:** wdce@tmcc.edu. **Website:** wdce.tmcc.edu. Estab. 1991.

COSTS $109 for a full-day seminar; $32 for a 10-minute one-on-one appointment with an agent or editor.

ACCOMMODATIONS The Silver Legacy, in downtown Reno, offers a special rate and shuttle service to the Reno/Tahoe International Airport, which is less than 20 minutes away.

ADDITIONAL INFORMATION "The conference is open to all writers, regardless of their level of experience. Brochures are available online and mailed in January. Send inquiries via e-mail."

WRITERS STUDIO AT UCLA EXTENSION

1010 Westwood Blvd., Los Angeles CA 90024. (310)825-9415. **E-mail:** writers@uclaextension.edu. **Website:** www.uclaextension.edu/writers. **Contact:** Katy Flaherty. Estab. 1997.

COSTS Feeis $775/$700 (early enrollment). Information on overnight accommodations is available.

ADDITIONAL INFORMATION For more information, call or e-mail.

NORTHWEST

CLARION WEST WRITERS WORKSHOP

P.O. Box 31264, Seattle WA 98103-1264. (206)322-9083. **E-mail:** info@clarionwest.org. **Website:** www.clarionwest.org. **Contact:** Leslie Howle, workshop director.

COSTS $3200 (for tuition, housing, most meals). Limited scholarships are available based on financial need.

ACCOMMODATIONS Workshop tuition, dormitory housing and most meals: $3,200. Students stay on-site in workshop housing at one of the University of Washington's sorority houses. "Students write their own stories every week while preparing critiques of all the other students' work for classroom sessions. This gives participants a more focused, professional approach to their writing. The core of the workshop remains speculative fiction, and short stories (not novels) are the focus." Conference information available in Fall. For brochure/guidelines send SASE, visit website, e-mail or call. Accepts inquiries by e-mail, phone, SASE. Limited scholarships are available, based on financial need. Students must submit 20-30 pages of ms with 4-page biography and $40 fee ($30 if received prior to Feb. 10) for applications sent by mail or e-mail to qualify for admission.

ADDITIONAL INFORMATION This is a critique-based workshop. Students are encouraged to write a story every week; the critique of student material produced at the workshop forms the principal activity of the workshop. Students and instructors critique mss as a group. Conference guidelines are available for a SASE. Visit the website for updates and complete details.

FLATHEAD RIVER WRITERS CONFERENCE

P.O. Box 7711, Kalispell MT 59904-7711. **E-mail:** answers@authorsoftheflathead.org. **Website:** www.authorsoftheflathead.org. Estab. 1990.

ACCOMMODATIONS Rooms are available at a discounted rate.

ADDITIONAL INFORMATION Come prepared to learn from renowned speakers and enjoy this spectacular area near Glacier National Park. Confirmed presenters for Oct. 1-2, 2011: Agents Deborah Herman of The Jeff Herman Agency, Katharine Sand of the Sarah Jane Freymann Literary Agency, children's book author Kathi Appelt, best-selling memoir author Laura Munson. Watch our website for additional speakers and other details. Register early as seating is limited.

THE GLEN WORKSHOP

Image, 3307 Third Ave. W., Seattle WA 98119. (206)281-2988. **Fax:** (206)281-2335. **E-mail:** glenworkshop@imagejournal.org; jmullins@imagejournal.org. **Website:** www.imagejournal.org/glen. Estab. 1991. Registration for the 2010 Glen Workshop is open until the deadline of June 1. Some workshops are already full, so consider registering soon to ensure a place in your workshop of choice. Writing classes. Art classes. A seminar on arts and aesthetics. A retreat option. The Glen Workshop combines an intensive learning experience with a lively festival of the arts. It takes place in the stark, dramatic beauty of the Sangre de Cristo mountains and within easy reach of the rich cultural, artistic, and spiritual traditions of northern New Mexico. Estab. 1991. Annual. Held first full week in August. 2010: August 1-8, Santa Fe, NM. Theme: Creativity from the Margins: Art as Witness. Conference duration: 1 week. Average attendance: 150-200. Workshop focuses on "fiction, poetry, spiritual writing, songwriting, playwriting, painting, drawing, and mixed media. Run by Image, a literary journal with a religious focus. The Glen welcomes writers who practice or grapple with religious faith." Site: features "presentations and readings by the faculty." Faculty has included Lauren F. Winner (spiritual writing), B.H. Fairchild and Marilyn Nelson (poetry), Mark St. Germain (playwriting), and Over the Rhine (songwriting).

COSTS See costs online. A limited number of partial scholarships are available.

ACCOMMODATIONS Offers dorm rooms, dorm suites, and apartments.

ADDITIONAL INFORMATION Like *Image*, the Glen is grounded in a Christian perspective, but its tone is informal and hospitable to all spiritual wayfarers. Depending on the teacher, participants may need to submit workshop material prior to arrival (usually 10-25 pages).

HEART TALK

Women's Center for Ministry, Western Seminary, 5511 SE Hawthorne Blvd., Portland OR 97215-3367. (800)517-1800, ext. 1931. **Fax:** (503)517-1889. **E-mail:** wcm@westernseminary.edu. **Website:** www.western-seminary.edu/women. Estab. 1998.

ACCOMMODATIONS Western Seminary has a chapel and classrooms to accommodate various size groups. The campus has a peaceful, park-like setting with beautiful lawns, trees, and flowers, plus an inviting fountain and pond. Please check website for further details as they become available.

ADDITIONAL INFORMATION Conference information is available online, by e-mail, phone, or fax.

JACKSON HOLE WRITERS CONFERENCE

PO Box 1974, Jackson WY 83001. (307)413-3332. **E-mail:** nicole@jacksonholewritersconference.com. **Website:** www.jacksonholewritersconference.com. Estab. 1991.

COSTS $355-385, includes all workshops, speaking events, cocktail party, BBQ, and goodie bag with dining coupons. $75 spouse/guest registration; $50 ms evaluation; $75 extended ms evaluation. "You must register for conference to be eligible for ms evaluation."

ADDITIONAL INFORMATION Held at the Center for the Arts in Jackson, Wyoming and online.

NORTH CASCADES INSTITUTE 2011 WRITING RETREATS

North Cascades Institute, 810 Highway 20, Secro-Wooley WA 98284-9394. (360)856-5700 ext. 209. **Fax:** (360)859-1934. **E-mail:** nci@ncascades.org. **Website:** www.ncascades.org. **Contact:** Deb Martin, registrar. Estab. 1999.

COSTS North Cascades Environmental Learning Center. Cost ranges from $275-515 depending on accommodations.

OUTDOOR WRITERS ASSOCIATION OF AMERICA ANNUAL CONFERENCE

615 Oak St., Suite 201, Missoula MT 59801. (406)728-7434. **E-mail:** info@owaa.org; rginer@owaa.org. **Website:** http://owaa.org. **Contact:** Rboin Giner, meeting planner.

WILLAMETTE WRITERS CONFERENCE

2108 Buck St., Portland OR 97068. (503)305-6729. **Fax:** (503)452-0372. **E-mail:** wilwrite@willamette-writers.com. **Website:** www.willamettewriters.com. Estab. 1981.

COSTS Pricing schedule available online.

ACCOMMODATIONS If necessary, arrangements can be made on an individual basis. Special rates may be available.

ADDITIONAL INFORMATION Brochure/guidelines are available for a catalog-sized SASE.

CANADA

BLOODY WORDS MYSTERY CONFERENCE

12 Roundwood Court, Toronto ON M1W 1Z2 Canada. (416)497-5293. **E-mail:** soles@sff.net. **Website:** www.bloodywords.com. **Contact:** Caro Soles, chair. Estab. 1999.

COSTS $175 (Includes the banquet and all panels, readings, dealers' room and workshop.)

ACCOMMODATIONS Offers block of rooms in hotel; list of optional lodging available. Check website for details.

ADDITIONAL INFORMATION Sponsors short mystery story contest—5,000 word limit; judges are experienced editors of anthologies; fee is $5 (entrants must be registered). Conference information is available now. For brochure visit website. Accepts inquiries by e-mail and phone. Agents and editors participate in conference. "This is a conference for both readers and writers of mysteries, the only one of its kind in Canada. We also run 'The Mystery Cafe,' a chance to get to know a dozen or so authors, hear them read and ask questions (half hour each)."

BOOMING GROUND ONLINE WRITERS STUDIO

Buch E-462, 1866 Main Mall, UBC, Vancouver BC V6T 1Z1 Canada. **Fax:** (604)648-8848. **E-mail:** contact@boomingground.com. **Website:** www.booming-ground.com. **Contact:** Jordan Hall, director.

MARITIME WRITERS' WORKSHOP

UNB College of Extended Learning, P.O. Box 4400, Fredericton NB E3B 5A3 Canada. (506)458-7106. **E-mail:** bpaynter@unb.ca. **Website:** www.unb.ca/cel/programs/creative/maritime-writers/index.html. **Contact:** Beth Paynter, coordinator.

SAGE HILL WRITING EXPERIENCE

Box 1731, Saskatoon SK S7K 2Z4 Canada. (306)652-7395. **E-mail:** sage.hill@sasktel.net. **Website:** www.sagehillwriting.ca. **Contact:** Paula Jane Remlinger.

COSTS Summer program: $1,095 (includes instruction, accommodation, meals). Fall Poetry Colloquium: $1,375. Scholarships and bursaries are available.

ACCOMMODATIONS Located at Lumsden, 45 kilometers outside Regina.

ADDITIONAL INFORMATION For Introduction to Creative Writing, send a 5-page sample of your writing or a statement of your interest in creative writing and a list of courses taken. For workshop and colloquium programs, send a résumé of your writing career and a 12-page sample of your work, plus 5 pages of published work. Guidelines are available for SASE. Inquire via e-mail or fax.

○ SASKATCHEWAN FESTIVAL OF WORDS

217 Main St. N., Moose Jaw SK S6J 0W1 Canada. **Website:** www.festivalofwords.com. Estab. 1997.

ACCOMMODATIONS Available at www.templegardens.sk.ca, campgrounds, and bed and breakfast establishments. Complete information about festival presenters, events, costs, and schedule available on website.

INTERNATIONAL

DINGLE WRITING COURSES

Ballintlea, Ventry Co Kerry Ireland. (353)(66)915-9815. **E-mail:** info@dinglewritingcourses.ie. **Website:** www.dinglewritingcourses.ie. Estab. 1996.

COSTS 420-445 euros. Some bursaries are available from county arts officers.

ACCOMMODATIONS Provides overnight accommodations.

ADDITIONAL INFORMATION Some workshops require material to be submitted in advance. Accepts inquiries by e-mail, phone, and fax.

PUBLISHERS & THEIR IMPRINTS

///

The publishing world is in constant transition. With all the buying, selling, reorganizing, consolidating, and dissolving, it's hard to keep publishers and their imprints straight. To help make sense of these changes, here's a breakdown of major publishers (and their divisions)—who owns whom and which imprints are under each company umbrella. Keep in mind that this information changes frequently. The website of each publisher is provided to help you keep an eye on this ever-evolving business.

HACHETTE BOOK GROUP USA

www.hachettebookgroup.com

CENTER STREET

FAITHWORDS

GRAND CENTRAL PUBLISHING

- Business Plus
- 5 Spot
- Forever
- Forever Yours
- GCP African American
- Grand Central Life & Style
- Twelve
- Vision

HACHETTE BOOK GROUP DIGITAL MEDIA

Hachette Audio

LITTLE, BROWN AND COMPANY

- Back Bay Books
- Bulfinch
- Mulholland Books
- Reagan Arthur Books

LITTLE, BROWN BOOKS FOR YOUNG READERS

- LB Kids
- Poppy

ORBIT

YEN PRESS

HARLEQUIN ENTERPRISES

www.harlequin.com

HARLEQUIN

Harlequin American Romance

Harlequin Bianca

Harlequin Blaze

Harlequin Deseo

Harlequin Historical

Harlequin Intrigue

Harlequin Tiffany

Harlequin Teen

Harlequin Medical Romance

Harlequin NASCAR

Harlequin Presents

Harlequin Romance

Harlequin Superromance

Harlequin eBooks

Harlequin Special Releases

Harlequin Nonfiction

Harlequin Historical Undone

HQN BOOKS

LUNA

MIRA

KIMANI PRESS

Kimani Press Arabesque

Kimani Press Kimani Romance

Kimani Press Kimani TRU

Kimani Press New Spirit

Kimani Press Sepia

Kimani Press Special Releases

Kimani Press eBooks

RED DRESS INK

SILHOUETTE

Silhouette Desire

Silhouette Nocturne

Silhouette Nocturne Bites

Silhouette Romantic Suspense

Silhouette Special Edition

Silhouette eBooks

SPICE

SPICE Books

SPICE Briefs

STEEPLE HILL

Steeple Hill Café©

Steeple Hill Love Inspired

Steeple Hill Love Inspired Historical

Steeple Hill Love Inspired Suspense

Steeple Hill Women's Fiction

Steeple Hill eBooks

WORLDWIDE LIBRARY

Rogue Angel

Worldwide Mystery

Worldwilde Library eBooks

HARLEQUIN CANADA

HARLEQUIN U.K.

Mills & Boon

HARPERCOLLINS

www.harpercollins.com

HARPERCOLLINS GENERAL BOOKS GROUP

Amistad

Avon

Avon Inspire

Avon Red

Broadside Books

Caedmon

Collins Design

Ecco

Harper

Harper Business

Harper Design

Harper Luxe

Harper paperbacks

Harper Perennial

Harper Perennial Modern Classics

Harper Voyager

HarperAudio

HarperBibles

HarperCollins e-Books

HarperOne

ItBooks

Rayo

William Morrow

HARPERCOLLINS CHILDREN'S BOOKS

Amistad

Balzer + Bray

Collins

Greenwillow Books

HarperCollins Children's Audio

HarperFestival

HarperTeen

Rayo

Katherine Tegen Books

Walden Pond Press

HARPERCOLLINS U.K.

Fourth Estate

HarperPress

HarperPerennial

The Friday Project

HarperThorsons/Element

HarperNonFiction

HarperTrue

HarperSport

HarperFiction

Voyager

Blue Door

Angry Robot

Avon U.K.

HarperCollins Childrens Books

Collins

Collins Geo

Collins Education

Collins Language

HARPERCOLLINS CANADA

HarperCollinsPublishers

Collins Canada

HarperPerennial Canada

HarperTrophyCanada

Phyllis Bruce Books

HARPERCOLLINS AUSTRALIA

HarperCollins

Angus & Robertson

HarperSports

Fourth Estate

Harper Perennial

Collins

Voyager

HARPERCOLLINS INDIA

HARPERCOLLINS NEW ZEALAND

HarperCollins

HarperSports

Flamingo

Voyager

Perennial

ZONDERVAN

Zonderkids

Editorial Vida

Youth Specialties

MACMILLAN US (HOLTZBRINCK)

http://us.macmillan.com

MACMILLAN

Farrar, Straus & Giroux

Faber and Faber, Inc

Farrar, Straus

Hill & Wang

HENRY HOLT & CO.

Henry Holt Books for Young Readers

Holt Paperbacks

Metropolitan

Times

MACMILLAN CHILDREN'S

Feiwel & Friends

Farrar, Straus and Giroux Books
    for Young Readers

Kingfisher

Holt Books for Young Readers

Priddy Books

Roaring Brook Press

First Second

Square Fish

PICADOR

PALGRAVE MACMILLAN

TOR/FORGE BOOKS

Tor

Forge

Orb

Tor/Seven Seas

ST. MARTIN'S PRESS

Minotaur Press

Thomas Dunne Books

BEDFORD, FREEMAN & WORTH
PUBLISHING GROUP

BEDFORD/ST. MARTIN'S

HAYDEN-MCNEIL

W.H. FREEMAN

WORTH PUBLISHERS

MACMILLAN KIDS

YOUNG LISTENERS

MACMILLAN AUDIO

PENGUIN GROUP (USA), INC.

www.penguingroup.com

PENGUIN ADULT DIVISION

Ace

Alpha

Amy Einhorn Books/Putnam

Avery

Berkley

Blue Rider Press

Current

Dutton

G.P. Putnam's Sons

Gotham

HP Books

Hudson Street Press

Jove

NAL

Pamela Dorman Books

Penguin

Penguin Press

Perigree

Plume

Portfolio

Prentice Hall Press

RIVERHEAD

Sentinel

Tarcher

Viking Press

Price Stern Sloan

YOUNG READERS DIVISION

Dial Books for Young Readers

Dutton Children's Books

Firebird

Frederick Warne

G.P. Putnam's Sons Books for Young Readers

Grosset & Dunlap

Philomel

PUFFIN BOOKS

Razorbill

Speak

Viking Books for Young Readers

RANDOM HOUSE, INC. (BERTELSMANN)

www.randomhouse.com

CROWN PUBLISHING GROUP

Amphoto Books

Backstage Books

Billboard Books

Broadway Business

Clarkson Potter

Crown

Crown Archetype

Crown Business

Crown Forum

Doubleday Religion

Harmony

Image Books

Potter Craft

Potter Style

Ten Speed Press

Three Rivers Press

Waterbrook Multnomah

Watson-Guptill

KNOPF DOUBLEDAY PUBLISHING GROUP

Alfred A. Knopf

Anchor Books

Doubleday

Everyman's Library

Nan A. Talese

Pantheon Books

Schocken Books

Vintage

RANDOM HOUSE PUBLISHING GROUP

Ballantine Books

Bantam

Del Rey

Del Rey/Lucas Books

Del Rey/Manga

Delacorte

Dell

The Dial Press

The Modern Library

One World

Presidio Press

Random House Trade Group

Random House Trade Paperbacks

Spectra

Spiegel and Grau

Triumph Books

Villard Books

RANDOM HOUSE AUDIO PUBLISHING GROUP

Listening Library

Random House Audio

RANDOM HOUSE CHILDREN'S BOOKS

Kids@Random

Golden Books

Princeton Review

Sylvan Learning

RANDOM HOUSE DIGITAL PUBLISHING GROUP

Books on Tape

Fodor's Travel

Living Language

Listening Library

Random House Audio

RH Large Print

RANDOM HOUSE INTERNATIONAL
- RH Australia
- RH of Canada Limited
- RH India
- RH Mondadori
- RH New Zealand
- RH South America
- RH Group (UK)
- Transworld Ireland
- Verlagsgruppe RH

SIMON & SCHUSTER

www.simonandschuster.com

SIMON & SCHUSTER ADULT PUBLISHING
- Atria Books/Beyond Words
- Folger Shakespeare Library
- Free Press
- Gallery Books
- Howard Books
- Pocket Books
- Scribner
- Simon & Schuster
- Threshold Editions
- The Touchstone & Fireside Group
- Pimsleur
- Simon & Schuster Audioworks

SIMON & SCHUSTER CHILDREN'S PUBLISHING
- Aladdin Paperbacks
- Atheneum Books for Young Readers
- Bench Lane Books
- Little Simon®
- Margaret K. McElderry Books
- Paula Wiseman Books
- Simon & Schuster Books for Young Readers
- Simon Pulse
- Simon Spotlight®

SIMON & SCHUSTER INTERNATIONAL
- Simon & Schuster Australia
- Simon & Schuster Canada
- Simon & Schuster UK

GLOSSARY

ADVANCE. Payment by a publisher to an author prior to the publication of a book, to be deducted from the author's future royalties.

ADVENTURE STORY. A genre of fiction in which action is the key element, overshadowing characters, theme, and setting. The conflict in an adventure story is often man against nature. A secondary plot that reinforces this kind of conflict is sometimes included.

ALL RIGHTS. The rights contracted to a publisher permitting a manuscript's use anywhere and in any form, including movie and book club sales, without additional payment to the writer.

AMATEUR SLEUTH. The character in a mystery, usually the protagonist, who does the detection but is not a professional private investigator or police detective.

ANTHOLOGY. A collection of selected writings by various authors.

ASSOCIATION OF AUTHORS' REPRESENTATIVES (AAR). An organization for literary agents committed to maintaining excellence in literary representation.

AUCTION. Publishers sometimes bid against each other for the acquisition of a manuscript that has excellent sales prospects.

BACKLIST. A publisher's books not published during the current season but still in print.

BIOGRAPHICAL NOVEL. A life story documented in history and transformed into fiction through the insight and imagination of the writer. This type of novel melds the elements of biographical research and historical truth into the framework of a novel, complete with dialogue, drama, and mood. A biographical novel resembles historical fiction, save for one aspect: Characters in a historical novel may be fabricated and then placed into an authentic setting; characters in a biographical novel have actually lived.

BOOK PRODUCER/PACKAGER. An organization that may develop a book for a publisher based upon the publisher's idea or may plan all elements of a book, from its initial concept to writing and marketing strategies, and then sell the package to a book publisher and/or movie producer.

CLIFFHANGER. Fictional event in which the reader is left in suspense at the end of a chapter or episode, so that interest in the story's outcome will be sustained.

CLIP. Sample, usually from a newspaper or magazine, of a writer's published work.

CLOAK-AND-DAGGER. A melodramatic, romantic type of fiction dealing with espionage and intrigue.

COMMERCIAL. Publishers whose concern is salability, profit, and success with a large readership.

CONTEMPORARY. Material dealing with popular current trends, themes, or topics.

CONTRIBUTOR'S COPY. Copy of an issue of a magazine or published book sent to an author whose work is included.

COPUBLISHING. An arrangement in which the author and publisher share costs and profits.

COPYEDITING. Editing a manuscript for writing style, grammar, punctuation and factual accuracy.

COPYRIGHT. The legal right to exclusive publication, sale, or distribution of a literary work.

COVER LETTER. A brief letter sent with a complete manuscript submitted to an editor.

"COZY" (OR "TEACUP") MYSTERY. Mystery usually set in a small British town, in a bygone era, featuring a somewhat genteel, intellectual protagonist.

ELECTRONIC RIGHTS. The right to publish material electronically, either in book or short story form.

ELECTRONIC SUBMISSION. A submission of material by e-mail or on computer disk.

ETHNIC FICTION. Stories whose central characters are black, Native American, Italian-American, Jewish, Appalachian, or members of some other specific cultural group.

EXPERIMENTAL FICTION. Fiction that is innovative in subject matter and style; avant-garde, non-formulaic, usually literary material.

EXPOSITION. The portion of the story line, usually the beginning, where background information about character and setting is related.

E-ZINE. A magazine that is published electronically.

FAIR USE. A provision in the copyright law that says short passages from copyrighted material may be used without infringing on the owner's rights.

FANZINE. A noncommercial, small-circulation magazine usually dealing with fantasy, horror or science-fiction literature and art.

FICTIONAL BIOGRAPHY. The biography of a real person that goes beyond the events of a person's life by being fleshed out with imagined scenes and dialogue. The writer of fictional biographies strives to make it clear that the story is, indeed, fiction and not history.

FIRST NORTH AMERICAN SERIAL RIGHTS. The right to publish material in a periodical before it appears in book form, for the first time, in the United States or Canada.

FLASH FICTION. See short short stories.

GALLEYS. The first typeset version of a manuscript that has not yet been divided into pages.

GENRE. A formulaic type of fiction such as romance, western, or horror.

GOTHIC. This type of category fiction dates back to the late 18th and early 19th centuries. Contemporary gothic novels are characterized by atmospheric, historical settings and feature young, beautiful women who win the favor of handsome, brooding heroes—simultaneously dealing successfully with some life-threatening menace, either natural or supernatural. Gothics rely on mystery, peril, romantic relationships, and a sense of foreboding for their strong, emotional effect on the reader. A classic early gothic novel is Emily Bronte's *Wuthering Heights*.

GRAPHIC NOVEL. A book (original or adapted) that takes the form of a long comic strip or heavily illustrated story of 40 pages or more, produced in paperback. Though called a novel, these can also be works of nonfiction.

HARD-BOILED DETECTIVE NOVEL. Mystery novel featuring a private eye or police detective as the protagonist; usually involves a murder. The emphasis is on the details of the crime, and the tough, unsentimental protagonist usually takes a matter-of-fact attitude toward violence.

HARD SCIENCE FICTION. Science fiction with an emphasis on science and technology.

HIGH FANTASY. Fantasy with a medieval setting and a heavy emphasis on chivalry and the quest.

HISTORICAL FICTION. A fictional story set in a recognizable period of history. As well as telling the stories of ordinary people's lives, historical fiction may involve political or social events of the time.

HORROR. Howard Phillips (H.P.) Lovecraft, generally acknowledged to be the master of the horror tale in the 20th century and the most important American writer of this genre since Edgar Allan Poe, maintained that "the oldest and strongest emotion of mankind is fear, and the oldest and strongest kind of fear is fear of the unknown. These facts few psychologists will dispute, and their admitted truth must establish for all time the genuineness and dignity of the weirdly horrible tale as a literary form." Lovecraft distinguishes horror literature from fiction based entirely on physical fear and the merely gruesome. It is that atmosphere—the creation of a particular sensation or emotional level—that, according to Lovecraft, is the most important element in the creation of horror literature. Contemporary writers enjoying considerable success in horror fiction include Stephen King, Robert Bloch, Peter Straub, and Dean Koontz.

HYPERTEXT FICTION. A fictional form, read electronically, which incorporates traditional elements of storytelling with a nonlinear plot line, in which the reader determines the direction of the story by opting for one of many author-supplied links.

IMPRINT. Name applied to a publisher's specific line (e.g. Owl, an imprint of Henry Holt).

INTERACTIVE FICTION. Fiction in book or computer-software format where the reader determines the path the story will take by choosing from several alternatives at the end of each chapter or episode.

INTERNATIONAL REPLY COUPON (IRC). A form purchased at a post office and enclosed with a letter or manuscript to an international publisher, to cover return postage costs.

JUVENILES, WRITING FOR. This includes works intended for an audience usually between the ages of 2 and 18. Categories of children's books are usually divided in this way: (1) picture books and storybooks (ages 2 to 8); (2) young readers or easy-to-read books (ages 5 to 8); (3) middle readers or middle grade (ages 9 to 11); (4) young adult books (ages 12 and up).

LIBEL. Written or printed words that defame, malign, or damagingly misrepresent a living person.

LITERARY AGENT. A person who acts for an author in finding a publisher or arranging contract terms on a literary project.

LITERARY FICTION. The general category of fiction that employs more sophisticated technique, driven as much or more by character evolution than action in the plot.

MAINSTREAM FICTION. Fiction that appeals to a more general reading audience, versus literary or genre fiction. Mainstream is more plot-driven than literary fiction and less formulaic than genre fiction.

MALICE DOMESTIC NOVEL. A mystery featuring a murder among family members, such as the murder of a spouse or a parent.

MANUSCRIPT. The author's unpublished copy of a work, usually typewritten, used as the basis for typesetting.

MASS MARKET PAPERBACK. Softcover book on a popular subject, usually around 4×7, directed to a general audience and sold in drugstores and groceries as well as in bookstores.

MIDDLE READER. Also called *middle grade*. Juvenile fiction for readers aged 9 to 11.

MS(S). Abbreviation for *manuscript(s)*.

MULTIPLE SUBMISSION. Submission of more than one short story at a time to the same editor. Do not make a multiple submission unless requested.

MYSTERY. A form of narration in which one or more elements remain unknown or unexplained until the end of the story. The modern mystery story contains elements of the serious novel: a convincing account of a character's struggle with various physical and psychological obstacles in an effort to achieve his goal, good characterization, and sound motivation.

NARRATION. The account of events in a story's plot as related by the speaker or the voice of the author.

NARRATOR. The person who tells the story, either someone involved in the action or the voice of the writer.

NEW AGE. A term including categories such as astrology, psychic phenomena, spiritual healing, UFOs, mysticism, and other aspects of the occult.

NOIR. A style of mystery involving hard-boiled detectives and bleak settings.

NOM DE PLUME. French for "pen name"; a pseudonym.

NONFICTION NOVEL. A work in which real events and people are written [about] in novel form, but are not camouflaged, as they are in the roman à clef. In the nonfiction novel, reality is presented imaginatively; the writer imposes a novelistic structure on the actual events, keying sections of narrative around moments that are seen (in retrospect) as symbolic. In this way, he creates a coherence that the actual story might not have had. *The Executioner's Song*, by Norman Mailer, and *In Cold Blood*, by Truman Capote, are notable examples of the nonfiction novel.

NOVELLA (ALSO NOVELETTE). A short novel or long story, approximately 20,000-50,000 words.

#10 ENVELOPE. 4×9½ envelope, used for queries and other business letters.

OFFPRINT. Copy of a story taken from a magazine before it is bound.

ONETIME RIGHTS. Permission to publish a story in periodical or book form one time only.

OUTLINE. A summary of a book's contents, often in the form of chapter headings with a few sentences outlining the action of the story under each one; sometimes part of a book proposal.

OVER THE TRANSOM. A phrase referring to unsolicited manuscripts, or those that come in "over the transom.'"

PAYMENT ON ACCEPTANCE. Payment from the magazine or publishing house as soon as the decision to print a manuscript is made.

PAYMENT ON PUBLICATION. Payment from the publisher after a manuscript is printed.

PEN NAME. A pseudonym used to conceal a writer's real name.

PERIODICAL. A magazine or journal published at regular intervals.

PLOT. The carefully devised series of events through which the characters progress in a work of fiction.

POPULAR FICTION. Generally, a synonym for category or genre fiction; i.e., fiction intended to appeal to audiences for certain kinds of novels. Popular, or category, fiction is defined as such primarily for the convenience of publishers, editors, reviewers, and booksellers who must identify novels of different areas of interest for potential readers.

PRINT ON DEMAND (POD). Novels produced digitally one at a time, as ordered. Self-publishing through print on demand technology typically involves some fees for the author.

Some authors use POD to create a manuscript in book form to send to prospective traditional publishers.

PROOFREADING. Close reading and correction of a manuscript's typographical errors.

PROOFS. A typeset version of a manuscript used for correcting errors and making changes, often a photocopy of the galleys.

PROPOSAL. An offer to write a specific work, usually consisting of an outline of the work and one or two completed chapters.

PROTAGONIST. The principal or leading character in a literary work.

PSYCHOLOGICAL NOVEL. A narrative that emphasizes the mental and emotional aspects of its characters, focusing on motivations and mental activities rather than on exterior events. The psychological novelist is less concerned about relating what happened than about exploring why it happened. The term is most often used to describe 20th-century works that employ techniques such as interior monologue and stream of consciousness. Two examples of contemporary psychological novels are Judith Guest's *Ordinary People* and Mary Gordon's *The Company of Women*.

PUBLIC DOMAIN. Material that either was never copyrighted or whose copyright term has expired.

PULP MAGAZINE. A periodical printed on inexpensive paper, usually containing lurid, sensational stories or articles.

QUERY. A letter written to an editor to elicit interest in a story the writer wants to submit.

READER. A person hired by a publisher to read unsolicited manuscripts.

READING FEE. An arbitrary amount of money charged by some agents and publishers to read a submitted manuscript.

REGENCY ROMANCE. A subgenre of romance, usually set in England between 1811 and 1820.

REMAINDERS. Leftover copies of an out-of-print book, sold by the publisher at a reduced price.

REPORTING TIME. The number of weeks or months it takes an editor to report back on an author's query or manuscript.

REPRINT RIGHTS. Permission to print an already published work whose rights have been sold to another magazine or book publisher.

ROMAN À CLEF. French "novel with a key." A novel that represents actual living or historical characters and events in fictionalized form.

ROMANCE NOVEL. A type of category fiction in which the love relationship between a man and a woman pervades the plot. The story is often told from the viewpoint of the heroine, who meets a man (the hero), falls in love with him, encounters a conflict that hinders their relationship, then resolves the conflict. Romance is the overriding element in this kind of story: The couple's relationship determines the plot and tone of the book.

ROYALTIES. A percentage of the retail price paid to an author for each copy of the book that is sold.

SAE. Self-addressed envelope.

SASE. Self-addressed stamped envelope.

SCIENCE FICTION [VS. FANTASY]. It is generally accepted that, to be science fiction, a story must have elements of science in either the conflict or setting (usually both). Fantasy, on the other hand, rarely utilizes science, relying instead on magic, mythological and neomythological beings, and devices and outright invention for conflict and setting.

SECOND SERIAL (REPRINT) RIGHTS. Permission for the reprinting of a work in another periodical after its first publication in book or magazine form.

SELF-PUBLISHING. In this arrangement, the author keeps all income derived from the book, but he pays for its manufacturing, production, and marketing.

SERIAL RIGHTS. The rights given by an author to a publisher to print a piece in one or more periodicals.

SERIALIZED NOVEL. A book-length work of fiction published in sequential issues of a periodical.

SETTING. The environment and time period during which the action of a story takes place.

SHORT SHORT STORY. A condensed piece of fiction, usually under 1,000 words.

SIMULTANEOUS SUBMISSION. The practice of sending copies of the same manuscript to several editors or publishers at the same time. Some editors refuse to consider such submissions.

SLANT. A story's particular approach or style, designed to appeal to the readers of a specific magazine.

SLICE OF LIFE. A presentation of characters in a seemingly mundane situation that offers the reader a flash of illumination about the characters or their situation.

SLUSH PILE. A stack of unsolicited manuscripts in the editorial offices of a publisher.

SOCIAL FICTION. Fiction written with the purpose of bringing positive changes in society.

SOFT/SOCIOLOGICAL SCIENCE FICTION. Science fiction with an emphasis on society and culture versus scientific accuracy.

SPACE OPERA. Epic science fiction with an emphasis on good guys versus bad guys.

SPECULATION (OR SPEC). An editor's agreement to look at an author's manuscript with no promise to purchase.

SPECULATIVE FICTION (SPECFIC). The all-inclusive term for science fiction, fantasy, and horror.

SUBSIDIARY. An incorporated branch of a company or conglomerate (e.g. Alfred Knopf, Inc., a subsidiary of Random House, Inc.).

SUBSIDIARY RIGHTS. All rights other than book publishing rights included in a book contract, such as paperback, book club, and movie rights.

SUBSIDY PUBLISHER. A book publisher who charges the author for the cost of typesetting, printing, and promoting a book. Also called a *vanity publisher*.

SUBTERFICIAL FICTION. Innovative, challenging, nonconventional fiction in which what seems to be happening is the result of things not so easily perceived.

SUSPENSE. A genre of fiction where the plot's primary function is to build a feeling of anticipation and fear in the reader over its possible outcome.

SYNOPSIS. A brief summary of a story, novel or play. As part of a book proposal, it is a comprehensive summary condensed in a page or page and a half.

TABLOID. Publication printed on paper about half the size of a regular newspaper page (e.g. the *National Enquirer*).

TEARSHEET. Page from a magazine containing a published story.

THEME. The dominant or central idea in a literary work; its message, moral, or main thread.

THRILLER. A novel intended to arouse feelings of excitement or suspense. Works in this genre are highly sensational, usually focusing on illegal activities, international espionage, sex, and violence. A thriller is often a detective story in which the forces of good are pitted against the forces of evil in a kill-or-be-killed situation.

TRADE PAPERBACK. A softbound volume, usually around 5x8, published and designed for the general public, available mainly in bookstores.

TRADITIONAL FANTASY. Fantasy with an emphasis on magic, using characters with the ability to practice magic, such as wizards, witches, dragons, elves, and unicorns.

UNSOLICITED MANUSCRIPT. A story or novel manuscript that an editor did not specifically ask to see.

URBAN FANTASY. Fantasy that takes magical characters, such as elves, fairies, vampires, or wizards, and places them in modern-day settings, often in the inner city.

VANITY PUBLISHER. See subsidy publisher.

VIEWPOINT. The position or attitude of the first- or third-person narrator or multiple narrators, which determines how a story's action is seen and evaluated.

WESTERN. Genre with a setting in the West, usually between 1860 and 1890, with a formula plot about cowboys or other aspects of frontier life.

WHODUNIT. Genre dealing with murder, suspense, and the detection of criminals.

WORK-FOR-HIRE. Work that another party commissions you to do, generally for a flat fee. The creator does not own the copyright and therefore cannot sell any rights.

YOUNG ADULT. The general classification of books written for readers 12 and up.

ZINE. Often one- or two-person operations run from the home of the publisher/editor. Themes tend to be specialized, personal, experimental, and often controversial.

GENRE GLOSSARY

Definitions of Fiction Subcategories

//

The following were provided courtesy of The Extended Novel Writing Workshop, created by the staff of Writers Online Workshops (www.writersonlineworkshops.com).

MYSTERY SUBCATEGORIES

The major mystery subcategories are listed below, each followed by a brief description and the names of representative authors, so you can sample each type of work. Note that we have loosely classified "suspense/thriller" as a mystery category. While these stories do not necessarily follow a traditional "whodunit" plot pattern, they share many elements with other mystery categories.

AMATEUR DETECTIVE. As the name implies, the detective is not a professional detective (private or otherwise), but is almost always a professional something. This professional association routinely involves the protagonist in criminal cases (in a support capacity), gives him or her a special advantage in a specific case, or provides the contacts and skills necessary to solve a particular crime. (Jonathan Kellerman, Patricia Cornwell, Jan Burke)

CLASSIC MYSTERY (WHODUNIT). A crime (almost always a murder) is solved. The detective is the viewpoint character; the reader never knows any more or less about the crime than the detective, and all the clues to solving the crime are available to the reader.

COURTROOM DRAMA. The action takes place primarily in the courtroom; protagonist is generally a defense attorney out to prove the innocence of his or her client by finding the real culprit.

COZY. A special class of the amateur detective category that frequently features a female protagonist. (Agatha Christie's Miss Marple stories are the classic example.) There is less onstage violence than in other categories, and the plot is often wrapped up in a final scene where the detective identifies the murderer and explains how the crime was solved. In contemporary stories, the protagonist can be anyone from a chronically curious housewife to a mystery-buff clergyman to a college professor, but he or she is usually quirky, even eccentric. (Susan Isaacs, Andrew Greeley, Lillian Jackson Braun)

ESPIONAGE. The international spy novel is less popular since the end of the cold war, but stories can still revolve around political intrigue in unstable regions. (John le Carré, Ken Follett)

HEISTS AND CAPERS. The crime itself is the focus. Its planning and execution are seen in detail, and the participants are fully drawn characters that may even be portrayed sympathetically. One character is the obvious leader of the group (the ``brains''); the other members are often brought together by the leader specifically for this job and may or may not have a previous association. In a heist, no matter how clever or daring the characters are, they are still portrayed as criminals, and the expectation is that they will be caught and punished (but not always). A caper is more lighthearted, even comedic. The participants may have a noble goal (something other than personal gain) and often get away with the crime. (Eric Ambler, Tony Kenrick, Leslie Hollander)

HISTORICAL. May be any category or subcategory of mystery, but with an emphasis on setting, the details of which must be diligently researched. But beyond the historical details (which must never overshadow the story), the plot develops along the lines of its contemporary counterpart. (Candace Robb, Caleb Carr, Anne Perry)

JUVENILE/YOUNG ADULT. Written for the 8-12 age group (Middle Grade) or the 12 and up age group (Young Adult), the crime in these stories may or may not be murder, but it is serious. The protagonist is a kid (or group of kids) in the same age range as the targeted reader. There is no graphic violence depicted, but the stories are scary and the villains are realistic. (Mary Downing Hahn, Wendy Corsi Staub, Cameron Dokey, Norma Fox Mazer)

MEDICAL THRILLER. The plot can involve a legitimate medical threat (such as the outbreak of a virulent plague) or the illegal or immoral use of medical technology. In the former scenario, the protagonist is likely to be the doctor (or team) who identifies the virus and procures the antidote; in the latter he or she could be a patient (or the relative of a victim) who uncovers the plot and brings down the villain. (Robin Cook, Michael Palmer, Michael Crichton, Stanley Pottinger)

POLICE PROCEDURALS. The most realistic category, these stories require the most meticulous research. A police procedural may have more than one protagonist since cops rarely work alone. Conflict between partners, or between the detective and his or her superiors, is a common theme. But cops are portrayed positively as a group, even though there may be a couple of bad or ineffective law enforcement characters for contrast and conflict. Jurisdictional disputes are still popular sources of conflict as well. (Lawrence Treat, Joseph Wambaugh, Ridley Pearson, Julie Smith)

PRIVATE DETECTIVE. When described as "hard-boiled," this category takes a tough stance. Violence is more prominent, characters are darker, the detective—while almost always licensed by the state—operates on the fringes of the law, and there is often open resentment between the detective and law enforcement. More "enlightened" male detectives and a crop of contemporary females have brought about new trends in this category. (For female P.I.s—Sue Grafton, Sara Paretsky; for male P.I.s—John D. MacDonald, Lawrence Sanders)

SUSPENSE/THRILLER. Where a classic mystery is always a whodunit, a suspense/thriller novel may deal more with the intricacies of the crime, what motivated it, and how the villain (whose identity may be revealed to the reader early on) is caught and brought to justice. Novels in this category frequently employ multiple points of view and have a broader scope than a more traditional murder mystery. The crime may not even involve murder—it may be a threat to global economy or regional ecology; it may be technology run amok or abused at the hands of an unscrupulous scientist; it may involve innocent citizens victimized for personal or corporate gain. Its perpetrators are kidnappers, stalkers, serial killers, rapists, pedophiles, computer hackers, or just about anyone with an evil intention and the means to carry it out. The protagonist may be a private detective or law enforcement official, but is just as likely to be a doctor, lawyer, military officer, or other individual in a unique position to identify the villain and bring him or her to justice. (James Patterson, John J. Nance)

TECHNO-THRILLER. These are replacing the traditional espionage novel, and feature technology as an integral part of not just the setting, but the plot as well.

WOMAN IN JEOPARDY. A murder or other crime may be committed, but the focus is on the woman (and/or her children) currently at risk, her struggle to understand the nature of the danger, and her eventual victory over her tormentor. The protagonist makes up for her lack of physical prowess with intellect or special skills, and solves the problem on her own or with the help of her family (but she runs the show). Closely related to this category is the Romantic Suspense. But, while the heroine in a romantic suspense is certainly a "woman in jeopardy,"' the mystery or suspense element is subordinate to the romance. (Mary Higgins Clark, Mary Stewart, Jessica Mann)

ROMANCE SUBCATEGORIES

These categories and subcategories of romance fiction have been culled from the *Romance Writer's Sourcebook* (Writer's Digest Books) and Phyllis Taylor Pianka's *How to Write Romances* (Writer's Digest Books). We've arranged the "major" categories below with the subcategories beneath them, each followed by a brief description and the names of authors who write in each category, so you can sample representative works.

CATEGORY OR SERIES. These are published in "lines" by individual publishing houses (such as Harlequin and Silhouette); each line has its own requirements as to word length, story content, and amount of sex. (Debbie Macomber, Nora Roberts, Glenda Sanders)

CHRISTIAN. With an inspirational, Christian message centering on the spiritual dynamic of the romantic relationship and faith in God as the foundation for that relationship; sensuality is played down. (Janelle Burnham, Ann Bell, Linda Chaikin, Catherine Palmer, Dee Henderson, Lisa Tawn Bergen)

GLITZ. So called because they feature (generally wealthy) characters with high-powered positions in careers that are considered to be glamorous—high finance, modeling/acting, publishing, fashion—and are set in exciting or exotic (often metropolitan) locales, such as Monte Carlo, Hollywood, London, or New York. (Jackie Collins, Judith Krantz)

HISTORICAL. Can cover just about any historical (or even prehistorical) period. Setting in the historical is especially significant, and details must be thoroughly researched and accurately presented. For a sampling of a variety of historical styles, try Laura Kinsell (*Flowers from the Storm*), Mary Jo Putney (*The Rake and the Reformer*) and Judy Cuevas (*Bliss*). Some currently popular periods/themes in historicals are:

- **GOTHIC:** historical with a strong element of suspense and a feeling of supernatural events, although these events frequently have a natural explanation. Setting plays an important role in establishing a dark, moody, suspenseful atmosphere. (Phyllis Whitney, Victoria Holt)

- **HISTORICAL FANTASY:** with traditional fantasy elements of magic and magical beings, frequently set in a medieval society. (Amanda Glass, Jayne Ann Krentz, Kathleen Morgan, Jessica Bryan, Taylor Quinn Evans, Carla Simpson, Karyn Monk)

- **EARLY AMERICAN:** usually Revolution to Civil War, set in New England or the South, but "frontier" stories set in the American West are quite popular as well. (Robin Lee Hatcher, Elizabeth Lowell, Heather Graham)

- **NATIVE AMERICAN:** where one or both of the characters are Native Americans; the conflict between cultures is a popular theme. (Carol Finch, Elizabeth Grayson, Karen Kay, Kathleen Harrington, Genell Dellim, Candace McCarthy)

- **REGENCY:** set in England during the Regency period from 1811 to 1820. (Carol Finch, Elizabeth Elliott, Georgette Heyer, Joan Johnston, Lynn Collum)

MULTICULTURAL. Most currently feature African-American or Hispanic couples, but editors are looking for other ethnic stories as well. Multiculturals can be contemporary or historical, and fall into any subcategory. (Rochelle Alers, Monica Jackson, Bette Ford, Sandra Kitt, Brenda Jackson)

PARANORMAL. Containing elements of the supernatural or science fiction/fantasy. There are numerous subcategories (many stories combine elements of more than one) including:

- **TIME TRAVEL:** One or more of the characters travels to another time—usually the past—to find love. (Jude Devereaux, Linda Lael Miller, Diana Gabaldon, Constance O'Day Flannery)
- **SCIENCE FICTION/FUTURISTIC:** S/F elements are used for the story's setting: imaginary worlds, parallel universes, Earth in the near or distant future. (Marilyn Campbell, Jayne Ann Krentz, J.D. Robb [Nora Roberts], Anne Avery)
- **CONTEMPORARY FANTASY:** From modern ghost and vampire stories to "New Age" themes such as extraterrestrials and reincarnation. (Linda Lael Miller, Anne Stuart, Antoinette Stockenberg, Christine Feehan)

ROMANTIC COMEDY. Has a fairly strong comic premise and/or a comic perspective in the author's voice or the voices of the characters (especially the heroine). (Jennifer Crusie, Susan Elizabeth Phillips)

ROMANTIC SUSPENSE. With a mystery or psychological thriller subplot in addition to the romance plot. (Mary Stewart, Barbara Michaels, Tami Hoag, Nora Roberts, Linda Howard, Catherine Coulter)

SINGLE TITLE. Longer contemporaries that do not necessarily conform to the requirements of a specific romance line and therefore feature more complex plots and nontraditional characters. (Mary Ruth Myers, Nora Roberts, Kathleen Gilles Seidel, Kathleen Korbel)

YOUNG ADULT. Focus is on first love with very little, if any, sex. These can have bittersweet endings, as opposed to the traditional romance happy ending, since first loves are often lost loves. (YA historical—Nancy Covert Smith, Louise Vernon; YA contemporary—Kathryn Makris)

SCIENCE FICTION SUBCATEGORIES

Peter Heck, in his article "Doors to Other Worlds: Trends in Science Fiction and Fantasy," which appears in the 1996 edition of *Science Fiction and Fantasy Writer's Sourcebook* (Writer's Digest Books), identifies some science fiction trends that have distinct enough characteristics to be defined as categories. These distinctions are frequently the result of marketing decisions as much as literary ones, so understanding them is important in deciding where your novel idea belongs. We've supplied a brief description and the names of authors who write in each category. In those instances where the author writes in more than one category, we've included titles of appropriate representative works.

ALTERNATE HISTORY. Fantasy, sometimes with science fiction elements, that changes the accepted account of actual historical events or people to suggest an alternate view of history. (Ted Mooney, *Traffic and Laughter*; Ward Moore, *Bring the Jubilee*; Philip K. Dick, *The Man in the High Castle*)

CYBERPUNK. Characters in these stories are tough outsiders in a high-tech, generally near-future society where computers have produced major changes in the way society functions. (William Gibson, Bruce Sterling, Pat Cadigan, Wilhelmina Baird)

HARD SCIENCE FICTION. Based on the logical extrapolation of real science to the future. In these stories the scientific background (setting) may be as, or more, important than the characters. (Larry Niven)

MILITARY SCIENCE FICTION. Stories about war that feature traditional military organization and tactics extrapolated into the future. (Jerry Pournelle, David Drake, Elizabeth Moon)

NEW AGE. A category of speculative fiction that deals with subjects such as astrology, psychic phenomena, spiritual healing, UFOs, mysticism, and other aspects of the occult. (Walter Mosley, *Blue Light*; Neil Gaiman)

SCIENCE FANTASY. Blend of traditional fantasy elements with scientific or pseudoscientific support (genetic engineering, for example, to "explain" a traditional fantasy creature like the dragon). These stories are traditionally more character driven than hard science fiction. (Anne McCaffrey, Mercedes Lackey, Marion Zimmer Bradley)

SCIENCE FICTION MYSTERY. A cross-genre blending that can either be a more-or-less traditional science fiction story with a mystery as a key plot element, or a more-or-less traditional whodunit with science fiction elements. (Philip K. Dick, Lynn S. Hightower)

SCIENCE FICTION ROMANCE. Another genre blend that may be a romance with science fiction elements (in which case it is more accurately placed as a subcategory within the romance genre) or a science fiction story with a strong romantic subplot. (Anne McCaffrey, Melanie Rawn, Kate Elliot)

SOCIAL SCIENCE FICTION. The focus is on how the characters react to their environments. This category includes social satire. (George Orwell's *1984* is a classic example.) (Margaret Atwood, *The Handmaid's Tale*; Ursula K. Le Guin, *The Left Hand of Darkness*; Marge Piercy, *Woman on the Edge of Time*)

SPACE OPERA. From the term "horse opera," describing a traditional good-guys-versus-bad-guys western, these stories put the emphasis on sweeping action and larger-than-life characters. The focus on action makes these stories especially appealing for film treatment. (The Star Wars series is one of the best examples; also Samuel R. Delany.)

STEAMPUNK. A specific type of alternate history science fiction set in Victorian England in which characters have access to 20th-century technology. (William Gibson; Bruce Sterling, *The Difference Engine*)

YOUNG ADULT. Any subcategory of science fiction geared to a YA audience (12-18), but these are usually shorter novels with characters in the central roles who are the same age as (or slightly older than) the targeted reader. (Jane Yolen, Andre Norton)

FANTASY SUBCATEGORIES

Before we take a look at the individual fantasy categories, it should be noted that, for purposes of these supplements, we've treated fantasy as a genre distinct from science fiction. While these two are closely related, there are significant enough differences to warrant their separation for study purposes. We have included here those science fiction categories that have strong fantasy elements, or that have a significant amount of crossover (these categories appear in both the science fiction and the fantasy supplements), but "pure" science fiction categories are not included below. If you're not sure whether your novel is fantasy or science fiction, consider this definition by Orson Scott Card in *How to Write Science Fiction and Fantasy* (Writer's Digest Books):

"Here's a good, simple, semi-accurate rule of thumb: If the story is set in a universe that follows the same rules as ours, it's science fiction. If it's set in a universe that doesn't follow our rules, it's fantasy.

Or in other words, science fiction is about what could be but isn't; fantasy is about what couldn't be."

But even Card admits this rule is only "semi-accurate." He goes on to say that the real boundary between science fiction and fantasy is defined by how the impossible is achieved: "If you have people do some magic, impossible thing [like time travel] by stroking a talisman or praying to a tree, it's fantasy; if they do the same thing by pressing a button or climbing inside a machine, it's science fiction."

Peter Heck, in his article "Doors to Other Worlds: Trends in Science Fiction and Fantasy," which appears in the 1996 edition of the *Science Fiction and Fantasy Writer's Sourcebook* (Writer's Digest Books), does note some trends that have distinct enough characteristics to be defined as separate categories. These categories are frequently the result of marketing decisions as much as literary ones, so understanding them is important in deciding where your novel idea belongs. We've supplied a brief description and the names of authors who write in each category, so you can sample representative works.

ARTHURIAN. Reworking of the legend of King Arthur and the Knights of the Round Table. (T.H. White, *The Once and Future King*; Marion Zimmer Bradley, *The Mists of Avalon*)

CONTEMPORARY (ALSO CALLED "URBAN") FANTASY. Traditional fantasy elements (such as elves and magic) are incorporated into an otherwise recognizable modern setting. (Emma Bull, *War for the Oaks*; Mercedes Lackey, *The SERRAted Edge*; Terry Brooks, the Knight of the Word series)

DARK FANTASY. Closely related to horror, but generally not as graphic. Characters in these stories are the "darker" fantasy types: vampires, witches, werewolves, demons, etc. (Anne Rice; Clive Barker, *Weaveworld*, *Imajica*; Fred Chappell)

FANTASTIC ALTERNATE HISTORY. Set in an alternate historical period (in which magic would not have been a common belief) where magic works, these stories frequently feature actual historical figures. (Orson Scott Card, *Alvin Maker*)

GAME-RELATED FANTASY. Plots and characters are similar to high fantasy, but are based on a particular role-playing game. (Dungeons and Dragons; Magic: The Gathering; Dragonlance Chronicles; Forgotten Realms; Dark Sun)

HEROIC FANTASY. The fantasy equivalent to military science fiction, these are stories of war and its heroes and heroines. (Robert E. Howard, the Conan the Barbarian series; Elizabeth Moon, *Deed of Paksenarion*; Michael Moorcock, the Elric series)

HIGH FANTASY. Emphasis is on the fate of an entire race or nation, threatened by an ultimate evil. J.R.R. Tolkien's Lord of the Rings trilogy is a classic example. (Terry Brooks, David Eddings, Margaret Weis, Tracy Hickman)

HISTORICAL FANTASY. The setting can be almost any era in which the belief in magic was strong; these are essentially historical novels where magic is a key element of the plot and/or setting. (Susan Schwartz, *Silk Road and Shadow*; Margaret Ball, *No Earthly Sunne*; Tim Powers, *The Anubis Gates*)

JUVENILE/YOUNG ADULT. Can be any type of fantasy, but geared to a juvenile (8-12) or YA audience (12-18); these are shorter novels with younger characters in central roles. (J.K. Rowling, Christopher Paolini, C.S. Lewis)

SCIENCE FANTASY. A blend of traditional fantasy elements with scientific or pseudoscientific support (genetic engineering, for example, to "explain" a traditional fantasy creature like the dragon). These stories are traditionally more character driven than hard science fiction. (Anne McCaffrey, Mercedes Lackey, Marion Zimmer Bradley)

HORROR SUBCATEGORIES

Subcategories in horror are less well defined than in other genres and are frequently the result of marketing decisions as much as literary ones. But being familiar with the terms used to describe different horror styles can be important in understanding how your own novel might be best presented to an agent or editor. What follows is a brief description of the most commonly used terms, along with names of authors and, where necessary, representative works.

DARK FANTASY. Sometimes used as a euphemistic term for horror in general, but also refers to a specific type of fantasy, usually less graphic than other horror subcategories, that features more ``traditional'' supernatural or mythical beings (vampires, werewolves, zombies, etc.) in either contemporary or historical settings. (Contemporary: Stephen King, *Salem's Lot*; Thomas Tessier, *The Nightwalker*. Historical: Brian Stableford, *The Empire of Fear*; Chelsea Quinn Yarbro, *Werewolves of London*.)

HAUNTINGS. "Classic" stories of ghosts, poltergeists, and spiritual possessions. The level of violence portrayed varies, but many writers in this category exploit the reader's natural fear of the unknown by hinting at the horror and letting the reader's imagination supply the details. (Peter Straub, *Ghost Story*; Richard Matheson, *Hell House*)

JUVENILE/YOUNG ADULT. Can be any horror style, but with a protagonist who is the same age as, or slightly older than, the targeted reader. Stories for middle grades (eight to 12 years old) are scary, with monsters and violent acts that might best be described as "gross," but stories for young adults (12-18) may be more graphic. (R.L. Stine, Christopher Pike, Carol Gorman)

PSYCHOLOGICAL HORROR. Features a human monster with horrific, but not necessarily supernatural, aspects. (Thomas Harris, *The Silence of the Lambs*, *Hannibal*; Dean Koontz, *Whispers*)

SPLATTERPUNK. Very graphic depiction of violence—often gratuitous—popularized in the 1980s, especially in film. (*Friday the 13th*, *Halloween*, *Nightmare on Elm Street*, etc.)

SUPERNATURAL/OCCULT. Similar to the dark fantasy, but may be more graphic in its depiction of violence. Stories feature satanic worship, demonic possession, or ultimate evil incarnate in an entity or supernatural being that may or may not have its roots in traditional mythology or folklore. (Ramsey Campbell; Robert McCammon; Ira Levin, *Rosemary's Baby*; William Peter Blatty, *The Exorcist*; Stephen King, *Pet Sematary*)

TECHNOLOGICAL HORROR. "Monsters" in these stories are the result of science run amok or technology turned to purposes of evil. (Dean Koontz, *Watchers*; Michael Crichton, *Jurassic Park*)

PROFESSIONAL ORGANIZATIONS

AGENTS' ORGANIZATIONS

ASSOCIATION OF AUTHORS' AGENTS (AAA), David Higham Associates Ltd., 5-8 Lower John Street, Golden Square, London W1F 9HA. (020) 7434 5900. E-mail: anthonygoff@davidhigham.co.uk. Website: www.agentsassoc.co.uk.

ASSOCIATION OF AUTHORS' REPRESENTATIVES (AAR). E-mail: info@aar-online.org. Website: www.aar-online.org.

ASSOCIATION OF TALENT AGENTS (ATA), 9255 Sunset Blvd., Suite 930, Los Angeles CA 90069. (310)274-0628. Fax: (310)274-5063. E-mail: shellie@agentassociation.com. Website: www.agentassociation.com.

WRITERS' ORGANIZATIONS

ACADEMY OF AMERICAN POETS 584 Broadway, Suite 604, New York NY 10012-5243. (212)274-0343. Fax: (212)274-9427. E-mail: academy@poets.org. Website: www.poets.org.

AMERICAN CRIME WRITERS LEAGUE (ACWL), 17367 Hilltop Ridge Dr., Eureka MO 63205. Website: www.acwl.org.

AMERICAN MEDICAL WRITERS ASSOCIATION (AMWA), 30 West Gude Drive, Suite 525, Rockville MD 20850-4347. (301)294-5303. Fax: (301)294-9006. E-mail: amwa@amwa.org. Website: www.amwa.org.

AMERICAN SCREENWRITERS ASSOCIATION (ASA), 269 S. Beverly Dr., Suite 2600, Beverly Hills CA 90212-3807. (866)265-9091. E-mail: asa@goasa.com. Website: www.asascreenwriters.com.

AMERICAN TRANSLATORS ASSOCIATION (ATA), 225 Reinekers Lane, Suite 590, Alexandria VA 22314. (703)683-6100. Fax: (703)683-6122. E-mail: ata@atanet.org. Website: www.atanet.org.

EDUCATION WRITERS ASSOCIATION (EWA), 2122 P St., NW, Suite 201, Washington DC

20037. (202)452-9830. Fax: (202)452-9837. E-mail: ewa@ewa.org. Website: www.ewa.org.

GARDEN WRITERS ASSOCIATION (GWA), 10210 Leatherleaf Ct., Manassas VA 20111. (703)257-1032. Fax: (703)257-0213. E-mail: info@gardenwriters.org. Website: www.gardenwriters.org.

HORROR WRITERS ASSOCIATION (HWA), 244 Fifth Ave., Suite 2767, New York NY 10001. E-mail: hwa@horror.org. Website: www.horror.org.

THE INTERNATIONAL WOMEN'S WRITING GUILD (IWWG),P.O. Box 810, Gracie Station, New York NY 10028-0082. (212)737-7536. Fax: (212)737-9469. E-mail: dirhahn@aol.org. Website: www.iwwg.com.

MYSTERY WRITERS OF AMERICA (MWA), 1140 Broadway, Suite 1507, New York NY 10001. (212)888-8171. Fax: (212)888-8107. E-mail: mwa@mysterywriters.org. Website: www.mysterywriters.org.

NATIONAL ASSOCIATION OF SCIENCE WRITERS (NASW), P.O. Box 7905, Berkeley, CA 94707. (510)647-9500. E-mail: LFriedmann@nasw.org. website: www.nasw.org.

NATIONAL ASSOCIATION OF WOMEN WRITERS (NAWW), 24165 IH-10 W., Suite 217-637, San Antonio TX 78257. Phone/Fax: (866)821-5829. Website: www.naww.org.

ORGANIZATION OF BLACK SCREENWRITERS (OBS). Golden State Mutual Life Insurance Bldg., 1999 West Adams Blvd., Rm. Mezzanine Los Angeles, CA 90018. Website: www.obswriter.com.

OUTDOOR WRITERS ASSOCIATION OF AMERICA (OWAA), 121 Hickory St., Suite 1, Missoula MT 59801. (406)728-7434. Fax: (406)728-7445. E-mail: krhoades@owaa.org. Website: www.owaa.org.

POETRY SOCIETY OF AMERICA (PSA), 15 Gramercy Park, New York NY 10003. (212)254-9628. website: www.poetrysociety.org. Poets & Writers, 90 Broad St., Suite 2100, New York NY 10004. (212)226-3586. Fax: (212)226-3963. Website: www.pw.org.

ROMANCE WRITERS OF AMERICA (RWA), 114615 Benfer Road, Houston TX 77069. (832)717-5200. Fax: (832)717-5201. E-mail: info@rwanational.org. Website: www.rwanational.org.

SCIENCE FICTION AND FANTASY WRITERS OF AMERICA (SFWA), P.O. Box 877, Chestertown MD 21620. E-mail: execdir@sfwa.org. Website: www.sfwa.org.

SOCIETY OF AMERICAN BUSINESS EDITORS & WRITERS (SABEW), University of Missouri, School of Journalism, 30 Neff Annex, Columbia MO 65211. (602) 496-7862. E-mail: sabew@sabew.org. Website: www.sabew.org.

SOCIETY OF AMERICAN TRAVEL WRITERS (SATW), 7044 S. 13 St., Oak Creek WI 53154. (414)908-4949. Fax: (414)768-8001. E-mail: satw@satw.org. Website: www.satw.org.

SOCIETY OF CHILDREN'S BOOK WRITERS & ILLUSTRATORS (SCBWI), 8271 Beverly Blvd., Los Angeles CA 90048. (323)782-1010. Fax: (323)782-1892. E-mail: scbwi@scbwi.org. Website: www.scbwi.org.

AMERICAN INDEPENDENT WRITERS (AIW), 1001 Connecticut Ave. NW, Suite 701, Washington DC 20036. (202)775-5150. Fax: (202)775-5810. E-mail: info@aiwriters.org. Website: www.americanindependentwriters.org.

WESTERN WRITERS OF AMERICA (WWA). E-mail: spiritfire@kc.rr.com. Website: www.westernwriters.org.

INDUSTRY ORGANIZATIONS

AMERICAN BOOKSELLERS ASSOCIATION (ABA), 200 White Plains Rd., Suite 600, Tarrytown NY 10591. (914)591-2665. Fax: (914)591-2720. E-mail: info@bookweb.org. Website: www.bookweb.org.

AMERICAN SOCIETY OF JOURNALISTS & AUTHORS (ASJA), 1501 Broadway, Suite 302, New York NY 10036. (212)997-0947. Fax: (212)937-2315. E-mail: director@asja.org. Website: www.asja.org.

ASSOCIATION FOR WOMEN IN COMMUNICATIONS (AWC), 3337 Duke St., Alexandria VA 22314. (703)370-7436. Fax: (703)342-4311. E-mail: info@womcom.org. Website: www.womcom.org.

ASSOCIATION OF AMERICAN PUBLISHERS (AAP), 71 Fifth Ave., 2nd Floor, New York NY 10003. (212)255-0200. Fax: (212)255-7007. Or, 50 F St. NW, Suite 400, Washington DC 20001. (202)347-3375. Fax: (202)347-3690. Website: www.publishers.org.

THE ASSOCIATION OF WRITERS & WRITING PROGRAMS (AWP), Mail Stop 1E3, George Mason University, Fairfax VA 22030. (703)993-4301. Fax: (703)993-4302. E-mail:

services@awpwriter.org. website: www.awpwriter.org.

THE AUTHORS GUILD, INC., 31 E. 32nd St., 7th Floor, New York NY 10016. (212)563-5904. Fax: (212)564-5363. E-mail: staff@authorsguild.org. website: www.authorsguild.org.

CANADIAN AUTHORS ASSOCIATION (CAA), P.O. Box 581, Stn. Main Orilla ON L3V 6K5 Canada. (705)653-0323. Fax: (705)653-0593. E-mail: admin@canauthors.org. Website: www.canauthors.org.

CHRISTIAN BOOKSELLERS ASSOCIATION (CBA), P.O. Box 62000, Colorado Springs CO 80962-2000. (800)252-1950. Fax: (719)272-3510. E-mail: info@cbaonline.org. website: www.cbaonline.org.

THE DRAMATISTS GUILD OF AMERICA, 1501 Broadway, Suite 701, New York NY 10036. (212)398-9366. Fax: (212)944-0420. Website: www.dramatistsguild.com.

NATIONAL LEAGUE OF AMERICAN PEN WOMEN (NLAPW), 1300 17th St. NW, Washington DC 20036-1973. (202)785-1997. Fax: (202)452-8868. E-mail: nlapw1@verizon.net. Website: www.americanpenwomen.org.

NATIONAL WRITERS ASSOCIATION (NWA), 10940 S. Parker Rd., #508, Parker CO 80134. (303)841-0246. Fax: (303)841-2607. E-mail: natlwritersassn@hotmail.com. Website: www.nationalwriters.com

NATIONAL WRITERS UNION (NWU), 256 West 38th Street, Suite 703, New York, NY 10018. (212)254-0279. Fax: (212)254-0673. E-mail: nwu@nwu.org. Website: www.nwu.org.

PEN AMERICAN CENTER, 588 Broadway, Suite 303, New York NY 10012-3225. (212)334-1660. Fax: (212)334-2181. E-mail: pen@pen.org. Website: www.pen.org.

THE PLAYWRIGHTS GUILD OF CANADA (PGC), 215 Spadina Ave., Suite #210, Toronto ON M5T 2C7 Canada. (416)703-0201. Fax: (416)703-0059. E-mail: info@playwrightsguild.ca. Website: www.playwrightsguild.com.

VOLUNTEER LAWYERS FOR THE ARTS (VLA), One E. 53rd St., 6th Floor, New York NY 10022. (212)319-2787. Fax: (212)752-6575. Website: www.vlany.org.

WOMEN IN FILM (WIF), 6100 Wilshire Blvd., Suite 710, Los Angeles CA 90048. (323)935-2211. Fax: (323)935-2212. E-mail: info@wif.org. Website: www.wif.org.

WOMEN'S NATIONAL BOOK ASSOCIATION (WNBA), P.O. Box 237, FDR Station, New York NY 10150. (212)208-4629. Fax: (212)208-4629. E-mail: publicity@bookbuzz.com. Website: www.wnba-books.org.

WRITERS GUILD OF ALBERTA (WGA), 11759 Groat Rd., Edmonton AB T5M 3K6 Canada. (780)422-8174. Fax: (780)422-2663. E-mail: mail@writersguild.ab.ca. Website: writersguild.ab.ca.

WRITERS GUILD OF AMERICA-EAST (WGA), 555 W. 57th St., Suite 1230, New York NY 10019. (212)767-7800. Fax: (212)582-1909. e-mail: info@wgaeast.org. Website: www.wgaeast.org.

WRITERS GUILD OF AMERICA-WEST (WGA), 7000 W. Third St., Los Angeles CA 90048. (323)951-4000. Fax: (323)782-4800. Website: www.wga.org.

WRITERS UNION OF CANADA (TWUC), 90 Richmond St. E., Suite 200, Toronto ON M5C 1P1 Canada. (416)703-8982. Fax: (416)504-9090. E-mail: info@writersunion.ca. Website: www.writersunion.ca.

LITERARY AGENTS SPECIALITIES INDEX

CATEGORY
INDEX

HORROR

HUMOR/SATIRE

SHORT STORY COLLECTIONS

SCIENCE FICTION

MAGAZINES

ADVENTURE

CHILDREN'S/JUVENILE

COMICS/GRAPHIC NOVELS

EROTICA

WESTERN

YOUNG ADULT/TEEN

GENERAL INDEX